W9-AUD-376

PRENTICE HALL

PRE-ALGEBRA

TOOLS FOR A CHANGING WORLD

Prentice
Hall

Needham, Massachusetts
Upper Saddle River, New Jersey
Glenview, Illinois

REVIEWERS

Chandler Cox
White Knoll Middle School
West Columbia, South Carolina

Fred Ferguson
Yough High School
Herminie, Pennsylvania

Nancy Hughes
Indian Hills Middle School
Shawnee Mission, Kansas

Dorothy (Dot) Johnson-Manning
Siwell Road Middle School
Jackson, Mississippi

Ellice P. Martin, Ed.D.
Lanier County Middle School
Lakeland, Georgia

Desireé Marcelin McNeal
Susan Miller Dorsey High School
Los Angeles, California

CONSULTANTS

READING CONSULTANT

Bonnie B. Armbruster, Ph.D.
Department of Curriculum and Instruction
University of Illinois at Champaign-Urbana
Champaign, Illinois

CONTENT CONSULTANTS

Elizabeth Cunningham
Mathematics
Prentice Hall National Consultant
Mansfield, Texas

Bridget Hadley
Mathematics
Director, Prentice Hall National Consultants
Hopkinton, Massachusetts

Shawyn Jackson
Mathematics
Prentice Hall National Consultant
Bayshore, New York

Sandra Mosteller
Mathematics
Prentice Hall National Consultant
Anderson, South Carolina

Loretta Rector
Mathematics
Prentice Hall National Consultant
Foresthill, California

Copyright © 2001 by Prentice-Hall, Inc., Upper Saddle River, New Jersey 07458.
All rights reserved. Printed in the United States of America. This publication is
protected by Copyright, and permission should be obtained from the publisher prior to
any prohibited reproduction, storage in a retrieval system, or transmission in any form
or by any means, electronic, mechanical, photocopying, recording, or likewise. For
information regarding permission(s), write to: Rights and Permissions Department.

ISBN 0-13-437331-6
11 12   04 03

AUTHORS

David M. Davison
Eastern Montana College
Billings, Montana

Marsha S. Landau
Formerly, National-Louis University
Evanston, Illinois

Leah McCracken
Lockwood Junior High School
Billings, Montana

Linda Thompson
Warrenton, Oregon

CONTENTS

CHAPTER 1

Algebraic Expressions and Integers

Problem Solving and Connections

CHAPTER PROJECT 1

CURE FOR THE COMMON CODE

CHAPTER

2

Solving One-Step Equations and Inequalities

Problem Solving and Connections

Language	81
Astronomy	88
Number Theory	96
Math at Work	97
Nutrition	101

. . . and More!

CHAPTER PROJECT 2

DON'T LOSE YOUR BALANCE!

Decimals and Equations

Problem Solving and Connections

CHAPTER PROJECT 3

CURRENCY EVENTS

Factors, Fractions, and Exponents

Problem Solving and Connections

Operations with Fractions

Ratios, Proportions, and Percents

Problem Solving and Connections

CHAPTER PROJECT 6

CHAPTER 7

Solving Equations and Inequalities

Problem Solving and Connections

CHAPTER PROJECT 7

THE INTENSITY OF DENSITY

Linear Functions and Graphing

**Problem Solving
and Connections**

Spatial Thinking

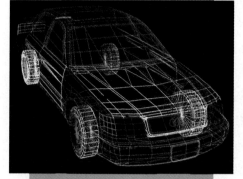

Problem Solving and Connections

CHAPTER

11

Right Triangles in Algebra

Problem Solving and Connections

Data Analysis and Probability

CHAPTER 13

Nonlinear Functions and Polynomials

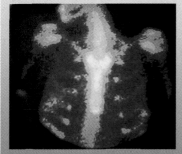

Problem Solving and Connections

CHAPTER PROJECT 13

PRISM BUILDING

Reading and Writing Math

As you work through Prentice Hall's *Pre-Algebra,* you will notice places in the text that say "Reading Math" and "Writing Math." These tips and useful facts will help you understand the language of mathematics. The examples below show how to read an equation and how to go from words to math symbols.

The equation $\frac{x}{-9} = -3$ is read as "x divided by negative nine equals negative three."

When you go from words to an equation, the order of the math symbols may be different from the order of the words:

- ten fewer than $n \rightarrow$ $n - 10$
- eight less than $r \rightarrow r - 8$
- n times $5 \rightarrow 5n$

Pay particular attention to vocabulary words. Some words may be familiar to you, and some you may not have seen before. Some words are used very differently in math than they are in everyday English. You need to be alert for these differences. The examples below explain *percent* and *bisect*.

Percent means "per hundred." The root *cent* shows up in many other words, such as centimeter, century, and centipede. In money, a cent is $\frac{1}{100}$ of a dollar, or $.01.

To *bisect* means to divide into two equal parts. Therefore a segment bisector divides a segment into two congruent parts.

Remember, reading is not a spectator sport. When you are actively involved in thinking before, during, and after reading, you will find math easier to read, understand, and learn!

Making Decisions: Using a Calculator

Touch this dot with your fingertip.

Now move your finger slowly from the dot to the end of your nose.

As you watch your finger approach your nose (slowly), think of the incredible amount of *information processing* and *decision making* that goes on in your brain to control the path of your fingertip.

Your brain is the finest computer you will ever use.

The computer inside your head has a data bank with a lifetime of information—enough to allow for continuous routine background (unconscious) processing. Nonroutine (conscious) problem solving, however, requires organized thinking by you, its user. Sometimes you may want to use an outside machine, like a calculator, for additional information. Your job is to manage the linked system of mind and machine as efficiently and productively as possible. Here are some guidelines.

Use your brain	*Use a calculator*
1. to do a multi-step problem with manageable steps.	1. to do a multi-step problem with complicated steps.
2. to compute when only estimates are needed.	2. to compute to more than two decimal places of precision.
3. to extend a simple pattern to the next two or three terms.	3. to extend a pattern to large numbers, or to many terms.
4. to find square roots of perfect squares.	4. to find square roots of non-perfect squares.
5. to find one-digit factors.	5. to test for factors.
6. to solve proportion problems using simple integers.	6. to find trigonometric ratios.

In general, the more you can extend both lists, the better equipped you will be for this course.

Tools for Problem Solving

An Overview

CONTENTS

To the Student:

The key to your success in math is your ability to use math in the real world—both now and in the future. To succeed, you need math skills and some problem solving tools, too. In this Problem Solving Overview, you'll learn how to use a four-step plan for problem solving, how to choose strategies for solving problems, how to evaluate your solutions, and how to apply strategies to standardized tests.

As you work through the book, you'll find plenty of opportunities to improve your problem solving and reasoning skills. Some of the problems you'll work through are simple and routine, so you can practice and develop your skills. Other problems are more complex and require more time and thought to complete. No matter what, you'll find plenty of opportunities to use your skills in everyday life as well as in theoretical situations.
Good luck!

Problem Solving Strategies

Account for All
  Possibilities
Draw a Diagram
Look for a Pattern
Make a Model
Make a Table
Simplify a Problem
Simulate a Problem
Solve by Graphing
Try, Test, Revise
Use Multiple Strategies
Work Backward
Write an Equation
Write a Proportion

The Four-Step Approach

When *Apollo 13* was damaged in space, the three astronauts on board had to modify some of the equipment to get back to Earth safely. They could use only materials that were on the spacecraft, including plastic bags, cardboard, and tape. The solution required problem solving abilities and creativity.

You solve problems every day, both in and outside of school. Having an organized way to tackle problems can help you sort through information and find an effective solution strategy. Many successful problem solvers use a four-step method developed by the mathematician George Polya.

Polya's Four-Step Approach

1. Read and understand the problem.
2. Plan how to solve the problem.
3. Solve the problem.
4. Look back.

■ SAMPLE PROBLEM

The Smiths' minivan averaged 24 mi/gal on a recent camping trip. They took the same route to and from the campsite, traveling a total of 480 mi. Because of heavy traffic, they averaged only 40 mi/h on the way to the campsite. The total driving time for the trip was 10 h. What was their average speed on the return trip?

 Read

Read the problem, and ask yourself questions.

What information am I given?

> The van gets 24 mi/gal.
> The distance was 480 mi round trip.
> The van's speed on the way to the campsite was 40 mi/h.
> The total driving time was 10 h.

What am I being asked to find?

I want to find the average speed traveled on the way home.

Is any of the given information not needed?

Since the problem does not ask about the amount of gas used, the fact that the van gets 24 mi/gal is not needed.

 Plan

Consider the strategies you know. Could you use one of them? Have you ever solved a similar problem? If so, try the same approach.

You have probably solved problems involving distance, speed, and time. In general, speed × time traveled = distance traveled. You can use the distance formula to solve the problem in three steps:

1. Determine the distance of the return trip.
2. Determine how long the return trip took.
3. Find the van's speed for the return trip.

 **Solve**

The total distance for the trip was 480 mi, so the return trip was 480 mi ÷ 2 = 240 mi.

Going to the campsite, the van traveled 240 mi at a speed of 40 mi/h. Since 240 ÷ 40 = 6, the trip took 6 h. Since the total driving time was 10 h, the return trip must have taken 10 h − 6 h = 4 h.

You now know that, on the way home, the van traveled 240 mi in 4 h. Its average speed was 240 mi ÷ 4 hr = 60 mi/h.

Look Back

This is an important step in solving problems. Ask yourself

Did I answer the question asked? Reread the problem to be sure.

Does my answer make sense? Substitute your answer into the original problem.

Could I have solved the problem another way? Sometimes you can confirm your answer by using another method.

If the Smiths traveled 40 mi/h on the way to the campsite and 60 mi/h on the way back, then the total driving time in hours would be 240 ÷ 40 + 240 ÷ 60 = 6 + 4 = 10. So the answer is correct.

Exercises

Use George Polya's four-step method to solve each problem. Remember that there are many ways to solve problems.

1. Nikki and Jing collect action figures. Together, they have 48 figures. Jing has six fewer figures than twice the number Nikki has. How many action figures does each girl have?

2. Yolanda's Yogurt Shoppe is having a special on sundaes. How many different sundaes are possible?

Yolanda's Sundae Special
Only $1.69
Choose one item from each list.

Yogurt	**Toppings**	**Nuts 'n Stuff**
Vanilla	Strawberries	Mixed Nuts
Chocolate	Bananas	Granola
Peach		Sprinkles
Raspberry		

3. **Number Sense** What is the ones digit of 3^{18}?

4. Amelia, Brian, and Cody have three bicycles. One bike is blue, one is green, and one is red. Amelia's brother rides a red bike. Brian does not have a blue bike. Cody's bike is either red or green. Cody is not related to Amelia. Who owns the red bike?

5. **Language** In another language, *desa tra* means "green pepper," *dro tra dam* means "big green house," and *tresti dam* means "big dog." What is the word for "house" in this language?
   A. *dam*   B. *desa*   C. *dro*   D. *tra*

6. **Number Sense** Mr. Lopez is packing the muffins he made for the school bake sale. He finds that whether he puts four, five, or six muffins in each bag, he has two muffins left over. What is the least number of muffins Mr. Lopez could have?

7. Jakob and Tom are the same age. Jakob is older than Clarisse. Clarisse is younger than Miko. Is Jakob older or younger than Miko, or can this not be determined from the information?

8. **Landscaping** A landscaper bought decorative fencing to enclose the flower bed at the right. The fencing cost $24.95/ft. How much did the landscaper spend on fencing?

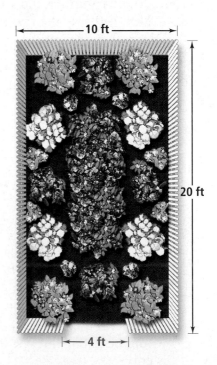

Using Strategies

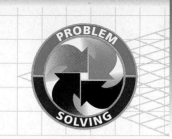

When you need to solve a problem, it helps to be familiar with several solution strategies. Most problems can be solved in several different ways, and for some problems a combination of strategies works best.

Here are some strategies to consider when you are planning to solve a problem.

> Draw a Diagram
> Look for a Pattern
> Make a Table
> Simplify a Problem
> Try, Test, Revise
> Write an Equation

▌ SAMPLE PROBLEM

Ana is organizing a tennis tournament at her town's recreation center. Each participant will play each of the other participants exactly once. Six people have signed up for the tournament. How many games does Ana need to schedule?

Solution 1

STRATEGIES: *Simplify a Problem* and *Look for a Pattern*

You can start by using the strategy *Simplify a Problem*. Figure out the number of games needed for tournaments with two, three, and four players. Then use the strategy *Look for a Pattern* to find the number of games for a six-person tournament.

What if only two players, A and B, sign up for the tournament? Then only one game would be played, A against B. You can use the notation AB to represent this game.

Now a third player, C, signs up. This adds two more games, since C must play both A and B. So a total of three games would be played: AB, AC, and BC.

If a fourth player, D, signed up for the tournament, then three more games would be needed, since D would need to play A, B, and C. A total of six games would be played: AB, AC, BC, AD, BD, and CD.

Do you see a pattern?

> 2 players: 1 game
>
> 3 players: 1 + 2 = 3 games
>
> 4 players: 1 + 2 + 3 = 6 games

You can extend the pattern and find the number of games for a six-player tournament.

> 6 players: 1 + 2 + 3 + 4 + 5 = 15 games

Solution 2

STRATEGIES: *Draw a Diagram*

You can also use the strategy *Draw a Diagram* to solve this problem. Use dots, labeled A to F, to represent the players. Use segments connecting the dots to represent the games.

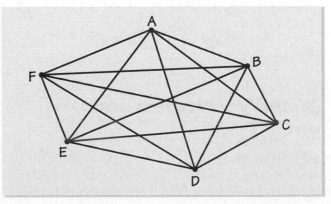

There are a total of 15 segments, so Ana needs to schedule 15 games.

Exercises

1. Roger has band practice every other day, meets with a math tutor every fourth day, and volunteers at a children's hospital once a week. Today, Roger had practice, met with his tutor, and worked at the hospital. In how many days will Roger have all three activities on the same day again?

2. **Patterns** If the pattern below continues, how many squares will be in Stage 23?

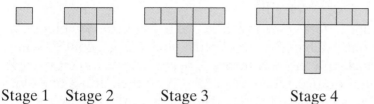

   Stage 1   Stage 2   Stage 3   Stage 4

3. **Fund-raising** The basketball team is selling calendars to raise money for new uniforms. Wall calendars sell for $7 each and desk calendars sell for $5 each. On Saturday, Maya sold 11 calendars for a total of $67 dollars. How many calendars of each type did she sell?

4. **Maps** Rama and Dan are using a trail map to plan a backpacking trip. On the first day, they plan to hike from the trail head to Miller's Pond—a map distance of about 4 in. The key on the map says that 1.25 in. represents 2.5 mi. About how many miles will Rama and Dan hike the first day?

5. **Geometry** How can you arrange 24 identical square tiles, without stacking, to create a shape with the least possible perimeter?

6. **Number Sense** Rose has forgotten the combination to her gym locker. She knows it has the digits 1, 3, 5, 7, and 9, but she doesn't remember the order of the digits. She decides to try every possible order until she finds the right one. How many five-digit numbers does Rose have to try?

7. **Geography** Suppose you are walking west. You come to a corner and turn right. You then come to another corner and turn right again. At the next corner you turn left. Which direction are you now facing—north, south, east, or west?

8. How many letters are in either the rectangle or the square at the right, but not in both?

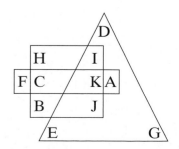

Using Rubrics

A *rubric* is a type of scoring guide. Rubrics are often used to grade projects or to score problems that require you to show your work or explain your thinking.

■ SAMPLE PROBLEM

The Mixing Colors game involves two bags of colored blocks. Bag 1 contains one red block and two blue blocks. Bag 2 contains one yellow block and two red blocks. A player guesses a color—red, yellow, blue, orange, green, or purple—and then draws one block from each bag without looking. The colors of the blocks are "mixed" according the following rules:

red + red = red	blue + blue = blue
yellow + yellow = yellow	red + blue = purple
red + yellow = orange	blue + yellow = green

If the mixture color matches the guess, the player wins a prize.

What color should a player guess to have the best chance of winning the game? Show your work and explain how you found your answer.

Solutions to this problem are scored from a high of 3 points to a low of 0 points according to the rubric below.

Rubric

3 You correctly state that the player should choose purple and give a clear, logical explanation for your answer.

2 You correctly answer the question but provide a weak explanation, *or* you use correct reasoning but make a minor mistake that leads to an incorrect answer.

1 You give the correct answer but provide no explanation *or* give the correct answer or an incorrect answer with a flawed explanation.

0 You give an incorrect answer with no explanation *or* fail to attempt an answer.

Sample Answer 1

The table shows all the possible color combinations. Purple happens the most, so the player should choose purple to have the best chance of winning a prize.

		Bag 1		
		R	B	B
Bag 2	Y	O	G	G
	R	R	P	P
	R	R	P	P

This response scores a 3. The student gives the correct answer with a clear, logical explanation.

Sample Answer 2

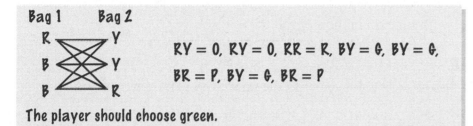

Bag 1   Bag 2
R   Y
B   Y
B   R

RY = O, RY = O, RR = R, BY = G, BY = G,
BR = P, BY = G, BR = P

The player should choose green.

This response scores a 2. The strategy is a good one, but the student gets the incorrect answer because of listing the contents for Bag 2 incorrectly. The student also does not list one of the color combinations.

Sample Answer 3

Bag 1 + Bag 2 = Mixture
blue + red = purple
blue + red = purple
red + yellow = orange

Purple happens 2 out of 3 times. The player should choose purple.

This response scores a 1. The student gives the correct answer but uses faulty reasoning.

Exercises

Use the given rubric to score each sample answer. Explain how you decided which score to give.

One baseball and two bats cost $51. Two baseballs and five bats cost $125. Find the price of a baseball and the price of a bat. Explain how you found your answers.

Rubric

3 You correctly state that a baseball costs $5 and a bat costs $23, and you give a clear, logical explanation for your answer.

2 You correctly answer the question but provide a weak explanation, *or* you make a minor mistake that leads to the incorrect answer.

1 You give the correct answer but provide no explanation, *or* you give an incorrect answer with a flawed explanation.

0 You give the incorrect answer with no explanation *or* fail to attempt an answer.

---

1. Sample answer 1:

Ball $5   Bat $23

2. Sample answer 2:

1 ball + 2 bats cost $51. Doubling everything, I get 2 balls + 4 bats cost $102. Adding 1 more bat makes 2 balls + 5 bats, which cost $125. So a bat costs $23.

2 bats cost $46 and 2 bats + 1 ball cost $51. So a ball costs $5.

3. Sample answer 3:

1 ball and 2 bats cost $51, and 2 balls and 5 bats cost $125.

Combining everything: 3 balls and 7 bats cost $176. Guess: Bat costs $20. Then, 7 bats cost $140. So 3 balls cost $36. or 1 ball costs $12. Test: 3(12) + 7(20) = 176 ✓

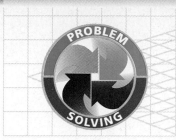

Standardized Test Prep

You can use problem solving skills to answer multiple-choice questions. By thinking logically or using estimation, you can eliminate some of the answer choices.

■ SAMPLE PROBLEM 1

Sandra conducted a survey to find the type of movie that students in her school liked best. Of the students surveyed, one fourth preferred action movies and one third preferred dramas. The remaining 30 students said they like comedies best. How many students took part in Sandra's survey?

A. 28   **B.** 67   **C.** 72   **D.** 80   **E.** 84

 **Read**

Read the problem carefully. You need to find the total number of students Sandra surveyed.

> The number of students Sandra surveyed must be greater than 30 and be divisible by 3 and by 4.

 Plan

You can think logically to eliminate some of the choices and then *Work Backward* to see which remaining answer choice fits the information given in the problem.

 **Solve**

Think about the choices you can eliminate easily.

> Sandra surveyed more than 30 students, so you can eliminate choice A.

> The number of students in each category must be a whole number. Since $67 \div 4 = 16.75$ and $80 \div 3 \approx 26.7$, you can eliminate choices B and D.

Only choices C and E remain. *Work Backward* to see which answer fits the information in the problem.

> Try choice C, 72:
>
> $72 \div 4 = 18$ and $72 \div 3 = 24$
> $72 - 18 - 24 = 30$ ✔
>
> Choice C is correct.

![Look Back icon] **Look Back**

Check your answer by making sure choice E is *not* correct.

> $84 \div 4 = 21$ and $84 \div 3 = 28$
> $84 - 21 - 28 = 35 \neq 30$ ✘
>
> Choice E is not correct.

When *Not here* is a choice, you need to check each of the other choices before choosing *Not here*.

■ SAMPLE PROBLEM 2

The mean of four numbers is 68. Three of the numbers are 74, 66, and 82. What is the fourth number?
A. 280   **B.** 73   **C.** 67   **D.** 50   **E.** Not here

Think Logically Since the three given numbers are even and the mean is even, the fourth number must be even as well.

> You can eliminate choices B and C because they are odd.

Since the mean of the four numbers is 68, the sum of the four numbers must be $4 \times 68 = 272$.

> $280 > 272$, so you can eliminate choice A.

Work Backward Only choices D and E remain. Check choice D.

> $74 + 66 + 82 + 50 = 272$
> $272 \div 4 = 68$ ✔
>
> Choice D is the correct answer.

Look Back Since one of the answer choices works in the original problem, choice E, *Not here,* is not correct.

Exercises

Use problem solving strategies to choose the best answer.

1. Desmond made a sketch of his dog Frankie. He used a photocopy machine to reduce his drawing to 75% of its original size. He then reduced the copy to 50% of its size. In the final copy, the distance from Frankie's nose to her tail was 10.5 cm. What was the distance from nose to tail in the original sketch?
   A. 3.5 cm   **B.** 9 cm   **C.** 21 cm   **D.** 28 cm   **E.** 135.5 cm

2. Tracy's father is three times as old as Tracy. Six years ago, he was five times as old as Tracy. How old is Tracy?
   A. 18   **B.** 15   **C.** 12   **D.** 10   **E.** 6

3. The square and the rectangle below have the same area. What is the value of x?

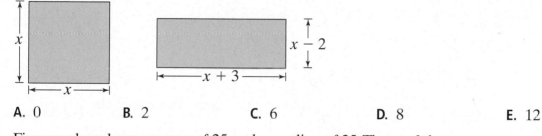

   A. 0   **B.** 2   **C.** 6   **D.** 8   **E.** 12

4. Five numbers have a mean of 25 and a median of 25. Three of the numbers are 20, 24, and 30. What are the other two numbers?
   A. 21 and 26   **B.** 23 and 25   **C.** 25 and 26   **D.** 25 and 28   **E.** 28 and 32

5. In a pile of dimes and quarters, there are twice as many quarters as dimes. The total value of the coins is $7.80. How many dimes are in the pile?
   A. 15   **B.** 13   **C.** 11   **D.** 9   **E.** Not here

6. One day last week, Suzanne ate lunch with Tommy, went to the library and borrowed two books, saw a photography exhibit at the museum, and had a cavity filled. Tommy was out of town on Monday. The library is closed on weekends. The museum is open only on Tuesdays, Wednesdays, and Fridays. The dentist has office hours on Mondays, Thursdays, and Fridays. On which day last week did Suzanne do all these things?
   A. Monday   **B.** Tuesday   **C.** Wednesday   **D.** Thursday   **E.** Friday

7. **Number Sense** Given the numbers 1 and 4, it is *not* reasonable to conclude that
   A. the difference is less than the sum.   **B.** the sum is greater than the product.
   C. the quotient is less than the sum.   **D.** the product is greater than the sum.

Skills You Need for Chapter 1

▶ Adding and subtracting whole numbers

Use before Lessons 1-2, 1-5, and 1-6.

Find each sum or difference.

1. $7 - 6$
2. $9 + 2$
3. $15 - 4$
4. $11 + 8$
5. $20 - 7$
6. $32 + 8$
7. $32 - 15$
8. $26 + 17$
9. $67 + 109$
10. $82 - 54$
11. $44 + 122$
12. $91 - 16$

▶ Comparing whole numbers

Use before Lessons 1-2 and 1-4.

Compare. Use >, <, or = to complete each statement.

13. $5 \blacksquare 2$
14. $1 \blacksquare 0$
15. $14 \blacksquare 17$
16. $6 + 12 \blacksquare 7 + 13$
17. $10 - 2 \blacksquare 27 - 18$
18. $4 \times 7 \blacksquare 2 \times 14$

▶ Multiplying and dividing whole numbers

Use before Lessons 1-2 and 1-9.

Find each product or quotient.

19. $36 \div 3$
20. 10×3
21. $7(4)$
22. $25 \div 5$
23. $12 \cdot 8$
24. $7\overline{)35}$
25. $20 \cdot 10$
26. $9\overline{)720}$
27. $124 \div 4$
28. $12\overline{)156}$
29. $4 \cdot 12 \cdot 10$
30. $132 \div 11$

▶ Reading numbers on a number line

Use before Lesson 1-4.

What is the distance of each point from zero on the number line?

31. A
32. B
33. C
34. D

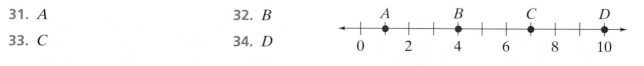

Algebraic Expressions and Integers

What you'll learn in this chapter:

- How to use variables and variable expressions

- How to perform operations with integers

- How to graph points in the coordinate plane

Cure for the Common Code

A special sculpture stands outside the headquarters of the United States Central Intelligence Agency (CIA) in Langley, Virginia. Carved in the copper sculpture is a message in secret code. The code is so complex that for many years even CIA agents could not figure it out. The sculptor, James Sanborn, provided the secret agents with a challenge they could appreciate.

Invent a Secret Code For the chapter project, you will decode computer writing and write in a code used by Julius Caesar. Then you'll invent a code of your own.

Steps to help you complete the project

p. 16   ACTIVITY: READING

p. 33   ACTIVITY: WRITING

p. 54   ACTIVITY: CREATING

p. 55   FINISHING THE CHAPTER PROJECT

Web Extension
www.phschool.com

How to solve a problem by looking for a pattern

Variables and Expressions

What You'll Learn

1. To identify variables, numerical expressions, and variable expressions

2. To write variable expressions for word phrases

. . . And Why

To use the language of algebra to model real-world problems

Gas Mileage How many miles can you drive on ten gallons of gas? The answer depends on the type of vehicle you drive. The table shows some typical data.

Vehicle Type	Miles	Gallons	Miles per Gallon
Subcompact	330	10	$330 \div 10$
Compact	300	10	$300 \div 10$
Mid-size sedan	245	10	$245 \div 10$
Sport utility vehicle	175	10	$175 \div 10$
Pickup truck	160	10	$160 \div 10$

The last column gives a *numerical expression* for each vehicle's miles per gallon.

If you don't know the number of miles, you can use a *variable* to stand for the number. Then you can write a *variable expression* for miles per gallon.

variable → m ← miles on 10 gallons

variable expression → $m \div 10$ ← miles per gallon

A **variable** is a letter that stands for a number. A **variable expression** is a mathematical phrase that uses variables, numerals, and operation symbols.

■ EXAMPLE 1

Identify each expression as a *numerical expression* or a *variable expression*. For a variable expression, name the variable.

a. $50 - 5$
numerical expression

b. $c - 5$
Variable expression; c is the variable.

1. $8 \div x$ **2.** 100×6 **3.** $d + 43 - 9$

PART
2 Writing Variable Expressions

You can translate word phrases into variable expressions.

Word Phrase	Variable Expression
Nine more than a number y	$y + 9$
4 less than a number n	$n - 4$
A number z times three	$z \cdot 3$ or $3z$ or $3(z)$
A number a divided by 12	$a \div 12$ or $\frac{a}{12}$
5 times the quantity 4 plus a number c	$5 \cdot (4 + c)$ or $5(4 + c)$

Writing Math

You can translate many words for operations into symbols.

total	$+$
more than	$+$
increased by	$+$
difference	$-$
fewer than	$-$
less than	$-$
decreased by	$-$
product	$\times$ or $\cdot$ or ( )
times	$\times$ or $\cdot$ or ( )
quotient	$\div$ or —
divided by	$\div$ or —

REAL-WORLD 🌎 **CONNECTION**

■ **EXAMPLE 2**

Science **The fastest dinosaur may have been *Ornithomimus*, which could run about 60 ft in a second. Write a variable expression for the distance *Ornithomimus* could run.**

Words   60   times   number of seconds

⬇   Let s = number of seconds.

Expression   60   · s

The variable expression $60 \cdot s$, or $60s$, describes the distance in feet *Ornithomimus* could run.

Ornithomimus was an ostrich-like oviraptor about 7 ft tall. Its long tail acted as a counterbalance and as a stabilizer during fast turns.

■ **TRY THIS**

4. Bagels cost \$.50 each. Write a variable expression for the cost of b bagels.

5. *Measurement* Write a variable expression for the number of hours in m minutes.

Exercises

CHECK UNDERSTANDING

Identify each expression as a *numerical expression* or a *variable expression*. For a variable expression, name the variable.

1. $b + 6$

2. $80 \div 8$

3. $14 - n$

Write an expression for each number of eggs.

4. two dozen eggs

5. five dozen eggs

6. d dozen eggs

Write an expression for each word phrase.

7. 16 more than m

8. 6 divided by z

9. the product of c and 3

PRACTICE AND PROBLEM SOLVING

Identify each expression as a *numerical expression* or a *variable expression*. For a variable expression, name the variable.

10. 14×14

11. $d + 53$

12. $\frac{g}{9}$

13. $100x$

14. $8 + 8 + 8 + 8$

15. $92 - 16 - p$

Write a variable expression for each word phrase.

16. m more than nineteen

17. 8 less than z

18. n divided by 3

19. 3 divided by n

20. the sum of five and a

21. thirty-two times g

22. two less than a number x

23. x less than 2

24. s divided by fifty-four

25. twelve times a number v

26. the product of 10 and a number p

27. a number m increased by 250

28. six subtracted from a number k

29. the quotient of 100 divided by a number z

Write an expression for each quantity.

30. the number of days in 4 weeks

31. the number of days in w weeks

32. the value in cents of 7 nickels

33. the value in cents of n nickels

34. the number of feet in 100 inches

35. the number of feet in i inches

Modeling In each model, the red line represents a variable expression. Match each expression with its model.

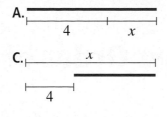

A.

4   x

B.

x   x   x   x

C.

x

4

D.

x

36. $4x$

37. $4 + x$

38. $\frac{x}{4}$

39. $x - 4$

40. *Writing* How are numerical expressions and variable expressions similar? How are they different?

41. Mia has $20 less than Brandi. Brandi has d dollars. Write a variable expression for the amount of money Mia has.

42. **TEST PREP** Pam is 15 years old. Which expression gives Pam's age p years ago?
   A. $p - 15$ **B.** $p + 15$ **C.** $15 - p$ **D.** $\frac{p}{15}$

Use the calorie chart for Exercises 43 and 44.

43. Write a variable expression for the number of calories in e eggs and one slice of bread.

44. Write a variable expression for the number of calories in a fruit salad made from a apples and b bananas.

45. There are twice as many sophomores as freshmen.
   a. If there are f freshmen, how many sophomores are there?
   b. If there are s sophomores, how many freshmen are there?

46. *Error Analysis* A student wrote the variable expression $n - 5$ for the word phrase *n less than five*. Explain the student's error.

Mathematical Reasoning **A hot air balloon is at an altitude of m meters. Write a word phrase for each expression.**

47. $m + 34$ **48.** $m - 2,000$ **49.** $3m$

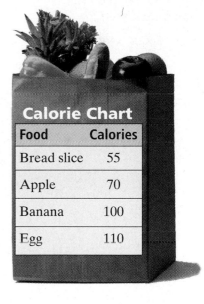

Calorie Chart

Food	Calories
Bread slice	55
Apple	70
Banana	100
Egg	110

▶ **MIXED REVIEW**

Compute. *(Previous Course)*

50. $105 + 25 + 95$ **51.** $3 \times 6 \times 4$ **52.** $8 + 1 - 1$

53. $648 - 573$ **54.** $169 \div 13$ **55.** $22,534 - 12,971$

56. *Choose a Strategy* A customer buys orange juice for $.95 and two apples for $.55 each. She gives the cashier a five-dollar bill. How much change should the cashier give the customer?

1-2

The Order of Operations

What You'll Learn

1 To use the order of operations

2 To use grouping symbols

...And Why

To find the value of an expression with more than one operation

Investigate

············· EXPERIMENTING WITH ORDER ·····················

In most languages, the meaning of words depends on their order. For example, "sign the check" is not the same as "check the sign."

Similarly, order is important in the language of mathematics.

1. **Mental Math** Find the value of the expression $3 + 5 \times 2$.

2. **Analyze** What answer do you get to Question 1 if you multiply before adding? If you add before multiplying?

3. **Critical Thinking** How does the order in which you do the operations affect your answer?

PART
1 **Using the Order of Operations**

The order in which you perform operations can affect the value of an expression. To avoid confusion, mathematicians have agreed on an **order of operations.** Multiply and divide first. Then add and subtract.

To *simplify* an expression means to replace the expression with the simplest name for its value.

■ EXAMPLE 1

Simplify $4 + 15 \div 3$.

$$4 + 15 \div 3$$

$$4 + 5 \qquad \text{First divide.}$$

$$9 \qquad \text{Then add.}$$

■ **TRY THIS** Simplify each expression.

4. $2 + 5 \times 3$ **5.** $12 \div 3 - 1$ **6.** $10 - 1 \cdot 7$

When operations have the same rank in the order of operations, do them from left to right.

■ EXAMPLE 2

Simplify 3 · 5 − 8 ÷ 4 + 6.

$3 \cdot 5 - 8 \div 4 + 6$

$15 \quad - \quad 2 \quad + \quad 6$ **Multiply and divide from left to right.**

$13 + 6$ **Add and subtract from left to right.**

19 **Add.**

■ **TRY THIS** Simplify each expression.

7. $4 - 1 \cdot 2 + 6 \div 3$ **8.** $5 + 6 \cdot 4 \div 3 - 1$

PART 2 Using Grouping Symbols

Grouping symbols, such as parentheses, ( ), and brackets, [ ], indicate order. A fraction bar also is a grouping symbol, since $\frac{4 + 2}{3} = (4 + 2) \div 3$. Always work inside grouping symbols first.

Order of Operations
1. Work inside grouping symbols.
2. Multiply and divide in order from left to right.
3. Add and subtract in order from left to right.

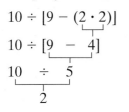

Calculator HINT

Many calculators use the order of operations. To test yours, enter $10 - 4 \div 2$.

If the answer is 8, then your calculator uses the order of operations.

If the answer is 3, then your calculator does *not* use the order of operations.

■ EXAMPLE 3

Simplify 10 ÷ [9 − (2 · 2)].

$10 \div [9 - (2 \cdot 2)]$

$10 \div [9 - 4]$ **Multiply within parentheses.**

$10 \div 5$ **Subtract within brackets.**

2 **Divide.**

■ **TRY THIS** Simplify each expression.

9. $2[(13 - 4) \div 3]$ **10.** $1 + \frac{10 - 2}{4}$

You can use the order of operations to find the area of an irregular figure by more than one method.

■ Different Ways to Solve a Problem

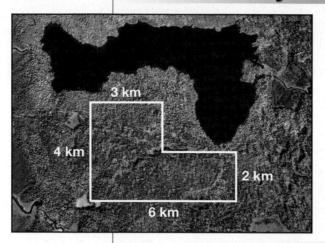

3 km

4 km

2 km

6 km

Urban Planning Some urban planners specialize in planning entire new towns. These towns are designed for livability, with plenty of open space. The sketch shows the dimensions for a new town called Panorama. Find Panorama's area.

Method 1

Divide the figure into rectangles. Then add their areas.

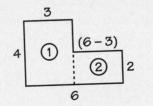

$$\text{Area} = \text{Area ① + Area ②}$$
$$= 4 \cdot 3 + (6 - 3) \cdot 2$$
$$= 4 \cdot 3 + 3 \cdot 2$$
$$= 12 + 6$$
$$= 18$$

Panorama's area is 18 km².

Method 2

Visualize the figure as a small rectangle within a large rectangle. Then subtract the small area from the large area.

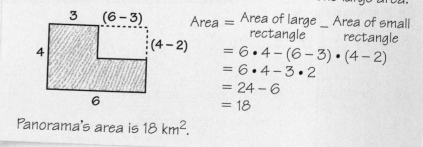

$$\text{Area} = \begin{array}{c}\text{Area of large} \\ \text{rectangle}\end{array} - \begin{array}{c}\text{Area of small} \\ \text{rectangle}\end{array}$$
$$= 6 \cdot 4 - (6 - 3) \cdot (4 - 2)$$
$$= 6 \cdot 4 - 3 \cdot 2$$
$$= 24 - 6$$
$$= 18$$

Panorama's area is 18 km².

Choose a Method

1. Which method would you use to find the town's area? Explain.
2. Can you think of another way to solve the problem? Explain.

Exercises

Which operation would you perform first? Explain.

1. $35 \cdot 98 - 50$ **2.** $115 - 87 + 29$ **3.** $4(67 \div 6)$

Simplify each expression.

4. $6 - 6 \div 3$ **5.** $21 - 13 + 8$ **6.** $7 + 3 \cdot (8 \div 4)$

7. $2(15 - 9) \cdot 9$ **8.** $[2 + (6 \cdot 8)] - 1$ **9.** $6 + \dfrac{6 + 2}{4}$

PRACTICE AND PROBLEM SOLVING

Mental Math **Simplify each expression.**

10. $12 - 8 \div 2$ **11.** $21 \div 7 + 14$ **12.** $6 \cdot 2 + 4$

13. $4(4) - 2$ **14.** $3(7 + 4)$ **15.** $2(6) + \dfrac{15}{3}$

Simplify each expression.

16. $14 + 5 \times 2$ **17.** $60 \div 4 + 9$ **18.** $16 \div 8 \times 2$

19. $12 \div 3 \times 4$ **20.** $2 + 3 \cdot 24$ **21.** $12 \div 3 - 2 + 1$

22. $2 \cdot 2 + 0 \cdot 4$ **23.** $36 - 27 \div 9 \div 1$ **24.** $4 \div 4 \cdot 4 + 4 - 4$

25. $(56 - 5) \div 17$ **26.** $440 \div (2 + 18)$ **27.** $(21 + 3) \div 4 \div 2$

28. $[6(4 + 1) - 5]$ **29.** $\dfrac{21 + 15}{3 + 6}$ **30.** $2[8 + (5 - 3)] - 8$

Compare. Use $>$, $<$, or $=$ to complete each statement.

31. $15 \cdot 3 - 2 \ \blacksquare\ 15 \cdot (3 - 2)$ **32.** $8 + 12 \div 4 \ \blacksquare\ (8 + 12) \div 4$

33. $12 \div 3 + 9 \cdot 4 \ \blacksquare\ 12 \div (3 + 9) \cdot 4$ **34.** $(19 - 15) \div (3 + 1) \ \blacksquare\ 19 - 15 \div 3 + 1$

35. **TEST PREP** Which expression has a value of 18?
    A. $3 \cdot 2 + 4$ **B.** $(18 - 10) \div 4 + 15$ **C.** $4 \cdot 2 + 3 - 2$
    D. $27 - 13 \cdot 2 + 17(6 - 5)$ **E.** Not here

Insert grouping symbols to make each number sentence true.

36. $7 + 4 \cdot 6 = 66$ **37.** $7 \cdot 8 - 6 + 3 = 17$

38. $3 + 8 - 2 \cdot 5 = 45$ **39.** $2 \cdot 3 - 8 - 5 \cdot 2 = 0$

40. A part-time employee worked 4 hours on Monday and 7 hours each day for the next 3 days. Write and simplify an expression that shows the total number of hours worked.

41. *Writing* Why do we need to agree on an order of operations?

42. *Error Analysis* A student found the value of the expression $30 \div 6 - 1$ to be 6. Explain the student's error.

Write a numerical expression for each phrase. Then simplify.

43. five added to the product of four and nine

44. twenty-one minus the sum of fifteen and five

45. seventeen minus the quotient of twenty-five and five

46. **TEST PREP** A music club member ordered three CDs at $14 each and four tapes at $8 each. The shipping charge for the entire order was $5. Which expression shows the total cost of the order?
  A. $3 \cdot 14 + 4 \cdot 8 + 5$ **B.** $3(14 + 5) + 4(8 + 5)$
  C. $(3 + 4) \cdot (14 + 8)$ **D.** $3 \cdot 14 + 4 \cdot 8$

Write two expressions you could use to find the area of each shaded figure. Find the area.

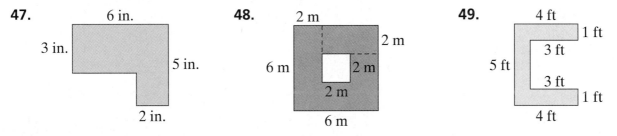

47. 6 in. 3 in. 5 in. 2 in.

48. 2 m 2 m 6 m 2 m 2 m 6 m

49. 4 ft 1 ft 3 ft 5 ft 3 ft 1 ft 4 ft

50. *Open-ended* Write a word problem for the numerical expression $3(4 + 3) + 2$. Then simplify the expression.

51. *Number Sense* Use the digits 1–9 in order. Insert operation signs and grouping symbols to get a value of 100.

▶ MIXED REVIEW

Write a variable expression for each word phrase. *(Lesson 1-1)*

52. the product of a number n and 8

53. k divided by 20

54. six less than a number h

55. the value, in cents, of d dimes

56. A telephone call costs c cents per minute. Write a variable expression for the cost of a 15-minute call. *(Lesson 1-1)*

See also Extra Practice section.

Evaluating Expressions

PART 1 Evaluating Variable Expressions

You can **evaluate** a variable expression by replacing each variable with a number. Then use the order of operations to simplify.

■ EXAMPLE 1

Evaluate $4y - 15$ for $y = 9$.

$$
\begin{aligned}
4y - 15 &= 4(9) - 15 && \text{Replace } y \text{ with 9.} \\
&= 36 - 15 && \text{Multiply.} \\
&= 21 && \text{Subtract.}
\end{aligned}
$$

■ TRY THIS Evaluate each expression.

1. $63 - 5x$, for $x = 7$ **2.** $4(t + 3) + 1$, for $t = 8$

Sometimes expressions have more than one variable.

■ EXAMPLE 2

Evaluate $3ab + \frac{c}{2}$ for $a = 2$, $b = 5$, and $c = 10$.

$$
\begin{aligned}
3ab + \frac{c}{2} &= 3 \cdot 2 \cdot 5 + \frac{10}{2} && \text{Replace the variables.} \\
&= 3 \cdot 2 \cdot 5 + 5 && \text{Work within grouping symbols.} \\
&= 6 \cdot 5 + 5 && \text{Multiply from left to right.} \\
&= 30 + 5 && \text{Multiply.} \\
&= 35 && \text{Add.}
\end{aligned}
$$

■ TRY THIS Evaluate each expression.

3. $6(g + h)$, for $g = 8$ and $h = 7$

4. $2xy - z$, for $x = 4$, $y = 3$, and $z = 1$

5. $\frac{r + s}{2}$, for $r = 13$ and $s = 11$

What You'll Learn

1 To evaluate variable expressions

2 To solve word problems by evaluating expressions

. . . And Why

To solve real-world problems involving packaging and shopping

Writing Math

The × sign looks a lot like the variable *x*. To avoid confusion, use · or ( ) for multiplication.

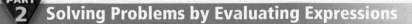

You can write and evaluate variable expressions to solve problems.

REAL-WORLD CONNECTION

■ EXAMPLE 3

Purchasing **Refer to the photo. (a) Write a variable expression for the number of cases a store should order to get *b* bottles of energy drinks. (b) Evaluate the expression for 120 bottles.**

a. *b* bottles

$$\frac{b}{24}$$

b. 120 bottles

$$\frac{b}{24} = \frac{120}{24} \qquad \text{Evaluate for } b = 120.$$

$$= 5 \qquad \text{Divide.}$$

The store should order five cases to get 120 bottles.

■ TRY THIS

6. The store in Example 3 pays $29 for each case of energy drinks. Write a variable expression for the cost of *c* cases. Evaluate the expression to find the cost of five cases.

These bottled energy drinks come in cases of 24.

REAL-WORLD CONNECTION

■ EXAMPLE 4

Online Shopping **An online music store charges $14 for each CD. Shipping costs $6 per order. Write a variable expression for the cost of ordering CDs. Find the cost of ordering four CDs.**

| **Words** | $14 | for each | CD | plus | $6 shipping |

Let *n* = number of CDs.

| **Expression** | 14 | · | *n* | + | 6 |

Evaluate the expression for $n = 4$.

$$14 \cdot n + 6 = 14 \cdot 4 + 6 \qquad \text{Replace } n \text{ with 4.}$$

$$= 56 + 6 \qquad \text{Multiply.}$$

$$= 62 \qquad \text{Add.}$$

It costs $62 to order four CDs.

■ TRY THIS

7. Evaluate the expression in Example 4 to find the cost of ordering seven CDs.

Writing Math

The phrase *for each* implies multiplication. So *$14 for each CD* means "$14 times the number of CDs."

Exercises

Evaluate each expression for $x = 2$, $y = 3$, and $z = 10$.

1. $x + 5$ **2.** $16 - z$ **3.** $4y$

4. $8 \div x$ **5.** $2z - 4$ **6.** $x + z$

7. $y + 5y$ **8.** xyz **9.** $8y \div x$

10. An office assistant types 55 words per minute. How many words does the office assistant type in m minutes? In 20 minutes?

Mental Math **Evaluate each expression.**

11. $7b$, for $b = 5$ **12.** $5 - c$, for $c = 3$ **13.** $x \div 8$, for $x = 40$

14. $3n + 2$, for $n = 7$ **15.** $41 - 4h$, for $h = 10$ **16.** $5a + 7$, for $a = 20$

Evaluate each expression.

17. $12a$, for $a = 2$ **18.** $x - 6$, for $x = 16$

19. $2a + 5$, for $a = 5$ **20.** $105z$, for $z = 7$

21. $6 \div a + 8$, for $a = 2$ **22.** $19 - (a - 4)$, for $a = 8$

23. $13ab$, for $a = 1$ and $b = 7$ **24.** $16 - 4mn$, for $m = 0$ and $n = 3$

25. $3(a + b)$, for $a = 7$ and $b = 9$ **26.** rst, for $r = 5$, $s = 5$ and $t = 5$

27. $\dfrac{150}{z + y}$, for $y = 25$ and $z = 50$ **28.** $\dfrac{x - y}{4}$, for $x = 52$ and $y = 12$

29. $4a - b + \dfrac{b}{2}$, for $a = 3$ and $b = 4$ **30.** $j(5 + k)$, for $j = 11$ and $k = 4$

31. *Data Analysis* Use the chart to find how many calories a 100-lb person uses in an hour of moderate walking.
   a. Write an expression for the number of calories a 100-lb person uses in moderate walking for h hours.
   b. Evaluate the expression to find the number of calories a 100-lb person uses in moderate walking for 2 hours.

32. *Error Analysis* Your friend evaluates $(10 - k) \div 5$ for $k = 5$, and gets 9 for an answer. Explain your friend's error.

Calories Per Hour Used by a 100-lb Walker

Type of Walking	Calories
Slow	110
Moderate	153
Brisk	175
Racing	295

Source: www.nutristrategy.com

33. **Marine Biology** Write an expression for the number of kilometers a dolphin travels in *h* hours swimming at 8 km/h. Then find the number of kilometers the dolphin travels in 3 hours.

34. A fitness club requires a $100 initiation fee and dues of $25 each month. Write an expression for the cost of membership for *n* months. Then find the cost of membership for one year.

35. **Vital Statistics** Every minute about 145 babies are born in the world. About how many babies are born in *m* minutes? In 6 minutes? In one day?

36. A carnival charges $5 for admission plus $2 per ride.
    a. Write an expression for the cost of admission plus *r* rides.
    b. Find the cost of admission plus six rides.
    c. How many rides can you afford if you have $15 to spend?

37. **Writing** Write a word problem that could be solved by evaluating the expression $3x - 5$ for $x = 5$.

By *porpoising*, (jumping clear of the water), dolphins can travel as fast as 26 km/h.

▶ MIXED REVIEW

Simplify each expression. *(Lesson 1-2)*

38. $(60 - 6) \div 9$

39. $80 \div 2 + 13$

40. $5 \div 5 \cdot 5 - 5$

Write a variable expression for each word phrase. *(Lesson 1-1)*

41. *t* fewer than 19

42. the sum of 8 and *n*

43. *d* divided by 20

44. **Error Analysis** Valerie has test grades of 96, 82, 78, and 76. Using a calculator, she found her average grade to be 275. Is Valerie's answer reasonable? Explain how she got her answer.

CHAPTER PROJECT 1   ACTIVITY 1 READING

American Standard Code for Information Interchange (ASCII) is a code used by computers. In ASCII, a number represents each English character. Use the tables below to decode the ASCII message at the right.

7765847269776584736783
3273833284726932766578
7185657169327970328472
6932857873866982836946

ASCII Number	32	46	65	66	67	68	69	70	71	72	73	74	75	76
English Character	space	.	A	B	C	D	E	F	G	H	I	J	K	L

ASCII Number	77	78	79	80	81	82	83	84	85	86	87	88	89	90
English Character	M	N	O	P	Q	R	S	T	U	V	W	X	Y	Z

Integers and Absolute Value

PART 1 **Comparing Integers**

Antifreeze is mixed with the water in a car's radiator to prevent the water from freezing. Pure water freezes at about 32 degrees Fahrenheit (°F) *above* zero. A mixture of equal parts water and antifreeze freezes at about 32 degrees *below* zero.

Freezing Points

Substance	Freezing Temperature (°F)
Water	32
Antifreeze and water	−32
Seawater	28
Gasoline	−36

What You ll Learn

1 To represent, graph, and order integers

2 To find opposites and absolute values

...And Why

To represent real-world quantities that are less than zero, such as cold temperatures

You can write 32 degrees above zero as +32°F or 32°F. You can write 32 degrees below zero as −32°F. Read the numbers 32 and −32 as "*positive* 32" and "*negative* 32."

MEASUREMENT CONNECTION

▌ EXAMPLE 1

Temperature **Write a number to represent the temperature shown by the thermometer.**

The temperature of the liquid in the thermometer is 4 degrees Celsius below zero, or −4°C.

▌ TRY THIS

1. *Temperature* Seawater freezes at about 28°F, or about 2 degrees Celsius below zero. Write a number to represent the Celsius temperature.

You can graph positive and negative numbers on a number line. A number line helps you compare numbers and arrange them in order.

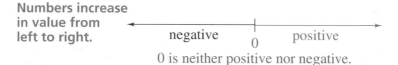

Numbers increase in value from left to right.

0 is neither positive nor negative.

■ **EXAMPLE 2**

Graph −1, 4, and −5 on a number line. Order the numbers from least to greatest.

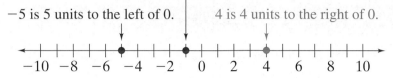

−1 is 1 unit to the left of 0.

−5 is 5 units to the left of 0.

4 is 4 units to the right of 0.

The numbers from least to greatest are −5, −1, and 4.

■ **TRY THIS**

2. Graph 0, 2, and −6 on a number line. Order the numbers from least to greatest.

PART 2 Finding Absolute Value

Numbers that are the same distance from zero on a number line but in opposite directions are called **opposites.**

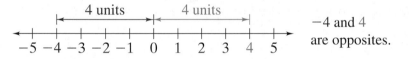

−4 and 4 are opposites.

Integers are the whole numbers and their opposites. A number's distance from zero on the number line is called its **absolute value.** You write *the absolute value of 3* as $|3|$.

■ **EXAMPLE 3**

Use a number line to find $|-3|$ and $|3|$.

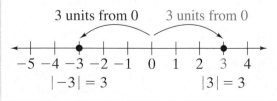

3 units from 0   3 units from 0

$|-3| = 3$ $|3| = 3$

■ **TRY THIS**

3. Write $|-10|$ in words. Then find $|-10|$.

Exercises

CHECK UNDERSTANDING

Write an integer to represent each quantity.

1. a profit of $250

2. 18°C below zero

3. 45 s before launch

Write the integer represented by each point on the number line.

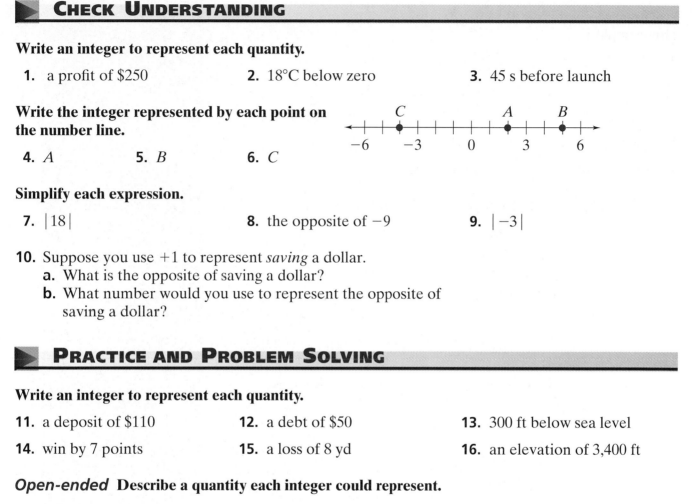

4. A **5.** B **6.** C

Simplify each expression.

7. $|18|$

8. the opposite of -9

9. $|-3|$

10. Suppose you use $+1$ to represent *saving* a dollar.
  a. What is the opposite of saving a dollar?
  b. What number would you use to represent the opposite of saving a dollar?

PRACTICE AND PROBLEM SOLVING

Write an integer to represent each quantity.

11. a deposit of $110

12. a debt of $50

13. 300 ft below sea level

14. win by 7 points

15. a loss of 8 yd

16. an elevation of 3,400 ft

Open-ended **Describe a quantity each integer could represent.**

17. $-1,000$

18. 28

19. -126

Graph each set of numbers on a number line. Then order the numbers from least to greatest.

20. $-2, 8, -9$

21. $-3, -12, -9$

22. $0, 6, -6$

Write the integer represented by each point.

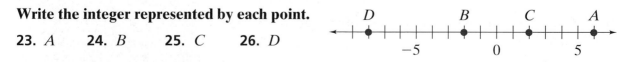

23. A **24.** B **25.** C **26.** D

Simplify each expression.

27. the opposite of 6

28. $|-7|$

29. $|0|$

30. $|-1,000|$

31. the opposite of -2

32. $-|-13|$

33. **TEST PREP** Which statement is *not* true?
   A. −1 is less than 3.   **B.** −3 is greater than −1.
   C. 1 is greater than −3.   **D.** −3 is less than 1.

Use numerals and absolute value symbols to represent each phrase. Then simplify.

34. the absolute value of negative six

35. the absolute value of the opposite of ninety

36. the opposite of the absolute value of negative 9

37. the opposite of the opposite of eight

38. the absolute value of the opposite of $|-1,000|$

Graph each integer and its opposite on a number line.

39. 1   **40.** −2   **41.** −8

42. −7   **43.** 6   **44.** −4

Compare. Use >, <, or = to complete each statement.

45. −8 ■ 0   **46.** 4 ■ −25   **47.** −9 ■ −2

48. $|-1|$ ■ $|50|$ **49.** $|-6|$ ■ $|-12|$ **50.** $|10|$ ■ $|-10|$

Open-ended **Name two integers between the given integers.**

51. −6, 2   **52.** 0, −4   **53.** −8, −12

Finding Famous Ships

Scientist-explorer Robert D. Ballard led the expeditions that found two famous ships deep in the North Atlantic Ocean.
    In 1912, the luxury passenger liner *Titanic* struck an iceberg. It came to rest 12,500 ft below sea level. *Titanic* was 882 ft long and 92 ft wide.

    In 1941, the mighty warship *Bismarck* sank in battle. *Bismarck* was 823 ft long and 118 ft wide.
    Star Hercules, only 269 ft long, towed the underwater camera sled that found *Bismarck* under 15,617 ft of water.

Math in the Media **Use the article above and the graph at the right for Exercises 54 and 55.**

54. Write integers that represent the positions of *Titanic*, *Bismarck*, and *Star Hercules*.

55. ***Error Analysis*** A friend says that *Bismarck's* resting place is higher than *Titanic's*, since 15,617 is higher than 12,500. Explain your friend's error.

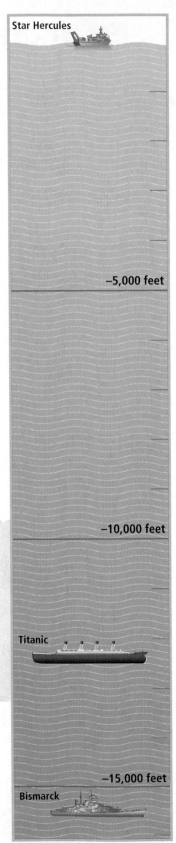

Star Hercules

−5,000 feet

−10,000 feet

Titanic

−15,000 feet

Bismarck

Complete each sentence with a word that makes it true.

56. An integer is negative, positive, or ___?___.

57. All ___?___ integers are less than zero.

58. The opposite of a ___?___ number is negative.

59. The absolute value of an integer is never ___?___.

60. a. *Data Analysis* Use a number line to graph the temperatures in the chart. Label each temperature with the name of the state where it was recorded.
   b. Which state recorded the lowest temperature?

61. *Writing* How can you use integers to describe water levels at high tide and low tide?

62. *Critical Thinking* Is $|x + y|$ the same as $|x| + |y|$? Explain.

Record Low Temperatures for Three States

State	Temperature (°C)
California	−43
Nevada	−46
Georgia	−27

SOURCE: *The World Almanac*

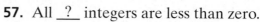

MIXED REVIEW

Evaluate each expression. *(Lesson 1-3)*

63. $p - 5$, for $p = 19$

64. $3d + 3$, for $d = 7$

65. $55y$, for $y = 8$

Compare. Use >, <, or = to complete each statement. *(Lesson 1-2)*

66. $5 + 10 \div 5 \ \blacksquare\ (5 + 10) \div 5$

67. $(9 - 6) \div (2 + 1) \ \blacksquare\ 9 - 6 \div 2 + 1$

68. Suppose you have c CDs. Your friend has 6 more CDs than you do. Write an expression for the number of CDs your friend has. *(Lesson 1-1)*

CHECKPOINT 1
Lessons 1-1 through 1-4

Write a variable expression for each word phrase.

1. 23 more than f

2. g divided by 34

3. the product of 9 and p

Simplify each expression.

4. $17 + 16 - 13$

5. $70 \div 5(3 + 4)$

6. $9 \times 6 \div 3 + 1$

Evaluate each expression for $x = 4$, $y = 6$, and $z = 12$.

7. $2x - 8$

8. $3(z + y)$

9. $4y - z + \frac{z}{x}$

10. *Temperature* On Monday the average temperature was $-10°F$. On Tuesday it was $-15°F$. On Wednesday it was $-13°F$. On Thursday it was $0°F$. Graph the temperatures on a number line. Write the days in order from coldest to warmest.

MATH TOOLBOX

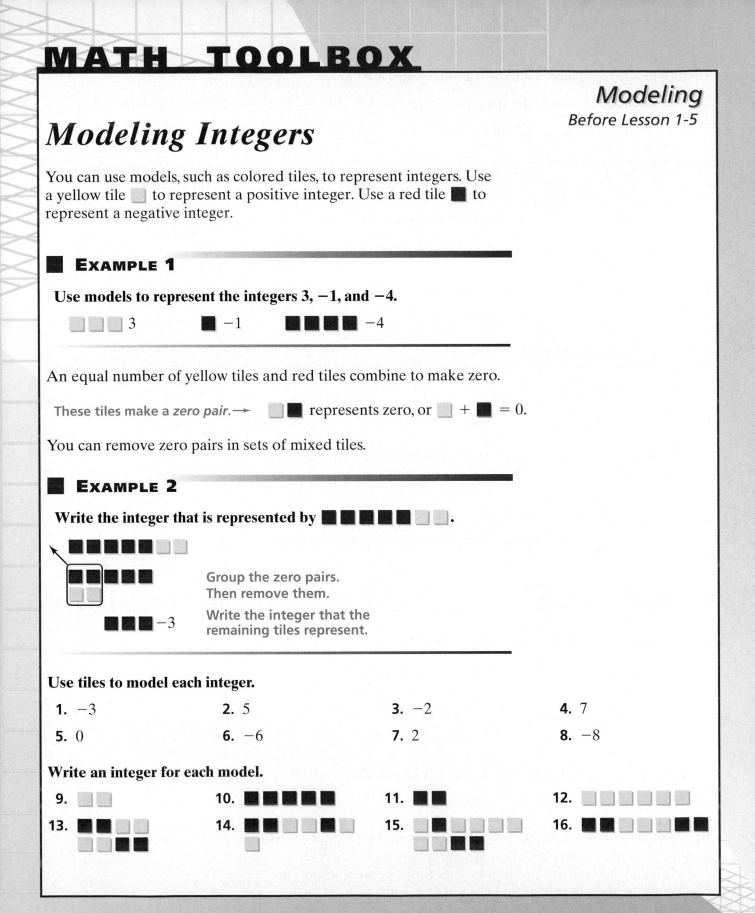

Modeling Integers

You can use models, such as colored tiles, to represent integers. Use a yellow tile ☐ to represent a positive integer. Use a red tile ■ to represent a negative integer.

EXAMPLE 1

Use models to represent the integers 3, −1, and −4.

☐☐☐ 3   ■ −1   ■■■■ −4

An equal number of yellow tiles and red tiles combine to make zero.

These tiles make a *zero pair.*→   ☐■ represents zero, or ☐ + ■ = 0.

You can remove zero pairs in sets of mixed tiles.

EXAMPLE 2

Write the integer that is represented by ■■■■■☐☐.

■■■■■☐☐

Group the zero pairs.
Then remove them.

■■■ −3

Write the integer that the remaining tiles represent.

Use tiles to model each integer.

1. −3	**2.** 5	**3.** −2	**4.** 7
5. 0	**6.** −6	**7.** 2	**8.** −8

Write an integer for each model.

9. ☐☐   **10.** ■■■■■   **11.** ■■   **12.** ☐☐☐☐☐☐

13. ■■☐
☐☐■■   **14.** ■■☐■☐
☐   **15.** ☐■■■☐☐
☐☐■■   **16.** ■■☐☐☐■■

Adding Integers

PART 1 Using Models to Add Integers

If a car goes forward 20 ft and then backs up 20 ft, it ends where it started. Using opposite integers, you can represent this situation as $20 + (-20) = 0$.

When you add two opposites, their sum is zero. So opposites are also called *additive inverses*.

Addition of Opposites

The sum of an integer and its opposite is zero.

Arithmetic	**Algebra**
$1 + (-1) = 0$	$x + (-x) = 0$
$-1 + 1 = 0$	$-x + x = 0$

You can use tiles to add integers. One positive tile and one negative tile combine to make a zero pair, since ▢ + ■ = 0.

To add integers with tiles, combine tiles and remove the zero pairs.

■ EXAMPLE 1

Modeling Use tiles to find $2 + (-5)$.

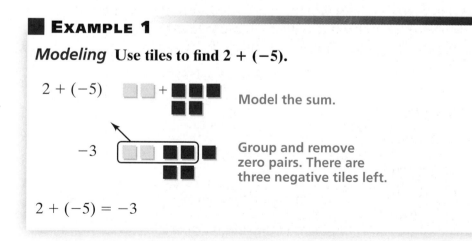

$2 + (-5)$ Model the sum.

-3 Group and remove zero pairs. There are three negative tiles left.

$2 + (-5) = -3$

■ **TRY THIS** Use tiles to find each sum.

1. $-1 + 4$ **2.** $7 + (-3)$ **3.** $-2 + (-2)$

What You'll Learn

1 To use models to add integers

2 To use rules to add integers

. . . And Why

To use integers to solve real-world problems in sports and Earth science

A number line is another model you can use to add integers.

■ **EXAMPLE 2**

On two plays, a football team loses 8 yd and then gains 3 yd. Find −8 + 3 to find the result of the two plays.

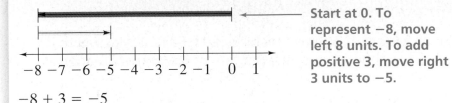

Start at 0. To represent −8, move left 8 units. To add positive 3, move right 3 units to −5.

$-8 + 3 = -5$

The result of the two plays is a loss of 5 yd.

■ **TRY THIS** Use a number line to find each sum.

4. $2 + (-6)$ **5.** $-4 + 9$ **6.** $-5 + (-1)$

PART 2   Using Rules to Add Integers

You can also use rules to find the sum of two integers.

Adding Integers

Same Sign The sum of two positive integers is positive. The sum of two negative integers is negative.

Different Signs To add two integers with different signs, find the difference of their absolute values. The sum has the sign of the integer with the greater absolute value.

■ **EXAMPLE 3**

Find each sum.

a. $-12 + (-31)$
$$-12 + (-31) = -43$$
Since both integers are negative, the sum is negative.

b. $7 + (-18)$
$$|-18| - |7| = 18 - 7$$
Find the difference of the absolute values.
$$= 11$$
Simplify.
$$7 + (-18) = -11$$
Since −18 has the greater absolute value, the sum is negative.

■ TRY THIS Find each sum.

7. $-22 + (-16)$ **8.** $60 + (-13)$ **9.** $-125 + 35$

■ EXAMPLE 4

Earth Science The earthquake monitor in Hockley, Texas, is located in a salt mine at an elevation of -416 m. The elevation of the monitor in Albuquerque, New Mexico, is 2,156 m higher than the one in Hockley. Find the elevation of the monitor in Albuquerque.

$-416 + 2,156$ Write an expression.

$|2,156| - |-416| = 2,156 - 416$ Find the difference of the absolute values.

$= 1,740$ Simplify.

$-416 + 2,156 = 1,740$ Since 2,156 has the greater absolute value, the sum is positive.

The elevation of the monitor in Albuquerque is 1,740 m.

A worldwide network of monitors keeps track of earthquake activity. Here technicians check the monitor in Albuquerque.

■ TRY THIS

10. The elevation of a monitor in Pinon Flat, California, is 1,696 m higher than the monitor in Hockley, Texas. Find the elevation of the monitor in Pinon Flat.

To add several integers, use the order of operations.

■ EXAMPLE 5

Find $-12 + (-6) + 15 + (-2)$.

$-12 + (-6) + 15 + (-2)$ Add from left to right.

$-18 \quad + \quad 15 + (-2)$ The sum of two negative integers is negative.

$-3 \quad + \quad (-2)$ $|-18| - |15| = 3$. Since -18 has the greater absolute value, the sum is negative.

-5 The sum of two negative integers is negative.

$-12 + (-6) + 15 + (-2) = -5$

■ TRY THIS Find each sum.

11. $1 + (-3) + 2 + (-10)$ **12.** $-250 + 200 + (-100) + 220$

Exercises

CHECK UNDERSTANDING

Modeling Write an expression for each model. Find the sum.

1. ■■■■ + ☐☐☐☐☐☐☐

2. ☐☐☐☐☐ + ☐■

3.
$$-2 \qquad -4$$

-6 -5 -4 -3 -2 -1 0

4.
$$-8$$
$$3$$

-6 -5 -4 -3 -2 -1 0 1 2 3 4

Modeling Draw a model and find each sum.

5. $2 + (-5)$

6. $-5 + 2$

7. $5 + (-2)$

8. $-5 + (-2)$

Find each sum.

9. $-26 + (-39)$

10. $-40 + 93$

11. $235 + (-420)$

12. $100 + (-100)$

PRACTICE AND PROBLEM SOLVING

Modeling Draw a model and find each sum.

13. $-6 + 1$

14. $-3 + (-6)$

15. $7 + (-4)$

16. $-3 + 2$

Without adding, tell whether each sum is positive, negative, or zero. Explain your reasoning.

17. $-4 + (-10)$

18. $11 + (-3)$

19. $-8 + 5$

20. $6 + (-6)$

Use rules to find each sum.

21. $14 + (-11)$

22. $0 + (-9)$

23. $-6 + (-7)$

24. $-18 + 4$

25. $450 + (-350)$

26. $-193 + 225$

27. $-18 + 7 + 45$

28. $30 + (-25) + (-15)$

29. $19 + (-9) + 45$

30. $-3 + 2 + (-7) + 7 + 13$

31. $-94 + 68 + (-22)$

32. $-20 + (-89) + 112 + 9$

Mental Math Find each sum.

33. $-5 + 20$

34. $6 + (-6)$

35. $10 + (-3)$

36. $-1 + (-8) + 2$

37. $-5 + 5 + 16$

38. $-4 + (-2) + (-2)$

39. $-120 + 100 + (-20)$

Evaluate each expression for $n = -15$.

40. $n + 7$ **41.** $n + (-7)$ **42.** $15 + n$ **43.** $n + (-15)$

Compare. Use >, <, or = to complete each statement.

44. $-6 + 1 \blacksquare 5 + 1$ **45.** $0 + 3 \blacksquare -2 + 0$ **46.** $10 + (-2) \blacksquare -4 + 12$

47. $-1 + 1 \blacksquare -2 + 0$ **48.** $49 + (-21) \blacksquare |-18|$ **49.** $|-20| + (-7) \blacksquare -11 + (-11)$

50. A football team gained 4 yd, lost 2 yd, gained 11 yd, lost 8 yd, and then lost 9 yd. Find the net gain or loss.

51. *Error Analysis* A friend says that the value of $-17 + 5$ is -22. Explain how your friend may have made this error.

52. *Open-ended* Write and solve a word problem that uses the integers $-10, 3, 5,$ and -6.

Write a numerical expression for each of the following. Then find the sum.

53. negative two plus negative seven

54. twelve plus the absolute value of nine

55. positive three plus the opposite of eight

56. one hundred added to negative nineteen

57. You borrow $20, and then pay back $18.

58. You save $200, and then spend $75.

59. A man deposits $120, and then writes a check for $25.

60. A submarine at 35 ft below sea level moves up 10 ft.

61. The temperature starts at $-10°F$, drops $2°$, rises $8°$, drops $5°$, drops $13°$, and rises $1°$.

62. **TEST PREP** Refer to the map at the right. The lowest temperature recorded in South America is 54 degrees higher than the lowest temperature recorded in North America. What is the lowest temperature recorded in South America?
   A. $-135°F$ **B.** $-27°F$ **C.** $-17°F$ **D.** $-138°F$

63. Maria had $123. She spent $35, loaned $20 to a friend, and received her $90 paycheck. How much does she have now?

Lowest Recorded Temperatures

North America $-81°F$

Europe $-67°F$

Africa $-11°F$

South America $\blacksquare°F$

Source: *The World Almanac*

Tell whether each sum is positive or negative. Then find each sum.

64. $4.8 + (-6.2)$ **65.** $-0.6 + 1.0$ **66.** $-72.5 + 36.4$ **67.** $-9.35 + (-2.84)$

68. *Writing* A friend is having trouble finding the sum of -84 and 28. What explanation would you give to help your friend?

Mathematical Reasoning **Refer to the number line. Is each sum positive or negative?**

```
←+─┼─●─┼─┼─┼─┼─●─┼─┼─┼─┼─●─┼─┼─┼─+→
      a         b   0         c
```

69. $a + b$

70. $b + c$

71. $a + a$

72. $|a + b + c|$

73. *Critical Thinking* Which statement is an example of additive inverses?

A. $xy = yx$

B. $x[(y + (-y)] = x(0)$

C. $x + y = y + x$

D. $x\left(\dfrac{y}{y}\right) = x(1)$

Journal

Summarize what you have learned about adding integers. Include examples.

▶ MIXED REVIEW

Compare. Use >, <, or = to complete each statement. *(Lesson 1-4)*

74. $-9 \ \blacksquare\ -6$

75. $-2 \ \blacksquare\ -7$

76. $|-15| \ \blacksquare\ -15$

77. $0 \ \blacksquare\ -8$

78. $-45 \ \blacksquare\ -44$

79. $100 \ \blacksquare\ |-101|$

80. Write a numerical expression for the phrase *one hundred thirty added to the difference of one hundred sixteen and eight.* Then simplify the expression. *(Lesson 1-2)*

81. A repair center charges a $25 flat fee plus $10 per hour for labor. Write an expression for the cost of a repair that takes *n* hours. Then evaluate the expression to find the cost of an oven repair that takes 3 hours. *(Lesson 1-3)*

Math at Work
Weaver

A sturdy four-shaft floor loom, a 10-dent reed, a ski shuttle, two boat shuttles—these are some of the tools and terms of the ancient craft of weaving. Weavers use yarn, ribbon, and thread. They design and make colorful, unique items such as rugs, tapestries, and handbags. Like a pattern in algebra, each design has rules that must be followed for the desired result.

For more information about weaving, visit the Prentice Hall Web site.

www.phschool.com

Subtracting Integers

PART 1 Using Models to Subtract Integers

You can use tiles to help you understand subraction of integers.

What You'll Learn

1 To use models to subtract integers

2 To use a rule to subtract integers

. . . And Why

To use integers to solve real-world problems involving weather

■ EXAMPLE 1

Find $-6 - (-2)$.

Start with 6 negative tiles.

Take away 2 negative tiles.
There are 4 negative tiles left.

$-6 - (-2) = -4$

■ **TRY THIS** Use tiles to find each difference.

1. $-7 - (-2)$ **2.** $-4 - (-3)$ **3.** $-8 - (-5)$

You can use zero pairs to subtract a larger integer from a smaller integer.

■ EXAMPLE 2

Find $3 - 5$.

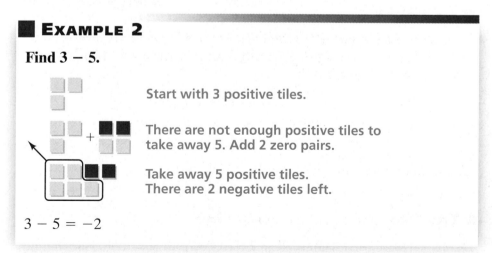

Start with 3 positive tiles.

There are not enough positive tiles to take away 5. Add 2 zero pairs.

Take away 5 positive tiles.
There are 2 negative tiles left.

$3 - 5 = -2$

■ **TRY THIS** Use tiles to find each difference.

4. $4 - 8$ **5.** $-1 - 5$ **6.** $-2 - (-7)$

You can use models to show the relationship between adding and subtracting integers.

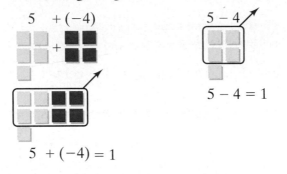

$5 + (-4) = 1$

$5 - 4 = 1$

Both $5 + (-4)$ and $5 - 4$ equal 1. So, $5 + (-4) = 5 - 4$.

The models suggest the following rule for subtracting integers.

Subtracting Integers

To subtract an integer, add its opposite.

Arithmetic	**Algebra**
$2 - 5 = 2 + (-5) = -3$	$a - b = a + (-b)$
$2 - (-5) = 2 + 5 = 7$	$a - (-b) = a + b$

REAL-WORLD CONNECTION

■ EXAMPLE 3

Weather **In January 1916 the temperature in Browning, Montana, fell 100 degrees overnight. The initial temperature was 44°F. What was the final temperature?**

$44 - 100$	Write an expression.
$44 - 100 = 44 + (-100)$	To subtract 100, add its opposite.
$= -56$	Simplify.

The final temperature was $-56°$F.

The lowest temperature ever recorded on Earth was –89°C (–129°F) in Vostok, Antarctica. Scientists there are taking ice core samples to depths of –3,600 m.

■ **TRY THIS** Find each difference.

7. $32 - (-3)$ **8.** $-40 - 66$ **9.** $2 - 48$

10. The lowest temperature ever recorded in Antarctica was $-89°$C. The lowest temperature ever recorded on the moon was about $-170°$C. Estimate the difference in the temperatures.

Exercises

▶ CHECK UNDERSTANDING

Model each situation. Then simplify.

1. You have $3. You owe $10.

2. You are $2 in debt. You borrow $4 more.

Write each difference as a sum. Then simplify.

3. $6 - 2$

4. $6 - (-2)$

5. $-6 - 2$

6. $-6 - (-2)$

7. $2 - 6$

8. $2 - (-6)$

9. $-2 - 6$

10. $-2 - (-6)$

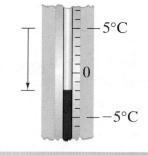

11. a. *Writing* A thermometer is like a vertical number line. Explain how to use the one at the right to model a subtraction problem.
   b. Write and simplify a numerical expression for the model.

▶ PRACTICE AND PROBLEM SOLVING

Write a number sentence for each model.

12.

13.

Modeling **Draw a model and find each difference.**

14. $2 - 3$
15. $-5 - (-6)$
16. $-9 - (-7)$
17. $-2 - 3$
18. $-7 - (-9)$
19. $-10 - 2$

Use a rule to find each difference.

20. $-16 - (-9)$

21. $5 - 11$

22. $-8 - (-3)$

23. $75 - (-25)$

24. $22 - (-7)$

25. $87 - (-9)$

26. $35 - (-15)$

27. $100 - (-91)$

28. $-49 - 75$

29. $-65 - 15$

30. $-92 - (-9)$

31. $16 - (-3)$

32. $120 - (-50)$

33. $-81 - (-13)$

34. $989 - 76$

35. $-59 - (-17)$

36. $-90 - (-80) - 20$

37. $810 - 30 - (-70)$

Mental Math **Find each difference.**

38. $-6 - (-8)$

39. $-45 - 15$

40. $-7 - (-7) + (-7)$

41. $100 - (-50)$

42. $20 - (-10) - 20$

43. $-11 + 22 - (-55)$

44. **TEST PREP** Which expression has a value different from the others?
A. $6 + (-4)$ B. $6 - 4$ C. $|4 - 6|$
D. $-6 - 4$ E. They all have the same value.

Open-ended Use positive and negative integers to write two different subtraction number sentences for each difference.

SAMPLE $\blacksquare - \blacksquare = -5$ $\blacksquare - \blacksquare = -5$
        $-20 - (-15) = -5$ $17 - 22 = -5$

45. $\blacksquare - \blacksquare = 0$ **46.** $\blacksquare - \blacksquare = 10$ **47.** $\blacksquare - \blacksquare = -6$

48. $\blacksquare - \blacksquare = -15$ **49.** $\blacksquare - \blacksquare = |-3|$ **50.** $\blacksquare - \blacksquare = |11|$

Estimation Round each number. Then estimate each sum or difference.

SAMPLE $-216 - 88 \approx -220 - 90 = -310$

51. $-41 - (-86)$ **52.** $-227 - 49$ **53.** $-398 - 67$

54. $-186 - 122$ **55.** $88 - 592$ **56.** $821 - (-924)$

Write a numerical expression for each phrase. Then simplify.

57. A plane climbs 3,000 ft and then descends 600 ft.

58. The temperature increases 15 degrees Fahrenheit and then drops 25 degrees.

59. *Meteorology* The graph shows how temperature changes with altitude.
 a. As the altitude increases, what happens to the temperature?
 b. By how much does the temperature change from 1,500 m to 6,000 m?
 c. What is the change in temperature for every 1,500-m increase in altitude?

60. Suppose you have a score of 35 in a game. You get a 50-point penalty. What is your new score?

61. *Weather* How much warmer is a temperature of 20°C than a temperature of $-7°C$?

62. a. *Mathematical Reasoning* When is $|a - b| = |a| - |b|$? Give an example.
 b. When is $|a - b| > |a| - |b|$? Give an example.
 c. When is $|a - b| < |a| - |b|$?

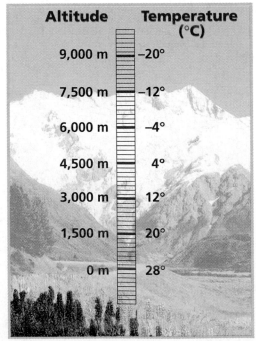

Altitude	Temperature (°C)
9,000 m	−20°
7,500 m	−12°
6,000 m	−4°
4,500 m	4°
3,000 m	12°
1,500 m	20°
0 m	28°

63. a. Patterns Copy and complete. The first one is done for you.

$8 - (-4) = 12$
$12 - (-4) = \blacksquare$
$16 - (-4) = \blacksquare$
$20 - (-4) = \blacksquare$
$24 - (-4) = \blacksquare$

  b. If you begin at 8 and subtract -4 five times, the result is $\blacksquare$.
  c. Begin at 0 and subtract -4 six times. What is the result?

**In a magic square, each row, column, and diagonal has the same sum.
Copy and complete each magic square.**

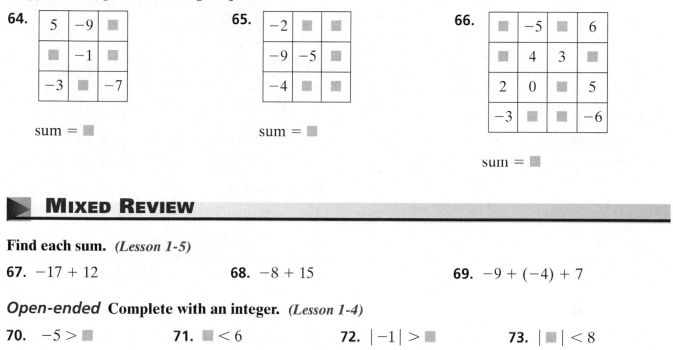

64.

5	−9	■
■	−1	■
−3	■	−7

sum = ■

65.

−2	■	■
−9	−5	■
−4	■	■

sum = ■

66.

■	−5	■	6
■	4	3	■
2	0	■	5
−3	■	■	−6

sum = ■

▶ MIXED REVIEW

Find each sum. *(Lesson 1-5)*

67. $-17 + 12$ **68.** $-8 + 15$ **69.** $-9 + (-4) + 7$

Open-ended Complete with an integer. *(Lesson 1-4)*

70. $-5 > \blacksquare$ **71.** $\blacksquare < 6$ **72.** $|-1| > \blacksquare$ **73.** $|\blacksquare| < 8$

74. Write an expression for the phrase *one hundred plus the product of six and nine.* Simplify the expression. *(Lesson 1-2)*

CHAPTER PROJECT 1
ACTIVITY 2 WRITING

A cipher is a secret code. To decode it, you must know the key. Caesar Cipher, used by Julius Caesar, substitutes one letter for another by shifting each letter in the alphabet three places: *A* becomes *D, B* becomes *E,* and so on. In Caesar Cipher, *dog* is written *grj.* Write a letter to a friend in Caesar Cipher.

Standardized Test Prep

Multiple Choice

Choose the best answer.

1. The temperature rose from −6°C to 6°C. Find the increase in temperature.
   A. 0°C   **B.** −12°C   **C.** 12°C   **D.** 6°C

2. A stray dog ran back and forth down a straight street. First he ran 6 blocks west, then he ran 4 blocks east, and finally he ran 7 blocks west. Where did the dog finish in relation to his starting point?
   F. 17 blocks west   **G.** 9 blocks west
   H. 13 blocks west   **J.** 17 blocks east

3. Simplify $5 + 10 \div 5 \cdot 4$.
   A. 12   **B.** 13   **C.** 24   **D.** 35

4. Evaluate $3(2d + 8)$ for $d = 7$.
   F. 66   **G.** 150   **H.** 51   **J.** 60

5. One inch is about 2.5 centimeters. Which expression would you use to find the length in centimeters of a 7-inch pencil?
   A. $7 \cdot 2.5$ **B.** $7 + 2.5$
   C. $7 \div 2.5$ **D.** $7 - 2.5$

6. Sean borrowed $4 from his brother. He paid back $3. Then he borrowed two times the original amount. Which expression does *not* represent the amount Sean owes his brother?
   F. $3 - 12$ **G.** $-(4 + 8) + 3$
   H. $4 - 3 - 2(4)$ **J.** $-4 + 3 + (-8)$

7. The stack consists of boxes that are all the same size. How many boxes are in the stack?

   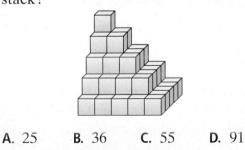

   A. 25   **B.** 36   **C.** 55   **D.** 91

8. A mountain rises 7,000 ft from its base. The temperature at the base is 60°F. It decreases by 5°F every 1,000 ft. What is the temperature at the mountain's top?
   F. 30°F   **G.** 25°F   **H.** 95°F   **J.** 40°F

9. The average 100-lb walker uses 175 calories for every hour of brisk walking. How many calories would an average 100-lb walker use for a 2-h brisk walk?
   A. 175   **B.** 350   **C.** 750   **D.** 1,750

10. Two enchiladas contain 732 calories. Suppose you use 175 cal/h by walking. How long would you need to walk to use the calories from two enchiladas?
    F. about 2 h   **G.** about 3 h
    H. about 4 h   **J.** about 5 h

Free Response

For Exercises 11–13, show your work.

11. A runner takes 8 min for each mile. Write a variable expression for the number of miles the runner completes in m min. Evaluate the expression to find the distance completed in 40 min.

12. A number machine uses a rule to change numbers into other numbers.

    $2 \rightarrow$ (IN → OUT) $\rightarrow -2$

    $-5 \rightarrow$ (IN → OUT) $\rightarrow -9$

    $39 \rightarrow$ (IN → OUT) $\rightarrow 35$

    This machine changed 2 into −2, −5 into −9, and 39 into 35. What number will 0 be changed into?

13. **Open-ended** The factors of x include 4 and 5. Write three possible values for x.

Inductive Reasoning

PART 1 Writing Rules for Patterns

Inductive reasoning is making conclusions based on patterns you observe. A conclusion by inductive reasoning is a **conjecture**.

GEOMETRY CONNECTION

■ **EXAMPLE 1**

Visual Patterns Use inductive reasoning. Make a conjecture about the next figure in the pattern. Then draw the figure.

Observation: The shaded triangle is rotating clockwise around the square.

Conjecture: The next figure will have a shaded triangle in the bottom right corner.

■ **TRY THIS**

1. Make a conjecture about the next figure in the pattern at the right. Then draw the figure.

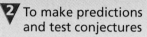

For a number pattern, a conjecture can be a rule that explains how to make and continue the pattern.

■ **EXAMPLE 2**

Number Patterns Write a rule for the number pattern 640, 320, 160, 80, . . . Find the next two numbers in the pattern.

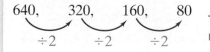

The first number is 640. The next numbers are found by dividing by 2.

The rule is *Start with 640 and divide by 2.* The next two numbers in the pattern are $80 \div 2 = 40$ and $40 \div 2 = 20$.

What You'll Learn

1 To write rules for patterns

2 To make predictions and test conjectures

. . . And Why

To use inductive reasoning in finding patterns and in making conjectures about economic data

The three dots in a pattern tell you that the pattern continues.

2. Write a rule for the pattern $1, 3, 5, 7, \ldots$ Find the next two numbers in the pattern.

■ **EXAMPLE 3**

Write a rule for each number pattern.

a. $30, 25, 20, 15, \ldots$ Start with 30 and subtract 5 repeatedly.

b. $2, -2, 2, -2, \ldots$ Alternate 2 and its opposite.

c. $1, 3, 4, 12, 13, \ldots$ Start with 1. Alternate multiplying by 3 and adding 1.

■ **TRY THIS**   Write a rule for each pattern.

3. $4, 9, 14, 19, \ldots$ **4.** $3, 9, 27, 81, \ldots$ **5.** $1, 1, 2, 3, 5, 8, \ldots$

PART 2 Predictions and Counterexamples

With sufficient information, you can make predictions based on reasonable conjectures. Such predictions will probably—but not necessarily—turn out to be accurate.

DATA ANALYSIS CONNECTION

■ **EXAMPLE 4**

Statistics **See the graph below. Is a conjecture that average hourly earnings in the year 2000 will be about $13 reasonable?**

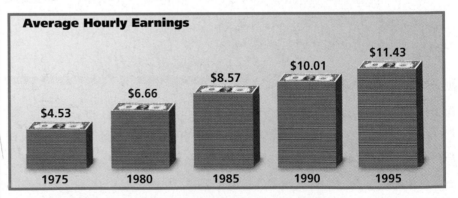

Average hourly earnings appear to increase by $1.50 to $2.00 every five years. The conjecture of $13 in 2000 is reasonable, since it is about $1.50 more than the earnings for 1995.

■ **TRY THIS**

6. You flip a coin four times, and it comes up heads each time. Is the conjecture *The coin will come up heads on every flip* reasonable? Explain.

An example that proves a statement false is a **counterexample.** You need only one counterexample to prove that a conjecture is incorrect.

■ **EXAMPLE 5**

Inductive Reasoning **Is each conjecture correct or incorrect? If it is incorrect, give a counterexample.**

a. **Every four-sided figure is a rectangle.**
   The conjecture is incorrect. The figure below has four sides, but it is not a rectangle.

b. **The absolute value of any integer is positive.**
   The conjecture is incorrect. The absolute value of zero is zero, which is neither positive nor negative.

c. **The next figure in the pattern below has 15 dots.**

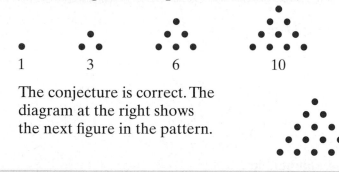

   1   3   6   10

   The conjecture is correct. The diagram at the right shows the next figure in the pattern.

■ **TRY THIS** Is each conjecture correct or incorrect? If it is incorrect, give a counterexample.

7. The last digit of the product of 5 and a whole number is either 0 or 5.

8. A number and its absolute value are always opposites.

Exercises

CHECK UNDERSTANDING

Geometry Describe the next figure in each pattern. Then
draw the figure.

1. 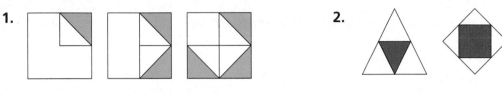 2.

Write a rule for each pattern. Find the next two numbers in
each pattern.

3. $100, 85, 70, 55, \ldots$ **4.** $5, 20, 80, 320, \ldots$ **5.** $1, 2, 5, 6, 9, \ldots$

Is each statement correct or incorrect? If it is incorrect, give a
counterexample.

6. All birds can fly.

7. Every square is a rectangle.

8. The product of two numbers is never less than
either of the numbers.

PRACTICE AND PROBLEM SOLVING

Geometry Describe the next figure in each pattern. Then
draw the figure.

9. 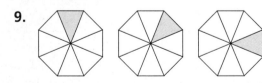 10.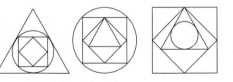

Write a rule for each pattern. Find the next three numbers in
the pattern.

11. $-10, -4, 2, 8, \ldots$ **12.** $1, 4, 7, 10, \ldots$

13. $1, 1.5, 2, 2.5, 3, \ldots$ **14.** $-1, 1, -2, 2, -3, 3, \ldots$

15. $1, 4, 10, 22, 46, 94, \ldots$ **16.** $1, -2, 4, -5, 7, -8, \ldots$

17. a. _Data Analysis_ Use the graph at the right. Make a conjecture about the unemployment rate in 1998. Justify your reasoning.
   b. How could you test your conjecture?

U.S. Unemployment Rate

Is each conjecture correct or incorrect? If it is incorrect, give a counterexample.

18. A clover always has three leaves.

19. The sum of two numbers is always greater than either of the two numbers.

20. A whole number is divisible by 3 if the sum of its digits is divisible by 3.

21. Mario caught a cold on each of his last three visits with his cousin. Is it reasonable for Mario to conclude that his catching a cold is the result of visiting his cousin? Explain.

22. **TEST PREP** Select the block that continues the given pattern.

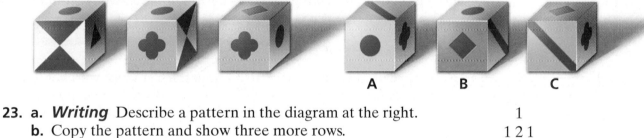

A   B   C

23. a. _Writing_ Describe a pattern in the diagram at the right.
   b. Copy the pattern and show three more rows.
   c. What is the sum of the numbers in each row?
   d. Predict the sum of the numbers in the ninth row.

```
        1
      1 2 1
    1 2 3 2 1
  1 2 3 4 3 2 1
1 2 3 4 5 4 3 2 1
```

▶ **MIXED REVIEW**

Find each difference. _(Lesson 1-6)_

24. $1 - 8$ **25.** $3 - (-6)$ **26.** $-4 - (-9)$ **27.** $86 - (-17)$

Evaluate each expression for $x = -1$ and $y = -3$. _(Lesson 1-5)_

28. $x + y$ **29.** $y + x + 2$ **30.** $-4 + x + y$

31. _Science_ The water in a stream flows at the rate of 1,500 gal/h.
   a. Write a variable expression for the amount of water that flows in n hours.
   b. Evaluate your expression for $n = 24$. _(Lesson 1-3)_

1-8

Look for a Pattern

Math Strategies in Action

What do songs on the radio, computer code, and your body's DNA have in common?

All are based on patterns. Radio uses patterns of electromagnetic waves. Computer code consists of patterns of numbers. Your DNA is made up of molecules that repeat in special patterns.

You can solve many types of problems by finding and using patterns. Making predictions from patterns is a form of inductive reasoning.

■ SAMPLE PROBLEM

News spreads quickly at Riverdell High. Each student who hears a story repeats it 15 minutes later to two students who have not yet heard it, and then tells no one else.

Suppose one student hears some news at 8:00 A.M. How many students will know the news at 9:00 A.M.?

 Read

1. How many students does each student tell?

2. How long does the news take to reach the second and third students?

 Plan

Make a table to organize the numbers. Then look for a pattern.

3. How many *new* students hear the news at 8:15 A.M.?

4. How many 15-minute periods are there between 8:00 A.M. and 9:00 A.M.?

 **Solve**

The pattern is to add the number of new students to the number who already know.

$$1 + 2 = 3 \quad \text{the number who know at 8:15}$$
$$3 + 4 = 7 \quad \text{the number who know at 8:30}$$

Make a table and extend the pattern to 9:00.

Time	8:00	8:15	8:30	8:45	9:00
Number of new students told	1	2	4	8	16
Number of students who know	1	1 + 2 = 3	3 + 4 = 7	7 + 8 = 15	15 + 16 = 31

By 9:00 A.M., 31 students know the news.

 **Look Back**

One way to check a solution is to solve the problem by another method. You can use a *tree diagram* to show the pattern visually.

	Time	New Students	Students Who Know
	8:00	1	1
	8:15	2	3
	8:30	4	7
	8:45	8	15
	9:00	16	31

5. Describe two ways to find the number of students who know the news at 9:15 A.M.

6. Suppose you want to continue the pattern beyond 9:15. Which would work better, a table or a tree diagram? Explain.

7. There are 251 students at Riverdell High. By what time will every student know the news?

Exercises

> ### CHECK UNDERSTANDING

Solve by looking for a pattern.

1. *Data Analysis* Caroline is training for a swim meet. The graph shows the number of laps per day she swims each week. If she keeps to this training pattern, how many laps per day will Caroline swim in week 8?

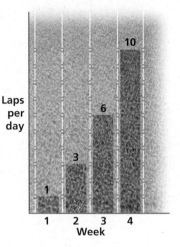

2. *Patterns* Students are to march in a parade. There will be one first-grader, two second-graders, three third-graders, and so on through the twelfth grade. How many students will march in the parade?

3. **a.** *Number Sense* Complete. Then look for a pattern.

$2 \cdot 2 = $ ■	$3 \cdot 3 = $ ■
$1 \cdot 3 = $ ■	$2 \cdot 4 = $ ■
Difference = ■	Difference = ■
$4 \cdot 4 = $ ■	$5 \cdot 5 = $ ■
$3 \cdot 5 = $ ■	$4 \cdot 6 = $ ■
Difference = ■	Difference = ■

   b. Which is greater, $10 \cdot 12$ or $11 \cdot 11$? How much is the difference?

   c. *Mathematical Reasoning* Suppose you know that $47 \cdot 47 = 2{,}209$. Use this to find $46 \cdot 48$.

   d. Suppose you know that $64 \cdot 66 = 4{,}224$. Use this to find $65 \cdot 65$.

4. Suppose that every day you save twice as many pennies as you saved the day before. You start by saving one penny on January 1. How much money will you have in all by January 10?

> ### PRACTICE AND PROBLEM SOLVING

Solve using any strategy.

5. Roland has an appointment tomorrow at 8:45 A.M. He wants to arrive at least fifteen minutes early. It takes him one hour to get ready and 45 minutes to drive to the appointment. At what time should Roland plan to get up?

6. **Geometry** You can cut a pizza into two pieces with one straight cut. With two cuts you can get four pieces. Three cuts give a maximum of seven pieces. What is the maximum number of pieces with four cuts? With five cuts?

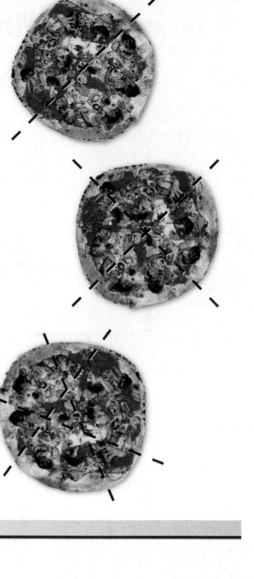

7. A restaurant offers a buffet dinner at group prices. It costs $10 for one person, $20 for two, $29 for three, $37 for four, $44 for five, and so on.
   a. How much does a buffet dinner for 8 cost? How much does a group of eight save if its members eat together rather than alone?
   b. The buffet costs the restaurant $6 per person. How large a group can the restaurant serve without losing money?

8. Jayne has 3 quarters, 2 dimes, a nickel, and 2 pennies in her pocket. How many different amounts of money can she make using some or all of these coins?

9. One edition of *Alice's Adventures in Wonderland* has 352 pages. How many 4's were used in the page numbers?

10. A woman jogging at 6 mi/h passes a man biking in the opposite direction at 12 mi/h. If they maintain their speeds, how far from each other will they be 10 min after passing?

▶ MIXED REVIEW

Geometry Describe the next figure in each pattern. Then draw the figure. *(Lesson 1-7)*

11.

12.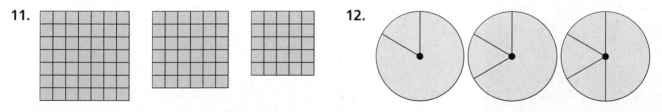

Evaluate each expression for $m = 1$ **and** $n = 4$. *(Lesson 1-3)*

13. $4m - n$

14. $4(n + 2) + m$

15. $11n - 5$

16. $mn + 13$

17. **Weather** At midnight, the temperature was $-5°F$. By dawn, the temperature had risen 14 degrees. What was the temperature at dawn? *(Lesson 1-5)*

1-9

Multiplying and Dividing Integers

What You'll Learn

1 To multiply integers using repeated addition, patterns, and rules

2 To divide integers

...And Why

To solve real-world problems involving deep-sea exploration and currency

Investigate

· PREPARING TO MULTIPLY INTEGERS ·

1. Copy and complete the table. The first row is done for you.

Multiplication	Repeated Addition	Sum
$3 \cdot (-5)$	$-5 + (-5) + (-5)$	-15
$5 \cdot (-4)$	■	■
$2 \cdot (-8)$	■	■
$4 \cdot (-10)$	■	■

2. What do you notice about the signs of the sums?

3. *Inductive Reasoning* What does the pattern suggest about the product of a positive integer and a negative integer?

PART 1 Multiplying Integers

You can think of multiplication as repeated addition.

REAL-WORLD CONNECTION

■ EXAMPLE 1

Deep Sea Exploration **After it is launched from a boat, *Deep Rover* descends 60 ft/min. Where is it in relation to sea level 3 min after its launch?**

Use a number line to show repeated addition.

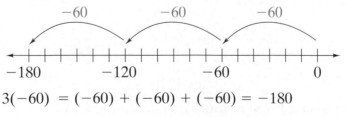

$3(-60) = (-60) + (-60) + (-60) = -180$

Deep Rover is at -180 feet, or 180 feet below sea level.

■ **TRY THIS** Simplify each product.

4. $2(-6)$ **5.** $4(-3)$ **6.** $7(-2)$

Scientists explore the deep waters of the Pacific Ocean in *Deep Rover*, a submersible designed for research.

You can use patterns to simplify the product of a negative number and a positive number, or the product of two negative numbers.

■ EXAMPLE 2

Patterns **Use a pattern to find each product.**

a. −2(5)

$2(5) = 10$	**Start with products you know.**
$1(5) = 5$	
$0(5) = 0$	
$-1(5) = -5$	**Continue the pattern.**
$-2(5) = -10$	

b. −2(−5)

$2(-5) = -10$
$1(-5) = -5$
$0(-5) = 0$
$-1(-5) = 5$
$-2(-5) = 10$

Writing Math

Symbols for multiplication:

$\times$	-2×2
$\cdot$	$-2 \cdot 2$
( )	$-2(3)$
*	$-2 * 3$

■ TRY THIS

7. *Patterns* Use a pattern to simplify $-3(-4)$.

By inductive reasoning, the patterns from Example 2 suggest rules for multiplying integers.

Multiplying Integers

The product of two integers with the same sign is positive.
The product of two integers with different signs is negative.
The product of zero and any integer is zero.

Examples

$3(4) = 12$	$3(-4) = -12$
$-3(-4) = 12$	$-3(4) = -12$
$3(0) = 0$	$-4(0) = 0$

■ EXAMPLE 3

Multiply $-3 \cdot 5(-4)$.

$-3 \cdot 5(-4) = -15(-4)$ **Multiply from left to right. The product of a negative integer and a positive integer is negative.**

$= 60$ **Multiply. The product of two negative integers is positive.**

■ TRY THIS Simplify each product.

8. $-4 \cdot 8(-2)$ **9.** $6(-3)(5)$ **10.** $-7 \cdot (-14) \cdot 0$

The rules for dividing integers are similar to those for multiplying.

Dividing Integers

The quotient of two integers with the same sign is positive.
The quotient of two integers with opposite signs is negative.
Remember that division by zero is undefined.

Examples $\qquad$ $12 \div 3 = 4$ $\qquad$ $12 \div (-3) = -4$

$\qquad\qquad\qquad$ $-12 \div (-3) = 4$ $\qquad$ $-12 \div 3 = -4$

DATA ANALYSIS CONNECTION

■ EXAMPLE 4

Currency **Find the average of the differences in the values of a Canadian dollar and a U.S. dollar for 1994–1998.**

Value of Dollars (U.S. cents)

Year	Canadian Dollar	U.S. Dollar	Difference
1994	73	100	−27
1995	73	100	−27
1996	74	100	−26
1997	72	100	−28
1998	68	100	−32

SOURCES: Bank of Canada; *The World Almanac*

$\dfrac{-27 + (-27) + (-26) + (-28) + (-32)}{5}$ $\qquad$ Write an expression for the average.

$= \dfrac{-140}{5}$ $\qquad$ Use the order of operations. The fraction bar acts as a grouping symbol.

$= -28$ $\qquad$ The quotient of a negative integer and a positive integer is negative.

For 1994–1998, the average difference was −28¢. The Canadian dollar was worth an average of 28¢ less than the U.S. dollar.

■ **TRY THIS** Simplify each quotient.

11. $-32 \div 8$ $\qquad$ **12.** $-48 \div (-6)$ $\qquad$ **13.** $-56 \div (-4)$

14. Find the average of $4, -3, -5, 2,$ and -8.

Exercises

▶ **CHECK UNDERSTANDING**

Write each sum as a product. Find the product.

1. $(-9) + (-9) + (-9) + (-9)$

2. $(-5) + (-5) + (-5) + (-5) + (-5)$

Without computing, tell whether each product or quotient is *positive* **or** *negative***. Explain your reasoning.**

3. $-6(-20)$

4. $7(-83)$

5. $39 \div (-3)$

6. $-3(8)(-24)$

Simplify each expression.

7. $-3 \cdot 10$

8. $-25 \div 5$

9. $4(-11)$

10. $-90 \div (-9)$

11. a. What is the product of -6 and -1?
　　b. How are that product and -6 related?
　　c. *Inductive Reasoning* Complete: The product of any integer and -1 is the __?__ of the integer.

▶ **PRACTICE AND PROBLEM SOLVING**

Mental Math **Find each product or quotient.**

12. $-5(-3)$

13. $-6 \cdot 10$

14. $-10 \cdot 0$

15. $24 \div (-24)$

16. $18 \div (-1)$

17. $-120 \div 12$

Choose **Use repeated addition, patterns, or rules to find each product or quotient.**

18. $24(-16)(-32)$

19. $-9(-8)(-5)$

20. $0(-12) \cdot 4$

21. $|-2| \cdot (-7)$

22. $-59(-79)$

23. $243(-88)$

24. $8 \cdot 3(-4)$

25. $-38 \div (-2)$

26. $-200 \div 25$

27. $-18(-12)$

28. $38(-2)$

29. $-72 \div 6$

30. $1,000 \div (-50)$

31. $-33 \div 11$

32. $225 \div (-15)$

33. $-58 \div (-1)$

34. $-72 \div (-8)$

35. $5,959 \div (-101)$

36. $\dfrac{-1,225}{35}$

37. $\dfrac{3,132}{-36}$

38. $\dfrac{-56 \cdot 12}{-24}$

39. Write a number sentence for the product shown on the number line.

Name the point on the number line that is the graph of each product.

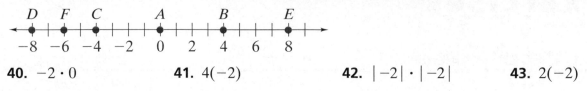

40. $-2 \cdot 0$ **41.** $4(-2)$ **42.** $|-2| \cdot |-2|$ **43.** $2(-2)$

Compare. Use >, <, or = to complete each statement.

44. $(-9)(-6)$ ■ $8(-10)$ **45.** $5(-2)$ ■ $(-6)(-1)$

46. $-10 \div (-2)$ ■ $25 \div (-5)$ **47.** $-(-15 \div 5)$ ■ $-100 \div (-20)$

48. $|-25| \div |-5|$ ■ $|-25 \div (-5)|$ **49.** $-|-28| \div 7$ ■ $-28 \div (-7)$

Open-ended **Simplify each pair of expressions. Then write an integer whose value is between the values of the expressions.**

50. $-2 \cdot (-2)$ and $2 \cdot 4$ **51.** $10 + (-7)$ and $10 \div (-5)$

52. $121 \div (-11)$ and $|-7| - |7|$ **53.** $50 + (-48)$ and $80 \div (-20)$

For each group, find the average.

54. temperatures: $-9°C, -12°C, 9°C, 4°C, -2°C$

55. football yardage: $10, -5, 7, 9, -11$

56. golf scores: $-3, 4, 2, 1, -4, -1, 3, -2$

57. bank balances: $\$200, -\$85, \$120, \$200, \$280$

58. feet above and below sea level: $135, -56, 92, -29, -88, -60$

59. ***Weather*** The temperature dropped 5 degrees each hour for 7 h. Use an integer to represent the total change in temperature.

60. ***Investing*** The price of one share of a stock fell $3 each day for 12 days.
    a. What was the total change in price of a share of the stock?
    b. The original stock price was $76 per share. What was the price after the drop?

61. a. ***Inductive Reasoning*** Will the sign be positive or negative for the product of three negative integers? Of four negative integers? Of five negative integers?
    b. ***Writing*** Use inductive reasoning to write a rule for the sign of the product of more than two negative integers.

62. A scuba diver descended to a depth of 50 feet in 25 seconds. Write an integer to represent the average number of feet per second the diver traveled.

63. What integer multiplied by -8 equals -96?

64. What integer multiplied by 9 equals -135?

65. What two integers have a sum of negative ten and a product of negative seventy-five?

66. *Mathematical Reasoning* If a and b are positive integers, and x and y are negative integers, what is the sign of $\frac{a + b}{x + y}$? Explain.

▶ MIXED REVIEW

Compare. Use $>$, $<$, or $=$ to complete each statement. *(Lessons 1-5 and 1-6)*

67. $-3 + (-8)$ ■ $12 - (-6)$ **68.** $-9 + 13$ ■ $24 - 30$ **69.** $|-6| - |12|$ ■ $-8 + |-12|$

Write a variable expression for each word phrase. *(Lesson 1-1)*

70. the product of y and 60 **71.** 50 decreased by a number **72.** the quotient of d and 5

73. *Choose a Strategy* How many whole numbers between 10 and 200 have exactly two identical digits?

◢ CHECKPOINT 2   Lessons 1-5 through 1-9

Simplify each expression.

1. $3 + (-11)$ **2.** $12 - (-8)$ **3.** $-9 \cdot 5$

4. $-64 \div (-8)$ **5.** $-8(-3)(3)$ **6.** $|-3| \cdot 8 \div (-2)$

Open-ended **Use integers to complete each equation.**

7. ■ $+$ ■ $= -7$ **8.** ■ $- (-20) =$ ■   **9.** ■ $\cdot$ ■ $= -40$

Patterns **Find the next three numbers in each pattern.**

10. $-7, -2, 3, 8,$ ■, ■, ■   **11.** $1, 3, 9, 27,$ ■, ■, ■

12. [TEST PREP] What is the average temperature for the five days?

Day	Mon.	Tue.	Wed.	Thu.	Fri.
Temperature	$-3°F$	$2°F$	$1°F$	$-4°F$	$-6°F$

  A. $-2°F$ **B.** $-1°F$ **C.** $2°F$ **D.** $1°F$

1-10

The Coordinate Plane

What You'll Learn

1 To name coordinates and quadrants in the coordinate plane

2 To graph points in the coordinate plane

...And Why

To use a graph to define locations of points

PART 1 Naming Coordinates and Quadrants

A **coordinate plane** is formed by the intersection of two number lines. The horizontal number line is called the **x-axis** and the vertical number line is called the **y-axis.**

The *x*- and *y*-axes divide the coordinate plane into four **quadrants.**

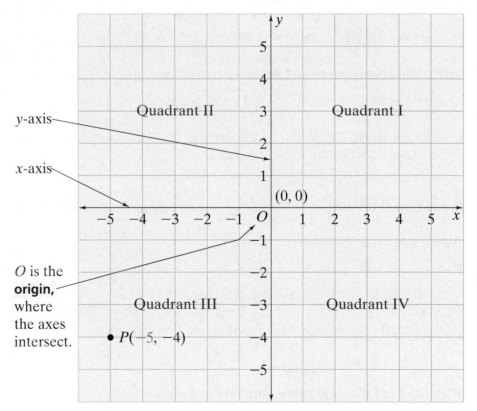

An **ordered pair** gives the coordinates and location of a point. The ordered pair $(-5, -4)$ identifies point P in Quadrant III above.

(−5, −4)

The **x-coordinate** shows the position left or right of the *y*-axis.

The **y-coordinate** shows the position above or below the *x*-axis.

■ EXAMPLE 1

Write the coordinates of point *A*. In which quadrant is point *A* located?

Point *A* is located 2 units to the left of the *y*-axis. So the *x*-coordinate is –2. The point is 1 unit above the *x*-axis. So the *y*-coordinate is 1.

The coordinates of point *A* are $(-2, 1)$. Point *A* is located in Quadrant II.

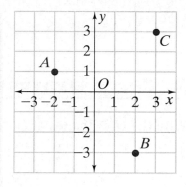

■ TRY THIS

1. Use the graph in Example 1. Write the coordinates of *B* and *C*.

2. Identify the quadrants in which *B* and *C* are located.

◤ PART 2 ⬛ Graphing Points

To graph a point $A(x, y)$ in a coordinate plane, you graph the ordered pair (x, y).

■ EXAMPLE 2

Graph point *R*(3, –5).

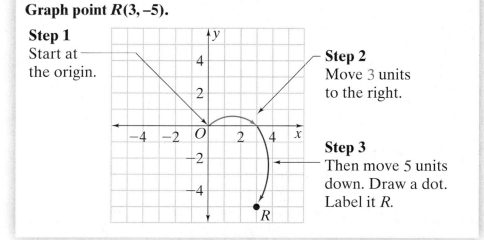

Step 1
Start at the origin.

Step 2
Move 3 units to the right.

Step 3
Then move 5 units down. Draw a dot. Label it *R*.

■ TRY THIS

3. **a.** Graph these points on one coordinate plane: $K(3, 1)$, $L(-2, 1)$, and $M(-2, -4)$.
   b. *Geometry* Draw lines to connect points *K*, *L,* and *M*. Describe the figure that results.

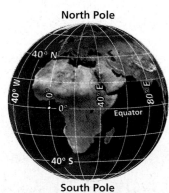

North Pole

South Pole

Geography Latitude and longitude are measurements in a coordinate system that locates every point on Earth's surface.

Exercises

CHECK UNDERSTANDING

Write the coordinates of each point.

1. T
2. V
3. M
4. K

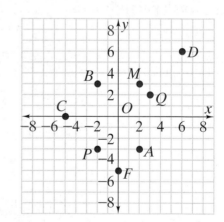

Name the point with the given coordinates.

5. $(-3, -4)$
6. $(3, 0)$
7. $(-2, 4)$
8. $(-4, -2)$

9. What ordered pair names the origin?

Draw a coordinate plane. Graph each point.

10. $A(-1, 3)$
11. $B(-4, -1)$
12. $C(2, 5)$
13. $D(2, -2)$
14. $F(0, 6)$
15. $G(6, 0)$

PRACTICE AND PROBLEM SOLVING

Name the point with the given coordinates.

16. $(3, 2)$
17. $(0, -5)$
18. $(2, 3)$
19. $(-2, -3)$

Write the coordinates of each point.

20. A
21. B
22. C
23. D

Mental Math Write the coordinates of each point.

24. the point 5 units to the left of the y-axis and 2 units below the x-axis

25. the point on the y-axis 4 units below the x-axis

26. the point on the x-axis 3 units to the right of the origin

Mental Math In which quadrant does $P(x, y)$ lie?

27. x is positive and y is negative.
28. x is positive and y is positive.
29. x is negative and y is positive.
30. x is negative and y is negative.

31. **TEST PREP** Fill in the blanks: $P(a, b)$ is in quadrant III.
The value of a must be __?__ . The value of b must be __?__ .
A. positive; positive   **B.** positive; negative
C. negative; positive   **D.** negative; negative

In which quadrant or on which axis does each ordered pair lie?

32. $(13, 25)$

33. $(-17, -2)$

34. (x, y) if $x = 0, y > 0$

35. (x, y) if $x > 0, y < 0$

36. (x, y) if $x < 0, y > 0$

37. $(0, |-2|)$

Draw a coordinate plane. Graph each point.

38. $F(-3, 2)$

39. $G(-5, -2)$

40. $H(1, 7)$

41. $K(5, -6)$

42. $L(0, 0)$

43. $N(7, 0)$

44. $P(-1, -3)$

45. $Q(1, 1)$

46. $R(0, -4)$

Geometry **Graph and connect the points in the order given.**
Connect the last point to the first. Name the figure.

47. $(2, 2), (2, -1), (-5, -1), (-5, 2)$

48. $(-4, 1), (1, 1), (-3, -1)$

49. $(2, -4), (7, -1), (4, 4), (-1, 1)$

50. $(-1, 2), (1, 5), (7, 5), (5, 2)$

Geometry ***PQRS*** **is a square. Find the coordinates of *S*.**

51. $P(-5, 0), Q(0, 5), R(5, 0), S(\blacksquare, \blacksquare)$

52. $P(-1, 3), Q(4, 3), R(4, -2), S(\blacksquare, \blacksquare)$

Geography **On a map, coordinates are given in degrees of longitude**
and latitude. Use the map below for Exercises 53–55.

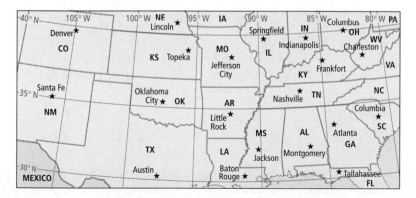

SAMPLE The longitude of Little Rock, Arkansas, is about 92° W
and the latitude is about 34° N.

53. Find the longitude and latitude of Jackson, Mississippi.

54. Find the longitude and latitude of Topeka, Kansas.

55. What city is located near 85° W, 38° N?

56. *Mathematical Reasoning* Assume that $a \neq b$. Do (a, b) and (b, a) describe the same point? Explain.

57. Write the coordinates of four points in the coordinate plane that are 3 units from the origin. Graph the points.

58. *Open-ended* Draw a dot-to-dot picture on a coordinate grid. Write the coordinates of the points in order. Exchange coordinates with a classmate and draw the other's picture.

Geometry Use one coordinate plane for Exercises 59–61.

59. Graph the points $(-2, 1), (-2, 3), (1, 3),$ and $(1, 1)$. Connect them in the order given. Connect the last point to the first.

60. Transform the coordinates of Exercise 59 as described below. Graph and connect each new set of coordinates. Use a different color for each set.
  a. Multiply each x-coordinate by -1.
  b. Multiply each y-coordinate by -1.
  c. Multiply each coordinate by -1.
  d. Multiply each coordinate by 2.

61. *Writing* Compare each figure in Exercise 60 to the figure in Exercise 59. Write a short paragraph describing your results.

Journal

Describe how to graph Q(4, −3) and four other points, each 1 unit from Q.

▶ MIXED REVIEW

Find each product or quotient. *(Lesson 1-9)*

62. $-11 \cdot 11$

63. $-432 \div 48$

64. $\dfrac{0}{-56}$

Write the value of each expression. *(Lesson 1-4)*

65. $|-8|$

66. $-|-95|$

67. the opposite of 12

68. A submarine at sea level dives 800 ft and then another 125 ft. Find the submarine's final depth. *(Lesson 1-5)*

CHAPTER PROJECT 1 **ACTIVITY 3 CREATING**

Codes don't always use numbers or letters. In "The Adventure of the Dancing Men," the detective Sherlock Holmes used deductive reasoning to decipher the code at the right. It substitutes stick figures for letters. Using the substitution symbols of your choice, invent a cipher. Use it to write a message. Don't forget to provide the key!

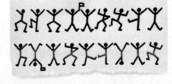

See also Extra Practice section.

Cure for the Common Code

Invent a Secret Code The Project Activities on pages 16, 33, and 54 will help you complete your project. Here is a checklist to help you gather the different parts.

✔ your decoding of the ASCII message

✔ your letter in Caesar Cipher

✔ a cipher of your own creation, including a message and key

Make a poster to display the cipher you invented. Explain how it works. Include a sample of the cipher and its English translation. You may wish to use a table to illustrate the cipher's key.

Reflect and Revise

Ask a friend or someone at home to review your poster. Are your explanations and illustrations clear? If necessary, make changes to improve your poster.

Web Extension

Visit Prentice Hall's Web site. You'll find some interesting links and ideas related to codes. You'll also be able to share information about your project.

www.phschool.com

Wrap Up

■ Key Terms

absolute value (p. 18)
conjecture (p. 35)
coordinate plane (p. 50)
counterexample (p. 37)
evaluate (p. 13)
integers (p. 18)

inductive reasoning (p. 35)
opposites (p. 18)
order of operations (p. 8)
ordered pair (p. 50)
origin (p. 50)
quadrants (p. 50)

variable (p. 4)
variable expression (p. 4)
x-axis (p. 50)
x-coordinate (p. 50)
y-axis (p. 50)
y-coordinate (p. 50)

■ Graphic Organizer

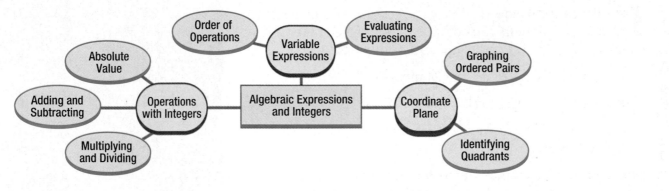

■ Variables and Expressions   1-1

Summary A **variable** is a letter that stands for a number. A **variable expression**
is a mathematical phrase that uses variables, numerals, and operation
symbols.

Write a variable expression for each word phrase.

1. twenty-five less than x

2. the product of n and 3

3. two more than y

4. ten decreased by t

5. a number n increased by 5

6. a number x divided by 4

■ The Order of Operations   1-2

Summary To simplify a numerical expression, follow the **order of operations.**
   1. Work inside grouping symbols.
   2. Multiply and divide in order from left to right.
   3. Add and subtract in order from left to right.

Simplify each expression.

7. $3 \cdot 7 + 6 \div 2$

8. $(4 + 8) \div 2 \cdot 2$

9. $9 \cdot 5 - 4(12 \div 6)$

■ Evaluating Expressions

Summary To **evaluate** a variable expression, substitute a number for each variable. Use the order of operations to simplify.

Evaluate each expression.

10. $3x + 4$ for $x = 5$

11. $15 + 10 \div n$ for $n = 5$

12. $(y - 6)2$ for $y = 16$

13. $4(4 + m)$ for $m = 6$

14. $15t \cdot 10$ for $t = 3$

15. $z + [15 - (z - 1)]$ for $z = 4$

■ Integers and Absolute Value

Summary **Integers** are the set of whole numbers and their **opposites.** The **absolute value** of an integer is its distance from zero on a number line. On a number line, the integer farther to the right is the greater integer.

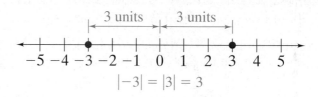

$|-3| = |3| = 3$

Simplify each expression.

16. the opposite of 17

17. $|-1,000|$

18. the absolute value of negative nine

19. the opposite of the absolute value of 12

Compare. Use $>, <,$ or $=$ to complete each statement.

20. $-7 \ \blacksquare \ -9$

21. $0 \ \blacksquare \ -3$

22. $|-5| \ \blacksquare \ |5|$

23. $-6 \ \blacksquare \ 2$

24. *Writing* Explain how you would use integers to describe the changing elevation of a hot-air balloon.

■ Adding and Subtracting Integers

Summary To add integers with the *same* sign, add their absolute values. The sum has the same sign as the integers. To add integers with *different* signs, find the difference of their absolute values. The sum has the sign of the integer with the greater absolute value. To subtract an integer, add its opposite.

Simplify each expression.

25. $8 + (-15)$

26. $-9 + 21$

27. $9 - (-5)$

28. $-7 - 4$

29. $-62 - (-59) - 24$

30. $14 + (-9) + (-20)$

31. $-4 + 12 + (-3) + (-6)$

■ Inductive Reasoning

Summary **Inductive reasoning** is making conclusions based on patterns you observe. A conclusion reached by inductive reasoning is a **conjecture**.

Write a rule for each pattern. Find the next three numbers in the pattern.

32. $0, 6, 12, 18, \ldots$
33. $-18, -9, 0, 9, \ldots$
34. $\frac{1}{2}, 1, 1\frac{1}{2}, 2, \ldots$

■ Look for a Pattern

Summary You can use patterns to solve problems.

35. Suppose you plan to save $12 per week. You have already saved $7.50. In how many weeks will you have saved at least $100?

36. A four-line classified ad costs $28 for a week. Each additional line costs $10.50. What is the weekly cost of a 12-line ad?

■ Multiplying and Dividing Integers

Summary To multiply or divide integers, multiply or divide the absolute values of the integers. If the integers have the same sign, the product or quotient is positive. If the integers have different signs, the product or quotient is negative.

Multiply or divide.

37. $7(-6)$
38. $250 \div (-50)$
39. $(-9)(-8)$
40. $-56 \div (-8)$

41. $-120 \div 40$
42. $-15(11)$
43. $\frac{-64}{8}$
44. $(-5)(-7)$

■ Graphing in the Coordinate Plane

Summary A **coordinate plane** is formed by the intersection of two number lines. The ***x*-axis** and the ***y*-axis** divide the coordinate plane into four **quadrants**. An **ordered pair** gives the coordinates of a point. The ***x*-coordinate** shows the position left or right of the *y*-axis. The ***y*-coordinate** shows the position above or below the *x*-axis.

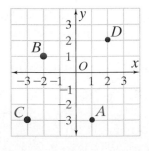

Write the coordinates of each point.

45. *A*
46. *B*
47. *C*
48. *D*

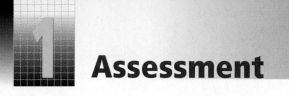

Assessment

Write an expression for each phrase.

1. a number n increased by nineteen

2. ten less than negative three

3. the product of x and negative five

4. 5 more than the opposite of y

Evaluate each expression for the given values of the variables.

5. $3a + 5$, for $a = -5$

6. $5m + 9 + 7n$, for $m = 8$ and $n = 1$

7. $3|x - y| + x$, for $x = 1$ and $y = 8$

8. $20 - 2(a - b)$, for $a = 3$ and $b = 2$

Simplify each expression.

9. $|-5|$
10. opposite of -9
11. opposite of 7
12. $|15|$

Use >, <, or = to complete each sentence.

13. $-6 \; \blacksquare \; -5$
14. $8 \; \blacksquare \; -10$
15. $-3 \; \blacksquare \; 3$
16. $0 \; \blacksquare \; -7$

Simplify each expression.

17. $15 + (-7)$
18. $-8 - (-12)$
19. $-9(-7)$
20. $54 \div (-6)$
21. $-6 \cdot 48$
22. $\frac{-56}{-7}$
23. $119 - (-24)$
24. $-47 + (-21)$
25. $-83 + 17$
26. $5(-12)(-3)(-1)$
27. $2|14 - (-9)|$
28. $8 \cdot 6 \div (2 + 1)$
29. $4 + 7 \cdot 2 + 8$
30. $16 - 2 \cdot (5 + 3)$

In which quadrant or on which axis does each point lie?

31. $(-5, 7)$
32. $(0, -4)$
33. $(-8, -6)$

Write the coordinates of each point.

34. F
35. G
36. H
37. J

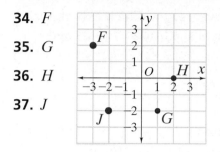

38. A shirt costs $15 and jeans cost $25.
    a. Write an expression for the cost of j jeans and s shirts.
    b. Evaluate the expression to find the cost of three pairs of jeans and five shirts.
    c. How many pairs of jeans can you buy for $60?

39. Which statement is *always* true?
    A. The absolute value of an integer is equal to the opposite of the integer.
    B. The absolute value of an integer is greater than zero.
    C. An integer is greater than its opposite.
    D. A positive integer is greater than a negative integer.

40. A submarine was 250 m below sea level. It rose 75 m. Use an integer to describe the new depth of the submarine.

41. Write a rule for the pattern below. Find the next two numbers in the pattern.

    $100, 90, 85, 75, 70, 60, \ldots$

42. You are in an elevator on the seventh floor. You go down 4 floors, and then up 8 floors. Then you go down 3 floors and up 9 floors. The elevator goes down again, and you get off. According to the pattern, on which floor are you now?

43. *Writing* Describe how to order the integers $2, -6, 9, 0,$ and -13 from least to greatest.

Choose the best answer.

1. A bridge is *t* years old. Which expression gives the age of the bridge 5 years ago?
   A. $t - 5$
   B. $5 - t$
   C. $t + 5$
   D. $\frac{t}{5}$

2. A florist sold five plants for $7 each and two wreaths for $12 each. Which expression gives the sales total?
   F. $(5 + 7) \cdot (2 + 12)$
   G. $(5 \cdot 7)(2 + 12)$
   H. $5 \cdot 7 + 2 \cdot 12$
   J. $5 \cdot (7 + 12)$

3. Evaluate $12a$ for $a = 4$.
   A. 8   B. 16
   C. 48   D. 3

4. Which statement is true?
   F. -2 is less than 2.
   G. -6 is greater than -4.
   H. $|-5|$ is greater than 6.
   J. -7 is greater than $|-6|$.

5. Find the sum of -4 and -3.
   A. -7 B. 1
   C. 7   D. -1

6. Which expression has a value that is different from the value of the other expressions?
   F. $9 - 3$
   G. $|3 - 9|$
   H. $-9 - 3$
   J. $9 + (-3)$

7. Find $-10 + (-18)$.
   A. -28 B. -8
   C. 8   D. 28

8. Find $-20 - (-9)$.
   F. -11 G. -29
   H. 29   J. 11

9. Which statement is *not* true?
   A. $|-3| > |-2|$
   B. $|-5| < |1 - 7|$
   C. $|-6 + 2| = |4|$
   D. $|-1| < 0$

10. In which quadrant does the point with the coordinates $(-3, -4)$ lie?
    F. I
    G. II
    H. III
    J. IV

For Exercises 11–19, show your work.

11. Write a rule for the pattern $1, -2, 4, -8, \ldots$ Find the next two numbers in the pattern.

12. The number of boys *b* on the swim team is one fifth of the number of girls. Write a variable expression for the number of girls on the team.

13. Simplify $6 \cdot 2 - 5 - (2 + 2) - 1$.

14. Insert grouping symbols to make the number sentence true.
    $3 \cdot 4 + 6 - 2 \cdot 3 = 24$

15. On a number line, graph $|-5|, -2, 0, |-3|$, and 1.

16. Evaluate $\frac{c + a}{2}$ for $a = 3$ and $c = 8$.

17. Find $|-3| \cdot (-4)$.

18. Find $-44 \div 2$.

19. Write the coordinates of points *A*, *B*, and *C*.

Skills You Need for Chapter 2

► Order of operations with integers

Use before Lesson 2-2.

Simplify each expression.

1. $5 \cdot 2 + 5 \cdot 3$
2. $7(6 - 2)$
3. $10 \cdot 3 - 5 \cdot 3$
4. $-(34 + 76)$
5. $4(6) + 4(3)$
6. $-4(12 - 16)$
7. $7(8) - 10(8)$
8. $11 \cdot 9 - 6 \cdot 9$
9. $-2 \cdot 3 - 2 \cdot 7$
10. $6 \cdot (-9) - 3(-9)$
11. $4(12) + 4(6)$
12. $12(-14 + 8)$
13. $(24 - 15)(-2)$
14. $-5(3) - (-5)(2)$
15. $(72 - 81)(5)$

► Inverse operations

Use before Lessons 2-5 and 2-6.

Complete the related equations.

16. $\blacksquare + 5 = 8$ $8 - \blacksquare = 5$
17. $20 - \blacksquare = 9$ $9 + \blacksquare = 20$
18. $-2 + \blacksquare = 3$ $3 - \blacksquare = -2$
19. $90 - \blacksquare = 55$ $55 + \blacksquare = 90$
20. $20 - \blacksquare = 23$ $23 + \blacksquare = 20$
21. $\blacksquare + 12 = -7$ $-7 - \blacksquare = 12$
22. $5 \cdot \blacksquare = 30$ $30 \div \blacksquare = 5$
23. $3 \cdot \blacksquare = 75$ $75 \div \blacksquare = 3$
24. $72 \div \blacksquare = 12$ $12 \cdot \blacksquare = 72$
25. $100 \div 20 = \blacksquare$ $20 \cdot \blacksquare = 100$
26. $2 \cdot \blacksquare = -14$ $-14 \div \blacksquare = 2$
27. $-36 \div \blacksquare = -6$ $-6 \cdot \blacksquare = -36$
28. $\blacksquare \cdot (-10) = -70$ $-70 \div \blacksquare = -10$
29. $52 \div \blacksquare = 4$ $4 \cdot \blacksquare = 52$

► Comparing numbers

Use before Lesson 2-8.

Compare. Use >, <, or = to complete each statement.

30. $6 \ \blacksquare \ 16$
31. $5 \ \blacksquare \ -5$
32. $36 \ \blacksquare \ 15$
33. $-52 \ \blacksquare \ -21$
34. $0 \ \blacksquare \ -8$
35. $-7 \ \blacksquare \ 3$
36. $12 + 3 \ \blacksquare \ 19 - 4$
37. $5(4) \ \blacksquare \ 7$
38. $18 - 27 \ \blacksquare \ -34 + 12$
39. $27 \div 9 \ \blacksquare \ 6 \cdot 2$
40. $-2 \cdot 6 \ \blacksquare \ 4 \cdot (-3)$
41. $-8 \div 2 \ \blacksquare \ 9 \div 3$
42. $8(-5) \ \blacksquare \ 100 - 65$
43. $3(-2)(-4) \ \blacksquare \ 4(-3)(2)$
44. $6 \div (10 - 8) \ \blacksquare \ 1 + 5$

CHAPTER 2

Solving One-Step Equations and Inequalities

What you'll learn in this chapter:

- How to use the Distributive Property

- How to write and solve equations

- How to write, solve, and graph inequalities

DON'T LOSE YOUR BALANCE!

Have you ever used a balance in your science class? Balances make very precise measurements in science, industry, and government. The United States Mint, for example, ensures that the coins it produces meet exact specifications. You can make your own version of a balance and use it to compare the masses of different objects.

Make a Balance Scale For the chapter project, you will make a simple balance scale. You will use it to write and solve equations and inequalities for the masses of different coins.

Steps to help you complete the project

Web Extension
www.phschool.com

How to solve a problem by Try, Test, Revise

2-1

Properties of Numbers

PART 1 **Identifying Properties**

What You'll Learn

1 To identify properties of addition and multiplication

2 To use properties to solve problems

. . . And Why

To find answers quickly using mental math

The sum of 6 and 4 is the same as the sum of 4 and 6. Similarly, the product of 9 and 5 is the same as the product of 5 and 9. These suggest the following properties.

Commutative Properties of Addition and Multiplication

Changing the order of the values you are adding or multiplying does not change the sum or product.

Arithmetic	Algebra
$6 + 4 = 4 + 6$	$a + b = b + a$
$9 \cdot 5 = 5 \cdot 9$	$a \cdot b = b \cdot a$

You can also change the grouping of numbers before you add or multiply them.

Associative Properties of Addition and Multiplication

Changing the grouping of the values you are adding or multiplying does not change the sum or product.

Arithmetic	Algebra
$(2 + 7) + 3 = 2 + (7 + 3)$	$(a + b) + c = a + (b + c)$
$(9 \cdot 4)5 = 9(4 \cdot 5)$	$(ab)c = a(bc)$

REAL-WORLD CONNECTION

■ **EXAMPLE 1**

Carlos rented a set of golf clubs for $7 and a golf cart for $12. He paid a greens fee of $23. Find his total cost.

You can use the Associative Property of Addition to find the total cost in two different ways.

$(7 + 12) + 23 = 19 + 23 = 42$ **Add 7 and 12 first.**

$7 + (12 + 23) = 7 + 35 = 42$ **Add 12 and 23 first.**

Carlos's total cost was $42.

When you use the order of operations, you do operations within grouping symbols first.

■ TRY THIS

1. You go out with friends. You spend $6 for dinner, $8 for a movie, and $4 for popcorn. Find your total cost. Explain which property or properties you used.

When you add a number and 0, the sum equals the original number. The **additive identity** is 0. When you multiply a number and 1, the product equals the original number. The **multiplicative identity** is 1.

Identity Properties of Addition and Multiplication

The sum of any number and zero is the original number. The product of any number and 1 is the original number.

Arithmetic	Algebra
$12 + 0 = 12$	$a + 0 = a$
$10 \cdot 1 = 10$	$a \cdot 1 = a$

■ EXAMPLE 2

Name each property shown.

a. $5 \cdot 7 = 7 \cdot 5$ — Commutative Property of Multiplication
b. $c \cdot 1 = c$ — Identity Property of Multiplication
c. $7 + a = a + 7$ — Commutative Property of Addition
d. $5(xy) = (5x)y$ — Associative Property of Multiplication

■ TRY THIS Name each property shown.

2. $3 + 6 = 6 + 3$ **3.** $8 = 1 \times 8$ **4.** $(3z)m = 3(zm)$

PART 2 Using Properties

You can use properties and mental math to help you find sums.

■ EXAMPLE 3

Use mental math to simplify $(81 + 6) + 9$.

$(81 + 6) + 9$
$= (6 + 81) + 9$ Use the Commutative Property of Addition.
$= 6 + (81 + 9)$ Use the Associative Property of Addition.
$= 6 + 90$ Add within parentheses.
$= 96$ Add.

Test Prep TIP

Look for combinations that equal 10 or a multiple of 10, since they are easier to use in calculating mentally.

■ **TRY THIS** Use mental math to simplify each expression.

5. 6 + 27 + 14

6. 8 + 0 + 2 + (−7)

7. 5 + 12 + 18 + 5

8. 19 + (−30) + 21

REAL-WORLD CONNECTION

$.85

$.35

$1.65

■ **EXAMPLE 4**

Suppose you buy the school supplies shown at the left. Use mental math to find the cost of these supplies.

1.65 + 0.85 + 0.35

    = 0.85 + 1.65 + 0.35   **Use the Commutative Property of Addition.**

    = 0.85 + (1.65 + 0.35)   **Use the Associative Property of Addition.**

    = 0.85 + 2.00   **Add within parentheses.**

    = 2.85   **Add.**

The cost of the school supplies is $2.85.

Need Help? For help with adding decimals, see Skills Handbook, p. 730.

■ **TRY THIS**

9. Use the supermarket receipt and mental math to find the cost of the groceries.

You can also use mental math to help you find products.

```
   SOUTH STREET
      MARKET
     527-5817
DATE 08.03.00    THU
1 GALLON MILK  $2.30
BREAD          $1.80
APPLES         $2.20
```

■ **EXAMPLE 5**

Use mental math to simplify (4 · 9) · 5.

(4 · 9) · 5 = (9 · 4) · 5   **Use the Commutative Property of Multiplication.**

         = 9 · (4 · 5)   **Use the Associative Property of Multiplication.**

         = 9 · 20   **Multiply within parentheses.**

         = 180   **Multiply.**

■ **TRY THIS** Use mental math to simplify each expression.

10. 25 · (3 · 4)

11. 3 · 1 · 5 · 8

12. 2(−8)(15)

13. 5 · 9 · 6 · (−2)

Exercises

CHECK UNDERSTANDING

Name each property shown.

1. $27 + 6 = 6 + 27$

2. $0 + 8 = 8$

3. $(6 \cdot 15)2 = 6(15 \cdot 2)$

4. $(12r)s = 12(rs)$

5. $999 \cdot 1 = 999$

6. $\bullet \cdot \blacktriangle = \blacktriangle \cdot \bullet$

Which two numbers would you combine first? Explain.

7. $5 + 36 + 95$

8. $5 \cdot 17 \cdot 2$

9. $50(-2)43$

Mental Math **Simplify each expression.**

10. $10 \cdot 13 \cdot (-10)$

11. $23 + (-15) + 85$

12. $25 + 157 + (-75)$

13. $(5)(-20)(66)$

14. $140 + 17 + (-60)$

15. $30 \cdot 30 \cdot 6$

16. ***Critical Thinking*** How do reordering and regrouping help you to add mentally? Include examples.

PRACTICE AND PROBLEM SOLVING

Name each property shown.

17. $\bullet + \blacktriangle = \blacktriangle + \bullet$

18. $8(3 \cdot 2) = (8 \cdot 3)2$

19. $5 + 8 = 8 + 5$

20. $(6x)y = 6(xy)$

21. $6 \cdot 1 = 6$

22. $ab = ba$

23. $999 + 0 = 999$

24. $(3 \cdot 4)(25) = 3(4 \cdot 25)$

25. $a \cdot 1 = 1 \cdot a$

26. $(6 + 5) + x = 6 + (5 + x)$

27. $(3 + 2)(4 + 5) = (4 + 5)(3 + 2)$

Mental Math **Simplify each expression.**

28. $62 + 3 + 7$

29. $25 \cdot 4 \cdot 8$

30. $24 + 0 + (-16)$

31. $10 \cdot 37 \cdot 10$

32. $35 + 15 + (-8)$

33. $5 \cdot 1 \cdot 20$

34. $730 + 693 + 270$

35. $5 \cdot 50 \cdot 20 \cdot (-2)$

36. $15 + 13 + (-25) + 12$

37. $125 + 18 + 75 + 162$

38. $4 \cdot 6 \cdot 25 \cdot 50 \cdot 2$

39. $17 + 17 + (-2) + 3$

Mental Math **Evaluate each expression.**

40. $x(y \cdot z)$, for $x = 4, y = -7,$ and $z = 5$

41. $t(u)(-v)$, for $t = 3, u = -10,$ and $v = 8$

42. $a + b + c$, for $a = 14, b = -52,$ and $c = 26$

43. $d(v)(d)$, for $d = 5$ and $v = -4$

44. *Mathematical Reasoning* Are there commutative and associative properties for subtraction and division? Justify your answer.

45. **TEST PREP** Which equation shows the Associative Property of Addition?
A. $8 + 6 + 7 = 8 + 7 + 6$
B. $10 + 5 + 15 + 6 = 10 + (5 + 15) + 6$
C. $9 + 0 + (-1) = 9 + (-1)$
D. $17 \cdot (-2) \cdot 1 \cdot 9 = 17 \cdot (-2) \cdot 9$

46. *Critical Thinking* As the first step in evaluating the expression $3 \cdot 4 + 2 \div (-2)$, can you use the Associative Property of Addition to find $4 + 2$? Explain.

Math in the Media **Use the article below for Exercises 47 and 48. Write an expression and simplify it.**

A Fair Fare in Alaska

Railroads are a popular means of transportation in Alaska. One scenic train route travels 356 miles from Anchorage to Fairbanks. It includes a stop in Denali Park, where you can see the tallest mountain in the United States, Mount McKinley. A one-way fare for the 12-hour trip is $154 in the summer and $120 in the spring and fall. A one-way fare for the 7.5-hour trip from Anchorage to Denali Park is $102 in the summer, and $84 in the spring and fall. Children's fares are half the fares for adults.

47. *Mental Math* A family with two adults and two children plans to travel round trip from Anchorage to Fairbanks. How much will the trip cost in the summer? In the fall?

48. a. A group of three adults and two children plan to travel round trip from Anchorage to Denali Park. How much will the trip cost in the fall?
   b. How much more would the trip cost them in the summer?

▶ MIXED REVIEW

In which quadrant of a coordinate plane does the graph of each ordered pair lie? *(Lesson 1-10)*

49. $(5, 3)$ **50.** $(-1, 4)$ **51.** $(-6, -3)$ **52.** $(8, -1)$ **53.** $(-4, 17)$ **54.** $(1, -3)$

Simplify each expression. *(Lesson 1-2)*

55. $3 \cdot 5 + 3 \cdot 15$ **56.** $4 \cdot 7 + 4 \cdot 11$ **57.** $5 \cdot 22 - 5 \cdot 2$

58. Lin worked 4 hours per day for 3 days to build a model bridge. How many hours did she spend on the project? *(Lesson 1-9)*

The Distributive Property

Investigate

∙∙∙∙∙∙∙∙∙∙∙∙∙∙∙∙∙∙∙∙∙∙∙∙ **EXPLORING THE DISTRIBUTIVE PROPERTY** ∙∙∙∙∙∙∙∙∙∙∙∙∙∙∙∙∙∙∙∙∙∙

You can find the total area of two rectangles by two methods.

1. Method 1: Find the area of each rectangle. Then find the sum of the areas.

2. Method 2: Combine the two into one large rectangle. Find its length. Find its width. Then find its area.

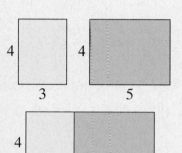

3. On a piece of paper, draw and label the dimensions of two rectangles with the same width and different lengths. Repeat Method 1 and Method 2 with your pair of rectangles. What do you notice about your results?

What You'll Learn

1 To use the Distributive Property with numerical expressions

2 To use the Distributive Property with algebraic expressions

...And Why

To solve real-world multiplication problems using mental math

---

PART 1 Numerical Expressions

The Investigate above shows different ways to find the sum of the areas of two rectangles. This shows the *Distributive Property*, which combines multiplication with addition or subtraction.

Distributive Property

To multiply a sum or difference, multiply each number within the parentheses by the number outside the parentheses.

Arithmetic	Algebra
$3(2 + 6) = 3(2) + 3(6)$	$a(b + c) = ab + ac$
$(2 + 6)3 = 2(3) + 6(3)$	$(b + c)a = ba + ca$
$6(7 - 4) = 6(7) - 6(4)$	$a(b - c) = ab - ac$
$(7 - 4)6 = 7(6) - 4(6)$	$(b - c)a = ba - ca$

You can use the Distributive Property to multiply mentally.

■ EXAMPLE 1

Use the Distributive Property to find 20(102) mentally.

$$20(102) = 20(100 + 2)$$ **Write 102 as (100 + 2).**

$$20(100 + 2) = 20 \cdot 100 + 20 \cdot 2$$ **Use the Distributive Property.**

$$= 2{,}000 + 40$$ **Multiply.**

$$= 2{,}040$$ **Add.**

■ **TRY THIS** Find each product mentally.

4. (53)50   **5.** $30 \cdot 104$ **6.** $9 \cdot 199$

REAL-WORLD CONNECTION

■ EXAMPLE 2

The PTA served 397 people at a pancake breakfast. How many pancakes did the PTA serve?

$$(397)4 = (400 - 3)4$$ **Write 397 as (400 − 3).**

$$= 400 \cdot 4 - 3 \cdot 4$$ **Use the Distributive Property.**

$$= 1{,}600 - 12$$ **Multiply.**

$$= 1{,}588$$ **Subtract.**

The PTA served 1,588 pancakes.

PTA PANCAKE BREAKFAST

$5

4 pancakes
blueberries
and strawberries
juice and milk

■ **TRY THIS**

7. Your club sold calendars for $7. Club members sold 204 calendars. How much money did they raise?

■ EXAMPLE 3

Simplify 8(15) − 8(5).

$$8(15) - 8(5) = 8(15 - 5)$$ **Use the Distributive Property.**

$$= 8(10)$$ **Subtract within parentheses.**

$$= 80$$ **Multiply.**

■ **TRY THIS** Simplify each expression.

8. $7(21) + 7(9)$ **9.** $12(52) - 12(62)$ **10.** $(16)7 - (11)7$

You can use algebra tiles to model the Distributive Property with variable expressions. Use a green rectangular tile to represent a variable.

EXAMPLE 4

Use models to multiply 3(2x + 5).

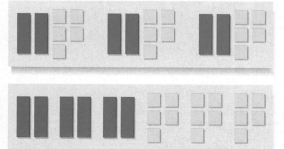

Model three groups of 2x + 5.

Use the Commutative Property of Addition.

So $3(2x + 5) = 6x + 15$.

Quick Review
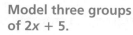
□ represents 1.
■ represents −1.

■ **TRY THIS** Use models to multiply.

11. $4(2x - 3)$ **12.** $3(x + 4)$ **13.** $(3x + 1)2$

In Example 4, notice that 3 multiplies both $2x$ and 5.
That is, $3(2x + 5) = 3(2x) + 3(5)$.

EXAMPLE 5

Multiply.

a. $-5(4x - 3)$

$-5(4x - 3) = -5(4x) - (-5)(3)$ Use the Distributive Property.

$\qquad\qquad = -20x - (-15)$ Multiply.

$\qquad\qquad = -20x + 15$ Simplify.

b. $(2x + 5)7$

$(2x + 5)7 = (2x)7 + (5)7$ Use the Distributive Property.

$\qquad\qquad = 14x + 35$ Multiply.

Reading Math

When a teacher distributes paper to the students in a class, each student gets some. Similarly, when a number is distributed over a sum or difference, each value within the parentheses is multiplied by the number.

■ **TRY THIS** Multiply.

14. $2(7 + 3d)$ **15.** $(6m + 1)(3)$ **16.** $-3(5t - 2)$

Exercises

▶ CHECK UNDERSTANDING

Copy and complete each statement.

1. $12(3 + 5) = \blacksquare \cdot 3 + \blacksquare \cdot 5$

2. $(y - 6)z = y \cdot \blacksquare - 6 \cdot \blacksquare$

3. $a(3 - b) = \blacksquare 3 - \blacksquare b$

4. $6 \cdot b + 12 \cdot b = (6 + 12)\blacksquare$

Mental Math **Use the Distributive Property to simplify.**

5. $6(23)$　　　　**6.** $7(48)$　　　　**7.** $5(18)$　　　　**8.** $13(101)$

▶ PRACTICE AND PROBLEM SOLVING

Mental Math **Use the Distributive Property to simplify.**

9. $6(52)$　　**10.** $(104)(9)$　　**11.** $8(98)$　　**12.** $(6)(83)$　　**13.** $(208)4$　　**14.** $5(1,005)$

15. $7(3) + 7(5)$　　　　**16.** $2(9) - 3(9)$　　　　**17.** $6(4) + 6(8)$

18. $9(3) - (2)(3)$　　　　**19.** $(-4)(7) + (-4)(-9)$　　　　**20.** $3(9) - 3(5) + 3(6)$

21. $12 \cdot 27 - 12 \cdot 24$　　　　**22.** $3 \cdot 5 + 27 \cdot 5$　　　　**23.** $(8) \cdot 11 + (-13) \cdot 11$

24. $13 \cdot (-3) - 7 \cdot (-3)$　　　　**25.** $-32 \cdot 6 + 29 \cdot 6$　　　　**26.** $4 \cdot 19 - 4 \cdot (11)$

Write an expression using parentheses for each model. Then multiply.

27.

28.

Use models to multiply.

29. $7(t - 5)$　　　　**30.** $(v - 3)4$　　　　**31.** $2(7z + 3)$　　　　**32.** $(2 + 3d)5$

Use the Distributive Property to multiply.

33. $4(b + 5)$　　**34.** $9(2h - 1)$　　**35.** $-3(2t + 6)$　　**36.** $-7(-3n + 2)$

37. $-8(6 - c)$　　**38.** $3(5 - 3w)$　　**39.** $(4 - t)(-7)$　　**40.** $-5(-m + 6)$

Name each property shown.

41. $m[t + (-t)] = mt + m(-t)$　　**42.** $m[t + (-t)] = m(-t + t)$　　**43.** $m[t + (-t)] = [t + (-t)]m$

Solve using mental math.

44. A theater sold out its evening performances four nights in a row. The theater has 294 seats. How many people attended the theater in the four nights?

45. *Geography* If you drove from Atlanta, Georgia, to Los Angeles, California, and back, how many miles would you travel?

46. You rent three videos for $2.95 each. How much do you pay in all?

47. *Writing* Explain how to use the Distributive Property to multiply $6(3r + 4s)$.

48. *Error Analysis* Suppose your friend wrote $7(2m + t) = 14m + t$. What error did your friend make?

49. *Open-ended* Use three integers to write an expression that you can simplify using the Distributive Property. Then simplify your expression.

50. *Mathematical Reasoning* Explain why $c(a + b) = (a + b)c$.

▶ MIXED REVIEW

Name the property shown. *(Lesson 2-1)*

51. $3(6 \cdot 2) = 3(2 \cdot 6)$ **52.** $8 = 8 + 0$ **53.** $4(8 \cdot 3) = (4 \cdot 8)3$ **54.** $1 \cdot 3 = 3$

Evaluate each expression. *(Lesson 1-3)*

55. $7 - m$, for $m = 6$ **56.** $6t + 1$, for $t = -2$ **57.** $c \div 3 - 5$, for $c = 6$

58. You have $120 in your checking account. In one month, you deposit $30, write a check for $21, withdraw $20, and deposit $45. Find your balance at the end of the month. *(Lessons 1-5 and 1-6)*

CHAPTER
PROJECT
2 **ACTIVITY 1 CREATING**

U se a ruler and a pencil to make a simple balance scale like the one pictured. Find the balance point near the center of the ruler. Label it *Zero*. Label points four inches in each direction from the balance point *Mass 1* and *Mass 2*. Practice using your balance scale by placing one penny at Mass 1 and another at Mass 2.

2-3

Simplifying Variable Expressions

PART 1 Identifying Parts of a Variable Expression

The diagram shows the possible parts of a variable expression.

A **term** is a number or the product of a number and variable(s).

$$7a + 4a + 3b - 6 \leftarrow \text{A \textbf{constant} is a term that has no variable.}$$

Like terms have identical variables.

A **coefficient** is a number that multiplies a variable.

When you have a variable expression that includes subtraction, you can rewrite the expression using only addition. This will help you find the coefficient(s) and constant(s).

$5x - 3y + z - 2$

$= 5x + (-3y) + z + (-2)$ **Rewrite subtraction as adding opposites.**

$= 5x + (-3y) + 1z + (-2)$ **Identity Property of Multiplication**

Rewriting the expression using addition shows that the coefficients are $5, -3,$ and 1. The constant is -2. Notice that the sign between terms in the original expression determines whether a coefficient or constant is positive or negative.

■ EXAMPLE 1

Name the coefficients, the like terms, and the constants in $3m - 2n + n - 4$.

Coefficients: $3, -2,$ and 1 Like terms: $-2n$ and n Constant: -4

■ **TRY THIS**   Name the coefficients, any like terms, and constants.

1. $6 + 2s + 4s$ **2.** $-4x$ **3.** $9m + 2r - 2m + r$

PART 2 Simplifying Variable Expressions

You **simplify** a variable expression by replacing it with an equivalent expression that has as few terms as possible.

EXAMPLE 2

Simplify $2x + 4 + 3x$.

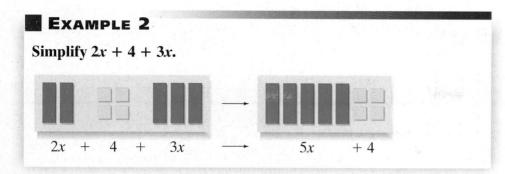

$2x$ + 4 + $3x$ $\longrightarrow$ $5x$ + 4

■ **TRY THIS**

4. Use tiles to simplify $3a + 2 + 4a - 1$.

You can also use the Distributive Property to combine like terms.

EXAMPLE 3

Simplify $5y + y$.

$$
\begin{aligned}
5y + y &= 5y + 1y & \text{Use the Identity Property of Multiplication.} \\
&= (5 + 1)y & \text{Use the Distributive Property.} \\
&= 6y & \text{Simplify.}
\end{aligned}
$$

■ **TRY THIS** Simplify each expression.

5. $8a + 5a$ **6.** $3b - b$ **7.** $-4m - 9m$

Deductive reasoning is the process of reasoning logically from given facts to a conclusion. As you use properties, rules, and definitions to justify the steps in a problem, you are using deductive reasoning.

EXAMPLE 4

Simplify $4g + 3(3 + g)$.

$$
\begin{aligned}
4g + 3(3 + g) &= 4g + 9 + 3g & \text{Use the Distributive Property.} \\
&= 4g + 3g + 9 & \text{Use the Commutative Property of Addition.} \\
&= (4 + 3)g + 9 & \text{Use the Distributive Property to combine like terms.} \\
&= 7g + 9 & \text{Simplify.}
\end{aligned}
$$

■ **TRY THIS** Simplify each expression. Justify each step.

8. $6y + 4m - 7y + m$ **9.** $4x + 3 - 2(5 + x)$

Exercises

▶ CHECK UNDERSTANDING

Name the coefficients, any like terms, and any constants.

1. $3x + 5y - 3$ **2.** $2x - 7$ **3.** $4x - 7x + 3x$ **4.** $6xy - 5xy$

Copy and complete each equation.

5. $6a + 4a + 7 = (6\blacksquare + 4\blacksquare) + 7$
$= (6 + 4)\blacksquare + 7$
$= 10\blacksquare + 7$

6. $8m - 3 - 9m = 8m - 9\blacksquare - 3$
$= (8 - 9)\blacksquare - 3$
$= -1\blacksquare - 3$

Simplify each expression.

7. $2r - 5 + 6r$ **8.** $12a + a$ **9.** $2x + 5x + 3$ **10.** $4 + 2m - m$

▶ PRACTICE AND PROBLEM SOLVING

Name the coefficients, any like terms, and any constants.

11. $5a + 8a$ **12.** $6a - 2b + b$ **13.** $-3x - 8$

14. $6ab + 8 + ab$ **15.** $12 - 4x + 7w - 9x - w$ **16.** $a + 2a + 3a - 4a$

Write an expression for each model. Simplify the expression.

17.

18.

Simplify each expression.

19. $4a - 3 + 5a$ **20.** $t - 3t + 2t + 4$ **21.** $5 + y - 3y$

22. $4 + 3a + 2$ **23.** $4m + 3 - 5m + m$ **24.** $r + 3 - 6r + r$

25. $8z + 8y + 3z$ **26.** $-4(a + 3) - a$ **27.** $3(g + 5) + 2g$

28. $4(w + 2x) + 9(-4w)$ **29.** $(2t + 4)3 + 6(-5t) - (-8)$ **30.** $-12(5x) + 3(-7x) - x$

Mathematical Reasoning **Justify each step.**

31. $3x + 2 + 5x - 3 = 3x + 5x + 2 - 3$
$= (3 + 5)x + 2 - 3$
$= 8x + 2 - 3$
$= 8x - 1$

32. $6(2x + y) + 2y = 12x + 6y + 2y$
$= 12x + (6 + 2)y$
$= 12x + 8y$

Simplify each expression. Justify each step.

33. $3a + 2a + a$

34. $w + 3w + 4$

35. $18 + 6(9k - 13)$

Write an expression for each situation. Simplify if possible.

36. Juan bought supplies for his new gecko. He bought four plants for p dollars each. He also bought a 10-gallon tank for $10 and a water dish for $3.

37. Jaleesa bought three folders for b cents each and two report covers for c cents each. She also bought a binder for $1.89.

38. *Writing* The expression $10bc$ has two variables. Explain why $10bc$ is not two terms.

39. **TEST PREP** Which expression has exactly two like terms?
   A. $3t + 1 - t$ **B.** $7 + 2m$ **C.** $8q + 3p$ **D.** $6r + r - 9r$

40. *Error Analysis* Your friend simplified $x + y + xy$ to $2xy$. What error did your friend make?

41. *Open-ended* Use the variables r and s to write a variable expression. Evaluate your expression for $r = 2$ and $s = -5$.

▶ **MIXED REVIEW**

Mental Math **Use the Distributive Property to find each product.** *(Lesson 2-2)*

42. $8(102)$

43. $54 \cdot 6$

44. $19(30)$

45. $(41)(9)$

46. *Choose a Strategy* A pair of rock climbers start up a 1,000-ft cliff. After one hour, they have gone up 160 ft. After two hours, they have gone up 320 ft. If they continue at this pace, how far will they have gone after five hours?

✓ **CHECKPOINT 1**   **Lessons 2-1 through 2-3**

Name each property shown.

1. $3 \cdot (-6) = -6 \cdot 3$ **2.** $(3a)b = 3(ab)$ **3.** $17 \cdot 1 = 17$ **4.** $6 + 0 = 0 + 6$

5. $(3 + 2)(4 - 7) = (4 - 7)(3 + 2)$ **6.** $4(3 - 12) = 4 \cdot 3 - 4 \cdot 12$

Simplify each expression.

7. $3(a + 2a)$ **8.** $9y - 3y + 12y$ **9.** $7(2w) + 2(w - 3)$

10. **TEST PREP** Which expression simplifies to $3xy + z$?
   A. $3x + z + 3y$ **B.** $2xy + z + xy$ **C.** $3xyz$ **D.** $3(x + y) + z$

2-4

Variables and Equations

What You'll Learn

1 To classify types of equations

2 To check equations using substitution

. . . And Why

To check solutions of equations

An **equation** is a mathematical sentence with an equal sign. Here are three of the ways you will see equations in this book.

$9 + 2 = 11$	a numerical expression equal to a numerical expression
$x + 7 = 37$	a variable expression equal to a numerical expression
$a + (-3) = 2a + 5$	a variable expression equal to a variable expression

An equation with a numerical expression equal to another numerical expression is either *true* or *false*. An equation with one or more variables is an **open sentence**.

■ EXAMPLE 1

Is each equation *true, false,* or an *open sentence?*

a. **6 + 12 = 18**   true, because $18 = 18$

b. **6 = 4 + 3**   false, because $6 \neq 7$

c. **6y = −3 + 5y**   an open sentence, because there is a variable

■ **TRY THIS**   Is each equation *true, false,* or an *open sentence?*

1. $9 - 7 = 3$ **2.** $8 + x = 2$ **3.** $4 \cdot 5 = 20$

You can write a mathematical word sentence as an equation.

■ EXAMPLE 2

Write an equation for *Nine times the opposite of five is forty-five.* Is the equation true, false, or an open sentence?

Words	nine	times	the opposite of five	is	forty-five
	9	times	−5	is	45
Equation	9	·	(−5)	=	45

Since $9 \cdot (-5) = -45$ and $-45 \neq 45$, the equation is false.

The phrases *is equal to* and *equals* indicate you should use the equal sign. The verb *is* often indicates you should use the equal sign also.

4. Write an equation for *Twenty minus x is three.* Is the equation true, false, or an open sentence?

PART 2 — Checking Equations Using Substitution

A **solution** is a value for a variable that makes an equation true. You substitute a number for a variable to determine whether the number is a solution of the equation.

■ EXAMPLE 3

Is 30 a solution of the equation $170 + x = 200$?

$170 + x = 200$

$170 + 30 \stackrel{?}{=} 200$ **Substitute 30 for x.**

$200 = 200$

Yes, 30 is a solution of the equation.

■ **TRY THIS** Is the given number a solution of the equation?

5. $8 + t = 2t; 1$ 6. $9 - m = 3; 6$

REAL-WORLD 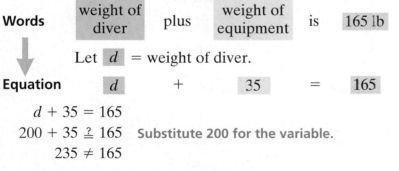 CONNECTION

■ EXAMPLE 4

A diver's equipment weighs 35 lb. The diver plus the equipment weighs 165 lb. Can the diver's weight be 200 lb?

Words	weight of diver	plus	weight of equipment	is	165 lb

Let d = weight of diver.

Equation	d	+	35	=	165

$d + 35 = 165$

$200 + 35 \stackrel{?}{=} 165$ **Substitute 200 for the variable.**

$235 \neq 165$

No, the diver's weight cannot be 200 lb.

■ **TRY THIS**

7. A tent weighs 6 lb. Your backpack and the tent weigh 33 lb. Use an equation to find whether the backpack weighs 27 lb.

A scuba tank can hold 63 ft^3 of compressed air. It weighs 29 lb when full.

Exercises

Determine whether each statement is true or false. Explain.

1. An equation can be false.

2. $3w - 7$ is an open sentence.

3. An open sentence must contain a variable.

4. $4 + 2x = 12$ is an open sentence.

Is each equation _true, false,_ or an _open sentence_?

5. $15 = 3 \cdot 5$

6. $4x - 8 = 25$

7. $3(-9) = -36 + 6$

Replace _c_ with −2. State whether the resulting equation is true or false.

8. $c + 5 = 3$

9. $24 = 2c + 29$

10. $c \div 2 - 8 = 3(-3)$

PRACTICE AND PROBLEM SOLVING

Is each equation _true, false,_ or an _open sentence_?

11. $6 - 10 = 22 - 18$

12. $18 = -3(-6)$

13. $20 + 3x = 42$

14. $4c - 12 = 20$

15. $37 - 17 = 2 \cdot 10$

16. $36 \div 6 + 1 = 5 + 3$

17. $6[-3 - (-5)] = 2(-4 + 10)$ **18.** $-24(-2) = 18(4 + 2)$

19. $-9 + x = 50 \div 10 + 3$

Is the given number a solution of the equation?

20. $4 + d = 6; 2$

21. $12 = 26 \div x; 14$

22. $-x - 5 = 6; 1$

23. $20 - c = 12; 8$

24. $8 = 2a + 3; 0$

25. $3 + 2t = 7; 4$

26. $3b \div 18 = 2; 12$

27. $3a = 12 + a; 6$

28. $2m = m + 6; 4$

Write an equation for each sentence. Is the equation _true, false,_ or an _open sentence_?

29. Four times the opposite of five equals negative twenty.

30. The product of negative twenty and nine is negative eleven.

31. The sum of fifteen and a number _n_ is fifty.

32. Forty-eight divided by twelve equals three.

33. Twenty-five equals a number _v_ plus fifteen.

Number Sense **Which of the numbers are reasonable substitutions for each variable? Justify your reasoning.**

34. Let p represent the number of passengers on a fifty-passenger school bus. Can p be 30? $27\frac{1}{2}$? -5? 48?

35. Let c represent the number of coins with a value of one dollar. Can c be 5 quarters? 10 dimes? 100 pennies? 17 nickels?

36. Let d represent the day of a month. Can d be 15? 56? 28? 0?

Write an equation. Is the given value a solution?

37. A veterinarian weighs 140 lb. When she steps on a scale carrying a husky, the scale shows 192 lb. Let d represent the weight of the dog. Does the dog weigh 52 lb?

38. A recipe calls for 4 c of flour. You have 20 c of flour. Let r represent the flour you have left after making the recipe. Is the remaining amount of flour 18 c?

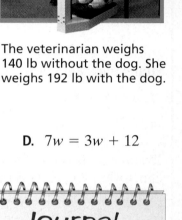

The veterinarian weighs 140 lb without the dog. She weighs 192 lb with the dog.

39. **TEST PREP** Which equation is false?
  A. $3 + (-7) = 10$ **B.** $6 \div 2 = 3$ **C.** $8 \cdot 2 - 15 = 1$ **D.** $7w = 3w + 12$

40. *Writing* Equations can be true or false. Can an expression be true or false? Explain.

41. *Language* Some word sentences are similar to equations.
  a. The sentence *Abraham Lincoln was an American president* is true. Write two other true sentences.
  b. The sentence *Eleanor Roosevelt was an American president* is false. Write two other false sentences.
  c. The sentence *He is a professional baseball player* is open. It is not clear to whom the word *he* refers. Write two other open sentences.

Journal

Explain the difference between an expression and an equation.

▶ MIXED REVIEW

Simplify each expression. *(Lesson 2-3)*

42. $6m + 7 - 2m + 1$ **43.** $-8t + 4t - 19$ **44.** $3w + 5k - 4w + k$

Evaluate each expression for $a = 3$ and $b = 2$. *(Lesson 1-3)*

45. $a + 2b$ **46.** $a - b + 15$ **47.** $(3b - 2a) \div 4$ **48.** $3(b + 2) - 4$

49. *Choose a Strategy* Larissa ran 15 mi per week before she decided to train for a marathon. The first week of training she ran 17 mi. The second week she ran 19 mi. If she continued her pattern, how far did she run the fifth week?

MATH TOOLBOX

Modeling
Before Lesson 2-5

Using Models with Equations

You can model an equation using algebra tiles. Use a green rectangular tile to represent the variable. Here are some examples.

Equation 1

$$x + 3 = 4$$

Equation 2

$$x + 3 = -3$$

Model each equation.

1. $x + 3 = 5$
2. $z + 2 = -6$
3. $y + 1 = 4$
4. $-3 = a - 4$
5. $2b + 2 = 8$
6. $3 + 3x = -6$

To solve an equation, get the variable alone on one side of the equal sign. Often you can do this by removing the same number of tiles from each side.

Here's how to solve $x + 3 = 7$.

Model the equation.

Solve by removing 3 tiles from each side.

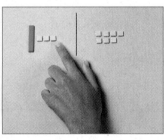

$$x = 4$$

Check $x + 3 = 7$
$4 + 3 \stackrel{?}{=} 7$ **Replace x with 4.**
$7 = 7$ ✔

Model and solve each equation.

7. $x + 3 = 6$
8. $m + 2 = 8$
9. $1 = 1 + d$
10. $-4 + y = -7$
11. $-1 + p = -5$
12. $w - 2 = -3$

Modeling **Write and solve the equation for each model.**

13.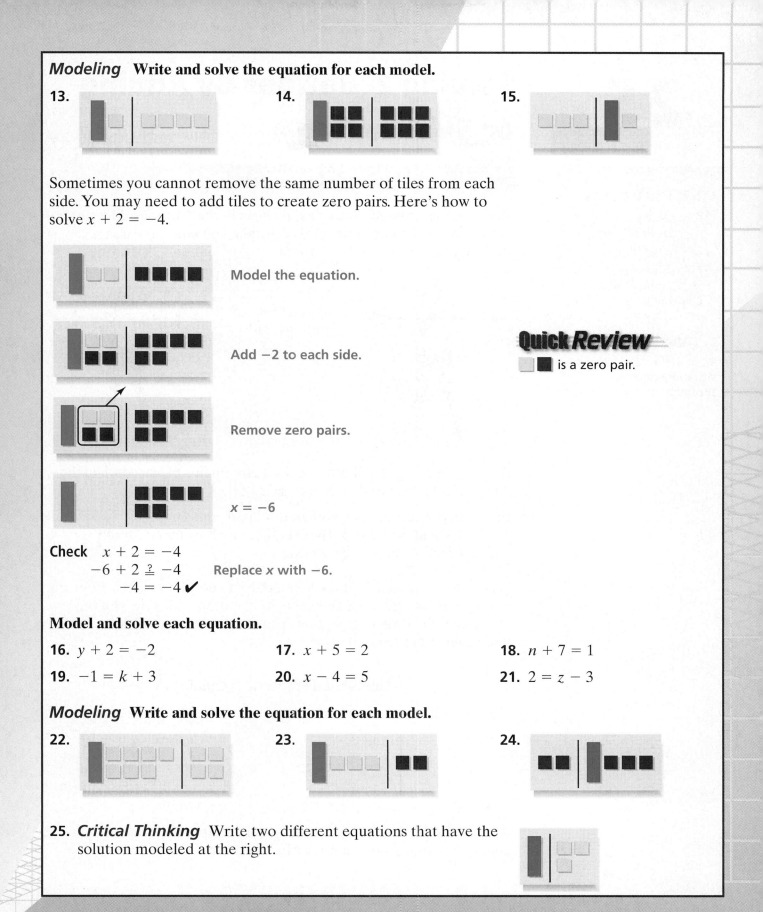

14.

15.

Sometimes you cannot remove the same number of tiles from each side. You may need to add tiles to create zero pairs. Here's how to solve $x + 2 = -4$.

Model the equation.

Add -2 to each side.

Quick Review

is a zero pair.

Remove zero pairs.

$x = -6$

Check $x + 2 = -4$

$-6 + 2 \stackrel{?}{=} -4$ Replace *x* with -6.

$-4 = -4$ ✔

Model and solve each equation.

16. $y + 2 = -2$

17. $x + 5 = 2$

18. $n + 7 = 1$

19. $-1 = k + 3$

20. $x - 4 = 5$

21. $2 = z - 3$

Modeling **Write and solve the equation for each model.**

22.

23.

24.

25. *Critical Thinking* Write two different equations that have the solution modeled at the right.

2-5

Solving Equations by Adding or Subtracting

PART 1 Using Subtraction to Solve Equations

What You'll Learn

1 To solve one-step equations using subtraction

2 To solve one-step equations using addition

...And Why

To model real-world situations such as problems involving health

Balancing an equation is like balancing a barbell. If you add weight to or subtract weight from one side of the bar, you must do the same on the other side.

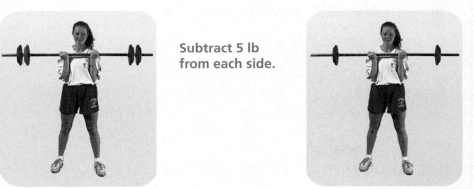

Subtract 5 lb from each side.

As you can see in the photos, the barbell remains balanced when the same weight is removed from each side.

In previous math courses, you used related equations like $3 + 5 = 8$ and $8 - 3 = 5$. These equations show that addition and subtraction undo each other.

When you solve an equation, your goal is to get the variable alone on one side of the equation. The value on the other side tells you the solution of the original equation. You use **inverse operations,** which undo each other to get the variable alone.

Subtraction Property of Equality

You can subtract the same number from each side of an equation.

Arithmetic	**Algebra**
$10 = 2(5)$	If $a = b$,
$10 - 5 = 2(5) - 5$	then $a - c = b - c$.

After you solve an equation, check your result in the original equation to make sure your solution is correct.

EXAMPLE 1

Solve $x + 6 = 4$.

Method 1

$$x + 6 = 4$$
$$x + 6 - 6 = 4 - 6 \qquad \text{Subtract 6 from each side.}$$
$$x = -2 \qquad \text{Simplify.}$$

Method 2

$$x + 6 = 4$$
$$\underline{ - 6 \quad -6}$$
$$x = -2$$

Check $\quad x + 6 = 4$

$$-2 + 6 \stackrel{?}{=} 4 \qquad \text{Replace } x \text{ with } -2.$$
$$4 = 4 \checkmark$$

■ **TRY THIS** Solve each equation.

1. $x + 8 = 3$ **2.** $5 = d + 1$ **3.** $c + (-4) = -5$

You can write and solve equations describing real-world situations. To help check, decide whether your solution is reasonable using the original problem.

REAL-WORLD CONNECTION

■ EXAMPLE 2

Health **Fred's target heart rate is 130 beats/min. This is 58 beats/min more than his resting heart rate. Find his resting heart rate.**

Words	target rate	is	58	more than	resting rate

Let r = resting heart rate.

Equation	130	=	58	+	r

$$130 = 58 + r$$
$$130 - 58 = 58 + r - 58 \qquad \text{Subtract 58 from each side.}$$
$$130 - 58 = r + 58 - 58 \qquad \text{Use the Commutative Property of Addition.}$$
$$72 = r \qquad \text{Simplify.}$$

Fred's resting heart rate is 72 beats per minute.

Check Is the answer reasonable? The resting heart rate plus 58 beats per minute should be 130 beats per minute. $72 + 58 = 130$. The answer is reasonable.

Here is one method for estimating your target heart-rate range: Begin by subtracting your age from 220. Then multiply the result by 0.6 and 0.8 to find the lower and upper limits of your heart-rate range.

■ **TRY THIS**

4. Cora measures her heart rate at 123 beats per minute. This is 55 beats per minute more than her resting heart rate r. Write and solve an equation to find Cora's resting heart rate.

When you solve an equation involving subtraction, *add* the same number to each side of the equation.

Addition Property of Equality

You can add the same number to each side of an equation.

Arithmetic	Algebra
$8 = 2(4)$	If $a = b$,
$8 + 3 = 2(4) + 3$	then $a + c = b + c$.

■ EXAMPLE 3

Solve $b - 12 = -49$.

$$b - 12 = -49$$
$$b - 12 + 12 = -49 + 12 \quad \text{Add 12 to each side.}$$
$$b = -37 \quad \text{Simplify.}$$

■ TRY THIS Solve each equation.

5. $y - 5 = 8$ **6.** $p - 30 = 42$ **7.** $98 = x - 14$

REAL-WORLD CONNECTION

■ EXAMPLE 4

Your friend's VCR cost $328 less than her TV. Her VCR cost $179. How much did her TV cost?

Words | cost of VCR | was | $328 | less than | cost of TV

Let t = the cost of the TV.

Equation | 179 | = | t | − | 328

$$179 = t - 328$$
$$179 + 328 = t - 328 + 328 \quad \text{Add 328 to each side.}$$
$$507 = t \quad \text{Simplify.}$$

Your friend's TV cost $507.

■ TRY THIS Write and solve an equation for this situation.

8. A softcover book costs $17 less than its hardcover edition. The softcover costs $5. How much does the hardcover cost?

Writing Math

When you go from words to an equation, the order of the math symbols may be different from the order of the words:

• ten fewer than n →
  $n - 10$
• eight less than r → $r - 8$
• n times 5 → $5n$

Exercises

Copy and complete the steps for solving each equation.

1.
$$x + 8 = 15$$
$$x + 8 - \blacksquare = 15 - \blacksquare$$
$$x = \blacksquare$$

2.
$$y - 3 = -5$$
$$y - 3 + \blacksquare = -5 + \blacksquare$$
$$y = \blacksquare$$

State the first step in solving each equation.

3. $a + 8 = 12$

4. $54 + x = 98$

5. $34 = c - 19$

Solve each equation.

6. $6 + b = 9$

7. $x + 35 = 15$

8. $3 = n + 4$

9. $d - 4 = -7$

10. $c - 34 = 20$

11. $-25 = q - 10$

12. **Open-ended** Write two word problems that can be solved using the equation $x + 15 = -18$.

Solve each equation.

13. $c + 9 = 37$

14. $b + 24 = 19$

15. $65 = n + 34$

16. $47 = 7 + y$

17. $450 = a + 325$

18. $h + 35 = 15$

19. $298 + n = 924$

20. $-45 = x + (-3)$

21. $89 + y = 112$

22. $e + (-43) = -45$

23. $a - 4 = -5$

24. $r - 3 = 8$

25. $x - 366 = -415$

26. $-27 = w - 14$

27. $z - 100 = 100$

28. $n - 29 - 16 = 246$

29. $34 + p + 112 = 78 - 7$

30. $183 + k - 20 = -15$

Mental Math Use mental math to solve each equation.

31. $5 = d - 1$

32. $40 = g - 20$

33. $b + 15 = -5$

34. $130 = 30 + s$

35. $x + 800 = 500$

36. $100 = x - 25$

Write and solve an equation for each sentence.

37. Negative six plus y equals eighteen.

38. Twelve equals the sum of n and twenty-three.

39. Negative five equals x minus eight.

40. The number a minus five is negative eight.

41. TEST PREP This year, the Newville Tigers won six games more than the Wilton Panthers won. The Tigers won 22 games. Which equation *cannot* be used to find the number of games the Panthers won?

A. $b + 6 = 22$ **B.** $22 - b = 6$ **C.** $22 = 6 + b$ **D.** $b - 6 = 22$

Use the table at the right for Exercises 42 and 43.

42. *Astronomy* The average distance from the sun to Jupiter is 550 million km greater than the average distance from the sun to Mars. Write and solve an equation to find Mars's average distance d from the sun.

43. *Astronomy* The distance from Venus to the sun is 42 million km less than Earth's average distance from the sun. Write and solve an equation to find Earth's average distance d from the sun.

Planet	Approximate Distance from Sun (millions of kilometers)
Mercury	58
Venus	108
Earth	■
Mars	■
Jupiter	778
Saturn	1,429
Uranus	2,871
Neptune	4,504
Pluto	5,914

44. *Error Analysis* A student solved the equation $x - 6 = -6$. His solution was -12. What error did the student make?

45. *Writing* To solve $x + 25 = -22$, one student subtracted 25 from each side. Another student added -25 to each side. Will both methods work? Explain.

46. In 1996, 487 million people across the world spoke English. This was 512 million people fewer than the number who spoke Mandarin Chinese. Write and solve an equation to find the number of people n who spoke Mandarin Chinese.

47. *Physics* The speed of sound through steel is 5,200 meters per second (m/s). This is 2,520 m/s faster than the speed of sound through silver. Write and solve an equation to find the speed s of sound through silver.

▶ MIXED REVIEW

Is each equation *true, false,* or an *open sentence*? *(Lesson 2-4)*

48. $x + 2 = 4$ **49.** $4 = 6 - 2$ **50.** $5 - 3 = 7 - 4$

Evaluate. *(Lesson 1-3)*

51. $6n$, for $n = 8$ **52.** $\frac{k}{20}$, for $k = 140$ **53.** $50x$, for $x = 8$

54. *Patterns* Deric studied math for 1 min the first week of school, and then doubled his study time each week. How many minutes did he study in the tenth week? *(Lesson 1-7)*

Solving Equations by Multiplying or Dividing

PART 1   Using Division to Solve Equations

Division and multiplication are inverse operations. You can solve an equation that involves multiplication by using the Division Property of Equality.

Division Property of Equality

If you divide each side of an equation by the same nonzero number, the two sides remain equal.

Arithmetic	**Algebra**
$6 = 3(2)$	If $a = b$ and $c \neq 0$,
$\dfrac{6}{3} = \dfrac{3(2)}{3}$	then $\dfrac{a}{c} = \dfrac{b}{c}$.

What You'll Learn

1 To solve one-step equations using division

2 To solve one-step equations using multiplication

...And Why

To model real-world situations such as population growth

DATA ANALYSIS CONNECTION

■ EXAMPLE 1

Statistics **The United States population in 1998 was twice the population in 1943. Find the 1943 population in millions.**

Words   1998 population   was   twice   1943 population

Let p = population in 1943.

Equation   270   =   2 · p

$270 = 2p$

$\dfrac{270}{2} = \dfrac{2p}{2}$ Divide each side by 2.

$135 = p$ Simplify.

The United States population in 1943 was 135 million people.

Check Is the answer reasonable? Twice the 1943 population should be the 1998 population. Since $135 \cdot 2 = 270$, the answer is reasonable.

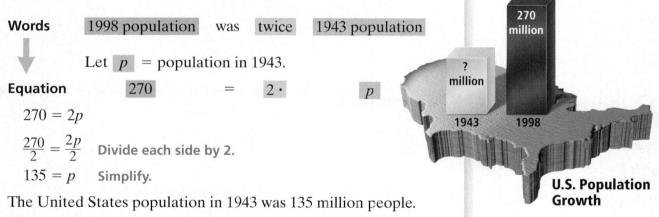

U.S. Population Growth

■ TRY THIS   Solve each equation.

1. $4x = 84$ **2.** $91 = 7y$ **3.** $12w = 108$

■ **EXAMPLE 2**

Solve $5r = -20$.

$$5r = -20$$
$$\frac{5r}{5} = \frac{-20}{5} \qquad \text{Divide each side by 5.}$$
$$r = -4 \qquad \text{Simplify.}$$

Check
$$5r = -20$$
$$5 \cdot (-4) \overset{?}{=} -20 \qquad \text{Replace } r \text{ with } -4.$$
$$-20 = -20 \checkmark$$

■ **TRY THIS** Solve each equation.

4. $-3b = 24$ **5.** $96 = -8n$ **6.** $-4d = -56$

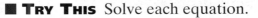

PART 2   Using Multiplication to Solve Equations

When you multiply each side of an equation by the same number, the two sides remain equal.

Multiplication Property of Equality

You can multiply each side of an equation by the same number.

Arithmetic	Algebra
$12 = 3(4)$	If $a = b$,
$12 \cdot 2 = 3(4) \cdot 2$	then $ac = bc$.

Reading Math

The equation $\frac{x}{-9} = -3$ is read as "x divided by negative nine equals negative three."

■ **EXAMPLE 3**

Solve $\frac{x}{-9} = -3$.

$$\frac{x}{-9} = -3$$
$$-9\left(\frac{x}{-9}\right) = -9(-3) \qquad \text{Multiply each side by } -9.$$
$$x = 27 \qquad \text{Simplify.}$$

■ **TRY THIS** Solve each equation.

7. $\frac{r}{-5} = 10$ **8.** $\frac{s}{-6} = 54$ **9.** $-30 = \frac{t}{20}$

Exercises

State the first step in solving each equation.

1. $6x = 96$

2. $32 = c \cdot 3$

3. $\frac{r}{-5} = -4$

Solve each equation.

4. $8x = -48$

5. $108 = 9x$

6. $-75 = -15x$

7. $\frac{v}{3} = 14$

8. $-6 = \frac{n}{4}$

9. $\frac{m}{-2} = -20$

10. *Critical Thinking* You can divide each side of an equation by the same *nonzero* value. Explain what would result from the equation $4 \cdot 0 = 5 \cdot 0$ if you could divide each side by zero and if $\frac{0}{0} = 1$.

PRACTICE AND PROBLEM SOLVING

Mental Math **Is −3 a solution of each equation? Explain.**

11. $-6 = 2m$

12. $\frac{b}{-3} = 1$

13. $\frac{-18}{k} = -6$

14. $3t = 9$

Solve each equation.

15. $4a = 28$

16. $-2b = 30$

17. $-45 = 9a$

18. $15c = 90$

19. $5w = 95$

20. $-28 = 7m$

21. $-10d = 100$

22. $125 = 25d$

23. $\frac{m}{4} = 13$

24. $\frac{b}{-6} = 20$

25. $-2 = \frac{d}{8}$

26. $\frac{v}{3} = -4$

27. $-50 = \frac{n}{-6}$

28. $9 = \frac{n}{8}$

29. $\frac{w}{12} = -2$

30. $\frac{r}{9} = -8$

Mental Math **Solve each equation.**

31. $20b = 2{,}000$

32. $75m = -7{,}500$

33. $\frac{v}{-50} = 300$

34. $3{,}823 = \frac{s}{100}$

For what values of *x* is each equation true?

35. $|x| = 7$

36. $2|x| = 8$

37. $-3|x| = -9$

38. $\frac{|x|}{3} = 2$

Solve for *x*.

39. $x - a = b$

40. $a + x = b$

41. $ax = b$

42. $\frac{x}{a} = b$

Write an equation for each sentence. Solve for the variable.

43. The product of negative twenty and y is one hundred.

44. Negative six multiplied by q equals one hundred eight.

45. Thirteen equals the quotient of x divided by three.

46. Use the table at the right. The number of students in grades 1–8 is four times the number of students in kindergarten. Write and solve an equation to find the number of students s in kindergarten.

47. One of the world's tallest office buildings is in Malaysia. The building has 88 stories. The height of the 88 stories is 1,232 ft. What is the height of one story?

48. *Writing* How are the procedures to solve $3x = 9$ and $x + 3 = 9$ alike? How are they different?

49. *Open-ended* Write a question that can be solved using the equation $5x = 45$.

U.S. School Enrollment

Grades	Millions of Students
Kindergarten	■
1–8	32
9–12	16

SOURCE: U.S. Bureau of the Census

▶ MIXED REVIEW

Solve each equation. *(Lesson 2-5)*

50. $-4 = a + 7$ **51.** $n - 5 = 12$ **52.** $t - (-4) = -15$ **53.** $y + 10 = 12$

Write a variable expression for each word phrase. *(Lesson 1-1)*

54. three less than a

55. 7 times a number n

56. Suppose you start hiking from a point 92 ft below sea level and break for lunch on a hilltop that is 1,673 ft above sea level. What is your change in elevation? *(Lesson 1-5)*

CHAPTER PROJECT 2 **ACTIVITY 2 CALCULATING**

Place a nickel at Mass 1 on your balance scale. At Mass 2, place as many pennies as you need to balance the scale. The nickel has a mass of about 5 g. Write and solve an equation to find the mass of a penny.

Multiple Choice

Choose the best answer.

1. The graph shows life expectancies in selected countries. Which conclusion is reasonable?

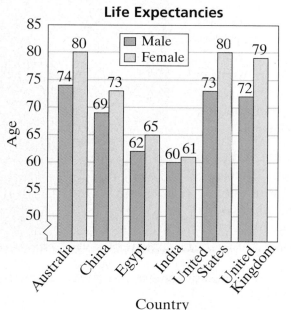

Life Expectancies

Country

A. The country in which a person lives has little influence on life expectancy.
B. A female in Australia lives about as long as a male in China.
C. The oldest male known to live in India is 60, while the oldest female is 61.
D. Females live longer than males.

2. Use the graph above. Which conjecture is *false?*
   F. A male in Egypt lives half as long as a female in Australia.
   G. A male in India lives almost as long as a female in India.
   H. Males in the United States and in the United Kingdom have about the same life expectancy.
   J. Females in the United States and in Australia have the same life expectancy.

3. During the riverside cleanup Marisa filled three times the number of bags Kevin filled. If b represents the number of bags Kevin filled, which expression gives the number of bags Marisa filled?
   A. $3b$ B. $b - 3$ C. $b + 3$ D. $\frac{b}{3}$

4. Which expression is *not* equivalent to $m(p + q)$?
   F. $mp + q$ G. $m(q + p)$
   H. $(p + q)m$ J. $mp + mq$

5. Which expression gives the area of the figure?
   A. $(3 \cdot 3) + (9 \cdot 3)$
   B. $(6 \cdot 9) - (3 \cdot 3)$
   C. $(3 \cdot 3) + (6 \cdot 9)$
   D. $6 + 3 + 3 + 6 + 3 + 9$

   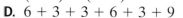
   3 m
   3 m
   6 m
   9 m

6. Which statement is true for the expression $5a - 3b - b - 1$?
   F. The expression is equivalent to $5a - 2b - 1$.
   G. The coefficients are all negative.
   H. The expression has three terms and two variables.
   J. The coefficients are 5, −3, and −1.

Free Response

For Exercises 7–9, show your work.

7. Use the pattern below.
   $$1 \cdot 8 + 1 = 9$$
   $$12 \cdot 8 + 2 = 98$$
   $$123 \cdot 8 + 3 = 987$$
   $$1{,}234 \cdot 8 + 4 = 9{,}876$$
   Find the value of $123{,}456{,}789 \cdot 8 + 9$.

8. Show two ways to simplify $8(5 + 4)$.

9. **Open-ended** Write an expression with four terms using variables t and z. Evaluate your expression for $t = -3$ and $z = 7$.

2-7

 Read | Plan | Look Back | Solve

Try, Test, Revise

Problem Solving Strategies

Account for All
    Possibilities

Draw a Diagram

Look for a Pattern

Make a Model

Make a Table

Simplify a Problem

Simulate a Problem

Solve by Graphing

Try, Test, Revise

Use Multiple Strategies

Work Backward

Write an Equation

Write a Proportion

Math Strategies in Action Did you know that meteorologists use weather balloons to collect data? They use the temperature, humidity, and other data in mathematical models to bring you the daily weather forecast. As more data become available—from weather balloons and satellites, for example— the models, and therefore the weather reports, become more accurate.

Similarly, in math problems, you can make an initial conjecture. You can test your conjecture. If it is not the right answer, you can use what you learn from your first conjecture to make a better second conjecture.

■ SAMPLE PROBLEM

The theater club at school put on a play. For one performance, it sold 133 tickets and raised $471. Tickets cost $4 for adults and $3 for students. How many student tickets and how many adult tickets did the club sell?

Read

Look at the given information to make an informed conjecture.

1. How much does each type of ticket cost?

2. How many tickets did the club sell for the performance?

3. How much money did the club raise from ticket sales for this performance?

Plan

Make a conjecture, and then test it. Use what you learn from your conjecture to make a better second conjecture.

4. When you make a conjecture for how many adult tickets were sold, how can you use your conjecture to find how many student tickets could have been sold?

5. By what number do you multiply your conjecture of adult tickets sold to find how much money was made on adult tickets?

 **Solve**

You can organize conjectures in a table. As a first conjecture, try making about half the tickets adult tickets.

Adult Tickets	Student Tickets	Total Money (in dollars)	
60	133 − 60 = 73	60(4) + 73(3) = 240 + 219 = 459	The total is too low. Increase the number of adult tickets.
80	133 − 80 = 53	80(4) + 53(3) = 320 + 159 = 479	The total is too high. Decrease the number of adult tickets.
70	133 − 70 = 63	70(4) + 63(3) = 280 + 189 = 469	The total is very close. Increase the number of adult tickets.
72	133 − 72 = 61	72(4) + 61(3) = 288 + 183 = 471	The total is correct.

There were 72 adult tickets and 61 student tickets sold.

Look Back

Is it possible to solve the problem in another way? Consider using logical reasoning.

- The less expensive ticket is \$3. So the theater club would get $133 \cdot \$3 = \$399$ if all the tickets sold were student tickets.

- $\$471 - \$399 = \$72$. The theater club actually raised \$72 more than if they had sold only student tickets.

- Since adult tickets are \$1 more than student tickets, there must have been 72 adult tickets sold.

- $133 - 72 = 61$. There were 61 student tickets sold.

- Since $72 \cdot 4 + 61 \cdot 3 = 471$, the solution 72 adult tickets and 61 student tickets is correct.

6. Suppose the club sold the same number of tickets, but raised \$452. How many tickets of each type did the theater club sell?

Exercises

► CHECK UNDERSTANDING

Use the *Try, Test, Revise* strategy to solve each problem.

1. Bonnie has 16 coins in her pocket worth $1.50. What are two different combinations of coins she could have in her pocket?

2. A cashier's drawer has some $5 bills, some $10 bills, and some $20 bills. There are 15 bills worth a total of $185. How many $5 bills, $10 bills, and $20 bills are there?

3. The Smiths have two children. The sum of their ages is 23. The product of their ages is 132. How old are the children?

► PRACTICE AND PROBLEM SOLVING

Solve using any strategy.

4. A movie theater sells senior and child tickets for $3, and other tickets for $6.50. One day, the theater sold 445 tickets. It made $2,518. How many of each kind of ticket did it sell?

5. *Geometry* A rectangular vegetable garden has a length of 5 ft and a width of 8 ft. The length is increased by 2 ft. By how many square feet does the area increase?

6. Trains leave New York for Boston every 40 min. The first train leaves at 5:20 A.M. What departure time is closest to 12:55 P.M.?

7. Lovell is 16 years old. Lovell's age is the same as Rafi's age divided by three. How old is Rafi?

8. *Number Theory* A number multiplied by itself and then by itself again gives −1,000. What is the number?

9. In a group of quarters and nickels, there are four more nickels than quarters. How many nickels and quarters are there if the coins are worth $2.30?

10. *Biology* A certain bacteria doubles the number of its cells every 20 min. A scientist puts 50 cells in a culture disk. How many cells will be in the culture dish after 2 h?

11. The sum of the page numbers on two facing pages is 245. The product of the numbers is 15,006. What are the page numbers?

12. A student bought some compact discs for $12 each and some books for $5 each. She spent $39 in all on five items. How many of each item did she buy?

13. Two runners ran as a team in a 5,000 m relay race. The first runner ran 500 m farther than the second runner. How many meters did each run?

▶ MIXED REVIEW

Solve each equation. *(Lesson 2-6)*

14. $\frac{m}{4} = 52$ **15.** $-32 = -16y$ **16.** $63 = \frac{t}{-3}$ **17.** $3x = -18$

Identify each property shown. *(Lessons 2-1 and 2-2)*

18. $8 + (-6 + 17) = [8 + (-6)] + 17$ **19.** $1,879 \cdot 1 = 1,879$

20. $8(52 - 37) = 8(52) - 8(37)$ **21.** $-19 + 37 + (-31) = -19 + (-31) + 37$

22. *Weather* The sound of thunder travels about one mile in five seconds. Suppose a bolt of lightning strikes 3 mi away from you. How long does it take for the sound of the thunder to reach you? *(Lesson 1-9)*

Math at Work

Nurse

Anyone who has been in a hospital knows that nurses are patients' principal caregivers. Nurses dispense medication, monitor patients' progress, and tend to patients' daily medical needs.

Mathematics plays an important role in a nurse's duties. The nurse compares a patient's blood pressure reading against established norms and draws a conclusion about the result. Nurses also solve math problems when they convert one unit of measure of medication to another, and then calculate the total amount of various medications needed for a patient in their care.

For more information about careers in nursing, visit the Prentice Hall Web site.
www.phschool.com

MATH TOOLBOX

Technology
Before Lesson 2-8

Data and Graphs

Sometimes a graph will help you analyze data. You can use a spreadsheet program to create different types of graphs. First, enter the data in a spreadsheet. Then use a graphing tool to create an appropriate graph.

■ EXAMPLE 1

The spreadsheet gives the voting-age populations in thousands for two states. Graph the data in the spreadsheet.

	A	B	C
1	Year	Arizona	Georgia
2	1988	2,610	4,631
3	1990	2,696	4,791
4	1992	2,812	5,006
5	1994	2,923	5,159
6	1996	3,094	5,396

Row 3 contains voting-age populations of both states in 1990.

Cell B3 contains the voting-age population of Arizona in 1990.

└ **Column B contains the voting-age population of Arizona.**

Choose an appropriate type of graph from your spreadsheet program. Line graphs are often useful to display changes in data over a period of time. Since the data show changes over time for two states, use a double line graph.

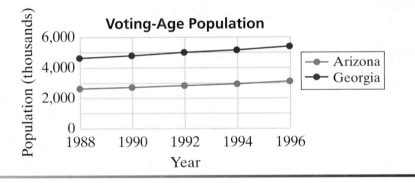

1. Use a spreadsheet to graph the data below.

Average Prices Farmers Received

Year	1990	1991	1992	1993	1994	1995	1996	1997
Price for Turkey (¢/lb)	39.4	38.4	37.7	39.0	40.4	41.6	43.3	39.9
Price for Chicken (¢/lb)	32.6	30.8	31.8	34.0	35.0	34.4	38.1	37.7

SOURCE: U.S. Department of Agriculture

EXAMPLE 2

**The spreadsheet gives population data for five states.
Graph the data in the spreadsheet.**

	A	B	C
1		Age 25 to 34	Age 75 to 84
2	California	5,285	1,229
3	Florida	1,968	958
4	Illinois	1,764	517
5	New York	2,767	825
6	Texas	2,882	638

Bar graphs are often useful in comparing amounts. Since the
data in the spreadsheet show populations for two age ranges,
use a double bar graph.

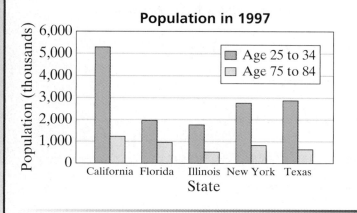

2. a. Use a spreadsheet to make a graph of the postage rate
data below.

Postage Rates

Sent from the United States to	First Class 1-oz Letter (¢)	Postcard (¢)
United States	33	20
Canada	52	40
Mexico	46	35
All other countries	100	50

Source: U.S. Postal Service

b. *Data Analysis* Use the graph you made in part (a). Which
bar is tallest? Explain why.

3. *Writing* Explain when you would use a line graph and when you
would use a bar graph to display a data set.

2-8 Inequalities and Their Graphs

What You'll Learn

1 To graph inequalities

2 To write inequalities

. . . And Why

To model real-world situations such as problems involving nutrition

---

PART 1 Graphing Inequalities

An **inequality** is a mathematical sentence that contains $>$, $<$, $\geq$, $\leq$, or $\neq$. Some inequalities contain a variable. Any number that makes an inequality true is a **solution of the inequality.** For example, -4 is a solution of $y \geq -5$ because $-4 \geq -5$.

You can graph the solutions of an inequality on a number line.

■ EXAMPLE 1

Graph the solutions of each inequality on a number line.

a. $y < 3$

An open dot shows that 3 is *not* a solution.

Shade all the points to the left of 3.

b. $x > -1$

An open dot shows that -1 is *not* a solution.

Shade all the points to the right of -1.

c. $a \leq -2$

A closed dot shows that -2 *is* a solution.

Shade all the points to the left of -2.

d. $-6 \leq g$

A closed dot shows that -6 *is* a solution.

Shade all the points to the right of -6.

Reading Math

Read $>$ as "is greater than."

Read $<$ as "is less than."

Read $\geq$ as "is greater than or equal to."

Read $\leq$ as "is less than or equal to."

■ **TRY THIS** Graph the solutions of each inequality.

1. $z < -2$ **2.** $4 > t$ **3.** $a \leq -5$ **4.** $2 \geq c$

You can write an inequality for a graph.

◼ EXAMPLE 2

Write the inequality shown in each graph.

a.
$$x > 0$$

b.
$$x \le -1$$

◼ TRY THIS

5. Write an inequality for the graph below.

You can write an inequality to describe a real-world situation. Keep in mind that *at most* means "less than or equal to" and *at least* means "greater than or equal to."

DATA ANALYSIS CONNECTION

◼ EXAMPLE 3

Nutrition **Food can be labeled *low sodium* only if it meets the requirement established by the federal government. Use the table to write an inequality for this requirement.**

Label	Definition
Sodium-free food	Less than 5 mg per serving
Very low sodium food	At most 35 mg per serving
Low-sodium food	At most 140 mg per serving

Words

| a serving of low-sodium food | has at most | 140 mg sodium |

Let s = number of milligrams of sodium in a serving of low-sodium food.

Inequality

| s | $\le$ | 140 |

◼ TRY THIS

6. Use the table in Example 3. A food is labeled sodium free. Write an inequality for n, the number of milligrams of sodium in a serving of sodium-free food.

Exercises

CHECK UNDERSTANDING

Match each inequality with its graph.

1. $x \geq -4$ **2.** $x \leq -4$ **3.** $x > -4$ **4.** $x < -4$

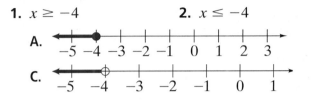

A.

B.

C.

D.

Write an inequality for each sentence.

5. x is less than 5. **6.** y is more than -3. **7.** b is less than or equal to 8.

8. *Critical Thinking* Explain how you know whether the endpoint of the graph of an inequality should be a solid dot or an open dot.

PRACTICE AND PROBLEM SOLVING

Graph the solutions of each inequality on a number line.

9. $x < 7$ **10.** $y > 2$ **11.** $a < 3$ **12.** $c < 1$

13. $z > -3$ **14.** $x > 1$ **15.** $m \leq -4$ **16.** $b \geq 6$

17. $p \leq 4$ **18.** $a \geq -2$ **19.** $j \geq -1$ **20.** $j \leq 0.6$

Write an inequality for each graph.

21.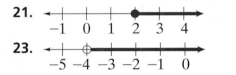

22.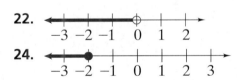

23.

24.

Write an inequality for each sentence.

25. A number c is at least twelve. **26.** The total t is greater than seven.

27. The price p is not more than $30. **28.** A number n is positive.

29. **TEST PREP** Which inequality represents *A number t is greater than or equal to -8?*
A. $-8 \leq t$ B. $t > -8$ C. $t \leq -8$ D. $-8 \geq t$

30. *Mathematical Reasoning* Compare. Use $>$ or $<$ to complete each statement.
a. If $a < b$, then b ▨ a.   b. If $x > y$, and $y > z$, then x ▨ z.

Write an inequality for each situation.

31. Fewer than 45 people attended a show. Let n be the number of people who attended the show.

32. *Nutrition* High-fiber foods have at least 5 g of fiber per serving. Let f be the number of grams of fiber per serving of high-fiber food.

33. A student pays for three movie tickets with a twenty-dollar bill and gets change back. Let t be the cost of a movie ticket.

Use a variable to write an inequality for each situation.

34.

35.

36.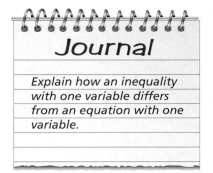

37. *Writing* Explain why graphing the solutions of an inequality is more efficient than listing all the solutions of the inequality.

38. *Critical Thinking* No more than 50 students walked in a walkathon. Let s be the number of students. Determine which numbers are reasonable values for s: 40, $45\frac{1}{2}$, 50, and 55.

39. *Open-ended* Describe a situation that you could represent with an inequality. Then write the inequality.

Journal

Explain how an inequality with one variable differs from an equation with one variable.

► **MIXED REVIEW**

Solve each equation. *(Lessons 2-5 and 2-6)*

40. $x - 5 = 29$ **41.** $7y = 35$ **42.** $t \div 12 = 6$ **43.** $8 + m = -3$

Simplify each expression. *(Lesson 2-3)*

44. $6 - 5s + 4s + 3$ **45.** $n + (n + 2) + (n + 4)$

46. Write a variable expression for the number of weeks in y years. *(Lesson 1-1)*

2-9

Solving One-Step Inequalities by Adding or Subtracting

PART 1 Solving Inequalities by Subtracting

What You'll Learn

1 To solve one-step inequalities using subtraction

2 To solve one-step inequalities using addition

...And Why

To model problems involving computers

Solving an inequality is similar to solving an equation. You want to get the variable alone on one side of the inequality.

You can see from the number line that if you subtract 2 from each side of the inequality $-1 < 2$, the resulting inequality $-3 < 0$ is still true.

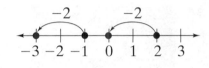

Subtraction Property of Inequality

You can subtract the same number from each side of an inequality.

Arithmetic	**Algebra**
$7 > 4$, so $7 - 3 > 4 - 3$	If $a > b$, then $a - c > b - c$.
$6 < 9$, so $6 - 2 < 9 - 2$	If $a < b$, then $a - c < b - c$.

■ EXAMPLE 1

Solve each inequality. Graph the solutions.

a. $n + 8 \geq 19$

$$n + 8 \geq 19$$
$$n + 8 - 8 \geq 19 - 8 \quad \text{Subtract 8 from each side.}$$
$$n \geq 11 \quad \text{Simplify.}$$

b. $-26 > y + 14$

$$-26 > y + 14$$
$$-26 - 14 > y + 14 - 14 \quad \text{Subtract 14 from each side.}$$
$$-40 > y \text{ or } y < -40 \quad \text{Simplify.}$$

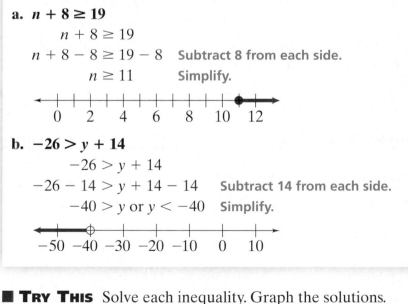

Test Prep TIP

You can use the related equation to check that you solved an inequality correctly. For example, use $-26 = y + 14$ for $-26 > y + 14$. Substitute the boundary point, -40, into the equation. Since $-26 = -40 + 14$, you solved correctly. You must also check that the inequality symbol in your solution is correct.

■ **TRY THIS** Solve each inequality. Graph the solutions.

1. $m + 3 > 6$ **2.** $8 + t < 15$ **3.** $-3 \leq x + 7$

■ EXAMPLE 2

Nearly 32 megabytes (MB) of memory are available for running your computer. If its basic systems require 12.1 MB, how much memory is available for other programs?

Words	memory for basic systems	plus	memory for other programs	is less than	total memory

Let m = memory available for other programs.

Inequality	12.1	+	m	<	32

$$12.1 + m < 32$$
$$12.1 - 12.1 + m < 32 - 12.1 \quad \text{Subtract 12.1 from each side.}$$
$$m < 19.9 \quad \text{Simplify.}$$

Less than 19.9 MB of memory is available for other programs.

You can increase the memory of a computer by adding more memory chips. These chips have multiples of 8 megabytes of extra memory.

■ TRY THIS

4. An airline lets you check up to 65 lb of luggage. One suitcase weighs 37 lb. How much can another suitcase weigh?

PART 2 Using Addition to Solve Inequalities

To solve an inequality involving subtraction, use addition.

Addition Property of Inequality

You can add the same number to each side of an inequality.

Arithmetic	Algebra
$7 > 3$, so $7 + 4 > 3 + 4$	If $a > b$, then $a + c > b + c$.
$2 < 5$, so $2 + 6 < 5 + 6$	If $a < b$, then $a + c < b + c$.

■ EXAMPLE 3

Solve $n - 15 < 3$.

$$n - 15 < 3$$
$$n - 15 + 15 < 3 + 15 \quad \text{Add 15 to each side.}$$
$$n < 18 \quad \text{Simplify.}$$

■ TRY THIS Solve each inequality.

5. $m - 13 > 29$ **6.** $v - 4 \leq 7$ **7.** $t - 5 \geq 11$

Exercises

CHECK UNDERSTANDING

What was done to the first inequality to get the second inequality?

1. $x - 5 \geq 6; x \geq 11$

2. $x + 8 \leq 11; x \leq 3$

Solve each inequality. Graph the solutions.

3. $n - 12 \leq 3$

4. $x - 8 > -2$

5. $w + 5 < 12$

6. $2 > 9 + a$

7. *Discussion* Explain how you know whether to add or subtract a number from each side to solve an inequality.

PRACTICE AND PROBLEM SOLVING

Solve each inequality. Graph the solutions.

8. $x + 6 \geq 7$

9. $2 + m \leq 2$

10. $6 < y + 19$

11. $18 \leq 20 + w$

12. $5 + x > -7$

13. $16 + t < 42$

14. $7.1 + r > 10.8$

15. $9 < b + 3.7$

16. $r - 4 \leq 3$

17. $x - 7 < -15$

18. $c - 9 > -5$

19. $6 \leq h - 10$

20. $w - 8 < -3$

21. $3 \leq y - 5$

22. $u - 3.5 \geq 8.9$

Mathematical Reasoning **Justify each step.**

23. $4 + a + 3 > 16$
$4 + 3 + a > 16$
$7 + a > 16$
$7 - 7 + a > 16 - 7$
$a > 9$

24. $m - 2(8 - 5) \leq -9$
$m - 2(3) \leq -9$
$m - 6 \leq -9$
$m - 6 + 6 \leq -9 + 6$
$m \leq -3$

Write an inequality for each sentence. Then solve the inequality.

25. Thirteen plus a number n is greater than fifteen.

26. The sum of a number w and three is less than or equal to ten.

27. Eleven subtracted from a number b is less than negative twelve.

28. The total weight limit for a truck is 100,000 lb. The truck weighs 36,000 lb empty. What is the most that the truck's load w can weigh?

29. Writing Are $m > -2$ and $-2 < m$ both solutions to $m + 4 > 2$? Explain.

30. **TEST PREP** If x and y are positive and $x > y$, which is true?

A. $x > \dfrac{x + y}{2}$ **B.** $y > \dfrac{x + y}{2}$ **C.** $x = \dfrac{x + y}{2}$ **D.** $x < \dfrac{x + y}{2}$

31. Budgeting You are saving to buy a bicycle that will cost at least $120. Your parents give you $45 toward the bicycle. Write an inequality to find how much money m you will have to save.

32. Use the table at the right. Suppose your computer's basic system uses at least 12 MB of memory.
   a. You want to have your e-mail active while you work on a paper with your word processor. How much memory m must your computer have?
   b. If you also want to search the Web for data at the same time, how much memory m must your computer have?

Computer Memory

Application	Memory Requirement
Word processor	11.2 MB
Spreadsheet	5.3 MB
Web browser	9.3 MB
E-mail	4.4 MB

▶ MIXED REVIEW

Graph the solutions of each inequality. *(Lesson 2-8)*

33. $x < 2$ **34.** $x \geq -5$ **35.** $y \leq 4$ **36.** $m > 0$

Simplify each expression. *(Lesson 2-3)*

37. $4x + 6 - 2x + 7$ **38.** $9 - 5r + 2(r - 3)$ **39.** $-4 - 5t + t - 10$

40. Write an integer to represent a debt of $35. *(Lesson 1-4)*

✓ CHECKPOINT 2   Lessons 2–4 through 2–9

Is each equation *true, false,* or an *open sentence*?

  1. $4 + 15 = 27 - 8$ **2.** $-30 = 9w$ **3.** $|9 - 10| = 8 - 9$

Solve each equation or inequality.

  4. $y - 3 = -7$ **5.** $x + 4 = 8$ **6.** $7t = 42$ **7.** $m \div 8 = -4$

  8. $-90 = 10f$ **9.** $m + 5 > -4$ **10.** $r - 12 < 7$ **11.** $9 \leq 3 + a$

12. Open-ended Describe a situation that can be modeled using an inequality. Write the inequality.

13. Choose a Strategy You have some quarters, dimes, and pennies. You have eight coins worth $.77 altogether. How many of each type of coin do you have?

2-10

Solving One-Step Inequalities by Multiplying or Dividing

What You'll Learn

1 To solve one-step inequalities using division

2 To solve one-step inequalities using multiplication

...And Why

To model real-world problems involving transportation

Investigate

·········· SOLVING INEQUALITIES ··········

Explore what happens when you divide each side of an inequality by a number.

1. Simplify each expression at the right. Replace each ■ with > or <.

2. *Patterns* Does the direction of the inequality symbol stay the same as you divide each side of an inequality by the given numbers? Explain your reasoning.

$$6 \div 3 \ \blacksquare \ 12 \div 3$$
$$6 \div 2 \ \blacksquare \ 12 \div 2$$
$$6 \div 1 \ \blacksquare \ 12 \div 1$$
$$6 \div (-1) \ \blacksquare \ 12 \div (-1)$$
$$6 \div (-2) \ \blacksquare \ 12 \div (-2)$$
$$6 \div (-3) \ \blacksquare \ 12 \div (-3)$$

PART 1 **Solving Inequalities Using Division**

You can solve an inequality that involves multiplication by dividing each side of the inequality by a nonzero number.

Division Properties of Inequality

If you divide each side of an inequality by a positive number, the direction of an inequality symbol is unchanged.

Arithmetic	**Algebra**
$3 < 6$, so $\frac{3}{3} < \frac{6}{3}$	If $a < b$ and c is positive, then $\frac{a}{c} < \frac{b}{c}$.
$8 > 2$, so $\frac{8}{2} > \frac{2}{2}$	If $a > b$ and c is positive, then $\frac{a}{c} > \frac{b}{c}$.

If you divide each side of an inequality by a negative number, *the direction of the inequality symbol is reversed.*

Arithmetic	**Algebra**
$6 < 12$, so $\frac{6}{-3} > \frac{12}{-3}$	If $a < b$ and c is negative, then $\frac{a}{c} > \frac{b}{c}$.
$16 > 8$, so $\frac{16}{-4} < \frac{8}{-4}$	If $a > b$ and c is negative, then $\frac{a}{c} < \frac{b}{c}$.

EXAMPLE 1

Engineering **An elevator can carry up to 2,500 lb. Suppose the weight of an average adult is 150 lb. At most how many average-sized adults can safely ride the elevator at the same time?**

Words | the number of adults | times | 150 lb | is less than or equal to | 2,500 lb

Let x = number the number of adults.

Inequality | x | $\cdot$ | 150 lb | $\leq$ | 2,500

$150x \leq 2,500$

$\dfrac{150x}{150} \leq \dfrac{2,500}{150}$ Divide each side by 150.

$x \leq 16.\overline{6}$ Simplify. Round the answer down to find a whole number of people.

At most 16 average adults can safely ride an elevator at one time.

Check Is the answer reasonable? The total weight of 16 average adults is $16(150) = 2,400$ lb, which is less than 2,500 lb but so close that another adult could not ride. The answer is reasonable.

Express elevators can travel as fast as 1,800 ft/min.

STATE INSPECTION CERTIFICATE
Department of Public Safety
Certificate for Use of Elevator
LOCATION: 221 Pat Street
SPEED: 150 ft. per min.
CAPACITY: 2,500 lb.
ISSUED ON: 08/06/00
EXPIRES: 08/06/01

■ **TRY THIS** Solve each inequality.

3. $4x > 40$ **4.** $-21 \geq 3m$ **5.** $36 \geq -9t$

PART 2 | **Solving Inequalities Using Multiplication**

You can solve inequalities that involve division.

Multiplication Properties of Inequality

If you multiply each side of an inequality by a positive number, the direction of the inequality symbol is unchanged.

Arithmetic	**Algebra**
$3 < 4$, so $3(5) < 4(5)$	If $a < b$ and c is positive, then $ac < bc$.
$7 > 2$, so $7(6) > 2(6)$	If $a > b$ and c is positive, then $ac > bc$.

If you multiply each side of an inequality by a negative number, *the direction of the inequality symbol is reversed.*

Arithmetic	**Algebra**
$6 < 9$, so $6(-2) > 9(-2)$	If $a < b$ and c is negative, then $ac > bc$.
$7 > 5$, so $7(-3) < 5(-3)$	If $a > b$ and c is negative, then $ac < bc$.

Test
Prep TIP

You can check whether the inequality symbol in your solution is correct. For example, for the inequality $\frac{t}{-4} \geq 7$, choose a number that is less than -28, such as -32. Substitute -32 into the original inequality. Since $\frac{-32}{-4} = 8$ and 8 is greater than 7, the inequality symbol in the solution is correct.

■ EXAMPLE 2

Solve $\frac{t}{-4} \geq 7$.

$$\frac{t}{-4} \geq 7$$

$$-4\left(\frac{t}{-4}\right) \leq -4(7) \qquad \text{Multiply each side by } -4 \text{ and reverse the inequality symbol.}$$

$$t \leq -28 \qquad \text{Simplify.}$$

■ **TRY THIS** Solve each inequality.

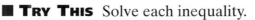

6. $\frac{m}{4} \geq 2$ **7.** $\frac{t}{-3} < 7$ **8.** $5 < \frac{r}{7}$

■ Different Ways to Solve a Problem

Solve $-3x < 12$.

Method 1

Divide each side by -3 and reverse the direction of the inequality symbol.

$$-3x < 12$$
$$\frac{-3x}{-3} > \frac{12}{-3}$$
$$x > -4$$

Method 2

Rewrite the inequality so the coefficient of the variable is positive.

$$-3x < 12$$
$$-3x + 3x < 12 + 3x$$
$$0 < 12 + 3x$$
$$0 - 12 < 3x + 12 - 12$$
$$-12 < 3x$$
$$\frac{-12}{3} < \frac{3x}{3}$$
$$-4 < x, \text{ or } x > -4$$

Choose a Method

1. Which method would you use to solve this inequality? Explain.

2. Solve $18 < -6x$ using Method 1 or Method 2.

Exercises

CHECK UNDERSTANDING

What happens to the inequality symbol when you do the following to each side of an inequality?

1. subtract a negative number

2. multiply by a positive number

3. divide by a negative number

4. multiply by a negative number

What was done to the first inequality to get the second?

5. $4x \geq 48; x \geq 12$

6. $8 > -4x; -2 < x$

7. $\frac{1}{3}x \leq 18; x \leq 54$

Solve each inequality.

8. $-2x < 14$

9. $3t > 21$

10. $\frac{x}{-6} > 3$

11. $\frac{m}{6} \leq -18$

12. **Critical Thinking** The rules for multiplying and dividing both sides of an inequality do not mention zero. Discuss why.

PRACTICE AND PROBLEM SOLVING

Solve each inequality.

13. $6m > 24$

14. $-4x \leq -16$

15. $9x \leq 27$

16. $-3x < 0$

17. $18 < -2m$

18. $64 \leq -8k$

19. $7m > 28$

20. $-r \geq 21$

21. $\frac{1}{2}x \geq -3$

22. $\frac{x}{3} \geq 5$

23. $\frac{y}{4} > 3$

24. $\frac{r}{-4} > 2$

25. $\frac{b}{3} \geq -31$

26. $6 > \frac{q}{-3}$

27. $20 < \frac{v}{6}$

28. $-3 \geq \frac{g}{-7}$

Mathematical Reasoning Justify each step.

29. $-7m \leq -28$

$\frac{-7m}{-7} \geq \frac{-28}{-7}$

$m \geq 4$

30. $\frac{a}{3} > 12$

$(\frac{a}{3})(3) > 12(3)$

$a > 36$

31. **Error Analysis** Your friend solved $3x > -12$ as shown at the right. What error did your friend make?

32. Determine whether each number is a solution of $-2x \leq -4$.

    a. 3   **b.** -2 **c.** 0   **d.** 10

$3x > -12$

$\frac{3x}{3} < \frac{-12}{3}$

$x < -4$

Write an inequality for each sentence. Then solve the inequality.

33. The product of negative two and a number a is greater than ten.

34. A number t multiplied by seven is less than or equal to twenty-one.

35. A number b divided by four is greater than or equal to three.

36. The quotient of a number v divided by negative five is less than nine.

37. **Open-ended** Write a problem that you would solve using the inequality $5m \le 15$.

38. **TEST PREP** Which inequality has the same solutions as $\frac{a}{4} < -20$?

   A. $4d > 80$ B. $\frac{m}{-2} < -40$ C. $-2r < -40$

   D. $\frac{z}{-2} > 40$ E. $4c < -80$

39. **Writing** Explain how solving $-4t < 32$ is different from solving $4t < -32$.

40. In Georgia, for every 18 four-year-old children in day care there must be at least one teacher. At one day care center, 56 four-year-olds are signed up for next year. At least how many teachers must the center have to teach four-year-olds next year?

▶ MIXED REVIEW

Solve each inequality. *(Lesson 2-9)*

41. $6 + t > 17$ 42. $m - 4 \le 6$ 43. $-9 \ge r + 5$ 44. $11 > v - 12$

Name each property shown. *(Lessons 2-1 and 2-2)*

45. $-12(100 - 3) = -12(100) - 12(-3)$ 46. $102 + 34 + 98 = 102 + 98 + 34$

47. **Weather** The high temperature one day in January was $34°F$, and the low temperature was $-7°F$. What was the difference between the high and the low temperatures that day? *(Lesson 1-6)*

CHAPTER PROJECT 2

ACTIVITY 3 GRAPHING

On your balance scale, place two quarters at Mass 1 and two nickels at Mass 2. Write and solve an inequality for the mass of a quarter. Then add another nickel at Mass 2. Write and solve a second inequality for the mass of a quarter. Graph your two solutions on one number line.

DON'T LOSE YOUR BALANCE!

Make a Balance Scale The Activities on pages 73, 92, and 112 will help you complete your project. Here is a checklist to help you gather the different parts.

✔ your balance scale

✔ your equation and solution for the mass of a penny

✔ your inequalities, solutions, and graph for the mass of a quarter

Draw diagrams to show your balance scale and your balancing experiments. For each diagram, include the names of the coins, the equation or inequality you solved, and the solution. For the inequalities, include your graph.

Reflect and Revise

Ask a friend or someone at home to review your diagrams. Are they clearly labeled? Are the equation, inequalities, graph, and solutions correct? If necessary, make changes to improve your diagrams.

Web Extension

Visit Prentice Hall's Web site. You'll find some interesting links and ideas related to scales. You'll also be able to share information about your project.

www.phschool.com

2 Wrap Up

■ Key Terms

Addition Property
  of Equality (p. 86)
  of Inequality (p. 105)
additive identity (p. 65)
Associative Properties of
  Addition and
  Multiplication (p. 64)
coefficient (p. 74)
Commutative Properties of
  Addition and
  Multiplication (p. 64)
constant (p. 74)
deductive reasoning (p. 75)

Distributive Property (p. 69)
Division Property
  of Equality (p. 89)
  of Inequality (p. 108)
equation (p. 78)
Identity Properties
  of Addition and
  Multiplication (p. 65)
inequality (p. 100)
inverse operations (p. 84)
like terms (p. 74)

Multiplication Property
  of Equality (p. 90)
  of Inequality (p. 109)
multiplicative identity (p. 65)
open sentence (p. 78)
simplify (p. 74)
solution (p. 79)
solution of the inequality
  (p. 100)
Subtraction Property
  of Equality (p. 84)
  of Inequality (p. 104)
term (p. 74)

■ Graphic Organizer

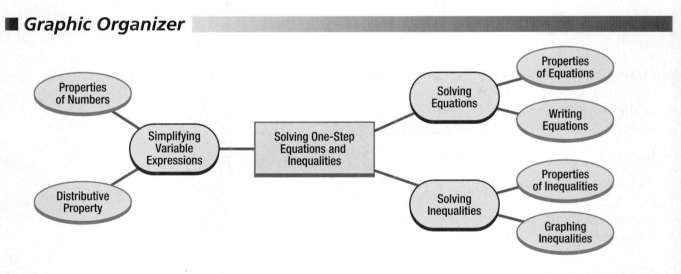

■ Properties of Numbers

2-1

Summary Use the **Commutative Property** to change order. Use the **Associative Property** to change grouping. Adding zero to an expression does not change its value. Multiplying an expression by 1 does not change its value.

Simplify each expression. Justify each step.

1. $58 + 16 + 2 + 4$

2. $4 \cdot 7 \cdot 25 \cdot 1$

3. $125 + 347 + 75$

4. $(20 \cdot 65) \cdot 5$

5. $10 \cdot 15 \cdot 2$

6. $37 + 0 + (5 + 63)$

■ The Distributive Property

Summary Use the **Distributive Property** to multiply a number outside parentheses by each term of a sum or difference.

Mental Math Use the Distributive Property to simplify.

7. $9(96)$ **8.** $8(62)$ **9.** $(43)(9)$

Use the Distributive Property to multiply.

10. $4(w + 9)$ **11.** $(2 + 4a)12$ **12.** $-7(6 - 2m)$

13. **TEST PREP** Which product equals $3t - 12$?
     A. $4(t - 3)$ **B.** $(3 - t)4$ **C.** $(4 - t)3$ **D.** $3(t - 4)$

■ Simplifying Variable Expressions

Summary To **simplify** a variable expression, replace it with an equivalent expression with as few terms as possible.

Simplify each expression.

14. $8a + 7 - 11a$ **15.** $3(w + 3) + 4w$ **16.** $6 + x - 4x + 3$

17. $19 - 4(5n + 1) - 4n$ **18.** $10 + 7k - 2(3k + 5)$ **19.** $-7(2r - 1) + 3(8 - r)$

20. *Writing* Explain how to determine whether terms are like terms.

■ Variables and Equations

Summary You can write an **equation** to model a situation. An equation with numerical expressions is true or false. An equation with at least one variable is an **open sentence**. A **solution** of an open sentence is a value of a variable that makes the equation true.

Write an equation for each sentence. Is each equation *true, false,* or an *open sentence*?

21. Thirty-two plus five equals the product of six and six.

22. A number t divided by seventeen equals the opposite of three.

23. The product of four and twenty equals eighty.

24. The admission price to an art museum increased by \$1.75 to \$6.50. Let p be the original admission price. Write an equation to model the situation.

■ Solving One-Step Equations

Summary To solve an equation, use an **inverse operation** and the **properties of equality** to get the variable alone on one side of the equation.

Solve each equation.

25. $6 + y = 17$

26. $-2 = a - 10$

27. $3x = -15$

28. $\frac{m}{9} = 3$

29. $\frac{w}{4} = 32$

30. $40 = -5b$

■ Try, Test, Revise

Summary You can solve some problems by trying an answer. Use each incorrect conjecture to make a better estimate of the correct answer.

31. Marcella and Danilo went to a bookstore. Marcella bought 2 notebooks and 3 pens for $14.50. Danilo bought 1 notebook and 2 pens for $7.50. How much does 1 notebook cost?

■ Inequalities and Their Graphs

Summary To graph an **inequality,** use a number line. Use an open dot for $>$ and $<$. Use a closed dot for $\geq$ and $\leq$.

Graph the solutions of each inequality.

32. $m > 5$

33. $t \geq -2$

34. $0 < r$

35. $w \leq 6$

Write an inequality for each sentence.

36. The temperature t is less than zero degrees.

37. The height h is greater than twelve feet.

■ Solving One-Step Inequalities

Summary To solve a one-step inequality, use inverse operations and the **properties of inequality** to get the variable alone on one side of the inequality. When multiplying or dividing each side of an inequality by a negative number, *reverse* the direction of the inequality symbol.

Solve each inequality.

38. $n - 4 > 10$

39. $t + 6 \geq 3$

40. $-3 < r + 5$

41. $-5 \leq k - 7$

42. $6s \leq 18$

43. $\frac{m}{3} < -2$

44. $-d > 14$

45. $\frac{c}{-4} \geq -9$

2 Assessment

Is each equation *true, false,* or an *open sentence?*

1. $24 = 3(-8)$

2. $5x + 28 = 153$

3. $18(-7 \div 7) = (-2)(9)$

4. $-6 + 15 = (120 \div 20) - (5 - 8)$

Simplify. Use the Commutative and the Associative Properties.

5. $50 \cdot 38 \cdot 2$ **6.** $45 + 62 + 55$

7. $2 \cdot 27 \cdot 5$ **8.** $99 + (-7) + 101$

9. **TEST PREP** Which property does $3 + (7 + 2) = (3 + 7) + 2$ show?
  A. Commutative Property of Addition
  B. Identity Property of Addition
  C. Distributive Property
  D. Commutative Property of Multiplication
  E. Associative Property of Addition

Simplify each expression.

10. $2(x + y) - 2y$

11. $5a + 2b + 3a - 7b$

12. $3(2r - 5) + 8(r + 2)$

13. $(-2c + 3d)(-5) + 3(-2c) - (-8d)$

Solve each equation.

14. $k - 23 = 17$ **15.** $\frac{t}{-5} = 15$

16. $y \div 12 = -3$ **17.** $7w = -217$

18. $-9 + a = 11$ **19.** $n - 2 = 13$

20. $120 = 38 + p$ **21.** $w \cdot (-2) = 14$

22. $r + 6 = 30$ **23.** $m - 7 = -3$

24. $9t = 18$ **25.** $-3f = -42$

26. $5 = \frac{s}{-7}$ **27.** $\frac{h}{12} = 12$

For Exercises 28 and 29, write and solve an equation.

28. *Architecture* The length of a room is 4 m greater than the width. The perimeter of the room is 28 m. Find the width of the room.

29. Brian bought a used bike for $25 less than its original price. He paid a total of $88 for the bike. What was the original price of the bike?

30. *Writing* How are the rules for solving inequalities similar to those for solving equations? How are they different?

Write an inequality for each situation. Graph the solutions.

31. The total t is greater than 5.

32. The perimeter p is less than 64.

33. The number of passengers p on the bus is no more than 45.

34. The number of students s that ran in the road race was not less than 55.

35. The number of questions q answered correctly is at most 49.

Solve each inequality.

36. $5 \le x + 1$ **37.** $3a > 4$

38. $y - 6 < 9$ **39.** $-2n \le 10$

40. $\frac{b}{3} \ge \frac{1}{3}$ **41.** $\frac{p}{-2} < -5$

42. $r + 8 > 12$ **43.** $j - 7 \le 24$

44. $h - 5 \ge -16$ **45.** $8 + b < -3$

46. $3k \le -27$ **47.** $\frac{h}{4} > 16$

48. $9 < \frac{a}{6}$ **49.** $-7z < 21$

Choose the best answer.

1. You make $8.00 per hour. Each week you work n hours. Which expression describes your weekly pay?
   A. $\frac{n}{8}$
   B. $8 - n$
   C. $n + 8$
   D. $8n$

2. Which equation shows the Associative Property of Addition?
   A. $9 + 7 + 8 = 9 + 8 + 7$
   B. $(8 + 3) + 13 = 8 + (3 + 13)$
   C. $12 + (-4) + 0 = 12 + (-4)$
   D. $19 \cdot (-3) \cdot 1 = 19 \cdot (-3)$

3. Mara ordered 5 bags of seed for $7 each and 3 wildflower seed kits for $9 each. She also paid a $13 shipping fee. Which expression shows the total cost?
   A. $5 + 7 + 3 + 9 + 13$
   B. $(5 \cdot 7) + (3 \cdot 9) + 13$
   C. $(5 + 3)16 + 13$
   D. $(5 \cdot 7 + 13) + (3 \cdot 9 + 13)$

4. Solve $r + 43 = -45$.
   A. -2
   B. 2
   C. 88
   D. -88

5. Evaluate $5(n + m)$ for $n = 12$ and $m = 6$.
   A. 30
   B. 66
   C. 90
   D. 810

6. Which integer is *not* a solution of $p + 12 < 16$?
   A. 4
   B. 3
   C. -4
   D. -28

7. Which group is in order from least to greatest?
   A. $4, 2, -2, -4$
   B. $|-3|, |-4|, -5, 6$
   C. $-7, 1, 4, |-12|$
   D. $-3, 4, -5, 6, -7$

8. Find $-23 + (-12)$.
   A. -11
   B. 11
   C. 35
   D. -35

9. Which symbol makes the statement true?
   $11 - (-4) \blacksquare -6 - 12$
   A. $>$
   B. $<$
   C. $=$
   D. $\leq$

10. **Writing** Simplify $25 \cdot 7 \cdot 4$. Explain how you can use the Commutative and Associative Properties to multiply mentally.

Use the Distributive Property to simplify each expression.

11. $7(58)$
12. $6(92)$
13. $5(1,002)$

Simplify each expression.

14. $3c - 4c + 1$
15. $6(t + 7) + t$
16. $-5(n + 9) - n$
17. $8 - 4(s + 2) - s$

Write an expression for each situation. Then simplify.

18. Lana bought juice for $3.25 and some fruit for $5.25. She also bought five beach passes for x dollars each.

19. Chung bought six brushes for b dollars each and two tubes of paint for p dollars each. He also bought paper for $7.59.

Is each equation *true, false,* or an *open sentence*?

20. $8(8 \div 2) = 32$
21. $18 = (2 \cdot 7) + 6$
22. $5x = 3 + 2x$
23. $14 - 1 = 52 \div 4$

Solve each equation.

24. $b - 7 = 21$
25. $18 + n = 37$
26. $\frac{c}{7} = 8$
27. $-9r = 108$

Graph each inequality.

28. $j < 4$
29. $t \geq -3$

Solve each inequality.

30. $24 > b + 17$
31. $x - 9 < -14$
32. $\frac{r}{13} \geq 3$
33. $-4s \geq -56$

Skills You Need
for Chapter 3

▶ Rounding numbers

Use before Lessons 3-1 and 3-2.

Round each number to the nearest ten.

1. 37
2. 12
3. 9
4. 2
5. 49
6. 105
7. 207
8. 602
9. 834
10. 6,009
11. 3
12. 45

▶ Comparing and ordering decimals

Use before Lesson 3-3.

Compare. Use >, <, or = to complete each statement.

13. 10.5 ■ 1.05
14. 8.792 ■ 8.972
15. 12.74 ■ 12.751
16. 0.96 ■ 1.32
17. 7.641 ■ 7.593
18. 6.3 ■ 6.38
19. 5.001 ■ 5.02
20. −9.871 ■ −10.3
21. −27.619 ■ −27.7
22. 14.0352 ■ 14.3052
23. 1.956 ■ 2.989
24. −24 ■ −23.68

Order each group of decimals from least to greatest.

25. 3.25, 4.19, 3.8, 4.91
26. 8.35, 8.349, 8.351, 9.25
27. 12.09, 12.01, 12.9, 12.1
28. 0.02, 0.017, 0.201, 0.0201
29. −1.4, −1.04, −1.401, −14.1
30. −2.3, −3.2, −3.19, −2.8

▶ Operations with decimals

Use before Lessons 3-5 and 3-6.

Simplify.

31. $3.4 + 8.09$
32. $9.32 - 7.65$
33. $5.6 + 9.3$
34. $8 - 4.93$
35. $0.59 + 3.06$
36. $5.8 - 4.92$
37. $10.579 + 4.638$
38. $2.19 - 0.984$
39. $3.4 \cdot 2.1$
40. $\frac{14.4}{1.2}$
41. $(1.001)(6.7)$
42. $16.25 \div 2.5$
43. $(6.1)(8.7)$
44. $40.02 \div 5.8$
45. $10.4 \cdot 5.3$
46. $\frac{77.38}{7.3}$

▶ Multiplying and dividing by multiples of 10

Use before Lesson 3-7.

Simplify.

47. $9.87 \cdot 10$
48. $5.32 \cdot 100$
49. $0.3 \cdot 1,000$
50. $15.407 \cdot 10,000$
51. $0.8 \div 10$
52. $8.42 \div 100$
53. $16.1 \div 1,000$
54. $12.09 \div 10,000$
55. $0.087 \cdot 10$
56. $157.4 \cdot 100$
57. $1,430 \div 10$
58. $1.89 \div 100$

Decimals and Equations

What you'll learn in this chapter:

- How to estimate with decimals
- How to solve equations with decimals
- How to convert metric units of measure

CURRENCY EVENTS

When you are shoppping, of course you want to know how much an item costs before you decide to buy it! When you travel in another country, you need to "translate" the cost into its value in U.S. dollars.

Compare Currencies For the chapter project, you will research currency exchange rates and calculate prices in different currencies. You will make a poster that shows prices in U.S. dollars and in the currencies of three other countries.

Steps to help you complete the project

Internet Connection

Web Extension
www.phschool.com

How to solve a problem by simplifying the problem

3-1

Rounding and Estimating

What You'll Learn

1 To round decimals

2 To estimate sums and differences

...And Why

To understand and apply appropriate estimation strategies in a variety of situations

Investigate

· **ESTIMATING IN THE REAL WORLD** ·

Some real-world problems require only an estimate for an answer. Others require an exact answer. Decide whether each situation needs an estimate or an exact answer. Explain your reasoning.

1. a headline noting the number of people living in China

2. the amount of money a babysitter charges per hour

3. the width of a window screen

4. the distance from Earth to the moon

PART 1 **Rounding Decimals**

You can round decimal numbers when you don't need exact values.

Quick *Review*

Ones	.	Tenths	Hundredths	Thousandths	Ten-thousandths
4	.	2	6	8	3

■ EXAMPLE 1

a. Round 4.2683 to the nearest tenth.

b. Round 4.2683 to the nearest integer.

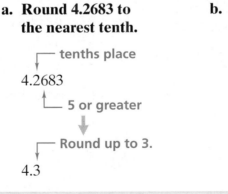

■ **TRY THIS** Identify the underlined place value. Then round each number to that place value.

5. 38.4<u>1</u>

6. <u>0</u>.7772

7. 7,098.<u>5</u>6

8. 274.94<u>3</u>4

9. 5.<u>0</u>25

10. 9.8<u>5</u>1

You can estimate an answer before you calculate it to make sure your answer is reasonable. If the answer is close to the estimate, then you know it is probably correct.

The symbol ≈ means "is approximately equal to."

Write $126   ≈ $130

Read $126 is approximately equal to $130.

One way to estimate is to round all numbers to the same place value.

Need Help? For help with decimal place value or adding and subtracting decimals, see Skills Handbook, pp. 727 and 730.

■ EXAMPLE 2

Estimate to find whether each answer is reasonable.

a.
Calculation		Estimate
$135.95	≈	$140
$15.90	≈	$20
+$24.05	≈	+$20
$275.90		$180

The answer is not close to the estimate. It is *not* reasonable.

b.
Calculation		Estimate
464.90	≈	460
−125.73	≈	−130
339.17		330

The answer is close to the estimate. It is reasonable.

■ **TRY THIS** Estimate.

11. 355.302 + 204.889

12. 453.56 − 230.07

A *front-end estimate* is often closer to the exact sum than an estimate you find by rounding. First add the front-end digits. Round to estimate the sum of the remaining digits. Then combine estimates.

REAL-WORLD 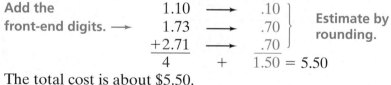 CONNECTION

■ EXAMPLE 3

The carrots cost $2.71, the red peppers cost $1.73, and the broccoli cost $1.10. Estimate the total cost of the vegetables.

Add the front-end digits. →

1.10	→	.10	⎫ Estimate by
1.73	→	.70	⎬ rounding.
+2.71	→	.70	⎭
4	+	1.50 = 5.50	

The total cost is about $5.50.

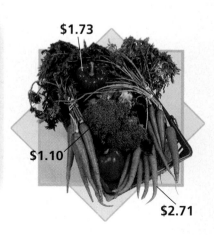

$1.73

$1.10

$2.71

■ **TRY THIS** Estimate using front-end estimation.

13. 6.75 + 2.2 + 9.58

14. $1.07 + $2.49 + $7.40

You can also use *clustering* to estimate the sum of several numbers that are close to one value.

REAL-WORLD  CONNECTION

EXAMPLE 4

Telephone Service **Estimate the total long-distance charge for the months of May, June, July, and August shown at the left.**

four months
↓
The values cluster around $15. ⟶ $15 \cdot 4 = 60$

The long-distance charge is about $60.00.

■ **TRY THIS** Estimate using clustering.

15. $4.50 + $5.20 + $5.55

16. 26.7 + 26.2 + 24.52 + 25.25 + 23.9

In this lesson, you have seen several methods for finding a reasonable estimate. Here are two methods used for the same situation.

■ Different Ways to Solve a Problem

Estimate the total cost of four items priced at $4.39, $3.75, $4.96, and $2.40.

Method 1

Round each price to the nearest dollar. Then add.

$4.39 + $3.75 + $4.96 + $2.40
$4   + $4   + $5   + $2   = $15

Method 2

Use front-end estimation.

$4.39	⟶	$.40
3.75	⟶	.80
4.96	⟶	1.00
+2.40	⟶	.40
$13	+	$2.60 = $15.60

Choose a Method

1. Which method would you use to estimate the cost of the items? Explain.

2. Find the exact cost. Which estimate is nearer the exact cost?

Exercises

Round to the underlined place value.

1. 27.3<u>8</u>56

2. 0.91<u>22</u>

3. 1,04<u>5</u>.98

4. 345.<u>6</u>78

Estimate by rounding.

5. $37.99 − $27.32

6. 1.58 + 17.0244

7. 72.98 − 28.301

Estimate using front-end estimation.

8. $6.04 + $3.45 + $4.43

9. $5.92 + $4.07

10. 9.89 + 2.43 + 8.37

Estimate by clustering.

11. 44.87 + 42.712 + 43.5

12. $9.50 + $8.45 + $9.08

13. 0.18 + 0.23 + 0.19

14. *Open-ended* Describe a situation in which a rounded answer is appropriate. Then describe one in which an exact answer is necessary.

PRACTICE AND PROBLEM SOLVING

Round to the underlined place value.

15. 1.<u>5</u>28

16. 4,652.9<u>8</u>7

17. <u>0</u>.5834

18. 33.3<u>0</u>4

Estimate by rounding.

19. $4.89
     + $3.87

20. 8.974
     + 2.154

21. $16.81
     + $11.49

22. 102.44
     + 48.35

23. $5.65 − $2.25

24. 600 − 209.52

25. 0.08 + 17.02

26. 27.4 − 16.02

Estimate using front-end estimation.

27. 14.39
     + 79.102

28. $38.59
     + $15.28

29. 78.87
     + 11.49

30. $412.44
     + $72.23

31. 7.04 + 2.45

32. 7.54 + 3.02

33. 2.298 + 7.750

34. 6.79 − 4.041

Estimate by clustering.

35. $7.43 + $7.05 + $6.95 + $7.29

36. 15.4 + 16 + 15.9 + 16.25 + 15.7

37. 800 + 810.5 + 807.35 + 803.9

38. 54.23 + 56.12 + 57.98 + 55.55

Estimate. State the method you used.

39. $8.99 + $8.01

40. 2.3 + 2.3 + 4.56

41. $89.90 − $49.29

42. 102.54 − 74.75

43. 20.55 − 1.48

44. $11.97 − $2.29

45. $19.01 + $10.99 + $7.49

46. 6.57 + 5.99 + 5.70 + 6.25

47. *Statistics* In 1990, the population of the state of Georgia was 6.8 million. In 1950, the population was 3.44 million. About how much greater was Georgia's population in 1990 than in 1950?

48. *Geography* Lake Superior, the largest of the Great Lakes, has an area of 31,760 mi². Lake Erie, the smallest of the Great Lakes, has an area of 9,920 mi². About how much larger is Lake Superior than Lake Erie?

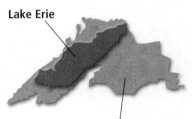

Lake Erie

Lake Superior

49. *Weather* Mobile, Alabama, has an average annual rainfall of 63.96 in. The average annual rainfall in San Francisco, California, is 19.70 in. About how much more rain falls each year in Mobile than in San Francisco?

50. *Error Analysis* You used a calculator to find 383.8 − 21.9. Your estimate was 360, but your display reads 164.8. How could you have gotten 164.8 on your calculator?

51. *Writing* You have $11.50 to buy two presents. You find one item that costs $7.43. Another item costs $4.41. What estimation strategy will help you decide whether you have enough money to buy both? Explain.

52. TEST PREP Choose the phrase that best completes the statement. The sum of $12.45 and $7.65 is __?__.
A. less than $20.00 **B.** greater than $20.00 **C.** an integer **D.** greater than $25.00

▶ MIXED REVIEW

Solve each inequality. *(Lesson 2-10)*

53. $9x \leq 27$

54. $4x < 16$

55. $-6k > -24$

56. $-3y \leq 0$

Simplify. *(Lesson 1-9)*

57. $(-2)(-2)$

58. $4(-3)$

59. $6(-5)$

60. $-8 \div 2$

61. *Choose a Strategy* Ming's model vehicle collection contains 4-wheeled trucks and 2-wheeled bikes. She owns an even number of vehicles, and they have 26 wheels in all. If Ming has a little more than twice as many bikes as trucks, how many of each does she own?

See also Extra Practice section.

Estimating Decimal Products and Quotients

PART 1 Estimating Products

You can use mental math to estimate products and quotients. It is a good idea to estimate answers to check your calculations.

■ EXAMPLE 1

Estimate 7.65 · 3.2.

$7.65 \approx 8$ $3.2 \approx 3$ **Round to the nearest integer.**

   $8 \cdot 3 = 24$ **Multiply.**

$7.65 \cdot 3.2 \approx 24$

■ **TRY THIS** Estimate each product.

1. $4.72 \cdot 1.8$ **2.** $17.02 \cdot 3.78$ **3.** $8.25 \cdot 19.8$

REAL-WORLD  CONNECTION

■ EXAMPLE 2

Arlene bought 6 yd of fabric to make a Lone Star quilt. The fabric cost $6.75/yd. The sales clerk charged Arlene $45.90 before tax. Did the clerk make a mistake? Explain.

$6.75 \approx 7$ **Round to the nearest dollar.**

$7 \cdot 6 = 42$ **Multiply 7 times 6, the number of yards of fabric.**

The sales clerk made a mistake. Since $6.75 < 7$, the actual cost should be less than the estimate. The clerk should have charged Arlene less than $42.00 before tax.

■ TRY THIS

4. You buy 8 rolls of film for your camera. Each roll costs $4.79. Estimate the cost of the film before tax.

The quilter is working on a Lone Star quilt. The quilt is 7.8 ft wide and 8.5 ft long.

When dividing, remember these names for the parts of a division sentence.

dividend

$6 \div 3 = 2$ — quotient

divisor

When dividing, you can use *compatible numbers* to estimate quotients. **Compatible numbers** are numbers that are easy to divide mentally. When you estimate a quotient, first round the divisor, and then round the dividend to a compatible number.

REAL-WORLD CONNECTION

▌EXAMPLE 3

5.61 kg

1.57 kg

Measurement **A bowling ball has a mass of 5.61 kg. A bowling pin has a mass of 1.57 kg. How many bowling pins are about equal in mass to one bowling ball? Estimate 5.61 ÷ 1.57.**

$1.57 \approx 2$ **Round the divisor.**

$5.61 \approx 6$ **Round the dividend to a multiple of 2 that is close to 5.61.**

$6 \div 2 = 3$ **Divide.**

The mass of three bowling pins is about equal to that of one bowling ball.

▌**TRY THIS** Estimate each quotient.

5. $38.9 \div 1.79$ **6.** $11.95 \div 2.1$ **7.** $82.52 \div 4.25$

You can estimate to determine the reasonableness of results.

▌EXAMPLE 4

Number Sense **Is 2.15 a reasonable quotient for 17.931 ÷ 8.34?**

$8.34 \approx 8$ **Round the divisor.**

$17.931 \approx 16$ **Round the dividend to a multiple of 8 that is close to 17.931.**

$16 \div 8 = 2$ **Divide.**

Since 2.15 is close to the estimate 2, it is reasonable.

▌**TRY THIS** Use estimation. Is each quotient reasonable?

8. $1.564 \div 2.3 = 0.68$ **9.** $26.0454 \div 4.98 = 52.3$

 *Test Prep TIP*

You can sometimes use estimation to eliminate possible responses on a multiple choice test.

Solve $8.19 \div 2.1$.

A. 39   **B.** 3.9

C. 4.1   **D.** 0.041

If you estimate $8 \div 2 \approx 4$, then you know you can eliminate choices A and D.

Exercises

▶ CHECK UNDERSTANDING

Estimate each product.

1. $4.562 \cdot 7.02$

2. $11.15 \cdot 4.44$

3. $6.3 \cdot 9.2$

4. $24.5 \cdot 4.2$

Estimate each quotient using compatible numbers.

5. $3.9 \div 2.1$

6. $0.33 \div 0.14$

7. $19.56 \div 0.71$

8. $\$585 \div 11.75$

9. *Number Sense* Explain how you would find a reasonable estimate for $14.90 \div 4.56$.

▶ PRACTICE AND PROBLEM SOLVING

Estimate each product or quotient.

10. $329.08 \cdot 56$

11. $0.98 \cdot 40.05$

12. $92.81 \cdot 48.33$

13. $16.2 \cdot 9.21$

14. $32.57 \cdot 4.2$

15. $193.7 \cdot 1.78$

16. $876.66 \cdot 39.34$

17. $16.33 \cdot 3.5$

18. $120.32 \div 4.948$

19. $\$2.97 \div 0.64$

20. $9.418 \div 1.583$

21. $7.95 \div 2.1$

22. $9.392 \div 2.9$

23. $\$32.43 \div 4.68$

24. $-483.09 \div 72$

25. $-7.75 \div (-1.97)$

Determine whether each product or quotient is reasonable. If it is not reasonable, find a reasonable result.

26. $7.008 \cdot 3.2 = 22.4256$

27. $102.6 \div 22.5 = 45.6$

28. $\$32.40 \div 4.80 = \$67.50$

29. $-46.82(-1.5) = 702.3$

30. $6.009(-11.9) = -71.5071$

31. $1.76(0.18) = 3.168$

32. *Open-ended* Write an expression that includes a product of decimals. Estimate the value of your expression.

33. *Gas Mileage* Shari is planning a 450-mi car trip. Her car can travel about 39 mi on a gallon of gasoline. Gasoline costs $\$1.19$/gal. About how much will the gas cost for her trip?

34. **TEST PREP** Greta ran the 400-m dash in 49.07 s. If Greta ran at a constant rate, how many meters did she run in one second?
   A. between 9 m and 10 m
   B. between 10 m and 11 m
   C. between 8 m and 9 m
   D. between 11 m and 12 m

35. *Writing* Two people estimate the product $\$1.99 \cdot 8.5$. Is it necessary that they get the same estimate? Explain.

36. **Consumer Awareness** You review your sales slip after buying 4 CDs that cost $14.95 each. Before tax, the total was $77.80. Is this total correct? Explain.

Data Analysis Use the table below for Exercises 37–39.

Hospital Staff Wages (40-h week)

Occupation	Dallas, TX	Washington, DC
Physical Therapist	$733.20	$655.20
Pharmacist	$793.60	$851.60
Nurse	$606.80	$714.80

SOURCE: *The American Almanac of Jobs and Salaries*

37. Estimate the hourly wage for each staff position.

38. Estimate the yearly salary for each staff position.

39. How much more per hour does a physical therapist in Dallas, Texas make than a physical therapist in Washington, D.C.?

40. **Health** Humans breathe about 15 breaths in a minute. The average breath at rest contains 0.76 liters of air. About how many liters of air will you breathe while at rest for 25 minutes?

41. **Mathematical Reasoning** You estimate $21.2 \div 3.75$ to be 5. Your friend estimates the quotient to be 7. Explain how the two estimates can be different and yet both be reasonable.

Journal

Describe a real-world situation in which you would use estimation to check the reasonableness of a calculation.

▶ MIXED REVIEW

Estimate each sum or difference. *(Lesson 3-1)*

42. $2.99 + $6.01

43. $12.3 + 12.3 + 14.56$

44. $25.90 − $5.79

45. $1,242.24 − 24.05$

46. $18.95 − 7.48$

47. $7.47 − $5.50

In which quadrant or on which axis of a coordinate plane does each ordered pair lie? *(Lesson 1-10)*

48. $(2, 4)$

49. $(-5, -3)$

50. $(8, -6)$

51. $(0, 8)$

52. $(-9, -2)$

53. $(-5, 0)$

54. **Choose a Strategy** A bus trip from Sacramento to Los Angeles takes 7 h 40 min. If the bus leaves Sacramento at 11:40 A.M., at what time will it arrive in Los Angeles?

See also **Extra Practice** section.

Mean, Median, and Mode

PART 1 Finding Mean, Median, and Mode

Mean, *median*, and *mode* are **measures of central tendency** of a collection of data. Consider the data 2, 3, 4, 5, 8, 8, and 12.

The **mean** is the sum of the data items divided by the number of data items.

$$\text{mean} = \frac{2 + 3 + 4 + 5 + 8 + 8 + 12}{7}$$
$$= \frac{42}{7}$$
$$\text{mean} = 6$$

The **median** is the middle number when data items are written in order and there are an odd number of data items. For an even number of data items, the median is the mean of the two middle numbers.

2   3   4   5   8   8   12
median

The **mode** is the data item that occurs most often. There can be one mode, more than one mode, or no mode.

2   3   4   5   8   8   12
mode

What You'll Learn

1 To find mean, median, and mode

2 To choose mean, median, or mode to describe data

. . . And Why

To apply different averages to consumer issues

REAL-WORLD CONNECTION

■ EXAMPLE 1

Six elementary students are participating in a one-week Readathon to raise money for a good cause. Use the graph at the right. Find the (a) mean, (b) median, and (c) mode.

a. Mean: $\dfrac{\text{sum of data items}}{\text{number of data items}} = \dfrac{40 + 45 + 48 + 50 + 50 + 59}{6}$

$$= \frac{292}{6}$$
$$= 48.66 \ldots$$

Rounded to the nearest tenth, the mean is 48.7.

b. Median: 40 45 48 50 50 59   Write the data in order.

$\dfrac{48 + 50}{2} = 49$ Find the mean of the two middle numbers.

The median is 49.

c. Mode: Find the data item that occurs most often.
The mode is 50.

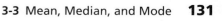

■ **TRY THIS** Find the mean, median, and mode.

1. 12 14 26 37 8 14 **2.** 2.3 4.3 3.2 2.9 2.7 2.3

■ EXAMPLE 2

How many modes, if any, does each have?

a. **$1.50 $2.00 $2.25 $2.40 $3.50 $4.00**

No values are the same, so there is no mode.

b. **2 3 6 <u>8</u> <u>8</u> 10 11 12 <u>14</u> <u>14</u> 18 20**

Both 8 and 14 appear more often than the other data items. Since they appear the same number of times, there are two modes.

c. **grape, grape, banana, nectarine, <u>strawberry</u>, <u>strawberry</u>, <u>strawberry</u>, orange, watermelon**

Strawberry appears most often. There is one mode.

■ **TRY THIS** Find the number of modes.

3. 11 9 7 7 8 8 13 11 **4.** 38.5 55.4 45.3 38.5 68.4

An **outlier** is a data value that is much higher or lower than the other data values. An outlier can affect the mean of a group of data.

DATA ANALYSIS CONNECTION

■ EXAMPLE 3

Use the data in the Central America map at the left.

a. Which data value is an outlier?

The data value for El Salvador, 27%, is an outlier. It is an outlier because it is 12% away from the closest data value.

b. How does the outlier affect the mean?

$\frac{78}{7} \approx 11.1$ Find the mean with the outlier.

$\frac{51}{6} = 8.5$ Find the mean *without* the outlier.

$11.1 - 8.5 = 2.6$

The outlier raises the mean about 2.6 points.

Percent of Land That Can Be Farmed in Central American Countries

Guatemala 12%

Belize 2%

Honduras 15%

Nicaragua 9%

El Salvador 27%

Costa Rica 6%

Panama 7%

SOURCE: *The New York Times Almanac*

■ **TRY THIS** Find an outlier in each group of data below and tell how it affects the mean. Round to the nearest tenth.

5. 9 10 12 13 8 9 31 9 **6.** 1 17.5 18 19.5 16 17.5

One measure of central tendency may be better than another to describe data. For example, consider the wages of the employees shown at the right. Here are the measures of central tendency.

Employees' Hourly Wages	
$5.50	$6.20
$5.50	$6.30
$5.50	$8.00
$6.00	$17.00

Mode: $5.50
Mean: $7.50
Median: $6.10

The mode is the lowest wage listed. So the mode does not describe the data well.

The mean is above the hourly wage of all but two workers. The mean is influenced by the outlier, $17.

The median is the best measure of central tendency here since it is not influenced by the outlier.

EXAMPLE 4

Which measure of central tendency best describes each situation? Explain.

a. the favorite movies of students in the eighth grade

Mode; since the data are not numerical, the mode is the appropriate measure. When determining the most frequently chosen item, or when the data are not numerical, use the mode.

b. the daily high temperatures during a week in July

Mean; since daily high temperatures in July are not likely to have an outlier, mean is the appropriate measure. When the data have no outliers, use the mean.

c. the distances students in your class travel to school

Median; since one student may live much farther from school than the majority of students, the median is the appropriate measure. When an outlier may significantly influence the mean, use the median.

Reading Math

To help you recall that *median* means "middle number," think of the green, grassy *median strip* in the middle of a divided highway.

TRY THIS

7. **a.** *Comparison Shopping* Toshio found the following prices for sport shirts: $20, $26, $27, $28, $21, $42, $18, and $20. Find the mean, median, and mode for the shirt prices.
   b. *Reasoning* Which measure of central tendency best describes the data? Justify your reasoning.

Exercises

► CHECK UNDERSTANDING

Find the mean, median, and mode. When the answer is not an integer, round to the nearest tenth. Identify any outliers.

1. 37 4 7 3 11 9 13 5

2. 126 123 115 125 123

Find the mean, median, and mode. Which measure of central tendency best describes the data? Explain.

3. minutes on the Internet
50 63 59 85 367 48

4. heights of students in inches
51 45 47 48 50 50 50 52

► PRACTICE AND PROBLEM SOLVING

Find the mean, median, and mode. When the answer is not an integer, round to the nearest tenth. Identify any outliers.

5. 47 56 57 63 89 44 56

6. 3,456 560 435 456

7. 4 5 2 3 2 3 3 3 1 1 3

8. 5.6 6.8 1.2 6.5 7.9 6.5

Which measure of central tendency best describes each situation? Explain.

9. numbers of apples in 2-lb bags

10. favorite brands of jeans of 14-year-olds

11. ages of students in a fifth-grade classroom

12. most common shoe color in a classroom

13. widths of computer screens at a bank

14. number of pets owned by your classmates

Find the mean, median, and mode. When the answer is not an integer, round to the nearest tenth. Which measure of central tendency best describes the data? Explain.

15. weight of backpacks in pounds
14.5 7 13.5 15 15 16 13.5

16. resting heart rate in beats per minute
79 72 80 81 40 72

17. numbers of raisins in cookies
20 1 18 19 14 18

18. temperatures (°F) on race days
53° 53° 55° 45° 47° 51° 57° 58°

19. **TEST PREP** The average cost of a meal at the Grand Plaza is $20. Which of the following statements *cannot* be true?
A. The cost of four meals is greater than $20. **B.** Some meals cost less than $10.
C. Each meal costs exactly $20. **D.** Each meal costs more than $20.

Use the table at the right for Exercises 20–22. Round your answers to the nearest tenth where necessary.

Fat and Calorie Content
(per 2-tablespoon serving)

Seed or Nut	Fat (g)	Calories
Peanut	8.9	104
Pecan	9.1	90
Pistachio	7.9	92
Pumpkin	7.9	93
Sunflower	8.9	102
Walnut	7.7	80

SOURCE: *The T-Factor Fat Gram Counter*

20. **Data Analysis** You make a mixture using the same amount of each kind of seed and nut.
    a. What is the mean number of grams of fat in a 2-tablespoon serving of the mixture?
    b. What is the mean number of calories in a 2-tablespoon serving of the mixture?

21. a. **Writing** Describe two different mixtures that use a total of 8 tablespoons.
    b. **Open-ended** Which recipe has the lower mean fat content for a 2-tablespoon serving?

22. **Nutrition** A mixture of equal amounts of pumpkin seeds, sunflower seeds, and pistachios contains 12 tablespoons in all. How many grams of fat and how many calories does the mixture contain?

▶ **MIXED REVIEW**

Estimate each product or quotient. *(Lesson 3-2)*

23. $9.01 ÷ $1.42   **24.** 7.5 · 89.1   **25.** 37.32 ÷ 5.99   **26.** 12.56 · $2.99

Simplify each expression. *(Lesson 2-3)*

27. $6x + 8 + 2$ **28.** $5z + 4x + 3z$ **29.** $x - 4t + 2t + 5$

30. **Choose a Strategy** Karen sells children's hats for $4 and adults' hats for $7. On Saturday, she sold 120 hats, and she collected $720. How many adults' hats did she sell?

CHAPTER PROJECT 3   **ACTIVITY 1 ESTIMATING**

Suppose you visit Mexico, and you want to estimate the cost of a jacket in U.S. dollars. The jacket costs 1,258 pesos. The exchange rate is $.117 = 1 peso or 8.54 pesos = $1. The 1,258-peso jacket is worth $147.19. When you shop, you can estimate the price in dollars by either multiplying or dividing.

Multiply: 1,258 pesos · $.117/peso ≈ 1,258 · $.10 = $125.80
Divide: 1,258 pesos ÷ 8.54 pesos/dollar ≈ 1,200 ÷ 8/$1 = $150

Estimate the price in dollars of a shirt that costs 326 pesos and of a souvenir that costs 45 pesos.

Technology
After Lesson 3-3

Mean and Median on a Graphing Calculator

You can use a graphing calculator to find means and medians.

■ EXAMPLE

Find (a) the mean and (b) the median number of acres in Ohio zoos.

Zoos in Ohio

Zoo	Number of Acres	Number of Species
Cincinnati Zoo	70	712
Cleveland Metroparks Zoo	165	599
Columbus Zoo	90	650
Toledo Zoological Gardens	62	633

SOURCE: *The World Almanac*

a. To use the mean function, press
`2nd` `STAT` `▶` `▶` 3.

Then press `2nd` `(` and enter the data, separated by commas. End by pressing `2nd` `)` `)`.

Press `ENTER` to calculate the mean.

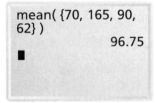

```
mean( {70, 165, 90,
62} )
            96.75
■
```

The mean is about 97 acres.

b. To use the median function, press
`2nd` `STAT` `▶` `▶` 4.

Then press `2nd` `(` and enter the data, separated by commas. End the list by pressing `2nd` `)` `)`.

Press `ENTER` to calculate the median.

```
median( {70, 165, 90,
62} )
              80
■
```

The median is 80 acres.

Use a calculator to find the mean and median.

1. number of species in Ohio zoos

2. 85°F, 79°F, 80°F, 75°F, 82°F

3. $3.75, $4.50, $9.25, $4.70, $5.90

4. 100, 95, 82, 102, 78, 76

5.

Miles of Atlantic Coastline by State

State	DE	FL	GA	ME	MD	MA	NH	NJ	NY	NC	RI	SC	VA
Miles	28	580	100	228	31	192	13	130	127	301	40	187	112

SOURCE: National Oceanic and Atmospheric Administration, U.S. Dept. of Commerce

Using Formulas

3-4

PART 1 Substituting into Formulas

A **formula** is an equation that shows a relationship between quantities that are represented by variables.

An important formula in math and science is $d = rt$, where d is the distance, r is the speed, and t is the time spent traveling.

REAL-WORLD CONNECTION

■ EXAMPLE 1

Suppose you travel 162 miles in 3 hours. Use the formula $d = rt$ to find your average speed.

$d = rt$ Write the formula.

$162 = (r)(3)$ Substitute 162 for d and 3 for t.

$\dfrac{162}{3} = \dfrac{3r}{3}$ Divide each side by 3.

$54 = r$ Simplify.

Your average speed is 54 mi/h.

■ **TRY THIS** Use the formula $d = rt$. Find d, r, or t.

1. $d = 273$ mi, $t = 9.75$ h   **2.** $d = 540.75$ in., $r = 10.5$ in./yr

REAL-WORLD CONNECTION

■ EXAMPLE 2

You can estimate the temperature outside using the chirps of a cricket. Use the formula $F = \frac{n}{4} + 37$, where n is the number of chirps a cricket makes in one minute, and F is the temperature in degrees Fahrenheit. Estimate the temperature when a cricket chirps 100 times in a minute.

$F = \dfrac{n}{4} + 37$ Write the formula.

$F = \dfrac{100}{4} + 37$ Replace n with 100.

$F = 25 + 37$ Divide.

$F = 62$ Add.

The temperature is about 62°F.

What You'll Learn

1 To substitute into formulas

2 To use the formula for the perimeter of a rectangle

. . . And Why

To use formulas to find perimeters, areas, and rates of speed

The chirping calls of crickets have been recorded at temperatures ranging from 45°F to 100°F.

■ **TRY THIS** Use the formula $F = \frac{n}{4} + 37$ to estimate the temperature in degrees Fahrenheit for each situation.

3. 96 chirps/min   **4.** 88 chirps/min   **5.** 66 chirps/min

PART 2   Using a Perimeter Formula

The **perimeter** of a figure is the distance around the figure. You can find the perimeter of a rectangle by adding the lengths of the four sides, or by using the formula $P = 2\ell + 2w$, where ℓ is the length and w is the width. For rectangles, it does not matter which dimension you choose to be the length or the width.

MEASUREMENT CONNECTION

■ **EXAMPLE 3**

Find the perimeter of the room. Use the formula for the perimeter of a rectangle, $P = 2\ell + 2w$.

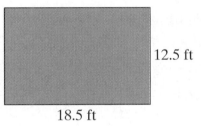

12.5 ft

18.5 ft

$P = 2\ell + 2w$ Write the formula.
$P = 2(18.5) + 2(12.5)$ Replace ℓ with 18.5 and w with 12.5.
$P = 37 + 25$ Multiply.
$P = 62$ Add.

The perimeter of the room is 62 ft.

■ **TRY THIS** Find the perimeter of each rectangle.

6.

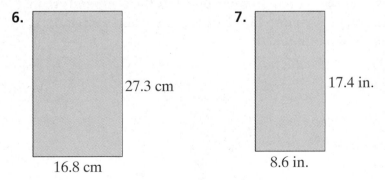

27.3 cm

16.8 cm

7.

17.4 in.

8.6 in.

Exercises

CHECK UNDERSTANDING

Use the formula $F = \frac{n}{4} + 37$ to find the temperature.

1. 120 chirps/min

2. 80 chirps/min

3. 92 chirps/min

4. 64 chirps/min

Use the formula $d = rt$. Find d, r, or t.

5. $r = 38.5$ m/h, $t = 12.5$ h

6. $d = 2{,}730$ mi, $t = 9.75$ h

7. $d = 596.39$ cm, $r = 2.3$ cm/s

8. $d = 10.2$ ft, $r = 0.5$ ft/h

9. The pronghorn antelope can run 0.73 mi/min. Use the formula $d = rt$ to find how far a pronghorn antelope can travel in 8 min at this speed.

PRACTICE AND PROBLEM SOLVING

Given that C is the temperature in degrees Celsius, use the formula $F = 1.8C + 32$ to find each temperature F in degrees Fahrenheit.

10. $C = 58$ **11.** $C = 14$ **12.** $C = -89$ **13.** $C = 56$ **14.** $C = 72$

Use the formula $P = 2\ell + 2w$. Find the perimeter of each rectangle.

15.

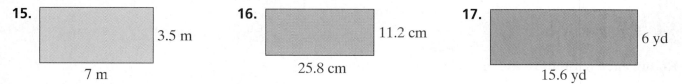

3.5 m

7 m

16.

11.2 cm

25.8 cm

17.

6 yd

15.6 yd

18. Use the formula for the area of a rectangle, $A = \ell w$. Find the area of each rectangle in Exercises 15–17.

19. *Geometry* The top surface of the world's longest rectangular strawberry shortcake was 175.33 ft long and 4 ft wide.
   a. Use the formula $A = \ell w$. Find the area of the top surface of the shortcake.
   b. What was the perimeter of the top surface of the shortcake?

20. *Measurement* The state of Colorado is nearly rectangular in shape. Find the approximate area of the state using the formula $A = \ell w$.

Colorado

270 mi

390 mi

Denver

21. A giant tortoise travels about 0.17mi/h on land. If a tortoise travels at a constant speed, how far can he travel in 2.5 h?

22. a. *Estimation* You can *estimate* a temperature in degrees Fahrenheit using the formula $F = 2 \cdot C + 30$, where C represents the temperature in degrees Celsius (°C). What is the approximate temperature in degrees Fahrenheit when it is 3°C? 5°C? 25°C?

   b. *Mathematical Reasoning* Is this formula better for estimating higher temperatures or lower temperatures? Explain.

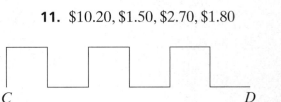

The weight of a giant tortoise hatchling is 0.001 of an adult's weight of 500 lb.

▶ MIXED REVIEW

Find the mean, median, and mode. When the answer is not an integer, round to the nearest integer. Which measure of central tendency best describes the data? *(Lesson 3-3)*

23. minutes of homework
8 125 154 120 105 125

24. number of mL per container
250 250 355 355 375 250

Solve each equation. *(Lesson 2-5)*

25. $c + 8 = 41$

26. $b + 32 = 19$

27. $98 = n + 42$

28. *Patterns* Which equation describes the relationship between the variables in the table? *(Lesson 1-7)*
   A. $n = t + 2$ **B.** $n = 2t$
   C. $t = n \cdot 2$ **D.** $t \div 2 = n$

n	14	16	18	20
t	7	8	9	10

✓ CHECKPOINT 1   Lessons 3-1 through 3-4

Round each number to the underlined place value.

1. 15.6<u>5</u>71

2. 0.89<u>1</u>4

3. 7,02<u>2</u>.56

4. 345.<u>6</u>78

Estimate.

5. $3.7 \cdot 8.06$

6. $17.25 + 6.66$

7. $8.7 - 9.6$

8. $4.21 \div 0.7$

Find the mean, median, and mode.

9. $47, 56, 58, 63$

10. $1, 4, 1, 3, 1, 2, 3, 2, 1, 2$

11. $\$10.20, \$1.50, \$2.70, \$1.80$

12. **TEST PREP** The path at the right is made of segments that are all the same length. The shortest distance from point C to point D is 7.2 m. What is the distance from point C to point D on the path shown?
   A. 6.2 m   **B.** 14.4 m   **C.** 21.6 m   **D.** 144.4 m

MATH TOOLBOX

Formulas in a Spreadsheet

You can use a computer spreadsheet to evaluate formulas. Look at the spreadsheet at the right. In the spreadsheet, the algebraic formula $d = rt$ is evaluated for $r = 50$ mi/h and $t = 3$ h.

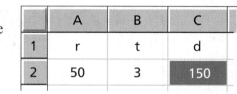

	A	B	C
1	r	t	d
2	50	3	150

The spreadsheet formula "=A2*B2" is used to calculate $d = rt$. The spreadsheet formula means that the value in cell C2 equals the value in cell A2 times the value in cell B2.

In spreadsheet formulas the asterisk symbol $*$ means multiply. The slash symbol $/$ means divide.

■ EXAMPLE

Use a spreadsheet and the formula $P = 2\ell + 2w$ to find the perimeter P of a rectangle. Evaluate the formula for a length ℓ of 7.8 in. and a width w of 2.6 in.

	A	B	C
1	ℓ	w	P
2	7.8	2.6	20.8

← Use the spreadsheet formula =2*A2+2*B2.

The perimeter is about 21 in.

Use a spreadsheet to find each perimeter.

1. $\ell = 5.6$ in., $w = 7.9$ in.   **2.** $\ell = 12.7$ in., $w = 15.6$ in.   **3.** $\ell = 0.2$ in., $w = 1.3$ in.

Use a spreadsheet to evaluate the formula $t = d \div r$ for the given values of d and r.

4. $d = 250$ mi, $r = 5$ mi/h   **5.** $d = 1,400$ mi, $r = 50$ mi/h   **6.** $d = 4,500$ mi, $r = 250$ mi/h

Write a spreadsheet formula for each algebraic formula.

7. to find A, using $A = 0.5bh$ **8.** to find P, using $P = 4a$ **9.** to find y, using $y = mx + b$

10. a. *Open-ended* Use a spreadsheet to evaluate the formula $A = \ell w$. How does the value of A change as you double the value of ℓ while keeping w unchanged?
   b. How does the value of A change as you double the values of both ℓ and w?

3-5

Solving Equations by Adding or Subtracting Decimals

What You'll Learn

1 To solve one-step decimal equations involving addition

2 To solve one-step decimal equations involving subtraction

. . . And Why

To model real-world situations in astronomy and money management

You can use the Subtraction Property of Equality to solve an equation. Remember to subtract the same number from each side of the equation.

■ EXAMPLE 1

Solve $n + 4.5 = -9.7$.

$$n + 4.5 = -9.7$$
$$n + 4.5 - 4.5 = -9.7 - 4.5 \quad \text{Subtract 4.5 from each side.}$$
$$n = -14.2 \quad \text{Simplify.}$$

Check
$$n + 4.5 = -9.7$$
$$-14.2 + 4.5 \stackrel{?}{=} -9.7 \quad \text{Replace } n \text{ with } -14.2.$$
$$-9.7 = -9.7 ✔$$

■ **TRY THIS** Solve each equation.

1. $x + 4.9 = 18.8$ **2.** $14.73 = -24.23 + b$

MEASUREMENT CONNECTION

■ EXAMPLE 2

Astronomy **A communications satellite is circling Earth. Use the diagram below to find the approximate distance from the satellite to the moon.**

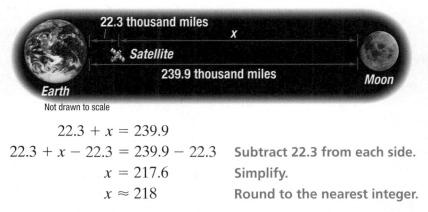

22.3 thousand miles

x

Satellite

239.9 thousand miles

Earth

Moon

Not drawn to scale

$$22.3 + x = 239.9$$
$$22.3 + x - 22.3 = 239.9 - 22.3 \quad \text{Subtract 22.3 from each side.}$$
$$x = 217.6 \quad \text{Simplify.}$$
$$x \approx 218 \quad \text{Round to the nearest integer.}$$

The distance from the satellite to the moon is about 218 thousand mi.

A communications satellite follows a circular path that is 22.3 thousand miles above Earth, orbiting above the equator. This *geostationary* orbit allows the satellite to maintain a fixed position above Earth.

■ **TRY THIS**

3. *Analyzing Markup* A store's cost plus markup is the price you pay for an item. Suppose a pair of shoes costs a store $35.48. You pay $70. Write and solve an equation to find the store's markup.

PART 2 Using Addition to Solve Equations

You can also use the Addition Property of Equality to solve equations. Remember to add the same number to each side of the equation.

■ **EXAMPLE 3**

Solve $k - 14.4 = -18.39$.

$$k - 14.4 = -18.39$$
$$k - 14.4 + 14.4 = -18.39 + 14.4 \quad \text{Add 14.4 to each side.}$$
$$k = -3.99 \quad \text{Simplify.}$$

Need Help? For help with adding and subtracting decimals, see Skills Handbook, p. 730.

■ **TRY THIS** Solve each equation.

4. $n - 5.85 = 15.25$ 5. $-10 = c - 2.6$

REAL-WORLD 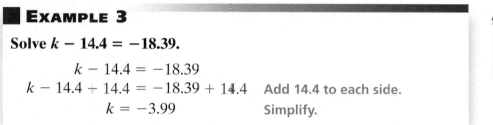 CONNECTION

■ **EXAMPLE 4**

Personal Finance Danzel wrote a check for $76.85. His new account balance is $235.00. What was his previous balance?

| Words | previous balance | minus | check | is | new balance |

Let p = previous balance.

| Equation | p | $-$ | 76.85 | $=$ | 235 |

$$p - 76.85 = 235$$
$$p - 76.85 + 76.85 = 235 + 76.85 \quad \text{Add 76.85 to each side.}$$
$$p = 311.85 \quad \text{Simplify.}$$

Danzel had $311.85 in his account before he wrote the check.

■ **TRY THIS**

6. You spent $14.95 for a new shirt. You now have $12.48. Write and solve an equation to find how much money you had before you bought the shirt.

Exercises

CHECK UNDERSTANDING

Complete the steps for each equation.

1.
$$x + 1.2 = 15$$
$$x + 1.2 - \blacksquare = 15 - \blacksquare$$
$$x = \blacksquare$$

2.
$$y - 3.33 = 12.42$$
$$y - 3.33 + \blacksquare = 12.42 + \blacksquare$$
$$y = \blacksquare$$

State the first step in solving each equation.

3. $a + 8.5 = 12.53$

4. $54.2 + x = 98$

5. $3.4 = c - 1.9$

Solve each equation.

6. $6.35 + b = 9.89$

7. $x + 0.035 = 0.915$

8. $12.13 = n + 1.4$

9. $d - 4.9 = 18.8$

10. $c - 19.2 = 24$

11. $-2.5 = q - 1.7$

12. *Critical Thinking* Do the equations $x + 2.4 = 1.5$ and $x + 24 = 15$ have the same solution? Explain.

PRACTICE AND PROBLEM SOLVING

Mental Math Use mental math to solve each equation.

13. $1.60 = 0.40 + s$

14. $x + 8.8 = 9.9$

15. $5.5 = x - 5.5$

Solve each equation.

16. $c + 9 = 3.7$

17. $b + 7.6 = 23$

18. $43.6 = n + 17.5$

19. $-5.6 = y - 8$

20. $4.035 = a - 3.25$

21. $h - (-1.5) = 1.5$

22. $n + (-7) = -7.08$

23. $-32 = x + (-8.05)$

24. $9.03 + y = 1.12$

25. $e + (-7.8) = -6.7$

26. $a - 108.8 = -203$

27. $r - 0.832 = 8.67$

28. $4.093 = d - 12$

29. $4.3 = g - 1$

30. $b - (-1.5) = -9$

Mathematical Reasoning Justify each step. Write the property or operation used to complete each step.

31.
$$p + 8.9 + (-7.2) = 54$$
$$p + 1.7 = 54$$
$$p + 1.7 - 1.7 = 54 - 1.7$$
$$p = 52.3$$

32.
$$81.3 + k - 4.13 = -15$$
$$k + 81.3 - 4.13 = -15$$
$$k + 77.17 = -15$$
$$k + 77.17 - 77.17 = -15 - 77.17$$
$$k = -92.17$$

33. *Error Analysis* A student solved an equation as shown at the right. Explain the student's error.

$$x - 1.6 = -6$$
$$x - 1.6 + 1.6 = -6 - 1.6$$
$$x = -7.6$$

34. **TEST PREP** Mira sold a basketball card for $12.30. This was $2.50 more than the price she paid for the card. Which equation *cannot* be used to find the original price p of the card?

A. $p + 2.50 = 12.30$ **B.** $p - 2.50 = 12.30$

C. $12.30 = 2.50 + p$ **D.** $12.30 - 2.50 = p$

35. *Writing* Explain how you would use the Addition Property of Equality to solve $x + 1.8 = -4.7$.

Math in the Media **Use the cartoon below for Exercise 36.**

Dilbert by Scott Adams

SOURCE: ©1993 United Features Syndicate, Inc.

36. a. *Critical Thinking* You can find the amount of money the clerk owes Dilbert by solving the equation $1.89 + x = 7.14. How much does the clerk owe Dilbert?

b. *Open-ended* Dilbert did not want to receive change that included pennies. What was another amount of money Dilbert could have given the cashier?

▶ MIXED REVIEW

Use the formula $A = \ell w$. Find A. *(Lesson 3-4)*

37. $\ell = 23.4$ in., $w = 15.8$ in.

38. $\ell = 5.5$ cm, $w = 7$ cm

Solve each equation. *(Lesson 2-6)*

39. $6a = 24$ **40.** $-2b = 60$ **41.** $-81 = 9a$ **42.** $3c = 39$

43. A large juice costs $.83. A small juice costs $.57. Ida buys one juice each school day. If Ida buys small juices instead of large juices, how much money will she save each week? *(Lesson 2-2)*

3-6

Solving Equations by Multiplying or Dividing Decimals

PART 1 **Using Division to Solve Equations**

What You'll Learn

1 To solve one-step decimal equations involving multiplication

2 To solve one-step decimal equations involving division

...And Why

To model real-world situations in business

Division undoes multiplication. You can solve an equation involving multiplication by dividing.

■ EXAMPLE 1

Solve $0.9r = -5.4$.

$0.9r = -5.4$

$\dfrac{0.9r}{0.9} = \dfrac{-5.4}{0.9}$ Divide each side by 0.9.

$r = -6$ Simplify.

Check $0.9r = -5.4$

$0.9(-6) \stackrel{?}{=} -5.4$ Replace r with -6.

$-5.4 = -5.4$ ✔

■ **TRY THIS** Solve each equation.

1. $0.8x = -1.6$ **2.** $1.15 = 2.3x$ **3.** $-81.81 = -0.9n$

REAL-WORLD CONNECTION

■ EXAMPLE 2

An oil field produces an average of 16.8 thousand barrels of crude oil per day. About how many days will it take to produce 200 thousand barrels?

Words	daily barrel production	times	number of days	equals	200 thousand barrels

Let d = number of days.

Equation	16.8	·	d	=	200

$16.8d = 200$

$\dfrac{16.8d}{16.8} = \dfrac{200}{16.8}$ Divide each side by 16.8.

$d = 11.904\ldots$ Simplify.

$d \approx 12$ Round to the nearest integer.

The field will take about 12 days to produce 200 thousand barrels.

■ TRY THIS

4. You paid $7.70 to mail a package that weighed 5.5 lb. Write and solve an equation to find the cost per pound.

PART 2 **Using Multiplication to Solve Equations**

To solve an equation involving division, multiply each side by the same nonzero number.

■ EXAMPLE 3

Solve $\frac{m}{-7.2} = -12.5$.

$$\frac{m}{-7.2} = -12.5$$

$$\frac{m}{-7.2}(-7.2) = -12.5(-7.2) \quad \text{Multiply each side by } -7.2.$$

$$m = 90 \quad \text{Simplify.}$$

■ TRY THIS Solve each equation.

5. $\frac{r}{-6.0} = 0.5$ 　　　6. $\frac{s}{2.5} = 5$ 　　　7. $-80 = \frac{t}{4.5}$

DATA ANALYSIS CONNECTION

■ EXAMPLE 4

Batting Averages The 1923 baseball season was one of Babe Ruth's best years. He was at bat 522 times and had a batting average of 0.393, rounded to the nearest thousandth. The batting average formula is $a = \frac{h}{n}$, where a is the batting average, h is the number of hits, and n is the number of times at bat. Use the formula to find the number of hits Babe Ruth made.

$$a = \frac{h}{n}$$

$$0.393 = \frac{h}{522} \quad \text{Replace } a \text{ with 0.393 and } n \text{ with 522.}$$

$$(0.393)(522) = \frac{h}{522}(522) \quad \text{Multiply each side by 522.}$$

$$h = 205.146 \quad \text{Simplify.}$$

$$h \approx 205 \quad \text{Since } h \text{ (hits) represents an integer, round to the nearest integer.}$$

Babe Ruth made 205 hits.

During his professional career Babe Ruth was at bat 8,399 times and had a batting average of 0.342. About how many hits did he have?

■ TRY THIS

8. Suppose your batting average is 0.222. You have batted 54 times. How many hits do you have?

Exercises

> ## CHECK UNDERSTANDING

Complete the steps for each equation.

1.
$$0.8x = 1.5$$
$$(0.8x) \div \blacksquare = 1.5 \div \blacksquare$$
$$x = \blacksquare$$

2. $\dfrac{d}{4.5} = -3$
$$\blacksquare \dfrac{d}{4.5} = \blacksquare(-3)$$
$$d = \blacksquare$$

State the first step in solving each equation.

3. $0.9x = -0.54$ **4.** $\dfrac{y}{0.6} = 1.2$ **5.** $1.5 = d \div 15$ **6.** $-1.2 = -0.4m$

Solve each equation.

7. $-0.5y = -0.73$ **8.** $0.8x = 0.448$ **9.** $\dfrac{n}{2.3} = -4.8$ **10.** $0.97 = \dfrac{c}{-2}$

11. a. *Error Analysis* Harry found 324.8 as a solution for the equation $4x = 81.2$. What was Harry's error?
  b. How could Harry have used estimation to check whether his answer was reasonable?

> ## PRACTICE AND PROBLEM SOLVING

Solve each equation.

12. $2x = -4.88$ **13.** $-0.3y = 7.53$ **14.** $6.4x = 0.2816$ **15.** $-5.1z = -11.73$

16. $1.92 = 1.6s$ **17.** $0.004m = 0.12$ **18.** $3.2n = 27.52$ **19.** $2.21 = 1.7w$

20. $\dfrac{n}{1.7} = 0.22$ **21.** $\dfrac{k}{2.01} = 0.04$ **22.** $4.5 = m \div (-3.3)$ **23.** $-33.04 = \dfrac{z}{-0.03}$

24. $-0.45 = x \div 12$ **25.** $\dfrac{m}{0.89} = 3{,}488$ **26.** $\dfrac{w}{-3.4} = -25.5$ **27.** $120 = \dfrac{v}{3.8}$

Mental Math **Solve each equation.**

28. $0.7x = 2.8$ **29.** $9 = \dfrac{a}{1.5}$ **30.** $\dfrac{m}{7.08} = -100$ **31.** $10{,}000r = 483.08$

Write an equation for each sentence. Solve for the variable.

32. The product of a number n and -7.3 is 30.66. Find the value of n.

33. The quotient of a number n divided by -4.5 equals 200.6. Find the value of n.

34. A number n divided by -2.35 equals 400.9. Find the value of n.

35. *Measurement* If you know a length ℓ in meters, you can multiply the length by 3.28 to find the length in feet f.
   a. Write an equation to model this situation.
   b. A tree is 7.5 m tall. Use your equation to find this height in feet.
   c. A bookshelf is 6 ft tall. What is this height in meters?
   d. A room in your home is 12 ft long and 15 ft wide. Use your equation and the formula for the area of a rectangle to find the area of the room in square meters. Round your answer to the nearest tenth.

36. *Number Sense* The weight of a record-setting onion was 12.25 lb. An average-sized onion weighs 0.5 lb. About how many average-sized onions have a total weight equal to the record-setting onion? Round your answer to the nearest integer.

37. a. Your batting average is 0.244, and you have been at bat 82 times. How many hits do you have?
   b. *Writing* Why is it necessary to round your answer in part (a) to the nearest integer?

38. *Mathematical Reasoning* Find values for x and y that satisfy $xy = 0.42$ and $x + y = 1.3$.

▶ **MIXED REVIEW**

Solve each equation. *(Lesson 3-5)*

39. $c + 9 = 3.7$ **40.** $b + 7.6 = 23$ **41.** $43.6 = n + 17.5$

42. $-5.6 = y - 8$ **43.** $4.035 = a - 3.25$ **44.** $h - (-3.5) = 1.5$

Is the given number a solution of the equation? *(Lesson 2-4)*

45. $20 - c = 12; c = 8$ **46.** $8 = 2a + 3; a = 0$ **47.** $2m = m + 6; m = 4$

48. a. *Patterns* Multiply $99 \cdot 24, 99 \cdot 25$, and $99 \cdot 26$. *(Lesson 1-7)*
   b. Describe the pattern you found in part (a).
   c. Use the pattern to evaluate $99 \cdot 27$.

CHAPTER PROJECT 3 **ACTIVITY 2 RESEARCHING**

In the business section of a newspaper or on the Internet, find today's foreign currency exchange rates. Keep the chart to use for your project.

Cut out advertisements from a newspaper for two items. Make sure the advertisements include the costs of the items.

3-7

Using the Metric System

PART 1 Identifying Appropriate Metric Measures

What You'll Learn

1 To identify appropriate metric measures

2 To convert metric units

...And Why

To understand metric measures and to measure everyday objects

Knowing the approximate size of each metric unit of measure will allow you to choose an appropriate unit.

Metric Units of Measurement

Type	Unit	Reference Example
Length	millimeter (mm)	about the thickness of a dime
	centimeter (cm)	about the width of a thumbnail
	meter (m)	about the distance from a doorknob to the floor
	kilometer (km)	a little more than one half mile
Capacity	milliliter (mL)	about 5 drops of water
	liter (L)	a little more than a quart of milk
Mass	milligram (mg)	about the mass of a speck of sawdust
	gram (g)	about the mass of a paper clip
	kilogram (kg)	about one half the mass of this math book

■ EXAMPLE 1

Choose an appropriate metric unit.

a. height of a classroom chalkboard

Meter; the height of a chalkboard is about twice the distance from the floor to a doorknob.

b. mass of a backpack filled with books

Kilogram; a backpack filled with books is many times the mass of this textbook.

c. capacity of a birdbath

Liter; several quart bottles of water would fill a birdbath.

■ **TRY THIS** Choose an appropriate metric unit. Explain your choice.

1. length of a broom

2. the mass of an energy bar

3. mass of a horse

4. capacity of a car's gas tank

■ EXAMPLE 2

Estimation Choose a reasonable estimate. Explain your choice.

a. **capacity of a juice box: 200 mL or 200 L**

200 mL; the juice box holds less than a quart of milk.

b. **length of a new pencil: 15 cm or 15 m**

15 cm; the length of a pencil would be about 15 widths of a thumbnail.

c. **mass of a small tube of toothpaste: 100 g or 100 kg**

100 g; the mass is about the same as a box of paper clips.

■ **TRY THIS** Choose a reasonable estimate.

5. distance between two cities: 50 mm or 50 km

6. amount of liquid that an eyedropper holds: 10 mL or 10 L

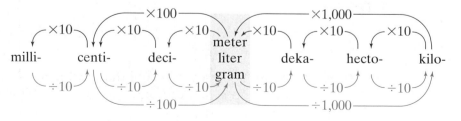

PART 2 Converting Units

The metric system uses a decimal system to relate different units to each other. Look down the metric units chart below. The units highlighted in yellow are the units most often used. As you read from left to right, each unit is 10 times the size of the unit before it.

	milli-	centi-	deci-	UNIT	deka-	hecto-	kilo-
Length	millimeter (mm)	centimeter (cm)	decimeter (dm)	meter (m)	dekameter (dam)	hectometer (hm)	kilometer (km)
Capacity	milliliter (mL)	centiliter (cL)	deciliter (dL)	liter (L)	dekaliter (daL)	hectoliter (hL)	kiloliter (kL)
Mass	milligram (mg)	centigram (cg)	decigram (dg)	gram (g)	dekagram (dag)	hectogram (hg)	kilogram (kg)

You can convert from one unit to another by multiplying or dividing by 10; 100; 1,000 and so on.

To convert from one unit to another in the metric system, find the relationship between the two units. Remember to multiply if you are going from a larger unit to a smaller unit (there will be more of the smaller units) and to divide if you are going from a smaller unit to a larger unit (there will be fewer of the larger units).

Need Help? For help with multiplying and dividing decimals by powers of 10, see Skills Handbook, p. 734.

■ EXAMPLE 3

Mental Math **Complete each statement.**

a. 4.35 L = ▩ mL

$4.35 \cdot 1,000 = 4,350$ To convert liters to milliliters, multiply by 1,000.

$4.35 \text{ L} = 4,350 \text{ mL}$

b. 914 cm = ▩ m

$914 \div 100 = 9.14$ To convert centimeters to meters, divide by 100.

$914 \text{ cm} = 9.14 \text{ m}$

■ TRY THIS   Complete each statement.

7. 35 mL = ▩ L   **8.** ▩ g = 250 kg   **9.** ▩ cm = 68 m

REAL-WORLD 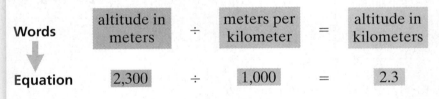 CONNECTION

■ EXAMPLE 4

Geography **The ancient Incan city of Machu Picchu is located in Peru. Its altitude is about 2,300 m above sea level. What is Machu Picchu's altitude in kilometers?**

Words	altitude in meters	÷	meters per kilometer	=	altitude in kilometers
Equation	2,300	÷	1,000	=	2.3

Machu Picchu is about 2.3 km above sea level.

■ TRY THIS

10. The record for the highest a kite has flown is 3.8 km. Find the height of the kite in meters.

11. *Number Sense* You have a recipe that requires 0.25 L of milk. Your measuring cup is marked only in milliliters. How many milliliters of milk do you need?

The ancient city of Machu Picchu (c. 1450–1550) is located in Peru's Andes Mountains. One of the few major pre-Columbian ruins found nearly intact, Machu Picchu was designated a World Heritage site in 1983.

Exercises

Match each quantity with an appropriate metric measurement.

1. length of your thumb
2. mass of a book
3. length of a soccer field
4. amount of water in a fishbowl
5. mass of a sewing needle
6. amount of fluid in a straw

A. 1 g
B. 100 m
C. 6 cm
D. 15 mL
E. 4 L
F. 1 kg

Mental Math **Complete each statement.**

7. 54 m = ■ cm
8. ■ L = 234 mL
9. 12 g = ■ kg
10. ■ m = 3.01 km

11. *Geography* The shortest street in the world is Elgin Street, in Bacup, England. It is 518 cm long. How many meters long is it?

PRACTICE AND PROBLEM SOLVING

Choose an appropriate metric unit of measure. Explain your choice.

12. mass of a banana
13. depth of Lake Michigan
14. length of a small calculator
15. mass of a car
16. width of a highway
17. quantity of water in a spoon

Choose a reasonable estimate. Explain your choice.

18. the mass of a small dog: 5 g or 5 kg

19. amount of liquid you should drink daily: 2,000 mL or 2,000 L

20. the mass of a box of cereal: 350 mg or 350 g

21. the width of a sidewalk: 150 cm or 150 m

22. the length of 24 city blocks: 2 m or 2 km

23. the mass of a thumbtack: 1 mg or 1 g

Write the metric unit that makes each statement true.

24. 9.03 ■ = 9,030 mm
25. 890 cm = 8.9 ■
26. 130,000 ■ = 1.3 km

Mental Math Complete each statement.

27. 0.25 m = ■ cm

28. ■ mL = 7.3 L

29. 595 g = ■ kg

30. 900,500 mL = ■ L

31. 35 m = ■ km

32. ■ m = 875 cm

33. 9,120 mg = ■ g

34. 900 km = ■ m

35. 5 g = ■ kg

36. ■ cm = 13 km

37. ■ km = 562,300 cm

38. 301 kg = ■ mg

Number Sense Match each measurement in the first column with its equivalent measurement in the second column.

39. 0.015 km

A. 15,000 mL

40. 1,500 cm

B. 150 cm

41. 150,000 mg

C. 150 g

42. 0.15 L

D. 1.5 kg

43. 15 L

E. 15 m

44. 1,500 g

F. 150 mL

G. 150 kg

H. 0.15 mL

45. ***Earth Science*** The flow of water over Niagara Falls averages 6,008,835,000 mL/s. On average, about how many liters of water flow over Niagara Falls each second?

46. The world's longest model train has 650 cars and is 0.695 km long. How many meters long is the train?

47. ***Nutrition*** A world-record grapefruit had a mass of 3,068 g. What was its mass in kilograms?

48. ***Zoology*** A hippopotamus is so large that it has a stomach 304.8 cm long, yet it is agile enough to outrun a human. How long is the stomach of a hippopotamus in meters?

49. ***Error Analysis*** One of the world's largest pearls had a mass of 6,392 g. Camille wrote in her report that the pearl had a mass of 6,392,000 kg. What was her error?

50. **TEST PREP** The albatross has the greatest wingspan of any bird. A reasonable wingspan for an albatross would be __?__ .
A. 335 km **B.** 335 m **C.** 335 cm **D.** 3.35 cm

51. ***Writing*** The prefix *kilo-* means "one thousand," and the prefix *milli-* means "one thousandth." What do the prefixes tell you about *kilometer* and *kilogram,* and *milliliter* and *milligram?*

52. ***Measurement*** What part of a second is a millisecond?

One of the world's first hydroelectric power plants was built at Niagara Falls. The present-day plant is capable of producing 2,100,000 kilowatts of electricity. A 100-watt light bulb, left on for ten hours, uses 1 kilowatt-hour.

53. a. *Physical Fitness* You walk about 3 mi/h. Approximately how many kilometers can you walk in an hour?

    b. How many meters can you walk in an hour?

▶ MIXED REVIEW

Estimate each product or quotient. *(Lesson 3-2)*

54. $28.134 \div 3.75$ **55.** $8.517 \cdot 9.82$ **56.** $101.49 \div 9.51$

Solve each inequality. *(Lessons 2-9 and 2-10)*

57. $a - 5 \geq 16$ **58.** $n + 8 < -7$ **59.** $-3r \leq 21$

60. *Data Analysis* Clinton Bailey, Sr., holds the record for knot tying. He tied six different rope knots in 8.1 s. Write and solve an equation to find his average time per knot. *(Lesson 3-6)*

◢ CHECKPOINT 2   Lessons 3-5 through 3-7

Solve each equation.

1. $0.5m = 0.125$ **2.** $y - 135.43 = -5.43$ **3.** $d \div 0.3 = 28.5$

4. $12.2 = 4x$ **5.** $29.25 = 4.5w$ **6.** $k + 870.9 = 1{,}000.5$

Choose the most reasonable estimate. Explain your choice.

7. height of a standard house window: 1.5 cm or 1.5 m

8. capacity of a shampoo bottle: 500 mL or 500 L

Complete each statement.

9. 95 mL = ■ L   **10.** ■ cm = 76.5 km   **11.** ■ km = 675 m   **12.** 7.1 kg = ■ g

13. The world's smallest horse had a mass of only 9.1 kg. What was the mass of the horse in grams?

CHAPTER PROJECT 3

ACTIVITY 3 CALCULATING

U se the foreign currency exchange rate chart and the advertisements you found for Activity 2. Find the cost of each item in the currencies of three countries other than the United States.

Precision and Significant Digits

The pin at the right measures about 5 cm. A more precise measurement is 4.5 cm. An even more precise measurement is 46 mm. The smaller the units on the scale of a measuring instrument, the more precise the measurement is.

■ EXAMPLE 1

Choose the more precise measurement.

a. 5 g or 8 mg
Since a milligram is a smaller unit of measure than a gram, 8 mg is more precise than 5 g.

b. 2.72 m or 3.5 m
A hundredth of a meter is a smaller unit of measure than a tenth of a meter. So 2.72 m is more precise than 3.5 m.

Choose the more precise measurement.

1. 3 m or 5.2 m   **2.** 8 mL or 9.5 L   **3.** 1.89 km or 8.7 cm   **4.** 1.9 kg or 1.87 kg

5. *Error Analysis* Your friend says that 4.35 km is more precise than 5.2 cm because a hundredths unit is a smaller unit than a tenths unit. What mistake did your friend make?

A calculation will be only as precise as the least precise measurement used in the calculation. So, round your results to match the precision of the least precise measurement.

■ EXAMPLE 2

Add the lengths 6.31 m, 5.447 m, and 2.8 m.

6.31 + 5.447 + 2.8 = 14.557   **The least precise measurement**
Rounded to tenths ≈ 14.6 m   **is 2.8 m. Round the sum to the**
                                 nearest tenth of a meter.

Find each sum or difference. Round to the place value of the less precise measurement.

6. 5.6 g + 8 g   **7.** 8.35 kg + 6.2 kg   **8.** 8.2 km − 1.75 km   **9.** 9 cm − 2.3 cm

Digits that represent an actual measurement are *significant digits*.
Nonzero digits (1–9) are always significant. The rules below will help
you decide whether a zero is a significant digit.

Type of Number	Which Zeros Are Significant	Example
decimal numbers between 0 and 1	Zeros to the left of *all* the nonzero digits are not significant. All other zeros are significant.	significant digits 0.006040 not significant digits
positive integers	Zeros to the right of *all* the nonzero digits are not significant. Zeros between nonzero digits are significant.	significant digits 203,400 not significant digits
noninteger decimal numbers greater than 1	All zeros are significant.	significant digits 350.07050

■ **EXAMPLE 3**

How many significant digits are in 0.0504 m?

The 5 and the 4 are significant. The zero between them is significant.
The other zeros are not significant. There are three significant digits.

Determine the number of significant digits in each measurement.

10. 0.069 m **11.** 100.5 L **12.** 3,400 kL **13.** 5.2100 km

When you multiply or divide measurements, round your answer to
match the least number of significant digits in the problem.

■ **EXAMPLE 4**

**A survey of a plot for a new house measures 152.6 m by 121 m.
What is the area of the plot? Use significant digits.**

┌─ 3 significant digits

152.6 · 121 = 18,464.6 ◄─── Multiply.

└─ 4 significant digits

The area is 18,500 m². ◄───Round the area to 3 significant digits.

Find each product or quotient. Use significant digits.

14. 1,234 in. · 31 in. **15.** 0.0702 ft · 227 ft **16.** 16,250 m ÷ 14.5 s **17.** 132.5 cm · 43.2 cm

Multiple Choice

Choose the best answer.

1. Every year Tyrone gets a raise as shown in the table.

Year	Hourly Wage
1997	$10.15
1998	$10.75
1999	$11.35
2000	$11.95

   The best prediction of Tyrone's hourly wage for the year 2001 is __?__.
   A. $12.55   B. $13.15
   C. $12.35   D. $12.15

2. Five men on the same team ran the 100-m dash. Their times were 11.6 s, 10.2 s, 9.9 s, 10.6 s, and 11.9 s. What was the mean time for the team members?
   F. 10.84 s   G. 10.5 s
   H. 54.2 s   J. 13.55 s

3. A number t divided by -2.35 is equal to 400.9. Find t.
   A. 170.596   B. -942.115
   C. -170.596 D. 942.115

4. Ms. Manfre's drive from Middletown took 4.5 hours. Her average speed was 60 mi/h and she used one of the roads shown. To which town did she drive?

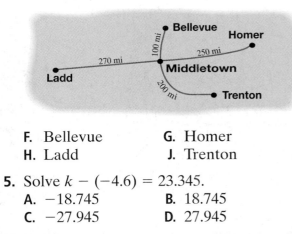

   F. Bellevue   G. Homer
   H. Ladd   J. Trenton

5. Solve $k - (-4.6) = 23.345$.
   A. -18.745 B. 18.745
   C. -27.945 D. 27.945

6. With a $20 bill, you buy 2 dozen bagels at $5.49 per dozen and 3 containers of cream cheese for $2.75 each. How much change should you receive?
   F. $19.23   G. $2.27
   H. $.77   J. $1.26

7. In 1998, Mary Meagher set the women's world swimming record for the 100-m butterfly. She swam the distance in 57.93 s. On average, how long did she take to swim 10 m?
   A. between 4 s and 5 s
   B. between 5 s and 6 s
   C. between 6 s and 7 s
   D. between 7 s and 8 s

8. What is the greatest precision that can be measured using this ruler?

   F. nearest meter
   G. nearest centimeter
   H. nearest millimeter
   J. nearest tenth of a millimeter

Free Response

For Exercises 9–11, show your work.

9. Mario had d dollars in his bank account when he wrote a check for $40.65. He now has $182.33 in his account. Write and solve an equation to find how much money Mario originally had in his bank acount.

10. The sum of two numbers is 14. The product of the numbers is 24. Find the two numbers.

11. **Open-ended** Describe two situations in which an estimate would be preferred over an exact amount.

Simplify a Problem

3-8

Math Strategies in Action

Scientists often encounter problems that are very complicated. When they work to develop a new vaccine or develop a new method to fight disease, they usually work on smaller or simpler pieces of the problem first. Sometimes when you solve a problem, it helps to solve other problems that have similar conditions. Here is a well-known problem that shows you how to use this strategy.

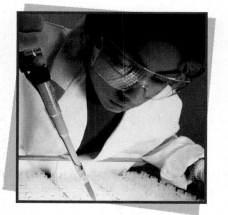

Problem Solving Strategies

Account for All
Possibilities

Draw a Diagram

Look for a Pattern

Make a Model

Make a Table

Simplify a Problem

Simulate a Problem

Solve by Graphing

Try, Test, Revise

Use Multiple Strategies

Work Backward

Write an Equation

Write a Proportion

■ SAMPLE PROBLEM

A snail is trying to escape from a well 10 ft deep. The snail can climb 2 ft each day, but each night it slides back 1 ft. How many days will the snail take to climb out of the well?

Read

A snail needs to climb 10 ft to escape from a well. It can climb 2 ft per day. At night the snail slides back 1 ft.

1. How far up the well will the snail be after the first day and the first night?

2. How far up the well will the snail be after the second day?

3. How far up the well will the snail be after the second day and the second night?

Plan

At first you might think that the snail progresses 1 ft each day and will therefore take 10 days to escape. This answer is wrong, however, because it leaves out an important part of the problem.

Try to solve a simpler problem. Change the problem to a simpler one based on a 3-ft well, and then try a 4-ft well to see if there is a pattern.

 **Solve**

Time	3-ft Well	4-ft Well
Day 1	Up 2 ft from bottom	Up 2 ft from bottom
Night 1	Up 1 ft from bottom	Up 1 ft from bottom
Day 2	Up 3 ft from bottom; OUT!	Up 3 ft from bottom
Night 2		Up 2 ft from bottom
Day 3		Up 4 ft from bottom; OUT!

4. Using the information from the simpler 3-ft well and 4-ft well problems, describe the pattern.

5. How many days will the snail take to escape from the 10-ft well?

 **Look Back**

You can check your answer by drawing a diagram.

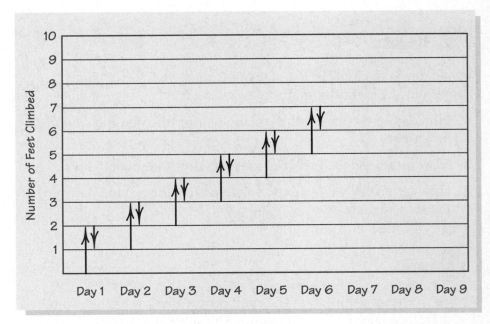

6. Copy and complete the diagram to check your answer.

Exercises

▶ CHECK UNDERSTANDING

Solve by simplifying each problem.

1. You decide to number the 58 pages in your journal from 1 to 58. How many digits do you have to write?

2. **Sports** In a tennis tournament, each athlete plays one match against each of the other athletes. There are 12 athletes scheduled to play in the tournament. How many matches will be played?

3. **Geometry** What is the total number of triangles in the figure at the right?

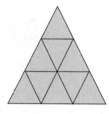

▶ PRACTICE AND PROBLEM SOLVING

Solve using any strategy.

4. What is the total number of squares in the figure at the right?

5. There are 10 girls and 8 boys at a party. A cartoonist wants to sketch a picture of each boy with each girl. How many cartoon sketches are required?

6. A rancher wants to build a fence for a square lot with dimensions of 50 yd by 50 yd. He wants to install a fence post every 5 yd. How many fence posts will he need?

7. **Construction** To accommodate a wheelchair, a builder installed counter tops that are 0.75 ft lower than the original ones. The new counter tops are 2.5 ft high. How high were the original counter tops?

Metal type is set upside down and from right to left in a composing stick. It would have taken a typesetter about 66 seconds to set the type for one line of this page.

8. **Writing** The houses on your street are numbered 1 to 120. No numbers are skipped. How many house numbers contain at least one digit 5? Explain your strategy.

9. Before the use of computers, typesetters used metal pieces of type to print each letter in a word and each digit in a number. For example, three pieces of type—1, 4, and 8—were used to create the page number 148. How many pieces of type would be needed to set the page numbers 1 through 476?

161

10. The school store buys pencils for $.20 each. It sells the pencils for $.25 each. How much profit does the store make if it sells five dozen pencils?

11. **Population** The population of Rancho Cucamonga, California, is 117,000 people. The area of Rancho Cucamonga is 37.8 mi^2. Find the population density, the number of people per square mile.

12. You are hiking with three friends. You pass a group of six hikers going the other way. Each person in one group greets each person in the other group. How many greetings are there?

▶ MIXED REVIEW

Measurement **Complete each statement.** (*Lesson 3-7*)

13. 27 cm = ■ m

14. 5,200 km = ■ m

15. 2,000 mg = ■ g

16. 0.5 L = ■ mL

17. 3 m = ■ cm

18. 6 kg = ■ mg

Estimate using front-end estimation. (*Lesson 3-1*)

19. $3.75 + $25.50 + $17.23

20. $9.54 + $1.25

21. **Choose a Strategy** Your test scores so far this semester are 100, 90, 82, 96, and 78. You have one more test to take. After you complete the last test, what is your highest possible average?

Math at Work
Woodworker

Woodworkers cut, shape, assemble, and finish wood to create tables, chairs, and other types of furniture. To create these items, woodworkers must plan and carry out many individual steps in sequence.

Machines used in professional woodworking shops cut and shape wood with great precision. The most sophisticated machines use computer-controlled programs. Woodworkers can enhance their skills by taking mathematics and computer courses that develop their ability to think three-dimensionally.

For more information about woodworking, visit the Prentice Hall Web site.
www.phschool.com

See also Extra Practice section.

CURRENCY EVENTS

Compare Currencies The Project Activities on pages 135, 149, and 155 will help you complete your project. Here is a checklist to help you gather the different parts.

✔ the cost of a shirt and a souvenir, in U.S. dollars and Mexican pesos

✔ a currency exchange rate chart

✔ two advertisements that include prices in U.S. dollars

✔ your calculations of the costs of the advertised items in the currencies of other countries

Make a poster that displays your results. Include a title. Identify the name of each currency you used, its exchange rate, and the country in which the currency is used.

Reflect and Revise

Have a friend review your poster. Does it have all the information listed above? Is it organized and easy to interpret? Are your calculations accurate? If necessary, make changes to improve your work.

Web Extension

Visit Prentice Hall's Web site. You'll find some interesting links and ideas related to currency exchange rates. You'll also be able to share information about your project.
www.phschool.com

Wrap Up

■ Key Terms

compatible
  numbers (p. 128)
formula (p. 137)

mean (p. 131)
measures of central
  tendency (p. 131)

median (p. 131)
metric system (p. 150)
mode (p. 131)

perimeter (p. 138)
outlier (p. 132)

■ Graphic Organizer

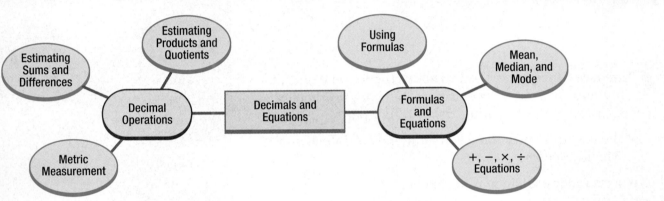

■ Rounding and Estimating   3-1

Summary You can estimate the sum of decimals by rounding, front-end
estimating, or clustering.

You can estimate the difference of decimals by rounding.

Estimate each sum or difference. State which method you used.

1. $3.14 + 6.952$

2. $10.2538 - 6.095$

3. $14.451 + 9.736$

4. $14.27 - 4.268$

5. $20.681 + 19.39 + 20.56$

6. $12.814 - 6.3791$

7. $9.0426 + 2.7182$

8. $21.9384 - 15.639$

9. $6.257 + 6.129 + 6.34$

10. **Writing** Explain when you would use each method to estimate a
sum of decimals. Use examples.

11. **TEST PREP** Which strategy is not appropriate to estimate
$5.57 + 5.021 + 4.98$?
A. $5.57 + 5.021 + 4.98 \approx 5 \cdot 3 = 15$
B. $5.57 + 5.021 + 4.98 \approx 6 + 5 + 5 = 16$
C. $5.57 + 5.021 + 4.98 \approx 10.591 + 4 = 14.591$
D. $5.57 + 5.021 + 4.98 \approx 14 + 0.6 + 0 + 1 = 15.6$

■ Estimating Decimal Products and Quotients

Summary You can estimate a product by rounding. You can estimate a quotient of two decimals by using **compatible numbers**.

Estimate each product or quotient.

12. 8.15(6.04)

13. 19.28 ÷ 5.439

14. 1.9 · 4.92

15. 25.1 ÷ 4.87

16. 12.497 · 0.894

17. 59.3581 ÷ 11.5304

18. 3.59(−2.3291)

19. −17.45 ÷ 3.059

20. (−2.0936)(−5.6892)

■ Mean, Median, and Mode

Summary You can use a **measure of central tendency** to describe a collection of data. The **mean** is the sum of the data items divided by the number of data items. The **median** is the middle value or the mean of the two middle values when the data are written in order. The **mode** is the data item that occurs most often. An **outlier** is a data item that is much greater or much less than the rest of the data items.

Find the mean, median, and mode. When an answer is not an integer, round to the nearest tenth. Identify any outliers.

21. 2, 3, 6, 2, 8, 9, 5, 10, 4, 5

22. 16.1, 16.3, 15.9, 16.2, 16.3, 16.3, 15.8

23. 32, 35, 31, 57, 33, 30, 34

24. 0.1, 7.9, 0.2, 0.3, 0.1, 0.2, 0.1, 0.1, 0.3

Which measure of central tendency best describes each situation? Explain.

25. the favorite radio stations of teenagers in your neighborhood

26. the numbers of videos owned by students in your class

27. the prices of 8-oz containers of yogurt at six local grocery stores

■ Using Formulas

Summary A **formula** is an equation that shows a relationship between quantities that are represented by variables. You can use formulas to find such things as **perimeter**, area, and distance.

Evaluate each formula for the values given.

28. distance: $d = rt$
when $r = 35$ mi/h and $t = 2$ h

29. area of a rectangle: $A = \ell w$
when $\ell = 16$ mm and $w = 24$ mm

30. Circumference: $C = 2\pi r$
when $r = 6$ in. Use 3.14 for π.

31. perimeter of a square: $P = 4s$
when $s = 13$ cm

■ Solving One-Step Equations with Decimals   3-5 and 3-6

Summary To solve a one-step equation, use an inverse operation and the properties of equality to get the variable alone on one side of the equation.

Solve each equation.

32. $n + 3.8 = 10.9$

33. $y - 6.72 = 2.53$

34. $h + 0.67 = -1.34$

35. $t - 2.7 = -3.5$

36. $12.9 + x = 3.8$

37. $5.7 = b - 4.9$

38. $6.3m = 15.75$

39. $a \div 4.9 = 8.33$

40. $v \cdot 7.1 = 80.23$

41. $c \div 12.5 = 77.5$

42. $-5.7z = 110.58$

43. $d \div 4.75 = -38.95$

44. **TEST PREP** Which equation has the solution 3.2?
A. $-2x = 6.4$ **B.** $5.1 + a = 1.9$ **C.** $t - 1.56 = 1.64$
D. $w \div 0.8 = 2.56$ **E.** Not here

■ *Using the Metric System*   3-7

Summary The **metric system** of measurement uses a decimal system to relate units to one another. To measure, you must choose an appropriate unit of measure.

Choose an appropriate metric unit of measure. Explain each choice.

45. height of a building

46. mass of a bicycle

47. amount of milk in a glass

Mental Math **Complete each statement.**

48. $0.85 \text{ m} = \blacksquare \text{ cm}$

49. $160 \text{ mL} = \blacksquare \text{ L}$

50. $2.3 \text{ m} = \blacksquare \text{ cm}$

51. $1.6 \text{ kg} = \blacksquare \text{ g}$

52. $0.62 \text{ L} = \blacksquare \text{ mL}$

53. $80 \text{ g} = \blacksquare \text{ kg}$

54. **TEST PREP** Which unit is appropriate to measure the height of a mature oak tree?
A. centimeter   **B.** kilogram   **C.** liter   **D.** meter

■ *Simplify a Problem*   3-8

Summary When a problem is complicated, you can solve related simpler problems to better understand the problem.

55. A school's lockers are numbered 1 to 100. One hundred students enter the school one at a time. The first student opens the lockers. The second student closes the even-numbered lockers. The third student either closes or opens every third locker, and so on. After all the students have passed the lockers, which lockers are open?

Assessment

Estimate.

1. $6.43 - 4.079$
2. $2.06 + 3.91$
3. $5.97 - 1.674$
4. $6.025 + 0.35$
5. $8.54 + 2.3$
6. $6.25 \cdot 9.87$
7. $12.89 \div 3.04$
8. $1.76 \cdot 3.93$
9. $4.96 \div 2.49$
10. $3.2 \cdot 14.69$

Find the mean, median, and mode. When an answer is not an integer, round to the nearest tenth. Identify any outliers.

11. $11, 12, 9, 13, 10, 12, 11, 14, 12$
12. $5.3, 5.6, 5.2, 5.0, 5.4, 5.6, 5.1, 5.0$
13. $10.6, 9.8, 11.6, 29.1, 3.4, 11.4, 12.7$
14. $8.7, 8.5, 8.7, 8.5, 8.6, 8.5, 8.7, 8.6$

Evaluate each formula for the given values.

15. area of a rectangle: $A = \ell w$
    when $\ell = 3.8$ in. and $w = 1.5$ in.
16. perimeter of a square: $P = 4s$
    when $s = 4.7$ cm
17. perimeter of a rectangle: $P = 2\ell + 2w$
    when $\ell = 2.9$ m and $w = 6.05$ m

Solve each equation.

18. $x + 7.8 = 12.5$
19. $n - 5.9 = 0.5$
20. $4.1 + c = -1.2$
21. $d - 6.3 = 11$
22. $-9.7 + h = 10.3$
23. $m \div 2.7 = 14.58$
24. $h \cdot 4.7 = 30.55$
25. $b \div (-7.8) = -79.56$
26. $-3.4t = 30.94$

Write an appropriate metric unit of measure for each quantity.

27. the height of a truck
28. the capacity of a standard shampoo bottle
29. the mass of a pineapple
30. the width of a paperback book

Complete.

31. $4.5 \text{ m} = \blacksquare \text{ cm}$
32. $68 \text{ mL} = \blacksquare \text{ L}$
33. $90 \text{ kg} = \blacksquare \text{ g}$
34. $6,700 \text{ cm} = \blacksquare \text{ m}$
35. $4 \text{ L} = \blacksquare \text{ mL}$
36. $50.2 \text{ g} = \blacksquare \text{ kg}$

For exercises 37 and 38, write an equation, and then solve.

37. You have a $20 bill. You buy gloves for $6.50. How much money do you now have?

38. The fastest speed recorded for a reptile on land is 9.7 m/s for a spiny-tailed iguana. At this rate, how far could a spiny-tailed iguana travel in 12 s?

39. *Geography* Madrid and Barcelona are cities in Spain. The distance between them is 636,000 m. What is this in kilometers?

40. You have an 18-ft metal pipe. How many cuts must you make to cut the pipe into 2-ft-long pieces?

41. *Data Analysis* Which measure of central tendency best describes the weights of the dogs in one neighborhood?
    15 lb, 20 lb, 18 lb, 27 lb, 15 lb, 70 lb
    A. mean
    B. median
    C. mode
    D. all of the above

42. *Writing* Explain how the outlier in the data set affects the mean.
    $3, 2, 6, 3, 5, 4, 15, 4, 3$

Choose the best answer.

1. Find the value of $4 \cdot 6 + 2 \div 2$.
   A. 24
   B. 13
   C. 25
   D. 16

2. Evaluate $4a + \frac{c}{4}$ for $a = 5$ and $c = 20$.
   F. 12
   G. 84
   H. 36
   J. 25

3. Simplify $-4(-15 + 5)$.
   A. -80
   B. -40
   C. 40
   D. 80

4. What replacement for a will make the equation $4a - 8 = 24$ true?
   F. -4
   G. 4
   H. -8
   J. 8

5. Which is an expression for the total area of the figure?

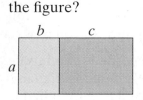

   A. $a \cdot (b \cdot c)$
   B. $a + (b + c)$
   C. $a(b + c)$
   D. $2a + 2c + 2c$

6. What is the first step in solving $\frac{x}{-9} = -3$?
   F. Multiply each side by -3.
   G. Divide each side by -3.
   H. Multiply each side by -9.
   J. Divide each side by -9.

7. Which inequality matches the sentence *A number y is less than or equal to 6?*
   A. $6 < y$
   B. $6 \le y$
   C. $y \ge 6$
   D. $y \le 6$

8. Find the mean.
   250, 280, 240, 230, 270,
   240, 270, 240, 230, 250
   F. 250
   G. 245
   H. 240
   J. 230

9. Round 6.55901 to the nearest tenth.
   A. 6.5
   B. 6.6
   C. 6.55
   D. 6.56

10. Use the formula $d = rt$. Find d when $r = 48$ mi/h and $t = 3.5$ h.
    F. 168 mi
    G. 13.71 mi
    H. 0.073 mi
    J. 192 mi

11. Solve $x - 2.5 = -5$.
    A. -2.5
    B. 7.5
    C. -7.5
    D. 12.5

12. Solve $2.8t = 56.98$.
    F. 2.035
    G. 20.35
    H. 159.544
    J. 15.95

13. Solve $5.6 = x + 3.5$.
    A. 9.1
    B. 2.1
    C. 9.2
    D. 8.5

14. Your car engine needs about 1.5 L of oil. A can of oil contains 946 mL. How many cans should you buy?
    F. 1 can
    G. 2 cans
    H. 3 cans
    J. 4 cans

15. A Swedish coin minted in 1644 has a mass of 19,750 g. What is the coin's mass in kilograms?
    A. 19,750,000 kg
    B. 197.5 kg
    C. 19.75 kg
    D. 1,975,000 kg

For Exercises 16–18, show your work.

16. A number x divided by six is equal to three hundred. Write and solve an equation to find x.

17. Grapes cost $1.99/lb. Explain how you can estimate the total cost of three bunches of grapes that weigh 1.3 lb, 2.6 lb, and 1.9 lb.

18. *Writing* Are all formulas equations? Are all equations formulas? Explain.

Skills You Need

for Chapter 4

▶ Dividing whole numbers

Use before Lesson 4-1.

Find each quotient.

1. $720 \div 8$
2. $7200 \div 8$
3. $6\overline{)132}$
4. $3\overline{)147}$
5. $\frac{189}{9}$
6. $\frac{450}{10}$
7. $424 \div 2$
8. $5\overline{)135}$
9. $10\overline{)1300}$
10. $700 \div 5$
11. $\frac{273}{3}$
12. $92 \div 4$

▶ Multiplying three or more factors

Use before Lesson 4-2.

Find each product.

13. $12 \cdot 12 \cdot 12$
14. $8 \cdot 8 \cdot 8$
15. $9 \cdot 9 \cdot 9 \cdot 9$
16. $5 \cdot 5 \cdot 5 \cdot 5 \cdot 5 \cdot 5$
17. $(-4)(-4)(-4)$
18. $(-2)(-2)(-2)(-2)(-2)(-2)$

▶ Recalling multiplication facts

Use before Lesson 4-3.

Write two numbers that, when multiplied, result in each product.

19. 12
20. 45
21. 18
22. 63
23. 24
24. 50
25. 32
26. 81
27. 54
28. 60
29. 28
30. 56
31. 44
32. 36
33. 72

▶ Reading and writing fractions

Use before Lesson 4-4.

Write two fractions to describe each model.

34. 
35. 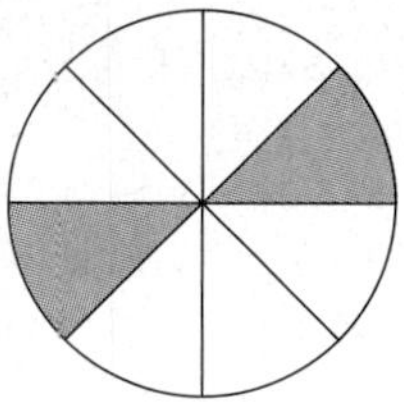
36.

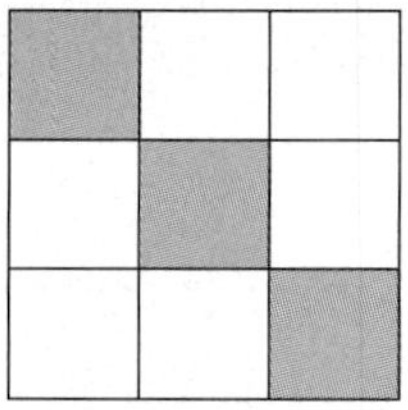

Factors, Fractions, and Exponents

What you'll learn in this chapter:

- How to simplify expressions with exponents

- How to simplify fractions

- How to write and calculate in scientific notation

TIME AFTER TIME

On the morning of the summer solstice, the sun rises directly over one of the stones at Stonehenge in southern England. Just as a sundial tells the time of day, Stonehenge tells the time of year.

A calendar may involve several astronomical events. For example, our day is based on Earth's rotation, while our year is based on Earth's movement around the sun. Over the centuries, people have come up with many different calendars.

Design a Calendar For the chapter project, you will investigate calendars and adjustments to calendars. Then you will design your own calendar. Your final project will be a sample of your calendar and an explanation of your calendar.

Steps to help you complete the project

Web Extension
www.phschool.com

How to solve problems by accounting for all possibilities

4-1

Divisibility and Factors

What You'll Learn

1 To use divisibility tests

2 To find factors

. . . And Why

To use divisibility tests to quickly find factors of numbers

PART 1 Using Divisibility Tests

One integer is **divisible** by another if the remainder is 0 when you divide. Because $18 \div 3 = 6$, 18 is divisible by 3. You can test for divisibility using mental math.

Divisibility Rules for 2, 5, and 10

An integer is divisible by

- 2 if it ends in 0, 2, 4, 6, or 8.
- 5 if it ends in 0 or 5.
- 10 if it ends in 0.

Even numbers end in 0, 2, 4, 6, or 8 and are divisible by 2.
Odd numbers end in 1, 3, 5, 7, or 9 and are not divisible by 2.

■ EXAMPLE 1

Is the first number divisible by the second?

a. 567 by 2   No, 567 doesn't end in 0, 2, 4, 6, or 8.
b. 1,015 by 5   Yes, 1,015 ends in 5.
c. 111,120 by 10   Yes, 111,120 ends in 0.

■ **TRY THIS** Is the first number divisible by the second? Explain.

1. 160 by 5   **2.** 56 by 10   **3.** 53 by 2   **4.** 1,118 by 2

To see a pattern for divisibility by 3 and 9, look at the following table.

Number	Sum of digits	Is the sum divisible by 3?	9?	Is the number divisible by 3?	9?
282	$2 + 8 + 2 = 12$	Yes	No	Yes	No
468	$4 + 6 + 8 = 18$	Yes	Yes	Yes	Yes
215	$2 + 1 + 5 = 8$	No	No	No	No
1,017	$1 + 0 + 1 + 7 = 9$	Yes	Yes	Yes	Yes

The pattern suggests the following rules for divisibility by 3 and 9.

Divisibility Rules for 3 and 9

An integer is divisible by

- 3 if the sum of its digits is divisible by 3.
- 9 if the sum of its digits is divisible by 9.

■ EXAMPLE 2

Is the first number divisible by the second?

a. 567 by 3   Yes, $5 + 6 + 7 = 18$; 18 is divisible by 3.

b. 1,015 by 9   No, $1 + 0 + 1 + 5 = 7$; 7 is not divisible by 9.

■ **TRY THIS** Is the first number divisible by the second? Explain.

5. 64 by 9   **6.** 472 by 3   **7.** 174 by 3   **8.** 43,542 by 9

PART 2 **Finding Factors**

The photo at the right shows all the rectangles you can form with 12 squares. Each of the rectangles has an area of 12 square units. Their dimensions, 1, 2, 3, 4, 6, and 12, are the *factors* of 12. One integer is a **factor** of another integer if it divides that integer with remainder zero.

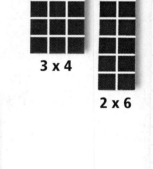

3 x 4

2 x 6

1 x 12

REAL-WORLD CONNECTION

■ EXAMPLE 3

There are 20 choral students singing at a school concert. Each row of singers must have the same number of students. If there are at least 5 students in each row, what are all the possible arrangements?

$1 \cdot 20,\ 2 \cdot 10,\ 4 \cdot 5$ Find the factors of 20.

There can be 1 row of 20 students, 2 rows of 10 students, or 4 rows of 5 students.

■ **TRY THIS** List the positive factors of each number.

9. 10   **10.** 21   **11.** 24   **12.** 31

13. What are the possible arrangements for Example 3 if there are 36 students singing at the concert?

Exercises

Test whether each number is divisible by 2, 3, 5, 9, or 10.

1. 20   **2.** 37   **3.** 45   **4.** 99   **5.** 240   **6.** 333

7. a. Which of the following numbers are divisible by both 2 and 3?

     10   66   898   4,710   975

    b. Which of the numbers above are divisible by 6?

    c. Using your results, write a divisibility rule for 6.

List the positive factors of each number.

8. 8   **9.** 16   **10.** 23   **11.** 54   **12.** 75   **13.** 68

PRACTICE AND PROBLEM SOLVING

Test whether each number is divisible by 2, 3, 5, 9, or 10.

14. 10   **15.** 23   **16.** 75   **17.** 90   **18.** 111   **19.** 131

20. 288   **21.** 300   **22.** 52   **23.** 891   **24.** 4,805   **25.** 437,684

26. a. Copy and complete the table.

Number	Last two digits	Are the last two digits divisible by 4?	Is the number divisible by 4?
136	36	Yes	Yes
1,268	68	Yes	Yes
314	14	No	No
1,078	■	■	■
696	■	■	■

    b. *Critical Thinking* Write a divisibility rule for 4.

Write the missing digit to make each number divisible by 9.

27. 22■,034   **28.** 3■,817   **29.** 2,03■,371   **30.** 1■,111

List the positive factors of each number.

31. 4   **32.** 1   **33.** 6   **34.** 14   **35.** 15   **36.** 17

37. 22   **38.** 25   **39.** 28   **40.** 32   **41.** 35   **42.** 37

43. 50   **44.** 53   **45.** 72   **46.** 108   **47.** 144   **48.** 157

49. *Mathematical Reasoning* If *a* is divisible by 2, what can you conclude about $a + 1$? Justify your answer.

50. *Writing* If a number is divisible by 9, is it also divisible by 3? Explain how you reached your conclusion.

51. *Open-ended* Deandrea has a trick for remembering her PIN (personal identification number), the secret number used with a bank card. The number formed by the first two digits is divisible by 3. The number formed by the last two digits is divisible by 5. Write two four-digit numbers that could be Deandrea's PIN.

52. There are 126 people in a workshop. The leader wants to put people into groups. Each group needs to have the same number of people. There must be at least 5 groups but not more than 20 groups. List the possible numbers of groups and the number of people in each group.

53. John made oatmeal cookies for a class bake sale. The cookies need to be distributed evenly on 2 or more plates. If each plate gets at least 7 cookies, what are the possible combinations for the totals below?
    a. 42 cookies   **b.** 56 cookies   **c.** 60 cookies

▶ MIXED REVIEW

Complete each statement. (*Lesson 3-7*)

54. 240 ■ = 24,000 mg   **55.** 18.2 km = 1,820,000 ■   **56.** 3.8 ■ = 0.0038 g

Evaluate. (*Lesson 1-3*)

57. $3y + 3$, for $y = 8$ **58.** $4(2 + a)$, for $a = 10$ **59.** xyz, for $x = 3$, $y = 7$, and $z = 2$

60. You have $5 to spend at the grocery store. You need $2.89 for a gallon of milk. Write an inequality to show how much money *m* you can spend on a box of cereal. (*Lesson 2-9*)

CHAPTER PROJECT 4

ACTIVITY 1 INVESTIGATING

The ancient Egyptian calendar divided a year into 12 months of 30 days each, with 5 extra days at the end. Why do you think the Egyptians based their calendar on 360, rather than 365? What are some other ways they could have organized a 360-day year into months? Why do you think the Egyptians chose 12 months of 30 days?

4-2 Exponents

What You'll Learn

1 To use exponents

2 To use the order of operations with exponents

. . . And Why

To use exponents as an efficient way of writing products of a repeated factor, for example $5 \cdot 5 \cdot 5$ as 5^3

PART 1 Using Exponents

You can use **exponents** to show repeated multiplication.

$$\overset{\text{exponent}}{\underset{\text{power}}{\text{base} \rightarrow \underbrace{2^6}}} = \underbrace{2 \cdot 2 \cdot 2 \cdot 2 \cdot 2 \cdot 2}_{\text{The base is used as a factor six times.}} = 64 \leftarrow \text{the value of the expression}$$

A **power** has two parts, a base and an exponent. The expression 2^6 is read as "two to the sixth power."

Power	Verbal Expression	Value
12^1	*Twelve to the first power*	12
6^2	*Six to the second power, or six squared*	$6 \cdot 6 = 36$
$(0.2)^3$	*Two tenths to the third power, or two tenths cubed*	$(0.2)(0.2)(0.2) = 0.008$
-7^4	*The opposite of the quantity seven to the fourth power*	$-(7 \cdot 7 \cdot 7 \cdot 7) = -2,401$
$(-8)^5$	*Negative eight to the fifth power*	$(-8)(-8)(-8)(-8)(-8) = -32,768$

■ EXAMPLE 1

Write using exponents.

a. $(-5)(-5)(-5)$

$(-5)^3$ Include the negative sign within parentheses.

b. $-2 \cdot a \cdot b \cdot a \cdot a$

$-2 \cdot a \cdot a \cdot a \cdot b$ Rewrite the expression using the commutative and associative properties.

$-2a^3b$ Write $a \cdot a \cdot a$ using exponents.

■ **TRY THIS** Write using exponents.

1. $6 \cdot 6 \cdot 6$ **2.** $(-3)(-3)(-3)(-3)$ **3.** $4 \cdot y \cdot x \cdot y$

Reading Math

Words in mathematics often have quite different everyday meanings. The word *base* can refer to the foundation of a building, or a starting point in a board game. How are these meanings similar to the use of the word *base* you see in this lesson?

■ EXAMPLE 2

Science A microscope can magnify a specimen 10^3 times. How many times is that?

$$10^3 = 10 \cdot 10 \cdot 10 \qquad \text{The exponent indicates that the base 10 is used as a factor 3 times.}$$

$$= 1{,}000 \qquad \qquad \text{Multiply.}$$

Human blood cells are shown here magnified (A)10^2 times, (B) 10^3 times, and (C) 10^4 times.

A.

B.

C.

■ TRY THIS

4. Simplify 6^2.

5. Evaluate $-a^4$ and $(-a)^4$, for $a = 2$.

PART 2 Using the Order of Operations with Exponents

You can extend the order of operations to include exponents.

Order of Operations

1. Work inside grouping symbols.
2. Simplify any terms with exponents.
3. Multiply and divide in order from left to right.
4. Add and subtract in order from left to right.

■ EXAMPLE 3

a. Simplify $4(3 + 2)^2$.

$$\begin{aligned} 4(3 + 2)^2 &= 4(5)^2 \qquad \text{Work within parentheses first.} \\ &= 4 \cdot 25 \qquad \text{Simplify } 5^2. \\ &= 100 \qquad \text{Multiply.} \end{aligned}$$

b. Evaluate $-2x^3 + 4y$, for $x = -2$ and $y = 3$.

$$\begin{aligned} -2x^3 + 4y &= -2(-2)^3 + 4(3) \qquad \text{Replace } x \text{ with } -2 \text{ and } y \text{ with 3.} \\ &= -2(-8) + 4(3) \qquad \text{Simplify } (-2)^3. \\ &= 16 + 12 \qquad \text{Multiply from left to right.} \\ &= 28 \qquad \text{Add.} \end{aligned}$$

Reading Math

The expression $4(3 + 2)^2$ is read as "four times the square of the quantity three plus two."

■ TRY THIS

6. Simplify $2 \cdot 5^2 + 4 \cdot (-3)^3$.

7. Evaluate $3(a)^2 + 6$, for $a = -5$.

Exercises

Write using exponents.

1. $8 \cdot 8 \cdot 8$

2. $r \cdot r \cdot r \cdot r \cdot s \cdot s$

3. $-7 \cdot a \cdot a \cdot 3 \cdot b$

Simplify each expression.

4. 4^3

5. 0.5^2

6. -3^2

7. $3(4+2)^2$

8. $49 - (4 \cdot 2)^2$

Evaluate each expression.

9. b^2, for $b = 9$

10. $(x + 4)^2$, for $x = 3$

11. $2m^2 + n$, for $m = -3$ and $n = 4$

12. *Critical Thinking* Are -6^2 and $(-6)^2$ equal? Explain.

▶ **PRACTICE AND PROBLEM SOLVING**

Write using exponents.

13. $5 \cdot 5 \cdot a \cdot a$

14. $x \cdot x \cdot y \cdot y \cdot z$

15. $-5 \cdot x \cdot x \cdot 3 \cdot y \cdot y$

16. $(-7)(-7)(-7)$

17. $c \cdot b \cdot 4 \cdot b \cdot b$

18. d cubed

Simplify each expression.

19. 5^3 and 3^5

20. 10^3 and 10^6

21. -1^8 and $(-1)^8$

22. -2^4 and $(-2)^3$

23. $-3^2 + 5 \cdot 2^3$

24. $2(9 - 4)^2$

25. $(-4)(-6)^2(2)$

26. $25 - (3 \cdot 2)^2$

27. $15 + (4 + 6)^2 \div 5$

28. $(12 - 3)^2 \div (2^2 - 1^2)$

29. $(4 + 8)^2 \div 4^2$

Evaluate each expression.

30. a^2, for $a = 8$

31. r^2, for $r = 0.6$

32. h^3, for $h = -4$

33. $(-x)^5$, for $x = -1$

34. b^2, for $b = -0.9$

35. $-6m^2$, for $m = 2$

36. $3a^2 - 2$, for $a = 5$

37. $5k^2$, for $k = 1.2$

38. $c^3 + 4$, for $c = -6$

39. xy^2, for $x = 3$ and $y = 4$

40. $8 - x^3$, for $x = -2$

41. $3(2m + 5)^2$, for $m = 2$

42. $4(2y - 3)^2$, for $y = 5$

43. $y^2 + 2y + 5$, for $y = -6$

44. *Mental Math* Given that $2^{10} = 1{,}024$, find 2^{11} mentally.

45. TEST PREP Which expression equals 1?

    A. -1^2
    B. $(-1)^3$
    C. $-(-1)^2$
    D. $|-1|^3$

46. Read the word phrase that follows:
the square of a increased by the sum of twice a and 3.
a. Write a variable expression for the word phrase.
b. Evaluate the expression for $a = 7$.

47. *Error Analysis* A student gives ab^3 as an answer when
asked to write the expression $ab \cdot ab \cdot ab$ using exponents.
What is the student's error?

48. a. Copy and complete the table at the right.
b. For what value(s) of n is each sentence true?
$$4^n = n^4 \qquad 4^n < n^4 \qquad 4^n > n^4$$

n	$4n$	4^n	n^4
1	▪	▪	▪
2	▪	▪	▪
3	▪	▪	▪
4	▪	▪	▪

49. *Inductive Reasoning* Evaluate $(-1)^m$ for $m = 2$,
4, and 6. Then, evaluate $(-1)^m$ for $m = 1, 3,$ and 5.
Write a conjecture about the sign of an even power
of a negative number. Then write a conjecture about
the sign of an odd power of a negative number.

Geometry Use the diagrams at the right.

50. A square has sides of length 5 in. What is its area?

51. A cube has a side length of 6 in. What is its volume?

52. What is the length of a side of a square with an
area of 64 in.^{2}?

53. What is the side length of a cube with a volume
of 64 in.^{3}?

54. *Language* Why do you think *squared* and *cubed* are
used to indicate the second power and the third power?

55. *Mathematical Reasoning* Are $5x^2y$ and $5xy^2$ the same for all
values of x and y? Justify your answer.

SAMPLE

$s = 3$ in.
Area $= s^2$
$= 9$ in.^{2}

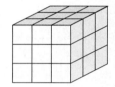

$s = 3$ in.
Volume $= s^3$
$= 27$ in.^{3}

MIXED REVIEW

Test whether each number is divisible by 2, 3, 5, 9, or 10. *(Lesson 4-1)*

56. 36   **57.** 135   **58.** 171   **59.** 190   **60.** 253

Simplify each expression. *(Lesson 2-3)*

61. $3x - 2y + x$ **62.** $w + 8 - 4w - 15$ **63.** $9a + 2(a - 5) + 3$

64. Sara's grades are 79, 83, 74, 86, and 93. What is the mean? *(Lesson 3-3)*

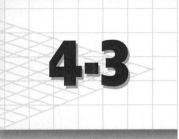

4-3

Prime Factorization and Greatest Common Factor

What You'll Learn

1 To find the prime factorization of a number

2 To find the greatest common factor (GCF) of two or more numbers

...And Why

To compute with fractions

Investigate

•••••••••••••••••••• EXPLORING PRIME NUMBERS ••••••••••••••••••••

The diagram shows the only rectangle you can make with integer side lengths and an area of 5 square units. Work with a partner. Find the number of rectangles you can make with each number of unit squares: 2, 3, 4, 5, 6, 7, 8, 9, and 10.

1. For which numbers of squares is only one rectangle possible?

2. For which numbers of squares is more than one rectangle possible?

3. List the dimensions of the rectangles you can make with each of the following numbers of unit squares: 13, 15, 17, 19, and 21.

PART 1 Finding Prime Factorizations

Test Prep TIP

To check whether a number is prime, look for prime factors in order, starting with 2. When you get to a prime whose square is greater than the original number, you can stop. For 23, check 2 and 3. Then stop at 5, since $5^2 > 23$. Since 2, 3, and 5 are not factors of 23, 23 is prime.

A **prime number** is a positive integer greater than 1 with exactly two factors, 1 and the number itself. The numbers 2, 3, 5, and 7 are prime numbers.

A **composite number** is a positive integer greater than 1 with more than two factors. The numbers 4, 6, 8, 9, and 10 are composite numbers. The number 1 is neither prime nor composite.

■ EXAMPLE 1

Tell whether each number is *prime* or *composite*.

a. 23 Prime; it has only 2 factors, 1 and 23.

b. 129 Composite; it has more than two factors, 1, 3, 43, and 129.

■ TRY THIS

4. Which numbers from 10 to 20 are prime? Are composite?

Writing a composite number as a product of its prime factors shows the **prime factorization** of the number. You can use a *factor tree* to find prime factorizations. Write the final factors in increasing order from left to right. Use exponents to indicate repeated factors.

■ EXAMPLE 2

Use a factor tree to write the prime factorization of 825.

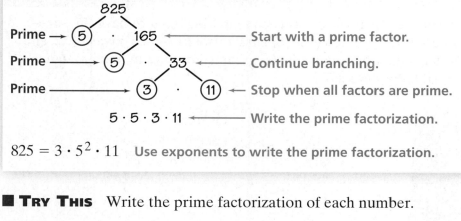

$825 = 3 \cdot 5^2 \cdot 11$ Use exponents to write the prime factorization.

■ **TRY THIS**   Write the prime factorization of each number.

5. 72   **6.** 150   **7.** 225   **8.** 236

PART 2
Finding the Greatest Common Factor

Any factors that are the same for two or more numbers are *common factors.* The greatest of these common factors is called the **greatest common factor (GCF).** You can use prime factorization to find the GCF of two or more numbers or expressions. If there are no prime factors in common, the GCF is 1.

■ EXAMPLE 3

Find the GCF of each pair of expressions.

a. 40 and 60

$40 = 2^3 \cdot 5$
$60 = 2^2 \cdot 3 \cdot 5$

Write the prime factorizations.

Find the common factors. Use the lesser power of the common factors.

GCF = $2^2 \cdot 5$
    = 20

The GCF of 40 and 60 is 20.

b. $6a^3b$ and $4a^2b$

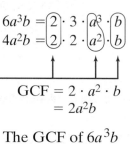

$6a^3b = 2 \cdot 3 \cdot a^3 \cdot b$
$4a^2b = 2 \cdot 2 \cdot a^2 \cdot b$

GCF = $2 \cdot a^2 \cdot b$
    = $2a^2b$

The GCF of $6a^3b$ and $4a^2b$ is $2a^2b$.

■ TRY THIS Use prime factorizations to find each GCF.

9. $8, 20$ **10.** $12, 87$ **11.** $12r^3, 8r$ **12.** $15m^2n, 45m$

You can find the GCF of two or more numbers or expressions by listing factors or by using prime factorizations.

■ Different Ways to Solve a Problem

> A parade organizer wants each marching band to have the same number of band members in each row. The bands have 48, 32, and 56 band members. What is the greatest number of band members possible for each row?

A parade organizer wants bands with 90 members, 108 members, and 72 members to have the same number of members in each row. What is the greatest number of members possible for each row?

Method 1

List the factors of each number. Then find the greatest factor the numbers have in common.

48: 1, 2, 3, 4, 6, ⑧ 12, 16, 24, 48

32: 1, 2, 4, ⑧ 16, 32

56: 1, 2, 4, 7, ⑧ 14, 28, 56

The GCF of 48, 32, and 56 is 8. The greatest possible number of band members in each row is 8.

Method 2

Find the prime factorization of each number. Then find the least power of all common prime factors.

48: $2^4 \cdot 3$

32: 2^5

56: $2^3 \cdot 7$

The GCF of 48, 32, and 56 is 2^3, or 8. The greatest possible number of band members in each row is 8.

Choose a Method

1. Which method do you prefer to find the GCF? Explain why.
2. Which method would you use to find the GCF of 4, 8, and 24? Of 54, 27, and 36? Explain why.

Exercises

CHECK UNDERSTANDING

Is each number *prime* or *composite*? For each composite number, write the prime factorization.

1. 27   **2.** 19   **3.** 31   **4.** 38   **5.** 45

6. 53   **7.** 87   **8.** 93   **9.** 125   **10.** 360

Find each GCF.

11. 10, 45   **12.** 6, 8, 12   **13.** 42, 65   **14.** $14c^2, 35c$ **15.** $3y^2, 24y^3$

16. *Critical Thinking* To find the prime factorization of 225, one student started by using the prime factor 3. Another started by using the prime factor 5. Does starting with different numbers make any difference in the prime factorization? Explain.

PRACTICE AND PROBLEM SOLVING

Is each number *prime, composite,* or *neither*? For each composite number, write the prime factorization.

17. 8   **18.** 17   **19.** 2   **20.** 34   **21.** 1   **22.** 29

23. 115   **24.** 186   **25.** 49   **26.** 621   **27.** 253   **28.** 1,575

Find each GCF.

29. 14, 21   **30.** 25, 100   **31.** 57, 84   **32.** 54, 144

33. 8, 16, 20   **34.** 12, 18, 21   **35.** 90, 900   **36.** 143, 169

37. z, z^2 **38.** $5a, 35a$ **39.** $18c^3, 24c^3$ **40.** $180a^2, 210a$

41. $48r^2s, 63s$ **42.** $6m^3n, 8mn^2$ **43.** $27x^2y^3, 46x^2y$ **44.** $25b^2c, 42bc$

45. *Puzzle* Find the integers that fit the following conditions:
- They are between 44 and 53.
- The sums of their digits are prime.
- They have more than three factors.

46. *Writing* Explain how to find the prime factorization of 50.

47. **TEST PREP** For which expressions is the GCF 12?

     A. 3 and 4   **B.** $24x^2$ and $36y$ **C.** $12xy$ and $24y$ **D.** $3x$ and $12x$

48. *Open-ended* The GCF of 36 and x is 6. What are two possible values for x?

Two numbers are *relatively prime* if their GCF is 1. Is each pair of numbers relatively prime? Explain.

SAMPLE 8, 17 Yes, 8 and 17 are relatively prime. The GCF is 1.
　　　　 7, 35 No, 7 and 35 are not relatively prime. The GCF is 7.

49. 3, 20 　　　　**50.** 9, 42 　　　　**51.** 13, 52 　　　　**52.** 24, 47 　　　　**53.** 52, 65

54. Simon is covering a wall with equal-sized tiles that can't be cut into smaller pieces. The area he wishes to cover is 66 in. high by 72 in. wide. What is the largest square tile that Simon can use?

55. A math teacher and a science teacher combine their first-period classes for a group activity. The math class has 24 students and the science class has 16 students. The teachers need to divide the students into groups of the same size. Each group must have the same number of math students. Find the greatest number of groups possible.

56. A photography club is practicing developing techniques. One set of negatives contains 32 negatives and another contains 48 negatives. Each set can be divided equally among the members present. List all the possible numbers of members present. What is the greatest possible number?

57. Organizers for a high school graduation have set up chairs in two sections. They put 126 chairs for graduates in the front section and 588 chairs for guests in the back section. If all rows have the same number of chairs, what is the greatest number of chairs possible for a row?

◤ MIXED REVIEW

Evaluate for $x = 2$ and $y = 5$. (*Lesson 4-2*)

58. $x^2 y$ 　　　　**59.** xy^2 　　　　**60.** $x^2 + y^2$ 　　　　**61.** $x^4 - y$

Solve each equation. (*Lesson 3-6*)

62. $3x = 5.4$ 　　　　**63.** $-0.5a = 4.35$ 　　　　**64.** $4.32 = 1.6y$ 　　　　**65.** $-8m = -74.4$

66. *Choose a Strategy* A store manager ordered three times as many books as magazines. She ordered a total of 108 books and magazines. How many books did she order?

MATH TOOLBOX

Venn Diagrams

You can use a *Venn diagram* to show relationships among collections of objects or numbers. Each collection is represented by a circle. The *intersection*, or overlap, of two circles indicates what is common to both collections.

■ EXAMPLE 1

School coaches plan to send notices to all students playing fall or winter sports. How many notices do they need to send?

Students in Sports

Season	Students
Fall	155
Winter	79
Both fall and winter	28

number who played
only a fall sport
155 − 28 = 127

Fall   **Winter**

127 28 51

↑
Both fall and winter

number who played
only a winter sport
79 − 28 = 51

Add all three numbers to find the number of notices needed.

127 + 28 + 51 = 206

The coaches need to send 206 notices.

---

1. In a class of 38 students, 32 are wearing jeans, 21 are wearing T-shirts, and 15 are wearing both. Find how many students are wearing jeans and something other than a T-shirt.

You can use a Venn diagram to find the GCF of two numbers.

■ EXAMPLE 2

Find the GCF of 30 and 84.

Include the common prime factors of 30 and 84 in the intersection.

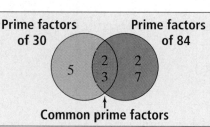

Prime factors of 30   **Prime factors of 84**

5   2 3   2 7

↑
Common prime factors

The GCF is the product of the factors in the intersection.

The GCF is 2 · 3, or 6.

Draw a Venn diagram to find each GCF.

2. 24, 56   3. 35, 49   4. 36, 84   5. 72, 108

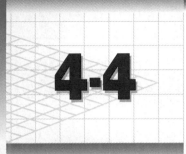

4-4 Simplifying Fractions

What You'll Learn

1 To find equivalent fractions

2 To write fractions in simplest form

...And Why

To recognize equivalent forms of a fraction, such as $\frac{24}{30}$ and $\frac{4}{5}$

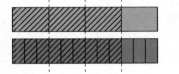

PART 1 Finding Equivalent Fractions

Each fraction bar below represents one whole. The blue bar is divided into four equal parts. The orange bar is divided into twelve equal parts.

$\frac{3}{4}$ of the bar is shaded.

$\frac{9}{12}$ of the bar is shaded.

$\frac{3}{4} = \frac{3 \cdot 3}{4 \cdot 3} = \frac{9}{12}$

The fraction bars show that $\frac{3}{4} = \frac{9}{12}$. The fractions $\frac{3}{4}$ and $\frac{9}{12}$ are **equivalent fractions** because they describe the same part of a whole.

You can find equivalent fractions by multiplying or dividing the numerator and denominator by the same nonzero factor.

Reading Math

Most fraction names are made by adding *th* or *ths* to the denominator. You read $\frac{1}{4}$ as "one fourth," $\frac{2}{5}$ as "two fifths," and $\frac{8}{10}$ as "eight tenths." Halves and thirds are two exceptions.

■ EXAMPLE 1

Find two fractions equivalent to $\frac{4}{12}$.

a. $\frac{4}{12} = \frac{4 \cdot 3}{12 \cdot 3}$

$= \frac{12}{36}$

b. $\frac{4}{12} = \frac{4 \div 4}{12 \div 4}$

$= \frac{1}{3}$

The fractions $\frac{12}{36}$ and $\frac{1}{3}$ are both equivalent to $\frac{4}{12}$.

■ **TRY THIS** Find two fractions equivalent to each fraction.

1. $\frac{5}{15}$ **2.** $\frac{10}{12}$ **3.** $\frac{14}{20}$

PART 2 Writing Fractions in Simplest Form

A fraction is in **simplest form** when the numerator and the denominator have no factors in common other than 1. You can use the GCF to write a fraction in simplest form.

■ **EXAMPLE 2**

Statistics **You survey your friends about their favorite sandwich and find that 8 out of 12, or $\frac{8}{12}$, prefer peanut butter. Write this fraction in simplest form.**

The GCF of 8 and 12 is 4.

$$\frac{8}{12} = \frac{8 \div 4}{12 \div 4} \qquad \text{Divide the numerator and denominator by the GCF, 4.}$$

$$= \frac{2}{3} \qquad \text{Simplify.}$$

The favorite sandwich of $\frac{2}{3}$ of your friends is peanut butter.

The average American child will eat 1,500 peanut butter and jelly sandwiches by the time she or he graduates from high school.

■ **TRY THIS** Write each fraction in simplest form.

4. $\frac{6}{8}$ **5.** $\frac{9}{12}$ **6.** $\frac{28}{35}$

You can simplify fractions that contain variables. In this book, assume that no expression for a denominator equals zero.

■ **EXAMPLE 3**

Write in simplest form.

a. $\frac{y}{xy}$

$$\frac{y}{xy} = \frac{\cancel{y}^1}{xy_1} \qquad \text{Divide the numerator and denominator by the common factor, } y.$$

$$= \frac{1}{x} \qquad \text{Simplify.}$$

b. $\frac{3ab^2}{12ac}$

$$\frac{3ab^2}{12ac} = \frac{3 \cdot a \cdot b \cdot b}{2 \cdot 2 \cdot 3 \cdot a \cdot c} \qquad \text{Write as a product of prime factors.}$$

$$= \frac{\cancel{3}^1 \cdot \cancel{a}^1 \cdot b \cdot b}{2 \cdot 2 \cdot {}_1\cancel{3} \cdot {}_1\cancel{a} \cdot c} \qquad \text{Divide the numerator and denominator by the common factors.}$$

$$= \frac{b \cdot b}{2 \cdot 2 \cdot c} \qquad \text{Simplify.}$$

$$= \frac{b \cdot b}{4 \cdot c} \qquad \text{Simplify.}$$

$$= \frac{b^2}{4c}$$

Test Prep TIP

You will see the directions *write in lowest terms* on some tests. This is another way of saying "write in simplest form."

■ **TRY THIS** Write in simplest form.

7. $\frac{b}{abc}$ **8.** $\frac{2mn}{6m}$ **9.** $\frac{24x^2y}{8xy}$

Exercises

▶ CHECK UNDERSTANDING

Find two fractions equivalent to each fraction.

1. $\frac{2}{8}$ **2.** $\frac{8}{10}$ **3.** $\frac{3}{9}$ **4.** $\frac{8}{36}$ **5.** $\frac{15}{30}$

Write in simplest form.

6. $\frac{3}{9}$ **7.** $\frac{4}{10}$ **8.** $\frac{12}{48}$ **9.** $\frac{2x}{3x}$ **10.** $\frac{4km^2}{12k}$

11. Write the numerator and denominator of $\frac{24}{32}$ as products of prime factors. Then use the prime factors to write $\frac{24}{32}$ in simplest form.

▶ PRACTICE AND PROBLEM SOLVING

Find two fractions equivalent to each fraction.

12. $\frac{4}{8}$ **13.** $\frac{4}{10}$ **14.** $\frac{5}{20}$ **15.** $\frac{10}{16}$ **16.** $\frac{18}{20}$ **17.** $\frac{25}{100}$

Write in simplest form.

18. $\frac{2}{10}$ **19.** $\frac{4}{12}$ **20.** $\frac{6}{15}$ **21.** $\frac{15}{25}$ **22.** $\frac{8}{14}$ **23.** $\frac{18}{32}$

24. $\frac{20}{30}$ **25.** $\frac{12}{16}$ **26.** $\frac{14}{42}$ **27.** $\frac{3b}{5b}$ **28.** $\frac{6m}{15m}$ **29.** $\frac{24x}{16}$

30. $\frac{8pr}{12p}$ **31.** $\frac{14a^2}{24a}$ **32.** $\frac{4bc}{16b}$ **33.** $\frac{40ab}{5ab}$ **34.** $\frac{5t}{10t^2}$ **35.** $\frac{x^2y}{3yz}$

36. You share a fishing tackle box with some friends. Of the 20 fishing lures in the box, 5 belong to you. What fraction of the lures belong to you? Write in simplest form.

37. *Error Analysis* A student claims $\frac{65}{91}$ is in simplest form. What prime factor do the numerator and denominator still have in common?

38. *Writing* Does $\frac{1}{2}$ of one pizza represent the same amount as $\frac{1}{2}$ of another pizza? Justify your answer.

39. *Open-ended* Write two fractions whose simplest form is $\frac{3x}{5}$.

40. **TEST PREP** Which fraction is equivalent to $\frac{ab}{5}$?

  A. $\frac{10ab}{50a}$ **B.** $\frac{15a^2b}{75a}$ **C.** $\frac{25ab^2}{5b}$ **D.** $\frac{45a^3b}{15a^2}$

41. _Health_ Doctors suggest that most people need about 8 h of sleep each night to stay healthy. What fraction of the day is this? Write your answer in simplest form.

Data Analysis Use the table at the right. Write each fraction in simplest form.

42. In 1997, what fraction of U.S. households had PCs (personal computers)?

43. In 1997, what fraction of U.S. households had PCs and modems?

44. In 1998, what fraction of U.S. households with PCs were on-line? (Assume a household must have a PC in order to be on-line.)

PC and On-Line Households in the U.S. (millions)

Households	1997	1998	Projected	
			1999	2000
Total households	100	101	102	103
Households with PCs	44	48	52	55
Households with PCs and modems	36	42	48	51
On-line households	21	27	33	36

SOURCE: _The Wall Street Journal Almanac 1999_

▶ MIXED REVIEW

Find each GCF. (_Lesson 4-3_)

45. $10, 12$ **46.** $28, 60$ **47.** $14a, 21a$ **48.** $24x^2, 40x^3$

Solve each equation. (_Lesson 3-5_)

49. $y + 3.23 = 5.85$ **50.** $b - 2.13 = 9.9$ **51.** $12.8 + z = 6.47$

52. _Estimation_ A damaged oil tanker spilled 34.7 million gallons of crude oil over 4 days. On average, about how many gallons did the tanker spill each day? (_Lesson 3-2_)

✓ CHECKPOINT 1   Lessons 4-1 through 4-4

Test whether each number is divisible by 2, 3, 5, 9, or 10.

1. 30 **2.** 54 **3.** 48 **4.** 161 **5.** $2{,}583$

Evaluate each expression.

6. x^2, for $x = 8$ **7.** a^3, for $a = 5$ **8.** $-2z^2$, for $z = -3$

Write in simplest form.

9. $\frac{8}{16}$ **10.** $\frac{14}{21}$ **11.** $\frac{16}{28}$ **12.** $\frac{3a}{12a}$ **13.** $\frac{2xy}{x}$

14. _Open-ended_ Write two expressions whose GCF is $5a^2$.

See also Extra Practice section.

4-5

Read Plan
Look Solve
Back

Account for All Possibilities

Math Strategies in Action Have you ever lost something that you just couldn't find anywhere? Don't you usually discover that you didn't check *every* place you could, even when you thought you had?

Even for a situation like losing a TV remote control, making a list of places to search might help.

In some problems, you need to count the possibilities. To solve these problems, you need to be sure that you have found every possible combination. Organized lists and diagrams help you to keep track of possibilities as you find them.

▮ SAMPLE PROBLEM

Mandy, Jim, Keisha, Darren, Lin, Chris, and Jen are friends. They want to take pictures of themselves with two people in each picture. How many pictures do they need to take?

Read

1. What do you need to find?

2. How many people are there in all?

3. How many people will be in each photograph?

Plan

To make sure that you account for everyone, make an organized list.

Solve

First pair Mandy with each of her six friends. Next, pair Jim with each of the five friends left. Since Mandy and Jim have already been paired, you don't need to count them again.

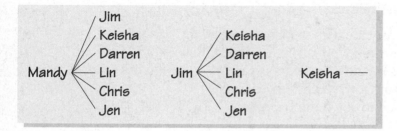

4. Copy and complete the list of paired friends.

5. What pattern do you see?

6. How many pictures do they need to take?

7. Suppose Mandy and nine friends paired up for pictures. Using the pattern suggested above, find how many pictures there would be.

Look Back

Another way to solve this problem is to use a diagram. Draw line segments to show all possible pairs of friends.

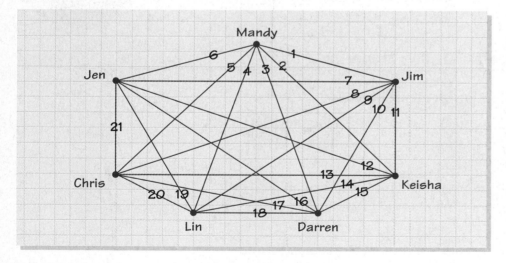

There are 21 line segments. This shows there are 21 pairs of friends.

Exercises

CHECK UNDERSTANDING

Solve each problem by accounting for all possibilities.

1. A sandwich shop serves turkey, ham, tuna, chicken, and egg salad
   sandwiches. You can have any sandwich using white, wheat, or rye
   bread. Suppose you eat there every day. For how many days can
   you order a sandwich that is different from any you have ordered
   before? Copy and complete the list below to solve the problem.

   white — turkey, ham, tuna, chicken, egg salad

   wheat — turkey

2. You throw three darts at the target shown at the right.
   If each dart hits the target, what possible point totals
   can you score?

3. *Patterns* Eight people are at a party. Everyone
   shakes hands once with everyone else. How many
   handshakes are there altogether?

4. You have one penny, one nickel, one dime, and one quarter.
   How many different amounts of money can you make using
   one or more of these coins?

PRACTICE AND PROBLEM SOLVING

Solve each problem by accounting for all possibilities.

5. You have pepperoni, mushrooms, onions, and green peppers.
   How many different pizzas can you make by using one, two,
   three, or four of the toppings?

6. There are seven softball teams in a league. Each team plays
   each of the other teams twice. What is the total number of
   games played?

7. Four candidates run for president of the student council. Three
   other candidates run for vice-president. How many different ways
   can the two offices be filled?

Solve using any strategy.

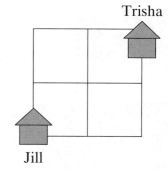

Trisha

Jill

8. Copy the diagram at the right. Using the paths shown, Jill can walk to Trisha's house in many different ways. Draw each route that is four blocks long. How can you be sure that you have found all possible routes?

9. **Geometry** You have 24 feet of fence to make a rectangular garden. Each side will measure a whole number of feet. How many different-sized rectangular gardens can you make?

10. **TEST PREP** How many different rectangles are there with an area of 36 cm² if the side lengths, in centimeters, are integers?
    A. 1   **B.** 3   **C.** 4   **D.** 5

11. **a.** Five workers take 12 hours to do a job. The number of person-hours the job requires is the number of hours the job would take one person to do. How many person-hours does the job require?
    b. In how many hours could 20 workers do the job?

12. **Patterns** The bottom row of a stack of blocks contains 11 blocks. The row above it contains 9 blocks. The next higher row contains 7 blocks. The rows continue in this pattern, and the top row contains a single block. How many blocks does the stack contain in all?

▶ **MIXED REVIEW**

Write in simplest form. *(Lesson 4-4)*

13. $\frac{6}{12}$

14. $\frac{10}{40}$

15. $\frac{6a^2}{15}$

16. $\frac{14a^3}{28a^2}$

Write a rule for each pattern. *(Lesson 1-7)*

17. $10, 20, 30, \ldots$

18. $8, 5, 2, -1, \ldots$

19. $2, 6, 18, 54, \ldots$

20. **Choose a Strategy** Elki has read the first 60 pages of a book. When he has read 35 more pages, he will have read half the book. How many pages are in the book?

CHAPTER PROJECT 4

ACTIVITY 2 ANALYZING

No calendar uses the exact solar year, which is 365 days, 5 hours, 48 minutes, 46 seconds. What problems arise from rounding a year to 365 days? A *leap year* has an extra day to adjust for the rounding. Explain why leap years occur at four-year intervals.

4-6

Rational Numbers

What You'll Learn

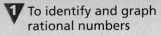

1 To identify and graph rational numbers

2 To evaluate fractions containing variables

. . . And Why

To use rational numbers in real-world situations, such as problems involving rates

PART 1 Identifying and Graphing Rational Numbers

A **rational number** is any number you can write as a quotient $\frac{a}{b}$ of two integers, where b is not zero. The diagram below shows rational numbers.

Notice that all integers are rational numbers. This is true because you can write any integer a as $\frac{a}{1}$.

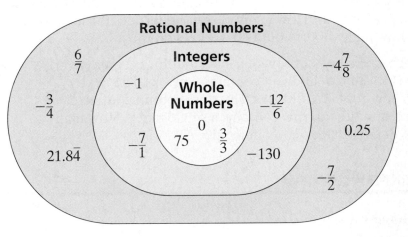

Here are three ways you can write a negative rational number.

$$-\frac{7}{9} = \frac{-7}{9} = \frac{7}{-9}$$

For each rational number, there are an unlimited number of equivalent fractions.

The quotient of two integers with the same sign is positive.

The quotient of two integers with opposite signs is negative.

■ **EXAMPLE 1**

Write two lists of fractions equivalent to $\frac{1}{2}$.

$\frac{1}{2} = \frac{2}{4} = \frac{3}{6} = \cdots$ Numerators and denominators are positive.

$\frac{1}{2} = \frac{-1}{-2} = \frac{-2}{-4} = \cdots$ Numerators and denominators are negative.

■ **TRY THIS** Write three fractions equivalent to each fraction.

1. $\frac{1}{3}$ **2.** $-\frac{4}{5}$ **3.** $\frac{5}{8}$ **4.** $-\frac{1}{2}$

You can graph rational numbers on a number line.

EXAMPLE 2

Graph each rational number on a number line.

a. $\frac{1}{2}$ b. $-\frac{8}{10}$ c. 1   d. -0.2

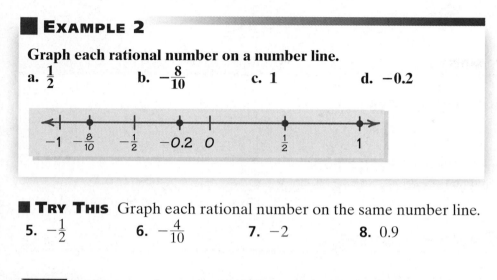

TRY THIS Graph each rational number on the same number line.

5. $-\frac{1}{2}$ 6. $-\frac{4}{10}$ 7. -2 8. 0.9

PART 2 Evaluating Fractions Containing Variables

To evaluate fractions with variables, remember that a fraction bar is a grouping symbol. First, substitute for the variables and simplify the expressions in the numerator and denominator. Then, write the fraction in simplest form.

Simplify the numerator. ⟶ $\dfrac{1 + 9 + 2}{2 - 5} = \dfrac{12}{-3} = -4$
Simplify the denominator. ⟶

REAL-WORLD CONNECTION

EXAMPLE 3

Science The speed of a car changes from 37 ft/s to 102 ft/s in five seconds. What is its acceleration in feet/second² (ft/s²)? Use the formula $a = \dfrac{f - i}{t}$, where a is acceleration, f is final speed, i is initial speed, and t is time.

$a = \dfrac{f - i}{t}$ Use the acceleration formula.

$= \dfrac{102 - 37}{5}$ Substitute.

$= \dfrac{65}{5}$ Subtract.

$= 13$ Write in simplest form.

The car's acceleration is 13 ft/s².

The world's fastest car, the Thrust SSC, can go from 0 ft/s to 1,119 ft/s in thirty seconds. What is its acceleration in ft/s²?

TRY THIS Evaluate each expression for $a = 6$ and $b = -5$.

9. $\dfrac{a + b}{-3}$ 10. $\dfrac{7 - b}{3a}$ 11. $\dfrac{a + 9}{b}$

Exercises

CHECK UNDERSTANDING

Write three fractions equivalent to each fraction.

1. $\frac{1}{6}$

2. $\frac{3}{5}$

3. $-\frac{5}{9}$

4. $\frac{2}{8}$

5. $-\frac{4}{4}$

Evaluate for $a = -4$ and $b = -6$. Write in simplest form.

6. $\frac{a}{b}$

7. $\frac{a+9}{b}$

8. $\frac{b+a}{3a}$

9. $\frac{2a+b}{20}$

PRACTICE AND PROBLEM SOLVING

Write three fractions equivalent to each fraction.

10. $\frac{3}{4}$

11. $-\frac{2}{5}$

12. $\frac{4}{12}$

13. $-\frac{12}{27}$

14. $\frac{7}{11}$

Graph the rational numbers below on the same number line.

15. $\frac{1}{10}$

16. $-\frac{3}{5}$

17. 2

18. -0.3

Evaluate. Write in simplest form.

19. $\frac{m}{n}$, for $m = -2$ and $n = 8$

20. $\frac{m-n}{-12}$, for $m = -3$ and $n = 6$

21. $\frac{3m-11}{n}$, for $m = 7$ and $n = 14$

22. $\frac{y}{-x}$, for $x = 5$ and $y = -4$

23. $\frac{-2y}{x^2}$, for $x = 9$ and $y = 3$

24. $\frac{y(xy-7)}{10}$, for $x = 6$ and $y = 2$

25. Which of the following rational numbers are equivalent to $-\frac{4}{5}$?
$$\frac{4}{-5}, \frac{-12}{15}, -\frac{16}{20}, \frac{-4}{-5}$$

26. a. *Open-ended* Write two rational numbers between 0 and $\frac{1}{2}$.

    b. *Critical Thinking* Is there any limit to the number of rational numbers between 0 and $\frac{1}{2}$? Explain.

27. *Writing* Can two different fractions that are written in simplest form be equivalent to each other? Explain.

28. *Mathematical Reasoning* What are three fractions equivalent to $\frac{a}{b}$? Justify your answers.

29. *Science* The formula $s = \frac{1,600}{d^2}$ gives the strength s of a radio signal at a distance d miles from the transmitter. What is the strength at 5 mi? Write your answer in simplest form.

What is the strength of a radio signal at 10 miles from a transmitter?

Write the opposite and the absolute value of each number.

SAMPLE   Find the opposite and absolute value of $-\frac{3}{5}$.

Opposite:

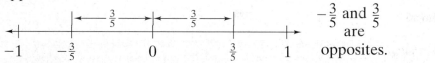

$-\frac{3}{5}$ and $\frac{3}{5}$ are opposites.

Absolute value:

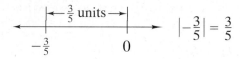

$\left|-\frac{3}{5}\right| = \frac{3}{5}$

30. $-\frac{5}{6}$ **31.** $\frac{2}{3}$ **32.** $\frac{-4}{5}$ **33.** $\frac{1}{4}$

Mathematical Reasoning **For positive integers a and b, tell whether each statement is *always* true. If the statement is not always true, give a counterexample.**

34. $\dfrac{a^2}{b} > \dfrac{a}{b}$ **35.** $\dfrac{3a}{3b} = \dfrac{a}{b}$ **36.** $\dfrac{a^2}{b^2} > \dfrac{a}{b}$

37. *Open-ended* Write two rational numbers between -3 and -2.

> **Journal**
>
> Explain why a whole number is an integer and an integer is a rational number.

▶ **MIXED REVIEW**

Write the integer represented by each point on the number line. *(Lesson 1-4)*

38. *A*   **39.** *B*   **40.** *C*   **41.** *D*

Multiply or divide. *(Lesson 1-9)*

42. $-7 \cdot 4$ **43.** $19(-5)$ **44.** $-124 \div (-4)$ **45.** $-204 \div 6$

46. *Choose a Strategy* Lucia has 4 pairs of pants, 5 shirts, and 2 sweaters. How many different three-piece outfits can she make?

CHAPTER PROJECT 4   ACTIVITY 3 DESIGNING

Design your own calendar. Use what you have learned about multiples and factors to decide how to divide your calendar year into shorter periods. Will your calendar have months? Weeks? Justify your decisions.

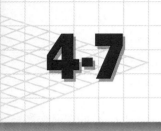

4-7

Exponents and Multiplication

What You'll Learn

1 To multiply powers with the same base

2 To find a power of a power

. . . And Why

To efficiently simplify expressions with exponents

$3 = 3^1$

$a = a^1$

PART 1 **Multiplying Powers with the Same Base**

In Lesson 4-2 you learned how to use exponents to indicate repeated multiplication. What happens when you multiply two powers with the same base, such as 7^2 and 7^3?

$$7^2 \cdot 7^3 = (7 \cdot 7) \cdot (7 \cdot 7 \cdot 7) = 7^5$$

Notice that $7^2 \cdot 7^3 = 7^{2+3} = 7^5$. In general, when you multiply powers with the same base, you can add the exponents.

Multiplying Powers with the Same Base

To multiply numbers or variables with the same base, add the exponents.

Arithmetic	**Algebra**
$2^3 \cdot 2^4 = 2^{3+4} = 2^7$	$a^m \cdot a^n = a^{m+n}$, for positive integers m and n.

You *simplify* an expression by doing as many of the indicated operations as possible.

■ EXAMPLE 1

Simplify each expression.

a. $3 \cdot 3^3$

$3^1 \cdot 3^3 = 3^{1+3}$ Add the exponents of powers with the same base.

$= 3^4$

$= 81$ Simplify.

b. $a^5 \cdot a \cdot b^2$

$a^5 \cdot a^1 \cdot b^2 = a^{5+1}b^2$ Add the exponents of powers with the same base.

$= a^6 b^2$ Simplify.

■ **TRY THIS** Simplify each expression.

1. $2^2 \cdot 2^3$ **2.** $m^5 \cdot m^7$ **3.** $x^2 \cdot x^3 \cdot y \cdot y^4$

EXAMPLE 2

Simplify $-2x^2 \cdot 3x^5$.

$-2x^2 \cdot 3x^5 = -2 \cdot 3 \cdot x^2 \cdot x^5$ **Use the Commutative Property of Multiplication.**

$= -6x^{2+5}$ **Add the exponents.**

$= -6x^7$ **Simplify.**

■ **TRY THIS** Simplify each expression.

4. $6a^3 \cdot 3a$ **5.** $-5c^2 \cdot -3c^7$ **6.** $4x^2 \cdot 3x^4$

Test Prep TIP

When in doubt, write it out! If you are unsure about the rules for multiplying powers, write the powers out. For instance, write $x^2 \cdot x^5$ as $(x \cdot x) \cdot (x \cdot x \cdot x \cdot x \cdot x)$. This simplifies to x^7.

PART 2 **Finding a Power of a Power**

You can find the power of a power by using the rule for Multiplying Powers with the Same Base.

$(7^2)^3 = (7^2) \cdot (7^2) \cdot (7^2)$ **7^2 is used as a base 3 times.**

$= 7^{2+2+2}$ **When multiplying powers with the same base, add the exponents.**

$= 7^6$

Notice that $(7^2)^3 = 7^{2 \cdot 3} = 7^6$. You can raise a power to a power by multiplying the exponents.

Finding a Power of a Power

To find a power of a power, multiply the exponents.

Arithmetic

$(2^3)^4 = 2^{3 \cdot 4} = 2^{12}$

Algebra

$(a^m)^n = a^{m \cdot n}$, for positive integers m and n.

EXAMPLE 3

Simplify each expression.

a. $(3^2)^3$

$(3^2)^3 = (3)^{2 \cdot 3}$ ←Multiply the exponents.

$= (3)^6$ ←Simplify the exponent.

$= 729$ ←Simplify.

b. $(a^6)^2$

$(a^6)^2 = a^{6 \cdot 2}$

$= a^{12}$

Reading Math

You read $(3^2)^3$ as "three squared to the third power." You read $(a^6)^2$ as "a to the sixth power squared."

■ **TRY THIS** Simplify each expression.

7. $(2^4)^2$ **8.** $(c^5)^4$ **9.** $(m^3)^2$

Exercises

CHECK UNDERSTANDING

Simplify each expression.

1. $4^2 \cdot 4$

2. $a^2 \cdot a^5$

3. $x^4 \cdot y \cdot x^5 \cdot y$

4. $7b^3 \cdot 4b^4$

5. $-9c^2 \cdot (-2c^8)$

6. $(10^3)^2$

7. $(x^3)^4$

8. $(m^6)^4$

9. **Critical Thinking** Can $x^6 y^7$ be simplified? Explain.

PRACTICE AND PROBLEM SOLVING

Simplify each expression.

10. $10^2 \cdot 10^5$

11. $2^2 \cdot 2^5$

12. $x^4 \cdot x^4$

13. $a^{10} \cdot a \cdot a^2$

14. $(x^2)(y^5)(x)$

15. $m^{50} \cdot m^2$

16. $5x^3 \cdot 2x^6$

17. $4y^7 \cdot 6y^4$

18. $(-2a^2)(-2a^2)$

19. $9b^2 \cdot (-4b)^2$

20. $-7x^6 \cdot -5x^8$

21. $(2^2)^3$

22. $(3^2)^4$

23. $(c^2)^8$

24. $(x^5)^7$

25. $(m^5)^5$

Complete each equation.

26. $8^2 \cdot 8^{\blacksquare} = 8^9$

27. $5^6 \cdot 5^{\blacksquare} = 5^{14}$

28. $c^{\blacksquare} \cdot c^4 = c^{11}$

29. $x^{\blacksquare} \cdot x^{12} = x^{15}$

30. $(2^2)^{\blacksquare} = 2^6$

31. $(9^{\blacksquare})^4 = 9^{16}$

32. $(a^{\blacksquare})^9 = a^{27}$

33. $(y^7)^{\blacksquare} = y^{35}$

Compare. Use >, <, or = to complete each statement.

34. $5^5 \ \blacksquare \ (5^3)^2$

35. $7^2 \cdot 7^5 \ \blacksquare \ (7^6)^2$

36. $(2^3)^3 \ \blacksquare \ 2^6$

37. $25^2 \ \blacksquare \ (5^2)^2$

38. $(2^7)^7 \ \blacksquare \ (2^{25})^2$

39. $(4^3 \cdot 4^2)^3 \ \blacksquare \ 4^9$

40. **TEST PREP** Which expression is equivalent to 2^{13}?

    A. $(2^3)^{10}$ **B.** $2^5 \cdot 2^8$ **C.** $2^1 \cdot 2^{13}$ **D.** 8,190

41. **Mathematical Reasoning** Are $-(2^3)^2$ and $(-2^3)^2$ equivalent? Justify your answer.

42. **Open-ended** A megabyte is 2^{20} bytes. Use exponents to write 2^{20} in four different ways.

43. **Writing** Explain why $x^8 \cdot x^2$ is equivalent to $x^5 \cdot x^5$.

44. **Error Analysis** Marcos thinks that $x^4 + x^4$ simplifies to $2x^4$. Doug thinks that $x^4 + x^4$ simplifies to x^8. Which result is correct? Explain.

45. *Critical Thinking* Is 2^{30} or 2^{16} twice the value of 2^{15}? Explain.

Geometry **Find the area of each rectangle.**

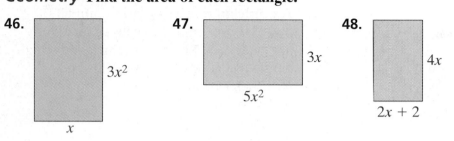

46. $3x^2$ — x

47. $3x$ — $5x^2$

48. $4x$ — $2x + 2$

▶ **MIXED REVIEW**

Evaluate. Write in simplest form. *(Lesson 4-6)*

49. $\dfrac{a}{b+1}$, for $a = -4$ and $b = 7$ **50.** $\dfrac{x-5}{y+8}$, for $x = -7$ and $y = 10$ **51.** $\dfrac{mn}{m-6}$, for $m = 4$ and $n = 2$

Graph the solutions of each inequality on a number line. *(Lesson 2-8)*

52. $x < -3$ **53.** $a > 0$ **54.** $y \le -4$ **55.** $b > -2$

56. The Scotts are getting ready for a barbeque. They buy 8 lb of hamburger at \$1.50/lb and 10 lb of chicken at \$1.25/lb. Write and simplify an expression that shows the total cost. *(Lesson 1-2)*

Math at Work

Geophysicist

Geophysicists study Earth's surface, including the history of Earth's crust and rock formations. They search for oil, natural gas, minerals, and underground water. They also work to solve environmental problems. In addition, they study what makes up Earth's interior, as well as its magnetic, electrical, and gravitational forces. They often study earthquakes and volcanoes.

Geophysicists use physics and mathematics in their studies. Much of their work involves measurement. They use instruments to track sound waves, gravity, energy waves, and magnetic fields. Exponents appear in the data that geophysicists gather because they often work with very large numbers.

For more information about careers in geophysics, visit the Prentice Hall Web site.
www.phschool.com

Standardized Test Prep

Multiple Choice

Choose the best answer.

1. Which is the prime factorization of 90?
   A. $2 \cdot 3^2 \cdot 5$ B. $2 \cdot 5 \cdot 9$
   C. $3 \cdot 3 \cdot 5^2$ D. $2 \cdot 45$

2. Which equation is true?
   F. $(3 \cdot 6)^2 = (3 \cdot 6)(3 \cdot 6)(3 \cdot 6)$
   G. $(3 \cdot 6)^2 = 3^2 \cdot 6^2$
   H. $(3 + 6)^2 = 3^2 + 6^2$
   J. $(3 - 6)^2 = 3^2 - 6^2$

3. A rectangular skateboard park has 5 curbs, 2 ramps, and a perimeter of 480 yd. The width of the park is $2s$ and the length is $3s$, where s equals 48 yd. What are the width and length of the park?
   A. 48 yd and 72 yd   B. 96 yd and 144 yd
   C. 120 yd and 2 yd   D. 60 yd and 40 yd

4. The diagram below shows the numbers of students in the school play, the comedy troupe, and the debate club.

   S: students

   P: play members

   C: comedy troupe members

   D: debate club members

   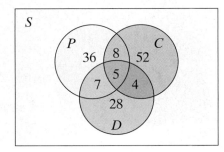

   How many students are in the play and the debate club but *not* in the comedy troupe?
   F. 4 students   G. 5 students
   H. 7 students   J. 12 students

5. A musician receives a "platinum CD" award if one million copies of an album are sold. A CD is 1.5 mm thick. How high would a stack of 1 million CDs be?
   A. 1,500,000 cm
   B. 150,000 m
   C. 1.5 km
   D. 15 km

6. What is the total number of squares in the figure below?

   F. 6   G. 7
   H. 8   J. 9

Free Response

For Exercises 7–10, show your work.

7. Complete the pattern.

Gold Measure	Gold Content
24-karat	$\frac{24}{24} = 1$
22-karat	$\frac{22}{24} = \frac{11}{12}$
18-karat	$\frac{18}{24} = \frac{3}{4}$
14-karat	$\frac{14}{24} = \blacksquare$
9-karat	$\blacksquare = \frac{3}{8}$

8. **Open-ended** The GCF of three numbers is 6. What are three possible values for the numbers?

9. Explain why -5^4 and $(-5)^4$ are not equal.

10. Choose an even number between 10 and 20 and an odd number between 50 and 60. Find the difference between the two numbers. Will the digit in the ones place of the difference be even or odd? Explain.

Exponents and Division

PART 1 Dividing Expressions Containing Exponents

In Lesson 4-7, you learned that you add exponents to multiply powers with the same base. To divide powers with the same base, you subtract exponents. Here's why.

$$\frac{7^8}{7^3} = \frac{7 \cdot 7 \cdot 7 \cdot 7 \cdot 7 \cdot 7 \cdot 7 \cdot 7}{7 \cdot 7 \cdot 7}$$ Expand the numerator and denominator.

$$= \frac{7^1 \cdot 7^1 \cdot 7^1 \cdot 7 \cdot 7 \cdot 7 \cdot 7 \cdot 7}{{}_1 7 \cdot {}_1 7 \cdot {}_1 7}$$ Divide common factors.

$$= 7^5$$

Notice that $\frac{7^8}{7^3} = 7^{8-3}$, or 7^5. This suggests the following rule.

What You'll Learn

1 To divide expressions containing exponents

2 To simplify expressions with integer exponents

...And Why

To divide and simplify expressions with exponents efficiently

---

Dividing Powers with the Same Base

To divide numbers or variables *with the same nonzero base,* you subtract exponents.

Arithmetic	**Algebra**
$\dfrac{4^5}{4^2} = 4^{5-2} = 4^3$	$\dfrac{a^m}{a^n} = a^{m-n}$, for $a \neq 0$ and positive integers m and n.

■ EXAMPLE 1

Simplify each expression.

a. $\dfrac{3^8}{3^5}$ **b.** $\dfrac{a^4}{a^2}$

$$\frac{3^8}{3^5} = 3^{8-5}$$ ← Subtract the exponents. → $\dfrac{a^4}{a^2} = a^{4-2}$

$$= 3^3$$ ← Simplify the exponent. → $= a^2$

$$= 27$$ ← Simplify.

■ **TRY THIS** Simplify each expression.

1. $\dfrac{10^7}{10^4}$ **2.** $\dfrac{x^{25}}{x^{18}}$ **3.** $\dfrac{12m^5}{3m}$

What happens when you divide powers with the same base and get zero as an exponent? Consider $\frac{3^4}{3^4}$.

$$\frac{3^4}{3^4} = 3^{4-4} = 3^0 \qquad \frac{3^4}{3^4} = \frac{\overset{1}{\cancel{3}} \cdot \overset{1}{\cancel{3}} \cdot \overset{1}{\cancel{3}} \cdot \overset{1}{\cancel{3}}}{\underset{1}{\cancel{3}} \cdot \underset{1}{\cancel{3}} \cdot \underset{1}{\cancel{3}} \cdot \underset{1}{\cancel{3}}} = \frac{1}{1} = 1$$

Notice that $\frac{3^4}{3^4} = 3^0$ and $\frac{3^4}{3^4} = 1$. This suggests the following rule.

Zero as an Exponent	
Arithmetic	**Algebra**
$3^0 = 1$	$a^0 = 1$, for $a \neq 0$.

▌ EXAMPLE 2

Simplify each expression.

a. $\dfrac{(-8)^2}{(-8)^2}$

$\dfrac{(-8)^2}{(-8)^2} = (-8)^{2-2}$ Subtract the exponents.

$\qquad\qquad = (-8)^0$

$\qquad\qquad = 1$ Simplify.

b. $\dfrac{6b^3}{18b^3}$

$\dfrac{6b^3}{18b^3} = \dfrac{1}{3}b^0$ Subtract the exponents. Simplify $\frac{6}{18}$.

$\qquad\quad = \dfrac{1}{3} \cdot 1$ Simplify b^0.

$\qquad\quad = \dfrac{1}{3}$ Multiply.

▌ **TRY THIS** Simplify each expression.

4. 43^0 **5.** $\dfrac{5^2 x^6}{5x^6}$ **6.** $\dfrac{x^5 y^6}{x^5 y^3}$ **7.** $5x^0$

What happens when you divide powers with the same base and get a negative exponent? Consider $\frac{3^2}{3^4}$.

$$\frac{3^2}{3^4} = 3^{2-4} = 3^{-2} \qquad \frac{3^2}{3^4} = \frac{\overset{1}{\cancel{3}} \cdot \overset{1}{\cancel{3}}}{\underset{1}{\cancel{3}} \cdot \underset{1}{\cancel{3}} \cdot 3 \cdot 3} = \frac{1}{3^2}$$

Notice $\frac{3^2}{3^4} = 3^{-2}$ and $\frac{3^2}{3^4} = \frac{1}{3^2}$. This suggests the following rule.

Negative Exponents	
Arithmetic	**Algebra**
$3^{-2} = \frac{1}{3^2}$	$a^{-n} = \frac{1}{a^n}$, for $a \neq 0$

A hummingbird has a mass of about 10^{-2} kg, or $\frac{1}{10^2}$ kg. To *simplify* 10^{-2}, you write $\frac{1}{100}$ or 0.01. So the hummingbird has a mass of 0.01 kg. When you simplify an expression such as x^{-2}, you write it as $\frac{1}{x^2}$, using no negative exponents.

■ EXAMPLE 3

Simplify each expression.

a. $\dfrac{5^6}{5^8}$

$\dfrac{5^6}{5^8} = 5^{6-8}$ ←Subtract the exponents.→

$= 5^{-2}$

$= \dfrac{1}{5^2}$ ←Write with a positive exponent.→

$= \dfrac{1}{25}$ ←Simplify.

b. $\dfrac{m^2}{m^5}$

$\dfrac{m^2}{m^5} = m^{2-5}$

$= m^{-3}$

$= \dfrac{1}{m^3}$

Hummingbirds may range from 0.0022 kg to 0.02 kg in mass.

■ TRY THIS Simplify each expression.

8. $\dfrac{4^5}{4^7}$

9. $\dfrac{a^4}{a^6}$

10. $\dfrac{3y^8}{9y^{12}}$

You can also write an expression such as $\frac{1}{x^2}$ so that there is no fraction bar.

■ EXAMPLE 4

Write $\dfrac{x^2 y^3}{x^3 y}$ **without a fraction bar.**

$\dfrac{x^2 y^3}{x^3 y} = x^{2-3} y^{3-1}$ Use the rule for Dividing Powers with the Same Base.

$= x^{-1} y^2$ Subtract the exponents.

■ TRY THIS Write each expression without a fraction bar.

11. $\dfrac{b^3}{b^9}$

12. $\dfrac{m^3 n^2}{m^6 n^8}$

13. $\dfrac{x y^5}{x^5 y^3}$

Exercises

CHECK UNDERSTANDING

Simplify each expression.

1. $\dfrac{2^5}{2^2}$ 2. $\dfrac{h^6}{h^2}$ 3. $\dfrac{6y^7}{10y^2}$ 4. $\dfrac{m^4 n^3}{m^6 n^2}$ 5. $(-4)^0$

6. $\dfrac{10b^8}{2b^8}$ 7. $\dfrac{m^2}{m^6}$ 8. 2^{-3} 9. $\dfrac{4a^3}{20a^6}$ 10. $\dfrac{x^5 y^4}{x^2 y^9}$

Write each expression without a fraction bar.

11. $\dfrac{y^4}{y^7}$ 12. $\dfrac{a^2 b^4}{a^8 b^2}$ 13. $\dfrac{m^5 n^6}{m^7 n^8}$ 14. $\dfrac{x y^2}{x^4 y^9}$ 15. $\dfrac{b^{12} c^5}{b^6 c^{10}}$

PRACTICE AND PROBLEM SOLVING

Simplify each expression.

16. $\dfrac{6^2}{6^1}$ 17. $\dfrac{11^5}{11^3}$ 18. $\dfrac{(-2)^{14}}{(-2)^{11}}$ 19. $\dfrac{x^7}{x^3}$ 20. $\dfrac{b^3}{b^2}$

21. $\dfrac{a^{27}}{a^{19}}$ 22. $\dfrac{200m^{200}}{100m^{100}}$ 23. $\dfrac{18x^{20}}{36x^{12}}$ 24. $\dfrac{w^{12} z^{15}}{w^8 z^8}$ 25. $\dfrac{42a^6 b^7}{7a^3 b^3}$

26. 3^0 27. $\dfrac{b^5}{b^8}$ 28. $\dfrac{5^3}{5^3}$ 29. 8^{-1} 30. $\dfrac{7^3}{7^5}$

31. a^{-4} 32. $\dfrac{6^7}{6^{11}}$ 33. $\dfrac{(-2)^4}{(-2)^4}$ 34. $(-2)^0$ 35. $\dfrac{a^2}{a^7}$

36. $\dfrac{6x^2}{x^4}$ 37. $\dfrac{2y^3}{8y^7}$ 38. $x^{-3} y^2$ 39. $\dfrac{5x^2}{10x^{-5}}$ 40. $5b^{-7}$

Complete each equation.

41. $\dfrac{4^{\blacksquare}}{4^3} = 4^5$ 42. $\dfrac{x^6}{x^{\blacksquare}} = x^4$ 43. $\dfrac{14x^5}{7x^3} = 2x^{\blacksquare}$ 44. $\dfrac{10^5}{10^{\blacksquare}} = 1$

45. $\dfrac{1}{8^2} = 8^{\blacksquare}$ 46. $\dfrac{1}{a^3} = a^{\blacksquare}$ 47. $\dfrac{y^{\blacksquare}}{y^9} = y^{-4}$ 48. $\dfrac{1}{-27} = (-3)^{\blacksquare}$

Write each expression without a fraction bar.

49. $\dfrac{x^3}{x^5}$ 50. $\dfrac{a^9 b^3}{a^7 b^8}$ 51. $\dfrac{m^9 n^3}{m^2 n^{10}}$ 52. $\dfrac{x^4 y}{x^8 y^3}$ 53. $\dfrac{b^{14} c^2}{b^9 c^{11}}$

54. **Writing** Explain why 3^{-2} is not a negative number.

55. **Error Analysis** A student wrote that $-5^0 = 1$. What was the student's error?

56. **Open-ended** Write three different quotients that equal 5^{-7}.

57. Science The *magnitude* of an earthquake is a measure of the amount of energy released. An earthquake of magnitude 6 releases about 30 times as much energy as an earthquake of magnitude 5.

The magnitude of the 1989 earthquake in Loma Prieta, California, was about 7. The magnitude of the 1933 earthquake in Sanriku, Japan, was about 9. Simplify $\frac{30^9}{30^7}$ to find how many times as much energy was released in the Sanriku earthquake.

The photo shows damage from the Loma Prieta, California, earthquake of October 17, 1989.

▶ MIXED REVIEW

Simplify each expression. *(Lesson 4-7)*

58. $5^2 \cdot 5$

59. $x^7 \cdot x^2$

60. $(y^{12})(y^8)$

61. $2a^9 \cdot 8a^7$

Estimate using front-end estimation. *(Lesson 3-1)*

62. $5.68 + 3.24$

63. $17.86 + 2.321$

64. $20.2 + 5.8$

65. $42.8 + 7.6$

66. *Choose a Strategy* The sum of three consecutive integers is 264. What are the three integers?

✓ CHECKPOINT 2　　　　　　　　　　　　　Lessons 4-5 through 4-8

Write three fractions equivalent to each fraction.

1. $\frac{3}{12}$

2. $\frac{12}{36}$

3. $\frac{49}{70}$

4. $\frac{18}{28}$

5. $\frac{4}{5}$

Evaluate for $a = 4$ and $b = -6$. Write in simplest form.

6. $\frac{a}{2b}$

7. $\frac{b + a}{a}$

8. $\frac{a - b}{15}$

9. $\frac{b - a}{a^2}$

10. $\frac{3a + b}{24}$

Graph the rational numbers below on the same number line.

11. -0.8

12. $\frac{1}{2}$

13. 0.6

14. $-\frac{2}{10}$

15. $\frac{9}{10}$

Simplify each expression.

16. $2^3 \cdot 2^4$

17. $(x^5)^{10}$

18. $\frac{18a^4}{3a^2}$

19. $\frac{x^3}{x^8}$

20. $\frac{a^3b^5}{a^9b^5}$

21. **TEST PREP** What is the simplest form of $\frac{12a^{35}}{36a^{50}}$?

A. $\frac{1}{3}a^{85}$

B. $\frac{1}{3a^{85}}$

C. $\frac{1}{3a^{15}}$

D. $\frac{1}{3}a^{15}$

22. If 12 of 16 students vote to do a project, what fraction of the students is this? Write the fraction in simplest form.

4-9

Scientific Notation

What You'll Learn

1 To write and evaluate numbers in scientific notation

2 To calculate with scientific notation

...And Why

To use scientific notation for recording very large or very small numbers, such as the weight of the Great Pyramid or the mass of a hydrogen atom

Investigate

·························· EXPLORING SCIENTIFIC NOTATION ··························

1. Copy and complete the chart below.

5×10^4	$= 5 \times 10,000$	$= 50,000$
5×10^3	$= 5 \times 1,000$	$= \blacksquare$
5×10^2	$= 5 \times \blacksquare$	$= \blacksquare$
5×10^1	$= 5 \times \blacksquare$	$= \blacksquare$
5×10^0	$= 5 \times \blacksquare$	$= \blacksquare$
$5 \times 10^{-1} = 5 \times \frac{1}{10}$	$= 5 \times 0.1$	$= 0.5$
$5 \times 10^{-2} = 5 \times \blacksquare$	$= 5 \times 0.01$	$= 0.05$
$5 \times 10^{-3} = 5 \times \blacksquare$	$= 5 \times \blacksquare$	$= 0.005$
$5 \times 10^{-4} = 5 \times \blacksquare$	$= 5 \times \blacksquare$	$= \blacksquare$

2. *Patterns* Describe the pattern you see in your chart.

3. a. Based on the pattern you see, simplify 5×10^7.
   b. Simplify 5×10^{-6}.

PART 1 Writing and Evaluating Scientific Notation

Scientific notation is a shorthand way of writing numbers using powers of 10. You write a number in scientific notation as the product of two factors.

Need Help? For help with multiplying by powers of ten, see Skills Handbook, p. 734.

Second factor is a power of 10.

$$7,500,000,000,000 = 7.5 \times 10^{12}$$

First factor is greater than or equal to 1, but less than 10.

Scientific notation lets you know the size of a number without having to count digits. For example, if the exponent of 10 is 6, the number is in the millions. If the exponent is 9, the number is in the billions.

■ EXAMPLE 1

About 4,200,000 people visit the Statue of Liberty every year. Write this number in scientific notation.

4,200,000 Move the decimal point to get a decimal
6 places greater than 1 but less than 10.

4.2 Drop the zeros after the 2.

4.2×10^6 The decimal point moved **6** places to the left. Use 6 as the exponent of 10.

■ **TRY THIS** Write each number in scientific notation.

4. 54,500,000   **5.** 723,000   **6.** 602,000,000,000

In scientific notation, you use a negative exponent to write a number between 0 and 1.

The total weight of the Statue of Liberty is about 450,000 lb. Write this number in scientific notation.

■ EXAMPLE 2

Write 0.000079 in scientific notation.

0.000079 Move the decimal point to get a decimal
5 places greater than 1 but less than 10.

7.9 Drop the zeros before the 7.

7.9×10^{-5} The decimal point moved **5** places to the right. Use −5 as the exponent of 10.

■ **TRY THIS** Write each number in scientific notation.

7. 0.00021   **8.** 0.00000005   **9.** 0.0000000000803

You can change expressions from scientific notation to **standard notation** by simplifying the product of the two factors.

■ EXAMPLE 3

Write each number in standard notation.

a. 8.9×10^5 **b.** 2.71×10^{-6}

8.90000 Add zeros while moving the decimal point. 000002.71

890,000 Rewrite in standard notation. 0.00000271

■ **TRY THIS** Write each number in standard notation.

10. 3.21×10^7 **11.** 5.9×10^{-8} **12.** 1.006×10^{10}

For a number to be in scientific notation, the digit in front of the decimal must be between 1 and 10.

▌ EXAMPLE 4

Write each number in scientific notation.

a. 0.37×10^{10}

$\quad 0.37 \times 10^{10} = 3.7 \times 10^{-1} \times 10^{10}$ Write 0.37 as 3.7×10^{-1}.

$\quad\quad\quad\quad\quad\quad = 3.7 \times 10^9$ Add the exponents.

b. 453.1×10^8

$\quad 453.1 \times 10^8 = 4.531 \times 10^2 \times 10^8$ Write 453.1 as 4.531×10^2.

$\quad\quad\quad\quad\quad = 4.531 \times 10^{10}$ Add the exponents.

■ **TRY THIS** Write each number in scientific notation.

13. 16×10^5 **14.** 0.203×10^6 **15.** $7{,}243 \times 10^{12}$

You can compare and order numbers using scientific notation. First compare the powers of 10, and then compare the decimals.

▌ EXAMPLE 5

Order 0.064×10^8, 312×10^2, and 0.58×10^7 from least to greatest.

Write each number in scientific notation.

0.064×10^8 $\quad\quad$ 312×10^2 $\quad\quad$ 0.58×10^7

$\quad\quad\downarrow$ $\quad\quad\quad\quad\quad\quad\downarrow$ $\quad\quad\quad\quad\quad\downarrow$

6.4×10^6 $\quad\quad$ 3.12×10^4 $\quad\quad$ 5.8×10^6

Order the powers of 10. Arrange the decimals with the same power of 10 in order.

3.12×10^4 $\quad\quad$ 5.8×10^6 $\quad\quad$ 6.4×10^6

Write the original numbers in order.

$312 \times 10^2, 0.58 \times 10^7, 0.064 \times 10^8$

■ **TRY THIS** Order from least to greatest.

16. $526 \times 10^7, 18.3 \times 10^6, 0.098 \times 10^9$

17. $8 \times 10^{-9}, 14.7 \times 10^{-7}, 0.22 \times 10^{-10}$

Calculating with Scientific Notation

You can multiply numbers in scientific notation using the rule for Multiplying Powers with the Same Base.

■ EXAMPLE 6

Multiply 3×10^{-7} and 9×10^3. Express the result in scientific notation.

$$(3 \times 10^{-7})(9 \times 10^3) = 3 \times 9 \times 10^{-7} \times 10^3 \qquad \text{Use the Commutative Property of Multiplication.}$$
$$= 27 \times 10^{-7} \times 10^3 \qquad \text{Multiply 3 and 9.}$$
$$= 27 \times 10^{-4} \qquad \text{Add the exponents.}$$
$$= 2.7 \times 10^1 \times 10^{-4} \qquad \text{Write 27 as } 2.7 \times 10^1.$$
$$= 2.7 \times 10^{-3} \qquad \text{Add the exponents.}$$

■ **TRY THIS** Multiply. Express each result in scientific notation.

18. $(4 \times 10^4)(6 \times 10^6)$ **19.** $(7.1 \times 10^{-8})(8 \times 10^4)$

Computations with scientific notation often occur in real-world situations that involve very large or very small numbers.

REAL-WORLD CONNECTION

■ EXAMPLE 7

Measurement The Great Pyramid of Giza in Egypt contains about 2.3×10^6 blocks of stone. On average, each block weighs about 5×10^3 lb. About how many pounds of stone does the Great Pyramid contain?

$$(2.3 \times 10^6)(5 \times 10^3) \qquad \text{Write a multiplication problem.}$$
$$= 2.3 \times 5 \times 10^6 \times 10^3 \qquad \text{Use the Commutative Property of Multiplication.}$$
$$= 11.5 \times 10^6 \times 10^3 \qquad \text{Simplify.}$$
$$= 11.5 \times 10^9 \qquad \text{Add the exponents.}$$
$$= 1.15 \times 10^1 \times 10^9 \qquad \text{Write 11.5 as } 1.15 \times 10^1.$$
$$= 1.15 \times 10^{10} \qquad \text{Add the exponents.}$$

The Great Pyramid contains more than 1.15×10^{10} lb of stone.

■ **TRY THIS**

20. *Chemistry* A hydrogen atom has a mass of 1.67×10^{-27} kg. What is the mass of 6×10^3 hydrogen atoms? Express the result in scientific notation.

Exercises

▶ CHECK UNDERSTANDING

Write each number in scientific notation.

1. 8,900,000,000
2. 0.000631
3. 555,900,000
4. 0.09×10^{12}

Write each number in standard notation.

5. 5.94×10^7
6. 2.104×10^{-8}
7. 1.2×10^5
8. 7.2×10^{-4}

Order from least to greatest.

9. $16 \times 10^9, 2.3 \times 10^{12}, 0.065 \times 10^{11}$
10. $253 \times 10^{-9}, 3.7 \times 10^{-8}, 12.9 \times 10^{-7}$

Multiply. Express each result in scientific notation.

11. $(5 \times 10^6)(6 \times 10^2)$
12. $(4.3 \times 10^3)(2 \times 10^8)$
13. $(9 \times 10^3)(7 \times 10^8)$

▶ PRACTICE AND PROBLEM SOLVING

Write each number in scientific notation.

14. 55,000
15. 0.000006
16. 0.00209
17. 52.8×10^9

18. Pluto is 5 billion km from the sun.
19. A nanometer is 0.000000001 meter.

20. A house spider weighs about 0.0001 kg.
21. The length of a grain of salt is about 0.004 in.

Write each number in standard notation.

22. 9×10^2
23. 8.43×10^6
24. 2×10^{-4}
25. 6.02×10^{-7}

26. One light year is 5.88×10^{12} mi.
27. Fingernails grow 7.14×10^{-3} cm per day.

28. The most venomous scorpion delivers 9×10^{-6} oz of venom per bite.

Order from least to greatest.

29. $10^9, 10^{-8}, 10^5, 10^{-6}, 10^0$
30. $65 \times 10^4, 432 \times 10^3, 2.996 \times 10^4$

31. $55.8 \times 10^{-5}, 782 \times 10^{-8}, 9.1 \times 10^{-5}, 1,009 \times 10^2, 0.8 \times 10^{-4}$

32. $0.16 \times 10^7, 1,600 \times 10^6, 1.6 \times 10^5, 160 \times 10^8, 0.0016 \times 10^6$

Multiply. Express each result in scientific notation.

33. $(3 \times 10^2)(2 \times 10^2)$
34. $(6 \times 10^3)(4 \times 10^1)$
35. $(8 \times 10^{-3})(2.5 \times 10^{-2})$

36. Gold leaf is pure gold hammered to a thickness of 0.0000035 in. Write this number in scientific notation.

Solve. Write each result in scientific notation.

37. *Zoology* An ant weighs about 2×10^{-5} lb. There are about 10^{15} ants on Earth. How many pounds of ants are on Earth?

38. *Statistics* The population density of India is about 8.33×10^2 people per square mile. The area of India is 1.2×10^6 mi^2. What is the approximate population of India?

39. *Health Care* In the year 2005, the population of the United States will be about 296 million. Health expenditures will be about $7,350 per person. In total, about how much will the United States spend on health care in 2005?

The dome of the Georgia State Capitol building has had two applications of gold leaf for a total of 103 oz. of 23-karat gold.

Math in the Media Use the article for Exercises 40–41.

40. Express the moon's distance from Earth in scientific notation.

41. a. Express the distance from Earth to the moon in meters, using scientific notation.
 b. How many 0.5-meter footsteps are there from here to the moon? Express in scientific notation.

42. *Open-ended* Describe a situation where you would use standard notation for a large number instead of scientific notation. Explain the reason for your choice.

43. *Writing* Explain how to write each number in scientific notation.
 a. 0.00043
 b. 523.4×10^5

One Giant Leap

On July 20, 1969, Neil Armstrong and Edwin "Buzz" Aldrin, Jr. were the first people to set foot on the moon. With his first step, Armstrong announced over the radio, "That's one small step for a man, one giant leap for mankind."

The moon is about 380,000 km from Earth. The footsteps the astronauts left on the moon will probably be visible for at least 10 million years.

▶ MIXED REVIEW

Simplify each expression. *(Lesson 4-8)*

44. $\dfrac{10^7}{10^9}$ **45.** $\dfrac{x^3 y}{xy}$ **46.** $\dfrac{15b^2}{10b^5}$ **47.** $\dfrac{9m^7}{3m^5 n}$

Use the formula $d = rt$. Find d, r, or t. *(Lesson 3-4)*

48. $r = 46.2$ m/h, $t = 2.75$ h   **49.** $d = 4.68$ ft, $t = 5.2$ h   **50.** $d = 988$ cm, $r = 6.5$ cm/s

51. A chime clock strikes once at one o'clock, twice at two o'clock, and so on. In a twelve-hour period, what is the total number of chimes the clock strikes?

Scientific Notation with Calculators

When you enter a number with more digits than a calculator can display, the calculator translates the number into scientific notation. E11 in the output below means "$\times 10^{11}$."

112,345,678,999 [ENTER] → *1.12345679E11* **The display shows the number rounded.**

You can use a calculator to calculate with numbers in scientific notation.

■ EXAMPLE 1

Use a calculator to find $(9.8 \times 10^5)(4.56 \times 10^4)$.

```
9.8E5*4.56E4

           4.4688E10
```

Use [2nd] [EE] to multiply by a power of 10.

The product is 4.4688×10^{10}.

■ EXAMPLE 2

Use a calculator to find $3.9 \times 10^{-7} + 4.7 \times 10^{-8}$.

```
3.9E-7+4.7E-8

           4.37E-7
```

Use [(−)] to enter a negative sign.

The sum is 4.37×10^{-7}.

Use a calculator to add, subtract, multiply, or divide.

1. $1.5 \times 10^{11} - 2.4 \times 10^8$ **2.** $6.97 \times 10^5 + 4.8 \times 10^{10}$ **3.** $(1.02 \times 10^9)(1.98 \times 10^7)$

4. $(5.1 \times 10^3) \div (3.64 \times 10^{10})$ **5.** $(2.8 \times 10^{13})(3.335 \times 10^{10})$ **6.** $9.807 \times 10^7 + 7.08 \times 10^{10}$

7. $7.1 \times 10^{-5} - 9.1 \times 10^{-6}$ **8.** $3.5 \times 10^{-6} + 6.76 \times 10^{-4}$ **9.** $(2.43 \times 10^{-3})(4.9 \times 10^{-10})$

10. $(1.08 \times 10^4) \div (7.3 \times 10^{-7})$ **11.** $(5.01 \times 10^{-3})(8.5 \times 10^{-8})$ **12.** $1.99 \times 10^{-5} - 3.81 \times 10^{-4}$

TIME AFTER TIME

Design a Calendar The Project Activity sections on pages 175, 193, and 197 will help you complete your project. Here is a checklist to help you gather the different parts.

✔ investigation of Egyptian calendar

✔ analysis of leap years

✔ your calendar design

Calendars are usually displayed in table form. You could also use a graph, a spreadsheet, a number line, or another format. Prepare a sample of your calendar and a written description of your design for presentation to your class.

Reflect and Revise

Ask a friend to review your calendar and your presentation. Is your calendar workable? Is it attractively presented? Are your explanations clear? If necessary, make changes to improve your calendar and presentation.

Web Extension

Visit Prentice Hall's Web site. You'll find some interesting links and ideas related to calendars. You'll also be able to share information about your project.
www.phschool.com.

Wrap Up

■ Key Terms

base (p. 176)
composite number (p. 180)
divisible (p. 172)
equivalent fractions (p. 186)
exponents (p. 176)

factor (p. 173)
greatest common
    factor (GCF) (p. 181)
power (p. 176)
prime number (p. 180)

prime factorization (p. 181)
rational number (p. 194)
scientific notation (p. 208)
simplest form (p. 186)
standard notation (p. 209)

■ Graphic Organizer

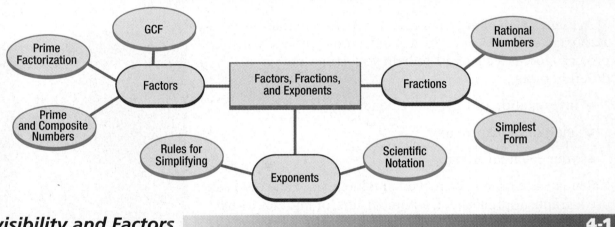

■ Divisibility and Factors

4-1

Summary One integer is **divisible** by another if the remainder is 0 when you divide. Divisibility tests help you find factors. One integer is a **factor** of another integer if it divides that integer with remainder zero.

List the positive factors of each number.

1. 12   **2.** 30   **3.** 42   **4.** 72   **5.** 111   **6.** 252

■ Exponents

4-2

Summary To simplify an expression that has an **exponent,** remember the **base** is the number used as a factor. The exponent shows the number of times the base is used as a factor.

Simplify each expression.

7. 2^3 **8.** $3(10 - 7)^2$ **9.** $28 + (1 + 5)^2 \cdot 4$ **10.** -5^2

Evaluate each expression.

11. x^2, for $x = 11$ **12.** $7m^2 - 5$, for $m = 3$ **13.** $(2a + 1)^2$, for $a = -4$ **14.** b^2, for $b = -4$

■ Prime Factorization and Greatest Common Factor `4-3`

Summary A **prime number** is a positive integer greater than 1 with only two factors, 1 and itself. A positive integer greater than 1 with more than two factors is a **composite number.** The **prime factorization** of a composite number is the product of its prime factors.

The **greatest common factor (GCF)** of two or more expressions is the greatest factor the expressions have in common. You can list factors or use prime factorization to find the GCF of two or more expressions.

Is each number *prime, composite,* or *neither?* For each composite number, write the prime factorization. Use exponents where possible.

15. 13   **16.** 20   **17.** 73   **18.** 110   **19.** 87

Find the GCF.

20. 16, 60   **21.** 36, 81, 27   **22.** 15, 17, 30   **23.** $3x^2y, 9x^2$ **24.** $8a^2b, 14ab^2$

25. ***Writing*** Why is the GCF of two or more positive integers never greater than the least of the numbers?

■ Simplifying Fractions `4-4`

Summary **Equivalent fractions** describe the same part of a whole. A fraction is in **simplest form** when the numerator and the denominator have no factors in common other than 1. You can use the GCF of the numerator and denominator to write a fraction in simplest form.

Write in simplest form.

26. $\frac{3}{15}$ **27.** $\frac{10}{20}$ **28.** $\frac{16}{52}$ **29.** $\frac{28}{40}$ **30.** $\frac{21}{33}$ **31.** $\frac{9}{54}$

32. $\frac{xy}{y}$ **33.** $\frac{25m}{5m}$ **34.** $\frac{2y}{8y}$ **35.** $\frac{2c}{5c}$ **36.** $\frac{9x^2}{27x}$ **37.** $\frac{36bc}{9c}$

■ Account for All Possibilities `4-5`

Summary To account for all possibilities in a word problem, make an organized list or a diagram to keep track of possibilities as you find them.

38. ***School*** Every day in class, Mike, Don, Tameka, and Rosa sit in the four desks in the last row of desks. Each day they sit in a different order. How many days can they do this before they repeat a previous pattern?

■ Rational Numbers

Summary A **rational number** is any number you can write as a quotient $\frac{a}{b}$ of two integers, where b is not zero.

Graph the rational numbers below on the same number line.

39. 2

40. -0.6

41. $-\frac{5}{10}$

42. $\frac{2}{10}$

Evaluate each expression for $a = -5$ and $b = -2$. Write in simplest form.

43. $\frac{b}{a}$

44. $\frac{a+b}{4b}$

45. $\frac{b-a}{a-b}$

46. $\frac{b^2}{a}$

■ Properties of Exponents

Summary To multiply numbers or variables with the same base, add the exponents. To raise a power to a power, multiply the exponents. To divide numbers or variables with the same nonzero base, subtract the exponents.

Simplify each expression.

47. $2^4 \cdot 2^3$

48. $7a^4 \cdot 3a^2$

49. $b \cdot c^2 \cdot b^6 \cdot c^2$

50. $(x^3)^5$

51. $(y^4)^5$

52. $\frac{4^8}{4^2}$

53. $\frac{b^2}{b^4}$

54. $\frac{28xy^7}{32xy^{12}}$

■ Scientific Notation

Summary **Scientific notation** is a way to write numbers as the product of two factors, a power of 10 and a decimal greater than or equal to 1, but less than 10. To multiply numbers in scientific notation, multiply the decimals, multiply the powers of ten, and then put the result in scientific notation.

Write each number in scientific notation.

55. $2{,}000{,}000$

56. $458{,}000{,}000$

57. 0.0000007

58. 0.0000000059

Write each number in standard notation.

59. 8×10^{11}

60. 3.2×10^{-6}

61. 1.119×10^7

62. 5×10^{-12}

Order from least to greatest.

63. $3{,}644 \times 10^9, 12 \times 10^{11}, 4.3 \times 10^{10}$

64. $58 \times 10^{-10}, 8 \times 10^{-10}, 716 \times 10^{-10}$

Multiply. Express each result in scientific notation.

65. $(4 \times 10^9)(6 \times 10^6)$

66. $(5 \times 10^7)(3.6 \times 10^3)$

218 Chapter 4 Wrap Up

4 Assessment

Test whether each number is divisible by 2, 3, 5, 9, or 10.

1. 36   **2.** 100   **3.** 270

4. 84   **5.** 555   **6.** 49

List all the factors of each number.

7. 16   **8.** 30   **9.** 41

10. 23   **11.** 55   **12.** 64

Simplify each expression.

13. 5^3 **14.** $2^0 \cdot 2^3$ **15.** $3^2 + 3^3$

16. $4^2 \cdot 1^3$ **17.** $(-9)^2$ **18.** $(7-6)^4$

19. $-2(3+2)^2$ **20.** $12 - 4^2$

21. *Writing* A number written in scientific notation is doubled. Must the exponent of the power of 10 change? Explain.

Evaluate for $a = -2$ and $b = 3$.

22. $(a \cdot b)^2$ **23.** $a^2 b$ **24.** $b^3 \cdot b^0$

25. $(a+b)^5$ **26.** $b^2 - a$ **27.** $2(a^2 + b^3)$

Is each number *prime* or *composite*? For each composite number, write the prime factorization.

28. 24   **29.** 17   **30.** 42

31. 54   **32.** 72   **33.** 100

Find each GCF.

34. 56, 96   **35.** 36, 60   **36.** 14, 25

37. $15x, 24x^2$ **38.** $14a^2 b^3, 21ab^2$

Simplify.

39. $\frac{4}{16}$ **40.** $\frac{44}{52}$ **41.** $\frac{15}{63}$

42. $\frac{a^3}{a^2}$ **43.** $\frac{5b^4}{b}$ **44.** $\frac{8m^4 n^2}{40mn}$

Graph the numbers on the same number line.

45. $\frac{1}{10}$ **46.** -0.3 **47.** $-\frac{1}{2}$ **48.** 1

49. A car manufacturer offers exterior colors of white, blue, red, black, and silver. The manufacturer offers interior colors of black and silver. How many different styles are there?

Evaluate for $x = 4$ and $y = -3$. Write in simplest form.

50. $\frac{2y}{x^2}$ **51.** $\frac{xy}{5x}$ **52.** $\frac{(x+y)^3}{x}$

53. $\frac{x+3y}{10}$ **54.** $\frac{y^2 - x}{5}$ **55.** $\frac{x-y}{x+y}$

Simplify each expression.

56. $a^4 \cdot a$ **57.** $(y^3)^6$ **58.** $x^3 \cdot x^6 \cdot y^2$

59. $(a^3)^2$ **60.** $6b^7 \cdot 5b^2$ **61.** $\frac{9^8}{9^2}$

62. $\frac{6a^7}{15a^3}$ **63.** $\frac{b^8}{b^{11}}$ **64.** $\frac{2x^2 y^5}{8x^3 y^5}$

Write each number in scientific notation.

65. 43,000,000   **66.** 6,000,000,000

67. 0.0000032   **68.** 0.00000000099

Write each number in standard notation.

69. 5×10^5 **70.** 3.812×10^{-7}

71. 9.3×10^8 **72.** 1.02×10^{-9}

Order from least to greatest.

73. $3 \times 10^{10}, 742 \times 10^7, 0.006 \times 10^{12}$

74. $85 \times 10^{-7}, 2 \times 10^{-5}, 0.9 \times 10^{-8}$

Multiply. Express each result in scientific notation.

75. $(3 \times 10^{10})(7 \times 10^8)$

76. $(8.3 \times 10^6)(3 \times 10^5)$

Choose the best answer.

1. Simplify $2(11 + 7 \cdot 2)$.
   A. 72
   B. 50
   C. 36
   D. 78

2. What is the opposite of -3?
   F. -9
   G. 9
   H. 0.3
   J. 3

3. Simplify $-8 + (-8) - (-8)$.
   A. -16
   B. 8
   C. -8
   D. -24

4. Simplify $(4c - 5c) + (7 - 2)$.
   F. $c + 5$
   G. $-c + 5$
   H. $9c + 5$
   J. $c - 5$

5. Which integer is *not* a solution of $25 + t < 19$?
   A. -6
   B. -43
   C. -7
   D. -8

6. Which sentence is true?
   F. $16 \geq 2 \cdot 9$
   G. $-36 - 10 = 4(5)$
   H. $5[-6 - (-2)] = 2 \cdot (-5)2$
   J. $32 - (-4 \cdot 6) \leq 54$

7. Which number is divisible by both 3 and 9?
   A. 95,500
   B. 36,089
   C. 24,000
   D. 45,288

8. Which expression is equivalent to $-8 \cdot n \cdot n \cdot n \cdot 4 \cdot t$?
   F. $-32n^3 t$
   G. $-8n^3 + 4t$
   H. $-32 \cdot 3n \cdot t$
   J. $-32nt^3$

9. Which expression is the GCF of $24x^3$ and $64x$?
   A. $1{,}536x^4$
   B. $4x^4$
   C. $40x^2$
   D. $8x$

10. Which expression is equal to x^{12}?
    F. $x^6 + x^6$
    G. $(x^4)^8$
    H. $x^2 \cdot x^6$
    J. $x^6 \cdot x^6$

11. Which expression is equivalent to $\frac{x^3 y^7}{x^5 y^2}$?
    A. $x^{-2} y^5$
    B. $x^2 y^5$
    C. $x^{-2} y^{-5}$
    D. $x^2 y^{-5}$

12. Evaluate $\frac{3m - 12}{n}$, for $m = 8$ and $n = 4$.
    F. 0
    G. 3
    H. 4
    J. $\frac{24m - 12}{4}$

13. Which symbol makes $7^2 \cdot 7^5 \ \blacksquare \ (7^5)^2$ true?
    A. $>$
    B. $<$
    C. $=$
    D. $\geq$

14. Simplify $x^5 \cdot y \cdot x^5 \cdot y$.
    F. $(x^{25})(2y)$
    G. $x^5 y^2$
    H. $2x^5 y$
    J. $x^{10} y^2$

15. Simplify $\frac{w^{12} y^{15} z}{w^9 y^7}$.
    A. $w^3 y^8 z$
    B. $w^{21} y^{22} z$
    C. $\frac{w^{21} y^{22} z}{wz}$
    D. $\frac{w^3 y^8 z}{wz}$

16. Simplify 2^{-3}.
    F. -6
    G. $\frac{1}{8}$
    H. -8
    J. 6

For Exercises 17–20, show your work.

17. Write a variable expression for the length of the red segment. Then find the length of the segment for $a = 7$.

    | a | a | a | a |

18. The product of negative 6.2 and a number k is negative seventy and sixty-eight hundredths. Write and solve an equation to find k.

19. List the positive factors of 54.

20. The school store sells erasers for $.05, $.10, and $.15. List all the ways that you could spend exactly $.45 on erasers.

Skills You Need

for Chapter 5

▶ **Reading and writing fractions**   Use before Lesson 5-1.

Write two equivalent fractions to describe each model.

1.

2.

3.

4.

▶ **Writing fractions and decimals**   Use before Lesson 5-2.

Write each fraction in simplest form.

5. $\frac{10}{12}$　　6. $\frac{8}{20}$　　7. $-\frac{32}{16}$　　8. $\frac{25}{200}$　　9. $-\frac{120}{125}$　　10. $\frac{15}{45}$

11. $\frac{-20}{-75}$　　12. $\frac{16}{124}$　　13. $-\frac{18}{81}$　　14. $-\frac{10}{65}$　　15. $\frac{14}{84}$　　16. $\frac{55}{77}$

Divide. Write each quotient as a decimal.

17. $27 \div 5$　　18. $6 \div 10$　　19. $10 \div 16$　　20. $9 \div 12$　　21. $15 \div 40$

▶ **Solving equations**   Use before Lessons 5-2, 5-7 and 5-8.

Solve each equation.

22. $x + 1.8 = 3$　　　　23. $n - 41 = 19$　　　　24. $27.2 = 3.5 + y$

25. $a \div (-3) = 15$　　　26. $-19 = p + 21$　　　27. $6t = 9$

28. $40 = z - 34$　　　　29. $8d = 64$　　　　　30. $-0.89 = \frac{x}{2}$

▶ **Finding the greatest common factor**   Use before Lesson 5-3.

Find the GCF of each group of numbers.

31. $3, 15$　　32. $16, 20$　　33. $12, 36$　　34. $11, 30$　　35. $30, 500$

36. $45, 80$　　37. $27, 72$　　38. $55, 121$　　39. $30, 40, 210$　　40. $14, 28, 84$

Operations with Fractions

What you'll learn in this chapter:

- How to perform operations with fractions

- How to solve equations with fractions

- How to find powers of products and quotients

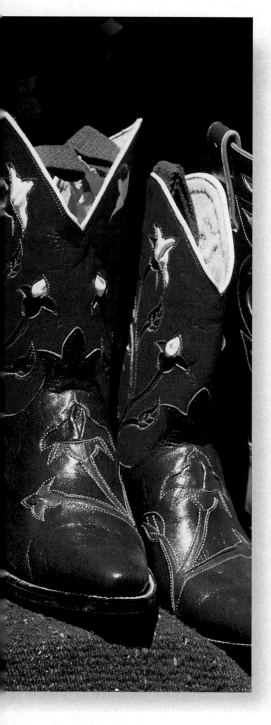

If the Shoe Fits

What size shoe do you wear? As you grow, your shoe size can change rapidly. If your foot grows half an inch, does that mean you should get shoes that are a half-size larger?

The scale we use for sizing shoes is from the *duodecimal*, or base 12, number system. For that reason, a size chart could come in handy.

Make a Comparison Chart For the chapter project, you will make measurements and calculations that relate women's shoe sizes, men's shoe sizes, and shoe lengths. Your final project will be a convenient comparison chart that you can distribute to your friends and family and to shoe stores.

Steps to help you complete the project

Web Extension
www.phschool.com

How to solve problems by working backward

5-1

Comparing and Ordering Fractions

PART 1 Finding the Least Common Multiple

What You'll Learn

1 To find the least common multiple

2 To compare fractions

...And Why

To understand how fractions are used in real-world situations, such as comparing team records

A **multiple** of a number is the product of that number and any nonzero whole number.

Multiples of 4: 4, 8, ⑫, 16, 20, ㉔, 28, 32, ㊱, ...

Multiples of 6: 6, ⑫, 18, ㉔, 30, ㊱, 42, ...

The numbers 12, 24, and 36 are *common multiples* of 4 and 6. The common multiple 12 is their **least common multiple (LCM).**

REAL-WORLD CONNECTION

■ EXAMPLE 1

Today both the school baseball and school soccer teams had games. The baseball team plays every 6 days. The soccer team plays every 5 days. When will both teams have games on the same day again?

6, 12, 18, 24, ㉚, 36, ...   List the multiples of 6.

5, 10, 15, 20, 25, ㉚, ...   List the multiples of 5.

The LCM is 30. In 30 days both teams will have games again.

■ TRY THIS Find the LCM.

1. 3, 4   **2.** 4, 5   **3.** 3, 4, 5

You can also use prime factorization to find the LCM.

■ EXAMPLE 2

Find the LCM of 12 and 40.

$12 = 2^2 \cdot ③$

$40 = ②^3 \cdot ⑤$ Write the prime factorizations.

$\text{LCM} = 2^3 \cdot 3 \cdot 5$ Use the greatest power of each factor.

$= 120$ Multiply.

The LCM of 12 and 40 is 120.

■ TRY THIS Use prime factorization to find the LCM.

4. $6, 16$ **5.** $9, 15$ **6.** $12, 15, 18$

You can find the LCM of a variable expression.

■ EXAMPLE 3

Find the LCM of $6a^2$ and $18a^3$.

$$6a^2 = \circled{2} \cdot 3 \cdot a^2$$
$$18a^3 = 2 \cdot \circled{3^2} \cdot \circled{a^3}$$

Write the prime factorizations.

$$\text{LCM} = 2 \cdot 3^2 \cdot a^3$$ **Use the greatest power of each factor.**
$$= 18a^3$$ **Multiply.**

The LCM of $6a^2$ and $18a^3$ is $18a^3$.

■ TRY THIS Find the LCM.

7. $12x, 15xy$ **8.** $8m^2, 14m^4$ **9.** $25y^2, 15x$

PART 2 Comparing Fractions

You can use a number line to compare fractions.

■ EXAMPLE 4

Graph and compare each pair of fractions.

a. $\dfrac{9}{11}, \dfrac{6}{11}$

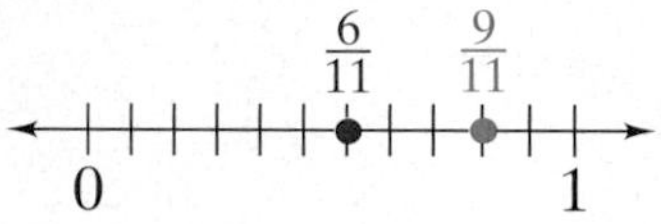

$\dfrac{9}{11}$ is to the right of $\dfrac{6}{11}$, so $\dfrac{9}{11} > \dfrac{6}{11}$.

b. $-\dfrac{1}{2}, -\dfrac{1}{10}$

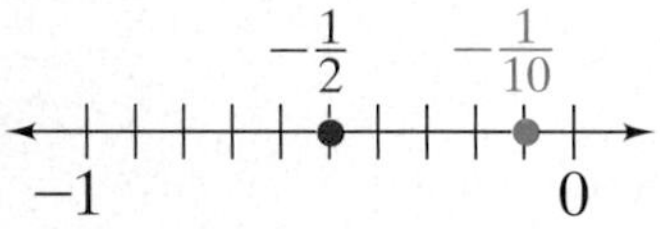

$-\dfrac{1}{2}$ is to the left of $-\dfrac{1}{10}$, so $-\dfrac{1}{2} < -\dfrac{1}{10}$.

■ TRY THIS Use a number line to compare each pair of fractions.

10. $\dfrac{4}{9}, \dfrac{2}{9}$ **11.** $-\dfrac{4}{9}, -\dfrac{2}{9}$ **12.** $-\dfrac{4}{9}, \dfrac{2}{9}$

When fractions have different denominators, rewrite the fractions with a common denominator. Then compare the numerators. The **least common denominator (LCD)** of two or more fractions is the LCM of the denominators.

REAL-WORLD CONNECTION

EXAMPLE 5

The math team won $\frac{5}{8}$ of its competitions and the debate team won $\frac{7}{10}$ of its competitions. Which team won the greater fraction of competitions?

Step 1 Find the LCM of 8 and 10.
$$8 = 2^3 \qquad \text{and} \qquad 10 = 2 \cdot 5$$
$$\text{LCM} = 2^3 \cdot 5 = 40$$

Step 2 Write equivalent fractions with a denominator of 40.
$$\frac{5 \cdot 5}{8 \cdot 5} = \frac{25}{40}$$
$$\frac{7 \cdot 4}{10 \cdot 4} = \frac{28}{40}$$

Step 3 Compare the fractions.
$$\frac{25}{40} < \frac{28}{40}, \text{ so } \frac{5}{8} < \frac{7}{10}.$$

The debate team won the greater fraction of competitions.

High school debate teams can have as few as 8 debates and as many as 20 debates in a school year. If the school in Example 5 had 20 debates, how many did they win?

■ **TRY THIS** Compare each pair of fractions.

13. $\frac{6}{7}, \frac{4}{5}$ **14.** $\frac{2}{3}, \frac{3}{4}$ **15.** $\frac{3}{4}, \frac{7}{10}$

EXAMPLE 6

Order $\frac{1}{2}, \frac{3}{4}$, and $\frac{2}{5}$ from least to greatest.

$$\left.\begin{array}{l} \frac{1}{2} = \frac{1 \cdot 10}{2 \cdot 10} = \frac{10}{20} \\[1em] \frac{3}{4} = \frac{3 \cdot 5}{4 \cdot 5} = \frac{15}{20} \\[1em] \frac{2}{5} = \frac{2 \cdot 4}{5 \cdot 4} = \frac{8}{20} \end{array}\right\}$$

The LCM of 2, 4, and 5 is 20. Use 20 as the common denominator.

$$\frac{8}{20} < \frac{10}{20} < \frac{15}{20}, \text{ so } \frac{2}{5} < \frac{1}{2} < \frac{3}{4}.$$

■ **TRY THIS** Order from least to greatest.

16. $\frac{2}{3}, \frac{1}{6}, \frac{5}{12}$ **17.** $\frac{3}{10}, \frac{1}{5}, \frac{1}{2}, \frac{7}{12}$

Exercises

CHECK UNDERSTANDING

Find the LCM of each pair of numbers.

1. $10, 45$ **2.** $6, 9$ **3.** $12, 20$ **4.** $5, 9$

Compare. Use >, <, or = to complete each statement.

5. $\frac{5}{8} \ \blacksquare \ \frac{3}{4}$ **6.** $\frac{7}{15} \ \blacksquare \ \frac{2}{3}$ **7.** $\frac{1}{2} \ \blacksquare \ \frac{4}{8}$ **8.** $-\frac{5}{18} \ \blacksquare \ -\frac{1}{3}$

Order from least to greatest.

9. $\frac{7}{9}, \frac{3}{9}, \frac{5}{9}$ **10.** $\frac{1}{2}, \frac{1}{3}, \frac{1}{4}$ **11.** $\frac{2}{5}, \frac{2}{3}, \frac{2}{7}$ **12.** $\frac{2}{5}, \frac{3}{7}, \frac{1}{3}, \frac{2}{4}$

13. You need $\frac{5}{8}$ yd of fabric for a craft project. You find a piece marked $\frac{2}{3}$ yd. Is the piece long enough? Explain.

PRACTICE AND PROBLEM SOLVING

Find the LCM of each group of numbers or expressions.

14. $10, 36$ **15.** $20, 36$ **16.** $7, 12$ **17.** $5, 6$

18. $5, 6, 7$ **19.** $45, 120, 150$ **20.** $8, 14, 20$ **21.** $2, 5, 12, 15$

22. $12x, 40$ **23.** $8x, 25y$ **24.** $6a^3, 8a$ **25.** $16a, 18ab, 21a^2$

Mental Math **Compare. Use >, <, or = to complete each statement.**

26. $-\frac{3}{19} \ \blacksquare \ \frac{1}{200}$ **27.** $\frac{(-1) \cdot (-1)}{3} \ \blacksquare \ \frac{1}{3}$ **28.** $\frac{9}{11} \ \blacksquare \ \frac{7}{11}$ **29.** $\frac{-2}{-7} \ \blacksquare \ \frac{4}{14}$

30. $\frac{8}{8} \ \blacksquare \ \frac{3}{3}$ **31.** $\frac{2}{10} \ \blacksquare \ \frac{2}{100}$ **32.** $\frac{2}{5} \ \blacksquare \ 3\frac{2}{5}$ **33.** $\frac{-4}{-17} \ \blacksquare \ -\frac{5}{2}$

Compare. Use >, <, or = to complete each statement.

34. $\frac{7}{14} \ \blacksquare \ \frac{3}{6}$ **35.** $\frac{5}{6} \ \blacksquare \ \frac{3}{4}$ **36.** $\frac{6}{8} \ \blacksquare \ \frac{7}{9}$ **37.** $\frac{1}{6} \ \blacksquare \ \frac{1}{8}$

38. $-\frac{7}{9} \ \blacksquare \ -\frac{2}{3}$ **39.** $-\frac{19}{24} \ \blacksquare \ -\frac{5}{6}$ **40.** $\frac{8}{5} \ \blacksquare \ \frac{3}{2}$ **41.** $-\frac{3}{8} \ \blacksquare \ -\frac{6}{16}$

42. $\frac{1}{3} \ \blacksquare \ \frac{3}{4}$ **43.** $-\frac{1}{5} \ \blacksquare \ -\frac{1}{7}$ **44.** $\frac{2}{3} \ \blacksquare \ \frac{3}{4}$ **45.** $\frac{10}{11} \ \blacksquare \ \frac{4}{5}$

46. $\frac{3}{8} \ \blacksquare \ \frac{15}{24}$ **47.** $\frac{3}{8} \ \blacksquare \ \frac{5}{12}$ **48.** $\frac{1}{2} \ \blacksquare \ \frac{2}{4}$ **49.** $-\frac{7}{12} \ \blacksquare \ -\frac{28}{48}$

50. The manager of Frank's Snack Shop buys hot dogs in packages of 36. He buys hot dog buns in packages of 20. He cannot buy part of a package. What is the least number of packages of each product he can buy to have an equal number of hot dogs and buns?

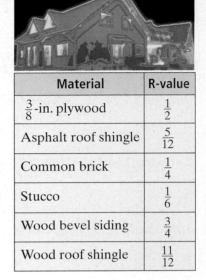

51. *Construction* The *R-value* of a building material measures how well the material keeps heat in or out. The greater the R-value, the better the insulating capability. Use the table at the right. List the materials in order from greatest to least R-value.

52. *Geometry* You have tiles that measure 4 in. by 5 in. What is the smallest square region you can cover without cutting or overlapping the tiles?

53. Suppose you and your brother shared two 12-in. pizzas, a mushroom pizza cut into 8 slices and a cheese pizza cut into 6 slices. If you ate 5 slices of the mushroom pizza, and your brother ate 3 slices of the cheese pizza, who ate more pizza?

Material	R-value
$\frac{3}{8}$-in. plywood	$\frac{1}{2}$
Asphalt roof shingle	$\frac{5}{12}$
Common brick	$\frac{1}{4}$
Stucco	$\frac{1}{6}$
Wood bevel siding	$\frac{3}{4}$
Wood roof shingle	$\frac{11}{12}$

► MIXED REVIEW

Write in scientific notation. *(Lesson 4-9)*

54. 5,000,000   **55.** 0.001394   **56.** 8,900,000   **57.** 0.000005

Find each GCF. *(Lesson 4-3)*

58. 24, 42   **59.** 16, 52   **60.** $25c, 55c^2$ **61.** $90xy, 45x^2$

62. *History* The first modern Olympics took place in 1896 in Athens, Greece. One hundred years later, 197 nations participated in the Olympics in Atlanta, Georgia. This was 184 more nations than at the first Olympics. Solve the equation $x + 184 = 197$ to find the number of nations participating in the first Olympics. *(Lesson 2-5)*

CHAPTER PROJECT 5   ■ **ACTIVITY 1 RESEARCHING**

We still use the *duodecimal*, or base 12, system. For example, 12 in. = 1 ft. Research some other examples of the duodecimal system. Describe how they appear in your everyday life.

Fractions and Decimals

PART 1 Writing Fractions as Decimals

You can write a fraction as a decimal by dividing the numerator by the denominator. When the division ends with a remainder of zero, the quotient is called a **terminating decimal.**

$$\frac{5}{8} \text{ or } 5 \div 8 \longrightarrow
\begin{array}{r}
0.625 \quad \leftarrow \text{quotient} \\
8\overline{)5.000} \\
-4\,8 \\ \hline
20 \\
-16 \\ \hline
40 \\
-40 \\ \hline
0 \quad \leftarrow \text{remainder}
\end{array}$$

The quotient of $5 \div 8$ ends with a remainder of zero. So 0.625 is a terminating decimal.

What You'll Learn

1 To write fractions as decimals

2 To write terminating and repeating decimals as fractions

...And Why

To use fractions and decimals in real-world situations, such as buying food

---

REAL-WORLD CONNECTION

■ EXAMPLE 1

Consumer Issues **A customer at a delicatessen asks for $\frac{3}{4}$ lb of potato salad. The scale reads 0.75. Is the customer getting the amount of potato salad she requested?**

$$\frac{3}{4} = 3 \div 4 = 0.75$$

Since $\frac{3}{4} = 0.75$, the customer is getting the right amount of potato salad.

■ **TRY THIS** Write each fraction or mixed number as a decimal.

1. $\frac{1}{4}$ **2.** $1\frac{7}{8}$

3. $3\frac{3}{10}$ **4.** $\frac{3}{5}$

When the same block of digits in a decimal repeats without end, the decimal is called a **repeating decimal.** The block of digits that repeats can be one digit or more than one digit.

Calculator HINT

Enter 2 ÷ 3 into your calculator. If the last digit in the display is 7, your calculator rounds. If the last digit in the display is 6, your calculator doesn't round.

EXAMPLE 2

Write each fraction as a decimal. State the block of digits that repeats.

a. $\frac{2}{3}$

$2 \div 3 = 0.66666\ldots$ ← Divide. →

$= 0.\overline{6}$ ← Place a bar over the digit or block of digits that repeats. →

$\frac{2}{3} = 0.\overline{6}$; the digit that repeats is 6.

b. $\frac{15}{11}$

$15 \div 11 = 1.36363\ldots$

$= 1.\overline{36}$

$\frac{15}{11} = 1.\overline{36}$; the block of digits that repeats is 36.

■ **TRY THIS** Write each fraction as a decimal. State whether the decimal is *terminating* or *repeating*. If the decimal repeats, state the block of digits that repeats.

5. $\frac{7}{9}$ **6.** $\frac{21}{22}$ **7.** $\frac{11}{8}$ **8.** $\frac{8}{11}$

When you compare and order decimals and fractions, it may be helpful to write the fractions as decimals first.

EXAMPLE 3

Write the numbers from least to greatest.
$$\frac{1}{4}, -0.2, -\frac{3}{5}, 1.1$$

$\left.\begin{array}{l} 1 \div 4 = 0.25 \\ -3 \div 5 = -0.6 \end{array}\right\}$ **Change the fractions to decimals.**

$-0.6 < -0.2 < 0.25 < 1.1$ **Compare the decimals.**

From least to greatest, the numbers are $-\frac{3}{5}, -0.2, \frac{1}{4}$, and 1.1.

■ **TRY THIS** Order from least to greatest.

9. $0.2, \frac{4}{5}, \frac{7}{10}, 0.5$ **10.** $-\frac{1}{8}, -0.75, -\frac{1}{4}, -0.375$

Reading a decimal correctly provides a way to write a fraction.

Decimal	Read	Fraction
0.43	"forty-three hundredths"	$\frac{43}{100}$

If a decimal is greater than 1, you can write it as a mixed number.

■ EXAMPLE 4

Write 1.12 as a mixed number in simplest form.

$1.12 = 1\frac{12}{100}$ Keep the whole number 1. Write twelve hundredths as a fraction.

$= 1\frac{12 \div 4}{100 \div 4}$ Divide the numerator and denominator of the fraction by the GCF, 4.

$1.12 = 1\frac{3}{25}$ Simplify.

■ **TRY THIS** Write each decimal as a mixed number in simplest form.

11. 1.75   **12.** 3.004   **13.** 2.32

You can use algebra to write a repeating decimal as a fraction.

■ EXAMPLE 5

Write $0.\overline{72}$ as a fraction in simplest form.

$n = 0.\overline{72}$ Let the variable n equal the decimal.

$100n = 72.\overline{72}$ Because 2 digits repeat, multiply each side by 10^2, or 100.

$\begin{array}{r} 100n = 72.\overline{72} \\ -n = -0.\overline{72} \\ \hline 99n = 72 \end{array}$ The Subtraction Property of Equality allows you to subtract an equal quantity from each side of an equation. So, subtract to eliminate $0.\overline{72}$.

$\frac{99n}{99} = \frac{72}{99}$ Divide each side by 99.

$n = \frac{72 \div 9}{99 \div 9}$ Divide the numerator and denominator by the GCF, 9.

$= \frac{8}{11}$ Simplify.

As a fraction in simplest form, $0.\overline{72} = \frac{8}{11}$.

■ **TRY THIS** Write each decimal as a fraction in simplest form.

14. $0.\overline{7}$ **15.** $0.\overline{54}$ **16.** $0.\overline{213}$

Quick Review

The properties of equality allow you to perform the same operation on each side of an equation.

Exercises

CHECK UNDERSTANDING

Write each fraction as a decimal.

1. $\frac{7}{25}$
2. $\frac{3}{5}$
3. $-\frac{5}{8}$
4. $-\frac{1}{6}$
5. $\frac{2}{9}$
6. $\frac{16}{24}$

Compare. Use >, <, or = to complete each statement.

7. $\frac{1}{2}$ ■ 1.2
8. $\frac{7}{8}$ ■ 0.875
9. $\frac{3}{5}$ ■ 0.25
10. $\frac{1}{8}$ ■ 0.375

Write each decimal as a fraction or mixed number in simplest form.

11. 0.1
12. 5.36
13. 2.55
14. $0.\overline{5}$
15. $2.\overline{15}$

16. In the school band, $\frac{6}{27}$ of the members play the clarinet. Write $\frac{6}{27}$ as a fraction in simplest form and as a decimal.

PRACTICE AND PROBLEM SOLVING

Write each fraction or mixed number as a decimal.

17. $\frac{9}{20}$
18. $5\frac{3}{8}$
19. $2\frac{5}{16}$
20. $6\frac{1}{4}$
21. $\frac{1}{25}$

22. $3\frac{4}{5}$
23. $-\frac{31}{100}$
24. $\frac{33}{22}$
25. $\frac{1}{3}$
26. $\frac{7}{11}$

27. $\frac{13}{20}$
28. $-\frac{3}{11}$
29. $\frac{4}{9}$
30. $-\frac{11}{12}$
31. $\frac{3}{50}$

Order from least to greatest.

32. $1.2, \frac{3}{5}, -0.5, \frac{9}{10}$
33. $\frac{1}{2}, \frac{3}{2}, \frac{5}{2}, 0.3$
34. $-\frac{1}{4}, -\frac{1}{8}, -0.75, -0.625$

35. $\frac{2}{3}, \frac{2}{5}, \frac{5}{6}, 0.\overline{06}$
36. $-\frac{7}{10}, -\frac{8}{10}, -0.77, -0.\overline{77}$
37. $2.1, \frac{22}{10}, 2.01, \frac{22}{11}$

Write as a fraction or mixed number in simplest form.

38. 0.35
39. 6.8
40. 0.05
41. −3.9
42. 0.27
43. 0.272727

44. $0.\overline{27}$
45. $-0.\overline{3}$
46. $-0.\overline{8}$
47. $1.1\overline{9}$
48. $0.0\overline{6}$
49. $0.1\overline{83}$

50. **Number Sense** The number of digits that repeat in a repeating decimal is called the *period* of the decimal. The period of $0.\overline{3}$ is 1.
   a. Write $\frac{5}{7}, \frac{4}{13}$, and $\frac{7}{15}$ as decimals.
   b. What is the period of each decimal you wrote in part (a)?

51. **Zoology** In 1995, there were about 70,200 cats registered with the Cat Fancier's Association. Of these, about 44,700 were Persians. What part of the registered cats were Persians? Write your answer as a fraction in simplest form and as a decimal rounded to the nearest hundredth.

52. Batting averages are usually expressed as decimals. Sarah got 32 hits in 112 times at bat. Lizzie got 26 hits in 86 times at bat.
   a. Find their batting averages, to the nearest thousandth.
   b. Based on their batting averages, who is more likely to get a hit? Explain.

53. **Number Sense** Copy and complete the tables of some commonly used fractions and decimals. Write the fractions in simplest form.

Test Prep TIP
You can work faster during a test if you memorize the decimals for commonly used fractions.

Fraction	■	■	$\frac{3}{8}$	$\frac{1}{2}$	■	$\frac{3}{4}$	$\frac{7}{8}$
Decimal	0.125	0.25	■	■	0.625	■	■

Fraction	$\frac{1}{5}$	■	■	$\frac{4}{5}$
Decimal	■	0.4	■	0.8

54. **Carpentry** A carpenter has a bolt with diameter $\frac{5}{32}$ in. Will the bolt fit in a hole made by a drill bit with diameter 0.2 in.? Justify your reasoning.

55. **Writing** Is 3.010010001... a repeating decimal? Explain.

56. **Critical Thinking** Seth had just finished a division problem on his calculator when the telephone rang. He got distracted. When he looked back at the calculator, all he could see was the display 0.04040404. What might have been the numbers Seth divided? Explain.

▶ **MIXED REVIEW**

Write each group of fractions from least to greatest. *(Lesson 5-1)*

57. $-\frac{1}{3}, \frac{2}{3}, -\frac{5}{6}, \frac{1}{6}$
58. $\frac{5}{8}, \frac{3}{8}, \frac{1}{5}, \frac{3}{5}, \frac{1}{8}$
59. $-\frac{4}{7}, -\frac{1}{14}, -\frac{3}{14}, -\frac{6}{7}$

Change each number to an improper fraction. *(Previous course)*

60. $3\frac{2}{3}$
61. $1\frac{5}{6}$
62. $10\frac{3}{7}$
63. $7\frac{5}{8}$
64. $4\frac{7}{10}$

65. **Geography** Lake Mead Reservoir, located between Arizona and Nevada, has a capacity of 34,850,000,000 m³. Write this number in scientific notation. *(Lesson 4-9)*

See also Extra Practice section.

MATH TOOLBOX

Estimating with Fractions and Mixed Numbers

You can round to estimate sums and differences involving fractions and mixed numbers. In one method, you round the fraction or fraction part of a mixed number to $0, \frac{1}{2},$ or 1.

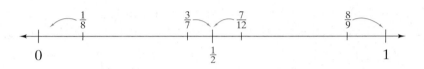

Round to 0 when the numerator is less than half of the denominator.

Round to $\frac{1}{2}$ when the numerator is about half the denominator.

Round to 1 when the numerator and denominator are almost equal.

EXAMPLE 1

a. Estimate $\frac{5}{6} + \frac{5}{12}$.

$$\frac{5}{6} \approx 1$$
$$+ \frac{5}{12} \approx \frac{1}{2}$$
$$\overline{\hspace{1.5cm}}$$
$$1\frac{1}{2}$$

⟵ **Round each fraction.** ⟶

⟵ **Add or subtract.** ⟶

b. Estimate $\frac{9}{20} - \frac{1}{5}$.

$$\frac{9}{20} \approx \frac{1}{2}$$
$$- \frac{1}{5} \approx 0$$
$$\overline{\hspace{1.5cm}}$$
$$\frac{1}{2}$$

You can get reasonable estimates when multiplying by rounding to the nearest whole number. For division, use compatible numbers.

EXAMPLE 2

a. Estimate $16\frac{1}{5} \div 2\frac{3}{4}$.

$16\frac{1}{5} \div 2\frac{3}{4}$ $2\frac{3}{4}$ rounds to 3. A number compatible with 3 and close to $16\frac{1}{5}$ is 15.

$\downarrow$ $\downarrow$

$15 \div 3 = 5$ **Divide.**

b. Estimate $4\frac{1}{8} \cdot 1\frac{9}{10}$.

$4\frac{1}{8} \cdot 1\frac{9}{10}$ If the fractional part is greater than $\frac{1}{2}$, round up.

$\downarrow$ $\downarrow$

$4 \cdot 2 = 8$ **Multiply.**

Estimate the value of each expression.

1. $\frac{2}{3} + \frac{7}{8}$ **2.** $5\frac{1}{12} - 2\frac{7}{9}$ **3.** $\frac{1}{5} + 3\frac{5}{8}$ **4.** $4\frac{11}{24} - \frac{7}{12}$

5. $\frac{11}{12} \cdot 4$ **6.** $6\frac{8}{9} \div 1\frac{1}{5}$ **7.** $10\frac{1}{10} \div 4\frac{7}{8}$ **8.** $2\frac{4}{5} \cdot 5$

Adding and Subtracting Fractions

Investigate

······· **USING MODELS TO ADD FRACTIONS** ·······

Use the models to answer each question below.

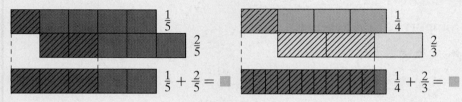

1. a. Refer to the model for $\frac{1}{5} + \frac{2}{5}$. What fraction does $\frac{1}{5} + \frac{2}{5}$ equal?
  b. *Mathematical Reasoning* Write a conjecture about how to find the numerator and denominator of a fraction that is the sum of two fractions with the same denominator.

2. a. Refer to the model for $\frac{1}{4} + \frac{2}{3}$. What fraction does $\frac{1}{4} + \frac{2}{3}$ equal?
  b. Can you add the numerators to find the sum? Explain.
  c. Can you add the denominators to find the sum? Explain.

What You'll Learn

1 To add or subtract fractions

2 To add or subtract mixed numbers

. . . And Why

To apply fraction skills to a variety of situations, such as cooking

---

PART 1 **Adding and Subtracting Fractions**

In the model for $\frac{1}{5} + \frac{2}{5}$ above, you can see that the sum (or difference) of fractions with the same denominator is the sum (or difference) of the numerators. The denominators do not change.

■ EXAMPLE 1

Find each sum or difference.

a. $\frac{1}{8} + \frac{3}{8}$

$$\frac{1}{8} + \frac{3}{8} = \frac{1+3}{8}$$ Add or subtract the numerators.

$$= \frac{4}{8} = \frac{1}{2}$$ Simplify.

b. $\frac{9}{x} - \frac{7}{x}$

$$\frac{9}{x} - \frac{7}{x} = \frac{9-7}{x}$$

$$= \frac{2}{x}$$

■ **TRY THIS** Find each sum or difference.

3. $\frac{3}{7} + \frac{1}{7}$ **4.** $\frac{2}{k} + \frac{3}{k}$ **5.** $\frac{7}{10} - \frac{3}{10}$ **6.** $\frac{11}{y} + \left(-\frac{5}{y}\right)$

Before you can add or subtract fractions with unlike denominators, first write the fractions with a common denominator. The method shown below works with subtraction also.

Arithmetic $\frac{2}{3} + \frac{1}{5}$

$$\frac{2}{3} \cdot \frac{5}{5} + \frac{1}{5} \cdot \frac{3}{3}$$

$$\frac{10}{15} + \frac{3}{15}$$

$$\frac{13}{15}$$

Algebra $\frac{a}{b} + \frac{c}{d}$

$$\frac{a}{b} \cdot \frac{d}{d} + \frac{c}{d} \cdot \frac{b}{b}$$

$$\frac{ad}{bd} + \frac{bc}{bd}$$

$$\frac{ad + bc}{bd}$$

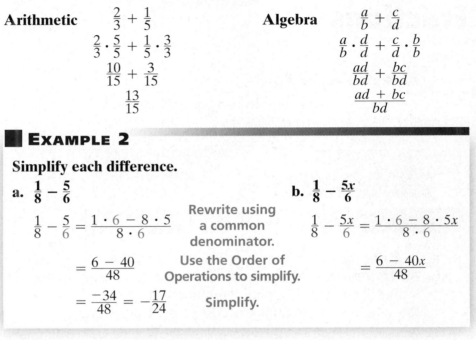

■ **EXAMPLE 2**

Simplify each difference.

a. $\frac{1}{8} - \frac{5}{6}$

$$\frac{1}{8} - \frac{5}{6} = \frac{1 \cdot 6 - 8 \cdot 5}{8 \cdot 6}$$ Rewrite using a common denominator.

$$= \frac{6 - 40}{48}$$ Use the Order of Operations to simplify.

$$= \frac{-34}{48} = -\frac{17}{24}$$ Simplify.

b. $\frac{1}{8} - \frac{5x}{6}$

$$\frac{1}{8} - \frac{5x}{6} = \frac{1 \cdot 6 - 8 \cdot 5x}{8 \cdot 6}$$

$$= \frac{6 - 40x}{48}$$

Quick Review

$$\frac{-17}{24} = -\frac{17}{24}$$

■ **TRY THIS** Write each sum or difference in simplest form.

7. $\frac{2}{3} - \frac{1}{5}$ **8.** $-\frac{7}{8} + \frac{3}{4}$ **9.** $\frac{3}{7} + \frac{2}{m}$

PART 2 **Adding and Subtracting Mixed Numbers**

Before you add or subtract mixed numbers, write the mixed numbers as improper fractions.

REAL-WORLD CONNECTION

■ **EXAMPLE 3**

Suppose you hiked $2\frac{2}{3}$ mi near Mt. Shasta and then another $1\frac{3}{4}$ mi to your campsite. How far did you hike in all?

$$2\frac{2}{3} + 1\frac{3}{4} = \frac{8}{3} + \frac{7}{4}$$ Write mixed numbers as improper fractions.

$$= \frac{8 \cdot 4 + 3 \cdot 7}{3 \cdot 4}$$ Rewrite using a common denominator.

$$= \frac{32 + 21}{12}$$ Use the Order of Operations to simplify.

$$= \frac{53}{12} = 4\frac{5}{12}$$ Write as a mixed number.

You hiked $4\frac{5}{12}$ mi in all.

Mt. Shasta, in northern California, is 14,162 ft high. The Avalanche Gulch route up the mountain is 6 mi long from Bunny Flat to the summit, and the elevation gain is more than 7,000 ft.

■ **TRY THIS** Find each sum.

10. $5\frac{3}{4} + \frac{7}{8}$ **11.** $25\frac{1}{3} + 3\frac{5}{6}$ **12.** $2\frac{3}{8} + \frac{7}{16}$

13. A recipe for punch calls for $1\frac{1}{2}$ qt of orange juice, $1\frac{1}{4}$ qt of ginger ale, and $\frac{3}{4}$ qt of cranberry juice. How many quarts of punch will the recipe make?

Need Help? For help with mixed numbers and improper fractions, see Skills Handbook, page 738.

You can subtract mixed numbers in more than one way.

■ Different Ways to Solve a Problem

You are making banana bread for a bake sale, using the recipe at the right. You have $1\frac{3}{4}$ c of sugar left in a bag of sugar. How much more sugar do you need?

Method 1

You write both mixed numbers as improper fractions.

$$2\frac{1}{2} - 1\frac{3}{4} = \frac{5}{2} - \frac{7}{4}$$
$$= \frac{5 \cdot 4 - 2 \cdot 7}{2 \cdot 4}$$
$$= \frac{20 - 14}{8}$$
$$= \frac{\cancel{6}^{3}}{\cancel{8}_{4}} = \frac{3}{4}$$

You need $\frac{3}{4}$ c more sugar.

Banana Bread

5 ripe bananas	$3\frac{1}{2}$ cups flour
4 eggs	2 tsp baking soda
1 cup shortening	1 tsp salt
$2\frac{1}{2}$ cups sugar	$1\frac{1}{2}$ cups chopped walnuts, optional
3 tsp vanilla	

Method 2

You write $2\frac{1}{2}$ as $2\frac{2}{4}$, and then rewrite it as $1\frac{6}{4}$ before subtracting.

$$2\frac{1}{2} - 1\frac{3}{4} = 2\frac{2}{4} - 1\frac{3}{4}$$
$$= 1\frac{6}{4} - 1\frac{3}{4}$$
$$= \frac{3}{4}$$

You need $\frac{3}{4}$ c more sugar.

Choose a Method

1. For the problem above, which method do you prefer? Explain.

2. Which method would you use to find $2\frac{4}{7} - 1\frac{9}{14}$? Which method would you use to find $-2\frac{1}{2} - 1\frac{3}{4}$? Explain your choices.

Exercises

Find each sum or difference.

1. $\frac{3}{16} + \frac{7}{16}$

2. $\frac{3}{4} - \frac{2}{3}$

3. $\frac{7m}{3} + \frac{5m}{3}$

4. $\frac{5x}{7} - \frac{2x}{7}$

5. $5\frac{3}{4} - 2\frac{1}{8}$

6. $\frac{4}{16} + 1\frac{3}{8}$

7. $10\frac{1}{8} + 3\frac{3}{4}$

8. $1\frac{7}{9} - \frac{17}{18}$

9. **Crafts** A dollmaker cuts a piece of lace $8\frac{5}{8}$ in. long from a piece $10\frac{1}{2}$ in. long. How many inches of lace are left?

► **PRACTICE AND PROBLEM SOLVING**

Find each sum or difference.

10. $\frac{5}{11} + \frac{4}{11}$

11. $\frac{11}{12} - \frac{7}{12}$

12. $\frac{7}{8} + \frac{5}{8}$

13. $\frac{3}{10} - \frac{7}{10}$

14. $\frac{9}{10} + \frac{3}{4}$

15. $\frac{2}{x} + \frac{3}{x}$

16. $-\frac{3}{10} - \frac{5}{100}$

17. $\frac{12}{15} + \frac{1}{2}$

18. $\frac{3}{n} - \frac{3}{10}$

19. $\frac{7}{d} + \frac{2d}{3}$

20. $\frac{12}{20} - \frac{1}{4}$

21. $\frac{5}{8y} - \frac{2}{8y}$

22. $\frac{x}{6} + \frac{2x}{12}$

23. $3\frac{3}{4} + 2\frac{1}{4}$

24. $1\frac{5}{9} - 1\frac{2}{9}$

25. $3\frac{5}{8} + 2\frac{7}{12}$

26. $-6\frac{1}{6} + \left(-2\frac{2}{9}\right)$

27. $1\frac{3}{4} - 2\frac{7}{8}$

28. $1\frac{5}{8} - \frac{3}{5} + 2\frac{1}{4}$

Estimation **Estimate each sum or difference.**

29. $2\frac{1}{3} + 7\frac{1}{8}$

30. $25\frac{5}{18} - 9\frac{11}{17}$

31. $-4\frac{7}{8} + 15\frac{1}{10}$

32. $15\frac{3}{4} + 31\frac{1}{2}$

Mental Math **Find each sum.**

33. $\frac{3}{4} + \frac{3}{8} + \frac{1}{4}$

34. $2\frac{5}{7} + 1\frac{2}{5} + 3\frac{2}{7}$

35. $\frac{2}{7} + \frac{x}{2} + \left(-\frac{2}{7}\right)$

Use prime factors to simplify each expression.

SAMPLE $\frac{1}{14} + \frac{1}{4} = \frac{1}{2 \cdot 7} + \frac{1}{2^2} = \frac{1 \cdot 2}{2 \cdot 7 \cdot 2} + \frac{1 \cdot 7}{2^2 \cdot 7} = \frac{2}{2^2 \cdot 7} + \frac{7}{2^2 \cdot 7} = \frac{2 + 7}{2^2 \cdot 7} = \frac{9}{28}$

36. $\frac{5}{6} + \frac{7}{9}$

37. $\frac{7}{24} - \frac{15}{90}$

38. $\frac{-5}{63} + \frac{-7}{99}$

39. $\frac{2}{28} + \frac{1}{49}$

40. **TEST PREP** Which sum or difference is greater than 0?

A. $-\frac{7}{8} + \frac{3}{4}$ B. $-\frac{7}{8} - \frac{3}{4}$ C. $-\frac{7}{8} + \left(-\frac{3}{4}\right)$ D. $\frac{7}{8} + \left(-\frac{3}{4}\right)$

41. **Error Analysis** Explain how the error in $\frac{3}{8} + \frac{2}{8} = \frac{5}{16}$ was made. Tell how the sum should be found.

42. First-class postage in the United States costs 33¢ for 1 oz. Your letter weighs $\frac{3}{4}$ oz. Do you need extra postage to include a newspaper clipping that weighs $\frac{3}{8}$ oz? Explain.

43. Yesterday a fisherman caught a fish that weighed $6\frac{3}{4}$ lb. Today he caught a fish that weighs $8\frac{1}{4}$ lb. How much heavier is today's fish than yesterday's fish?

44. *Weather* There were three snowstorms last winter. The storms dropped $3\frac{1}{2}$ in., $6\frac{1}{2}$ in., and $10\frac{3}{4}$ in. of snow. What was the combined snowfall of the three storms?

45. *Algebra* Dora and Paul have a collection of x marbles. Dora has $\frac{x}{3}$ of the marbles. What fraction of the marbles does Paul have?

Journal

Describe why estimating a sum or difference before adding or subtracting is useful.

▶ **MIXED REVIEW**

Order from least to greatest. *(Lesson 5-2)*

46. $\frac{5}{8}, \frac{4}{7}, \frac{3}{6}$ **47.** $\frac{2}{3}, 0.6, 0.66$ **48.** $\frac{10}{9}, \frac{9}{10}, -\frac{9}{10}, -\frac{10}{9}$

Simplify each expression. *(Lesson 4-7)*

49. $x \cdot x^2$ **50.** $y^3 \cdot y^5$ **51.** $(x^3)^4$

52. *Data Analysis* Use the data at the right. Find the mean, median, and mode of the annual salaries. Which statistic would you use to encourage someone to take a job at Company A? *(Lesson 3-3)*

10 Salaries at Company A	
$26,000	$62,000
$30,000	$22,000
$22,000	$26,000
$50,000	$21,000
$22,000	$65,000

✓ **CHECKPOINT 1**   **Lessons 5-1 through 5-3**

Find the LCM of each pair of numbers.

1. 30 and 50   **2.** 10 and 100   **3.** 1 and 5   **4.** 15 and 20   **5.** 27 and 32

Compare. Use >, <, or = to complete each statement.

6. $\frac{2}{3} \blacksquare \frac{2}{5}$ **7.** $\frac{1}{4} \blacksquare 0.36$ **8.** $-1.65 \blacksquare -1\frac{5}{8}$ **9.** $-\frac{1}{5} \blacksquare -\frac{1}{8}$ **10.** $2\frac{2}{3} \blacksquare 2\frac{4}{6}$

Write each fraction or mixed number as a decimal and each decimal as a fraction in simplest form.

11. $\frac{51}{100}$ **12.** 0.012 **13.** $1\frac{1}{4}$ **14.** $0.\overline{3}$ **15.** $\frac{5}{6}$ **16.** $0.\overline{51}$

17. **TEST PREP** Which expression is equal to $\frac{1}{3} + \frac{1}{6}$?

A. $\frac{1}{2} + \frac{2}{4}$ B. $\frac{1}{4} + \frac{2}{8}$ C. $\frac{1}{5} + \frac{2}{10}$ D. $\frac{1}{7} + \frac{2}{14}$

5-4

Multiplying and Dividing Fractions

What You'll Learn

1 To multiply fractions

2 To divide fractions

...And Why

To use fractions in finding area

Investigate

·············· **MODELING MULTIPLICATION OF FRACTIONS** ··············

Use paper folding to find $\frac{2}{3}$ of $\frac{1}{4}$, or $\frac{2}{3} \cdot \frac{1}{4}$.

1. Fold a sheet of paper into fourths as shown. Shade $\frac{1}{4}$ of it.

2. Now unfold the paper and fold it into thirds as shown in the second picture. Shade $\frac{2}{3}$ of it.

3. **a.** Count the total number of rectangles.
   b. How many did you shade twice?
   c. What fraction of all the rectangles is this?

4. Use your model to complete:
   $\frac{2}{3} \cdot \frac{1}{4} = \frac{\blacksquare}{\blacksquare}$

5. *Modeling* Use paper folding and shading to find $\frac{3}{4} \cdot \frac{1}{2}$.

PART 1 Multiplying Rational Numbers

To multiply fractions, first multiply their numerators and multiply their denominators. Then write the result in simplest form.

EXAMPLE 1

Find $\frac{3}{7} \cdot \frac{4}{5}$.

$\frac{3}{7} \cdot \frac{4}{5} = \frac{3 \cdot 4}{7 \cdot 5}$ ⟵ Multiply the numerators.
⟵ Multiply the denominators.

$= \frac{12}{35}$ Simplify.

TRY THIS Find each product.

6. $\frac{2}{5}\left(\frac{1}{3}\right)$ 7. $-\frac{5}{6} \cdot \frac{2}{3}$ 8. $\frac{7}{8} \cdot \frac{5}{9}$ 9. $-\frac{1}{4}\left(-\frac{3}{8}\right)$

When a numerator and a denominator have common factors, you can simplify before multiplying.

■ **EXAMPLE 2**

a. Find $\frac{9}{15} \cdot \frac{5}{9}$.

$$\frac{9}{15} \cdot \frac{5}{9} = \frac{\overset{1}{\cancel{9}}}{\underset{3}{\cancel{15}}} \cdot \frac{\overset{1}{\cancel{5}}}{\underset{1}{\cancel{9}}} \qquad \text{Divide the common factors.}$$

$$= \frac{1}{3} \qquad \text{Multiply.}$$

b. Find $\frac{y}{4} \cdot \frac{8}{11}$.

$$\frac{y}{4} \cdot \frac{8}{11} = \frac{y}{\underset{1}{\cancel{4}}} \cdot \frac{\overset{2}{\cancel{8}}}{11} \qquad \text{Divide the common factors.}$$

$$= \frac{2y}{11} \qquad \text{Multiply.}$$

■ **TRY THIS** Find each product.

10. $\frac{2}{3} \cdot \frac{6}{7}$ **11.** $-\frac{5}{14} \cdot \frac{21}{25}$ **12.** $\frac{2x}{9} \cdot \frac{3}{4}$

To multiply mixed numbers, first write them as improper fractions. Then simplify before multiplying, if possible.

REAL-WORLD 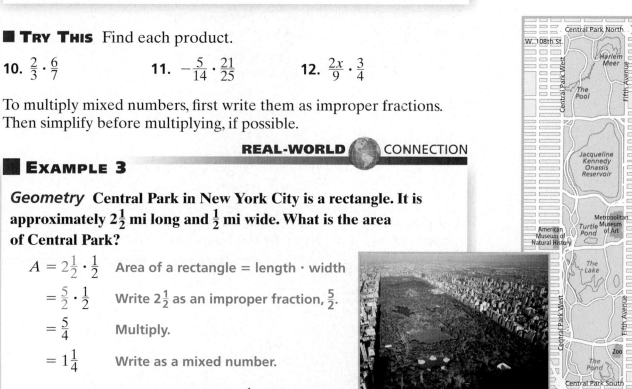 CONNECTION

■ **EXAMPLE 3**

Geometry Central Park in New York City is a rectangle. It is approximately $2\frac{1}{2}$ mi long and $\frac{1}{2}$ mi wide. What is the area of Central Park?

$$A = 2\frac{1}{2} \cdot \frac{1}{2} \qquad \text{Area of a rectangle = length} \cdot \text{width}$$

$$= \frac{5}{2} \cdot \frac{1}{2} \qquad \text{Write } 2\frac{1}{2} \text{ as an improper fraction, } \frac{5}{2}.$$

$$= \frac{5}{4} \qquad \text{Multiply.}$$

$$= 1\frac{1}{4} \qquad \text{Write as a mixed number.}$$

The area of Central Park is about $1\frac{1}{4}$ mi².

Central Park is a rectangle. The angle of the photo makes two sides appear not to be parallel.

■ **TRY THIS** Find each product.

13. $3\frac{3}{4} \cdot \frac{2}{5}$ **14.** $\frac{2}{3} \cdot 1\frac{2}{7}$ **15.** $\left(-2\frac{5}{6}\right) \cdot 1\frac{3}{5}$

Asking "What is $3 \div \frac{1}{2}$?" is the same as asking "How many halves are in three wholes?" Look at the oranges below.

$$3 \div \frac{1}{2} = 3 \cdot 2 = 6$$

↑

divisor

Reading Math

Reciprocals are also called *multiplicative inverses*.

Numbers like $\frac{1}{2}$ and 2 $\left(\text{or } \frac{2}{1}\right)$ are **reciprocals** because their product is 1. To divide fractions, rewrite the division as a related multiplication in which you multiply by the reciprocal of the divisor.

■ EXAMPLE 4

a. Find $\frac{2}{9} \div \frac{2}{5}$.

$$\frac{2}{9} \div \frac{2}{5} = \frac{2}{9} \cdot \frac{5}{2}$$ Multiply by the reciprocal of the divisor.

$$= \frac{2^1}{9} \cdot \frac{5}{\underset{1}{2}}$$ Divide the common factors.

$$= \frac{5}{9}$$ Simplify.

b. Find $\frac{x}{3} \div \frac{x}{4}$.

$$\frac{x}{3} \div \frac{x}{4} = \frac{x}{3} \cdot \frac{4}{x}$$

$$= \frac{x^1}{3} \cdot \frac{4}{\underset{1}{x}}$$

$$= \frac{4}{3} = 1\frac{1}{3}$$

■ TRY THIS Find each quotient.

16. $\frac{5}{8} \div \frac{2}{3}$ **17.** $-\frac{1}{4} \div \frac{1}{2}$ **18.** $\frac{5x}{9} \div \frac{10x}{27}$

To divide mixed numbers, change the mixed numbers to improper fractions before multiplying by the reciprocal of the divisor.

■ EXAMPLE 5

Find $1\frac{3}{4} \div \left(-2\frac{5}{8}\right)$.

$$1\frac{3}{4} \div \left(-2\frac{5}{8}\right) = \frac{7}{4} \div \left(-\frac{21}{8}\right)$$ Change to improper fractions.

$$= \frac{7}{4} \cdot \left(-\frac{8}{21}\right)$$ Multiply by $-\frac{8}{21}$, the reciprocal of $-\frac{21}{8}$.

$$= \frac{^1 7}{_1 4} \cdot -\frac{^2 8}{_3 21} = -\frac{2}{3}$$ Divide the common factors. Simplify.

■ TRY THIS Find each quotient.

19. $1\frac{1}{3} \div \frac{5}{6}$ **20.** $-1\frac{3}{5} \div 1\frac{1}{5}$ **21.** $12\frac{1}{2} \div 1\frac{2}{3}$

Exercises

► ## CHECK UNDERSTANDING

Find each product.

1. $\frac{2}{3} \cdot \frac{1}{5}$

2. $-\frac{1}{2}\left(\frac{3}{8}\right)$

3. $5\frac{7}{8} \cdot \frac{6}{7}$

4. $2\frac{3}{4} \cdot 1\frac{1}{5}$

5. $\left(-\frac{7}{8}\right)\left(-\frac{4}{5}\right)$

6. $3\frac{2}{5} \cdot 1\frac{2}{3}$

7. $\frac{12y}{25} \cdot \frac{5}{6}$

8. $\frac{9}{10} \cdot \frac{15x}{3}$

Find each quotient.

9. $\frac{1}{2} \div \frac{1}{3}$

10. $\frac{5}{8} \div \frac{3}{4}$

11. $-\frac{3}{4} \div \frac{1}{3}$

12. $\frac{11}{12} \div \left(-\frac{7}{8}\right)$

13. $12\frac{2}{3} \div \frac{3}{4}$

14. $1\frac{3}{8} \div 2\frac{1}{16}$

15. $-1\frac{7}{11} \div \frac{9}{11}$

16. $-3\frac{2}{3} \div \left(-2\frac{4}{9}\right)$

17. One granola bar weighs $1\frac{1}{2}$ oz. How much does a box of 6 granola bars weigh?

► ## PRACTICE AND PROBLEM SOLVING

Find each product.

18. $\frac{4}{7} \cdot \frac{3}{5}$

19. $\frac{5}{9}\left(\frac{9}{10}\right)$

20. $1\frac{2}{5} \cdot 2\frac{2}{7}$

21. $\frac{6x}{7} \cdot \frac{1}{3}$

22. $\left(-\frac{2}{3}\right)\left(\frac{11}{13}\right)$

23. $-1\frac{1}{4} \cdot 6\frac{2}{3}$

24. $\frac{8}{9} \cdot \frac{15}{28}$

25. $-\frac{2}{3} \cdot \frac{9}{10}$

26. $\frac{4}{t} \cdot \frac{3t}{8}$

27. $\frac{4a}{9} \cdot \frac{3}{10}$

28. $1\frac{3}{5} \cdot \left(-2\frac{1}{2}\right)$

29. $\left(-\frac{7}{12}\right)\left(-\frac{5}{6}\right)$

Find each quotient.

30. $\frac{3}{4} \div \frac{8}{9}$

31. $\frac{3}{4} \div \frac{1}{2}$

32. $3\frac{1}{2} \div \frac{4}{21}$

33. $\frac{1}{x} \div \frac{3}{x}$

34. $-\frac{1}{2} \div \frac{2}{3}$

35. $\frac{10}{13} \div \frac{15}{26}$

36. $\frac{2t}{5} \div \frac{2}{5}$

37. $-\frac{5}{6} \div \frac{4}{9}$

38. $\frac{4}{9x} \div \frac{2}{3x}$

39. $1\frac{4}{5} \div \left(-1\frac{1}{2}\right)$

40. $6\frac{2}{3} \div \frac{8}{9}$

41. $\frac{2}{5} \div \frac{15}{16}$

Choose Use paper and pencil or mental math to simplify each expression.

42. $\frac{1}{2} \cdot \frac{2}{5}$

43. $\frac{1}{2} \div \frac{2}{5}$

44. $10 \cdot \frac{1}{4}$

45. $10 \div \frac{1}{4}$

46. $\frac{5}{8} \cdot \frac{3}{5}$

47. $\frac{5}{8} \div \frac{3}{5}$

48. $\frac{2}{7} \cdot \frac{12}{49}$

49. $\frac{2}{7} \div \frac{12}{49}$

50. Suppose you charge \$4.50/h for baby-sitting. How much will you earn baby-sitting for $3\frac{1}{2}$ hours?

51. *Construction* A cable television crew has to install cable along a road $1\frac{1}{2}$ mi long. The crew takes a day to install each $\frac{1}{4}$ mi of cable. How many days will the installation take?

52. A cheetah can run as fast as 64 mi/h. At that speed, how far could a cheetah run in $\frac{1}{16}$ h? $\frac{1}{30}$ h?

53. You are hiking along a trail that is $13\frac{1}{2}$ mi long. You plan to rest every $2\frac{1}{4}$ mi. How many rest stops will you make?

54. a. *Patterns* Find each quotient: $\frac{1}{2} \div 2, \frac{1}{2} \div 3, \frac{1}{2} \div 4,$ and $\frac{1}{2} \div 5.$
b. *Writing* Explain what happens to the quotients as the divisor increases in value.

55. *Critical Thinking* Write a multiplication equation and a division equation that you could use to show the result of cutting four melons into eight equal slices each.

56. *Open-ended* Find two fractions greater than $\frac{1}{2}$ with a product less than $\frac{1}{2}$.

57. **TEST PREP** Which quotient does *not* equal 1?
A. $2\frac{3}{4} \div \frac{11}{4}$ **B.** $\frac{3}{8} \div 0.375$ **C.** $\frac{7}{8} \div \frac{7}{8}$ **D.** $-1\frac{2}{3} \div \left(-\frac{3}{5}\right)$

58. a. Write an expression for the following: The product of $\frac{1}{2}a$ and 3 is decreased by the quotient $a \div (-4)$.
b. Evaluate your expression for $a = 3$.

Quick Review

divisor
↓
6 ÷ 2 = 3
↑ ↑
dividend quotient

▶ **MIXED REVIEW**

Add or subtract. *(Lesson 5-3)*

59. $\frac{4}{5} + \frac{6}{7}$ **60.** $\frac{10}{13} - \frac{25}{26}$ **61.** $-\frac{3}{10} + \frac{3}{5}$ **62.** $\frac{16}{21} - \frac{5}{7}$

Simplify each fraction. *(Lesson 4-4)*

63. $\frac{10}{12}$ **64.** $\frac{24}{40}$ **65.** $\frac{45}{10}$ **66.** $\frac{12}{50}$ **67.** $\frac{34}{51}$ **68.** $\frac{105}{135}$

69. *Choose a Strategy* You spent $\frac{1}{4}$ of your money on lunch. After lunch, you gave half of what you had left to a friend, and then you spent \$3 on a book. You have \$4.50 left. How much money did you have before lunch?

Using Customary Units of Measurement

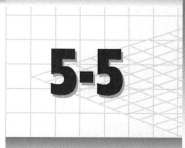

PART 1 Identifying Appropriate Units of Measure

Most people in the United States use the *customary system* of measurement.

Customary Units of Measure

Type	Length	Capacity	Weight
Unit	Inch (in.) Foot (ft) Yard (yd) Mile (mi)	Fluid ounce (fl oz) Cup (c) Pint (pt) Quart (qt) Gallon (gal)	Ounce (oz) Pound (lb) Ton (t)
Equivalents	1 ft = 12 in. 1 yd = 3 ft 1 mi = 5,280 ft	1 c = 8 fl oz 1 pt = 2 c 1 qt = 2 pt 1 gal = 4 qt	1 lb = 16 oz 1 t = 2,000 lb

In order to measure an object, you should choose an appropriate unit of measure.

■ EXAMPLE 1

Choose an appropriate unit of measure. Explain your choice.

a. weight of a truck   Measure its weight in tons because a truck is very heavy.

b. length of a hallway rug   Measure its length in feet or yards because the length is too great to measure in inches.

■ TRY THIS   Choose an appropriate unit of measure. Explain.

1. capacity of a swimming pool

2. weight of a baby

3. length of a pencil

4. capacity of an eyedropper

Test Prep TIP

You can work faster during tests if you memorize common conversions.

You can use *conversion factors* to change from one unit of measure to another. The process of analyzing units to decide which conversion factors to use is called **dimensional analysis.** You use equivalent units to write a conversion factor. For example, since 12 in. = 1 ft, the fraction $\frac{12 \text{ in.}}{1 \text{ ft}} = 1$. You can use $\frac{12 \text{ in.}}{1 \text{ ft}}$ to convert from feet to inches.

▪ EXAMPLE 2

Use dimensional analysis to convert 10 quarts to gallons.

$$10 \text{ qt} = \frac{10 \text{ qt}}{1} \cdot \frac{1 \text{ gal}}{4 \text{ qt}}$$ Use a conversion factor that changes quarts to gallons.

$$= \frac{\overset{5}{\cancel{10}} \text{ qt} \cdot 1 \text{ gal}}{\underset{2}{\cancel{4}} \text{ qt}}$$ Divide the common factors and units.

$$= \frac{5}{2} \text{ gal}$$ Simplify.

$$= 2\frac{1}{2} \text{ gal}$$ Write as a mixed number.

There are $2\frac{1}{2}$ gal in 10 qt.

▪ TRY THIS   Complete each statement.

5. 14 oz = ▪ lb   **6.** 14 in. = ▪ ft   **7.** 14 pt = ▪ qt

Converting units can help you make comparisons.

REAL-WORLD CONNECTION

▪ EXAMPLE 3

Consumer Issues At Store A, a $4\frac{1}{4}$-lb bag of cashews costs $15.99. Store B charges the same price for a 76-oz bag of cashews. Which store gives you more for your money?

$$4\frac{1}{4} \text{ lb} = \frac{17}{4} \text{ lb} \cdot \frac{16 \text{ oz}}{1 \text{ lb}}$$ Use a conversion factor that changes pounds to ounces.

$$= \frac{17}{\underset{1}{\cancel{4}}} \cancel{\text{lb}} \cdot \frac{\overset{4}{\cancel{16}} \text{ oz}}{1 \cancel{\text{lb}}}$$ Divide the common factors and units.

$$= 68 \text{ oz}$$ Multiply.

Since 76 oz > 68 oz, Store B gives you more for your money.

▪ TRY THIS   Complete each statement.

8. $3\frac{1}{2}$ lb = ▪ oz   **9.** $3\frac{1}{2}$ yd = ▪ ft   **10.** $3\frac{1}{2}$ pt = ▪ c

Exercises

Estimation **Match each situation with a possible measure.**

1. height of a 7-year-old
2. weight of a bag of apples
3. width of your palm
4. amount of water in a vase
5. weight of a peach
6. amount of juice in a child's cup

A. 4 fl oz
B. 4 lb
C. 4 ft
D. 4 c
E. 4 oz
F. 4 in.

Mental Math **Complete each equation.**

7. $1{,}000 \text{ lb} = \blacksquare \text{ t}$
8. $\frac{1}{2} \text{ yd} = \blacksquare \text{ ft}$
9. $3 \text{ qt} = \blacksquare \text{ gal}$
10. $16{,}000 \text{ oz} = \blacksquare \text{ lb}$
11. $\frac{1}{2} \text{ mi} = \blacksquare \text{ ft}$
12. $3 \text{ gal} = \blacksquare \text{ qt}$

13. You have a 24-fl oz bottle of water and a 2-pt bottle of water. How much water do you have altogether?

PRACTICE AND PROBLEM SOLVING

Should each item be measured by *length*, *weight*, or *volume*?

14. a hair ribbon
15. a package of meat
16. a bottle of juice
17. a bag of oranges
18. a zipper
19. the contents of an eyedropper

Choose an appropriate unit of measure. Explain your choice.

20. weight of a paper clip
21. volume of a baby bottle
22. distance to Australia
23. length of a sports field
24. volume of a cooking pot
25. weight of a medium-sized fish

Is each measurement reasonable? If not, give a reasonable measurement.

26. A textbook weighs 2 oz.
27. You drink about 10 gal of liquid per day.
28. The street is 25 ft wide.
29. A sewing needle is about 2 ft long.

Number Sense Match each measurement from the first group with an equivalent amount from the second group.

30. 15 mi

31. 15 t

32. 15 in.

33. 15 fl oz

34. 15 c

35. 15 lb

36. 15 pt

A. 30,000 lb

B. $\frac{3}{400}$ t

C. $1\frac{1}{4}$ ft

D. $7\frac{1}{2}$ pt

E. $7\frac{1}{2}$ qt

F. $1\frac{7}{8}$ c

G. 79,200 ft

Choose Use estimation, mental math, or paper and pencil to convert from one unit to the other.

37. 9 lb 2 oz = ■ oz

38. 4 ft = ■ in.

39. 28 in. = ■ ft

40. 5 c = ■ pt

41. 5 t = ■ lb

42. 3 gal = ■ qt

43. 2,640 ft = ■ mi

44. 3,000 lb = ■ t

45. $10\frac{1}{2}$ lb = ■ oz

46. $5\frac{1}{2}$ mi = ■ ft

47. $7\frac{1}{2}$ c = ■ fl oz

48. 3 yd 2 ft = ■ ft

49. $6\frac{1}{4}$ gal = ■ qt

50. $\frac{3}{4}$ lb = ■ oz

51. 13 pt = ■ qt

52. 70 fl oz = ■ c

53. 1 ft 9 in. = ■ in.

54. 18 qt = ■ gal

55. 50 oz = ■ lb

56. $3\frac{1}{2}$ qt = ■ pt

57. 12 pt = ■ c

58. 20 c = ■ qt

59. $1\frac{1}{3}$ yd = ■ in.

60. $\frac{1}{5}$ t = ■ oz

Complete each equation.

61. $2\frac{1}{4}$ yd = $6\frac{3}{4}$ ■

62. 6 qt = $1\frac{1}{2}$ ■

63. 100 lb = $\frac{1}{20}$ ■

64. 6 c = 48 ■

65. **TEST PREP** The great white shark is the world's largest predatory fish. A reasonable measurement for its length would be __?__.
A. 18 in.   **B.** 18 ft   **C.** 18 yd   **D.** 18 mi

66. a. *Geography* The Mississippi River is about 19,747,200 ft long. What is a better unit of measure?
b. Find the length of the Mississippi using the unit of measure you named in part (a).

67. *Error Analysis* Suzanne claims a quarter-pound hamburger is heavier than a 6-oz hamburger. Explain why she is incorrect.

68. *Hiking* You are hiking a 2-mi-long trail. You pass by a sign showing that you have hiked 1,000 ft. How many feet are left?

69. *Reasoning* A student converted 8 cups to pints. His answer was 16 pints. Use dimensional analysis to determine whether the student's answer is reasonable.

70. *History* People once measured length in *handbreadths, spans,* and *rods.*
   a. *Open-ended* Measure the length of an object. Give the length in *handbreadths, spans,* and *rods.*
   b. *Writing* Consider the measurements you made in part (a). Which unit of measure is the most appropriate for the item you chose? Explain.

> **Historical Measures**
> 1 handbreadth = 3 in.
> 1 span = 9 in.
> 1 rod = $16\frac{1}{2}$ ft

▶ MIXED REVIEW

Multiply or divide. *(Lesson 5-4)*

71. $\frac{9}{11} \div 2\frac{7}{11}$ **72.** $1\frac{5}{7} \cdot 1\frac{1}{2}$ **73.** $\frac{9}{10} \div \frac{3}{4}$ **74.** $2\frac{2}{5} \cdot 3\frac{2}{3}$

Simplify each expression. *(Lesson 2-3)*

75. $3x + (-2x) + 3y$ **76.** $10 - 3t - 4t$ **77.** $2y - 5y$

78. *Choose a Strategy* In a single-elimination softball tournament each team plays until it loses. Eight teams are playing in a single-elimination tournament. How many games must be played?

Math at Work
Technical Artist

Technical artists prepare the drawings used by manufacturing and construction workers. The drawings give visual guidelines and technical details of products, buildings, and structures. Technical artists specify dimensions and materials to be used in the building process, and state procedures and processes to be followed. Many technical artists use computer-aided design (CAD) systems to prepare plans. Since they draw technical plans to scale, fractions and operations with fractions are an important part of their work.

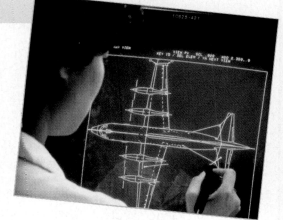

For more information about careers in design, visit the Prentice Hall Website.
www.phschool.com

MATH TOOLBOX

Greatest Possible Error

Extension

After Lesson 5-5

Measurement is not exact. To the
nearest centimeter, each segment
at the right measures 3 cm.

When a measurement is rounded to the nearest centimeter, it can
vary from the actual length by as much as one half centimeter.
The *greatest possible error* of a measurement is half the unit used
for measuring.

■ EXAMPLE

Find the greatest possible error for each measurement.

a. $1\frac{1}{2}$ **in.**   The measurement is to the nearest $\frac{1}{2}$ in.

Since $\frac{1}{2} \cdot \frac{1}{2} = \frac{1}{4}$, the greatest possible error is $\frac{1}{4}$ in.

b. **15.6 L**   The measurement is to the nearest tenth of a liter.
Since $\frac{1}{2} \cdot 0.1 = 0.05$, the greatest possible error is 0.05 L.

c. **3.004 mm**   The measurement is to the nearest 0.001 mm.
Since $\frac{1}{2} \cdot 0.001 = 0.0005$, the greatest possible error is 0.0005 mm.

Find the greatest possible error for each measurement.

1. 45.98 mg   **2.** $12\frac{1}{4}$ in.   **3.** 54.4 cm   **4.** $1\frac{3}{4}$ c

5. 3 ft   **6.** 9 g   **7.** 12.3 L   **8.** 15.575 mm

9. $24\frac{1}{2}$ yd   **10.** 500 m   **11.** $10\frac{1}{8}$ oz   **12.** $3\frac{1}{16}$ in.

13. *Geometry* A rectangle measures 12 cm by 10.5 cm. What is the
greatest possible error for each measurement?

14. *Carpentry* A carpenter is cutting a table leg that is $2\frac{1}{4}$ ft long.
   a. What is the greatest possible error?
   b. *Writing* Is the greatest possible error acceptable in this
   situation? Explain.

Work Backward

Math Strategies in Action In England in the 1800s, many wealthy people had mazes made of hedges constructed in their gardens. Some of the mazes still exist today. The hedges are so high you can't see over them unless you stand on a bench. You have to remember the path you followed to get to the center of the maze and work backward to get out.

Problem Solving Strategies

Account for All
  Possibilities

Draw a Diagram

Look for a Pattern

Make a Model

Make a Table

Simplify a Problem

Simulate a Problem

Solve by Graphing

Try, Test, Revise

Use Multiple Strategies

Work Backward

Write an Equation

Write a Proportion

Working backward from known information will sometimes help you solve a problem.

▌ SAMPLE PROBLEM

You are planning to go to a baseball game that starts at 1:00 P.M. You want to arrive half an hour early. Your walk to the train station is about 10 minutes long. The train ride to the city takes $\frac{3}{4}$ of an hour. After you arrive in the city, you will need to walk for about 10 more minutes to get to the stadium. What time should you plan to leave?

 Read

Think about the information you are given.

1. What do you want to find?

2. What is your arrival time?

3. How much time will you spend walking to the train?

4. How much time will you spend on the train?

5. How much time will you spend walking from the train?

Plan

You know that the series of events must end at 1:00 P.M. Work backward to find when the events must begin.

Solve

Move the hands of a clock to find your departure time.

6. Write the starting time for each event.

You should leave home at 11:25 A.M.

Look Back

Check the departure time. Find the total time needed.

10 min + 45 min + 10 min + 30 min = 95 min

Add 95 minutes to your departure time.

$$\begin{array}{r} 11: \ 25 \\ + \ 0: \ 95 \\ \hline 11:120 \end{array}$$ **120 min = 2 h**

11:120 = 2 hours after 11:00, or 1:00 P.M.

Since the game starts at 1 P.M., your departure time is correct.

Exercises

Work backward to solve each problem.

1. Eduardo wants to finish mowing lawns at 3:00 P.M. on Saturday. It takes $1\frac{1}{2}$ h to mow the first lawn, and twice as long to mow the lawn next door. The lawn across the street takes $1\frac{1}{2}$ h to mow. Eduardo plans to take a $\frac{1}{2}$-h break between the second and third lawns. What time should he plan to start mowing?

2. Siobhan's family is planning a trip to the Grand Canyon. It will take 5 h of driving. In addition, her family is planning to make three $\frac{1}{2}$-h stops. They want to arrive at 3:30 P.M. What time should they plan to leave?

3. Korin is going to a movie. The movie begins at 1:00 P.M. She has a 15-minute walk to the bus from her home and a 5-minute walk from the bus to the movie. The bus ride takes 38 min. What is the latest bus she can take to make the movie?

BUS DEPARTURE TIMES

10:10 A.M.	12:05 P.M.
10:30 A.M.	12:15 P.M.
11:00 A.M.	12:25 P.M.
11:35 A.M.	12:40 P.M.

Solve using any strategy.

4. You have two nickels, three dimes, and a quarter. Using at least one of each coin, how many different amounts of money can you make?

5. *Geometry* Zach's rectangular garden measures 12 ft by 10 ft. He puts a stake in each corner and one every 2 ft along each side. How many stakes are there in all?

6. You spent half of your money at the amusement park and had $15 left. How much money did you have originally?

7. *Patterns* Describe the pattern of the numbers below. Then find the next three numbers in the pattern.

$\frac{2}{3}, 1\frac{5}{12}, 2\frac{1}{6}, 2\frac{11}{12}, \blacksquare, \blacksquare, \blacksquare, \ldots$

8. Several freshmen tried out for the school track team.

After Round 1, $\frac{1}{2}$ of the freshmen were eliminated.

After Round 2, $\frac{1}{3}$ of those remaining were eliminated.

After Round 3, $\frac{1}{4}$ of those remaining were eliminated.

After Round 4, $\frac{1}{5}$ of those remaining were eliminated.

After Round 5, $\frac{1}{6}$ of those remaining were eliminated.

The 10 freshmen who remained made it onto the track team. How many freshmen originally tried out?

9. *Number Sense* Use the equation at the right and the numbers 1, 1, 1, 2, 3, 5, and 6. Make four different true equations.

10. Pump A can fill a tank in 12 min. Pump B can fill the same tank in 20 min.
   a. How many tanks can each pump fill in 60 min?
   b. How many tanks can the two pumps fill in 60 min?
   c. Working together, how long would it take the two pumps to fill one tank?

▶ **MIXED REVIEW**

Simplify each expression. *(Lessons 5-4 and 1-9)*

11. $\frac{1}{3} \div \frac{5}{6}$ **12.** $1\frac{2}{3} \div 1\frac{1}{9}$ **13.** $\frac{2}{5} \cdot (-20)$ **14.** $\frac{4}{9} \cdot \frac{5}{12}$

15. $\frac{3}{4} \div 8$ **16.** $-\frac{1}{6} \cdot (-12)$ **17.** $-8 \cdot 5$ **18.** $2 \cdot 3 \cdot (-4) \cdot 5$

19. $-1(-1)$ **20.** $-56 \div 8$ **21.** $100 \div (-2)$ **22.** $-100 \div (-10)$

23. *Estimation* You want to buy three shirts for $15.95 each. Estimate the total cost of the shirts. *(Lesson 3-2)*

CHAPTER PROJECT 5   **ACTIVITY 2 CREATING**

S hoes come in whole and half sizes. Shoe sizes for men and women are different, however. For shoes of equal length, a woman's shoe is one size larger than a man's shoe. Make a chart that compares men's and women's shoe sizes, including half sizes, from 1 to 15.

Solving Equations by Adding or Subtracting Fractions

PART 1 Using Subtraction to Solve Equations

You solve equations with fractions the same way you solve equations with integers and decimals, by using inverse operations.

REAL-WORLD CONNECTION

■ EXAMPLE 1

Recycling In 1995 the average household in the United States recycled about $\frac{1}{4}$ of its solid waste. The Environmental Protection Agency (EPA) has set a goal of recycling about $\frac{1}{3}$ of solid waste. By how much would the average U.S. household need to increase its recycling to meet the EPA goal?

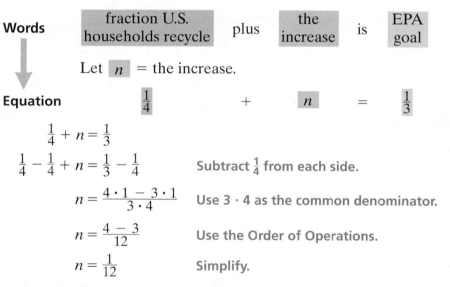

Words

| fraction U.S. households recycle | plus | the increase | is | EPA goal |

Let n = the increase.

Equation $\frac{1}{4}$ $+$ n $=$ $\frac{1}{3}$

$\frac{1}{4} + n = \frac{1}{3}$

$\frac{1}{4} - \frac{1}{4} + n = \frac{1}{3} - \frac{1}{4}$ Subtract $\frac{1}{4}$ from each side.

$n = \frac{4 \cdot 1 - 3 \cdot 1}{3 \cdot 4}$ Use $3 \cdot 4$ as the common denominator.

$n = \frac{4 - 3}{12}$ Use the Order of Operations.

$n = \frac{1}{12}$ Simplify.

To meet the EPA goal, the average U.S. household needs to recycle $\frac{1}{12}$ more of its waste.

Check Is the answer reasonable? The present fraction of solid waste that is recycled plus the increase must equal the goal. Since $\frac{1}{4} + \frac{1}{12} = \frac{3}{12} + \frac{1}{12} = \frac{4}{12} = \frac{1}{3}$, the answer is reasonable.

What You'll Learn

1 To solve equations by subtracting fractions

2 To solve equations by adding fractions

... And Why

To solve equations in real-world situations, such as recycling

In 1996, people in the United States generated 209.7 million tons of solid waste, or 4.3 lb per person per day. The same year, 57.3 million tons of solid waste were recycled, or 1.2 lb per person per day.

SOURCE: Environmental Protection Agency

■ **TRY THIS** Solve and check each equation.

1. $y + \frac{8}{9} = \frac{5}{9}$ **2.** $\frac{2}{3} = u + \frac{3}{5}$ **3.** $c + \frac{3}{10} = \frac{11}{15}$

You can use addition to solve equations involving subtraction.

■ EXAMPLE 2

Solve $n - \frac{3}{4} = -\frac{5}{8}$.

$$n - \frac{3}{4} = -\frac{5}{8}$$

$$n - \frac{3}{4} + \frac{3}{4} = -\frac{5}{8} + \frac{3}{4}$$ Add $\frac{3}{4}$ to each side.

$$n = \frac{-5 \cdot 4 + 8 \cdot 3}{8 \cdot 4}$$ Use 8 · 4 as the common denominator.

$$n = \frac{-20 + 24}{32}$$ Use the Order of Operations.

$$n = \frac{\overset{1}{4}}{\underset{8}{32}}$$ Divide the common factors.

$$n = \frac{1}{8}$$ Simplify.

■ **TRY THIS** Solve and check each equation.

4. $a - \frac{3}{5} = \frac{1}{5}$ **5.** $\frac{6}{7} = x - \frac{2}{7}$

You can use the same methods for equations with mixed numbers.

■ EXAMPLE 3

Solve $p - 1\frac{3}{5} = 2\frac{1}{4}$.

$$p - 1\frac{3}{5} = 2\frac{1}{4}$$

$$p - 1\frac{3}{5} + 1\frac{3}{5} = 2\frac{1}{4} + 1\frac{3}{5}$$ Add $1\frac{3}{5}$ to each side.

$$p = \frac{9}{4} + \frac{8}{5}$$ Write mixed numbers as improper fractions.

$$p = \frac{9 \cdot 5 + 4 \cdot 8}{4 \cdot 5}$$ Use 4 · 5 as the common denominator.

$$p = \frac{45 + 32}{20}$$ Use the Order of Operations.

$$p = \frac{77}{20}$$ Simplify.

$$p = 3\frac{17}{20}$$ Write as a mixed number.

■ **TRY THIS** Solve and check each equation.

6. $c - 2\frac{1}{6} = 5\frac{1}{4}$ **7.** $3\frac{7}{18} = z - 1\frac{1}{3}$

Exercises

CHECK UNDERSTANDING

Solve each equation.

1. $a - \frac{1}{8} = \frac{5}{8}$

2. $t - \frac{2}{3} = \frac{4}{9}$

3. $c - \frac{9}{10} = \frac{1}{3}$

4. $x + 1\frac{1}{4} = 4\frac{3}{4}$

5. $5\frac{1}{4} = w + 2\frac{1}{2}$

6. $y + 4\frac{7}{8} = 2$

7. *Health* At the end of the school year Jamie's height was $62\frac{1}{2}$ in. During the school year she had grown $1\frac{5}{8}$ inches. What was her height at the beginning of the school year?

PRACTICE AND PROBLEM SOLVING

Mental Math **Solve each equation.**

8. $b + \left(-\frac{4}{5}\right) = 6$

9. $z - 7\frac{5}{9} = -7\frac{5}{9}$

10. $g - \frac{9}{10} = -\frac{7}{10}$

11. $c - 2\frac{1}{12} = 3\frac{1}{12}$

12. $10\frac{1}{2} = x + 1\frac{1}{2}$

13. $a + \frac{3}{5} = \frac{4}{5}$

Solve each equation.

14. $m - \frac{3}{4} = \frac{1}{4}$

15. $p - 3\frac{2}{3} = 1\frac{1}{3}$

16. $n - \frac{5}{8} = 6\frac{1}{3}$

17. $a - \frac{5}{8} = \frac{7}{12}$

18. $1\frac{3}{8} = b + 2\frac{1}{6}$

19. $y - 4\frac{7}{8} = \frac{3}{4}$

20. $k + 2\frac{1}{9} = 1\frac{1}{3}$

21. $\frac{5}{16} = c + \frac{3}{16}$

22. $t + \frac{1}{4} = \frac{5}{9}$

23. $f + 4\frac{5}{12} = 5\frac{3}{8}$

24. $g + 8\frac{4}{9} = 3\frac{1}{6}$

25. $n + \frac{5}{8} = -3$

26. $h + 2\frac{1}{2} = 5\frac{7}{10}$

27. $6\frac{1}{4} = a + \frac{5}{8}$

28. $2\frac{1}{16} = d + 5\frac{7}{16}$

Number Sense **Without solving each equation, tell whether *x* is** *positive,* *negative,* **or** *equal to zero.* **Justify your reasoning.**

29. $x + \frac{1}{2} = \left(-3\frac{4}{5}\right)$

30. $x + 2\frac{9}{11} = 2\frac{9}{11}$

31. $x - 5\frac{7}{9} = 6\frac{1}{4}$

32. $x + \frac{9}{10} = \frac{1}{2}$

33. $x + 4\frac{1}{5} = 5\frac{1}{2}$

34. $x + \left(-\frac{3}{4}\right) = -3\frac{3}{4}$

35. **TEST PREP** A tree is $10\frac{1}{2}$ ft tall. Which equation can you use to find the height of the tree before last spring's growth of 8 in.?

A. $t + \frac{8}{12} = 10\frac{1}{2}$ **B.** $t - \frac{8}{12} = 10\frac{1}{2}$ **C.** $t + 10\frac{1}{2} = \frac{8}{12}$ **D.** $t - 10\frac{1}{2} = \frac{8}{12}$

Write an equation to solve each problem.

36. A restaurant chef needs $8\frac{1}{2}$ lb of salmon. To get a good price, she buys more than she needs. She ends up with $4\frac{7}{8}$ lb too much. How much salmon did she buy?

37. Carpentry A carpenter used $3\frac{3}{16}$ lb of nails for a job. After the job was over, the remaining nails weighed $1\frac{1}{16}$ lb. How many pounds of nails did the carpenter have at the beginning of the job?

38. A cookie recipe calls for $1\frac{1}{4}$ c of oatmeal. You have $\frac{3}{8}$ c of oatmeal. How much more oatmeal do you need?

39. Environment During a recent wet spell, the water level in Jasper's Pond rose $2\frac{3}{4}$ in. The depth of the pond was then 10 ft 3 in. What was the depth of the water in the pond before the wet spell?

40. Writing Write a problem that you could solve with the equation $y + \frac{1}{2} = 7$. Solve the problem.

41. Error Analysis Below is a student's work for solving the equation $x - (-\frac{1}{2}) = 3$. What is the student's error?

$$x - (-\tfrac{1}{2}) = 3$$
$$x - (-\tfrac{1}{2}) + \tfrac{1}{2} = 3 + \tfrac{1}{2}$$
$$x = 3\tfrac{1}{2}$$

In 1998, the average weight of an Alaskan Coho salmon was about $7\frac{9}{10}$ lb.

SOURCE: ADF&G Commercial Fisheries

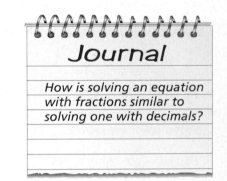

Journal

How is solving an equation with fractions similar to solving one with decimals?

▶ **MIXED REVIEW**

Complete each statement. (*Lesson 5-5*)

42. $2\frac{2}{3}$ ft = 32 ▦

43. $1\frac{1}{2}$ ▦ = 12 fl oz

44. 9 pt = $4\frac{1}{2}$ ▦

45. $\frac{1}{2}$ ▦ = $\frac{1}{4}$ qt

46. 750 lb = $\frac{3}{8}$ ▦

47. $1\frac{2}{3}$ ▦ = 5 ft

Solve each equation. (*Lesson 3-6*)

48. $3.5t = 8.75$

49. $\frac{b}{4} = -38$

50. $y \div 7.5 = -3.75$

51. $1.7x = 8.5$

52. a. Jobs Your job is to paint $\frac{1}{4}$ of the lockers in the school. Your friend agrees to share the job equally with you. What fraction of the lockers will each of you paint?

b. If the job of painting all of the lockers in the school pays $1,100, how much will you earn? (*Lesson 5-4*)

Solving Equations by Multiplying Fractions

PART 1 — Using Multiplication to Solve Equations

You know how to undo multiplication by dividing each side of an equation by the same number. You can also multiply each side of an equation by the same fraction to undo multiplication.

What You'll Learn

1 To solve equations by multiplying fractions

2 To solve equations by multiplying mixed numbers

... And Why

To solve equations with fractions in real-world situations, such as carpentry

■ EXAMPLE 1

Solve $5a = \frac{1}{7}$.

$$5a = \frac{1}{7}$$

$$\frac{1}{5} \cdot (5a) = \frac{1}{5} \cdot \frac{1}{7} \qquad \text{Multiply each side by } \tfrac{1}{5}, \text{ the reciprocal of 5.}$$

$$a = \frac{1}{35} \qquad \text{Simplify.}$$

■ **TRY THIS** Solve each equation.

1. $8x = \frac{5}{7}$ **2.** $2y = \frac{7}{9}$ **3.** $3a = \frac{4}{5}$

When fractions have common factors, you can simplify before multiplying.

■ EXAMPLE 2

Solve $\frac{4}{5}m = \frac{9}{10}$.

$$\frac{4}{5}m = \frac{9}{10}$$

$$\frac{5}{4} \cdot \frac{4}{5}m = \frac{5}{4} \cdot \frac{9}{10} \qquad \text{Multiply each side by } \tfrac{5}{4}, \text{ the reciprocal of } \tfrac{4}{5}.$$

$$m = \frac{\overset{1}{5}}{4} \cdot \frac{9}{\underset{2}{10}} \qquad \text{Divide common factors.}$$

$$m = \frac{9}{8} \qquad \text{Simplify.}$$

$$m = 1\frac{1}{8} \qquad \text{Write as a mixed number.}$$

■ **TRY THIS** Solve each equation.

4. $\frac{2}{9}t = \frac{5}{6}$ **5.** $\frac{3}{4}s = \frac{8}{9}$ **6.** $\frac{5}{4}d = \frac{5}{4}$

Remember, the reciprocal of a negative fraction is also negative.

EXAMPLE 3

Solve $-\frac{14}{25}k = \frac{8}{15}$.

$$-\frac{14}{25}k = \frac{8}{15}$$

$$-\frac{25}{14}\left(-\frac{14}{25}k\right) = -\frac{25}{14}\left(\frac{8}{15}\right)$$ 　Multiply each side by $-\frac{25}{14}$, the reciprocal of $-\frac{14}{25}$.

$$k = -\frac{\overset{5}{25} \cdot \overset{4}{8}}{\underset{7}{14} \cdot \underset{3}{15}} = -\frac{20}{21}$$ 　Divide common factors and simplify.

TRY THIS Solve each equation.

7. $-\frac{6}{7}r = \frac{3}{4}$ 　　　　**8.** $-\frac{10}{13}b = -\frac{2}{3}$ 　　　　**9.** $-6n = \frac{3}{7}$

PART 2 Solving Equations with Mixed Numbers

To solve equations involving mixed numbers, change them to improper fractions before multiplying.

REAL-WORLD CONNECTION

EXAMPLE 4

Carpentry Your teacher needs a shelf to hold a set of textbooks each $1\frac{5}{8}$ in. wide. How many books fit on a 26-in.-long shelf?

Words	width of each book	times	the number of books	is	width of bookshelf

Let n = the number of books.

Equation	$1\frac{5}{8}$	$\cdot$	n	$=$	26

$$1\frac{5}{8} \cdot n = 26$$

$$\frac{13}{8}n = 26$$ 　Write $1\frac{5}{8}$ as $\frac{13}{8}$.

$$\frac{8}{13} \cdot \frac{13}{8}n = \frac{8}{13} \cdot 26$$ 　Multiply each side by $\frac{8}{13}$, the reciprocal of $\frac{13}{8}$.

$$n = \frac{8 \cdot \overset{2}{26}}{\underset{1}{13} \cdot 1} = 16$$ 　Divide common factors and simplify.

Your teacher can fit 16 books on the shelf.

TRY THIS Solve each equation.

10. $3\frac{1}{2}n = 28$ 　　　　**11.** $1\frac{1}{6}r = -\frac{7}{20}$ 　　　　**12.** $-2\frac{3}{4}h = -12\frac{1}{2}$

Exercises

CHECK UNDERSTANDING

Solve each equation.

1. $\frac{5}{8} = 6p$

2. $\frac{1}{5}x = \frac{2}{3}$

3. $\frac{2}{3}k = \frac{5}{6}$

4. $\frac{7}{8}z = 3\frac{1}{2}$

5. $\frac{8}{9} = -6d$

6. $2\frac{1}{3}m = \frac{7}{12}$

7. $\frac{1}{15} = -1\frac{1}{10}t$

8. $-1\frac{6}{78}g = -\frac{13}{15}$

9. Construction A sheet of plywood is $\frac{3}{4}$ in. thick. Write and solve an equation to find how many sheets of plywood are in a stack 9 in. high.

PRACTICE AND PROBLEM SOLVING

Mental Math **Solve each equation.**

10. $8d = 16$

11. $\frac{1}{3}y = 2$

12. $\frac{5}{8} = \frac{5}{8}k$

13. $\frac{3}{7}x = 1$

14. $-\frac{2}{3}t = -2$

15. $-5s = \frac{5}{7}$

16. $3 = 1\frac{1}{2}b$

17. $2\frac{1}{2}x = \frac{2}{5}$

Solve each equation.

18. $7c = \frac{3}{4}$

19. $9y = \frac{5}{7}$

20. $\frac{5}{9} = \frac{1}{8}h$

21. $\frac{1}{7}x = \frac{4}{7}$

22. $\frac{3}{4}d = \frac{3}{8}$

23. $\frac{10}{27} = \frac{5}{9}t$

24. $\frac{2}{7}a = \frac{5}{8}$

25. $-\frac{1}{9}p = \frac{5}{6}$

26. $-\frac{5}{7}x = \frac{9}{10}$

27. $\frac{9}{13} = -\frac{6}{11}s$

28. $\frac{2}{3}x = -8$

29. $-3b = \frac{2}{3}$

30. $-\frac{12}{13} = -\frac{1}{4}w$

31. $2\frac{1}{8}k = 7$

32. $3\frac{1}{9}a = \frac{3}{7}$

33. $1\frac{1}{2}n = 3\frac{4}{9}$

34. $2\frac{3}{4} = -6\frac{3}{5}y$

35. $1\frac{1}{2}m = 1\frac{3}{4}$

36. $-9\frac{1}{3} = -1\frac{1}{4}t$

37. $3\frac{3}{5}p = -4\frac{4}{9}$

Number Sense **Without solving each equation, tell whether x is** ***positive, negative,*** **or** ***equal to zero.*** **Justify your reasoning.**

38. $17x = -\frac{11}{30}$

39. $\frac{1}{57}x = 2$

40. $\frac{4}{13}x = 0$

41. $-\frac{3}{4}x = -6$

42. $\frac{5}{8}x = -1\frac{1}{2}$

43. $\frac{-5}{-7}x = -\frac{3}{5}$

44. $3\frac{1}{2}x = -7$

45. $-6\frac{1}{2}x = 0$

46. Critical Thinking By what would you multiply each side of the equation $ax = 27$ to solve for x? By what would you multiply each side of the equation $\frac{1}{a}x = 27$ to solve for x?

Use the article below for Exercises 47 and 48.

Paper Recycling on the Rise

During the 1990s, recycling in the United States steadily increased. In 1996, people in the United States recycled about nine twentieths of their paper waste. This amounted to 42.3 million tons of paper, or about 295 lb/person. Only one year earlier, Americans recycled just over two fifths of their paper waste, a total of about 32.7 million tons of paper.

47. Solve the equation $\frac{2}{5}p = 32.7$ to find the amount of paper waste produced in the United States in 1995.

48. Write and solve an equation to find the amount of paper waste produced in the United States in 1996.

Write an equation to solve each probem.

49. *Biology* In ideal conditions, the kudzu plant can grow at least $1\frac{3}{20}$ ft per week. At this rate, how many weeks would it take a kudzu plant to grow 23 ft?

50. *Weather* Based on annual rainfall, about $\frac{18}{25}$ in. of rain falls each day in Buenaventura, Colombia. At this rate, in how many days does 8 in. of rain fall?

51. A sailfish can swim about $11\frac{1}{3}$ mi in 10 min. About how many miles can a sailfish swim per minute? At that speed, about how many miles can a sailfish swim per hour?

52. *Astronomy* The Chandra satellite telescope views X-rays in space. It orbits as much as 87,000 miles above Earth. This is about $\frac{1}{3}$ of the distance to the moon. About how far away is the moon?

53. A small airplane coming in for a landing descends $\frac{5}{66}$ mi/min. About how long does it take to descend 4,000 ft? (*Hint:* 1 mi = 5,280 ft)

A native of China and Japan, kudzu was brought to the United States in 1876. Left alone, it grows over trees, telephone poles, and abandoned houses and cars.

54. *Error Analysis* A student solved the equation $-\frac{7}{10}h = 5\frac{3}{5}$ and found the solution 8. What was the student's error?

55. **TEST PREP** Which equation has a solution greater than 1?
   A. $-5x = \frac{5}{8}$ **B.** $-\frac{5}{8}x = 5$ **C.** $\frac{5}{8}x = 5$ **D.** $5x = \frac{5}{8}$

56. *Writing* Describe how you would solve the equation $\frac{2}{3}x = 3x$.

Solve each equation or inequality. *(Lessons 5-7 and 2-9)*

57. $j + \frac{3}{4} = \frac{7}{8}$ **58.** $\frac{4}{5} < y - \frac{3}{5}$ **59.** $6\frac{1}{2} = m + 2\frac{7}{8}$ **60.** $t - 1\frac{1}{2} \geq -\frac{5}{6}$

Simplify each expression. *(Lessons 4-7 and 4-8)*

61. $3r \cdot r^4$ **62.** $\frac{6x^3}{2x}$ **63.** $10s^2 \cdot 10s^3$ **64.** $\frac{20a^5}{4a^2}$ **65.** $x^3 \cdot x^{10}$

66. One bag of popcorn holds $1\frac{5}{8}$ oz. Another holds $1\frac{3}{4}$ oz. Which bag holds more popcorn, and how much more? *(Lesson 5-3)*

◢ CHECKPOINT 2   Lessons 5-4 through 5-8

Multiply or divide.

1. $\frac{2}{3}(21)$ **2.** $\frac{4}{5} \cdot \frac{5}{8}$ **3.** $-\frac{4}{9}\left(\frac{1}{3}\right)$ **4.** $\frac{2}{5} \div \frac{3}{10}$ **5.** $-\frac{3}{4} \div \frac{3}{8}$ **6.** $8\frac{1}{2} \div \frac{1}{4}$

Complete each statement.

7. ■ t = 4,500 lb   **8.** $2\frac{1}{2}$ yd = ■ in.   **9.** 24 oz = ■ lb   **10.** ■ mi = 1,760 ft

Solve each equation.

11. $y + \frac{2}{5} = \frac{3}{5}$ **12.** $t - \frac{3}{4} = \frac{7}{8}$ **13.** $x - 4\frac{1}{2} = 6\frac{3}{4}$ **14.** $5\frac{1}{3} + v = -12$

15. $\frac{5}{7}y = \frac{1}{3}$ **16.** $4t = \frac{24}{35}$ **17.** $-\frac{8}{9}g = \frac{3}{5}$ **18.** $\frac{9}{10} = \frac{1}{4}w$

19. *Choose a Strategy* You spend $\frac{1}{3}$ of your money on lunch. Your friend then pays back a loan of $2.50. Later, you spend $4 on a movie ticket and $1.25 for a snack. You have $5.25 left. How much money did you have before lunch?

20. *Open-ended* Describe an object you might measure using the customary system of measurement. Choose a unit of measure and estimate the measurement of the object using that unit.

CHAPTER PROJECT 5 ◢ **ACTIVITY 3 INVESTIGATING**

Measure the length of your shoe to the nearest $\frac{1}{4}$ in. Calculate the size of your shoe, using L as the length of your shoe. Compare your calculation to the size on the label of your shoe.

Finding Shoe Sizes
Women's shoe sizes
$3L - 23\frac{3}{4}$
Men's shoe sizes
$3L - 24\frac{3}{4}$

Standardized Test Prep

Multiple Choice

Choose the best answer.

1. Use the line graph below. Which statement is true?

Tires Bought

SOURCE: *Statistical Abstract of the United States*

   A. The greatest increase was between 1993 and 1994.
   B. The least decrease was between 1993 and 1994.
   C. The most car tires were bought in 1992.
   D. There were fewer tires bought in 1994 than in 1990.

2. Which equation would you use to solve the following problem?

   A walkathon route is 20 mi long. There is a water station every $1\frac{1}{4}$ mi. How many water stations w are along the route?

   F. $20w = 1\frac{1}{4}$

   G. $w - 1\frac{1}{4} = 20$

   H. $1\frac{1}{4} + w = 20$

   J. $1\frac{1}{4}w = 20$

3. The price of one share of a stock is $16\frac{3}{8}$. What is the price in decimal form?
   A. 16.38   B. 16.83
   C. 16.375   D. 16.335

4. A recipe for soup includes 1 pt of tomato juice. Suppose Martin plans to double the recipe. How many cups of tomato juice does he need?
   F. 1 c   G. 2 c   H. 4 c   J. 8 c

5. Michael drove at 30 mi/h for $\frac{1}{2}$ h, and 50 mi/h for 1 h. Find his mean speed to the nearest mile per hour.
   A. 40 mi/h   B. 43 mi/h
   C. 45 mi/h   D. 47 mi/h

6. Suppose you are building a tree house. You have a board that is 6 ft $5\frac{3}{4}$ in. long, but you need one 5 ft $6\frac{1}{2}$ in. long. How much should you cut off?
   F. $11\frac{1}{4}$ in.   G. $11\frac{3}{4}$ in.
   H. $12\frac{3}{4}$ in.   J. $13\frac{1}{4}$ in.

Free Response

For Exercises 7–9, show your work.

7. Shana had $40 before she went shopping. She bought three books for $7.24 each including tax, and a pair of earrings for $8.99, including tax. How much money did she have left at the end of her shopping trip?

8. What is the area of the shaded region in the figure below?

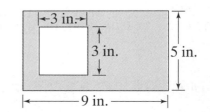

9. **Open-ended** Find two fractions for which the product is greater than 1 and the quotient is less than 1.

Powers of Products and Quotients

PART 1 Finding Powers of Products

What You'll Learn

1 To find powers of products

2 To find powers of quotients

...And Why

To extend your knowledge of the properties of exponents

You can use the Commutative and Associative Properties of Multiplication to find a pattern in products raised to a power.

$$(4 \cdot 2)^3 = (4 \cdot 2) \cdot (4 \cdot 2) \cdot (4 \cdot 2)$$ Write the factors.

$$= 4 \cdot 4 \cdot 4 \cdot 2 \cdot 2 \cdot 2$$ Use the Commutative Property to arrange the factors.

$$= (4 \cdot 4 \cdot 4) \cdot (2 \cdot 2 \cdot 2)$$ Use the Associative Property to group the factors.

$$= 4^3 \cdot 2^3$$ Write the powers.

This result suggests a rule for simplifying products raised to a power.

Rule for Raising a Product to a Power
To raise a product to a power, raise each factor to the power.

    Arithmetic   **Algebra**

$$(5 \cdot 3)^4 = 5^4 \cdot 3^4 \qquad (ab)^m = a^m b^m,$$
$$\text{for any positive integer } m$$

Remember, to simplify an expression, you write it with no like terms or parentheses.

■ EXAMPLE 1

Simplify $(4x^2)^3$.

$$(4x^2)^3 = 4^3 \cdot (x^2)^3$$ Raise each factor to the power 3.

$$= 4^3 \cdot x^{2 \cdot 3}$$ Use the Rule for Raising a Power to a Power.

$$= 4^3 \cdot x^6$$ Multiply exponents.

$$= 64x^6$$ Simplify.

Quick Review

exponent ⌐

$$2^3 = 2 \cdot 2 \cdot 2$$

⌐base

Quick Review

$(a^m)^n = a^{m \cdot n}$

■ TRY THIS Simplify each expression.

1. $(2(3))^3$ **2.** $(2p)^4$ **3.** $(xy^2)^5$ **4.** $(5x^3)^2$

The location of a negative sign affects the value of an expression.

EXAMPLE 2

a. **Simplify $(-5x)^2$.**
$$(-5x)^2 = (-5)^2(x)^2$$
$$= 25x^2$$

b. **Simplify $-(5x)^2$.**
$$-(5x)^2 = (-1)(5x)^2$$
$$= (-1)(5)^2(x)^2$$
$$= -25x^2$$

■ **TRY THIS** Simplify each expression.

5. $(-2y)^4$ 6. $-(2y)^4$ 7. $(-5a^2b)^3$

PART 2 **Finding Powers of Quotients**

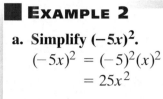
Reading Math

You read $\left(\frac{2}{3}\right)^5$ as "two thirds to the fifth power." You read $\frac{2}{3^5}$ as "two divided by three to the fifth power."

You can use repeated multiplication to write a power of a quotient.
$$\left(\frac{4}{5}\right)^3 = \left(\frac{4}{5}\right)\left(\frac{4}{5}\right)\left(\frac{4}{5}\right) = \frac{4 \cdot 4 \cdot 4}{5 \cdot 5 \cdot 5} = \frac{4^3}{5^3}$$

Raising a Quotient to a Power

To raise a quotient to a power, raise both the numerator and denominator to the power.

Arithmetic
$$\left(\frac{2}{3}\right)^4 = \frac{2^4}{3^4}$$

Algebra
$$\left(\frac{a}{b}\right)^m = \frac{a^m}{b^m},$$

for $b \neq 0$ and any positive integer m

GEOMETRY CONNECTION

EXAMPLE 3

Find the area of the square tile.

$$A = s^2 \qquad s = \text{length of a side}$$
$$= \left(\frac{3}{b}\right)^2$$
$$= \frac{3^2}{b^2} = \frac{9}{b^2}$$

The area of the tile is $\frac{9}{b^2}$ square units.

■ **TRY THIS** Simplify each expression.

8. $\left(\frac{1}{2}\right)^3$ 9. $\left(-\frac{2}{3}\right)^4$ 10. $\left(\frac{2x^2}{3}\right)^3$

Exercises

CHECK UNDERSTANDING

Simplify each expression.

1. $(3 \cdot 5)^2$
2. $(4a^5)^2$
3. $(2c^2)^5$
4. $(-10x^3)^4$
5. $\left(\frac{2}{5}\right)^2$
6. $\left(-\frac{2}{5}\right)^3$
7. $\left(\frac{4}{7y}\right)^2$
8. $\left(\frac{3x^2}{10}\right)^4$

Complete each equation.

9. $(5 \cdot 2)^{\blacksquare} = 25 \cdot 4$
10. $(a^2)^{\blacksquare} = a^2$
11. $(4m)^{\blacksquare} = 256m^4$
12. $\left(-\frac{1}{2}\right)^{\blacksquare} = -\frac{1}{8}$
13. $\left(\frac{b^{\blacksquare}}{5}\right)^2 = \frac{b^{10}}{25}$
14. $\left(\frac{3}{7}\right)^{\blacksquare} = \frac{27}{343}$

15. **Geometry** Find the area of a square with side length $4c$.

PRACTICE AND PROBLEM SOLVING

Simplify each expression.

16. $(3 \cdot 4)^3$
17. $(-2 \cdot 5)^2$
18. $-(xy)^2$
19. $(2x^2)^3$
20. $(-5b)^3$
21. $-(3x)^2$
22. $(a^2b^4)^3$
23. $(5c^3)^2$
24. $(2ab^3)^2$
25. $-(x^2y^2)^2$
26. $(3a^4b)^3$
27. $(m^2 \cdot n)^4$
28. $\left(\frac{4}{9}\right)^2$
29. $\left(-\frac{3}{7}\right)^2$
30. $\left(-\frac{5}{8}\right)^3$
31. $\left(-\frac{2}{x^3}\right)^5$
32. $\left(\frac{2c}{7d}\right)^2$
33. $\left(-\frac{3a}{b^2}\right)^3$
34. $\left(-\frac{2x}{7y}\right)^2$
35. $\left(\frac{2c}{d^2}\right)^4$
36. $\left(-\frac{m}{b^3}\right)^6$
37. $\left(-\frac{xy}{2xy^4}\right)^5$
38. $\left(\frac{x^3}{2y^4}\right)^5$
39. $\left(\frac{1}{3x^2}\right)^4$

Complete each equation.

40. $(4 \cdot (-7))^{\blacksquare} = 64 \cdot (-343)$
41. $(2b^{\blacksquare})^2 = 4b^8$
42. $(gh^2)^{\blacksquare} = g^3h^6$

Evaluate for $a = -1$, $b = 3$, and $c = \frac{1}{2}$.

43. $(2a^5)^3$
44. $(-b^2)^2$
45. $(c^3)^2$
46. $\left(\frac{a}{b}\right)^3$
47. $(2b)^3$
48. $(ac^2)^2$
49. $(4c^2)^2$
50. $(a^2b)^2$

51. **Geometry** A square has sides $3x^2$ units long. Write an expression for the area of the square. Simplify your expression.

52. *Error Analysis* What is the error in the following computation?
$$(3y)^7 = 3y^7$$

53. *Open-ended* Write a^{36} as a power of the form $(a^m)^n$ in two different ways.

54. *Writing* Explain why $\left(-\frac{1}{7}\right)^2 = \left(\frac{1}{7}\right)^2$.

Geometry Use the formula $V = s^3$, where s is the length of a side, to find the volume of each cube.

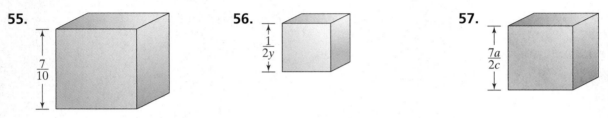

55. $\frac{7}{10}$

56. $\frac{1}{2}y$

57. $\frac{7a}{2c}$

▶ MIXED REVIEW

Solve each equation. *(Lesson 5-8)*

58. $\frac{2}{7}h = \frac{7}{8}$

59. $6\frac{3}{4}c = 1\frac{5}{9}$

60. $\frac{5}{8} = \frac{10}{12}x$

61. $10\frac{3}{4} = -5\frac{1}{2}y$

Use the coordinate plane at the right. Write the coordinates of each point named below. Write the name of each point with the coordinates given below. *(Lesson 1-10)*

62. A

63. $(4, -2)$

64. C

65. $(-4, 0)$

66. F

67. $(0, 4)$

68. Delia bought three plants for $5.99, $12.99 and x dollars. She paid a total of $34.97 for the plants. How much did the third plant cost? *(Lesson 3-5)*

CHAPTER PROJECT 5

ACTIVITY 4 CALCULATING

Extend your shoe-size chart by adding a column for shoe length. Calculate the length in inches of each whole and half size. Use the expression in the table at the right, where s is the shoe size. Put the results in your chart.

Finding Shoe Lengths
Women's shoe lengths: $\frac{s}{3} + 7\frac{11}{12}$
Men's shoe lengths: $\frac{s}{3} + 8\frac{1}{4}$

See also Extra Practice section.

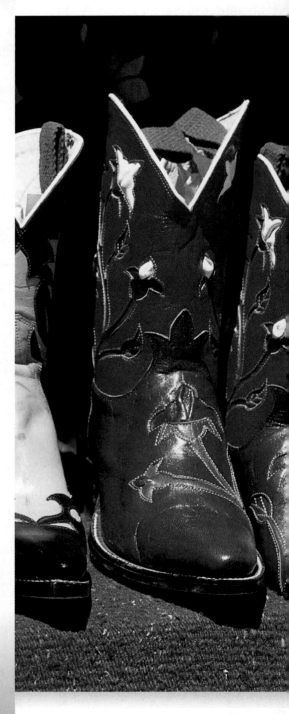

If the Shoe Fits

Make a Comparison Chart The Project Activities on pages 228, 254, 263, and 268 will help you complete your project. Here is a checklist to help you gather the different parts.

- ✔ examples of the duodecimal system in everyday life
- ✔ comparison of calculated size to labeled size
- ✔ calculations of shoe lengths
- ✔ shoe-size comparison chart

Manufacturers often distribute helpful charts to retailers as a form of advertising. Assume that your comparison chart will be distributed to shoe stores. Your chart should be easy to read and simply presented, so that anyone can use it.

Reflect and Revise

Ask a friend to review your chart and your calculations. Is your chart accurate? Is it presented attractively? If necessary, make changes to improve your chart.

Web Extension

Visit Prentice Hall's Web site. You'll find some interesting links and ideas related to sizes. You'll also be able to share information about your project.

www.phschool.com

Wrap Up

■ Key Terms

dimensional analysis (p. 246)
least common denominator
  (LCD) (p. 226)

least common multiple
  (LCM) (p. 224)
multiple (p. 224)

repeating decimal (p. 230)
reciprocals (p. 242)
terminating decimal (p. 229)

■ Graphic Organizer

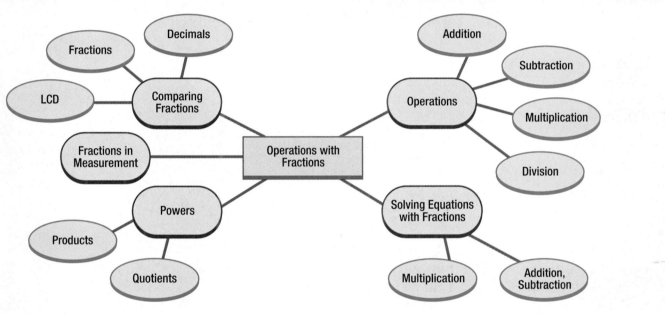

■ Comparing and Ordering Fractions

5-1

Summary A **multiple** of a number is the product of that number and any whole number. A *common multiple* of any group of numbers is a number that is a multiple of all the numbers. The common multiple with the least value is the **least common multiple (LCM)** of the numbers.

To compare fractions, use the LCM as the **least common denominator (LCD)** and write equivalent fractions.

Find the LCM of each group of numbers or expressions.

1. $12, 18$ **2.** $8m^2, 14m$ **3.** $3, 5, 7$ **4.** $6x, 15y$

Compare. Use $>, <,$ or $=$ to complete each statement.

5. $\frac{5}{9} \blacksquare \frac{5}{11}$ **6.** $\frac{2}{3} \blacksquare \frac{3}{4}$ **7.** $-\frac{4}{5} \blacksquare -\frac{7}{8}$ **8.** $\frac{1}{3} \blacksquare \frac{4}{12}$

■ Fractions and Decimals

Summary To write a fraction as a decimal, divide the numerator by the denominator. If the division has a remainder of zero, the decimal is a **terminating decimal.** If the division produces a repeating block of digits, the decimal is a **repeating decimal.** The repeating part of the decimal is written with an overbar.

Reading a decimal correctly provides one way to write it as a fraction. To write a repeating decimal as a fraction, use algebra to eliminate the repeating part.

Write each fraction as a decimal.

9. $\frac{3}{5}$ **10.** $\frac{1}{6}$ **11.** $\frac{5}{8}$ **12.** $\frac{3}{10}$ **13.** $\frac{7}{100}$

Write each decimal as a fraction or mixed number.

14. 0.25 **15.** $0.8\overline{3}$ **16.** 5.6 **17.** $2.\overline{04}$

■ Adding and Subtracting Fractions

Summary To add or subtract fractions and mixed numbers, write them with a common denominator. Then you can add or subtract the numerators. Change a mixed number to an improper fraction before adding or subtracting.

Add or subtract.

18. $2\frac{1}{3} + \frac{3}{4}$ **19.** $16\frac{4}{5} - 9\frac{2}{3}$ **20.** $\frac{6}{x} + \frac{3}{5}$ **21.** $1\frac{1}{2} - \frac{5}{8}$

22. An upholsterer cuts a piece of cording $1\frac{2}{3}$ ft long from a piece $2\frac{1}{4}$ ft long. How much cording is left?

■ Multiplying and Dividing Fractions

Summary To multiply fractions, multiply their numerators and their denominators. To divide fractions, multiply the first fraction by the **reciprocal** of the second fraction.

To multiply or divide mixed numbers, write them as improper fractions before multiplying or dividing.

Find each product or quotient.

23. $\frac{1}{4} \cdot \frac{7}{10}$ **24.** $-\frac{2}{3} \div \frac{5}{6}$ **25.** $1\frac{3}{5} \cdot \frac{3}{4}$ **26.** $5\frac{1}{4} \div 2\frac{3}{5}$ **27.** $\frac{3x}{5} \div \frac{6x}{5}$

■ Using Customary Units of Measure

Summary To convert units of measure in the customary system of measurement, use **dimensional analysis.**

Complete each statement.

28. 30 in. = ■ ft

29. ■ lb = 54 oz

30. 20 yd = ■ ft

31. ■ fl oz = $1\frac{1}{2}$ pt

32. 12 gal = ■ pt

33. $2\frac{3}{4}$ t = ■ lb

■ Work Backward

Summary To solve some problems, you have to work backward.

34. Your family is planning a 4-h car trip. Along the way, you are planning to make five $\frac{1}{2}$-h stops. At what time should you leave home to arrive at the destination by 8:00 P.M.?

35. Buses bound for Los Angeles leave the station every hour from 6:00 A.M. to 8:00 P.M. How many buses is that in one day?

36. *Writing* Explain how solving a problem by working backward is similar to solving an equation.

■ Solving Equations

Summary To solve equations with fractions, use inverse operations to undo addition or subtraction. You can undo multiplication by multiplying each side of the equation by the same fraction.

Solve each equation.

37. $\frac{1}{8} + x = 2\frac{1}{2}$

38. $x - \frac{1}{3} = \frac{4}{5}$

39. $x + 4\frac{2}{3} = 6$

40. $6x = \frac{1}{9}$

41. $-\frac{3}{4}x = \frac{2}{7}$

42. $2\frac{3}{4}x = \frac{14}{33}$

■ Powers of Products and Quotients

Summary To raise a product to a power, raise each factor to the power. To raise a quotient to a power, raise both the numerator and the denominator to the power.

Simplify each expression.

43. $(2d)^4$

44. $(-3(2))^2$

45. $(a^2b)^5$

46. $\left(-\frac{1}{2}\right)^3$

47. $\left(\frac{x}{3}\right)^2$

48. $\left(\frac{2a}{c^2}\right)^4$

Find the LCM of each group of numbers.

1. 24, 36   **2.** 50, 100

3. $3x, 2y$ **4.** 16, 20

Compare. Use $>$, $<$, or $=$ to complete each statement.

5. $\frac{7}{8} \blacksquare \frac{7}{9}$ **6.** $\frac{2}{3} \blacksquare \frac{10}{15}$

7. $\frac{7}{10} \blacksquare 0.71$ **8.** $2\frac{3}{5} \blacksquare 2\frac{2}{3}$

9. $-0.87 \blacksquare -\frac{7}{8}$ **10.** $\frac{3}{4} \blacksquare \frac{14}{20}$

Order from least to greatest.

11. $0.5, \frac{1}{10}, 0, -\frac{1}{4}$ **12.** $-\frac{3}{5}, -0.\overline{6}, \frac{1}{6}, \frac{2}{3}$

Write each decimal as a fraction.

13. 0.4   **14.** $0.\overline{7}$ **15.** $12.\overline{36}$

16. 5.2   **17.** 0.002   **18.** $7.\overline{1}$

Write each fraction as a decimal.

19. $\frac{4}{15}$ **20.** $-\frac{2}{3}$ **21.** $\frac{3}{8}$

22. $\frac{1}{2}$ **23.** $\frac{6}{7}$ **24.** $\frac{5}{9}$

Add or subtract.

25. $\frac{1}{8} + \frac{3}{4}$ **26.** $\frac{2}{3} - \frac{1}{9}$

27. $-\frac{1}{6x} + \frac{1}{4}$ **28.** $11\frac{5}{6} - 5\frac{3}{8}$

29. $\frac{2}{3} - \left(-\frac{8y}{9}\right)$ **30.** $2\frac{1}{5} - \frac{3}{4}$

Multiply or divide.

31. $\frac{3}{5} \cdot \frac{1}{2}$ **32.** $-\frac{3}{4} \cdot \frac{5}{8}$

33. $\frac{5}{8x} \div \frac{7}{16}$ **34.** $\frac{4}{m} \div \frac{5m}{9}$

35. $3\frac{3}{4} \cdot 2\frac{4}{5}$ **36.** $-1\frac{1}{3} \div \left(-\frac{5}{9}\right)$

Complete each statement.

37. 10 yd = $\blacksquare$ ft   **38.** 20 oz = $\blacksquare$ lb

39. $\blacksquare$ lb = $1\frac{3}{4}$ t   **40.** 6 pt = $\blacksquare$ qt

41. $3\frac{1}{2}$ qt = $\blacksquare$ c   **42.** $\blacksquare$ in. = $1\frac{3}{4}$ yd

Solve each equation.

43. $m - \frac{2}{3} = \frac{1}{4}$ **44.** $h + \frac{3}{5} = \frac{9}{10}$

45. $x - \frac{5}{6} = -\frac{5}{6}$ **46.** $\frac{3}{5}a = 9$

47. $n + \frac{7}{8} = \frac{1}{3}$ **48.** $2\frac{1}{2}n = 3\frac{3}{4}$

49. $-5b = 3\frac{1}{3}$ **50.** $\frac{3}{8}y = -15$

Simplify each expression.

51. $(3(4))^2$ **52.** $(2a)^3$ **53.** $\left(\frac{3}{4}\right)^3$

54. $(3x^2)^3$ **55.** $-(2x^2y)^4$ **56.** $\left(\frac{2y}{5x}\right)^3$

Solve.

57. *Number Sense* Suppose you take a number, subtract 8, multiply by 7, add 10, and divide by 5. The result is 9. What is the original number?

58. You spend $\frac{3}{4}$ of your money on clothes and have $21 left. How much did you have before you bought the clothes?

59. *Writing* Write a word problem for the equation $x - 1\frac{1}{4} = 5$.

60. Two packages each weigh $1\frac{7}{8}$ lb. How much do they weigh altogether?

61. You rode your bicycle a mile and a half to school. Then you rode to a friend's house. Altogether you rode $2\frac{1}{10}$ mi. Write and solve an equation to find how far it is from school to your friend's house.

Choose the best answer.

1. Which group of numbers is in order from least to greatest?

   A. $0.583, \frac{7}{12}, \frac{5}{8}, 0.635$

   B. $\frac{7}{12}, 0.583, \frac{5}{8}, 0.635$

   C. $\frac{5}{8}, 0.583, \frac{7}{12}, 0.635$

   D. $\frac{5}{8}, 0.583, 0.635, \frac{7}{12}$

2. Which statement is *not* true about the expression below?
$$\frac{5}{16}m + \frac{7}{11}t - mt^2$$

   F. The expression has no constants.
   G. The coefficient of m is less than the coefficient of t.
   H. The expression has no like terms.
   J. The coefficient of m is less than the coefficient of mt^2.

3. Find the sum of $\frac{2}{5}, \frac{3}{10},$ and $\frac{3}{4}$ in simplest form.

   A. $1\frac{9}{20}$ B. $\frac{30}{20}$ C. $1\frac{23}{30}$ D. $\frac{18}{200}$

4. Which expression is equivalent to $8b^4$?

   F. $2^3(b^2 + b^2)$
   G. $(4 + 4)(b^2)^2$
   H. $(2 \cdot 2 \cdot 2)(b + b + b + b)$
   J. $(2b)^4$

5. What is the prime factorization of 750?
   A. $2 \cdot 5^2 \cdot 7$ B. $3 \cdot 5^3 \cdot 7$
   C. $2 \cdot 3 \cdot 5^3$ D. $15 \cdot 50$

6. A student bought 3 pens for p cents each, 4 notebooks for n cents each, and a ruler for \$1.29. Which expression models this situation?
   F. $3p + 4n + 1.29$
   G. $3n + 4p + 129$
   H. $0.3p + 0.4n + 1.29$
   J. $3p + 4n + 129$

Add or subtract.

7. $4 - (-7)$ 8. $-9 + 3.5$

9. $\frac{5}{8} + \frac{1}{8}$ 10. $\frac{3}{4} + \frac{3}{5}$

11. $\frac{7}{11} - \frac{2}{5}$ 12. $-\frac{6}{7} + \frac{3}{14}$

13. $1\frac{1}{9} - \frac{3}{4}$ 14. $10\frac{4}{5} - 9\frac{1}{2}$

Complete each statement.

15. $5\frac{1}{2}$ yd = ■ ft   16. 3 c = ■ pt

17. 4 fl oz = ■ c   18. ■ gal = 3 qt

19. ■ ft = $1\frac{1}{2}$ mi   20. 18 in. = ■ ft

Write each decimal as a fraction in simplest form.

21. 0.56 22. $0.\overline{45}$ 23. 0.18

Simplify each expression.

24. $\frac{2}{3}(8 - 5)^3$ 25. $3\left(\frac{6 + 4}{2}\right)^2$

26. $\frac{7}{12} \cdot \frac{6}{21} \div \frac{2}{3}$ 27. $\frac{1}{2} \div \left(\frac{3}{4} + \frac{1}{8}\right)$

Evaluate each expression for $c = -3$ and $d = \frac{1}{4}$.

28. $4c + 3d$ 29. $6d^2 - 9$

30. $c^2 + 2c^3$ 31. $5 + 7d - c$

Simplify each expression.

32. $(6 \cdot 3)^3$ 33. $\left(\frac{4}{5}\right)^2$ 34. $\left(\frac{2}{3}\right)^4$

35. $\left(\frac{3x}{y}\right)^3$ 36. $\left(-\frac{x}{2}\right)^5$ 37. $(4y)^2$

38. **Patterns** Write a rule for the pattern below. Find the next three terms.
$$\frac{1}{1}, \frac{1}{2}, \frac{1}{4}, \frac{1}{8}, \cdots$$

Skills You Need
for Chapter 6

▶ **Simplifying fractions** Use before Lessons 6-1, 6-2, and 6-4.

Write each fraction in simplest form.

1. $\frac{2}{8}$ 2. $\frac{6}{24}$ 3. $\frac{12}{15}$ 4. $\frac{6}{16}$

5. $\frac{18}{42}$ 6. $\frac{25}{200}$ 7. $\frac{80}{96}$ 8. $\frac{40}{1,000}$

▶ **Solving equations by multiplying or dividing** Use before Lessons 6-2, 6-3, and 6-7.

Solve each equation.

9. $3x = 48$ 10. $94.5 = 7r$ 11. $\frac{3}{7}t = \frac{3}{8}$

12. $0.5y = 1.25$ 13. $\frac{4}{5}x = 1$ 14. $38.5 = 1.4m$

▶ **Writing fractions and decimals** Use before Lesson 6-5.

Write each fraction as a decimal. Write each decimal as a fraction or a mixed number in simplest form.

15. $\frac{7}{20}$ 16. 0.06 17. $\frac{30}{8}$ 18. 0.35

19. 0.875 20. $3\frac{3}{5}$ 21. 1.07 22. $\frac{12}{18}$

23. $11\frac{1}{9}$ 24. $0.\overline{3}$ 25. $\frac{100}{16}$ 26. 3.98

▶ **Writing percents** Use before Lessons 6-5, 6-6, 6-7, and 6-8.

Write each of the following as a percent with the % symbol.

27. 5 percent   28. 50 percent   29. 5 tenths of a percent

30. 17 hundredths percent   31. 1 and 7 tenths percent   32. 17 percent

Ratios, Proportions, and Percents

What you'll learn in this chapter:

- How to find and use ratios and unit rates

- How to write and solve proportions

- How to find and use percents

STRING BAND

Guitars, fiddles, harps . . . people have been enjoying stringed instruments for thousands of years. The music from a stringed instrument follows rules of mathematics that you will learn in this chapter.

Make a Musical Instrument For the chapter project, you will construct and play a simple stringed instrument. You will make measurements that can be applied to a real instrument. Your final project will consist of drawings that show how to play notes on both instruments.

Steps to help you complete the project

Web Extension
www.phschool.com

How to solve a
problem by making
a table

6-1

Ratios and Unit Rates

What You'll Learn

1 To write and simplify ratios

2 To find rates and unit rates

...And Why

To use and compare measures such as unit prices, gas mileage, and speed

PART 1 **Writing Ratios**

Statistics In the United States, about 10 out of every 15 people eligible to vote are registered to vote. The numbers 10 and 15 form a *ratio.*

Ratio
A **ratio** is a comparison of two quantities by division. You can write a ratio in different ways.

Arithmetic	**Algebra**
10 to 15 10 : 15 $\frac{10}{15}$	a to b $a : b$ $\frac{a}{b}$, for $b \neq 0$

DATA ANALYSIS CONNECTION

■ EXAMPLE 1

Students were asked in a survey whether they had after-school jobs. Write each ratio as a fraction in simplest form.

a. students with jobs to students without jobs

$$\frac{\text{students with jobs}}{\text{students without jobs}} = \frac{40}{60}$$

$$= \frac{2}{3}$$

After-School Jobs

Response	Number
Have a Job	40
Don't Have a Job	60
Total	100

b. students without jobs to all students surveyed

$$\frac{\text{students without jobs}}{\text{all students surveyed}} = \frac{60}{100}$$

$$= \frac{3}{5}$$

■ **TRY THIS** Write each ratio as a fraction in simplest form.

1. students with jobs to all students surveyed

2. students without jobs to students with jobs

A **rate** is a ratio that compares quantities in different units. A **unit rate** is a rate that has a denominator of 1. Examples of unit rates include unit prices, gas mileage, and speed.

DATA ANALYSIS CONNECTION

■ EXAMPLE 2

Unit Prices **The table shows prices for different sizes of the same dish detergent. Which size has the lowest unit price?**

Mini: $\dfrac{\text{price} \rightarrow}{\text{volume} \rightarrow} \dfrac{\$1.20}{12 \text{ fl oz}} = \$.10/\text{fl oz}$

Family: $\dfrac{\text{price} \rightarrow}{\text{volume} \rightarrow} \dfrac{\$2.24}{28 \text{ fl oz}} = \$.08/\text{fl oz}$ **Find the unit prices.**

Economy: $\dfrac{\text{price} \rightarrow}{\text{volume} \rightarrow} \dfrac{\$3.60}{40 \text{ fl oz}} = \$.09/\text{fl oz}$

The Family size has the lowest unit price.

Dish Detergent Prices

Size	Volume (fl oz)	Price
Mini	12	$1.20
Family	28	$2.24
Economy	40	$3.60

■ TRY THIS Find each unit rate.

3. Two liters of spring water costs $1.98.

4. A car goes 425 mi on 12.5 gal of gas.

You can use dimensional analysis to choose conversion factors for converting rates.

■ EXAMPLE 3

Convert 10 mi/h to feet per minute.

$10 \text{ mi/h} = \dfrac{10 \text{ mi}}{1 \text{ h}} \cdot \dfrac{5{,}280 \text{ ft}}{1 \text{ mi}} \cdot \dfrac{1 \text{ h}}{60 \text{ min}}$ **Use conversion factors that convert miles to feet and hours to minutes.**

$= \dfrac{{}^{1}\cancel{10 \text{ mi}}}{1 \cancel{\text{h}}} \cdot \dfrac{\overset{880}{\cancel{5{,}280 \text{ ft}}}}{1 \cancel{\text{mi}}} \cdot \dfrac{1 \cancel{\text{h}}}{\underset{6_{1}}{\cancel{60}} \text{ min}}$ **Divide the common factors and units.**

$= \dfrac{880 \text{ ft}}{\text{min}}$ **Simplify.**

10 mi/h equals 880 ft/min.

■ TRY THIS Complete each statement.

5. 3.5 qt/min = ▩ gal/h   **6.** 12 cm/s = ▩ m/h

Exercises

Write each ratio as a fraction in simplest form.

1. 9 : 27

2. 12 to 8

3. 10 out of 16

4. 2 to 18

5. 6 : 50

6. $\frac{1,000}{10,000}$

Find the unit rate for each situation.

7. A sprinter runs 200 m in 25 s.

8. A keyboarder types 1,575 words in 25 min.

Complete each statement.

9. 720 m/day = ■ m/min

10. 1.5 gal/min = ■ qt/h

11. $9/h = ■ ¢/min

PRACTICE AND PROBLEM SOLVING

Write each ratio as a fraction in simplest form.

12. 3 : 8

13. 7 to 9

14. 8 out of 11

15. $\frac{14}{18}$

16. 15 : 25

17. 36 to 48

18. 60 to 24

19. 16 : 12

For each situation, write a ratio as a fraction in simplest form.

20. 3 out of 12 people live in a rural area.

21. In one class, there are 6 girls for every 10 boys.

22. 98 homes in 100 have a TV.

23. 70 homes out of 125 have a personal computer.

Find each unit rate.

24. 20 mi in 5 h

25. 42 gal in 7 min

26. a fall of 144 ft in 3 s

27. 245 mi in 56 h

28. 676 mi in 13 h

29. 20 gal flowing in 4 min

Complete each statement.

30. $29/kg = ■ ¢/g

31. 32 yd/min = ■ in./s

32. 0.85 km/s = ■ m/min

33. 80 mi/h = ■ ft/s

34. 20 fl oz/min = ■ qt/day

35. $\frac{90 \text{ m}}{4 \text{ s}}$ = ■ km/h

36. *Mathematical Reasoning* A student claims that a ratio remains unchanged if 1 is added to both the numerator and the denominator of the fraction. Does $\frac{a}{b}$ equal $\frac{a+1}{b+1}$? Explain, and give an example or a counterexample.

37. a. For each class, write the ratio of the number of boys to the total number of students.
   b. Which class has the greater ratio of boys to students?

Boys in Two Classes

Class	Number of Boys	Number of Students
A	6	30
B	4	24

38. A bookstore sells hardbacks, paperbacks, and magazines. The store sells 5 magazines for every 3 hardbacks. It sells 20 paperbacks for every 10 magazines. Write a ratio for each pair of sales categories.
   a. hardbacks to magazines
   b. magazines to paperbacks
   c. hardbacks to all publications (*Hint:* First find the number of hardbacks sold for every 10 magazines.)

39. *Science* Density is the ratio of a substance's mass to its volume. A volume of 20 cubic centimeters of gold has a mass of 386 grams. Express the density of gold as a unit rate.

40. *Error Analysis* A student converts 100 ft/min to 500 in./s. Use dimensional analysis to explain why the student's result is not reasonable.

A Sappy Story

Connecticut has more than 100 farms that produce maple syrup. Sugarers collect sap and boil it down to syrup. In a good year, one small sugarer in Connecticut collects 300 gallons of sap from 200 trees. The sap boils down to just seven gallons of syrup. The syrup is sold for $4.50 per half pint or $44 per gallon.

Math in the Media **Refer to the article above.**

41. Write the ratio of sap to syrup in three different ways.

42. Calculate the unit prices for syrup sold by the half-pint and syrup sold by the gallon. Which has the lower unit price?

▶ MIXED REVIEW

Simplify each expression. (*Lesson 5-9*)

43. $(-3 \cdot 4)^3$

44. $(2x^2y)^4$

45. $\left(-\dfrac{ab^3}{a^2b}\right)^3$

Compare. Use >, <, or = to complete each statement. (*Lesson 5-2*)

46. $\dfrac{7}{8}$ ▇ $\dfrac{14}{24}$

47. $\dfrac{4}{12}$ ▇ $\dfrac{10}{30}$

48. $\dfrac{13}{20}$ ▇ 0.6

49. *Choose a Strategy* Three friends shared the driving on a long trip. Marla drove 7 mi more than Guido. Guido drove five times as far as Juanita did. Juanita drove 112 mi. How long was the trip?

MATH TOOLBOX

Converting between Measurement Systems

You can use conversion factors to convert a unit of measure from one system to another. For example, since 1 mi ≈ 1.61 km, you can use $\frac{1 \text{ mi}}{1.61 \text{ km}}$ and $\frac{1.61 \text{ km}}{1 \text{ mi}}$ as conversion factors.

The table shows some useful conversion factors.

Customary Units and Metric Units	Conversion Factor
1 in. = 2.54 cm	$\frac{1 \text{ in.}}{2.54 \text{ cm}}$ or $\frac{2.54 \text{ cm}}{1 \text{ in.}}$
1 mi ≈ 1.61 km	$\frac{1 \text{ mi}}{1.61 \text{ km}}$ or $\frac{1.61 \text{ km}}{1 \text{ mi}}$
1.06 qt ≈ 1 L	$\frac{1.06 \text{ qt}}{1 \text{ L}}$ or $\frac{1 \text{ L}}{1.06 \text{ qt}}$
1 oz ≈ 28.4 g	$\frac{1 \text{ oz}}{28.4 \text{ g}}$ or $\frac{28.4 \text{ g}}{1 \text{ oz}}$
2.20 lb ≈ 1 kg	$\frac{2.20 \text{ lb}}{1 \text{ kg}}$ or $\frac{1 \text{ kg}}{2.20 \text{ lb}}$

You can use dimensional analysis to decide which conversion factor to use.

■ EXAMPLE 1

The longest track event at the Olympics is the 50-km walk. How long is the race in miles?

$50 \text{ km} \approx 50 \text{ km} \cdot \frac{1 \text{ mi}}{1.61 \text{ km}}$ Use a conversion factor that changes kilometers to miles.

$= 50 \text{ k\cancel{m}} \cdot \frac{1 \text{ mi}}{1.61 \text{ \cancel{km}}}$ Divide the common units.

$= \frac{50 \text{ mi}}{1.61}$ Multiply.

$\approx 31 \text{ mi}$ Divide.

The 50-km walk is about 31 mi long.

Convert. Where necessary, round to the nearest tenth.

1. 16 cm = ■ in.   **2.** ■ mi = 20 km   **3.** ■ km = 100 mi   **4.** ■ L = 50 qt

5. ■ g = 15 oz   **6.** 15 L = ■ qt   **7.** ■ lb = 14 kg   **8.** 44 lb = ■ kg

You can estimate using conversion factors.

■ EXAMPLE 2

About how many ounces are in 60 grams?

$60 \text{ g} \approx 60 \text{ g} \cdot \dfrac{1 \text{ oz}}{28.4 \text{ g}}$ Use the conversion factor that changes grams to ounces.

$\approx 60 \text{ g} \cdot \dfrac{1 \text{ oz}}{30 \text{ g}}$ Round the conversion factor to a number compatible with 60.

$= \overset{2}{\cancel{60}} \text{ g} \cdot \dfrac{1 \text{ oz}}{\underset{1}{\cancel{30 \text{ g}}}}$ Divide the common factors and units.

$= 2 \text{ oz}$ Simplify.

There are about 2 ounces in 60 grams.

Sometimes you may need to use two or more conversion factors.

■ EXAMPLE 3

A punch recipe calls for a gallon of sparkling water. How many 2-L bottles should you buy?

$1 \text{ gal} \approx 1 \text{ gal} \cdot \dfrac{4 \text{ qt}}{1 \text{ gal}} \cdot \dfrac{1 \text{ L}}{1.06 \text{ qt}}$ Use conversion factors that change gallons to quarts and quarts to liters.

$= 1 \cancel{\text{ gal}} \cdot \dfrac{4 \cancel{\text{ qt}}}{1 \cancel{\text{ gal}}} \cdot \dfrac{1 \text{ L}}{1.06 \cancel{\text{ qt}}}$ Divide the common units.

$= \dfrac{4 \text{ L}}{1.06}$ Multiply numerators and multiply denominators.

$= 3.8 \text{ L}$ Divide.

Now find the number of bottles you need for 3.8 L.

$\dfrac{3.8}{2} = 1.9$ Divide by 2, since there are 2 L per bottle.

You need about 1.9 bottles. You should buy two bottles.

Convert. Where necessary, round to the nearest tenth.

9. $100 \text{ oz} = \blacksquare \text{ kg}$

10. $\blacksquare \text{ L} = 212 \text{ pt}$

11. $500 \text{ g} = \blacksquare \text{ lb}$

12. $1,000 \text{ mm} = \blacksquare \text{ in.}$

13. $\blacksquare \text{ gal} = 20 \text{ L}$

14. $\blacksquare \text{ km/h} = 10 \text{ mi/h}$

15. *Home Economics* A recipe calls for 8 oz of figs. The figs come in packages of 100 g. How many packages should you buy?

16. *Writing* Explain how you would estimate the number of kilometers in 19 miles.

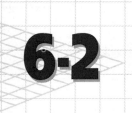
Proportions

What You'll Learn

1 To solve proportions

2 To use proportions to solve problems

...And Why

To solve real-world problems involving science

A **proportion** is an equality of two ratios—for example, $\frac{6}{9} = \frac{8}{12}$. You can use the Multiplication Property of Equality to show an important property of all proportions.

If $\frac{a}{b} = \frac{c}{d}$

then $\frac{a}{b} \cdot bd = \frac{c}{d} \cdot bd$ **Multiplication Property of Equality**

$$\frac{ab^1d}{\underset{1}{b}} = \frac{cbd^1}{\underset{1}{d}} \qquad \frac{b}{b} = 1 \text{ and } \frac{d}{d} = 1$$

and $ad = cb$, or $ad = bc$.

The products ad and bc are called the **cross products** of the proportion $\frac{a}{b} = \frac{c}{d}$.

Reading Math

Read the proportion $\frac{6}{9} = \frac{8}{12}$ as "the ratio of 6 to 9 equals the ratio of 8 to 12," or as "6 is to 9 as 8 is to 12."

Cross Products
In a proportion, the cross products are equal.

Arithmetic

$$\frac{6}{9} = \frac{8}{12}$$

$6 \cdot 12 = 9 \cdot 8 = 72$

Algebra

$$\frac{a}{b} = \frac{c}{d}$$

$ad = bc$

To solve a proportion that contains a variable, you find the value that makes the equation true.

■ EXAMPLE 1

Solve $\frac{x}{9} = \frac{4}{6}$.

Method 1 Multiplication Property of Equality

$$\frac{x}{9} = \frac{4}{6}$$

$$\frac{x}{9} \cdot 9 = \frac{4}{6} \cdot 9$$

$$x = \frac{36}{6}$$

$$x = 6$$

Method 2 cross products

$$\frac{x}{9} = \frac{4}{6}$$

$$x \cdot 6 = 9 \cdot 4$$

$$6x = 36$$

$$\frac{6x}{6} = \frac{36}{6}$$

$$x = 6$$

■ **TRY THIS** Solve each proportion

1. $\frac{h}{9} = \frac{2}{3}$ **2.** $\frac{4}{5} = \frac{t}{55}$ **3.** $\frac{22}{d} = \frac{6}{21}$

Two ratios form a proportion if their cross products are equal.

■ **EXAMPLE 2**

Do the ratios $\frac{4}{6}$ and $\frac{10}{14}$ form a proportion?

$\frac{4}{6} \stackrel{?}{=} \frac{10}{14}$ **Test by writing as a proportion.**

$4 \cdot 14 \stackrel{?}{=} 6 \cdot 10$ **Write cross products.**

$56 \neq 60$ **Simplify.**

No, the ratios do not form a proportion.

■ **TRY THIS** Tell whether each pair of ratios forms a proportion.

4. $\frac{6}{9}, \frac{4}{6}$ **5.** $\frac{15}{20}, \frac{5}{7}$ **6.** $\frac{7}{12}, \frac{17.5}{30}$

PART 2 **Using Proportions to Solve Problems**

You can write and solve proportions for many real-world problems.

MEASUREMENT CONNECTION

■ **EXAMPLE 3**

Navigation **One hundred nautical miles equals about 115 standard, or statute, miles. To the nearest mile, how far in statute miles is 156 nautical miles?**

Let d = distance in statute miles.

$\dfrac{\text{distance in nautical miles} \longrightarrow}{\text{distance in statute miles} \longrightarrow} \dfrac{100}{115} = \dfrac{156}{d} \dfrac{\longleftarrow \text{distance in nautical miles}}{\longleftarrow \text{distance in statute miles}}$

$100d = 115(156)$ **Write cross products.**

$d = \dfrac{115(156)}{100}$ **Divide each side by 100.**

$d \approx 179$ **A calculator may be useful.**

156 nautical miles is about 179 statute miles.

■ **TRY THIS**

7. To the nearest mile, how far in nautical miles is 100 statute miles?

Sailors and astronauts measure distances in *nautical miles*. This photo of the Great Lakes was taken from the space shuttle at an altitude of 156 nautical miles.

Exercises

CHECK UNDERSTANDING

Solve each proportion.

1. $\frac{2}{v} = \frac{1}{8}$

2. $\frac{z}{42} = \frac{25}{70}$

3. $\frac{4}{11} = \frac{x}{16.5}$

Tell whether each pair of ratios forms a proportion.

4. $\frac{2}{3}$ and $\frac{10}{20}$

5. $\frac{80}{25}$ and $\frac{16}{5}$

6. $\frac{3.9}{5.4}$ and $\frac{13}{18}$

Write a proportion for each situation. Then solve.

7. Four ounces of orange juice contain 50 calories. Fourteen ounces contain c calories.

8. A lion has 12 heartbeats in 16 s, and h heartbeats in 60 s.

9. *Mathematical Reasoning* If $\frac{a}{b} = \frac{c}{d}$, will $\frac{a}{c} = \frac{b}{d}$? Assume that $b \neq 0$, $c \neq 0$, and $d \neq 0$. Explain your reasoning.

PRACTICE AND PROBLEM SOLVING

Mental Math **Solve by mental math.**

10. $\frac{1}{6} = \frac{a}{72}$

11. $\frac{h}{4} = \frac{10}{8}$

12. $\frac{16}{4} = \frac{8}{s}$

13. $\frac{2}{9} = \frac{r}{36}$

14. $\frac{n}{12} = \frac{12}{2}$

15. $\frac{1}{15} = \frac{3}{p}$

16. $\frac{120}{24} = \frac{y}{2}$

17. $\frac{10}{v} = \frac{3}{1.5}$

Solve each proportion. Where necessary, round to the nearest tenth.

18. $\frac{4}{15} = \frac{a}{75}$

19. $\frac{4}{3} = \frac{b}{21}$

20. $\frac{13}{c} = \frac{39}{60}$

21. $\frac{3}{6} = \frac{7}{d}$

22. $\frac{6}{25} = \frac{e}{80}$

23. $\frac{4}{9} = \frac{f}{15}$

24. $\frac{3}{8} = \frac{50}{g}$

25. $\frac{24}{17} = \frac{108}{h}$

26. $\frac{7}{9} = \frac{j}{22.5}$

27. $\frac{11}{18} = \frac{k}{49.5}$

28. $\frac{6}{13} = \frac{7.8}{m}$

29. $\frac{20}{27} = \frac{1.1}{n}$

Estimation **Estimate the solution of each proportion.**

30. $\frac{w}{20} = \frac{6}{23}$

31. $\frac{3}{2} = \frac{29}{d}$

32. $\frac{20}{3.9} = \frac{s}{6}$

33. $\frac{1.5}{p} = \frac{2.1}{4.1}$

34. $\frac{f}{4} = \frac{12}{49}$

35. $\frac{60}{g} = \frac{24.1}{8.1}$

36. $\frac{b}{19} = \frac{13}{6}$

37. $\frac{9}{4.4} = \frac{x}{19}$

Tell whether each pair of ratios forms a proportion.

38. $\frac{4}{7}$ and $\frac{20}{25}$

39. $\frac{3}{2}$ and $\frac{16}{10}$

40. $\frac{3}{4}$ and $\frac{12}{15}$

41. $\frac{8}{3}$ and $\frac{56}{21}$

42. $\frac{9}{24}$ and $\frac{15}{40}$

43. $\frac{32}{20}$ and $\frac{20}{12}$

44. $\frac{40}{24}$ and $\frac{75}{45}$

45. $\frac{120}{144}$ and $\frac{145}{75}$

For Exercises 46–51, write a proportion for each phrase. Then solve. Where necessary, round to the nearest hundredth.

46. 3 oz for $1.65; 5 oz for x dollars

47. 20 lb for $27.50; 12 lb for x dollars

48. 5 km in 18 min 36 s; 8 km in v min

49. 25 yd in $2\frac{1}{2}$ s; 100 yd in x seconds

50. 96 oz for $2; y pounds for $10

51. 4 oz for $1.85; 1 lb for t dollars

52. Three posters cost $9.60. At that rate, how many posters can you buy for $48?

53. Three tea bags are needed to make a gallon of iced tea. How many tea bags are needed to make four gallons?

54. At the Copy Shoppe, 18 copies cost $1.08. At that rate, how much will 40 copies cost?

55. At the rate shown in the cartoon, how much would five potatoes cost?

56. *Quality Control* A microchip inspector found three defective chips in a batch containing 750 chips. At that rate, how many defective chips would there be in 10,000 chips?

57. *Geometry* A rectangle that is 20 cm long and 28 cm wide is the same shape as one that is 9 cm long and z cm wide. Find z.

58. **TEST PREP** An artist makes purple paint by mixing red and blue paint in the ratio of 2 parts red to 3 parts blue. What is the ratio of red paint to purple paint?
   A. 3 : 2 **B.** 3 : 5 **C.** 2 : 3 **D.** 2 : 5

59. *Exchange Rates* On a recent day, the exchange rate for U.S. dollars to French francs was 0.16 dollars per franc. On that day, how many francs would you get for 25 dollars?

60. *Writing* A truck driver estimates that it will take him 12 h to drive 1,160 km. After 5 h, he has driven 484 km. Is he on schedule? Explain.

61. *Error Analysis* Fancy ribbon costs $3 for 15 in. Your friend wants to find the cost of 3 ft of ribbon. He uses the proportion $\frac{3}{15} = \frac{x}{3}$ and gets an answer of $.60. Explain your friend's error.

REAL LIFE ADVENTURES by Gary Wise and Lance Aldrich

If the people who own the shops at the airport owned other things.

Use the table for Exercises 62–65.

62. How many times does an adult's heart beat in 270 s?

63. In how many seconds will a newborn's heart beat 35 times?

64. In how many seconds will a 12-year-old's heart beat 17 times?

65. In 45 s, how many more times does a newborn's heart beat than a 6-year-old's heart?

Human Heart Rates

Age (years)	Beats per Minute
newborn	140
1	120
6	100
10	90
12	85
adult	80

66. On Monday, the ratio of Tara's pocket money to her brother Seth's pocket money was $\frac{3}{1}$. On Tuesday, Tara gave $5 to Seth. Then the ratio of Tara's money to Seth's was $\frac{2}{1}$.

    a. Let $3x$ equal the amount Tara had on Monday and x equal the amount Seth had on Monday. Write two ratios that show $\frac{\text{Tara's money on Tuesday}}{\text{Seth's money on Tuesday}}$.

    b. Use the ratios to write a proportion. Solve for x. Then find the amount of money each person had on Monday.

▶ MIXED REVIEW

Write each ratio as a fraction in simplest form. *(Lesson 6-1)*

67. ten per thousand   **68.** 30 to 55   **69.** $125 : 70$

Tell whether each equation is true or false. *(Lessons 1-3 and 5-3)*

70. $\left| -2\frac{1}{4} \right| - \left| 2\frac{1}{4} \right| = 0$ **71.** $\left| -2\frac{1}{4} \right| + \left| 2\frac{1}{4} \right| = 0$ **72.** $-\left| -\frac{9}{4} \right| + \left| 2\frac{1}{4} \right| = 0$

73. *Choose a Strategy* On Saturday afternoon, a student bought two music tapes for $8.95 each and a sweater for $24.95. She received $20 for mowing a lawn. On Saturday night, she had $45.12. How much money did the student have on Saturday morning?

CHAPTER PROJECT 6

◢ ACTIVITY 1 CREATING

Put pencil at 10-in. mark.

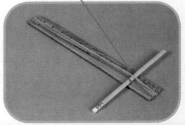

Use a 12-in. ruler, a pencil, and two rubber bands to make a simple stringed instrument like the one at the right. Pluck a string and listen to the resulting sound. Then press the string down against the ruler somewhere between 0 and 10. Using your other hand, pluck the string again. Describe how the resulting sound differs from the first sound.

     See also Extra Practice section.

Similar Figures and Scale Drawings

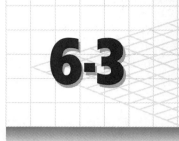

PART 1 Using Similar Figures

Similar figures have the same shape, but not necessarily the same size. Similar figures have *corresponding angles* and *corresponding sides*.

The symbol ~ means *is similar to*. At the right, $\triangle ABC \sim \triangle XYZ$.

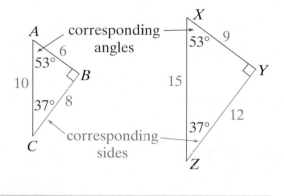

corresponding angles

corresponding sides

What You'll Learn

1 To solve problems that involve similar figures

2 To solve problems that involve scale drawings

...And Why

To apply proportions to geometry and measurement

Similar Figures

Similar figures have two properties.

- The corresponding angles have equal measures.
- The lengths of corresponding sides are in proportion.

GEOMETRY CONNECTION

■ EXAMPLE 1

Parallelogram $ABCD$ ~ parallelogram $EFGH$. Find the value of x.

Write a proportion for corresponding sides.

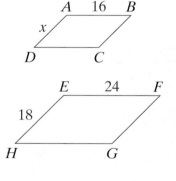

Side *DA* corresponds to side *HE*.	$\dfrac{x}{18} = \dfrac{16}{24}$	Side *AB* corresponds to side *EF*.
	$x \cdot 24 = 18 \cdot 16$	Write cross products.
	$\dfrac{24x}{24} = \dfrac{18 \cdot 16}{24}$	Divide each side by 24.
	$x = 12$	Simplify.

■ TRY THIS

1. Parallelogram *KLMN* is similar to parallelogram *ABCD* in Example 1. Find the value of *y*.

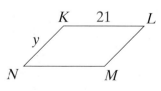

You can use similar figures to compute distances that are difficult to measure directly. This method is called **indirect measurement.**

▐ EXAMPLE 2

Indirect Measurement **A tree casts a shadow 10 ft long. A 5-ft woman casts a shadow 4 ft long. The triangle shown for the woman and her shadow is similar to the triangle shown for the tree and its shadow. How tall is the tree?**

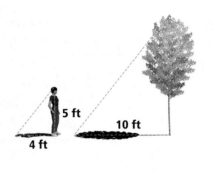

5 ft

4 ft

10 ft

$\dfrac{4}{10} = \dfrac{5}{x}$ **Corresponding sides of similar triangles are in proportion.**

$4x = 10 \cdot 5$ **Write cross products.**

$\dfrac{4x}{4} = \dfrac{10 \cdot 5}{4}$ **Divide each side by 4.**

$x = 12.5$ **Simplify.**

The tree is 12.5 ft tall.

▐ TRY THIS

2. *Indirect Measurement* A building 70 ft high casts a 150-ft shadow. A nearby flagpole casts a 60-ft shadow. Draw a diagram. Use similar triangles to find the height of the flagpole.

PART 2   Using Scale Drawings

A **scale drawing** is an enlarged or reduced drawing that is similar to an actual object or place. The ratio of a distance in the drawing to the corresponding actual distance is the *scale* of the drawing.

▐ EXAMPLE 3

Maps **The scale of the map is 1 in. : 40 mi. About how far from Atlanta is Athens?**

Map distance = $1\frac{1}{2}$ in., or 1.5 in.   **Measure the map distance.**

$\dfrac{\text{map (in.)}}{\text{actual (mi)}} \rightarrow \quad \dfrac{1}{40} = \dfrac{1.5}{d} \quad \leftarrow \dfrac{\text{map (in.)}}{\text{actual (mi)}}$ **Write a proportion.**

$1 \cdot d = 40 \cdot 1.5$ **Write cross products.**

$d = 60$ **Simplify.**

Athens is about 60 mi from Atlanta.

▐ TRY THIS

3. *Maps* Find the approximate distance from Atlanta to Macon.

Exercises

CHECK UNDERSTANDING

Trapezoid *EFGH* ~ trapezoid *MNOP.* Find each length.

1. length *EF*

2. length *OP*

3. A scale drawing has a scale of 1 in. : 10 ft. What is the distance on the drawing for an actual distance of 20 ft? Of 45 ft?

4. *Critical Thinking* A note at the bottom of a map says "not to scale." Explain why that is important information.

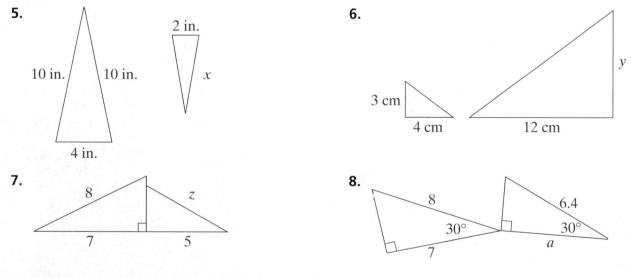

PRACTICE AND PROBLEM SOLVING

Each pair of triangles is similar. Find the missing length. Round to the nearest tenth where necessary.

5.

6.

7.

8.

The scale of a map is 2 cm : 15 km. Find the actual distance for each map distance.

9. 6 cm

10. 2.1 cm

11. 10 mm

12. 17.4 cm

A scale drawing has a scale of $\frac{1}{2}$ in. : 10 ft. Find the length on the drawing for each actual length.

13. 40 ft

14. 5 ft

15. 35 ft

16. $3\frac{1}{2}$ ft

17. An image on a slide is similar to its projected image. A slide is 35 mm wide and 21 mm high. Its projected image is 85 cm wide. To the nearest centimeter, how high is the image?

18. *Indirect Measurement* A tree casts a shadow 8 ft long. A 6-ft man casts a shadow 4 ft long. The triangle formed by the tree and its shadow is similar to the triangle formed by the man and his shadow. How tall is the tree?

19. *Open-ended* Give some examples of similar figures you find in everyday life.

20. *Writing* Are all squares similar? Explain.

21. *Architecture* The actual length of a room is 16 ft. The scale of a blueprint is $\frac{1}{2}$ in. : 1 ft. Find the room's length in the blueprint.

22. *Geography* The cities of Jackson, Mississippi, and Carson City Nevada, are 1,750 mi apart.
 a. A map of the United States has a scale of 1 in. : 250 mi. How far apart on the map are the cities?
 b. On another map, the cities are 5 in. apart. What is the scale of the map?

The length of each piece in a model railroad built on the HO scale is $\frac{1}{87}$ of the actual length. Another popular model is the N scale, for which the scale is $\frac{1}{160}$.

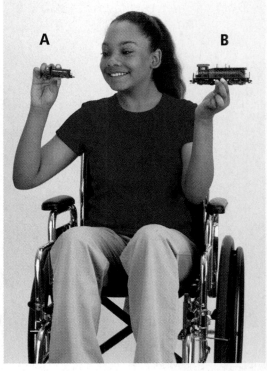

23. The student in the photograph is holding an HO model and an N model. Which type of model is labeled *A?* Which type of model is labeled *B?*

24. Each car on a full-size passenger train is 80 ft long. What is the length in inches of a model passenger car in the HO scale? In the N scale?

25. A diesel locomotive is 60 ft long. How long is a model of the locomotive in the N scale?

26. In the O scale, the length of a model is $\frac{1}{48}$ of an actual length. An O-scale locomotive is 1.05 ft long. How long is the actual locomotive?

27. A boxcar on a freight train is 40 ft long. A model boxcar is 3 in. long. In which scale was the model built?

28. You are building a display shelf for your model train. You have 12 cars. Each car is 1.2 ft long. You want 1.2 in. of space between cars. How long must the shelf be?

Architecture **A 2-in. length in the scale drawing represents an actual length of 20 ft.**

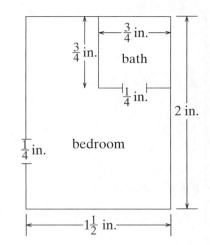

29. What is the scale of the drawing?

30. What are the actual dimensions of the bath?

31. Find the actual width of the doorways that lead into the bedroom and the bathroom.

32. Find the actual area of the bedroom.

33. Can a bed 6 ft long and 3 ft wide fit into the narrow section of the bedroom? Justify your answer.

34. You want to design a rectangular dance floor 90 ft long and 75 ft wide. You want to make a drawing with a scale of 1 in. : 9 ft. Can you fit the drawing on a piece of paper $8\frac{1}{2}$ in. by 11 in.? Justify your answer.

▶ MIXED REVIEW

Solve each proportion. *(Lesson 6-2)*

35. $\frac{x}{5} = \frac{32}{80}$ **36.** $\frac{3}{8} = \frac{r}{15}$ **37.** $\frac{40}{w} = \frac{50}{3}$ **38.** $\frac{24}{16} = \frac{204}{c}$

Find the mean, median, and mode. *(Lesson 3-3)*

39. 12, 10, 11, 7, 9, 8, 10, 5   **40.** 4.5, 3.2, 6.3, 5.2, 5, 4.8, 6, 3.9

Write each fraction as a decimal. *(Lesson 5-2)*

41. $\frac{3}{8}$ **42.** $\frac{4}{9}$ **43.** $\frac{7}{16}$ **44.** $\frac{5}{12}$

45. *Gas Mileage* A car travels 264 mi on 12 gal of gas. Find the unit rate in miles per gallon. *(Lesson 6-1)*

CHAPTER PROJECT 6

ACTIVITY 2 INVESTIGATING

By experimenting with your stringed instrument, learn to play the notes of "The Star Spangled Banner" that correspond to the words *say, can, you,* and *see.* Use the full string length for *say.* For the other notes, press the string down against the ruler. For each note, measure the string length, which is the distance between your finger and the pencil. Record the results.

MATH TOOLBOX

Dilations

You can use geometry software to make a scale drawing, or *dilation*, of a figure. First choose the Dilate command. Then choose a center of dilation and a scale, which is also known as a *scale factor*.

■ EXAMPLE

Draw a triangle. Then draw a dilation with scale factor 3.

Use geometry software to draw △*ABC*. Draw a point *D* on one side of the triangle. Choose *D* as the center of a dilation with scale factor 3. The result is an image like the one at the right. Each side of the dilation is 3 times as long as the corresponding side of △*ABC*.

If you move point *D*, the dilation also will move. If instead you move *A*, *B*, or *C*, the dilation will change as △*ABC* changes.

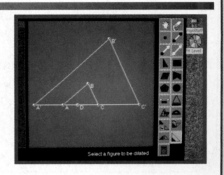

Use geometry software to draw △*PQR*.

1. **a.** Draw a point *S outside* △*PQR*. Draw a dilation of △*PQR* with center *S* and scale factor 2.5. Label the dilation △*XYZ*. △*XYZ* is similar to △*PQR*. Angle *X* corresponds to angle *P*, angle *Y* corresponds to angle *Q*, and angle *Z* corresponds to angle *R*.
   b. Compare the location of △*XYZ* to the location of △*PQR*. Does the dilation lie inside the original triangle? Outside the triangle? Do the triangles overlap?
   c. Now move *S* to be *inside* △*PQR*. Once again, compare the locations of the two triangles. How did moving the center of dilation change the relative locations of the triangles?

2. Change the location of point *S* so that △*PQR* and △*XYZ* have the given number of points in common. Print an example of each case.
   a. 0   **b.** 1   **c.** 2   **d.** more than 2

3. With *S* inside △*PQR*, change the scale factor to 0.5. Describe the relative locations of the two triangles.

4. **a.** Keep the scale factor of the dilation at 0.5. Use the Area tool to find the area of △*PQR*. Use the Area tool again to find the area of △*XYZ*. Write a ratio to compare the areas.
   b. Move *P*, *Q*, or *R* to see how the area of △*XYZ* changes as the area of △*PQR* changes. Does the ratio of the areas change?
   c. ***Mathematical Reasoning*** What do your results suggest about the areas of similar triangles that have a scale factor of 0.5?

Probability

Investigate

········· EXPLORING PROBABILITY ·········

Many board games involve rolling two number cubes and then adding the numbers on the cubes. Are certain sums more likely than others? The table shows the possible rolls and their sums.

1. Copy and complete the table.

2. What is the number of times each sum appears in the chart?

3. Which sum appears most frequently?

4. There are a total of 36 sums in the table. Use your answer to Question 3 to write the ratio $\frac{\text{number of times the most frequent sum appears}}{\text{total number of sums}}$.

Sums of 2 Number Cubes

	1	2	3	4	5	6
1	2	3	4	■	6	7
2	3	4	5	6	■	8
3	4	5	■	7	8	9
4	5	■	7	8	9	10
5	6	7	8	9	10	■
6	■	8	9	10	11	12

What You'll Learn

1 To find probability

2 To find odds

. . . And Why

To understand the likelihood of everyday events, such as rolling a number on a number cube or being a twin

PART 1 Finding Probability

Outcomes are the possible results of an action. There are six outcomes for rolling a single number cube: 1, 2, 3, 4, 5, and 6.

An **event** is any outcome or group of outcomes. In the activity above, for example, rolling a sum of 4 is an event corresponding to three different outcomes.

Three different outcomes result in the event *a sum of 4.*

The outcomes for rolling two number cubes are *random* and therefore *equally likely* to occur. When outcomes are equally likely, you can use a ratio to find the *probability of an event*.

probability of an event = $P(\text{event}) = \frac{\text{number of favorable outcomes}}{\text{number of possible outcomes}}$

You can read the probability $\frac{3}{6}$ as "three in six" or "three out of six."

EXAMPLE 1

Find P(rolling an even number) with one number cube.

$$\frac{\text{number of favorable outcomes}}{\text{number of possible outcomes}} = \frac{3}{6} \quad \leftarrow \quad \textbf{3 even-number outcomes}$$
$$\qquad\qquad\qquad\qquad\qquad\qquad \leftarrow \quad \textbf{6 possible outcomes}$$

$$P(\text{rolling an even number}) = \frac{3}{6}, \text{ or } \frac{1}{2}$$

■ **TRY THIS** Find each probability for rolling one number cube.

5. P(odd number)   **6.** P(2)   **7.** P(5 or 6)

All probabilities range from 0 to 1.

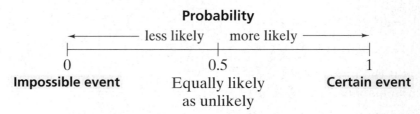

Probability

less likely   more likely

0   0.5   1

Impossible event   **Equally likely as unlikely**   **Certain event**

The **complement** of an event is the opposite of that event. The events *no rain* and *rain* are complements of each other. The probability of an event plus the probability of its complement always equals 1.

DATA ANALYSIS CONNECTION

EXAMPLE 2

Vital Statistics **In the United States, the probability that a child is a twin is 2 in 90, or $\frac{2}{90}$. Find P(not a twin).**

$P(\text{twin}) + P(\text{not a twin}) = 1$	Write an equation.
$\frac{2}{90} + P(\text{not a twin}) = 1$	Substitute.
$\frac{2}{90} - \frac{2}{90} + P(\text{not a twin}) = 1 - \frac{2}{90}$	Subtract $\frac{2}{90}$ from each side.
$P(\text{not a twin}) = \frac{88}{90} = \frac{44}{45}$	Simplify.

The probability that a child is not a twin is $\frac{44}{45}$.

■ **TRY THIS**

8. When you roll a number cube, what is P(not 2)?

9. What is the complement of an impossible event?

You can think of probability as a ratio of $\frac{\text{part}}{\text{whole}}$. You can also use
a $\frac{\text{part}}{\text{part}}$ ratio, called *odds*, to describe the likelihood of an event.

odds in favor of an event $= \dfrac{\text{number of } \textit{favorable} \text{ outcomes}}{\text{number of } \textit{unfavorable} \text{ outcomes}}$

odds against an event $= \dfrac{\text{number of } \textit{unfavorable} \text{ outcomes}}{\text{number of } \textit{favorable} \text{ outcomes}}$

REAL-WORLD CONNECTION

■ **EXAMPLE 3**

**The reverse sides of five quarters are shown below. What are the
odds that a quarter chosen at random from these has at least one
human figure on its reverse?**

odds in favor $= \dfrac{3}{2}$ ←3 have a human figure.
←2 do not.

The odds are $\dfrac{3}{2}$, or 3 to 2, in favor.

Reading Math

Reads odds of $\frac{3}{2}$ as "three
to two."

■ **TRY THIS**

10. What are the odds that a quarter chosen at random from the
five shows a horse? What are the odds that it shows no horse?

11. Consider the event of randomly choosing a quarter that shows
the outline of a state.
  a. What are the odds in favor of the event?
  b. What are the odds against the event?

Exercises

Suppose you select a letter at random from the word ARKANSAS.

1. What is the probability of selecting the letter A?

2. What is the probability of *not* selecting the letter A?

3. What is the probability of selecting the letter C?

4. What are the odds in favor of selecting a vowel?

5. a. *Critical Thinking* Can a probability be greater than 1? Explain.
   b. Can a probability be less than 0? Explain.

PRACTICE AND PROBLEM SOLVING

Find each probability for one roll of a number cube.

6. $P(3)$

7. $P(3 \text{ or } 4)$

8. $P(1, 2, \text{ or } 3)$

9. $P(7)$

10. $P(\text{not } 2, 3, \text{ or } 6)$

11. $P(\text{greater than } 2)$

12. $P(\text{less than } 3)$

13. $P(\text{not } 1, 3, 4, \text{ or } 5)$

Find each probability for choosing a letter at random from the word MATHEMATICS.

14. $P(\text{consonant})$

15. $P(M)$

16. $P(\text{not E})$

17. $P(K)$

18. $P(\text{one of the letters that occurs more than once})$

A student is chosen at random from a class of 10 boys and 15 girls. Find the odds in favor of each event.

19. A girl is chosen.

20. A boy is chosen.

21. A boy is not chosen.

22. A girl is not chosen.

23. Neither a girl nor a boy is chosen.

A set of 36 flash cards is numbered from 1 to 36. A card is chosen at random. Find the odds against each selection.

24. an even number

25. a number greater than 20

26. a multiple of 3

27. a multiple of both 2 and 3

28. a multiple of 2 or 3

29. a prime number

30. **TEST PREP** Refer to the spinner. Find the probability of the complement of *stopping on red or yellow*.

   A. $\frac{3}{8}$ B. $\frac{3}{4}$ C. $\frac{1}{4}$ D. Not here

31. *Mathematical Reasoning* The table describes the loose socks in Lola's drawer. One morning Lola pulls a sock from the drawer without looking. It is white. She pulls out another sock without looking. Find the probability that it also is white.

Lola's Socks

Color	Number of Socks
Pink	6
White	4
Green	3
Purple	2

32. *Open-ended* Give an example of an event for which the probability equals 1. Justify your answer.

33. *Number Sense* A number is chosen at random from the whole numbers less than 100. Find the odds in favor of each event.
    a. It has only one digit.   **b.** It has more than one digit.

34. *Error Analysis* Your friend is flipping a coin. He says that heads and tails are equally likely outcomes, so the probability of getting heads is $\frac{50}{50}$. Explain your friend's error.

35. *Writing* Explain how you can use odds to find probability. Include an example.

▶ MIXED REVIEW

The scale of a map is 3 in. : 20 mi. Find the actual distance for each map distance. *(Lesson 6-3)*

36. 6 in.   **37.** 1 in.   **38.** 4.2 in.   **39.** $10\frac{1}{2}$ in.

Write each decimal as a fraction or mixed number in simplest form. *(Lesson 5-2)*

40. 0.25   **41.** $0.\overline{6}$ **42.** 0.8125   **43.** 5.15

44. Students paid $855 for tickets to a dance. Each ticket cost $5. Write and solve an equation to find the number of tickets the students purchased. *(Lesson 2-6)*

✔ CHECKPOINT 1

Lessons 6-1 through 6-4

Write each phrase as a unit rate.

1. 20 mi in 5 h   2. 42 gal in 7 min   3. a fall of 144 ft in 3 s

4. *Geometry* The figures are similar. Find the missing length.

5. A person blinks 112 times in 4 min. At that rate, how many times does the person blink in 1.5 min?

6. **TEST PREP** Suppose you roll a number cube. Which event has the same probability as P(not 1, 2, or 3)?
   A. P(3 or 4)   **B.** P(less than 5)   **C.** P(more than 4)
   D. P(not an odd number)   **E.** Not here

See also Extra Practice section.

6-4 Probability**299**

Fractions, Decimals, and Percents

PART 1 | Writing Percents as Fractions and Decimals

What You'll Learn

1 To write percents as fractions and decimals

2 To write decimals and fractions as percents

. . . And Why

To use percents to report data such as the number of families who own pets

A **percent** is a ratio that compares a number to 100. Therefore, you can write a percent as a fraction with a denominator of 100.

▮ EXAMPLE 1

Write each percent as a fraction or a mixed number.

a. 5%

$\frac{5}{100}$ ← Write as a fraction with a denominator of 100. → $\frac{125}{100}$

$\frac{1}{20}$ ← Simplify. → $\frac{5}{4}$

Write as a mixed number. → $1\frac{1}{4}$

b. 125%

▮ **TRY THIS** Write each percent as a fraction or mixed number in simplest form.

1. 58% **2.** 72% **3.** 144%

Percent means "per hundred." The root *cent* shows up in many other words, such as centimeter, century, and centipede. In money, a cent is $\frac{1}{100}$ of a dollar, or $.01.

To write a percent as a decimal, write the percent as a fraction with a denominator of 100. Then divide to convert the fraction to a decimal.

▮ EXAMPLE 2

Write 9.7% as a decimal.

$9.7\% = \frac{9.7}{100}$ Write as a fraction with a denominator of 100.

$= 009.7$ Divide by moving the decimal point two places to the left. You may need to add one or more zeros.

$= 0.097$

▮ **TRY THIS** Write each percent as a decimal.

4. 16% **5.** 62.5% **6.** 120%

7. *Biology* About 45% of the people in the United States have type O blood. Express this percent as a decimal and as a fraction in simplest form.

To write a decimal as a percent, rewrite the decimal as a fraction with a denominator of 100. Then write the fraction as a percent.

Another way to change a decimal to a percent is to move the decimal point two places to the right and add a percent sign.

■ EXAMPLE 3

Express 0.333 as a percent.

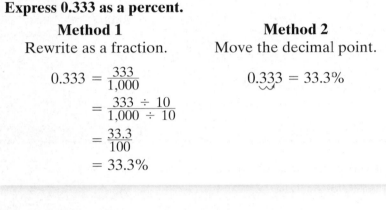

Method 1	**Method 2**
Rewrite as a fraction.	Move the decimal point.

$$0.333 = \frac{333}{1,000}$$

$$= \frac{333 \div 10}{1,000 \div 10}$$

$$= \frac{33.3}{100}$$

$$= 33.3\%$$

$$0.333 = 33.3\%$$

■ **TRY THIS** Write each decimal as a percent.

8. 0.4   **9.** 0.023   **10.** 1.75

To write a fraction as a percent, divide the numerator by the denominator. Then convert the decimal quotient to a percent.

DATA ANALYSIS CONNECTION

■ EXAMPLE 4

Five out of sixteen families in the United States own dogs. What percent of families own dogs?

$\frac{5}{16}$	Write a fraction.
0.3125	Divide the numerator by the denominator.
31.25%	Write as a percent.

About 31% of families own dogs.

■ **TRY THIS**

11. Three out of eleven families in the United States own cats. To the nearest percent, what percent of families own cats?

There are about 55 million dogs and 61 million cats in the United States. What percent of the total number of dogs and cats are cats?

Exercises

▶ CHECK UNDERSTANDING

Write each percent as a fraction in simplest form and as a decimal.

1. 40%　　　　**2.** 28%　　　　**3.** 39%　　　　**4.** 55%

Write each decimal or fraction as a percent.

5. 1.68　　　　**6.** 0.36　　　　**7.** 0.70　　　　**8.** 0.002

9. $\frac{23}{100}$　　　**10.** $\frac{1}{4}$　　　**11.** $\frac{11}{20}$　　　**12.** $\frac{1}{6}$

13. *Critical Thinking* Explain why 0.25 is different from 0.25%.

▶ PRACTICE AND PROBLEM SOLVING

Write each percent as a fraction or mixed number in simplest form.

14. 20%　　　　**15.** 6%　　　　**16.** 45%　　　　**17.** 98%

18. 65%　　　　**19.** 36%　　　　**20.** 220%　　　**21.** 0.4%

Write each percent as a decimal.

22. 1%　　　　**23.** 19.25%　　　**24.** 0.06%　　　**25.** 6.3%

26. 133%　　　**27.** 79.7%　　　**28.** 350.5%　　**29.** $4\frac{1}{2}$%

Write each decimal or fraction as a percent. Round to the nearest tenth of a percent where necessary.

30. 0.33　　　　**31.** 0.85　　　　**32.** 0.06　　　　**33.** 0.0075

34. 1.88　　　　**35.** 2.59　　　　**36.** $\frac{79}{100}$　　　**37.** $\frac{26}{50}$

38. $\frac{7}{20}$　　　**39.** $\frac{2}{9}$　　　**40.** $\frac{5}{6}$　　　**41.** $\frac{111}{100}$

Estimation **About what percent of each flag is red?**

42.　　　　　　**43.**　　　　　　**44.**

Tennessee　　　　Arizona　　　　North Carolina

Probability Find each probability for one roll of a number cube. Write the probability as a percent. Where necessary, round to the nearest tenth of a percent.

45. $P(6)$ **46.** $P(\text{even})$ **47.** $P(1 \text{ or } 2)$ **48.** $P(\text{not } 1)$

Copy and complete the table.

	Fraction	Decimal	Percent
49.	$\frac{4}{5}$	▇	▇
50.	▇	0.10	▇
51.	▇	0.5	▇
52.	$\frac{3}{4}$	▇	▇
53.	▇	▇	67
54.	▇	▇	25

Compare. Use >, <, or = to complete each statement.

55. 0.05% ▇ 50% **56.** $\frac{7}{12}$ ▇ 60% **57.** 0.0325 ▇ 32.5%

58. $\frac{7}{8}$ ▇ 68% **59.** 0.1756 ▇ 176% **60.** $\frac{140}{130}$ ▇ 104%

61. Maps A map has a scale of 0.01%. Express the scale as a fraction.

Critical Thinking For Exercises 62–65, does each sentence make sense? Explain.

62. About 17% of Americans go camping. That means about 83% do not go camping.

63. A student correctly answered 200% of the items on a test.

64. Today a runner ran 150% of the distance she ran yesterday.

65. On a test, a student missed 12 items and correctly answered 96% of all items.

66. Open-ended Use a percent to describe an everyday event. Then write the percent as a fraction and as a decimal.

67. Statistics In the United States, about one person in eight lives in California. Complete: About ▇% of the people in the United States live in California.

Each year, about 45 million Americans go camping. How many do not go camping?

68. **TEST PREP** In a free-throw contest, three players take the same number of shots. Player A makes 30 of 35 shots. Player B makes 0.84 of his shots. Player C makes 87% of her shots. Who wins?
 A. Player A **B.** Player B **C.** Player C **D.** A and C tie.

69. Jeanette answered 32 questions correctly on a 45-question test. The passing grade was 70%. Did Jeanette pass? Justify your answer.

70. *Scale Drawings* A scale drawing has a scale of 1.12. Express the scale as a percent.

71. A crowd filled the 8,000 seats in a stadium. There were 1,400 children and 4,800 men present. Write a ratio and a percent to describe how many seats were filled by each group.
 a. men   **b.** children   **c.** women

72. *Writing* Explain how to write a decimal as a percent. Give examples.

What percent of her shots did Player A make?

▶ MIXED REVIEW

Find each probability for choosing a letter at random from the word PROBABLE. *(Lesson 6-4)*

73. $P(B)$ **74.** $P(\text{vowel})$ **75.** $P(R)$ **76.** $P(\text{not L or R})$

Solve each equation. *(Lesson 3-6)*

77. $0.85x = 39.95$ **78.** $4.8y = -0.84$ **79.** $100 = \dfrac{a}{13.2}$ **80.** $\dfrac{b}{-25} = 1.8$

81. *Choose a Strategy* The average of three test scores is 85. One test score is 90. Another is 72. What is the third?

CHAPTER PROJECT 6

ACTIVITY 3 CALCULATING

Use your results from Activity 2. For each note, calculate the ratio of the string length to 10 in., the string length for the note *say*. Put your results in a table like the one at the right.

Note	String Length (in.)	Ratio to *say*'s Length
can	■	$\dfrac{■}{10}$
you	■	$\dfrac{■}{10}$
see	■	$\dfrac{■}{10}$

Proportions and Percents

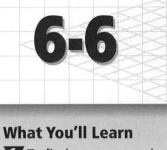
PART 1 **Finding Part of a Whole**

PART 1 **Finding Part of a Whole**

You can solve a percent problem by writing and solving a proportion.

A model can help you write a proportion. This model shows that 30 is 75% of 40.

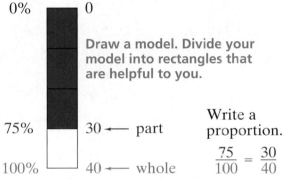

Draw a model. Divide your model into rectangles that are helpful to you.

Write a proportion.

$$\frac{75}{100} = \frac{30}{40}$$

EXAMPLE 1

Find 65% of 245.

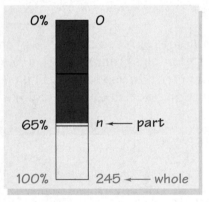

$\dfrac{65}{100} = \dfrac{n}{245}$ Write a proportion.

$65(245) = 100n$ Write cross products.

$\dfrac{65(245)}{100} = \dfrac{100n}{100}$ Divide each side by 100.

$159.25 = n$ Simplify.

65% of 245 is 159.25.

■ **TRY THIS** Draw a model and write a proportion. Then solve.

1. 25% of 124 is ■.   **2.** 43% of 230 is ■.   **3.** 12.5% of 80 is ■.

■ EXAMPLE 2

What percent of 60 is 52? Round to the nearest tenth of a percent.

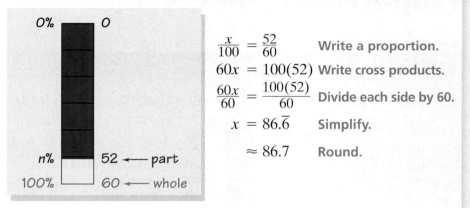

$\dfrac{x}{100} = \dfrac{52}{60}$ Write a proportion.

$60x = 100(52)$ Write cross products.

$\dfrac{60x}{60} = \dfrac{100(52)}{60}$ Divide each side by 60.

$x = 86.\overline{6}$ Simplify.

≈ 86.7 Round.

52 is approximately 86.7% of 60.

■ **TRY THIS**   Round to the nearest tenth of a percent.

4. What percent of 250 is 138?   **5.** 14 is what percent of 15?

PART 2   **Finding a Whole Amount**

Sometimes you know the percent that a part represents, and you want to find the whole amount. For example, your class fundraising committee might announce, "We've collected $207 so far, which is 46% of our goal!" You can use a proportion to calculate the goal.

■ EXAMPLE 3

207 is 46% of what number?

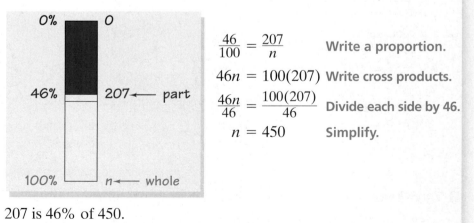

$\dfrac{46}{100} = \dfrac{207}{n}$ Write a proportion.

$46n = 100(207)$ Write cross products.

$\dfrac{46n}{46} = \dfrac{100(207)}{46}$ Divide each side by 46.

$n = 450$ Simplify.

207 is 46% of 450.

■ TRY THIS Round to the nearest tenth.

6. 19 is 75% of what number? **7.** 310 is 99% of what number?

■ EXAMPLE 4

In 1998, the number of drive-in movie screens in the United States was only about 21% of the number in 1980. About how many drive-in screens were there in 1980?

Drive-In Movies

Year	Number of Screens
1980	▪
1990	915
1998	748

SOURCE: Motion Picture Association of America

$\dfrac{21}{100} = \dfrac{748}{n}$ Write a proportion.

$21n = 100(748)$ Write cross products.

$\dfrac{21n}{21} = \dfrac{100(748)}{21}$ Divide each side by 21.

$n \approx 3,562$ Round.

There were about 3,562 screens in 1980.

Check Is the answer reasonable? The original problem says that the number of screens in 1998 was about 21% of those in 1980. Check by estimating:
21% of 3,562 ≈ 0.2 × 3,600 = 720, which is close to 748, the number for 1998. So the answer is reasonable.

■ TRY THIS

8. Refer to the table in Example 4. In 1990, the number of drive-in movie screens was about 32.4% of the number in 1985. Find the number of drive-in screens in 1985.

The table below summarizes how to use proportions to solve percent problems.

Percents and Proportions		
Finding the Percent	**Finding the Part**	**Finding the Whole**
What percent of 40 is 6?	What number is 15% of 40?	6 is 15% of what number?
$\dfrac{n}{100} = \dfrac{6}{40}$ ← part ← whole	$\dfrac{15}{100} = \dfrac{n}{40}$ ← part ← whole	$\dfrac{15}{100} = \dfrac{6}{n}$ ← part ← whole

Exercises

> ## CHECK UNDERSTANDING

Write a proportion. Then solve. Where necessary, round to the nearest tenth or tenth of a percent.

1. Find 80% of 20.
2. Find 300% of 50.
3. What percent of 40 is 30?
4. What percent of 20 is 40?
5. What is 40% of 60?
6. What is 53% of 70?
7. 25% of what number is 8?
8. 18% of ■ is 14.4.
9. 250% of t is 50. What is t?

10. *Mathematical Reasoning* Do $a\%$ of b and $b\%$ of a represent the same amount? Justify your answer.

> ## PRACTICE AND PROBLEM SOLVING

Write and solve a proportion.

11.   12.   13.

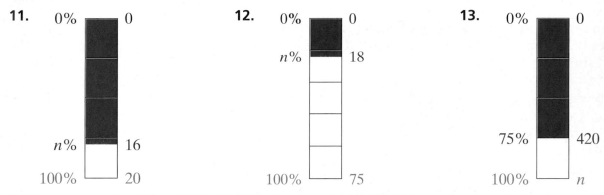

Write a proportion. Then solve. Where necessary, round to the nearest tenth or tenth of a percent.

14. What percent of 25 is 13?
15. Find 18% of 150.
16. Find 116% of 75.
17. Find 60% of 15.
18. 75 is ■ percent of 250.
19. Find 92% of 625.
20. Find 53% of 76,550.
21. What percent of 92 is 17?
22. Find 9.3% of 47.89.
23. Find 98% of 6.1.
24. Find $33\frac{1}{3}\%$ of 54.
25. 14 is 35% of ■.
26. 1 is 2% of what number?
27. 35% of ■ is 52.5.
28. 49% of ■ is 31.85.
29. 2.5% of ■ is 912.5.
30. $12\frac{1}{2}\%$ of ■ is 6.
31. 116% of a is 125. What is a?

32. A bicycle cost $250 last year. The same bike costs $200 this year. What percent of last year's cost is this year's cost?

33. **Statistics** The population of Alaska was about 129,000 in 1950. The population was about 614,000 in 1998. The 1950 population was about what percent of the 1998 population?

34. **Sales Tax** The table shows sales tax rates for different states.
    a. For each state, find the amount of sales tax on a $15,000 car.
    b. For each state, find the car's total cost.

State	Sales Tax Rate
Georgia	7%
Kansas	4.9%
Pennsylvania	6%
South Carolina	5%

35. **Writing** At Pineapples, all books and posters are marked 30% off. At Avocados, the same items are marked $\frac{1}{3}$ off. Which store offers the greater discount rate? Explain.

36. A student pole-vaulted 5 ft yesterday. Today she vaulted 20% higher. How high was her vault today?

37. **TEST PREP** Which proportion would you use to solve *42 is 60% of n?*
    A. $\frac{60}{100} = \frac{42}{n}$ B. $\frac{42}{100} = \frac{60}{n}$ C. $\frac{n}{100} = \frac{60}{42}$ D. $\frac{60}{100} = \frac{n}{42}$

38. **Profit** You invested some money and made a profit of $55. Your profit was 11% of your investment. How much did you invest?

39. Nineteen members, or 38%, of the ski club are going on a ski trip. Find the total number of members in the club.

40. **Error Analysis** Your class has 26 students, which represents 5% of your school's enrollment. Your friend uses the proportion $\frac{5}{100} = \frac{n}{26}$ to find the number of students in your school. Explain your friend's error.

41. **Open-ended** Write and solve a word problem involving percents.

▶ MIXED REVIEW

Write each number as a percent. (*Lesson 6-5*)

42. 0.08   43. 0.523   44. $\frac{7}{12}$ 45. 4.56

Order from least to greatest. (*Lesson 4-9*)

46. $10^3, 10^{-2}, 10^{-1}, 10^0$ 47. $2.3 \times 10^4, 2.03 \times 10^5, 2.03 \times 10^4, 2.4 \times 10^3$

48. Peter has four cousins. Paul has *c* cousins fewer than Peter. Write an expression for the number of Paul's cousins. (*Lesson 1-1*)

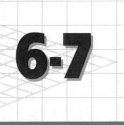

6-7

Percents and Equations

What You'll Learn

1 To write and solve percent equations

2 To use equations in solving percent problems

... And Why

To solve problems involving surveys and earnings from commissions

PART 1 Writing and Solving Percent Equations

You can solve a percent problem by writing and solving an equation. When you use a percent in an equation, write it as a decimal.

Percent Equations		
Finding the Percent	**Finding the Part**	**Finding the Whole**
What percent of 40 is 6?	What is 15% of 40?	6 is 15% of what?
$n \quad\quad \cdot 40 = 6$	$n = 0.15 \cdot 40$	$6 = 0.15 \cdot \quad n$

■ EXAMPLE 1

What is 85% of 62?

$n = 0.85 \cdot 62$ Write an equation. Write the percent as a decimal.

$n = 52.7$ Simplify.

85% of 62 is 52.7.

You can write and solve an equation to find a percent greater than 100%.

■ EXAMPLE 2

What percent of 48 is 54?

$n \cdot 48 = 54$ Write an equation.

$\dfrac{48n}{48} = \dfrac{54}{48}$ Divide each side by 48.

$n = 1.125$ Simplify.

$= 112.5\%$ Change the decimal to a percent.

54 is 112.5% of 48.

■ TRY THIS   Write and solve an equation.

1. What is 45.5% of 20?

2. 380 is 125% of what number?

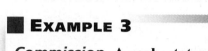
Some sales jobs pay an amount based on how much you sell. This amount is called a **commission.**

REAL-WORLD CONNECTION

■ EXAMPLE 3

Commission **A real estate agent makes a 4.5% commission on property she sells. How much does she make on the sale of a house for $132,500?**

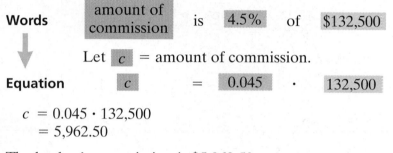

Words   amount of commission   is   4.5%   of $132,500

Let c = amount of commission.

Equation c =   0.045   ·   132,500

$$c = 0.045 \cdot 132{,}500$$
$$= 5{,}962.50$$

The broker's commission is $5,962.50.

■ TRY THIS

3. *Royalties* A singer receives a 5% royalty on each CD sale. To the nearest cent, find his royalty for a CD that sells for $16.99.

DATA ANALYSIS CONNECTION

■ EXAMPLE 4

The graph shows the results of a survey. There were 1,023 people who answered yes. How many people were surveyed?

Words   1,023   is   93%   of   number surveyed

Let n = number surveyed.

Equation   1,023   =   0.93   · n

$$0.93n = 1{,}023$$
$$\frac{0.93n}{0.93} = \frac{1{,}023}{.93}$$
$$n = 1{,}100$$

1,100 people were surveyed.

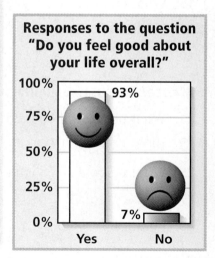

Responses to the question "Do you feel good about your life overall?"

■ TRY THIS

4. In a survey, 922 people, or about 68.6%, preferred smooth peanut butter to chunky. How many people were surveyed?

Exercises

Write and solve an equation.

1. Find 30% of 30.

2. What percent of 40 is 25?

3. 120 is 15% of what number?

4. Find 150% of 90.

5. *Commission* A real estate agent received a $7,000 commission for a sale of $175,000. Find the percent of commission.

6. *Critical Thinking* Describe a situation in which you would use a percent greater than 100%.

PRACTICE AND PROBLEM SOLVING

Write and solve an equation. Where necessary, round to the nearest tenth or tenth of a percent.

7. What percent of 20 is 11?

8. Find 56% of 75.

9. 135% of t is 63. What is t?

10. What percent of 25 is 17?

11. Find 500% of 12.

12. 85% of z is 106,250. What is z?

13. What percent of 4 is 9?

14. Find 5.5% of 44.

15. What percent of 150 is 96?

16. What percent of 45 is 24?

17. Find 15% of 150.

18. What percent of 8 is 20?

19. Find 225% of 3.6.

20. 3.5% of d is 0.105. What is d?

Mental Math **Use mental math.**

21. What percent of 60 is 30?

22. Find 20% of 20.

23. 100% of t is 100. What is t?

24. What percent of 3 is 30?

25. What percent of 55 is 11?

26. Find 5% of 10.

27. Find 15% of 12.

28. What percent of 70 is 140?

29. Find 150% of 200.

30. 50% of g is 24. What is g?

Estimation **For each restaurant bill, estimate a 15% tip for the server.**

31. $3.52

32. $9.95

33. $20.14

34. $13.88

35. In 1985, daily newspaper circulation in the United States was about 63 million. In 1995, it was about 58 million. About what percent of the 1985 circulation was the 1995 circulation?

36. *Commission* A salesperson receives 5.4% commission. On one sale, she received $6.48. What was the amount of the sale?

Use the table at the right for Exercises 37–39.

United States Households with VCRs

Year	Households (millions)
1980	1
1985	18
1990	63
1995	■

SOURCE: *Statistical Abstract of the United States*

37. a. The number of households with VCRs in 1985 was about 23.4% of the number with VCRs in 1995. About how many households had VCRs in 1995?
b. The number of households with VCRs in 1991 was about 106% of the number with VCRs in 1990. About how many households had VCRs in 1991?

38. **TEST PREP** There were about 92 million households in the United States in 1990. About what percent of them had VCRs?
A. 68%　　**B.** 146%　　**C.** 92%　　**D.** 63%

39. *Critical Thinking* Is each statement true or false? Explain.
a. The number of households with VCRs in 1985 was less than 10% of the number of households with VCRs in 1990.
b. The number of households with VCRs in 1985 was more than 1,000% of the number in 1980.

40. *Writing* Explain why someone taking a survey might be more interested in the percent than in the actual number of people who responded in each category.

41. Polly got a 20% discount on a computer that regularly cost x dollars. She paid sales tax of 5%. Later she sold the computer for 70% of what she paid for it. Write an expression for the amount Polly received for the computer.

Journal

Which approach do you prefer to use in solving percent problems—the approach you learned in this lesson, or the one you learned in Lesson 6-6? Explain.

▶ MIXED REVIEW

Write a proportion. Then solve. *(Lesson 6-6)*

42. ■% of 360 is 45.　　**43.** 35% of 60 is ■.　　**44.** 45 is 1.5% of ■.

Simplify each expression. *(Lesson 4-7)*

45. $10^2 \cdot 10^4$　　**46.** $9y^4 \cdot y^5$　　**47.** $(x^3)^7$

48. *Choose a Strategy* Ernest started writing a story on a Friday. He worked on the story for $\frac{1}{2}$ h each day. He took 7 h to finish it. On what day did Ernest finish his story?

6-8

Percent of Change

What You'll Learn

▼**1** To find percent of increase

▼**2** To find percent of decrease

...And Why

To use percent of change in real-world applications, such as environmental management

Investigate

·············· **EXPLORING PERCENT OF CHANGE** ··············

1. Find the change in population from 1980 to 1990 for each state.

2. Which state had the greater change in population?

Populations of Two States

State	1980	1990
California	23,668,000	29,786,000
Nevada	800,000	1,202,000

3. Write the ratio $\frac{\text{change in population}}{\text{1980 population}}$ for each state. Then write each ratio as a percent.

4. Compare the two percents. Which state had the greater population change in terms of percent?

PART 1 ▶ **Finding Percent of Increase**

The percent a quantity increases or decreases from its original amount is the **percent of change.**

$$\text{percent of change} = \frac{\text{amount of change}}{\text{original amount}}$$

■ EXAMPLE 1

Find the percent of increase from 4 to 7.5.

amount of increase $= 7.5 - 4 = 3.5$

percent of increase $= \dfrac{\text{amount of increase}}{\text{original amount}}$

$= \dfrac{3.5}{4}$

$= 0.875 = 87.5\%$

The percent of increase from 4 to 7.5 is 87.5%.

■ **TRY THIS** Find each percent of increase.

5. from 100 to 114   6. from 2.0 to 3.2   7. from 4,000 to 8,500

■ EXAMPLE 2

Environmental Management The annual production of municipal solid waste in the United States has more than doubled since 1960. Find the percent of increase from 1960 to 1990.

amount of increase $= 205 - 88 = 117$

$\text{percent of increase} = \dfrac{\text{amount of increase}}{\text{original amount}}$

$= \dfrac{117}{88}$

$= 1.329\overline{54} \approx 133\%$

The percent of increase from 1960 to 1990 was about 133%.

Municipal Solid Waste

88 million tons — 1960
121 million tons — 1970
132 million tons — 1980
205 million tons — 1990
222* million tons — 2000

SOURCE: Environmental Protection Agency   *projected

■ TRY THIS

8. *Environmental Management* Find the percent of increase in solid waste production from 1970 to 1980. Round to the nearest percent.

PART
2 Finding Percent of Decrease

You can also find percent of decrease.

■ EXAMPLE 3

Find the percent of decrease from 1,500 to 1,416.

amount of decrease $= 1,500 - 1,416 = 84$

$\text{percent of decrease} = \dfrac{\text{amount of decrease}}{\text{original amount}}$

$= \dfrac{84}{1,500}$

$= 0.056 = 5.6\%$

■ **TRY THIS** Find each percent of decrease. Where necessary, round to the nearest tenth of a percent.

9. from 9.6 to 4.8   10. from 202 to 192   11. from 854.5 to 60.6

12. A computer that cost $1,099 last year costs $999 this year. Find the percent of decrease to the nearest percent.

Exercises

▶ CHECK UNDERSTANDING

Find each percent of change. Tell whether the change is an increase or a decrease.

1. from 30 to 39

2. from 55 to 176

3. from 48 to 60

4. from 60 to 48

5. from 96 to 78

6. from 240 to 90

7. *Error Analysis* Eva's first step in finding the percent of change from 7 to 8 was to write $\frac{8-7}{8} = \frac{1}{8}$. Explain Eva's error.

▶ PRACTICE AND PROBLEM SOLVING

Find each percent of change. Round to the nearest tenth of a percent. Tell whether the change is an increase or a decrease.

8. from 50 to 66

9. from 80 to 95

10. from 32 to 76

11. from 45 to 105

12. from 38 to 95

13. from 27 to 72

14. from 90 to 75

15. from 64 to 24

16. from 120 to 95

17. from 280 to 126

18. from 111 to 74

19. from 180 to 54

Choose **Use mental math or pencil and paper to find each percent of change. Round to the nearest tenth of a percent. Tell whether the change is an increase or a decrease.**

20. from 25 to 30

21. from 40 to 45

22. from 50 to 45

23. from 87 to 108

24. from 59 to 127

25. from 77 to 13

26. from 132 to 46.2

27. from 1,800 to 1,000

28. from 100 to 101.1

29. *Statistics* In the United States in the 20th century, average life expectancy increased from about 47 years to about 77 years. Find the percent of increase to the nearest percent.

30. **TEST PREP** Percent of sales tax is an example of percent of increase. The retail price of an item is $5.99. With sales tax, the total cost of the item is $6.35. Find the percent of sales tax.
 A. 3%   **B.** 4%   **C.** 5%   **D.** 6%

31. *Economics* The average cost of a gallon of gasoline was $1.29 in 1997 and $1.12 in 1998. Find the percent of decrease to the nearest percent.

32. **Zoology** Refer to the photo. Find the percent of increase for each given period. Round to the nearest percent.
    a. After one month, Ganesh weighed 300 lb.
    b. After one year, Ganesh weighed 1,061 lb.

Ganesh was the first baby elephant born at the Cincinnati Zoo. At birth, he weighed 213 lb.

33. The population of Growtown increased from 10,000 to 13,000 in one year. In the same year, the population of Slowtown decreased from 30,000 to 24,000.
    a. Find each town's percent of increase or decrease in population.
    b. If each town maintains the same rate of change, within how many years will the population of Growtown exceed that of Slowtown?

34. a. **Mathematical Reasoning** 100 is increased by 10%. The result is decreased by 10%. Is the final result 100? Explain.
    b. Compare the final result in part (a) to 100, the original number. Find the percent of change.

▶ **MIXED REVIEW**

Evaluate each expression. (*Lesson 4-2*)

35. $3x^2$ for $x = -5$

36. $[(3 + 12)(8 \div 2)]^2$

37. $(7 + 4y)^2$ for $y = -2$

Find each sum or difference. (*Lesson 5-3*)

38. $5\frac{3}{4} - 2\frac{5}{8}$

39. $-4\frac{1}{3} + 2\frac{1}{2}$

40. $-6\frac{1}{3} - 6\frac{1}{3}$

41. **Astronomy** The Space Surveillance Center in Colorado tracks about 8,500 objects in orbit around Earth. All but about 500 objects are junk from past space missions. What percent are junk? Round to the nearest percent. (*Lesson 6-7*)

CHAPTER PROJECT 6 **ACTIVITY 4 CALCULATING**

$\mathcal{S}$uppose you want to play your notes on a real cello. A cello string is about 24 in. long from the bridge to the nut. Using a full string length for *say*, how far from the bridge should you press down the string to play the notes for *can, you,* and *see*?

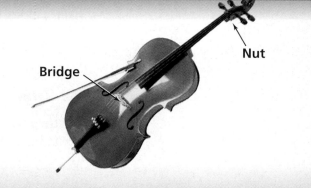

Nut

Bridge

6-9

Markup and Discount

What You'll Learn

▼ **1** To find markups

▼ **2** To find discounts

...And Why

To understand how markups and discounts are used in pricing consumer products

PART 1 Finding Markups

To make a profit, stores charge more for merchandise than they pay for it. The amount of increase is called the **markup.** The percent of increase is the *percent of markup*.

REAL-WORLD CONNECTION

■ EXAMPLE 1

A music store's percent of markup is 67%. A CD costs the store $10.15. Find the markup.

$$\text{markup} = \text{percent of markup} \cdot \text{store's cost}$$
$$= 0.67 \cdot 10.15$$
$$\approx 6.80 \quad \textbf{Simplify. Round to the nearest cent.}$$

The markup is $6.80.

■ TRY THIS

1. A clothing store pays $56 for a jacket. The store's percent of markup is 75%. Find the markup for the jacket.

The store's cost plus the markup equals the *selling price*.

REAL-WORLD CONNECTION

■ EXAMPLE 2

Retailing **A computer store pays $6 for a computer mouse. The percent of markup is 75%. Find the mouse's selling price.**

$$0.75 \cdot 6 = 4.50 \qquad \textbf{Multiply to find the markup.}$$
$$6.00 + 4.50 = 10.50 \quad \textbf{store's cost + markup = selling price}$$

The selling price is $10.50.

■ TRY THIS

2. A store pays $5 for a baseball cap. The percent of markup is 70%. Find the selling price of the cap.

When an item goes on sale, the amount of the price decrease is called the **discount.** The percent of decrease is the *percent of discount.* The original price minus the discount is the *sale price.*

Here are two ways to use percent of discount to find a sale price.

■ Different Ways to Solve a Problem

A video game that regularly sells for $39.95 is on sale for 20% off. What is the sale price?

Reading Math

20% off means a discount of 20%.

Method 1

Find the discount. Then find the sale price.

discount = percent of discount · original price
= 0.20 · 39.95
= 7.99
sale price = original price − discount
= 39.95 − 7.99
= 31.96

The sale price is $31.96.

Method 2

Find the sale price directly. The sale price equals 100% of the original price minus 20% of the original price.

sale price = (100% − 20%) · original price
= 80% · original price
= 0.80(39.95)
= 31.96

The sale price is $31.96.

Choose a Method

1. Which method do you prefer? Explain.

2. Find the sale price if the percent of discount is 25%. Round to the nearest cent.

Exercises

Find each markup.

1. cost: $1.50
   percent of markup: 70%

2. cost: $38
   percent of markup: 58%

3. cost: $111.00
   percent of markup: 50%

Find each discount.

4. regular price: $100
   percent of discount: 27%

5. regular price: $24.50
   percent of discount: 20%

6. regular price: $700
   percent of discount: 30%

PRACTICE AND PROBLEM SOLVING

Find each selling price. Round to the nearest cent where necessary.

7. cost: $6
   percent of markup: 75%

8. cost: $2.66
   percent of markup: 50%

9. cost: $149.99
   percent of markup: 100%

Find each sale price. Round to the nearest cent where necessary.

10. regular price: $180
    percent of discount: 40%

11. regular price: $14.99
    percent of discount: 15%

12. regular price: $180
    percent of discount: 75%

13. A beach store pays $11.40 for each beach umbrella. The store's percent of markup is 75%. Find the markup.

14. A record store buys a CD for $9.99 and marks it up by 60%. Find the markup and the selling price.

15. A pair of shoes regularly sells for $49 at the shop in the photo.
    a. Find the discount.
    b. Find the sale price.

16. Software that regularly sells for $60 is on sale for 15% off. Find the sale price.

17. **Mathematical Reasoning** A store buys an item for $x and sells it for $y.
    a. Write an expression for the markup.
    b. Write an expression for the percent of markup.

18. **Choose a Method** An $11 shirt is on sale for 10% off.
    a. Describe two different methods of finding the sale price.
    b. Use one of the methods to calculate the sale price.

19. Store A is selling a video for 20% off the store's regular price of \$25.95. Store B is selling the same video for 30% off the store's regular price of \$29.50. Which store's sale price is lower? How much lower is it?

20. ***Estimation*** Suppose you want to buy the three books shown in the table. The bookstore is having a $\frac{1}{4}$-off sale. Your state charges sales tax of 5% of an item's final price. You have \$20. Do you have enough money? Justify your answer.

Title	Regular Price
Variable Blues	\$6.95
Math Moments	\$9.95
City of Angles	\$10.95

21. ***Writing*** Identical sweaters are on sale in two different stores. In the first store, the sale price is 30% off the regular price of \$25. In the second store, the sale price is 40% off the regular price of \$30. Which sweater is the better buy? Explain.

MIXED REVIEW

Find each percent of decrease. Round to the nearest tenth of a percent. ***(Lesson 6-8)***

22. from 90 to 70
23. from 44.4 to 14.8
24. from 1,750 to 1,125

Draw a coordinate plane. Graph each point. ***(Lesson 1-10)***

25. $A(1, 0)$
26. $B(-2, 3)$
27. $C(-1, 2)$

28. ***Recipes*** A bread recipe calls for $6\frac{1}{2}$ cups of flour. You have $4\frac{3}{4}$ cups. How much more flour do you need? ***(Lesson 5-3)***

CHECKPOINT 2

Lessons 6-5 through 6-9

Compare. Use >, <, or = to complete each statement.

1. $\frac{14}{25}$ ■ 56%
2. 1.1% ■ 0.11
3. $\frac{3}{11}$ ■ 27%

Write and solve an equation.

4. Find 33% of 120.
5. Find 125% of 42.
6. What percent of 5.6 is 1.4?
7. 15% of q is 9.75. What is q?
8. What percent of 500 is 1,375?
9. 80% of w is 120. What is w?

10. A car originally priced at \$12,000 is sold at a 20% discount. Find the sale price.

11. ***Open-ended*** Choose an item you buy that has changed in price. Give the original and new prices. Find the percent of change.

See also Extra Practice section.

Multiple Choice

Choose the best answer.

1. Suppose you pick one of the chips below at random. What is the probability of picking an even-numbered chip?

   A. $\frac{7}{10}$ **B.** $\frac{7}{12}$ **C.** $\frac{1}{2}$ **D.** $\frac{5}{12}$

2. Only 12% of an iceberg's mass is above water. If the mass above water is 9,000,000 kg, what is the mass of the entire iceberg?
   F. 108,000 kg
   G. 1,080,000 kg
   H. 75,000,000 kg
   J. 120,000,000 kg

3. The scale drawing below is for a billboard 21 ft wide and 10.5 ft high. Measure the drawing. What is its scale?

   FALL FOLIAGE
   Peaks October 14th!

   A. 1 in. : 21 ft   **B.** 1.5 in. : 21 ft
   C. 2 ft : 1 in.   **D.** 1 in. : 10.5 ft

4. A 50-lb bag of Glossy Coat Horse Feed costs $23.50. A 25-lb bag costs $15.50. How much money per pound would you save by buying the bag with the lower unit price?
   F. $.47   **G.** $.62
   H. $.32   **J.** $.15

5. Diego paid $1.25 in sales tax for an item he purchased. The sales tax rate was 5%. What was the price of the item before tax?
   A. $25.00   **B.** $26.25
   C. $2.50   **D.** $6.25

6. Last week $\frac{9}{10}$ of the students in a class had perfect attendance. Three students were absent. How many students had perfect attendance?
   F. 30   **G.** 27   **H.** 18   **J.** 33

7. A $59.50 coat is on sale for $36.50. Find the percent of discount.
   A. about 39%
   B. $23.00
   C. more than half off
   D. about 63%

8. Karla and her dad were nailing up plywood. They started at 10:00. Karla drove 30 nails in 10 min, the time it took her dad to drive 50 nails. At that rate, when did they finish driving 392 nails?
   F. 10:30   **G.** 10:39
   H. 10:45   **J.** 10:49

Free Response

For each exercise, show all your work.

9. Chan's team won 70% of the 20 games it played. Latisha's team played 15 games and won 80% of them. Whose team won the greater number of games? Explain.

10. Twenty-five students voted for Tim, 25% voted for Gina, $\frac{2}{5}$ voted for Lee, and the remaining 45 students voted for Ronnie. Who won? Explain, including the number of votes each person received.

Copy and complete the table.

	Sale	Percent of Commission	Amount of Commission
11.	$270.00	8%	■
12.	$566.50	10%	■
13.	■	12%	$97.86
14.	■	15%	$410.25
15.	$12,348.00	■	$2,346.12

Make a Table

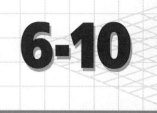

Math Strategies in Action

Have you ever watched a baseball game at a field that doesn't have a scoreboard? It's hard to keep track of the score!

A scoreboard is a type of table. You can use tables to organize information. Tables are particularly helpful in solving problems that require several steps.

Problem Solving Strategies

Account for All
  Possibilities

Draw a Diagram

Look for a Pattern

Make a Model

Make a Table

Simplify a Problem

Simulate a Problem

Solve by Graphing

Try, Test, Revise

Use Multiple Strategies

Work Backward

Write an Equation

Write a Proportion

■ SAMPLE PROBLEM

Population Prediction At the beginning of the year 2000, the population of the United States was about 273.5 million. The rate of population growth was about 0.85% per year. If that rate continues, what will the population be at the beginning of 2010?

 Read

Read the problem carefully.

1. What information are you asked to find?

2. What information will you need to use to solve the problem?

Plan

Decide on a strategy. You can use the percent of increase to predict the population increase for each year from 2000 to 2010. You can make a table to organize your predictions for each year.

3. How can you find the increase in population from the beginning of 2000 to the end of that year?

4. How can you find the population at the beginning of 2001?

5. The percent of increase is the same each year. Does that mean that the increase in population also will be the same each year? Explain your reasoning.

 **Solve**

Copy and complete the table below.

6. Find the numbers for Column 4 by multiplying the numbers in Columns 2 and 3. Round to the nearest tenth of a million.

7. Find the numbers for Column 5 by adding the numbers in Columns 2 and 4.

1	2	3	4	5
Year	Population at Beginning of Year (millions)	Rate of Increase (0.85%)	Increase in Population (millions)	Population at End of Year (millions)
2000	273.5	0.0085	2.3	275.8
2001	275.8	0.0085	2.3	278.1
2002	278.1	0.0085	2.4	280.5
2003	280.5	0.0085	2.4	282.9
2004	282.9	0.0085	2.4	285.3
2005	285.3	0.0085	2.4	287.7
2006	287.7	0.0085	2.4	290.1
2007	290.1	0.0085	■	■
2008	■	0.0085	■	■
2009	■	0.0085	■	■
2010	■			

8. Sometimes the number in Column 4 changes from one year to the next, and sometimes it does not change. Explain.

9. What is your prediction for population at the beginning of 2010?

 **Look Back**

10. Your friend says that she knows a quicker way to find the answer. Simply multiply 273.5 · 0.0085 · 10 to find the increase for the ten-year period 2000 to 2010. Do you agree with your friend's approach? Explain your reasoning.

11. Suppose the annual percent of increase in population is 0.9%. At that rate, what will the population be at the beginning of 2010?

Exercises

CHECK UNDERSTANDING

Make a table to solve each problem.

1. **Biology** A microbe population increases 100% every 10 min. If you start with 1 microbe, how many will you have at the end of 1 h?

2. Cher has forgotten the combination to her locker. She knows it consists of three numbers—3, 5, and 9—but she can't remember the order. She decides to try every possible order until she gets the right one. How many possible orders are there?

3. In how many ways can you make 40¢ in change without using pennies?

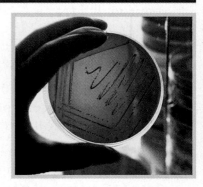

Scientists grow microbe cultures on agar gel in petri dishes.

PRACTICE AND PROBLEM SOLVING

Make a table to solve each problem.

4. **Population** The population of a town increases at the rate of 1% each year. Today the town's population is 8,500. What will the population be in five years? Round to the nearest person.

5. Paco has four pairs of jeans and four T-shirts. How many outfits of a T-shirt and a pair of jeans can Paco make?

6. **Related Rates** A train leaves a station at noon and averages 45 mi/h. Another train leaves the same station an hour after the first and averages 60 mi/h in the same direction. At what time will the second train catch up with the first? How far from the station will the trains be?

7. A family went to the movies. Tickets cost $4 for each child and $6 for each adult. The total admission charge for the family was $26. List all the possible numbers of adults and children in the family.

Use any strategy to solve each problem.

8. A class sold tickets for a pancake breakfast. One hundred twenty people came. They accounted for 60% of the tickets sold. How many tickets were sold?

9. **Geometry** The length of a rectangle is twice the width. The perimeter of the rectangle is 42 cm. Find the length and width.

10. **Number Sense** The difference of two numbers is 18. The sum of the two numbers is 34. What are the two numbers?

11. **Capacity** You fill a container $\frac{3}{4}$ full of water. The amount of water now in the container is 6 quarts. How much can the container hold?

12. **Number Sense** A number n is multiplied by $\frac{5}{8}$. The product is subtracted from $\frac{2}{3}$. The result is $\frac{7}{12}$. What is n?

13. At a local high school, 60% of the students are girls. Of these girls, 75% own cassette players. What percent of all students are girls who do *not* own cassette players?

14. **Water Resources** Water for irrigation is measured in *acre-feet*. One acre-foot is the volume of water that would cover one acre of land to a depth of one foot. How many acre-feet of water would it take to cover 600 acres to a depth of one inch?

Journal

Describe how you could use indirect measurement to estimate the height of your school.

▶ MIXED REVIEW

Find each sale price. *(Lesson 6-9)*

15. regular price: $5
    percent of discount: 34%

16. regular price: $39
    percent of discount: 30%

17. regular price: $159.95
    percent of discount: 20%

Write in simplest form. *(Lesson 4-4)*

18. $\frac{16}{36}$

19. $\frac{10x}{65x}$

20. $\frac{8ab}{2bc}$

21. **Probability** What is the probability that a digit selected at random from the number 364,892 is a multiple of 3? *(Lesson 6-4)*

Math at Work
Caterer

A caterer provides food for parties, weddings, and other events. Caterers plan the menu, buy the ingredients, and cook the food. Often they provide seating and music. For each event, a caterer determines the cost per guest.

The catering business requires a thorough knowledge of ratios, proportions, and percents.

For more information about careers in catering, visit the Prentice Hall Web site.
www.phschool.com

STRING BAND

Make a Musical Instrument The Project Activities on pages 288, 293, 304, and 317 will help you complete your project. Here is a checklist to help you gather the different parts.

- ✔ your stringed instrument
- ✔ measurements of string lengths for different notes
- ✔ table of ratios of string lengths
- ✔ calculations of locations of notes on a cello

Make a drawing of the stringed instrument you constructed. On the drawing, label the locations of the points that correspond to the notes for *can, you,* and *see.* Make and label a similar drawing of a cello.

Reflect and Revise

Ask a friend to review your drawings and your calculations. Are they accurate? Are they clearly drawn and labeled? If necessary, make changes to improve your drawings.

Web Extension

Visit Prentice Hall's Web site. You'll find some interesting links and ideas related to musical instruments. You'll also be able to share information about your project.
www.phschool.com

6 Wrap Up

Key Terms

commission (p. 311)
complement (p. 296)
cross products (p. 284)
discount (p. 319)
event (p. 295)

indirect measurement
  (p. 289)
markup (p. 318)
odds (p. 297)
outcome (p. 295)

percent (p. 300)
percent of
  change (p. 314)
probability (p. 295)
proportion (p. 284)

rate (p. 279)
ratio (p. 278)
scale drawing (p. 290)
similar figures (p. 289)
unit rate (p. 279)

Graphic Organizer

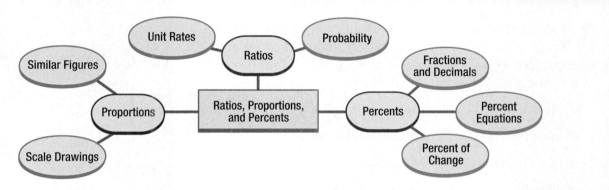

Ratios and Unit Rates   6-1

Summary A **ratio** is a comparison of two quantities by division. A **rate** is a ratio
that compares quantities in different units. A **unit rate** is a rate that
has a denominator of 1.

Write each ratio as a fraction in simplest form.

1. $9 : 24$ **2.** $20 : 35$ **3.** $15 : 20$ **4.** $100 : 130$

Write each ratio as a unit rate.

5. 150 mi in 3 h   **6.** 270 words in 3 min   **7.** $9.45 for 5 lb

Proportions   6-2

Summary A **proportion** is an equality of ratios. To solve a proportion, write the
cross products, and then solve.

Solve. Round to the nearest tenth where necessary.

8. $\frac{5}{6} = \frac{n}{42}$ **9.** $\frac{53}{2} = \frac{18}{x}$ **10.** $\frac{15}{a} = \frac{30}{98}$ **11.** $\frac{m}{150} = \frac{21}{25}$

■ Similar Figures and Scale Drawings 6-3

Summary **Similar figures** have the same shape, but not necessarily the same size. In similar figures, the corresponding angles have equal measures and the corresponding sides are proportional.

A **scale drawing** is an enlarged or reduced drawing of an object.

Each pair of figures is similar. Find x.

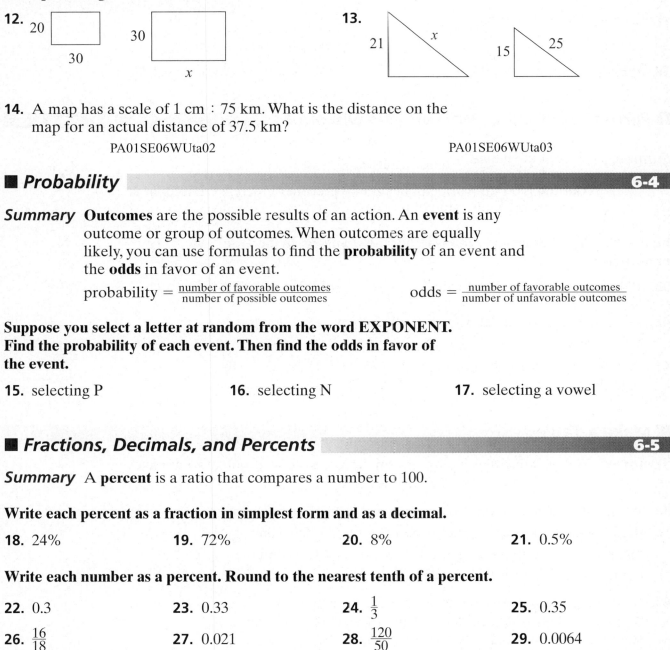

12. 20 / 30 / 30 / x

13. 21 / x / 15 / 25

14. A map has a scale of 1 cm : 75 km. What is the distance on the map for an actual distance of 37.5 km?

PA01SE06WUta02   PA01SE06WUta03

■ Probability 6-4

Summary **Outcomes** are the possible results of an action. An **event** is any outcome or group of outcomes. When outcomes are equally likely, you can use formulas to find the **probability** of an event and the **odds** in favor of an event.

$$\text{probability} = \frac{\text{number of favorable outcomes}}{\text{number of possible outcomes}} \qquad \text{odds} = \frac{\text{number of favorable outcomes}}{\text{number of unfavorable outcomes}}$$

Suppose you select a letter at random from the word EXPONENT. Find the probability of each event. Then find the odds in favor of the event.

15. selecting P   **16.** selecting N   **17.** selecting a vowel

■ Fractions, Decimals, and Percents 6-5

Summary A **percent** is a ratio that compares a number to 100.

Write each percent as a fraction in simplest form and as a decimal.

18. 24%   **19.** 72%   **20.** 8%   **21.** 0.5%

Write each number as a percent. Round to the nearest tenth of a percent.

22. 0.3   **23.** 0.33   **24.** $\frac{1}{3}$ **25.** 0.35

26. $\frac{16}{18}$ **27.** 0.021   **28.** $\frac{120}{50}$ **29.** 0.0064

■ Finding Percents

Summary Solve percent problems by using a proportion or an equation.

Write and solve a proportion.

30. Find 15% of 48.

31. 20% of x is 30. What is x?

32. What percent of 300 is 90?

33. 125% of y is 100. What is y?

Write and solve an equation.

34. 35% of a is 70. What is a?

35. Find 68% of 300.

36. What percent of 180 is 9?

37. What percent of 56 is 3.5?

■ Percent of Change, Markup, and Discount

Summary percent of change $= \dfrac{\text{amount of change}}{\text{original amount}}$

Markup is a real-world application of percent of increase. **Discount** is a real-world application of percent of decrease.

Find each percent of change. Tell whether the change is an increase or decrease.

38. 120 to 90

39. 148 to 37

40. 285 to 342

41. 1,000 to 250

42. A cap that cost a retailer $5 was marked up by 75%. Find the selling price.

43. Peaches that are usually priced at $2/lb are on sale for 15% off. Find the sale price.

■ Make a Table

Summary Make a table to organize information or to solve problems that have several steps.

44. Alicia bikes 25% of a 100-mi trip on the first day. She bikes $\frac{1}{3}$ of the remaining distance on the second day. On the third day, she bikes 40% of the remaining distance. Make a table to find the number of miles left in Alicia's trip.

45. ***Writing*** Describe how you could use the strategy *Make a Table* together with another problem solving strategy that you have studied. Justify your answer with an example.

Find each unit rate.

1. A car travels 84 mi on 3 gal of gas.

2. A car travels 220 mi in 4 h.

Write = or ≠ to complete each statement.

3. $\frac{7}{8} \blacksquare \frac{42}{40}$

4. $\frac{3}{5} \blacksquare \frac{45}{75}$

5. $\frac{12}{18} \blacksquare \frac{18}{12}$

6. $\frac{5}{9} \blacksquare \frac{25}{81}$

Solve each proportion.

7. $\frac{x}{8} = \frac{90}{120}$

8. $\frac{0.8}{90} = \frac{5.6}{y}$

Write a proportion to describe each situation. Then solve.

9. Three cans of dog food sell for 99¢. Find the cost of 15 cans.

10. A photo that measures 5 in. by 7 in. is enlarged to 7.5 in. by b in.

11. A student reads 45 pages in 2 h and x pages in 3 h.

The length of the kitchen in the drawing below is $1\frac{1}{4}$ in. The actual length is 20 ft. Use the drawing for Exercises 12–14.

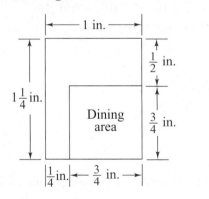

12. What is the scale of the drawing?

13. What is the actual width of the kitchen?

14. What are the actual length and width of the dining area?

Find each probability for one roll of a number cube.

15. $P(1)$

16. $P(1 \text{ or } 2)$

17. $P(\text{not } 2 \text{ or } 6)$

18. $P(\text{greater than } 1)$

Write each decimal as a percent.

19. 0.37

20. 0.005

21. 1.02

Write each fraction as a percent.

22. $\frac{5}{8}$

23. $\frac{7}{16}$

24. $\frac{5}{4}$

Solve.

25. What percent of 400 is 20?

26. Find 45% of 12.

27. 20% of c is 24. What is c?

28. What percent of 3 is 15?

29. Find 125% of 50.

30. 60% of y is 75.

Find each percent of change. Tell whether the change is an increase or decrease. Round to the nearest tenth of a percent.

31. from 60 to 36

32. from 18 to 24

33. from 15 to 25

34. from 85 to 50

35. from 8.8 to 30

36. from 1.2 to 0.2

37. A salesperson made a $128 commission selling merchandise. His commission rate was 5%. Find the dollar amount of his sales.

38. A bicycle that usually sells for $230 is on sale for 15% off. Find the sale price.

39. **Writing** Explain the difference between a markup and a discount.

40. In how many ways can you make change for $.35 without using pennies?

Choose the best answer.

1. Evaluate $6x - 9$ for $x = -11$.
   A. 57 B. -59
   C. -75 D. 75

2. -4 is a solution of which equation?
   F. $9z = 36$ G. $\frac{-36}{z} = -9$
   H. $z + 9 = 5$ J. $z - 9 = -5$

3. Simplify $(-1)^7 \cdot (-2)^0$.
   A. 2 B. -1
   C. -14 D. 14

4. Solve $y + 0.5 = 3$.
   F. 2.5 G. 1.5
   H. 3.5 J. -2.5

5. Write 56,500,000,000 in scientific notation.
   A. $5.65 \cdot 10^8$ B. $56.5 \cdot 10^{10}$
   C. $5.65 \cdot 10^{10}$ D. $565 \cdot 10^9$

6. Solve $\frac{2}{3}x = 2\frac{2}{9}$.
   F. $\frac{3}{10}$ G. $7\frac{2}{3}$ H. $2\frac{5}{8}$ J. $3\frac{1}{3}$

7. Complete $\left|2\frac{4}{5}\right|$ ■ $\left|-\frac{9}{4}\right|$.
   A. $>$ B. $<$ C. $=$ D. $\leq$

8. What is the unit rate for a ball moving 252 ft in 4 s?
   F. $252 : 4$ G. 63 ft/s
   H. 252 ft/s J. 1,008 ft/s

9. What percent of 63 is 41?
   A. about 41% B. about 82%
   C. about 65% D. about 0.65%

10. Find 40% of 40.
    F. 20 G. 15 H. 4 J. 16

11. Which has the lowest unit price?
    A. 30 oz for $.87
    B. 10 oz for $.30
    C. $.56 for 20 oz
    D. $1.16 for 40 oz

For Exercises 12–33, show your work.

12. The figures below are similar. Write a proportion. Then solve for x.

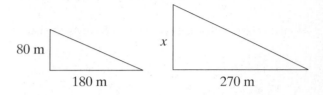

Find the sale price. Round to the nearest cent where necessary.

13. regular price: $58
    percent of discount: 45%

14. regular price: $15.98
    percent of discount: 80%

Write each number as a percent.

15. 0.84 16. $\frac{16}{20}$ 17. $\frac{33}{55}$

18. $\frac{6}{22}$ 19. $\frac{524}{200}$ 20. 0.045

Find each probability for one roll of a number cube.

21. $P(5 \text{ or } 6)$ 22. $P(\text{less than } 4)$

The scale on a map is 1 in. = 5 mi. Find the actual distance for each map distance.

23. 5.5 in. 24. 12 in. 25. 9.75 in.

Solve each proportion.

26. $\frac{5}{8} = \frac{15}{n}$ 27. $\frac{28}{x} = \frac{14}{2.5}$

28. $\frac{n}{9} = \frac{40}{12}$ 29. $\frac{6}{21} = \frac{s}{70}$

Write each ratio as a fraction in simplest form.

30. $20 : 45$ 31. $8 : 96$

32. $30 : 36$ 33. $120 : 80$

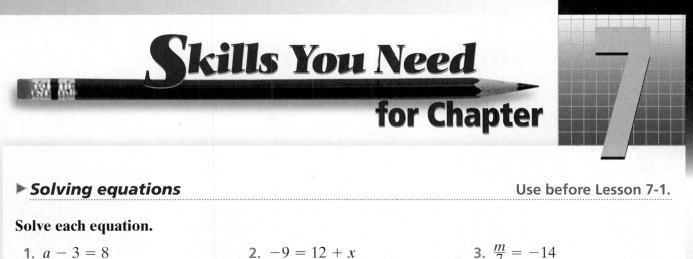

Skills You Need
for Chapter 7

▶ **Solving equations** Use before Lesson 7-1.

Solve each equation.

1. $a - 3 = 8$
2. $-9 = 12 + x$
3. $\frac{m}{7} = -14$
4. $-10 = -2b$
5. $y \div 2 = 4$
6. $6.8 = c - 2.2$
7. $\frac{x}{-4} = 8$
8. $-40 = 5a$
9. $x + 16 = 4$

▶ **Simplifying expressions** Use before Lessons 7-2, 7-3, 7-4, and 7-5.

Simplify each expression.

10. $3n + n$
11. $5b + 10 - 8b$
12. $6x + x - 4x + 5x$
13. $12c + 9 + 7c + 4$
14. $3x + 2y - 7y - 10x$
15. $2(a + 3)$
16. $9(6 - 4b)$
17. $5(m - 7) + 4m$
18. $-5y + 2(x + y)$

▶ **Writing variable expressions** Use before Lesson 7-3.

Write a variable expression for each situation.

19. three more than p points
20. six fewer than q questions
21. the number of months in y years
22. the value in cents of d dimes
23. twice as many as b baskets
24. eight fewer than n nickels

▶ **Solving inequalities** Use before Lesson 7-5.

Solve and graph each inequality.

25. $c + 6 \geq 7$
26. $y - 8 < -6$
27. $\frac{a}{2} < 5$
28. $5b < 20$
29. $-3x < 0$
30. $12 \leq x + 18$
31. $-m > 17$
32. $-\frac{x}{3} \geq -5$
33. $b - 15 \leq 4$
34. $24 > -8a$
35. $\frac{m}{4} \geq 20$
36. $16y \geq -16$

CHAPTER 7

Solving Equations and Inequalities

What you'll learn in this chapter:

- How to write and solve multi-step equations

- How to write and solve two-step inequalities

- How to find simple interest and compound interest

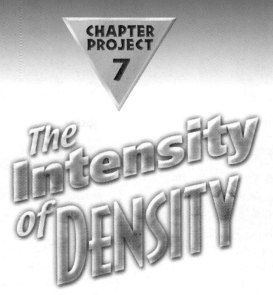

The Intensity of DENSITY

Have you ever wondered why some objects sink while others float? People float in the salt water of the Dead Sea. Pebbles sink when tossed into a river. The densities of a liquid and an object influence whether the object sinks or floats in the liquid. Similarly, the densities of two liquids influence whether they combine or separate.

Find the Densities of Liquids For the chapter project, you will measure the masses and volumes of several liquids. You will use your measurements and an equation to calculate the density of each liquid.

Steps to help you complete the project

Internet Connection

Web Extension
www.phschool.com

PROBLEM SOLVING

How to solve problems by writing equations

7·1

Solving Two-Step Equations

PART 1 Using Properties to Solve Two-Step Equations

What You'll Learn

1 To solve two-step equations

2 To use two-step equations to solve problems

. . . And Why

To solve problems involving savings

Algebra tiles can help you understand the algebra behind solving the equation $2x + 1 = 5$.

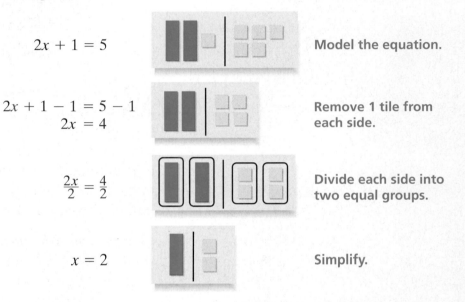

$2x + 1 = 5$ — Model the equation.

$2x + 1 - 1 = 5 - 1$
$2x = 4$ — Remove 1 tile from each side.

$\dfrac{2x}{2} = \dfrac{4}{2}$ — Divide each side into two equal groups.

$x = 2$ — Simplify.

To solve a two-step equation, first undo addition or subtraction. Then undo multiplication or division.

■ EXAMPLE 1

Solve $3n - 6 = 15$.

$$3n - 6 = 15$$
$$3n - 6 + 6 = 15 + 6 \quad \text{Add 6 to each side.}$$
$$3n = 21 \quad \text{Simplify.}$$
$$\frac{3n}{3} = \frac{21}{3} \quad \text{Divide each side by 3.}$$
$$n = 7 \quad \text{Simplify.}$$

Check $\quad 3n - 6 = 15$
$$3(7) - 6 \overset{?}{=} 15 \quad \text{Replace } n \text{ with 7.}$$
$$21 - 6 \overset{?}{=} 15 \quad \text{Multiply.}$$
$$15 = 15 ✔ \quad \text{Subtract.}$$

■ **TRY THIS** Solve each equation. Explain each step.

1. $15x + 3 = 48$ **2.** $\frac{t}{4} - 10 = -6$ **3.** $9g + 11 = 2$

■ **EXAMPLE 2**

Solve $5 - x = 17$.

$$5 - x = 17$$
$$-5 + 5 - x = -5 + 17 \quad \text{Add } -5 \text{ to each side.}$$
$$0 - x = 12 \quad \text{Simplify.}$$
$$-x = 12 \quad 0 - x = -x$$
$$-1(-x) = -1(12) \quad \text{Multiply each side by } -1.$$
$$x = -12 \quad \text{Simplify.}$$

■ **TRY THIS** Solve each equation.

4. $-a + 6 = 8$ **5.** $-9 - \frac{y}{7} = -12$ **6.** $13 - 6f = 31$

PART 2 Solving Problems with Two-Step Equations

You can use two-step equations to model real-world situations.

REAL-WORLD CONNECTION

■ **EXAMPLE 3**

Lynne saves $45 each week. She now has $180. She plans to save for a trip to Puerto Rico. To find how many weeks w she will take to save $900, solve $180 + 45w = 900$.

$$180 + 45w = 900$$
$$180 + 45w - 180 = 900 - 180 \quad \text{Subtract 180 from each side.}$$
$$45w = 720 \quad \text{Simplify.}$$
$$\frac{45w}{45} = \frac{720}{45} \quad \text{Divide each side by 45.}$$
$$w = 16 \quad \text{Simplify.}$$

Lynne will take 16 weeks to save $900.

■ **TRY THIS**

7. Jacob bought four begonias in 6-in. pots and a $19 fern at a fund-raiser. He spent a total of $83. Solve the equation $4p + 19 = 83$ to find the price p of each begonia.

If you flew to San Juan, Puerto Rico, in December 1999, it could have cost you $186 to leave from New York City, $590 to leave from San Francisco, $914 to leave from Reno, Nevada, or $1,392 to leave from Dallas, Texas.

Exercises

▶ **CHECK UNDERSTANDING**

State the first step in solving each equation.

1. $2b + 9 = 3$

2. $\frac{a}{3} - 4 = 9$

3. $-6t + (-3) = 14$

Solve each equation.

4. $\frac{h}{6} + 9 = 21$

5. $4b - 6 = -18$

6. $5 = -\frac{x}{3} + 10$

7. $-8c + 1 = -3$

8. $2d - 8 = -10$

9. $12 - 11a = 45$

10. Thomas, Ardell, and Nichole baked muffins, which they shared equally. Nichole ate a muffin on the way home. She then had 14 muffins left. Solve the equation $\frac{m}{3} - 1 = 14$ to find the number of muffins m that Thomas, Ardell, and Nichole baked.

▶ **PRACTICE AND PROBLEM SOLVING**

Solve and check each equation.

11. $9x - 15 = 39$

12. $10 = 3 + \frac{b}{2}$

13. $-35 = 4h + 1$

14. $\frac{x}{3} + 2 = 0$

15. $18 = -a + 2$

16. $4 - \frac{m}{5} = 18$

17. $-75 - k = -95$

18. $4 - \frac{z}{3} = -17$

19. $3n - 5 = -23$

20. $\frac{b}{2} - 8 = -10$

21. $15 = -11b + 4$

22. $9 - 3p = -27$

23. $21 = 6 - \frac{t}{5}$

24. $12y - 6 = 138$

25. $-\frac{d}{7} + 14 = 0$

Mental Math **Solve each equation.**

26. $2x + 3 = 15$

27. $\frac{n}{6} + 2 = -8$

28. $4a - 1 = 27$

29. $\frac{n}{6} + 3 = 6$

30. You bought a CD for $16.95 and eight blank video tapes. The total cost was $52.55 before the sales tax was added. Solve the equation $8t + 16.95 = 52.55$ to find the cost of each blank video tape.

31. You had $235 in your savings account nine weeks ago. You withdrew the same amount each week for eight weeks. Your balance was then $75. Solve the equation $235 - 8m = 75$ to find how much money m you withdrew each week.

32. **TEST PREP** A reasonable estimate of the solution to the equation $28x + 52 = 183$ would be ▪.

A. 6 **B.** 10 **C.** 25 **D.** 100

33. **Construction** A building contractor buys 525 metal bars. Because he is buying more than 500 bars, the wholesaler gives him a discount of $420. The total price is $3,780. Solve the equation $525b - 420 = 3,780$ to find the cost of each metal bar.

34. Carmela wants to buy a digital camera for $249. She has $24 and is saving $15 each week. Solve the equation $15w + 24 = 249$ to find how many weeks w she will take to save enough to buy the digital camera.

35. **Nutrition** A soccer player wants to eat 700 calories at a meal that includes a Reuben sandwich and pickles. The sandwich has 464 calories, and the pickles have 7 calories each.
   a. Solve the equation $464 + 7f = 700$ to find the number of pickles the soccer player can eat.
   b. Suppose the soccer player drinks a 200-calorie sports drink with the meal. Solve the equation $664 + 7f = 700$ to find the number of pickles the soccer player can eat now.

36. **Error Analysis** A student solved the equation $\frac{x}{4} + 5 = 1$ without showing all the work. The student's solution is incorrect. What error did the student make?

$$\frac{x}{4} + 5 = 1$$
$$\frac{x}{4} = -4$$
$$x = -1$$

37. **Open-ended** Write a word problem for which you could use the equation $3g + 4 = 16$.

Journal

Explain how to solve the equation $2x - 5 = 19$.

38. **Writing** Explain how the process of solving $\frac{x}{4} - 2 = 8$ is different from the process of solving $\frac{x}{4} = 8$.

▶ MIXED REVIEW

Find each percent of markup. *(Lesson 6-9)*

39. wholesale price: $12.00
selling price: $18.00

40. wholesale price: $34
selling price: $42.50

41. wholesale price: $45.95
selling price: $82.71

Simplify each expression. *(Lesson 2-3)*

42. $3x + 8 - 5x$

43. $a + 3b + 9a$

44. $2(c + 4) - 5c$

45. **Probability** A student is chosen at random from a class of 20 boys and 15 girls. Find the odds that a girl is chosen. *(Lesson 6-4)*

See also Extra Practice section.

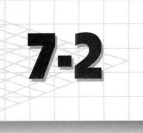

7-2

Solving Multi-Step Equations

What You'll Learn

1 To combine like terms to simplify an equation

2 To use the distributive property to simplify an equation

. . . And Why

To solve problems involving consecutive integers

Investigate

· USING PROPERTIES TO SIMPLIFY EQUATIONS ·

The tiles model the equation $2x + 7 + x = 16$.

1. How does this equation differ from others you have seen?

2. **a.** Group the tiles so that all the x tiles are together. This is the same as combining like terms. Write an equation to represent the tiles once the x tiles are grouped together.

   b. Solve your equation. Check your solution.

PART 1 **Combining Like Terms**

Combine like terms to simplify an equation before you solve it.

REAL-WORLD 🌐 CONNECTION

EXAMPLE 1

Jake and Suki collect model airplanes. Suki has four fewer than twice as many model airplanes as Jake. Together they have 14 models. Solve the equation $m + 2m - 4 = 14$. Find the number of models each person has.

$$m + 2m - 4 = 14$$
$$3m - 4 = 14 \qquad \text{Combine like terms.}$$
$$3m - 4 + 4 = 14 + 4 \quad \text{Add 4 to each side.}$$
$$3m = 18 \qquad \text{Simplify.}$$
$$\frac{3m}{3} = \frac{18}{3} \qquad \text{Divide each side by 3.}$$
$$m = 6 \qquad \text{Simplify.}$$

Jake has 6 models. Suki has $2(6) - 4 = 8$ models.

Check Is the solution reasonable? Jake and Suki have a total of 14 models. Since $6 + 8 = 14$, the solution is reasonable.

3. One basketball team defeated another by 13 points. The total number of points scored by both teams was 171. Solve the equation $p + p - 13 = 171$ to find the number of points p scored by the winning team.

When you count by ones from any integer, you are counting **consecutive integers.**

two consecutive integers

$\overbrace{120, 121}$

three consecutive integers

$\overbrace{-5, -4, -3}$

■ **EXAMPLE 2**

Number Sense The sum of three consecutive integers is 96. Find the integers.

Words   sum of three consecutive integers   is   96

Let n = the least integer.
Then $n + 1$ = the second integer,
and $n + 2$ = the third integer.

Equation $n + (n + 1) + (n + 2)$ =   96

$n + (n + 1) + (n + 2) = 96$
$(n + n + n) + (1 + 2) = 96$ Use the Commutative and Associative Properties of Addition to group like terms together.

$3n + 3 = 96$ Combine like terms.

$3n + 3 - 3 = 96 - 3$ Subtract 3 from each side.

$3n = 93$ Simplify.

$\dfrac{3n}{3} = \dfrac{93}{3}$ Divide each side by 3.

$n = 31$ Simplify.

If $n = 31$, then $n + 1 = 32$, and $n + 2 = 33$. The three integers are 31, 32, and 33.

Check Is the solution reasonable? Yes, because $31 + 32 + 33 = 96$.

■ **TRY THIS**

4. *Number Sense* Find four consecutive integers with a sum of 358.

5. For *consecutive even integers,* the first is n, and the second is $n + 2$. Find two consecutive even integers with a sum of 66.

The Distributive Property

$5(a + 4) = 5a + 20$

$3(6b - 2) = 18b - 6$

Sometimes you may need to use the Distributive Property when you solve a multi-step equation.

EXAMPLE 3

Solve each equation.

a. $2(5x - 3) = 14$

$2(5x - 3) = 14$	
$10x - 6 = 14$	Use the Distributive Property.
$10x - 6 + 6 = 14 + 6$	Add 6 to each side.
$10x = 20$	Simplify.
$\frac{10x}{10} = \frac{20}{10}$	Divide each side by 10.
$x = 2$	Simplify.

b. $38 = -3(4y + 2) + y$

$38 = -3(4y + 2) + y$	
$38 = -12y - 6 + y$	Use the Distributive Property.
$38 = -12y + y - 6$	Use the Commutative and Associative Properties of Addition to group like terms together.
$38 = -11y - 6$	Combine like terms.
$38 + 6 = -11y - 6 + 6$	Add 6 to each side.
$44 = -11y$	Simplify.
$\frac{44}{-11} = \frac{-11y}{-11}$	Divide each side by −11.
$-4 = y$	Simplify.

■ **TRY THIS** Solve each equation.

6. $-3(m - 6) = 4$ **7.** $3(x + 12) - x = 8$

Useful Steps for Solving a Multi-Step Equation

Step 1	Use the Distributive Property, if necessary.
Step 2	Combine like terms.
Step 3	Undo addition or subtraction.
Step 4	Undo multiplication or division.

Exercises

CHECK UNDERSTANDING

Simplify the left side of each equation. (Do not solve.)

1. $8a + 4a = 144$

2. $5b + 11 - 2b = 50$

3. $-2(x - 7) = 8$

Solve each equation.

4. $9x - 2x = -42$

5. $4a + 1 - a = 19$

6. $18 = b - 7b$

7. $3(n - 2) = 36$

8. $-3(2y + 7) = -18$

9. $-2(a + 3) - a = 0$

10. *Number Sense* Which equation can you use to find four consecutive integers with a sum of 50?
   A. $n + n + n + n = 50$
   B. $n + 2n + 3n + 4n = 50$
   C. $50 = n + 4$
   D. $n + (n + 1) + (n + 2) + (n + 3) = 50$

PRACTICE AND PROBLEM SOLVING

Solve and check each equation.

11. $d + 3d = 20$

12. $5x - x = -12$

13. $-6 = a + a + 4$

14. $y + 2 - 3y = -8$

15. $-9 - b + 8b = -23$

16. $36 = y - 5y - 12$

17. $7 = 2(a + 6)$

18. $4(y - 1) = 36$

19. $16 = 2(x - 1) - x$

20. $9(2c + 5) + 3c = -75$

21. $21 = 2(4a + 2)$

22. $8 - 3(x - 4) = 4$

23. $15 = -8(b - 1) + 9$

24. $\frac{1}{3}(x - 12) = 8$

25. $3 = \frac{1}{4}(m - 4) + \frac{1}{4}m$

26. *Error Analysis* A student solved the equation $7x - 5 - 5x = 15$ and found $x = 5$. What might be the student's error?

Number Sense **Write and solve an equation for each situation.**

27. Two consecutive integers sum to 33.

28. Four consecutive even integers sum to -92.

29. *Construction* A carpenter is building a fence around a swimming pool. One side of the pool is next to the house and does not need fencing. The carpenter has 120 feet of fencing and plans to use it all. Solve the equation $w + 76 + w = 120$ to find the unknown dimension of the enclosed rectangular area.

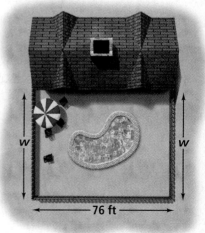

30. Bill and his younger sister Jasmine collect glass marbles. Together, they have 94 marbles. Bill calculated he has 4 more than twice as many marbles as Jasmine. If Jasmine has m marbles, then Bill has $(2m + 4)$ marbles. Solve the equation $m + (2m + 4) = 94$. Find how many glass marbles each has.

31. *Number Sense* Two numbers are w and $3w - 5$. Their sum is 23. Solve the equation $w + 3w - 5 = 23$. Find the numbers.

32. *Writing* Explain how to solve $3(9 + 4a) - 19 = 32$.

33. Together, Donal, Yolanda, and Iris made 28 birdhouses for a school fair. Yolanda made n birdhouses. Donal made one more birdhouse than Yolanda, and Iris made one more than Donal. Solve the equation $n + (n + 1) + (n + 1 + 1) = 27$. Find the number of birdhouses each one made.

Geometry **For each rectangle, the area is 20 cm².Find the value of x.**

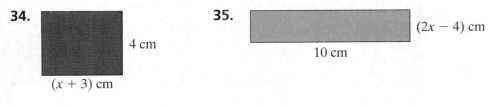

34.

4 cm

$(x + 3)$ cm

35.

10 cm

$(2x - 4)$ cm

▶ **MIXED REVIEW**

Solve each equation. *(Lesson 7-1)*

36. $10a - 32 = -28$

37. $5 - 2d = 15$

38. $\frac{c}{4} - 7 = 5$

Solve each equation. *(Lessons 3-5 and 5-8)*

39. $\frac{7}{10}a = \frac{3}{5}$

40. $\frac{4}{5}x = 8$

41. $5.3 + k = 23.9$

42. $z - 3.2 = 7$

43. *Measurement* If you take $\frac{2}{3}$ c of flour from a bowl containing $2\frac{1}{2}$ c of flour, how much flour is left in the bowl? *(Lesson 5-5)*

CHAPTER PROJECT 7 **ACTIVITY 1 MEASURING**

You'll need a beaker or measuring cup marked in milliliters and a scale that measures mass. Measure and record the mass of the empty beaker. Add 250 mL of water to the beaker. Measure and record the total mass of the beaker and water. Find the mass of the water.

See also Extra Practice section.

Multi-Step Equations with Fractions and Decimals

PART 1 Solving Multi-Step Equations with Fractions

Remember, when the coefficient of a variable in an equation is a fraction, you can use reciprocals to solve the equation.

$$\frac{4}{5}x = 12$$

$$\frac{5}{4} \cdot \frac{4}{5}x = \frac{5}{4} \cdot 12 \quad \textbf{Multiply each side by } \tfrac{5}{4}, \textbf{ because } \tfrac{5}{4} \cdot \tfrac{4}{5} = 1.$$

$$x = 15$$

When you have a multi-step equation and the coefficient of the variable is a fraction, gather the variables on one side of the equation and the constants on the other before multiplying by the reciprocal.

What You'll Learn

1 To solve multi-step equations with fractions

2 To solve multi-step equations with decimals

. . . And Why

To solve problems involving cost of phone service

■ EXAMPLE 1

Solve $\frac{2}{3}n - 6 = 22$.

$$\frac{2}{3}n - 6 = 22$$

$$\frac{2}{3}n - 6 + 6 = 22 + 6 \quad \textbf{Add 6 to each side.}$$

$$\frac{2}{3}n = 28 \quad \textbf{Simplify.}$$

$$\frac{3}{2} \cdot \frac{2}{3}n = \frac{3}{2} \cdot 28 \quad \textbf{Multiply each side by } \tfrac{3}{2}, \textbf{ the reciprocal of } \tfrac{2}{3}.$$

$$1n = \frac{3 \cdot 28^{14}}{{}_1 2} \quad \textbf{Divide common factors.}$$

$$n = 42 \quad \textbf{Simplify.}$$

Check $\quad \frac{2}{3}n - 6 = 22$

$$\frac{2}{3}(42) - 6 \stackrel{?}{=} 22 \qquad \textbf{Replace } n \textbf{ with 42.}$$

$$\frac{2 \cdot 42^{14}}{{}_1 3} - 6 \stackrel{?}{=} 22 \qquad \textbf{Divide common factors.}$$

$$28 - 6 \stackrel{?}{=} 22 \qquad \textbf{Multiply.}$$

$$22 = 22 \ ✔$$

Need Help? For more help with fractions and reciprocals, see Skills Handbook, page 740.

■ **TRY THIS** Solve each equation.

1. $-\frac{7}{10}k + 14 = -21$

2. $\frac{2}{3}(m - 6) = 3$

You can use the Multiplication Property of Equality to make equations involving fractions easier to solve. Use the LCM of the denominators to clear the equation of fractions.

REAL-WORLD CONNECTION

■ **EXAMPLE 2**

A student has two test scores of 93 and 80. Solve the equation $\frac{93 + 80 + t}{3} = 90$ to find what the student would have to score on a third test to average 90.

$$\frac{93 + 80 + t}{3} = 90$$

$3\left(\frac{93 + 80 + t}{3}\right) = 3(90)$ **Multiply each side by 3.**

$93 + 80 + t = 270$ **Simplify each side of the equation.**

$173 + t = 270$ **Add.**

$173 - 173 + t = 270 - 173$ **Subtract 173 from each side.**

$t = 97$ **Simplify.**

The student would have to score 97 on a third test to average 90.

■ **TRY THIS** Solve each equation.

3. $-\frac{12 + x}{2} = 13$ **4.** $\frac{4}{7}(a + 6) = 2$

■ **EXAMPLE 3**

Solve $\frac{2}{5}x + 2 = \frac{3}{4}$.

$$\frac{2}{5}x + 2 = \frac{3}{4}$$

$20\left(\frac{2}{5}x + 2\right) = 20\left(\frac{3}{4}\right)$ **Multiply each side by 20, the LCM of 5 and 4.**

$20 \cdot \frac{2}{5}x + 20 \cdot 2 = 20\left(\frac{3}{4}\right)$ **Use the Distributive Property.**

$8x + 40 = 15$ **Simplify.**

$8x + 40 - 40 = 15 - 40$ **Subtract 40 from each side.**

$8x = -25$ **Simplify.**

$\frac{8x}{8} = \frac{-25}{8}$ **Divide each side by 8.**

$x = -3\frac{1}{8}$ **Simplify.**

■ **TRY THIS** Solve each equation.

5. $-\frac{5}{8}y + y = \frac{1}{8}$ **6.** $\frac{1}{3}b - 1 = \frac{5}{6}$

You can solve multi-step equations containing decimals by calculating with the decimals or by multiplying by a power of 10 to clear the equation of decimals.

■ Different Ways to Solve a Problem

For local telephone service, the McNeils pay $9.95/month plus $.035/min for local calls. Last month, they paid $12.75 for local service. To find the minutes m of local calls, solve the equation $0.035m + 9.95 = 12.75$.

Method 1

You can work with decimals as you have before.

$$0.035m + 9.95 = 12.75$$
$$0.035m + 9.95 - 9.95 = 12.75 - 9.95$$
$$0.035m = 2.8$$
$$\frac{0.035m}{0.035} = \frac{2.8}{0.035}$$
$$m = 80$$

The McNeils made 80 min of local calls.

Method 2

Use multiplication to clear the decimals. Use the decimal with the greatest number of decimal places to decide what power of 10 to use.

$$0.035m + 9.95 = 12.75$$
$$1,000(0.035m + 9.95) = 1,000(12.75)$$
$$35m + 9,950 = 12,750$$
$$35m + 9,950 - 9,950 = 12,750 - 9,950$$
$$35m = 2,800$$
$$\frac{35m}{35} = \frac{2,800}{35}$$
$$m = 80$$

The McNeils made 80 min of local calls.

The telephone company also offers monthly rate of $32.95 for unlimited local calls. How many minutes of local calls can the McNeils make before the monthly rate of $32.95 becomes the better deal?

Choose a Method

1. For the problem above, which method do you prefer? Explain.

2. In Method 2, why was 1,000 used to multiply each side of the equation?

Exercises

State the first step in solving each equation. (Do not solve.)

1. $\frac{1}{4}x + 3 = 2$

2. $16 = 2.8y - 1.5$

3. $\frac{7}{9}w - w = \frac{1}{9}$

Solve each equation.

4. $\frac{3}{4}b + 5 = 14$

5. $\frac{7}{10}c - 10 = \frac{2}{5}$

6. $-\frac{1}{3}(x - 9) = -1$

7. $2.25x - 6.1 = 14.15$

8. $1.2n + 3.4 = 10$

9. $-0.8k - 3.1 = -8.3$

10. *Weather* On three days in August 1999, the high temperatures in Jackson, Mississippi, were 96°F, 96°F, and x°F. The average high temperature for the three days was 97°F. Solve the equation $\frac{96 + 96 + x}{3} = 97$ to find the high temperature on the third day.

By what number would you multiply each equation to get an equation without denominators or decimals? Do not solve.

11. $\frac{1}{8}h - 1 = \frac{3}{8}$

12. $\frac{1}{5}y + 3 = \frac{2}{3}$

13. $6.25f - 3.5 = 24.5$

Solve and check each equation.

14. $\frac{1}{4}c + 2 = \frac{3}{4}$

15. $\frac{2}{3}(a - 3) = -\frac{1}{3}$

16. $\frac{5}{8}(p - 4) = 2$

17. $\frac{2}{7}n + n = \frac{5}{9}$

18. $8 - \frac{w}{10} = \frac{3}{5}$

19. $p + \frac{1}{3}p = \frac{2}{3}$

20. $-\frac{3}{4}y + \frac{1}{4} = \frac{1}{2}$

21. $\frac{x}{4} - \frac{3x}{2} = -\frac{1}{2}$

22. $\frac{2}{7}k - \frac{1}{14}k = -3$

23. $2.4b + 5.6 = -11.2$

24. $4x + 2 = -28.4$

25. $0.07x + 9.95 = 12.47$

26. $0.9x + 2.3x = -6.4$

27. $-0.5x + 4 + 2x = 9$

28. $0.4(a + 2) = 2$

29. $1.2c + 2.6c = 4.56$

30. $12p - 6.5p + 7 = -15$

31. $5(t - 0.4) + 6t = 0$

32. **TEST PREP** What is the solution of $\frac{1}{2}(x - 1) = \frac{1}{2}$?

    A. -1 **B.** 0 **C.** 1 **D.** 2

33. Six friends hire a raft and guide to go white-water rafting in Colorado. Each person also buys a souvenir photo of the trip for $25.75. The total each person pays is $90.30. To find the cost c of the raft and guide, solve the equation $\frac{c}{6} + 25.75 = 90.3$.

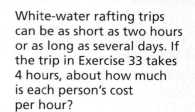

34. A pair of athletic shoes is on sale for $\frac{1}{4}$ off the original cost. The sale price is $49.95. Solve the equation $c - \frac{1}{4}c = 49.95$ to find the original cost c of the shoes.

35. Dwayne is taking a drawing class. The drawing pencils cost $.97 apiece, and a sketchbook costs $5.95. Dwayne spent a total of $11.77. Solve the equation $0.97n + 5.95 = 11.77$ to find the number n of pencils he bought.

White-water rafting trips can be as short as two hours or as long as several days. If the trip in Exercise 33 takes 4 hours, about how much is each person's cost per hour?

36. a. A student has grades of 65, 80, 78 and 92 on four tests. Use s to represent the student's grade on the next test. Write an expression for the average of the five tests.
  b. The student wants to have an average of 80 after the fifth test. Use the expression you wrote in part (a) to write an equation.
  c. Solve the equation to find the grade the student must earn on the fifth test to have an average of 80 for the class.

37. _Writing_ At a 15%-off sale, a customer pays $11.01 for a video. Explain how to solve the equation $p - 0.15p = 11.01$ to find the original price p of the video.

38. _Geometry_ Use the rectangle at the right.
  a. Find the value of x if the area is 15 square units.
  b. Find the value of x if the perimeter is 24 units.

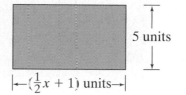

5 units

$\left|\leftarrow(\frac{1}{2}x + 1)\text{ units}\rightarrow\right|$

▶ **MIXED REVIEW**

Solve each equation. (*Lesson 7-2*)

39. $-9 = 3(y + 4)$ **40.** $5(t - 8) = 10$ **41.** $x + 7 - 3x = 7$

Write using exponents. (*Lesson 4-2*)

42. $4 \cdot 4 \cdot 4$ **43.** $(-7) \cdot (-7)$ **44.** $c \cdot c \cdot c \cdot c \cdot d$ **45.** $9 \cdot a \cdot a \cdot 2$

46. _Choose a Strategy_ Mrs. Milton travels 60 mi round-trip to work. She works five days a week. Her car gets about 25 mi/gal of gasoline. About how many gallons of gasoline does Mrs. Milton's car use during her weekly commute?

7-4

Write an Equation

Math Strategies in Action You probably recognize Albert Einstein's famous formula, $E = mc^2$. Many scientists write and use equations and formulas every day. Banks use equations to calculate interest and loan information. Statisticians use equations to find sports and population statistics. Doctors use equations to calculate correct doses of medicines.

You have written one-step equations for word problems. Now you will extend your skills to more complex situations.

■ SAMPLE PROBLEM

A moving van rents for \$29.95 a day plus \$.12/mi. Ms. Smith's bill for a two-day rental was \$70.46. How many miles did she drive?

 Read

1. What is the goal of this problem?

2. For how long did Ms. Smith rent the van?

3. What does the van cost without mileage?

4. What is the mileage charge?

Plan

Write an equation.

Words

| two days | · $29.95/d | + | $.12/mi | · | number of miles | = | $70.46 |

Let m = the number of miles Ms. Smith drove the van.

Equation 2 · 29.95 + 0.12 · m = 70.46

Solve

Solve the equation.

$$2 \cdot 29.95 + 0.12 \cdot m = 70.46$$

$59.9 + 0.12m = 70.46$	**Multiply 2 and 29.95.**
$59.9 - 59.9 + 0.12m = 70.46 - 59.9$	**Subtract 59.9 from each side.**
$0.12m = 10.56$	**Simplify.**
$\dfrac{0.12m}{0.12} = \dfrac{10.56}{0.12}$	**Divide each side by 0.12.**
$m = 88$	**Simplify.**

Ms. Smith drove the van 88 mi.

Look Back

5. A student suggested that another way to solve the gas mileage problem was to use the strategy *Try, Test, Revise*. Suppose that Ms. Smith's bill for the two-day rental was $76.34. How many miles did she drive the van?

   a. Copy and complete the table below to keep track of your trials.

Miles	Cost	High/Low?
75	$2 \cdot 29.95 + 75 \cdot 0.12 = $ ■	low
100	$2 \cdot 29.95 + $ ■ $\cdot 0.12 = $ ■	■

   b. Extend the table to find the solution to the problem.
   c. Check your solution by writing and solving an equation.

6. *Reasoning* Which method do you prefer for solving this type of problem? Explain.

Exercises

▶ CHECK UNDERSTANDING

Write an equation. Then solve.

1. The sale price of a sweater is $48. The price is 20% less than the original price. What was the original price?

2. **Budgeting** Elena has $240 in the bank. She withdraws $15 each week to pay for piano lessons. How many lessons can she afford with her savings?

3. **Geometry** The perimeter of a rectangle is 64 cm. The length is 4 cm less than twice the width. Find the length and width.

▶ PRACTICE AND PROBLEM SOLVING

Solve using any strategy.

4. Lamar's summer job is mowing lawns for a landscaper. His pay is $7.50/h. Lamar also makes $11.25/h for any time over 40 h that he works in one week. He worked 40 h last week plus *n* overtime hours and made $339.38. How many hours overtime did he work?

5. Cathy has a collection of dimes and quarters. The number of dimes equals the number of quarters. She has a total of $2.80. How many of each coin does Cathy have? (*Hint:* Let n = the number of dimes. Since each dime has a value of 10¢, the value of n dimes is $10n$. Since the number of quarters is also n, the value of n quarters is $25n$. Also change the value of $2.80 to its value in cents.)

6. **Number Sense** Find two whole numbers with a sum of 15 and a product of 54.

7. A farmer is building a square pen 21 ft on each side. He puts one post at each corner and one post every 3 ft in between. How many posts will he use?

8. **Physics** The weight of an object on Venus is about $\frac{9}{10}$ of its weight on Earth. The weight of an object on Jupiter is about $\frac{13}{5}$ times its weight on Earth.
   a. If a rock weighs 23 lb on Venus, how much would it weigh on Earth?
   b. If the same rock were on Jupiter, how much would it weigh?

9. a. It takes 8 painters 6 hours to paint the walls of a gymnasium. How many person-hours does this job require?

   b. How many hours will 12 painters take to paint the gymnasium?

10. Ladonna and Jane are renting an apartment. They pay the landlord the amount of the first month's rent, the same amount for the last month's rent, and half of a month's rent for a security deposit. The total is $1,625. What is the monthly rent?

11. Jackson, Petra, and Tyrone went to the beach and collected seashells over the weekend. Jackson collected s seashells. Petra and Tyrone each collected thirteen less than twice the number of seashells Jackson collected. At the end of the weekend, they had 94 seashells. How many seashells did each person collect?

▶ **MIXED REVIEW**

Solve each equation. *(Lesson 7-3)*

12. $\frac{3}{5}k + \frac{1}{5}k = 4$ $\qquad$ **13.** $1.4x + 8.8 = 92.8$ $\qquad$ **14.** $\frac{1 + x + 7}{5} = 7$

Write each percent as a fraction in simplest form and as a decimal. *(Lesson 6-5)*

15. 52% $\qquad$ **16.** 20.5% $\qquad$ **17.** 0.5% $\qquad$ **18.** 205%

19. You can buy 12 pencils for $.80. At this rate, how much will you pay for 27 pencils? *(Lesson 6-1)*

■ **CHECKPOINT 1** $\qquad\qquad$ **Lessons 7-1 through 7-4**

Solve each equation.

1. $12n + 60 = 300$ $\qquad$ **2.** $5y - 9 - 3y = 13$ $\qquad$ **3.** $-44 = 3x + 10$

4. $\frac{a}{4} - \frac{3}{4} = \frac{1}{4}$ $\qquad$ **5.** $\frac{4}{7}x - 3 = 13$ $\qquad$ **6.** $-\frac{x}{6} - 7 = 0$

7. $0.6x + 1.9x = 5$ $\qquad$ **8.** $10(5 + m) = 63$ $\qquad$ **9.** $2c + 4 + 3c = -26$

10. $\frac{1}{5}(x + 10) = 2$ $\qquad$ **11.** $7(2y - 1) = 7$ $\qquad$ **12.** $3a + 9 = 27$

Write an equation for each situation. Solve.

13. Wendy bought a drill at a 10%-off sale. The sale price was $75.60. Find the original price p.

14. *Number Sense* Three consecutive integers have a sum of 132. Find the integers.

Multiple Choice

Choose the best answer.

1. At Store A, a $5\frac{1}{2}$-lb bag of carrots costs $4.40. Store B charges the same price for an 84-oz bag of carrots. Which expression will help you find the number of ounces in a $5\frac{1}{2}$-lb bag of carrots?

   A. $\frac{11}{2}$lb $\cdot \frac{16 \text{ oz}}{1 \text{ lb}}$ B. $4.40 $\div \frac{16 \text{ oz}}{1 \text{ lb}}$

   C. $84 \text{ oz} - \frac{16 \text{ oz}}{2 \text{ lb}}$ D. $\frac{11}{2}$ lb $\div 16$ oz

2. The sides of square W are three times the sides of square Z. How many times the area of square Z is the area of square W?

   F. 2 times   G. 4 times
   H. 6 times   J. 9 times

3. The Sullivans rented a large truck for $49.95 plus $.60/mi. Before returning the truck, they filled the gas tank, which cost $9.00. The total cost for renting the truck, including gasoline, was $93.23. Find the number of miles the truck was driven to the nearest mile.
   A. 20 mi   B. 57 mi
   C. 72 mi   D. 155 mi

4. One third of the businesses bordering the Fir River donated money for its cleanup. One half of the businesses that donated money supplied volunteers as well. About what percent of the businesses supplied volunteers?
   F. 6%   G. 13%
   H. 17%   J. 50%

5. Which of the following equals $2 \cdot 2 \cdot 2 \cdot a \cdot a$?
   A. $2a2^3$ B. $6a^2$
   C. 2^3a^2 D. $8a^3$

6. A video rental company rents movies for $3.95 for the first day. Each additional day costs $1.25. Sara paid a total of $7.70 for renting a movie. For how many additional days did Sara keep the movie?
   F. 6 days   G. 5 days
   H. 4 days   J. 3 days

7. The area of a rectangle is 64 in.^{2}. If the area is increased by 25%, which of these could be the dimensions of the new rectangle?
   A. 10 in. by 8 in.   B. 8 in. by 8 in.
   C. 6 in. by 8 in.   D. 10 in. by 10 in.

8. Suppose you drop a ball from the ledge of a third-story window. Each bounce of the ball reaches one half the height of the previous bounce. On the third bounce the ball reaches a height of 3 ft and is caught. The total vertical distance traveled by the ball is 63 ft. What is the height of the window ledge?
   F. 22 ft   G. 11 ft
   H. 24 ft   J. 48 ft

Free Response

For Exercises 9–12, show all your work.

9. Solve $-\frac{x}{7} + 3 = -2$.

10. The sum of three consecutive integers is 57. What are the integers?

11. You eat three meals a day for seven days each week. About how many meals will you eat in 25 years?

12. **Open-ended** Write an equation involving one variable and two or more consecutive integers. Solve your equation.

Solving Equations with Variables on Both Sides

Investigate

• • • • • • • • • • • • • • • • USING MODELS TO SOLVE EQUATIONS • • • • • • • • • • • • • • • •

Work in pairs.

1. Write an equation for the model at the right.

2. **a.** You must do the same thing to each side of the model. What can you do to get all of the green tiles on only one side?
   b. Show what the model will look like when green tiles are on only one side. Write the new equation.
   c. Solve your new equation.

What You'll Learn

1 To solve equations with variables on both sides

2 To use equations with variables on both sides

. . . And Why

To solve problems that involve time and distance

PART 1 Solving Equations with Variables on Both Sides

To solve an equation with variables on both sides, use addition or subtraction to get the variable on only one side of the equation.

■ EXAMPLE 1

Solve $9a + 2 = 4a - 18$.

$$9a + 2 = 4a - 18$$
$$9a - 4a + 2 = 4a - 4a - 18 \qquad \text{Subtract } 4a \text{ from each side.}$$
$$5a + 2 = -18 \qquad \text{Combine like terms.}$$
$$5a + 2 - 2 = -18 - 2 \qquad \text{Subtract 2 from each side.}$$
$$5a = -20 \qquad \text{Simplify.}$$
$$\frac{5a}{5} = \frac{-20}{5} \qquad \text{Divide each side by 5.}$$
$$a = -4 \qquad \text{Simplify.}$$

Check $\qquad 9a + 2 = 4a - 18$
$$9(-4) + 2 \stackrel{?}{=} 4(-4) - 18 \qquad \text{Substitute } -4 \text{ for } a.$$
$$-36 + 2 \stackrel{?}{=} -16 - 18 \qquad \text{Multiply.}$$
$$-34 = -34 \checkmark$$

■ **TRY THIS** Solve and check each equation.

3. $4x + 4 = 2x + 36$ **4.** $-15 + 6b = -8b + 13$

You may need to use the Distributive Property to simplify one or both sides of an equation before you can get the variable alone on one side.

REAL-WORLD CONNECTION

■ **EXAMPLE 2**

Beth leaves home on her bicycle, riding at a steady rate of 8 mi/h. Her brother Ted leaves home on his bicycle half an hour later, following Beth's route. He rides at a steady rate of 12 mi/h. How long after Beth leaves home will Ted catch up?

distance Beth travels = distance Ted travels

Words 8 mi/h · Beth's time = 12 mi/h · Ted's time

Let x = Beth's time.

Then $x - \frac{1}{2}$ = Ted's time.

Equation 8 · x = 12 · $\left(x - \frac{1}{2}\right)$

$$8x = 12\left(x - \frac{1}{2}\right)$$

$8x = 12x - 6$ Use the Distributive Property.

$8x - 12x = 12x - 12x - 6$ Subtract 12x from each side.

$-4x = -6$ Combine like terms.

$\frac{-4x}{-4} = \frac{-6}{-4}$ Divide each side by −4.

$x = \frac{6}{4}$ or $1\frac{1}{2}$ Simplify.

Ted will catch up with Beth $1\frac{1}{2}$ h after she leaves home.

Check Test the solution. At 8 mi/h, Beth will ride 12 mi in $1\frac{1}{2}$ h. Ted's time is $\frac{1}{2}$ h less than Beth's. He rides for 1 h. At 12 mi/h, he travels 12 mi in all. Since Beth and Ted each travel 12 mi, the answer checks.

An estimated 80.6 million people in the United States ride bicycles. About 14.5% of the nation's bicycle riders live in California.

SOURCE: Bicycle Market Research Institute

■ **TRY THIS**

5. Car A leaves Eastown traveling at a steady rate of 50 mi/h. Car B leaves Eastown 1 h later following Car A. It travels at a steady rate of 60 mi/h. How long after Car A leaves Eastown will Car B catch up?

Exercises

CHECK UNDERSTANDING

Copy and complete the steps to solve each equation.

1.
$$-2a + 7 = a - 8$$
$$-2a + 7 - a = a - 8 - \blacksquare$$
$$\blacksquare + 7 = -8$$
$$\blacksquare + 7 - 7 = -8 - 7$$
$$\blacksquare = -15$$
$$\blacksquare = \frac{-15}{-3}$$
$$a = \blacksquare$$

2.
$$2(x + 8) = -x - 5$$
$$2x + \blacksquare = -x - 5$$
$$2x + 16 + \blacksquare = -x - 5 + \blacksquare$$
$$\blacksquare + 16 = -5$$
$$3x + 16 - \blacksquare = -5 - \blacksquare$$
$$\blacksquare = -21$$
$$\frac{\blacksquare}{3} = \frac{-21}{3}$$
$$x = \blacksquare$$

Solve each equation.

3. $3y - 20 = 8y$

4. $x - 7 = 2x - 6$

5. $2(x - 4) = 3x$

6. A jet airplane leaves an airport traveling at a steady rate of 600 km/h. Another jet leaves the same airport $\frac{3}{4}$ h later traveling at 800 km/h in the same direction. How long will the second jet take to overtake the first?

PRACTICE AND PROBLEM SOLVING

Solve each equation.

7. $5x + 8 = 7x$

8. $3a = a + 22$

9. $20.6 + 2.1x = -8.2x$

10. $2a + 6 = -a - 8$

11. $4w + 8 = 6w - 4$

12. $7a = 2(a - 10)$

13. $5(n - 3) = 2n - 6$

14. $4(8 - y) = 2y + 16$

15. $-2(y + 6) = y + 3 + 2y$

16. $b + b + 18 = 4b$

17. $q + q + q = q + 6$

18. $\frac{1}{2}(4d - 2) = d + 5$

19. $m - 14 = 3m + 18 + 2m$

20. $6(g + 3) = -2(g + 31)$

21. $7a - 4 + 2a = 3a - 2$

22. $3(2y - 0.3) = 19.4 - y$

23. $9 - (2k - 3) = k$

24. $2\left(2a + \frac{1}{2}\right) = 3\left(a - \frac{2}{3}\right)$

25. *Mental Math* Is the solution to $5b = 2b - 42 - 3b$ positive or negative? Explain.

26. *Open-ended* Write a problem that you can represent with an equation with variables on both sides. Write and solve the equation.

Write an equation for each situation. Solve.

27. *Number Sense* If a number n is subtracted from 18, the result is four less than n. What is the value of n?

28. A cellular phone company charges a $27.95 monthly fee and $.12/min for local calls. Another company charges $12.95 a month and $.32/min for local calls. For what number of minutes of local calls is the cost of the plans the same?

29. A group of campers and one group leader left a campsite in a canoe traveling at a steady 8 km/h. One hour later, the other group leader left the campsite in a motorboat with all of the supplies. The motorboat followed the canoe at a steady 20 km/h. How long after the canoe left the campsite did the motorboat overtake it?

30. A video store offers two types of rental cards. Each rental card is good for six months. The gold rental card costs $25 plus $1.75/rental. The silver rental card costs $10 plus $3.25/rental. For what number of videos is the total cost of the rental cards the same?

Math in the Media Use the article below for Exercises 31 and 32.

The Father of Algebra

Diophantus was a Greek mathematician who lived in the third century. He was one of the first mathematicians to use algebraic symbols.

Most of what is known about Diophantus's life comes from an algebraic riddle from around the early sixth century. The riddle states, "Diophantus's youth lasted one sixth of his life. He grew a beard after one twelfth more. After one seventh more of his life he married. Five years later he and his wife had a son. The son lived exactly one half as long as his father, and Diophantus died four years after his son. All of this adds up to the years Diophantus lived." The riddle, the "facts" of which may or may not be true, results in the following equation:

$$\tfrac{1}{6}a + \tfrac{1}{12}a + \tfrac{1}{7}a + 5 + \tfrac{1}{2}a + 4 = a$$

where a is Diophantus's age at the time of his death.

31. Solve the equation in the article to determine how many years Diophantus lived.

32. How old was Diophantus when he married?

33. a. _Reasoning_ Would you solve the equation $\frac{5}{8}b = 10 - b$ by multiplying each side by $\frac{8}{5}$ as your first step? Why or why not?

b. Solve the equation.

34. _Writing_ Describe the steps you would use to solve the equation $5(2a - 3) = 20 + a$.

35. _Error Analysis_ The student who solved the equation at the right made an error. Find the error. State the correct solution.

$$8x + 36 = 4(7 - x)$$
$$8x + 36 = 28 - 4x$$
$$4x + 36 = 28$$
$$4x = -8$$
$$x = -2$$

▶ MIXED REVIEW

Solve and graph each inequality. _(Lesson 2-10)_

36. $-4x < 32$

37. $\frac{a}{-9} \geq -3$

38. $-12 < 3y$

39. $12 \leq -2y$

Find each discount or markup. _(Lesson 6-9)_

40. $15; 25\%$ discount

41. $88; 32\%$ markup

42. $24; 72\%$ markup

43. $110; 75\%$ discount

44. _Choose a Strategy_ In a collection of dimes and quarters, there are seven more quarters than there are dimes. How many dimes and quarters are there if the collection is worth $3.50?

Math at Work
City Planner

City planners, also called urban planners or regional planners, determine the best use of a community's land and resources for homes, businesses, and recreation. They also work on community problems such as traffic congestion and air pollution. They study the effects of proposed changes in a community, such as the addition of a bus line or a new highway. Planners use mathematical analysis to evaluate different courses of action and to predict the impact of each course on a community.

Internet Connection

For more information about city planners, visit the Prentice Hall Web site.
www.phschool.com

See also Extra Practice section.

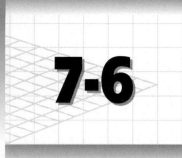

7-6

Solving Two-Step Inequalities

What You'll Learn

1 To solve two-step inequalities

2 To use two-step inequalities to solve problems

...And Why

To solve problems involving camping and jobs

PART
1 Solving Two-Step Inequalities

PART
1 Solving Two-Step Inequalities

Solving two-step inequalities involves the same steps as solving two-step equations.

■ EXAMPLE 1

Solve and graph $2y - 3 \leq -5$.

$$2y - 3 \leq -5$$
$$2y - 3 + 3 \leq -5 + 3 \qquad \text{Add 3 to each side.}$$
$$2y \leq -2 \qquad \text{Simplify.}$$
$$\frac{2y}{2} \leq \frac{-2}{2} \qquad \text{Divide each side by 2.}$$
$$y \leq -1 \qquad \text{Simplify.}$$

```
 ←——+——+——+——●——+——+——+——+——+——+——+——→
   -6    -4    -2    0    2    4    6
```

■ TRY THIS Solve and graph each inequality.

1. $5a - 9 > 11$ **2.** $-10 \geq 2x - 6$ **3.** $17 + \frac{1}{2}c < 14$

Remember to reverse the direction of the inequality symbol when you multiply or divide by a negative number.

■ EXAMPLE 2

Solve $-9 > -\frac{1}{3}x + 6$.

$$-9 > -\frac{1}{3}x + 6$$
$$-9 - 6 > -\frac{1}{3}x + 6 - 6 \qquad \text{Subtract 6 from each side.}$$
$$-15 > -\frac{1}{3}x \qquad \text{Simplify.}$$
$$-3(-15) < -3\left(-\frac{1}{3}x\right) \qquad \text{Multiply each side by } -3. \text{ Reverse the direction of the inequality symbol.}$$
$$45 < x \text{ or } x > 45 \qquad \text{Simplify.}$$

Quick *Review*

If $a > b$, then $a + c > b + c$.

If $a > b$, then $a - c > b - c$.

If $a > b$ and $c > 0$, then $ac > bc$.

If $a > b$ and $c > 0$, then $\frac{a}{c} > \frac{b}{c}$.

If $a > b$ and $c < 0$, then $ac < bc$.

If $a > b$ and $c < 0$, then $\frac{a}{c} < \frac{b}{c}$.

■ **TRY THIS** Solve each inequality.

4. $\frac{m}{-5} + 4 \le 7$ **5.** $6 - x > 3$ **6.** $8.3 < -0.5b - 2.7$

Now that you know how to solve two-step inequalities, you can use them to solve real-world problems.

REAL-WORLD  CONNECTION

■ **EXAMPLE 3**

An expedition leader estimates that a group of hikers can carry less than 550 lb of food and equipment. The group must carry 336 lb of equipment as well as 25 lb of food for each climber. What is the greatest possible number of people in the expedition?

A pint of water weighs 1 lb. You need about a gallon of water per person per day. About how much does water weigh for eight people for four days?

Words $\boxed{\begin{array}{c}336 \text{ lb of} \\ \text{equipment}\end{array}} + \boxed{\begin{array}{c}25 \text{ lb of} \\ \text{food/} \\ \text{person}\end{array}}$ times $\boxed{\begin{array}{c}\text{number of} \\ \text{people}\end{array}}$ is less than $\boxed{550 \text{ lb}}$

Let $\boxed{p}$ = number of people in the expedition.

Inequality 336 + $\boxed{25}$ · $\boxed{p}$ < $\boxed{550}$

$336 + 25p < 550$

$336 + 25p - 336 < 550 - 336$ **Subtract 336 from each side.**

$25p < 214$ **Simplify.**

$\dfrac{25p}{25} < \dfrac{214}{25}$ **Divide each side by 25.**

$p < 8.56$ **Simplify.**

Since p is the number of people, p must be a whole number. The greatest number of people in the expedition is 8.

Check Is the answer reasonable? The original problem states that the total of the equipment plus 25 lb of food per person is less than 550 lb. Since $336 + 25(8) = 536$, the equipment plus the food is less than 550 lb. The answer is reasonable.

■ **TRY THIS**

7. *Commissions* A stereo salesperson earns a salary of $1,200 per month, plus a commission of 4% of sales. The salesperson wants to maintain a monthly income of at least $1,500. How much must the salesperson sell each month?

Exercises

CHECK UNDERSTANDING

**Tell what you can do to the first inequality in order to get the second.
Be sure to list *all* the steps.**

1. $4x - 2 \leq 6; x \leq 2$

2. $\frac{1}{2}a - 1 < 3; a < 8$

3. $2 - 3y > 20; y < -6$

Solve each inequality.

4. $-2x - 1 < 11$

5. $10 + 4a < -6$

6. $-\frac{b}{7} + 7 \leq 6$

7. $2.1 - 0.6y \geq 0.9$

8. *Number Sense* You divide a number x by -3. Then you subtract 1 from the quotient. The result is at most 5. Write and solve an inequality to find all possible solutions.

PRACTICE AND PROBLEM SOLVING

Solve and graph each inequality.

9. $2m + 8 > 0$

10. $-\frac{x}{5} + 2 > 3$

11. $-9c + 3 \geq 21$

12. $6 + 3y > 5$

13. $-2a + 18 < 0$

14. $4x - 9 > -7$

15. $11 - 3b > 5$

16. $\frac{1}{3}a - 4 \geq -1$

Solve each inequality.

17. $10 \leq -8x - 6$

18. $-5y + 3 \geq 28$

19. $3.4 < 1 + 0.8p$

20. $4 + 7a \geq 32$

21. $1.6 - 0.4b > -6.4$

22. $-\frac{1}{9}c + 13 \geq 5$

23. $-21 - 3m < 0$

24. $\frac{x}{3} + 11 < 31$

25. $-\frac{x}{6} - 2 < 4$

26. $6y - 10 - y > 14$

27. $-4(2a + 7) \leq -12$

28. $\frac{1}{2}c - \frac{1}{4} < -\frac{3}{4}$

29. *Error Analysis* A student solved and graphed the inequality $-12x + 40 > 4$. What error did the student make?

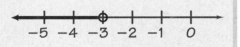

30. **TEST PREP** Which graph shows the solution of $-15 < -2x - 7$?

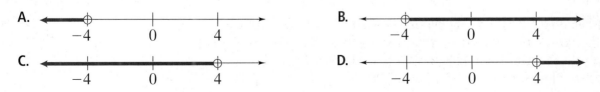

A.
  −4   0   4

B.
  −4   0   4

C.
  −4   0   4

D.
  −4   0   4

31. *Writing* A friend was absent from class today. Write a letter to your friend telling how to solve two-step inequalities.

Write an inequality for each situation. Then solve the inequality.

32. *Data Analysis* Maureen is ordering photographic reprints and enlargements. She can spend at most $11. She wants to order an 11-in. × 14-in. enlargement and some 3-in. × 5-in. reprints. How many reprints can she order using the price list at the right?

Photo Price List	
Size	Price
3 in. x 5 in.	$.40
4 in. x 6 in.	$.45
5 in. x 7 in.	$1.95
8 in. x 10 in.	$4.95
8 in. x 12 in.	$6.45
11 in. x 14 in.	$7.00
16 in. x 20 in.	$13.95
20 in. x 30 in.	$16.95

33. You want to spend at most $10 for a taxi ride. Before you go anywhere, the taxi driver sets the meter at the initial charge of $2. The meter then adds $1.25 for every mile driven. If you plan on a $1 tip, what is the farthest you can go?

34. Students in a math class need an average of at least 90 points to earn an A. One student's test scores are 88, 91, and 85. What must the student score on the next test to earn an A?

35. Corey wants to go on a school music trip to Florida in the spring. His parents agree to lend him $162 if Corey will pay them back at least $18 per month. How long will it take Corey to pay the money he owes to his parents?

▶ **MIXED REVIEW**

Solve each equation. *(Lesson 7-2)*

36. $a - 81 = 9a + 7$ **37.** $8x - 15 + 4x = 5x + 6$ **38.** $4(5m - 7) = 10m + 2$

Use the distance formula, $d = rt$. Find each missing value. *(Lesson 3-4)*

39. $r = 45$ mi/h, $t = 3.25$ h   **40.** $d = 351$ mi, $r = 54$ mi/h   **41.** $d = 12$ cm, $t = 0.25$ h

42. *Sales Tax* A stereo costs $262.99. The sales tax rate is 5%. What is the total cost of the stereo? *(Lesson 6-6)*

CHAPTER PROJECT 7
ACTIVITY 2 CALCULATING

Y ou can use the formula $D = \frac{M}{V}$ to find the density of a liquid, where D is density, M is the mass of the liquid, and V is the volume of the liquid. Substitute your values from Activity 1 for M and V to find the density of water.

Compound Inequalities

Compound inequalities are two inequalities joined by the word *and* or the word *or*.

$x > 4$ and $x \leq 6$

$x \leq -2$ or $x > 3$

A solution of a compound inequality joined by *and* is any number that makes both inequalities true.

A solution of a compound inequality joined by *or* is any number that makes at least one of the inequalities true.

■ EXAMPLE

Graph each compound inequality on a number line.

a. $2 \leq x$ and $x < 6$

A closed circle shows 2 is a solution.

An open circle shows 6 is not a solution.

b. $z > 4$ or $z \leq 1$

closed circle   open circle

Graph each compound inequality.

1. $x \geq 0$ and $x \leq 7$ **2.** $z < -2$ and $z \geq -4$ **3.** $5 > a$ and $a \geq -6$

4. $b < -1$ or $b > 4$ **5.** $c < 2$ or $c > 3.5$ **6.** $y \geq 1$ or $y < -3$

7. $x \leq 4$ and $x \geq 3$ **8.** $n \leq -5$ or $n > 0$ **9.** $3 > m$ and $m > -3$

10. *Writing* Explain why there are no solutions of the compound inequality $x > 2$ and $x \leq -2$.

Transforming Formulas

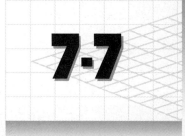

PART 1 Solving Formulas for a Given Variable

Remember that a formula shows the relationship between two or more quantities. You can use the properties of equality to transform a formula to represent one quantity in terms of another.

GEOMETRY CONNECTION

■ EXAMPLE 1

Solve the area formula $A = \ell w$ for ℓ.

$A = \ell w$

$\dfrac{A}{w} = \dfrac{\ell w}{w}$ Use the Division Property of Equality.

$\dfrac{A}{w} = \ell$ or $\ell = \dfrac{A}{w}$ Simplify.

■ **TRY THIS** Solve for the variable indicated in red.

1. $p = s - c$ **2.** $h = \dfrac{k}{j}$ **3.** $I = prt$

Sometimes you may need to use more than one step.

GEOMETRY CONNECTION

■ EXAMPLE 2

Solve the perimeter formula $P = 2\ell + 2w$ for ℓ.

$P = 2\ell + 2w$

$P - 2w = 2\ell + 2w - 2w$ Subtract $2w$ from each side.

$P - 2w = 2\ell$ Simplify.

$\dfrac{P - 2w}{2} = \dfrac{2\ell}{2}$ Divide each side by 2.

$\ell = \dfrac{P - 2w}{2}$ Simplify.

■ **TRY THIS** Solve for the variable indicated in red.

4. $5a + 7 = b$ **5.** $P = 2\ell + 2w$ **6.** $y = \dfrac{x}{3} + 8$

What You'll Learn

1 To solve a formula for a given variable

2 To use formulas to solve problems

...And Why

To find distance or area in real-world situations

You can transform formulas to solve real-world problems.

REAL-WORLD CONNECTION

EXAMPLE 3

You plan a 425-mi trip to Bryce Canyon National Park. You estimate you will average 50 mi/h. To find about how long the trip will take, solve the distance formula $d = rt$ for t. Then substitute to find the time.

$d = rt$

$\dfrac{d}{r} = \dfrac{rt}{r}$ Divide each side by r.

$\dfrac{d}{r} = t$ or $t = \dfrac{d}{r}$ Simplify.

$t = \dfrac{425}{50} = 8.5$ Replace d with 425 and r with 50. Simplify.

It will take you about 8.5 h to complete the trip.

■ TRY THIS

7. Solve the distance formula in Example 3 for r.

REAL-WORLD CONNECTION

EXAMPLE 4

Temperature **An exchange student in your class wants to know the Celsius equivalent of 77°F. First solve the formula $F = \frac{9}{5}C + 32$ for C. Then substitute to find the temperature.**

$F = \frac{9}{5}C + 32$

$F - 32 = \frac{9}{5}C + 32 - 32$ Subtract 32 from each side.

$F - 32 = \frac{9}{5}C$ Simplify.

$\frac{5}{9}(F - 32) = \frac{5}{9} \cdot \frac{9}{5}C$ Multiply each side by $\frac{5}{9}$.

$\frac{5}{9}(F - 32) = C$ or $C = \frac{5}{9}(F - 32)$ Simplify and rewrite.

$C = \frac{5}{9}(77 - 32) = 25$ Replace F with 77. Simplify.

77°F is 25°C.

■ TRY THIS

8. Solve the batting average formula, $a = \frac{h}{n}$, for h. Find the number of hits h a batter needs in 40 times at bat n to have an average of 0.275.

Wind and water, rushing along stone plateaus, erode the stone and create shapes called "fins" and "hoodoos" in Bryce Canyon, Utah. Each year, more than 1.5 million people visit the national park.

Exercises

Complete the steps to solve each equation for the variable indicated in red.

1.
$$a = 6c + 3$$
$$a - \blacksquare = 6c + 3 - 3$$
$$a - \blacksquare = 6c$$
$$\frac{a - 3}{\blacksquare} = \frac{6c}{\blacksquare}$$
$$\frac{a - 3}{\blacksquare} = \blacksquare$$

2.
$$g = \frac{h}{j}$$
$$\blacksquare g = j\left(\frac{h}{j}\right)$$
$$jg = \blacksquare$$
$$\frac{jg}{\blacksquare} = \frac{h}{g}$$
$$\blacksquare = \frac{h}{g}$$

Choose the correct transformation for the variable indicated in red.

3. $z = xy$ ⠀⠀ **A.** $x = \frac{z}{y}$ ⠀⠀ **B.** $x = \frac{y}{z}$ ⠀⠀ **C.** $x = yz$

4. $r = 2s - 8$ ⠀⠀ **A.** $s = \frac{r + 2}{8}$ ⠀⠀ **B.** $s = r + 4$ ⠀⠀ **C.** $s = \frac{r + 8}{2}$

5. $\frac{2}{3}m - 5 = n$ ⠀⠀ **A.** $m = \frac{2}{3}(n + 5)$ ⠀⠀ **B.** $m = \frac{3}{2}(n + 5)$ ⠀⠀ **C.** $m = \frac{3}{2}n + 5$

Solve for the variable indicated in red.

6. $V = \ell w h$ ⠀⠀ **7.** $P = 4s$ ⠀⠀ **8.** $V = \frac{1}{3}\ell w h$ ⠀⠀ **9.** $m = \frac{a + b}{2}$

10. $q = \frac{p}{d}$ ⠀⠀ **11.** $A = \frac{1}{2}bh$ ⠀⠀ **12.** $d^2 = \frac{3}{2}h$ ⠀⠀ **13.** $T = 2h + 3k$

14. Commission LaTanya sells business suits and gets a 4% commission on her sales. Last week, she received a paycheck that included $19.60 in commissions. Solve the formula $C = 0.04s$ for s, where C is the amount of commission and s is the amount of sales. Substitute to find LaTanya's sales.

15. a. Geometry You can use the formula $C = \pi d$ to find the circumference C of a circle when you know the diameter. Solve the formula for d.
b. The circumference of a circle is 15.7 in. Use 3.14 for π. Find the diameter.

16. Writing The formula for the perimeter of a rectangle is $P = 2\ell + 2w$. Explain how you would find the width of the rectangle if you knew the perimeter and the length.

17. **a.** *Construction* Bricklayers use the formula $N = 7LH$ to estimate the number N of bricks needed in a wall. L is the length of the wall and H is the height. Solve the formula for H.
   b. If 1,134 bricks are used to build a wall that is 18 ft long, how high is the wall?

18. **a.** *Economics* Joe uses the formula $p = wh + 1.5wv$ to figure his weekly pay. In the formula, p is the weekly pay, w is the hourly wage, h is the number of regular hours, and v is the number of overtime hours. Solve the formula for v.
   b. Joe's hourly wage is \$6.25/h. If he earned \$282.81 last week working 40 regular hours plus overtime, how many hours overtime did he work?

▶ MIXED REVIEW

Solve each inequality. (*Lesson 7-5*)

19. $3x - 12 > -6$　　**20.** $17 \le -4a + 5$　　**21.** $-\frac{b}{2} + 9 < -3$　　**22.** $\frac{1}{3}y - 7 \ge 2$

Write and solve an equation. Where necessary, round to the nearest tenth or tenth of a percent. (*Lesson 6-7*)

23. What percent of 20 is 15?　　**24.** Find 35% of 45.　　　　**25.** 80% of what number is 25?

26. *Budgeting* Audrey wants to buy a dress for \$54. She has \$6 already and plans to save \$8 each week. In how many weeks will she be able to buy the dress? (*Lesson 7-1*)

✔ CHECKPOINT 2　　　　　　　　　　　　　Lessons 7-5 through 7-7

Solve each equation or inequality.

1. $-8a - 6 = 10$　　　　**2.** $9b + 42 = -12$　　　　**3.** $2c + 6 + 7c = 8$

4. $18y = 12y + 24$　　　**5.** $2x + 5 = 9x - 16$　　　**6.** $12(m - 4) = 3m - 3$

7. $15 - 10y < 24$　　　　**8.** $23 > -\frac{x}{2} - 5$　　　**9.** $1.8x - 3.4 > 5.6$

Solve for the variable indicated in red.

10. $s = g + h$　　　**11.** $3r + 4 = k$　　　**12.** $I = prt$　　　**13.** $M = \frac{4h}{1.5}$

14. | TEST PREP | A school car wash charged \$5 per car. Supplies for the car wash cost \$23. The total of extra donations was \$35. The treasurer says at least \$150 was made at the car wash. What was the least possible number of cars washed?
   A. 18 cars　　**B.** 19 cars　　**C.** 27 cars　　**D.** 28 cars

Simple and Compound Interest

7-8

PART 1 Simple Interest

When you first deposit money in a savings account, your deposit is called **principal.** The bank takes the money and invests it. In return, the bank pays you **interest** based on the **interest rate.** **Simple interest** is interest paid only on the principal.

What You'll Learn

1 To solve simple interest problems

2 To solve compound interest problems

. . . And Why

To find interest paid on investments using simple and compound interest

Simple Interest Formula

$$I = prt,$$
where I is the interest, p is the principal,
r is the interest rate per year, and t is the time in years.

REAL-WORLD CONNECTION

■ EXAMPLE 1

Banking **Suppose you deposit $400 in a savings account. The interest rate is 5% per year.**

a. **Find the interest earned in six years. Find the total of principal plus interest.**

$I = prt$	Use the simple interest formula.
$I = 400 \cdot 0.05 \cdot 6$	Replace p with 400, r with 0.05, and t with 6.
$I = 120$	Simplify.
total $= 400 + 120 = 520$	Find the total.

The account will earn $120 in six years. There will be $520 in the account at the end of six years.

b. **Find the interest earned in three months. Find the total of principal plus interest.**

$t = \frac{3}{12} = \frac{1}{4} = 0.25$	Write the months as part of a year.
$I = prt$	Use the simple interest formula.
$I = 400 \cdot 0.05 \cdot 0.25$	Replace p with 400, r with 0.05, and t with 0.25.
$I = 5$	Simplify.
total $= 400 + 5 = 405$	Find the total.

The account will earn $5 in three months. The balance at the end of three months will be $405.

■ **TRY THIS** Find the simple interest.

1. principal = $250
   interest rate = 4%
   time = 3 years

2. principal = $250
   interest rate = 3.5%
   time = 6 months

PART 2 Compound Interest

When a bank pays interest on the principal *and* on the interest an account has earned, the bank is paying **compound interest.** The principal plus the interest is the **balance,** which becomes the principal on which the bank figures the next interest payment.

REAL-WORLD ● CONNECTION

■ **EXAMPLE 2**

Banking **You deposit $400 in an account that earns 5% interest compounded annually (once per year). What is the balance in your account after 4 years? In your last calculation, round to the nearest cent.**

Principal at Beginning of Year	Interest	Balance
Year 1: $400.00	$400.00 \cdot 0.05 = 20.00$	$400 + 20 = 420.00$
Year 2: $420.00	$420.00 \cdot 0.05 = 21.00$	$420 + 21 = 441.00$
Year 3: $441.00	$441.00 \cdot 0.05 = 22.05$	$441 + 22.05 = 463.05$
Year 4: $463.05	$463.05 \cdot 0.05$ $= 23.1525$	$463.05 + 23.1525$ ≈ 486.20

After four years, the balance is $486.20.

■ **TRY THIS** Make a table and find the balance. The interest is compounded annually.

3. principal = $500
   interest rate = 3%
   time = 2 years

4. principal = $625
   interest rate = 2%
   time = 4 years

You can find a balance using compound interest in one step with the compound interest formula and a calculator. An *interest period* is the length of time over which interest is calculated. The interest period can be a year or less than a year.

Compound Interest Formula

$$B = p(1 + r)^n,$$

where B is the final balance, p is the principal,
r is the interest rate for each interest period, and
n is the number of interest periods.

You can use this formula to solve Example 2.

$B = p(1 + r)^n$

$B = 400(1 + 0.05)^4$ Replace p with 400, r with 0.05, and n with 4.

$B \approx 486.20$ Use a calculator. Round to the nearest cent.

The balance is $486.20. Using the formula means there are fewer calculations and fewer chances for mistakes.

When interest is compounded semiannually (twice per year), you must *divide* the interest rate by the number of interest periods, which is 2.

$$\frac{6\% \text{ annual}}{\text{interest rate}} \div \frac{2 \text{ interest}}{\text{periods}} = \frac{3\% \text{ semiannual}}{\text{interest rate}}$$

To find the number of payment periods, *multiply* the number of years by the number of interest periods per year.

Calculator HINT

Remember to use the parentheses on your calculator when evaluating the compound interest formula.

REAL-WORLD CONNECTION

■ EXAMPLE 3

Banking **Find the balance on a deposit of $1,000, earning 6% interest compounded semiannually for 5 years.**

The interest rate r for compounding semiannually is $0.06 \div 2$, or 0.03. The number of payment periods n is 5 years $\times$ 2 interest periods per year, or 10.

$B = p(1 + r)^n$ Use the compound interest formula.

$B = 1,000(1 + 0.03)^{10}$ Replace p with 1,000, r with 0.03, and n with 10.

$B \approx 1,343.92$ Use a calculator. Round to the nearest cent.

The balance is $1,343.92.

■ **TRY THIS** Find the balance for each account.
Amount deposited: $900, annual interest rate: 2%, time: 3 years

5. compounding annually   **6.** compounding semiannually

Exercises

▶ CHECK UNDERSTANDING

Find the simple interest.

1. $200 deposited at an interest rate of 7% for 2 years

2. $870 deposited at an interest rate of 6% for 9 months

Find the balance.

3. $495 at 8% compounded annually for 2 years

4. $1,280 at 13% compounded annually for 3 years

5. $2,000 at 5% compounded semiannually for 2 years

6. $15,600 at 10% compounded semiannually for 3 years

7. **Mental Math** Calculate the amount of simple interest on $9,000 deposited at an interest rate of 5% for 2 years.

▶ PRACTICE AND PROBLEM SOLVING

Find the simple interest.

8. $500 deposited at an interest rate of 3% for 4 years

9. $35 deposited at an interest rate of 2.5% for 1 year

10. $900 deposited at an interest rate of 8% for 3 months

Complete each table. Compound the interest annually.

11. $3,000 at 4% for 3 years

Principal at Beginning of Year	Interest	Balance
Year 1: $3,000	▦	▦
Year 2: ▦	▦	▦
Year 3: ▦	▦	▦

12. $10,000 at 6% for 3 years

Principal at Beginning of Year	Interest	Balance
Year 1: $10,000	▦	▦
Year 2: ▦	▦	▦
Year 3: ▦	▦	▦

Find each balance.

13. $3,000 at 14% compounded annually for 4 years

14. $8,900 at 9% compounded semiannually for 5 years

15. $54,500 at 3% compounded semiannually for 9 years

16. **Banking** You deposit $600 in a savings account for 3 years. The account pays 8% annual interest compounded quarterly.
    a. What is the quarterly interest rate?
    b. What is the number of payment periods?
    c. Find the final balance in the account.

17. Banking Leroy borrows $800 at 10% annual interest compounded semiannually. He makes no payments.
 a. How much will he owe after four years?
 b. How much interest will he owe in four years?

18. [TEST PREP] Matthew invests $5,000 at 14% simple interest. About how much interest will he earn in eight months?
 A. $467   **B.** $700   **C.** $1,050   **D.** $5,467

19. Open-ended Choose an amount of money to be invested and an interest rate. Find the value of the investment after 5 years if the interest is simple interest; if the interest is compounded annually.

20. Writing Explain the difference between simple interest and compound interest.

21. Banking Ling invests $1,000 in an account paying 8% interest.
 a. Compare the account balances after 5 years of simple interest and after 5 years of interest compounded annually.
 b. After how many years of compounded interest will the account balance be about twice Ling's initial investment?
 c. Critical Thinking What would the simple interest rate on Ling's investment have to be for the investment to double in the same amount of time?

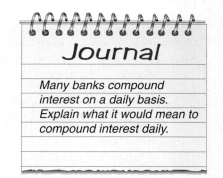

Journal

Many banks compound interest on a daily basis. Explain what it would mean to compound interest daily.

► MIXED REVIEW

Solve for the variable indicated in red. *(Lesson 7-6)*

22. $f = \frac{15m}{a}$ **23.** $E = mc^2$ **24.** $y = 4x - 9$ **25.** $d = \frac{5}{8}k + 1$

Graph each point on a coordinate plane. *(Lesson 1-10)*

26. $A(-2, 0)$ **27.** $B(2, 3)$ **28.** $C(-4, -5)$ **29.** $D(1, -3)$

30. Architecture A floor plan has a scale of $\frac{1}{4}$ in. : 5 ft. Find the length on the drawing for an actual length of 60 ft. *(Lesson 6-3)*

CHAPTER PROJECT 7

ACTIVITY 3 CALCULATING

Measure and record the mass of 250 mL of each of these liquids: vinegar, vegetable oil, and corn syrup. Use the formula from Activity 2 to calculate the density of each liquid. Compare the density of each liquid to the density of water.

MATH TOOLBOX

Credit Card Interest

When you use a credit card, you are charged interest each month on the balance in your account. You can use a spreadsheet to investigate the interest charged on a credit card account.

You use a credit card to buy a $450 airline ticket. You are charged 1.8% monthly interest on your account balance, and you make a $40 payment each month. Using a spreadsheet program, create a spreadsheet with the formulas shown in red.

	A	B	C	D	E	F
1	Month	Balance	Planned Monthly Payment	Interest	New Balance	Total Interest
2	1	450	40	=B2*0.018	=B2+D2−C2	=D2
3	=A2+1	=E2				=F2+D3
4						

The arrows indicate you should use the Fill Down feature of your spreadsheet program. This will calculate successive months for you.

Use your spreadsheet. Round any totals to the nearest cent.

1. **a.** In which month is the balance less than the monthly payment?
    b. Your last payment is the balance plus the interest in the month you found in part (a). What is the amount of the last payment?
    c. What is the total interest paid on this account?

2. **a.** Change the monthly payment to $60 a month. In which month is the balance less than the monthly payment?
    b. What is the total interest paid on this account?

3. **a.** Create a new spreadsheet using a beginning balance of $1,200, 2.1% monthly interest, and a monthly payment of $100. What is the total interest paid on this account in 5 months?
    b. Change the monthly payment to $200. What is the total interest paid on this account in 5 months?
    c. *Critical Thinking* What can you conclude about the relationship between the amount of monthly payments and the amount of interest charges?

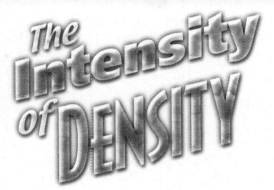

The Intensity of DENSITY

Find the Densities of Liquids The Project Activities on pages 344, 363, and 373 will help you complete your project. Here is a checklist to help you gather the different parts.

✔ your measurements of the mass and volume of water

✔ your calculation of the density of water

✔ your measurements and calculations for the densities of other liquids

Write a report that summarizes your activities and presents your results. Which liquid has the greatest density? Make a prediction about what would happen if you poured two of the liquids into one jar or beaker. Use diagrams and tables as needed to illustrate the report.

Reflect and Revise

Ask a friend or someone at home to review your calculations and your report. Are they accurate and clear? If necessary, make changes to improve them.

Web Extension

Visit Prentice Hall's Web site. You'll find some interesting links and ideas related to density. You'll also be able to share information about your project.

www.phschool.com

7 Wrap Up

■ Key Terms

balance (p. 370)
compound interest (p. 370)
consecutive integers (p. 341)

interest (p. 369)
interest rate (p. 369)

principal (p. 369)
simple interest (p. 369)

■ Graphic Organizer

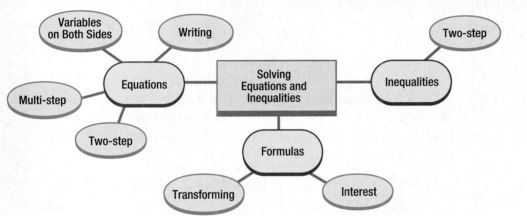

■ Two-Step Equations
7-1

Summary To solve two-step equations, undo addition and subtraction, then undo multiplication and division.

Solve each equation.

1. $2a - 7 = -15$

2. $3 = -6x + 15$

3. $\frac{c}{4} + 10 = 22$

4. $1.5y + 3.4 = 7.9$

5. $\frac{2}{3}y - 9 = 5$

6. $8 = 9x - 7$

■ Multi-Step Equations
7-2 and 7-3

Summary To solve multi-step equations, remove grouping symbols and combine like terms first. Then follow the steps for solving two-step equations.

Solve each equation.

7. $8m - 3m = 4$

8. $6 - 2y - y = 12$

9. $\frac{2}{3}q + 5 = \frac{3}{4}$

10. $\frac{1}{4}(b - 7) = 8$

11. $3(2x + 5) = -39$

12. $-2(5 + 6c) + 16 = -90$

13. Number Sense Find four consecutive integers with a sum of -66.

■ *Write an Equation*

Summary One strategy for solving problems is to write an equation and then solve the equation.

Write an equation. Solve.

14. A pair of jeans is on sale for 15% off the original price. The sale price of the jeans is $29.74. What was the original price?

15. A bank teller is counting his money and notices that he has an equal number of tens and twenties. He also has $147 in other bills. If the total value of the bills he has is $1,167, how many tens and twenties does he have?

16. *Finance* Jalisha invested some money and made an 8% profit. The current value of her investment is $1,308. How much did she invest initially?

■ *Equations with Variables on Both Sides*

Summary To solve equations with variables on both sides, first simplify both sides of the equation. Then use properties of equality to get the variable alone on one side of the equation.

Solve each equation.

17. $7x = 33 - 4x$ 18. $2a - 24 - 3a = 5a$ 19. $5x + 7 = -5x + 19$

20. $4x - 26 = 5(2 - x)$ 21. $8(b + 3) = 4b - 4$ 22. $2x - (9 - 3x) = 8x - 11$

23. A refrigerated truck leaves a rest stop traveling at a steady rate of 56 mi/h. A car leaves the same rest stop $\frac{1}{4}$ h later following the truck at a steady rate of 64 mi/h. How long after the truck leaves the rest stop will the car overtake the truck?

■ *Two-Step Inequalities*

Summary Solving two-step inequalities involves the same steps as solving two-step equations. Reverse the direction of the inequality symbol when you multiply or divide by a negative number.

Solve and graph each inequality.

24. $2a - 3 > 11$ 25. $9y + 13 \le -14$ 26. $-6c + 12 \ge 8$ 27. $23 < 7 - 4x$

28. $\frac{8}{9}x + 5 < -3$ 29. $-\frac{b}{2} + 14 > 13$ 30. $-17 > \frac{x}{3} - 19$ 31. $x + 4x + 9 \ge 6$

32. Last year's personal computer model is on sale for $799. You can add more memory to the computer. Each chip of 8 megabytes of memory costs $25. How many megabytes of memory can you add if you have at most $1,000 to spend? Write and solve an inequality.

■ Transforming Formulas 7-7

Summary Use the properties of equality to transform a formula.

Solve for the variable indicated in red.

33. $r = 6km$

34. $8x = 6y$

35. $Q = gp$

36. $a = b - 2c$

37. $w = 3a + 5n$

38. $e = \frac{h}{6} + 11$

■ Simple and Compound Interest 7-8

Summary You can calculate **simple interest** using the formula $I = prt$, where I is the interest, p is the **principal** (original amount deposited), r is the **interest rate** per year, and t is the time in years.

Compound interest is interest paid on both the principal and interest. It is found using the formula $B = p(1 + r)^n$, where B is the final **balance**, p is the principal, r is the interest rate for each interest period, and n is the number of interest periods.

Find the simple interest.

39. $150 deposited at an interest rate of 9% for 2 years

40. $2,525 deposited at an interest rate of 2.5% for 4 years

41. $6,500 deposited at an interest rate of 3% for 6 months

Find each balance.

42. $8,000 at 12% compounded annually for 3 years

43. $17,500 at 17% compounded annually for 6 years

44. $22,000 at 6% compounded semiannually for 8 years

45. $33,800 at 18% compounded semiannually for 5 years

46. *Writing* The more interest periods there are, the more interest you make on an investment. Do you agree with this statement? Explain why or why not.

Assessment

Solve each equation.

1. $3x + 4 = 19$

2. $5 + \frac{c}{9} = -31$

3. $2y - 15 = 11$

4. $8a + 3 = -12.2$

5. $\frac{3}{5}b - 8 = 4$

6. $\frac{m}{2} - 5 = 7$

7. $-83 = 9x - 2$

8. $18 - \frac{a}{4} = -5$

9. $\frac{3}{5}y + \frac{2}{5} = \frac{4}{5}$

10. $-23 - c = -19$

11. $3x + 4x = 21$

12. $\frac{1}{2}(10y + 4) = 17$

13. $2(7b - 6) - 4 = 12$

14. $2m - 6 = m$

15. $\frac{2}{3}a - 5 + \frac{8}{9}a = -19$

16. $0.015x + 3.45 = 4.65$

17. $12y + 3 = 9y - 15$

18. $3(2b + 6) = 2(4b - 8)$

Write an equation. Solve.

19. *Number Sense* Find three consecutive integers with a sum of 267.

20. A rental car company charges $35 a day plus $.15/mi for a mid-size car. A customer owes $117.25 for a three-day rental. How many miles did the customer drive?

21. A moving truck leaves a house and travels at a steady rate of 40 mi/h. The family leaves the house 1 h later following the same route in a car. They travel at a steady rate of 60 mi/h. How long after the moving truck leaves the house will the car catch up with the truck?

22. The Jaspers have a jar where they collect nickels, dimes, and quarters. When they count the change in the jar, there are twice as many nickels as there are quarters. If there is $15.30 in dimes and $74.80 in all, how many quarters are there?

Solve and graph each inequality.

23. $7m - 8 > 6$

24. $2x - 6 \geq -9$

25. $-9a - 1 \leq 26$

26. $22 < 6c + 4$

27. $\frac{b}{3} + 12 > -3$

28. $-\frac{2}{3}x + 8 \leq 2$

29. $11 > -3y + 2$

30. $16 - 4a \geq 18$

31. *Commissions* An insurance salesperson earns a salary of $1,200 per month plus a commission of 3% of sales. How much must the salesperson sell to have a monthly income of at least $1,500?

32. *Writing* How is solving a two-step inequality different from solving a two-step equation?

Solve for the variable indicated in red.

33. $H = 3w$

34. $g = cst$

35. $R = 6n + 4p$

36. $y = \frac{x}{5} - 4$

Find the simple interest.

37. $800 deposited at an interest rate of 1.5% for 3 years

38. $1,050 deposited at an interest rate of 2% for 9 months

39. $2,500 deposited at an interest rate of 8% for 5 years

Find each balance.

40. $12,000 at 8% compounded annually for 4 years

41. $1,950 at 5% compounded annually for 2 years

42. $18,500 at 9% compounded semiannually for 5 years

43. $75,000 at 15% compounded semiannually for 8 years

Choose the best answer.

1. Complete $43(2) - (-3)$ ■ $-58 + (-4)12$.
   A. >   B. <   C. =   D. ≤

2. Simplify $3(a + 2b) - 3a$.
   F. $-6a + 6b$ G. $3a + 6b$
   H. $2b$ J. $6b$

3. Use the batting average formula $a = \frac{h}{n}$ for $a = 0.254$ and $n = 25$. Find the number of hits h. Round to the nearest integer.
   A. 98   B. 7   C. 6   D. 0

4. Find the GCF of $4a^3b^2$ and $12ab^3$.
   F. $4ab^2$ G. $12a^3b^3$ H. $3a^2b$ J. $16a^2b^4$

5. Which expression is equal to $1\frac{1}{2}$?
   A. $2\frac{5}{8} - 1\frac{1}{4}$ B. $\frac{-3}{-2} - \frac{1}{2}$
   C. $3\frac{1}{s} - 1\frac{3}{s}, s = 4$ D. $\frac{b - 1.5}{3.5 - b}, b = \frac{1}{2}$

6. Scott jumped 15 ft $6\frac{3}{8}$ in. The school record for the long jump is 15 ft $8\frac{7}{8}$ in. How much shorter was Scott's jump?
   F. $2\frac{1}{2}$ in.   G. $1\frac{1}{2}$ in.   H. $2\frac{1}{8}$ in.   J. $2\frac{1}{4}$ in.

7. Which statement is *not* true?
   A. $\frac{5}{8} > 40\%$ B. $0.09\% < \frac{1}{10}$
   C. $100\% = 1$ D. $0.125 > 20\%$

8. Sixteen of the 50 members of the rock climbing club are going climbing today. What percent of the club is going?
   F. 33%   G. 32%   H. 3.125%   J. 0.32

9. Which graph shows the solutions of $-15 > 7x + 20$?

   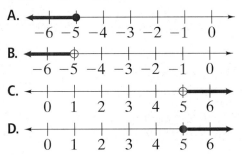

10. A recipe requires 2.5 cups of juice concentrate for every 4 cups of water. How much juice concentrate is required to fill a 20-cup punch bowl?
    F. 12.5 cups   G. 10 cups
    H. 50 cups   J. 8 cups

11. A magazine telemarketer receives a weekly salary of $240 plus $3.00 for each magazine subscription she sells. She uses the formula $p = 240 + 3n$ where p is total pay and n is the number of subscriptions sold. Solve the formula for n.
    A. $n = p + 240$ B. $n = \frac{240 + p}{3}$
    C. $n = 240 + 3p$ D. $n = \frac{p - 240}{3}$

12. Use the formula you found for Exercise 11 to find the number of subscriptions for total pay p of $360.
    F. 30   G. 40   H. 90   J. 120

For Exercises 13–22, show your work.

13. A savings account earns 10% simple interest. How much interest does an $800 deposit earn in four years?

14. a. Greg deposits $800 into a savings account that earns 10% interest compounded annually. What is Greg's balance after four years?
    b. How much interest did Greg's account earn?

Solve each equation.

15. $4x - 2 = 18$ 16. $3(n - 5) = 12$

17. $\frac{1}{2}(4a + 16) = 5$ 18. $5.2 = 3.8h + 7.1$

19. $\frac{2}{5}m + 4 = -\frac{3}{5}$ 20. $14 - \frac{m}{3} = \frac{7}{9}$

21. $14n + 12 = 5n - 6$

22. $6(k - 2) = 3k - 6$

Skills You Need
for Chapter 8

► **Transforming equations**   Use before Lesson 8-2.

Solve each equation for y.

1. $4x + y = 3$
2. $y - 4 = -2x$
3. $8x - 4y = 24$
4. $8 + y + 6x = 0$
5. $12 - y = x$
6. $2y + x = 5$
7. $5y - 20 = x$
8. $3x + 4y = 12$

► **Graphing points**   Use before Lessons 8-2, 8-3, 8-4, and 8-7.

Write the coordinates of each point.

9. A
10. B
11. C
12. D
13. E
14. F

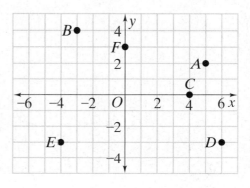

Draw a coordinate plane. Graph each point.

15. $G(3, 0)$
16. $H(-2, 4)$
17. $J(6, 1)$
18. $K(5, -3)$
19. $L(-4, -3)$
20. $M(0, -2)$

► **Simplifying ratios**   Use before Lesson 8-3.

Write each ratio in simplest form.

21. $\dfrac{6 - 2}{3 - 1}$
22. $\dfrac{8 - 5}{4 - 2}$
23. $\dfrac{7 - (-1)}{10 - 2}$
24. $\dfrac{-3 - 5}{4 - 0}$
25. $\dfrac{-5 - (-4)}{12 - (-6)}$
26. $\dfrac{15 - (-12)}{17 - 8}$
27. $\dfrac{-4 - 1}{-7 - (-2)}$
28. $\dfrac{4.3 - 3.5}{7.1 - 4.7}$

► **Describing number patterns**   Use before Lesson 8-6.

Write the next two numbers in each pattern.

29. $-3, -5, -7, -9, \ldots$
30. $7, 12, 17, 22, \ldots$
31. $8, 5, 2, -1, \ldots$
32. $43, 37, 31, 25, \ldots$
33. $4.5, 6, 7.5, 9, \ldots$
34. $27, 41, 55, 69, \ldots$

Linear Functions and Graphing

What you'll learn in this chapter:

■ How to determine whether a relation is a function

■ How to solve linear equations

■ How to solve systems of linear equations and inequalities

Rental Math

Your school is planning its graduation ceremony. Hundreds of people will be coming, and they need a place to sit. Your school has some chairs, but not enough for this crowd! Better call a rental company.

Compare Prices For the chapter project, you will research the cost of renting folding chairs. You do not yet know how many chairs you will need, so you will investigate the price per chair, as well as delivery charges. For your report to the graduation committee, you will write and graph equations to show the total costs of renting chairs from different companies.

Steps to help you complete the project

Web Extension
www.phschool.com

How to solve a problem by graphing

Relating Graphs to Events

You can use graphs to show real-world relationships visually.
Labels can help explain the parts of a graph.

■ EXAMPLE 1

Transportation **The graph at the right shows one trip from home to school and back. The trip combines walking and getting a ride from a neighbor. Tell what the graph shows by labeling each part.**

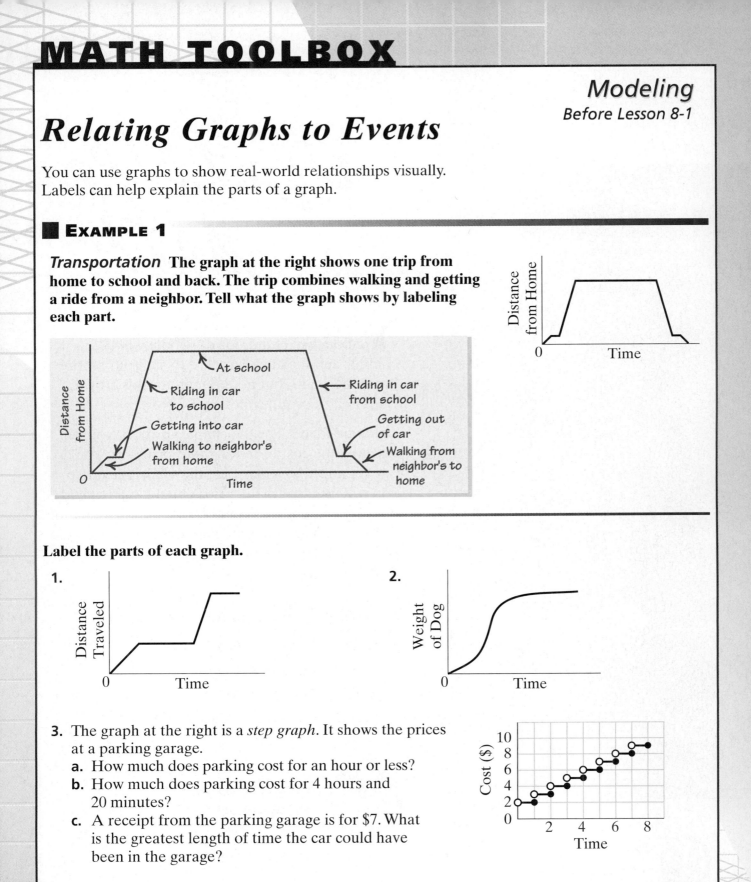

Label the parts of each graph.

1.

2.

3. The graph at the right is a *step graph*. It shows the prices at a parking garage.
   a. How much does parking cost for an hour or less?
   b. How much does parking cost for 4 hours and 20 minutes?
   c. A receipt from the parking garage is for $7. What is the greatest length of time the car could have been in the garage?

4. **Critical Thinking** Use the graph below. Jolene and Tamika were sprinting. Which girl ran faster? Explain.

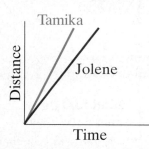

When you draw a graph without actual data, you are making a sketch. A sketch can help you visualize relationships.

■ EXAMPLE 2

You go to an amusement park and ride a moving horse on a carousel. Sketch a graph to show your height above the ground. Identify your axes and include labels for each part.

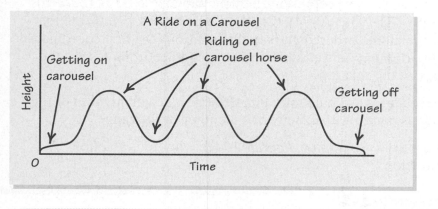

Sketch a graph for each situation. Identify your axes and include labels for each part.

5. the temperature outside during one 24-hour period

6. your speed as you take a trip on a train

7. the total distance you travel as you go to a concert and return home

8. the distance above ground of a pole vaulter's feet at a track meet

9. You pour water at a constant rate into the container shown at the right. Sketch a graph of the water level as you fill the container.

8-1

Relations and Functions

What You'll Learn

1 To determine whether a relation is a function

2 To graph relations and functions

...And Why

To model everyday activities in which one quantity depends on another, such as cooking a turkey

The table shows the results of a canned food drive.

You can write the data in the table as a **relation,** a set of ordered pairs. The first coordinate of each ordered pair is the number of students in a homeroom. The second coordinate is the number of cans the students in that homeroom collected.

Food for Life Canned Food Drive

Homeroom	Number of Students	Number of Cans
101	25	133
102	22	216
103	24	148
104	22	195
105	20	74
106	21	150

Here is the relation represented by the table: {(25, 133), (22, 216), (24, 148), (22, 195), (20, 74), (21, 150)}. The braces, {}, indicate that these are all the ordered pairs in this relation. The first coordinates are the **domain** of the relation. The second coordinates are the **range** of the relation.

Some relations are functions. In a **function,** each member of the domain is paired with exactly one member of the range.

You can draw a *mapping diagram* to see whether a relation is a function.

■ EXAMPLE 1

Is each relation a function? Explain.

a. {(0, 1), (1, 2), (1, 3), (2, 4)}

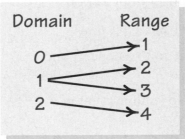

List the domain values and the range values in order.

Draw arrows from the domain values to their range values.

There are two range values for the domain value 1. This relation is not a function.

b. {(0, 1), (1, 2), (2, 2), (3, 4)}   **c.** {(0, 1), (1, 3), (2, 2), (3, 4)}

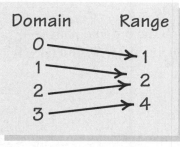

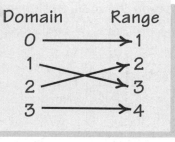

There is one range value
for each domain value.
This relation is a function.

There is one range value
for each domain value.
This relation is a function.

■ **TRY THIS** Is each relation a function? Explain.

1. {(−2, 3), (2, 2), (2, −2)}   **2.** {(−5, −4), (0, −4), (5, −4)}

Functions can model many everyday situations when one quantity
depends on another. One quantity *is a function of* the other.

REAL-WORLD CONNECTION

■ **EXAMPLE 2**

Cooking **Is the time needed to cook a turkey a function of the
weight of the turkey? Explain.**

The time the turkey cooks (range value) is determined by the
weight of the turkey (domain value). This relation is a function.

You can estimate the
cooking time of a turkey:
20 minutes per pound
unstuffed, or 30 minutes
per pound stuffed.

■ **TRY THIS**

3. For the United States Postal Service, is package weight a
function of the postage paid to mail the package? Explain.

4. Is the cost of postage a function of package weight? Explain.

PART 2 **Graphing Relations and Functions**

Graphing a relation on a coordinate plane gives you a visual way to tell
whether the relation is a function. If the relation is a function, then any
vertical line can pass through only one point on the graph. If you can
find a vertical line that passes through two points on the graph, then the
relation is *not* a function. This is the **vertical-line test.**

a. Graph the relation shown in the table.

x-coordinates   *y*-coordinates

Domain Value	Range Value
−4	−3
2	0
2	3
4	3
5	−4

Graph the ordered pairs (−4, −3), (2, 0), (2, 3), (4, 3), and (5, −4).

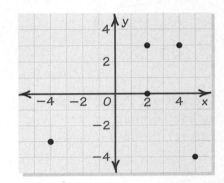

Quick Review

The first value in an ordered pair is the *x*-coordinate, which shows horizontal position.

The second value in an ordered pair is the *y*-coordinate, which shows vertical position.

b. Use the vertical-line test. Is the relation a function? Explain.

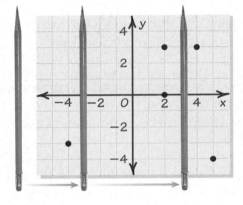

Pass a pencil across the graph as shown. Keep the pencil vertical (parallel to the *y*-axis) to represent a vertical line.

The pencil held vertically would pass through both (2, 0) and (2, 3), so the relation is *not* a function.

■ **TRY THIS** Graph each relation. Use the vertical-line test to tell whether the relation is a function.

5.

x	y
−6	−5
−3	−2
0	−2
1	0
4	3
5	7

6.

x	y
−7	4
−2	6
−1	−1
−1	3
0	5
1	5

7.

x	y
−5	4
−4	4
−3	4
0	0
1	4
2	4

Exercises

CHECK UNDERSTANDING

For each relation, list the members of the domain. Then list the members of the range.

1. $\{(0, 1), (3, 5), (2, 2), \left(-\frac{1}{2}, \frac{4}{5}\right)\}$

2. $\{(-1, 2), (-2, 2), (-2, 3), (0, 2)\}$

Is each relation a function? Explain.

3. $\{(3, -1), (3, 0), (-3, 4), (3, 8), (-2, 8)\}$

4. $\{(-3, -2), (-1, 0), (1, 0), (5, -2), (6, 4)\}$

5. Domain Range

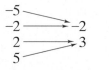

6. Domain Range

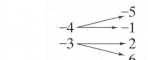

7. **8.**

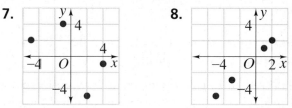

9. Is age a function of height?

10. Is the time you take to walk to the library a function of the distance to the library?

11. Is the price of a piece of cloth a function of the length of the cloth?

PRACTICE AND PROBLEM SOLVING

Is each relation a function? Explain.

12. $\{(-1, 9), (0, -1), (-1, 4), (4, 9)\}$

13. $\{(-12, 7), (-3, -6), (0, -6), (8, 7)\}$

14. $\{(4, -8), (4, -6), (1, 2), (1, 5), (1, -6)\}$

15. $\{(-1.2, 1.5), (1.5, -1.2), (0.37, -0.37)\}$

16. Domain Range

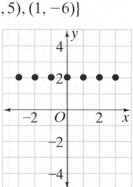

17. **18.** **19.**

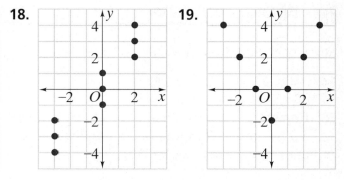

Graph each relation. Is the relation a function? Explain.

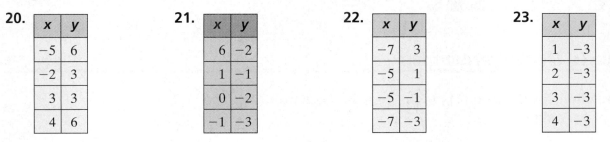

20.

x	y
−5	6
−2	3
3	3
4	6

21.

x	y
6	−2
1	−1
0	−2
−1	−3

22.

x	y
−7	3
−5	1
−5	−1
−7	−3

23.

x	y
1	−3
2	−3
3	−3
4	−3

Patterns In each function below, there is a pattern to how the range values relate to the domain values. Describe the pattern.

24. $\{(-7, -5), (-2, 0), (0, 2), (3, 5), (8, 10)\}$

25. $\{(-5, 5), (-1, 1), (0, 0), (3, 3), (9, 9)\}$

26. $\{(-4, -2), (-1, -0.5), (2, 1), (7, 3.5)\}$

27. $\{(1, 1), (2, 4), (3, 9), (4, 16), (5, 25)\}$

28. Is the number of students on a field trip a function of the number of buses used? Explain.

29. Is the number of buses used for a field trip a function of the number of students on the field trip? Explain.

30. *Writing* Is every relation a function? Is every function a relation? Explain.

31. *Geometry* Explain why the area of a square is a function of the length of a side of the square.

32. a. *Open-ended* Write two different relations for which the domain is $\{-1, 0, 1\}$ and the range is $\{1, 2\}$.
　　b. Graph your relations. Use the vertical-line test to tell whether each relation is a function.

33. *Error Analysis* Your friend says that a relation is not a function when two ordered pairs have the same *y*-coordinate. Explain your friend's error.

◤ **MIXED REVIEW**

Solve each equation. *(Lessons 7-1 and 7-3)*

34. $-42 + 3c = -6$　　**35.** $\frac{3}{2}t - 4 = \frac{1}{2}$　　　　**36.** $2m - 4.9 = -3.6$　　**37.** $-4x + 7 = -5$

38. *Banking* Suppose you invest $1,200 in an account that earns 3.5% interest compounded annually. Find the account balance after four years. *(Lesson 7-8)*

　　　　　　　　　　　　　　　　See also Extra Practice section.

Equations with Two Variables

PART 1 Finding Solutions

In previous chapters you solved equations like $2x + 5 = 7x$, which has only one variable. In this chapter, you will find solutions of equations like $y = 3x + 4$, which has two variables. An ordered pair that makes an equation in two variables a true statement is a **solution** of the equation.

EXAMPLE 1

Find the solution of $y = 3x + 4$ for $x = -1$.

$y = 3x + 4$

$y = 3(-1) + 4$ Replace x with -1.

$y = -3 + 4$ Multiply.

$y = 1$ Add.

A solution of the equation is $(-1, 1)$.

TRY THIS Find the solution of each equation for $x = -3$.

1. $y = 2x + 1$ **2.** $y = -4x + 3$ **3.** $y = 0x - 4$

You can use two-variable equations to model real-world situations.

REAL-WORLD CONNECTION

EXAMPLE 2

Meteorology **The equation $t = 21 - 0.01n$ models the normal low July temperature in degrees Celsius at Mt. Rushmore, South Dakota. In the equation, t is the temperature at n meters above the base of the mountain. Find the normal low July temperature at 300 m above the base.**

$t = 21 - 0.01n$

$t = 21 - 0.01(300)$ Replace n with 300.

$t = 21 - 3$ Multiply.

$t = 18$ Subtract.

A solution of the equation is $(300, 18)$. The normal low July temperature at 300 m above the base of the mountain is 18°C.

What You'll Learn

1 To find solutions of linear equations with two variables

2 To graph linear equations with two variables

...And Why

To investigate relationships in meteorology and oceanography

Mt. Rushmore is 1,745 meters tall.

4. Find the normal low July temperature at 700 m above the base of Mt. Rushmore.

PART 2 | **Graphing Equations with Two Variables**

An equation with two variables can have many solutions. One way to show these solutions is to graph them, which also gives a graph of the equation. A **linear equation** is any equation whose graph is a line. All the equations in this lesson are linear equations.

■ **EXAMPLE 3**

Graph $y = -\frac{1}{2}x + 3$.

Make a table of values to show ordered-pair solutions.

x	$-\frac{1}{2}x + 3$	(x, y)
-2	$-\frac{1}{2}(-2) + 3 = 1 + 3 = 4$	$(-2, 4)$
0	$-\frac{1}{2}(0) + 3 = 0 + 3 = 3$	$(0, 3)$
4	$-\frac{1}{2}(4) + 3 = -2 + 3 = 1$	$(4, 1)$

Graph the ordered pairs. Draw a line through the points.

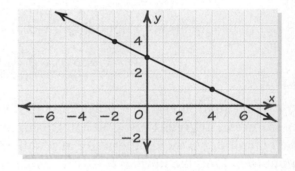

Quick Review

The expression $-\frac{1}{2}x$ means "the opposite of $\frac{1}{2}x$." So when the value of x is -2, the expression $-\frac{1}{2}x$ represents the opposite of one half of -2, which is 1.

■ **TRY THIS** Graph each linear equation.

5. $y = 2x + 1$ **6.** $y = 3x - 2$ **7.** $y = -\frac{1}{2}x + 4$

If you use the vertical-line test on the graph in Example 3, you see that every x-value has exactly one y-value. This means that the relation $y = -\frac{1}{2}x + 3$ is a function. A linear equation is a function *unless* its graph is a vertical line.

EXAMPLE 4

Graph each equation. Is the equation a function?

a. $y = 2$

For every value of x, $y = 2$.

This is a horizontal line. The graph of $y = 2$ is a function.

b. $x = 2$

For every value of y, $x = 2$.

This is a vertical line. The graph of $x = 2$ is *not* a function.

■ **TRY THIS** Graph each equation. Is the equation a function?

8. $x = 1$ **9.** $y = -4$ **10.** $x = 0$

You may find it helpful to solve an equation for y before you find solutions and graph the equation.

EXAMPLE 5

Solve $3x + y = -5$ for y. Then graph the equation.

Solve the equation for y.

$$3x + y = -5$$
$$3x + y - 3x = -5 - 3x \qquad \text{Subtract } 3x \text{ from each side.}$$
$$y = -3x - 5 \qquad \text{Simplify.}$$

Make a table of values.

x	$-3x - 5$	(x, y)
-2	$-3(-2) - 5 = 1$	$(-2, 1)$
-1	$-3(-1) - 5 = -2$	$(-1, -2)$
0	$-3(0) - 5 = -5$	$(0, -5)$

Graph.

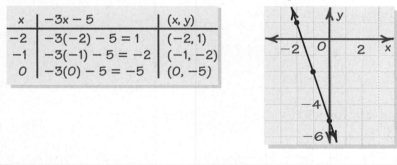

■ **TRY THIS** Solve each equation for y. Then graph the equation.

11. $2x + y = 3$ **12.** $y - x = 5$ **13.** $-3x + 2y = 6$

Exercises

CHECK UNDERSTANDING

Is each ordered pair a solution of $4x - 3y = 6$?

1. $(3, 2)$ **2.** $(-3, -2)$ **3.** $(0, 2)$ **4.** $(2, 0)$ **5.** $(1.5, 0)$

Solve each equation for y.

6. $-4x + y = 16$ **7.** $-3y = 3x - 9$ **8.** $2x - 4y = 12$

Graph each equation.

9. $y = x - 3$ **10.** $-1 = y$ **11.** $4x + y = -3$

PRACTICE AND PROBLEM SOLVING

Find the solutions of each equation for $x = -2, 1$, and 4.

12. $y = 4x - 5$ **13.** $y = -2x$ **14.** $y = 2x - 1$ **15.** $y = 7 - 3x$

16. $y = x + 4$ **17.** $y = -x + 32$ **18.** $y = \frac{1}{4}x + 6$ **19.** $y = \frac{3}{5}x - 6$

Graph each equation.

20. $y = x + 3$ **21.** $y = x - 10$ **22.** $y = 2x - 1$ **23.** $y = 0.5x - 6$

24. $y = -3x + 7$ **25.** $y = -6$ **26.** $y = -x - 2$ **27.** $-3x = 2y$

28. $x = 7$ **29.** $y = \frac{3}{2}x + 5$ **30.** $x - 2y = 8$ **31.** $x - 2y = -2$

32. **TEST PREP** Which ordered pair is *not* a solution of $-4y = 3x - 1$?

    A. $(0, -1)$ **B.** $\left(\frac{2}{3}, -\frac{1}{4}\right)$ **C.** $(-1.5, 1.375)$ **D.** $(0.\overline{3}, 0)$

33. a. For the equation $y = 3x - 2$, make a table of values
    for $x = 1, 2, 3, 4$, and 5.
    b. *Patterns* Describe the number pattern formed by the
    y-coordinates.

34. *Error Analysis* A student solved $3x + 4y = 12$ for y. Her work is
at the right. What error did the student make?

35. *Writing* Explain how you can determine from a linear equation
whether the solutions of the equation form a function.

> $3x + 4y = 12$
>
> $4y = 12 - 3x$
>
> $y = 3 - 3x$

Math in the Media Use the article for Exercise 36.

36. The equation $y = 14.7 + 0.44x$ gives the pressure y in pounds per square inch at a depth of x feet below sea level.
    a. **Open-ended** Find four solutions of this equation.
    b. Find the pressure at the depth of the record dive.

37. If you swim the backstroke, you burn 9 cal/min (calories per minute). If you swim the butterfly stroke, you burn 12 cal/min. The equation $9x + 12y = 360$ models how you can burn 360 cal by swimming the backstroke for x min and the butterfly for y min.
    a. Find the solutions of the equation for $x = 0$ and $y = 0$. Explain what your solutions mean.
    b. Graph the solutions you found in part (a). Draw a line through the two points.
    c. **Language** The solutions you found in part (a) are the *y-intercept* and the *x-intercept* of the graph. Explain why these names are appropriate.
    d. Use your graph from part (b). If you swim the butterfly stroke for 10 min, how long should you swim the backstroke to burn a total of 360 calories?

> **Mountains Under the Sea**
>
> There is a mountain range in the Pacific Ocean far beneath the surface. Jacques Piccard and Donald Walsh made a record dive in these mountains in a submersible. Piccard and Walsh descended to 35,814 ft.
>
> The depth of the dive is remarkable because of the tremendous of pressure at these depths. The pressure of the air at sea level is 14.7 lb/in.^{2}, and the pressure increases about 0.44 lb/in.^{2} for every foot an object descends below sea level.

▶ MIXED REVIEW

Is each relation a function? Explain. *(Lesson 8-1)*

38. $\{(2, 4), (3, 6), (-3, 6), (1, 2)\}$ 39. $\{(0, 3), (2, 1), (-7, 2), (1, 1)\}$ 40. $\{(3, 4), (2.3, 6), (3, -7)\}$

Write each decimal or fraction as a percent. *(Lesson 6-5)*

41. 0.62   42. $\frac{3}{8}$ 43. 1.2   44. 3.507   45. $\frac{17}{20}$ 46. $\frac{11}{10}$

47. **Astronomy** The sun orbits the Milky Way galaxy at about 135 mi/s. How far does the sun travel in an hour? In a week? Write your answers in scientific notation. *(Lessons 4-9 and 5-5)*

CHAPTER PROJECT 8

ACTIVITY 1 RESEARCHING

Contact two or three rental companies in your area. Find out the price per chair for renting plastic folding chairs. Also find out the delivery charge. Organize the information in a table like the one at the right.

Company	Price per Chair	Delivery Charge
▩	▩	▩
▩	▩	▩

Extension
After Lesson 8-2

Direct Variation

A *direct variation* is a linear function modeled by the equation $y = kx$, where $k \neq 0$. The coefficient k is the slope, or the *constant of variation*. In a direct variation, you can find k from one ordered pair (x, y). The graph of a direct variation always includes the origin.

■ EXAMPLE 1

Write an equation for the direct variation that includes $A(-3, 5)$.

Step 1 First find the value of k.

$y = kx$ Use the equation for a direct variation.

$5 = k(-3)$ Replace y with 5 and x with -3.

$k = -\frac{5}{3}$ Solve for k.

Step 2 Write the equation using the value of k.

$y = kx$ Use the equation for a direct variation.

$y = -\frac{5}{3}x$ Replace k with $-\frac{5}{3}$.

Write an equation for a direct variation that includes each point.

1. $(4, 3)$ **2.** $(4, -3)$ **3.** $(-4, 3)$ **4.** $(-4, -3)$

You can write a direct variation to find the conversion factor between two measurement systems.

■ EXAMPLE 2

Measurement A segment measures 5 in. or 12.7 cm. Let x represent inches and let y represent centimeters. Write a direct variation to convert inches to centimeters. Then convert 24 in. to centimeters.

$y = kx$ Use the equation for a direct variation.

$12.7 = k(5)$ Replace x with 5 and y with 12.2.

$2.54 = k$ Solve for k.

$y = 2.54x$ Replace k with 2.54 to write a direct variation.

$y = 2.54(24)$ Solve for $x = 24$.

$y = 60.96$ Multiply.

A length that measures 24 in. is 60.96 cm.

5. *Measurement* A carton indicates that it contains 2 qt of juice or 1.89 L of juice. Write a direct variation for the relationship between quarts and liters. Find the number of liters in 8 quarts.

Slope and y-intercept

Investigate
.... UNDERSTANDING SLOPE ....

1. **a.** Graph $y = x$, $y = 2x$, and $y = 3x$ on one coordinate plane.
   b. *Writing* How do the graphs change as the coefficient of x increases?
   c. Graph $y = -x$ on the same coordinate plane.
   d. How are the graphs of $y = x$ and $y = -x$ alike? Different?

What You'll Learn

1 To find the slope of a line

2 To use slope-intercept form in graphing a linear equation

... And Why

To describe features of common objects, such as the incline of a ramp or the slant of a roof

---

PART 1 Finding the Slope of a Line

The ratio that describes the tilt of a line is its slope. If a line slants upward from left to right, it has positive slope. If it slants downward, it has negative slope. To calculate slope, you use this ratio.

$$\textbf{slope} = \frac{\text{vertical change}}{\text{horizontal change}} = \frac{\text{rise}}{\text{run}}$$

Rise shows vertical change. Up is positive; down is negative. Run shows horizontal change. Right is positive; left is negative.

■ EXAMPLE 1

Find the slope of each line.

a.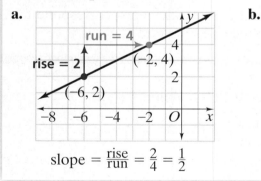

$$\text{slope} = \frac{\text{rise}}{\text{run}} = \frac{2}{4} = \frac{1}{2}$$

b.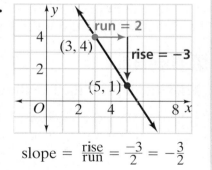

$$\text{slope} = \frac{\text{rise}}{\text{run}} = \frac{-3}{2} = -\frac{3}{2}$$

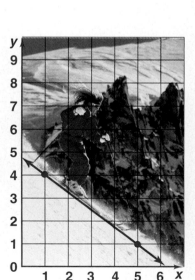

■ TRY THIS

2. What is the slope of the ski trail at the right?

Horizontal and vertical lines are special cases for slope.

■ EXAMPLE 2

Find the slope of each line.

a.
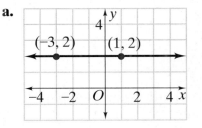

$$\text{slope} = \frac{\text{rise}}{\text{run}} = \frac{0}{4} = 0$$

Slope is 0 for a
horizontal line.

b.
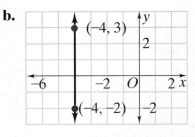

$$\text{slope} = \frac{\text{rise}}{\text{run}} = \frac{-5}{0}$$

Division by zero is undefined.
Slope is *undefined* for a
vertical line.

Test
Prep TIP

You may say that a vertical
line has *no slope*. But be sure
that you do not confuse *no
slope* with *slope 0*.

■ TRY THIS Find the slope of each line.

3.

4.

If you know two points of a line, you can find the slope of the line
using the following formula.

$$\text{slope} = \frac{\text{difference in } y\text{-coordinates}}{\text{difference in } x\text{-coordinates}}$$

The *y*-coordinate you use first in the numerator must correspond to
the *x*-coordinate you use first in the denominator.

■ EXAMPLE 3

Find the slope of the line through $C(-2, 6)$ and $D(4, 3)$.

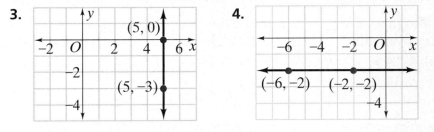

$$\text{slope} = \frac{\text{difference in } y\text{-coordinates}}{\text{difference in } x\text{-coordinates}} = \frac{3 - 6}{4 - (-2)} = \frac{-3}{6} = \frac{-1}{2}$$

■ TRY THIS Find the slope of the line through each pair of points.

5. $V(8, -1), Q(0, -7)$ **6.** $S(-4, 3), R(-10, 9)$

Here is the graph of $y = -\frac{1}{2}x + 3$.

The slope of the line is $\frac{-2}{4}$ or $-\frac{1}{2}$.

The **y-intercept** of the line is the point where the line crosses the y-axis. The constant in the equation is the same as the y-intercept.

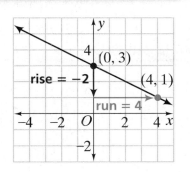

$$y = -\frac{1}{2}x + 3$$

↑   ↑
slope   y-intercept

Slope-Intercept Form

The equation $y = mx + b$ is the slope-intercept form. In this form, m is the slope of the line, and b is the y-intercept.

You can use slope-intercept form to help you graph a function.

REAL-WORLD CONNECTION

■ EXAMPLE 4

Engineering **A ramp slopes from a warehouse door down to a street. The function $y = -\frac{1}{3}x + 2$ models the ramp, where x is the distance in feet from the door and y is the height in feet above the street. Graph the function.**

Step 1 Since the y-intercept is 2, graph $(0, 2)$.

Step 2 Since the slope is $-\frac{1}{3}$ or $\frac{-1}{3}$, move 1 unit down from $(0, 2)$. Then move 3 units right to graph a second point.

Step 3 Draw a line through the points.

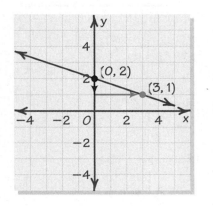

■ **TRY THIS** Graph each equation.

7. $y = 2x - 3$ **8.** $y = -x + 4$

Exercises

CHECK UNDERSTANDING

Find the slope of each line.

1.

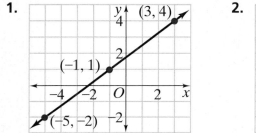

2.

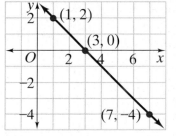

3.

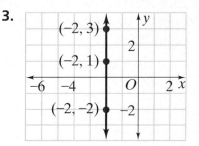

Find the slope of the line through each pair of points.

4. $A(2, 6), B(8, 1)$

5. $R(-4, 5), S(-1, 5)$

6. $W(-10, -2), Z(2, -10)$

Identify the slope and the *y*-intercept of the graph of each equation. Then graph each equation.

7. $y = 7x + 3$

8. $y = -x - 4$

9. $y = \frac{1}{2}x - 8$

PRACTICE AND PROBLEM SOLVING

Find the slope of each line.

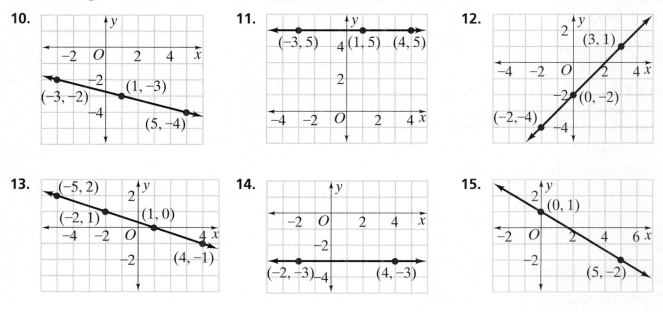

Find the slope of the line through each pair of points.

16. $C(2, 1), D(3, 1)$ **17.** $J(-2, 5), K(-2, -1)$

18. $G(3, 4), H(6, 10)$ **19.** $N(-5, 2), Q(1, -4)$

20. $E(1, -2), F(4, -8)$ **21.** $L(-1, 15), M(3, 5)$

Identify the slope and the *y*-intercept of the graph of each equation.

22. $y = 2x + 4$ **23.** $y = 5x - 3$ **24.** $y = -x + 1$ **25.** $y = -\frac{2}{3}x + 1$

26. $y = x - \frac{3}{4}$ **27.** $y = -\frac{2}{5}x - 2$ **28.** $y = \frac{1}{2}x$ **29.** $y = -3$

Graph each equation.

30. $y = 2x + 1$ **31.** $y = -x$ **32.** $y = -3x - 1$ **33.** $y = -\frac{1}{4}x - 12$

34. $y = 4$ **35.** $y = \frac{2}{3}x + 5$ **36.** $3x + y = 3$ **37.** $2y + 3x = 12$

Graph each line.

38. slope 5, through $(-4, -5)$ **39.** no slope, through $(4, -2)$ **40.** slope $\frac{2}{3}$, through $(0, -4)$

41. *Construction* The slope of a roof is its *pitch*. You indicate the pitch of a roof by a ratio $a : b$, where a is the number of feet of rise for every b feet of run. In the photos at the right, which house has a roof with steeper pitch? Explain.

42. *Error Analysis* A student said that the slope of the line through $(8, 4)$ and $(2, 2)$ is 3. What error could this student have made?

43. a. Graph the three groups of equations on three coordinate planes.

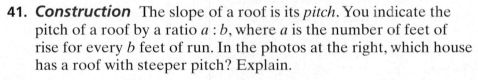

Group 1	Group 2	Group 3
$y = 2x - 5$	$y = -3x - 1$	$y = -6$
$y = 2x$	$y = -3x$	$y = 1$
$y = 2x + 3$	$y = -3x + 4$	$y = 4.5$

    b. *Writing* How are the lines in each group related to each other? Explain.

    c. *Critical Thinking* What is the coefficient of x in the equation of a graph that has slope 0?

44. *Construction* The slope of a road is its *grade*. What do you think it means for the grade of a road to be 4%? (*Hint:* Write the percent as a fraction.)

45. **TEST PREP** The slope of a line is -1. Which two points could this line contain?

    A. $(0, 1), (0, -1)$ **B.** $(0, 1), (1, 0)$ **C.** $(0, 1), (-1, 0)$ **D.** Not here

46. *Critical Thinking* Find the slope of the line at the right using two points. Then find the slope using two other points. Are the slopes the same? Explain.

47. *Open-ended* Write equations for five different lines that intersect at $(0, 3)$.

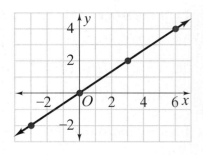

▶ **MIXED REVIEW**

Find each percent of change. Tell whether the change is an increase or a decrease. *(Lesson 6-8)*

48. from 12 to 15   **49.** from 10 to 9   **50.** from 20 to 30   **51.** from 52 to 39

Solve and graph each inequality. *(Lesson 7-6)*

52. $4x + 5 < 17$ **53.** $18 \leq 5 - 2x$ **54.** $-x + 6 > 31$ **55.** $9 + \frac{1}{2}x \geq -3$

56. a. During the 1998–1999 season, New York theatergoers bought 11.7 million tickets for $588.5 million. To the nearest dollar, what was the mean price for a theater ticket in New York? *(Lesson 3-6)*

   b. The box office receipts for New York shows were up 5.5% from the year before. What were the New York receipts for the 1997–1998 season? *(Lesson 6-7)*

Math at Work

Movie Camera Operator

Lights . . . camera . . . action! These are familiar words for movie camera operators. When the action begins, movie camera operators are responsible for capturing the action on film. One scene in a movie can cost hundreds of thousands of dollars, so a scene has to be filmed correctly in as few tries as possible. Camera operators are trained in the effective use of lighting, lens filters, and camera angles. The operators determine the precise movements of the camera and its platform and the camera angles in advance of the actual shooting. It takes a good understanding of algebra and coordinate geometry to do that!

For more information about movie camera operators, see the Prentice Hall Web site. www.phschool.com

MATH TOOLBOX

Technology
After Lesson 8-3

Graphing Lines

You can use a graphing calculator to graph equations in slope-intercept form and find solutions.

■ EXAMPLE

Graph $y = 3x - 2$.

Step 1 Press the Y= key. Enter $3x - 2$.

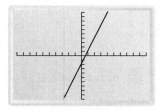

Step 2 Press ZOOM 6 to graph your equation with the standard viewing window.

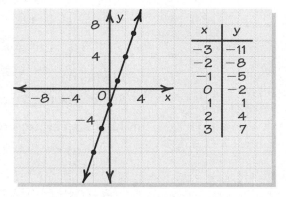

Step 3 Press TABLE to see solutions.

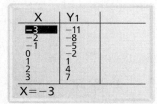

Step 4 Sketch your graph and copy the table of solutions.

Graph each equation.

1. $y = 2x + 1$ **2.** $y = x - 4$ **3.** $y = 3x + 2$

4. $y = -x$ **5.** $y = -x + 4$ **6.** $y = 4x - 3$

7. $y = -3x - 2$ **8.** $y = \frac{1}{2}x - 5$ **9.** $y = -\frac{1}{2}x + 2$

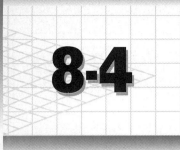

8-4

Writing Rules for Linear Functions

What You'll Learn

1 To write a function rule for a word relationship

2 To write a function rule by analyzing a table or graph

...And Why

To model everyday tasks such as converting measurements or finding the cost of a mail order

You can write a function using **function notation,** where you use $f(x)$ instead of y. You read $f(x)$ as "f of x." You can think of a domain value as an *input* and the resulting range value as the *output*. A **function rule** is an equation that describes a function.

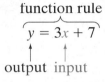

$$\overbrace{y = 3x + 7}^{\text{function rule}}$$

output input

$$\overbrace{f(x) = 3x + 7}^{\text{function rule}}$$

output input

REAL-WORLD CONNECTION

■ EXAMPLE 1

Sales Commissions **Paulo works at a local store. Each week he earns a $300 salary plus a 3% commission on his sales.**

a. Write a function rule that relates total earnings to sales.

| Words | total earnings | are | $300 | plus | 3% | of | sales |

Let s = the amount of his sales.

Let $t(s)$ = total earnings, a function of his sales.

| Rule | $t(s)$ | = | 300 | + | 0.03 | · | s |

A rule for the function is $t(s) = 300 + 0.03s$.

b. Find his earnings for one week if his sales are $2,500.

$t(s) = 300 + 0.03s$

$t(2,500) = 300 + 0.03(2,500)$ **Replace s with 2,500.**

$t(2,500) = 300 + 75$ **Multiply.**

$t(2,500) = 375$ **Add.**

Paulo earns $375 if his sales are $2,500.

■ TRY THIS

1. Scrumptious Snack Mix is sold by mail order. It costs $3/lb, plus $4 for shipping and handling. Write a function rule for the total cost $c(p)$ based on the number of pounds p bought. Use your function to find the total cost of 5 lb of snack mix.

To write a function rule from a table, look for a pattern. The formula $y = mx + b$ in function notation is $f(x) = mx + b$. The slope m is $\frac{\text{difference in } f(x)\text{-values}}{\text{difference in } x\text{-values}}$, and b is the value of $f(x)$ when $x = 0$.

■ EXAMPLE 2

Write a rule for the linear function in the table below.

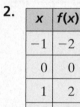

x	f(x)
−2	−5
0	1
2	7
4	13

+2 +6
+2 +6
+2 +6

As the *x* values increase by 2, the *f(x)* values increase by 6. So $m = \frac{6}{2} = 3$. When $x = 0$, $f(x) = 1$. So $b = 1$.

A rule for the function is $f(x) = 3x + 1$.

■ TRY THIS Write a rule for each linear function.

2.

x	f(x)
−1	−2
0	0
1	2
2	4

3.

x	f(x)
−3	6
0	0
3	−6
6	−12

4.

x	y
−6	−11
−4	−7
−2	−3
0	1

You can use slope-intercept form, $f(x) = mx + b$ or $y = mx + b$, when you write a rule for a linear function.

■ EXAMPLE 3

Write a rule for the linear function graphed below.

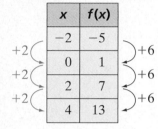

$$\text{slope} = \frac{1 - (-1)}{4 - 0} = \frac{2}{4} = \frac{1}{2}$$

y-intercept $= -1$

A rule for the function is $f(x) = \frac{1}{2}x - 1$.

■ TRY THIS

5. Write a rule for the function graphed at the right.

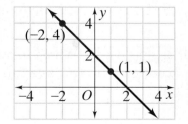

Exercises

1. **Money** Suppose you give a salesperson $20 for a purchase. Write a function rule to express the amount of change $a(c)$ that you receive as a function of the cost c.

Write a rule for each linear function.

2.

x	f(x)
−9	−18
0	−9
9	0
18	9

3.

x	f(x)
−4	4
−2	2
0	0
2	−2

4.

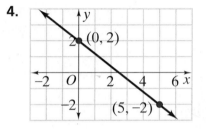

▶ **PRACTICE AND PROBLEM SOLVING**

Write a function rule for each situation.

5. **Science** The temperature k in degrees *Kelvin* is 273.15 less than the temperature c in degrees *Celsius*.

6. **Physics** The force of gravity is less on Mars than it is on Earth. As a result, the weight of an object on Mars m is 40% of its weight on Earth w.

7. **Measurement** Write a rule that expresses the number of quarts q of a liquid as a function of each of the following.
   a. the number of pints p **b.** the number of fluid ounces f

8. **a. Measurement** Express the number of inches $n(d)$ as a function of the number of yards d.
   b. Use your function to find the number of inches in 4 yards.

9. **a. Geometry** Write a rule that expresses the perimeter $p(s)$ of a square as a function of the length s of one side.
   b. Use your function to find the perimeter of a square with side length 7 cm.

10. **TEST PREP** Which function rule describes the number of centimeters $c(m)$ as a function of a number of millimeters m?
    A. $c(m) = 10m$ **B.** $c(m) = 0.1m$ **C.** $c(m) = 100m$ **D.** $c(m) = 0.01m$

Quick Review

8 fluid ounces = 1 cup
2 cups = 1 pint
2 pints = 1 quart
4 quarts = 1 gallon

Write a rule for each function.

11.

x	f(x)
2	−2.4
4	−4.8
6	−7.2
8	−9.6

12.

x	y
−3	2
0	2
3	2
6	2

13.

x	f(x)
−5	−7
−1	−3
0	−2
8	6

14.

x	f(x)
−6	−15
1	−1
7	11
11	19

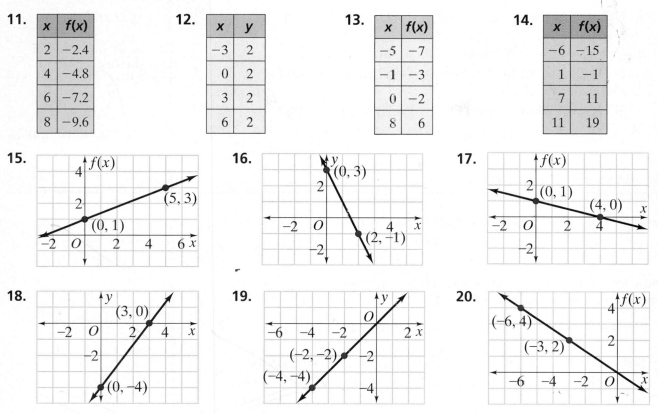

15.   16.   17.

18.   19.   20.

21. **Writing** Describe the advantages you see in using a rule for a function rather than listing function values in a table. Describe the disadvantages.

Data Analysis Use the data at the right for Exercises 22–24.

22. Write a function rule for the total monthly charge to a customer who has electric space heating. (*Hint:* Remember to write the rule either in dollars or in cents.)

23. **a.** Write a function rule for the total monthly charge to a residential customer.
    b. Suppose a residential customer received a monthly bill for $22.52. How many kilowatt-hours did the customer use that month?

24. **Critical Thinking** Write a rule to describe how much a customer saves by being a residential customer rather than a customer who uses electricity for space heating.

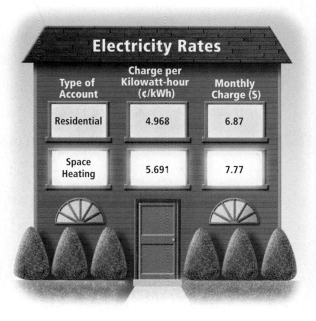

Electricity Rates

Type of Account	Charge per Kilowatt-hour (¢/kWh)	Monthly Charge ($)
Residential	4.968	6.87
Space Heating	5.691	7.77

25. *Patterns* The rule for a function is $y = \frac{3}{2}x$.

a. Use the domain $\{-6, -4, -2, 0, 2, 4\}$ to make a function table.

b. Complete this statement: As the domain values in the table in part (a) increase by 2, the corresponding range values __?__ .

c. How is the pattern from part (b) related to the slope of the line with equation $y = \frac{3}{2}x$?

Journal

Summarize the different ways you can represent a function.

▶ MIXED REVIEW

Find the slope of the line through each pair of points. *(Lesson 8-3)*

26. $C(0, -2), D(2, 1)$ **27.** $J(-3, 1), K(-6, -1)$ **28.** $G(12, 8), H(6, 2)$

Find each probability for choosing a letter at random from the word FUNCTION. *(Lesson 6-4)*

29. $P(\text{N or C})$ **30.** $P(\text{consonant})$ **31.** $P(\text{not T})$

32. *Sports* In 1999, Hicham El Guerrouj of Morocco broke the former world record for running the mile by 1.26 seconds. The previous record was 3 min, 44.39 sec, set in 1993. Write and solve an equation to find the 1999 record time. *(Lesson 3-5)*

◩ CHECKPOINT 1   Lessons 8-1 through 8-4

1. Find three solutions of $9x - 2y = 18$.

2. Graph $3x - y = 5$ on a coordinate plane.

3. Is $\{(-2, 0), (-1, 3), (0, -2), (3, -1)\}$ a function? Explain.

4. ***Writing*** Explain how to use the vertical-line test to determine whether a relation is a function.

Find the slope of the line through the given points.

5. $A(1, 5), B(3, 15)$ **6.** $D(-2, -4), F(0, -6)$ **7.** $G(-3, 4), H(-3, -6)$

8. What are the slope and the y-intercept of $y = -2x + 5$?

9. ***Measurement*** Write a rule to describe the number of pounds $p(t)$ as a function of a number of tons t.

10. **TEST PREP** Which rule is the same function as $x + y = 6$?

    A. $y = x + 6$ **B.** $y = x - 6$ **C.** $y = 6 - x$ **D.** Not here

Scatter Plots

Investigate

·········· **MAKING SCATTER PLOTS** ··········

1. *Data Collection* For each person in your group, measure the height and *hand span*, the greatest distance possible between the tips of the thumb and little finger on one hand.

2. Graph the lengths as ordered pairs (height, hand span).

3. **a.** Share your data with the class. Make a graph of the class data.
   b. *Critical Thinking* Compare the two graphs you made. Does one graph show a relationship between height and hand span more clearly than the other? Explain.

What You'll Learn

▼**1** To interpret and draw scatter plots

▼**2** To use scatter plots for finding trends

. . . And Why

To investigate trends in income, climate, and sports

PART 1
Interpreting and Drawing Scatter Plots

A **scatter plot** is a graph that shows the relationship between two sets of data. To make a scatter plot, graph the data as ordered pairs.

REAL-WORLD 🌐 CONNECTION

■ EXAMPLE 1

Income The scatter plot shows education and income data.

a. **Describe the person represented by point *A*.**
This person has 12 years of education and earns $20,000 each year.

b. **How many years of education did the person who earns $100,000 finish?**
The point (16, 100) has income coordinate 100. The person earning $100,000 each year has 16 years of education.

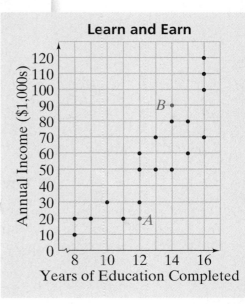

■ **TRY THIS** Use the scatter plot in Example 1.

4. Describe the person represented by point *B*.

5. How many people have exactly 12 years of education?

◼ EXAMPLE 2

Climate **Use the table to make a scatter plot of the latitude and temperature data.**

Climate Data

City	Location (degrees north latitude)	Daily Mean Temperature (°F)	Mean Annual Precipitation (inches)
Atlanta, GA	34	61	51
Boston, MA	42	51	42
Chicago, IL	42	49	36
Duluth, MN	47	39	30
Honolulu, HI	21	77	22
Houston, TX	30	68	46
Juneau, AK	58	41	54
Miami, FL	26	76	56
Phoenix, AZ	33	73	8
Portland, ME	44	45	44
San Diego, CA	33	64	10
Wichita, KS	38	56	29

SOURCES: *The World Almanac* and *Statistical Abstract of the United States*

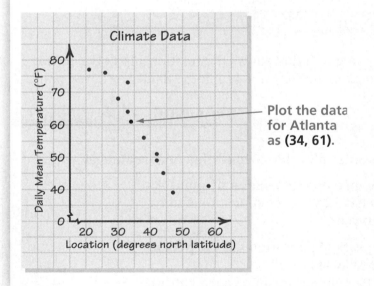

Plot the data for Atlanta as **(34, 61)**.

◼ TRY THIS

6. Use the table in Example 2. Make a scatter plot of the latitude and precipitation data.

7. Use the table in Example 2. Make a scatter plot of the temperature and precipitation data. Plot temperature along the horizontal axis of the graph.

You can use scatter plots to look for trends. The next three scatter plots show the types of relationships two sets of data may have.

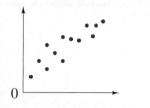

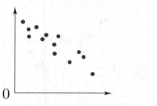

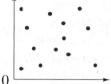

Positive correlation
As one set of values increases, the other set tends to increase.

Negative correlation
As one set of values increases, the other set tends to decrease.

No correlation
The values show no relationship.

REAL-WORLD CONNECTION

■ EXAMPLE 3

Sports Use the scatter plot below. Is there a *positive correlation*, a *negative correlation*, or *no correlation* between the year and the winning time? Explain.

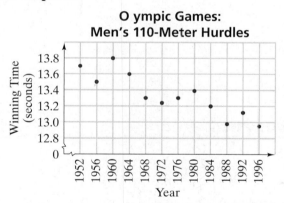

Olympic Games:
Men's 110-Meter Hurdles

Since 1952, the winning time has generally decreased. There is a negative correlation.

■ TRY THIS

8. *Sports* Use the scatter plot at the right. Is there a *positive correlation*, a *negative correlation*, or *no correlation* between the year and the winning distance? Explain.

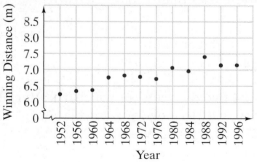

Olympic Games: Women's Long Jump

Exercises

Statistics The scatter plot at the right shows the average time fifteen students spent watching television and the average time they spent on physical activity in a day.

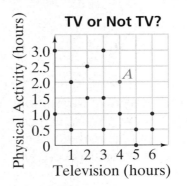

TV or Not TV?

1. Describe the student represented by point *A*.

2. How many students had one hour of physical activity or less?

3. How many students spent four or more hours watching television?

Is there a *positive correlation*, a *negative correlation*, or *no correlation* between the sets of data in each scatter plot? Explain.

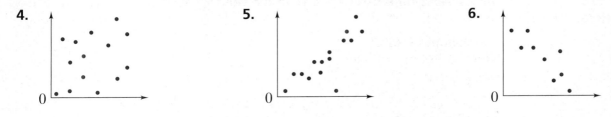

4.   5.   6.

PRACTICE AND PROBLEM SOLVING

Data Analysis The scatter plot at the right shows the relationship between distance from school and the time it takes to get to school for the students in one class.

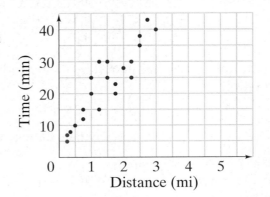

7. How long does the student who lives 0.5 mi from school take to get to school?

8. How many students live closer than 1 mi from school?

9. How many students take longer than 35 min to get to school?

10. *Open-ended* Describe two data sets for which a scatter plot would be an appropriate way to look for a correlation.

Is there a *positive correlation*, a *negative correlation*, or *no correlation* between the two data sets in each scatter plot? Explain.

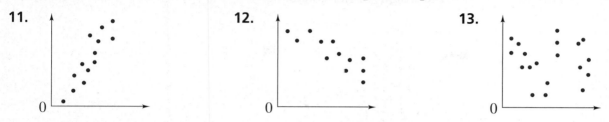

11.

12.

13.

Would you expect a *positive correlation*, a *negative correlation*, or *no correlation* between the two sets of data? Explain.

14. the shoe sizes and the shirt sizes for men

15. the time candles take to burn and their original height

16. the number of students in a school and the number of stores near a school

Nutrition Use the data in the table for Exercises 17–20.

Nutritional Values for 100 Grams of Food

Food	Fat (grams)	Protein (grams)	Carbohydrate (grams)	Energy (calories)
Bread	4	8	50	267
Cheese	33	25	1	403
Chicken	4	31	0	165
Eggs	11	13	1	155
Ground beef	19	27	0	292
Milk	3	3	5	61
Peanuts	49	26	16	567
Pizza	5	12	33	223
Tuna	1	26	0	116

SOURCE: U. S. Department of Agriculture Nutrient Database for Standard Reference

17. Make a scatter plot of the data for calories and grams of fat. Graph the calories on the horizontal axis.

18. Make a scatter plot of the data for calories and grams of protein. Graph the calories on the horizontal axis.

19. Make a scatter plot of the data for calories and grams of carbohydrates. Graph the calories on the horizontal axis.

20. *Data Analysis* Use your graphs for Exercises 17–19. Is there a *positive correlation*, a *negative correlation*, or *no correlation* between the numbers of calories and grams of each nutrient?
    a. fat   b. protein   c. carbohydrate

21. **TEST PREP** Which scatter plot shows that as the number of pages in a magazine increases, the weight of the magazine increases?

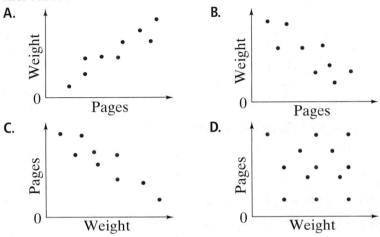

A.

Weight

0   Pages

B.

Weight

0   Pages

C.

Pages

0   Weight

D.

Pages

0   Weight

22. The table at the right shows the average price of a movie ticket and the number of movie admissions.
   a. Make a scatter plot of the data in the table. Graph the price of a movie ticket on the horizontal axis.
   b. *Data Analysis* Is there a *positive correlation*, a *negative correlation*, or *no correlation* between the number of admissions and the price of a ticket?
   c. *Critical Thinking* Would your answer to part (b) be the same or different if you graphed the price of a movie ticket on the vertical axis instead? Explain.

Year	Number of Admissions (millions)	Average Ticket Price
1990	1,189	$4.23
1992	1,173	$4.15
1994	1,292	$4.18
1996	1,339	$4.42
1998	1,481	$4.69

SOURCE: Motion Picture Association of America

▶ MIXED REVIEW

Write a rule for each function. (*Lesson 8-5*)

23.

x	y
−4	−10
−2	−5
0	0
2	5

24.

x	y
−6	5
−3	3
0	1
3	−1

25.

x	f(x)
−2	9
1	6
4	3
7	0

26.

x	f(x)
−5	2
−4	4
−3	6
−2	8

Solve each formula for the variable indicated in red. (*Lesson 7-7*)

27. $A = \frac{1}{2}(b + c)h$ **28.** $V = \frac{1}{3}Bh$ **29.** $S = \frac{a}{1 - r}$ **30.** $c = \frac{p}{h}$

31. *Choose a Strategy* Ms. Jimenez earns $27,000 per year. She is paid weekly. She puts 8% of her salary in a retirement fund. How much money goes into this fund each week?

See also Extra Practice section.

Standardized Test Prep

Multiple Choice

Choose the best answer.

1. Which ordered pair names the coordinates of a point on the line at the right?
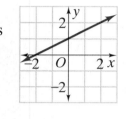
   A. $(0, 1)$
   B. $(2, -2)$
   C. $(-2, -2)$
   D. $(1, -1)$

2. A ball is dropped from different heights. The height of the bounce is measured each time the ball is dropped. Which statement describes the data in the graph?

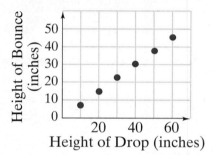

   F. The height of a bounce is about $1\frac{1}{3}$ of the height from which the ball is dropped.
   G. The height of a bounce is about 6 inches less than the height from which the ball is dropped.
   H. The height of a bounce is about 6 inches greater than the height from which the ball is dropped.
   J. The height of a bounce is about $\frac{3}{4}$ of the height from which the ball is dropped.

3. The ordered pair $(4, 6)$ is *not* a solution of which equation?
   A. $x - y = -2$
   B. $-10 = -x - y$
   C. $y - x = 2$
   D. $x - y = 2$

4. Classify the slope of the line below.
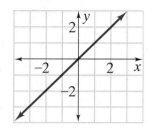
   F. positive
   G. negative
   H. zero
   J. undefined

5. What is the slope of a line through the points $(-2, 4)$ and $(6, 3)$?
   A. $-\frac{1}{8}$ B. $\frac{4}{7}$ C. $\frac{7}{4}$ D. -8

6. The slope of a line is -1. Through which two points could this line pass?
   F. $(0, 3)$ and $(0, -3)$
   G. $(0, 3)$ and $(3, 0)$
   H. $(0, 3)$ and $(-3, 0)$
   J. $(-3, 0)$ and $(3, 0)$

7. Which rule describes the function in the table?
   A. $f(x) = x + 8$
   B. $f(x) = 4x + 8$
   C. $f(x) = x - 1$
   D. $f(x) = x + 17$

x	f(x)
-3	-4
0	8
3	20
6	32

Free Response

For Exercises 8–10, show your work.

8. Each point in Quadrant I has a positive x-coordinate and a positive y-coordinate. Describe the signs of the coordinates for points in Quadrants II, III, and IV.

9. Find the value of n that makes $(-3, 3)$ a solution of the equation $x + ny = 6$.

10. Is the relation $\{(3, 4), (-3, 2), (5, 1), (2, 2)\}$ a function? Explain.

8-6

Read | Plan
Look Back | Solve

Solve by Graphing

Problem Solving Strategies

Account for All
   Possibilities

Draw a Diagram

Look for a Pattern

Make a Model

Make a Table

Simplify a Problem

Simulate a Problem

Solve by Graphing

Try, Test, Revise

Use Multiple Strategies

Work Backward

Write an Equation

Write a Proportion

Math Strategies in Action

Businesses and government agencies use scatter plots to look for trends and make predictions. For example, the park service at Isle Royale, Michigan, surveys the moose and wolf populations each spring. They use a scatter plot to show the relationship between them. Then they draw a **trend line** that closely fits the data points in the scatter plot. Using the trend line, they can predict the size of one population from the size of the other.

■ SAMPLE PROBLEM

Wildlife Use the data in the table below. Suppose there were 18 wolves one year. About how many moose would you expect to be on the island that year?

Isle Royale Populations

Year	Wolf	Moose	Year	Wolf	Moose	Year	Wolf	Moose
1982	14	700	1988	12	1,653	1994	15	1,800
1983	23	900	1989	11	1,397	1995	16	2,400
1984	24	811	1990	15	1,216	1996	22	1,200
1985	22	1,062	1991	12	1,313	1997	24	500
1986	20	1,025	1992	12	1,600	1998	14	700
1987	16	1,380	1993	13	1,880	1999	25	750

SOURCE: Isle Royale National Park Service

 Read

1. What are the two variables?

2. What are you trying to predict?

Plan

You can graph the data in a scatter plot. If the points show a correlation, you can draw a trend line. You can then use the line to predict other data values.

Solve

Step 1 Make a scatter plot by graphing the (wolf, moose) ordered pairs. Use the *x*-axis for wolves and the *y*-axis for moose.

Step 2 Sketch a trend line. The line should be as close as possible to each data point. There should be about as many points above the trend line as below it.

Step 3 To predict the number of moose when there are 18 wolves, find 18 along the horizontal axis. Look up to find the

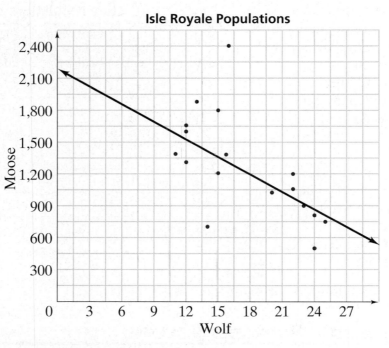

point on the trend line that corresponds to 18 wolves. Then look across to the value on the vertical axis, which is 1,200.

There will be about 1,200 moose when there are 18 wolves.

Look Back

You can write an equation for a trend line. You can use the equation to make predictions.

3. a. What is the *y*-intercept of the trend line above?
  b. Locate one other point on the trend line. Then find the slope of the trend line.
  c. Write an equation for the trend line in slope-intercept form.
  d. Use the equation you wrote in part (c). Find the solution of the equation when $x = 18$.

Exercises

CHECK UNDERSTANDING

Statistics **The table shows the populations of some states and the numbers of cars registered in those states. Use the data for Exercises 1 and 2.**

1. a. Use the data to make a scatter plot of the data. Use the population data for the horizontal axis.

    b. Draw a trend line.

    c. Predict how many cars are registered by the 32.2 million people in California.

    d. Write an equation for your trend line. Predict the number of cars registered by the 7.3 million people in North Carolina.

State Populations and Cars

State	Population (millions)	Registered Cars (millions)	State	Population (millions)	Registered Cars (millions)
FL	14.4	7.2	NY	18.1	7.9
GA	7.3	3.8	OH	11.2	6.6
IL	11.8	6.2	PA	12.0	5.9
KS	2.6	1.2	SC	3.7	1.8
ME	1.2	0.6	TN	5.3	3.0
MS	2.7	1.3	TX	19.1	7.4
NV	1.6	0.6	WA	5.5	2.6

SOURCE: *Statistical Abstract of the United States*

2. Describe the correlation between the two sets of data.

PRACTICE AND PROBLEM SOLVING

Solve using any strategy.

3. A delivery van travels 240.8 mi on the highway using 10.6 gal of gasoline. Its gas tank holds 13.6 gal. How many highway miles can the driver expect the van to travel on a full tank of gasoline? Round your answer to the nearest mile.

4. *Data Analysis* Use the data in the table below. Predict the number of gallons bought for $12.

Gasoline Purchases

Dollars Spent	10	11	9	10	8	5	8	6
Gallons Bought	8.3	8.7	6.5	7.1	6.7	3.6	5.6	4.1

5. Four candidates are running for president of the student council. Three other candidates are running for vice-president. How many different ways can the two offices be filled?

6. **Physics** As the weight held by a spring increases, the length of the spring also increases proportionally. Suppose a 2-lb weight stretches a spring to 15 in., and a 12-lb weight stretches the same spring to 20 in. What is the length of the spring with no weight attached?

7. **Engineering** To provide wheelchair access, a ramp with a slope of $\frac{1}{15}$ is being built to a door of a building. Suppose that the bottom of the door is 3 ft above street level. How far will the ramp extend from the building?

8. A plumber charges $45 for a service call, plus $70/h for her time.
   a. Find the cost of a two-hour service call.
   b. How long was a service call that cost $150?

9. **Business** A supermarket charges $1.19 for a 12-oz jar of salsa and $1.89 for a 20-oz jar. Now the producer is introducing a 16-oz jar of the same salsa. What do you think would be a fair price for this new size? Justify your answer.

▶ MIXED REVIEW

Find the solutions of each equation for $x = -3, 0,$ and 2. *(Lesson 8-2)*

10. $y = 2x - 1$ **11.** $y = -3x$ **12.** $y = \frac{1}{3}x + 4$ **13.** $y = 0.5x - 2$

Solve each equation. *(Lessons 7-2 and 7-5)*

14. $3x + 7 = 4x - 12$ **15.** $7t + 3 - 4t = -6$ **16.** $8(2 - c) - 12 = -3c$

17. About 150 million of the 20 billion hot dogs that are eaten in the United States each year are eaten during the Fourth of July weekend. What percent of the hot dogs are eaten during the Fourth of July weekend? *(Lesson 6-6)*

CHAPTER PROJECT 8 **ACTIVITY 2 GRAPHING**

Refer to your results from Activity 1. For each rental company, write an equation in the form $y = Px + D$, where y is the total cost of the chairs, P is the price per chair, x is the number of chairs, and D is the delivery charge. Graph the equations on the same coordinate plane for values of x from 0 to 500.

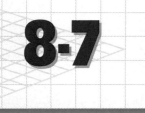

8-7

Solving Systems of Linear Equations

What You'll Learn

1 To solve systems of linear equations by graphing

2 To solve problems by solving systems of linear equations

... And Why

To model real-world problems involving carpentry

Two or more linear equations form a **system of linear equations.** A *solution of the system* is any ordered pair that is a solution of each equation in the system.

You can solve some systems of equations by graphing the equations on a coordinate plane and identifying the point(s) of intersection.

■ EXAMPLE 1

Solve the system $y = -x + 1$ and $y = 2x + 4$ by graphing.

Step 1 Graph each line.

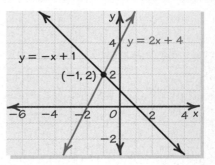

Step 2 Find the point of intersection.

The lines intersect at one point, $(-1, 2)$. The solution is $(-1, 2)$.

Check See whether $(-1, 2)$ makes both equations true.

$$y = -x + 1 \qquad\qquad\qquad\qquad y = 2x + 4$$

$$2 \overset{?}{=} -(-1) + 1 \leftarrow \overset{\text{Replace } x \text{ with } -1}{\text{and } y \text{ with } 2.} \rightarrow 2 \overset{?}{=} 2(-1) + 4$$

$$2 = 2 \; ✔ \qquad \text{The solution checks.} \qquad 2 = 2 \; ✔$$

■ TRY THIS Solve each system of equations by graphing.

1. $y = x - 6$
    $y = -2x$

2. $y = 3x - 3$
    $x + y = 1$

When the graphs of two equations are parallel, there is no point of intersection. The system has *no solution*.

When the graphs of two equations are the same line, all the points on the line are solutions. The system has *infinitely many solutions*.

EXAMPLE 2

Solve each system by graphing.

a. $x + y = 1; y = -x + 3$

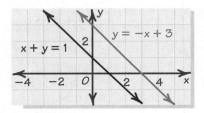

The lines are parallel.
They do not intersect.
There is no solution.

b. $x - 2y = 4; 2x - 4y = 8$

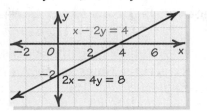

The graphs are the same line.
There are infinitely many
solutions.

Graphing Calculator HINT

You can use a graphing
calculator to check your
solution of a system.
Write the equations in slope-
intercept form, press **Y=** ,
and enter them as Y1 and Y2.
Then use the **CALC** menu to
find the coordinates of the
intersection point.

■ **TRY THIS** Solve each system by graphing.

3. $y = x - 6; x - y = 6$

4. $y = x + 4; y = 2x$

PART 2 Writing Systems of Linear Equations

You can write and graph systems of equations to solve problems.

EXAMPLE 3

Find two numbers with a sum of 6 and a difference of 4.

Step 1 Write equations.

Let x = the greater number.
Let y = the lesser number.

Equation 1 Sum   is   6.
$$x + y = 6$$

Equation 2 Difference is 4.
$$x - y = 4$$

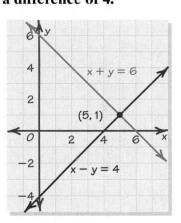

Step 2 Graph the equations.

The lines intersect at $(5, 1)$.
The numbers are 5 and 1.

Check Since the sum of 5 and 1 is 6 and the difference of 5 and 1 is
4, the answer is correct.

■ **TRY THIS**

5. Find two numbers with a difference of 2 and a sum of -8.

You can solve some problems involving two variables by writing and graphing a system of equations, or you may be able to use one variable to write and solve an equation.

Different Ways to Solve a Problem

Carpenter **A carpenter cuts an 8-ft board into two pieces. One piece is three times as long as the other. What is the length of each piece?**

Method 1

Write and graph a system of equations.
Let x = length of longer piece; y = length of shorter piece.

Equation 1   Longer piece is three times shorter piece.
$$x = 3 \cdot y$$

Equation 2   Sum of lengths is eight.
$$x + y = 8$$

Graph the equations.

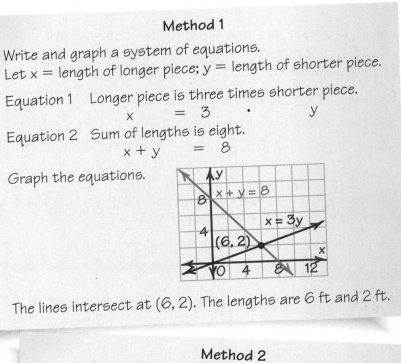

The lines intersect at $(6, 2)$. The lengths are 6 ft and 2 ft.

Method 2

Write a one-variable equation.
Let x = length of shorter piece; $3x$ = length of longer piece.

Equation   Shorter piece plus longer piece is 8 feet.
$$x + 3x = 8$$
$$4x = 8$$
$$x = 2$$

The shorter piece is 2 ft, and the longer piece is $3(2) = 6$ ft.

Choose a Method

1. Which method would you use to find the lengths? Explain.
2. In Method 1, suppose x = length of shorter piece. What difference would this make in the equations and the graph?

Exercises

CHECK UNDERSTANDING

Use the graph to find the solution of each system. Check each solution.

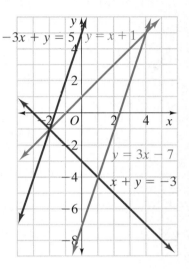

1. $y = x + 1$
$y = 3x - 7$

2. $y = x + 1$
$x + y = -3$

3. $-3x + y = 5$
$y = 3x - 7$

Is $(-1, 5)$ a solution of each system? Show your work.

4. $x + y = 4$
$x - y = 6$

5. $y = -2x + 3$
$y = x - 4$

6. $2x = y - 7$
$2y = -x + 9$

Solve each system by graphing.

7. $y = x + 1$
$y = -x - 3$

8. $y = -x - 3$
$y = -x + 2$

9. $y = -6 - 2x$
$2x + y = -6$

10. Cliff is six years older than his sister Claire. Two years from now, Cliff's age will be twice Claire's age.
   a. Let $x =$ Cliff's present age, and let $y =$ Claire's present age. Write an equation relating their ages now, and another equation relating their ages two years from now.
   b. Graph the system of equations you wrote in part (a).
   c. What are Cliff's and Claire's present ages?

PRACTICE AND PROBLEM SOLVING

Is each ordered pair a solution of the given system? Show your work.

11. $y = x + 2$
$x - 3y = 4; (-5, -3)$

12. $x + y = 2$
$-x + y = -4; (3, 1)$

13. $2x + 5y = 3$
$y = 7.5x; (1.5, 0.2)$

Solve each system by graphing. Check your solution.

14. $y = x + 5$
$y = -2x + 8$

15. $y = x - 4$
$y = 3x$

16. $y = 2x - 2$
$y = 6$

17. $y = -x + 1$
$y = 2x - 5$

18. $x = -2$
$y = -0.5x + 7$

19. $y = x$
$y = 4x - 9$

20. $x + y = 3$
$2x = 10 - 2y$

21. $x - y = -4$
$x + y = 6$

22. $y = 2x - 4$
$4x - 2y = 8$

23. $2x - 4y = 4$
$y = 0.5x - 1$

24. $y = x - 2$
$x + 3y = 6$

25. $3y - 2x = 3$
$6y = 4x + 6$

Open-ended **Write a system of equations with the given solutions.**

26. no solutions

27. one solution

28. infinitely many solutions

29. There are 16 questions on a test. Each question is worth either 5 points or 10 points. The total is 100 points.
  a. Let x = the number of 5-point questions.
  Let y = the number of 10-point questions.
  Write a system of equations to find the number of each type of question.
  b. Solve the system by graphing.
  c. How many questions of each type are on the test?

30. *Geometry* A four-foot-long wooden rod is cut into two pieces to make a kite. One piece is three times as long as the other.
  a. Let x = the length of the longer piece.
  Let y = the length of the shorter piece.
  Write a system of equations to find the length of each piece.
  b. Solve the system by graphing.
  c. What are the lengths of the pieces?

Solve each problem using a system of linear equations.

31. Find two numbers with a sum of -8 and a difference of 4. Let x be the greater number and y be the lesser number.

32. The difference of two numbers is 5. The result when the greater number is decreased by twice the lesser is 9. Let x be the greater number and y be the lesser number. Find the numbers.

33. *Geometry* The perimeter of a rectangle is 24 ft. Its length is five times its width. Let x be the length and y be the width. What is the area of the rectangle?

34. There are eleven animals in a barnyard. Some are chickens and some are cows. There are 38 legs in all. Let x be the number of chickens and y be the number of cows. How many of each animal are in the barnyard?

35. a. *Mathematical Reasoning* Graph each system of equations on a separate coordinate plane.

$y = 3x + 1$ $y = -2x - 1$
$y = 3x - 2$ $y = -2x + 4$

  b. *Writing* Use the graphs of systems of equations with the same slope. Make a conjecture about the number of solutions of these systems.

36. **TEST PREP** Use the system $x + y = -6$, and $x - y = 2$. What is the relationship of the x-coordinate and the y-coordinate of the solution of the system?
  A. $x > y$ **B.** $x < y$ **C.** $x = y$ **D.** cannot be determined

37. Solve the system $y = x + 2$, $y = 4x + 11$, and $y = -2x - 7$.

38. *Geometry* The graphs of $y = 3$, $y = 7$, $x = 2$, and $x = 5$ contain the sides of a rectangle. Find the area of the rectangle.

39. *Open-ended* Write a system of two linear equations that has $(-2, 8)$ as its solution.

▶ MIXED REVIEW

40. *Movies* Use the scatter plot at the right. *(Lesson 8-5)*
   a. How many hours did the person who saw four movies spend?
   b. How many people saw more than three movies?
   c. How many people spent less than three hours watching movies?

Solve each inequality. *(Lessons 2-9, 2-10, 7-6)*

41. $6x < -12$ **42.** $m + 4 > -10$

43. $3t - 1 \leq 17$ **44.** $-2c + 5 \geq 3$

Find each probability for one roll of a number cube. *(Lesson 6-4)*

45. $P(2)$ **46.** $P(6 \text{ or } 5)$ **47.** $P(-1)$ **48.** $P(4, 2, \text{ or } 5)$

(Scatter plot: vertical axis "Time Spent Watching (hours)" marked 2, 4, 6, 8; horizontal axis "Number of Movies Seen" marked 2, 4, 6.)

✓ CHECKPOINT 2
                                       Lessons 8-5 through 8-7

1. a. *Statistics* Use the table at the right. Make a scatter plot relating newspaper circulation and television sets.
   b. Is there is a *positive correlation*, a *negative correlation*, or *no correlation* between daily newspaper circulation and the number of television sets in homes? Explain.
   c. *Data Analysis* Draw a trend line on your scatter plot. Use the trend line to predict the number of television sets when newspaper circulation is 55 million.

Solve each system by graphing.

2. $y = -4x$
   $y = -x + 6$

3. $x - y = 1$
   $x + y = -7$

4. $6x + 2y = 12$
   $y = 3x$

Media in the United States

Year	Daily Newspaper Circulation (millions)	Television Sets in Homes (millions)
1980	62	128
1985	63	155
1990	62	193
1991	61	193
1992	60	192
1993	60	201
1994	59	211
1995	57	217
1996	57	223

SOURCE: *Statistical Abstract of the United States*

5. *Measurement* One gallon of liquid occupies 231 cubic inches. Write a rule that expresses the number of gallons $g(c)$ as a function of the number of cubic inches c.

6. Find two numbers with a sum of -4 and a difference of 10. Let x be the greater number and y be the lesser number.

8-8

Graphing Linear Inequalities

What You'll Learn

1 To graph linear inequalities

2 To graph systems of linear inequalities

...And Why

To model real-world situations such as grocery shopping and earnings from jobs

Quick Review

$<$ is less than

$>$ is greater than

$\leq$ is less than or equal to

$\geq$ is greater than or equal to

PART 1 Graphing Linear Inequalities

If you replace the equal sign in a linear equation with $>$, $<$, $\geq$, or $\leq$, the result is a **linear inequality.** The graph of a linear inequality is a region of the coordinate plane bounded by a line. Every point in the region is a solution of the inequality.

■ EXAMPLE 1

Graph each inequality on a coordinate plane.

a. $y \leq x + 2$ **b.** $y < -2x$

Step 1 Graph the boundary line.

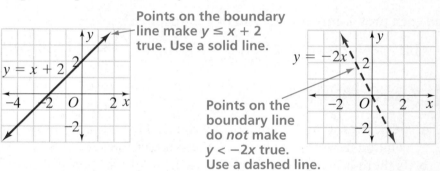

Points on the boundary line make $y \leq x + 2$ true. Use a solid line.

Points on the boundary line do *not* make $y < -2x$ true. Use a dashed line.

Step 2 Test a point not on the boundary line.

Test $(0, 0)$ in the inequality.

$y \leq x + 2$

$0 \leq 0 + 2$ Substitute.

$0 \leq 2$ ✔ true

Test $(1, 1)$ in the inequality.

$y < -2x$

$1 < -2(1)$ Substitute.

$1 < -2$ ✘ false

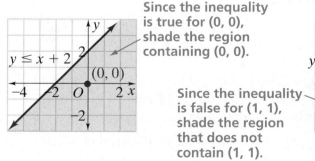

Since the inequality is true for (0, 0), shade the region containing (0, 0).

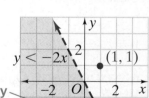

Since the inequality is false for (1, 1), shade the region that does not contain (1, 1).

■ **TRY THIS** Graph each inequality on a separate coordinate plane.

1. $y \geq 3x - 1$ **2.** $y > -x + 3$ **3.** $y < 2x - 4$

REAL-WORLD  CONNECTION

■ **EXAMPLE 2**

Apricots cost $3/lb. Tomatoes cost $1/lb. You plan to spend no more than $10. How many pounds of each can you buy?

Step 1 Write an inequality.

| Words | cost of apricots | plus | cost of tomatoes | is at most | ten dollars |

Let x = number of pounds of apricots.

Let y = number of pounds of tomatoes.

| Inequality | $3x$ | + | y | $\leq$ | 10 |

Step 2 Write the equation of the boundary line in slope-intercept form.
$$3x + y = 10$$
$$\longrightarrow y = -3x + 10$$

Step 4 Test $(1, 1)$.
$$y \leq -3x + 10$$
$$1 \leq -3(1) + 10$$
$$1 \leq 7 \; ✔$$

The inequality is true. $(1, 1)$ is a solution.

Step 3 Graph $y = -3x + 10$ in Quadrant I since weight is not negative.

Step 5 Shade the region containing $(1, 1)$.

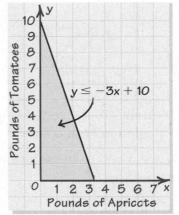

The graph shows the possible solutions. For example, you could buy 1 pound of apricots and 5 pounds of tomatoes.

4. Adult tickets to the school play cost $4. Children's tickets cost $2. Your goal is to sell tickets worth at least $30. Let x be the number of children's tickets and y be the number of adult tickets. Graph a linear inequality to show how many of each type of ticket you must sell to reach your goal.

PART 2 Graphing Systems of Linear Inequalities

Two or more linear inequalities form a **system of linear inequalities.** A *solution of a system of linear inequalities* is any ordered pair that makes each inequality in the system true. To solve a system, graph the inequalities on one coordinate plane.

■ EXAMPLE 3

Solve the system $y > x$ and $y \leq -x + 2$ by graphing.

Step 1 Graph $y > x$ on a coordinate plane.

Step 2 Graph $y \leq -x + 2$ on the same coordinate plane.

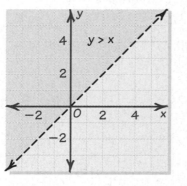
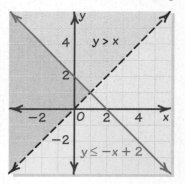

The solutions are the coordinates of all the points in the region that is shaded in both colors.

Check See whether the solution $(-1, 0)$ makes both of the inequalities true.

$y > x$		$y \leq -x + 2$
$0 > -1$	Replace x with -1 and y with 0.	$0 \leq -(-1) + 2$
$0 > -1$ ✔	The solution checks.	$0 \leq 3$ ✔

■ **TRY THIS** Solve each system by graphing.

5. $y \leq -2x - 5$
   $y < \frac{1}{2}x$

6. $y > x - 1$
   $y < 3x + 4$

Exercises

CHECK UNDERSTANDING

Solve each inequality for *y*.

1. $4x + y < -3$

2. $-y \leq 2x$

3. $2x + 3y \leq 7$

Graph each inequality on a separate coordinate plane.

4. $y \geq 3x - 1$

5. $x - y > 10$

6. $y \leq 5$

Solve each system by graphing.

7. $y > -x$
$y < x + 6$

8. $2x + y \leq 4$
$y + 1 \geq -2x$

9. $x + y > -3$
$x - y < 5$

10. a. *Income* You can earn \$6/h mowing lawns and \$3/h baby-sitting. You want to earn at least \$45. Let x = number of hours mowing lawns and y = number of hours baby-sitting. Write a linear inequality to model this situation.
b. Graph the linear inequality.
c. If you baby-sit for 6 hours, what is the number of hours you will need to mow lawns to earn \$45?

PRACTICE AND PROBLEM SOLVING

TEST PREP Choose a linear inequality to match each graph.

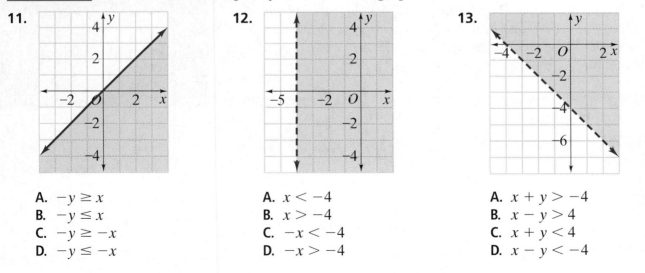

11.

A. $-y \geq x$
B. $-y \leq x$
C. $-y \geq -x$
D. $-y \leq -x$

12.

A. $x < -4$
B. $x > -4$
C. $-x < -4$
D. $-x > -4$

13.

A. $x + y > -4$
B. $x - y > 4$
C. $x + y < 4$
D. $x - y < -4$

Write the equation of each boundary line in slope-intercept form. Tell whether the boundary line is solid or dashed.

14. $2x + y \geq 3$ **15.** $y - 2 < 3x$ **16.** $-y > 4x$ **17.** $-y \leq -\frac{1}{2}x$

18. $x + y < -3$ **19.** $x - y \geq 7$ **20.** $5x + 3y \leq 9$ **21.** $4x - 2y > 10$

Graph each inequality on a separate coordinate plane.

22. $y > x - 6$ **23.** $y \leq -x + 8$ **24.** $y \geq -\frac{2}{3}x$ **25.** $y < 4x - 3$

26. $y \leq 2x + 1$ **27.** $y > x + 2$ **28.** $9x + 3y < 3$ **29.** $x - 2y \geq -12$

Solve each system by graphing. Use a separate coordinate plane for each system.

30. $y \leq x$
    $y \geq -x - 4$

31. $y > -x$
    $y > 2x + 3$

32. $x < 6$
    $y \leq 2x$

33. $y < 4$
    $x > -5$

34. $y \leq -x + 1$
    $y > x - 5$

35. $y > x - 4$
    $y \leq x + 2$

36. $-2x + y > 1$
    $x + 2y < 2$

37. $3x + y > 5$
    $y \geq -2$

For Exercises 38–41 show all the solutions of each problem by graphing a linear inequality.

38. Find two numbers with a sum greater than three.

39. A number is greater than or equal to three times another number. What are the numbers?

40. Use the prices shown in the photo at the right. Let x be the number of medium drinks sold and y be the number of large drinks sold. How many drinks must the vendor sell to have at least $60 in sales?

41. Melissa has a collection of dimes and nickels with a total face value of less than one dollar. Let x be the number of dimes and y be the number of nickels. How many of each type of coin does she have?

42. *Writing* Explain why the graph of $y < -x$ is different from the graph of $-y < x$.

43. **TEST PREP** Which inequality has the same solutions as $y \geq -2x + 1$?
    A. $2x + y \leq 1$ **B.** $2x + y \geq 1$
    C. $2x - y \leq 1$ **D.** $2x - y \geq 1$

44. *Open-ended* Write a system of inequalities that has no solutions.

45. Critical Thinking Write a system of linear inequalities to describe each graph.

a.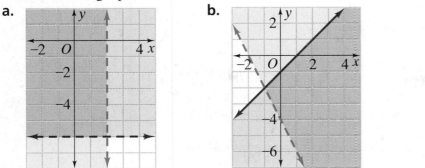

b.

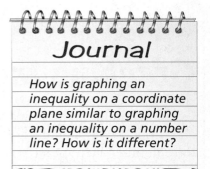

Journal

How is graphing an inequality on a coordinate plane similar to graphing an inequality on a number line? How is it different?

▶ MIXED REVIEW

Solve each system of equations by graphing. *(Lesson 8-7)*

46. $y = x + 3$
$y = -2x - 3$

47. $x + y = 8$
$x - y = -2$

48. $y = 2x - 1$
$2x - y = 3$

49. $3y = -2x - 3$
$3y = x - 12$

Solve each equation. *(Lessons 5-7, 5-8)*

50. $m - \frac{2}{3} = \frac{1}{6}$

51. $\frac{5}{4}c = \frac{3}{2}$

52. $\frac{3}{4} + w = \frac{9}{10}$

53. $\frac{5}{9}p = \frac{5}{12}$

Evaluate each expression for $c = 4$ and $m = -3$. *(Lesson 4-6)*

54. $\frac{c + m}{5}$

55. $\frac{m - c}{2}$

56. $\frac{2c - m}{-4}$

57. $\frac{4m}{2 - c}$

58. Animals In 1999, there were 162 California condors. Of these birds, 113 were in captivity, 29 were living free in California, and 20 were living free in Arizona. *(Lesson 6-6)*
   a. What percent of the condors were living free in Arizona? Round your answer to the nearest tenth of a percent.
   b. What percent of the condors were living free in all? Round your answer to the nearest tenth of a percent.

CHAPTER PROJECT 8 ▼ **ACTIVITY 3 ANALYZING**

Analyze your graph from Activity 2. What does the slope of each line represent? What does the y-intercept of each line represent? Do the lines intersect at any point? Explain the significance of such an intersection. Which company will charge the least? Will the number of chairs you rent affect your answer? Explain.

MATH TOOLBOX

Technology
After Lesson 8-8

Graphing Inequalities

Graphing an inequality on a calculator is similar to graphing an equation. If your calculator does not graph dashed lines, you have to remember the type of boundary line you need for the inequality.

■ EXAMPLE

Graph $y > -x + 4$.

Step 1 Press the [Y=] key. Enter $-x + 4$.

Step 2 Press ◄ to move to the left of Y1. Press [ENTER] twice when y is greater than the right side of the equation, or press [ENTER] three times when y is less than the right side of the equation.

Step 3 Press [ZOOM] 6 to graph the inequality using the standard viewing window. Then sketch the inequality.

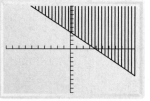

x scale: 1   *y* scale: 1

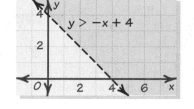

Graph each inequality. Be sure to graph the boundary line appropriately.

1. $y > 3x + 1$ **2.** $y \le 2x$ **3.** $y < -x - 5$ **4.** $y \ge 4x + 6$

5. $y \le -2x - 4$ **6.** $y < x + 7$ **7.** $y > -3x + 4$ **8.** $y \ge -\frac{2}{5}x + 1$

9. Graph the inequalities $y > -x + 7$ and $y \ge 2x - 3$. Sketch the system of inequalities.

Rental Math

Compare Prices The Project Activities on pages 395, 419, and 431 will help you complete your project. Here is a checklist to help you gather the different parts.

- ✔ your table of prices
- ✔ your equations and graphs
- ✔ your analysis of the graphs

Write a report that presents your results. Make a recommendation to the graduation committee about which rental company to hire.

Reflect and Revise

Ask a friend or someone at home to review your report. Are your equations and graphs correct? Do they support your recommendation? If necessary, make changes to improve your report.

Web Extension

Visit Prentice Hall's Web site. You'll find some links related to renting furniture and equipment for celebrations. You'll also be able to share information about your project.
www.phschool.com

■ Key Terms

domain (p. 386)
function (p. 386)
function notation (p. 404)
function rule (p. 404)
linear equation (p. 392)
linear inequality (p. 426)
negative correlation (p. 411)
no correlation (p. 411)

positive correlation (p. 411)
range (p. 386)
relation (p. 386)
scatter plot (p. 409)
slope (p. 397)
slope-intercept form (p. 399)
solution (p. 391)

system of linear
    equations (p. 420)
system of linear
    inequalities (p. 428)
trend line (p. 416)
vertical-line test (p. 387)
y-intercept (p. 399)

■ Graphic Organizer

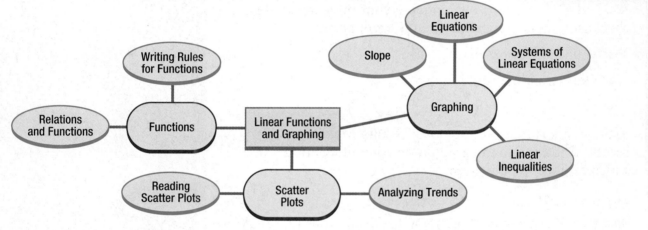

■ Relations and Functions

8-1

Summary Any set of ordered pairs is a **relation**. The **domain** of a relation is the set of first coordinates of the ordered pairs. The **range** is the set of second coordinates. A **function** is a relation in which no two ordered pairs have the same first coordinate.

Is each relation a function? Explain.

1. $\{(2, 3), (4, 3), (0, 1), (-2, 3)\}$

2.
x	-3	4	-1	-4
y	0	2	0	1

3. Domain   Range

4. ***Writing*** Is the amount of a long-distance telephone bill a function of time spent talking on the telephone? Explain.

■ Equations with Two Variables   8-2

Summary A solution of an equation with two variables is any ordered pair that makes the equation true. The graph of a **linear equation** is a line.

Find the solutions of each equation for $x = -3, 0,$ and 2.

5. $y = x + 5$ **6.** $y = -4x$ **7.** $y = \frac{1}{2}x + 3$ **8.** $y = 6 - 2x$

■ Slope and y-intercept   8-3

Summary **Slope** is a measure describing the tilt of a line, which you can calculate using the ratio $\frac{\text{vertical change}}{\text{horizontal change}}$, or $\frac{\text{difference in } y\text{-coordinates}}{\text{difference in } x\text{-coordinates}}$.
One form of a linear equation is the slope-intercept form, $y = mx + b$, where m is the slope and b is the y-intercept.

Identify the slope and y-intercept of each equation. Then graph each equation.

9. $x + y = 7$ **10.** $x - y = -2$ **11.** $2x + 5y = 10$ **12.** $3x - 2y = 12$

Write the slope of each line.

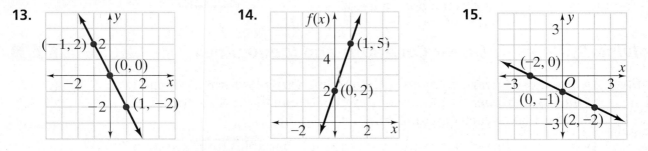

13.   **14.**   **15.**

■ Writing Rules for Linear Functions   8-4

Summary You can write a **function rule** from a verbal description, from a table of values, or from a graph.

Write a rule for each function.

16.

x	f(x)
-2	2
-1	1
0	0
1	-1

17.

x	y
-3	-5
-2	-3
-1	-1
0	1

18.

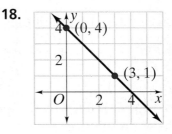

19. Tickets to a play cost $14 each by mail, plus a $2 processing fee for each order of one or more tickets. Write a rule to describe total cost $c(t)$ as a function of the number of tickets t.

■ *Scatter Plots and Trend Lines* 8-5 and 8-6

Summary A **scatter plot** is a graph that shows the relationship between two sets of data. A scatter plot can help you find trends between sets of data.

Use the scatter plot at the right.

20. How long did the person who used 240 calories ride a bicycle?

21. How many calories did the person who bicycled 50 minutes use?

22. ***Data Analysis*** Is there a positive correlation, a negative correlation, or no correlation between the time spent bicycling and the calories used? Explain.

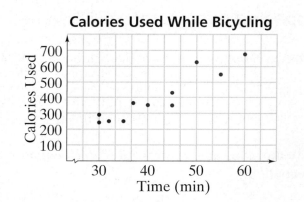

Calories Used While Bicycling

23. a. ***Data Analysis*** Copy the scatter plot and draw a trend line.
  b. A person went for a 70-min bicycle ride. Use the trend line to predict how many calories the person used.

■ *Solving Systems of Linear Equations and Inequalities* 8-7 and 8-8

Summary Two or more linear equations with the same variables form a **system of linear equations**. A solution of a system of equations is any ordered pair that makes each equation true.

Two or more linear inequalities with the same variables form a **system of linear inequalities**. A solution of a system of inequalities is any ordered pair that makes both inequalities true. You can solve a system by graphing.

Graph each inequality.

24. $y > 2x + 5$ **25.** $y \le -x + 1$ **26.** $y \ge \frac{1}{2}x - 3$ **27.** $y < 3x - 2$

Solve each system by graphing.

28. $y = \frac{1}{2}x - 3$ **29.** $3x + 2y = 6$ **30.** $y = x - 5$ **31.** $y < 3x + 2$
  $y = -\frac{1}{2}x + 1$ $x + 4y = -8$ $y = -2x + 1$ $y > 3x - 1$

32. ***Writing*** Explain why it is possible for a system of linear equations to have no solutions.

Is each relation a function? Explain.

1. $\{(-2, -12), (-2, 0), (-2, 4), (-2, 11)\}$

2. $\{(8, 1), (4, 1), (0, 1), (-15, 1)\}$

3. $\{(-4, -6), (-3, -2), (1, -2), (1, 0), (1, 3)\}$

4. $\{(0, 1), (0, 2), (1, 2), (1, 3), (3, 1), (4, 2)\}$

Graph each equation.

5. $y = 2x$

6. $y = -x - 2$

7. $2x - y = 4$

8. $3y = x - 6$

Find the slope of the line through each pair of points.

9. $C(0, 1)$ and $D(-5, 1)$

10. $M(-4, 1)$ and $N(6, 3)$

11. $J(-1, -2)$ and $K(2, 7)$

12. $P(4, 9)$ and $Q(-6, 12)$

Write a rule for each function.

13.
x	f(x)
-2	-3
-1	-5
0	-7
1	-9

14.
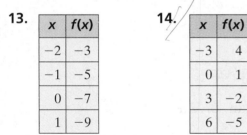
x	f(x)
-3	4
0	1
3	-2
6	-5

Is there a *positive correlation*, a *negative correlation*, or *no correlation* between the sets of data in each scatter plot? Explain.

15.
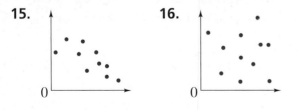

16.

Graph each inequality.

17. $y \geq 3x - 1$

18. $y < -x + 5$

Solve each system by graphing.

19. $y = x - 1$
    $x = 2y$

20. $x + y = 4$
    $2x + 2y = 8$

21. $x + y = 3$
    $y = x - 5$

22. $y \leq 3x - 2$
    $y > x + 4$

23. **Writing** Is the amount of sales tax paid a function of the labeled price of a taxable item? Explain.

24. **Writing** Is a person's age a function of his or her height? Explain.

25. Use the data in the table below.

New York Thruway Tolls

Distance (miles)	Toll (dollars)	Distance (miles)	Toll (dollars)
112	3.50	125	3.90
137	3.75	100	3.10
112	3.40	22	0.70
69	1.65	58	1.80
69	2.15	137	4.25
169	5.70	43	1.80
90	2.80	84	3.05
188	5.85	164	5.10

a. Make a (distance, toll) scatter plot.

b. Draw a trend line. Predict the toll if a car travels 200 mi on the toll road.

c. Use your trend line to predict how far a car traveled on the toll road if there was a $4.50 toll.

d. Write an equation of your trend line.

26. **Open-ended** The slope of a line through the origin is $-\frac{2}{3}$. Find the coordinates of two points on the line.

Choose the best answer.

1. An empty pot weighs 1 lb 11 oz. With oatmeal in it, the pot weighs 3 lb 7 oz. How much does the oatmeal weigh?
   A. 5 lb 2 oz   B. 2 lb 3 oz
   C. 1 lb 12 oz   D. 1 lb 4 oz

2. ***Probability*** The probability that a couple will give birth to a pair of twins is 1 in 90. About how many pairs of twins would you expect to find in 250,000 births?
   F. 280   G. 2,778   H. 1,316   J. 22,500

3. Which equation has a solution of 8?
   A. $8x + 8 = 64$ B. $\frac{b}{2} + 7 = 10$
   C. $2z + 5 = 11$ D. $5n - 13 = 27$

4. Four friends split the cost of renting a car for a snorkeling trip. Each person also rents a snorkel for $2. Each person pays a total of $15. Which equation will help find the cost c of renting the car?
   F. $\frac{c}{4} + 2 = 15$ G. $15 - 2^4 = c$
   H. $15 - 4c = 2$ J. $\frac{c}{2} + 4 = 15$

5. Sara and Juan collect soccer cards. Sara has 6 fewer than three times the number of cards Juan has. Together they have 42 cards. Solve $c + (3c - 6) = 42$ to find the number of cards each student has.
   A. Sara has 9 cards; Juan has 33 cards.
   B. Sara has 33 cards; Juan has 9 cards.
   C. Sara has 12 cards; Juan has 30 cards.
   D. Sara has 30 cards; Juan has 12 cards.

6. Which ordered pair is *not* a solution of $4x + 2y = 16$?
   F. $(-2, 12)$ G. $(5, -2)$
   H. $(2, 5)$ J. $(1, 6)$

7. Which function represents the number of kilograms $k(g)$ as a function of the number of grams g?
   A. $k(g) = 100g$ B. $k(g) = 0.01g$
   C. $k(g) = 1,000g$ D. $k(g) = 0.001g$

8. Find the slope of the line through $(3, 2)$ and $(1, -2)$.
   F. -2 G. 2   H. 1   J. 3

9. ***Data Analysis*** In the scatter plot below, each point represents an athlete who ran in the 100-m race. Greg won the race. How old is Greg?

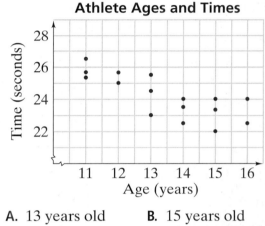

   Athlete Ages and Times

   A. 13 years old   B. 15 years old
   C. 14 years old   D. 16 years old

10. Which point is a solution of the system $y = x + 2$ and $y = 2x - 2$?
    F. $(6, 4)$ G. $(1, 3)$
    H. $(4, 6)$ J. no solution

11. Solve $-2(x - 1) \le -6$.
    A. $x \le 3$ B. $x \le -3$
    C. $x \ge 3$ D. Not here

Find the solutions of each equation for $x = -3, 0,$ and 2.

12. $y = x + 12$ 13. $4x - 4y = 8$

Write each equation in slope-intercept form. Then find the slope and y-intercept of each equation.

14. $x + \frac{1}{2}y = 4$ 15. $6x - 3y = 6$

16. Are the earnings in dollars for an hourly worker a function of the number of hours worked? Explain.

Skills You Need
for Chapter 9

▶ **Naming polygons**   Use before Lesson 9-3.

Match each polygon to its name.

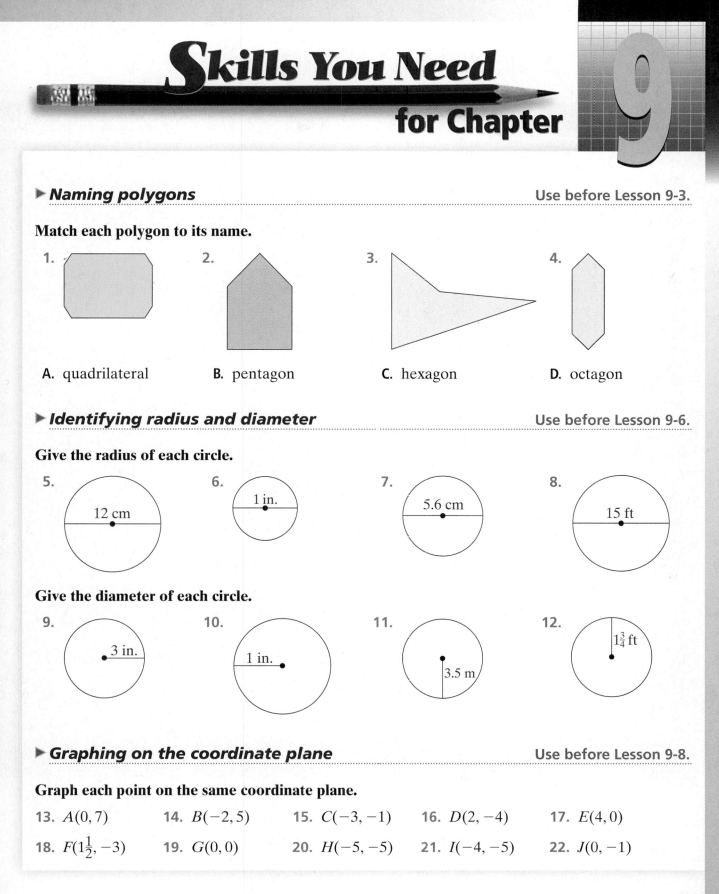

1.

2.

3.

4.

A. quadrilateral   **B.** pentagon   **C.** hexagon   **D.** octagon

▶ **Identifying radius and diameter**   Use before Lesson 9-6.

Give the radius of each circle.

5. 12 cm   6. 1 in.   7. 5.6 cm   8. 15 ft

Give the diameter of each circle.

9. 3 in.   10. 1 in.   11. 3.5 m   12. $1\frac{3}{4}$ ft

▶ **Graphing on the coordinate plane**   Use before Lesson 9-8.

Graph each point on the same coordinate plane.

13. $A(0, 7)$ 14. $B(-2, 5)$ 15. $C(-3, -1)$ 16. $D(2, -4)$ 17. $E(4, 0)$

18. $F(1\frac{1}{2}, -3)$ 19. $G(0, 0)$ 20. $H(-5, -5)$ 21. $I(-4, -5)$ 22. $J(0, -1)$

Spatial Thinking

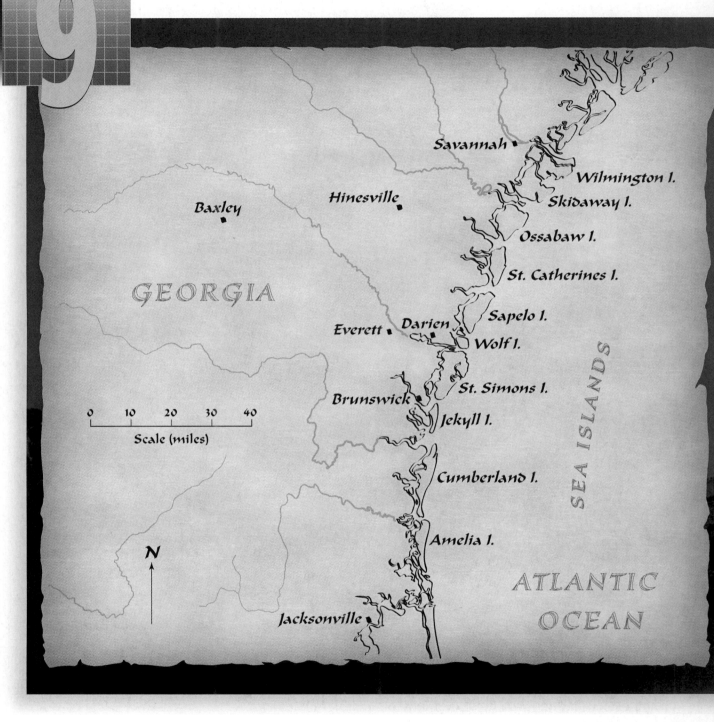

What you'll learn in this chapter:

■ How to use properties of figures to solve problems

■ How to classify geometric figures

■ How to construct figures

A mysterious map has come into your possession. The map shows the Sea Islands off the coast of Georgia. But that's not all! The map also contains three clues that tell where a treasure is supposedly buried.

Draw a Treasure Map Your project for this chapter will be to find the location of the treasure. Trace the map on the page at the left. Then follow the clues in the activities.

Steps to help you complete the project

Web Extension
www.phschool.com

How to solve a problem by drawing a diagram

Introduction to Geometry: Points, Lines, and Planes

What You'll Learn

1 To name basic geometric figures

2 To recognize intersecting lines, parallel lines, and skew lines

...And Why

To build a basic vocabulary in geometry and to solve problems in architecture

Geometric shapes are evident in many man-made and natural structures. Notice the hexagonal shape of each cell of the honeycomb in the photo below. Two other examples of geometry in nature are the spiral structure of a snail's shell and the shape of a snowflake.

Basic Geometric Figures

Name	Sample	Symbolic Name	Description
Point	• A	Point A	A **point** is a location in space. It has no size.
Line	A B n	$\overleftrightarrow{AB}$, $\overleftrightarrow{BA}$, or n	A **line** is a series of points that extends in two directions without end. A line can be named with a lower case letter.
Plane	A B M D C	$ABCD$ or M	A **plane** is a flat surface. It has no thickness. It continues without end in all directions.
Line segment or segment	Q P	$\overline{PQ}$, or $\overline{QP}$	A **segment** is a part of a line. It has two endpoints. The length of $\overline{PQ}$ is written as PQ.
Ray	C R	$\overrightarrow{CR}$	A **ray** is a part of a line. It has exactly one endpoint. Name its endpoint first.

You can combine the basic geometric figures to create many other geometric figures.

■ EXAMPLE 1

Name each figure in the diagram.

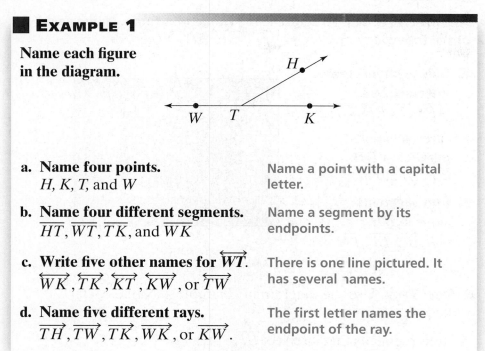

a. **Name four points.**
$H, K, T,$ and W

Name a point with a capital letter.

b. **Name four different segments.**
$\overline{HT}, \overline{WT}, \overline{TK},$ and $\overline{WK}$

Name a segment by its endpoints.

c. **Write five other names for $\overleftrightarrow{WT}$.**
$\overleftrightarrow{WK}, \overleftrightarrow{TK}, \overleftrightarrow{KT}, \overleftrightarrow{KW},$ or $\overleftrightarrow{TW}$

There is one line pictured. It has several names.

d. **Name five different rays.**
$\overrightarrow{TH}, \overrightarrow{TW}, \overrightarrow{TK}, \overrightarrow{WK},$ or $\overrightarrow{KW}$.

The first letter names the endpoint of the ray.

■ **TRY THIS** Name each figure in the diagram.

1. three points

2. two segments

3. two rays

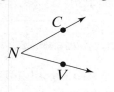

PART 2 Intersecting, Parallel, and Skew Lines

Two lines *intersect* if they have exactly one point in common. Two lines that lie in the same plane and do not intersect are **parallel.** You use the symbol ∥ to indicate "is parallel to." Segments and rays are parallel if they lie in parallel lines.

Skew lines are lines that do not lie in the same plane. They are not parallel and they do not intersect. Skew segments must be parts of skew lines.

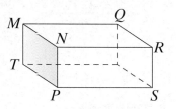

$\overline{MN}$ intersects $\overline{NP}$.
$\overline{MN} \parallel \overline{QR}$
$\overline{MN}$ is skew to $\overline{RS}$.

EXAMPLE 2

Architecture **This structure is the frame of a room. Name each of the following.**

a. **four segments that intersect $\overline{DH}$**
$\overline{AD}, \overline{CD}, \overline{EH}, \overline{GH}$

b. **three segments parallel to $\overline{DH}$**
$\overline{AE}, \overline{BF}, \overline{CG}$

c. **four segments skew to $\overline{DH}$**
$\overline{AB}, \overline{BC}, \overline{EF}, \overline{FG}$

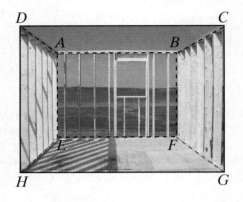

■ **TRY THIS** Use the diagram in Example 2. Name each of the following.

4. four segments that intersect $\overline{EF}$

5. three segments parallel to $\overline{EF}$

6. four segments skew to $\overline{EF}$

EXAMPLE 3

Draw a figure containing two parallel lines. Then draw a segment that intersects the parallel lines.

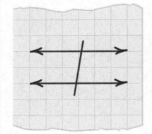

Use the lines on a piece of notebook paper or graph paper to create parallel lines. Then draw a segment that intersects the other two lines.

■ **TRY THIS**

7. Use notebook paper or graph paper. Draw a figure containing three segments that are parallel to each other. Draw a ray that intersects the parallel segments.

Exercises

Use the figure at the right.

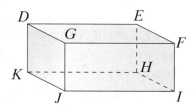

1. Name the line in three ways.

2. Name three different segments.

3. Name four different rays.

Use the figure at the right. Find each of the following.

4. all segments that intersect $\overline{DE}$

5. all segments parallel to $\overline{DE}$

6. all segments skew to $\overline{DE}$

Name all points, segments, lines, and rays shown.

7.

8.

9.

10.

11.

12.

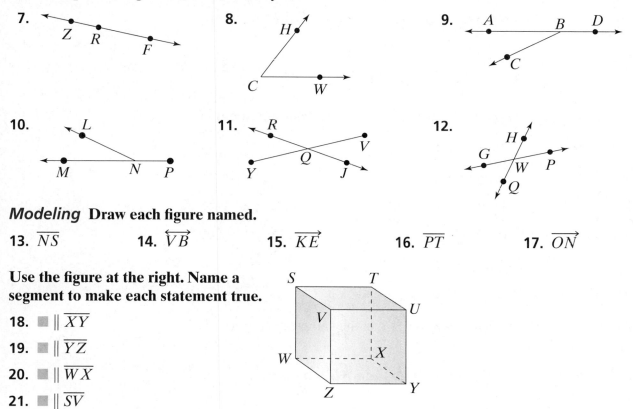

Modeling **Draw each figure named.**

13. $\overline{NS}$

14. $\overleftrightarrow{VB}$

15. $\overrightarrow{KE}$

16. $\overline{PT}$

17. $\overrightarrow{ON}$

Use the figure at the right. Name a segment to make each statement true.

18. ▩ ∥ $\overline{XY}$

19. ▩ ∥ $\overline{YZ}$

20. ▩ ∥ $\overline{WX}$

21. ▩ ∥ $\overline{SV}$

Decide whether each pair of objects are usually *intersecting, parallel,* or *skew*. Justify your answer.

22. stop sign pole, street curb **23.** two rungs of a ladder

24. fence post, fence wire **25.** sidewalk, telephone pole

Use the figure at the right. Name each of the following.

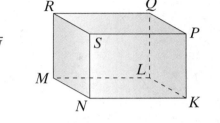

26. four segments that intersect $\overline{MN}$

27. three segments parallel to $\overline{MN}$

28. three segments skew to $\overline{MN}$

29. a. Suppose a town installs a mailbox at point *P*. How many straight roads can the town build leading to *P*?
   b. Suppose a town installs mailboxes at points *P* and *R*. How many straight roads might the town build that pass by both mailboxes?

30. Draw $\overleftrightarrow{CD}$ so that it intersects two segments, $\overline{FG}$ and $\overline{HJ}$.

31. Draw two parallel rays.

Algebra **Write an equation, and then find the length of each segment.**

32.

$2x$	3

|← $8x$ →|

33.

6	$5x$	$4x+1$

|← $12x+1$ →|

Complete with *always, sometimes,* or *never* to make a true statement.

34. $\overrightarrow{AB}$ and $\overrightarrow{BC}$ are __?__ on the same line.

35. $\overrightarrow{AB}$ and $\overrightarrow{AC}$ are __?__ the same ray.

36. $\overline{AX}$ and $\overline{XA}$ are __?__ the same segment.

37. $\overleftrightarrow{TQ}$ and $\overleftrightarrow{QT}$ are __?__ the same line.

38. Skew lines are __?__ in the same plane.

39. Two lines in the same plane are __?__ parallel.

40. ***Error Analysis*** A student says that $\overrightarrow{AB}$ is the same ray as $\overrightarrow{BA}$. Explain the student's error.

41. ***Writing*** Explain what the symbols $\overline{AB}$ and AB represent. Use an example.

42. a. On a coordinate plane, draw a line through $(-1, -2)$ and $(2, 3)$. Then draw a line through $(-2, 2)$ and $(1, 7)$.
   b. What appears to be true of the two lines that you drew in part (a)?
   c. Find the slope of each line.
   d. *Inductive Reasoning* Make a conjecture based on your answer to parts (b) and (c).

43. *City Planning* Use the map at the right. Judging from appearance, tell whether each pair of streets is parallel or intersecting.
   a. N.W. Highway and Fifth Avenue
   b. C Street and A Street
   c. B Street and C Street
   d. N.W. Highway and B Street
   e. C Street and Main Street

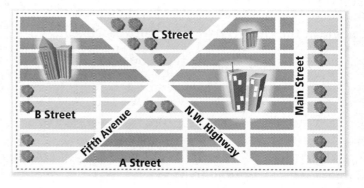

C Street

Main Street

B Street

Fifth Avenue

N.W. Highway

A Street

▶ **MIXED REVIEW**

Graph each inequality. Use different coordinate planes. *(Lesson 8-8)*

44. $y \geq -2x + 6$ **45.** $y > x + 1$ **46.** $x \leq -4$

Simplify each expression. *(Lessons 5-3 and 5-4)*

47. $\dfrac{3}{8} + \dfrac{7}{12}$ **48.** $2\dfrac{3}{4} - 1\dfrac{5}{6}$ **49.** $\dfrac{5}{8} \cdot \dfrac{3}{4}$ **50.** $2\dfrac{2}{3} \div \dfrac{3}{8}$

Math at Work
Choreographer

Choreographers are usually experienced dancers whose hard work and dedication have earned them the opportunity to create original dances. Choreographers have an excellent sense of timing and spatial positioning.

Many choreographed dance numbers reflect geometric shapes such as triangles and quadrilaterals. Next time you see a dance group perform, be on the lookout for geometry—it will help you think like a choreographer!

For more information about choreographers, visit the Prentice Hall Web site.
www.phschool.com

MATH TOOLBOX

Drawing and Measuring Angles

An *angle* is formed by two rays with a common endpoint. The rays are the *sides* of the angle. The common endpoint is the *vertex*. You can name the angle at the right ∠*ABC*, ∠*CBA*, ∠*B*, or ∠1.

You can classify angles using their measures.

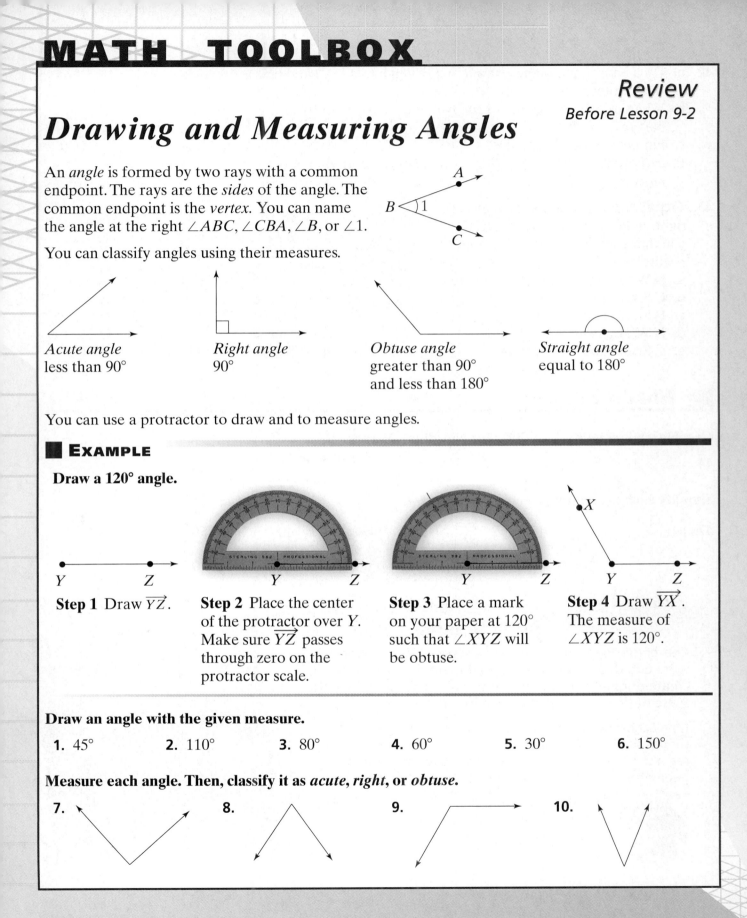

Acute angle
less than 90°

Right angle
90°

Obtuse angle
greater than 90°
and less than 180°

Straight angle
equal to 180°

You can use a protractor to draw and to measure angles.

■ EXAMPLE

Draw a 120° angle.

Y *Z*

Step 1 Draw $\overrightarrow{YZ}$.

Step 2 Place the center of the protractor over *Y*. Make sure $\overrightarrow{YZ}$ passes through zero on the protractor scale.

Step 3 Place a mark on your paper at 120° such that ∠*XYZ* will be obtuse.

Step 4 Draw $\overrightarrow{YX}$. The measure of ∠*XYZ* is 120°.

Draw an angle with the given measure.

1. 45°   **2.** 110°   **3.** 80°   **4.** 60°   **5.** 30°   **6.** 150°

Measure each angle. Then, classify it as *acute*, *right*, or *obtuse*.

7.   **8.**   **9.**   **10.**

Angle Relationships and Parallel Lines

PART 1   Adjacent and Vertical Angles

What You'll Learn

1 To identify adjacent and vertical angles

2 To find the relationships of angles formed by parallel lines

. . . And Why

To use the relationships of angles formed by parallel lines in real-world situations, such as setting leaded window panes

In this lesson you will learn to identify special pairs of angles.

Adjacent angles share a vertex and a side but no points in their interiors.

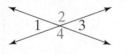

Common side

$\angle AXB$ and $\angle BXC$ are adjacent angles.

$\angle AXC$ and $\angle BXC$ not adjacent angles.

Vertical angles are formed by two intersecting lines and are opposite each other. Vertical angles have the same measure.

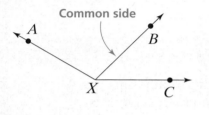

$\angle 1$ and $\angle 3$ are vertical angles.
$\angle 2$ and $\angle 4$ are vertical angles.

Angles that have the same measure are **congruent angles.** In the diagram $\angle 1$ is congruent to $\angle 3$. You can write this as $\angle 1 \cong \angle 3$. You can write *the measure of* $\angle 1$ as $m\angle 1$. Since $\angle 1 \cong \angle 3$, $m\angle 1 = m\angle 3$.

If the sum of the measures of two angles is 180°, the angles are **supplementary.**

If the sum of the measures of two angles is 90°, the angles are **complementary.**

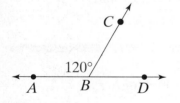

$\angle ABC$ and $\angle CBD$ are supplementary.

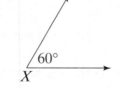

$\angle X$ and $\angle ABC$ are supplementary.
$\angle X$ and $\angle RQS$ are complementary.

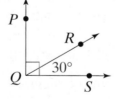

$\angle RQS$ and $\angle PQR$ are complementary.

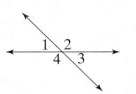

EXAMPLE 1

Find the measure of $\angle 1$ if $m\angle 4 = 135°$.

$$m\angle 1 + m\angle 4 = 180° \qquad \angle 1 \text{ and } \angle 4 \text{ are supplementary.}$$
$$m\angle 1 + 135° = 180° \qquad \text{Replace } m\angle 4 \text{ with } 135°.$$
$$m\angle 1 + 135° - 135° = 180° - 135° \qquad \text{Solve for } m\angle 1.$$
$$m\angle 1 = 45°$$

■ TRY THIS

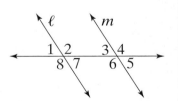

1. If $m\angle 8 = 20°$, find the measures of $\angle 5$, $\angle 6$, and $\angle 7$.

PART 2 Relating Angles and Parallel Lines

A line that intersects two other lines in different points is a **transversal.** Some pairs of angles formed by transversals and two lines have special names.

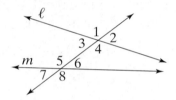

Corresponding angles lie on the same side of the transversal and in corresponding positions. $\angle 1$ and $\angle 5$, $\angle 3$ and $\angle 7$, $\angle 2$ and $\angle 6$, and $\angle 4$ and $\angle 8$ are corresponding angles.

Alternate interior angles are in the interior of a pair of lines and on opposite sides of the transversal. $\angle 3$ and $\angle 6$, and $\angle 4$ and $\angle 5$ are alternate interior angles.

When a transversal intersects two parallel lines, each pair of corresponding angles is congruent. Each pair of alternate interior angles is also congruent.

EXAMPLE 2

In the diagram, $\ell \parallel m$. Identify each of the following.

a. congruent corresponding angles

$\angle 1 \cong \angle 3$, $\angle 2 \cong \angle 4$, $\angle 8 \cong \angle 6$, $\angle 7 \cong \angle 5$

b. congruent alternate interior angles

$\angle 3 \cong \angle 7$, $\angle 2 \cong \angle 6$

■ TRY THIS

2. In the diagram $a \parallel b$. Name four pairs of congruent corresponding angles and two pairs of congruent alternate interior angles.

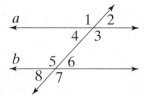

When solving a problem that involves parallel lines, you can often choose whether to use corresponding angles or alternate interior angles.

■ Different Ways to Solve a Problem

The windowpanes at the right are held in place by parallel strips of lead. Lines q, r, and s indicate lead stripping; $s \parallel r$. If $m\angle 1 = 65°$, what is $m\angle 4$?

Method 1

Use corresponding angles.

$\angle 1 \cong \angle 3$ because they are corresponding angles.
So $m\angle 3 = 65°$. $\angle 3$ and $\angle 4$ are supplementary.
So $m\angle 3 + m\angle 4 = 180°$.

$$m\angle 3 + m\angle 4 = 180°$$
$$65° + m\angle 4 = 180°$$
$$65° + m\angle 4 - 65° = 180° - 65°$$
$$m\angle 4 = 115°$$

Method 2

Use alternate interior angles.

$\angle 1$ and $\angle 2$ are supplementary.

$$m\angle 1 + m\angle 2 = 180°$$
$$65° + m\angle 2 = 180°$$
$$65° + m\angle 2 - 65° = 180° - 65°$$
$$m\angle 2 = 115°$$

Since $\angle 2$ and $\angle 4$ are alternate interior angles, they are congruent. If $m\angle 2 = 115°$, then $m\angle 4 = 115°$.

Choose a Method

1. Which method do you prefer? Explain why.

2. What is another way to solve the problem?

Exercises

1. Find the sum of the measures of ∠1, ∠2, and ∠3 in the figure at the right.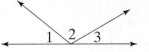

2. Fill in the blank. The sum of the measures of two angles is 90°. The angles are __?__ angles.

Name the angle vertical to ∠1. Name an angle adjacent to ∠1. Then find m∠1.

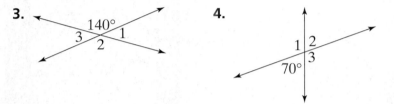

3.

4.

5.

Use the figure at the right for Exercises 6–8.

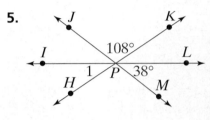

6. Name four pairs of corresponding angles.

7. Name the alternate interior angles.

8. Suppose $\overleftrightarrow{AB} \parallel \overleftrightarrow{MN}$. Name all angles congruent to ∠8.

PRACTICE AND PROBLEM SOLVING

9. a. *Algebra* Write an equation and find the value of x.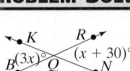
   b. Find $m\angle KQB$.
   c. Find $m\angle KQR$.

10. a. In the figure at the right, $x \parallel y$. List all angles that are congruent to ∠1.
    b. If $m\angle 5 = 45°$, what are the measures of the other angles?

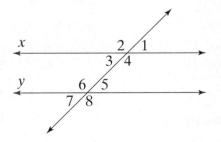

11. Find the measures of ∠1, ∠2, and ∠3 if $m\angle 4 = 100°$.

12. **Writing** Describe how you will keep from confusing the definitions of supplementary angles and complementary angles.

Algebra In each figure find the measures of ∠1 and ∠2.

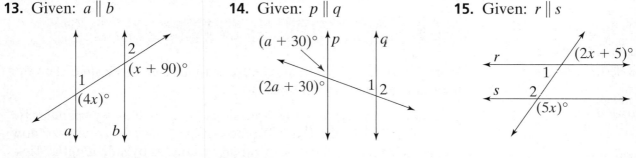

13. Given: $a \parallel b$

14. Given: $p \parallel q$

15. Given: $r \parallel s$

Math in the Media Use the article below and the map for Exercises 16 and 17.

New Road Approved

The Middleton City Board approved the proposal for a new road parallel to Highway 10. This new road, to be called Leeway Road, will help ease traffic flow in downtown Middleton during rush hour. Leeway Road will intersect both Sand Avenue and Piper Street.

16. When Leeway Road is built, what should be $m\angle 1$?

17. **Error Analysis** A surveyor stated that $m\angle 2$ should be 130°. Explain the surveyor's error.

18. **Mathematical Reasoning** Angles on the "outside" of two lines and on opposite sides of a transversal are called *alternate exterior angles*. The transversal q intersects two parallel lines m and n. If $m\angle 1 = 85°$, what is the measure of ∠5? Explain your reasoning.

▶ MIXED REVIEW

Draw each figure. *(Lesson 9-1)*

19. $\overline{AB}$

20. $\overrightarrow{CD}$

21. $\overrightarrow{DC}$

22. $\overleftrightarrow{EF}$

23. ∠*GHI*

Find the sale price. *(Lesson 6-9)*

24. $25 at 10% discount

25. $55 at 5% discount

26. $324 at 20% discount

27. **Choose a Strategy** In a single elimination tournament a team plays until it loses. Eight teams play in a tournament. How many games must be played?

9-3 Classifying Polygons

PART 1 Classifying Triangles

What You'll Learn

1 To classify triangles

2 To classify quadrilaterals

... And Why

To use polygons in real-world situations involving design and construction

A **polygon** is a *closed* plane figure with at least three *sides*. The sides meet only at their endpoints.

A triangle is a polygon with three sides. You can classify triangles by angle measures. In the Math Toolbox on page 448 you reviewed how to classify angles. You can also classify triangles by side lengths. Tick marks are used to indicate congruent sides of a figure.

Acute triangle
three acute angles

Right triangle
one right angle

Obtuse triangle
one obtuse angle

Equilateral triangle
three congruent sides

Isosceles triangle
at least two congruent sides

Scalene triangle
no congruent sides

The piano lid and its support shown here determine a scalene triangle.

■ EXAMPLE 1

Classify the triangle by its sides and angles.

The triangle has two congruent sides and one right angle.

The triangle is an isosceles right triangle.

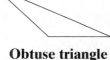

■ **TRY THIS** Judging by appearance, classify each triangle by its sides and angles.

1.   2.   3.

You can also classify quadrilaterals by their sides and angles.

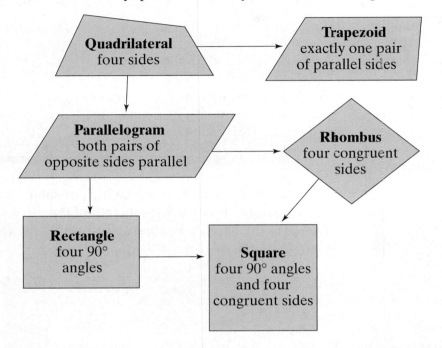

■ EXAMPLE 2

Name the types of quadrilaterals that have both pairs of opposite sides parallel.

All parallelograms have opposite sides parallel. Parallelograms include rectangles, rhombuses, and squares.

■ TRY THIS

4. Name the types of quadrilaterals that have four right angles.

In later math courses, you will prove that a parallelogram has opposite sides congruent and opposite angles congruent.

Polygons are named using their vertices. Start at one vertex and list them in consecutive order.

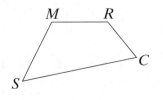

Starting from *M*, the name of this figure is quadrilateral *MRCS* or quadrilateral *MSCR*.

Reading Math

The plural of *vertex* is *vertices*.

A **regular polygon** has all sides congruent and all angles congruent. Some regular polygons are shown below.

Triangle

Square

Pentagon

Hexagon

You can use algebra to write a formula for the perimeter of a regular polygon.

PA01SE0903ta11

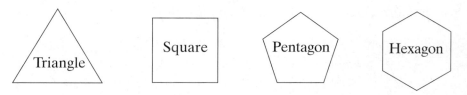
REAL-WORLD CONNECTION

■ **EXAMPLE 3**

Construction **A contractor is framing a regular octagonal gazebo. Write a formula to find the perimeter of the gazebo. Evaluate the formula for a side length of 4 ft.**

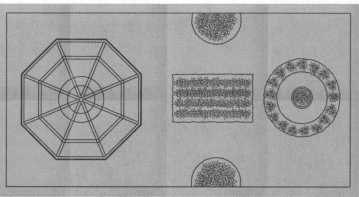

Most gazebos are regular hexagons or regular octagons.

To write a formula, let $x =$ the length of each side. The perimeter of the regular octagon is $x + x + x + x + x + x + x + x$. Therefore the formula for the perimeter is $P = 8x$.

$P = 8x$ Write the formula.

$\quad = 8(4)$ Substitute 4 for x.

$\quad = 32$ Simplify.

For a side length of 4 ft, the perimeter is 32 ft.

■ **TRY THIS**

5. Write a formula to find the perimeter of a regular pentagon. Use the formula to find the perimeter if one side is 16 cm.

Exercises

► CHECK UNDERSTANDING

Open-ended **Sketch each figure.**

1. an isosceles right triangle

2. a scalene obtuse triangle

3. an isosceles obtuse triangle

Find the perimeter of each figure.

4.

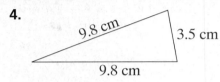

5. an equilateral triangle that has a side of 36 yd

6. a square that has a side of 5.1 cm

7. Draw a parallelogram without a right angle but with four congruent sides. What is another name for this figure?

8. Draw a regular quadrilateral.

► PRACTICE AND PROBLEM SOLVING

Judging by appearance, classify each triangle by its sides and angles.

9.

10.

11.

Write a formula to find the perimeter of each figure. Use the formula to find the perimeter.

12. an equilateral triangle with one side 3.5 cm

13. a square with one side 12.5 in.

14. a regular hexagon with one side $\frac{5}{8}$ in.

15. a regular pentagon with one side $1\frac{2}{3}$ yd

Name three different figures in each flag.

16.

Flag of Antigua

17.

Flag of Philippines

Open-ended Sketch each figure.

18. an isosceles acute triangle   **19.** a scalene right triangle   **20.** an equilateral triangle

Name all quadrilaterals that have each of the named properties.

21. exactly one pair of parallel sides

22. four congruent sides

23. two pairs of parallel sides

24. opposite sides congruent

25. supplementary angles

26. opposite angles congruent

27. *Mathematical Reasoning* Two sides of an isosceles triangle are 10 cm and 12 cm. Explain why the perimeter could be either 32 cm or 34 cm.

28. a. A decagon is a polygon with 10 sides. Write a formula for the perimeter of a regular decagon.
  b. Find the perimeter of a regular decagon that has a side 14.5 m long.
  c. Find the length of a side of a regular decagon that has a perimeter of 22 ft.

Journal

Are all equilateral triangles isosceles? Are all isosceles triangles equilateral? Explain.

▶ **MIXED REVIEW**

29. A transversal intersects two parallel lines, forming eight angles. One angle measures 60°. Sketch a diagram showing the measures of all eight angles. *(Lesson 9-2)*

Solve each equation. *(Lessons 7-2 and Lesson 7-5)*

30. $x + 20 + 2x = 41$ **31.** $53 - 6x = 13 - 2x$ **32.** $3y - 10 + 5y = 6$

33. *Choose a Strategy* A town parade included modern and antique cycles. The modern cycles had two wheels and the antique cycles had three wheels. Altogether there were 64 wheels on the 28 cycles. How many of the cycles had three wheels?

CHAPTER PROJECT 9 **ACTIVITY 1 DRAWING**

Here is the first clue: *Draw a line from Baxley to Savannah. From Savannah, draw a southwesterly line that forms a 60° angle with the first line. The treasure is on an island that lies along the second line.* On which islands could the treasure be buried?

MATH TOOLBOX

Angles of a Polygon

In previous courses, you learned that the sum of the measures of the angles of a triangle is 180°. Now you have the tools to prove that this is true with deductive reasoning.

In the figure, $\overleftrightarrow{AC} \parallel \overleftrightarrow{DE}$. If two parallel lines are cut by a transversal, then alternate interior angles are congruent. Therefore, $\angle 1 \cong \angle 4$, or $m\angle 1 = m\angle 4$. Similarly, $m\angle 3 = m\angle 5$. $\angle ABC$ is a straight angle. So $m\angle 1 + m\angle 2 + m\angle 3 = 180°$. When you substitute $m\angle 4$ for $m\angle 1$ and $m\angle 5$ for $m\angle 3$, you get $m\angle 4 + m\angle 2 + m\angle 5 = 180°$. These are the angles of $\triangle BDE$.

You can use triangles to find the sum of the measures of the angles of any polygon.

■ EXAMPLE

Find the sum of the measures of the angles of a hexagon.

The hexagon has **6** vertices.
From vertex A, there are **5** segments to the other vertices.
The segments determine **4** triangles.

sum of measures of angles of hexagon	=	number of triangles	·	number of degrees in a triangle
720°	=	4	·	180°

Find the sum of the measures of the angles of each polygon.

1. a quadrilateral   **2.** a decagon (10 sides)

3. an octagon   **4.** a dodecagon (12 sides)

5. *Mathematical Reasoning* Write a formula for the sum of the measures of the angles of an *n*-gon (*n* sides).

6. Find the value of *x* in the figure at the right.

7. *Writing* The sum of the measures of the angles of a polygon is 1,260°. Explain how you can find the number of sides of the polygon.

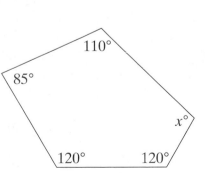

9-4

Draw a Diagram

Math Strategies in Action

Car designers rely on computer design programs to create, test, and modify their plans. The process of drawing a diagram helps them to discover any problems they may have and to see possible solutions.

Drawing a diagram is an important problem solving tool.

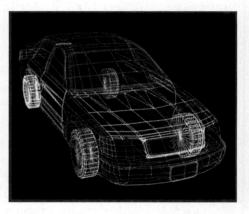

■ SAMPLE PROBLEM

How many diagonals does an octagon have?

Read

In reading the problem, make sure you understand the meanings of all of the terms.

1. What is an octagon?

2. What is a diagonal?

Plan

One strategy for solving this problem is to draw a diagram and count the diagonals. An octagon has eight sides. You can draw five diagonals from one vertex of an octagon.

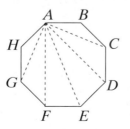

$\overline{AG}, \overline{AF}, \overline{AE}, \overline{AD}$, and $\overline{AC}$ are some of the diagonals.

Start at one vertex, draw all diagonals from that vertex, and count them.

3. There are 5 diagonals drawn from vertex *A*. Copy the diagram on the previous page. Now find the number of diagonals you can draw from vertex *B*.

4. How many new diagonals can you draw from vertex *C*?

 **Solve**

It may be helpful to organize your results as you count the diagonals. Make a table similar to the one below and fill in the number of diagonals from each vertex. Do not count a diagonal twice. (The segment from *A* to *C* is the same segment as the one from *C* to *A*.) Then find the sum of the diagonals.

Vertex	Number of Diagonals
A	5
B	5
C	4
D	▩
E	▩
F	▩
G	▩
H	▩
Total	▩

 **Look Back**

Recounting the diagonals after they have all been drawn is not an easy task. To check your results, you may want to try a different approach. Start with figures with fewer sides and see whether there is a pattern of diagonals as you increase the number of sides.

Figure	Number of Sides	Number of Diagonals
Triangle	3	0
Quadrilateral	4	2
Pentagon	5	5
Hexagon	6	9

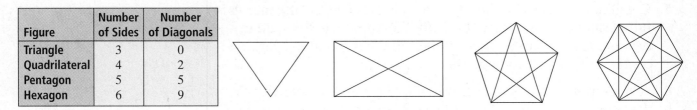

Notice that the number of diagonals increases as you increase the number of sides of the polygon. First the number increases by 2, then by 3, and then by 4. Continue this pattern to check your results.

Exercises

► CHECK UNDERSTANDING

Solve by drawing a diagram.

1. A furniture delivery truck leaves the store at 8 A.M. It travels 6 miles east, then 4 miles south, then 2 miles west, and then 4 miles north. At the end of this route, how far is the truck from the store?

2. Bill is older than Jim and younger than Jose. Jose is older than Chris and younger than Tandala. Chris is older than Jim. Bill is younger than Tandala. Chris is older than Bill. Who is youngest?

3. *Geometry* How many triangles can you form in a hexagon if you draw all of the diagonals from only one vertex?

► PRACTICE AND PROBLEM SOLVING

Solve by drawing a diagram.

4. Eight soccer teams are to play each other two times in a season. How many games will be played?

5. There are 25 students in a math class. Ten students are members of the math club. Twelve students are in the band. Five students are in both. How many students in the math class are members of neither club?

6. *Coordinate Geometry* Snoozles are always born as twins, and each snoozle always moves in the opposite direction from its twin. Twin snoozles are at the origin. One follows the path $(0, 0)$ to $(1, 3)$ to $(2, 2)$ to $(4, 7)$. What path will its twin travel?

Solve using any strategy.

7. Container A has twice the capacity of container B. Container A is full of sand and container B is empty. Suppose $\frac{1}{8}$ of the sand in container A is poured into container B. What fractional part of container B will contain sand?

8. A student was standing in the middle of a line. Twenty-three students were ahead of her. How many students were in the line?

9. *Writing* Suppose you want to find the thickness of one sheet of paper. Describe the problem solving method you would use.

10. Points P, Q, R, and S appear in that order on a line. The ratio $PQ : QR$ is $3 : 4$, and the ratio $QR : RS$ is $2 : 5$. The length PQ is 6 in. Find the length PS.

11. Shana has three pets, a dog, a cat, and a bird. One of them is named Sammy. Noodles is younger than both the bird and the dog. Fluffy is green. Which pet has the name Sammy?

12. *Geometry* You can draw one segment to connect two points and three distinct segments to connect three named points. How many segments can you draw to connect five points if no three of the points lie on the same line?

13. *Writing* What are the next three numbers in the sequence $1, 3, 6, 10, 15, 21, \ldots$? Describe the pattern.

14. Two friends rented a canoe for 10 days. One friend used the canoe for 6 days. The other friend used the canoe for 4 days. How much of the $150 rental fee should each friend pay?

15. *Measurement* Maureen cut a 20-cm ribbon into exactly three pieces. The first piece is 3 cm shorter than the second piece. The third piece is 4 cm shorter than the second piece. Find the length of the shortest piece.

16. **TEST PREP** A coin collector has 53 rare coins. This is 12 fewer than 5 times the number he had a year ago. Choose the equation that you could use to find how many coins the collector had a year ago.
   A. $12 - 5x = 53$
   B. $53 - 5x = 12$
   C. $53 - 12 = 5x$
   D. $53 = 5x - 12$

▶ **MIXED REVIEW**

Classify each triangle by its sides and angles. *(Lesson 9-3)*

17. no congruent sides and one right angle

18. three congruent sides

19. one obtuse angle and no congruent sides

20. a 90° angle and two congruent sides

Write each decimal as a fraction in simplest form and as a percent. *(Lesson 6-5)*

21. 0.14   **22.** 4.5   **23.** 0.11   **24.** 0.02   **25.** 0.125

26. Adult tickets for the school musical sell for $8 and student tickets sell for $5 each. Let x be the number of adult tickets sold and y be the number of student tickets sold. The school hopes to make at least $1,000. Write a linear inequality to model the situation. Show all of the solutions by graphing the linear inequality. *(Lesson 8-8)*

9-5

Congruence

What You'll Learn

1 To identify corresponding parts of congruent triangles

2 To determine whether triangles are congruent

...And Why

To use congruent figures for finding distance

Investigate

•••••••••••••••••• **EXPLORING CONGRUENCE** ••••••••••••••••••

1. Have each member of your group cut plastic straws 3 cm, 6 cm, and 7 cm long. String an 18-cm string through the three straws. Tie the string just tight enough to form a strong triangle without bending any straws.

2. Hold the triangles up to one another to compare. Are they the same size and shape? Describe how the angle measures compare.

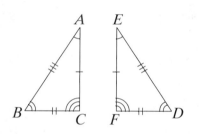

$\triangle ABC \cong \triangle EDF$

$\angle A \cong \angle E$	$\overline{AB} \cong \overline{ED}$
$\angle B \cong \angle D$	$\overline{BC} \cong \overline{DF}$
$\angle C \cong \angle F$	$\overline{AC} \cong \overline{EF}$

PART 1 | **Identifying Corresponding Parts**

When two polygons are congruent, their corresponding parts have the same measure. The triangles at the left are congruent. You can use tick marks to indicate congruent segments and arcs to indicate congruent angles. You can write a congruence statement by listing the corresponding angles in the same order.

You can use corresponding parts of congruent polygons to find distances.

REAL-WORLD CONNECTION

EXAMPLE 1

Measurement In the figure at the left, $\triangle AMN \cong \triangle ABC$.

a. **Name the corresponding congruent angles.**
   $\angle M \cong \angle B, \angle N \cong \angle C, \angle MAN \cong \angle BAC$

b. **Name the corresponding congruent sides.**
   $\overline{MN} \cong \overline{BC}, \overline{NA} \cong \overline{CA}, \overline{MA} \cong \overline{BA}$

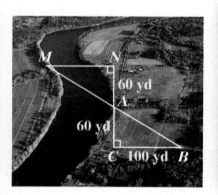

c. **Find the distance across the river from *M* to *N*.**
   Since $\overline{MN} \cong \overline{BC}$ and $BC = 100$ yd, $MN = 100$ yd.

3. $\triangle ABC \cong \triangle DEC$. List all pairs of congruent corresponding sides and angles. Then find AC.

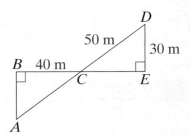

You use corresponding parts of triangles to identify congruent triangles. Below are three of the ways to show that two triangles are congruent.

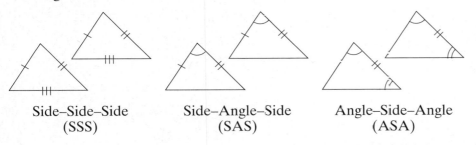

Side–Side–Side
(SSS)

Side–Angle–Side
(SAS)

Angle–Side–Angle
(ASA)

■ **EXAMPLE 2**

List the congruent corresponding parts of each pair of triangles. Write a congruence statement for the triangles.

a.

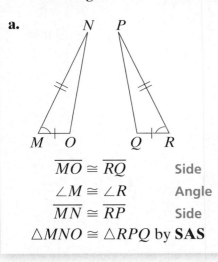

$\overline{MO} \cong \overline{RQ}$	Side
$\angle M \cong \angle R$	Angle
$\overline{MN} \cong \overline{RP}$	Side

$\triangle MNO \cong \triangle RPQ$ by **SAS**

b.

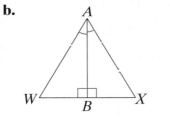

$\angle WAB \cong \angle XAB$	Angle
$\overline{AB} \cong \overline{AB}$	Side
$\angle ABW \cong \angle ABX$	Angle

$\triangle WAB \cong \triangle XAB$ by **ASA**

■ **TRY THIS**

4. List the congruent corresponding parts of the pair of triangles. Write a congruence statement for the triangles.

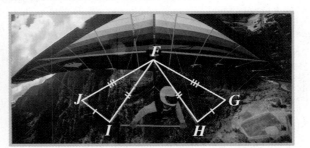

Exercises

CHECK UNDERSTANDING

1. Assume that $\triangle ABC \cong \triangle XYZ$. Write six congruence statements involving corresponding sides and angles.

List the congruent corresponding parts of each pair of triangles. Write a congruence statement for the triangles.

2.

3.

4.

PRACTICE AND PROBLEM SOLVING

Given that $\triangle ABC \cong \triangle DEF$, complete the following.

5. $\angle A \cong \blacksquare$ **6.** $\angle B \cong \blacksquare$ **7.** $\angle C \cong \blacksquare$

8. $m\angle C = \blacksquare$ **9.** $m\angle B = \blacksquare$ **10.** $m\angle A = \blacksquare$

11. $\overline{AC} \cong \blacksquare$ **12.** $\overline{EF} \cong \blacksquare$ **13.** $\overline{BA} \cong \blacksquare$

14. $AB = \blacksquare$ **15.** $AC = \blacksquare$ **16.** $FE = \blacksquare$

17. $\triangle CBA \cong \blacksquare$

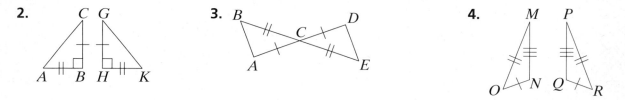

List the congruent corresponding parts of each pair of triangles. Write a congruence statement for the triangles.

18.

19.

20.

21.

22.

23.

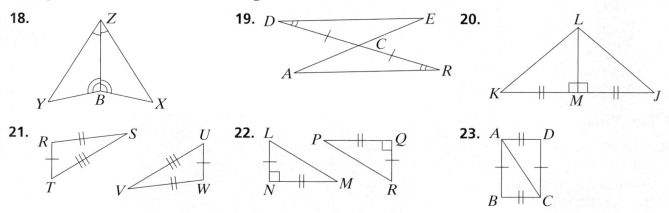

Explain why each pair of triangles is congruent. Then find the missing measures in each diagram.

24.

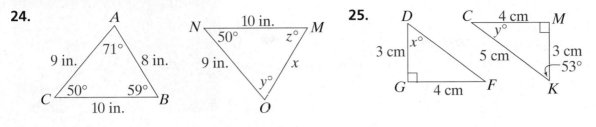

25.

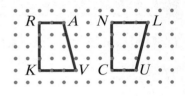

Error Analysis The two figures in the diagram are congruent. Explain why each congruence statement in Exercises 26–31 is or is not correct.

26. $RAVK \cong NLUC$

27. $RKVA \cong ULNC$

28. $ARKV \cong CULN$

29. $\overline{NL} \cong \overline{KV}$

30. $\angle V \cong \angle C$

31. $\angle VAR \cong \angle LUC$

32. **TEST PREP** If $\triangle MFQ \cong \triangle DRW$, which of the following is *not necessarily* true?

A. $\angle M \cong \angle W$ B. $\overline{MQ} \cong \overline{DW}$ C. $\angle MFQ \cong \angle DRW$ D. $m\angle F = m\angle R$

33. *Mathematical Reasoning* $\triangle KWR$ is *equiangular* (all angles are congruent). $\triangle ABJ$ is also equiangular. Can you use Angle-Angle-Angle (**AAA**) to show that two triangles are congruent? Use diagrams to justify your conclusion.

34. *Writing* $\triangle ABC \cong \triangle XYZ$. What can you conclude about the perimeters of the triangles? Explain.

35. *Geometric Patterns* In the quilt design below name the triangles that appear to be congruent.

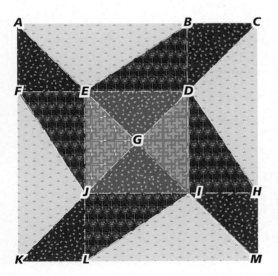

36. The end of the packing crate at the right is rectangular. The diagonals are congruent and intersect at point H. $\overline{HB} \cong \overline{HD}$ and $\overline{AH} \cong \overline{CH}$.

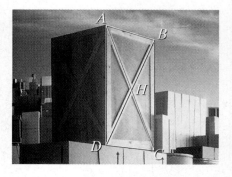

  a. Which triangle is congruent to $\triangle ABH$? How can you show that the triangles are congruent?

  b. Which triangle is congruent to $\triangle ADC$? How can you show that the triangles are congruent?

▶ MIXED REVIEW

Order from least to greatest. *(Lesson 5-1)*

37. $\dfrac{1}{2}, \dfrac{5}{6}, \dfrac{3}{8}, \dfrac{2}{3}$ **38.** $\dfrac{3}{8}, \dfrac{2}{3}, \dfrac{3}{4}, \dfrac{4}{5}$ **39.** $\dfrac{1}{6}, \dfrac{1}{5}, \dfrac{1}{7}, \dfrac{1}{4}$

Write and solve an equation. *(Lesson 6-7)*

40. What percent of 50 is 20? **41.** 15% of what number is 12? **42.** Find 125% of 200.

43. Students are evenly spaced as they sit around a round table. The fourth student is directly across from the 11th student. How many students are seated at the table? *(Lesson 9-4)*

✔ CHECKPOINT 1   Lessons 9-1 through 9-5

Name the figure that has the properties described.

1. a part of a line with one endpoint

2. a series of points that extends in two directions without end

3. a location in space

4. two rays with a common endpoint

5. *Algebra* In the diagram at the right, $a \parallel b$.
  a. Write an equation to find x.
  b. Find $m\angle TAV$.
  c. Find $m\angle TAN$.
  d. Find $m\angle DNK$.

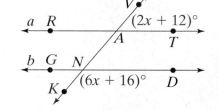

6. *Open-ended* Draw a triangle that is scalene and has a right angle.

7. **TEST PREP** Which of the following must be true if $\triangle AND \cong \triangle PCK$?
  A. $\overline{AN} \cong \overline{PK}$ **B.** $\angle AND \cong \angle PKC$
  C. $\angle N \cong \angle C$ **D.** $\overline{ND} \cong \overline{PC}$

Circles

Investigate

················· EXPLORING PI ·················

1. Work in groups. Each member of your group should have a ruler, string, and several circular objects, such as jar lids. Make a chart similar to the chart below. Record your results.

Object	Diameter	Circumference	Ratio $\frac{\text{Circumference}}{\text{Diameter}}$
▪	▪	▪	▪
▪	▪	▪	▪

2. Measure the diameter of each circle to the nearest millimeter.

3. Find the circumference of each circle by wrapping a string around the outside of the circle. Then straighten the string and measure its length to the nearest millimeter.

4. Calculate the ratio $\frac{\text{circumference}}{\text{diameter}}$ to the nearest tenth.

5. Make a conjecture about the relationship between the circumference of a circle and its diameter.

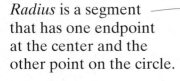
PART 1 **Finding Circumference**

A **circle** is the set of all points that are the same distance from a given point, called the center of the circle.

Radius is a segment that has one endpoint at the center and the other point on the circle.

Circumference is the distance around the circle.

Diameter is a chord that passes through the center of a circle.

Chord is a segment whose endpoints are on the circle.

The ratio of every circle's circumference C to its diameter d is the same. It has a special symbol, π, which is pronounced "pie." Both 3.14 and $\frac{22}{7}$ are good approximations for this ratio. Use $\frac{22}{7}$ for π when calculations involve fractions, and use 3.14 when they do not.

If you multiply both sides of the equation $\frac{C}{d} = \pi$ by d, you get $C = \pi d$, which is a formula for the circumference of a circle.

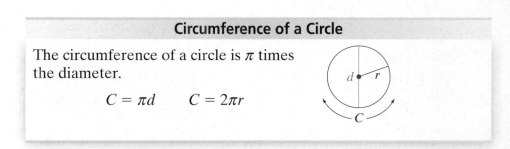

Circumference of a Circle

The circumference of a circle is π times the diameter.

$$C = \pi d \qquad C = 2\pi r$$

■ EXAMPLE 1

Find the circumference of the circle at the right.

$\begin{aligned} C &= \pi d & &\text{Write the formula.} \\ C &\approx (3.14)6 & &\text{Substitute 3.14 for } \pi \text{ and 6 for } d. \\ &= 18.84 & &\text{Simplify.} \end{aligned}$

6 ft

The circumference of the circle is about 18.84 ft.

■ **TRY THIS** Find the circumference of each circle.

6. diameter = 200 mi   **7.** radius = 30 mm   **8.** diameter = $2\frac{4}{5}$ in.

PART 2 Making Circle Graphs

To make a circle graph, you find the measure of each *central angle*. A **central angle** is an angle whose vertex is the center of a circle. There are 360° in a circle.

REAL-WORLD CONNECTION

■ EXAMPLE 2

Budget **Make a graph for Juan's weekly budget shown at the left.**

Use proportions to find the measures of the central angles.

$$\frac{25}{100} = \frac{\ell}{360} \qquad \frac{20}{100} = \frac{r}{360} \qquad \frac{15}{100} = \frac{c}{360} \qquad \frac{40}{100} = \frac{s}{360}$$

$$\ell = 90° \qquad r = 72° \qquad c = 54° \qquad s = 144°$$

Juan's Weekly Budget

Lunch (ℓ)	25%
Recreation (r)	20%
Clothes (c)	15%
Savings (s)	40%

Use a compass to draw a circle. Draw the central angles with a protractor. Label each section. Add a title and necessary information.

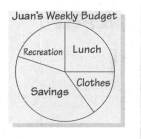

Juan's Weekly Budget

Recreation | Lunch | Clothes | Savings

■ TRY THIS

9. Draw a circle graph for the data. Round the measure of each central angle to the nearest degree.

Blood Types of Population

Type A	Type B	Type AB	Type O
40%	12%	5%	43%

REAL-WORLD CONNECTION

■ EXAMPLE 3

National Parks **Draw a circle graph of the data at the right.**

First add to find the total number of visits (in millions).

$$0.3 + 0.4 + 1.3 + 1.8 = 3.8$$

Use proportions to find the measures of the central angles.

$$\frac{0.3}{3.8} = \frac{a}{360°} \qquad \frac{0.4}{3.8} = \frac{b}{360°} \qquad \frac{1.3}{3.8} = \frac{c}{360°} \qquad \frac{1.8}{3.8} = \frac{d}{360°}$$

$$a \approx 28° \qquad b \approx 38° \qquad c \approx 123° \qquad d \approx 171°$$

Use a compass to draw a circle. Draw the central angles with a protractor. Label each section. Add a title and necessary information.

Visits to Kentucky's National Recreation Areas

Cumberland Gap 123° — Big South Fork 38° — Abe Lincoln 28° — Mammoth Caves 171°

Visits to Kentucky's National Recreation Areas

Site	Visits (millions)
Abraham Lincoln's Birthplace	0.3
Big South Fork	0.4
Cumberland Gap	1.3
Mammoth Caves	1.8

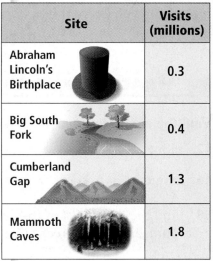

■ TRY THIS

10. Students at Western High School work in the following places: restaurants, 140; library, 15; auto shop, 60; retail stores, 75; and other places, 30. Draw a circle graph to show where students at Western High School work. Round the measures of the central angles to the nearest degree.

Exercises

CHECK UNDERSTANDING

Use the graph at the right.

1. **Personal Finance** Nancy spends a third of her salary on rent, a fifth on utilities, a fourth on food, 5% on transportation, and she saves a sixth. Which section of the graph represents rent? Utilities? Food? Transportation? Savings?

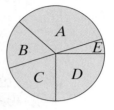

Find the circumference of each circle with the given radius or diameter.

2. radius = 3.5 cm
3. diameter = 100 in.
4. radius = $4\frac{2}{3}$ m
5. diameter = 0.1 m
6. radius = 18 in.
7. diameter = 2 mi

Find the measures of the central angles that you would draw to represent each percent in a circle graph. Round to the nearest degree.

8. 35%
9. 50%
10. 30%
11. 1%

PRACTICE AND PROBLEM SOLVING

Find the circumference of each circle with the given radius or diameter.

12. radius = 25 m
13. diameter = 46 yd
14. radius = 1,000 mi
15. diameter = 6.3 cm
16. radius = 90 ft
17. diameter = $\frac{1}{2}$ m

18. Find the measures of the central angles that you would draw to represent each percent in a circle graph.

What College Students Earn

Monthly Income from Jobs	No job	Less than $200	$200 to $399	$400 or over
Percent of Total Students	33%	14%	25%	28%

19. If the total number of college students surveyed in the table above was 10,000, how many students responded "no job"?

20. **Writing** Write a paragraph to a student who was not in class describing how to make a circle graph.

21. The data below show how a group of students travel to school each day. Draw a circle graph for the data.

How Students Travel to School

Transportation	Walk	Bicycle	Bus	Car	Other
Number of Students	55	80	110	40	15

22. A *tangent* to a circle is a line, segment, or ray in the same plane as the circle and that intersects the circle in exactly one point. A *secant* is a line, segment, or ray that intersects a circle in two points. Use the diagram to identify the following.

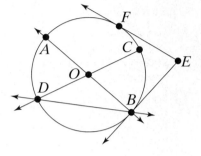

   a. one diameter   **b.** four radii   **c.** two secants

   d. three chords   **e.** two tangents

23. **TEST PREP** The radius of one circle is 7 m. A second circle has a radius twice the length of the radius of the first circle. How many times the circumference of the first circle is the circumference of the second circle?

   A. 2   **B.** 4   **C.** 7   **D.** 14

24. The data at the right represent the circumference and the diameter of four circles of different sizes.

   a. Graph the points on a coordinate plane. Use the diameter as the *x*-coordinate and the circumference as the *y*-coordinate.

   b. Connect the points with a line.

   c. Find the slope of the line.

   d. *Mathematical Reasoning* Explain the meaning of slope in this situation.

Diameter	Circumference
1 in.	3.14 in.
5 in.	15.7 in.
8 in.	25.1 in.
10 in.	31.4 in.

▶ **MIXED REVIEW**

List the congruent corresponding parts of each pair of triangles. Write a congruence statement for the triangles. *(Lesson 9-5)*

25.

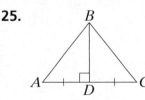

26.

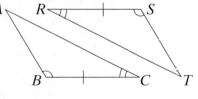

27.

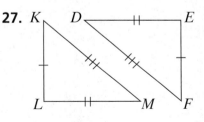

Is each relation a function? Explain. *(Lesson 8-1)*

28. $\left\{\left(4, \frac{1}{2}\right), \left(6, \frac{1}{2}\right), \left(-2, \frac{1}{2}\right)\right\}$ **29.** $\left\{(1, 0), (1, 5), \left(1, 3\frac{1}{4}\right)\right\}$ **30.** $\{(3, 7), (5, 11), (8, 17)\}$

31. While exercising, your heart beats 32 times in 15 sec. At this rate, how many times will it beat in 2 min? *(Lesson 6-2)*

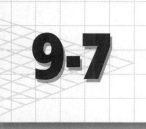

9-7

Constructions

What You'll Learn

1 To construct a segment or angle congruent to a given segment or angle

2 To construct segment bisectors and angle bisectors

. . . And Why

To construct precise drawings such as those that architects use

In constructions, you use only a *compass* and *straightedge* (an unmarked ruler) to accurately copy a segment or an angle. A compass is a tool used to draw circles or parts of circles. An *arc* is part of a circle.

■ EXAMPLE 1

Construct a segment congruent to $\overline{AB}$.

A • ———— • B

Step 1 Draw a ray with endpoint C.

C • ————————→

Step 2 Open the compass to the length of $\overline{AB}$.

Step 3 With the *same* compass setting, put the compass tip on C. Draw an arc that intersects the ray. Label the intersection D.

$$\overline{CD} \cong \overline{AB}$$

To work with a compass easily, here is one way of holding it.

■ TRY THIS

1. Draw a segment. Construct a segment twice the length of the segment you drew.

■ EXAMPLE 2

Construct an angle congruent to ∠E.

Step 1 Draw a ray with endpoint Q.

Step 2 With the compass point at E, draw an arc that intersects the sides of ∠E. Label the intersection points F and G.

Step 3 With the *same* compass setting, put the compass tip at Q. Draw an arc intersecting the ray at point P.

Step 4 Open the compass to the length of $\overline{FG}$. Using this setting, put the compass tip at P. Draw an arc to determine the point R. Draw $\overrightarrow{QR}$.

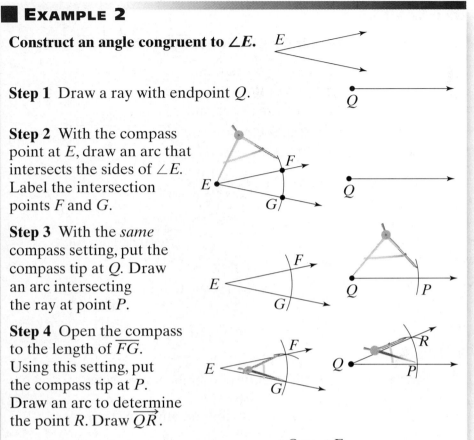

$$\angle Q \cong \angle E$$

■ TRY THIS

2. Draw an obtuse angle. Construct an angle congruent to the angle you drew.

PART 2 Constructing Bisectors

The figures below show some special relationships intersecting lines may have.

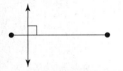

Perpendicular lines, segments, or rays intersect to form right angles.

A **segment bisector** is a line, segment, or ray that divides a segment into two congruent segments.

A **perpendicular bisector** is a line, segment, or ray that is perpendicular to the segment it bisects.

> ### Reading Math
> To *bisect* means to divide into two equal parts. Therefore a segment bisector divides a segment into two congruent parts.

P   Q

■ EXAMPLE 3

Construct the perpendicular bisector of $\overline{PQ}$ at the left.

Step 1 Open the compass to more than half of the length of $\overline{PQ}$. Put the compass tip at P. Draw an arc above and below $\overline{PQ}$. With the same compass setting, repeat from point Q.

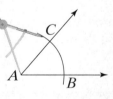

Step 2 Label the points of intersection S and T. Draw $\overleftrightarrow{ST}$. Label the intersection of $\overleftrightarrow{ST}$ and $\overline{PQ}$ point M.

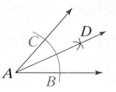

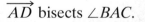

$\overleftrightarrow{ST}$ bisects $\overline{PQ}$.

■ TRY THIS

3. Draw a segment. Construct its perpendicular bisector.

An **angle bisector** is a ray that divides an angle into two congruent angles.

■ EXAMPLE 4

Construct the bisector of $\angle A$ at the left.

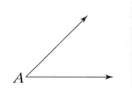

Step 1 Put the compass tip at A. Draw an arc that intersects the sides of $\angle A$. Label the points of intersection B and C.

Step 2 Put the compass tip at B. Draw an arc. With the same compass setting, repeat with the compass tip at C. Make sure the arcs intersect. Label the intersection of the arcs D. Draw $\overrightarrow{AD}$.

$\overrightarrow{AD}$ bisects $\angle BAC$.

■ TRY THIS

4. Draw an obtuse angle. Construct its angle bisector.

Exercises

CHECK UNDERSTANDING

Draw a diagram similar to the one at the right. Then construct each figure.

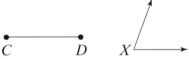

1. $\overline{EF}$ congruent to $\overline{XY}$
2. $\overline{GH}$ half the length of $\overline{XY}$
3. $\angle D$ congruent to $\angle A$
4. $\angle I$ so that $m\angle I = 2m\angle A$
5. $\triangle RST$ with two sides congruent to $\overline{XY}$ and an angle formed by the two sides congruent to $\angle A$.
6. Draw $\overline{DE}$ at least 4 in. long. Then construct its perpendicular bisector.

PRACTICE AND PROBLEM SOLVING

For Exercises 7–11, draw a figure like the ones at the right. Then construct each figure.

7. $\overline{PQ}$ congruent to $\overline{CD}$
8. $\overline{MN}$ three times the length of $\overline{CD}$
9. $\angle Y$ congruent to $\angle X$
10. $\angle T$ half the measure of $\angle X$
11. $\triangle ABF$ with two angles congruent to $\angle X$
12. Construct a 90° angle.
13. Construct a 45° angle.
14. **Writing** How are constructing a segment bisector and constructing an angle bisector alike?
15. The bisector of $\angle XYZ$ is $\overrightarrow{YN}$. If the measure of $\angle XYN$ is 55°, what is the measure of $\angle XYZ$?
16. $\overleftrightarrow{BC}$ is the perpendicular bisector of $\overline{RP}$ at point N. Name two congruent segments.
17. $\overrightarrow{DB}$ is the bisector of $\angle CDE$. Name two congruent angles.
18. **Open-ended** Use your compass to create a design. Decorate your design.

19. To construct a perpendicular line (or segment) from a point to a line, start by placing your compass tip at the point. Open your compass far enough to draw an arc that intersects the line in two points. Construct the perpendicular bisector of the segment between the two arcs.

   a. Draw a point and a line. Construct the perpendicular segment from the point to the line.

   b. An *altitude* of a triangle is a perpendicular segment from a vertex to a line containing the side opposite the vertex. Draw a large acute triangle. Construct the three altitudes of the triangle.

20. Draw $\triangle PQR$. To construct $\triangle ABC$ congruent to $\triangle PQR$, first construct $\overline{AB}$ congruent to $\overline{PQ}$. Use a compass setting the length of $\overline{PR}$. Draw an arc with the compass tip at A. Then use a compass setting the length of $\overline{QR}$. With the compass tip at B draw an arc that intersects the first arc. Label the intersection C. Draw $\overline{AC}$ and $\overline{BC}$.

▶ MIXED REVIEW

Find the measure of the central angle that would represent each percent in a circle graph. Round your answer to the nearest degree. *(Lesson 9-6)*

21. 12%   **22.** 45%   **23.** 5%   **24.** 25%

Find the simple interest. *(Lesson 7-8)*

25. $1,000 deposited at an interest rate of 2% for 3 years

26. $150 deposited at an interest rate of 4% for 6 months

27. Find two numbers with a sum of 25 and with a difference of 15. *(Lesson 8-7)*

CHAPTER
PROJECT
9 **ACTIVITY 2 CONSTRUCTING**

H ere is the second clue: *The treasure is on an island 22 miles from Everett.* Construct a figure that contains all the points 22 miles from Everett. According to the first two clues, on which islands could the treasure be buried? Explain.

Translations

PART 1 Graphing Translations

You can move pattern blocks by sliding them, flipping them, or turning them. Each of these moves is a type of transformation. A **transformation** is a change of position or size of a figure.

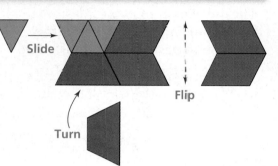

A **translation** is a transformation that moves points the same distance and in the same direction. A figure and its translated image are congruent. You can see examples of translations or slides in wallpaper, fabric, and wrapping paper.

The figure you get after a transformation is called the **image.** To name the image of a point, you use prime notation. The figure at the right shows the translation of A to its image A'.

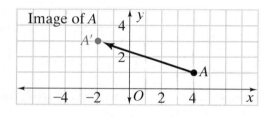

What You'll Learn

1 To graph translations

2 To describe translations

... And Why

To use translations in describing real-world situations, such as moves in a chess game

---

■ EXAMPLE 1

Graph the image of △KRT after a translation 5 units to the right and 3 units down.

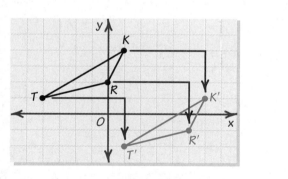

■ TRY THIS

1. On a coordinate plane, draw △KRT. Graph the image of △KRT after a translation 4 units to the left and 5 units down.

You can describe a transformation using arrow (→) notation, which describes the *mapping* of a figure onto its image.

■ EXAMPLE 2

The movement of point *P* is both horizontal and vertical. Use arrow notation to describe this translation.

The point moves from $P(-2, 2)$ to $P'(1, -1)$, so the translation is $P(-2, 2) \rightarrow P'(1, -1)$.

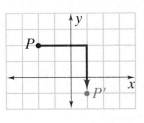

■ TRY THIS

2. Use arrow notation to describe a translation of $B(-1, 5)$ to $B'(3, 1)$.

You can also use arrow notation to write a general rule that describes a transformation. To write a rule for a translation, choose corresponding points on a figure and its image. Subtract the coordinates of the preimage from the coodinates of the image.

■ EXAMPLE 3

Write a rule to describe the translation of $\triangle PQR$ to $\triangle P'Q'R'$.

Use $P(3, 2)$ and its image $P'(-2, 5)$ to find the horizontal and vertical translations.

Horizontal translation: $-2 - 3 = -5$
Vertical translation: $\quad\ \ 5 - 2 = 3$

The rule is $(x, y) \rightarrow (x - 5, y + 3)$.

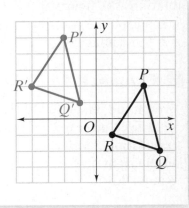

In chess, the move of a knight is a translation. The translation of piece *A* is $(x, y) \rightarrow (x + 1, y - 2)$.

■ TRY THIS

3. Write a rule to describe the translation of quadrilateral *ABCD* to quadrilateral *A'B'C'D'*.

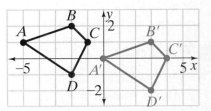

Exercises

> ### CHECK UNDERSTANDING

Complete with *horizontal* or *vertical* to make a true statement.

1. In a __?__ translation, the *y*-coordinate changes and the
   x-coordinate stays the same.

2. In a __?__ translation, the *x*-coordinate changes and the
   y-coordinate stays the same.

**The endpoints of a segment and a translation are given. Graph each
segment and its image.**

3. $A(0, 0)$, $B(0, 5)$; 2 units left   4. $C(0, 0)$, $D(0, 2)$; 2 units up   5. $E(0, 0)$, $F(2, 0)$; 4 units down

6. $G(0, 0)$, $H(-4, 0)$; 4 units up   7. $J(0, 0)$, $K(5, 5)$; 1 unit right   8. $L(-1, 3)$, $M(2, 1)$; 5 units left

Write a rule to describe each translation.

9.   10.   11.

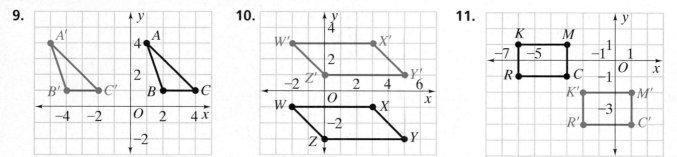

> ### PRACTICE AND PROBLEM SOLVING

**The endpoints of a segment and a translation are given. Graph each
segment and its image.**

12. $N(3, 3)$, $P(-3, 4)$; 2 units down   13. $Q(2, -1)$, $R(-2, 1)$; 2 units right

14. $S(4, 3)$, $T(1, -5)$; 4 units left   15. $U(-4, -5)$, $V(2, 1)$; 3 units right, 2 units down

16. The vertices of $\triangle HIJ$ are $H(0, 5)$, $I(-2, 4)$ and $J(-1, -3)$.
    Graph the triangle and its translation of 3 units to the right
    and 2 units down.

17. You translated a figure to the right 5 units and down 7 units.
    Complete the general rule to show how to find the image:
    $(x, y) \rightarrow (x + \blacksquare, y - \blacksquare)$.

A point and its image after a translation are given. Write a rule to describe each translation.

18. $A(7, -3), A'(-4, 1)$ **19.** $A(-7, 3), A'(4, 1)$ **20.** $A(7, 3), A'(-4, -1)$

21. $A(-7, -3), A'(-4, 1)$ **22.** $A(7, 3), A'(4, 1)$ **23.** $A(-7, -3), A'(-4, -1)$

Write a rule to describe each translation.

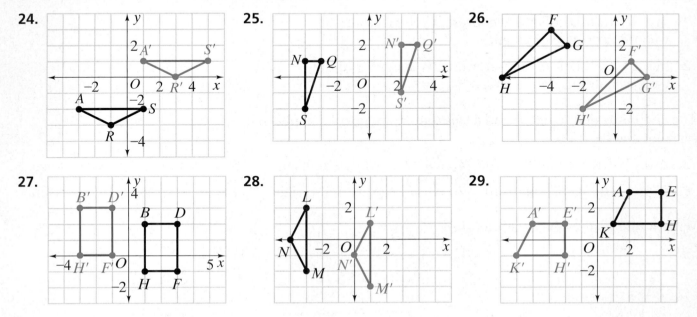

24.   **25.**   **26.**

27.   **28.**   **29.**

30. Quadrilateral $WXYZ$ has vertices $W(0, 0)$, $X(-4, 2)$, $Y(-4, 6)$, and $Z(0, 4)$. Quadrilateral $W'X'Y'Z'$ has vertices $W'(2, -3)$, $X'(-2, -1)$, $Y'(-2, 3)$, and $Z'(2, 1)$. Write a rule to describe the translation.

31. Translate point $T(2, 5)$ 2 units to the right and 6 units up. Translate its image, point T', 4 units to the left and 1 unit down. What are the coordinates of the image of point T''?

32. $\triangle CDE$ has coordinates $C(0, 2)$, $D(3, 4)$, and $E(5, 1)$. A translation maps C to $(-2, -2)$. What are the coordinates of D' and E'?

33. *Error Analysis* The image of $D(3, 4)$ is $D'(5, 4)$. A student described the translation as 2 units down. What error did the student make? What should the student have done?

34. *Writing* Explain why moving a figure a units horizontally and then $-a$ units horizontally results in the original position of the figure.

35. **TEST PREP** The graph of $y = 2x + 4$ is translated 3 units down and 4 units right. Find the slope of the graph of the image.

   A. $\frac{3}{4}$ **B.** $\frac{4}{3}$ **C.** -2 **D.** 2

36. *Art* You can use translations to draw three-dimensional figures. Design a figure on graph paper using the following steps.

SAMPLE

Step 1
Draw a figure on graph paper.

Step 2
Translate the figure.

Step 3
Connect each vertex with its image.

Step 4
Use dashes for sides that are not visible

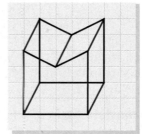
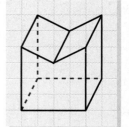

  a. Start with a rectangle. Draw a three-dimensional figure.
  b. Start with a triangle. Draw a three-dimensional figure.

▶ MIXED REVIEW

37. Draw an acute angle and construct its bisector. *(Lesson 9-7)*

Simplify each product. *(Lesson 5-4)*

38. $\frac{3}{7} \cdot \frac{7}{9}$

39. $\frac{1}{2} \cdot \frac{8}{11}$

40. $\frac{1}{2} \cdot \frac{1}{8}$

41. *Choose a Strategy* Amanda, Adam, and Antoine ate salad, chicken, or tofu for lunch. Amanda did not eat chicken or tofu. Antoine did not eat chicken. Each one had a different meal. What did each person eat?

✓ CHECKPOINT 2   Lessons 9-6 through 9-8

Use the circle graph at the right.

  1. Eighty people attended a catered meal. Twenty-eight people ordered fish, half ordered chicken, and twelve ordered the vegetarian meal. Which section represents each of the meals?

  2. Determine the measure of the central angle of each section in the circle graph.

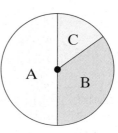

  3. *Open-ended* Draw a segment about 2 in. long. Construct an equilateral triangle with sides of this length.

  4. Graph $\overline{NR}$ with endpoints $N(2, 7)$ and $R(-4, 0)$. Then graph its image after a translation 4 units right and 3 units down.

Matrices and Translations

A matrix is a rectangular arrangement of numbers. Each number is a matrix entry. You can write the coordinates of the vertices of a figure as a matrix.

$$
\begin{array}{cccc}
 & A & B & C \\
x\text{-coordinate} & \begin{bmatrix} 0 & -1 & -4 \\ 0 & 4 & 0 \end{bmatrix} \\
y\text{-coordinate} &
\end{array}
$$

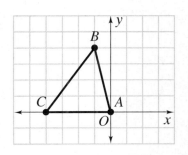

You can use matrices to translate figures.

■ EXAMPLE

Geometry Use a matrix to find the vertices of the image of quadrilateral *ABCD* using the rule $(x, y) \longrightarrow (x + 3, y - 2)$.

vertices of quadrilateral + translation matrix = vertices of image

Add 3 to each *x*-coordinate.
Add −2 to each *y*-coordinate.

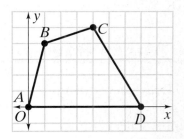

$$
\begin{array}{cccc}
A & B & C & D \\
\end{array}
\begin{bmatrix} 0 & 1 & 4 & 7 \\ 0 & 4 & 5 & 0 \end{bmatrix}
+
\begin{bmatrix} 3 & 3 & 3 & 3 \\ -2 & -2 & -2 & -2 \end{bmatrix}
=
\begin{array}{cccc} A' & B' & C' & D' \end{array}
\begin{bmatrix} 3 & 4 & 7 & 10 \\ -2 & 2 & 3 & -2 \end{bmatrix}
$$

The vertices of the image are $A'(3, -2)$, $B'(4, 2)$, $C'(7, 3)$, and $D'(10, -2)$.

Use matrix addition to find the vertices of the image of the given figure under each translation.

1. $\triangle TRI$ with vertices
   $T(-5, -5)$, $R(-3, -1)$, and $I(-1, -3)$
   translation: $(x, y) \longrightarrow (x + 6, y + 6)$

2. square *SQRE* with vertices
   $S(1, 2)$, $Q(4, 2)$, $R(4, 5)$, and $E(1, 5)$
   translation: $(x, y) \longrightarrow (x + 1, y - 3)$

3. $\triangle NGL$ with vertices
   $N(4, 4)$, $G(7, 4)$, and $L(5, 0)$

   translation matrix $\begin{bmatrix} -9 & -9 & -9 \\ -4 & -4 & -4 \end{bmatrix}$

4. square *RECT* with vertices
   $R(0, 0)$, $E(0, -4)$, $C(-4, -4)$, and $T(-4, 0)$

   translation matrix $\begin{bmatrix} -1 & -1 & -1 & -1 \\ 2 & 2 & 2 & 2 \end{bmatrix}$

5. **a.** What matrix would you use to translate a triangle 1 unit to the left and 4 units down?
   b. Use your answer from part (a) to translate $\triangle ABC$ with vertices $A(2, 2)$, $B(3, 5)$, and $C(3, 0)$.

Symmetry and Reflections

A figure has **reflectional symmetry** when one half is a mirror image of the other half. A **line of symmetry** divides a figure with reflectional symmetry into two congruent halves.

A pattern for the back of a shirt is shown below. To make a shirt, you place the pattern on a folded piece of material, with the dashed lines of the pattern on the fold. After cutting the material, the back of the shirt will look like this.

What You'll Learn

1 To identify a line of symmetry

2 To graph a reflection of a geometric figure

. . . And Why

To use symmetry and reflections in real-world situations, such as sewing

The fold is the line of symmetry.

The shirt has one line of symmetry.

It is possible for a figure to have more than one line of symmetry.

■ EXAMPLE 1

Identify the lines of symmetry.

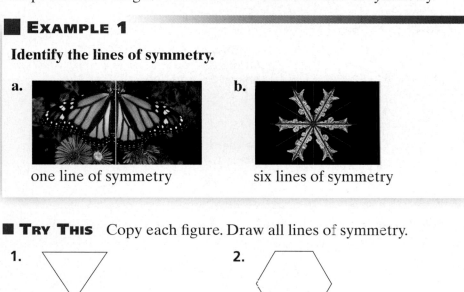

a.

one line of symmetry

b.

six lines of symmetry

■ **TRY THIS** Copy each figure. Draw all lines of symmetry.

1.

2.

A **reflection** flips a figure over a **line of reflection.** The reflected figure, or image, is congruent to the original figure. Together, an image and its reflection have line symmetry, the line of reflection being the line of symmetry.

■ **EXAMPLE 2**

Graph the image of △ABC after a reflection over the y-axis.

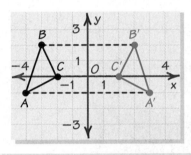

Since *A* is 4 units to the left of the *y*-axis, *A'* is 4 units to the right of the *y*-axis. Reflect the other vertices. Draw △*A'B'C'*.

■ **TRY THIS**

3. Graph the image of △*ABC* after a reflection over the *x*-axis.

You can reflect images over lines other than the axes.

■ **EXAMPLE 3**

Graph the image of △PQR after a reflection over y = 2.

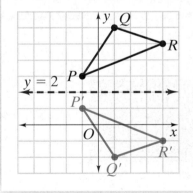

Graph *y* = 2. Since *P* is 1 unit above the red line, *P'* is 1 unit below the red line.

Reflect the other vertices. Draw △*P'Q'R'*.

■ **TRY THIS** Graph the image of △*ABC* with vertices $A(3, 0)$, $B(2, 3)$, and $C(5, -1)$ over each line.

4. $x = 2$ **5.** $y = -1$

Exercises

CHECK UNDERSTANDING

Draw each figure. Draw all the lines of symmetry.

1. rhombus   **2.** square   **3.** isosceles triangle

Graph each point and its image after a reflection over the given line.

4. $R(7, 1)$; x-axis   **5.** $S(5, -1)$; y-axis   **6.** $F(-2, 9)$; $y = 1$ **7.** $N(-4, -6)$; $x = 4$

The vertices of a triangle are listed. Reflect each triangle over the given line.

8. $A(0, 0)$, $B(6, 0)$, $C(0, -6)$; $y = 1$ **9.** $K(-1, 4)$, $L(3, 3)$, $M(0, 2)$; $y = 0$

PRACTICE AND PROBLEM SOLVING

Copy each figure. Draw all the lines of symmetry. If a figure has no line of symmetry, explain why.

10.   **11.**   **12.**   **13.**

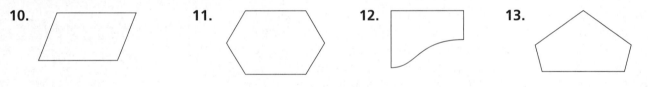

Graph each point and its image after a reflection over the given line. Name the coordinates of the image.

14. $H(-8, 3)$; $y = 4$ **15.** $J(-8, 3)$; $y = 2$ **16.** $V(5, 0)$; $x = -2$ **17.** $A(2, 5)$; $y = x$

The vertices of a polygon are listed. Graph each polygon and its image after a reflection over the given line. Name the coordinates of the image.

18. $F(0, 0)$, $G(6, 0)$, $H(8, 6)$, $I(2, 6)$; $x = 0$ **19.** $W(-1, -1)$, $X(0, 0)$, $Y(-5, 0)$; $y = 2$

20. **TEST PREP** Which figure always has exactly two lines of symmetry?
 A. parallelogram   B. trapezoid
 C. isosceles triangle   D. rhombus

21. *Writing* Will a reflection of an angle have a different measure than the original angle? Explain why or why not.

The given point is reflected over line 1. Then the image is reflected over line 2. Name the coordinates of the second image.

22. $A(3, -2)$
line 1: y-axis
line 2: x-axis

23. $B(-1, 5)$
line 1: x-axis
line 2: $y = 3$

24. $C(-5, -1)$
line 1: $x = 2$
line 2: y-axis

Critical Thinking **Decide whether each statement is *always* true, *sometimes* true, or *never* true.**

25. When a point is reflected over a horizontal line, the x–coordinate stays the same.

26. When a point is reflected over a vertical line, the y–coordinate stays the same.

27. The image of a polygon reflected over a line is congruent to the original polygon.

28. When corresponding points of an original figure and its reflection are connected, the resulting segments are all perpendicular to the line of reflection.

29. a. On a coordinate plane, graph the line $y = x$ and $\triangle ABC$ with vertices $A(5, 3)$, $B(6, -1)$, and $C(2, -1)$.
b. To graph the image of $\triangle ABC$ over the line $y = x$, trace the axes and $\triangle ABC$ on tracing paper. Fold the paper along $y = x$. Trace over the triangle so that it makes an impression on your original graph. Label $A'B'C'$ appropriately.
c. Connect A to A', B to B', and C to C'. What do you notice about these segments and the line $y = x$?
d. Complete the statement: The segment that connects a point to its image is __?__ to the line of reflection and forms a __?__ angle at the intersection.
e. Reflect $\triangle ABC$ over $y = x + 3$.

Journal

How many lines of symmetry does a circle have? Explain.

▶ **MIXED REVIEW**

The endpoints of a segment and a translation are given. Graph the segment and its image. Name the endpoints of the image. (*Lesson 9-8*)

30. $A(4, 3)$, $B(5, 7)$; 3 units left, 2 units down

31. $X(0, -1)$, $Y(2, 7)$; 2 units right, 3 units up

Graph each equation. (*Lesson 8-2*)

32. $x + 3 = y$

33. $y - 8 = x$

34. $2y = x + 10$

35. *Choose a Strategy* If six people meet, and each person shakes every other person's hand, how many handshakes are there in all?

See also Extra Practice section.

Standardized Test Prep

Multiple Choice

Choose the best answer.

1. Find the measure of the central angle that represents 46% in a circle graph. Round to the nearest degree.
   A. 46°   B. 83°
   C. 54°   D. 166°

2. Identify the rule that describes the translation of $B(3, 5)$ to $B'(1, 1)$.
   F. $(x + 2, y + 4)$ G. $(x - 2, y - 4)$
   H. $(x + 2, y - 4)$ J. $(x - 4, y - 2)$

3. Quadrilateral $JKLM \cong$ quadrilateral $PQRS$. Choose the correct congruence statement.
   A. $\overline{JK} \cong \overline{RS}$ B. $\overline{LM} \cong \overline{QR}$
   C. $\angle K \cong \angle Q$ D. $\angle M \cong \angle P$

4. Choose the correct congruence statement.

   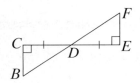

   F. $\triangle BCD \cong \triangle FED$ by **ASA**
   G. $\triangle BCD \cong \triangle FED$ by **SSS**
   H. $\triangle CDB \cong \triangle DEF$ by **ASA**
   J. $\triangle BDC \cong \triangle FED$ by **SAS**

5. A store receives a shipment of shirts. Each shirt costs the store $18.00. The store sells each shirt for $24.95. What is the percent of markup, to the nearest percent?
   A. 139%   B. 72%   C. 39%   D. 28%

6. Some taxicabs begin each trip by setting the meter to $1.50. The meter then adds $.40 for each $\frac{1}{4}$ mi traveled. If a trip costs $7.90, how far did the cab travel?
   F. 160 mi   G. 16 mi
   H. 8 mi   J. 4 mi

Use the figure below for Exercises 7–9.

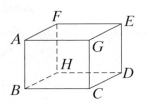

7. Name a segment skew to $\overline{AB}$.
   A. $\overline{BC}$ B. $\overline{CD}$
   C. $\overline{DE}$ D. $\overline{GC}$

8. Name a segment parallel to $\overline{ED}$.
   F. $\overline{BH}$ G. $\overline{AF}$
   H. $\overline{AB}$ J. $\overleftrightarrow{GE}$

9. Name a segment that does *not* intersect $\overline{AG}$.
   A. $\overline{AB}$ B. $\overline{GC}$
   C. $\overline{AF}$ D. $\overline{BC}$

Free Response

For each exercise, show your work.

10. Copy the segment below. Construct its perpendicular bisector.

11. Graph $\triangle XYZ$ with vertices $X(-2, 4)$, $Y(-3, 1)$ and $Z(-1, 5)$. Translate it 5 units to the right and 3 units down. Write the coordinates of the vertices of the translated image.

12. **Open-ended** Draw a net for a cylinder.

13. Company A charges $29 per day to rent a car. For the same car, Company B charges $19 per day and $.15 per mile driven. Under what circumstances would you pay less at Company A? Explain your reasoning.

14. How many diagonals does a hexagon have?

9-10

Rotations

What You'll Learn

1 To graph rotations

2 To identify rotational symmetry

. . . And Why

To use rotations in describing real objects

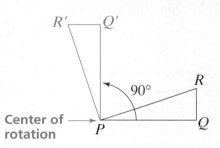

PART 1 Graphing Rotations

A **rotation** is a transformation that turns a figure about a fixed point called the **center of rotation.** The angle measure of the rotation is the **angle of rotation.**

In the figure, $\triangle QPR$ is rotated 90° about the center of rotation, point P. Notice that $m\angle QPQ' = 90°$ and $m\angle RPR' = 90°$. A figure and its rotation image are congruent.

In the diagram, the direction of the rotation is *counterclockwise.* All rotations in this book will be counterclockwise.

You can graph rotations on a coordinate plane.

■ EXAMPLE 1

Find the vertices of the image of $\triangle ABC$ after a rotation of 180° about the origin.

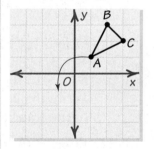 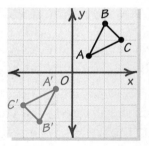

Step 1 Draw $\triangle ABC$. Place a piece of tracing paper over the graph. Trace the vertices of the triangle, the x-axis, and the y-axis. Then place your pencil at the origin to rotate the paper.

Step 2 Rotate the paper 180°. Make sure the axes line up. Mark the position of each vertex by pressing through the paper. Connect the vertices of the rotated triangle.

The vertices of the image are $A'(-1, -1)$, $B'(-2, -3)$, and $C'(-3, -2)$.

■ **TRY THIS**

1. Copy the graph of △*ABC*. Draw its image after a rotation of 90° about the origin. Name the coordinates of the vertices of the image.

PART 2 **Identifying Rotational Symmetry**

A figure has **rotational symmetry** if you can rotate it 180° or less so that its image matches the original figure. The angle that a figure rotates so that the image matches the original figure is the angle of rotation. When point *A* moves to point *A'* the wheel will look the same as it does now.

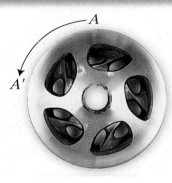

Since point *A* can move to five different positions in which the wheel matches the original figure, the angle of rotation is 360° ÷ 5, or 72°. The figure has rotational symmetry.

REAL-WORLD CONNECTION

■ **EXAMPLE 2**

Botany **Judging from appearance, tell whether the flower has rotational symmetry. If so, what is the angle of rotation?**

The flower can match itself in 3 positions.

The pattern repeats in 3 even intervals.
360° ÷ 3 = 120°

The figure has rotational symmetry. The angle of rotation is 120°.

■ **TRY THIS** Judging from appearance, tell whether each figure has rotational symmetry. If so, what is the angle of rotation?

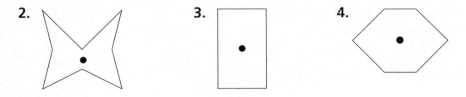

2.   3.   4.

Exercises

► CHECK UNDERSTANDING

Each figure below is an image formed by rotating the figure at the right. What is each angle of rotation?

1. 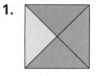 **2.** 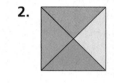 **3.**

Graph each point. Then rotate it the given number of degrees about the origin. What are the coordinates of the image?

4. $A(5, 5)$; $90°$ **5.** $B(0, -2)$; $180°$ **6.** $C(2, 4)$; $180°$ **7.** $D(-1, -3)$; $90°$

Judging from appearance, tell whether each figure has rotational symmetry. If so, what is the angle of rotation?

8.   **9.**   **10.**   **11.**

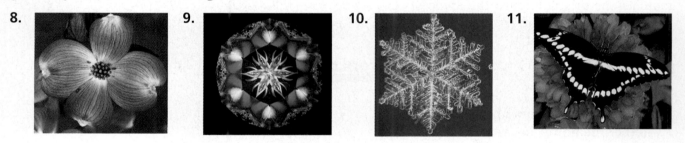

► PRACTICE AND PROBLEM SOLVING

The vertices of a triangle are given. On separate coordinate planes, graph each triangle and its image after a rotation of **(a) 90°** and **(b) 180°** about the origin.

12. $V(0, 0)$ **13.** $K(3, 0)$ **14.** $S(0, -4)$ **15.** $C(-2, 0)$ **16.** $G(-4, -1)$
    $W(2, 5)$ $L(2, 2)$ $T(-4, -4)$ $D(-3, 5)$ $H(-2, -5)$
    $X(1, -5)$ $M(2, 4)$ $U(-4, -3)$ $E(-1, 2)$ $I(-2, -1)$

17. $\triangle JKL$ has vertices $J(4, 4)$, $K(3, 2)$ and $L(5, 1)$.
   a. Graph its image after a rotation of $90°$ about the origin. Name the coordinates of the vertices of the image.
   b. Graph the image of $\triangle J'K'L'$ after a reflection over the y-axis.

18. Explain how translations, reflections, and rotations affect the positions of figures.

Judging from appearance, tell whether each figure has rotational symmetry. If so, what is the angle of rotation?

19. 20. 21. 22.

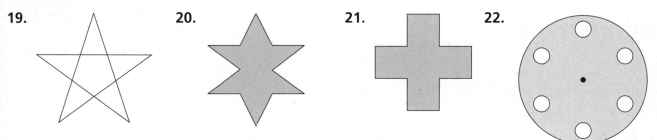

Does each figure have rotational symmetry? If so, what is the angle of rotation?

23. equilateral triangle   24. rectangle   25. regular pentagon   26. trapezoid

27. For Exercises 23–26, tell whether each figure has line symmetry.

28. *Writing* Describe something in your classroom that has rotational symmetry. What is the angle of rotation?

29. *Mathematical Reasoning* Is a rotation of 180° the same as a reflection across the *y*-axis? Justify your answer.

▶ **MIXED REVIEW**

The vertices of △ABC are A(5, 6), B(0, 3), and C(3, 2). Reflect △ABC over the following lines. *(Lesson 9-9)*

30. $x = -2$ 31. $y = -2$ 32. *x*-axis

Find the slope of the line through each pair of points. *(Lesson 8-3)*

33. $A(5, 9), B(5, 14)$ 34. $C(-2, 4), D(-7, 14)$ 35. $E(2, 1), F(8, 4)$

36. *Choose a Strategy* How many three-digit numbers greater than 500 can you form using the digits 2, 6, and 8 exactly once each?

CHAPTER PROJECT 9   ACTIVITY 3 CLASSIFYING

Here is the third clue: *An obtuse triangle connects Savannah, Everett, and the treasure island. The treasure is buried by the lighthouse on the island.* On which island is the treasure buried? Explain.

Tessellations

A *tessellation* is a repeating pattern of figures that completely covers a plane without gaps or overlaps. You can see tessellations in art, architecture, and nature.

You can use translations, rotations, and reflections to create a tessellation.

■ EXAMPLE

Show how the figure at the right forms a tessellation.

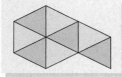

Rotate and translate the figure to cover the plane.

Make multiple copies of each figure on graph paper. Determine whether each figure can form a tessellation. If it does, show the tessellation.

1.
2.
3.
4.

5. ***Open-ended*** The diagram below shows how to create a shape to use as a repeating figure for a tessellation. Following the instructions shown, create your own tessellation.

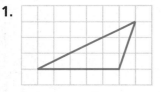

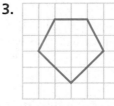

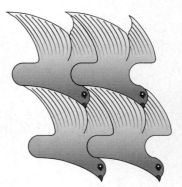

Cut
Slide
Cut
Slide
Slide
Cut

6. ***Critical Thinking*** Draw regular polygons with 3, 4, 5, 6, 7, and 8 sides. Which ones can you use to create a tessellation?

Draw a Treasure Map The Project Activities on pages 458, 478, and 493 will help you complete your project. Here is a checklist to help you gather the different parts.

✔ your drawing of the map, including the lines and figures defined in the activities

✔ your answers to the questions

✔ your explanations of your reasoning

Make a poster to display your map. Mark the location of the treasure. On the poster, include the clues you followed and an explanation of how your map relates to the clues.

Reflect and Revise

Ask a friend or someone at home to review your poster. Are your drawings neat and accurate? Are your explanations complete and clear? If necessary, make changes to improve your poster.

Web Extension

Visit Prentice Hall's Web site. You'll find some interesting links and ideas related to maps. You'll also be able to share information about your project.

www.phschool.com

9 Wrap Up

■ Key Terms

adjacent angles (p. 449)

alternate interior angles (p. 450)

angle bisector (p. 476)

angle of rotation (p. 490)

center of rotation (p. 490)

central angle (p. 470)

complementary angles (p. 449)

congruent angles (p. 449)

corresponding angles (p. 450)

image (p. 479)

line (p. 442)

line of reflection (p. 486)

line of symmetry (p. 485)

parallel (p. 443)

perpendicular bisector (p. 475)

perpendicular lines (p. 475)

plane (p. 442)

point (p. 442)

polygon (p. 454)

ray (p. 442)

reflection (p. 486)

reflectional symmetry (p. 485)

regular polygon (p. 456)

rotation (p. 490)

rotational symmetry (p. 491)

segment (p. 442)

segment bisector (p. 475)

skew (p. 443)

supplementary angles (p. 449)

transformation (p. 479)

translation (p. 479)

transversal (p. 450)

vertical angles (p. 449)

■ Graphic Organizer

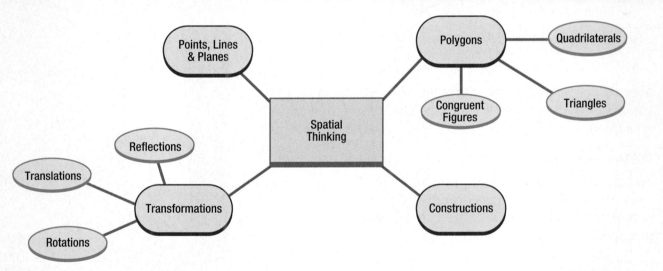

■ Points, Lines, and Planes

9-1

Summary A **point** is a position in space. All geometric figures are made up of points. A **line** is a series of points that extends in two directions without end. A **segment** is a part of a line and has two endpoints. A **ray** is a part of a line with exactly one endpoint. An angle is two rays that intersect at their endpoints.

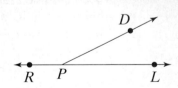

Name the following in the figure above.

1. three angles   **2.** three rays   **3.** four segments   **4.** four points   **5.** a line

■ Angle Relationships and Parallel Lines

Summary **Adjacent angles** share a vertex and a side but no points in their interiors. **Vertical angles** are formed by intersecting lines and are **congruent**. If parallel lines are crossed by a **transversal** their **corresponding angles** are congruent. **Alternate interior angles** of parallel lines are also congruent.

Use the diagram at the right. $m \parallel n$

6. Name all angles congruent to $\angle 1$.

7. Name two pairs of supplementary angles.

8. Name all pairs of corresponding angles.

9. Name all pairs of alternate interior angles.

10. If $m\angle 2 = 75°$, find the measures of all the other angles.

■ Classifying Polygons and Congruent Polygons

Summary A **polygon** is a closed figure with at least three sides. Polygons with the same size and shape are congruent. A triangle can be classified by its angles and its sides. You can show two triangles are congruent using **Side–Side–Side**, **Side–Angle–Side**, and **Angle–Side–Angle**. You can classify some quadrilaterals as parallelograms, rectangles, squares, rhombuses, or trapezoids.

Use the most precise name for each figure described.

11. a triangle with all sides congruent

12. a parallelogram with all sides congruent and four 90° angles

13. a triangle with all acute angles and exactly two congruent sides

14. a quadrilateral with exactly one pair of parallel sides

List the congruent corresponding parts of each of the triangles below.
Write a congruence statement for the triangles.

15.

16.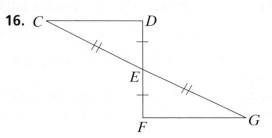

■ Draw a Diagram 9-4

Summary Drawing a diagram helps you visualize a problem.

17. A house is to be built on a lot 70 ft wide by 100 ft deep. The shorter side of the lot faces the street. The house must be set back from the street at least 25 ft. It must be 20 ft from the back lot line and 10 ft from each side lot line. What are the maximum length and width of the house?

■ Circles 9-6

Summary You can use these formulas to find the circumference of a circle:
$C = \pi \cdot d$ and $C = 2\pi r$.
There are 360° in a circle. An angle whose vertex is the center of a circle is a **central angle.**

18. Find the circumference of a circle with a diameter of 14 cm.

19. **Television Programming** Suppose a survey indicates that at 8 P.M. 40% of viewers watched channel X, 25% watched channel Y, and 35% watched channel Z. Make a circle graph of the data.

■ Constructions 9-7

Summary You can use a compass and straightedge to construct congruent segments, congruent angles, **segment bisectors,** and **angle bisectors**.

Draw $\triangle CDE$ with an obtuse $\angle D$.

20. Construct the bisector of $\angle D$.   21. Construct the perpendicular bisector of $\overline{DE}$.

■ Translations, Reflections, and Rotations 9-8, 9-9 and 9-10

Summary A **transformation** is a change of position or size of a figure. The figure after the transformation is called the **image**. You can transform figures in a plane by a **translation**, a **reflection**, or a **rotation**.

What is the image of point $A(7, -2)$ after each transformation?

22. 4 units right, 3 units up   23. reflection over the y-axis

24. rotation of 90° about the origin   25. reflection over the line $y = -1$

26. **Writing** How do translations, reflections, and rotations affect the size and shape of an image? Explain.

Use the diagram to name the following.

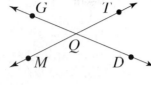

1. all segments containing point G

2. all vertical angles

3. all rays containing point M

4. a line containing point T

Use the diagram to name the following.

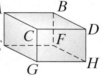

5. four segments that intersect $\overline{AB}$

6. three segments parallel to $\overline{AB}$

For Exercises 7 and 8, name all possible polygons for each description.

7. quadrilateral with at least one pair of parallel sides and at least two right angles

8. quadrilateral with one diagonal that divides it into two congruent equilateral triangles

9. Find the perimeter of an equilateral triangle that has a side measure of 60 cm.

10. Find the perimeter of a square that has a side measure of 60 cm.

11. The perimeter of a rectangle is 58 cm. One side is 18 cm. Find the lengths of the other three sides.

A segment has endpoints $A(-3, -6)$ and $M(-3, -4)$. Find the coordinates of the endpoints after each transformation.

12. a translation of 4 units right and 3 units up

13. a reflection over the y-axis

14. a rotation of 90° about the origin

15. Draw a segment. Construct its perpendicular bisector.

16. **Open-ended** Draw an obtuse angle. Construct its angle bisector.

Use the diagram for Exercises 17 and 18.

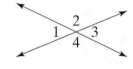

17. If $m\angle 2 = 130°$, find $m\angle 4$.

18. **Writing** Describe how you can find $m\angle 1$ if you know $m\angle 2$.

19. **Statistics** Forty two-year-old children were asked their favorite color. Five chose yellow, seven chose blue, and fourteen chose red. The rest chose other colors.
    a. To make a circle graph, what should be the measure of the central angle representing blue, red, and yellow? Round to the nearest degree.
    b. Create a circle graph for the information.

20. If $\overline{AB} \cong \overline{CD}$, $\angle A \cong \angle D$, and $\angle B \cong \angle C$, what method can you use to show that $\triangle ABE \cong \triangle DCF$?

21. **Open-ended** Draw and describe a figure that has rotational symmetry.

22. a. The measures of two angles of a triangle are 50° and 35°. What is the measure of the third angle?
    b. Classify the triangle by its angles.

23. $\triangle CAB \cong \triangle DEB$. Find as many angle measures and side lengths as you can.

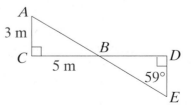

Cumulative Review

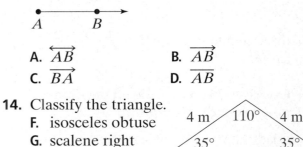

Preparing for Algebra

Choose the best answer.

1. Simplify $\frac{10 - 5(5 \cdot 2)}{10}$.

   A. 5   **B.** 4   **C.** −4   **D.** −1.5

2. Which expression simplifies to $x + 2$?

   F. $\frac{1}{2}(2x + 4)$ **G.** $10 - x - 8$

   H. $\frac{1}{2}(x + 10) - 3$ **J.** $12x - 10x + 2$

3. Find the mean of the following prices:
   $1.18, $1.17, $1.23, $1.22, $1.23, $1.23.

   A. $1.20   **B.** $1.21
   C. $1.22   **D.** $1.23

4. Which expression is equivalent
   to $-x \cdot x \cdot y \cdot y \cdot (-y) \cdot 2 \cdot 3$?

   F. $-6x^2y^3$ **G.** $(6)(-x^2)(-y^2)$
   H. $-6x^3y^2$ **J.** $6x^2y^3$

5. Simplify $3\frac{1}{2} - 1\frac{5}{8}$.

   A. $2\frac{2}{3}$ **B.** $2\frac{1}{8}$

   C. $1\frac{7}{8}$ **D.** $1\frac{2}{3}$

6. Which measure is equivalent to $\frac{1}{2}$ gal?

   F. 4 qt   **G.** 8 qt
   H. 8 pt   **J.** 4 pt

7. 200 is 40% of what number?

   A. 500   **B.** 80
   C. 5   **D.** 4,000

8. Solve $3(2x + 8) - 2x = 20$.

   F. 3   **G.** 7

   H. −1   **J.** $-\frac{2}{3}$

9. Find the slope of the line through
   $A(1, -4)$ and $B(3, 2)$.

   A. −3   **B.** $-\frac{1}{2}$

   C. 3   **D.** $\frac{1}{2}$

10. Two angles of a triangle have measures of
    159° and 5°. What is the measure of the
    third angle?

    F. 14°   **G.** 16°
    H. 159°   **J.** 164°

11. Angles 1 and 2 are supplementary.
    If $m\angle 1 = 40°$, what is $m\angle 2$?
    A. 180°   **B.** 140°
    C. 50°   **D.** 40°

12. Which statement may be *false* if
    $\triangle ABC \cong \triangle DEF$?

    F. $\angle A \cong \angle D$
    G. $\overline{BC} \cong \overline{EF}$
    H. $\overline{CA} \cong \overline{FD}$
    J. $\angle C \cong \angle E$

13. Name the figure.

    A. $\overleftrightarrow{AB}$ **B.** $\overrightarrow{AB}$
    C. $\overrightarrow{BA}$ **D.** $\overline{AB}$

14. Classify the triangle.
    F. isosceles obtuse
    G. scalene right
    H. isosceles acute
    J. equilateral right

For Exercises 15–17, use $\triangle STU$ with vertices $S(0, 0)$, $T(3, 4)$, and $U(3, -4)$.

15. Graph $\triangle STU$ and then graph the image of
    its translation 2 units left and 3 units up.

16. Graph the image of the reflection of
    $\triangle STU$ over the y-axis. List the vertices
    of the image.

17. Graph $\triangle STU$ and an image of $\triangle STU$
    rotated 90° about the origin.

For Exercises 18–20, show your work.

18. Write two fractions that are equivalent
    to $\frac{5x}{z}$.

19. The GCF of 18 and y is 1. Give two
    possible values of y.

20. Draw an acute angle. Construct its bisector.

Skills You Need for Chapter 10

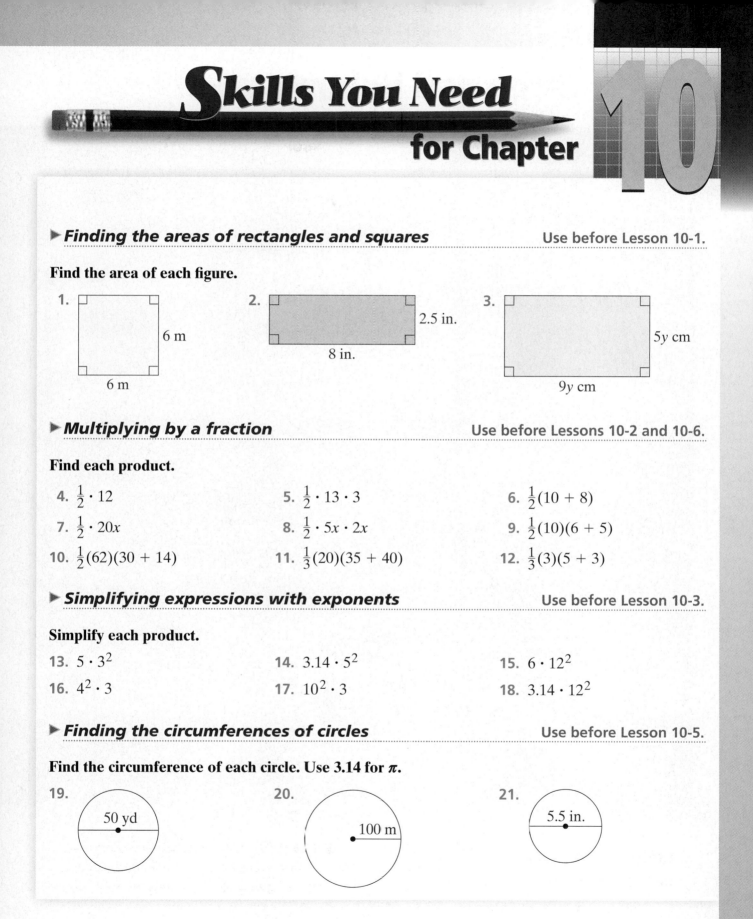

▶ **Finding the areas of rectangles and squares**　　　　Use before Lesson 10-1.

Find the area of each figure.

1.
6 m
6 m

2.
2.5 in.
8 in.

3.
5*y* cm
9*y* cm

▶ **Multiplying by a fraction**　　　　Use before Lessons 10-2 and 10-6.

Find each product.

4. $\frac{1}{2} \cdot 12$

5. $\frac{1}{2} \cdot 13 \cdot 3$

6. $\frac{1}{2}(10 + 8)$

7. $\frac{1}{2} \cdot 20x$

8. $\frac{1}{2} \cdot 5x \cdot 2x$

9. $\frac{1}{2}(10)(6 + 5)$

10. $\frac{1}{2}(62)(30 + 14)$

11. $\frac{1}{3}(20)(35 + 40)$

12. $\frac{1}{3}(3)(5 + 3)$

▶ **Simplifying expressions with exponents**　　　　Use before Lesson 10-3.

Simplify each product.

13. $5 \cdot 3^2$

14. $3.14 \cdot 5^2$

15. $6 \cdot 12^2$

16. $4^2 \cdot 3$

17. $10^2 \cdot 3$

18. $3.14 \cdot 12^2$

▶ **Finding the circumferences of circles**　　　　Use before Lesson 10-5.

Find the circumference of each circle. Use 3.14 for π.

19.
50 yd

20.
100 m

21.
5.5 in.

Area and Volume

What you'll learn in this chapter:

- How to find the areas of figures

- How to find the surface areas of space figures

- How to find the volumes of space figures

MAKING A
SPLASH

W hen you jump into a pool, or step into a bathtub, you cause the water level to rise. That's an example of water displacement. The volume of water displaced is equal to the volume of the object submerged—you.

Use Water Displacement to Find Volume For your chapter project you will build a prism and a cylinder. You will calculate their volumes by using formulas. Then you will find their volumes by using water displacement.

Steps to help you complete the project

Web Extension
www.phschool.com

How to solve a problem by making a model

10-1

Area: Parallelograms

What You'll Learn

▼**1** To find areas of rectangles

▼**2** To find areas of parallelograms

...And Why

To use formulas in finding areas of objects, such as the area of a banner

Investigate

......................**DISCOVERING AN AREA FORMULA**......................

1. Use a 3-in. by 5-in. index card. Find the area of the card.

2. Draw a line from one vertex to a point on another side to create a triangle. Cut along that line.

3. Use the pieces to form a parallelogram that is not a rectangle.

4. What is the area of your parallelogram? Explain.

PART 1 Finding Areas of Rectangles

The **area** of a figure is the number of square units it encloses. The rectangle outlined in red encloses 8 square units, each with area 1 cm² (1 square centimeter). So, the area of the rectangle is 8 cm².

You can use the formula $A = bh$ to find the area of a rectangle, where b is the length of one side and h is the length of the other. For the rectangle above, $A = 2 \cdot 4 = 8$. So, the area is 8 cm².

Before you find the area of a figure, make sure the dimensions are in the same unit.

REAL-WORLD  CONNECTION

■ EXAMPLE 1

Find the area of the rectangular banner at the left.

Step 1 Change the units so that they are the same.

$1 \text{ yd} = 3 \text{ ft}$ Change 1 yard to feet.

Step 2 Find the area.

$A = bh$ Use the formula for area of a rectangle.

$= (3)(7)$ Replace b and h with the dimensions 3 and 7.

$= 21$ Simplify.

The area of the banner is 21 ft².

■ **TRY THIS** Find the area of each rectangle.

5.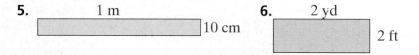

1 m

10 cm

6.

2 yd

2 ft

PART
2 **Finding Areas of Parallelograms**

A rectangle is a special kind of parallelogram. The formula for the area of a parallelogram follows from the formula for the area of a rectangle. The height *h* of a parallelogram is the length of the *altitude*. The **altitude** is a line segment drawn from the side opposite the base and perpendicular to the base *b* of the figure.

Area of a Parallelogram

The area of a parallelogram is the product of any base length *b* and the corresponding height *h*.

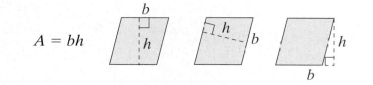

$A = bh$

■ **EXAMPLE 2**

Find the area of each parallelogram.

a.

9 cm

10 cm

$A = bh$ area formula
$= (9)(10)$ Substitute.
$= 90$ Simplify.
The area is 90 cm^2.

b.

8 in.

3.5 in.

$A = bh$
$= (3.5)(8)$
$= 28$
The area is 28 in.^{2}.

■ **TRY THIS** Find the area of each parallelogram.

7.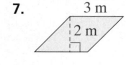

3 m

2 m

8.

8 in.

3 in.

10-1 Area: Parallelograms   **505**

Exercises

Find the area of each parallelogram.

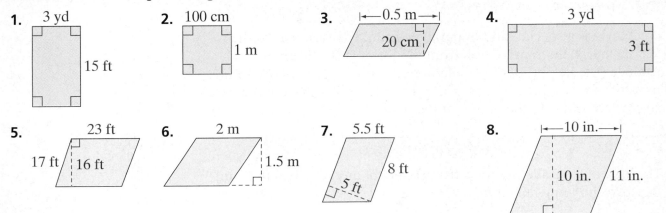

1. 3 yd, 15 ft

2. 100 cm, 1 m

3. 0.5 m, 20 cm

4. 3 yd, 3 ft

5. 23 ft, 17 ft, 16 ft

6. 2 m, 1.5 m

7. 5.5 ft, 8 ft, 5 ft

8. 10 in., 10 in., 11 in.

9. Find the area of a parallelogram with base length 3 m and height 50 cm.

Find the area of each parallelogram.

10. 4 ft, 1 yd

11. $3\frac{1}{2}$ yd, 4 yd

12. 10,560 ft, 2 mi

13. 5 m, 200 cm

14. 3 ft, 72 in.

15. 2 in., 4.5 in., 4 in.

16. 22 in., 30 in., 77 in.

17. 7 cm, 20 mm

Coordinate Geometry **The vertices of a parallelogram are given. Draw each parallelogram. Find its area.**

18. $A(0, 0)$ $B(3, 0), C(4, 3), D(1, 3)$

19. $W(-2, 0), X(-3, 3), Y(2, 0), Z(1, 3)$

---

506 Chapter 10 Area and Volume

Find the area of each shaded region. Assume that all angles that appear to be right angles are right angles.

20.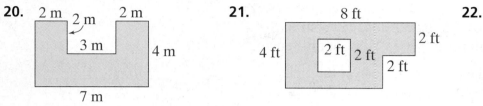

21.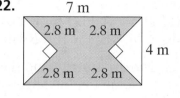

22.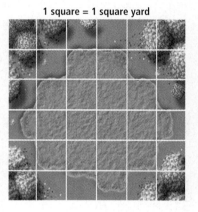

23. *Estimation* Estimate the area of the small pond at the right. Each square represents 1 yd^2.

1 square = 1 square yard

24. a. *Mathematical Reasoning* The bases of two parallelograms are the same length. The height of the first parallelogram is half the height of the second. What is the ratio of the area of the first parallelogram to the area of the second? Justify your answer.

b. Suppose both the height and the length of the base of a parallelogram are twice those of another parallelogram. What is the ratio of the area of the smaller parallelogram to the larger parallelogram? Justify your answer.

25. **TEST PREP** Square $ABCD$ has perimeter x units. What is its area in terms of x?

A. $\frac{x^2}{16}$ square units   **B.** $4x^2$ square units   **C.** $\frac{x^2}{4}$ square units   **D.** $\frac{x}{16}$ square units

Math in the Media Use the article below for exercises 26 and 27.

Sign Regulations Set for Political Campaign

The City Council issued the following regulations for political signs in the upcoming election:
1. Only one sign may be posted on a single lot of land.

2. Sign areas may not exceed 32 ft^2.
3. Signs cannot be more than 6 ft in height.
4. All signs must be removed no later than 7 days after the election.

26. You wish to display a sign that is 6 ft high. What is the greatest width it can have?

27. Draw rectangles to represent three different political signs that use the maximum possible area. Label the dimensions.

28. *Writing* At the right are two parallelograms with the same perimeter. Are the areas the same? Explain.

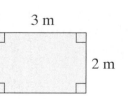

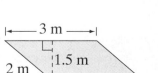

29. **Open-ended** You want to make a 400-ft² vegetable garden. You plan to build a fence to keep the rabbits out. To spend the least amount of money, you want to use as little fencing as possible.
   a. Draw and list three possible dimensions for your garden.
   b. Which of the three will need the least amount of fencing?

30. a. **Landscaping** Find the area of the yard at the right. Assume that all angles that appear to be right angles are right angles.
   b. How many square yards of sod would you need to cover the yard?
   c. One bag of fertilizer covers approximately 2,000 ft². How many bags should you buy to cover the yard? **3**

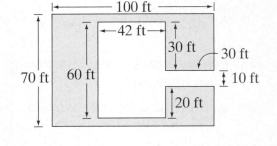

► MIXED REVIEW

The endpoints of a segment are given. Graph each segment and its image after a rotation of 90° about the origin. *(Lesson 9-10)*

31. $A(5, 8), B(2, 4)$ **32.** $C(0, 3), D(3, -5)$ **33.** $E(-2, -3), F(-2, 4)$

Simplify each expression. *(Lesson 5-4)*

34. $\frac{2}{5} \cdot 2\frac{1}{2}$ **35.** $\frac{2}{5} \div 2\frac{1}{2}$ **36.** $3\frac{2}{3} \cdot \frac{3}{4}$ **37.** $3\frac{2}{3} \div \frac{3}{4}$

38. **Choose a Strategy** Find the measures of two supplementary angles if the difference of their measures is 56°.

Math at Work
Pharmacist

Pharmacists dispense medications. They also talk to their customers about the possible side effects of medications. To do this, they must thoroughly understand how prescription drugs are made.

Sometimes a doctor prescribes a special medication that a pharmacist must mix. The pharmacist must measure the ingredients in the exact proportions that the patient needs. In a situation such as this, mathematics are essential.

For more information about pharmacists, visit the Prentice Hall Web site.
www.phschool.com

Area: Triangles and Trapezoids

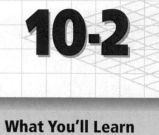

10-2

PART 1 Finding Areas of Triangles

A diagonal divides a parallelogram into two congruent triangles.

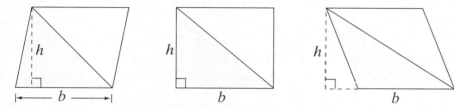

You can see that the area of a triangle is half the area of a parallelogram. An **altitude of a triangle** is the perpendicular segment from a vertex of a triangle to the line containing the opposite side. The height is the length of the altitude.

What You'll Learn

1 To find areas of triangles

2 To find areas of trapezoids

. . . And Why

To find areas in real-world situations, such as construction

Area of a Triangle

The area of a triangle equals half the product of any base length b and the corresponding height h.

$$A = \tfrac{1}{2}bh$$

■ EXAMPLE 1

Find the area of the triangle.

$A = \tfrac{1}{2}bh$ Use the formula for area of a triangle.

$= \tfrac{1}{2} \cdot 8 \cdot 3$ Replace b with 8 and h with 3.

$= 12$ Simplify.

The area is 12 cm^2.

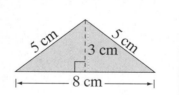

■ TRY THIS Find the area of each triangle.

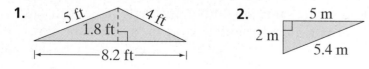

1. 5 ft   4 ft   1.8 ft   8.2 ft

2. 5 m   2 m   5.4 m

■ EXAMPLE 2

Construction **How much siding does a builder need to cover the side of the house shown at the left?**

Area of triangle	Area of rectangle
$A = \frac{1}{2}bh$	$A = bh$
$= \frac{1}{2} \cdot 16 \cdot 9$	$= 16 \cdot 10$
$= 72$	$= 160$

Add to find the total: $72 + 160 = 232$.

The builder needs 232 ft² of siding.

■ **TRY THIS** Find the area of the shaded figure.

3.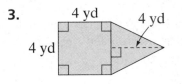

PART 2 Finding Areas of Trapezoids

A diagonal divides a trapezoid into two triangles. You can add the areas of the triangles to find the area of the trapezoid.

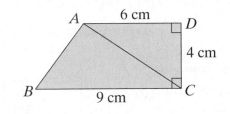

Area of $\triangle ABC$	Area of $\triangle ADC$
$A = \frac{1}{2}bh$	$A = \frac{1}{2}bh$
$= \frac{1}{2} \cdot 9 \cdot 4$	$= \frac{1}{2} \cdot 6 \cdot 4$
$= 18$	$= 12$

The areas of the two triangles are 18 cm² and 12 cm². The area of the trapezoid is the sum of the areas of the two triangles, 30 cm². Notice that the triangles have the same height but different bases. You can use this information to write a formula for the area of a trapezoid.

In a trapezoid, the parallel sides are its bases. For the figure at the right the bases are b_1 and b_2.

The area of the trapezoid is $\frac{1}{2}b_1h + \frac{1}{2}b_2h$.

By using the distributive property, you can see that $\frac{1}{2}b_1h + \frac{1}{2}b_2h$ is $\frac{1}{2}h(b_1 + b_2)$. So, the area of the trapezoid is $\frac{1}{2}h(b_1 + b_2)$.

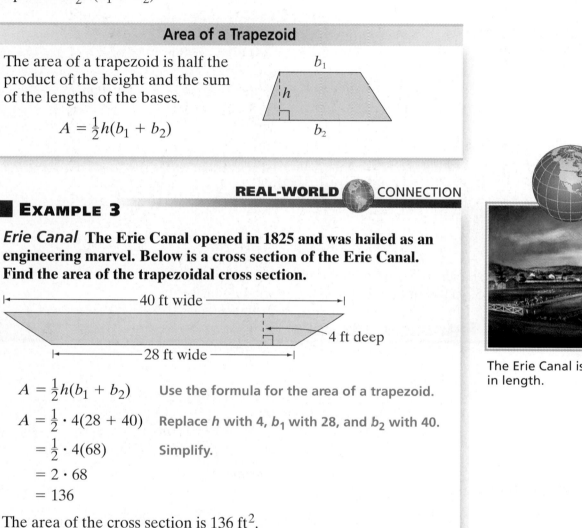

Area of a Trapezoid

The area of a trapezoid is half the product of the height and the sum of the lengths of the bases.

$$A = \frac{1}{2}h(b_1 + b_2)$$

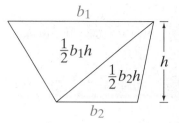

REAL-WORLD CONNECTION

■ EXAMPLE 3

Erie Canal **The Erie Canal opened in 1825 and was hailed as an engineering marvel. Below is a cross section of the Erie Canal. Find the area of the trapezoidal cross section.**

$A = \frac{1}{2}h(b_1 + b_2)$ **Use the formula for the area of a trapezoid.**

$A = \frac{1}{2} \cdot 4(28 + 40)$ **Replace h with 4, b_1 with 28, and b_2 with 40.**

$= \frac{1}{2} \cdot 4(68)$ **Simplify.**

$= 2 \cdot 68$

$= 136$

The area of the cross section is 136 ft^2.

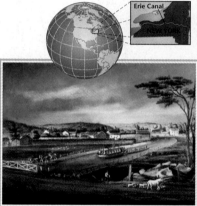

The Erie Canal is 363 miles in length.

■ **TRY THIS** Find the area of each trapezoid.

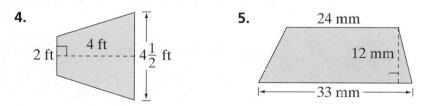

4.

5.

Exercises

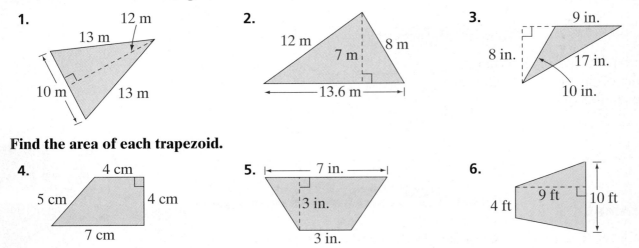

▶ **CHECK UNDERSTANDING**

Find the area of each triangle.

1. 12 m, 13 m, 10 m, 13 m

2. 12 m, 7 m, 8 m, 13.6 m

3. 9 in., 8 in., 17 in., 10 in.

Find the area of each trapezoid.

4. 4 cm, 5 cm, 4 cm, 7 cm

5. 7 in., 3 in., 3 in.

6. 9 ft, 10 ft, 4 ft

7. *Critical Thinking* A triangle and a parallelogram both have areas of 20 cm² and bases of 5 cm. What do you know about the heights?

▶ **PRACTICE AND PROBLEM SOLVING**

Find the area of each triangle.

8. 4 in., 4 in., 5.7 in.

9. 9.4 cm, 8 cm, 9.6 cm, 9 cm

10. 32 m, 80 m, 32 m

Find the area of each trapezoid.

11. 10 in., 20 in., 31 in.

12. 24.5 cm, 14 cm, 17.5 cm, 14 cm

13. 60 ft, 40 ft, 30 ft

14. 32 m, 12 m, 16 m

15. 25 mm, 15 mm, 30 mm

16. $2\frac{4}{5}$ mi, $\frac{4}{5}$ mi, $\frac{4}{5}$ mi

512 **Chapter 10** Area and Volume

Find the area of each shaded region.

17.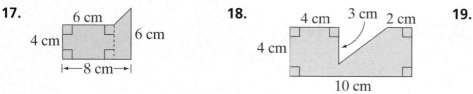

18.

19.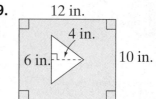

20. A trapezoid has area 50 in.^{2}. The two bases are 5 in. and 15 in. What is the height of the trapezoid?

21. Find the area of the yellow region in the figure at the right.

22. a. *Mathematical Reasoning* The bases of two triangles are the same length. The height of the first triangle is twice the height of the second. What is the ratio of the area of the second triangle to the area of the first? Justify your answer.
   b. Suppose the height and the base of a triangle are twice the length of the height and base of another triangle. What is the ratio of the area of the smaller triangle to the area of the larger triangle? Justify your answer.

23. *Open-ended* Sketch and label two different triangles, each with an area of 180 in.^{2}.

24. *Writing* Are $\left(\frac{1}{2} \cdot 3\right) \cdot 8$ and $3 \cdot \left(\frac{1}{2} \cdot 8\right)$ equal? Explain how this can help in finding the area of a triangle.

25. **TEST PREP** *ABCD* is a rectangle. What is the area of the shaded region?
   A. 15 cm^2 **B.** 20 cm^2 **C.** 35 cm^2 **D.** 50 cm^2

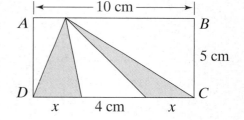

▶ MIXED REVIEW

Find the area of each parallelogram. *(Lesson 10-1)*

26.

27.

28.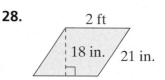

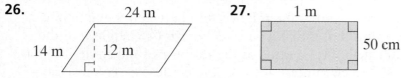

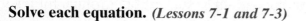

Solve each equation. *(Lessons 7-1 and 7-3)*

29. $13 + 3x = 7$ **30.** $16 + 2y = 9$ **31.** $5.5a + 2 = 10.5$ **32.** $\frac{1}{2}b - 10 = 24$

33. *Choose a Strategy* Suppose you bought two books for $15. The original price of the two books was the same, but you were able to buy one for full price and get the other for half price. What was the full price?

10-3

Area: Circles

What You'll Learn

1 To find areas of circles

2 To find areas of irregular figures that include parts of circles

...And Why

To use area formulas in real-world situations, such as finding the amount of grass seed needed to cover a circular region

Investigate

························· FINDING THE FORMULA FOR AREA OF A CIRCLE ·····················

1. Use your compass to draw a circle. Cut out the circle.

2. Fold the circle in half, and then in half again. Fold it in half a third and fourth time.

3. Cut out the 16 wedges that you have formed with the folds.

4. Arrange the wedges in a row as shown below.

5. Notice that the new shape resembles a parallelogram. How does the base of the parallelogram (the side shown in red) relate to the circumference of the circle? How does the height of the parallelogram relate to the radius of the circle?

6. Use the formula for the area of a parallelogram to estimate the area of your circle.

PART 1 Finding Areas of Circles

The diagram above shows the relationship between the area of a circle and a figure that is like a parallelogram. The height h of the parallelogram is about the same as the radius r of the circle. The base b is about half the circumference C of the circle. You can use the formula for the area of a parallelogram to suggest the formula for the area of a circle.

$A = bh$	Use the formula for area of a parallelogram.
$A = (\frac{1}{2}C)(r)$	Substitute $\frac{1}{2}C$ for b and r for h.
$A = \frac{1}{2}(2\pi r) \cdot r$	Substitute $2\pi r$ for C.
$A = \pi r^2$	Simplify.

Area of a Circle

The area of a circle equals the product of π and the square of the radius r.

$$A = \pi r^2$$

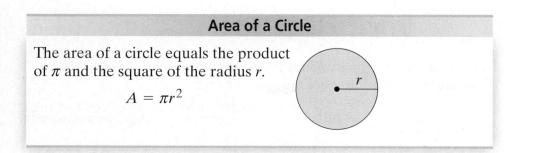

To find the *exact area* of a circle, you express the area using π.

■ EXAMPLE 1

Find the exact area of a circle with diameter 12 cm.

$$
\begin{aligned}
A &= \pi r^2 \\
&= \pi(6)^2 \qquad r = \tfrac{1}{2}d;\ r = 6 \\
&= 36\pi \qquad \text{Simplify.}
\end{aligned}
$$

The area is 36π cm^2.

■ TRY THIS

7. Find the exact area of a circle with diameter 100 in.

For real-world situations, you usually want an approximate value for the area of a circle. If you are finding an approximate area, use 3.14 for π.

REAL-WORLD 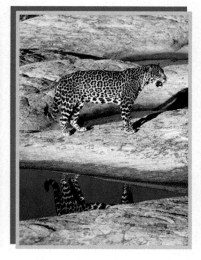 **CONNECTION**

■ EXAMPLE 2

Biology **The size of a jaguar's territory depends on how much food is available. In a situation where there is plenty of food, such as in a forest, the circular territory of the jaguar may be as small as 3 mi in diameter. Find the area of the region.**

$$
\begin{aligned}
A &= \pi r^2 \\
&= \pi(1.5)^2 \qquad r = \tfrac{1}{2}d;\ r = 1.5 \\
&= 2.25\pi \qquad \text{exact area} \\
&\approx (2.25)(3.14) \qquad \text{Use 3.14 for } \pi. \\
&= 7.065 \qquad \text{approximate area}
\end{aligned}
$$

The area of the region is about 7 mi^2.

During a drought a jaguar may need to search for food in a territory as large as 6 mi in diameter.

■ TRY THIS

8. Find the approximate area of a circle with diameter 6 mi.

To find the area of an irregular figure, you can sometimes separate it into figures with areas you know how to find.

REAL-WORLD CONNECTION

■ EXAMPLE 3

Landscaping A pound of grass seed covers approximately 675 ft². Find the area of the lawn below. Then find the amount of grass seed you need to buy to cover the lawn. Grass seed comes in 3-lb bags.

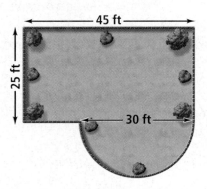

Area of region that is one half of a circle

area of circle = πr^2

area of half circle = $\frac{1}{2}\pi r^2$

$A \approx \frac{1}{2}(3.14)(15)^2$ **Replace π with 3.14 and r with 15.**

$A = 353.25$

Area of region that is a rectangle

area of rectangle = bh

$A = 45 \cdot 25$ **Replace b with 45 and h with 25.**

$A = 1,125$

The area of the lawn is about 353 ft² + 1,125 ft² = 1,478 ft².

$1,478 \div 675 \approx 2.19$ **Divide to find the amount of seed.**

You will need to buy one 3-lb bag of grass seed.

■ TRY THIS

9. Find the area of the shaded region to the nearest tenth.

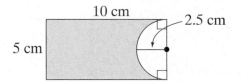

Exercises

▶ CHECK UNDERSTANDING

Find the area of each circle. Give an exact area and an approximate area to the nearest square unit.

1. $r = 3$ ft

2. $d = 10$ m

3. $r = 20$ cm

4.

5.

6.

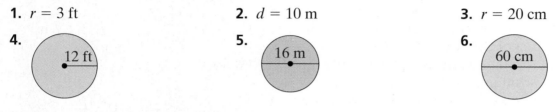

Find the area of each figure to the nearest square unit.

7.

8.

9. Which has a greater area, a circle with radius 2 m or a square with side length 2 m? Explain.

▶ PRACTICE AND PROBLEM SOLVING

Find the area of each circle. Give an exact area and an approximate area to the nearest tenth.

10. $r = 11$ mi

11. $r = \frac{1}{2}$ m

12. $d = 1.2$ in.

13. $r = 5\frac{1}{2}$ mi

14. $d = 3.2$ ft

15. $d = 8.4$ mm

Find the area of each shaded region to the nearest square unit.

16.

17.

18.

19.

20.

21.

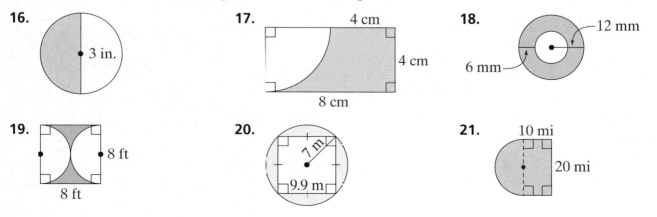

Number Sense **Match each object with the most reasonable area.**

22. dinner plate

A. 0.8 in.^{2}

23. quarter

B. 110 in.^{2}

24. circle at the center of a basketball floor

C. 7 in.^{2}

25. jar lid

D. 16,000 in.^{2}

26. 12 in. pizza

E. 80 in.^{2}

27. You need to carpet the border of the pool at the right.
   a. What is the area of the border in square feet?
   b. Carpet is sold by the square yard. How many square feet does a square yard contain?
   c. How many square yards of carpet should you buy?

28. ***Open-ended*** Describe a real-life situation, not used in this lesson, where you might use the formula for the area of a circle.

29. ***Manufacturing*** Lids of aluminum cans are cut from rectangular sheets of aluminum.

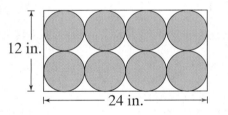

   a. What is the radius of each lid?
   b. How many square inches of aluminum do the lids require?
   c. How many square inches of aluminum are wasted?

30. a. ***Consumer Issues*** Each circle represents the area of a pizza. What is the area of each pizza?
   b. What is the price per square inch of each pizza?
   c. ***Critical Thinking*** Is the largest pizza the best buy? Explain.

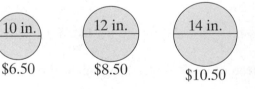

31. ***Writing*** Which has a greater area, four circles, each with the radius 1 m, or one circle with radius 4 m? Explain.

32. ***Critical Thinking*** What is the area of the largest circle that will fit in a square with area 64 cm^2?

33. How many circles with radius 2 cm will have the same total area as a circle with radius 4 cm?

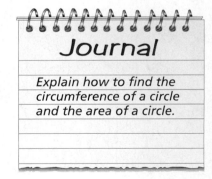

Journal

Explain how to find the circumference of a circle and the area of a circle.

Find the area of each triangle or trapezoid. *(Lesson 10-2)*

34.
5 mi

3 mi

$6\frac{1}{2}$ mi

35.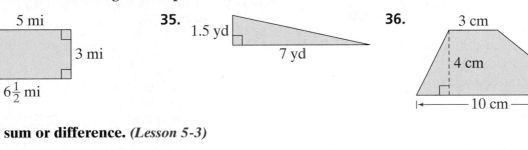
1.5 yd

7 yd

36.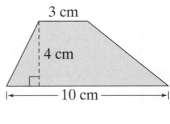
3 cm

4 cm

10 cm

Find each sum or difference. *(Lesson 5-3)*

37. $4\frac{3}{5} + 5\frac{2}{3}$ **38.** $5\frac{2}{3} - 4\frac{3}{5}$ **39.** $\frac{7}{8} + \frac{5}{6}$ **40.** $\frac{7}{8} - \frac{5}{6}$

41. Square *ABCD* has side length 8 in.
△*BXY* is isosceles. The congruent sides
have length 2 in. How many triangles
congruent to △*BXY* can be cut
from *ABCD*? *(Lesson 9-4)*

A   *X*   *B*

Y

D   *C*

✓ **CHECKPOINT 1**   **Lessons 10-1 through 10-3**

Find the area of each figure.

1.
20 yd

12 yd   13 yd

30 yd

2.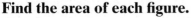
30 cm   35 cm

70 cm

3.
25 m

15 m

20 m

**Find the area of each figure. Give an exact answer and an
approximate answer to the nearest square unit.**

4.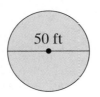
10 yd

5.
50 ft

6.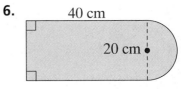
40 cm

20 cm

7. TEST PREP Which figure has an area that is about the same as
the area of a circle with a radius of 10 in.?

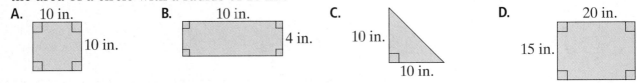

A.   10 in.

10 in.

B.   10 in.

4 in.

C.
10 in.

10 in.

D.   20 in.

15 in.

MATH TOOLBOX

Extension
Before Lesson 10-4

Three Views of an Object

A solid is a three-dimensional figure. Solids are often drawn in perspective to show that they are three-dimensional.

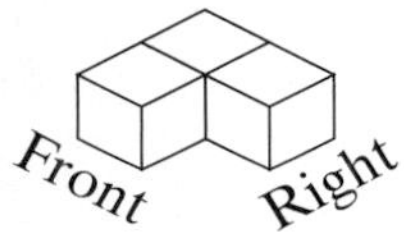

Isometric Dot

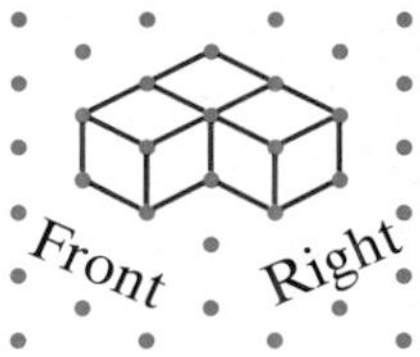

Solid lines are used for edges that show.

Isometric dot paper is helpful for drawing a corner view.

Rectangular Graph

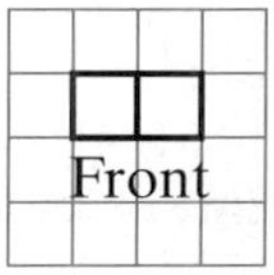

Rectangular graph paper is used for drawing the top, front, and side views.

EXAMPLE

Draw the top, front, and right-side views of the solid.

Isometric

Top

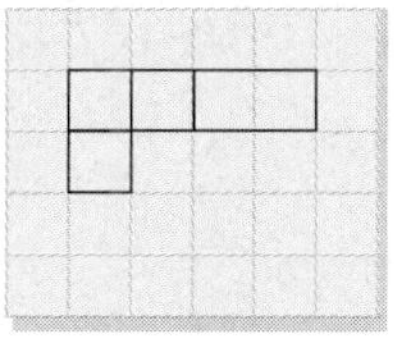

Front

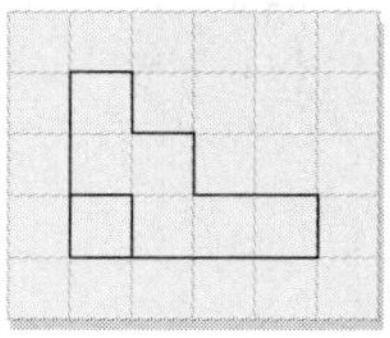

Right Side

Draw the top, front, and right-side views of each solid.

1.

2.

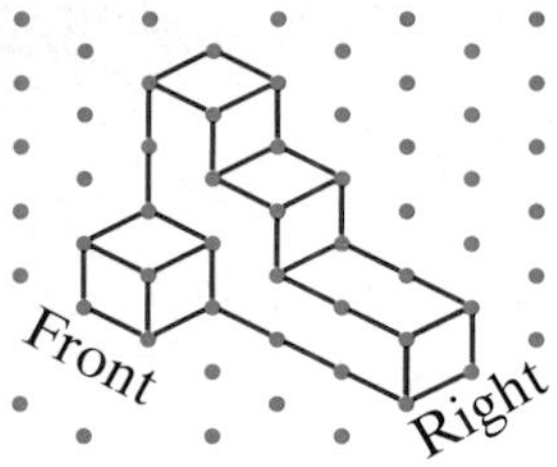

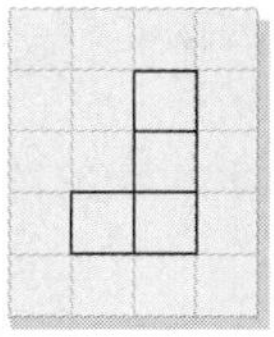

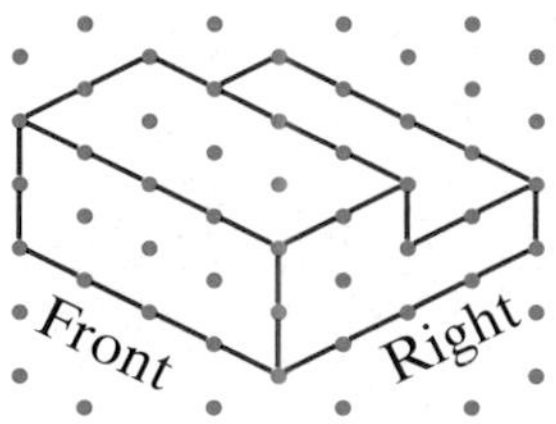

3.

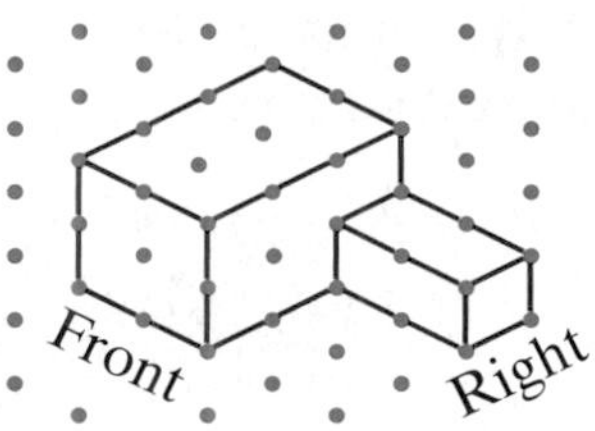

4.

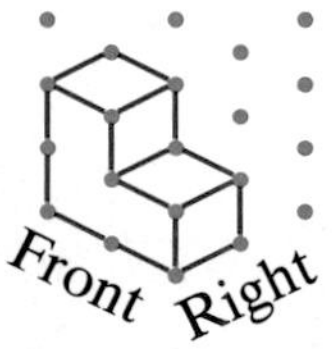

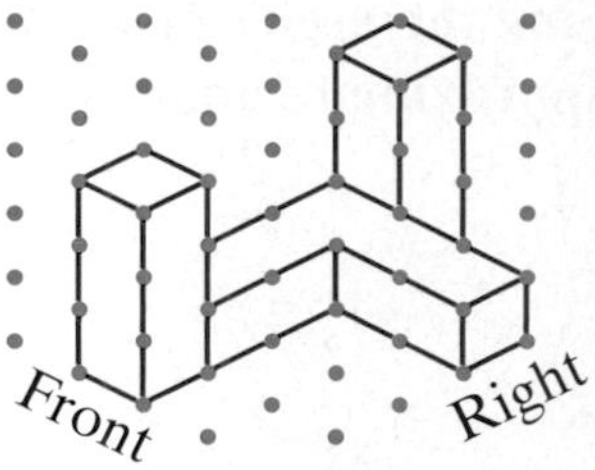

5. The top, front, and right-side views are given. Draw an isometric view on isometric dot paper.

Top

Front

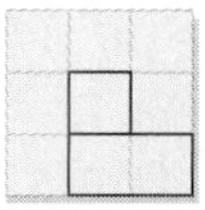

Right Side

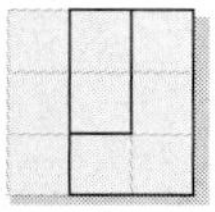

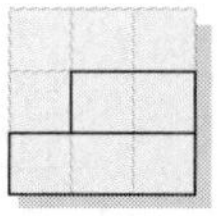

Space Figures

The figures below are common three-dimensional figures, also called **space figures** or solids. The space figures you will study in this book are prisms, pyramids, cylinders, cones, and spheres.

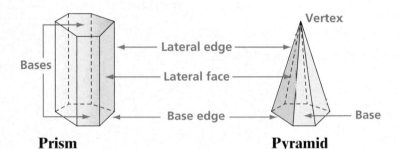

Prism

Pyramid

A **prism** has two parallel bases that are congruent polygons, and lateral faces that are parallelograms.

A **pyramid** has a base that is a polygon. The lateral faces are triangles.

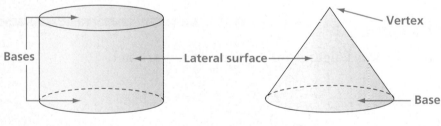

Cylinder

Cone

A **cylinder** has two parallel bases that are congruent circles.

A **cone** has one circular base and one vertex.

Sphere

A **sphere** is the set of all points in space that are a given distance from a given point called the center.

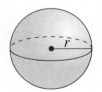

What You'll Learn

1 To identify common space figures

2 To identify nets of space figures

. . . And Why

To identify the space figures often used in constructing buildings

Reading Math

Lateral means "on the side." The lateral faces of a figure are the surfaces that connect the bases.

Describe the shapes that make up this tank.

You can use the shape of a base to help you name a space figure.

■ **EXAMPLE 1**

For each figure, describe the base and name the figure.

a.

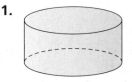

The bases are triangles.
The figure is a triangular prism.

b.

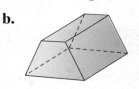

The bases of the prism are trapezoids. The figure is a trapezoidal prism.

■ **TRY THIS** Name each figure.

1.

2.

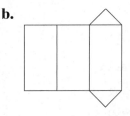

PART
2 Identifying Space Figures from Nets

A **net** is a pattern you can form into a space figure.

■ **EXAMPLE 2**

Name the space figure you can form from each net.

a.

With a hexagonal base and triangular sides, you can form a hexagonal pyramid.

b.

With two triangular bases and rectangular sides, you can form a triangular prism.

■ **TRY THIS** Name the space figure you can form from each net.

3.

4.

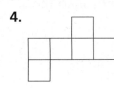

Exercises

CHECK UNDERSTANDING

For each figure, describe the base(s) and name the figure.

1.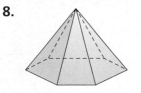

2.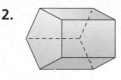

3.

Name the space figure you can form from each net.

4.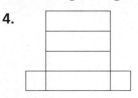

5.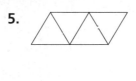

6.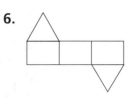

7. **Open-ended** Draw a net for a hexagonal prism.

PRACTICE AND PROBLEM SOLVING

For each figure, describe the base(s) and name the figure.

8.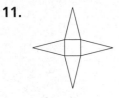

9.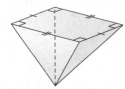

10.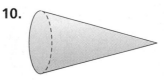

Name the space figure you can form from each net.

11.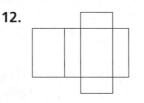

12.

13.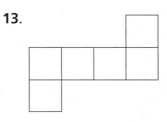

14. **Open-ended** Draw a net for a pentagonal pyramid.

15. **TEST PREP** Which of the following could be a net for a cylinder?

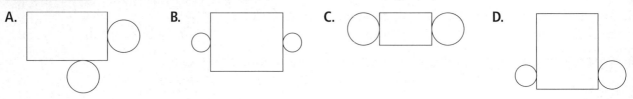

A.   B.   C.   D.

Match each container with the appropriate net.

16.   17.   18.

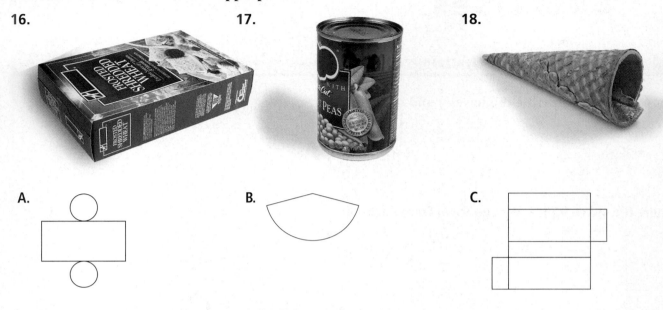

A.   B.   C.

19. **Error Analysis** A student explains that since each figure below has six square faces, each can be folded to make a cube. Explain the error the student might have made.

Figure A   Figure B   Figure C   Figure D

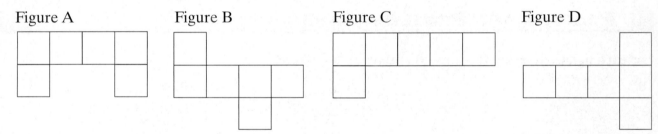

For Exercises 20–22, write the most precise name for each figure.

20. The figure has four lateral faces that are triangles.

21. The figure has three lateral faces that are rectangles.

22. The figure has one vertex and one circular base.

23. **Writing** Suppose you see a net for a rectangular prism and a net for a rectangular pyramid. Explain how you can match each net with its name.

24. Draw a net to represent a rectangular box that is 10 cm long, 8 cm wide, and 4 cm high. Label dimensions on the net.

25. What mathematical name does each object suggest?
    a. a shoe box   **b.** a teepee   **c.** a basketball

26. **Open-ended** Draw a net for an object you find in your classroom.

27. A rectangular solid with congruent sides, or cube, is one of the easiest objects to draw in *one-point perspective*. Follow the steps below to draw a cube.

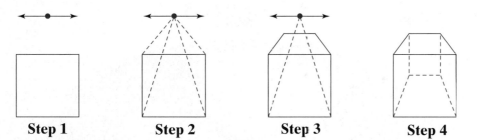

Step 1   Step 2   Step 3   Step 4

Step 1 Begin by drawing a square for the front. Draw a *horizon line* parallel to one horizontal edge of your square. Select a *vanishing point* on the horizon line.

Step 2 Draw lines, called *vanishing lines*, from the vertices of the square to the vanishing point.

Step 3 Draw a line segment parallel to the horizon line. Use this segment to determine the back edges.

Step 4 Draw dashed lines for the hidden back vertical and horizontal edges. Erase the horizon line and unnecessary parts of the vanishing lines.

28. Using the steps from exercise 27, draw a rectangular solid in one-point perspective.

▶ MIXED REVIEW

Find the exact area and the approximate area of each circle.
(Lesson 10-3)

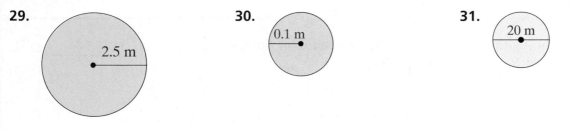

29.

2.5 m

30.

0.1 m

31.

20 m

Write each equation in slope-intercept form. *(Lesson 8-3)*

32. $3x - y = 6$ **33.** $2x - 2y = 10$ **34.** $-8y - 16 = 24x$

35. *Choose a Strategy* A rectangular yard is 20 ft by 40 ft. Your lawn mower will mow a 2-ft-wide path. What is the least number of turns you must make to mow the lawn?

Extension
Before Lesson 10-5

Cross Sections of Space Figures

The intersection of a plane and a space figure is a *cross section* of the space figure. This cross section of a block of cheese is a rectangle.

■ EXAMPLE

Sketch a plane intersecting a cube in three different ways to show a rectangular cross section.

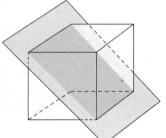 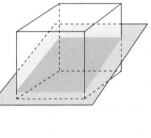 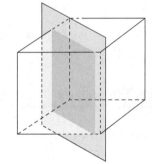

Use the name of a polygon to describe each cross section of the cube. Points *M, N, P, Q*, and *R* are midpoints of edges.

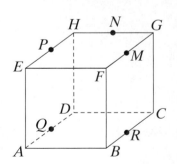

1. through *M, P, Q,* and *R*
2. through *E, A, C,* and *G*
3. through *B, E,* and *G*
4. through *M, N, D,* and *B*

Sketch a cube to show each cross section.

5. a scalene triangle
6. a rhombus
7. a square
8. an isosceles triangle
9. Describe the possible cross sections of a sphere.

Surface Area: Prisms and Cylinders

PART 1 Finding Surface Areas of Prisms

Prisms and cylinders can be *right* or *oblique*.

Right prism   Oblique prism   Right cylinder   Oblique cylinder

In this text, you may assume that prisms and cylinders are right unless otherwise stated.

Surface area (S.A.) is the sum of the areas of the base(s) and the lateral faces of a space figure. One way to find the surface area of a space figure is to find the area of its net. You measure surface area in square units.

What You'll Learn

1 To find surface areas of prisms

2 To find surface areas of cylinders

...And Why

To find the amount of material needed in packaging

◼ EXAMPLE 1

Find the surface area of the rectangular prism using a net.

8 in.
5 in.
20 in.

40 in.²	|←— 20 in. —→|	40 in.²	**Draw and label a net.**
8 in.	160 in.²	
5 in.	100 in.²	**Find the area of each rectangle in the net.**
8 in.	160 in.²	
5 in.	100 in.²	

$40 + 40 + 160 + 100 + 160 + 100 = 600$ **Add the areas.**

The surface area is 600 in.².

◼ TRY THIS

1. Find the surface area of the triangular prism at the right.

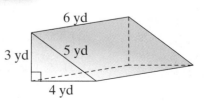

6 yd
3 yd   5 yd
4 yd

Another way to find the surface area of a prism is to use the *lateral area* and the base areas. **Lateral area (L.A.)** of a prism is the sum of the areas of the lateral faces.

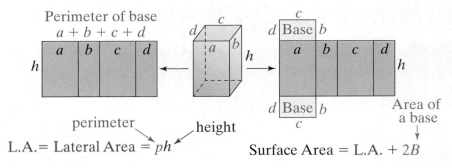

L.A.= Lateral Area = ph

Surface Area = L.A. + $2B$

When you find the surface area of a prism, it is a good idea to find the lateral area first.

Surface Area of a Prism

The lateral area of a prism is the product of the perimeter of the base and the height.

$$\text{L.A.} = ph$$

The surface area of a prism is the sum of the lateral area and the areas of the two bases.

$$\text{S.A.} = \text{L.A.} + 2B$$

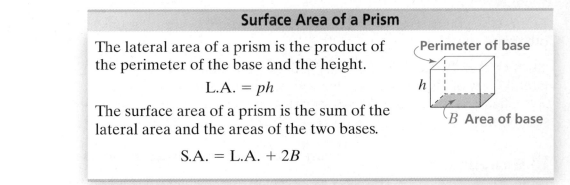

■ **EXAMPLE 2**

Find the surface area of the triangular prism at the left.

Step 1 Find the lateral area.

$\text{L.A.} = ph$ ⟶ Use the formula for lateral area.

$\quad = (5 + 5 + 6)12$ ⟶ $p = 5 + 5 + 6$ and $h = 12$

$\quad = 192$

Step 2 Find the surface area.

$\text{S.A.} = \text{L.A.} + 2B$

$\quad = 192 + 2(\frac{1}{2} \cdot 6 \cdot 4)$ ⟶ $\text{L.A.} = 192$ and $B = \frac{1}{2} \cdot 6 \cdot 4$

$\quad = 192 + 24$

$\quad = 216$

The surface area of the triangular prism is 216 cm².

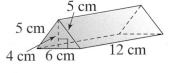

■ **TRY THIS**

2. Find the surface area of the figure at the left.

If you cut a label from a soup can, you will see that the label is a rectangle. The height of the rectangle is the height of the can. The base length of the rectangle is the circumference of the can.

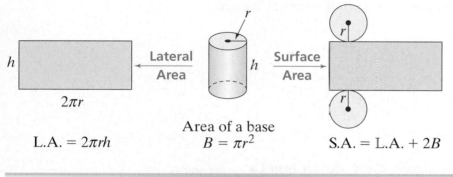

h

$\xleftarrow{\text{Lateral Area}}$ h $\xrightarrow{\text{Surface Area}}$

$2\pi r$

L.A. $= 2\pi rh$

Area of a base
$B = \pi r^2$

S.A. $=$ L.A. $+ 2B$

Surface Area of a Cylinder

The lateral area of a cylinder is the product of the circumference of the base and the height of the cylinder.

B is the area of a base.

$$\text{L.A.} = 2\pi rh$$

The surface area of a cylinder is the sum of the lateral area and the areas of the two bases.

$$\text{S.A.} = \text{L.A.} + 2B$$

■ EXAMPLE 3

Packaging **Find the surface area of the can at the right.**

3.5 cm

Step 1 Find the lateral area.

$\qquad$ L.A. $= 2\pi rh$ $\qquad$ Use the formula for lateral area.

$\qquad\qquad \approx 2(3.14)(3.5)(11.5)$

$\qquad\qquad \approx 253$

11.5 cm

Step 2 Find the surface area.

$\qquad$ S.A. $=$ L.A. $+ 2B$ $\qquad$ Use the formulas for surface areas.

$\qquad\qquad =$ L.A. $+ 2(\pi r^2)$

$\qquad\qquad \approx 253 + 2(3.14)(3.5)^2 = 329.93$

The surface area of the can is about 330 cm^2.

■ TRY THIS

3. Find the surface area of a can with radius 5 cm and height 20 cm.

Exercises

► CHECK UNDERSTANDING

For the space figure represented by each net, find the surface area to the nearest square unit.

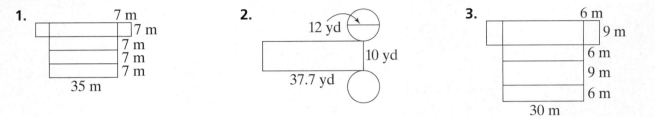

1. 7 m / 7 m / 7 m / 7 m / 7 m / 35 m

2. 12 yd / 10 yd / 37.7 yd

3. 6 m / 9 m / 6 m / 9 m / 6 m / 30 m

Find the surface area of each space figure. If the answer is not a whole number, round to the nearest tenth.

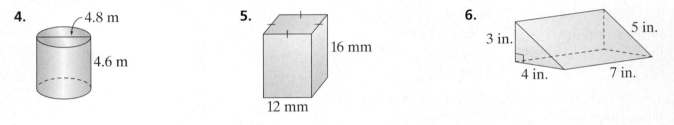

4. 4.8 m / 4.6 m

5. 16 mm / 12 mm

6. 3 in. / 4 in. / 5 in. / 7 in.

7. The base of a rectangular prism is 3 in. by 5 in., and the height is 11 in. Draw and label a net for the prism. Find its surface area.

► PRACTICE AND PROBLEM SOLVING

For the space figure represented by each net, find the surface area to the nearest square unit.

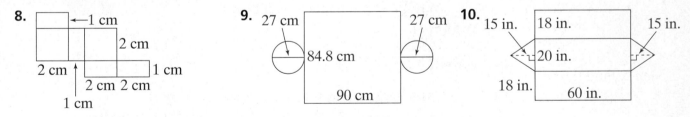

8. 1 cm / 2 cm / 2 cm / 1 cm / 2 cm / 2 cm / 1 cm

9. 27 cm / 27 cm / 84.8 cm / 90 cm

10. 15 in. / 18 in. / 15 in. / 20 in. / 18 in. / 60 in.

Find the surface area of each space figure. If the answer is not a whole number, round to the nearest tenth.

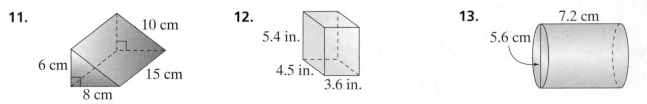

11. 10 cm / 6 cm / 15 cm / 8 cm

12. 5.4 in. / 4.5 in. / 3.6 in.

13. 7.2 cm / 5.6 cm

530 Chapter 10 Area and Volume

14. A cylinder has radius 8 ft and height 12 ft. Draw and label a net for the cylinder. Find its surface area.

15. Find the surface area of a square prism with base edge 7 m and height 15 m.

16. Find the area of the top and lateral surface of a cylindrical water tank with radius 20 ft and height 30 ft.

17. The camping tent at the right is similar to a triangular prism. Find the surface area of the tent, including the bottom.

18. Find the surface area of a cylinder with radius 8 cm and height 10 cm.

19. The neighborhood swimming pool needs to be painted. The pool is 40 ft by 60 ft. The depth of the pool is 6 ft throughout.
  a. How many sides need to be painted?
  b. What is the total number of square feet to be painted?
  c. The materials for painting the pool cost $1.50 per square yard. What is the cost of the materials for painting the pool?

20. *Error Analysis* A student explains that the two cylinders below have the same surface area. Explain the student's error.

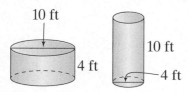

21. *Open-ended* Describe a real-world situation in which you need to know the surface area of a space figure.

22. *Critical Thinking* Use the cubes with side lengths of 1, 2, and 3 units to answer the following questions.

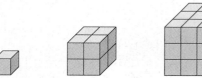

  a. Find the surface area of each cube.
  b. If the length of each side of a cube is doubled, how does that affect the surface area?
  c. If the length of each side of a cube is tripled, how does that affect the surface area?

23. *Mathematical Reasoning* Which has the greater effect on the surface area of a cylinder: doubling the base radius or doubling the height? Justify your answer.

24. **TEST PREP** Which figure would cost more to paint?
   A. the square prism
   B. the cylinder
   C. They would cost the same.

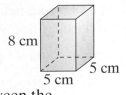

8 cm

5 cm

5 cm

10 cm

5 cm

25. *Writing* In a triangular prism, what is the difference between the height of a base and the height of the prism?

26. *Packaging* You have made two boxes with lids. Which box required more cardboard, a box 8 in. by 6.25 in. by 10.5 in., or a box 9 in. by 5.5 in. by 11.75 in.? Explain.

27. *Construction* The concrete figure at the right has a hole in it. The surface will be painted except for the inside of the hole. Find the total surface area to be painted to the nearest square foot.

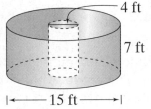

4 ft

7 ft

|← 15 ft →|

► MIXED REVIEW

Name each space figure. (*Lesson 10-4*)

28.

29.

30.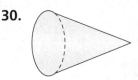

Graph each point and its image after a reflection over the given line.
(*Lesson 9-9*)

31. $A(0, 9)$; x-axis

32. $B(-3, 5)$; y-axis

33. $C(3, -1)$; $x = 2$

34. A recipe for 6 people calls for $\frac{1}{2}$ teaspoon of salt. In preparing this recipe for 25 people, how many teaspoons of salt should you use?
(*Lesson 6-2*)

CHAPTER PROJECT 10 ► **ACTIVITY 1 MEASURING**

Use centimeter cubes to make a prism. Measure the dimensions of the prism's base. Calculate the area of the base.

Stack some pennies or nickels to make a cylinder. Measure the diameter of the cylinder's base. Calculate the area of the base.

Keep your space figures for use in Activities 2 and 3.

Surface Area: Pyramids, Cones, and Spheres

PART 1 Finding Surface Areas of Pyramids

What You'll Learn

1. To find surface areas of pyramids

2. To find surface areas of cones and spheres

... And Why

To find surface areas of real-world objects, such as a basketball

In this text, all pyramids are *regular* pyramids. They have regular polygons for bases and congruent isosceles triangles for lateral faces.

You can use the **slant height** ℓ, the height of a face, to find the area of the lateral faces.

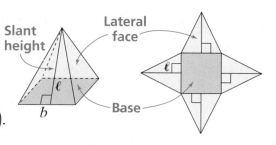

If n is the number of lateral triangular faces, L.A. is $n\left(\frac{1}{2}b\ell\right)$.

Surface Area of a Pyramid

The surface area of a pyramid is the sum of the lateral area and the area of the base.

$$\text{S.A.} = \text{L.A.} + B$$

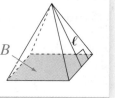

The entrance to the Louvre in Paris, France is a pyramid that is 66 ft tall.

■ EXAMPLE 1

Find the surface area of the square pyramid at the right.

$\text{L.A.} = 4\left(\frac{1}{2}b\ell\right)$ **There are 4 lateral faces.**

$\qquad = 4\left(\frac{1}{2} \cdot 12 \cdot 16\right) = 384$

$\text{S.A.} = \text{L.A.} + B$

$\qquad = 384 + 12^2$ **The base is a square.**

$\qquad = 384 + 144 = 528$

The surface area of the pyramid is 528 cm².

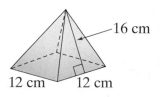

■ TRY THIS

1. A pyramid has a square base with edge 20 ft. The slant height is 8 ft. Find the surface area.

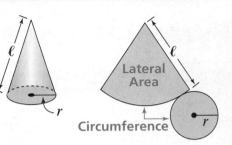

In this text, every cone is a right circular cone with the vertex of the cone directly over the center of the circular base.

L.A. is $\frac{1}{2}(2\pi r)\ell$ or L.A. $= \pi r \ell$.

Surface Area of a Cone

The surface area (S.A.) of a cone is the sum of the lateral area and base area, or S.A. $=$ L.A. $+ B$.

EXAMPLE 2

Find the surface area of the cone at the right.

$$\begin{aligned}
\text{L.A.} &= \pi r \ell \\
&\approx 3.14(4)(10) \quad \text{The radius is 4.} \\
&= 125.6 \quad \text{Simplify.}
\end{aligned}$$

$$\begin{aligned}
\text{S.A.} &= \text{L.A.} + B \\
&\approx 125.6 + 3.14(4)^2 \quad \text{The radius is 4.} \\
&= 175.84 \quad \text{Simplify.}
\end{aligned}$$

10 cm

4 cm

The total surface area of the cone is about 176 cm^2.

TRY THIS

2. Find the surface area of a cone with slant height 39 ft and diameter 14 ft.

The figure at the left suggests how the cover of a baseball may help you remember the formula for surface area of a sphere.

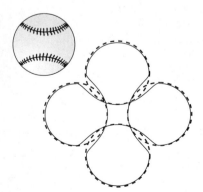

Surface Area of a Sphere

The surface area of a sphere of radius r is S.A. $= 4\pi r^2$.

EXAMPLE 3

Calculate the surface area of a basketball.

$$S.A. = 4\pi r^2 \qquad \text{surface area formula}$$
$$\approx 4(3.14)(5)^2 \quad \text{Replace } \pi \text{ with 3.14 and } r \text{ with 5.}$$
$$= 314 \qquad\quad \text{Simplify.}$$

The surface area of the basketball is about 314 in.^{2}.

$\vdash$————— 10 in. —————$\dashv$

You can find the surface area of a space figure that combines two or more of the figures you have studied.

Different Ways to Solve a Problem

Find the surface area of the silo formed by a half sphere and a cylinder. The diameter of the silo is 20 ft.

10 ft

72 ft

Method 1

Find the area of each space figure. Then find their sum.

One half sphere
$$S.A. = \frac{1}{2}(4\pi r^2)$$
$$\approx \frac{1}{2}(4)(3.14)(10^2)$$
$$= 628$$

Cylinder
$$L.A. = 2\pi rh$$
$$\approx 2(3.14)(10)(72)$$
$$= 4{,}521.6$$

Surface area of silo is 628 + 4,521.6, or 5,149.6 ft^2.

Method 2

Combine formulas before substituting values.

$$\begin{array}{ll} \text{Surface area} \\ \text{of silo} \end{array} = \frac{1}{2}\begin{array}{l}S.A.\\ \text{of sphere}\end{array} + \begin{array}{l}L.A.\\ \text{of cylinder}\end{array}$$

$$= \frac{1}{2}(4\pi r^2) + 2\pi rh$$
$$= 2\pi r^2 + 2\pi rh$$
$$\approx 2(3.14)(10^2) + 2(3.14)(10)(72)$$
$$= 5{,}149.6$$

Surface area of silo is 5,149.6 ft^2.

Choose a Method

1. Which method do you prefer? Explain.

Exercises

▶ **CHECK UNDERSTANDING**

Find the surface area of each space figure, to the nearest square unit.

1.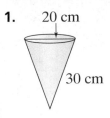
20 cm
30 cm

2.
9 cm

3.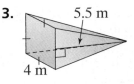
5.5 m
4 m

4. The base of a cone has radius 3 ft. Its slant height is 8 ft. Find the surface area of the cone.

5. The length of the base of a square pyramid is 5 cm. Its slant height is 8 cm. Find the surface area of the square pyramid.

6. *Mathematical Reasoning* Which has the greater surface area, a cylinder with height 2 in. and radius of base 2 in., or a sphere with radius 2 in.? Justify your answer.

▶ **PRACTICE AND PROBLEM SOLVING**

Find the surface area of each space figure, to the nearest square unit.

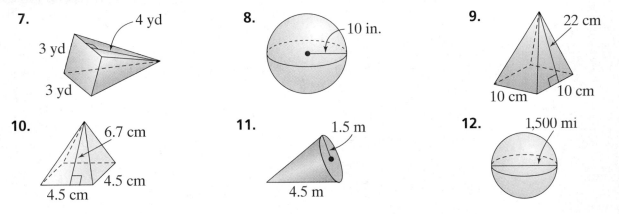

7.
4 yd
3 yd
3 yd

8.
10 in.

9.
22 cm
10 cm   10 cm

10.
6.7 cm
4.5 cm
4.5 cm

11.
1.5 m
4.5 m

12.
1,500 mi

13. *Error Analysis* A friend tells you that the surface area of a square prism with base length 4 m and height 5 m is the same as the area of a square pyramid with base length 4 m and height 5 m. Explain your friend's error.

Find the surface area of each figure. Give your answers to the nearest square unit.

14.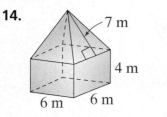
7 m
4 m
6 m 6 m

15.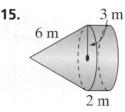
3 m
6 m
2 m

16.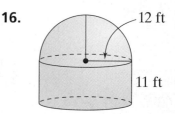
12 ft
11 ft

17. *Architecture* The American Museum of Natural History in New York City has built a spherical planetarium. The sphere measures 87 ft in diameter.
  a. What is the surface area of the sphere?
  b. The sphere is covered by 2,474 panels to absorb sound. What is the average area of each panel, to the nearest tenth of a square foot?

18. *Writing* Write a paragraph explaining how to find the surface area of a cone with slant height 10 in. and base radius 8 in.

19. **TEST PREP** What is the ratio of the surface area of a sphere with radius 2 ft to the area of a sphere with radius 5 ft?
  A. 2 to 5   **B.** 4 to 25   **C.** 16 to 125   **D.** 18 to 20

20. *Geography* Approximately 70% of Earth's surface is covered by water. If the diameter of the earth is approximately 13,000 km, find the approximate area *not* covered by water.

The American Museum of Natural History, New York City

► MIXED REVIEW

Find the surface area, to the nearest square unit. *(Lesson 10-5)*

21.
2 ft
3 ft
4 ft

22.
24 in.
12 in.

23.
22 cm
10 cm
14 cm

List all the factors of each number. *(Lesson 4-1)*

24. 21   **25.** 100   **26.** 25   **27.** 32   **28.** 65

29. Under rate plan A a new computer costs $200 down and $20 a month. Under rate plan B the computer costs $175 down and $25 a month. After how many months will the amount paid be the same for both plans? *(Lesson 8-7)*

10-7

What You'll Learn

1 To find volumes of prisms

2 To find volumes of cylinders

. . . And Why

To solve real-world problems, such as finding volumes of containers

Volume: Prisms and Cylinders

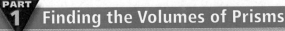

PART 1 Finding the Volumes of Prisms

The **volume** of a three-dimensional figure is the number of cubic units needed to fill it. A **cubic unit** is the space occupied by a cube with sides one unit long.

Consider filling the rectangular prism at the right with centimeter cubes.

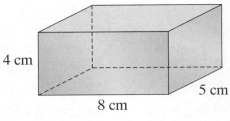

The bottom layer of the prism contains $8 \cdot 5 = 40$ centimeter cubes, or a volume of 40 cm^3.

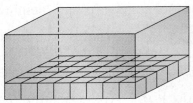

The prism has four layers of cubes, so it contains $4 \cdot 40$ or 160 centimeter cubes in all.

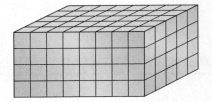

The volume of the prism is 160 cm^3.

The volume found for the rectangular prism above suggests the following formula.

Volume of a Prism

The volume V of a prism is the product of the base area B and the height h.

$$V = Bh$$

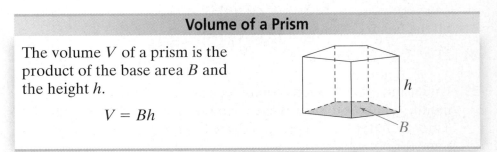

■ EXAMPLE 1

Find the volume of the triangular prism.

$V = Bh$ Use the formula for volume.

$\quad = 30 \cdot 21$ $B = \frac{1}{2} \cdot 10 \cdot 6 = 30$ cm^2

$\quad = 630$ Simplify.

The volume is 630 cm^3.

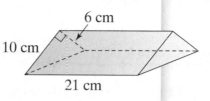

■ TRY THIS

1. Find the volume of the triangular prism at the right.

PART 2 **Finding the Volumes of Cylinders**

You can calculate the volume of a cylinder in much the same way that you calculate the volume of a prism.

Volume of a Cylinder

The volume V of a cylinder is the base area B times the height h.

$$V = Bh$$

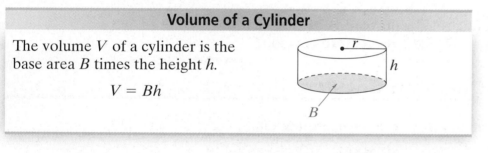

REAL-WORLD CONNECTION

■ EXAMPLE 2

Packaging **Find the volume of the juice can at the right to the nearest cubic centimeter.**

$V = Bh$ Use the formula for volume.

$V = \pi r^2 h$ $B = \pi r^2$.

$\quad \approx 3.14 \cdot 3.4^2 \cdot 12$ Replace π with 3.14, r with 3.4, and h with 12.

$\quad = 435.5808$ Simplify.

The volume is about 436 cm^3.

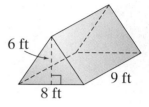

■ TRY THIS

2. Find the volume of the cylinder to the nearest cubic foot.

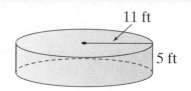

Exercises

Find the volume of each prism or cylinder to the nearest cubic unit.

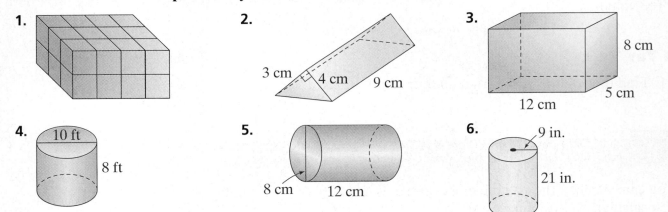

1.

2. 3 cm 4 cm 9 cm

3. 8 cm 12 cm 5 cm

4. 10 ft 8 ft

5. 8 cm 12 cm

6. 9 in. 21 in.

7. Wood for a fireplace is often sold by the cord. A cord is 8 ft by 4 ft by 4 ft. How many cubic feet are in a cord of wood?

Find the volume of each prism or cylinder to the nearest tenth.

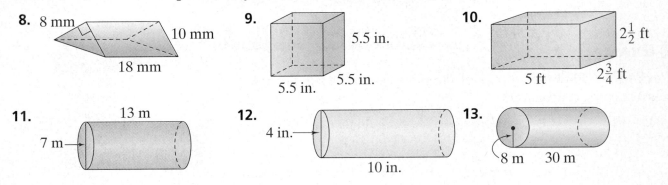

8. 8 mm 10 mm 18 mm

9. 5.5 in. 5.5 in. 5.5 in.

10. $2\frac{1}{2}$ ft 5 ft $2\frac{3}{4}$ ft

11. 13 m 7 m

12. 4 in. 10 in.

13. 8 m 30 m

14. **Open-ended** Name at least one real prism and one real cylinder for which you may need to know the volumes.

15. Concrete is sold by the yard, which means by the cubic yard. It costs $70 per yard. How many cubic feet are in a cubic yard? How much would it cost to pour a slab 14 ft by 16 ft by 6 in. for a patio?

16. A box measures 24 in. by 12 in. by 3 in. Find its volume to the nearest cubic centimeter (1 in. = 2.54 cm).

17. **Error Analysis** A student explains that a cylinder with radius 1 in. and height 3 in. has half the volume of one with radius 2 in. and height 3 in. Explain the student's error.

18. **Manufacturing** Table salt is usually packaged in cylinders.
   a. If a cylindrical box of salt has radius 4 cm and height 13.5 cm, what is its volume? What is its surface area?
   b. Would a rectangular prism 8 cm by 8 cm by 13.5 cm hold more or less salt than the cylindrical box? Explain.
   c. Would the rectangular prism need more or less cardboard to construct than the cylindrical box? Explain.
   d. Which type of box makes the more efficient use of cardboard? Explain.

19. **Critical Thinking** The two stacks of paper in the photo at the right contain the same number of sheets. The first stack forms an oblique prism; the second forms a right prism. The stacks have the same height, base, and volume. Use this information to find the volume of the oblique prism.

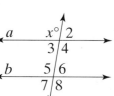

MIXED REVIEW

Find the surface area of each figure, to the nearest square unit. *(Lesson 10-6)*

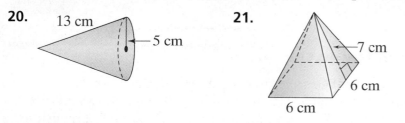

20. 13 cm — 5 cm

21. 7 cm / 6 cm / 6 cm

22. $1\frac{1}{2}$ in. / 5 in.

23. If $a \parallel b$, find the measures of the numbered angles in the figure at the right in terms of x. *(Lesson 9-2)*

24. **Choose a Strategy** Juan has $3.80 in coins in his pocket. He has 6 quarters and 12 dimes. The rest are nickels. How many nickels does he have?

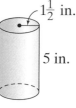

CHAPTER
PROJECT
10 **ACTIVITY 2 CALCULATING**

Measure the heights of the prism and the cylinder you made for Activity 1. Use the heights and your results from Activity 1 to calculate the volume of each figure.

10-8

Make a Model

Math Strategies in Action Architects build and use models when they plan. When they design buildings, they experiment with models. When they design packaging, they first create prototype models.

■ SAMPLE PROBLEM

A box company makes boxes to hold popcorn. Each box is made by cutting the square corners out of a rectangular sheet of cardboard. The rectangle is $8\frac{1}{2}$ in. by 11 in. What are the dimensions of the box that will hold the most popcorn if the square corners have side lengths 1 in., 2 in., 3 in., and 4 in.?

 Read

1. What is the goal of the problem?

2. What information do you have to help you build a model?

 Plan

To find the size that will hold the greatest amount of popcorn, you must find the dimensions that will give you the greatest volume.

Build four boxes using sheets of $8\frac{1}{2}$-in. by 11-in. paper. Test four whole-number lengths of cuts.

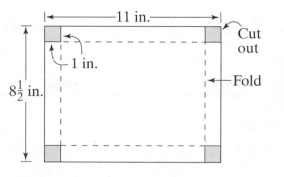

11 in.

Cut out

1 in.

Fold

$8\frac{1}{2}$ in.

3. a. What are the dimensions of the box with corners 1 in. by 1 in.?
   b. What is the volume of this box?

4. When you cut a 2-in. by 2-in. square from each corner, what effect does that have on the length, width, and height of the box?

 **Solve**

Measure to find the dimensions of each of your boxes. Then find the volume of each box.

5. Which box has the greatest volume?

6. Is it possible to create a box that has 5-in. by 5-in. corners? Explain.

 **Look Back**

A table is another way to organize your information and solve the problem. List the size of the cut, and then figure the length, width, and height of the box. Find each volume.

7.

Size of Cut	Length	Width	Height	Volume
1 in.	9 in.	6.5 in.	1 in.	58.5 in.^{3}
2 in.	■	■	■	■
3 in.	■	■	■	■
4 in.	■	■	■	■

Use a table to find the volume of a box if the square corners are $1\frac{1}{2}$ in., $2\frac{1}{2}$ in., or $3\frac{1}{2}$ in.

8. Did you find dimensions of a box that holds a greater volume than you did in Question 5? Which dimensions are they?

Exercises

► CHECK UNDERSTANDING

Explain how to model each situation.

1. You want to find how the length of a pendulum affects the time the pendulum takes to swing back and forth. Explain how you would model the situation.

2. Newspapers, books, and magazines often are printed in groups of 8, 16, or 32 pages, called signatures. The diagram at the right shows how pages should be positioned for an 8-page signature. The pages are positioned to print on both sides of the paper that is fed through the printing press. When the paper is folded, the pages are in order. Make a model to show one way to position the pages in a 16-page book.

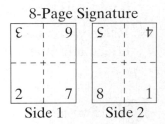

8-Page Signature

Side 1   Side 2

Solve by making a model.

3. *Packaging* A company packages snack mix in cylindrical tubes. Each tube will be made from a rectangle of cardboard. The bases of the cylinder will be plastic. The cardboard comes in $8\frac{1}{2}$-in. by 11-in. sheets. To hold the greatest amount of mix, should the longer side be the height, or should the shorter side? Justify your answer.

► PRACTICE AND PROBLEM SOLVING

Solve using any strategy.

4. You cut square corners off a piece of cardboard with dimensions 16 in. by 20 in. You then fold the cardboard to create a box with no lid. To the nearest inch, what dimensions will give you the greatest volume?

5. **TEST PREP** The figure at the right represents the net of an unfolded box with designs on several panels. Below are three drawings of boxes with designs. Select the box that matches the net.

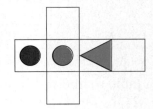

A.   B.   C.

6. A dog owner wants to use 200 ft of fencing to enclose the greatest possible area for his dog. He wants the fenced area to be rectangular. What dimensions should he use?

7. The length of a rectangle is twice its width. The perimeter of the rectangle is 90 cm. What are the length and width?

8. *Volume* The figure at the right shows a 3-by-3-by-3 cube.
   a. How many 1-by-1-by-1 cubes are there?
   b. How many 2-by-2-by-2-cubes are there?
   c. How many 3-by-3-by-3 cubes are there?
   d. How many 3-by-3-by-3 cubes would be in a 5-by-5-by-5 cube?

▶ MIXED REVIEW

Find the volume of each figure, to the nearest tenth. *(Lesson 10-7)*

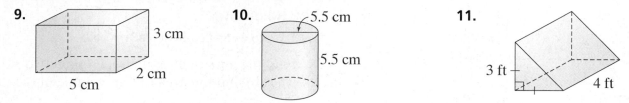

9. 3 cm, 2 cm, 5 cm

10. 5.5 cm, 5.5 cm

11. 3 ft, 4 ft

Find the solutions of each equation when *x* is 0, 1, and −1. *(Lesson 8-2)*

12. $2x - y = 10$ **13.** $5x + y = 15$ **14.** $2x + 3y = 6$

15. The wheels of a racing bike are about 70 cm in diameter. What is the circumference of the wheels? *(Lesson 9-6)*

✓ CHECKPOINT 2   Lessons 10-4 through 10-8

Name each space figure, and find its surface area, to the nearest square unit.

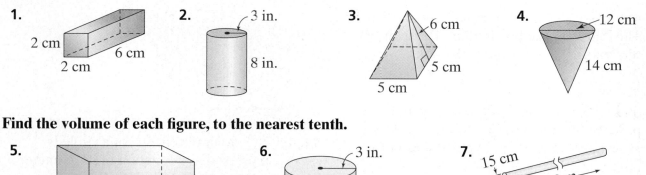

1. 2 cm, 6 cm, 2 cm

2. 3 in., 8 in.

3. 6 cm, 5 cm, 5 cm

4. 12 cm, 14 cm

Find the volume of each figure, to the nearest tenth.

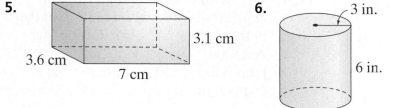

5. 3.1 cm, 3.6 cm, 7 cm

6. 3 in., 6 in.

7. 15 cm, 10 m

8. *Open-ended* Choose a space figure. Draw its net.

Standardized Test Prep

Multiple Choice

Choose the best answer.

1. Find the area of a circle that has a 7-ft diameter. Use 3.14 for π.
   - **A.** 38.465 ft^2
   - **B.** 153.86 ft^2
   - **C.** 76.93 ft^2
   - **D.** 21.98 ft^2

2. What is the area of the trapezoid?

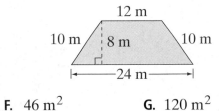

   - **F.** 46 m^2
   - **G.** 120 m^2
   - **H.** 144 m^2
   - **J.** 288 m^2

3. Each edge of a cube is 40 cm long. Find the surface area of the cube in square inches. Use 2.5 cm $\approx$ 1 in.
   - **A.** 3,840 in.^{2}
   - **B.** 9,600 in.^{2}
   - **C.** 256 in.^{2}
   - **D.** 1,536 in.^{2}

4. A cylinder has a height of 10 in. Its base has a radius of 2.5 in. Find the cylinder's surface area. Use 3.14 for π.
   - **F.** 215.875 in.^{2}
   - **G.** 235.5 in.^{2}
   - **H.** 188.4 in.^{2}
   - **J.** 196.25 in.^{2}

5. The volume of a rectangular box is 455 in.^{3} The length of the box is 13 in. The width of the box is 7 in. How tall is the box?
   - **A.** 364 in.^{3}
   - **B.** 5 in.
   - **C.** 6 in.
   - **D.** 5 in.^{3}

6. Shari's recipe calls for 8 oz of dry milk powder. She recalls that 1 oz equals 28.4 g. How many ounces are in a 210-g can of milk powder?
   - **F.** between 5 and 6
   - **G.** between 6 and 7
   - **H.** between 7 and 8
   - **J.** between 8 and 9

7. What is the surface area of the figure at the right?

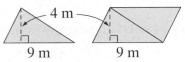

   - **A.** 2,150 in.^{2}
   - **B.** 3,200 in.^{2}
   - **C.** 3,000 in.^{2}
   - **D.** 2,600 in.^{2}

Free Response

For Exercises 8–11, show your work.

8. Find the area of each figure. Explain two ways to find the area of the second figure.

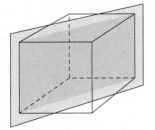

9. If the diameter of a circle is doubled, how are the area and the circumference of the circle affected? Use examples to explain.

10. The cube below shows a rectangular cross section. Copy the cube and draw the following cross-sections.
    - **a.** an equilateral triangle
    - **b.** a square

11. **a.** The circumference C of a circle is expressed as a function of its diameter d in the equation $C = \pi d$. Graph the equation.
    - **b.** Find the slope of the line.
    - **c.** Explain the significance of the slope.

Volume: Pyramids, Cones, and Spheres

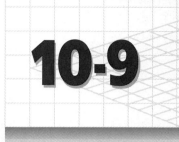

10-9

PART 1 Finding the Volumes of Cones and Pyramids

You can fill three cones with sand and pour the contents into a cylinder with the same height and radius. You will fill the cylinder evenly to the top.

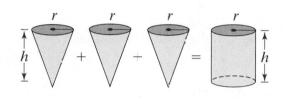

The volume of the cone is one third the volume of the cylinder. The same relationship is true of a pyramid and a prism with the same base and height.

What You'll Learn

1 To find the volumes of pyramids and cones

2 To find the volumes of spheres

... And Why

To find out how much water is displaced by a space figure

Volume of a Cone and of a Pyramid

The formula for volume of a cone or a pyramid is $\frac{1}{3}$ the base area B times the height h.

$$V = \frac{1}{3}Bh$$

■ EXAMPLE 1

Find the volume of the cone at the right.

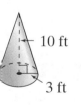

$V = \frac{1}{3}Bh$ Use the formula for volume.

$V = \frac{1}{3}\pi r^2 h$ $B = \pi r^2$.

$\approx \frac{1}{3}(3.14)(3)^2(10)$ Replace π with 3.14, r with 3, and h with 10.

$= 94.2$ Simplify.

The volume of the cone is about 94 ft^3.

10 ft

3 ft

■ TRY THIS

1. Find the volume, to the nearest cubic unit, of a cone with height 5 cm and radius of base 2 cm.

▣ EXAMPLE 2

Find the volume of the square pyramid.

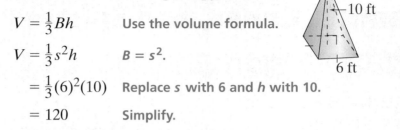

$V = \frac{1}{3}Bh$ **Use the volume formula.**

$V = \frac{1}{3}s^2h$ $B = s^2$.

$\quad = \frac{1}{3}(6)^2(10)$ **Replace s with 6 and h with 10.**

$\quad = 120$ **Simplify.**

The volume of the pyramid is 120 ft^3.

▣ TRY THIS

2. Find the volume of a square pyramid that has a side of 5 ft and a height of 20 ft.

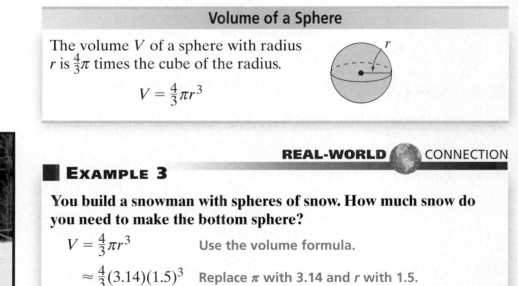

PART 2   **Finding the Volumes of Spheres**

Below is the formula for the volume of a sphere.

Volume of a Sphere

The volume V of a sphere with radius r is $\frac{4}{3}\pi$ times the cube of the radius.

$$V = \frac{4}{3}\pi r^3$$

REAL-WORLD   CONNECTION

▣ EXAMPLE 3

You build a snowman with spheres of snow. How much snow do you need to make the bottom sphere?

$V = \frac{4}{3}\pi r^3$ **Use the volume formula.**

$\quad \approx \frac{4}{3}(3.14)(1.5)^3$ **Replace π with 3.14 and r with 1.5.**

$\quad = 14.13$ **Simplify.**

The volume of the sphere of snow is about 14 ft^3.

▣ TRY THIS   Find the volume of each sphere.

3. radius = 15 m   4. diameter = 7,000 mi

3 ft

Exercises

Find the volume of each figure, to the nearest cubic unit.

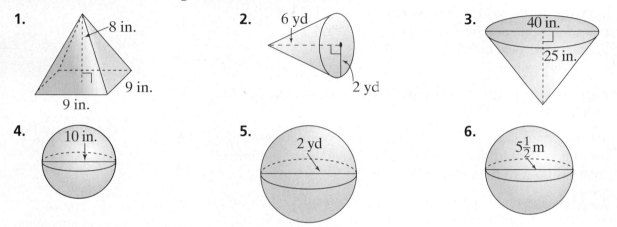

1. 8 in. 9 in. 9 in.

2. 6 yd 2 yd

3. 40 in. 25 in.

4. 10 in.

5. 2 yd

6. $5\frac{1}{2}$ m

7. How many cones of radius 1 m and height 1 m have total volume equal to the volume of a sphere with radius 1 m?

PRACTICE AND PROBLEM SOLVING

Find the volume of each figure, to the nearest cubic unit.

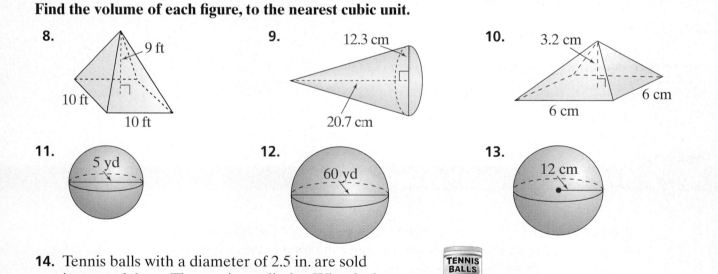

8. 9 ft 10 ft 10 ft

9. 12.3 cm 20.7 cm

10. 3.2 cm 6 cm 6 cm

11. 5 yd

12. 60 yd

13. 12 cm

14. Tennis balls with a diameter of 2.5 in. are sold in cans of three. The can is a cylinder. What is the volume of the space in the can not occupied by tennis balls? Assume the balls touch the can on the sides, top, and bottom.

TENNIS BALLS

15. You want to fill the top part of an hourglass $\frac{2}{3}$ full of salt. The height of the hourglass is 20 cm and the radius of the base is 8 cm. Find the volume of salt needed.

16. *Error Analysis* A student tells a class that if you double the radius of a sphere, the volume will be multiplied by 6. Explain the student's error.

17. The diameter of the world's largest ball of string is 13 ft $2\frac{1}{2}$ in. The string was collected between 1989 and 1991.
   a. What is the surface area?
   b. What is the volume?

18. How much frozen yogurt can you pack inside a cone that is 5 in. high with a radius of 1.25 in.?

19. *Physics* You place a steel ball with diameter 4 cm in a water-filled cylinder that is 5 cm in diameter and 10 cm high. What volume of water will spill out of the cylinder?

20. **TEST PREP** The eight segments from the center of a cube to the four corners of the cube form the edges of six pyramids. If one edge of the cube is 4 in., what is the volume of each pyramid?

   A. 8 in.^{3} **B.** $\frac{32}{3}$ in.^{3} **C.** $\frac{64}{3}$ in.^{3} **D.** 64 in.^{3}

Journal

Explain how you can remember the different formulas for finding volume.

> ## ▶ MIXED REVIEW

Simplify each expression. *(Lesson 5-9)*

21. $(3ab^2)^3$ **22.** $-(4x)^2$ **23.** $\left(-\frac{3}{8}\right)^2$ **24.** $\left(\frac{2x}{y^3}\right)^2$

Solve each equation. *(Lesson 7-5)*

25. $\frac{5}{6}x = \frac{1}{6}x + 12$ **26.** $3a + 10 = 12 - 2a$ **27.** $5y + 2 = 3y + 10$

CHAPTER PROJECT 10 **ACTIVITY 3 COMPARING**

Pour 50 mL of water into a graduated cylinder. Add the cubes of your prism to the graduated cylinder. Measure the total volume. Find the volume of the prism by subtracting the water's volume from the total volume. Compare this volume to the value you found in Activity 2. (Recall that 1 mL equals 1 cm^3.) Express the difference in volumes as a percent of change.

Repeat the steps above for your cylinder.

Use Water Displacement to Find Volume The Activities on pages 532, 541, and 550 will help you complete your project. Here is a checklist to help you gather the different parts.

✔ dimensions of your prism and cylinder

✔ volumes you found by using formulas

✔ volumes you found by using water displacement

Make a table to summarize your measurements and calculations. Write a paragraph in which you compare the values you found by different methods. Explain why the values are not exactly the same. Describe the advantages and disadvantages of each method.

Reflect and Revise

Ask a friend to review your table and your explanations. If necessary, make changes to improve your project.

Web Extension
Visit Prentice Hall's Web site. You'll find some interesting links and ideas related to volume. You'll also be able to share information about your project.
          www.phschool.com

Wrap Up

Key Terms

altitude (p. 505)	cylinder (p. 521)	slant height (p. 533)
altitude of a triangle (p. 509)	lateral area (p. 528)	space figure (p. 521)
area (p. 504)	net (p. 522)	sphere (p. 521)
cone (p. 521)	prism (p. 521)	surface area (p. 527)
cubic unit (p. 538)	pyramid (p. 521)	volume (p. 538)

Graphic Organizer

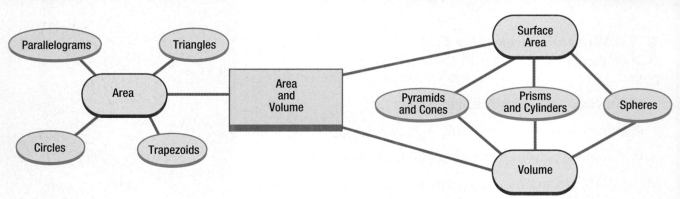

Areas of Parallelograms, Triangles, and Trapezoids

10-1 and 10-2

Summary   The **area** of a polygon is the number of square units enclosed by the polygon. To find the areas of parallelograms, triangles, or trapezoids, use the appropriate formulas.

parallelogram	triangle	trapezoid
$A = bh$	$A = \frac{1}{2}bh$	$A = \frac{1}{2}h(b_1 + b_2)$

Find the area of the shaded region in each figure.

1. Parallelogram   **2.** Trapezoid   **3.**   **4.**

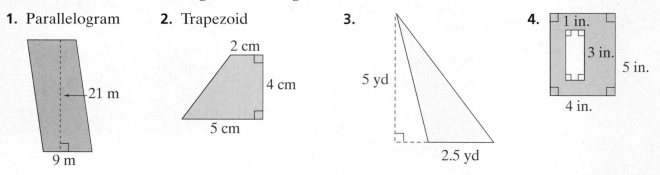

■ *Areas of Circles*

Summary To find the area of a circle, use the formula $A = \pi r^2$. Use 3.14 for π.

Find the area of each figure to the nearest square unit.

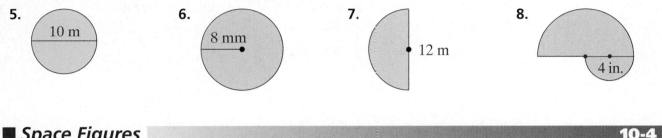

5. 10 m

6. 8 mm

7. 12 m

8. 4 in.

■ *Space Figures*

Summary Name **pyramids** and **prisms** by the shapes of their bases. A **cylinder** is a space figure with two circular bases. **Cones** have one circular base and one vertex. **Nets** are flat patterns for space figures.

Name the space figure represented by each net.

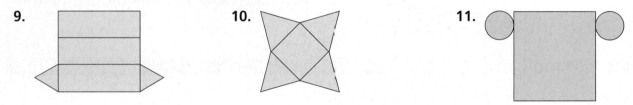

9.

10.

11.

■ *Surface Areas of Prisms and Cylinders*

Summary The **lateral area** of a prism is the sum of the areas of the lateral faces. The lateral area of a cylinder is the area of the curved surface. The **surface area** of a prism or a cylinder is the sum of the lateral area and the areas of the two bases.

To find surface area, use the appropriate formula.

prism
L.A. = ph
S.A. = L.A. + $2B$

cylinder
L.A. = $2\pi rh$
S.A. = L.A. + $2B$

Find the surface area to the nearest square unit.

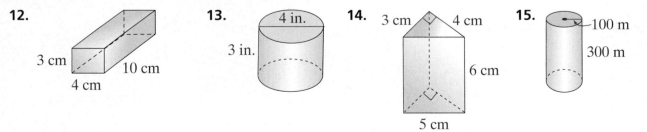

12. 3 cm, 10 cm, 4 cm

13. 4 in., 3 in.

14. 3 cm, 4 cm, 6 cm, 5 cm

15. 100 m, 300 m

■ Surface Areas of Pyramids, Cones, and Spheres

Summary For pyramids and cones, use **slant height** ℓ to find the lateral area. For a regular pyramid, if n is the number of lateral faces, you can find the area of one face, and then multiply by n. The lateral area of a cone is the area of the curved surface. The surface area of a pyramid or a cone is the sum of the lateral area and the base area.

To find surface area, use the appropriate formula.

pyramid
$$\text{L.A.} = n\left(\tfrac{1}{2}b\ell\right)$$
$$\text{S.A.} = \text{L.A.} + B$$

cone
$$\text{L.A.} = \pi r\ell$$
$$\text{S.A.} = \text{L.A.} + B$$

sphere

$$\text{S.A.} = 4\pi r^2$$

Find the surface area of each figure, to the nearest square unit.

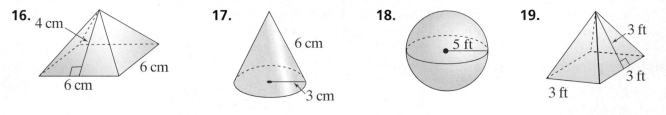

16. 4 cm, 6 cm, 6 cm

17. 6 cm, 3 cm

18. 5 ft

19. 3 ft, 3 ft, 3 ft

■ Make a Model

Summary To solve some problems, make a model.

20. A rectangular sheet of wrapping paper covers a gift box 6 in. by 6 in. by 6 in., without overlapping. What are the least possible dimensions of the sheet?

21. ***Writing*** A 12-m by 15-m rectangular garden has a walk 1 m wide around it. Describe how you would find the area of the walk.

■ Volume

Summary **Volume** is the measure of how much a space figure can hold.

To find volume, use the appropriate formula.

prisms and cylinders
$$V = Bh$$

pyramids and cones
$$V = \tfrac{1}{3}Bh$$

spheres
$$V = \tfrac{4}{3}\pi r^3$$

Find each volume to the nearest cubic unit.

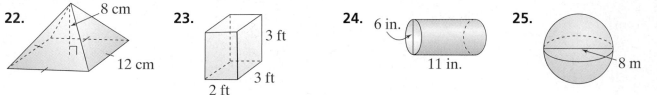

22. 8 cm, 12 cm

23. 3 ft, 2 ft, 3 ft

24. 6 in., 11 in.

25. 8 m

Find the area of each figure.

1.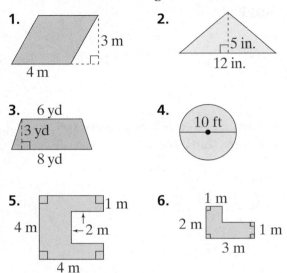
3 m
4 m

2.
5 in.
12 in.

3.
6 yd
3 yd
8 yd

4.
10 ft

5.
1 m
4 m ←2 m
4 m

6.
1 m
2 m 1 m
3 m

Find the missing measures.

7. circle
$d = 4$ cm
$A = \blacksquare$ cm^2

8. triangle
$b = 7$ m
$h = 4$ m
$A = \blacksquare$ m^2

Name the space figure for each net.

9.

10.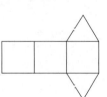

Find the surface area of each figure.

11.
12 m
10 m

12.
2 cm
4 cm

13.
15 m

14.
2.5 cm
1.9 cm

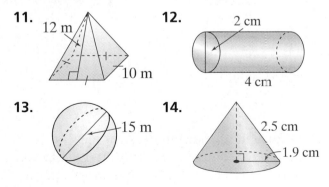

Find the volume of each figure.

15.
500 m

16.
5 ft
4 ft

17.
2 in.
2 in.
4 in.

18.
4 cm
2 cm

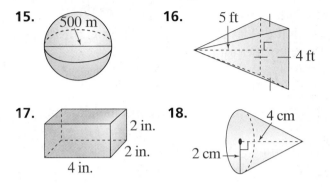

19. The height of a rectangle is doubled while the base is unchanged. How does this affect the area? Explain.

20. In cubic feet, how much greater is the volume of a cone with height 10 ft and radius 6 ft than the volume of a square pyramid with height 10 ft and length of base 6 ft?

21. The diameter of Mars is about 4,000 mi.
   a. Find the surface area.
   b. Find the volume.

22. A box is 25.5 cm by 17 cm by 5 cm.
   a. How much dry dishwashing detergent can it hold?
   b. Without overlap, how much cardboard is needed to make the box ?

23. *Writing* How is the formula for volume of a prism like the formula for volume of a pyramid? How are the formulas different?

24. A rectangular piece of sheet metal measures 26 in. by 20 in. A square measuring 2 in. by 2 in. is cut out of each corner, and the sides are folded to form a box. What is the volume of the box?

25. *Open-ended* Draw a net for a rectangular prism.

Cumulative Review

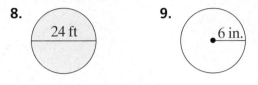

Preparing for Algebra

Choose the best answer.

1. The average nose has about 6,000,000 cells that detect odors. Write this number in scientific notation.
   A. $6 \cdot 10^5$ B. $6 \cdot 10^6$
   C. $6 \cdot 10^7$ D. $6 \cdot 10^8$

2. Which equation represents the statement *The sum of twice a number and five times another number is 40?*
   F. $40 = 2x + 5y$ G. $5y = \frac{40}{2x}$
   H. $2x \cdot 5y = 40$ J. $5y = \frac{1}{2}x + 40$

3. Two angles are supplementary if
   A. the sum of their measures is 180°.
   B. they share a vertex.
   C. the sum of their measures is 90°.
   D. they have the same measure.

4. What space figure can you form from the net below?

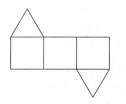

   F. square pyramid   G. triangular pyramid
   H. triangular prism   J. hexagonal prism

5. Figure *A* is a rectangle 10 in. long and 7.5 in. wide. Figure *B* is a parallelogram with height 12 in. and base length 7.5 in. Which statement is true?
   A. area of *A* > area of *B*
   B. area of *A* < area of *B*
   C. area of *A* = area of *B*
   D. Not here

Find the area of each figure.

6.
7.

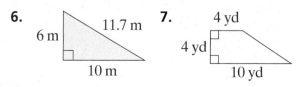

Find the approximate area of each circle to the nearest square unit.

8. 24 ft   9. 6 in.

Find the surface area of each figure to the nearest square unit.

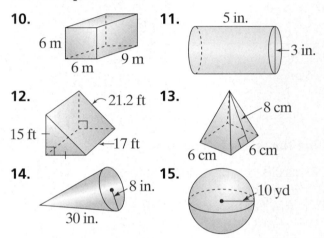

10. 6 m, 6 m, 9 m
11. 5 in., 3 in.
12. 15 ft, 21.2 ft, 17 ft
13. 8 cm, 6 cm, 6 cm
14. 8 in., 30 in.
15. 10 yd

Find the volume of each figure, to the nearest cubic unit.

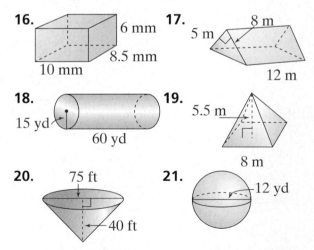

16. 6 mm, 8.5 mm, 10 mm
17. 5 m, 8 m, 12 m
18. 15 yd, 60 yd
19. 5.5 m, 8 m
20. 75 ft, 40 ft
21. 12 yd

22. Draw a net for a cylinder that has diameter 3 cm and height 6 cm. Label and find its surface area, to the nearest square centimeter.

Skills You Need
for Chapter

▶ **Simplifying numbers with exponents**　　　　　　Use before Lesson 11-1.

Simplify each expression.

1. 10^2
2. 6^2
3. 2^2
4. 9^2
5. 11^2

6. 0.2^2
7. 7^2
8. 2.3^2
9. 4^2
10. 5^2

▶ **Understanding coordinates**　　　　　　Use before Lesson 11-3.

Name the point with the given coordinates.

11. $(0, 3)$
12. $(1, -4)$

13. $(-2, 2)$
14. $(-5, -1)$

15. $(3, 5)$
16. $(6, -4)$

17. $(-3, 6)$
18. $(4, 2)$

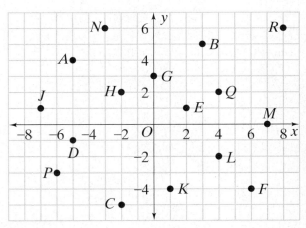

Write the coordinates of each point.

19. A
20. C

21. E
22. M

23. J
24. L

25. R
26. P

▶ **Solving proportions**　　　　　　Use before Lesson 11-4.

Solve each proportion.

27. $\frac{1}{3} = \frac{a}{12}$
28. $\frac{h}{5} = \frac{20}{25}$
29. $\frac{24}{6} = \frac{4}{x}$
30. $\frac{2}{7} = \frac{c}{35}$

31. $\frac{e}{5} = \frac{32}{80}$
32. $\frac{18}{g} = \frac{3}{10}$
33. $\frac{4}{11} = \frac{28}{m}$
34. $\frac{21}{13} = \frac{42}{a}$

35. $\frac{2}{15} = \frac{c}{75}$
36. $\frac{1}{4} = \frac{8}{x}$
37. $\frac{13}{p} = \frac{39}{51}$
38. $\frac{x}{20} = \frac{40}{100}$

39. $\frac{1}{12} = \frac{5}{m}$
40. $\frac{9}{a} = \frac{3}{21}$
41. $\frac{h}{5} = \frac{12}{20}$
42. $\frac{7}{17} = \frac{c}{51}$

Right Triangles in Algebra

What you'll learn in this chapter:

■ How to find the square roots of numbers

■ How to find the missing measures of right triangles

■ How to use the Distance and Midpoint Formulas

Tree Angles

A giant sequoia in California is the largest living thing on earth. It weighs about as much as 15 blue whales. What is the largest tree in your neighborhood? Maybe it is the largest of its species. You could nominate it to be in the National Register of Big Trees.

Measure a Big Tree The National Register of Big Trees has a formula to compare the sizes of trees of the same species: Big Tree Points $= C + H + \frac{S}{4}$, where C is the circumference in inches of the trunk at $4\frac{1}{2}$ feet above the ground, H is the tree's height in feet, and S is the average spread in feet of the tree's crown of branches.

For the chapter project, you will measure a tree and calculate its score in Big Tree Points.

Steps to help you complete the project

Web Extension
www.phschool.com

How to solve a
problem by writing
a proportion

11-1

Square Roots and Irrational Numbers

PART 1 Finding Square Roots

What You'll Learn

1 To find square roots of numbers

2 To classify real numbers

. . . And Why

To use square roots in real-world situations, such as finding the distance to the horizon

Consider the three squares at the right.

Each square has sides with integer length. The area of a square is the *square* of the length of a side. The square of an integer is a **perfect square.**

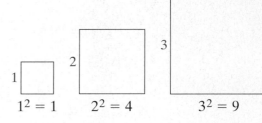

The inverse of squaring a number is finding a **square root.** The symbol $\sqrt{\ }$ indicates the nonnegative square root of a number. Assume that an expression under a radical is greater than or equal to 0.

■ EXAMPLE 1

Simplify each square root.

a. $\sqrt{64}$ **b.** $-\sqrt{121}$

$\sqrt{64} = 8$ $-\sqrt{121} = -11$

■ **TRY THIS** Simplify each square root.

1. $\sqrt{100}$ **2.** $-\sqrt{100}$ **3.** $\sqrt{16}$ **4.** $-\sqrt{16}$

The first thirteen perfect squares are 0, 1, 4, 9, 16, 25, 36, 49, 64, 81, 100, 121, and 144. Memorizing these will help you solve problems efficiently.

For an integer that is not a perfect square, you can estimate a square root. For example, 8 is between the perfect squares 4 and 9.

$\sqrt{8}$ is between $\sqrt{4}$ and $\sqrt{9}$.

Since 8 is closer to 9 than to 4, $\sqrt{8}$ is closer to 3 than to 2. So, $\sqrt{8} \approx 3$.

■ EXAMPLE 2

You can use the formula $d = \sqrt{1.5h}$ to estimate the distance d, in miles, to a horizon line. Here, h is the height, in feet, of the viewer's eyes above the ground. Estimate the distance to the horizon seen by a lifeguard whose eyes are 10 feet above the ground.

$d = \sqrt{1.5h}$	Use the formula.
$d = \sqrt{15}$	Replace h with 10 and multiply.
$\sqrt{9} < \sqrt{15} < \sqrt{16}$	Find perfect squares close to 15.
$\sqrt{16} = 4$	Find the square root of the closest perfect square.

The lifeguard can see about 4 miles to the horizon.

■ **TRY THIS** Estimate to the nearest integer.

5. $\sqrt{27}$ **6.** $-\sqrt{72}$ **7.** $\sqrt{50}$ **8.** $-\sqrt{22}$

PART 2 Classifying Real Numbers

You can express a rational number as the ratio of two integers $\frac{a}{b}$, where b is not zero. A number that *cannot* be expressed as such a ratio is **irrational.** In decimal form, rational numbers either terminate or repeat. Irrational numbers neither terminate nor repeat. If a positive integer is not a perfect square, its square root is irrational.

■ EXAMPLE 3

Identify each number as rational or irrational.

a. $\sqrt{18}$	irrational, because 18 is not a perfect square
b. $\sqrt{121}$	rational, because 121 is a perfect square
c. $-\sqrt{24}$	irrational, because 24 is not a perfect square
d. 432.8	rational, because it is a terminating decimal
e. 0.1212 . . .	rational, because it is a repeating decimal
f. 0.120120012 . . .	irrational, because it neither terminates nor repeats
g. π	irrational, because it cannot be represented as $\frac{a}{b}$, where a and b are integers

■ **TRY THIS** Identify each number as rational or irrational.

9. $\sqrt{2}$ **10.** $-\sqrt{81}$ **11.** 0.53   **12.** $\sqrt{42}$

Exercises

CHECK UNDERSTANDING

Simplify each square root.

1. $\sqrt{4}$
2. $-\sqrt{36}$
3. $\sqrt{64}$
4. $\sqrt{25}$
5. $-\sqrt{49}$

Estimate to the nearest integer.

6. $\sqrt{10}$
7. $-\sqrt{3}$
8. $\sqrt{61}$
9. $\sqrt{17}$
10. $-\sqrt{39}$

Identify each number as rational or irrational.

11. $\sqrt{0}$
12. $4.1010010001\ldots$
13. $\sqrt{87}$
14. $-\sqrt{16}$

15. **Critical Thinking** What number do you get when you square the square root of x?

PRACTICE AND PROBLEM SOLVING

Simplify each square root.

16. $\sqrt{81}$
17. $-\sqrt{9}$
18. $-\sqrt{64}$
19. $\sqrt{144}$
20. $\sqrt{\frac{4}{9}}$

Estimate to the nearest integer.

21. $\sqrt{7}$
22. $\sqrt{2}$
23. $\sqrt{42}$
24. $-\sqrt{80}$
25. $\sqrt{58}$
26. $\sqrt{43}$
27. $-\sqrt{98}$
28. $\sqrt{14}$
29. $-\sqrt{55}$
30. $\sqrt{105}$

Identify each number as rational or irrational.

31. $-0.\overline{3}$
32. $\sqrt{5}$
33. $2{,}222{,}222$
34. $\sqrt{144}$
35. $0.31311\ldots$

36. **Writing** A classmate was absent for today's lesson. Explain to him or her how to estimate $\sqrt{30}$.

37. a. **Patterns** You can create irrational numbers. For example, the number $1.010010001\ldots$ shows a pattern, yet it is irrational. What pattern do you see?
    b. **Open-ended** Name three irrational numbers between 9 and 10.

38. **TEST PREP** The floor of a square room has an area of 256 ft². What is the perimeter of the room?
    A. 16 ft
    B. 56 ft
    C. 64 ft
    D. 68 ft

Algebra Find two integers that make each equation true.

39. $a^2 = 9$ **40.** $b^2 = 25$ **41.** $y^2 = 100$ **42.** $m^2 = \frac{100}{25}$

Algebra Write a simplified expression for each product. Then simplify each expression.

SAMPLE $\sqrt{8} \cdot \sqrt{2} = \sqrt{8 \cdot 2} = \sqrt{16} = 4$

43. $\sqrt{3} \cdot \sqrt{27}$ **44.** $\sqrt{50} \cdot \sqrt{2}$ **45.** $\sqrt{36} \cdot \sqrt{4}$

46. *Geometry* Find the length of a side of a square with an area of 81 cm².

47. *Geometry* The area of a circle is 12 in.². Estimate its radius to the nearest inch.

48. The observation windows at the top of the Washington Monument in Washington, D.C. are 500 ft from the ground. Using the formula $d = \sqrt{1.5h}$, estimate the distance a visitor can see to the horizon from the observation windows.

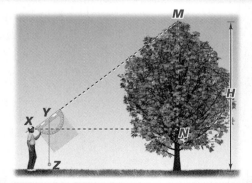

▶ MIXED REVIEW

Find the volume of each figure. *(Lesson 10-9)*

49. sphere with $r = 0.03$ m

50. cone with $r = 4$ cm and $h = 10$ cm

List all the factors of each number. *(Lesson 4-1)*

51. 18   **52.** 22   **53.** 33   **54.** 45   **55.** 50   **56.** 90

57. Shannon scored 17 correct on a 25-item test. The passing grade was 65%. Did Shannon pass? *(Lesson 6-5)*

CHAPTER PROJECT 11

ACTIVITY 1 CREATING

An *inclinometer* is an instrument for measuring angles. You can build one from a piece of cardboard, a drinking straw, a protractor, a piece of string, and a washer. Practice using your inclinometer, reading it at the point where the string crosses the protractor. This reading measures $\angle XYZ$.

11-2

The Pythagorean Theorem

What You'll Learn

1 To use the Pythagorean Theorem

2 To identify right triangles

. . . And Why

To use the Pythagorean Theorem in real-world situations, such as carpentry

Investigate

• EXPLORING RIGHT TRIANGLES •

1. On graph paper, create right triangles with legs a and b. Measure the length of the third side c with another piece of graph paper. Copy and complete the table below.

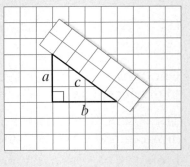

a	b	c	a^2	b^2	c^2
3	4	■	9	16	■
5	12	■	25	144	■
9	12	■	81	144	■

2. Based on your table, use $>$, $<$, or $=$ to complete the following statement.

$$a^2 + b^2 \;■\; c^2$$

Quick *Review*

A right triangle is a triangle with a 90° angle.

PART 1 | **Using the Pythagorean Theorem**

In a right triangle, the two shortest sides are **legs.** The longest side, which is opposite the right angle, is the **hypotenuse.** The Pythagorean Theorem shows how the legs and hypotenuse of a right triangle are related.

Pythagorean Theorem

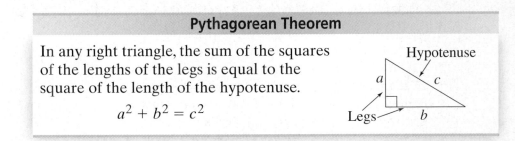

In any right triangle, the sum of the squares of the lengths of the legs is equal to the square of the length of the hypotenuse.

$$a^2 + b^2 = c^2$$

You will prove the Pythagorean Theorem in a future math class. For now, you will use the theorem to find the length of a leg or the length of a hypotenuse.

■ EXAMPLE 1

Find *c*, the length of the hypotenuse, in the triangle at the right.

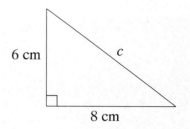

$c^2 = a^2 + b^2$ Use the Pythagorean Theorem.

$c^2 = 6^2 + 8^2$ Replace *a* with 6 and *b* with 8.

$c^2 = 100$ Simplify.

$c = \sqrt{100} = 10$ Find the positive square root of each side.

The length of the hypotenuse is 10 cm.

■ **TRY THIS** The lengths of two sides of a right triangle are given. Find the length of the third side.

3. legs: 3 ft and 4 ft   **4.** leg: 12 m; hypotenuse: 15 m

You can use a calculator or a table of square roots to find approximate values for square roots.

■ EXAMPLE 2

Find the value of *x* in the triangle at the right. Round to the nearest tenth.

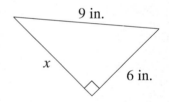

$a^2 + b^2 = c^2$ Use the Pythagorean Theorem.

$6^2 + x^2 = 9^2$ Replace *a* with 6, *b* with *x*, and *c* with 9.

$36 + x^2 = 81$ Simplify.

$x^2 = 45$ Subtract 36 from each side.

$x = \sqrt{45}$ Find the positive square root.

Then, use one of the two methods below to approximate $\sqrt{45}$.

Method 1 Use a calculator.

A calculator value for $\sqrt{45}$ is 6.708203932.

$x \approx 6.7$ Round to the nearest tenth.

Method 2 Use a table of square roots.

Use the table on page 746. Find 45 in the *N* column. Then find the corresponding value in the $\sqrt{N}$ column. It is 6.708.

$x \approx 6.7$ Round to the nearest tenth.

The value of *x* is about 6.7 in.

■ **TRY THIS**

5. In a right triangle the length of the hypotenuse is 15 m and the length of a leg is 8 m. What is the length of the other leg, to the nearest tenth of a meter?

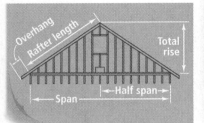

■ EXAMPLE 3

Carpentry **The carpentry terms** *span,* *rise,* **and** *rafter length* **are illustrated in the diagram at the left. A carpenter wants to make a roof that has a span of 24 ft and a rise of 8.5 ft. What should the rafter length be?**

$c^2 = a^2 + b^2$	Use the Pythagorean Theorem.
$c^2 = 12^2 + 8.5^2$	Use half the span, 12 ft. Replace *a* with 12 and *b* with 8.5.
$c^2 = 144 + 72.25$	Square 12 and 8.5.
$c^2 = 216.25$	Add.
$c = \sqrt{216.25}$	Find the positive square root.
$c \approx 14.70544117$	Approximate the square root.

The rafter length should be about 14.7 ft.

■ TRY THIS

6. ***Carpentry*** What is the rise of a roof if the span is 22 feet and the rafter length is 14 feet? Round to the nearest tenth of a foot.

PART 2   Identifying Right Triangles

The *Converse of the Pythagorean Theorem* allows you to substitute the lengths of the sides of a triangle into the equation $a^2 + b^2 = c^2$ to check whether a triangle is a right triangle. It *is* a right triangle if the equation is true. It *is not* a right triangle if the equation is not true.

■ EXAMPLE 4

Is a triangle with sides 12 m, 15 m, and 20 m a right triangle?

$a^2 + b^2 = c^2$	Write the equation for the Pythagorean Theorem.
$12^2 + 15^2 \stackrel{?}{=} 20^2$	Replace *a* and *b* with the shorter lengths and *c* with the longest length.
$144 + 225 \stackrel{?}{=} 400$	Simplify.
$369 \neq 400$	

The triangle is not a right triangle.

■ TRY THIS Can you form a right triangle with the three lengths given? Explain.

7. 7 in., 8 in., 9 in.   8. 5 mm, 6 mm, 10 mm

Exercises

CHECK UNDERSTANDING

Find each square root. Use tables or a calculator. Round to the nearest tenth.

1. $\sqrt{63}$ 2. $\sqrt{12}$ 3. $\sqrt{32}$ 4. $\sqrt{95}$ 5. $\sqrt{51}$ 6. $\sqrt{8}$

Name the legs and the hypotenuse.

7.
8.
9.

Find each missing length to the nearest tenth of a unit.

10.
11.
12.

13. **Mental Math** Is a triangle with side lengths of $\sqrt{12}$ cm, $\sqrt{7}$ cm, and $\sqrt{5}$ cm a right triangle?

PRACTICE AND PROBLEM SOLVING

Find each missing length to the nearest tenth of a unit.

14.
15.
16.

17.
18.
19.

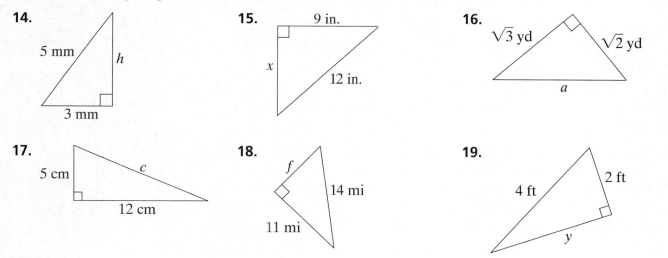

Can you form a right triangle with the three lengths given? Show your work.

20. 4 m, 6 m, 7 m

21. 5 cm, 12 cm, 13 cm

22. 7 in., 24 in., 25 in.

23. 1 ft, 3 ft, $\sqrt{12}$ ft

24. 4 mi, 5 mi, 6 mi

25. 1 m, 0.54 m, 0.56 m

26. 8 in., 10 in., 12 in.

27. $\sqrt{5}$ yd, $\sqrt{3}$ yd, $\sqrt{2}$ yd

28. $3p$ ft, $4p$ ft, $5p$ ft

Use the triangle at the right. Find the missing length to the nearest tenth of a unit.

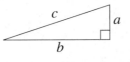

29. $a = 2$ in., $b = 4$ in., $c = $ ■

30. $a = 1.4$ m, $b = 2.8$ m, $c = $ ■

31. $a = 3$ ft, $c = 5$ ft, $b = $ ■

32. $b = 2.7$ km, $c = 3.4$ km, $a = $ ■

Algebra **Find the value of *n* in each diagram. Give your answer as a square root.**

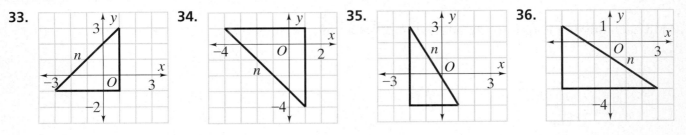

33. **34.** **35.** **36.**

Any three positive integers that make $a^2 + b^2 = c^2$ true form a *Pythagorean triple*. Three sets of Pythagorean triples are given below. For each set, multiply each number by 2. Do the new numbers form a Pythagorean triple? Verify your answer.

37. 3, 4, 5

38. 7, 24, 25

39. 5, 12, 13

In Exercises 40–42, draw a sketch, and then solve.

40. The diagonals for a quilting frame must be the same length to ensure the frame is rectangular. What should the lengths of the diagonals be for a quilting frame 86 in. by 100 in.?

41. An 11-ft ladder is placed against a house by a painter. The base of the ladder is 3 ft from the house. How high on the house does the ladder reach?

42. Jim works for a landscaping company. He must plant and stake a tree. The stakes are 2 ft from the base of the tree and they are connected to wires that attach to the trunk at a height of 5 ft. If there is 6 in. of extra length at the ends of each wire, how long must each wire be, to the nearest tenth of a foot?

43. **Geometry** In the rectangular prism at the right, d_1 is the diagonal of the base of the prism, and d_2 is the *diagonal of the prism*.
   a. Find d_1.
   b. The triangle formed by d_1, d_2, and the side that is 4 in. is a right triangle. Use your answer to part (a) to find d_2.
   c. Find the diagonal of a rectangular prism with dimensions 9 in., 12 in., and 5 in.

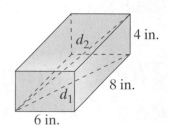

44. **Geometry** A circle has radius 6 in. What is the length of a diagonal of a square that has all four vertices on the circle?

45. **TEST PREP** The lengths of the two legs of a right triangle are in the ratio 3 : 4. The perimeter of the triangle is 60 m. What is the length of the hypotenuse?
   A. 15 m   **B.** 20 m   **C.** 25 m   **D.** 30 m

▶ **MIXED REVIEW**

Identify each number as rational or irrational. *(Lesson 11-1)*

46. $\sqrt{36}$ **47.** $0.\overline{6}$ **48.** $-\sqrt{12}$ **49.** -33.3 **50.** $0.654654\ldots$

Simplify each expression. *(Lesson 5-9)*

51. $(bc)^5$ **52.** $(2x^2)^4$ **53.** $(-3b)^3$ **54.** $(a^5b^2)^4$ **55.** $\left(\frac{3m}{5}\right)^2$

56. Greenland is the world's largest island and has an area of 2,175,600 km². Express this area in scientific notation. *(Lesson 4-9)*

Math at Work
Air Traffic Controller

When we think of airline safety, many of us think of pilots. But there is also a network of people, the air traffic controllers, who work hard to ensure the safe operation of aircraft. Using radar and visual observation, they closely monitor the location of each plane. They coordinate the movement of air traffic to make certain that aircraft stay a safe distance apart. They also coordinate landings and takeoffs to keep delays at a minimum.

In their jobs, air traffic controllers use angle measurements in some of the same ways you do when you solve problems in algebra and geometry.

Internet Connection

For more information about air traffic controllers, visit the Prentice Hall Web site.
www.phschool.com

MATH TOOLBOX

The Pythagorean Theorem and Circles

Follow the steps below to discover a characteristic of chords and their perpendicular bisectors.

Step 1 With a compass, construct a large circle. Label the center O.

Step 2 Draw a chord $\overline{AB}$ that is not a diameter.

Step 3 Construct the perpendicular bisector of the chord with a compass and straightedge or by folding the circle so that A lies on B.

Step 4 Label the point where the perpendicular bisector intersects the chord D.

1. Write a conjecture about the perpendicular bisector of a chord and the center of the circle.

2. Classify $\triangle AOD$ by its angles.

The distance from the center of a circle to a chord is the length of the perpendicular segment with endpoints at the center and on the chord. You can use the radius of a circle and the length of a chord to find the distance from the center of a circle to the chord.

▪ EXAMPLE 1

Circle O has a radius of 10 cm. Chord FG is 12 cm long. How far is $\overline{FG}$ from O?

$MG = 6$ cm. Use the Pythagorean Theorem to find the distance x from the center to the chord.

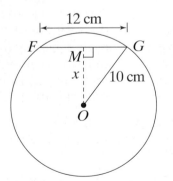

$$10^2 = x^2 + 6^2$$
$$100 = x^2 + 36$$
$$100 - 36 = x^2 + 36 - 36$$
$$64 = x^2$$
$$8 = x$$

The distance from the center to the chord is 8 cm.

Find x, the distance from the center O of each circle to chord $\overline{JK}$. Round to the nearest tenth.

3.

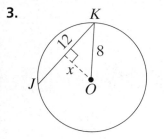

4.

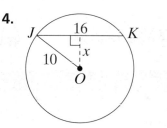

5.

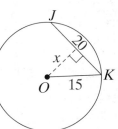

For a given circle, you can also find the length of a chord or the length of the radius if you know two other lengths.

■ EXAMPLE 2

Chord PT is 24 in. long and 5 in. from the center O of the circle. Find the length of the radius.

Use the Pythagorean Theorem to find the radius r.

$PM = \frac{1}{2}(PT) = 12$

$r^2 = 12^2 + 5^2$

$r^2 = 144 + 25$

$r^2 = 169$

$r = 13$

The radius is 13 in.

Find the length of x in each circle O. If your answer is not an integer, round to the nearest tenth.

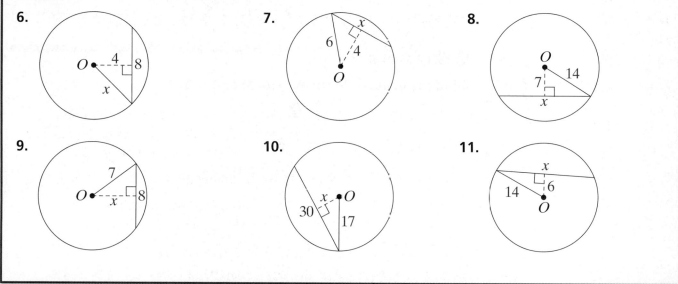

11-3

Distance and Midpoint Formulas

PART 1 **Finding Distance**

What You'll Learn

1 To find the distance between two points using the Distance Formula

2 To find the midpoint of a segment using the Midpoint Formula

... And Why

To find the perimeters of figures on the coordinate plane

In the graph at the right, you can draw a point $C(7, 1)$ to form a right triangle with points $A(2, 1)$ and $B(7, 3)$. Using the Pythagorean Theorem, you can find AB.

$$(AB)^2 = (AC)^2 + (BC)^2$$

$$(AB)^2 = (7 - 2)^2 + (3 - 1)^2$$ *AC* equals the difference in *x*-values.
                                    BC equals the difference in *y*-values.

$$(AB)^2 = 5^2 + 2^2$$ Subtract.

$$AB = \sqrt{25 + 4} = \sqrt{29} \approx 5.4$$ Find the square root.

You can use the Pythagorean Theorem to find the length of a segment on a coordinate plane, or you can use the *Distance Formula*. The Distance Formula is based on the Pythagorean Theorem.

Reading Math

The long square root sign in the Distance Formula indicates that you subtract, square, and add before you take the square root.

Distance Formula
You can find the **distance** d between any two points (x_1, y_1) and (x_2, y_2): $$d = \sqrt{(x_2 - x_1)^2 + (y_2 - y_1)^2}$$

■ EXAMPLE 1

Find the distance between $A(6, 3)$ and $B(1, 9)$.

$$d = \sqrt{(x_2 - x_1)^2 + (y_2 - y_1)^2}$$ Use the Distance Formula.

$$d = \sqrt{(1 - 6)^2 + (9 - 3)^2}$$ Replace (x_2, y_2) with (1, 9) and (x_1, y_1) with (6, 3).

$$d = \sqrt{(-5)^2 + 6^2}$$ Simplify.

$$d = \sqrt{61}$$ Find the exact distance.

$$d \approx 7.8$$ Round to the nearest tenth.

The distance between A and B is about 7.8 units.

■ **TRY THIS** Find the distance between each pair of points. Round to the nearest tenth.

1. $(3, 8), (2, 4)$ **2.** $(10, -3), (1, 0)$

You can also use the Distance Formula to solve geometry problems. Wait until the last step to round your answer.

■ **EXAMPLE 2**

Find the perimeter of $ABCD$.

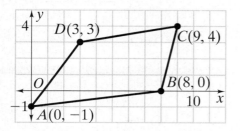

Use the Distance Formula to find the side lengths.

$AB = \sqrt{(8 - 0)^2 + (0 - (-1))^2}$ **Replace (x_2, y_2) with (8, 0) and (x_1, y_1) with (0, −1).**

$\quad = \sqrt{64 + 1} \ = \sqrt{65}$ **Simplify.**

$BC = \sqrt{(9 - 8)^2 + (4 - 0)^2}$ **Replace (x_2, y_2) with (9, 4) and (x_1, y_1) with (8, 0).**

$\quad = \sqrt{1 + 16} \ = \sqrt{17}$ **Simplify.**

$CD = \sqrt{(3 - 9)^2 + (3 - 4)^2}$ **Replace (x_2, y_2) with (3, 3) and (x_1, y_1) with (9, 4).**

$\quad = \sqrt{36 + 1} \ = \sqrt{37}$ **Simplify.**

$DA = \sqrt{(0 - 3)^2 + ((-1) - 3)^2}$ **Replace (x_2, y_2) with (0, −1) and (x_1, y_1) with (3, 3).**

$\quad = \sqrt{9 + 16} \ = \sqrt{25} = 5$ **Simplify.**

perimeter $= \sqrt{65} + \sqrt{17} + \sqrt{37} + 5 \ \approx 23.2681259$

The perimeter is about 23.3 units.

■ **TRY THIS**

3. Find the perimeter of $\triangle DEF$ at the right. Round to the nearest tenth.

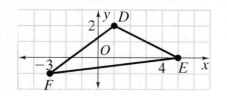

The **midpoint** of a segment $\overline{AB}$ is the point M on $\overline{AB}$ halfway between the endpoints A and B where $AM = MB$.

Midpoint Formula

You can find the midpoint of a line segment with endpoints $A(x_1, y_1)$ and $B(x_2, y_2)$:

$$M\left(\frac{x_1 + x_2}{2}, \frac{y_1 + y_2}{2}\right)$$

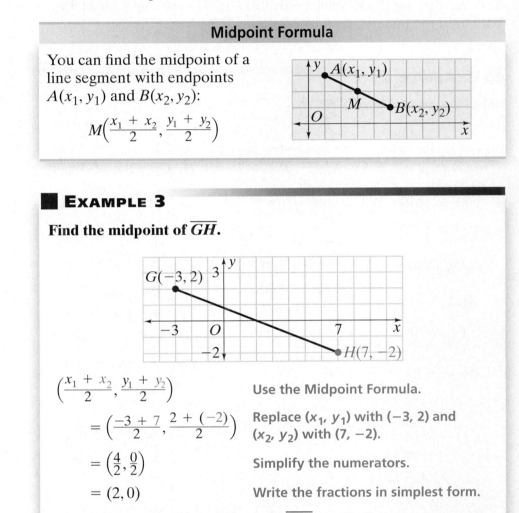

■ EXAMPLE 3

Find the midpoint of $\overline{GH}$.

$$\left(\frac{x_1 + x_2}{2}, \frac{y_1 + y_2}{2}\right)$$ Use the Midpoint Formula.

$$= \left(\frac{-3 + 7}{2}, \frac{2 + (-2)}{2}\right)$$ Replace (x_1, y_1) with $(-3, 2)$ and (x_2, y_2) with $(7, -2)$.

$$= \left(\frac{4}{2}, \frac{0}{2}\right)$$ Simplify the numerators.

$$= (2, 0)$$ Write the fractions in simplest form.

The coordinates of the midpoint of $\overline{GH}$ are $(2, 0)$.

■ TRY THIS Find the midpoint of each segment.

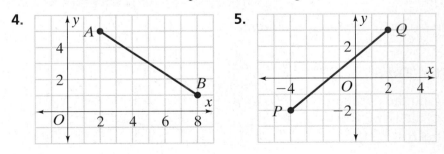

4.

5.

Exercises

Find the distance between each pair of points.

1.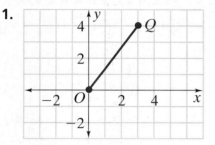

2.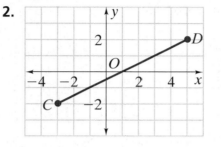

3.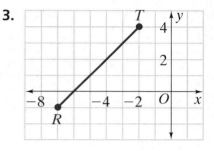

Find the midpoint of each segment with the given endpoints.

4. $P(4, 2)$ and $F(10, 0)$

5. $L(6, -3)$ and $T(1, -7)$

6. $G(-4, 9)$ and $K(-8, 10)$

7. **Critical Thinking** When you use the Distance Formula, does it matter which point you use as (x_2, y_2)? Explain.

PRACTICE AND PROBLEM SOLVING

**Find the distance between each pair of points.
Round to the nearest tenth.**

8. $(1, 5), (5, 2)$

9. $(6, 0), (-6, 5)$

10. $(-5, 10), (11, -7)$

11. $(-6, 12), (-3, -7)$

12. $(8, -1), (-5, 11)$

13. $(12, 3), (-12, 4)$

Find the midpoint of each segment with the given endpoints.

14. $Z(3, 5)$ and $W(5, -3)$

15. $G(-2, 0)$ and $J(7, -8)$

16. $S(9, 12)$ and $U(-9, -12)$

17. $B(10, -8)$ and $E(7, -7)$

18. $K(23, 4)$ and $W(-2, 16)$

19. $D(3.4, 6.5)$ and $P(-2.1, 3)$

Geometry Find the perimeter of each figure.

20.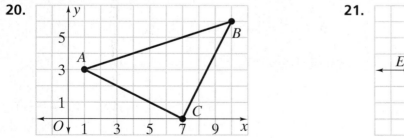

21.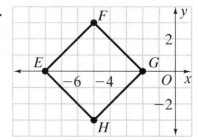

22. Error Analysis A student's
calculation of the midpoint of the
segment with endpoints $A(-4, 2)$
and $B(6, 6)$ is shown at the right.
What mistake did the student make?

$$\left(\frac{6-(-4)}{2}, \frac{6-2}{2}\right)$$
$$= \left(\frac{10}{2}, \frac{4}{2}\right)$$
$$= (5, 2)$$

23. Critical Thinking The midpoint of
$\overline{AB}$ is $(3, 5)$. The coordinates of A are
$(-6, 1)$. What are the coordinates of B?

24. Geometry The three vertices of a triangle have coordinates
$P(-3, 1)$, $Q(2, -5)$, and $R(4, 6)$. Determine whether the triangle
is scalene, isosceles, or equilateral.

25. a. Find the midpoint M of the line segment with endpoints
$A(-3, 5)$ and $B(2, 1)$.
b. Use the distance formula to verify that $AM = MB$.

Journal

Explain how using the midpoint formula is like finding an average.

▶ MIXED REVIEW

Can you form a right triangle with the three lengths given? *(Lesson 11-2)*

26. 8 cm, 15 cm, 17 cm

27. 5 in., 8 in., 5 in.

28. 20 yd, 12 yd, 16 yd

Solve each proportion. *(Lesson 6-2)*

29. $\frac{3}{8} = \frac{a}{24}$

30. $\frac{11}{c} = \frac{66}{72}$

31. $\frac{5}{6} = \frac{n}{15}$

32. $\frac{b}{1.9} = \frac{7}{9.5}$

33. Geometry Draw a net to represent a rectangular box that is
4 in. long, 3 in. wide, and 2 in. high. Label dimensions on the net. *(Lesson 10-4)*

✓ CHECKPOINT 1
Lessons 11-1 through 11-3

Estimate to the nearest integer.

1. $-\sqrt{3}$

2. $\sqrt{14}$

3. $\sqrt{27}$

4. $\sqrt{90}$

5. $-\sqrt{45}$

6. $\sqrt{105}$

**The lengths of two legs of a right triangle are given. Find the length of
the hypotenuse. Round to the nearest tenth of a unit.**

7. 6 ft, 8 ft

8. 8 m, 14 m

9. 7 yd, 24 yd

10. 5 cm, 5 cm

**Find the length of $\overline{AB}$ and the midpoint of $\overline{AB}$. Round the length of
$\overline{AB}$ to the nearest tenth.**

11. $A(0, -2)$ and $B(-6, -9)$

12. $A(8, 11)$ and $B(-5, 2)$

13. $A(-14, 12)$ and $B(-4, -7)$

14. Open-ended Name three irrational numbers between 10 and 20.

See also Extra Practice section.

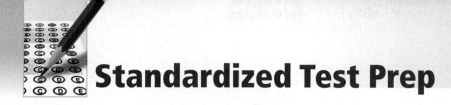

Standardized Test Prep

Multiple Choice

Choose the best answer.

1. Which statement is *false*?

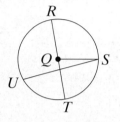

   A. $\overline{QT}$ is a radius of circle Q.
   B. $\overline{SU}$ is a radius of circle Q.
   C. $\overline{SU}$ is a chord of circle Q.
   D. $\overline{RT}$ is a diameter of circle Q.

2. The cost for a one-page advertisement at newspaper A is \$37 plus \$6.60 per week. newspaper B charges a single fee of \$14 per week. Which inequality can help you decide how many weeks an ad must run for newspaper A to be less expensive than newspaper B?
   F. $37 + 6.60x > 14x$
   G. $37 + 6.60x \geq 14x$
   H. $37 + 6.60x \leq 14x$
   J. $37 + 6.60x < 14x$

3. Find x.

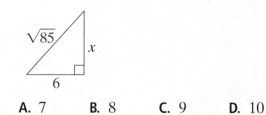

   A. 7   **B.** 8   **C.** 9   **D.** 10

4. A rectangle's length is 60 mm, and its perimeter is 160 mm. What is the area of the rectangle in *square centimeters*?
   F. 12 cm^2 **G.** 30 cm^2
   H. $1{,}200 \text{ cm}^2$ **J.** $3{,}000 \text{ cm}^2$

5. Name the coordinates of the image of polygon $ABCD$ reflected over the y-axis.

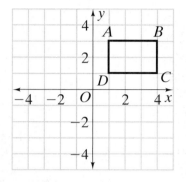

   A. $A'(1, -1), B'(4, -1), C'(4, -3), D'(1, -3)$
   B. $A'(-1, 3), B'(-4, 3), C'(-4, 1), D'(-1, 1)$
   C. $A'(-4, 3), B'(-1, 3), C'(-1, 1), D'(-4, 1)$
   D. $A'(1, -3), B'(4, -3), C'(4, -1), D'(1, -1)$

6. A scale model of a house has a flat rectangular roof 1 foot by 2 feet. Each inch on the model corresponds to 39 inches on the actual house. What is the area of the actual roof?
   F. 468 in.^2 **G.** 936 in.^2
   H. $3{,}042 \text{ ft}^2$ **J.** $36{,}504 \text{ ft}^2$

Free Response

For Exercises 7 and 8, show your work.

7. a. Express the number of centimeters as a function $n(d)$ of the number of meters d.
   b. Graph the function.
   c. Find the slope of the line you graphed.
   d. Explain the significance of the slope.

8. The area of Nevada is greater than the area of Utah by about what percent? Explain your reasoning.

11-4

Read Plan Look Back Solve

Write a Proportion

Problem Solving Strategies

Account for All Possibilities

Draw a Diagram

Look for a Pattern

Make a Model

Make a Table

Simplify a Problem

Simulate a Problem

Solve by Graphing

Try, Test, Revise

Use Multiple Strategies

Work Backward

Write an Equation

Write a Proportion

Math Strategies in Action You can't measure distance across the Grand Canyon with a tape measure. Yet, distances across it have been measured. How were they measured?

Surveyors sometimes find such distances indirectly using similar triangles. You learned about similar figures and proportions in Lesson 6-3. Now let's see how you can use similar right triangles to find measurements indirectly.

■ SAMPLE PROBLEM

To find the distance from Q to P across a canyon, a surveyor picks points R and S such that $\overline{RS}$ is perpendicular to $\overline{RP}$. He locates point T on $\overline{SP}$ such that $\overline{QT}$ is perpendicular to $\overline{RP}$. The two triangles, $\triangle PRS$ and $\triangle PQT$, are similar. He then measures $\overline{RS}$, $\overline{RQ}$, and $\overline{QT}$. What is the distance QP across the canyon?

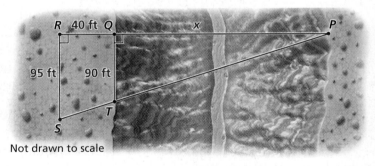

Not drawn to scale

 Read

1. What information is given?

2. What are you asked to find?

Plan

Since $\triangle PQT \sim \triangle PRS$, and you know three lengths, writing and solving a proportion is a good strategy to use. It is helpful to draw the triangles as separate figures.

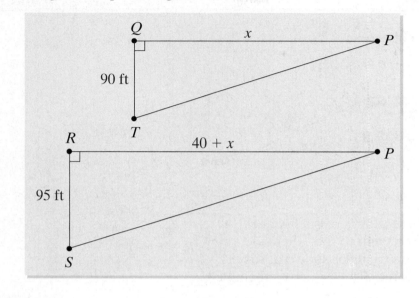

 **Solve**

Write a proportion using the legs of the similar right triangles.

$$\frac{x}{40 + x} = \frac{90}{95} \qquad \text{Write a proportion.}$$

$$95x = 90(40 + x) \qquad \text{Write cross products.}$$

$$95x = 3{,}600 + 90x \qquad \text{Use the Distributive Property.}$$

$$5x = 3{,}600 \qquad \text{Subtract } 90x \text{ from each side.}$$

$$x = 720 \qquad \text{Divide each side by 5.}$$

The distance QP across the canyon is 720 ft.

 **Look Back**

Solving problems that involve indirect measurement often makes use of figures that *overlap*. Use the diagram on page 578 to answer the following questions.

3. Which segments overlap?

4. A common error students make is to use part of a side in a proportion. For example, some students might think $\frac{40}{95}$ is equal to $\frac{x}{90}$. How does drawing the triangles as separate figures help you avoid this error?

Exercises

CHECK UNDERSTANDING

Write a proportion and find the value of each *x*.

1. $\triangle PQT \sim \triangle PRS$

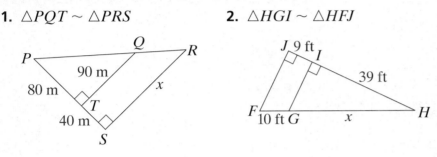

2. $\triangle HGI \sim \triangle HFJ$

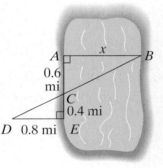

3. A swimmer needs to know the distance *x* across a lake to help her decide whether it is safe to swim to the other side. She estimates the distance using the triangles shown at the right. $\triangle ABC \sim \triangle EDC$. How far is the distance across the lake?

PRACTICE AND PROBLEM SOLVING

Write a proportion, and find the value of each *x*.

4. $\triangle ABE \sim \triangle ACD$

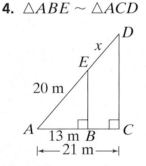

5. $\triangle GHI \sim \triangle KJI$

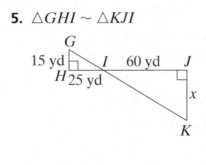

6. To estimate the height of a tree, Milton positions a mirror on the ground so he can see the top of the tree reflected in it. His height, his distance from the mirror, and his line of sight to the mirror determine a triangle. The tree's height, its distance from the mirror, and the distance from the top of the tree to the mirror form a similar triangle. Use the measurements at the right to determine the height of the tree.

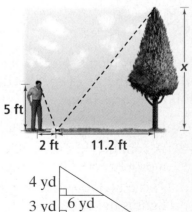

7. A landscaper needs to find the distance *x* across a piece of land. He estimates the distance using the similar triangles at the right. What is the distance?

Solve using any strategy.

8. The height of the Eiffel Tower is 984 ft. A souvenir model of the tower is 6 in. tall. At 5 P.M. in Paris, the shadow of the souvenir model is 8 in. long. The Eiffel Tower and its shadow determine two legs of a right triangle that are similar to the two legs of a right triangle determined by the souvenir model and its shadow. About how long is the shadow of the Eiffel Tower?

9. There are 30 students in a math class. Twelve belong to the computer club, and eight belong to the photography club. Three belong to both clubs. How many belong to neither club?

10. Jake spent $\frac{3}{8}$ of his money on a videotape and $\frac{1}{2}$ of what was left on a cassette tape. He now has $6.25. How much money did he start with?

11. Hai takes 12 minutes to walk to school. He wants to get there 15 minutes early to meet with his lab partner. What time should he leave his house if school starts at 8:10 A.M.?

12. **Number Sense** Christa thought of a number. She added 4, multiplied the sum by -5, and subtracted 12. She then doubled the result and got -34. What number did Christa start with?

13. Madison Square Garden in New York City is built in the shape of a circle. Its diameter is 404 ft and it accommodates 20,234 spectators. To the nearest tenth of a square foot, how much area is there for each spectator?

14. A tennis ball is served from one end of a tennis court, 39 ft from the net. The ball is hit 9 ft above the ground, travels in a straight path down the middle of the court, and just clears the top of the 3-ft net. This is illustrated in the figure at the right. $\triangle PQR \sim \triangle MQS$. How far from the net does the ball land?

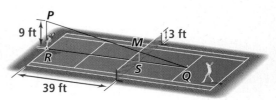

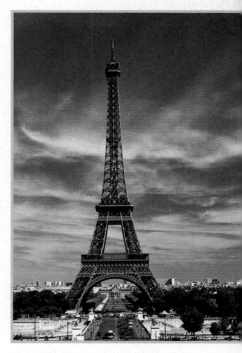

The Eiffel Tower was named for its designer, Gustave Eiffel. He was the same engineer who designed the framework of the Statue of Liberty.

▶ **MIXED REVIEW**

Find the midpoint of each segment with the given endpoints. *(Lesson 11-3)*

15. $A(2, 3)$ and $B(4, 7)$

16. $X(-1, 2)$ and $Y(2, 6)$

17. $L(6, -5)$ and $M(-3, -8)$

Sketch each figure. *(Lesson 9-3)*

18. isosceles right triangle

19. equilateral triangle

20. scalene obtuse triangle

21. Keith collected twice as much money as Lucy for a walkathon. Together they collected $120. How much money did each person collect? *(Lesson 7-4)*

11-5

Special Right Triangles

What You'll Learn

1 To use the relationships in 45°-45°-90° triangles

2 To use the relationships in 30°-60°-90° triangles

...And Why

To find distances in real-world situations, such as in sports

The Pythagorean Theorem requires that you understand square roots. The rule for Multiplying Square Roots will help you work with square roots more efficiently.

Multiplying Square Roots

For nonnegative numbers, the square root of a product equals the product of the square roots.

Arithmetic

$$\sqrt{9 \cdot 2} = \sqrt{9} \cdot \sqrt{2}$$

Algebra

If $a \geq 0$ and $b \geq 0$,

then $\sqrt{ab} = \sqrt{a} \cdot \sqrt{b}$.

The rule for Multiplying Square Roots is especially useful with an isosceles right triangle, which is also known by its angle measures as a 45°-45°-90° triangle.

For the figure at the left, you can use the Pythagorean Theorem to find the length of the hypotenuse.

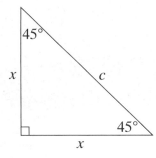

$c^2 = a^2 + b^2$	Use the Pythagorean Theorem.
$c^2 = x^2 + x^2$	Replace a and b with x.
$c^2 = 2x^2$	Simplify.
$c = \sqrt{2x^2}$	Find the square root.
$c = \sqrt{2} \cdot \sqrt{x^2}$	Use the rule for Multiplying Square Roots.
$c = \sqrt{2} \cdot x$, or $x\sqrt{2}$	Simplify.

This shows the special relationship of the hypotenuse and the legs of a 45°-45°-90° triangle.

45°-45°-90° Triangles

In a 45°-45°-90° triangle, the legs are congruent and the length of the hypotenuse is the length of a leg times $\sqrt{2}$.

$$\text{hypotenuse} = \text{leg} \cdot \sqrt{2}$$

■ EXAMPLE 1

Find the length of the hypotenuse in the figure at the right.

$$\text{hypotenuse} = \text{leg} \cdot \sqrt{2}$$

$x = 6 \cdot \sqrt{2}$ **The length of the leg is 6.**

≈ 8.5 **Use a calculator.**

The length of the hypotenuse is about 8.5 in.

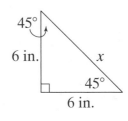

■ TRY THIS

1. The length of the legs of an isosceles right triangle is 4.2 cm.
   Find the length of the hypotenuse. Round to the nearest tenth.

You can use 45°-45°-90° triangles in real-world situations.

REAL-WORLD CONNECTION

■ EXAMPLE 2

A baseball diamond is a square. The distance from any base to the next is 90 ft. How far is it from home plate to second base?

$\text{hypotenuse} = \text{leg} \cdot \sqrt{2}$ **Use the 45°-45°-90° relationship.**

$= 90 \cdot \sqrt{2}$ **The length of the leg is 90.**

≈ 127.28 **Use a calculator.**

The distance from home plate to second base is about 127 ft.

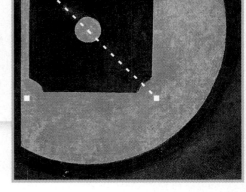

■ TRY THIS

2. Gymnasts use mats that are 12 m by 12 m for floor exercises.
   A gymnast does cartwheels across the diagonal of a mat.
   What is the length of the diagonal to the nearest meter?

PART 2   Using 30°-60°-90° Triangles

Another special right triangle is the 30°-60°-90° triangle. You can
form two congruent 30°-60°-90° triangles by bisecting an angle of
an equilateral triangle. This is shown in the diagram at the right.

In the diagram, the length of the hypotenuse of each 30°-60°-90°
triangle is twice the length of the shorter leg. You can use the
Pythagorean Theorem to find the length of the longer leg.

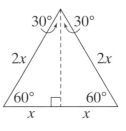

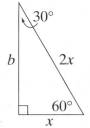

For the figure at the left, find the length of the longer leg.

$$(2x)^2 = x^2 + b^2 \qquad \text{Use the Pythagorean Theorem.}$$
$$4x^2 = x^2 + b^2 \qquad \text{Simplify.}$$
$$3x^2 = b^2 \qquad \text{Subtract } x^2 \text{ from each side.}$$
$$\sqrt{3x^2} = b \qquad \text{Find the square root.}$$
$$\sqrt{3} \cdot \sqrt{x^2} = b \qquad \text{Use the rule for Multiplying Square Roots.}$$
$$b = \sqrt{3} \cdot x, \text{ or } x\sqrt{3} \qquad \text{Simplify.}$$

This shows the special relationship of the hypotenuse and the legs in a 30°-60°-90° triangle.

30°-60°-90° Triangle

In a 30°-60°-90° triangle, the length of the hypotenuse is 2 times the length of the shorter leg. The length of the longer leg is $\sqrt{3}$ times the length of the shorter leg.

$$\text{hypotenuse} = 2 \cdot \text{shorter leg}$$
$$\text{longer leg} = \text{shorter leg} \cdot \sqrt{3}$$

■ EXAMPLE 3

Find the missing lengths in the triangle at the left.

$$\text{hypotenuse} = 2 \cdot \text{shorter leg}$$
$$x = 2 \cdot 5 \qquad \text{The length of the shorter leg is 5.}$$
$$x = 10 \qquad \text{Simplify.}$$
$$\text{longer leg} = \text{shorter leg} \cdot \sqrt{3}$$
$$y = 5 \cdot \sqrt{3} \qquad \text{The length of the shorter leg is 5.}$$
$$y \approx 8.7 \qquad \text{Use a calculator.}$$

The length of the hypotenuse is 10 ft, and the length of the longer leg is about 8.7 ft.

■ **TRY THIS** Find the missing lengths in each 30°-60°-90° triangle.

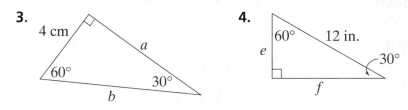

3.

4.

Exercises

CHECK UNDERSTANDING

Tell whether a triangle with sides of the given lengths could be
45°-45°-90° or 30°-60°-90°. Explain.

1. $6, 8, 10$

2. $5, 5, 5\sqrt{2}$

3. $15, 7.5\sqrt{3}, 7.5$

Find the missing lengths.

4.
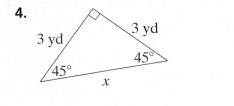

5.
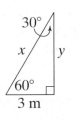

6.
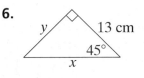

7. *Mathematical Reasoning* The smaller angles of a 30°-60°-90°
triangle are in the ratio $1:2$. Are the shorter sides also in the ratio
$1:2$? Explain.

PRACTICE AND PROBLEM SOLVING

The length of one side of the triangle is given in each row of the table.
Find the missing lengths for that triangle.

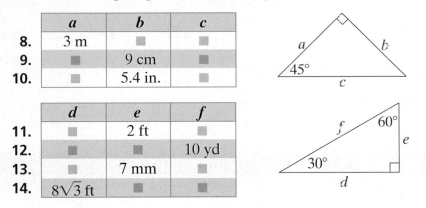

	a	*b*	*c*
8.	3 m	■	■
9.	■	9 cm	■
10.	■	5.4 in.	■

	d	*e*	*f*
11.	■	2 ft	■
12.	■	■	10 yd
13.	■	7 mm	■
14.	$8\sqrt{3}$ ft	■	■

15. *Writing* Explain how to find the lengths of the longer leg and
hypotenuse of a 30°-60°-90° triangle if the shorter leg is 10 ft.

16. *Error Analysis* A student says that a right triangle with a
hypotenuse of length $2\sqrt{2}$ in. has to be an isosceles right
triangle. What mistake might the student have made?

17. Geometry A polygon is inscribed in a circle if all of its vertices lie on the circle. To find the area of the hexagon inscribed in a circle with a diameter of 8 in., answer each of the following.

a. The segments shown form 6 congruent equilateral triangles. What is the length of each side of each triangle?

b. What is the height of one triangle?

c. What is the area of one triangle?

d. What is the area of the hexagon?

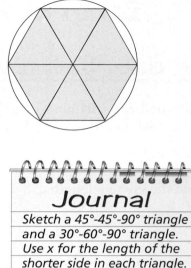

18. Geometry You can inscribe a regular hexagon in a circle using a compass and straightedge.

a. Use your compass to construct a circle. Keep the compass at the same setting. Place the tip of the compass on the circle. Mark an arc on the circle. Place the tip of the compass where the arc intersects the circle and mark another arc. Continue around the circle until you have six arcs on the circle. Join consecutive arcs with segments.

b. Measure the diameter of the circle. Use this measure and Exercise 17 to find the area of your hexagon.

> ## Journal
> Sketch a 45°-45°-90° triangle and a 30°-60°-90° triangle. Use x for the length of the shorter side in each triangle. Explain how to find the lengths of the other sides of each triangle.

▶ MIXED REVIEW

Is each relation a function? Explain. *(Lesson 8-1)*

19. $\{(-1, 3), (0, 4), (1, 5)\}$

20. $\{(2, 3), (3, 4), (4, 5), (5, 6)\}$

Find the circumference of each circle with the given radius or diameter. *(Lesson 9-6)*

21. radius = 4 in.   **22.** diameter = 6 m   **23.** radius = 2.5 ft

24. Surveying A surveyor needs to find the distance across a lake. He estimates the distance using the similar triangles at the right. What is the distance? *(Lesson 11-4)*

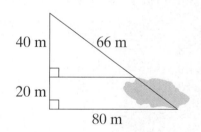

40 m   66 m
20 m
80 m

ACTIVITY 2 MEASURING

Choose a big tree in your neighborhood. Find the following:
- the measure of $\angle XYZ$ as explained in Activity 1 on page 563
- the distance you are from the tree when you measure $\angle XYZ$
- the circumference C, as explained on page 559
- s_1 and s_2, the maximum and minimum spread of the tree (See the diagram at the right.)
- S, the average of s_1 and s_2

MATH TOOLBOX

Square Roots of Expressions with Variables

You can simplify square roots of expressions that contain variables.
Assume that the value of each variable is not negative.

■ EXAMPLE 1

a. **Simplify $\sqrt{25x^2}$.**

$\sqrt{25x^2} = \sqrt{(5x)^2}$ Write $25x^2$ as the square of $5x$.

$= 5x$ Simplify.

b. **Simplify $\sqrt{p^6}$.**

$\sqrt{p^6} = \sqrt{(p^3)^2}$ Use the rule for the Power of a Power.

$= p^3$ Simplify.

Simplify each square root.

1. $\sqrt{49y^2}$
2. $\sqrt{100m^{12}}$
3. $-\sqrt{25x^6}$
4. $\sqrt{a^2b^{10}}$

You can also simplify expressions that have nonsquare factors by
using the rule for Multiplying Square Roots.

■ EXAMPLE 2

a. **Simplify $\sqrt{x^9}$.**

$\sqrt{x^9} = \sqrt{x^8 \cdot x}$ Use the rule for Multiplying Powers with the Same Base.

$= \sqrt{x^8} \cdot \sqrt{x}$ Use the rule for Multiplying Square Roots.

$= x^4\sqrt{x}$ Simplify.

b. **Simplify $\sqrt{48x}$.**

$\sqrt{48x} = \sqrt{16 \cdot 3x}$ Find a perfect square factor.

$= \sqrt{16} \cdot \sqrt{3x}$ Use the rule for Multiplying Square Roots.

$= 4\sqrt{3x}$ Simplify.

Simplify each square root.

5. $\sqrt{a^{12}}$
6. $\sqrt{36x^4}$
7. $\sqrt{81b^8}$
8. $-\sqrt{64a^{16}}$
9. $-\sqrt{x^4y^{12}}$
10. $\sqrt{c^7}$
11. $\sqrt{x^{23}}$
12. $-\sqrt{20m}$
13. $\sqrt{27b^{11}}$
14. $-\sqrt{72a^{19}}$

Sine, Cosine, and Tangent Ratios

What You'll Learn

1 To find trigonometric ratios in right triangles

2 To use trigonometric ratios to solve problems

...And Why

To find lengths that cannot be measured directly

Investigate

· · · · · · · · · · · **EXPLORING RATIOS IN SIMILAR RIGHT TRIANGLES** · · · · · · · · · ·

1. In the diagram at the right, $\triangle PQR \sim \triangle XYZ$. Find the length of the hypotenuse of each triangle.

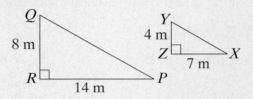

2. In the triangles above, $\angle P$ is the smallest angle of $\triangle PQR$ and $\angle X$ is the smallest angle of $\triangle XYZ$. For each figure, write the following ratios in simplest form.

   a. $\dfrac{\text{length of leg opposite smallest angle}}{\text{length of hypotenuse}}$

   b. $\dfrac{\text{length of leg adjacent to smallest angle}}{\text{length of hypotenuse}}$

   c. $\dfrac{\text{length of leg opposite smallest angle}}{\text{length of leg adjacent to smallest angle}}$

3. What do you notice about each pair of ratios you wrote for Question 2?

PART 1 **Finding Ratios in Right Triangles**

The word **trigonometry** means triangle measure. The ratio of two sides of a right triangle is a **trigonometric ratio.** To write trigonometric ratios, you must identify sides that are opposite and adjacent to the acute angles of a triangle.

Trigonometric Ratios

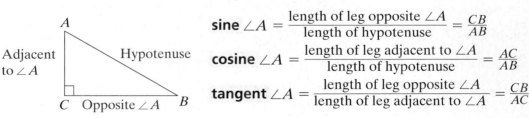

$$\textbf{sine } \angle A = \frac{\text{length of leg opposite } \angle A}{\text{length of hypotenuse}} = \frac{CB}{AB}$$

$$\textbf{cosine } \angle A = \frac{\text{length of leg adjacent to } \angle A}{\text{length of hypotenuse}} = \frac{AC}{AB}$$

$$\textbf{tangent } \angle A = \frac{\text{length of leg opposite } \angle A}{\text{length of leg adjacent to } \angle A} = \frac{CB}{AC}$$

You can use these abbreviations when you find trigonometric ratios for a given acute $\angle N$.

$$\sin N = \frac{\text{opposite}}{\text{hypotenuse}} \qquad \cos N = \frac{\text{adjacent}}{\text{hypotenuse}} \qquad \tan N = \frac{\text{opposite}}{\text{adjacent}}$$

■ EXAMPLE 1

For $\triangle XYZ$, find the sine, cosine, and tangent of $\angle X$.

$$\sin X = \frac{\text{opposite}}{\text{hypotenuse}} = \frac{5}{13}$$

$$\cos X = \frac{\text{adjacent}}{\text{hypotenuse}} = \frac{12}{13}$$

$$\tan X = \frac{\text{opposite}}{\text{adjacent}} = \frac{5}{12}$$

■ TRY THIS

4. For $\triangle XYZ$ in Example 1, find the sine, cosine, and tangent of $\angle Y$.

Trigonometric ratios are usually expressed in decimal form as approximations. If you know the measure of an acute angle of a right triangle, you can use a calculator or a table of trigonometric ratios to find approximate values for the sine, cosine, and tangent of the angle.

■ EXAMPLE 2

Find the trigonometric ratios of 42° using a scientific calculator or the table on page 747. Round to four decimal places.

$\sin 42° \approx 0.6691$ Scientific calculator: Enter 42 and press the key
$\cos 42° \approx 0.7431$ labeled SIN, COS, or TAN.
$\tan 42° \approx 0.9004$ Table: Find 42° in the first column. Look across to find the appropriate ratio.

Graphing Calculator HINT

If you are using a graphing calculator, the trigonometric ratio name is entered before the angle measure. Be sure the calculator is in degree mode.

■ TRY THIS Find each value. Round to four decimal places.

5. $\sin 10°$ **6.** $\cos 75°$ **7.** $\tan 53°$ **8.** $\cos 22°$

PART 2 Using Ratios to Solve Problems

You can use trigonometric ratios to find measures in right triangles indirectly. The advantage to using trigonometric ratios is that you need only an acute angle measure and the length of one side to find the lengths of the other two sides.

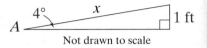

4° x

A 1 ft

Not drawn to scale

EXAMPLE 3

Ramps **The diagram at the left shows a wheelchair ramp for a school. What is the length of the ramp?**

You know the angle and the side opposite the angle. You want to find x, the length of the hypotenuse.

$\sin A = \dfrac{\text{opposite}}{\text{hypotenuse}}$	**Use the sine ratio.**
$\sin 4° = \dfrac{1}{x}$	**Substitute 4° for the angle and 1 for the height.**
$x(\sin 4°) = 1$	**Multiply each side by x.**
$x = \dfrac{1}{\sin 4°}$	**Divide each side by sin 4°.**
$x \approx 14.34$	**Use a calculator. Round to the nearest hundredth.**

The ramp is about 14.34 ft long.

■ TRY THIS

9. What is the length of the longer leg of the ramp in Example 3?

■ Different Ways to Solve a Problem

Ladders **Find x, the height the ladder reaches up the building.**

8 ft x

68°

3 ft

Method 1

Use the Pythagorean theorem.

$$3^2 + x^2 = 8^2$$
$$9 + x^2 = 64$$
$$x^2 = 55$$
$$x = \sqrt{55} \approx 7.4$$

The ladder reaches about 7.4 ft.

Method 2

Use a trigonometric ratio.

$$\sin 68° = \frac{x}{8}$$
$$8(\sin 68°) = x$$
$$7.4 \approx x$$

The ladder reaches about 7.4 ft.

Choose a Method

1. Which method do you prefer to use? Explain.

2. What information is not needed for Method 1? For Method 2?

Exercises

► CHECK UNDERSTANDING

Use △ABC for Exercises 1 and 2.

1. a. What is the length of the leg opposite ∠A?
   b. What is the length of the leg adjacent to ∠A?
   c. What is the length of the hypotenuse of △ABC?

2. Find the sine, cosine, and tangent of ∠A.

Find each value. Round to four decimal places.

3. tan 89°   4. sin 30°   5. cos 14°   6. sin 67°   7. tan 28°

Mental Math Use right triangles to find the ratios. Show your diagrams.

8. tan 45°   9. cos 60°   10. sin 30°

► PRACTICE AND PROBLEM SOLVING

Use △QRS for Exercises 11 and 12.

11. Find the sine, cosine, and tangent of ∠R.

12. Find the sine, cosine, and tangent of ∠S.

Find each value. Round to four decimal places.

13. cos 9°   14. tan 11°   15. sin 56°   16. tan 44°   17. sin 22°   18. cos 19°

19. sin 83°   20. cos 39°   21. tan 60°   22. tan 84°   23. cos 77°   24. sin 2°

25. A hot air balloon climbs continuously along a 30° angle to a height of 5,000 feet. To the nearest tenth of a foot, how far has the balloon traveled to reach 5,000 feet? Draw a sketch, and then solve.

26. *Writing* Tom says the missing length in the triangle at the right can be found using the tangent ratio. Jed says it can be found using the sine ratio. Who is correct? Explain.

27. *Mathematical Reasoning* Find the sine of an acute angle and the cosine of its complement. Do this for several angles. Make a conjecture based on your results.

Math in the Media **Use the article below for Exercises 28 and 29.**

The Tilting Tower

Building began on the bell tower at Pisa, Italy, in 1173. Shortly after that, the tower began to lean and has continued to lean even more over the centuries. In 1993, the tower had a tilt that was 5.5° from the vertical.

In the spring of 1999, engineering experts began to remove soil at the base to correct some of the lean. The team hopes to reduce the lean by about a tenth, which would stabilize the tower for the next 300 years.

28. From base to top, the height of the tower is about 55.9 m. About how many meters from the vertical was the top in 1993?

29. Determine how many meters the top will be from the vertical when the tilt is reduced by a tenth.

▶ MIXED REVIEW

Find the missing lengths. *(Lesson 11-5)*

30.
a
$45°$
4 m   4 m

31.
y 7 ft
$30°$

32.
x
13 in.
$60°$

Find the solutions of each equation for $x = -1, 0,$ and 3. *(Lesson 8-2)*

33. $y = 2x - 4$

34. $y = -3x + 2$

35. $x + y = 20$

36. $6x - 2y = 12$

37. *Geometry* $\overleftrightarrow{GT}$ is the perpendicular bisector of $\overline{RA}$ at point E. Name two congruent segments. *(Lesson 9-7)*

✔ CHECKPOINT 2   Lessons 11-4 through 11-6

Tell whether a triangle with sides of the given lengths is 45°-45°-90°, 30°-60°-90°, or neither.

1. $8, 8, 8\sqrt{2}$

2. $1, 2, \sqrt{3}$

3. $12\sqrt{3}, 12, 24$

Find each value. Round to four decimal places.

4. $\cos 61°$

5. $\tan 30°$

6. $\sin 32°$

7. $\sin 87°$

8. **TEST PREP** A wire from a radio tower is supported by a 23-ft brace. How high is the radio tower?
A. 46 ft   **B.** 69 ft   **C.** 83 ft   **D.** 176 ft

Brace
←— 90 ft —→ |45 ft|

MATH TOOLBOX

Finding the Angles of a Right Triangle

You can use a calculator or a trigonometric ratio table to find the degree measure of an acute angle of a right triangle if two sides of the triangle are known. If you are using a graphing calculator, be sure you are in degree mode.

■ EXAMPLE

You have a map charting a ship's course. The ship is traveling from the port along the course shown. What is the angle from due north of the ship's course?

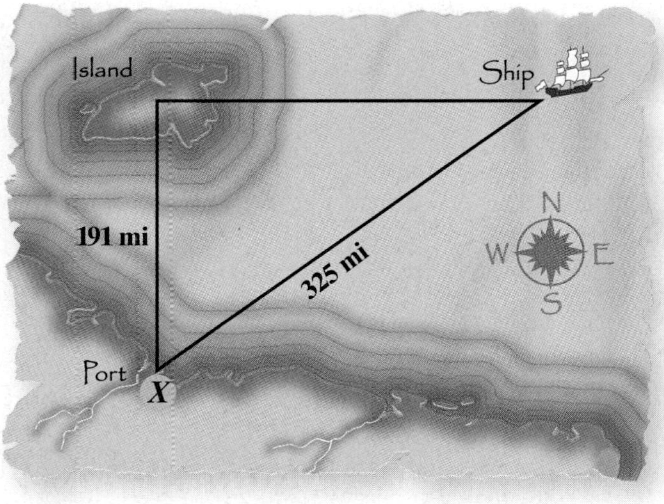

The angle formed by due north, the port, and the ship is the angle at which the ship is traveling. This is angle X.

$$\cos X = \frac{191}{325}$$

To find $m\angle X$ with a calculator:

Press 191 [÷] 325 [=] [2nd] [COS].

$m\angle X \approx 54°$

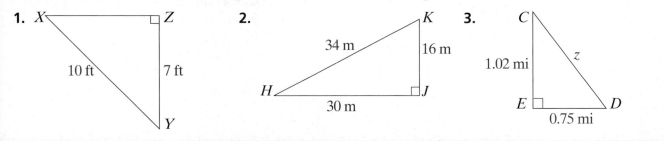

To find $m\angle X$ using the table of trigonometric ratios on p. 747:

$\cos X = \frac{191}{325} \approx 0.587692308$ Divide.

$m\angle X \approx 54°$ In the cosine column, find the decimal closest to 0.5877, which is 0.5878. Read the angle measure across from 0.5878.

The ship is traveling at a 54° angle from due north.

Find the measure of each acute angle. Round to the nearest degree.

1. Triangle with right angle at Z, X at top left, Y at bottom. XZ labeled 10 ft, ZY labeled 7 ft.

2. Triangle HJK with right angle at J. HK labeled 34 m, KJ labeled 16 m, HJ labeled 30 m.

3. Triangle CED with right angle at E. CE labeled 1.02 mi, CD labeled z, ED labeled 0.75 mi.

11-7

Angles of Elevation and Depression

What You'll Learn

1 To use trigonometry for finding angles of elevation

2 To use trigonometry for finding angles of depression

...And Why

To solve real-world problems in subjects such as surveying and navigation

Civil engineers and navigators use the terms *angle of elevation* and *angle of depression* to describe the angles at which they observe things. An **angle of elevation** is formed by a horizontal line and a line of sight above it. It is used when you must look up at an object.

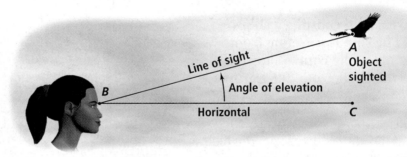

∠*ABC* is an angle of elevation.

REAL-WORLD CONNECTION

◼ EXAMPLE 1

Marcus is flying a kite. He lets out 40 yd of string and anchors it to the ground. He determines that the angle of elevation of the kite is 52°. What is the height *x* of the kite from the ground?

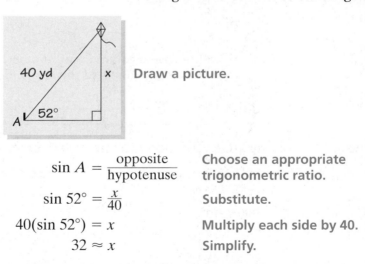

Draw a picture.

$$\sin A = \frac{\text{opposite}}{\text{hypotenuse}} \qquad \text{Choose an appropriate trigonometric ratio.}$$

$$\sin 52° = \frac{x}{40} \qquad \text{Substitute.}$$

$$40(\sin 52°) = x \qquad \text{Multiply each side by 40.}$$

$$32 \approx x \qquad \text{Simplify.}$$

The kite is about 32 yd from the ground.

1. The angle of elevation from a ship to the top of a lighthouse is 12°. The lighthouse is known to be 30 m tall. How far is the ship from the base of the lighthouse?

In real life, a person's line of sight is parallel to the ground at eye height. In some problems you must account for this.

REAL-WORLD CONNECTION

■ **EXAMPLE 2**

Felicia wants to determine the height of a tree. From her position 20 ft from the base of the tree, she sees the top of the tree at an angle of elevation of 73°. Felicia's eyes are 5 ft from the ground. How tall is the tree, to the nearest foot?

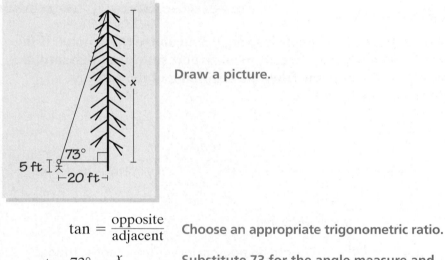

Draw a picture.

$$\tan = \frac{\text{opposite}}{\text{adjacent}}$$ Choose an appropriate trigonometric ratio.

$$\tan 73° = \frac{x}{20}$$ Substitute 73 for the angle measure and 20 for the adjacent side.

$$20(\tan 73°) = x$$ Multiply each side by 20.

$$65 \approx x$$ Use a calculator or a table.

$$65 + 5 = 70$$ Add 5 to account for the height of Felicia's eyes from the ground.

The tree is about 70 ft tall.

■ **TRY THIS**

2. A rock climber looks at the top of a vertical rock wall at an angle of elevation of 74°. He is standing 4.2 m from the base of the wall and his eyes are 1.5 m from the ground. How high is the wall, to the nearest tenth of a meter?

Angles of Depression

An **angle of depression** is formed by a horizontal line and a line of sight below it. It is used when you must look down at an object.

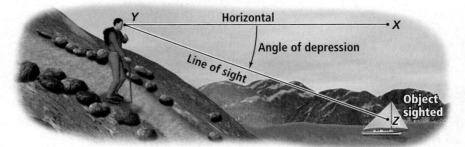

$\angle XYZ$ is an angle of depression.

REAL-WORLD CONNECTION

■ **EXAMPLE 3**

Navigation **An airplane is flying 0.5 mi above the ground. If the pilot must begin a 3° descent to an airport runway at that altitude, how far is the airplane from the beginning of the runway (in ground distance)?**

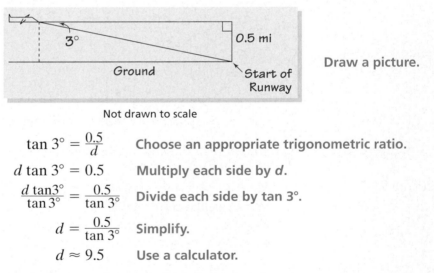

Draw a picture.

$\tan 3° = \dfrac{0.5}{d}$ Choose an appropriate trigonometric ratio.

$d \tan 3° = 0.5$ Multiply each side by d.

$\dfrac{d \tan 3°}{\tan 3°} = \dfrac{0.5}{\tan 3°}$ Divide each side by tan 3°.

$d = \dfrac{0.5}{\tan 3°}$ Simplify.

$d \approx 9.5$ Use a calculator.

The airplane is about 9.5 mi from the airport.

■ **TRY THIS**

3. A group of people in a hang-gliding class are standing on top of a cliff 70 m high. They spot a hang glider landing on the beach below them. The angle of depression from the top of the cliff to the hang glider is 72°. How far is the hang glider from the base of the cliff?

Exercises

CHECK UNDERSTANDING

Name the acute angles of elevation and depression in each figure.

1.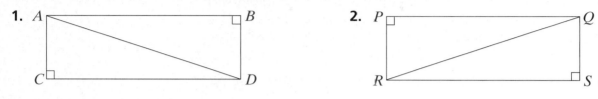

2.

Find x to the nearest tenth.

3.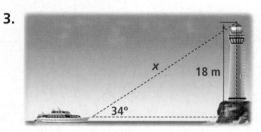

4.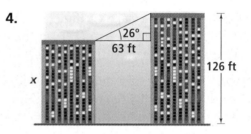

5. *Error Analysis* The drawing at the right was drawn by a student to solve an angle of depression problem. What mistake has the student made?

PRACTICE AND PROBLEM SOLVING

Find x to the nearest tenth.

6.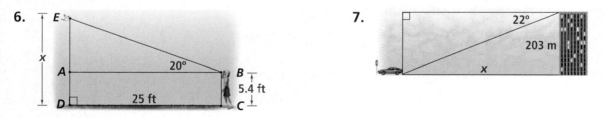

7.

Solve. If the answer is not a whole number, round to the nearest tenth.

8. *Navigation* The angle of elevation from a ship to the top of a lighthouse is 4°. If the top of the lighthouse is known to be 50 m above sea level, how far is the ship from the lighthouse?

9. *Meteorology* A meteorologist measures the angle of elevation of a weather balloon as 53°. A radio signal from the balloon indicates that it is 1,620 m from the meteorologist's location. How high above ground is the weather balloon?

10. **Astronomy** The figure at the right illustrates a method for determining depths of moon craters from observations on Earth. Astronomers calculate that the distance from R to H is 3 km when the angle of depression of the sun's rays is 12°. How high is the rim of the moon crater from the floor of the crater?

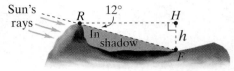

11. From an aerial photograph, rangers determine that a canyon is 9 km wide. From one rim of the canyon, the angle of depression to the floor of the canyon at the other rim is 20°. How deep is the canyon? Draw a sketch, and then solve.

12. **Writing** How do you decide which trigonometric ratio to use to solve a problem?

13. A rare bird is spotted in a tree by a bird watching group. The group is 9.5 yd from the base of the tree. The angle of elevation to the bird is 57°. How far is the bird from the group along the line of sight? Draw a sketch, and then solve.

14. **Navigation** The pilot of a helicopter at an altitude of 6,000 ft sees a second helicopter at an angle of depression of 43°. The altitude of the second helicopter is 4,000 ft. What is the distance from the first helicopter to the second along the line of sight?

▶ MIXED REVIEW

Find each value. Round to four decimal places. *(Lesson 11-6)*

15. $\tan 29°$ 16. $\sin 80°$ 17. $\cos 34°$ 18. $\sin 76°$ 19. $\tan 68°$

Find the area of each circle. Give an exact area and an approximate area to the nearest tenth. *(Lesson 10-3)*

20. $r = 8$ in.   21. $r = 1.9$ cm   22. $r = 10$ mm   23. $r = 4.5$ in.

24. A recipe that serves four people calls for $1\frac{1}{2}$ c of flour. How many cups of flour are needed to make enough to serve ten people? *(Lesson 6-2)*

CHAPTER PROJECT 11   **ACTIVITY 3 CALCULATING**

Refer to the diagram for Activity 1 on page 563. Use your measurement of $\angle XYZ$ from Activity 2 to find the angle of elevation. Then calculate H. Use your values for C, H, and S to find your tree's score in Big Tree Points using the formula on page 559.

Tree Angles

Measure a Big Tree The Project Activities on pages 563, 586, and 598 will help you complete your project. Here is a checklist to help you gather the different parts.

✔ your inclinometer

✔ your measurements for $\angle XYZ$, C, and S

✔ your calculation of H and of your tree's score in Big Tree Points

Create a display. Include your inclinometer, your calculations, and a diagram of your tree with its measurements. If possible, find out the species of your tree. Compare your tree's score to the scores of other trees of the same species, which are available at the Web address given below.

Reflect and Revise

Ask a friend or someone at home to review your display. Are your diagrams and calculations accurate and clear? If necessary, make changes to improve them.

Web Extension

Visit Prentice Hall's Web site. You'll find some interesting links and ideas related to angles and Big Trees. You'll also be able to share information about your project.
www.phschool.com

11 Wrap Up

Key Terms

angle of elevation (p. 594)
angle of depression (p. 596)
cosine (p. 588)
distance (p. 572)
hypotenuse (p. 564)

irrational number (p. 561)
legs (p. 564)
midpoint (p. 574)
perfect square (p. 560)
sine (p. 588)

square root (p. 560)
tangent (p. 588)
trigonometry (p. 588)
trigonometric ratio (p. 588)

Graphic Organizer

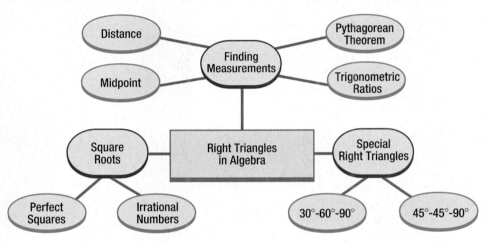

Square Roots and Irrational Numbers

11-1

Summary The square of an integer is a **perfect square.** The inverse of squaring a number is finding a **square root.** The symbol $\sqrt{}$ indicates the positive square root of a number. A number that cannot be expressed as the ratio of two integers $\frac{a}{b}$, where b is not zero, is **irrational.** If a positive integer is not a perfect square, its square root is irrational.

Simplify each square root.

1. $\sqrt{1}$ 2. $-\sqrt{16}$ 3. $\sqrt{49}$ 4. $\sqrt{64}$ 5. $-\sqrt{36}$

Estimate to the nearest integer.

6. $\sqrt{5}$ 7. $\sqrt{11}$ 8. $\sqrt{33}$ 9. $\sqrt{62}$ 10. $\sqrt{91}$

Identify each number as rational or irrational.

11. 0.55 12. $\sqrt{64}$ 13. $0.\overline{45}$ 14. $\sqrt{15}$ 15. $0.123123\ldots$

16. *Writing* Explain why 0.12122122212222 . . . is an irrational number.

■ *The Pythagorean Theorem* 11-2

Summary In a right triangle, the two shortest sides are the **legs.** The longest side, which is opposite the right angle, is the **hypotenuse.** The Pythagorean Theorem states that in any right triangle the sum of the squares of the lengths of the legs is equal to the square of the length of the hypotenuse ($a^2 + b^2 = c^2$).

Can you form a right triangle with the three lengths given? Show your work.

17. 1 mi, 3 mi, 3 mi   **18.** 9 yd, 12 yd, 15 yd   **19.** $\sqrt{6}$ ft, $\sqrt{10}$ ft, 4 ft   **20.** 30 m, 40 m, 50 m

■ *Distance and Midpoint Formulas* 11-3

Summary The Distance Formula states that the **distance** d between any two points (x_1, y_1) and (x_2, y_2) is $d = \sqrt{(x_2 - x_1)^2 + (y_2 - y_1)^2}$. The Midpoint Formula states that the **midpoint** of a line segment with endpoints $A(x_1, y_1)$ and $B(x_2, y_2)$ is $\left(\frac{x_1 + x_2}{2}, \frac{y_1 + y_2}{2}\right)$.

Find the distance between each pair of points. Round to the nearest tenth.

21. $(3, 0), (0, 2)$ **22.** $(-1, 7), (3, 10)$ **23.** $(4, -5), (-8, -1)$

24. $(-10, -12), (-8, -11)$ **25.** $(2, -14), (9, -20)$ **26.** $(10, 4), (-2, -2)$

Find the midpoint of each segment with the given endpoints.

27. $H(0, 1)$ and $J(4, 7)$ **28.** $K(2, 6)$ and $L(4, 2)$ **29.** $M(-7, 8)$ and $P(3, -4)$

30. $A(4, 9)$ and $B(5, 11)$ **31.** $X(-15, -12)$ and $Y(-9, -4)$ **32.** $D(20, 18)$ and $E(-15, -19)$

■ *Write a Proportion* 11-4

Summary You can write a proportion to solve indirect measurement problems using similar triangles.

33. *Engineering* An engineer needs to know what length to plan for a bridge across a river. She estimates the distance using the similar triangles $\triangle ABC$ and $\triangle DEC$ in the figure at the right. What is the distance across the river?

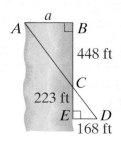

Summary In a 45°-45°-90° triangle, the length of the hypotenuse is the length of a leg times $\sqrt{2}$.

In a 30°-60°-90° triangle, the length of the hypotenuse is 2 times the length of the shorter leg and the length of the longer leg is $\sqrt{3}$ times the length of the shorter leg.

Find the values of the variables.

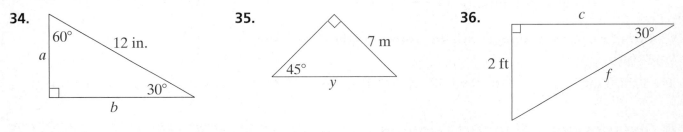

34. 60° 12 in. a 30° b

35. 7 m 45° y

36. c 30° 2 ft f

■ **Using Trigonometric Ratios**
                                                    11-6 and 11-7

Summary The ratios of the lengths of two sides of a right triangle are **trigonometric ratios.** Three trigonometric ratios are **sine, cosine,** and **tangent.** You can use these abbreviations when you find trigonometric ratios for a given acute $\angle N$.

$$\sin N = \frac{\text{opposite}}{\text{hypotenuse}} \qquad \cos N = \frac{\text{adjacent}}{\text{hypotenuse}} \qquad \tan N = \frac{\text{opposite}}{\text{adjacent}}$$

An **angle of elevation** is formed by a horizontal line and a line of sight above it. An **angle of depression** is formed by a horizontal line and a line of sight below it.

Find each value. Round to four decimal places.

37. $\sin 16°$ **38.** $\tan 82°$ **39.** $\cos 25°$ **40.** $\tan 3°$ **41.** $\sin 87°$

42. $\cos 73°$ **43.** $\cos 46°$ **44.** $\tan 45°$ **45.** $\sin 79°$ **46.** $\tan 13°$

Solve each problem. Round to the nearest unit.

47. A loading ramp forms a 28° angle with the ground. If the base of the ramp is 15 ft long, how high does the ramp reach?

48. Melanie is flying a kite and lets out 100 ft of string. Rosa determines that from Melanie's hands the angle of elevation of the kite is 71°. Melanie's hands are 4.3 ft from the ground. What is the height of the kite?

Assessment

Simplify each square root.

1. $\sqrt{25}$ **2.** $-\sqrt{81}$ **3.** $\sqrt{100}$

4. $-\sqrt{4}$ **5.** $\sqrt{16}$ **6.** $\sqrt{49}$

Estimate to the nearest integer.

7. $\sqrt{6}$ **8.** $\sqrt{12}$ **9.** $\sqrt{45}$

10. $\sqrt{78}$ **11.** $\sqrt{85}$ **12.** $\sqrt{118}$

Identify each number as rational or irrational.

13. $0.999\ldots$ **14.** $\sqrt{24}$

15. $\sqrt{100}$ **16.** $420,420$

Find each missing length to the nearest tenth of a unit.

17.
18.

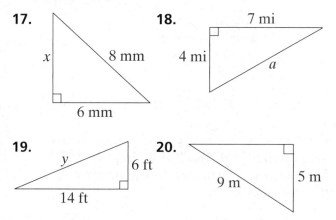

19.
20.

Find the distance between each pair of points. Round to the nearest tenth.

21. $(0,0), (4,6)$ **22.** $(5,-3), (-6,2)$

23. $(-8,-9), (1,2)$ **24.** $(-1,-3), (-4,-7)$

Find the midpoint of each segment with the given endpoints.

25. $C(5,0)$ and $D(3,6)$

26. $M(9,-4)$ and $P(2,8)$

27. To estimate the height of a tree, Joan positions a mirror on the ground so she can see the top of the tree reflected in it. Joan's height, her distance from the mirror, and her line of sight to the mirror determine a triangle. The tree's height, its distance from the mirror, and the distance from the top of the tree to the mirror determine a similar triangle. Use the measurements below to find the height of the tree.

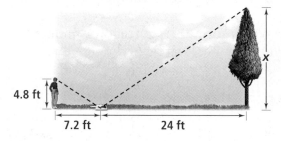

Find the missing lengths.

28.
29.

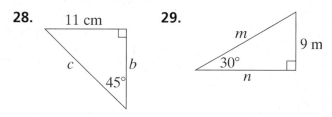

Find each value. Round to four decimal places.

30. $\sin 47°$ **31.** $\tan 75°$ **32.** $\cos 86°$

33. $\tan 29°$ **34.** $\cos 60°$ **35.** $\sin 67°$

36. *Writing* Explain how a trigonometric ratio can be used to find a measurement indirectly.

37. *Navigation* The captain of a ship sights the top of a lighthouse at an angle of elevation of 12°. The captain knows that the top of the lighthouse is 24 m above sea level. What is the distance from the ship to the lighthouse?

Choose the best answer.

1. What is the best description of the figure?

2 ft   2 ft

  A. obtuse equilateral triangle
  B. acute equilateral triangle
  C. obtuse isosceles triangle
  D. acute isosceles triangle

2. Which formula is correct for finding the area of a half circle?

  F. $A = \frac{\pi d}{2}$ **G.** $A = \frac{\pi d^2}{8}$

  H. $A = \pi r$ **J.** $A = \pi r^2$

3. Which expression represents the area of the figure below?

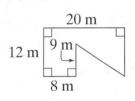

20 m

12 m   9 m

8 m

  A. $(20 \cdot 12) + \frac{1}{2}(12 \cdot 9)$

  B. $(20 \cdot 12) - \frac{1}{2}(12 \cdot 9)$

  C. $(12 \cdot 8) + \frac{1}{2}(12 \cdot 12)$

  D. $(12 \cdot 8) - \frac{1}{2}(12 \cdot 12)$

4. What is the surface area of a rectangular prism that is 8 in. long, $5\frac{1}{2}$ in. wide, and 3 in. tall?

  F. 132 in.^2 **G.** 99 in.^2

  H. 169 in.^2 **J.** $84\frac{1}{2} \text{ in.}^2$

5. Simplify $\sqrt{36x^6}$.

  A. $6x^3$ **B.** $\sqrt{6x^3}$

  C. $\sqrt{6x}$ **D.** $6x^6$

6. Find x.

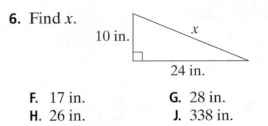

10 in. x

24 in.

  F. 17 in.   **G.** 28 in.
  H. 26 in.   **J.** 338 in.

7. Which could be the side lengths of a right triangle?
  A. 4 m, 4 m, 4 m   **B.** 8 m, 11 m, 14 m
  C. 3 m, 4 m, 6 m   **D.** 9 m, 12 m, 15 m

8. Which estimate is closest to the distance between A and B?

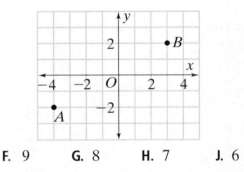

  F. 9   **G.** 8   **H.** 7   **J.** 6

For Exercises 9–15, use a calculator or the Trigonometric Ratios Table on page 747. Find each value. Round to the nearest ten thousandth.

9. $\sin 34°$ **10.** $\tan 79°$ **11.** $\cos 79°$

12. $\tan 22°$ **13.** $\cos 9°$ **14.** $\sin 75°$

15. In the diagram, the angle of depression between the parking lot and the ramp is 10°. Find the height h of the loading dock.

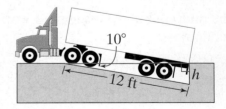

10°

12 ft h

Skills You Need for Chapter 12

► **Finding the median**   Use before Lesson 12-2.

Find the median.

1. 12, 14, 10, 9, 13, 12, 15, 12, 11   2. 55, 53, 67, 52, 50, 49, 51, 52, 52

3. 101, 100, 100, 105, 102, 101   4. 0.2, 0.5, 0.11, 0.25, 0.34, 0.19

► **Finding probability**   Use before Lessons 12-4, 12-5, and 12-7.

Find the probability for one roll of a number cube.

5. $P(2)$ 6. $P(5)$ 7. $P(2 \text{ or } 5)$ 8. $P(8)$

9. $P(1, 2, \text{ or } 3)$ 10. $P(\text{greater than } 4)$ 11. $P(\text{not } 3)$ 12. $P(\text{less than } 1)$

A student is chosen at random from a class of 15 boys and 18 girls.
Find each probability.

13. $P(\text{girl})$ 14. $P(\text{boy})$ 15. $P(\text{not a girl})$

► **Multiplying fractions**   Use before Lesson 12-5.

Find each product.

16. $\frac{2}{3} \cdot \frac{1}{2}$ 17. $\frac{7}{8} \cdot \frac{6}{7}$ 18. $\frac{9}{10} \cdot \frac{8}{9}$ 19. $\frac{5}{6} \cdot \frac{4}{5}$

20. $\frac{3}{4} \cdot \frac{2}{3}$ 21. $\frac{1}{2} \cdot \frac{1}{2} \cdot \frac{1}{2}$ 22. $\frac{7}{8} \cdot \frac{6}{7} \cdot \frac{5}{6}$ 23. $\frac{2}{5} \cdot \frac{1}{4}$

► **Fractions, decimals, and percents**   Use before Lessons 12-5 and 12-7.

Write each percent as a decimal.

24. 50%   25. 36%   26. 20%   27. 5%

Write each decimal or fraction as a percent.

28. $\frac{1}{5}$ 29. $\frac{7}{8}$ 30. 0.28   31. 0.3

Data Analysis and Probability

What you'll learn in this chapter:

■ How to use graphs to represent data

■ How to find theoretical probability and experimental probability

■ How to find permutations and combinations

The Good Times Poll

Do you participate in an organized extracurricular activity, such as a sport or a club? How much time do you devote to such activities each week? How does the amount of time you spend compare to the averages for students in your class and your school?

Conduct a Survey For the chapter project, you will do a survey of your class and a survey of your school. You will use graphs and statistical measures to display and analyze the results.

Steps to help you complete the project

Web Extension
www.phschool.com

How to solve
problems by doing
simulations

12-1

Frequency Tables and Line Plots

What You'll Learn

1 To display data in frequency tables

2 To display data in line plots

...And Why

To analyze data collected in surveys

Investigate

••••••••••••••••••••• EXPLORING FREQUENCY TABLES •••••••••••••••••••••

Surveys Many people have favorite colors. Do people also have favorite numbers? Take a survey of your classmates.

1. Ask each person to choose an integer from 0 to 9. Use a table to record the responses.

2. Which number was chosen most frequently? How many times was each of the other numbers chosen?

3. Suppose you want to continue your survey by asking more people. Looking back, would you use the same type of table you used for Question 1? Can you make improvements? Explain.

PART 1 Using Frequency Tables to Display Data

You can display data in a **frequency table,** which lists each data item with the number of times it occurs.

■ EXAMPLE 1

A number cube was rolled 20 times. The results are shown at the right. Display the data in a frequency table.

5 2 5 4 1 6 5 2 5 1
3 6 1 3 4 5 3 5 3 4

List the numbers on the cube in order. | Use a tally mark for each result. | Count the tally marks and record the frequency.

Number	Tally	Frequency
1					3
2				2
3						4
4					3
5							6
6				2

■ TRY THIS

4. Display the data below in a frequency table.
10 12 13 15 10 11 14 13 10 11 11 12 10 10 15

A **line plot** displays data with **X** marks above a number line.

The **range** of the data is the difference between the greatest and the least values in the data set.

REAL-WORLD CONNECTION

■ EXAMPLE 2

Surveys **Twenty-five students in a school hallway were asked how many books they were carrying. The frequency table at the right shows their responses. Display the data in a line plot. Then find the range.**

"How many books are you carrying?"

① Write a title that describes the data.

③ Mark an X for each response.

```
        X
        X   X
        X   X
        X   X       X
    X   X   X       X   X
    X   X   X   X   X   X
    X   X   X   X   X   X
  ───────────────────────────►
    0   1   2   3   4   5
```

② Draw a number line with the choices below it.

The greatest value in the data set is 5 and the least value is 0.
So the range is 5 − 0, or 5.

"How many books are you carrying?"

Number	Frequency
0	3
1	7
2	6
3	2
4	4
5	3

■ TRY THIS

5. Display the data below in a line plot. Then find the range.
miles from home to the mall: 2, 4, 3, 7, 3, 1, 4, 2, 2, 6, 3, 5, 1, 8, 3

6. What is the range of the data below?
prices of a gallon of regular gas at different gas stations:
$1.48, $1.32, $1.30, $1.35, $1.41, $1.29, $1.32, $1.43, $1.36

Reading Math

The word *range* is used in different ways in mathematics. The range of a data set is the difference between the greatest and the least values. The range of a function is its set of functional values.

Exercises

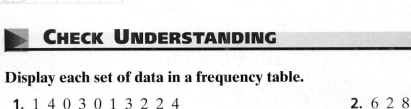

▶ **CHECK UNDERSTANDING**

Display each set of data in a frequency table.

1. 1 4 0 3 0 1 3 2 2 4

2. 6 2 8 7 9 3 5 4 8 2 4 6 4 1

Display each set of data in a line plot. Find the range.

3. 0 2 1 1 4 0 4 3 2

4. 5 0 2 1 4 3 4 0 2 5 4 3 2 0 4

5. *Critical Thinking* Describe a set of data that would be easier to display with a frequency table than with a line plot.

▶ **PRACTICE AND PROBLEM SOLVING**

Display each set of data in a frequency table.

6. 10 30 20 30 50 10 40 30 50 40 30 50

7. 25 29 28 28 30 25 26 28 27 29 26 30

8. rolls of a number cube: 4 1 3 4 2 1 2 5 2 3 5 1 6 1 3 5 6

9. test scores: 100 90 70 60 95 65 85 70 70 75 80 85 75 70 100 90

10. ages of club members: 14 16 14 16 14 13 12 15 16 12 12 15 14 15 15

11. heights of plants (inches): 25 25 20 25 16 20 25 30 25 31 26 28 30

Display each set of data in a line plot.

12. 5 2 1 3 3 6 4 5 4 2

13. 4 2 4 12 8 12 10 6 4 8 6 8 12

14. 7 11 10 10 8 11 9 7 9 8 11 11

15. 17 20 16 17 19 18 17 20 17 18 18 19 18 17

16. **TEST PREP** What is the range of the data below?
99.2 101.5 97.9 102.1 98.6 100.4 102.2 99.9
  A. 3.7   **B.** 3.9   **C.** 4.0   **D.** 4.2   **E.** Not here

Draw a line plot for each frequency table.

17.

Number	1	2	3	4	5	6
Frequency	2	5	7	8	4	3

18.

Number	1	2	3	4	5	6
Frequency	1	3	5	8	8	5

19.

Number	1	2	3	4	5	6
Frequency	7	5	3	2	6	7

20.

Number	1	2	3	4	5	6
Frequency	5	5	5	5	5	5

Construct a frequency table from each line plot.

21.
```
              ×
       × ×         ×
  ×    × × × ×
  1  2  3  4  5  6
```

22.
```
  ×              ×
  ×    ×     × ×
  × × × × × ×
  × × × × × ×
  15 16 17 18 19 20
```

23.
```
  ×    ×              ×
  × × × × × ×
  × × × × × ×
  × × × × × ×
  70 75 80 85 90 95
```

24. In the World Series, the first team to win four games is the champion. Sometimes the series lasts for seven games, but sometimes a team is able to win in fewer games. Below are data for 1970–1999. Make a frequency table and use it to find the mode.

Numbers of World Series Games, 1970–1999: 5, 7, 7, 7, 5, 7, 4, 6, 6, 7, 6, 6, 7, 5, 5, 7, 7, 7, 5, 4, 4, 7, 6, 6, 0, 6, 6, 7, 4, 4

25. Use a line plot to display the data at the right.

26. Below are the numbers of letters in each of the first twenty-five words of *Alice's Adventures in Wonderland* by Lewis Carroll.
4 3 10 5 3 9 2 3 4 5 2 7 2 3 6 2 3 4 3 2 6 7 2 2 4
   a. Draw a line plot for the data.
   b. Make a frequency table.
   c. Find the range.

27. Here are the weekly earnings in dollars of the employees at Industrial Enterprises: 320, 320, 320, 400, 400, 400, 400, 400, 400, 480, 480, 480, 720, 720, 720, 1000.
   a. Draw a line plot for the data.
   b. Make a frequency table.
   c. Find the range.

28. *Mathematical Reasoning* You are given a line plot of the results of a survey. Explain how you could use the line plot to find the number of people who answered the survey.

Distribution of Gold Medals 1998 Winter Olympics

Country	Medals
Germany	12
Norway	10
Russia	9
Canada	6
United States	6
Netherlands	5
Japan	5
Austria	3
Korea	3
Italy	2
Finland	2
Switzerland	2
France	2
Czech Republic	1
Bulgaria	1

SOURCE: *The World Almanac*

▶ **MIXED REVIEW**

Find the mean, the median, and the mode of each data set. *(Lesson 3-3)*

29. 12 13 14 16 16 17 18 18

30. 8 15 22 9 11 16 20 10

Given that $\triangle LMN \cong \triangle PQR$, **complete each statement.** *(Lesson 9-5)*

31. $\angle N \cong$ ■

32. $\overline{MN} \cong$ ■

33. $PQ =$ ■

34. *Measurement* The angle of elevation to the top of a tree from a point 10 ft from the tree's base is 70°. Find the height of the tree. *(Lesson 11-7)*

Making Histograms

A histogram shows the frequencies of data items as a graph.
You can use a graphing calculator to make a histogram.

■ EXAMPLE

Make a histogram of the data below.
21, 23, 20, 22, 23, 21, 24, 26, 23, 21, 20, 23, 21, 23, 20, 24

Step 1 Press STAT ENTER to set up lists for
the data. If necessary, press ▲ CLEAR ENTER
to clear an old list. Enter the data under L1,
pressing ENTER after each item.

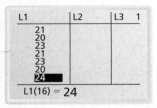

Step 2 Press 2nd Y= to use the StatPlot
feature. Press ENTER. Use the arrow keys and
ENTER to select **On** and to select a histogram in
the **Type:** row.

Step 3 Press ZOOM 9 to graph the histogram.

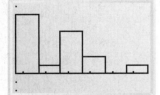

Step 4 To see the frequency of each number,
press WINDOW and set Xscl = 1. Then press
GRAPH. Sketch the histogram.

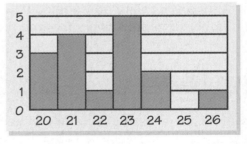

Use a graphing calculator to make a histogram of each set of data.
Then sketch the histogram.

1. 11, 12, 12, 11, 10, 12, 13, 15, 9, 10, 12, 13

2. 9, 7, 6, 9, 8, 5, 9, 2, 2, 5, 8, 4, 6, 3, 8, 7, 8, 5

3. 23, 26, 25, 26, 23, 25, 25, 24, 21, 21, 22, 23

4. 95, 90, 92, 91, 95, 94, 93, 92, 94, 93, 95, 91

Box-and-Whisker Plots

PART 1 Making Box-and-Whisker Plots

A **box-and-whisker plot** displays the distribution of data items along a number line. **Quartiles** divide the data into four equal parts. The median is the middle quartile.

Box-and-Whisker Plot

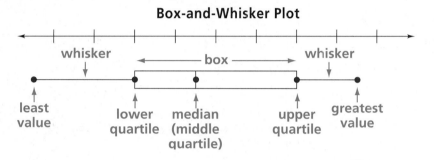

whisker — box — whisker

least value — lower quartile — median (middle quartile) — upper quartile — greatest value

What You'll Learn

1 To make box-and-whisker plots

2 To analyze data in box-and-whisker plots

. . . And Why

To analyze large data sets, such as crop acreages and animal weights

REAL-WORLD CONNECTION

■ EXAMPLE 1

Statistics **Use the data at the right to make a box-and-whisker plot for crops harvested in the years 1985–1997.**

Step 1 Arrange the data in order from least to greatest. Find the median.

293 298 308 314 316 317 318 318 321 322 326 333 342

Step 2 Find the lower quartile and upper quartile, which are the medians of the lower and upper halves.

293 298 308 314 316 317 318 318 321 322 326 333 342

lower quartile $= \dfrac{308 + 314}{2} = \dfrac{622}{2} = 311$

upper quartile $= \dfrac{322 + 326}{2} = \dfrac{648}{2} = 324$

Step 3 Draw a number line. Mark the least and greatest values, the median, and the quartiles. Draw a box from the first to the third quartiles. Mark the median with a vertical segment. Draw whiskers from the box to the least and greatest values.

Crops Harvested (millions of acres)

290 300 310 320 330 340 350

Crops Harvested in the United States

Year	Acres (millions)
1985	342
1986	316
1987	293
1988	298
1989	318
1990	322
1991	318
1992	317
1993	308
1994	321
1995	314
1996	326
1997	333

SOURCE: *Statistical Abstract of the United States*

■ TRY THIS

1. Draw a box-and-whisker plot for the distances of migration of birds (thousands of miles): 5, 2.5, 6, 8, 9, 2, 1, 4, 6.2, 18, 7.

You can compare two sets of data by making two box-and-whisker plots on one number line.

REAL-WORLD CONNECTION

■ EXAMPLE 2

Biology **Use box-and-whisker plots to compare orca whale masses and hippopotamus masses.**

Orca whale masses (kg)

3,900   2,750   2,600   3,100   4,200   2,600   3,700   3,000   2,200

Hippopotamus masses (kg)

1,800   2,000   3,000   2,500   3,600   2,700   1,900   3,100   2,300

Draw a number line for both sets of data. Use the range of data points to choose a scale.

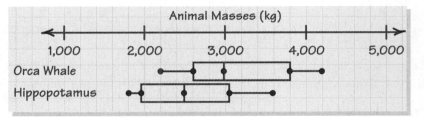

Draw the second box-and-whisker plot below the first one.

DNA evidence suggests that whales and hippopotamuses are closely related genetically.

■ TRY THIS

2. Compare annual video sales and album sales by making two box-and-whisker plots on one number line.

   videos (millions of units): 28, 24, 15, 21, 22, 16, 22, 30, 24, 17

   albums (millions of units): 16, 17, 22, 16, 18, 24, 15, 16, 25, 18

PART 2 Analyzing Box-and-Whisker Plots

Although you cannot see every data point in a box-and-whisker plot, you can use the quartiles and the greatest and least values to analyze a data set.

■ EXAMPLE 3

Describe the data in the box-and-whisker plot at the right.

The highest score is 90 and the lowest is 50. At least half of the scores are within 10 points of the median, 75. Since the median is not in the center of the box, the scores are not evenly distributed.

Exam Scores

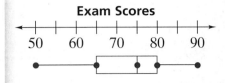

■ **TRY THIS** Describe the data in each box-and-whisker plot.

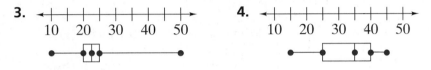

3.

4.

You can compare box-and-whisker plots to analyze two sets of data.

DATA ANALYSIS CONNECTION

■ EXAMPLE 4

Social Studies **The plots below compare the percents of the voting-age population who said they registered to vote in U.S. elections to the percents who said they voted. What conclusions can you draw?**

Percents of Population Who Registered and Voted, 1980–1996

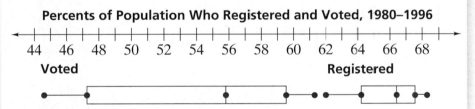

The percent registered was fairly constant, since the box-and-whisker plot is narrow. The percent who voted varied more, but it was always less than the percent who registered. Therefore, you can conclude that many who were registered did not vote.

■ **TRY THIS**

5. Use the box-and-whisker plots below. What conclusions can you draw about heights of Olympic basketball players?

Olympic Basketball Players' Heights (in.)

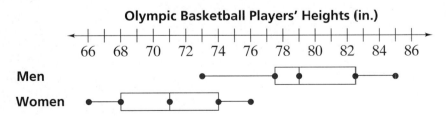

Exercises

CHECK UNDERSTANDING

Make a box-and-whisker plot for each set of data.

1. 16, 18, 59, 75, 30, 34, 25, 49, 27, 16, 21, 58, 71, 19, 50

2. 138, 149, 200, 101, 128, 196, 186, 150, 129, 176, 192, 190

Use the box-and-whisker plot to answer each question.

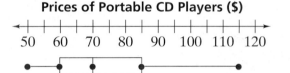

Prices of Portable CD Players ($)

3. What are the highest and lowest prices for the CD players?

4. What is the median price?

5. What is the lower quartile price?

6. What is the upper quartile price?

7. Are the prices evenly distributed? Explain.

PRACTICE AND PROBLEM SOLVING

Make a box-and-whisker plot for each set of data.

8. flamingo heights (cm):
92, 101, 96, 85, 126, 124, 116, 97, 109

9. wingspans of eagles (m):
2.3, 2, 2.5, 2.1, 1.9, 1.7, 2.2, 2.3, 2, 2.4

10. wingspans of butterflies (mm):
90, 100, 35, 90, 10, 30, 35, 60, 37, 63, 18, 38

11. numbers of pages in books:
205, 198, 312, 258, 185, 268, 279, 242, 356

Use box-and-whisker plots to compare data sets. Use a single number line for each comparison.

12. first set: 12, 16, 62, 48, 16, 59, 43
second set: 34, 92, 73, 71, 59, 68, 49

13. first set: 36, 9, 4, 3, 12, 29, 50, 16, 25, 21
second set: 18, 22, 7, 4, 11, 16, 40, 18, 33, 9

14. first set: 3, 7, 9, 12, 2, 1, 6, 5, 4, 3, 7, 10, 13, 8, 1, 9
second set: 9, 8, 1, 7, 6, 3, 7, 9, 8, 6, 4, 7, 8, 9, 10, 10

15. *Writing* Explain how you can find the quartiles of a set of data.

16. *Open-ended* Write a set of data that has a wide box and narrow whiskers.

17. **Biology** Use the data at the right to make a box-and-whisker plot for the maximum speeds of animals.

18. **Error Analysis** A student made a box-and-whisker plot. The student marked the greatest and least data values and then divided the distance between those points into four equal parts. What error did the student make?

19. Use the box-and-whisker plot below. What can you conclude about acreages of state parks?

Areas of State Parks (acres)

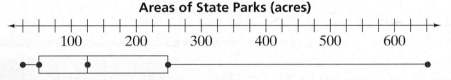

20. a. Use the data below to make two box-and-whisker plots on one number line.

    Ages of U.S. Olympic Soccer Team Players

    men: 22, 21, 22, 26, 20, 26, 23, 21, 22, 22, 22, 22, 21, 22, 23, 21, 20, 22

    women: 30, 27, 28, 25, 31, 24, 31, 24, 21, 23, 27, 18, 19, 24, 23, 20

    b. Compare the two box-and-whisker plots. What can you conclude?

21. **Mathematical Reasoning** Can you find the mean, median, and mode of a set of data by looking at a box-and-whisker plot? Explain.

Maximum Speeds of Animals for a Quarter Mile

Animal	Maximum Speed (mi/h)
Cheetah	70
Lion	50
Quarter horse	47.5
Coyote	43
Hyena	40
Rabbit	35
Giraffe	32
Grizzly bear	30
Cat (domestic)	30
Elephant	25
Squirrel	12

SOURCE: *The World Almanac*

▶ MIXED REVIEW

Display each set of data in a frequency table. *(Lesson 12-1)*

22. 6 8 7 6 5 8 5 6 4 8 7 5 4 7 6 8 6 7   23. 32 31 29 33 31 32 35 33 32 31 32 30

Find the distance between each pair of points. *(Lesson 11-3)*

24. $D(3, -2), S(-3, 2)$ 25. $A(0, 4), W(-7, -5)$ 26. $Y(6, 4), K(-1, 3)$ 27. $Z(9, 0), M(-8, 11)$

28. Lawns can have 850 blades of grass per square foot.
    a. A grass lawn is 3 yd by 6 yd. About how many blades of grass are in the yard? *(Lesson 10-1)*
    b. The area of all the lawns in the United States equals an area twice as large as that of Pennsylvania. Pennsylvania's area is 46,058 mi². Estimate the number of blades of grass in lawns in the United States. Write your answer in scientific notation. (*Hint:* A mile equals 5,280 feet.) *(Lesson 4-9)*

MATH TOOLBOX

Stem-and-Leaf Plots

A *stem-and-leaf plot* organizes data by showing each item in order. The leaf is the last digit to the right. The stem is the remaining digit or digits.

stem⟶ 15.7 ⟵leaf   stem⟶ 32 ⟵leaf

■ EXAMPLE 1

Use the table at the right to construct a stem-and-leaf plot. Then find the median, mode, and range.

Choose the stems. For this data set, use the values in the tens place. Draw a line to the right of the stems.

stems ⟶
```
2 |
3 |
```

Leaves are single digits, so for this data set the leaves will be the values in the ones place.

```
2 | 8 9
3 | 7 3 7 8 7 3   ◀── leaves
```

Broadway Productions

Season	New Shows
1990–1991	28
1991–1992	37
1992–1993	33
1993–1994	37
1994–1995	29
1995–1996	38
1996–1997	37
1997–1998	33

SOURCE: *The World Almanac*

Arrange the leaves on each stem from least to greatest. Include a key that shows how to read your stem-and-leaf plot.

Broadway Productions

```
2 | 8 9
3 | 3 3 7 7 7 8
    2 | 3 means 23   ◀── key
```

Since the data items are in order, the median is the midpoint. The median is the mean of the fourth and fifth items, or 35.

The mode corresponds to the most repeated leaf. The mode is 37.

The range is the difference of the greatest and least values, or 10.

---

1. *Biology* Use the table at the right.
   a. *Critical Thinking* What number should you use as the stem for the kangaroo and the opossum?
   b. Construct a stem-and-leaf plot.
   c. Find the median.
   d. Find the mode.
   e. Find the range.

Average Longevity

Animal	Years	Animal	Years
Grizzly bear	25	Hippopotamus	41
Kangaroo	7	Pig	10
Cow	15	Lion	15
Dog	12	Opossum	1
Giraffe	10	Cat	12
Gorilla	20	Zebra	15

SOURCE: *The World Almanac*

Make a stem-and-leaf plot for each set of data. Then find the median, the mode, and the range.

2. 15, 22, 25, 10, 36, 15, 28, 35, 18

3. 47, 41, 60, 75, 85, 53, 57, 76, 79, 81, 84, 86

4. 785, 785, 776, 772, 792, 788, 761, 768, 768

5. 4.5, 4.3, 0.8, 3.5, 2.6, 1.4, 0.2, 0.8, 4.3, 6.0

A back-to-back stem-and-leaf plot uses two sets of data. The side-by-side display makes the data easier to compare.

■ EXAMPLE 2

Draw a back-to-back stem-and-leaf plot for the winning times in the Olympic 100-m dash. Find each median and mode.

Use seconds for the stem and tenths of seconds for the leaves. Put the leaves in ascending order starting at the stem.

Winning Times, 100-m Dash

Men's Times (tenths of second)	Stem (seconds)	Women's Times (tenths of second)
9 9 8	9	
3 2 1 1 0 0 0	10	5 8 9
	11	0 0 0 1 1 1 4

means 10.1 ◀—— 1 │10│ 5 ——▶ means 10.5

The median of the times for men is 10.0 s. The median of the times for women is 11.0 s. The mode of the times for men is 10.0 s. The modes of the times for women are 11.0 s and 11.1 s.

Winning Times, 100-m Dash (seconds)

Year	Men	Women
1960	10.2	11.0
1964	10.0	11.4
1968	9.9	11.0
1972	10.1	11.1
1976	10.1	11.1
1980	10.3	11.1
1984	10.0	11.0
1988	9.9	10.5
1992	10.0	10.8
1996	9.8	10.9

SOURCE: *Sports Illustrated Sports Almanac*

Make a back-to-back stem-and-leaf plot for each pair of data sets. Then find each median and mode.

6. Set A: 9.1, 8.2, 7.3, 6.4, 7.3, 8.5   Set B: 7.6, 9.2, 8.2, 8.3, 9.7, 7.6

7. Set C: 236, 237, 241, 250, 242   Set D: 262, 251, 248, 243, 257

Use the stem-and-leaf plot at the right. The plot shows the time two classes spent on homework.

8. Which numbers are the stems?

9. What is the least time spent for each set of data?

10. What is the median for each set of data?

11. What is the mode for each set of data?

12. What is the range for each set of data?

Time Spent on Homework (min)

Class A		Class B
7 4 3	6	1 1 3 5 5
9 9 8 5 4 4	7	0 2 2 4
5 2 1 0	8	4 5 8 9
7 6 6 4 2	9	3 6 7 9 9 9

means 63 ◀—— 3 │6│1 ——▶ means 61

12-3

Using Graphs to Persuade

What You'll Learn

1 To recognize the use of breaks in the scales of graphs

2 To recognize the use of different scales

. . . And Why

To interpret graphical data correctly

PART 1 Using Breaks in Scales

You can use a graph to give different impressions by drawing it in different ways.

When you make a line or bar graph, you can use a break in the scale on one or both axes. Using a break lets you show more detail, but it can also give a distorted picture of the data.

REAL-WORLD CONNECTION

■ EXAMPLE 1

Population **Which title would be more appropriate for the graph below: "Los Angeles Overwhelms Chicago" or "Populations of Chicago and Los Angeles"? Explain.**

Because of the break in the vertical axis, the bar for Los Angeles appears to be about three times as tall as the bar for Chicago. Actually, the population of Los Angeles is a little less than 3.6 million, and the population of Chicago is about 2.7 million. So the population of Los Angeles is about 1.3 times that of Chicago.

The title "Los Angeles Overwhelms Chicago" could be misleading. "Populations of Chicago and Los Angeles" better describes the information in the graph.

■ TRY THIS

1. Use the data in the graph in Example 1. Redraw the graph without a break.

PART
2 Using Different Scales

You can use a graph to give different impressions by choosing longer or shorter spaces between units on the graph's axes.

REAL-WORLD CONNECTION

■ EXAMPLE 2

Cost of Living **Study the graphs below. Which graph gives the impression of a sharper increase in price? Explain.**

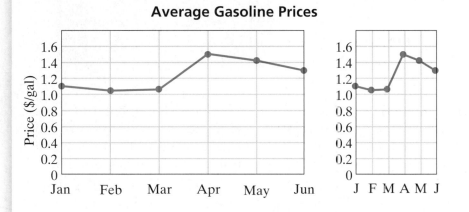

Average Gasoline Prices

In the graph at the right, the months are much closer together, so the line appears to climb more rapidly. This graph suggests that prices are going up faster than the graph at the left suggests.

■ **TRY THIS** Use the data in the table at the right.

2. Make a graph that suggests a rapid decrease in the total weight of fish caught.

3. Make a graph that suggests a slow decrease in the total weight of fish caught.

4. *Critical Thinking* A group is planning a campaign to protect the supply of fish. They are proposing a regulation that would limit the number of pounds of fish caught annually. Would they more likely use the graph from Question 2 or Question 3 in their proposal? Explain.

Fish Caught for Food in the U.S.

Year	Fish Caught (billions of pounds)
1993	8.2
1994	7.9
1995	7.7
1996	7.5

SOURCE: *Statistical Abstract of the United States*

Bar graphs can be misleading if their bars change in more than one dimension.

■ EXAMPLE 3

Critical Thinking **What makes the graph misleading? Explain.**

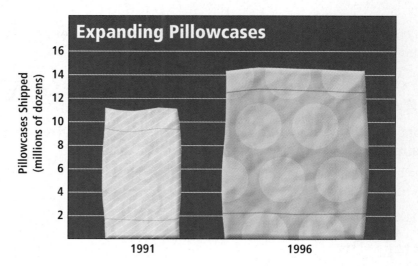

By reading the vertical axis, you can see that the number of pillowcases shipped increased by about one fourth. However, the bar on the right has not only increased in height, but has also nearly doubled in width. Since the area of the second bar is more than two times the area of the first bar, you might get the impression that the increase was much greater than it really was.

■ **TRY THIS** Use the data in the table below.

**Prices of Field-Grown Tomatoes
in the United States**

Year	Price of Tomatoes (cents per pound)
1990	86
1997	162

SOURCE: *Statistical Abstract of the United States*

5. Draw a graph that suggests that the price of tomatoes nearly doubled.

6. Draw a graph that suggests that the price of tomatoes more than doubled.

Exercises

CHECK UNDERSTANDING

Use the graph at the right for Exercises 1–4.

1. Which magazine *appears* to have about twice the circulation of *Circuitry Today?*

2. Which magazine *actually* has twice the circulation of *Circuitry Today?*

3. *Writing* Explain why the graph is misleading.

4. Improve the graph by redrawing it without a break.

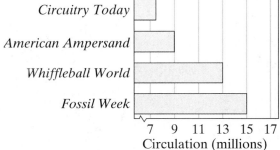

Magazine Circulation

5. a. *Statistics* Use the data below. Draw a graph with a break that suggests that the enrollment in 2000 was many times the enrollment in 1990.

U.S. College Enrollment

Year	Enrollment
1990	13.8 million
1995	14.2 million
2000	14.9 million

SOURCE: U.S. Education Department

b. Draw a second graph of the data, without using a break. Choose a scale that suggests that enrollment did not increase much from 1990 to 2000.

PRACTICE AND PROBLEM SOLVING

Use the graph at the right for Exercises 6–8.

6. The graph suggests that the number of students per computer in elementary schools is three times the number of students per computer in high schools. Is this true? Explain.

7. What does the graph suggest is the ratio of middle school students per computer to high school students per computer? What is the actual ratio?

8. Redraw the graph without a break. Describe the effect this has on what the graph suggests.

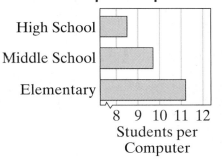

Average Number of Students per Computer

Statistics Use the graph at the right for Exercises 9 and 10.

9. Does the graph suggest that the percent of students using a computer at school is rising rapidly or rising slowly? How does it make that suggestion?

10. Redraw the graph to suggest less of an increase from 1989 to 1993.

Use the graph below for Exercises 11 and 12.

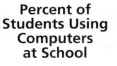

Percent of Students Using Computers at School

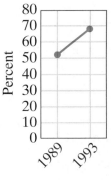

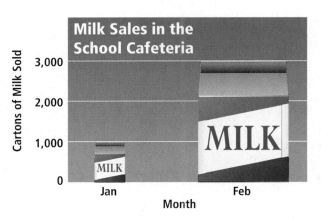

11. What impression does the graph give you about milk sales in the school cafeteria?

12. *Critical Thinking* Is the graph misleading? Explain.

Math in the Media Use the cartoon at the right for Exercises 13 and 14.

13. *Writing* Based on this sales presentation, would you buy stock in this company? Explain.

14. a. Explain how you could redraw the graph so it gives a better picture of the company's sales.
    b. Redraw the graph.

15. Use the data below to make two different graphs. Draw one of the graphs to suggest that the percent of low-fat milk sold in 1990 was double the percent in 1980.

Percent of Milk Sold That Was Low-Fat

Year	Percent
1980	38%
1990	59%

"As you can see, sales are booming!"

16. Use the data at the right. Draw a line graph that gives the impression that college costs increased sharply from 1984 to 1995.

17. *Open-ended* Find a graph in a newspaper or magazine that could be misleading. Explain why and how it could be misleading.

Average Annual Costs of College

Year	Cost
1984–1985	$4,563
1989–1990	$6,207
1994–1995	$8,306

SOURCE: *Wall Street Journal Almanac*

18. *Statistics* Use the graph below. Explain why the intervals on the horizontal axis could make the graph misleading.

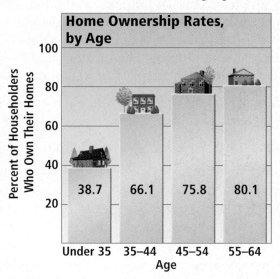

MIXED REVIEW

Make a box-and-whisker plot for each set of data. *(Lesson 12-2)*

19. 27, 25, 23, 29, 25, 28, 26, 27, 23, 21, 20, 24, 25, 28, 30, 19, 25

20. 2, 6, 3, 9, 15, 4, 9, 20, 6, 7, 2, 3, 8, 4, 1, 5, 6, 8, 5, 4, 9, 3, 2, 8, 7

21. 100, 95, 102, 101, 96, 100, 104, 115, 102, 108, 92, 97, 103, 106

Find each probability for choosing a letter at random from the word STATISTICS. *(Lesson 6-4)*

22. P(vowel)　　**23.** P(S)　　**24.** P(not T)　　**25.** P(A or C)

26. *Geometry* The Museum of Health and Medical Science in Houston, Texas, has one of the largest kaleidoscopes in the world. It is a cylinder 10 feet long and 22 inches in diameter. What is the surface area of the kaleidoscope? *(Lesson 10-5)*

12-4

Counting Outcomes and Theoretical Probability

What You'll Learn

1 To use a tree diagram and the Counting Principle to find the number of possible outcomes

2 To find theoretical probability by counting outcomes

...And Why

To find outcomes and probabilities in real-world problems

Investigate

·········· **EXPLORING POSSIBLE OUTCOMES** ··········

Congratulations! Your application to run the pizza stand at school home games has been accepted. Now you have to decide which pizzas to sell. You plan to offer two or three choices in each of three categories—size, crust, and topping. The more types of pizza the better, but you're limited by kitchen space to a total of 18 types.

1. Decide which types of pizza you will offer. Make a menu that shows your customers their options.

2. *Mathematical Reasoning* Suppose you decide to offer three choices of size and three choices of crust. How many toppings can you offer?

PART 1 Counting Possible Choices

You can use a tree diagram to display and count possible choices.

■ EXAMPLE 1

A school team sells caps in two colors (blue or white), two sizes (child or adult), and two fabrics (cotton or polyester). Draw a tree diagram to find the number of cap choices.

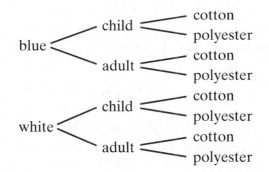

Each branch of the "tree" represents one choice—for example, blue-child-cotton.

There are 8 possible cap choices.

■ **TRY THIS**

3. Suppose the caps in Example 1 also come in black. Draw a tree diagram. How many cap choices are there?

Another way to count choices is to use the Counting Principle.

Counting Principle

If there are *m* ways of making one choice, and *n* ways of making a second choice, then there are $m \cdot n$ ways of making the first choice followed by the second.

Test Prep TIP

The Counting Principle is sometimes called the Multiplication Counting Principle.

The Counting Principle is particularly useful when a tree diagram would be too large to draw.

REAL-WORLD  CONNECTION

■ **EXAMPLE 2**

How many two-letter monograms are possible?

first letter		second letter		monograms
possible choices		possible choices		possible choices
26	·	26	=	676

There are 676 possible two-letter monograms.

A monogram is a figure made up of two or more letters, such as the initials of your name.

■ **TRY THIS**

4. How many three-letter monograms are possible?

PART 2 Counting Outcomes to Find Probability

You can count outcomes to help you find the **theoretical probability** of an event in which outcomes are equally likely.

Theoretical Probability

$$P(\text{event}) = \frac{\text{number of favorable outcomes}}{\text{number of possible outcomes}}$$

A **sample space** is a list of all possible outcomes. You can use a tree diagram to find a sample space. Then you can calculate probability.

EXAMPLE 3

Use a tree diagram to find the sample space for tossing two coins. Then find the probability of tossing two tails.

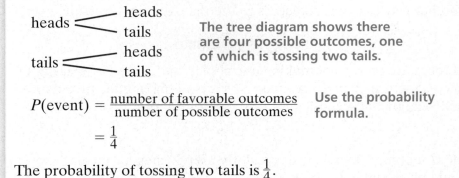

$P(\text{event}) = \dfrac{\text{number of favorable outcomes}}{\text{number of possible outcomes}}$ Use the probability formula.

$= \dfrac{1}{4}$

The probability of tossing two tails is $\dfrac{1}{4}$.

■ TRY THIS

5. You toss two coins. Find $P(\text{one head and one tail})$.

You can also use the Counting Principle to find probability.

REAL-WORLD CONNECTION

EXAMPLE 4

Many people play lottery games without knowing the probability of winning. In some state lotteries, the winning number is made up of four digits chosen at random. Suppose a player buys two tickets with different numbers. What is the probability that the player has a winning ticket?

First find the number of possible outcomes. For each digit, there are 10 possible outcomes, 0 through 9.

1st digit		2nd digit		3rd digit		4th digit		total
outcomes		outcomes		outcomes		outcomes		outcomes
10	·	10	·	10	·	10	=	10,000

Then find the probability when there are two favorable outcomes.

$P(\text{event}) = \dfrac{\text{number of favorable outcomes}}{\text{number of possible outcomes}} = \dfrac{2}{10,000}$

The probability is $\dfrac{2}{10,000}$, or $\dfrac{1}{5,000}$.

■ TRY THIS

6. A lottery uses five digits chosen at random. Find the probability of buying a winning ticket.

Exercises

CHECK UNDERSTANDING

1. There are 3 ways of performing Task A. There are 4 ways of performing Task B. Use a tree diagram to find the number of ways there are to perform Task A and then Task B.

2. There are 8 roads leading from Marsh to Taft and 7 roads leading from Taft to Polk. How many possible routes are there for driving from Marsh to Polk through Taft?

3. Find the probability of rolling a 3 on each of two number cubes.

PRACTICE AND PROBLEM SOLVING

4. You can buy a burrito made from a flour tortilla or a corn tortilla. You have a choice of five fillings: beef, chicken, bean, triple-cheese, or grilled vegetables. Draw a tree diagram. How many burrito choices do you have?

5. There are 6 roads leading from Seymour to Clarksville and 3 roads leading from Clarksville to Belleview. Use a tree diagram to find the number of possible routes from Seymour to Belleview through Clarksville.

6. **a.** A student has eight shirts and six pairs of pants. How many different shirt-pants outfits can he choose?
   b. The student also has three neckties. How many shirt-pants-tie outfits can he choose?

7. An automobile manufacturer makes four different car styles. Each style comes in 11 colors. Each car comes in one of five different interior styles and with an automatic or a manual transmission. A car dealer wants to order one of each kind of car. How many cars will the dealer order?

8. *Open-ended* Write a problem that you can solve by using the Counting Principle. Then solve the problem.

Find each sample space.

9. tossing 3 coins

10. tossing one coin and rolling one number cube

11. scheduling an appointment for a weekday during the morning or the afternoon

Find each event's probability.

12. You toss three coins and get three heads.

13. You toss three coins. You get one head and two tails.

14. You toss a coin and roll a number cube. You toss tails and roll an even number.

Use the table. You have one sweater for each possible color and style.

15. Find the sample space. How many sweaters do you have?

16. What is the probability of choosing a brown sweater at random?

17. What is the probability of choosing a cardigan at random?

18. *Mathematical Reasoning* You have a bag containing an equal number of nickels, dimes, and quarters. You reach into the bag and choose a coin. Are all outcomes equally likely? Explain.

Sweaters

Colors	Styles
Blue	Cardigan
Pink	Crewneck
Red	V-neck
Brown	
Black	

▶ MIXED REVIEW

Display each data set in a line plot. Find the range. *(Lesson 12-1)*

19. 3 4 5 4 7 7 3 6 5

20. 19 18 19 17 17 16 19 18 17 19

Find the midpoint of a segment with the given endpoints.
(Lesson 11-3)

21. $X(3, -2)$ and $Y(-3, 6)$ **22.** $A(-1, 0)$ and $B(2, 1)$

23. *Writing* Explain why the graph at the right could be misleading. *(Lesson 12-3)*

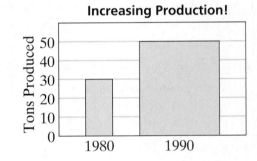
Increasing Production!

✓ CHECKPOINT 1   Lessons 12-1 through 12-4

1. Display the data below in a frequency table.
47 51 50 52 50 47 48 50 49 51 48 52

2. Make a box-and-whisker plot for the data below.
31, 33, 74, 90, 44, 49, 40, 64, 42, 31, 36, 73, 86, 34, 46, 65

3. *Open-ended* Use the data in the table.
   a. Draw a graph that could be misleading. Explain.
   b. Redraw the graph so it is not misleading.

4. Two numbers from 1 to 10 are chosen at random. Find the probability that both numbers are odd numbers.

Year	Hourly Minimum Wage
1996	$4.75
1997	$5.15

SOURCE: *Wall Street Journal Almanac*

Independent and Dependent Events

Investigate

···················· **EXPLORING PROBABILITY IN GAMES** ····················

You have four cards with an M written on them, two with an A, six with a T, and eight with an H.

1. You draw an M card at random and replace it. What is the probability that the next card you draw at random will also be an M card?

2. You draw an M card at random and do not replace the card. What is the probability that the next card you draw at random will also be an M card?

3. Make a table to find the probability of matching cards.

<table>
<tr><th colspan="2">Probability
With Replacement</th><th colspan="2">Probability
Without Replacement</th></tr>
<tr><th>First Card</th><th>Second Card
Matches</th><th>First Card</th><th>Second Card
Matches</th></tr>
<tr><td>$P(M) = \blacksquare$</td><td>$P(M) = \blacksquare$</td><td>$P(M) = \blacksquare$</td><td>$P(M) = \blacksquare$</td></tr>
<tr><td>$P(A) = \blacksquare$</td><td>$P(A) = \blacksquare$</td><td>$P(A) = \blacksquare$</td><td>$P(A) = \blacksquare$</td></tr>
<tr><td>$P(T) = \blacksquare$</td><td>$P(T) = \blacksquare$</td><td>$P(T) = \blacksquare$</td><td>$P(T) = \blacksquare$</td></tr>
<tr><td>$P(H) = \blacksquare$</td><td>$P(H) = \blacksquare$</td><td>$P(H) = \blacksquare$</td><td>$P(H) = \blacksquare$</td></tr>
</table>

4. *Critical Thinking* For any letter, why is the probability for selecting the second card with replacement of the first card different from the probability of selecting the second card without replacement of the first card?

PART 1 Independent Events

Suppose you select a card from a stack of cards. You then select a second card *after replacing* the first card. Your first selection does not affect your second selection. The cards available for the second selection are the same as those for the first.

Independent events are events in which the first event *does not* affect the second event.

Probability of Independent Events

For two independent events A and B, the probability of both events occurring is the product of the probabilities of each event occurring.

$$P(A \text{ and } B) = P(A) \cdot P(B)$$

■ EXAMPLE 1

You roll a number cube once. Then you roll it again. What is the probability that you get 2 on the first roll and a number greater than 4 on the second roll?

$P(2) = \frac{1}{6}$ There is one 2 among 6 numbers on a cube.

$P(\text{greater than 4}) = \frac{2}{6}$ There are two numbers greater than 4 on a cube.

$P(2 \text{ and greater than } 4) = P(2) \cdot P(\text{greater than } 4)$

$$= \frac{1}{6} \cdot \frac{2}{6}$$

$$= \frac{2}{36}, \text{ or } \frac{1}{18}$$

The probability of rolling 2 and then a number greater than 4 is $\frac{1}{18}$.

■ TRY THIS

5. You toss a coin twice. Find the probability of getting two heads.

You can use fractions, decimals, or percents to represent probabilities and to find the probability of two events occurring.

REAL-WORLD CONNECTION

■ EXAMPLE 2

Botany **Bluebonnets grow wild in the southwest United States. Under the best conditions, each bluebonnet seed has a 20% probability of growing. If you select two seeds at random, what is the probability that both will grow, under the best conditions?**

$P(\text{a seed grows}) = 20\%, \text{ or } 0.20$ Write the percent as a decimal.

$P(\text{two seeds grow}) = P(\text{a seed grows}) \cdot P(\text{a seed grows})$

$$= 0.20 \cdot 0.20$$ Substitute.

$$= 0.04 = 4\%$$ Multiply. Write 0.04 as a percent.

The probability that two seeds grow is 4%.

If you randomly select *three* bluebonnet seeds like those in Example 2, what is the probability that all three will grow?

6. *Botany* Chemically treated bluebonnet seeds have a 30% probability of growing. You select two such seeds at random. What is the probability that both will grow?

PART
2 **Dependent Events**

Suppose you select a card from a stack of cards. You then select a second card *without replacing* the first card. Your first selection affects your second selection because there is one card fewer in the stack when you select the second card.

Dependent events are events in which the first event *does* affect the second event.

Probability of Dependent Events

For two dependent events *A* and *B*, the probability of both events occurring is the product of the probability of the first event and the probability that, after the first event, the second event occurs.

$$P(A \text{ and } B) = P(A) \cdot P(B \text{ after } A)$$

■ **EXAMPLE 3**

Three girls and two boys volunteer to represent their class at a school assembly. The teacher selects one name and then another from a bag containing the five students' names. What is the probability that both representatives will be girls?

$$P(\text{girl}) = \frac{3}{5} \quad \text{Three of five students are girls.}$$

$$P(\text{girl after girl}) = \frac{2}{4} \quad \text{If a girl's name is drawn, two of the four remaining students are girls.}$$

$$P(\text{girl and girl}) = P(\text{girl}) \cdot P(\text{girl after girl})$$

$$= \frac{3}{5} \cdot \frac{2}{4} \quad \text{Substitute.}$$

$$= \frac{6}{20}, \text{ or } \frac{3}{10} \quad \text{Simplify.}$$

The probability that both representatives will be girls is $\frac{3}{10}$.

■ **TRY THIS**

7. For Example 3, find *P*(boy and girl).

Exercises

You pick a marble from a bag containing 1 green marble, 4 red marbles, 2 yellow marbles, and 3 black marbles. You replace the first marble and select a second one. Find each probability.

1. P(red and yellow)   **2.** P(black and black)   **3.** P(red and black)   **4.** P(yellow and black)

A student has 5 blue socks and 4 black socks. He selects one sock at random. Without replacing the sock, he selects a second sock at random. Find each probability.

5. P(blue and black)   **6.** P(black and blue)   **7.** P(black and black)   **8.** P(blue and blue)

Are the events independent or dependent? Explain.

9. You select a card. Without putting the card back, you select a second card.

10. You select a card. After putting it back, you select a second card.

11. You roll a number cube. You roll it again.

You roll a number cube twice. What is the probability that you roll each of the following pairs of numbers?

12. 6 and then 5

13. 6 and then 2 or 5

14. 6 and then a number less than 4

15. 1 and then 1

16. an even number and then 2 or 5

17. an even number and then an odd number

You select a card at random from those at the right. Without replacing the card, you select a second card. Find the probability of selecting each set of letters.

18. P and then G   **19.** E and then A   **20.** E and then a second vowel

21. G and then R or A   **22.** P or E and then A   **23.** a consonant and then a vowel

24. *Writing* Explain the difference between independent and dependent events.

25. ***Open-ended*** Give an example of dependent events different from the ones used in this lesson.

26. A refrigerator contains 12 orange drinks, 4 grape drinks, and 25 apple drinks. Ann is first in the line for drinks. Mark is second. What is the probability that Ann gets an apple drink and Mark gets a grape drink, if they are given drinks at random?

27. Mrs. Kendall's wallet contains 3 one-dollar bills, 2 five-dollar bills, and 3 ten-dollar bills. She randomly selects one bill and then another from the wallet. Find the probability that she selects the given bills.
    a. a one-dollar bill and then a ten-dollar bill
    b. a ten-dollar bill and then a five-dollar bill

28. On a multiple-choice test you randomly guess the answers to two questions. Each question has five choices.
    a. What is the probability that you get both answers correct?
    b. What is the probability that you get both answers incorrect?

29. ***Weather Forecasting*** Weather forecasters are accurate 91% of the time when predicting precipitation for the following day. What is the probability that a forecaster will make a correct precipitation prediction on Friday for the following Saturday, two weeks in a row?

▶ MIXED REVIEW

Find the sine, cosine, and tangent of angle *A* for each triangle. *(Lesson 11-6)*

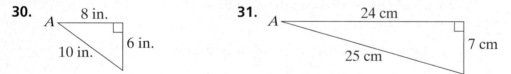

30. 8 in. / 6 in. / 10 in.   31. 24 cm / 7 cm / 25 cm

32. From Compt there are four ways to get to Murch. From Murch there are five ways to get to Toll. How many ways are there from Compt to Toll through Murch? *(Lesson 12-4)*

CHAPTER PROJECT 12
ACTIVITY 1 INTERVIEWING

Survey the members of your class. Ask each person how much time per week he or she spends on organized extracurricular activities. Record the results.

12-6

Permutations and Combinations

What You'll Learn

1 To use permutations

2 To use combinations

...And Why

To make choices in real-world problems involving sports and earth science

An arrangement in which order is important is a **permutation.** For the letters O, P, S, and T, the permutations *STOP* and *POTS* are different because the order of the letters is different. You can use the Counting Principle to find the number of possible permutations.

■ EXAMPLE 1

Find the number of permutations of the letters O, P, S, and T.

1st letter	2nd letter	3rd letter	4th letter
4 choices	3 choices	2 choices	1 choice

$$4 \quad \cdot \quad 3 \quad \cdot \quad 2 \quad \cdot \quad 1 \quad = \quad 24$$

There are 24 permutations of the letters O, P, S, and T.

■ TRY THIS

1. Use the Counting Principle to find the number of permutations possible for the letters W, A, T, E, and R.

A track team has seven members. In how many ways can four members line up for a relay race?

You can use *permutation notation* to represent this problem.

7 members — Choose 4.

$$_7P_4 = 7 \quad \cdot \quad 6 \quad \cdot \quad 5 \quad \cdot \quad 4 \quad = \quad 840$$

1st member   2nd member   3rd member   4th member

Four of seven team members can line up in 840 ways.

Permutation Notation

The expression $_nP_r$ stands for the number of permutations of n objects chosen r at a time.

EXAMPLE 2

In how many ways can you arrange five books out of nine books on a shelf?

9 books ——┐ ┌—— Choose 5.

$$_9P_5 = 9 \cdot 8 \cdot 7 \cdot 6 \cdot 5 = 15{,}120 \qquad \text{Simplify.}$$

Graphing Calculator HINT

You can use a calculator to evaluate $_9P_5$. Here are the keystrokes.

9 MATH ◁ 2 5 ENTER

The result is 15,120.

■ **TRY THIS** Simplify each expression.

2. $_5P_2$ **3.** $_5P_3$ **4.** $_5P_4$ **5.** $_5P_5$

PART 2   Combinations

Sometimes the order of a group of items is not important. For instance, a ham and cheese sandwich is the same as a cheese and ham sandwich. An arrangement in which order does not matter is a **combination.**

REAL-WORLD CONNECTION

EXAMPLE 3

Geography **In how many ways can you choose two countries from the table when you write reports about inland water?**

Make an organized list of all the combinations.

AC AE AI AT AU   Abbreviate by using the first
     CE CI CT CU   letter of each country's name.
         EI ET EU   First list all pairs containing
             IT IU   Australia. Continue until every
                TU   pair of countries is listed.

There are fifteen ways to choose two countries from a list of six.

Inland Water

Country	Water Area (mi²)
Australia	26,610
Canada	291,573
Ethiopia	46,680
India	121,391
Tanzania	22,799
United States	79,541

SOURCE: *The Top 10 of Everything*

■ **TRY THIS**

6. In how many ways can you choose three different items from a menu containing six items?

Combination Notation

The expression $_nC_r$ stands for the number of combinations of n objects chosen r at a time.

For combinations, a group with the same items as another is a *duplicate group*. For r items, the number of duplicate groups is $_rP_r$. The number of combinations equals the number of permutations divided by the number of duplicates of each group. So,

$$_nC_r = \frac{_nP_r}{_rP_r}.$$

Graphing Calculator HINT

You can use a calculator to evaluate $_5C_3$. Here are the keystrokes.

5 [MATH] [◁] 3 3 [ENTER]

The result is 10.

■ EXAMPLE 4

How many different sandwiches can you make if you can choose exactly three items out of five?

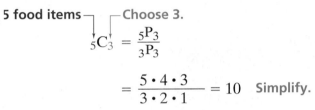

5 food items ⟶ ⌐ Choose 3.

$$_5C_3 = \frac{_5P_3}{_3P_3}$$

$$= \frac{5 \cdot 4 \cdot 3}{3 \cdot 2 \cdot 1} = 10 \quad \text{Simplify.}$$

You can make 10 different sandwiches.

■ TRY THIS Simplify each expression.

7. $_8C_2$ **8.** $_8C_3$ **9.** $_8C_4$ **10.** $_8C_5$

You can tell whether a problem requires permutations or combinations by asking yourself *Does order matter?* If the answer is *yes*, use permutations. If it is *no*, use combinations.

■ EXAMPLE 5

Tell which type of arrangement each problem involves.

a. How many different groups of three books can you choose from five books?
Combinations: the order of the books selected does not matter.

b. In how many different orders can you play three CDs?
Permutations: the order in which you play the CDs matters.

■ TRY THIS Tell which type of arrangement is involved.

11. A teacher selects a committee of 4 students from 25 students. How many different committees can the teacher select?

12. Class officers are president, vice-president, secretary, and treasurer. From a class of 25 students, how many different groups of officers can be chosen?

Exercises

Use the Counting Principle to find the number of permutations possible for each group of letters. Use all the letters.

1. S, I, T

2. W, O, R, L, D

3. D, E, C, I, M, A, L

Make a list to find the number of combinations using two different letters you can form from each group of letters.

4. C, A, T

5. M, A, T, H

6. V, A, L, U, E

Simplify each expression.

7. $_4P_2$

8. $_6P_4$

9. $_9P_4$

10. $_{10}P_8$

11. $_3P_2$

12. $_4C_2$

13. $_6C_4$

14. $_9C_4$

15. $_{10}C_8$

16. $_3C_2$

PRACTICE AND PROBLEM SOLVING

Use the Counting Principle to find the number of three-letter permutations possible for each group of letters.

17. P, L, U, S

18. F, A, C, T, O, R

19. T, R, I, A, N, G, L, E

Make a list to find the number of three-letter combinations you can form from each group of letters.

20. F, O, R, T, Y

21. S, I, X

22. E, I, G, H, T, Y

Simplify each expression.

23. $_6P_3$

24. $_2P_1$

25. $_{10}P_5$

26. $_7P_4$

27. $_{12}P_9$

28. $_6C_3$

29. $_2C_1$

30. $_{10}C_5$

31. $_7C_4$

32. $_{12}C_9$

33. Use the letters E, P, S, and T.
   a. How many possible arrangements of the letters are there?
   b. How many arrangements form real English words?
   c. *Probability* What is the probability that an arrangement of these letters chosen at random will form an English word?

34. *Writing* The lock at the right has a combination consisting of three whole numbers. Explain why it is not likely to be opened by someone who does not know the correct numbers.

35. _Open-ended_ Use the different letters from your last name.
   a. Find the number of two-letter permutations.
   b. Find the number of two-letter combinations.

36. Louisa May Alcott published 13 novels during her lifetime. In how many ways could you select three of these books?

Does each problem involve _permutations_ or _combinations_? Explain.

37. In how many different ways can three students form a line?

38. In how many orders can you play three different games?

39. **TEST PREP** Which question can you answer by evaluating $_{10}C_2$?
   A. In how many ways can you arrange 10 books on 2 shelves?
   B. In how many ways can 10 people line up 2 at a time?
   C. In how many ways can you choose 2 people from 10 for tennis?
   D. In how many ways can you choose first-place and second-place winners from 10 finalists?

Journal

Explain the difference between a permutation and a combination.

> ## MIXED REVIEW

On each of five cards there is one of the letters A, B, C, D, and E. You select two cards. Find each probability. _(Lesson 12-5)_

40. $P(A,$ then B with A replaced)

41. $P(A,$ then B without A replaced)

42. Find the area of the triangle at the right. _(Lessons 10-2 and 11-2)_

43. _Consumer Issues_ A coat is on sale for $80. Its original price was $120. What is the percent of discount? _(Lesson 6-9)_

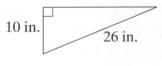
10 in. 26 in.

Math at Work
Wildlife Statistician

Wildlife statisticians study the growth or decline of plant and animal life in a geographical region. They make observations and collect data for a small portion, or sample, of an animal or plant population. Then they draw conclusions about the entire population. If you enjoy studying wildlife, this may be the job for you.

For more information about careers in wildlife statistics, visit the Prentice Hall Web site. **www.phschool.com**

See also Extra Practice section.

Multiple Choice

Choose the best answer.

1. You are writing a three-digit number. The first digit must be 2 or 8. The second digit must be 1, 3, or 9. The third digit must be 4, 5, 6, 7, or 8. Which expression can you use to determine how many different numbers you can write?
   A. $2 \cdot 3 \cdot 5$
   B. $5 \cdot 4 \cdot 3 \cdot 2 \cdot 1$
   C. $(1 \cdot 2) + (2 \cdot 3) + (3 \cdot 5)$
   D. $2 + 3 + 5$

2. Which expression shows the prime factorization of the numerator and denominator of $\left(\frac{42}{22}\right)\left(\frac{75}{63}\right)$?

   F. $\frac{42 \cdot 75}{22 \cdot 63}$

   G. $\frac{2 \cdot 3^2 \cdot 5^2 \cdot 7}{2 \cdot 3^2 \cdot 7 \cdot 11}$

   H. $2\frac{27}{100}$

   J. $\frac{6 \cdot 7 \cdot 5 \cdot 25}{2 \cdot 11 \cdot 7 \cdot 9}$

3. Name the figure.

   A. $\overleftrightarrow{AB}$
   B. $\overline{AB}$
   C. $\overrightarrow{AB}$
   D. $\angle AB$

4. Each solid has a height of 5 in. Which has the greatest volume?

   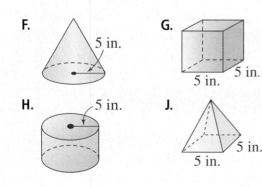

5. Which figure *cannot* be a net for the prism shown?

   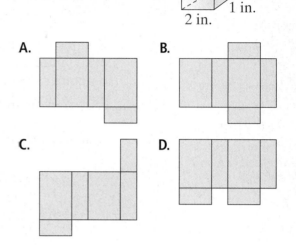

Free Response

For Exercises 6–8, show your work.

6. $\angle ABC$ is an acute angle. Write an inequality for x.

7. Explain how you can use the Pythagorean Theorem to find the height of an equilateral triangle with side length 12.

8. **a.** The table below shows the maximum life span of some mammals. Create a box-and-whisker plot for the data.
   b. Write the values of the lower quartile, the median, and the upper quartile.

Beaver	50 yr	Goat	18 yr
Black bear	36 yr	Horse	50 yr
Chimpanzee	53 yr	Mouse	6 yr
Chipmunk	8 yr	Squirrel	23 yr
Elephant	77 yr	Tiger	26 yr

12-7

Experimental Probability

Finding Experimental Probability

You have learned to find theoretical probability, which is the ratio of the number of favorable outcomes to the number of possible outcomes. You can also find probability based on experimental data, which is known as **experimental probability.**

Experimental Probability

$$P(\text{event}) = \frac{\text{number of times an event occurs}}{\text{number of times experiment is done}}$$

REAL-WORLD CONNECTION

■ EXAMPLE 1

Medical Science **A medical study tests a new medicine on 3,500 participants. It is effective for 3,010 participants. Find the experimental probability that the medicine is effective.**

$$P(\text{event}) = \frac{\text{number of times an event occurs}}{\text{number of times experiment is done}}$$

$$= \frac{3,010}{3,500} = 0.86$$

The experimental probability that the medicine is effective is 0.86, or 86%.

■ TRY THIS

1. Another medicine is effective for 1,183 of 2,275 participants. Find the experimental probability that the medicine is effective.

Simulating Events

A **simulation** is a model used to find experimental probability. Experimental probability found by simulation can differ from theoretical probability. The more trials you do in a simulation, the closer the two types of probability values are likely to be.

■ Different Ways to Solve a Problem

Use theoretical and experimental probabilities to find the probability of correctly guessing all 4 answers on a 4-question true-false quiz.

Method 1: Theoretical Probability

Each guess is an independent event. Find the probability of one correct guess. Then find the probability of four independent correct guesses.

$P(1 \text{ correct guess}) = \frac{1}{2}$

$P(4 \text{ correct guesses}) = \frac{1}{2} \cdot \frac{1}{2} \cdot \frac{1}{2} \cdot \frac{1}{2} = \frac{1}{16}$

The theoretical probability is $\frac{1}{16}$.

Method 2: Experimental Probability

Simulate the problem by tossing a coin. Let heads stand for a correct guess and tails for an incorrect guess. Use the results of 120 tosses given at the right.

Separate the results into 30 groups of 4. Count the groups with 4 heads. There are two.

HTTT	HTTT	HHHT	TTTT	TTHT	THTT
THHH	THHH	HTTT	TTHH	HTTT	HTHH
HTHH	THTT	TTHT	THTH	HHTT	THTH
HHHH	TTHT	HHHH	THTT	TTTH	HHHT
HHTT	HTTT	THTT	HHTT	HHTH	HTHH

Find the experimental probability.

$P(\text{event}) = \dfrac{\text{number of times an event occurs}}{\text{number of times experiment is done}}$

$= \dfrac{2}{30} = \dfrac{1}{15}$

The experimental probability is $\frac{1}{15}$.

120 Coin Tosses

H	T	T	T	H	T	T	T	H	H	H	T
T	T	T	T	T	H	T	T	H	T	T
T	H	H	H	T	H	H	H	H	T	T	T
T	T	H	H	H	T	T	T	H	T	H	H
H	T	H	H	T	H	T	T	T	T	H	T
T	H	T	H	H	H	T	T	T	H	T	H
H	H	H	H	T	T	H	T	H	H	H	H
T	H	T	T	T	T	H	H	H	H	T
H	H	T	T	H	T	T	T	T	H	T	T
H	H	T	T	H	H	T	H	H	T	H	H

For this simulation, the experimental probability is a little greater than the theoretical probability. Another simulation might give different results. As you do more trials, the experimental probability is likely to approach the theoretical probability.

Choose a Method

1. Which method would you use to solve the problem? Explain.

Exercises

CHECK UNDERSTANDING

Students were surveyed about the number of pencils in their bookbags. The table shows the results. Write each experimental probability as a fraction in simplest form.

Pencils in Students' Bookbags

Number of pencils	Number of students
0	4
1	16
2 or more	12

1. P(one pencil)

2. P(no pencils)

3. P(two or more pencils)

4. P(at least one pencil)

5. *Calendar* Design a simulation you could use to find the experimental probability of your birthday falling on a Saturday in a year chosen at random.

PRACTICE AND PROBLEM SOLVING

A student took a survey of some of the vehicles in a parking lot. Use the results in the table to find the experimental probability that a random vehicle in the lot is the given color. Write the probability as a percent, to the nearest tenth of a percent.

Color	Number of Vehicles
Black	9
Blue	10
Brown	13
Green	7
Red	12
White	11
Gray	6

6. red

7. white

8. black

9. blue or green

10. not black or gray

11. purple

12. **TEST PREP** A baseball manufacturer checked 250 of its baseballs and found that 8 were defective. Find the experimental probability that a baseball was *not* defective.
  A. 9.68%   **B.** 32%   **C.** 3.2%   **D.** 96.8%

13. a. How would you find the experimental probability of tossing three coins and getting three heads?
  b. *Mathematical Reasoning* How would you compare the experimental probability of getting three heads to the theoretical probability? Would you expect the probabilities to be equal? Explain.

14. You take a 5-question multiple-choice test. Each question has 4 choices. Use a simulation to find the experimental probability of guessing the correct answers to exactly 4 questions.

15. *Data Analysis* Roll a number cube 100 times. Record the results.
  a. Find the experimental probability of rolling an even number.
  b. Compare the experimental probability to the theoretical probability.

16. Two players played a game with a number cube. The table shows the results.

a. Find Probability(A wins) and Probability(B wins).

b. *Writing* A *fair game* is one in which each player has the same chance of winning. Do you think the game that A and B played is fair? Explain.

| Game Results | |
A Wins	B Wins

17. a. *Open-ended* Write a problem you can solve with a simulation.

b. Solve the problem.

18. *Error Analysis* A student wants to do a simulation to find the probability of correctly guessing a number from 1 to 5 two times in a row. He decides to roll a number cube 100 times, separating the results into 50 groups of two and letting a roll of 1 stand for a correct guess. Explain why the student's simulation will not give good results.

▶ MIXED REVIEW

Evaluate each expression. *(Lesson 12-6)*

19. $_4P_2$

20. $_{10}P_3$

21. $_4C_3$

22. $_6C_3$

Spatial Thinking **Write a rule to describe each translation.** *(Lesson 9-8)*

23.

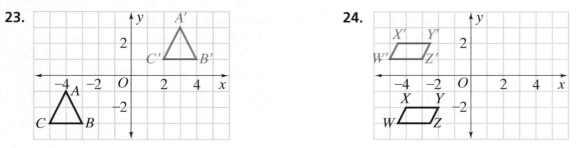

24.

25. *Geometry* Find the volume of a spherical globe with a diameter of 0.9 m. Use 3.14 for π. Round to the nearest tenth. *(Lesson 10-9)*

ACTIVITY 2 GRAPHING

Display your data from Activity 1 in a line plot and a box-and-whisker plot. Which type of graph is better for comparing the amount of time you spend on extracurricular activities to the class average? Explain.

Random Samples and Surveys

PART 1
Choosing Samples for Surveys

What You'll Learn

1 To choose a sample for a survey of a population

2 To make estimates about populations

. . . And Why

To solve problems involving recycling and quality control

How many books do you read each week? What are your hobbies? Statisticians use questions like these in surveys to get information about specific groups. A **population** is a group about which you want information. A **sample** is a part of the population you use to make estimates about the population. The larger your sample, the more reliable your estimates will be.

For a **random sample** each member of the population has an equal chance to be selected. A random sample is likely to be representative of the whole population.

REAL-WORLD CONNECTION

■ EXAMPLE 1

You want to find out whether students will participate if you start a recycling program at your school. Tell whether each survey plan describes a good sample.

a. **Interview every tenth teenager you see at a mall.**
   This sample will probably include students who do not go to your school. It is not a good sample because it is not taken from the population you want to study.

b. **Interview the students in your ecology class.**
   The views of students in an ecology class may not represent the views about recycling of students in other classes. This is not a good sample because it is not random.

c. **Interview every tenth student leaving a school assembly.**
   This is a good sample. It is selected at random from the population you want to study.

■ **TRY THIS** Explain whether each plan describes a good sample.

1. You want to know which bicycle is most popular. You plan to survey entrants in a bicycle race.

2. You want to know how often teens rent videos. You plan to survey teens going into the local video rental store.

3. You want to know the most popular breakfast cereal. You plan to survey people entering a grocery store.

PART 2 Making Estimates about Populations

You can use a sample to make an estimate about a population by writing and solving a proportion.

REAL-WORLD CONNECTION

■ EXAMPLE 2

Quality Control **From 20,000 calculators produced, a manufacturer takes a random sample of 500 calculators. The sample has 3 defective calculators. Estimate the total number of defective calculators.**

$$\frac{\text{defective sample calculators}}{\text{sample calculators}} = \frac{\text{defective calculators}}{\text{calculators}} \qquad \text{Write a proportion.}$$

$$\frac{3}{500} = \frac{n}{20{,}000} \qquad \text{Substitute.}$$

$$3(20{,}000) = 500n \qquad \text{Write cross products.}$$

$$\frac{3(20{,}000)}{500} = \frac{500n}{500} \qquad \text{Divide each side by 500.}$$

$$120 = n \qquad \text{Simplify.}$$

Estimate: About 120 calculators are defective.

■ **TRY THIS** Use the data in the table below.

Calculator Samples

Sample	Number Sampled	Number Defective
A	500	3
B	200	2
C	50	0

4. Using Sample B, how many of 20,000 calculators would you estimate to be defective?

5. *Mathematical Reasoning* Would you expect an estimate based on Sample C to be more accurate or less accurate than one based on Sample B? Explain.

6. Explain why you would take a sample rather than counting or surveying an entire population.

Exercises

▶ CHECK UNDERSTANDING

You want to find out how popular basketball is at your school. State whether each survey plan describes a good sample. Explain your reasoning.

1. You interview the 10 tallest students in the school.

2. You choose 20 student identification numbers at random to find students to interview.

3. You interview 30 students watching a basketball game.

4. *Quality Control* A worker takes 100 eggs at random from a shipment of 144,000 eggs. The worker finds that four eggs are bad. Estimate the total number of bad eggs.

▶ PRACTICE AND PROBLEM SOLVING

You want to find out which restaurants in your city are most popular. State whether each survey plan describes a good sample. Explain your reasoning.

5. You choose people to interview at random from the city telephone book.

6. You interview every fifth person leaving a restaurant in the city.

7. You interview all the restaurant critics in the state.

8. **TEST PREP** You want to find how many students in the local elementary school bring their lunches. Which group would be a good sample?
   A. the entire student population   **B.** one first-grade homeroom
   C. the cafeteria workers   **D.** students on one school bus

9. *Open-ended* Describe a survey question, a population, and a sample you could use to make an estimate.

10. *Estimation* Of 75 pairs of jeans, 7 have flaws. Estimate how many of 24,000 pairs of jeans are flawed.

11. *Writing* From 50,000 computer chips produced, the manufacturer samples 250 chips and finds 2 that are defective. Explain how you could estimate the total number of defective chips.

12. **Error Analysis** Eight of the 32 students in your math class have a cold. The school population is 450. A student estimates that 112 students in the school have a cold.
   a. Why is your math class not representative of the population?
   b. Describe a survey plan you could use to better estimate the number of students who have a cold.

▶ MIXED REVIEW

Use the survey data at the right. Write each experimental probability as a fraction in simplest form. *(Lesson 12-7)*

Students' Pets

Number of Pets	Number of Students
0	9
1	12
2 or more	5

13. P(no pets)

14. P(one pet)

15. P(two or more pets)

16. P(at least one pet)

Geometry Find the area of each circle. Give the exact area and an approximate area. *(Lesson 10-3)*

17. $r = 24$ cm

18. $d = 45$ in.

19. $r = 50$ mi

20. How many combinations of four flowers can you choose from a bouquet of one dozen different flowers? *(Lesson 12-6)*

◢ CHECKPOINT 2   Lessons 12-5 through 12-8

1. A bag contains 10 cards labeled 1–10. You draw one card and then another, without replacing the first card before drawing the second. Find the probability of drawing two even numbers.

  A. $\frac{1}{5}$ **B.** $\frac{5}{10}$ **C.** $\frac{9}{10}$ **D.** $\frac{2}{9}$

2. a. A club of 20 students chooses a president and a vice-president. How many different outcomes are possible?
   b. A club of 20 students chooses two committee members. How many different committees may be chosen?

3. A hockey player attempts 15 goals and makes 2.
   a. Find the experimental probability of the player's making a goal.
   b. Predict the number of goals the player will make in the next game if the player attempts 23 goals.
   c. Can the player expect to make the same percent of goals in each game? Explain.

4. An orange farmer picks 450 oranges. Of these, 85 are "premium." Estimate the number of premium oranges the farmer will pick from a crop of 50,000 oranges.

 Simulate a Problem

Math Strategies in Action
Do you dream of flying your own airplane? Can you picture yourself in a space shuttle? Flight simulators help pilots train for real flying. Simulators are models of the real experience.

You can use simulations to investigate real-world problems. First develop a model, and then conduct an experiment.

■ SAMPLE PROBLEM

As time is running out in the basketball game, your team is behind by one point. You are fouled and go to the free-throw line. If you miss the shot, your team loses. If you make it, the score is tied and you get another shot. If you miss the second shot, the game ends in a tie. If you make both shots, your team wins. Your average at free throws is four out of five. What is the experimental probability that you tie or win the game?

 Read

Think about the problem.

1. Based on your average, what is the probability of making one free throw?

2. What methods could you use to simulate the problem?

Plan

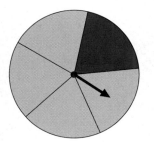

You can use a spinner to simulate the problem. Construct a spinner with five congruent sections. Make four of the sections blue and one of them red. The blue section represents *makes the shot* and the red section represents *misses the shot*. Each spin represents one shot.

3. How many spins will you make for each experiment?

4. How many experiments will you do?

 **Solve**

Use the results given in the table below. "B" stands for blue and "R" stands for red. Note that there is no second shot when the first shot is a miss (R).

Results of 100 Experiments

BR	BB	BB	BB	BB	BR	BB	BB	BB	BB
BR	BB	BR	BB	R	BB	R	BB	BR	BB
BB	BB	BB	R	BB	BB	BB	BB	BB	BB
BB	R	BB	BB	BB	BB	BB	BB	BB	BB
BB	R	BR	BR	BB	BB	BB	R	BB	BR
BB	BR	BB	BB	BB	R	BB	R	BB	BB
BB	R	BR	BB	BB	R	BB	BR	BB	R
BB	BB	BB	BB	BB	BB	BB	BR	BB	BB
BB	R	BR	BB	R	BB	BB	BB	R	BB
BR	BR	BB	R	BB	R	BB	BB	BB	BB

Make a frequency table.

Misses the first shot (R)	Makes the first shot and misses the second shot (BR)	Makes the first shot and makes the second shot (BB)
|||| |||| ||||		|||| |||| ||||	|||| |||| |||| |||| |||| |||| |||| |||| |||| |||| |||| |||| |||| ||||

5. Find each experimental probability.
  a. Your team wins the game.
  b. Your team ties the game.
  c. Your team wins or ties the game.

 **Look Back**

Simulations can give different results. You may find a different probability if you do another simulation. The more experiments you do, the closer the results of different simulations are likely to be.

6. Continue the simulation with another 100 experiments. Combine the results with the results of the first 100 experiments.

7. Based on the second simulation, what is the probability that your team wins?

Exercises

Solve by simulating the problem.

1. What is the probability that exactly three children in a family of five children will be boys? Assume that $P(\text{boy}) = P(\text{girl})$.

2. On a TV game show, you try to win a prize that is hidden behind one of three doors. After you choose a door, but before it is opened, the host opens one of the other doors, behind which there is no prize. You can then switch to the remaining closed door or stay with your original choice.
   a. Find the experimental probability of winning if your strategy is to stay with your original choice. (*Hint:* Simulate by using one marked index card and two unmarked index cards.)
   b. Find the experimental probability of winning if your strategy is to switch to the other door.
   c. *Writing* Should you stay or switch in this game? Explain.

PRACTICE AND PROBLEM SOLVING

Solve using any strategy.

3. You take a three-question multiple-choice test. Each question has four choices. You don't know any of the answers. What is the probability that you will guess exactly two out of three correctly?

4. Thirteen of 25 students are going on a field trip. Six students are traveling in a van. What is the theoretical probability that a student chosen at random from those going on the trip is *not* traveling in the van?

5. *Prices* The original cost of a jacket is $72. During a sale, the store reduces the jacket price by 25%. After the sale, the store raises the reduced jacket price by 25%. What is the price of the jacket after it is increased?

6. Each box of Tastycrunch cereal contains a prize. There are four possible prizes. The prizes are equally likely. You purchase 10 boxes of Tastycrunch. Find the probability that you will get all four prizes.

7. *Geometry* A farmer uses 24 yd of fencing to make a rectangular pen. The pen is 6 yd longer than it is wide. What are the dimensions of the pen?

8. A student draws a card at random from the cards below. What is the probability that the student will draw a card showing A or B?

9. You toss five coins. What is the probability that you will get five heads?

10. Many sweepstakes contests have an elimination round. In the elimination round, half of the entrants are chosen at random to go on to the final round. Then one person is chosen as the winner. What is the theoretical probability that a person who enters a contest with 10,000 entrants will be the winner?

11. The circumference of the peg is 3 in. Will the peg go through the hole? Explain.

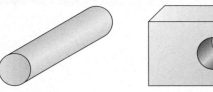
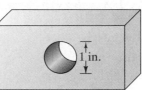

Journal

Explain the difference between experimental probability and theoretical probability.

▶ **MIXED REVIEW**

Estimate to the nearest integer. *(Lesson 11-1)*

12. $\sqrt{15}$ **13.** $\sqrt{10}$ **14.** $\sqrt{50}$ **15.** $-\sqrt{82}$

16. *Quality Control* Six out of every 80 wrenches are found to be defective. For a batch of 3,200 wrenches, estimate the number of wrenches that will *not* have any flaw. *(Lesson 12-8)*

17. *Geometry* You are building a kite in the shape of a square. Each side is 20 in. long. To the nearest inch, what length of wood do you need to make the diagonals? *(Lesson 11-2)*

CHAPTER PROJECT 12 — **ACTIVITY 3 COMPARING**

Design a survey plan for your entire school. The survey question will be the same as in Activity 1. Choose a sample and conduct the survey. Compare the results of your school survey to the results of your class survey by graphing them in a double box-and-whisker plot.

Using Random Numbers

Some calculators and computer programs can generate *random numbers*. You can use random numbers for simulations.

On a graphing calculator, the command *randInt* generates random integers. To create a list of random integers, press MATH ◄ 5. You will see **randInt(**. After the parenthesis, type "0,9999" and press ENTER to create a 4-digit random number. Each time you press ENTER you will get a different number. The calculator suppresses any zeros at the front of a number, so write 456, for example, as 0456.

■ EXAMPLE

There is a 30% probability of being stopped by a red light at each of four stoplights. Use a simulation to find the experimental probability of being stopped by at least two red lights.

Use your calculator to generate 20 random 4-digit numbers.

There is a 30% chance of a red light, so let three of the ten digits represent a red light. For this simulation let 1, 2, and 3 represent a red light. Let 4, 5, 6, 7, 8, 9, and 0 represent a yellow or green light.

5186	8918	4275	4285
8124	9619	2517	9964
0912	2759	2329	1666
8938	0357	6755	2227
0201	6325	1905	6885

Any group with two or more of the digits 1, 2, or 3 represents being stopped by at least two red lights. There are seven such groups in this list.

P(at least two red lights) $= \frac{7}{20}$, or 35%

1. Use the information in the Example. What is the probability of being stopped by exactly three red lights? By four red lights?

2. **a.** Create a new random number list by using randInt(0,999) in place of randInt(0,9999). How many digits are in each random number?
   b. How can you make a 6-digit random number?

3. *Writing* Suppose the probability of being stopped by a red light at each of four lights is 50%. Describe how you would use random numbers to find the probability of getting a red light at two or more lights.

4. About 20% of high school students in the United States say they would like to be President. Use random numbers to find the probability that at least three of the next five high school students you see would like to be President.

The Good Times POll

Conduct a survey The Project Activities on pages 635, 645, and 653 will help you complete your project. Here is a checklist to help you gather the different parts.

- ✔ the results of your class survey
- ✔ your graphs of the data from your class survey
- ✔ your double box-and-whisker plot comparing the results of your two surveys

Write a report that summarizes the results of your surveys. Include a description of your school survey plan and how you chose a sample. Also include your double box-and-whisker plot. Analyze the plot and write a paragraph that explains the conclusions you draw from your analysis.

Reflect and Revise

Ask a friend or someone at home to review your report. Are your graphs and explanations accurate and clear? If necessary, make changes to improve your report.

Web Extension

Visit Prentice Hall's Web site. You'll find some interesting links and ideas related to surveys. You'll also be able to share information about your project.

www.phschool.com

Wrap Up

■ Key Terms

box-and-whisker plot (p. 613)
combination (p. 637)
counting principle (p. 627)
dependent events (p. 633)
experimental probability
  (p. 642)

frequency table (p. 608)
independent events (p. 631)
line plot (p. 609)
permutation (p. 636)
population (p. 646)
quartile (p. 613)

random sample (p. 646)
range (p. 609)
sample (p. 646)
sample space (p. 627)
simulation (p. 642)
theoretical probability (p. 627)

■ Graphic Organizer

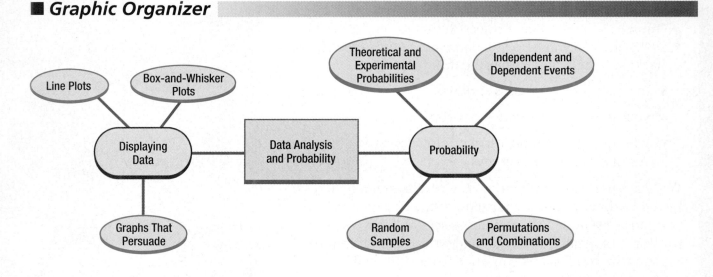

■ Frequency Tables and Line Plots

12-1

Summary You can show data in a **frequency table**, which lists each data item
with the number of times it occurs, or a **line plot**, which displays data
with **X** marks on a number line. The **range** is the difference between
the greatest and the least values in a set of data.

Display each set of data in a frequency table.

1. 11 10 12 10 12 11 13 12 11 9 12 10

2. 47 48 46 47 45 49 46 48 50 48 46 49

Draw a line plot for each frequency table. Find the range.

3.

Number	1	2	3	4	5	6
Frequency	6	4	5	2	3	1

4.

Number	1	2	3	4	5	6
Frequency	2	8	6	7	3	1

■ Box-and-Whisker Plots 12-2

Summary A **box-and-whisker plot** displays data items below a number line. **Quartiles** divide the data into four parts. The median is the middle quartile. You can compare two sets of related data by making two box-and-whisker plots on one number line.

Make a box-and-whisker plot for each set of data.

5. 6 9 6 5 8 2 3 9 4 8 5 7 12 9 4   **6.** 21 35 26 32 24 30 29 38 27 32 51

■ Using Graphs to Persuade 12-3

Summary Graphs can be misleading when a break is used in the scale or when the scale is distorted.

Use the graph at the right for Exercises 7 and 8.

7. *Writing* Explain why the graph could be misleading.

8. Explain how you could redraw the graph so that production seems to be increasing dramatically.

■ Counting Outcomes and Theoretical Probability 12-4

Summary A **sample space** is all the possible outcomes of an event. Use a tree diagram or the **Counting Principle** to count the number of outcomes. You can count outcomes to help find **theoretical probability**.

9. Volunteers have made a large number of sandwiches for a school party. The sandwiches come on white bread, whole wheat bread, or a roll. Each contains one of five fillings: turkey, chicken, egg salad, cheese, or peanut butter.
  a. How many different types of sandwich are possible?
  b. There are 20 of each type of sandwich. You receive one sandwich at random. Find the theoretical probability of getting a sandwich on bread with a meat filling.

■ Independent and Dependent Events 12-5

Summary **Independent events** are events in which one event *does not* affect the other event. If A and B are independent events, the probability of both A and B happening is $P(A \text{ and } B) = P(A) \cdot P(B)$.

Dependent events are events in which one event *does* affect the other event. If A and B are dependent events, the probability of both A and B happening is $P(A \text{ and } B) = P(A) \cdot P(B \text{ after } A)$.

You select a card at random from those at the right.
Find the probability of each event.

10. You select E, replace the card, and then select V.

11. You select T, do not replace the card, and then select N.

■ *Permutations and Combinations*

12-6

Summary An arrangement in which order is important is a **permutation**. An arrangement in which order does not matter is a **combination**.

**Tell whether each question is a *permutation* or a *combination*
problem. Explain. Then find each answer.**

12. In how many different ways can five people line up for a photo?

13. How many groups of three pens can you select from a box of twelve pens?

■ *Experimental Probability and Simulations*

12-7 and 12-9

Summary **Experimental probability** is based on experimental data. You can use a simulation to model real-world problems.

**Use the survey data at the right. Write each experimental
probability as a fraction in simplest form.**

**Notebooks in
Students' Lockers**

Number of Notebooks	Frequency
0	1
1	9
2	6
3 or more	4

14. P(one notebook)   **15.** P(at least two notebooks)

16. You take a 3-question multiple-choice quiz. Each question has 3 choices. You don't know any of the answers. Use a simulation to find the probability that you will guess 2 out of 3 correctly.

■ *Random Samples and Surveys*

12-8

Summary A **population** is a group about which you want information. A **sample** is a part of the population you use to make estimates for the population. In a **random sample** each member of the population has an equal chance to be selected.

**You want to find the favorite brand of in-line skates in your town.
Does each survey plan describe a good sample? Explain.**

17. You interview students in your homeroom.

18. You interview every tenth student entering the building.

19. You interview people skating at the local park.

Use the box-and-whisker plot for Exercises 1 and 2.

Test Grades

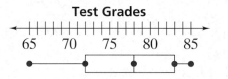

1. What is the median grade on the test?

2. What is the range in grades?

3. Make a box-and-whisker plot for the data.
75, 70, 80, 85, 85, 55, 60, 60, 65, 85, 75, 95, 50

4. Use the data below.
8, 4, 5, 1, 8, 4, 7, 9, 10, 5, 0, 5, 3, 4, 2
   a. Display the data in a frequency table.
   b. Display the data in a line plot.
   c. Find the range of the data.

The table shows the money spent on movie tickets. Use the table for Exercises 5 and 6.

Year	Dollars (billions)
1994	5.6
1995	6.0
1996	6.3

5. Draw a graph that emphasizes the increase in money spent over time.

6. Draw a graph to show that the money spent has not changed much over time.

Use the word TRAIN. Find the probability of each event when a letter is drawn at random.

7. selecting an R, replacing it, and then selecting an N

8. selecting an R, not replacing it, and then selecting an N

9. a. Find the sample space for tossing 3 coins.
   b. Find the theoretical probability of tossing 2 heads and 1 tail.

Simplify each expression.

10. $_3P_2$

11. $_5C_2$

Find the number of three-letter permutations you can make using each group of letters.

12. F, O, U, R

13. L, U, N, C, H

A student has 4 blue shirts and 2 white shirts. He selects one shirt at random. Without replacing the shirt, he selects a second shirt at random. Find each probability.

14. P(blue and white)

15. P(white and blue)

16. P(blue and blue)

17. P(white and white)

The table below shows the colors of a random sample of the bicycles in a rack at school. Use the table for Exercises 18–21.

Color	Number of Bicycles
Black	9
Blue	10
Red	14

Find each experimental probability for a bicycle chosen at random from the rack. Write each probability as a percent, to the nearest tenth of a percent.

18. P(red)

19. P(blue)

20. P(black)

21. How many bicycles would you expect to be black if there are 50 bicycles in the rack?

22. You roll a pair of number cubes once. What is the probability of rolling doubles?
   a. Find the sample space. Then find the theoretical probability.
   b. Use a simulation to find the experimental probability.
   c. *Writing* Should you expect your answers to (a) and (b) to be the same? Explain.

Choose the best answer.

1. $\overleftrightarrow{MN} \parallel \overleftrightarrow{OP}$. Which angles are supplementary?

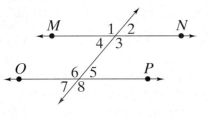

A. ∠1 and ∠3　　B. ∠4 and ∠6
C. ∠2 and ∠5　　D. ∠7 and ∠5

2. How many shaded triangles can fit inside the trapezoid?

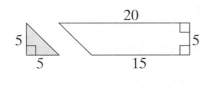

F. four　　　G. five
H. six　　　J. seven

3. Each of the six faces of a cube is painted either yellow or green. When the cube is tossed, the probability is $\frac{2}{3}$ that the cube will land with a green face up. How many faces are yellow?
A. one　　　B. two
C. three　　D. four

4. Simplify $_6P_3$.
F. 20　　G. 2　　H. 120　　J. 18

5. A student has 3 blue T-shirts and 2 white T-shirts. He selects one T-shirt at random. Without replacing the T-shirt, he selects another T-shirt at random. Find the probability that the student will pick a white T-shirt and then a blue T-shirt.
A. $\frac{3}{10}$　　B. $\frac{1}{6}$　　C. $\frac{1}{6}$　　D. $\frac{5}{6}$

6. A shoe manufacturer checks 150 pairs of walking shoes and finds three pairs to be defective. Find the probability that a pair of walking shoes is defective.
F. 2%　　G. 98%　　H. 148%　　J. 50%

For Exercises 7–11, show your work.

7. Make a box-and-whisker plot for the data.
55, 50, 60, 65, 65, 35, 40, 40, 45, 65, 55, 75, 30, 35, 55, 60, 45, 55

8. Use the data in the table. Make a graph that shows each situation.
a. sales decreasing sharply
b. sales staying about the same

Year	Sales (dollars)
1997	18.2 million
1998	17.9 million
1999	17.7 million
2000	17.5 million

9. You toss two coins.
a. Find the theoretical probability of tossing two tails.
b. Find the experimental probability of tossing two tails.
c. Summarize your results. Compare the two probabilities.

State whether each survey plan describes a good sample. Explain your reasoning.

10. You want to find out how many people who buy stamps are buying them for a stamp collection. You plan to survey people going into the post office.

11. You want to find out how popular the national women's soccer team is in your school. You survey all the young women in your school.

Skills You Need for Chapter 13

▶Equations with two variables   Use before Lessons 13-2 and 13-3.

Find the y values of each equation for $x = -2, 0,$ and 2.

1. $y = 3x - 4$ **2.** $y = -3x$ **3.** $y = 4x - 2$

4. $y = \frac{1}{2}x$ **5.** $y = \frac{3}{5}x - 5$ **6.** $y = 6 - 2x$

7. $y = -\frac{1}{4}x - 8$ **8.** $y = \frac{1}{4}x + 6$ **9.** $y = -3x - 1$

▶Evaluating expressions   Use before Lesson 13-4.

Evaluate each expression.

10. $8b$, for $b = 5$ **11.** $x - 5$, for $x = 16$ **12.** $104z$, for $z = 2$

13. $4a + 4$, for $a = 6$ **14.** $19 - (n - 6)$, for $n = 8$ **15.** $55 - 3mn$, for $m = 2, n = 5$

16. $c^2 + 5$, for $c = -4$ **17.** n^2, for $n = 0.8$ **18.** $(-h)^5$, for $h = 2$

19. $\frac{120}{s + r}$, for $s = 25$ and $r = 35$ **20.** $\frac{j - k}{9}$, for $j = 75$ and $k = 12$

▶Simplifying variable expressions   Use before Lesson 13-5.

Simplify each expression.

21. $5a - 4 + 6a$ **22.** $x - 4x + 3x + 5$ **23.** $g + 4 - 3g + g$

24. $5t + 5s + 5t$ **25.** $9b - 3d + 7d - 2b$ **26.** $-4(9c) + 2(-4c) - c$

▶Using the Distributive Property   Use before Lessons 13-6 and 13-7.

Simplify each expression.

27. $7(v + 3)$ **28.** $(d - 4)3$ **29.** $5(3x + 1)$ **30.** $-5(6 - 3t)$

31. $3(u - 8)$ **32.** $(p + 8)9$ **33.** $-4(-2y - 7)$ **34.** $4(-3d + 1)$

35. $10(5 - 3s)$ **36.** $-3(7 - 2w)$ **37.** $6(h + 9)$ **38.** $(9 - 2b)3$

Nonlinear Functions and Polynomials

What you'll learn in this chapter:

■ How to use arithmetic and geometric sequences

■ How to graph nonlinear functions

■ How to perform operations with polynomials

PRISM BUILDING

The prismatic shapes of the buildings at the left can be described using mathematical expressions such as $(a + b)^3$. Is $(a + b)^3$ equal to $a^3 + b^3$? No, but many students make that mistake. Sometimes it helps to have a concrete representation of a mathematical expression.

Make a 3-D Polynomial Model For the chapter project, you will make a three-dimensional model of a polynomial. You will analyze the model and its parts. You will use the model to see how polynomials can represent real-world objects.

Steps to help you complete the project

Internet Connection

Web Extension
www.phschool.com

How to solve a problem by using multiple strategies

13-1 Patterns and Sequences

What You'll Learn

1 To describe number patterns with arithmetic sequences

2 To describe number patterns with geometric sequences

...And Why

To use sequences in making predictions

Investigate

·············· DISCOVERING A PATTERN ··············

You win a contest and can choose one of two options for 30 days.

Option A	**Option B**
You receive $500 the first day, $550 the second, $600 the third, $650 the fourth, and so on.	You receive $1 the first day, $2 the second, $4 the third, $8 the fourth, and so on.

1. Make a table of values for both options for the first 10 days.
    a. Which option gives you more money in 10 days?
    b. Which option would you choose for 30 days? Explain.

PART 1 Arithmetic Sequences

Reading Math

In the phrase *arithmetic sequence*, the word *arithmetic* is pronounced "a rith MET ik." The third syllable, *met*, is emphasized.

A **sequence** is a set of numbers that follow a pattern. Each number in the sequence is a **term** of the sequence. You find a term of an **arithmetic sequence** by adding a fixed number to the previous term. This fixed number is called the **common difference.**

Term Number	1st	2nd	3rd	4th
Arithmetic Sequence	2	6	10	14
Common Difference		+4	+4	+4

■ EXAMPLE 1

What is the common difference in the sequence $4, 2, 0, -2, \ldots$?

    4   2   0 -2 **Find the common difference.**
      -2 -2 -2

The common difference is -2.

■ TRY THIS What is the common difference in each sequence?

2. $8, 13, 18, 23, \ldots$ **3.** $12, 9, 6, 3, \ldots$

You can continue a sequence and write a rule to describe it.

■ EXAMPLE 2

A runner training for a race runs 2 mi the first day, $2\frac{1}{4}$ mi the second day, $2\frac{1}{2}$ mi the third day, and so on. Find the next three terms of the sequence. Then write a rule to describe the sequence.

$$2 \quad 2\frac{1}{4} \quad 2\frac{1}{2} \quad 2\frac{3}{4} \quad 3 \quad 3\frac{1}{4}$$
$$+\frac{1}{4} \quad +\frac{1}{4} \quad +\frac{1}{4} \quad +\frac{1}{4} \quad +\frac{1}{4}$$

Find the common difference. Use it to find the next three terms.

The next three terms are $2\frac{3}{4}$, 3, and $3\frac{1}{4}$. The rule for the sequence is *Start with 2 and add $\frac{1}{4}$ repeatedly*.

■ TRY THIS

Find the next three terms of each sequence. Then write a rule to describe each sequence.

4. $23, 19, 15, 11, \ldots$ **5.** $-6, -4\frac{2}{3}, -3\frac{1}{3}, -2, \ldots$

During a two-mile run, a runner's feet strike the ground about 3,000 times. About how many times will the feet of the runner in Example 2 strike the ground on the fifth day?

PART 2   Geometric and Other Sequences

You find a term of a **geometric sequence** by *multiplying* the previous term by a fixed number called the **common ratio.**

Term Number	1st	2nd	3rd	4th
Geometric Sequence	2	6	18	54
Common Ratio		×3	×3	×3

You can find the common ratio for a geometric sequence by dividing a term by the previous term in the sequence.

Reading Math

The word *common* means "shared by all." The common ratio is called that because you get the same value when you divide each term in a geometric sequence by the previous term. The ratio is shared by every pair of consecutive terms.

■ EXAMPLE 3

Find the common ratio in the sequence 4, 8, 16, 32, … Find the next three terms of the sequence. Then write a rule to describe the sequence.

$$4 \quad 8 \quad 16 \quad 32 \quad 64 \quad 128 \quad 256$$
$$×2 \quad ×2 \quad ×2 \quad ×2 \quad ×2 \quad ×2$$

Find the common ratio. Use it to find the next three terms.

The next three terms are 64, 128, and 256. The rule for the sequence is *Start with 4 and multiply by 2 repeatedly*.

■ **TRY THIS** Find the common ratio and the next three terms of each sequence. Then write a rule to describe each sequence.

6. $2, 6, 18, 54, \ldots$ **7.** $4, 2, 1, 0.5, \ldots$

Not every sequence is arithmetic or geometric. You can determine whether any sequence of numbers *is* arithmetic or geometric by looking for a common difference or a common ratio. You can look for patterns to continue any sequence.

■ **EXAMPLE 4**

Tell whether each sequence is *arithmetic, geometric,* or *neither.* Find the next three terms of each sequence.

a. $4, 6, 8, 10, \ldots$

$$\begin{array}{ccccccc} 4 & 6 & 8 & 10 & 12 & 14 & 16 \\ +2 & +2 & +2 & +2 & +2 & +2 \end{array}$$

There is a common difference of 2. The sequence is arithmetic. The next three terms are 12, 14, and 16.

b. $4, 6, 9, 13\frac{1}{2}, \ldots$

$$\begin{array}{ccccccc} 4 & 6 & 9 & 13\frac{1}{2} & 20\frac{1}{4} & 30\frac{3}{8} & 45\frac{9}{16} \\ \times\frac{3}{2} & \times\frac{3}{2} & \times\frac{3}{2} & \times\frac{3}{2} & \times\frac{3}{2} & \times\frac{3}{2} \end{array}$$

The ratio determined by the first three terms is $\frac{6}{4}$ or $\frac{9}{6}$. These equal $\frac{3}{2}$, which is the common ratio. The sequence is geometric. The next three terms are $20\frac{1}{4}$, $30\frac{3}{8}$, and $45\frac{9}{16}$.

c. $4, 6, 9, 13, \ldots$

$$\begin{array}{ccccccc} 4 & 6 & 9 & 13 & 18 & 24 & 31 \\ +2 & +3 & +4 & +5 & +6 & +7 \end{array}$$

The sequence is neither arithmetic nor geometric. Following the pattern above, the next three terms are 18, 24, and 31.

■ **TRY THIS** Tell whether each sequence is *arithmetic, geometric,* or *neither.* Find the next three terms of each sequence.

8. $3, 9, 27, 81, \ldots$ **9.** $10, 13, 18, 25, \ldots$

10. $-12, 12, -12, 12, \ldots$ **11.** $50, 200, 350, 500, \ldots$

Exercises

CHECK UNDERSTANDING

What is the common difference of each arithmetic sequence?

1. $5, 4, 3, 2, \ldots$ **2.** $4, 11, 18, 25, \ldots$ **3.** $1, 1\frac{1}{2}, 2, 2\frac{1}{2}, \ldots$ **4.** $7, 1, -5, -11, \ldots$

What is the common ratio of each geometric sequence?

5. $45, 90, 180, 360, \ldots$ **6.** $3, 6, 12, 24, \ldots$ **7.** $5, 1, \frac{1}{5}, \frac{1}{25}, \ldots$ **8.** $-3, -15, -75, \ldots$

Find the next three terms of each sequence. Then write a rule to describe each sequence.

9. $1, 4, 16, 64, \ldots$ **10.** $-21, -18, -15, -12, \ldots$ **11.** $6.5, 6.7, 6.9, 7.1, \ldots$

PRACTICE AND PROBLEM SOLVING

What is the common difference of each arithmetic sequence?

12. $-6, -5, -4, -3, \ldots$ **13.** $3, 9, 15, 21, \ldots$ **14.** $80, 60, 40, 20, \ldots$ **15.** $5, 6.4, 7.8, 9.2, \ldots$

What is the common ratio of each geometric sequence?

16. $5, 10, 20, 40, \ldots$ **17.** $-4, 12, -36, 108, \ldots$ **18.** $8, 40, 200, 1{,}000, \ldots$ **19.** $12, 4, 1\frac{1}{3}, \frac{4}{9}, \ldots$

Find the next three terms of each sequence. Then write a rule to describe each sequence.

20. $0, 5, 10, 15, \ldots$ **21.** $9, 18, 36, 72, \ldots$ **22.** $2, 20, 200, 2{,}000, \ldots$ **23.** $21, 15, 9, 3, \ldots$

24. $25, 50, 75, 100, \ldots$ **25.** $80, 50, 20, -10, \ldots$ **26.** $3, 1, -1, -3, \ldots$ **27.** $2, 8, 32, 128, \ldots$

**Tell whether each sequence is *arithmetic, geometric,* or *neither.*
Find the next three terms of each sequence.**

28. $1, 3, 9, 27, \ldots$ **29.** $10, 5, 0, -5, \ldots$ **30.** $4.5, 4, 3.5, 3, \ldots$

31. $2, 2, 4, 6, \ldots$ **32.** $-1, 3, -9, 27, \ldots$ **33.** $\frac{1}{2}, \frac{5}{6}, 1\frac{1}{6}, 1\frac{1}{2}, \ldots$

34. $7, 7.03, 7.06, 7.09, \ldots$ **35.** $0, 5, 12, 21, \ldots$ **36.** $1, 10, 2, 20, \ldots$

37. $13, 12, 10, 7, \ldots$ **38.** $50, 150, 450, 950, \ldots$ **39.** $-\frac{1}{5}, -\frac{1}{10}, -\frac{1}{20}, -\frac{1}{40}, \ldots$

40. *Writing* The first two numbers of a sequence are 4 and 8. Can you tell what kind of sequence this is? Explain.

Math in the Media Use the article at the right for Exercise 41.

41. Write the data as a sequence. Then answer the questions below.
    a. Find the difference between each pair of consecutive terms of the sequence.
    b. Find the ratio between each pair of consecutive terms of the sequence.
    c. Does an arithmetic or a geometric sequence best model the data?
    d. Use your choice in part (c) to predict what the population will be in the year 2005.

> ## Population Watch
> The population of the United States in 1980 was about 226 million, in 1985 it was about 238 million, in 1990 it was about 249 million, and in 1995 it was about 263 million.

Evaluate each expression for $n = -2, -1, 0,$ and 1. Is the sequence formed *arithmetic, geometric,* or *neither*?

42. $3n$ **43.** $n(n + 1)$ **44.** 2^n **45.** $2n$ **46.** n^2

47. You open a savings account with $2,000. The account earns 4% interest compounded semiannually.
    a. Write the balance in the savings account after each interest payment for two years.
    b. Does the pattern of balances form an arithmetic or geometric sequence? Explain.

48. ***Patterns*** In the Fibonacci sequence $1, 1, 2, 3, 5, 8, \ldots$, you find each term (after the first two terms) by adding the two previous terms together. Write the next three terms of the sequence.

49. TEST PREP If the first term of an arithmetic sequence is 35 and the tenth term is 107, what is the third term?
    A. 50 **B.** 51 **C.** 52 **D.** 53

The formula for compound interest is $B = p(1 + r)^n$, where B is the balance, p is the principal, r is the interest rate for each interest period, and n is the number of interest periods. For interest that is compounded semiannually, the interest rate is $\frac{1}{2}$ the yearly rate.

▶ **MIXED REVIEW**

Find the circumference of each circle. (*Lesson 9-6*)

50. diameter = 14 cm **51.** radius = 5 in. **52.** radius = 8.5 m

53. List the congruent corresponding parts of the triangles at the right. Write a congruence statement for the triangles. (*Lesson 9-5*)

54. ***Surveys*** You want to find out which presidential candidate is most popular in your city. You plan to interview people who visit the city's art museum. State whether the survey plan describes a good sample. Explain your reasoning. (*Lesson 12-8*)

See also Extra Practice section.

Graphing Nonlinear Functions

Investigate

································ GRAPHING DATA ································

You can graph the area of a square as a function of the length of a side of the square.

1. Complete the table at the right.

2. Draw a graph of the data. Does your graph appear to be a linear function? Explain.

Side x	Area $f(x)$
1	1
2	■
3	■
4	■
5	■
6	36

What You'll Learn

1 To graph quadratic functions

2 To graph absolute value functions

...And Why

To use nonlinear functions in modeling real-world situations, such as finding the area of an enclosed space

---

PART 1 **Graphing Quadratic Functions**

In a **quadratic function,** the input variable is squared. The graph of a quadratic function is a U-shaped curve, called a *parabola*. The curve may open upward or downward.

Reading Math

A *nonlinear function* is a function that cannot be graphed as a line.

■ EXAMPLE 1

For the function $y = 2x^2$, make a table with integer values of x from -2 to 2. Then graph the function.

Make a table.

x	$2x^2 = y$	(x, y)
-2	$2(-2)^2 = 8$	$(-2, 8)$
-1	$2(-1)^2 = 2$	$(-1, 2)$
0	$2(0)^2 = 0$	$(0, 0)$
1	$2(1)^2 = 2$	$(1, 2)$
2	$2(2)^2 = 8$	$(2, 8)$

Make a graph.

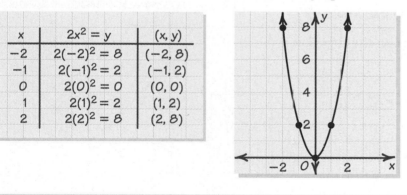

■ TRY THIS For each function, make a table with integer values of x from -2 to 2. Then graph each function.

3. $y = \frac{1}{2}x^2 + 3$

4. $y = -x^2 + 3$

■ **EXAMPLE 2**

The function $A = 10x - x^2$, where x is the width in yards, gives the area A of a goat pen in square yards. Graph the function. Use the graph to find the width that gives the greatest area.

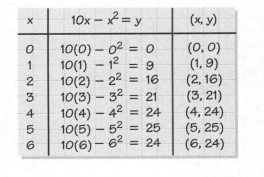

x	$10x - x^2 = y$	(x, y)
0	$10(0) - 0^2 = 0$	$(0, 0)$
1	$10(1) - 1^2 = 9$	$(1, 9)$
2	$10(2) - 2^2 = 16$	$(2, 16)$
3	$10(3) - 3^2 = 21$	$(3, 21)$
4	$10(4) - 4^2 = 24$	$(4, 24)$
5	$10(5) - 5^2 = 25$	$(5, 25)$
6	$10(6) - 6^2 = 24$	$(6, 24)$

Suppose the area of this kid's pen is 24 yd². What are the pen's width and length?

The ordered pair $(5, 25)$ shows what appears to be the highest point. So the width 5 yards gives the greatest area.

■ **TRY THIS** Graph each function.

5. $y = -2x^2$ 6. $y = 6x - x^2$

PART 2 **Graphing Absolute Value Functions**

The equation $y = |x|$ is an **absolute value function.** The graph of $y = |x|$ is V-shaped.

■ **EXAMPLE 3**

Graph the function $y = |x|$.

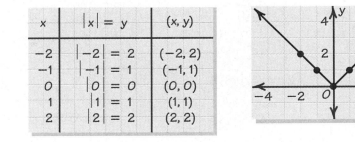

x	$|x| = y$	(x, y)
-2	$|-2| = 2$	$(-2, 2)$
-1	$|-1| = 1$	$(-1, 1)$
0	$|0| = 0$	$(0, 0)$
1	$|1| = 1$	$(1, 1)$
2	$|2| = 2$	$(2, 2)$

■ **TRY THIS** Graph each function.

7. $y = -|x| + 1$ 8. $y = 2|x|$

Exercises

► CHECK UNDERSTANDING

What is the shape of the graph of each function?

1. $y = |x| + 1$ **2.** $y = x^2 - 8$ **3.** $y = -4x^2$ **4.** $y = -|x| - 3$

For each function, make a table with integer values of x from -2 to 2. Then graph each function.

5. $y = x^2 + 1$ **6.** $y = |x| - 2$ **7.** $y = -x^2 + 2$ **8.** $y = -3|x|$

► PRACTICE AND PROBLEM SOLVING

TEST PREP   **Match each graph with an equation.**

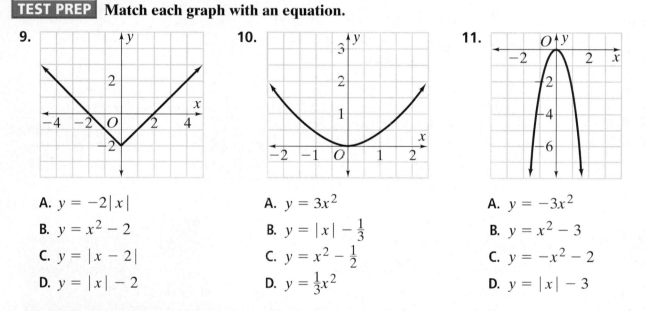

9.

A. $y = -2|x|$

B. $y = x^2 - 2$

C. $y = |x - 2|$

D. $y = |x| - 2$

10.

A. $y = 3x^2$

B. $y = |x| - \frac{1}{3}$

C. $y = x^2 - \frac{1}{2}$

D. $y = \frac{1}{3}x^2$

11.

A. $y = -3x^2$

B. $y = x^2 - 3$

C. $y = -x^2 - 2$

D. $y = |x| - 3$

For each function, make a table with integer values of x from -2 to 2. Then graph each function.

12. $y = x^2 - 2$ **13.** $y = x^2 + 4$ **14.** $y = 2x^2 - 2$ **15.** $y = -x^2 + 5$

16. $y = |x| + 3$ **17.** $y = |x| - 4$ **18.** $y = -|x| - 1$ **19.** $y = -2|x|$

20. *Open-ended* Write an absolute value function of your own. Graph the function.

21. *Mathematical Reasoning* For the function $y = x^3$, make a table with integer values of x from -2 to 2. Then graph the function. Is the function quadratic? Explain.

22. **a.** *Geometry* Make a table to show side lengths and volumes of four cubes. The four cubes have integer side lengths from 1 m to 4 m.
    b. Graph the ordered pairs from your table.
    c. Using your graph from part (b), estimate the volume of a cube with side length 3.5 m.

23. **a.** Graph $y = x^2$, $y = 2x^2$, and $y = \frac{1}{2}x^2$ on a coordinate plane.
    b. *Writing* Describe how the coefficient of x^2 affects the width of the graph of the functions.

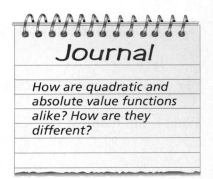

Journal

How are quadratic and absolute value functions alike? How are they different?

▶ MIXED REVIEW

Find the next three terms of each sequence. Then write a rule to describe each sequence. *(Lesson 13-1)*

24. $4, 11, 18, 25, \ldots$ 25. $12, 27, 42, 57, \ldots$ 26. $3, 6, 9, 12, \ldots$

Name all points, segments, lines, and rays shown. *(Lesson 9-1)*

27.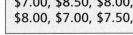
    $A\ B$ C

28. D E F

29. *Statistics* The data at the right show the prices of an evening movie at eighteen different movie theaters. Use the data to draw a frequency table. *(Lesson 12-1)*

Cost of a Movie

$7.00, $6.50, $7.50, $7.00, $7.50, $8.00, $7.00, $8.50, $8.00, $6.00, $7.00, $7.50, $8.00, $7.00, $7.50, $8.50, $7.50, $6.50

Math at Work
Computer Systems Analyst

Systems analysts are responsible for upgrading hardware and designing and installing new software. They also respond to problems users have with hardware or software. Logic skills are necessary for writing programs, isolating problems, and solving problems.

Systems analysts have backgrounds in computer programming. Since computer technology is constantly changing, they must continue their education throughout their careers.

For more information about systems analysts, visit the Prentice Hall Web site. www.phschool.com

Exponential Growth and Decay

PART 1 Exponential Growth

A function like $y = 2^x$ has input, or domain, values that are exponents. It models *exponential growth*. Its graph curves upward as input values increase.

REAL-WORLD CONNECTION

■ EXAMPLE 1

Biology **A warren of rabbits starts with one male and one female. The number of rabbits then doubles each month. The function $y = 2^x$ models the number of rabbits in the warren. For the function $y = 2^x$, make a table with integer values of x from 2 to 5. Then graph the function.**

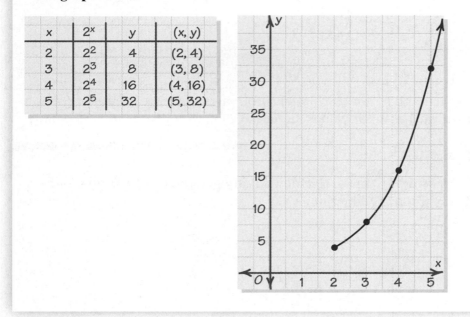

x	2^x	y	(x, y)
2	2^2	4	$(2, 4)$
3	2^3	8	$(3, 8)$
4	2^4	16	$(4, 16)$
5	2^5	32	$(5, 32)$

■ TRY THIS

1. For the function $y = 3^x$, make a table with integer values of x from 1 to 4. Then graph the function.

You can multiply the power in a function by a number. For example, in $y = 0.25(4^x)$, the power 4^x is multiplied by 0.25.

■ EXAMPLE 2

For the function $y = 0.25(4)^x$, make a table with integer values of x from 0 to 4. Then graph the function.

x	$0.25(4)^x$	y	(x, y)
0	$0.25(4)^0$	0.25	$(0, 0.25)$
1	$0.25(4)^1$	1	$(1, 1)$
2	$0.25(4)^2$	4	$(2, 4)$
3	$0.25(4)^3$	16	$(3, 16)$
4	$0.25(4)^4$	64	$(4, 64)$

■ TRY THIS

2. For $y = 0.5(2)^x$, make a table with integer values of x from 0 to 5. Then graph the function.

PART 2 — Exponential Decay

A function like $y = \left(\frac{1}{2}\right)^x$ models *exponential decay*. Its graph slopes downward as input values increase.

■ EXAMPLE 3

For $y = 60\left(\frac{1}{2}\right)^x$, make a table with integer values of x from 0 to 5. Then graph the function.

x	$60\left(\frac{1}{2}\right)^x$	y	(x, y)
0	$60\left(\frac{1}{2}\right)^0$	60	$(0, 60)$
1	$60\left(\frac{1}{2}\right)^1$	30	$(1, 30)$
2	$60\left(\frac{1}{2}\right)^2$	15	$(2, 15)$
3	$60\left(\frac{1}{2}\right)^3$	7.5	$(3, 7.5)$
4	$60\left(\frac{1}{2}\right)^4$	3.75	$(4, 3.75)$
5	$60\left(\frac{1}{2}\right)^5$	1.875	$(5, 1.875)$

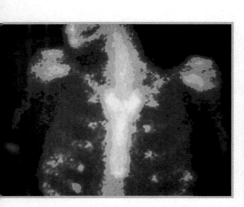

Doctors use the element technetium to make bone scans. Technetium decays exponentially. After 6 hours, only 15 mg of a 30-mg dose remains. After 12 hours, only 7.5 mg remains. How much remains after 18 h?

■ TRY THIS

3. For the function $y = 90\left(\frac{1}{3}\right)^x$, make a table with integer values of x from 0 to 5. Then graph the function.

Exercises

CHECK UNDERSTANDING

Complete the table for each function.

1. $f(x) = 0.5(2)^x$

x	0	1	2	3	4	5
f(x)	0.5	■	■	4	■	16

2. $y = 30\left(\frac{1}{3}\right)^x$

x	0	1	2	3	4	5
y	■	10	■	■	■	■

3. $y = 4(0.5)^x$

x	0	1	2	3	4	5
y	4	■	1	■	■	■

For each function, make a table with integer values of x from 0 to 5. Then graph each function.

4. $y = 3^x$

5. $g(x) = 3 \cdot 2^x$

6. $y = 100(0.6)^x$

PRACTICE AND PROBLEM SOLVING

Match each graph with an equation.

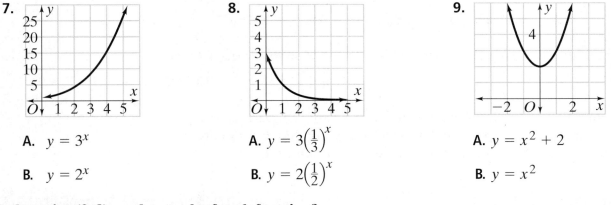

7.

A. $y = 3^x$

B. $y = 2^x$

8.

A. $y = 3\left(\frac{1}{3}\right)^x$

B. $y = 2\left(\frac{1}{2}\right)^x$

9.

A. $y = x^2 + 2$

B. $y = x^2$

Is the point (2, 8) on the graph of each function?

10. $y = 4x$

11. $y = 2^x$

12. $y = x^2$

13. $y = \left(\frac{1}{2}\right)^x$

For each function, make a table with integer values of x from 0 to 4. Then graph each function.

14. $y = 2 \cdot 3^x$

15. $f(x) = \frac{1}{2} \cdot 2^x$

16. $y = \frac{1}{5} \cdot 5^x$

17. $g(x) = 20\left(\frac{1}{2}\right)^x$

18. $y = 6(0.5)^x$

19. $y = 200(0.4)^x$

20. a. For the functions $y = 2x$, $y = x^2$, and $y = 2^x$, make tables with integer values of x from 0 to 5. Then graph the functions.

b. *Writing* Describe how the graphs are similar. Describe how they are different.

21. **Critical Thinking** Without graphing, predict whether each function shows exponential growth or exponential decay. Explain how you came to your conclusion.

    a. $y = 5^x$ **b.** $y = \left(\frac{1}{2}\right)^x$ **c.** $y = 3(0.2)^x$ **d.** $y = 3(2)^x$

22. **Biology** A bacteria culture starts with 10 cells and doubles every hour. The function $y = 10(2)^x$ models the number of cells y in the culture after x hours. How many bacteria are in the culture after 3 hours?

23. **Finance** You put $100 in a stock that has an annual return of 20% of its value. This is the same as 20% interest compounded annually. The function $b = 100(1.2)^x$ describes the balance b in the account after x years.

    a. Evaluate the function for $x = 2$. What does the value represent?

    b. For the function, make a table with integer values of x from 1 to 6. Graph the function.

    c. **Critical Thinking** Estimate how long it will take for the balance to be twice the initial investment.

▶ MIXED REVIEW

Graph each function. *(Lesson 13-2)*

24. $y = |x| + 2$ **25.** $f(x) = 3|x|$ **26.** $y = x^2 - 5$ **27.** $g(x) = -x^2 + 1$

Find the midpoint of each segment with the given endpoints. *(Lesson 11-3)*

28. $A(4, -6)$ and $B(-2, 5)$ **29.** $X(-3, -8)$ and $Y(1, 6)$ **30.** $Q(7, 9)$ and $R(-7, -9)$

31. Janelle is buying a sweatshirt. She has a choice of red, purple, or green; zipper or no zipper; and hooded or not hooded. How many different sweatshirt choices does she have? *(Lesson 12-4)*

✓ CHECKPOINT 1   Lessons 13-1 through 13-3

Find the next three terms of each sequence. Then write a rule to describe the sequence.

1. $100, 85, 70, 55, \ldots$ **2.** $17, 24, 31, 38, \ldots$ **3.** $13, 26, 52, 104, \ldots$

For each function, make a table with integer values of x from 0 to 4. Then graph each function.

4. $y = \frac{1}{4}x^2$ **5.** $f(x) = \frac{1}{4}|x|$ **6.** $y = 0.25(2)^x$ **7.** $f(x) = 0.5(3)^x$

8. **TEST PREP** The graph of which function has points in Quadrant IV?

    A. $y = x^2 + 2$ **B.** $y = 0.2(2)^x$ **C.** $y = |x| - 2$ **D.** $y = 2\left(\frac{1}{2}\right)^x$

Nonlinear Functions and Graphing Calculators

You can use a graphing calculator to graph nonlinear functions.
For the exponent 2, you can use the x^2 key or press $\wedge$ 2.

■ EXAMPLE

Graph $y = |3x|$.

Step 1 Press $\boxed{Y=}$ $\boxed{\text{MATH}}$ $\boxed{\blacktriangleright}$ $\boxed{\text{ENTER}}$ 5.
Then press 3 $\boxed{\text{X,T,}\theta,n}$ $\boxed{)}$.

```
Plot1  Plot2  Plot3
\Y1■abs(3X)
\Y2=
\Y3=
\Y4=
\Y5=
\Y6=
\Y7=
```

Step 2 Set your viewing window.

```
WINDOW
Xmin=-5
Xmax=5
Xscl=1
Ymin=-5
Ymax=5
Yscl=1
Xres=1
```

Step 3 Use $\boxed{\text{GRAPH}}$ to see your graph.

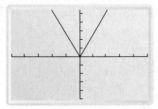

Step 4 Use the $\boxed{\text{TABLE}}$ feature to see solutions.

X	Y1
-4	12
-3	9
-2	6
-1	3
0	0
1	3
2	6

X=2

Graph each equation using a graphing calculator. For each function, use the solutions you see in the $\boxed{\text{TABLE}}$ feature to create a table with integer values of x from -5 to 5. Then sketch the graph.

1. $y = |2x|$

2. $y = -|2x|$

3. $y = |2x| + 1$

4. $y = x^2 - 1$

5. $y = -x^2 - 1$

6. $y = 3(2)^x$

7. $y = -3(2)^x$

8. $y = 3\left(\frac{1}{2}\right)^x$

9. $y = -3\left(\frac{1}{2}\right)^x$

10. *Open-ended* Write a nonlinear function that you can graph using a graphing calculator. Graph your function. Make a table of values and sketch your graph.

13-4 Polynomials

PART 1 Identifying Polynomials

What You'll Learn

1 To identify polynomials

2 To evaluate polynomials

...And Why

To model real-world applications in science

You have seen how mathematics uses algebraic expressions to represent real-world situations. Some of these expressions are monomials. A **monomial** is a real number, a variable, or a product of a real number and variables with whole-number exponents.

Monomials: 3 m $5xy$ $0.35bc^3$ $\frac{w}{9}$ $\frac{1}{4}p^2q$

Not monomials: $a - 8$ $\sqrt{m}$ y^{-1} (or $\frac{1}{y}$) $\frac{ab}{c}$

■ EXAMPLE 1

Is each expression a monomial? Explain.

a. $7x^2y$ Yes, the expression is the product of the real number 7 and the variables x and y.

b. $8 + a$ No, the expression is a sum.

c. $\frac{a}{7y}$ No, the denominator contains a variable.

d. $\frac{5x}{4}$ Yes, the expression is the product of the real number $\frac{5}{4}$ and the variable x.

■ **TRY THIS** Is each expression a monomial? Explain.

1. $\frac{6}{m}$ **2.** $\frac{m}{6}$ **3.** 45   **4.** $mx + b$

A **polynomial** is a monomial or a sum or difference of monomials. We call the monomials that make up a polynomial its *terms*. You can name a polynomial by the number of its terms.

Polynomial	Number of terms	Examples
Monomial	1	$4, 32, x, 2x^2$
Binomial	2	$x - 3, 5x + 1, x^3 - x$
Trinomial	3	$x^2 + x + 1, x^4 - 2x - 5$

EXAMPLE 2

Tell whether each polynomial is a *monomial*, a *binomial*, or a *trinomial*.

a. $x - y$

binomial

b. $8xyz$

monomial

c. $y^2 + 8y + 18$

trinomial

■ **TRY THIS** Tell whether each polynomial is a monomial, a binomial, or a trinomial.

5. 10

6. $9x^2 + xy$

7. $8 - y$

8. $5 + x - 3y$

PART 2 Evaluating Polynomials

You evaluate polynomials by substituting values for the variables.

EXAMPLE 3

Evaluate each polynomial for $m = 8$ and $p = -3$.

a. $2mp$

$2mp = 2(8)(-3)$ Replace m with 8 and p with −3.

$= -48$ Simplify.

b. $3m - 2p$

$3m - 2p = 3(8) - 2(-3)$

$= 24 + 6$

$= 30$

■ **TRY THIS** Evaluate each polynomial for $x = -2$ and $y = 5$.

9. $5xy$

10. $x + 3y$

11. $y^2 - 2y + x$

REAL-WORLD CONNECTION

EXAMPLE 4

Science The polynomial $-16t^2 + 140t$ gives the height, in feet, reached by fireworks in t seconds. If the fireworks explode 4 seconds after launch, at what height do they explode?

$-16t^2 + 140t$

$-16(4)^2 + 140(4)$ Replace t with 4.

304 Simplify.

The fireworks explode at 304 feet.

■ **TRY THIS**

12. Fireworks are set to explode 6 seconds after launch. At what height will they explode?

During a twenty-minute show, fireworks technicians can set off as many as 6,000 different fireworks. How many fireworks is that per minute?

Exercises

CHECK UNDERSTANDING

Is each expression a monomial? Explain.

1. $2 + x$ **2.** $18ab^2$ **3.** $\frac{4}{b}$ **4.** 1 **5.** pq^{-3} **6.** $0.82k$

Tell whether each polynomial is a *monomial*, a *binomial*, or a *trinomial*.

7. $3xy + 4y^2$ **8.** $5c - 2 + a$ **9.** $7y^2 + 2y - 9$ **10.** 658

Evaluate each polynomial for $a = 2$ and $b = -4$.

11. $a - 3b$ **12.** $5a + 7b$ **13.** $ab^2 + 5$ **14.** $2a^2 - b + 4$

15. *Open-ended* Write a trinomial.

PRACTICE AND PROBLEM SOLVING

Is each expression a monomial? Explain.

16. $2x$ **17.** $-0.3y$ **18.** $\frac{a}{3}$ **19.** 82 **20.** $\frac{3}{p}$ **21.** $10bc + b$

Tell whether each polynomial is a *monomial*, a *binomial*, or a *trinomial*.

22. $3x^2 + 2x$ **23.** 21 **24.** $7p^2$ **25.** $56 - x$

26. $x^2 + 7x + 4$ **27.** $15 + w$ **28.** abc **29.** $4.5 + 3.7m$

Evaluate each polynomial for $x = -5$ and $y = 3$.

30. $y - x$ **31.** $2x + 2y$ **32.** $7 + x^2y$ **33.** $7y^2 + 6x - 20$

34. $xy - y$ **35.** $3y + x$ **36.** $x^2 + 2x - 3$ **37.** $\frac{x^2}{5} + x$

38. a. *Writing* Name other words with the prefixes *mono, bi, tri*, and *poly*. How do the prefixes help you understand the meanings of the words?

   b. What would you call a polynomial with four terms?

Critical Thinking **Tell why each expression is not a polynomial.**

39. $x^2 + 2x + \frac{1}{x}$ **40.** $2ab + b^2 + \sqrt{a}$ **41.** $(y^2 + 4) \div y$

42. **TEST PREP** Which of the following statements is *not* true?
   A. A monomial is a polynomial.
   B. A binomial consists of two monomials.
   C. A polynomial must have more than one term.
   D. An integer is a monomial.

43. *Geometry* You can write an expression for the area of a trapezoid as $\frac{1}{2}b_1h + \frac{1}{2}b_2h$. What kind of polynomial is this?

44. a. The polynomial $34x^2 - 945x + 46{,}971$ models U.S. public school enrollment, in thousands, from 1970 to 1998. The value of x for 1970 is 1 and the value of x for 1998 is 29. How many students were enrolled in public schools in 1970? In 1998?
   b. Use the polynomial to predict enrollment in 2010.

45. *Geometry* A polygon is convex if no diagonal has points outside the polygon. The polynomial $\frac{n^2}{2} - \frac{3n}{2}$ gives the number of diagonals that you can draw in a convex polygon with n sides. How many diagonals does a 20-sided convex polygon have?

▶ **MIXED REVIEW**

For each function, make a table with integer values of x from 1 to 4. Then graph each function. *(Lesson 13-3)*

46. $y = 2 \cdot 2^x$

47. $f(x) = \frac{1}{3} \cdot 3^x$

48. $y = 18(0.2)^x$

Simplify each expression. *(Lesson 2-3)*

49. $m + 5 + 3m$

50. $2y - 12 + 6x + 5$

51. $-4a + 10b + 7a - 2$

52. *Navigation* A plane is flying 6.3 mi above the ground. The angle of depression to an airport is 14°. How far is the plane from the airport (in ground distance)? *(Lesson 11-7)*

CHAPTER PROJECT 13 ACTIVITY 1 CREATING

Use poster board to make two cubes, one with edge length a, and one with edge length b. You can use any values you choose for a and b. Next make six rectangular prisms, three with dimensions $a \times a \times b$, and three with dimensions $a \times b \times b$. Assemble the eight prisms into one large cube. Use tape to hold the prisms together. What is the edge length of the large cube, in terms of a and b?

Degree of a Polynomial

Just as you can get information about a polynomial by counting the number of terms, you can get other information by looking at the exponents. The *degree of a term* is the sum of the exponents of the variables in the term. The *degree of a polynomial* is the greatest degree of its terms.

polynomial $\longrightarrow x^3 + 4x^2 + xy - 5x + 9 \longleftarrow$ The degree of a nonzero constant is zero.

degree of each term $\longrightarrow$ 3   2   2   1   0

Degree of the polynomial is 3.

■ EXAMPLE 1

Identify each polynomial by name and by degree.

a. $2 - a$

   0   1 $\longleftarrow$ degree of each term

Greatest degree of the terms is 1.

The polynomial is a binomial of degree 1.

b. $3y^3x$

   4 $\longleftarrow$ Add the exponents: $3 + 1 = 4$.

Degree of the term is 4.

The polynomial is a monomial of degree 4.

c. $5x^2 + x + 4$

   2   1   0 $\longleftarrow$ degree of each term

Greatest degree of the terms is 2.

The polynomial is a trinomial of degree 2.

Identify each polynomial by name and by degree.

1. $9c + 5$ **2.** $12a^2b$ **3.** $6x^2 - 3x + 2$ **4.** p^2q^3

5. $d^4 + 6d$ **6.** $4a^3 + 8a^2 - 11$ **7.** $24x^3yz$ **8.** $15x - 2x^2$

When you write a polynomial with the terms in order of decreasing degree, the polynomial is in *standard form*. When terms need to be moved, first use the Commutative Property of Addition to reorganize terms that are subtracted. For example, you can write $4 - x^2$ as $4 + (-x^2)$. Then you can rewrite the polynomial as $-x^2 + 4$.

■ EXAMPLE 2

Write each polynomial in standard form.

a. $x^4 + 2 - x^2$

  4 0 2 ←—— degree of each term

standard form: $x^4 - x^2 + 2$

b. $-2y + y^3 + y^2 - 3$

  1 3 2 0 ←—— degree of each term

standard form: $y^3 + y^2 - 2y - 3$

Write each polynomial in standard form.

9. $8 + 5a$

10. $3y^2 + 16 + y$

11. $2c + 4c^2 - 7$

12. $5x - 4x^2 + 3$

13. $2b^2 - 2 + b^3 - b$

14. $11 + 6y^2 - y$

15. $4x^4 + 4x^5 + x^2 + 2x^3$

16. $p^6 - 4 + p + p^2 - 7p^3$

17. $9a - 5 + 6a^3 - 5a^2$

When you simplify a polynomial, you should write your answer in standard form.

■ EXAMPLE 3

Simplify each polynomial.

a. $5a + a^2 + 3a^2 + 2$

$5a + (1 + 3)a^2 + 2$ Combine like terms.

$5a + 4a^2 + 2$ Simplify.

$4a^2 + 5a + 2$ Write in standard form.

b. $3x - 8x + 2x^2 + 4x^2$

$(3 - 8)x + (2 + 4)x^2$

$-5x + 6x^2$

$6x^2 - 5x$

Simplify each polynomial.

18. $x + 3x^2 + x^2$

19. $3a + 5a^2 + 2a + 6$

20. $4m^2 + m^2 + 10 + 4m$

21. $6p - 5p^2 + 4p + 3p^2$

22. $c + 9c^2 - 7c - 8$

23. $-2x^2 + 5 + 3x^2 + 2x + 3$

24. $3b + 1 + 7b^2 - 3b - 2b^2$

25. $5m^3 + 8m^2 + 11m + 14$

26. $3a^4 - 5a^6 - 9a + 6$

27. $-11 - y^2 - 8y + 2y$

28. $6p + 8p^2 + 5p + 7p^2$

29. $22x + 18x^2 + 6 + 4x$

13-5

Adding and Subtracting Polynomials

PART 1 Adding Polynomials

What You'll Learn

1 To add polynomials

2 To subtract polynomials

. . . And Why

To solve problems involving area and volume

In Chapter 2 you saw models for variables and numbers. You can also model the square of a variable.

You can use models or properties to add polynomials.

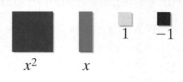

x^2 x

■ **EXAMPLE 1**

Simplify $(2x^2 + 3x + 1) + (x^2 + x + 3)$.

Method 1 Add using tiles.

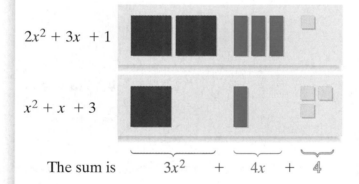

$2x^2 + 3x\ + 1$

$x^2 + x\ + 3$

The sum is $3x^2$ + $4x$ + 4

Quick *Review*

Like terms are terms with the same variable(s), raised to the same power(s). Like terms are combined by adding their coefficients.

$3b + 12b = (3 + 12)b$
$\qquad\qquad = 15b$

Method 2 Add by combining like terms.

$(2x^2 + 3x + 1) + (x^2 + x + 3)$

$= (2x^2 + x^2) + (3x + x) + (1 + 3)$ **Use the Commutative and Associative Properties of Addition to group like terms.**

$= (2 + 1)x^2 + (3 + 1)x + (1 + 3)$ **Use the Distributive Property to combine like terms.**

$= 3x^2 + 4x + 4$ **Simplify.**

■ **TRY THIS** Simplify.

  1. $(7d^2 + 7d) + (2d^2 + 3d)$ **2.** $(x^2 + 2x + 5) + (3x^2 + x + 12)$

You can also add polynomials in a column by aligning like terms and then adding their coefficients.

EXAMPLE 2

Find the sum of $z^2 + 5z + 4$ and $2z^2 - 5$.

Align like terms.

$$
\begin{array}{r}
z^2 + 5z + 4 \\
+ \quad 2z^2 \qquad - 5 \\
\hline
3z^2 + 5z - 1
\end{array}
$$

Add the terms in each column.

■ TRY THIS Simplify.

3. $\quad 4x + 9y$
$\quad + \quad 3x - 5y$

4. $\qquad a^2 + 6a - 4$
$\quad + \quad 8a^2 - 8a$

5. $(4g^2 - 2g + 2) + (2g^2 - 3)$

6. $(-2t^2 + t + 5) + (2t + 4)$

PART 2 Subtracting Polynomials

You subtract polynomials by adding the opposite of each term in the second polynomial.

EXAMPLE 3

Simplify $(5x^2 + 10x) - (3x - 12)$.

$(5x^2 + 10x) - (3x - 12)$

$= 5x^2 + 10x - 3x + 12$ Write the opposite of each term in the second polynomial.

$= 5x^2 + (10x - 3x) + 12$ Group like terms.

$= 5x^2 + (10 - 3)x + 12$ Use the Distributive Property.

$= 5x^2 + 7x + 12$ Simplify.

■ TRY THIS Simplify.

7. $(7a^2 - 2a) - (5a^2 + 3a)$

8. $(10z^2 + 6z + 5) - (z^2 - 8z + 7)$

9. $(3w^2 + 8 + v) - (5w^2 - 3 - 7v)$

Exercises

CHECK UNDERSTANDING

Write the sum modeled in each exercise. Then simplify the sum.

1.

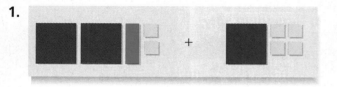

2.

Use a model to simplify each sum.

3. $(x^2 + 3x + 1) + (x^2 + x + 6)$

4. $(x^2 + 5x + 2) + (3x^2 + x + 1)$

Simplify each sum or difference.

5.
$$\begin{aligned} & 5a + 7b \\ + \ & {-3a + 2b} \end{aligned}$$

6.
$$\begin{aligned} & x^2 + 4x - 2 \\ + \ & 8x^2 - 3x + 7 \end{aligned}$$

7. $(5x + 9) - (2x + 1)$

8. $(-11a^2 + 2a - 1) - (7a^2 + 4a - 1)$

PRACTICE AND PROBLEM SOLVING

Use a model to simplify each sum.

9. $(3x + 2) + (-4x + 3)$

10. $(5x^2 + 3x + 7) + (7x - 2)$

Simplify each sum or difference.

11.
$$\begin{aligned} & x^4 + 3x^3 - x^2 + \ x - 2 \\ + \ & \qquad 7x^3 + x^2 - 5x - 9 \end{aligned}$$

12.
$$\begin{aligned} & xy + 5x - 2y + 4 \\ + \ & 2xy - 3x - 3y - 8 \end{aligned}$$

13.
$$\begin{aligned} & x^3 + 5x^2 + 3x - 2 \\ + \ & x^3 \qquad - 2x + 6 \end{aligned}$$

14.
$$\begin{aligned} & 4x^2 - 5xy \qquad + 7 \\ + \ & 8x^2 + 3xy - 3y - 4 \end{aligned}$$

15. $(3x - 2y) + (5x + 4y)$

16. $(x^2 + 3x - 7) + (x^2 - 6x - 9)$

17. $(-4x^2 + 2x - 1) + (x^2 - x + 8)$

18. $(ab - 4) + (3ab - 6)$

19. $(13a^2b - 3ab^2) + (2a^2b + 5ab^2)$

20. $(w^2 + 5w) + (2w - 6)$

21. $(2x^2 + 3x) - (x^2 + 2x)$

22. $(x^2 + 3x + 5) - (x^2 + x + 2)$

23. $(8j - 3k + 6m) - (-2j + 3m)$

24. $(3x^2 + x + 7) - (2x^2 + x + 2)$

25. $(6y - 8) - (2y + 7)$

26. $(x^2 - 3x - 9) - (5x - 4)$

Mathematical Reasoning Justify each step.

27. $(x^2 + 3x - 2) + (3x^2 + 2x + 4)$
$(x^2 + 3x^2) + (3x + 2x) + (-2 + 4)$
$(1 + 3)x^2 + (3 + 2)x + (-2 + 4)$
$4x^2 + 5x + 2$

28. $(x^2 + 2x + 1) - (2x^2 - 3x - 4)$
$(x^2 + 2x + 1) + -(2x^2 - 3x - 4)$
$(x^2 + 2x + 1) + (-2x^2) + 3x + 4$
$(x^2 + -2x^2) + (2x + 3x) + (1 + 4)$
$(1 + -2)x^2 + (2 + 3)x + (1 + 4)$
$-x^2 + 5x + 5$

Write the perimeter of each figure as a polynomial. Simplify.

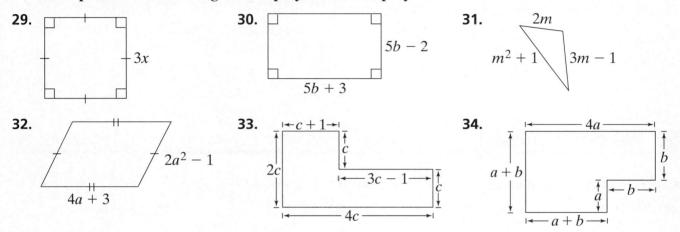

29. $3x$

30. $5b - 2$, $5b + 3$

31. $2m$, $m^2 + 1$, $3m - 1$

32. $2a^2 - 1$, $4a + 3$

33. $c + 1$, c, $2c$, $3c - 1$, c, $4c$

34. $4a$, b, $a + b$, a, b, $a + b$

35. *Error Analysis* Tian simplified $(5x^2 + 4x - 3) - (2x^2 - x)$ as shown below. What is his error?

$$5x^2 + 4x - 3$$
$$-\quad 2x^2 - x$$
$$\overline{\quad 3x^2 + 3x - 3\quad}$$

36. a. Write an expression for the sum of three consecutive numbers. Let x be the first number. Then simplify the expression.
   b. What three consecutive numbers have the sum 108?

37. a. *Geometry* The volume of a cube is $(3x^3 + 9)$ in.³. A smaller cube with volume $(x^3 - 3)$ in.³ is cut out of the cube. Write a polynomial for the remaining volume.
   b. Evaluate your polynomial for $x = 2$.
   c. *Reasoning* Will the original cube fit into a box with dimensions 10 in. $\times$ 9 in. $\times$ 15 in.? Explain.

38. a. *Critical Thinking* What polynomial is the opposite of $2x^2 + 3x - 5$?
   b. What is the sum of $2x^2 + 3x - 5$ and its opposite?

Geometry Find each missing length.

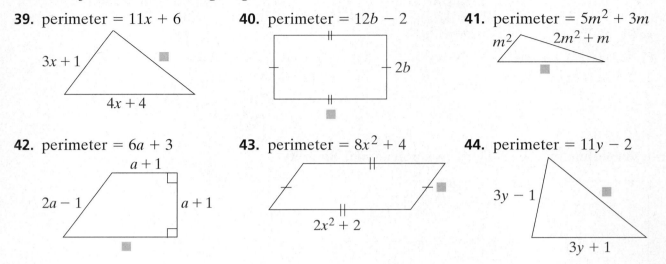

39. perimeter = $11x + 6$

$3x + 1$
$4x + 4$

40. perimeter = $12b - 2$

$2b$

41. perimeter = $5m^2 + 3m$

m^2 $2m^2 + m$

42. perimeter = $6a + 3$

$a + 1$
$2a - 1$ $a + 1$

43. perimeter = $8x^2 + 4$

$2x^2 + 2$

44. perimeter = $11y - 2$

$3y - 1$
$3y + 1$

▶ MIXED REVIEW

Evaluate each polynomial for $a = 2$, $b = -1$, and $c = \frac{1}{2}$. *(Lesson 13-4)*

45. $8ab + 1$ **46.** $5 + 4ab - c$ **47.** $a^2 + ab + b^2$ **48.** $5c - b - 1$

Find the area of each figure. *(Lesson 10-2)*

49.

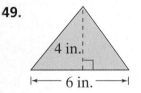

4 in.
6 in.

50.

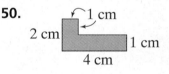

2 cm   1 cm
1 cm
4 cm

51.

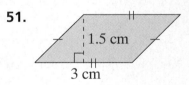

1.5 cm
3 cm

52. A student participated in a walk for charity. His friends pledged a total of $3.20 for each mile he walked. The student earned $22.40 for the charity. How many miles did he walk? *(Lesson 3-6)*

CHAPTER PROJECT 13 ▶ **ACTIVITY 2 WRITING**

For the area of one face of the large cube that you created in Activity 1, write a polynomial in terms of the cube's edge length. Then write a polynomial for the area of the face as the sum of the areas of the parts of the face. Write an equation that compares the two polynomials.

See also Extra Practice section.

Multiplying a Polynomial by a Monomial

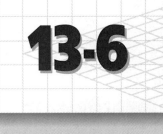

13-6

PART 1 Using an Area Model

You can model the product of a monomial and a polynomial using algebra tiles. You can find the area of a rectangle that is $2x$ units long and $(x + 4)$ units wide by counting the tiles.

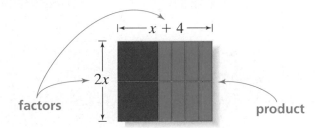

factors $2x$ product

The area is $2x^2 + 8x$. So $2x(x + 4) = 2x^2 + 8x$.

You can also use the Distributive Property to simplify a product of a monomial and a polynomial. Multiply each term of the polynomial by the monomial.

REAL-WORLD CONNECTION

■ EXAMPLE 1

Find the area of the garden. All measurements are in feet.

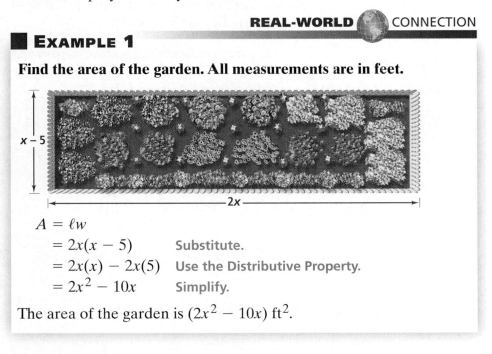

$$A = \ell w$$
$$= 2x(x - 5) \qquad \text{Substitute.}$$
$$= 2x(x) - 2x(5) \qquad \text{Use the Distributive Property.}$$
$$= 2x^2 - 10x \qquad \text{Simplify.}$$

The area of the garden is $(2x^2 - 10x)$ ft^2.

■ **TRY THIS** Simplify each product.

1. $3x(x + 4)$ **2.** $x(2x - 3)$

You can often use other properties to simplify the product of a monomial and a polynomial.

When multiplying powers with the same base, add exponents.

■ EXAMPLE 2

Simplify $3x^2(8x^2 - 5x + 2)$.

$3x^2(8x^2 - 5x + 2)$

$= 3x^2(8x^2) + 3x^2(-5x) + 3x^2(2)$ Use the Distributive Property.

    Use the Commutative

$= (3)(8)x^{2+2} + (3)(-5)x^{2+1} + (3)(2)x^2$ Property of Multiplication.

$= (3)(8)x^4 + (3)(-5)x^3 + (3)(2)x^2$ Add exponents.

$= 24x^4 - 15x^3 + 6x^2$ Simplify.

■ TRY THIS   Simplify each product.

3. $x(x^2 + 2x + 4)$ **4.** $2a^2(2a^3 - 3a^2 + 3)$

PART 2   Writing a Polynomial as a Product

The Distributive Property
$10a + 20 = 10(a + 2)$
$5y - y = (5 - 1)y$

You can sometimes use the Distributive Property to write a polynomial as the product of two factors. You will usually want to find the GCF of all the terms of a polynomial and use that as one of the factors.

■ EXAMPLE 3

Write $6x^3 + 3x^2 + 9x$ as a product of two factors.

$\left.\begin{array}{l} 6x^3 = 2 \cdot 3 \cdot x \cdot x \cdot x \\ 3x^2 = 3 \cdot x \cdot x \\ 9x = 3 \cdot 3 \cdot x \end{array}\right\}$ Write the prime factorization of each term.

GCF $= 3x$ Find the GCF.

Write each term as the product of $3x$ and another factor.

$6x^3 = 3x \cdot 2x^2$ $3x^2 = 3x \cdot x$ $9x = 3x \cdot 3$

$6x^3 + 3x^2 + 9x = 3x(2x^2 + x + 3)$ Use the Distributive Property.

■ TRY THIS   Use the GCF of the terms to write each expression as the product of two factors.

5. $2x^2 + x$ **6.** $2b^3 + 6b^2 - 12b$

Exercises

▶ CHECK UNDERSTANDING

Use an area model to simplify each product.

1. $3x(x + 1)$ **2.** $x(x + 5)$ **3.** $2x(x + 3)$ **4.** $2x(3x + 1)$

Use the Distributive Property to simplify each product.

5. $3x(x + 5)$ **6.** $-4x(2x - 3)$ **7.** $5x(-3x^2 + 2x)$

8. $x(5x^2 + x - 4)$ **9.** $3a(a^2 + 2a + 1)$ **10.** $3b(2b^2 - b + 4)$

Use the GCF of the terms to write each expression as the product of two factors.

11. $3d^4 + d^2$ **12.** $10x^5 - 5x^3 + 10x$ **13.** $4y^3 - 8y^2 - 12y$ **14.** $-9b^2 - 3b$

▶ PRACTICE AND PROBLEM SOLVING

Use an area model to simplify each product.

15. $2x(x + 6)$ **16.** $x(2x + 6)$ **17.** $2x(3x - 1)$ **18.** $3x(2x + 4)$

Simplify each product.

19. $2x(x + 4)$ **20.** $-4a(a - 9)$ **21.** $3y(y + 7)$

22. $-2b(3b - 1)$ **23.** $5x(x + 3)$ **24.** $7c(4 + c)$

25. $3y(4y - 1)$ **26.** $a(a^2 + 3)$ **27.** $x(2x - 5)$

28. $\frac{1}{2}b(b - 8)$ **29.** $-8y(2y + 3)$ **30.** $-3(2c^2 - 3c - 1)$

31. $12x^2(5x + 2)$ **32.** $a^3(a + a^2 + 5)$ **33.** $6y^2\left(y^2 - 2y - \frac{1}{3}\right)$

34. $7b^2(2b^2 + b - 3)$ **35.** $4x^2(x^3 + x^2 - x)$ **36.** $5c(c + 5 - c^2)$

37. $-14a(a^2 + 3a - 4)$ **38.** $17y(2y^2 - 8y + 9)$

39. $-3xy(2x^2y + xy + y^2 - 3)$ **40.** $4z(2z^6 - 3z^5 - 12z^2 + 8)$

Write an expression for the area of each shaded region.

41.

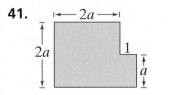

42.

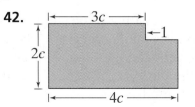

Use the GCF of the terms to write each expression as the product of two factors.

43. $7x^2 - 14x$

44. $24y^3 + 6y^2 - 20y$

45. $14a^2 + 7a - 7$

46. $7p^2 + p$

47. $5z^2 - 20z$

48. $15x^3 + 4x^2 - 7x$

49. $-4x^5 - 4x^4 + 8x^2$

50. $18g^7 - 6g^4 + 3g^2$

51. $12a^3 - 16a^2 - 4a$

52. $4m^9 + 6m^5 - 2m^2$

53. $2a^2 + ab$

54. $2m^3n - 6m^2n^2 + 8mn$

55. **Open-ended** Write a monomial and a polynomial with 4 terms. Multiply them and then simplify the product.

Geometry **Write an expression to represent the area of each figure. Then simplify the expression.**

56. The width of a rectangle is 7 more than $\frac{1}{2}$ its length.

57. The length of a rectangle is 5 less than 4 times its width.

58. The base length of a triangle is $8x$. The triangle's height is twice the base length plus 5.

59. The height of an isosceles triangle is 3 less than $\frac{1}{3}$ its base.

Journal

Explain how to use the GCF to write the polynomial $15a^3 + 20a^2 + 45a$ as the product of two factors.

► **MIXED REVIEW**

Find each sum or difference. *(Lesson 13-5)*

60. $(2x + 8) + (3x^2 + 5x - 2)$

61. $(-7x^2 - 8x + 4) - (2x^2 - 3x - 9)$

Display each set of data in a line plot. *(Lesson 12-1)*

62. $1.7, 2.1, 1.9, 2.1, 2.2, 2.4, 2.3, 2.1, 1.9$

63. $13, 17, 15, 14, 12, 14, 11, 13, 15$

64. **Choose a Strategy** A college student received a bank statement. The new balance was $200. It showed deposits of $400, interest of $1, and checks totaling $650. What was the beginning balance?

CHAPTER PROJECT 13 **ACTIVITY 3 WRITING**

For the volume of the large cube that you created in Activity 1, write a polynomial in terms of the cube's edge length. Then write and simplify a polynomial for the volume as the sum of the volumes of the parts of the cube. Write an equation that compares the two polynomials.

Multiple Choice

Choose the best answer.

1. In the figure,
   $m\angle LPN = 70°$,
   $m\angle MPO = 60°$, and
   $m\angle LPO = 100°$.
   Find $m\angle MPN$.

   A. 40°   **B.** 20°   **C.** 30°   **D.** 10°

2. U.S. car sales are shown in the graph below. Suppose the total number of cars sold was 8 million. How many luxury cars were sold?

   U.S. Car Sales

   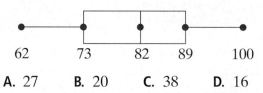

   9%   15%   27%   49%

   ☐ Luxury
   ☐ Small
   ☐ Midsize
   ☐ Large

   F. 1,200,000   **G.** 21,600,000
   H. 2,160,000   **J.** 120,000,000

3. The box-and-whisker plot represents the scores on a 100-point test. What is the difference between the upper quartile and lower quartile scores?

   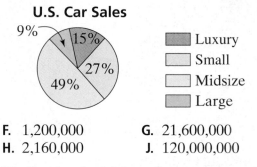

   62   73   82   89   100

   A. 27   **B.** 20   **C.** 38   **D.** 16

4. How many C boxes are needed to balance one A box?

   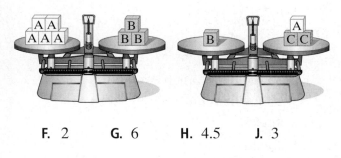

   F. 2   **G.** 6   **H.** 4.5   **J.** 3

Free Response

For Exercises 5–13, show your work.

5. A bird flying 200 ft above the ground drops a stick from its beak. The equation $d = 200 - 16t^2$ gives the height d, in feet, of the stick after t seconds.
   a. Make a table with integer values of t from 0 to 4. Then graph the function.
   b. Use your graph to estimate the height of the stick after $1\frac{1}{2}$ s.
   c. Estimate the time until the stick hits the ground.

Graph each linear equation or inequality.

6. $y = -2x$ 7. $y = 2x$

8. $y = 2x - 1$ 9. $y \leq 2x - 2$

The table lists the grams of fat and the number of calories in 1-oz servings of cheese.

Type of Cheese	Fat (g)	Calories
American	8.9	106
Blue	8.2	100
Cheddar	9.4	114
Colby	9.1	112
Limburger	7.7	93
Mozzarella	6.1	80
Provolone	7.6	100
Swiss	7.8	107

SOURCE: *The T-Factor Fat Gram Counter*

10. Make a (fat, calories) scatter plot.

11. Use the scatter plot to describe the correlation between the number of grams of fat and the number of calories.

For each function, make a table with integer values of x from 0 to 3. Then graph each function.

12. $y = -3(2)^x$ 13. $y = 2x^3$

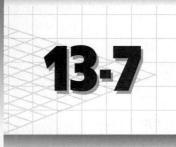

13-7

Multiplying Binomials

What You'll Learn

1 To use models in multiplying binomials

2 To multiply two binomials

...And Why

To find the areas of geometric figures

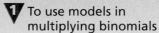

PART 1 Using Models

You can use tiles to find the product of two binomials.

■ EXAMPLE 1

Simplify $(x + 2)(x + 4)$.

$$(x + 2)(x + 4) = x^2 + 6x + 8$$

The area is $x^2 + 6x + 8$.

■ TRY THIS Simplify each product using models.

1. $(x + 2)(x + 3)$ **2.** $(y + 1)(y + 4)$

PART 2 Using the Distributive Property

You can use the Distributive Property to simplify the product of two binomials. If you think of one binomial as a single expression, you can use the distributive property twice to simplify the product.

■ EXAMPLE 2

Simplify $(x + 4)(x - 3)$.

$(x + 4)(x - 3)$

$= x(x - 3) + 4(x - 3)$ Use the Distributive Property.

$= x^2 - 3x + 4x - 12$ Use the Distributive Property again!

$= x^2 + x - 12$ Simplify.

■ **TRY THIS** Simplify each product.

3. $(x + 2)(x - 5)$ **4.** $(m + 2)(2m + 3)$

■Different Ways to Solve a Problem

Write a polynomial to express the area of the square at the right.

$(2x + 1)$ in.

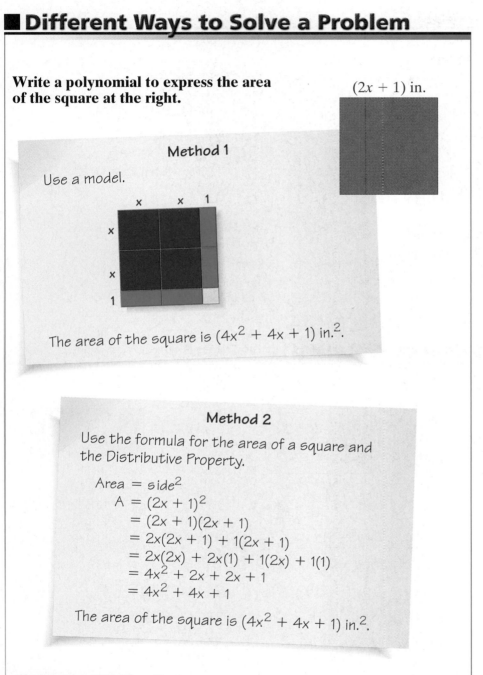

Method 1

Use a model.

The area of the square is $(4x^2 + 4x + 1)$ in.^{2}.

Method 2

Use the formula for the area of a square and the Distributive Property.

$$\text{Area} = \text{side}^2$$
$$A = (2x + 1)^2$$
$$= (2x + 1)(2x + 1)$$
$$= 2x(2x + 1) + 1(2x + 1)$$
$$= 2x(2x) + 2x(1) + 1(2x) + 1(1)$$
$$= 4x^2 + 2x + 2x + 1$$
$$= 4x^2 + 4x + 1$$

The area of the square is $(4x^2 + 4x + 1)$ in.^{2}.

Choose a Method

1. Which method do you prefer to use? Explain.

2. Which method would you use to simplify $(3x + 4)(3x + 4)$?

Exercises

CHECK UNDERSTANDING

Simplify each product using a model.

1. $(x + 2)(x + 1)$ 2. $(x + 2)(x + 2)$ 3. $(x + 3)(x + 1)$

4. $(x + 3)(x + 4)$ 5. $(x + 4)(x + 5)$ 6. $(x + 9)(x + 3)$

Simplify each product.

7. $(x + 2)(x - 1)$ 8. $(c + 7)(c + 9)$ 9. $(x - 5)(x + 3)$

10. $(a - 4)(a - 2)$ 11. $(x + 5)(x + 5)$ 12. $(b + 6)(b - 6)$

13. **Error Analysis** A student simplifies $(x + 5)(x - 3)$. Find the error in the work at the right.

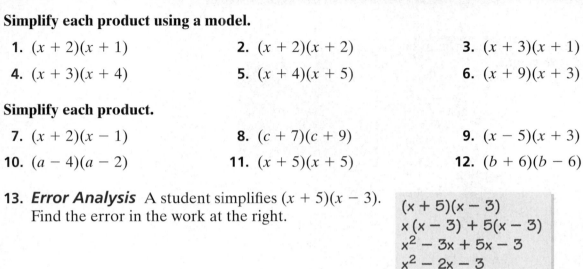

$$(x + 5)(x - 3)$$
$$x(x - 3) + 5(x - 3)$$
$$x^2 - 3x + 5x - 3$$
$$x^2 - 2x - 3$$

PRACTICE AND PROBLEM SOLVING

Find the area of each rectangle.

14.

$x + 3$

$2x + 1$

15.

$2c + 4$

$5c + 3$

16.

$4n - 5$

$3n + 1$

Simplify each product.

17. $(x + 3)(x + 6)$ 18. $(a - 7)(a + 5)$ 19. $(m + 1)(m + 6)$

20. $(c + 3)(c - 4)$ 21. $(x + 3)(x - 2)$ 22. $(y + 3)(y + 8)$

23. $(x + 4)(2x + 1)$ 24. $(n - 16)(n + 20)$ 25. $(x + 2)(x + 8)$

26. $(b + 1)(b + 12)$ 27. $(m - 8)(m - 3)$ 28. $(3 + x)(5 - x)$

29. $(3c + 1)(2c - 4)$ 30. $(2a + b)(4c - 2d)$ 31. $\left(\frac{1}{2}x + 9\right)(4x + 8)$

32. **Patterns** Simplify $(y + 2)^2, (y + 3)^2$, and $(y + 4)^2$. What pattern do you see?

33. **Patterns** Simplify $(y + 1)(y - 1), (y + 2)(y - 2)$, and $(y + 5)(y - 5)$. What pattern do you see?

34. *Writing* Explain the similarities between multiplying two binomials and multiplying a polynomial by a monomial.

35. *Geometry* The base of a parallelogram is $(w + 5)$ cm. The height is 2 cm less than the base. Find the area of the parallelogram.

36. **TEST PREP** Assume m is an even integer. What is the product of the next two consecutive even integers?

    A. $m^2 + 3m + 2$ **B.** $m^2 + 6m + 8$

    C. $m^2 + 2m$ **D.** $2m + 6$

▶ MIXED REVIEW

Find each product. *(Lesson 13-6)*

37. $7a(a + 5b + 2c)$ **38.** $-3xy(2x + 9y - 6)$ **39.** $8m^2(-4m^3 + mp + 2p^4)$

Make a box-and-whisker plot for the data. *(Lesson 12-2)*

40. $8, 9, 27, 39, 14, 17, 13, 25, 15, 8, 11, 29, 36, 10, 15, 25$

41. Does the problem below require *permutations* or *combinations*? Explain. *(Lesson 12-6)*

    You select three colors from a choice of eight colors to paint a picture. How many 3-color choices are possible?

▟ CHECKPOINT 2   Lessons 13–4 through 13–7

Tell whether each polynomial is a *monomial*, a *binomial*, or a *trinomial*.

  1. 178 **2.** $x + 15y$ **3.** $7pq$ **4.** $m^2 + 4m - 12$

Evaluate each polynomial for $x = -1$ and $y = 3$.

  5. $5x - y$ **6.** $x + 3y$ **7.** $-7x + x^2y$ **8.** $4y^2 + 11x - 16$

Simplify each expression.

  9. $(4a - b) + (3a + 5b)$ **10.** $(x^2 + 7x - 4) + (x^2 + 9)$

11. $2pq(5p + 8pq + 2)$ **12.** $(g + 6)(g + 4)$ **13.** $3m(-6m - 2m^2p - 10p)$

14. *Open-ended* Write a binomial expression for the length of the side of a square. Write a polynomial to express the area of the square.

Binomial Factors of a Trinomial

You can sometimes write a trinomial as the product of two binomial factors. You can use algebra tiles to find the factors. Use tiles to form a rectangle. The lengths of the sides of the rectangle are the factors of the trinomial.

◼ EXAMPLE

Write $x^2 + 4x + 3$ as the product of two binomial factors.

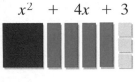

$x^2 + 4x + 3$

Model the trinomial.

Use the tiles to form a rectangle. The length is $(x + 3)$ and the width is $(x + 1)$.

$x^2 + 4x + 3 = (x + 3)(x + 1)$

Use tiles to find binomial factors of each trinomial.

1. $x^2 + 2x + 1$ **2.** $x^2 + 5x + 6$ **3.** $x^2 + 7x + 10$

4. $x^2 + 6x + 5$ **5.** $x^2 + 4x + 4$ **6.** $x^2 + 5x + 4$

7. $x^2 + 9x + 8$ **8.** $2x^2 + 5x + 3$ **9.** $2x^2 + 9x + 10$

10. *Critical Thinking* Complete $x^2 + \blacksquare x + 12$ with three different integers so that each trinomial has two binomial factors. For each trinomial, write the binomial factors.

11. a. What two numbers have a sum of 11 and a product of 30?
   b. *Mathematical Reasoning* Use your answer to part (a) to find the binomial factors of $x^2 + 11x + 30$.

Use Multiple Strategies

Math Strategies in Action

After a natural disaster such as an earthquake, a tornado, or a flood, relief workers help rescue survivors. They also bring food, clothing, and blankets to people who need them. Relief organizers use multiple strategies as they plan and coordinate their efforts.

In simple and complex situations in your own life, you already use multiple strategies. Remember when you learned how to ride a bike or fly a kite. The more you practiced, the less you had to think about the steps required to be successful.

Problem Solving Strategies

Account for All
    Possibilities

Draw a Diagram

Look for a Pattern

Make a Model

Make a Table

Simplify a Problem

Simulate a Problem

Solve by Graphing

Try, Test, Revise

Use Multiple Strategies

Work Backward

Write an Equation

Write a Proportion

In mathematics, you can use multiple strategies to solve problems. The more strategies you learn and the more you use them, the better problem solver you will be. Solving problems can become as easy as riding a bike or flying a kite!

■ SAMPLE PROBLEM

Suppose you receive instructions for building a kite. The writer of the instructions presents them as a puzzle:

> I fly above the clouds with my tail flowing behind me.
> My tail is 12 ft plus twice my length. Together, our
> length is 21 ft. How long am I? How long is my tail?

 **Read**

Read the problem carefully.

1. What do you want to find?

2. What is the relationship between the length of the kite's tail and the length of the kite's body?

Plan

To get a visual picture of the problem, draw a diagram. Then write an equation to solve the problem.

 **Solve**

Draw a diagram.

Let b = length of the body of the kite.

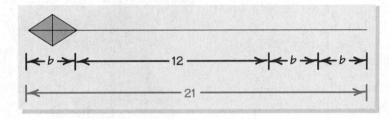

Write an equation.

$3b + 12 = 21$	Use the diagram to write an equation.
$3b + 12 - 12 = 21 - 12$	Subtract 12 from each side.
$3b = 9$	Simplify.
$\dfrac{3b}{3} = \dfrac{9}{3}$	Divide each side by 3.
$b = 3$	

The kite is 3 ft long. Now find the length of the tail.

length of tail $= 2b + 12$	Use the diagram to write an expression for the length of the tail.
$= 2(3) + 12$	Replace b with the length of the kite's body.
$= 18$	Simplify.

The tail is 18 ft long.

 **Look Back**

Check the answer using the original problem.

3. a. The original problem says that the tail must be 12 ft plus twice the length of the kite's body. Show that the lengths found meet this condition.
   b. The length of the kite's body plus the length of its tail must be 21 ft. Show that the lengths found meet this condition.

Exercises

► CHECK UNDERSTANDING

Use multiple strategies to solve each problem.

1. A bus traveling 40 mi/h left Freetown at noon. A car following the bus at 60 mi/h left Freetown at 1:30 P.M.
   a. At what time did the car catch up with the bus?
   b. How many miles were the car and the bus from Freetown when the car caught up with the bus?

2. A student playing a computer chess game gets 5 points every time he wins a round. The computer gets 3 points every time it wins a round. They play 64 rounds and end with a tie score. How many rounds did the computer win?

3. A kite and its tail total 36 ft in length. The tail is five times the length of the body. How long is the kite's tail?

► PRACTICE AND PROBLEM SOLVING

Solve using any strategy.

4. A student has $8 to spend on a phone call to a friend. The cost of a call is $.34 for the first minute and $.24 for each additional minute. How long can the student talk to his friend?

5. *Construction* A painter places an 8.5-ft-long ladder against a wall. The bottom of the ladder is 4 ft from the base of the wall. How high up the wall does the ladder reach?

6. *Geometry* There are 27 white cubes assembled to form a large cube. The outside surface of the large cube is painted red. The large cube is then separated into the 27 smaller cubes. How many of the small cubes will have red paint on exactly the following number of faces?
   a. three faces   **b.** two faces   **c.** one face   **d.** no face

7. A room has a floor area of 1,025 ft^2 and a 10-ft-high ceiling. Occupancy guidelines recommend at least 200 ft^3 per person. What is the maximum number of people allowed in the room?

8. A student weighs her hamsters two at a time. Sandy and White Ears weigh 209 g together. White Ears and Sport weigh 223 g together. Sandy and Sport weigh 216 g together. How much does each hamster weigh?

9. **Geometry** A circle has a circumference of 20 cm and a square has a perimeter of 20 cm.
   a. What is the area of the circle?
   b. What is the area of the square?
   c. Which figure has the greater area?

10. A student decided to purchase a new telephone. He could choose from 8 different models, 2 different cord lengths, and 4 different colors. How many possible choices did he have?

11. A clerk starts working at a beginning salary of $10,400 with an annual increase of $400. An assistant clerk who starts at the same time has a starting salary of $9,600 per year with an annual increase of $600.
    a. Who earns more after 3 years?
    b. After how many years will the assistant be earning more money than the clerk?

12. **Geometry** A lot measures 50 ft by 100 ft. The house on the lot measures 25 ft by 50 ft. What is the area of the lawn?

13. A student spends $\frac{1}{3}$ of her money on a movie and $\frac{1}{4}$ of the remaining amount on a snack after the movie. She now has $12 left. How much money did she originally have?

14. List the different ways you can give change from a $100 bill for a $78 purchase without using coins and without giving a customer more than seven singles.

15. Each face of a cube can be painted either red or yellow. How many different ways can you paint the cube?

▶ **MIXED REVIEW**

Simplify. (*Lesson 13-7*)

16. $(x + 1)(x - 3)$ 17. $(d + 2)(2d + 5)$ 18. $(x + 3)^2$

Make a list to find the number of two-letter combinations you can form from each group of letters. (*Lesson 12-6*)

19. G, O, A, T   20. A, P, E   21. H, Y, E, N, A

22. **Choose a Strategy** A boy jogs in the park every other day. His sister jogs every third day. They both jogged together on April 2. On how many more of the 30 days in April will they jog together if they maintain this schedule?

Make a 3-D Polynomial Model The Project Activities on pages 681, 688, and 692 will help you complete your project. Here is a checklist to help you gather the different parts.

✔ your prisms, assembled into a cube

✔ your equation of two polynomials for the area of a cube face

✔ your equation of two polynomials for the volume of the cube

Make a display for your polynomial model. Label the parts of the cube with their dimensions. Include an explanation of the connection between the cube's dimensions and your polynomial expressions.

Reflect and Revise

Ask a friend or someone at home to review your display. Are your polynomials correct? Are your explanations clear? If necessary, make changes to improve your display.

Web Extension

Visit Prentice Hall's Web site. You'll find some interesting links and ideas related to models. You'll also be able to share information about your project.

www.phschool.com

Wrap Up

■ Key Terms

absolute value function (p. 670)
arithmetic sequence (p. 664)
binomial (p. 678)
common difference (p. 664)

common ratio (p. 665)
geometric sequence (p. 665)
monomial (p. 678)
polynomial (p. 678)

quadratic function (p. 669)
sequence (p. 664)
term (p. 664)
trinomial (p. 678)

■ Graphic Organizer

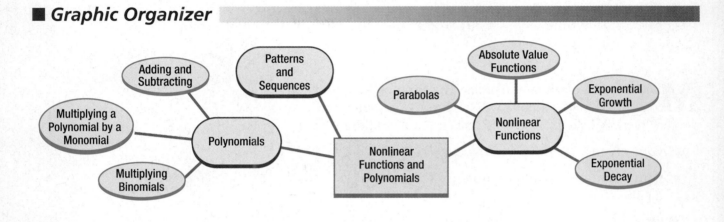

■ Patterns and Sequences

13-1

Summary A **sequence** is a set of numbers that follow a pattern. Each number in the sequence is a **term** of the sequence. You find a term of an **arithmetic sequence** by adding a fixed number, called the **common difference,** to the previous term.

You find a term of a **geometric sequence** by multiplying the previous term by a fixed number. This fixed number is called a **common ratio.**

Find the next three terms of each sequence. Then write a rule to describe each sequence.

1. $1, 5, 9, 13, \ldots$

2. $-60, -30, -15, -7.5, \ldots$

3. $100, 107, 114, 121, \ldots$

4. $0, -5, -10, -15, \ldots$

5. $26, 15, 4, -7, \ldots$

6. $\frac{1}{10}, \frac{1}{2}, 2.5, 12.5, \ldots$

Tell whether each sequence is *arithmetic, geometric,* or *neither.* Find the next three terms of each sequence.

7. $9, 13, 17, 21, \ldots$

8. $-8, -4, -2, -1, \ldots$

9. $3, 4, 5, 6, \ldots$

10. $-22, -11, 0, 11, \ldots$

11. $10, 1, 20, 2, \ldots$

12. $\frac{1}{200}, \frac{1}{100}, \frac{1}{50}, \frac{1}{25}, \ldots$

13. **Open-ended** Describe a situation that you can represent with an arithmetic sequence. Write a sequence of numbers for that situation and identify the common difference.

■ Graphing Nonlinear Functions

13-2 and 13-3

Summary Two types of nonlinear functions are **quadratic functions** and **absolute value functions.** The graph of a quadratic function is a U-shaped curve called a *parabola* that opens upward or downward. The graph of an absolute value function is V-shaped.

A function like $y = 2^x$ models *exponential growth*. Its graph curves upward as input values increase. A function like $y = \left(\frac{1}{2}\right)^x$ models *exponential decay*. Its graph slopes downward as input values increase.

For each function, make a table with integer values of x from -2 to 2. Then graph each function.

14. $y = \frac{1}{2}x^2$ 15. $y = 2|x|$ 16. $y = |x| + 1$ 17. $y = x^2 + 5$

18. $y = -|x|$ 19. $y = \frac{1}{2}|x|$ 20. $y = -x^2 - 3$ 21. $y = -x^2 + 4$

For each function, make a table with integer values of x from 0 to 4. Then graph each function.

22. $y = \left(\frac{1}{4}\right)^x$ 23. $y = \frac{1}{2} \cdot 2^x$ 24. $y = 3^x$ 25. $y = \left(\frac{1}{2}\right)^x$

■ Polynomials

13-4

Summary A **monomial** is a real number, a variable, or a product of a real number and variables with whole-number exponents. A **polynomial** is a monomial or a sum or difference of monomials. You can name a polynomial by the number of its terms. A **binomial** has two terms and a **trinomial** has three terms.

Tell whether each polynomial is a *monomial*, a *binomial*, or a *trinomial*.

26. $3x$ 27. $2x^2 - 1$ 28. $\frac{2}{3}x$ 29. $x^4 - x^3 + 2$ 30. 15

31. mn 32. $z^2 + z$ 33. $7d + f$ 34. $-2x^2 - 12$ 35. $3 + 2x - x^2$

Evaluate each polynomial for $x = -3$ and $y = 2$.

36. y^5 37. $x^2 - y$ 38. $y^2 - x - 1$ 39. $2xy$ 40. $3 - xy$

■ Adding and Subtracting Polynomials

Summary You can add polynomials by using models, combining like terms, or aligning like terms vertically and then adding their coefficients. You can subtract polynomials by adding the opposite of each term in the second polynomial.

Simplify each sum or difference.

41. $(a^2 + a + 1) + (2a^2 + a + 7)$

42. $(m^2 - 5m - 2) + (3m^2 + 3m - 10)$

43. $(3x^2 - 4) + (x^2 - 2x + 6)$

44. $(7p - 5q + 2) - (3p + 2q + 4)$

45. $(10w^2 + 6w) - (7w^2 - 3w + 5)$

46. $(9x - 3y) - (3x - 9y)$

■ Multiplying Polynomials

Summary You can use properties to simplify the product of a monomial and a polynomial. You can sometimes use the Distributive Property to write a polynomial as the product of two factors.

You can use tiles to model the product of two binomials. When you use the Distributive Property to find the product of two binomials, you use the Distributive Property twice.

Simplify each product.

47. $a(2a + 5)$

48. $4c(3c - 7)$

49. $-6y(5y + 3)$

50. $3x(x^2 - x - 5)$

51. $x^2(x + 7)$

52. $2x^2(x^2 - 3x - 6)$

53. $(x + 3)(x + 4)$

54. $(x + 1)(x - 5)$

55. $(x - 2)(x - 4)$

Use the GCF of the terms to write each expression as the product of two factors.

56. $x^2 - x$

57. $9p^2 + 27$

58. $3x^3 - 9x^2 + 6x$

59. $5b^5 + 20b^3 - 30$

60. $8x^3 + 2x^2 + 4x$

61. $28a^2 - 4ab$

■ Use Multiple Strategies

Summary You can use multiple strategies to solve problems.

62. A gardener plans to use 196 feet of fencing to enclose a garden. What is the largest possible area of the garden?

63. *Writing* Explain your choice of strategies for Exercise 62.

Find the next three terms of each sequence. Then write a rule to describe each sequence.

1. $5, 8, 11, 14, \ldots$ 2. $-1.5, -3, -6, -12, \ldots$

3. $50, 10, 2, 0.4, \ldots$ 4. $100, 93, 86, 79, \ldots$

Tell whether each sequence is *arithmetic*, *geometric*, or *neither*. Find the next three terms of the sequence.

5. $5, 2, -1, -4, \ldots$ 6. $1, 1, 2, 3, 5, \ldots$

7. $15, 13, 11, 9, \ldots$ 8. $-48, -12, -3, -\frac{3}{4}, \ldots$

9. $2, 4, 8, 16, \ldots$ 10. $0, 7, 14, 21, \ldots$

For each function, make a table with integer values of x from -2 to 2. Then graph each function.

11. $y = x^2$ 12. $y = x^2 - 1$

13. $y = -x^2 + 1$ 14. $y = -x^2 - 2$

15. $y = |x| - 1$ 16. $y = \frac{1}{2}|x|$

For each function, make a table with integer values of x from 0 to 4. Then graph each function.

17. $y = 2^x$ 18. $y = 3^x$

19. $y = 2\left(\frac{1}{2}\right)^x$ 20. $y = \left(\frac{1}{3}\right)^x$

Tell whether each polynomial is a *monomial*, a *binomial*, or a *trinomial*.

21. $4x - 1$ 22. $c^2 + c + 1$

23. xyz 24. $a^5 - 7$

25. $h^4 - h^3 - h$ 26. ab

Evaluate each polynomial for $x = 4$ and $y = 10$.

27. $x + y$ 28. $y - x^2$

29. $xy - 15$ 30. $x^2 + xy - y^2$

31. ***Open-ended*** Write a polynomial with two different variables. Assign a value to each variable. Evaluate your polynomial for those values.

Simplify each sum or difference.

32. $(x^2 + 4x + 3) + (x^2 - 3x + 7)$

33. $(2x^2 - 3) + (x + 4)$

34. $(3x^2 + 2x + 4) + (x^2 + 3)$

35. $(x^2 + 10x + 9) - (x^2 + x + 1)$

36. $(3x^2 - x + 3) - (2x^2 - 2x - 4)$

37. $(2x^2 - 4x) - (x^2 - 3x - 5)$

Simplify each product.

38. $x(x - 4)$

39. $2x(x^2 - x + 2)$

40. $x^2(3x^2 + 2x - 5)$

41. $(x + 2)(x + 4)$ 42. $(x + 1)(x + 5)$

43. $(x + 3)(x - 1)$ 44. $(x + 2)(x - 4)$

45. $(x - 1)(x - 6)$ 46. $(x - 2)(x - 3)$

Write each expression as the product of a monomial and a polynomial.

47. $2x^3 + 4x^2 + 12x$

48. $x^2 - x$

49. $9x^3 - 18x^2 - 3x$

50. ***Writing*** Explain how you can use the Distributive Property to write the expression $3x^2 + 6x$ as the product of a monomial and a polynomial.

51. A customer gives a clerk a $100 bill for a $76 purchase. In how many ways can the clerk give change without using coins?

Choose the best answer.

1. Solve $-3x + 1 < 25$.
   - **A.** $x > 8$
   - **B.** $x < -8$
   - **C.** $x > -8$
   - **D.** Not here

2. 32% of b is 8,000. Find b.
   - **F.** 2,560
   - **G.** 25,000
   - **H.** 250
   - **J.** 25,600

3. Find the distance Joe traveled if he drove for $2\frac{1}{2}$ h at a rate of 62 mi/h.
   - **A.** 24.8 mi
   - **B.** 124 mi
   - **C.** 154 mi
   - **D.** 155 mi

4. Which decimal is between $(-0.1)^2$ and 0.05?
   - **F.** 0.03
   - **G.** 0.2
   - **H.** 0.3
   - **J.** -0.02

5. Evaluate $\dfrac{a^5b^3c}{a^6b^2}$ for $a = 2$, $b = -3$, and $c = -4$.
   - **A.** 12
   - **B.** -6
   - **C.** 6
   - **D.** -2

6. An artist created this scale drawing of a lighthouse. What is the height of the actual lighthouse? Use your centimeter ruler.

   Scale:
   1 cm = 12 m

   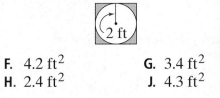

   - **F.** 36 m
   - **G.** 48 m
   - **H.** 72 m
   - **J.** 120 m

7. Which ordered pair is a solution of $x - 2y = 3$ and $3x + y = 2$?
   - **A.** $(1, -1)$
   - **B.** $(-1, 1)$
   - **C.** $(3, 2)$
   - **D.** $\left(2, -\frac{1}{2}\right)$

8. What number is next in the pattern $-1, \sqrt{1}, -2, \sqrt{4}, -3, \ldots$?
   - **F.** $\sqrt{3}$
   - **G.** $\sqrt{5}$
   - **H.** $\sqrt{7}$
   - **J.** $\sqrt{9}$

9. In $\triangle ABC$, $m\angle A = 55°$, and $m\angle C = 15°$. Name the triangle.
   - **A.** acute
   - **B.** equiangular
   - **C.** right
   - **D.** obtuse

10. $\triangle ABC \sim \triangle DEF$. Find AC.

    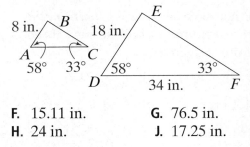

    - **F.** 15.11 in.
    - **G.** 76.5 in.
    - **H.** 24 in.
    - **J.** 17.25 in.

11. $ABCD$ is a rectangle. Which of the following is *not* true?

    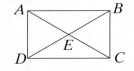

    - **A.** $\overline{AC} \cong \overline{DB}$
    - **B.** $\angle ADC \cong \angle CBA$
    - **C.** $\triangle DAE \cong \triangle BCE$
    - **D.** $\angle CBD \cong \angle DAB$

12. Find the volume of a cone in which $r = 4$ and $h = 12$.
    - **F.** 16π
    - **G.** 64π
    - **H.** 192π
    - **J.** 96π

13. Write an inequality for *The number t is at least 35*.
    - **A.** $t > 35$
    - **B.** $t < 35$
    - **C.** $t \geq 35$
    - **D.** $t \leq 35$

14. Find the area of the shaded region.

    - **F.** 4.2 ft^2
    - **G.** 3.4 ft^2
    - **H.** 2.4 ft^2
    - **J.** 4.3 ft^2

15. Find the area of $\triangle CDE$.

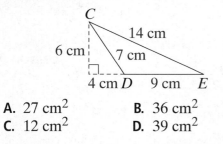

A. 27 cm^2 **B.** 36 cm^2
C. 12 cm^2 **D.** 39 cm^2

16. A bicycle company makes 3 different bicycle styles. Each style comes in 4 colors. Each style is made in 6 frame sizes with a choice of 2 types of seat. The bicycle shop would like to order one of each type of bicycle. How many bicycles is that?
F. 60 bicycles   **G.** 120 bicycles
H. 144 bicycles   **J.** 240 bicycles

17. In a box filled with 60 colored chips, $\frac{1}{6}$ are blue, $\frac{1}{12}$ are white, $\frac{1}{4}$ are yellow, and $\frac{1}{2}$ are purple. Find the probability of picking at random a purple chip or a white chip.
A. $\frac{2}{3}$ **B.** $\frac{1}{24}$ **C.** 35   **D.** $\frac{7}{12}$

18. If the first term in an arithmetic sequence is 15 and the tenth term is 69, what is the fourth term in the sequence?
F. 32   **G.** 33   **H.** 34   **J.** 35

19. Simplify $6z(4 - 2z^2)$.
A. $24z - 12z^3$ **B.** $24z - 12z^2$
C. $24z - 2z^2$ **D.** $24z + 12z^3$

20. Which expression is represented by the model shown below?

F. $2(x^2 + 2x) + 3$ **G.** $2x^2 + 2 + 3^2$
H. $x^2 + 2x + 3$ **J.** $2x^2 + 2x + 3$

21. Which phrase best describes the expression $9xyz$?
A. monomial   **B.** binomial
C. trinomial   **D.** Not here

22. Match the graph with an equation below.

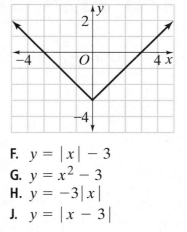

F. $y = |x| - 3$
G. $y = x^2 - 3$
H. $y = -3|x|$
J. $y = |x - 3|$

23. Find the sum.
$$\begin{array}{r} x^4 + 2x^3 - x^2 + x - 3 \\ + \quad 6x^3 + x^2 - 4x - 8 \\ \hline \end{array}$$
A. $x^4 + 4x^3 - 2x^2 - 5x - 5$
B. $x^4 + 8x^3 - 4x - 5$
C. $x^4 + 8x^3 + 2x^2 - 3x - 11$
D. $x^4 + 8x^3 - 3x - 11$

24. Find the difference.
$(5r - 4s) - (2r - s)$
F. $10r - 4s$ **G.** $3r - 3s$
H. $10r^2 - 4s^2$ **J.** $3r - 5s$

Write the perimeter of each figure as a polynomial. Simplify.

25.

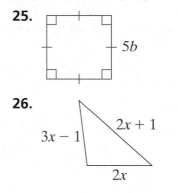
$5b$

26.
$3x - 1$ $2x + 1$
$2x$

For each function, make a table with integer values of x from 0 to 4. Then graph each function.

27. $y = 3^x$ **28.** $y = 20\left(\frac{1}{2}\right)^x$

CHAPTER

1 Extra Practice

Write a variable expression for each word phrase. Lesson 1-1

1. 6 less than x

2. y less than 12

3. the sum of z and 2

4. a number m increased by 34

5. the product of 8 and p

6. t divided by 5

Simplify each expression. Lesson 1-2

7. $15 + 20 \cdot 3$

8. $46 - 4(2 + 8)$

9. $16 \div 4 + 10 \div 2$

10. $100 \div (30 + 20)$

11. $5(8 + 4) \div 6 \div 2$

12. $9 \cdot 6 - 12 \div 2$

Evaluate each expression. Lesson 1-3

13. $3x + 6$, for $x = 12$

14. $15a - 2a$, for $a = 20$

15. $38 - 3y$, for $y = 9$

16. $25 - (t + 18)$, for $t = 7$

17. $\frac{x + y}{10}$, for $x = 35$ and $y = 65$

Compare. Use >, <, or = to complete each statement. Lesson 1-4

18. $-12 \;\blacksquare\; -9$

19. $|-4| \;\blacksquare\; |4|$

20. $-|-7| \;\blacksquare\; |-7|$

21. $0 \;\blacksquare\; -100$

Simplify each expression. Lessons 1-5 and 1-6

22. $-56 + 60$

23. $18 + -25$

24. $-34 + -36$

25. $19 - (-5)$

26. $80 - (-125)$

27. $-82 - (-50)$

28. $-7 + 35 + -22$

29. $-44 - 20 - 80$

30. $-8 + (-13) - (24)$

Write a rule for continuing each pattern. Find the next three numbers in the pattern. Lesson 1-7

31. $-12, -3, 6, 15, 24, \ldots$

32. $0.15, 0.3, 0.45, 0.6, \ldots$

33. $1, 1, 2, 3, 5, 8, 13, \ldots$

Simplify each expression. Lesson 1-9

34. $-4 \cdot 12$

35. $-15(-8)$

36. $30 \cdot (-5)$

37. $-1(-2)(-3)(-4)$

38. $-78 \div (-3)$

39. $-150 \div 25$

40. $\frac{120}{-15}$

41. $-1{,}125 \div (-125)$

Draw a coordinate plane. Graph each point. Lesson 1-10

42. $A(0, 9)$

43. $B(-3, -5)$

44. $C(-9, 5)$

45. $D(7, 2)$

46. $E(0, 0)$

47. $F(8, 0)$

48. $G(7, -8)$

49. $H(1, 1)$

50. $K(-2, -2)$

Simplify each expression. Justify each step. Lesson 2-1

1. $99 + (-46) + (-99) + 45$ **2.** $225 + 320 + 75$

3. $18 + 12 + (-25) + 13$ **4.** $5 \cdot 678 \cdot 2$

5. $58 \cdot 2 \cdot 50$ **6.** $20 \cdot 4 \cdot 5 \cdot 25$

Use the Distributive Property to simplify. Lessons 2-2 and 2-3

7. $7(5) - 3(5)$ **8.** $3 \cdot 6 + 7 \cdot 6$ **9.** $15 \cdot 32 - 12 \cdot 32$

10. $7b + 25 - 4b$ **11.** $3(a - 2c)$ **12.** $3q + 2(q + 1)$

13. $-3(4y - 1) + 5(7 - y)$ **14.** $41 - 2(m + 1) - m$ **15.** $12 + 5x - 2(3x + 5)$

Write an equation for each sentence. Is each equation *true*, *false*, or an *open sentence*? Lesson 2-4

16. Twice the sum of a number and one is twenty-two.

17. Negative three divided by negative one is three.

18. Forty-five plus five equals negative fifty.

Solve each equation. Lessons 2-5 and 2-6

19. $40 + x = 25$ **20.** $-5 = y - 12$ **21.** $z + (-23) = -47$

22. $14 = a - 9$ **23.** $t - 453 = -520$ **24.** $78 = b + 100$

25. $4k = 96$ **26.** $300 = -15j$ **27.** $-12c = 180$

28. $\frac{d}{7} = -14$ **29.** $-4 = \frac{w}{16}$ **30.** $\frac{k}{-9} = -20$

Graph the solutions of each inequality. Lesson 2-8

31. $x > -12$ **32.** $y \le 3$ **33.** $0 \ge z$

34. $p < -9$ **35.** $7 < n$ **36.** $f \le -3$

Solve each inequality. Lessons 2-9 and 2-10

37. $a + 3 < -1$ **38.** $-2 > b - 4$ **39.** $5 + x > -8$

40. $-12 < -2 + y$ **41.** $w - 32 \le 15$ **42.** $-20 \ge z - 13$

43. $\frac{c}{5} \le -3$ **44.** $8p \ge -96$ **45.** $0 < 8r$

46. $\frac{t}{-6} < -3$ **47.** $\frac{a}{11} > -22$ **48.** $-12k \ge -144$

3 Extra Practice

Estimate. State the method you used. Lesson 3-1

1. 5.35 + 7.953　　　　**2.** 25.68 − 3.7　　　　**3.** 6.877 + 3.521 + 8.5

4. 103.890 − 25.6　　　**5.** 42.875 + 36.982 + 45.7　　**6.** 42.651 − 12.8

Estimate each product or quotient. Lesson 3-2

7. 9.5(12.31)　　　　　　　　　　**8.** 24.8 ÷ 5.03

9. 2.8 · 6.11　　　　　　　　　　**10.** −5.78 ÷ 1.95

11. (−2.468)(−9.031)　　　　　　**12.** −19.32 ÷ 4.025

Find the mean, median, and mode. When the answer is not an integer, Lesson 3-3
round to the nearest tenth. Identify any outliers.

13. 10 13 10 15 12 11 12 19 14　　　**14.** 85 86 80 85 90 90 50 88

15. $25 $30 $32 $28 $30 $15 $28 $30　　**16.** 6.2 4.5 4.8 12.3 5.7 4.8 6.0

Evaluate each formula for the values given. Lesson 3-4

17. perimeter of a rectangle: $P = 2\ell + 2w$　　**18.** circumference of a circle: $C = 2\pi r$
when $\ell = 45$ yd and $w = 20$ yd　　　　　　when $r = 6.8$ in.; use 3.14 for π

19. distance traveled: $d = rt$　　　　　　　**20.** perimeter of a square: $P = 4s$
when $r = 50$ mi/h and $t = 3.5$ h　　　　　when $s = 12$ cm

Solve each equation. Lessons 3-5 and 3-6

21. $t + 4.5 = 17.2$　　　　**22.** $15.5 + y = 10.5$　　　　**23.** $x − 70.2 = 23.6$

24. $1.2b = 6$　　　　　　　**25.** $c \div 5.3 = 12$　　　　　　**26.** $−21.2 = p − 12.7$

27. $f \div 5.25 = 7.8$　　　　**28.** $6.4m = 38.4$　　　　　　**29.** $−3.1 = −31a$

30. $h + 25.8 = 76$　　　　**31.** $101.5 = j − 82.8$　　　　**32.** $−50.8 = d + 36.2$

33. $4.5v = 13.5$　　　　　**34.** $s \div 10.5 = 42$　　　　　**35.** $26.2 = z − 6.55$

Complete each statement. Lesson 3-7

36. 0.95 m = ▇ cm　　　　**37.** 250 mL = ▇ L　　　　**38.** 2.5 kg = ▇ g

39. 60 g = ▇ kg　　　　　　**40.** 0.54 L = ▇ mL　　　　**41.** 5.62 m = ▇ cm

42. 58 cm = ▇ m　　　　　**43.** 564 mm = ▇ m　　　　**44.** 345 g = ▇ mg

45. 36 mg = ▇ g　　　　　**46.** 234 cm = ▇ m　　　　**47.** 567 mg = ▇ g

List all the factors of each number.   Lesson 4-1

1. 60   **2.** 45   **3.** 64   **4.** 46   **5.** 36   **6.** 100

Evaluate each expression.   Lesson 4-2

7. x^2, for $x = 8$ **8.** $-2v^3$, for $v = 2$ **9.** $5t^2 - 4$, for $t = 4$

10. $a^3 + 10$, for $a = -5$ **11.** mn^2, for $m = 3$ and $n = 4$ **12.** $6(2r - 4)^2$, for $r = 7$

Is each number *prime*, *composite*, or *neither*? For each composite   Lesson 4-3
number, write the prime factorization. Use exponents where possible.

13. 25   **14.** 36   **15.** 47   **16.** 38   **17.** 1   **18.** 117

Find the GCF.   Lesson 4-3

19. 20, 30   **20.** 8, 12, 18   **21.** $5x, 40x$ **22.** $6y, 108$

Write in simplest form.   Lesson 4-4

23. $\frac{12}{20}$ **24.** $\frac{4}{20}$ **25.** $\frac{35}{80}$ **26.** $\frac{18}{36}$

27. $\frac{13}{52}$ **28.** $\frac{75}{100}$ **29.** $\frac{16}{50}$ **30.** $\frac{5x}{65x^2}$

31. $\frac{3x^2}{45x}$ **32.** $\frac{50a^2}{5a}$ **33.** $\frac{36x}{16}$ **34.** $\frac{100pq}{625q}$

Graph each rational number on one number line.   Lesson 4-6

35. 0.2   **36.** $\frac{3}{10}$ **37.** -2 **38.** -1 **39.** $-\frac{1}{2}$

Evaluate each expression for $a = 10$ and $b = -4$. Write in   Lesson 4-6
simplest form.

40. $\frac{a + b}{a}$ **41.** $\frac{b}{a}$ **42.** $\frac{a - b}{3a}$ **43.** $\frac{b^2}{a^2}$

Simplify each expression.   Lessons 4-7 and 4-8

44. $8a^2 \cdot 3a^4$ **45.** $3y^2 \cdot 2y^3$ **46.** $(p^5)^6$ **47.** $(x^3)(y)(x^5)$

48. $\frac{6x^2}{2x^5}$ **49.** $\frac{18t^{20}}{6t^5}$ **50.** $\frac{b^2}{b^3}$ **51.** 12^0

Multiply. Express each result in scientific notation.   Lesson 4-9

52. $(5 \times 10^4)(8 \times 10^9)$ **53.** $(1.1 \times 10^6)(6 \times 10^{10})$ **54.** $(3 \times 10^{12})(4 \times 10^8)$

CHAPTER
5 Extra Practice

Find the LCM of each group of numbers or expressions. Lesson 5-1

1. $15, 30$ **2.** $4, 8, 10$ **3.** $8x, 12y$ **4.** $3t^2, 5t$

Compare. Use >, <, or = to complete each statement. Lesson 5-1

5. $\frac{5}{8} \blacksquare \frac{3}{5}$ **6.** $\frac{3}{10} \blacksquare \frac{1}{3}$ **7.** $\frac{3}{4} \blacksquare \frac{6}{8}$ **8.** $-\frac{1}{5} \blacksquare -\frac{1}{4}$

Write each fraction or mixed number as a decimal. Lesson 5-2

9. $\frac{7}{8}$ **10.** $2\frac{3}{5}$ **11.** $\frac{3}{11}$ **12.** $\frac{16}{5}$ **13.** $-\frac{7}{10}$ **14.** $-2\frac{1}{9}$

Write each decimal as a fraction or mixed number in simplest form. Lesson 5-2

15. 1.3 **16.** 0.605 **17.** $0.\overline{6}$ **18.** $-0.\overline{15}$ **19.** 0.35 **20.** 5.4

Add or subtract. Lesson 5-3

21. $\frac{2}{5} + \frac{3}{5}$ **22.** $3\frac{3}{4} - 1\frac{5}{6}$ **23.** $-\frac{5}{8} + \frac{1}{4}$ **24.** $\frac{10}{x} - \frac{12}{x}$

25. $\frac{1}{2} - \frac{3}{4}$ **26.** $4\frac{5}{6} + 5\frac{2}{9}$ **27.** $\frac{5}{t} + \frac{3}{4}$ **28.** $5\frac{1}{3} - \frac{7}{8}$

Find each product or quotient. Lesson 5-4

29. $\frac{3}{5} \cdot \frac{2}{3}$ **30.** $\frac{5}{6} \div 1\frac{2}{3}$ **31.** $-\frac{7}{10} \cdot 1\frac{3}{7}$ **32.** $\frac{5y}{6} \div \frac{2y}{3}$ **33.** $-\frac{2}{3} \cdot \left(-\frac{9}{22}\right)$

34. $10\frac{5}{8} \div \frac{5}{8}$ **35.** $\frac{5x}{7} \cdot \frac{1}{5}$ **36.** $\left(-\frac{1}{2}\right)\left(-\frac{3}{4}\right)$ **37.** $\frac{2}{5} \div \left(-\frac{1}{5}\right)$ **38.** $\frac{6}{7} \cdot \frac{3}{7}$

Complete each statement. Lesson 5-5

39. $60 \text{ in.} = \blacksquare \text{ ft}$ **40.** $15 \text{ qt} = \blacksquare \text{ pt}$ **41.** $4 \text{ lb} = \blacksquare \text{ oz}$

Solve each equation. Lessons 5-7 and 5-8

42. $\frac{3}{5} + a = 1\frac{2}{3}$ **43.** $b - 3\frac{1}{2} = 5$ **44.** $-\frac{4}{5}c = \frac{7}{10}$

45. $5d = \frac{3}{4}$ **46.** $1\frac{4}{7} = f + \frac{3}{14}$ **47.** $\frac{7}{8} = g - \frac{2}{3}$

Simplify each expression. Lesson 5-9

48. $(8a^3)^2$ **49.** $(x^2y^3)^4$ **50.** $(-2v)^3$ **51.** $(abc^3)^5$ **52.** $(f^2g^3)^6$

53. $(2xy)^3$ **54.** $\left(\frac{2}{5}\right)^3$ **55.** $\left(\frac{2c}{d^3}\right)^2$ **56.** $\left(\frac{3t}{4v}\right)^2$ **57.** $\left(\frac{1}{4}\right)^3$

6 Extra Practice

Write each ratio as a fraction in simplest form.   Lesson 6-1

1. $15 : 30$ **2.** 25 to 10   **3.** 4 out of 16   **4.** $\frac{15}{35}$

Find each unit rate.   Lesson 6-1

5. $40\text{ mi/h} = \blacksquare \text{ ft/s}$ **6.** $8\text{ cm/s} = \blacksquare \text{ m/h}$ **7.** $5.5\text{ qt/min} = \blacksquare \text{ gal/h}$

Solve each proportion. Round to the nearest tenth where necessary.   Lesson 6-2

8. $\frac{3}{5} = \frac{a}{60}$ **9.** $\frac{8}{7} = \frac{96}{b}$ **10.** $\frac{8}{c} = \frac{40}{85}$ **11.** $\frac{d}{36} = \frac{2}{3}$

12. $\frac{105}{200} = \frac{x}{40}$ **13.** $\frac{8}{15} = \frac{y}{50}$ **14.** $\frac{z}{40} = \frac{11}{15}$ **15.** $\frac{t}{2} = \frac{1.5}{8}$

The scale of a map is 4 in. : 25 mi. Find the actual distance for each map distance. Round to the nearest tenth where necessary.   Lesson 6-3

16. 10 in.   **17.** 5.5 in.   **18.** $\frac{1}{2}$ in.   **19.** 3 in.

Find each probability for one roll of a number cube. Then find the odds in favor of the event.   Lesson 6-4

20. $P(4)$ **21.** $P(8)$ **22.** $P(\text{even number})$ **23.** $P(1\text{ or }2)$

Write each percent as a fraction in simplest form and as a decimal.   Lesson 6-5

24. 10%   **25.** 200%   **26.** 6%   **27.** 1.75%   **28.** 8.5%

Write each number as a percent. Where necessary, round to the nearest tenth of a percent.   Lesson 6-5

29. 0.15   **30.** 1.2   **31.** $\frac{5}{12}$ **32.** $\frac{1}{8}$ **33.** 0.345

Solve each percent problem by using a proportion or an equation.   Lessons 6-6 and 6-7

34. Find 12% of 80.   **35.** 30% of x is 12. What is x?

36. What percent of 50 is 2.5?   **37.** Find 30% of 121.

Find each percent of change. Tell whether the change is an increase or a decrease.   Lesson 6-8

38. 120 to 80   **39.** 40 to 100   **40.** 175 to 231   **41.** $4 to $3.50

Find each sale price.   Lesson 6-9

42. regular price, $100; discount, 20%   **43.** regular price, $60; discount, 25%

Solve and check each equation. Lessons 7-1, 7-2, 7-3, and 7-5

1. $10 - 5x = 15$ 2. $3y + 17 = -13$ 3. $62 = -12z + 14$

4. $6x - 2x = 12$ 5. $t + 5 - 2t = -10$ 6. $24 = 2(b - 2) - 4b$

7. $5 - 2(y - 5) = 27$ 8. $-56a + 90 + 58a = 92$ 9. $8 = 3(c + 8)$

10. $8 - \frac{t}{2} = 53$ 11. $75 = \frac{m}{3} + 10$ 12. $\frac{3}{5}p + 18 = 24$

13. $0.05x - 0.08 + x = 0.97$ 14. $2.5y + 3.5 = -1.5$ 15. $6.3p + 1.2p = 22.5$

16. $2x + 6 = 5x$ 17. $3a + 2 = a - 8$ 18. $3(b - 2) = 9b$

19. $8(f + 3) = 10f - 32$ 20. $\frac{1}{4}(x - 8) = \frac{3}{4}x$ 21. $4(w - 2.1) = w + 0.6$

Solve and graph each inequality. Lesson 7-6

22. $3x + 18 > 12$ 23. $4 + 9a \geq -23$ 24. $10.5 < -4y + 2.5$

25. $19 - 3x \geq -2$ 26. $-5(a - 3) \leq 45$ 27. $\frac{1}{2}(t - 6) \leq 22$

28. $\frac{y}{4} - 6 < -9$ 29. $-31.4 \leq 2x + 1$ 30. $5.8 > 1 + 0.2m$

Solve for the variable indicated in red. Lesson 7-7

31. $s = p + c$ 32. $x + y = 180$ 33. $a - b = c$ 34. $I = prt$

Find the simple interest. Lesson 7-8

35. $450 deposited at an interest rate of 2% for 4 years

36. $3,000 deposited at an interest rate of 3% for 10 years

37. $10,000 deposited at an interest rate of 9% for 5 years

Find each balance.

38. $9,000 at 6% compounded annually for 5 years

39. $25,000 at 7% compounded semiannually for 10 years

40. $12,000 at 3% compounded semiannually for 8 years

41. $1,000 at 4% compounded annually for 10 years

42. $500 at 1.5% compounded annually for 4 years

43. $2,000 at 5% compounded semiannually for 2 years

Is each relation a function? Explain.   Lesson 8-1

1. $\{(3, 5), (4, 7), (4, 8), (6, 10)\}$

2. $\{(0, -1), (1, 3), (-2, 4), (3, 6)\}$

3. $\{(4, 5), (5, 2), (1, -3), (-2, -3), (0, 2)\}$

4. $\{(1.5, 0.6), (1.5, 1.1), (2, 1.9), (1, 3.2)\}$

Find the solution of each equation for $x = -3, 0$, and 2.   Lesson 8-2

5. $y = 3x - 2$

6. $y = 2x + 5$

7. $y = \frac{1}{2}x + 8$

8. $x = 3 - y$

9. $y = -4$

10. $2y = 6x - 10$

11. $x - 2y = 3$

12. $y = -x - 1.5$

Find the slope and y-intercept of the graph of each equation.   Lesson 8-3

13. $y = 5x - 4$

14. $y = 10 - 3x$

15. $2y = 3x + 12$

16. $4x + y = 16$

17. $y = \frac{3}{5}x - 1$

18. $12x - 6y = 30$

19. $y = x - \frac{1}{2}$

20. $x - y = -2$

Graph each line.

21. slope 3, through $(0, -5)$

22. slope -1, through $(3, 5)$

23. no slope, through $(2, -1)$

24. $y = 2x + 1$

25. $x + y = 4$

26. $y = \frac{1}{2}x - 1$

Write a rule for each function.   Lesson 8-4

27.

x	y
0	-1
1	2
2	5
3	8

28.

x	y
-1	4
0	6
1	8
2	10

29.

x	y
-2	-6
0	4
2	14
4	24

Use the table to complete Exercises 30 and 31.   Lesson 8-5

30. Make a scatter plot of (time studying, test grade).

31. Is there a positive correlation, negative correlation, or no correlation between the sets of data? Explain.

Study Time

Time Spent Studying (minutes)	40	30	20	50	75
Test Grade	85	80	60	80	90

Solve each system by graphing.   Lessons 8-7 and 8-8

32. $y = x + 3$
    $3x - y = 1$

33. $x + y = -7$
    $x - y = 1$

34. $y > 2x - 4$
    $y < -3x + 6$

35. $x + y < 10$
    $x - y < -5$

Use the figure at the right.   Lesson 9-1

1. Name the line in three ways.

2. Name four different rays.

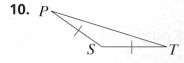

Use the figure at the right. Name each of the following.   Lesson 9-1

3. four segments that intersect $\overline{MR}$

4. three segments parallel to $\overline{MR}$

5. three segments skew to $\overline{MR}$

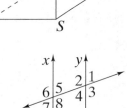

In the figure at the right, $x \parallel y$.   Lesson 9-2

6. List all angles that are congruent to $\angle 1$.

7. If $m\angle 5 = 67°$, what are the measures of the other angles?

Judging by appearances, classify each figure.   Lesson 9-3

8.

9.

10.

11. $\triangle XYZ \cong \triangle STU$. Which of the following must be true?   Lesson 9-5
    A. $\overline{YZ} \cong \overline{TU}$ **B.** $\angle X \cong \angle T$ **C.** $\overline{ZX} \cong \overline{TS}$
    D. $\angle YZX \cong \angle STU$ **E.** $\triangle YZX \cong \triangle UTS$

Find the circumference of each circle with the given radius   Lesson 9-6
or diameter.

12. radius = 4 in.   13. diameter = 25 ft   14. radius = 7.8 cm   15. diameter = 100 m

Draw $\triangle XYZ$ with acute $\angle Y$.   Lesson 9-7

16. Construct the angle bisector of $\angle Y$.   17. Construct a bisector of $\overline{XY}$.

Graph the image of $\triangle CDG$ with vertices $C(1, 3)$, $D(3, 5)$, and   Lessons 9-8, 9-9, and 9-10
$G(5, 1)$ after each transformation.

18. 3 units left, 2 units down   19. reflected over the x-axis   20. rotated 90° about the origin

Find the area of each figure.   Lessons 10-1 and 10-2

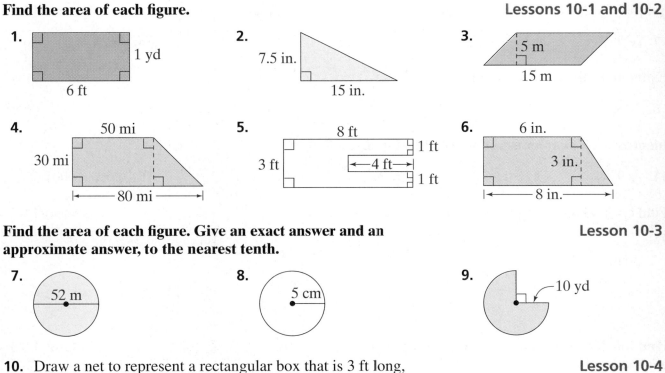

1.   2.   3.
1 yd   7.5 in.   5 m
6 ft   15 in.   15 m

4.   50 mi   5.   8 ft   6.   6 in.
30 mi   1 ft   3 in.
80 mi   3 ft ←4 ft→ 1 ft   8 in.

Find the area of each figure. Give an exact answer and an   Lesson 10-3
approximate answer, to the nearest tenth.

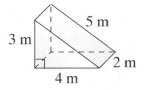

7.   8.   9.
52 m   5 cm   10 yd

10. Draw a net to represent a rectangular box that is 3 ft long,   Lesson 10-4
    5 ft wide, and 2 ft high. Label dimensions on the net and find
    the surface area.

Find the surface area and volume of each space figure,   Lessons 10-5, 10-6, 10-7, and 10-9
to the nearest tenth.

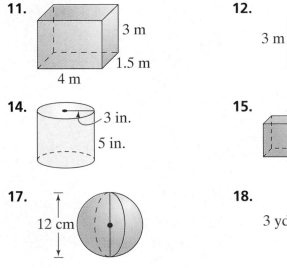
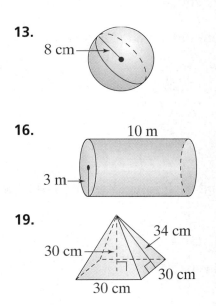

11.   12.   13.
3 m   5 m   8 cm
1.5 m   3 m
4 m   4 m   2 m

14.   15.   9 ft   16.   10 m
3 in.   5 ft
5 in.   4 ft   3 m

17.   18.   19.
12 cm   3 yd   3.6 yd   34 cm
                                  2 yd   30 cm
                                                       30 cm

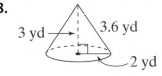

CHAPTER
11 Extra Practice

Simplify each square root.   Lesson 11-1

1. $\sqrt{4}$ **2.** $\sqrt{100}$ **3.** $-\sqrt{36}$ **4.** $\sqrt{121}$ **5.** $\sqrt{25}$

Estimate to the nearest integer.

6. $\sqrt{50}$ **7.** $\sqrt{12}$ **8.** $\sqrt{40}$ **9.** $\sqrt{105}$ **10.** $\sqrt{55}$

Identify each number as rational or irrational.

11. $\sqrt{9}$ **12.** 0.6 **13.** $\sqrt{5}$ **14.** $0.\overline{6}$ **15.** $0.010010001\ldots$

Find each missing length, to the nearest tenth of a unit.   Lesson 11-2

16.   **17.**   28 yd   **18.**   38.5 m

30 in. x 29 yd x a 45 m

40 in.

Find the distance between each pair of points. Round to the   Lesson 11-3
nearest tenth.

19. $(4, 6), (8, 2)$ **20.** $(0, -4), (-5, 1)$ **21.** $(20, -5), (10, -8)$

Find the midpoint of each segment with the given endpoints.

22. $A(5, 4)$ and $B(3, 0)$ **23.** $C(-2, -4)$ and $D(3, 1)$ **24.** $E(-1, 5)$ and $F(2, -1)$

Find the missing lengths.   Lesson 11-5

25.   **26.**   36 mm   **27.** x

y 45° x 60°   45°

32 cm x y y 15 mi

30°

Find each value. Round to four decimal places.   Lessons 11-6 and 11-7

28. $\sin 10°$ **29.** $\tan 85°$ **30.** $\cos 33°$

31. $\tan 5°$ **32.** $\sin 78°$ **33.** $\cos 65°$

34. $\cos 52°$ **35.** $\tan 50°$ **36.** $\sin 30°$

Display each set of data in a frequency table. Then draw a line plot for each frequency table. Find the range.   Lesson 12-1

1. 21 22 20 21 21 20 23 22 21 21   **2.** 95 100 95 95 90 80 85 80 95 100

Use box-and-whisker plots to compare data sets. Use a single number line.   Lesson 12-2

3. 1st set: 26 60 36 44 62 24 29 50 37 52 40 41 18 39 64 42
2nd set: 78 22 29 67 10 62 50 72 8 63 35 80 52 60 18 65 61

Use the graph at the right for Exercises 4 and 5.   Lesson 12-3

4. The graph suggests that the number of farms in 1982 was three times the number in 1992. Is this true? Explain.

5. Redraw the graph without a break.

Farms in the United States

6. A menu shows that you can pick one vegetable from four choices, one potato dish from five choices, and one main dish from two choices. How many different choices of meals do you have?   Lesson 12-4

You select letters at random from the word MATHEMATICS.   Lesson 12-5

7. Find the probability that you select A and, after replacing A, then select T.

8. Find the probability that you select A and, without replacing A, then select T.

Simplify each expression.   Lesson 12-6

9. $_3C_2$ **10.** $_3P_2$ **11.** $_5P_2$ **12.** $_7C_3$ **13.** $_{10}C_3$ **14.** $_8P_3$

Some students were surveyed about the number of books in their lockers. The table shows the results.   Lessons 12-7 and 12-8

15. Find the experimental probability that a locker will have 3 books.

16. In a school of 600 students, how many lockers would you expect to have one book?

Number of Books in Students' Lockers

Number of Books	1	2	3	4	5
Number of Students	12	21	10	7	10

CHAPTER
13 Extra Practice

Find the next three terms of each sequence. Then write a rule to describe each sequence.

Lesson 13-1

1. $100, 80, 60, 40, \ldots$

2. $6, 12, 18, 24, \ldots$

3. $8, 16, 24, 32, \ldots$

4. $50, 500, 5{,}000, 50{,}000, \ldots$

5. $-5, 25, -125, 625, \ldots$

6. $50, 10, -30, -70, \ldots$

Graph each function, for x values from -2 to 2.   **Lesson 13-2**

7. $y = x^2 - 1$ **8.** $y = -x^2 + 6$ **9.** $y = |x| - 3$ **10.** $y = -|x| + 2$

11. $y = -3x^2$ **12.** $y = -3|x| - 1$ **13.** $y = 2x^2 - 2$ **14.** $y = \frac{1}{2}|x|$

For each function, make a table with integer values of x from 0 to 4. Then graph each function.   **Lesson 13-3**

15. $y = 4^x$ **16.** $y = \frac{1}{2} \cdot 10^x$ **17.** $y = 10(0.5)^x$ **18.** $y = 2^x$

Tell whether each polynomial is a *monomial*, a *binomial*, or a *trinomial*.   **Lesson 13-4**

19. $2x^2 - 3x - 1$ **20.** $3xy$ **21.** $5x^3 - 15$ **22.** $10 - 2x + 5y$

23. xyz^2 **24.** $56 - y$ **25.** $3ab - a^2 - b$ **26.** 80

Simplify each sum or difference.   **Lesson 13-5**

27. $(5y - 12) + (2y + 10)$ **28.** $(x^2 + 3x + 4) + (2x^2 + x + 6)$

29. $(x^2 - 7x + 2) + (-x^2 + 6x - 2)$ **30.** $(4a^2 - 3a - 2) - (2a^2 + 5a + 10)$

31. $(5x - 3) + (6x^2 - 9)$ **32.** $(15y^2 + 12y) - (12y^2 - 20)$

33. $(3ab + a^2 + b^2) - (a^2 - 3b^2 - 5ab)$ **34.** $(10t - t^2 - 15) + (3t^2 + 12)$

Simplify each product.   **Lessons 13-6 and 13-7**

35. $2x(5x^2 + 6)$ **36.** $y^2(x + y)$ **37.** $6t^2(2t^2 - 3 + 8t)$

38. $(x - 8)(x + 1)$ **39.** $(y + 6)(2y + 4)$ **40.** $3b(5ab + 2ab^2 + 6b)$

Use the GCF of the terms to write each expression as the product of two factors.   **Lesson 13-7**

41. $4x^2 - 12$ **42.** $5z^2 - 20z + 30$ **43.** $2a^2b - 4a + 6b$

44. $t^2 - 3t$ **45.** $6xy + 2x + 3x^2y$ **46.** $5w^3 + 6w^2 - 3w$

Comparing and Ordering Whole Numbers

The numbers on a number line are in order from least to greatest.

You can use a number line to compare whole numbers. Use the symbols > (is greater than) and < (is less than).

■ EXAMPLE 1

Use > or < to compare the numbers.

a. **303 ■ 299**

303 is to the right of 299.
303 > 299

b. **301 ■ 305**

301 is to the left of 305.
301 < 305

The value of a digit depends on its place in a number. Compare digits starting from the left.

■ EXAMPLE 2

Use > or < to compare the numbers.

a. **12,060,012,875 ■ 12,060,012,675**

8 hundreds > 6 hundreds, so
12,060,012,875 > 12,060,012,675

b. **465,320 ■ 4,653,208**

0 millions < 4 millions, so
465,320 < 4,653,208

▶ EXERCISES

Use > or < to compare the numbers.

1. 3,660 ■ 360   **2.** 74,328 ■ 74,238   **3.** 88,010 ■ 8,101   **4.** 87,524 ■ 9,879

5. 295,286 ■ 295,826   **6.** 829,631 ■ 842,832   **7.** 932,401 ■ 932,701   **8.** 60,000 ■ 500,009

9. 1,609,372,002 ■ 609,172,002   **10.** 45,248,315,150 ■ 45,283,718,150

Write the numbers from least to greatest.

11. 3,747; 3,474; 3,774; 3,347; 3,734   **12.** 70,903; 70,309; 73,909; 73,090

13. 32,056,403; 302,056,403; 30,265,403; 30,256,403   **14.** 884,172; 881,472; 887,142; 881,872

Rounding Whole Numbers

You can use number lines to help you round numbers.

■ EXAMPLE 1

a. Round 7,510 to the nearest thousand.

7,510 is between 7,000 and 8,000.
7,510 rounds to 8,000.

b. Round 237 to the nearest ten.

237 is between 230 and 240.
237 rounds to 240.

To round a number to a particular place, look at the digit to the right of that place. If the digit is less than 5, round down. If the digit is 5 or more, round up.

■ EXAMPLE 2

Round to the place of the underlined digit.

a. 3,4<u>6</u>3,280

The digit to the right of the 6 is 3, so 3,463,280 rounds down to 3,460,000.

b. 28<u>9</u>,543

The digit to the right of the 9 is 5, so 289,543 rounds up to 290,000.

▶ EXERCISES

Round to the nearest ten.

1. 42   **2.** 89   **3.** 671   **4.** 3,482   **5.** 7,029   **6.** 661,423

Round to the nearest thousand.

7. 5,800   **8.** 3,100   **9.** 44,280   **10.** 9,936   **11.** 987   **12.** 313,591

13. 5,641   **14.** 37,896   **15.** 82,019   **16.** 808,155   **17.** 34,501   **18.** 650,828

Round to the place of the underlined digit.

19. 68,<u>8</u>52   **20.** <u>4</u>51,006   **21.** 3,40<u>6</u>,781   **22.** 2<u>8</u>,512,030   **23.** 71,2<u>2</u>5,003

24. 96,<u>3</u>59   **25.** 4<u>0</u>1,223   **26.** <u>8</u>,902   **27.** 3,6<u>7</u>7   **28.** 2,551,<u>7</u>50

29. 6<u>8</u>,663   **30.** 701,<u>8</u>03,229   **31.** 56<u>5</u>,598   **32.** 32,<u>8</u>10   **33.** 1,<u>4</u>46,300

Multiplying Whole Numbers

When you multiply by a two-digit number, first multiply by the ones and then multiply by the tens. Add the products.

■ EXAMPLE 1

Multiply 62 × 704.

Step 1	Step 2	Step 3
704	704	704
× 62	× 62	× 62
1408	1408	1 408
	42240	+ 42 240
		43,648

■ EXAMPLE 2

Find each product.

a. 93 × 6

```
   93
 ×  6
  558
```

b. 25 × 48

```
   48
 × 25
  240
+ 960
1,200
```

c. 80 × 921

```
    921
 ×   80
 73,680
```

▶ EXERCISES

Find each product.

1. 74 × 6	**2.** 35 × 9	**3.** 53 × 7	**4.** 80 × 8	**5.** 98 × 4	**6.** 65 × 8
7. 512 × 3	**8.** 407 × 9	**9.** 225 × 6	**10.** 340 × 5	**11.** 816 × 7	**12.** 603 × 3
13. 70 × 36	**14.** 41 × 55	**15.** 38 × 49	**16.** 601 × 87	**17.** 271 × 34	**18.** 450 × 67

19. 6 × 82   **20.** 405 × 5   **21.** 81 × 9   **22.** 3 × 274   **23.** 552 × 4

24. 60 × 84   **25.** 52 × 17   **26.** 31 × 90   **27.** 78 × 52   **28.** 43 × 66

29. 826 × 3   **30.** 702 × 4   **31.** 8 × 180   **32.** 6 × 339   **33.** 781 × 7

Dividing Whole Numbers

First estimate the quotient by rounding the divisor, the dividend, or both. When you divide, after you bring down a digit, you must write a digit in the quotient.

■ EXAMPLE

Find each quotient.

a. $741 \div 8$

Estimate:

$720 \div 8 \approx 90$

$$
\begin{array}{r}
92 \text{ R5} \\
8\overline{)741} \\
-72 \\
\hline
21 \\
-16 \\
\hline
5
\end{array}
$$

b. $838 \div 43$

Estimate:

$800 \div 40 \approx 20$

$$
\begin{array}{r}
19 \text{ R21} \\
43\overline{)838} \\
-43 \\
\hline
408 \\
-387 \\
\hline
21
\end{array}
$$

c. $367 \div 9$

Estimate:

$360 \div 9 \approx 40$

$$
\begin{array}{r}
40 \text{ R7} \\
9\overline{)367} \\
-360 \\
\hline
7
\end{array}
$$

▶ EXERCISES

Divide.

1. $4\overline{)61}$
2. $8\overline{)53}$
3. $7\overline{)90}$
4. $3\overline{)84}$
5. $6\overline{)81}$

6. $6\overline{)469}$
7. $3\overline{)653}$
8. $8\overline{)645}$
9. $9\overline{)231}$
10. $4\overline{)415}$

11. $60\overline{)461}$
12. $40\overline{)213}$
13. $70\overline{)517}$
14. $30\overline{)432}$
15. $80\overline{)276}$

16. $43\overline{)273}$
17. $52\overline{)281}$
18. $69\overline{)207}$
19. $38\overline{)121}$
20. $81\overline{)433}$

21. $94\overline{)1,368}$
22. $62\overline{)1,147}$
23. $55\overline{)2,047}$
24. $85\overline{)1,450}$
25. $46\overline{)996}$

26. $94 \div 4$
27. $66 \div 9$
28. $90 \div 5$
29. $69 \div 6$
30. $58 \div 8$

31. $323 \div 5$
32. $849 \div 7$
33. $404 \div 8$
34. $934 \div 3$
35. $619 \div 6$

36. $777 \div 50$
37. $528 \div 20$
38. $443 \div 70$
39. $312 \div 40$
40. $335 \div 60$

41. $382 \div 72$
42. $580 \div 68$
43. $279 \div 43$
44. $232 \div 27$
45. $331 \div 93$

46. $614 \div 35$
47. $423 \div 28$
48. $489 \div 15$
49. $1,134 \div 51$
50. $1,103 \div 26$

Decimals and Place Value

Each digit in a whole number or a decimal has both a place and a value. The value of any place is one tenth the value of the place to its left. The chart below can help you read and write decimals.

Billions	Hundred millions	Ten millions	Millions	Hundred thousands	Ten thousands	Thousands	Hundreds	Tens	Ones	.	Tenths	Hundredths	Thousandths	Ten-thousandths	Hundred-thousandths	Millionths
2	4	0	1	2	6	2	8	3	0	.	7	5	0	1	9	1

◾ EXAMPLE

a. What is the value of the digit 8 in the number above?
The digit 8 is in the hundreds place.
So, its value is 8 hundreds.

b. Write 2.006 in words.

The digit 6 is in the thousandths place.
So, 2.006 is read two and six thousandths.

c. Write five and thirty-four ten-thousandths as a decimal.
Ten-thousandths is 4 places to the right of the decimal point.
So, the decimal will have 4 places after the decimal point.
The answer is 5.0034.

▶ EXERCISES

Use the chart above. Write the value of each digit.

1. the digit 9

2. the digit 7

3. the digit 5

4. the digit 6

5. the digit 4

6. the digit 3

Write a decimal for the given words.

7. forty-one ten-thousandths

8. eighteen and five hundred four thousandths

9. eight millionths

10. seven and sixty-three hundred-thousandths

11. twelve thousandths

12. sixty-five and two hundred one thousandths

Write each decimal in words.

13. 0.06

14. 4.7

15. 0.00011

16. 0.9

17. 0.012

18. 0.000059

19. 0.0042

20. 6.029186

Comparing and Ordering Decimals

To compare two decimals, use the symbols > (is greater than), < (is less than), or = (is equal to). When you compare, start at the left and compare the digits.

■ EXAMPLE 1

Use >, <, or = to compare the decimals.

a. 0.1 ▨ 0.06

1 tenth > 0 tenths, so
0.1 > 0.06

b. 2.4583 ▨ 2.48

5 hundredths < 8 hundredths,
so 2.4583 < 2.48

c. 0.30026 ▨ 0.03026

3 tenths > 0 tenths, so
0.30026 > 0.03026

■ EXAMPLE 2

Draw number lines to compare the decimals.

a. 0.1 ▨ 0.06

b. 2.4583 ▨ 2.48

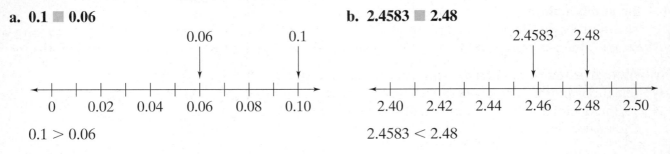

0.1 > 0.06

2.4583 < 2.48

▶ EXERCISES

Use >, <, or = to compare the decimals. Draw number lines if you wish.

1. 0.003 ▨ 0.02   **2.** 84.2 ▨ 842   **3.** 0.162 ▨ 0.106   **4.** 0.0659 ▨ 0.6059

5. 2.13 ▨ 2.99   **6.** 3.53 ▨ 3.529   **7.** 02.01 ▨ 02.010   **8.** 0.00072 ▨ 0.07002

9. 0.458 ▨ 0.4589   **10.** 8.627 ▨ 8.649   **11.** 0.0019 ▨ 0.0002   **12.** 0.19321 ▨ 0.19231

Write the decimals in order from least to greatest.

13. 2.31, 0.231, 23.1, 0.23, 3.21

14. 1.02, 1.002, 1.2, 1.11, 1.021

15. 0.02, 0.002, 0.22, 0.222, 2.22

16. 55.5, 555.5, 55.555, 5.5555

17. 0.07, 0.007, 0.7, 0.71, 0.72

18. 2.78, 2.7001, 2.701, 2.71, 2.7

19. 7, 7.3264, 7.3, 7.3246, 7.0324

20. 0.0101, 0.0099, 0.011, 0.00019

Rounding

When you round to a particular place, look at the digit to the right of that place. If it is 5 or more, the digit in the place you are rounding to will increase by 1. If it is less than 5, the digit in the place you are rounding to will stay the same.

■ EXAMPLE

a. **Round 1.627 to the nearest whole number.**
The digit to the right of the units place is 6, so 1.627 rounds up to 2.

b. **Round 12,034 to the nearest thousand.**
The digit to the right of the thousands place is 0, so 12,034 rounds down to 12,000.

c. **Round 2.7195 to the nearest hundredth.**
The digit to the right of the hundredths place is 9, so 2.7195 rounds up to 2.72.

d. **Round 0.060521 to the nearest thousandth.**
The digit to the right of the thousandths place is 5, so 0.060521 rounds up to 0.061.

▶ EXERCISES

Round to the nearest thousand.

1. 105,099　　**2.** 10,400　　**3.** 79,527,826　　**4.** 79,932　　**5.** 4,312,349

Round to the nearest whole number.

6. 135.91　　**7.** 3.001095　　**8.** 96.912　　**9.** 101.167　　**10.** 299.9

Round to the nearest tenth.

11. 82.01　　**12.** 4.67522　　**13.** 20.397　　**14.** 399.95　　**15.** 129.98

Round to the nearest hundredth.

16. 13.458　　**17.** 96.4045　　**18.** 0.699　　**19.** 4.234　　**20.** 12.09531

Round to the place of the underlined digit.

21. 7.0_6_15　　**22.** _5_.77125　　**23.** 1,5_2_2　　**24.** 0.919_5_2　　**25.** 4._2_43

26. 2_3_6.001　　**27.** _3_52　　**28.** 3.4953_6_6　　**29.** 8._0_7092　　**30.** _0_.6008

31. 4_0_9　　**32.** 23,_9_51,888　　**33.** 2.5_7_84　　**34.** 8_6_2　　**35.** 1_9_.32

36. _9_18　　**37.** 7,_7_35　　**38.** 25.66_0_47　　**39.** 9_8_3,240,631　　**40.** _2_7

41. 0.003_77_1　　**42.** 0._0_649　　**43.** 12._7_77　　**44.** 1,75_9_,230　　**45.** 2_0_,908

Adding and Subtracting Decimals

You add or subtract decimals just as you do whole numbers. You line up the decimal points and then add or subtract. If you wish, you can use zeros to make the columns even.

■ EXAMPLE

Find each sum or difference.

a. **37.6 + 8.431**

$$
\begin{array}{r} 37.6 \\ +\ 8.431 \\ \hline \end{array}
\rightarrow
\begin{array}{r} 37.600 \\ +\ 8.431 \\ \hline 46.031 \end{array}
$$

b. **8 − 4.593**

$$
\begin{array}{r} 8 \\ -\ 4.593 \\ \hline \end{array}
\rightarrow
\begin{array}{r} 8.000 \\ -\ 4.593 \\ \hline 3.407 \end{array}
$$

c. **8.3 + 2.99 + 17.5**

$$
\begin{array}{r} 8.3 \\ 2.99 \\ +\ 17.5 \\ \hline \end{array}
\rightarrow
\begin{array}{r} 8.30 \\ 2.99 \\ +\ 17.50 \\ \hline 28.79 \end{array}
$$

▶ EXERCISES

Find each sum or difference.

1. $\begin{array}{r} 39.7 \\ -\ 36.03 \\ \hline \end{array}$ 2. $\begin{array}{r} 1.08 \\ -\ 0.9 \\ \hline \end{array}$ 3. $\begin{array}{r} 6.784 \\ +\ 0.528 \\ \hline \end{array}$ 4. $\begin{array}{r} 5.01 \\ -\ 0.87 \\ \hline \end{array}$ 5. $\begin{array}{r} 13.02 \\ +\ 23.107 \\ \hline \end{array}$

6. $\begin{array}{r} 8.634 \\ +\ 1.409 \\ \hline \end{array}$ 7. $\begin{array}{r} 2.1 \\ -\ 0.5 \\ \hline \end{array}$ 8. $\begin{array}{r} 8.23 \\ -\ 3.1 \\ \hline \end{array}$ 9. $\begin{array}{r} 1.05 \\ +\ 12.9 \\ \hline \end{array}$ 10. $\begin{array}{r} 2.6 \\ +\ 0.003 \\ \hline \end{array}$

11. $\begin{array}{r} 0.1 \\ 58.21 \\ +\ 1.9 \\ \hline \end{array}$ 12. $\begin{array}{r} 12.2 \\ 3.06 \\ +\ 0.5 \\ \hline \end{array}$ 13. $\begin{array}{r} 9.42 \\ 3.6 \\ +\ 21.003 \\ \hline \end{array}$ 14. $\begin{array}{r} 15.22 \\ 7.4 \\ +\ 8.125 \\ \hline \end{array}$ 15. $\begin{array}{r} 3.7 \\ 20.06 \\ +\ 16.19 \\ \hline \end{array}$

16. 76.39 − 8.47   17. 8.7 + 17.03   18. 32.403 + 12.06   19. 20.5 + 11.45

20. 8.9 − 4.45   21. 1.245 + 5.8   22. 3.9 + 6.57   23. 14.81 − 8.6

24. 11.9 − 2.06   25. 3.45 + 4.061   26. 8.29 + 4.3   27. 7.06 − 4.235

28. 6.02 + 4.005   29. 7.05 − 3.5   30. 1.18 + 3.015   31. 2.304 − 0.87

32. 5.002 − 3.45   33. 6.8 + 3.57   34. 0.23 + 0.091   35. 0.5 − 0.18

36. 8.3 + 2.99 + 17.52   37. 9.5 + 12.32 + 6.4   38. 4.521 + 1.8 + 3.07

39. 3.602 + 9.4 + 24   40. 11.6 + 8.05 + 5.13   41. 7.023 + 1.48 + 3.9

42. 57 + 0.6327 + 189.007   43. 741 + 6.08 + 0.0309   44. 0.045 + 16.32 + 8.6

45. 4.27 + 6.18 + 0.91   46. 3.856 + 14.01 + 1.72   47. 11.45 + 3.79 + 23.861

Multiplying Decimals

Multiply decimals as you would whole numbers. Then place the decimal point in the product. To do this, add the number of decimal places in the factors.

■ EXAMPLE 1

Multiply 0.068 × 2.3.

Step 1   Multiply.

```
  0.068
× 2.3
─────
  204
+1360
─────
 1564
```

Step 2   Place the decimal point.

```
  0.068  ← three decimal places
× 2.3    ← one decimal place
─────
  204
+1360
─────
 0.1564  ← four decimal places
```

■ EXAMPLE 2

Find each product.

a. 3.12 × 0.9

```
  3.12
× 0.9
─────
 2.808
```

b. 5.75 × 42

```
   5.75
×  42
──────
  11 50
+230 00
──────
 241.50
```

c. 0.964 × 0.28

```
   0.964
×  0.28
───────
   7712
+19280
───────
 0.26992
```

► EXERCISES

Multiply.

1. 1.48 × 3.6	**2.** 191.2 × 3.4	**3.** 0.05 × 43	**4.** 0.27 × 5	**5.** 1.36 × 3.8
6. 6.23 × 0.21	**7.** 0.512 × 0.76	**8.** 0.04 × 7	**9.** 0.136 × 8.4	**10.** 3 × 0.05

11. 2.07×1.004 **12.** 0.12×6.1 **13.** 3.2×0.15 **14.** 0.74×0.23

15. 2.6×0.14 **16.** 0.77×51 **17.** 9.3×0.706 **18.** 71.13×0.4

19. 0.42×98 **20.** 6.3×85 **21.** 45×0.028 **22.** 76×3.3

23. 9×1.35 **24.** 4.56×7 **25.** 5×2.41 **26.** 704×0.3

27. 8.003×0.6 **28.** 42.2×0.9 **29.** 0.6×30.02 **30.** 0.05×11.8

Zeros in a Product

When you multiply with decimals, you may have to write one or more zeros to the left of a product before you can place the decimal point.

■ EXAMPLE 1

Multiply 0.06 × 0.015.

Step 1 Multiply.

$$\begin{array}{r} 0.015 \\ \times\ 0.06 \\ \hline 90 \end{array}$$

Step 2 Place the decimal point.

$$\begin{array}{r} 0.015 \\ \times\ 0.06 \\ \hline 0.00090 \end{array}$$

← The product should have 5 decimal places, so you must write three zeros before placing the decimal point.

■ EXAMPLE 2

a. 0.02 × 1.3

$$\begin{array}{r} 1.3 \\ \times\ 0.02 \\ \hline 00.026 \end{array}$$

b. 0.012 × 2.4

$$\begin{array}{r} 2.4 \\ \times\ 0.012 \\ \hline 48 \\ +\ 240 \\ \hline 0.0288 \end{array}$$

c. 0.022 × 0.051

$$\begin{array}{r} 0.051 \\ \times\ 0.022 \\ \hline 102 \\ +\ 1020 \\ \hline 0.001122 \end{array}$$

▶ EXERCISES

Multiply.

1. $\begin{array}{r} 0.03 \\ \times\ 0.9 \end{array}$	**2.** $\begin{array}{r} 0.06 \\ \times\ 0.5 \end{array}$	**3.** $\begin{array}{r} 2.4 \\ \times\ 0.03 \end{array}$	**4.** $\begin{array}{r} 7 \\ \times\ 0.01 \end{array}$	**5.** $\begin{array}{r} 0.05 \\ \times\ 0.05 \end{array}$
6. $\begin{array}{r} 0.016 \\ \times\ 0.12 \end{array}$	**7.** $\begin{array}{r} 0.031 \\ \times\ 0.08 \end{array}$	**8.** $\begin{array}{r} 0.03 \\ \times\ 0.2 \end{array}$	**9.** $\begin{array}{r} 0.27 \\ \times\ 0.033 \end{array}$	**10.** $\begin{array}{r} 0.014 \\ \times\ 0.25 \end{array}$

11. 0.003 × 0.55　　**12.** 0.01 × 0.74　　**13.** 0.47 × 0.08　　**14.** 0.76 × 0.1

15. 0.3 × 0.27　　**16.** 0.19 × 0.05　　**17.** 0.018 × 0.04　　**18.** 0.43 × 0.2

19. 0.03 × 0.03　　**20.** 4.003 × 0.02　　**21.** 0.5 × 0.08　　**22.** 0.06 × 0.7

23. 0.047 × 0.008　　**24.** 0.05 × 0.06　　**25.** 0.03 × 0.4　　**26.** 0.05 × 0.036

27. 0.4 × 0.23　　**28.** 0.3 × 0.017　　**29.** 0.3 × 0.24　　**30.** 0.67 × 0.09

31. 3.02 × 0.006　　**32.** 0.31 × 0.08　　**33.** 0.14 × 0.05　　**34.** 0.07 × 0.85

Dividing Decimals by Whole Numbers

When you divide a decimal by a whole number, the decimal point in the quotient goes directly above the decimal point in the dividend. You may need extra zeros to place the decimal point.

■ EXAMPLE 1

Divide 2.432 ÷ 32.

Step 1 Divide.

$$
\begin{array}{r}
76 \\
32\overline{)2.432} \\
-2\,24 \\
\hline
192 \\
-192 \\
\hline
0
\end{array}
$$

Step 2 Place the decimal point.

$$
\begin{array}{r}
0.076 \\
32\overline{)2.432} \\
-2\,24 \\
\hline
192 \\
-192 \\
\hline
0
\end{array}
$$

← Put extra zeros to the left. Then place the decimal point.

■ EXAMPLE 2

a. 37.6 ÷ 8

$$
\begin{array}{r}
4.7 \\
8\overline{)37.6} \\
-32 \\
\hline
5\,6 \\
-5\,6 \\
\hline
0
\end{array}
$$

b. 39.33 ÷ 69

$$
\begin{array}{r}
0.57 \\
69\overline{)39.33} \\
-34\,5 \\
\hline
4\,83 \\
-4\,83 \\
\hline
0
\end{array}
$$

c. 4.482 ÷ 54

$$
\begin{array}{r}
0.083 \\
54\overline{)4.482} \\
-4\,32 \\
\hline
162 \\
-162 \\
\hline
0
\end{array}
$$

► EXERCISES

Divide.

1. $7\overline{)17.92}$
2. $5\overline{)16.5}$
3. $9\overline{)6.984}$
4. $6\overline{)91.44}$
5. $4\overline{)35.16}$

6. $56\overline{)8.848}$
7. $22\overline{)2.42}$
8. $26\overline{)1,723.8}$
9. $83\overline{)15.272}$
10. $39\overline{)26.91}$

11. $14.49 \div 7$
12. $10.53 \div 9$
13. $17.52 \div 2$
14. $37.14 \div 6$

15. $0.1352 \div 8$
16. $0.0324 \div 9$
17. $0.0882 \div 6$
18. $0.8682 \div 6$

19. $12.342 \div 22$
20. $29.792 \div 32$
21. $22.568 \div 26$
22. $11.340 \div 36$

23. $45.918 \div 18$
24. $79.599 \div 13$
25. $58.5 \div 15$
26. $74.664 \div 12$

27. $2.1 \div 84$
28. $89.378 \div 67$
29. $0.0672 \div 48$
30. $171.031 \div 53$

Multiplying and Dividing by Powers of Ten

You can use shortcuts to multiply or divide by powers of ten.

When you multiply by	Move the decimal point	When you divide by	Move the decimal point
10,000	4 places to the right	10,000	4 places to the left
1,000	3 places to the right	1,000	3 places to the left
100	2 places to the right	100	2 places to the left
10	1 place to the right	10	1 place to the left
0.1	1 place to the left	0.1	1 place to the right
0.01	2 places to the left	0.01	2 places to the right
0.001	3 places to the left	0.001	3 places to the right

■ EXAMPLE

Multiply or divide.

a. 0.7 × 0.001

Move the decimal point 3 places to the left.
0.000.7

$0.7 \times 0.001 = 0.0007$

b. 0.605 ÷ 100

Move the decimal point 2 places to the left.
0.00.605

$0.605 \div 100 = 0.00605$

▶ EXERCISES

Multiply or divide.

1. $10,000 \times 0.056$ **2.** 0.001×0.09 **3.** 5.2×10 **4.** $0.03 \times 1,000$

5. $236.7 \div 0.1$ **6.** $45.28 \div 10$ **7.** $0.9 \div 1,000$ **8.** $1.07 \div 0.01$

9. 100×0.08 **10.** $1.03 \times 10,000$ **11.** 1.803×0.001 **12.** 4.1×100

13. $13.7 \div 0.001$ **14.** $203.05 \div 0.01$ **15.** $4.7 \div 10$ **16.** $0.05 \div 100$

17. 23.6×0.01 **18.** $1,000 \times 0.12$ **19.** 0.41×0.001 **20.** 0.01×6.2

21. $42.3 \div 0.1$ **22.** $0.4 \div 10,000$ **23.** $5.02 \div 0.01$ **24.** $16.5 \div 100$

25. $0.27 \div 0.01$ **26.** 1.05×0.001 **27.** 10×0.04 **28.** $2.09 \div 100$

29. 0.65×0.1 **30.** $0.03 \div 100$ **31.** $2.6 \div 0.1$ **32.** $12.6 \times 10,000$

33. $0.3 \div 1,000$ **34.** 0.01×6.7 **35.** 100×0.158 **36.** $23.1 \div 10$

Dividing Decimals by Decimals

To divide with a decimal divisor, multiply it by the smallest power of ten that will make the divisor a whole number. Then multiply the dividend by that same power of ten.

Skills Handbook

■ EXAMPLE

Find each quotient.

a. 3.348 ÷ 6.2
Multiply by 10.

$$
\begin{array}{r}
0.54 \\
6.2.\overline{)3.3.48} \\
-3\;1\;0 \\
\hline
2\;48 \\
-2\;48 \\
\hline
0
\end{array}
$$

b. 2.4885 ÷ 0.35
Multiply by 100.

$$
\begin{array}{r}
7.11 \\
0.35.\overline{)2.48.85} \\
-2\;45 \\
\hline
3\;8 \\
-3\;5 \\
\hline
35 \\
-35 \\
\hline
0
\end{array}
$$

c. 0.0576 ÷ 0.012
Multiply by 1,000.

$$
\begin{array}{r}
4.8 \\
0.012.\overline{)0.057.6} \\
-48 \\
\hline
96 \\
-96 \\
\hline
0
\end{array}
$$

▶ EXERCISES

Divide.

1. $3.2\overline{)268.8}$ **2.** $1.9\overline{)123.5}$ **3.** $0.3\overline{)135.6}$ **4.** $2.3\overline{)170.2}$ **5.** $7.9\overline{)252.8}$

6. $5.7\overline{)10.26}$ **7.** $2.3\overline{)71.53}$ **8.** $3.1\overline{)16.12}$ **9.** $7.8\overline{)24.18}$ **10.** $6.3\overline{)14.49}$

11. 134.42 ÷ 5.17   **12.** 89.96 ÷ 3.46   **13.** 160.58 ÷ 5.18   **14.** 106.59 ÷ 6.27

15. 62.4 ÷ 3.9   **16.** 260.4 ÷ 8.4   **17.** 316.8 ÷ 7.2   **18.** 162.4 ÷ 2.9

19. 1.512 ÷ 0.54   **20.** 3.225 ÷ 0.43   **21.** 2.484 ÷ 0.69   **22.** 511.5 ÷ 5.5

23. 0.992 ÷ 0.8   **24.** 4.53 ÷ 0.05   **25.** 3.498 ÷ 0.06   **26.** 59.2 ÷ 0.8

27. 2.198 ÷ 0.07   **28.** 14.28 ÷ 0.7   **29.** 1.98 ÷ 0.5   **30.** 26.36 ÷ 0.04

31. 3.922 ÷ 7.4   **32.** 23.52 ÷ 0.98   **33.** 71.25 ÷ 7.5   **34.** 114.7 ÷ 3.7

35. 0.832 ÷ 0.52   **36.** 1.125 ÷ 0.09   **37.** 9.666 ÷ 2.7   **38.** 1.456 ÷ 9.1

39. 0.4374 ÷ 1.8   **40.** 2.3414 ÷ 0.46   **41.** 0.07224 ÷ 0.021   **42.** 0.1386 ÷ 0.18

43. 0.16926 ÷ 0.091   **44.** 0.6042 ÷ 5.3   **45.** 2.3374 ÷ 0.62   **46.** 1.0062 ÷ 0.078

Zeros in Decimal Division

When you are dividing by a decimal, sometimes you need to use extra zeros in the dividend or the quotient, or both.

■ EXAMPLE 1

Divide 0.045 ÷ 3.6.

Step 1 Multiply by 10.

$$3.6\,\overline{)0.0.45}$$

Step 2 Divide.

$$
\begin{array}{r}
125 \\
3.6\,\overline{)0.0.4500} \\
-36 \\
\hline
90 \\
-72 \\
\hline
180 \\
-180 \\
\hline
0
\end{array}
$$

Step 3 Place the decimal point.

$$
\begin{array}{r}
0.0125 \\
3.6\,\overline{)0.0.4500} \\
-36 \\
\hline
90 \\
-72 \\
\hline
180 \\
-180 \\
\hline
0
\end{array}
$$

■ EXAMPLE 2

Find each quotient.

a. 0.4428 ÷ 8.2

Multiply by 10.

$$
\begin{array}{r}
0.054 \\
8.2\,\overline{)0.4.428}
\end{array}
$$

b. 0.00434 ÷ 0.07

Multiply by 100.

$$
\begin{array}{r}
0.062 \\
0.07.\,\overline{)0.00.434}
\end{array}
$$

c. 0.00306 ÷ 0.072

Multiply by 1,000.

$$
\begin{array}{r}
0.0425 \\
0.072.\,\overline{)0.003.0600}
\end{array}
$$

▶ EXERCISES

Divide.

1. $0.05\,\overline{)0.0023}$

2. $0.02\,\overline{)0.000162}$

3. $0.12\,\overline{)0.009}$

4. $2.5\,\overline{)0.021}$

5. $0.0019 \div 0.2$

6. $0.9 \div 0.8$

7. $0.000175 \div 0.07$

8. $0.142 \div 0.04$

9. $0.0017 \div 0.02$

10. $0.003 \div 0.6$

11. $0.0105 \div 0.7$

12. $0.034 \div 0.05$

13. $0.00056 \div 0.16$

14. $0.0612 \div 7.2$

15. $0.217 \div 3.1$

16. $0.052 \div 0.8$

17. $0.000924 \div 0.44$

18. $0.05796 \div 0.63$

19. $0.00123 \div 8.2$

20. $0.0954 \div 0.09$

21. $0.0084 \div 1.4$

22. $0.259 \div 3.5$

23. $0.00468 \div 0.52$

24. $0.104 \div 0.05$

25. $0.00063 \div 0.18$

26. $0.011 \div 0.25$

27. $0.3069 \div 9.3$

28. $0.00045 \div 0.3$

Writing Equivalent Fractions

If you multiply or divide both the numerator and the denominator of a fraction by the same number, you get an equivalent fraction.

◼ EXAMPLE 1

a. **Find the missing number in $\frac{5}{6} = \frac{20}{■}$.**

$$\overset{\times 4}{\curvearrowright}$$
$$\frac{5}{6} = \frac{20}{■}$$
$$\frac{5}{6} = \frac{20}{24}$$
$$\underset{\times 4}{\curvearrowright}$$

b. **Find the missing number in $\frac{12}{30} = \frac{■}{15}$.**

$$\overset{\div 2}{\curvearrowright}$$
$$\frac{12}{30} = \frac{■}{15}$$
$$\frac{12}{30} = \frac{6}{15}$$
$$\underset{\div 2}{\curvearrowright}$$

To write a fraction in simplest form, divide both the numerator and the denominator by the greatest common factor.

◼ EXAMPLE 2

a. **Write $\frac{6}{15}$ in simplest form.**

3 is the greatest common factor.

$$\frac{6}{15} = \frac{6 \div 3}{15 \div 3} = \frac{2}{5}$$

The simplest form of $\frac{6}{15}$ is $\frac{2}{5}$.

b. **Write $\frac{36}{42}$ in simplest form.**

6 is the greatest common factor.

$$\frac{36}{42} = \frac{36 \div 6}{42 \div 6} = \frac{6}{7}$$

The simplest form of $\frac{36}{42}$ is $\frac{6}{7}$.

▶ EXERCISES

Find each missing number.

1. $\frac{1}{3} = \frac{■}{6}$
2. $\frac{3}{4} = \frac{■}{16}$
3. $\frac{18}{30} = \frac{6}{■}$
4. $\frac{2}{3} = \frac{■}{21}$
5. $\frac{3}{4} = \frac{9}{■}$

6. $\frac{3}{10} = \frac{9}{■}$
7. $\frac{4}{5} = \frac{■}{30}$
8. $\frac{2}{3} = \frac{8}{■}$
9. $\frac{33}{55} = \frac{■}{5}$
10. $\frac{27}{72} = \frac{9}{■}$

11. $\frac{2}{3} = \frac{■}{24}$
12. $\frac{11}{12} = \frac{55}{■}$
13. $\frac{3}{5} = \frac{18}{■}$
14. $\frac{60}{72} = \frac{10}{■}$
15. $\frac{7}{8} = \frac{■}{24}$

Write each fraction in simplest form.

16. $\frac{12}{36}$
17. $\frac{25}{30}$
18. $\frac{14}{16}$
19. $\frac{27}{36}$
20. $\frac{21}{35}$
21. $\frac{40}{50}$

22. $\frac{24}{40}$
23. $\frac{32}{64}$
24. $\frac{15}{45}$
25. $\frac{27}{63}$
26. $\frac{44}{77}$
27. $\frac{45}{75}$

28. $\frac{60}{72}$
29. $\frac{77}{84}$
30. $\frac{12}{24}$
31. $\frac{24}{32}$
32. $\frac{7}{21}$
33. $\frac{18}{42}$

Mixed Numbers and Improper Fractions

A fraction, such as $\frac{10}{7}$, in which the numerator is greater than or equal to the denominator is an improper fraction. You can write an improper fraction as a mixed number that shows the sum of a whole number and a fraction.

Sometimes it is necessary to do the opposite and write a mixed number as an improper fraction.

■ EXAMPLE

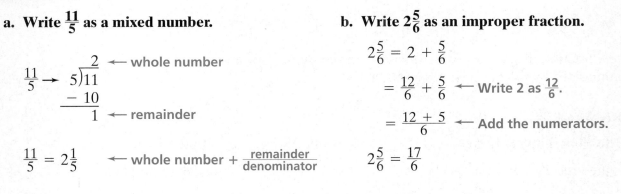

a. Write $\frac{11}{5}$ as a mixed number.

$$\frac{11}{5} \rightarrow \quad 5\overline{)11} \quad \leftarrow \text{whole number}$$
$$\underline{-10}$$
$$1 \quad \leftarrow \text{remainder}$$

$$\frac{11}{5} = 2\frac{1}{5} \quad \leftarrow \text{whole number} + \frac{\text{remainder}}{\text{denominator}}$$

b. Write $2\frac{5}{6}$ as an improper fraction.

$$2\frac{5}{6} = 2 + \frac{5}{6}$$
$$= \frac{12}{6} + \frac{5}{6} \quad \leftarrow \text{Write 2 as } \frac{12}{6}.$$
$$= \frac{12 + 5}{6} \quad \leftarrow \text{Add the numerators.}$$

$$2\frac{5}{6} = \frac{17}{6}$$

▶ EXERCISES

Write each improper fraction as a mixed number.

1. $\frac{7}{5}$ 2. $\frac{9}{2}$ 3. $\frac{13}{4}$ 4. $\frac{21}{5}$ 5. $\frac{13}{10}$ 6. $\frac{49}{5}$

7. $\frac{21}{8}$ 8. $\frac{13}{7}$ 9. $\frac{17}{5}$ 10. $\frac{49}{6}$ 11. $\frac{17}{4}$ 12. $\frac{5}{2}$

13. $\frac{27}{5}$ 14. $\frac{12}{9}$ 15. $\frac{30}{8}$ 16. $\frac{37}{12}$ 17. $\frac{8}{6}$ 18. $\frac{19}{12}$

19. $\frac{45}{10}$ 20. $\frac{15}{12}$ 21. $\frac{11}{2}$ 22. $\frac{20}{6}$ 23. $\frac{34}{8}$ 24. $\frac{21}{9}$

Write each mixed number as an improper fraction.

25. $1\frac{1}{2}$ 26. $2\frac{2}{3}$ 27. $1\frac{1}{12}$ 28. $3\frac{1}{5}$ 29. $2\frac{2}{7}$ 30. $4\frac{1}{2}$

31. $2\frac{7}{8}$ 32. $1\frac{2}{9}$ 33. $5\frac{1}{5}$ 34. $4\frac{7}{9}$ 35. $9\frac{1}{4}$ 36. $2\frac{3}{8}$

37. $7\frac{7}{8}$ 38. $1\frac{5}{12}$ 39. $3\frac{3}{7}$ 40. $6\frac{1}{2}$ 41. $3\frac{1}{10}$ 42. $4\frac{6}{7}$

Adding and Subtracting Fractions with Like Denominators

When you add or subtract fractions with the same denominator, add or subtract the numerators and then write the answer over the denominator.

■ EXAMPLE 1

Add or subtract. Write each answer in simplest form.

a. $\frac{5}{8} + \frac{7}{8}$

$\frac{5}{8} + \frac{7}{8} = \frac{5 + 7}{8} = \frac{12}{8} = 1\frac{4}{8} = 1\frac{1}{2}$

b. $\frac{11}{12} - \frac{2}{12}$

$\frac{11}{12} - \frac{2}{12} = \frac{11 - 2}{12} = \frac{9}{12} = \frac{3}{4}$

To add or subtract mixed numbers, add or subtract the fractions first.
Then add or subtract the whole numbers.

■ EXAMPLE 2

Add or subtract. Write each answer in simplest form.

a. $3\frac{4}{6} + 2\frac{5}{6}$

$$\begin{array}{r} 3\frac{4}{6} \\ + 2\frac{5}{6} \\ \hline 5\frac{9}{6} = 5 + 1 + \frac{3}{6} = 6\frac{1}{2} \end{array}$$

b. $6\frac{1}{4} - 1\frac{3}{4}$

$$\begin{array}{r} 6\frac{1}{4} \\ - 1\frac{3}{4} \\ \hline \end{array} \rightarrow \begin{array}{r} 5\frac{5}{4} \\ - 1\frac{3}{4} \\ \hline 4\frac{2}{4} = 4\frac{1}{2} \end{array}$$ ← Rewrite 1 unit as as $\frac{4}{4}$ and add it to $\frac{1}{4}$.

▶ EXERCISES

Add or subtract. Write each answer in simplest form.

1. $\frac{4}{5} + \frac{3}{5}$

2. $\frac{2}{6} - \frac{1}{6}$

3. $\frac{2}{7} + \frac{2}{7}$

4. $\frac{7}{8} + \frac{2}{8}$

5. $1\frac{2}{5} - \frac{1}{5}$

6. $\frac{3}{6} - \frac{1}{6}$

7. $\frac{6}{8} - \frac{3}{8}$

8. $\frac{2}{9} + \frac{1}{9}$

9. $\frac{4}{5} - \frac{1}{5}$

10. $\frac{5}{9} + \frac{7}{9}$

11. $9\frac{1}{3} - 8\frac{1}{3}$

12. $8\frac{6}{7} - 4\frac{2}{7}$

13. $3\frac{1}{10} + 1\frac{3}{10}$

14. $2\frac{2}{9} + 3\frac{4}{9}$

15. $4\frac{5}{12} - 3\frac{1}{12}$

16. $9\frac{5}{9} + 6\frac{7}{9}$

17. $5\frac{7}{8} + 2\frac{3}{8}$

18. $4\frac{4}{7} - 2\frac{1}{7}$

19. $9\frac{3}{4} + 1\frac{3}{4}$

20. $8\frac{2}{3} - 4\frac{1}{3}$

21. $8\frac{7}{10} + 2\frac{3}{10}$

22. $1\frac{4}{5} + 3\frac{3}{5}$

23. $7\frac{1}{5} - 2\frac{3}{5}$

24. $4\frac{1}{3} - 1\frac{2}{3}$

25. $4\frac{3}{8} - 3\frac{5}{8}$

26. $5\frac{1}{12} - 2\frac{7}{12}$

Multiplying and Dividing Fractions

To multiply fractions, multiply the numerators and the denominators.
To divide fractions, multiply by the reciprocal of the divisor.

■ EXAMPLE

Multiply. Write each answer in simplest form.

a. $\dfrac{8}{9} \times \dfrac{3}{10} = \dfrac{\overset{4}{\cancel{8}}}{\underset{3}{\cancel{9}}} \times \dfrac{\overset{1}{\cancel{3}}}{\underset{5}{\cancel{10}}} = \dfrac{4}{15}$

b. $3\dfrac{1}{8} \times 1\dfrac{3}{4} = \dfrac{25}{8} \times \dfrac{7}{4}$

$= \dfrac{175}{32} = 5\dfrac{15}{32}$ ← Rewrite as a mixed number.

Divide. Write each answer in simplest form.

c. $\dfrac{2}{3} \div \dfrac{4}{5} = \dfrac{2}{3} \times \dfrac{5}{4}$

$= \dfrac{\overset{1}{\cancel{2}}}{3} \times \dfrac{5}{\underset{2}{\cancel{4}}} = \dfrac{5}{6}$

d. $3\dfrac{1}{8} \div 1\dfrac{3}{4} = \dfrac{25}{8} \div \dfrac{7}{4}$

$= \dfrac{25}{\underset{2}{\cancel{8}}} \times \dfrac{\overset{1}{\cancel{4}}}{7} = \dfrac{25}{14} = 1\dfrac{11}{14}$ ← Rewrite as a mixed number.

► EXERCISES

Multiply. Write each answer in simplest form.

1. $\dfrac{3}{4} \times \dfrac{3}{5}$ **2.** $\dfrac{2}{3} \times \dfrac{3}{4}$ **3.** $6 \times \dfrac{2}{3}$ **4.** $\dfrac{3}{4} \times \dfrac{5}{6}$ **5.** $\dfrac{5}{8} \times \dfrac{2}{3}$

6. $\dfrac{9}{16} \times \dfrac{2}{3}$ **7.** $\dfrac{3}{10} \times \dfrac{2}{15}$ **8.** $\dfrac{3}{4} \times \dfrac{1}{6}$ **9.** $\dfrac{1}{4} \times \dfrac{5}{20}$ **10.** $\dfrac{9}{10} \times \dfrac{1}{3}$

11. $1\dfrac{1}{3} \times 2\dfrac{2}{3}$ **12.** $\dfrac{3}{5} \times 2\dfrac{3}{4}$ **13.** $2\dfrac{1}{4} \times 3\dfrac{1}{3}$ **14.** $\dfrac{1}{4} \times 3\dfrac{1}{3}$

15. $6\dfrac{1}{4} \times 7$ **16.** $1\dfrac{3}{4} \times 2\dfrac{1}{5}$ **17.** $2\dfrac{3}{4} \times \dfrac{1}{2}$ **18.** $3\dfrac{4}{5} \times 2\dfrac{1}{3}$

Divide. Write each answer in simplest form.

19. $\dfrac{5}{8} \div \dfrac{5}{7}$ **20.** $\dfrac{5}{7} \div \dfrac{5}{8}$ **21.** $\dfrac{3}{4} \div \dfrac{6}{11}$ **22.** $\dfrac{1}{9} \div \dfrac{1}{9}$ **23.** $\dfrac{1}{9} \div 9$

24. $\dfrac{9}{10} \div \dfrac{3}{5}$ **25.** $\dfrac{2}{3} \div \dfrac{1}{9}$ **26.** $\dfrac{4}{5} \div \dfrac{5}{6}$ **27.** $\dfrac{1}{5} \div \dfrac{8}{9}$ **28.** $\dfrac{7}{8} \div \dfrac{1}{3}$

29. $4\dfrac{1}{5} \div 2\dfrac{2}{5}$ **30.** $6\dfrac{1}{4} \div 4\dfrac{3}{8}$ **31.** $2\dfrac{1}{3} \div 5\dfrac{5}{6}$ **32.** $1\dfrac{1}{2} \div 4\dfrac{1}{2}$

33. $15\dfrac{2}{3} \div 1\dfrac{1}{3}$ **34.** $10\dfrac{1}{3} \div 2\dfrac{1}{5}$ **35.** $6\dfrac{1}{4} \div 1\dfrac{3}{4}$ **36.** $6\dfrac{2}{3} \div 3\dfrac{1}{8}$

Working with Integers

Quantities less than zero can be written using negative integers. For example, a temperature of 5 degrees below zero can be written as -5. Positive integers are used for quantities greater than zero.

■ EXAMPLE 1

Write an integer for each situation.

a. 10 degrees above zero
$+10$, or 10

b. a loss of $20
-20

c. 15 yards lost
-15

A number line can be used to compare integers. The integer to the right is greater.

$$\longleftarrow \; | \underset{-7}{} \; | \underset{-6}{} \; | \underset{-5}{} \; | \underset{-4}{} \; | \underset{-3}{} \; | \underset{-2}{} \; | \underset{-1}{} \; | \underset{0}{} \; | \underset{1}{} \; | \underset{2}{} \; | \underset{3}{} \; | \underset{4}{} \; | \underset{5}{} \; | \underset{6}{} \; | \underset{7}{} \; \longrightarrow$$

■ EXAMPLE 2

Compare. Use >, <, or = to complete each statement.

a. 0 ■ −3
0 is to the right, so it is greater.
$0 > -3$

b. −2 ■ −6
-2 is to the right, so it is greater.
$-2 > -6$

c. −7 ■ 3
-7 is to the left, so it is less.
$-7 < 3$

► EXERCISES

Write an integer for each situation.

1. 6 yards gained   **2.** 10 yards lost   **3.** 5 steps forward   **4.** 4 steps backward

5. find $3   **6.** lose $8   **7.** 12 floors up   **8.** 4 floors down

Compare. Use >, <, or = to complete each statement.

9. 0 ■ −1   **10.** −9 ■ 0   **11.** −3 ■ 3   **12.** 7 ■ −3   **13.** 0 ■ 1

14. 3 ■ 0   **15.** 1 ■ −4   **16.** −2 ■ −9   **17.** 6 ■ −1   **18.** 3 ■ −10

19. −7 ■ 3   **20.** 4 ■ 6   **21.** −16 ■ −25   **22.** −15 ■ −12   **23.** 7 ■ −8

24. 2 ■ 3   **25.** −7 ■ −8   **26.** 35 ■ −40   **27.** −30 ■ −20   **28.** 25 ■ −25

29. 9 ■ −9   **30.** −6 ■ −5   **31.** −23 ■ −15   **32.** −17 ■ −19   **33.** −15 ■ −25

Tables

Table 1 **Measures**

Metric

Length

10 millimeters (mm) = 1 centimeter (cm)

100 cm = 1 meter (m)

1,000 m = 1 kilometer (km)

Area

100 square millimeters (mm^2) =
  1 square centimeter (cm^2)

10,000 cm^2 = 1 square meter (m^2)

1,000,000 m^2 = 1 square kilometer (km^2)

Volume

1,000 cubic millimeters (mm^3) =
  1 cubic centimeter (cm^3)

1,000,000 cm^3 = 1 cubic meter (m^3)

Mass

1,000 milligrams (mg) = 1 gram (g)

1,000 g = 1 kilogram (kg)

Volume

1,000 milliliters (mL) = 1 liter (L)

1 mL = 1 cm^3

Customary

Length

12 inches (in.) = 1 foot (ft)

3 ft = 1 yard (yd)

36 in. = 1 yd

5,280 ft = 1 mile (mi)

1,760 yd = 1 mi

Area

144 square inches (in.^{2}) = 1 square foot (ft^2)

9 ft^2 = 1 square yard (yd^2)

4,840 yd^2 = 1 acre

Volume

1,728 cubic inches (in.^{3}) = 1 cubic foot (ft^3)

27 ft^3 = 1 cubic yard (yd^3)

Weight

16 ounces (oz) = 1 pound (lb)

2,000 lb = 1 ton (t)

Volume

8 fluid ounces (fl oz) = 1 cup (c)

2 c = 1 pint (pt)

2 pt = 1 quart (qt)

4 qt = 1 gallon (gal)

Time

1 minute (min) = 60 seconds (s)

1 hour (h) = 60 min

1 day (d) = 24 h

1 year (yr) = 365 d

Table 2   Symbols

$>$	is greater than	a^n	nth power of a
$<$	is less than	d	distance, diameter
$\geq$	is greater than or equal to	A'	image of A, A prime
$\leq$	is less than or equal to	A	Area
$=$	is equal to	b_1, b_2	base lengths of a trapezoid
$\neq$	is not equal to	b	base length
$\approx$	is approximately equal to	h	height
$\overset{?}{=}$	is this statement true?	p or P	perimeter
$+$	plus (addition)	ℓ	slant height, length
$-$	minus (subtraction)	w	width
$\pm$	plus or minus	C	circumference
$\times, \cdot$	times (multiplication)	S.A.	surface area
$\div, \overline{)}$	divide (division)	B	area of a base
$\sqrt{x}$	nonnegative square root of x	V	volume
$^\circ$	degrees	r	rate, radius
%	percent	$\overline{AB}$	segment AB
( )	parentheses for grouping	$\overrightarrow{AB}$	ray AB
$\lvert a \rvert$	absolute value of a	$\overleftrightarrow{AB}$	line AB
$a:b, \frac{a}{b}$	ratio of a to b	$\triangle ABC$	triangle with vertices A, B, and C
(a, b)	ordered pair with x-coordinate a and y-coordinate b	$\angle A$	angle with vertex A
$\cong$	is congruent to	$\angle ABC$	angle with sides $\overrightarrow{BA}$ and $\overrightarrow{BC}$
$\not\cong$	is not congruent to	$m\angle ABC$	measure of angle ABC
$\sim$	is similar to	AB	length of segment $\overline{AB}$
$\perp$	is perpendicular to	$\sin A$	sine of $\angle A$
$\parallel$	is parallel to	$\cos A$	cosine of $\angle A$
π	pi, an irrational number approximately equal to 3.14	$\tan A$	tangent of $\angle A$
$f(n)$	function value at n, f of n	$P(\text{event})$	probability of an event
b	y-intercept	$n!$	n factorial
m	slope of a line	$_nP_r$	permutations of n things taken r at a time
$\begin{bmatrix} 1 & 3 \\ 2 & 4 \end{bmatrix}$	matrix	$_nC_r$	combinations of n things taken r at a time
$-a$	opposite of a	$\wedge$	raised to a power (in a spreadsheet formula)
$\frac{1}{a}$	reciprocal of a	$*$	multiply (in a spreadsheet formula)
		$/$	divide (in a spreadsheet formula)

Tables

Table 3   Properties of Real Numbers

Unless otherwise stated, a, b, c, and d are real numbers.

Identity Properties

Addition $a + 0 = a$ and $0 + a = a$

Multiplication $a \cdot 1 = a$ and $1 \cdot a = a$

Commutative Properties

Addition $a + b = b + a$

Multiplication $a \cdot b = b \cdot a$

Associative Properties

Addition $(a + b) + c = a + (b + c)$

Multiplication $(a \cdot b) \cdot c = a \cdot (b \cdot c)$

Inverse Properties

Addition

$a + (-a) = 0$ and $-a + a = 0$

Multiplication

$a \cdot \frac{1}{a} = 1$ and $\frac{1}{a} \cdot a = 1 (a \neq 0)$

Distributive Properties

$a(b + c) = ab + ac$ $(b + c)a = ba + ca$

$a(b - c) = ab - ac$ $(b - c)a = ba - ca$

Properties of Equality

Addition   If $a = b$, then $a + c = b + c$.

Subtraction   If $a = b$, then $a - c = b - c$.

Multiplication If $a = b$, then $a \cdot c = b \cdot c$.

Division   If $a = b$, and $c \neq 0$, then $\frac{a}{c} = \frac{b}{c}$.

Substitution   If $a = b$, then b can replace a in any expression.

Reflexive $a = a$

Symmetric   If $a = b$, then $b = a$.

Transitive   If $a = b$ and $b = c$, then $a = c$.

Cross Product Property

$\frac{a}{b} = \frac{c}{d}$ is equivalent to $ad = bc$.

Zero-Product Property

If $ab = 0$ then $a = 0$ or $b = 0$.

Closure Property

$a + b$ is a unique real number.

ab is a unique real number.

Density Property

Between any two rational numbers, there is at least one other rational number.

Properties of Inequality

Addition   If $a > b$, then $a + c > b + c$.
                If $a < b$, then $a + c < b + c$.

Subtraction   If $a > b$, then $a - c > b - c$.
                If $a < b$, then $a - c < b - c$.

Multiplication

If $a > b$ and $c > 0$, then $ac > bc$.

If $a < b$ and $c > 0$, then $ac < bc$.

If $a > b$ and $c < 0$, then $ac < bc$.

If $a < b$ and $c < 0$, then $ac > bc$.

Division

If $a > b$ and $c > 0$, then $\frac{a}{c} > \frac{b}{c}$.

If $a < b$ and $c > 0$, then $\frac{a}{c} < \frac{b}{c}$.

If $a > b$ and $c < 0$, then $\frac{a}{c} < \frac{b}{c}$.

If $a < b$ and $c < 0$, then $\frac{a}{c} > \frac{b}{c}$.

Transitive   If $a > b$ and $b > c$, then $a > c$.

Comparison If $a = b + c$ and $c > 0$ then $a > b$.

Properties of Exponents

For any nonzero number a and any integers m and n:

Zero Exponent $a^0 = 1$

Negative Exponent $a^{-n} = \frac{1}{a^n}$

Product of Powers $a^m \cdot a^n = a^{m+n}$

Quotient of Powers $\frac{a^m}{a^n} = a^{m-n}$

Table 4   **Geometric Formulas**

Perimeter and Circumference

Rectangle
$P = 2\ell + 2w$

Circle
$C = \pi d$ or $C = 2\pi r$

Area

Square
$A = s^2$

Parallelogram and Rectangle
$A = bh$

Triangle
$A = \frac{1}{2}bh$

Trapezoid
$A = \frac{1}{2}h(b_1 + b_2)$

Circle
$C = \pi r^2$

Triangle Formulas

Pythagorean Theorem
In a right triangle with legs of lengths a and b and hypotenuse of length c, $a^2 + b^2 = c^2$.

Trigonometric Ratios
tangent of $\angle A = \dfrac{\text{length of leg opposite } \angle A}{\text{length of leg adjacent to } \angle A}$

sine of $\angle A = \dfrac{\text{length of leg opposite } \angle A}{\text{length of hypotenuse}}$

cosine of $\angle A = \dfrac{\text{length of leg adjacent to } \angle A}{\text{length of hypotenuse}}$

Triangle Angle Sum
For any $\triangle ABC$,
$m\angle A + m\angle B + m\angle C = 180°$.

Surface Area

Rectangular Prism
L.A. $= ph$
S.A. $=$ L.A. $+ 2B$

Cylinder
L.A. $= 2\pi rh$
S.A. $=$ L.A. $+ 2B$

Square Pyramid
L.A. $= n\left(\frac{1}{2}b\ell\right)$, where n is the number of faces
S.A. $=$ L.A. $+ B$

Cone
L.A. $= \pi r\ell$
S.A. $=$ L.A. $+ B$

Sphere
S.A. $= 4\pi r^2$

Volume

Prism
$V = Bh$

Cylinder
$V = Bh$ or $B = \pi r^2 h$

Pyramid
$V = \frac{1}{3}Bh$

Cone
$V = \frac{1}{3}Bh$ or $V = \frac{1}{3}\pi r^2 h$

Sphere
$V = \frac{4}{3}\pi r^3$

Tables

Table 5   Squares and Square Roots

N	N^2	$\sqrt{N}$	N	N^2	$\sqrt{N}$
1	1	1	51	2,601	7.141
2	4	1.414	52	2,704	7.211
3	9	1.732	53	2,809	7.280
4	16	2	54	2,916	7.348
5	25	2.236	55	3,025	7.416
6	36	2.449	56	3,136	7.483
7	49	2.646	57	3,249	7.550
8	64	2.828	58	3,364	7.616
9	81	3	59	3,481	7.681
10	100	3.162	60	3,600	7.746
11	121	3.317	61	3,721	7.810
12	144	3.464	62	3,844	7.874
13	169	3.606	63	3,969	7.937
14	196	3.742	64	4,096	8
15	225	3.873	65	4,225	8.062
16	256	4	66	4,356	8.124
17	289	4.123	67	4,489	8.185
18	324	4.243	68	4,624	8.246
19	361	4.359	69	4,761	8.307
20	400	4.472	70	4,900	8.367
21	441	4.583	71	5,041	8.426
22	484	4.690	72	5,184	8.485
23	529	4.796	73	5,329	8.544
24	576	4.899	74	5,476	8.602
25	625	5	75	5,625	8.660
26	676	5.099	76	5,776	8.718
27	729	5.196	77	5,929	8.775
28	784	5.292	78	6,084	8.832
29	841	5.385	79	6,241	8.888
30	900	5.477	80	6,400	8.944
31	961	5.568	81	6,561	9
32	1,024	5.657	82	6,724	9.055
33	1,089	5.745	83	6,889	9.110
34	1,156	5.831	84	7,056	9.165
35	1,225	5.916	85	7,225	9.220
36	1,296	6	86	7,396	9.274
37	1,369	6.083	87	7,569	9.327
38	1,444	6.164	88	7,744	9.381
39	1,521	6.245	89	7,921	9.434
40	1,600	6.325	90	8,100	9.487
41	1,681	6.403	91	8,281	9.539
42	1,764	6.481	92	8,464	9.592
43	1,849	6.557	93	8,649	9.644
44	1,936	6.633	94	8,836	9.695
45	2,025	6.708	95	9,025	9.747
46	2,116	6.782	96	9,216	9.798
47	2,209	6.856	97	9,409	9.849
48	2,304	6.928	98	9,604	9.899
49	2,401	7	99	9,801	9.950
50	2,500	7.071	100	10,000	10

Table 6   Trigonometric Ratios

Angle	Sine	Cosine	Tangent	Angle	Sine	Cosine	Tangent
1°	0.0175	0.9998	0.0175	46°	0.7193	0.6947	1.0355
2°	0.0349	0.9994	0.0349	47°	0.7314	0.6820	1.0724
3°	0.0523	0.9986	0.0524	48°	0.7431	0.6691	1.1106
4°	0.0698	0.9976	0.0699	49°	0.7547	0.6561	1.1504
5°	0.0872	0.9962	0.0875	50°	0.7660	0.6428	1.1918
6°	0.1045	0.9945	0.1051	51°	0.7771	0.6293	1.2349
7°	0.1219	0.9925	0.1228	52°	0.7880	0.6157	1.2799
8°	0.1392	0.9903	0.1405	53°	0.7986	0.6018	1.3270
9°	0.1564	0.9877	0.1584	54°	0.8090	0.5878	1.3764
10°	0.1736	0.9848	0.1763	55°	0.8192	0.5736	1.4281
11°	0.1908	0.9816	0.1944	56°	0.8290	0.5592	1.4826
12°	0.2079	0.9781	0.2126	57°	0.8387	0.5446	1.5399
13°	0.2250	0.9744	0.2309	58°	0.8480	0.5299	1.6003
14°	0.2419	0.9703	0.2493	59°	0.8572	0.5150	1.6643
15°	0.2588	0.9659	0.2679	60°	0.8660	0.5000	1.7321
16°	0.2756	0.9613	0.2867	61°	0.8746	0.4848	1.8040
17°	0.2924	0.9563	0.3057	62°	0.8829	0.4695	1.8807
18°	0.3090	0.9511	0.3249	63°	0.8910	0.4540	1.9626
19°	0.3256	0.9455	0.3443	64°	0.8988	0.4384	2.0503
20°	0.3420	0.9397	0.3640	65°	0.9063	0.4226	2.1445
21°	0.3584	0.9336	0.3839	66°	0.9135	0.4067	2.2460
22°	0.3746	0.9272	0.4040	67°	0.9205	0.3907	2.3559
23°	0.3907	0.9205	0.4245	68°	0.9272	0.3746	2.4751
24°	0.4067	0.9135	0.4452	69°	0.9336	0.3584	2.6051
25°	0.4226	0.9063	0.4663	70°	0.9397	0.3420	2.7475
26°	0.4384	0.8988	0.4877	71°	0.9455	0.3256	2.9042
27°	0.4540	0.8910	0.5095	72°	0.9511	0.3090	3.0777
28°	0.4695	0.8829	0.5317	73°	0.9563	0.2924	3.2709
29°	0.4848	0.8746	0.5543	74°	0.9613	0.2756	3.4874
30°	0.5000	0.8660	0.5774	75°	0.9659	0.2588	3.7321
31°	0.5150	0.8572	0.6009	76°	0.9703	0.2419	4.0108
32°	0.5299	0.8480	0.6249	77°	0.9744	0.2250	4.3315
33°	0.5446	0.8387	0.6494	78°	0.9781	0.2079	4.7046
34°	0.5592	0.8290	0.6745	79°	0.9816	0.1908	5.1446
35°	0.5736	0.8192	0.7002	80°	0.9848	0.1736	5.6713
36°	0.5878	0.8090	0.7265	81°	0.9877	0.1564	6.3138
37°	0.6018	0.7986	0.7536	82°	0.9903	0.1392	7.1154
38°	0.6157	0.7880	0.7813	83°	0.9925	0.1219	8.1443
39°	0.6293	0.7771	0.8098	84°	0.9945	0.1045	9.5144
40°	0.6428	0.7660	0.8391	85°	0.9962	0.0872	11.4301
41°	0.6561	0.7547	0.8693	86°	0.9976	0.0698	14.3007
42°	0.6691	0.7431	0.9004	87°	0.9986	0.0523	19.0811
43°	0.6820	0.7314	0.9325	88°	0.9994	0.0349	28.6363
44°	0.6947	0.7193	0.9657	89°	0.9998	0.0175	57.2900
45°	0.7071	0.7071	1.0000				

Tables

Glossary/Study Guide

A

Absolute value (p. 18) Absolute value is the distance of a number from zero on a number line. You write *the absolute value of −3* as $|-3|$.

The absolute value of −3 is 3 because −3 is 3 units from zero on a number line.

Absolute value function (p. 670) An absolute value function is a function with a graph that is V-shaped and opens up or down.

EXAMPLE This absolute value function is the graph of the equation $y = |x| - 3$.

Acute angle (p. 448) An acute angle is an angle with a measure less than 90°.

EXAMPLE $0° < m\angle 1 < 90°$

Acute triangle (p. 454) An acute triangle is a triangle with three acute angles.

EXAMPLE $\angle 1$, $\angle 2$, and $\angle 3$ are acute.

Addition Property of Equality (p. 86) If $a = b$, then $a + c = b + c$.

$8 = 2(4)$, so $8 + 3 = 2(4) + 3$

Addition Property of Inequality (p. 105) If $a > b$, then $a + c > b + c$. If $a < b$, then $a + c < b + c$.

$7 > 3$, so $7 + 4 > 3 + 4$
$2 < 5$, so $2 + 6 < 5 + 6$

Additive inverses (p. 23) Additive inverses are two numbers with a sum of zero.

23 and −23 are additive inverses because $-23 + 23 = 0$.

Additive identity (p. 65) The additive identity is zero. When you add a number and 0, the sum equals the original number.

$a + 0 = a$

Adjacent angles (p. 449) Adjacent angles are two angles that share a vertex and a side but no points in their interiors.

EXAMPLE $\angle 1$ and $\angle 2$ are adjacent angles.

Alternate interior angles (p. 450) Alternate interior angles are angles between two lines and on opposite sides of a transversal.

EXAMPLE $\angle 2$ and $\angle 3$ are alternate interior angles. $\angle 1$ and $\angle 4$ are also alternate interior angles.

Altitude (p. 505)   An altitude is any segment perpendicular to the line containing the base of a figure, and drawn from the side opposite the base.

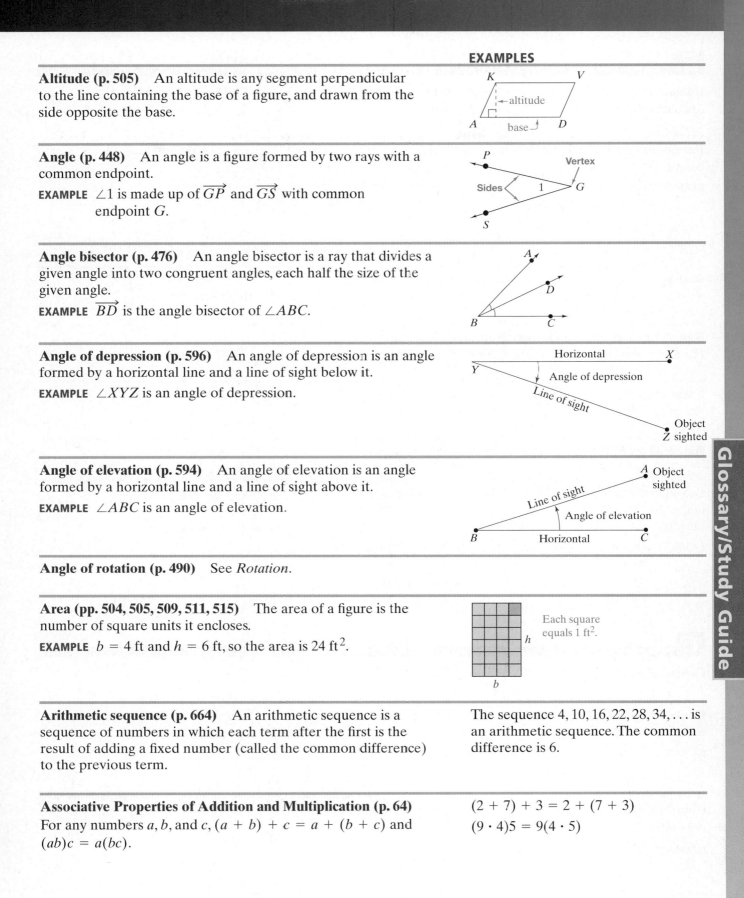

Angle (p. 448)   An angle is a figure formed by two rays with a common endpoint.

EXAMPLE $\angle 1$ is made up of $\overrightarrow{GP}$ and $\overrightarrow{GS}$ with common endpoint G.

Angle bisector (p. 476)   An angle bisector is a ray that divides a given angle into two congruent angles, each half the size of the given angle.

EXAMPLE $\overrightarrow{BD}$ is the angle bisector of $\angle ABC$.

Angle of depression (p. 596)   An angle of depression is an angle formed by a horizontal line and a line of sight below it.

EXAMPLE $\angle XYZ$ is an angle of depression.

Angle of elevation (p. 594)   An angle of elevation is an angle formed by a horizontal line and a line of sight above it.

EXAMPLE $\angle ABC$ is an angle of elevation.

Angle of rotation (p. 490)   See *Rotation*.

Area (pp. 504, 505, 509, 511, 515)   The area of a figure is the number of square units it encloses.

EXAMPLE $b = 4$ ft and $h = 6$ ft, so the area is 24 ft^2.

Arithmetic sequence (p. 664)   An arithmetic sequence is a sequence of numbers in which each term after the first is the result of adding a fixed number (called the common difference) to the previous term.

The sequence 4, 10, 16, 22, 28, 34, . . . is an arithmetic sequence. The common difference is 6.

Associative Properties of Addition and Multiplication (p. 64)
For any numbers a, b, and c, $(a + b) + c = a + (b + c)$ and $(ab)c = a(bc)$.

$(2 + 7) + 3 = 2 + (7 + 3)$
$(9 \cdot 4)5 = 9(4 \cdot 5)$

Glossary/Study Guide

B

Balance (p. 370)   The balance in an account is the principal plus the earned interest.

See *Compound interest.*

Bar graph (p. 99)   A bar graph is a graph that compares amounts.

EXAMPLE   This bar graph compares the numbers of students in grades 6, 7, and 8.

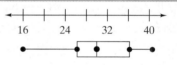

Base (p. 176)   The base is the repeated factor of a number written in exponential form.

$5^4 = 5 \cdot 5 \cdot 5 \cdot 5$
5 is the base.

Bases of two-dimensional figures (pp. 504, 509)   See *Parallelogram, Triangle,* and *Trapezoid.*

Bases of three-dimensional figures (p. 521)   See *Cone, Cylinder, Prism,* and *Pyramid.*

Binomial (p. 678)   A binomial is a polynomial with two terms.

$3x^2 - 1$ is a binomial.

Box-and-whisker plot (p. 613)   A box-and-whisker plot is a graph that shows the distribution of data along a number line. Quartiles divide the data into four equal parts.

EXAMPLE   The box-and-whisker plot at the right is for the data 16 19 26 27 27 29 30 31 34 35 37 39 40.

The lower quartile is 26.5. The median is 30. The upper quartile is 36.

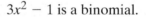

C

Center of rotation (p. 490)   See *Rotation.*

Central angle (p. 470)   A central angle is an angle whose vertex is the center of a circle.

EXAMPLE   In circle O, $\angle AOB$ is a central angle.

Chord (p. 469)   A chord of a circle is a segment whose endpoints are on the circle.

EXAMPLE $\overline{AB}$ is a chord of circle O.

Circle (p. 469) A circle is the set of all points that are equidistant from a given point, called the center.

EXAMPLE Circle O

Center

Circle graph (p. 470) A circle graph is a graph that represents parts of a whole. The total must be 100% or 1.

EXAMPLE This circle graph represents the different types of the plays that William Shakespeare wrote.

Shakespeare's Plays
Histories 26% — Tragedies 26%
Romances 13% — Comedies 35%

Circumference (p. 469) Circumference is the distance around a circle. You calculate the circumference of a circle by multiplying the diameter by π.

EXAMPLE The circumference of the circle is 10π cm, or approximately 31.4 cm.

10 cm, about 31.4 cm, O

Coefficient (p. 74) A coefficient is a number that multiplies a variable.

In the expression $2x + 3y - 16$, 2 is the coefficient of x and 3 is the coefficient of y.

Combination (p. 637) A combination is a group of items in which the order of the items is *not* important. You can use the notation $_nC_r$ to express the number of combinations of n objects chosen r at a time.

The combination (pots and pans) is the same as the combination (pans and pots).

Commission (p. 311) Commission is pay that is equal to a percent of sales.

A saleswoman received a 5% commission on sales of $120. Her commission was $6.

Common difference (p. 664) See *Arithmetic sequence.*

Common ratio (p. 665) See *Geometric sequence.*

Commutative Properties of Addition and Multiplication (p. 64) For any numbers $a, b,$ and $c, a + b = b + a$ and $ab = ba$.

$6 + 4 = 4 + 6$
$9 \cdot 5 = 5 \cdot 9$

Compass (p. 474) A compass is a geometric tool used to draw circles and arcs.

Compatible numbers (p. 128)   Compatible numbers are numbers that are close in value to the numbers you want to divide, and that are easy to divide mentally. Estimating quotients is easy to do mentally when you use compatible numbers.

Estimate $151 \div 14.6$.
$151 \approx 150$
$14.6 \approx 15$
$150 \div 15 = 10$
$151 \div 14.6 \approx 10$

Complement of an event (p. 296)   The complement of an event is the opposite of that event. The probability of an event plus the probability of its complement equals 1.

The event *no rain* is the complement of the event *rain*.

Complementary angles (p. 449)   Complementary angles are two angles whose measures add to 90°.

EXAMPLE $\angle BCA$ and $\angle CAB$ are complementary angles.

Composite number (p. 180)   A composite number is an integer greater than 1 with more than two factors.

24 is a composite number that has 1, 2, 3, 4, 6, 8, 12, and 24 as factors.

Compound inequalities (p. 364)   Compound inequalities are two inequalities joined by the word *and* or the word *or*.

$x > 4$ and $x \le 6$

$x \le -2$ or $x > 3$

Compound interest (p. 370)   Compound interest is interest paid on both the principal and the interest earned in previous interest periods. You can use the formula $B = p(1 + r)^n$ where B is the final balance, p is the principal, r is the interest rate for each interest period, and n is the number of interest periods.

You deposit $500 in an account earning 5% annual compound interest. The balance after six years is $500(1 + 0.05)^6$, or $670.05. The compound interest is $670.05 - 500$, or $170.05.

Cone (p. 521)   A cone is a space figure with one circular base and one vertex.

Congruent angles (p. 449)   Congruent angles are angles that have the same measure.

EXAMPLE $\angle B \cong \angle C$

Congruent figures (p. 464)   Congruent figures are figures that have the same size and shape. Congruent polygons have congruent corresponding sides and congruent corresponding angles. The symbol ≅ means "is congruent to."

EXAMPLE $\overline{AB} \cong \overline{QS}$, $\overline{CB} \cong \overline{RS}$, and $\overline{AC} \cong \overline{QR}$. $\angle A \cong \angle Q$, $\angle C \cong \angle R$, and, $\angle B \cong \angle S$. Triangles ABC and QSR are congruent. $\triangle ABC \cong \triangle QSR$

Congruent segments (p. 474)   Congruent segments are segments that have the same length.

EXAMPLE $\overline{AB} \cong \overline{WX}$

Conjecture (p. 35)   A conjecture is a conclusion reached through inductive reasoning.

Every clover has three leaves.

Consecutive integers (p. 341)   Consecutive integers are a sequence of integers obtained by counting by ones from any integer.

Three consecutive integers are -5, -4, and -3.

Constant (p. 74)   A constant is a term that has no variable.

In the expression $4x - 13y + 17$, 17 is the constant.

Constant of variation (p. 396)   A constant of variation is the coefficient k in a direct variation $y = kx$.

In the direct variation $y = 3x$, the constant of variation is 3.

Coordinate plane (p. 50)   The coordinate plane is the plane formed by two number lines that intersect at their zero points. The horizontal number line is called the x-axis. The vertical number line is called the y-axis. The two axes meet at the origin, $O(0,0)$, and divide the coordinate plane into four quadrants.

Coordinates (p. 50)   Coordinates are ordered pairs (x, y) that identify points in a coordinate plane. The x-coordinate (the first coordinate) shows the horizontal position. The y-coordinate (the second coordinate) shows the vertical position.

EXAMPLE The ordered pair $(-2, 1)$ describes the point that is found by moving 2 units to the left from the origin and one unit up from the x-axis.

Glossary/Study Guide

Correlation (p. 411)   A correlation is a relation between two sets of data. The data have a *positive correlation* if, as one set of values increases, the other set tends to increase. The data have a *negative correlation* if, as one set of values increases, the other set tends to decrease. The data have little or *no correlation* if the values show no relationship.

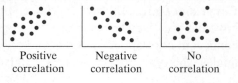

Positive correlation   Negative correlation   No correlation

Corresponding angles (p. 450)   Corresponding angles are pairs of nonadjacent angles that lie on the same side of a transversal of two lines and in corresponding positions.

EXAMPLE   ∠1 and ∠3 are corresponding angles. ∠2 and ∠4 are also corresponding angles.

Corresponding angles of polygons (p. 464)   Corresponding angles are matching angles of similar or congruent figures.

Corresponding angles of similar trapezoids   Corresponding angles of congruent triangles

Corresponding sides of polygons (p. 464)   Corresponding sides are matching sides of similar or congruent figures.

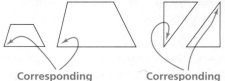

Corresponding sides of similar polygons   Corresponding sides of congruent triangles

Cosine (p. 588)   The cosine of an acute angle is the ratio of the length of the leg of a right triangle adjacent to the acute angle to the length of the hypotenuse.

See *Trigonometric ratios.*

Counterexample (p. 37)   A counterexample is an example that proves a statement false.

Statement: Motor vehicles have four wheels.

Counterexample: A motorcycle is a motor vehicle with two wheels.

Counting Principle (p. 627)   If there are m ways of making one choice and n ways of making a second choice, then there are $m \times n$ ways of making the first choice followed by the second.

There are 26 possible choices for each letter of a monogram. Thus, there are $26 \cdot 26$, or 676, possible two-letter monograms.

Cross products (p. 284)   Cross products are products formed from a proportion. They are the product of the numerator of the first ratio and the denominator of the second ratio, and the product of the denominator of the first ratio and the numerator of the second ratio. For a proportion, these products are equal.

The cross products for the proportion $\frac{3}{4} = \frac{6}{8}$ are $3 \cdot 8$ and $4 \cdot 6$.
$3 \cdot 8 = 24$ and $4 \cdot 6 = 24$

Cross section (p. 526)   A cross section is the intersection of a plane and a space figure.

Cube (p. 538)   A cube is rectangular prism with six congruent faces.

— Face

Cubic unit (p. 538)   A cubic unit is the amount of space occupied by a cube with sides one unit long.

Cylinder (p. 521)   A cylinder is a space figure with two circular, parallel, and congruent bases.

Bases

Height

D

Decagon (p. 458)   A decagon is a polygon with ten sides.

See *Polygon*.

Deductive reasoning (p. 75)   Deductive reasoning is the process of reasoning logically from given facts to a conclusion.

EXAMPLE Deductive reasoning is used to simplify the expression $4c + 3(3 + c)$.

$$4c + 3(3 + c) = 4c + 9 + 3c$$
$$= 4c + 3c + 9$$
$$= (4 + 3)c + 9$$
$$= 7c + 9$$

Dependent events (p. 633)   Dependent events are events for which the outcome of one event affects the outcome of a second event.

A bag contains 10 pieces of paper and on each piece is a different number from 1 to 10. A paper is picked and not returned to the bag. The outcome of picking a second piece is dependent on the outcome of the first pick.

Diagonal (p. 460)   A diagonal of a polygon is a segment that connects two nonconsecutive vertices.

EXAMPLE $\overline{BD}$ is a diagonal of quadrilateral $ABCD$.

Glossary/Study Guide

Diameter (p. 469) A diameter of a circle is a chord that passes through the center of the circle.

EXAMPLE $\overline{RS}$ is a diameter of circle O.

Dilation (p. 294) A dilation is a transformation that results in a size change. The scale factor describes the size of the change from the original figure to its image. If $r > 1$, the dilation is an enlargement. If $r < 1$, the dilation is a reduction.

EXAMPLE The blue triangle is an enlargement of the red triangle. The red triangle is a reduction of the blue triangle.

Dimensional analysis (p. 246) Dimensional analysis is a process of analyzing units to decide which conversion factors to use.

$0.5 \text{ mi} = \frac{0.5 \text{ mi}}{1} \cdot \frac{5{,}280 \text{ ft}}{1 \text{ mi}} = 2{,}640 \text{ ft}$

Direct variation (p. 396) A direct variation is a linear function modeled by the equation $y = kx$, where $k \neq 0$.

$y = 3x$

Discount (p. 319) A discount is the amount by which a price is decreased.

The price of a $10 book is reduced by a discount of $1.50 to sell for $8.50.

Distance Formula (p. 572) The distance d between any two points (x_1, y_1) and (x_2, y_2) is $d = \sqrt{(x_2 - x_1)^2 + (y_2 - y_1)^2}$.

The distance between $(6, 3)$ and $(1, 9)$ is d:

$$d = \sqrt{(1 - 6)^2 + (9 - 3)^2}$$
$$= \sqrt{(-5)^2 + 6^2}$$
$$= \sqrt{61}$$
$$\approx 7.8$$

Distributive Property (p. 69) For any numbers a, b, and c, $a(b + c) = ab + ac$ and $a(b - c) = ab - ac$.

$2\left(3 + \frac{1}{2}\right) = 2 \cdot 3 + 2 \cdot \frac{1}{2}$
$8(5 - 3) = 8(5) - 8(3)$

Divisible (p. 172) Divisible means that the remainder is 0 when you divide one integer by another.

15 is divisible by 5 because $15 \div 5 = 3$ with remainder 0.

Division Property of Equality (p. 89) If $a = b$ and $c \neq 0$, then $\frac{a}{c} = \frac{b}{c}$.

$6 = 3(2)$, so $\frac{6}{3} = \frac{3(2)}{3}$

Division Properties of Inequality (p. 108)   If $a < b$ and c is positive, then $\frac{a}{c} < \frac{b}{c}$. If $a > b$ and c is positive, then $\frac{a}{c} > \frac{b}{c}$.

If you divide each side of an inequality by a negative number, the direction of the inequality symbol is reversed.

If $a < b$ and c is negative, then $\frac{a}{c} > \frac{b}{c}$.

If $a > b$ and c is negative, then $\frac{a}{c} < \frac{b}{c}$.

$3 < 6$, so $\frac{3}{3} < \frac{6}{3}$

$8 > 2$, so $\frac{8}{2} > \frac{2}{2}$

$6 < 12$, so $\frac{6}{-3} > \frac{12}{-3}$

$16 > 8$, so $\frac{16}{-4} < \frac{8}{-4}$

Domain (p. 386)   A domain is the set of first coordinates of the ordered pairs of a relation.

In the relation $\{(0, 1), (-3, 2), (0, 2)\}$, the domain is $\{0, -3\}$.

E

Edge (p. 521)   An edge is the intersection of two faces of a space figure.

Faces
Edges

Equation (p. 78)   An equation is a mathematical sentence with an equal sign, $=$. An equation says that the side to the left of the equal sign has the same value as the side to the right of the equal sign.

$2(6 + 17) = 46$

Equilateral triangle (p. 454)   An equilateral triangle is a triangle with three congruent sides.

EXAMPLE $\overline{SL} \cong \overline{LW} \cong \overline{WS}$

Equivalent fractions (p. 186)   Equivalent fractions are fractions that describe the same part of a whole.

$\frac{3}{4}$ and $\frac{6}{8}$

Evaluate an expression (p. 13)   To evaluate an expression is to replace each variable with a number, and then follow the order of operations.

To evaluate the expression $3x + 2$ for $x = 4$, substitute 4 for x.

$3x + 2 = 3(4) + 2 = 12 + 2 = 14$

Event (p. 295)   An event is any outcome or group of outcomes.

In a game that includes tossing a coin and rolling a number cube, *tossing heads and rolling a 2* is an event.

Experimental probability (p. 642)   See *Probability*.

Exponent (p. 176)   An exponent is a number that shows how many times a base is used as a factor.

$3^4 = 3 \cdot 3 \cdot 3 \cdot 3$

Glossary/Study Guide

Exponential decay (p. 674) Exponential decay is any function of the form $y = b^x$, where $0 < b < 1$. The graph of the function slopes downward as input values increase.

EXAMPLE The function $y = 10\left(\frac{1}{2}\right)^x$ is graphed for integer values of x from 1 to 5.

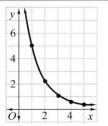

Exponential growth (p. 673) Exponential growth is any function of the form $y = b^x$, where $b > 1$. The graph of the function curves upward as input values increase.

EXAMPLE The function $y = 2^x$ is graphed for integer values of x from 0 to 4.

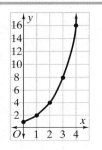

F

Face (p. 521) A face is a surface of a space figure.

Faces

Edges

Factor (p. 173) A factor is an integer that divides another integer with no remainder.

1, 2, 3, 4, 6, 9, 12, 18, and 36 are factors of 36.

Formula (p. 137) A formula is an equation that shows a relationship between quantities that are represented by variables.

The formula $P = 4s$ gives the perimeter of a square in terms of the length s of a side.

Frequency table (p. 608) A frequency table is a list of items that shows the number of times, or frequency, with which they occur.

EXAMPLE This frequency table shows the number of household telephones for the students in one school class.

Household Telephones

Phones	Tally	Frequency
1	卌				8
2	卌		6
3						4

Front-end estimation (p. 123) Front-end estimation is a way to estimate a sum. First add the front-end digits. Round to estimate the sum of the remaining digits. Then combine estimates.

Estimate $\$3.49 + \$2.29$.
$3 + 2 = 5$
$0.49 + 0.29 \approx 0.50 + 0.30 = 0.80$
$\$3.49 + \$2.29 \approx \$5 + \$0.80 = \$5.80$

Function (p. 386) A function is a relationship in which each member of the domain is paired with exactly one member of the range. A number of the domain is an input and the related number of the range is an output.

Earned income is a function of the number of hours worked (n). If you earn $\$5/h$, then your income is expressed by the function $f(n) = 5n$.

Function notation (p. 404) Function notation is notation that represents a function as $f(x)$ instead of y.

$f(x) = -2x + 1$

Function rule (p. 404) A function rule is an equation that describes a function.

$y = 2x + 5, f(x) = -4x + 3$

G

Geometric sequence (p. 665) A geometric sequence is a sequence of numbers in which each term after the first is the result of multiplying the previous term by a fixed number (called the common ratio).

The sequence $1, 3, 9, 27, 81, \ldots$ is a geometric sequence. The common ratio is 3.

Greatest common factor (GCF) (p. 181) The greatest common factor of two or more numbers is the greatest factor that the numbers have in common.

The greatest common factor (GCF) of 12 and 30 is 6.

Greatest possible error (p. 250) The greatest possible error of a measurement is half the unit used for measuring.

The measurement 400 kg is rounded to the nearest hundred kilograms. So, the greatest possible error is 50 kg.

H

Height of two-dimensional figures (pp. 505, 509, 510)
See *Parallelogram*, *Triangle*, and *Trapezoid*.

Height of three-dimensional figures (pp. 528, 529, 533, 534)
See *Cylinder* and *Prism*.

Hexagon (p. 456) A hexagon is a polygon with six sides.

See *Polygon*.

Histogram (p. 612) A histogram is a bar graph in which the heights of the bars give the frequencies of the data. There are no spaces between bars.

EXAMPLE This histogram gives the frequencies of board game purchases at a local toy store.

Board Game Purchases

Hypotenuse (p. 564) In a right triangle, the hypotenuse is the longest side, which is opposite the right angle.

See *Right triangle*.

Glossary/Study Guide

Identity Properties of Addition and Multiplication (p. 65) The sum of any number a and 0 is a. The product of any number a and 1 is a.

$a + 0 = a$
$a \cdot 1 = a$

Image (p. 479) An image is the result of the transformation of a point, line, or figure to a new set of coordinates.

See *Transformation*.

Improper fraction (p. 236) An improper fraction is a fraction with a numerator that is greater than or equal to the denominator.

$\frac{24}{15}$ and $\frac{16}{16}$ are improper fractions.

Independent events (p. 631) Independent events are events for which the outcome of one event does not affect the outcome of a second event.

When a number cube is rolled twice, the events (rolling 6, rolling 3) are independent.

Indirect measurement (p. 289) Indirect measurement is a method of determining length or distance without measuring directly.

EXAMPLE By using the distances shown in the diagram and using properties of similar figures, you can find the height of the taller tower.

$\frac{240}{540} = \frac{x}{1,192} \rightarrow x \approx 529.8$ ft

Inductive reasoning (p. 35) Inductive reasoning is making conclusions based on patterns you observe.

By inductive reasoning, the next number in the pattern 2, 4, 6, 8, ... is 10.

Inequality (p. 100) An inequality is a sentence that uses one of the symbols $>, <, \geq, \leq,$ or $\neq$.

$0 \leq 2, k > -3, 10 < t$

Integer (p. 18) The integers are the whole numbers and their opposites.

$-45, 0,$ and 289 are integers.

Interest (p. 369) See *Compound interest* and *Simple interest*.

Interest rate (p. 369) An interest rate is the percentage of the balance that an account or investment earns in a fixed period of time.

A savings account pays $2\frac{1}{4}$% per year.

Inverse operations (p. 84) Inverse operations are operations that undo each other.

Multiplication and division are inverse operations.

Irrational number (p. 561) An irrational number is a number that can be represented by a nonrepeating, nonterminating decimal.

The number π, which is approximately equal to 3.141592654, is an irrational number.

Isosceles triangle (p. 454) An isosceles triangle is a triangle with at least two congruent sides.

EXAMPLE $\overline{LM} \cong \overline{LB}$

$\triangle MLB$ is an isosceles triangle.

L

Lateral area (p. 528) The lateral area of a prism is the sum of the areas of the lateral faces.

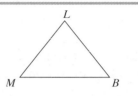

Lateral face (p. 534) See *Prism* and *Pyramid*.

Least common denominator (LCD) (p. 226) The least common denominator of two or more fractions is the least common multiple (LCM) of their denominators.

The least common denominator (LCD) of the fractions $\frac{3}{8}$ and $\frac{7}{10}$ is $2 \cdot 2 \cdot 2 \cdot 5$, or 40.

Least common multiple (LCM) (p. 224) The least common multiple (LCM) of two or more numbers is the least number that is a common multiple.

The least common multiple (LCM) of 6 and 15 is $2 \cdot 3 \cdot 5$, or 30.

Legs of a right triangle (p. 564) The legs of a right triangle are the two shorter sides of the triangle.

See *Right triangle.*

Like terms (p. 74) Like terms are terms with the same variable(s), raised to the same power(s).

$3b + 12b = (3 + 12)b$
$\qquad\qquad = 15b$

EXAMPLE $3b$ and $12b$ are like terms. Like terms can be combined by using the Distributive Property.

Line (p. 442) A line is a series of points that extends in two directions without end.

EXAMPLE $\overleftrightarrow{AB}, \overleftrightarrow{BA},$ or n is a line.

Glossary/Study Guide

Line graph (p. 98)   A line graph is a graph that shows changes over time.

EXAMPLE This line graph shows the change in the number of listeners to station KLZR during the day.

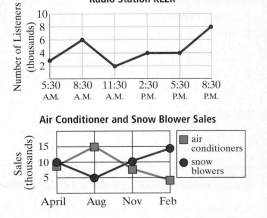

EXAMPLE This multiple line graph represents seasonal air conditioner and snowblower sales (in thousands) for a large chain of stores.

Line of reflection (p. 486)   A line of reflection is a line across which a figure is reflected.

See *Reflection.*

Line (of) symmetry (p. 485)   A line of symmetry is a line that divides a figure with reflectional symmetry into two congruent halves.

Line plot (p. 609)   A line plot is a graph that displays data by using X's above a number line.

EXAMPLE This line plot shows the heights in inches of the girls on a field hockey team.

Linear equation (p. 392)   A linear equation is any equation whose graph is a line.

EXAMPLE $y = \frac{1}{2}x + 3$ is linear because its graph is a line.

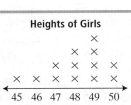
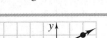
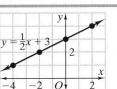

Linear inequality (p. 426)   A linear inequality is a number sentence in which the equal sign of a linear equation is replaced with $>$, $<$, $\geq$, or $\leq$.

$y \geq 2x + 3$
$y < -4x - 1$

Lower quartile (p. 613)   The lower quartile is the median of the lower half of a data set.

See *Box-and-whisker plot.*

Matrix (p. 484)   A matrix is a rectangular arrangement of numbers.

$$\begin{bmatrix} 0 & -1 & -4 \\ 0 & 4 & 0 \end{bmatrix}$$

Markup (p. 318)   Markup is the amount of increase in price. Markup is added to the cost of merchandise to arrive at the selling price.

A store buys a coat for $60 and sells it for $100. The markup is $40.

Mean (p. 131)   The mean of a collection of data is the sum of the data items divided by the number of data items.

The mean temperature (°F) for the temperatures 44, 52, 48, 55, 61, 67 and 58 is 55.

Measures of central tendency (p. 131)   Measures of central tendency in statistics are *mean*, *median*, and *mode*.

See *Mean*, *Median*, and *Mode*.

Median (p. 131)   The median of a collection of data is the middle number when there are an odd number of data items and they are written in order. For an even number of data items, the median is the mean of the two middle numbers.

The median temperature (°F) for the temperatures 44, 48, 52, 55, 58, 61, and 67 is 55.

Midpoint Formula (p. 574)   The midpoint of a line segment with endpoints $A(x_1, y_1)$ and $B(x_2, y_2)$ is $\left(\frac{x_1 + x_2}{2}, \frac{y_1 + y_2}{2} \right)$.

The midpoint of $A(-3, 2)$ and $B(7, -2)$ is $\left(\frac{-3 + 7}{2}, \frac{2 + -2}{2} \right)$, or $(2, 0)$.

Mixed number (p. 229)   A mixed number is the sum of a whole number and a fraction.

$3\frac{11}{16}$ is a mixed number.

$3\frac{11}{16} = 3 + \frac{11}{16}$

Mode (p. 131)   The mode of a collection of data is the data item that occurs most often. There can be no mode, one mode, or more than one mode.

The mode of the collection of numbers 3, 4, 1, 3, 2, 2, 5, 3 is 3.

Monomial (p. 678)   A monomial is a real number, a variable, or a product of a real number and variables with whole number exponents.

$5x$, -4, and y^3 are all monomials.

Multiple (p. 224)   A multiple of a number is the product of that number and any nonzero whole number.

The multiples of 13 are 13, 26, 39, 52, and so on.

Multiple line graph (p. 98)   A multiple line graph is a graph that shows more than one data set changing over time.

See *Line graph*.

Multiplication Property of Equality (p. 90)   If $a = b$, then $ac = bc$.

$12 = 3(4)$, so $12 \cdot 2 = 3(4) \cdot 2$

Multiplication Properties of Inequality (p. 109)   If $a < b$, and c is positive, then $ac < bc$. If $a > b$, and c is positive, then $ac > bc$.

$3 < 4$, so $3(5) < 4(5)$
$7 > 2$, so $7(6) > 2(6)$

If you multiply each side of an inequality by a negative number, the direction of the inequality symbol is reversed.

If $a < b$, and c is negative, then $ac > bc$. If $a > b$, and c is negative, then $ac < bc$.

$6 < 9$, so $6(-2) > 9(-2)$
$7 > 5$, so $7(-3) < 5(-3)$

Multiplicative identity (p. 65)   The multiplicative identity is one.

$a \cdot 1 = a$

Multiplicative inverse (p. 242)   The reciprocal of a number is its multiplicative inverse.

The multiplicative inverse of $\frac{4}{9}$ is $\frac{9}{4}$.

N

Negative correlation (p. 411)   See *Correlation*.

Net (p. 522)   A net is a pattern that can be folded to form a space figure.

EXAMPLE This net can be folded to form a cube.

No correlation (p. 411)   See *Correlation*.

O

Obtuse angle (p. 448)   An obtuse angle is an angle with a measure greater than 90° and less than 180°.

Obtuse triangle (p. 454)   An obtuse triangle is a triangle with one obtuse angle.

EXAMPLE $\triangle NJX$ is an obtuse triangle, since $\angle J$ is an obtuse angle.

Octagon (p. 460)   An octagon is a polygon with eight sides.

See *Polygon*.

Odds (p. 297)   Odds are a ratio that describe the likelihood of an event. Odds in favor of an event $= \frac{\text{number of favorable outcomes}}{\text{number of unfavorable outcomes}}$.

For the toss of a coin, the odds of tossing heads are 1 to 1.

Open sentence (p. 78)   An open sentence is an equation with one or more variables.

$3a = 5a + 8$

Opposites (p. 18)   Opposites are numbers that are the same distance from zero on the number line but in opposite directions.

-17 and 17 are opposites because they are both 17 units from zero on the number line.

Order of operations (pp. 9, 177)
1. Work inside grouping symbols.
2. Simplify any terms with exponents.
3. Multiply and divide in order from left to right.
4. Add and subtract in order from left to right.

$2^3(7 - 4) = 2^3(3) = 8 \cdot 3 = 24$

Ordered pair (p. 50)　An ordered pair is a pair of numbers that gives the location of a point in a coordinate plane. The first number is the x-coordinate and the second number is the y-coordinate.

See *Coordinates*.

Origin (p. 50)　The origin is the intersection of the x-axis and the y-axis in a coordinate plane. The ordered pair $(0, 0)$ describes the origin.

See *Coordinate plane*.

Outcomes (p. 295)　Outcomes are the possible results of an action.

Heads is an outcome of tossing a coin.

Outlier (p. 132)　An outlier is a data value that is much higher or lower than the other data values in a collection of data.

An outlier in the data $1, 1, 2, 3, 4, 4, 6, 7, 7, 52$, is 52.

P

Parabola (p. 669)　A parabola is the U-shaped graph of a quadratic function.

EXAMPLE This parabola is the graph of the equation $y = x^2 - 2$.

Parallel lines (p. 443)　Parallel lines are lines that lie in the same plane and do not intersect. The symbol ∥ means "is parallel to."

EXAMPLE $\overleftrightarrow{EF} \parallel \overleftrightarrow{HI}$

Parallelogram (p. 455)　A parallelogram is a quadrilateral with both pairs of opposite sides parallel.

EXAMPLE $KVDA$ is a parallelogram.

$\overline{KV} \parallel \overline{AD}$ and $\overline{AK} \parallel \overline{DV}$.

Pentagon (p. 456)　A pentagon is a polygon with five sides.

See *Polygon*.

Percent (p. 300)　A percent is a ratio that compares a number to 100. The symbol for percent is %.

$\frac{50}{100} = 50\%$

Glossary/Study Guide

	EXAMPLES

Percent of change (p. 314)   Percent of change is the percent something increases or decreases from its original amount.

A school's population increases from 500 to 520 students. The percent of change is $\frac{520 - 500}{500} = 4\%$.

Perfect square (p. 560)   A perfect square is the square of an integer.

$3^2 = 9$, so 9 is a perfect square.

Perimeter (p. 138)   The perimeter of a figure is the distance around the figure. To find the perimeter of a rectangle, find the sum of the lengths of all its sides, or use the formula $P = 2\ell + 2w$.

EXAMPLE The perimeter of $ABCD$ is 12 ft.

Permutation (p. 636)   A permutation is an arrangement of objects in a particular order. You can use the notation $_nP_r$ to express the number of permutations of n objects chosen r at a time.

The seating plans (Judith, Ann, Adrian) and (Ann, Judith, Adrian) are two different permutations.

Perpendicular bisector (p. 475)   A perpendicular bisector is a line, segment, or ray that is perpendicular to a segment.

Perpendicular lines (p. 475)   Perpendicular lines are lines that intersect to form right angles.

EXAMPLE $\overleftrightarrow{DE} \perp \overleftrightarrow{RS}$

Pi (p. 470)   Pi (π) is the name for the ratio of the circumference C to the diameter d of a circle.

$\pi = \frac{C}{d}$

Plane (p. 442)   A plane is a flat surface that has no thickness and continues without end in all directions.

EXAMPLE $ABCD$ or M is a plane.

Point (p. 442)   A point is a location in space that has no size.

EXAMPLE A is a point.

$\cdot A$

Polygon (p. 454)   A polygon is a closed plane figure with at least three sides.

Polynomial (p. 678)   A polynomial is a monomial or a sum or difference of monomials.

$4x^2 - 3x + 7$ is a polynomial.

Population (p. 646)   A population is a group about which you want information.

See *Sample*.

Positive correlation (p. 411)   See *Correlation*.

Power (p. 176)   A power is any expression in the form a^n. *Power* is also used to refer to the exponent.

5^4 is a power and can be read as "five to the fourth power."

Precision in measurement (p. 156)   The precision of a measurement is its exactness. A measurement cannot be more precise than the precision of the measuring tool used.

A hundredth of a meter is a smaller unit than a tenth of a meter. So, 2.72 m is more precise than 2.7 m.

Prime factorization (p. 181)   The prime factorization of a number is the expression of the number as the product of its prime factors.

The prime factorization of 30 is $2 \cdot 3 \cdot 5$.

Prime number (p. 180)   A prime number is an integer greater than 1 with only two factors, 1 and itself.

13 is a prime number because its only factors are 1 and 13.

Principal (p. 369)   The principal is the initial amount of an investment or loan.

See *Simple interest*.

Prism (p. 521)   A prism is a space figure with two parallel and congruent polygonal faces, called bases, and lateral faces that are parallelograms. A prism is named for the shape of its base.

Probability (pp. 296, 627, 642)   The *theoretical probability* of an event E is $P(E) = \frac{\text{number of favorable outcomes}}{\text{number of possible outcomes}}$ when outcomes are equally likely.

The experimental probability of an event E is $P(E) = \frac{\text{number of times an event occurs}}{\text{number of times experiment is done}}$. Experimental probability is based on experimental data.

The theoretical probability of spinning the number 4 is $\frac{1}{8}$.

In 100 trials, you spin the number 4 ten times. The experimental probability of spinning 4 is $\frac{10}{100}$, or $\frac{1}{10}$.

Proportion (p. 284)   A proportion is an equality of two ratios.

$\frac{3}{12} = \frac{12}{48}$ is a proportion.

Glossary/Study Guide

Pyramid (p. 521)   A pyramid is a space figure with triangular faces that meet at a vertex, and a base that is a polygon. A pyramid is named for the shape of its base.

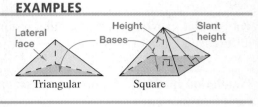

Pythagorean Theorem (p. 564)   In any right triangle, the sum of the squares of the lengths of the legs (a and b) is equal to the square of the length of the hypotenuse (c): $a^2 + b^2 = c^2$.

EXAMPLE The right triangle shown has leg lengths 3 and 4 and hypotenuse length 5: $3^2 + 4^2 = 5^2$.

Q

Quadrants (p. 50)   Quadrants are the four regions determined by the x- and y-axes of the coordinate plane.

See *Coordinate plane.*

Quadratic function (p. 669)   A quadratic function is a function based on squaring the input variable. The graph of a quadratic function is a parabola.

See *Parabola.*

Quadrilateral (p. 455)   A quadrilateral is a polygon with four sides.

See *Polygon.*

Quartiles (p. 611)   Quartiles are numbers that divide a data set into four equal parts.

See *Box-and-whisker plot.*

R

Radius (plural is radii) (p. 469)   A radius of a circle is a segment that has one endpoint at the center of the circle and the other endpoint on the circle.

EXAMPLE $\overline{OA}$ is a radius of circle O.

Random sample (p. 646)   A random sample is a sample of a population for which each member of the population has an equal chance of being selected.

For the population *customers at a mall*, a random sample could be every 20th customer entering for a 2-hour period.

Range of a relation (p. 386)   A range is the set of second coordinates of the ordered pairs of a relation.

In the relation $\{(0, 1), (-3, 2), (0, 2)\}$, the range is $\{1, 2\}$.

Range of a set of data (p. 609)   The range is the difference between the greatest and least values in a set of data.

The range of the data 7 9 15 3 18 2 16 14 14 20 is $20 - 2 = 18$.

Rate (p. 279)   A rate is a ratio that compares quantities measured in different units.

A student typed 1,100 words in 50 minutes for a typing rate of 1,100 words per 50 minutes, or 22 words/minute.

Ratio (p. 278)   A ratio is a comparison of two quantities by division.

There are three ways to write a ratio: 72 to 100, 72 : 100, and $\frac{72}{100}$.

Rational number (p. 194)   A rational number is any number you can write as a quotient of two integers $\frac{a}{b}$, where b is not zero.

$\frac{3}{5}, -8, 8.7, 0.333\ldots, -5\frac{3}{11}, 0,$ and $\frac{17}{4}$ are rational numbers.

Ray (p. 442)   A ray is a part of a line. It has exactly one endpoint. Its endpoint is named first.

EXAMPLE $\overrightarrow{SW}$ represents a ray.

Endpoint of $\overrightarrow{SW}$
S   W

Real number (p. 561)   A real number is a rational number or an irrational number.

$3, -5.25, 3.141592653\ldots,$ and $\frac{7}{8}$ are real numbers.

Reciprocal (p. 242)   Reciprocals are two numbers with a product of 1.

$\frac{4}{9}$ and $\frac{9}{4}$ are reciprocals. $\frac{4}{9} \cdot \frac{9}{4} = 1$.

Rectangle (p. 455)   A rectangle is a parallelogram with four right angles.

EXAMPLE $RSWH$ is a rectangle.

Reflection (p. 486)   A reflection is a transformation that flips a figure over a line of reflection.

EXAMPLE $K'L'M'N'$ is the reflection of $KLMN$ across the y-axis. The y-axis is the line of reflection.

Reflectional symmetry (p. 485)   A figure has reflectional symmetry when one half of the figure is a mirror image of the other half. The reflection line is also called the line of symmetry.

Regular polygon (p. 456)   A regular polygon is a polygon with all its sides congruent and all its angles congruent.

EXAMPLE $ABDFEC$ is a regular hexagon.

Relation (p. 386)   A relation is a set of ordered pairs.

$\{(0, 2), (-3, 2), (0, 1)\}$ is a relation.

Glossary/Study Guide

Relatively prime (p. 184) Two numbers are relatively prime if their GCF is 1.

9 and 20 are relatively prime.

Repeating decimal (p. 230) A repeating decimal is a decimal in which the same block of digits repeats without end. The symbol for a repeating decimal is a bar drawn over the digit or digits that repeat.

$0.8888\ldots = 0.\overline{8}$

Rhombus (p. 455) A rhombus is a parallelogram with four congruent sides.

EXAMPLE $GHJI$ is a rhombus.
$$GH = HJ = IJ = GI$$

Right angle (p. 448) A right angle is an angle with a measure of 90°.

EXAMPLE $\angle CDE$ is a right angle.

Right triangle (p. 454) A right triangle is a triangle with one right angle.

EXAMPLE $\triangle ABC$ is a right triangle, since $\angle B$ is a right angle.

Rotation (p. 490) A rotation is a transformation that turns a figure about a fixed point, called the center of rotation. The angle measure of the rotation is the angle of rotation.

EXAMPLE The image of $\triangle PQR$ after a 90° rotation is $\triangle PQ'R'$. Point P is the center of rotation.

Rotational symmetry (p. 491) A figure has rotational symmetry if the figure can be rotated 180° or less and match the original figure.

EXAMPLE This figure has a 60° rotational symmetry.

S

Sample (p. 646) A sample is a small part of a population.

A class of 25 students is a sample of the population of a large school.

Sample space (p. 627) A sample space is all possible outcomes of an experiment.

The sample space for tossing two coins is HH, HT, TH, TT.

Scale drawing (p. 290) A scale drawing is an enlarged or reduced drawing that is similar to an actual object or place.

A map is a scale drawing.

Scalene triangle (p. 454) A scalene triangle is a triangle with no congruent sides.

EXAMPLE $\triangle NPO$ is a scalene triangle.

Scatter plot (p. 409) A scatter plot is a graph that displays data from two related sets as ordered pairs.

EXAMPLE This scatter plot displays the amount various companies spent on advertising (in dollars) versus product sales (in thousands of dollars).

Scientific notation (p. 208) Scientific notation is a way of reexpressing a number. A number is expressed in scientific notation when it is written as the product of a number greater than or equal to 1 and less than 10, and a power of 10.

In scientific notation, 37,000,000 is written as 3.7×10^7.

Segment (p. 442) A segment is part of a line. It has two endpoints.

EXAMPLE $\overline{CB}$ represents the segment shown.

Segment bisector (p. 475) A segment bisector is a line, segment, or ray that separates a segment into two congruent segments.

Sequence (p. 664) A sequence is a set of numbers that follows a pattern.

$2, 2.3, 2.34, 2.345, \ldots$

Side (p. 448, 454) See *Angle* and *Polygon*.

Significant digits (p. 157) Significant digits are the digits that represent an actual measurement.

Similar figures (p. 289) Similar figures are figures with corresponding angles that have equal measures and corresponding sides that have proportional lengths. The symbol ~ means "is similar to."

EXAMPLE $\triangle ABC \sim \triangle RTS$

Simple interest (p. 369)   Simple interest is interest paid only on the principal, the initial amount of money invested or borrowed. The formula for simple interest is $I = prt$, where I is the interest, p is the principal, r is the interest rate per year, and t is the time in years.

The simple interest on $1,000 at 5% for 2 years is $1,000 \cdot 0.05 \cdot 2$, or $100.

Simplest form of a fraction (p. 186)   The simplest form of a fraction is the form in which the only common factor of the numerator and denominator is 1.

The simplest form of the fraction $\frac{15}{20}$ is $\frac{3}{4}$.

Simplify a variable expression (p. 74)   To simplify a variable expression is to replace it with an equivalent expression having as few terms as possible.

$2x + 5 + 4x$ simplifies to $6x + 5$.

Simulation (p. 642)   A simulation is a model used to find experimental probability.

Your baseball team has an equal chance of winning or losing each of its next five games. You can toss a coin to simulate the outcomes of the next five games.

Sine (p. 588)   The sine of an acute angle is the ratio of the length of the leg of a right triangle opposite the acute angle to the length of the hypotenuse.

See *Trigonometric ratios.*

Skew lines (p. 443)   Skew lines are lines in space that do not intersect and are not parallel. They do not lie in the same plane. Skew segments must be parts of skew lines.
EXAMPLE $\overleftrightarrow{MT}$ and $\overleftrightarrow{QR}$ are skew lines.

Slant height (p. 533)   See *Cone* and *Pyramid.*

Slope (pp. 397, 398)   Slope is a ratio that describes the tilt of a line.
$$\text{slope} = \frac{\text{vertical change}}{\text{horizontal change}} = \frac{\text{difference in } y\text{-coordinates}}{\text{difference in } x\text{-coordinates}}$$
EXAMPLE The slope of the given line is $\frac{2}{4}$ or $\frac{1}{2}$.

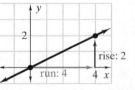

Slope-intercept form of an equation (p. 399)   The slope-intercept form of an equation is $y = mx + b$, where m is the slope and b is the y-intercept of the line.

The equation $y = 2x + 1$ is in slope-intercept form with $m = 2$ and $b = 1$.

Solid (p. 520)   A solid is a three-dimensional figure.

See *Space figure.*

Solution (p. 79, 100, 391, 420, 428)   A solution is any value or values that make an equation or an inequality true.

4 is the solution of $x + 5 = 9$.

$(8, 4)$ is a solution of $y = -1x + 12$ because $4 = -1(8) + 12$.

-4 is a solution of $2x < -3$, because $2 \cdot -4 < -3$.

$(-1, 3)$ is a solution of $y > x - 4$, because $3 > -1 - 4$.

Space figure (p. 521)   A space figure is a three-dimensional figure or solid.

EXAMPLE A cylinder, a cone, and a prism are space figures.

Sphere (p. 521)   A sphere is the set of points in space that are a given distance from a point, called the center.

Square (p. 455)   A square is a parallelogram with four right angles and four congruent sides.

EXAMPLE $QRTS$ is a square. $\angle Q, \angle R, \angle T$, and $\angle S$ are right angles.
$QR = RT = ST = SQ$

Square root (p. 560)   The square root of a given number is a number that when multiplied by itself equals the given number.

The symbol for the nonnegative square root of a number is $\sqrt{}$.

$\sqrt{25} = 5$ because $5^2 = 25$

Standard form (p. 683)   Standard form of a polynomial is the form in which the terms are in order of decreasing degree.

$3y^2 + 8y - 2$ is in standard form.

Standard notation (p. 209)   Standard notation is the usual form for representing a number.

The standard notation of 8.9×10^5 is 890,000.

Stem-and-leaf plot (p. 618)   A stem-and-leaf plot is a display that shows numeric data arranged in order. The leaf of each data item is its last digit. The stem is its other digits. The stems are stacked in order and the leaves are arranged in order to the side of each stem.

Stem	Leaf
27	7
28	5 6 8
29	6 9
30	8

27 | 7 means 27.7

EXAMPLE This stem-and-leaf plot displays recorded times in a race. The stem records the whole number of seconds. The leaf represents tenths of a second. So, 27 | 7 represents 27.7 seconds.

Glossary/Study Guide

Straight angle (p. 448)   A straight angle is an angle with a measure of 180°.

Subtraction Property of Equality (p. 84)   If $a = b$, then $a - c = b - c$.

$10 = 2(5)$, so $10 - 5 = 2(5) - 5$

Subtraction Property of Inequality (p. 104)   If $a > b$, then $a - c > b - c$. If $a < b$, then $a - c < b - c$.

$7 > 4$, so $7 - 3 > 4 - 3$
$6 < 9$, so $6 - 2 < 9 - 2$

Supplementary angles (p. 449)   Supplementary angles are two angles whose measures add to 180°.

EXAMPLE $\angle A$ and $\angle D$ are supplementary.

Surface area (pp. 527–529, 533, 534)   Surface area is the sum of the areas of the base(s) and lateral faces of a space figure.

EXAMPLE The surface area of the prism is the sum of the areas of its faces.
$(12 + 12 + 12 + 12 + 9 + 9)$ in.^{2} = 66 in.^{2}

Each square = 1 in.^{2}

System of linear equations (p. 420)   A system of linear equations is two or more linear equations.

$y = 3x + 1$ and $y = -2x - 3$ are a system of linear equations.

System of linear inequalities (p. 428)   A system of linear inequalities is two or more linear inequalities.

$y \geq 3x + 1$ and $y < -2x - 3$ are a system of linear inequalities.

T

Tangent (p. 588)   The tangent of an acute angle is the ratio of the length of the leg of a right triangle opposite the acute angle to the length of the leg adjacent to the angle.

See *Trigonometric ratios*.

Term of an expression (p. 74)   A term is a number, variable, or the product of a number and variable(s).

The expression $7x + 12 + (-9y)$ has three terms: $7x$, 12, and $-9y$.

Term of a sequence (p. 664)   A term of a sequence is any number in the sequence.

$1, 2, 3, 4, \ldots$

EXAMPLE In this sequence, 1 is the first term, 2 is the second term, 3 is the third term, and 4 is the fourth term.

Terminating decimal (p. 229)   A terminating decimal is a decimal with a finite number of digits.

Both 0.6 and 0.7265 are terminating decimals.

Tessellation (p. 494) A tessellation is a repeated pattern of figures that completely covers a plane without gaps or overlaps.

EXAMPLE This tessellation consists of small squares and large squares.

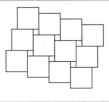

Theoretical Probability (p. 296) See *Probability*.

Three-dimensional figure (p. 521) A three-dimensional figure is a figure that does not lie in a plane.

See *Space figure*.

Transformation (p. 479) A transformation is a change of position or size of a figure. Four types of transformations are translations, reflections, rotations, and dilations.

EXAMPLE $K'L'M'N'$ is a reflection of $KLMN$ across the y-axis.

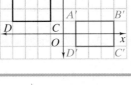

Translation (p. 479) A translation is a transformation that moves points the same distance and in the same direction.

EXAMPLE $A'B'C'D'$ is the translation image of $ABCD$.

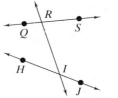

Transversal (p. 450) A transversal is a line that intersects two other lines in different points.

EXAMPLE $\overleftrightarrow{RI}$ is a transversal of $\overleftrightarrow{QS}$ and $\overleftrightarrow{HJ}$.

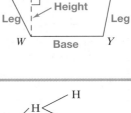

Trapezoid (p. 455) A trapezoid is a quadrilateral with exactly one pair of parallel sides.

EXAMPLE $UVYW$ is a trapezoid.
$\overleftrightarrow{UV} \parallel \overleftrightarrow{WY}$.

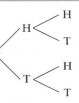

Tree diagram (p. 626) A tree diagram is a diagram that displays all the possible outcomes of an event.

EXAMPLE There are for 4 possible outcomes for tossing 2 coins: HH, HT, TH, and TT.

Trend line (p. 416) A trend line is a line that closely fits the data points in a scatter plot.

Glossary/Study Guide

Triangle (p. 454)   A triangle is a polygon with three sides.

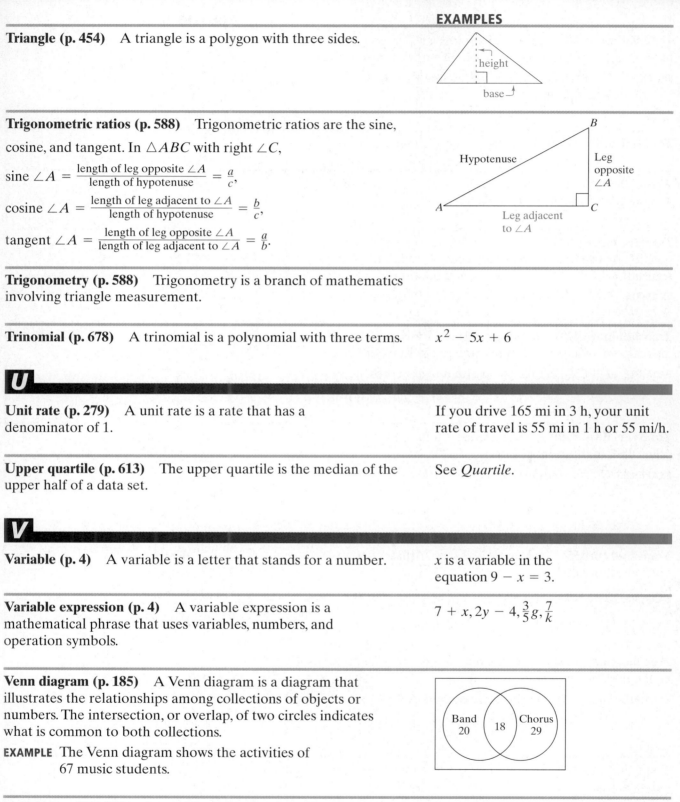

Trigonometric ratios (p. 588)   Trigonometric ratios are the sine, cosine, and tangent. In $\triangle ABC$ with right $\angle C$,

$$\text{sine } \angle A = \frac{\text{length of leg opposite } \angle A}{\text{length of hypotenuse}} = \frac{a}{c},$$

$$\text{cosine } \angle A = \frac{\text{length of leg adjacent to } \angle A}{\text{length of hypotenuse}} = \frac{b}{c},$$

$$\text{tangent } \angle A = \frac{\text{length of leg opposite } \angle A}{\text{length of leg adjacent to } \angle A} = \frac{a}{b}.$$

Trigonometry (p. 588)   Trigonometry is a branch of mathematics involving triangle measurement.

Trinomial (p. 678)   A trinomial is a polynomial with three terms.

$x^2 - 5x + 6$

U

Unit rate (p. 279)   A unit rate is a rate that has a denominator of 1.

If you drive 165 mi in 3 h, your unit rate of travel is 55 mi in 1 h or 55 mi/h.

Upper quartile (p. 613)   The upper quartile is the median of the upper half of a data set.

See *Quartile*.

V

Variable (p. 4)   A variable is a letter that stands for a number.

x is a variable in the equation $9 - x = 3$.

Variable expression (p. 4)   A variable expression is a mathematical phrase that uses variables, numbers, and operation symbols.

$7 + x, 2y - 4, \frac{3}{5}g, \frac{7}{k}$

Venn diagram (p. 185)   A Venn diagram is a diagram that illustrates the relationships among collections of objects or numbers. The intersection, or overlap, of two circles indicates what is common to both collections.

EXAMPLE   The Venn diagram shows the activities of 67 music students.

Vertex (pp. 448, 455)   See *Angle* and *Polygon*.

Vertical angles (p. 449)   Vertical angles are angles formed by two intersecting lines, and are opposite each other. Vertical angles are congruent.

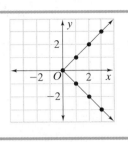

∠1 and ∠2 are vertical angles, as are ∠3 and ∠4.

Vertical-line test (p. 387)   The vertical line test is a test that allows you to describe graphically whether a relation is a function.

EXAMPLE Since the vertical line $x = 2$ passes through two points of the graph, the graphical relation is not a function.

Volume (pp. 538, 539, 547, 548)   The volume of a space figure is the number of cubic units needed to fill it.

EXAMPLE The volume of the rectangular prism is 36 in.^{3}. Each cube is 1 in.^{3}.

X

***x*-axis (p. 50)**   The *x*-axis is the horizontal number line that, together with the *y*-axis, establishes the coordinate plane.

See *Coordinate plane*.

***x*-coordinate (p. 50)**   The *x*-coordinate is the horizontal position of a point in the coordinate plane.

See *Coordinates*.

***x*-intercept (p. 395)**   The *x*-intercept of a line is the *x*-coordinate of the point where the line crosses the *x*-axis.

EXAMPLE The *x*-intercept is 2. The *y*-intercept is -3.

$6x - 4y = 12$

Y

***y*-axis (p. 50)**   The *y*-axis is the vertical number line that, together with the *x*-axis, forms the coordinate plane.

See *Coordinate plane*.

***y*-coordinate (p. 50)**   The *y*-coordinate is the vertical position of a point in the coordinate plane.

See *Coordinates*.

***y*-intercept (p. 399)**   The *y*-intercept of a line is the *y*-coordinate of the point where the line crosses the *y*-axis.

See *x-intercept*.

Z

Zero pair (p. 23)   A zero pair is a positive algebra tile paired with a negative algebra tile.

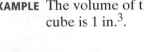
← A zero pair

▶TOOLS FOR PROBLEM SOLVING

The Four-Step Approach — page xxii

1. Nikki 18; Jing 30 **3.** 9 **5.** C **7.** cannot be determined

Using Strategies — page xxv

1. 28 days **3.** 6 wall, 5 desk **5.** in a 6 by 4 array **7.** north

Standardized Test Prep — page xxxi

1. D **3.** C **5.** B **7.** D

▶CHAPTER 1

Skills You Need — page 1

1. 1 **2.** 11 **3.** 11 **4.** 19 **5.** 13 **6.** 40 **7.** 17
8. 43 **9.** 176 **10.** 28 **11.** 166 **12.** 75 **13.** >
14. > **15.** < **16.** < **17.** < **18.** = **19.** 12
20. 30 **21.** 28 **22.** 5 **23.** 96 **24.** 5 **25.** 200
26. 80 **27.** 31 **28.** 13 **29.** 480 **30.** 12 **31.** 1
32. 4 **33.** 7 **34.** 10

Lesson 1-1 — pages 4–7

TRY THIS 1. Variable expression; x is the variable. **2.** numerical expression **3.** Variable expression; d is the variable. **4.** 0.50b **5.** $\frac{m}{60}$

CHECK UNDERSTANDING 1. Variable expression; b is the variable. **2.** numerical expression **3.** Variable expression; n is the variable. **4.** $2 \cdot 12$ **5.** $5 \cdot 12$ **6.** $d \cdot 12$ **7.** $m + 16$ **8.** $\frac{6}{z}$ **9.** $3c$

PRACTICE AND PROBLEM SOLVING
11. Variable expression; d is the variable.
13. Variable expression; x is the variable.
15. Variable expression; p is the variable.
17. $z - 8$ **19.** $\frac{3}{n}$ **21.** $32g$ **23.** $2 - x$ **25.** $12v$
27. $m + 250$ **29.** $\frac{100}{z}$ **31.** $7w$ **33.** $5n$
35. $\frac{i}{12}$ **37.** A **39.** C **41.** $d - 20$
43. $110e + 55$ **45a.** $2f$ **b.** $\frac{s}{2}$ **47.** The balloon rose 34 m. **49.** The balloon tripled its altitude.

MIXED REVIEW 51. 72 **53.** 75 **55.** 9,563

Lesson 1-2 — pages 8–12

TRY THIS 4. 17 **5.** 3 **6.** 3 **7.** 4 **8.** 12 **9.** 6 **10.** 3

CHECK UNDERSTANDING 1. Multiplication; multiplication comes before subtraction in the order of operations. **2.** Subtraction; when operations have the same rank in the order of operations, do them from left to right. **3.** Division; work within parentheses first. **4.** 4 **5.** 16 **6.** 13 **7.** 108 **8.** 49 **9.** 8

PRACTICE AND PROBLEM SOLVING 11. 17
13. 14 **15.** 17 **17.** 24 **19.** 16 **21.** 3 **23.** 33
25. 3 **27.** 3 **29.** 4 **31.** > **33.** > **35.** D
37. $7 \cdot (8 - 6) + 3 = 17$ **39.** $2 \cdot 3 - (8 - 5) \cdot 2 = 0$, or $2 \cdot [3 - (8 - 5)] \cdot 2 = 0$ **41.** We must agree on an order of operations to ensure that everyone gets the same value for an expression.
43. $4 \cdot 9 + 5$; 41 **45.** $17 - (25 \div 5)$; 12

MIXED REVIEW 53. $\frac{k}{20}$ **55.** $10d$

Lesson 1-3 — pages 13–16

TRY THIS 1. 28 **2.** 45 **3.** 90 **4.** 23 **5.** 12
6. $29c$; $145 **7.** $104

CHECK UNDERSTANDING 1. 7 **2.** 6 **3.** 12
4. 4 **5.** 16 **6.** 12 **7.** 18 **8.** 60 **9.** 12
10. $55m$; 1,100 words

PRACTICE AND PROBLEM SOLVING 11. 35
13. 5 **15.** 1 **17.** 24 **19.** 15 **21.** 11 **23.** 91
25. 48 **27.** 2 **29.** 10 **31a.** $153h$
b. 306 calories **33.** $8h$; 24 km **35.** $145m$;
870 babies; 208,800 babies

MIXED REVIEW 39. 53 **41.** $19 - t$ **43.** $\frac{d}{20}$

Lesson 1-4 — pages 17–21

TRY THIS 1. -2
2.

$-6, 0, 2$

3. the absolute value of negative ten; 10

CHECK UNDERSTANDING 1. 250 **2.** -18
3. -45 **4.** 2 **5.** 5 **6.** -4 **7.** 18 **8.** 9 **9.** 3
10a. spending a dollar **b.** -1

PRACTICE AND PROBLEM SOLVING 11. 110
13. −300 **15.** −8
21. 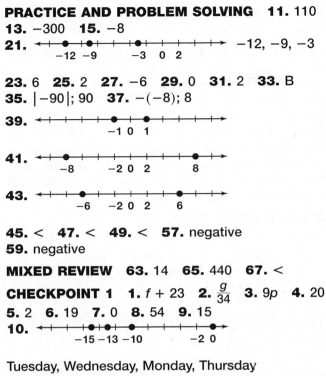 −12, −9, −3

23. 6 **25.** 2 **27.** −6 **29.** 0 **31.** 2 **33.** B
35. |−90|; 90 **37.** −(−8); 8

39.

41.

43.

45. < **47.** < **49.** < **57.** negative
59. negative

MIXED REVIEW 63. 14 **65.** 440 **67.** <

CHECKPOINT 1 1. $f + 23$ **2.** $\frac{g}{34}$ **3.** $9p$ **4.** 20
5. 2 **6.** 19 **7.** 0 **8.** 54 **9.** 15
10.

Tuesday, Wednesday, Monday, Thursday

9. 2 **11.** −2 **13.** 0 **15.** 4

TRY THIS 1. 3 **2.** 4 **3.** −4 **4.** −4 **5.** 5
6. −6 **7.** −38 **8.** 47 **9.** −90 **10.** 1,280 m
11. −10 **12.** 70

CHECK UNDERSTANDING 1. −4 + 7; 3
2. 5 + 0; 5 **3.** −4 + (−2); −6 **4.** 3 + (−8); −5
9. −65 **10.** 53 **11.** −185 **12.** 0

PRACTICE AND PROBLEM SOLVING
17. Negative; both numbers are negative.
19. Negative; the number with greater absolute
value is negative. **21.** 3 **23.** −13 **25.** 100
27. 34 **29.** 55 **31.** −48 **33.** 15 **35.** 7
37. 16 **39.** −40 **41.** −22 **43.** −30 **45.** >
47. > **49.** > **53.** −2 + (−7); −9 **55.** 3 + (−8);
−5 **57.** −20 + 18; −2 **59.** 120 + (−25); 95
61. −10 + (−2) + 8 + (−5) + (−13) + 1; −21
63. $158 **65.** positive; 0.4 **67.** negative; −12.19
69. negative **71.** negative **73.** B

MIXED REVIEW 75. > **77.** > **79.** <
81. 25 + 10n; $55

TRY THIS 1. −5 **2.** −1 **3.** −3 **4.** −4 **5.** −6
6. 5 **7.** 35 **8.** −106 **9.** −46 **10.** about 80°C

CHECK UNDERSTANDING 3. 6 + (−2); 4
4. 6 + 2; 8 **5.** −6 + (−2); −8 **6.** −6 + 2; −4
7. 2 + (−6); −4 **8.** 2 + 6; 8 **9.** −2 + (−6); −8
10. −2 + 6; 4 **11b.** 5 − 7; −2

PRACTICE AND PROBLEM SOLVING
13. −9 − (−2) = −7 **21.** −6 **23.** 100 **25.** 96
27. 191 **29.** −80 **31.** 19 **33.** −68 **35.** −42
37. 850 **39.** −60 **41.** 150 **43.** 66 **51.** 50
53. −470 **55.** −500 **57.** 3,000 − 600; 2,400
59a. It decreases. **b.** −24°C **c.** −8°C **61.** 27°C
63a. 8 − (−4) = 12 **b.** 28 **c.** 24

12 − (−4) = 16	**65.**	−2	−7	−6	−15
16 − (−4) = 20		−9	−5	−1	
20 − (−4) = 24		−4	−3	−8	
24 − (−4) = 28					

MIXED REVIEW 67. −5 **69.** −6

1. C **3.** B **5.** A **7.** C **9.** B **11.** $\frac{m}{8}$; 5 mi

TRY THIS 2. Start with 1 and add 2 repeatedly;
9, 11 **3.** Start with 4 and add 5 repeatedly.
4. Start with 3 and multiply by 3 repeatedly.
5. Add the previous two numbers. **6.** No; if the
coin toss is fair, the coin can come up tails on any
toss. **7.** correct **8.** Incorrect; 8 and |8| are not
opposites.

CHECK UNDERSTANDING
1. a square with four
corners shaded

2. a six-sided figure
with a six-sided figure
inside it

3. Start with 100 and subtract 15 repeatedly; 40, 25
4. Start with 5 and multiply by 4 repeatedly; 1,280,
5,120. **5.** Start with 1 and alternately add 1 and 3;
10, 13. **6.** Incorrect; an ostrich cannot fly.
7. correct **8.** Incorrect; 0.2 · 0.2 = 0.04, which is
less than 0.2.

Selected Answers

PRACTICE AND PROBLEM SOLVING
9. an eight-sided figure with bottom right eighth shaded

 11. Start with −10 and add 6 repeatedly; 14, 20, 26 **13.** Start with 1 and add 0.5 repeatedly; 3.5, 4, 4.5

15. Start with 1, add 3 initially, and then add the last added number multiplied by 2, repeatedly; 190, 382, 766. **19.** Incorrect; 8 + (−6) is 2, and 2 < 8.

23b.
```
          1
        1 2 1
      1 2 3 2 1
    1 2 3 4 3 2 1
  1 2 3 4 5 4 3 2 1
1 2 3 4 5 6 5 4 3 2 1
1 2 3 4 5 6 7 6 5 4 3 2 1
1 2 3 4 6 5 7 8 7 6 5 4 3 2 1
```
c. 1, 4, 9, 16, 25, 36, 49, 64 **d.** 81

MIXED REVIEW 25. 9 **27.** 103 **29.** −2
31a. 1,500n **b.** 36,000

Lesson 1-8   pages 40–43

READ 1. 2 students **2.** 15 min

PLAN 3. 2 students **4.** 4 periods

LOOK BACK 6. A table; it would be difficult to draw all the branches of the tree. **7.** 9:45 A.M.

CHECK UNDERSTANDING 1. 36 laps/day
2. 78 students
3a.
2 · 2 = 4	3 · 3 = 9
1 · 3 = 3	2 · 4 = 8
Difference = 1	Difference = 1
4 · 4 = 16	5 · 5 = 25
3 · 5 = 15	4 · 6 = 24
Difference = 1	Difference = 1

The differences are all 1. **b.** 11 · 11; 1 greater
c. 2,208 **d.** 4,225 **4.** $10.23

PRACTICE AND PROBLEM SOLVING
5. 6:45 A.M. **7a.** $59; $21 **b.** 10 people **9.** 75 4's

MIXED REVIEW 11. a 4 × 4 square;
13. 0 **15.** −1 **17.** 9°F

Lesson 1-9   pages 44–49

TRY THIS 4. −12 **5.** −12 **6.** −14 **7.** 12
8. 64 **9.** −90 **10.** 0 **11.** −4 **12.** 8 **13.** 14
14. −2

CHECK UNDERSTANDING 1. 4(−9); −36
2. 5(−5); −25 **3.** Positive; the integers have the same sign. **4.** Negative; the integers have opposite signs. **5.** Negative; the integers have opposite signs. **6.** Positive; the first product is negative, so the second product is of integers with

---

the same sign. **7.** −30 **8.** −5 **9.** −44 **10.** 10
11a. 6 **b.** They are opposites. **c.** opposite

PRACTICE AND PROBLEM SOLVING 13. −60
15. −1 **17.** −10 **19.** −360 **21.** −14
23. −21,384 **25.** 19 **27.** 216 **29.** −12
31. −3 **33.** 58 **35.** −59 **37.** −87
39. 5 · (−2) = −10 **41.** D **43.** C **45.** <
47. < **49.** < **55.** 2 yd **57.** $143 **59.** −35
61a. negative; positive; negative **b.** If there are an even number of negative integers, the sign of the product will be positive; otherwise, the sign will be negative. **63.** 12 **65.** −15, 5

MIXED REVIEW 67. < **69.** <
71. 50 − n **73.** 36

CHECKPOINT 2 1. −8 **2.** 20 **3.** −45
4. 8 **5.** 72 **6.** −12 **10.** 13, 18, 23
11. 81, 243, 729 **12.** A

Lesson 1-10   pages 50–54

TRY THIS 1. (2, −3); (3, 3) **2.** Quadrant IV; Quadrant I
3a–b.
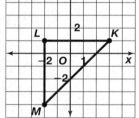
an isosceles triangle

CHECK UNDERSTANDING 1. (0, −7)
2. (−4, 1) **3.** (1, −4) **4.** (2, 6) **5.** J **6.** G **7.** R
8. Q **9.** (0, 0) **10–15.**
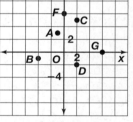

PRACTICE AND PROBLEM SOLVING 17. F
19. P **21.** (−2, 3) **23.** (6, 6) **25.** (0, −4)
27. IV **29.** II **31.** D **33.** III **35.** IV
37. (positive) y-axis

47.

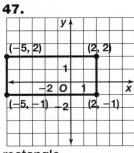

rectangle

49.

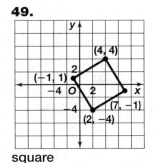

square

51. (0, −5)   **53.** about 90° W, 32° N
55. Frankfort, KY   **59.**
61. 60a shifts the figure right 1 unit; 60b shifts it down 4 units; 60c shifts it right 1 unit and down 4 units; 60d doubles its dimensions.

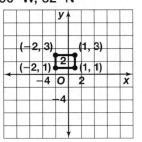

MIXED REVIEW
63. −9   **65.** 8   **67.** −12

Wrap Up	pages 56–58

1. x − 25   **2.** 3n   **3.** y + 2   **4.** 10 − t   **5.** n + 5
6. $\frac{x}{4}$ **7.** 24   **8.** 12   **9.** 37   **10.** 19   **11.** 17
12. 20   **13.** 40   **14.** 450   **15.** 16   **16.** −17
17. 1,000   **18.** 9   **19.** −12   **20.** >   **21.** >
22. =   **23.** <   **25.** −7   **26.** 12   **27.** 14
28. −11   **29.** −27   **30.** −15   **31.** −1   **32.** Start with 0 and add 6 repeatedly; 24, 30, 36.   **33.** Start with −18 and add 9 repeatedly; 18, 27, 36.
34. Start with $\frac{1}{2}$ and add $\frac{1}{2}$ repeatedly; $2\frac{1}{2}$, 3, $3\frac{1}{2}$.
35. 8 weeks   **36.** $112   **37.** −42   **38.** −5
39. 72   **40.** 7   **41.** −3   **42.** −165   **43.** −8
44. 35   **45.** (1, −3)   **46.** (−2, 1)   **47.** (−3, −3)
48. (2, 2)

Cumulative Review	page 60

1. A   **3.** C   **5.** A   **7.** A   **9.** D   **11.** Start with 1 and multiply by −2 repeatedly; 16, −32.   **13.** 2
15. (number line with points marked at −2, 0, 1, |−3|, |−5|)   **17.** −12

19. (−2, 3); (0, 0); (2, −2)

▶**CHAPTER 2**

Skills You Need	page 61

1. 25   **2.** 28   **3.** 15   **4.** −110   **5.** 36   **6.** 16
7. −24   **8.** 45   **9.** −20   **10.** −27   **11.** 72

---

12. −72   **13.** −18   **14.** −5   **15.** −45   **16.** 3; 3
17. 11; 11   **18.** 5; 5   **19.** 35; 35   **20.** −3; −3
21. −19; −19   **22.** 6; 6   **23.** 25; 25   **24.** 6; 6
25. 5; 5   **26.** −7; −7   **27.** 6; 6   **28.** 7; 7
29. 13; 13   **30.** <   **31.** >   **32.** >   **33.** <
34. >   **35.** <   **36.** =   **37.** >   **38.** >   **39.** <
40. =   **41.** <   **42.** <   **43.** >   **44.** <

Lesson 2-1	pages 64–68

TRY THIS   **1.** $18   **2.** Comm. Prop. of Add.
3. Ident. Prop. of Mult.   **4.** Assoc. Prop. of Mult.
5. 47   **6.** 3   **7.** 40   **8.** 10   **9.** $6.30   **10.** 300
11. 120   **12.** −240   **13.** −540

CHECK UNDERSTANDING   **1.** Comm. Prop. of Add.   **2.** Ident. Prop. of Add.   **3.** Assoc. Prop. of Mult.   **4.** Assoc. Prop. of Mult.   **5.** Ident. Prop. of Mult.   **6.** Comm. Prop. of Mult.   **7.** 5 and 95; they are easiest to add.   **8.** 5 and 2; they are easiest to multiply.   **9.** 50 and (−2); they are easiest to multiply.   **10.** −1,300   **11.** 93   **12.** 107
13. −6,600   **14.** 97   **15.** 5,400

PRACTICE AND PROBLEM SOLVING
17. Comm. Prop. of Add.   **19.** Comm. Prop. of Add.   **21.** Ident. Prop. of Mult.   **23.** Ident. Prop. of Add.   **25.** Comm. Prop. of Mult.   **27.** Comm. Prop. of Mult.   **29.** 800   **31.** 3,700   **33.** 100
35. −10,000   **37.** 380   **39.** 35   **41.** 240
43. −100   **45.** B   **47.** $924; $720

MIXED REVIEW   **49.** I   **51.** III   **53.** II
55. 60   **57.** 100

Lesson 2-2	pages 69–73

TRY THIS   **4.** 2,650   **5.** 3,120   **6.** 1,791
7. $1,428   **8.** 210   **9.** −120   **10.** 35
11. 8x − 12   **12.** 3x + 12   **13.** 6x + 2
14. 14 + 6d   **15.** 18m + 3   **16.** −15t + 6

CHECK UNDERSTANDING   **1.** 12, 12   **2.** z, z
3. a, a   **4.** b   **5.** 138   **6.** 336   **7.** 90   **8.** 1,313

PRACTICE AND PROBLEM SOLVING   **9.** 312
11. 784   **13.** 832   **15.** 56   **17.** 72   **19.** 8
21. 36   **23.** −55   **25.** −18   **27.** 4(x + 2); 4x + 8
29. 7t − 35   **31.** 14z + 6   **33.** 4b + 20
35. −6t − 18   **37.** −48 + 8c   **39.** −28 + 7t
41. Dist. Prop.   **43.** Comm. Prop. of Mult.
45. 3,888 mi

MIXED REVIEW   **51.** Comm. Prop. of Mult.
53. Assoc. Prop. of Mult.   **55.** 1   **57.** −3

Selected Answers

Lesson 2-3 — page 74–77

TRY THIS **1.** 2, 4; 2s, 4s; 6 **2.** −4; none; none
3. 9, 2, −2, 1; 9m and −2m, 2r and r; none
4. 7a + 1 **5.** 13a **6.** 2b **7.** −13m **8.** −y + 5m
9. 2x − 7

CHECK UNDERSTANDING **1.** 3; 5; none; −3
2. 2; none; −7 **3.** 4, −7, 3; 4x, − 7x, 3x; none
4. 6, −5; 6xy, −5xy; none **5.** a, a; a; a **6.** m; m;
m **7.** 8r − 5 **8.** 13a **9.** 7x + 3 **10.** 4 + m

PRACTICE AND PROBLEM SOLVING **11.** 5, 8;
5a, 8a; none **13.** −3; none; −8 **15.** −4, 7, −9, −1;
−4x and −9x, 7w and −w; 12 **17.** x + 2 + 3x +
5 + x + 3 + 2x; 7x + 10 **19.** 9a −3 **21.** −2y + 5
23. 3 **25.** 11z + 8y **27.** 5g + 15 **29.** −24t + 20
31. Comm. Prop. of Add.; Dist. Prop.; Add within
parentheses.; Simplify. **33.** 6a **35.** 54k − 60
37. 3b + 2c + 189 **39.** A

MIXED REVIEW **43.** 324 **45.** 369

CHECKPOINT 1 **1.** Comm. Prop. of Mult.
2. Assoc. Prop. of Mult. **3.** Ident. Prop. of Mult.
4. Comm. Prop. of Add. **5.** Comm. Prop. of Mult.
6. Dist. Prop. **7.** 9a **8.** 18y **9.** 16w − 6 **10.** B

Lesson 2-4 — pages 78–81

TRY THIS **1.** false **2.** open **3.** true
4. 20 − x = 3; open **5.** no **6.** yes **7.** b + 6 =
33; 27 + 6 = 33 ✔; Yes, the backpack weighs 27 lb.

CHECK UNDERSTANDING **1.** True; for example,
3 + 2 = 7. **2.** False; 3w − 7 is not an equation.
3. True; by definition, an open sentence is one that
contains a variable. **4.** True; it contains a variable.
5. true **6.** open **7.** false **8.** true **9.** false
10. true

PRACTICE AND PROBLEM SOLVING **11.** false
13. open **15.** true **17.** true **19.** open **21.** no
23. yes **25.** no **27.** yes **29.** 4(−5) = −20; true
31. 15 + n = 50; open **33.** 25 = v + 15; open
35. 10 dimes or 100 pennies; both have a value of
one dollar. **37.** 140 + d = 192; yes **39.** A

MIXED REVIEW **43.** −4t − 19 **45.** 7
47. 0 **49.** 25 mi

Math Toolbox — pages 82–83

1.

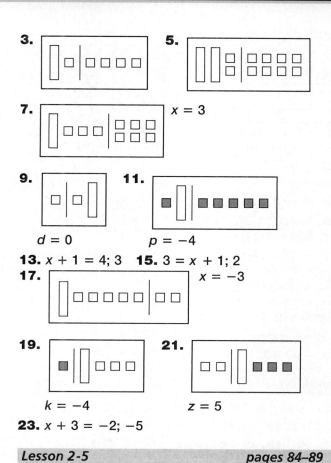

x = 3

d = 0   **p = −4**

13. x + 1 = 4; 3 **15.** 3 = x + 1; 2

x = −3

k = −4   **z = 5**

23. x + 3 = −2; −5

Lesson 2-5 — pages 84–89

TRY THIS **1.** −5 **2.** 4 **3.** −1
4. 123 = r + 55; 68 beats/min **5.** 13 **6.** 72
7. 112 **8.** h − 17 = 5; $22

CHECK UNDERSTANDING **1.** 8, 8; 7 **2.** 3, 3;
−2 **3.** Subtract 8 from each side. **4.** Subtract 54
from each side. **5.** Add 19 to each side. **6.** 3
7. −20 **8.** −1 **9.** −3 **10.** 54 **11.** −15

PRACTICE AND PROBLEM SOLVING **13.** 28
15. 31 **17.** 125 **19.** 626 **21.** 23 **23.** −1
25. −49 **27.** 200 **29.** −75 **31.** 6 **33.** −20
35. −300 **37.** −6 + y = 18; 24
39. −5 = x − 8; 3 **41.** D **43.** 108 = d − 42;
150 million km **45.** Yes; subtracting a number is
the same as adding its opposite.
47. 5,200 = s + 2,520; 2,680 m/s

MIXED REVIEW **49.** true **51.** 48 **53.** −400

Lesson 2-6 — pages 89–92

TRY THIS **1.** 21 **2.** 13 **3.** 9 **4.** −8 **5.** −12
6. 14 **7.** −50 **8.** −324 **9.** −600

CHECK UNDERSTANDING **1.** Divide each side by 6. **2.** Divide each side by 3. **3.** Multiply each side by −5. **4.** −6 **5.** 12 **6.** 5 **7.** 42 **8.** −24 **9.** 40

PRACTICE AND PROBLEM SOLVING **11.** yes; $-6 = 2(-3)$ **13.** no; $\frac{-18}{-3} \neq -6$ **15.** 7 **17.** −5 **19.** 19 **21.** −10 **23.** 52 **25.** −16 **27.** 300 **29.** −24 **31.** 100 **33.** −15,000 **35.** 7, −7 **37.** 3, −3 **39.** $b + a$ **41.** $\frac{b}{a}, a \neq 0$ **43.** $-20y = 100; -5$ **45.** $13 = \frac{x}{3}; 39$ **47.** 14 ft

MIXED REVIEW **51.** 17 **53.** 2 **55.** $7(w - 9)$

Standardized Test Prep   **page 93**

1. D **3.** A **5.** A **7.** 987,654,321

Lesson 2-7   **pages 94–97**

READ **1.** adult $4; student $3
2. 133 tickets **3.** $471

PLAN **4.** Subtract the number of adult tickets from 133. **5.** 4

LOOK BACK **6.** 53 adult tickets, 80 student tickets

CHECK UNDERSTANDING **2.** 1, 10, and 4, or 3, 7, and 5, or 5, 4, and 6, or 7, 1, and 7 **3.** 11 years and 12 years

PRACTICE AND PROBLEM SOLVING
5. 16 ft² **7.** 48 years **9.** 11 nickels, 7 quarters **11.** 122, 123 **13.** 2,750 m, 2,250 m

MIXED REVIEW **15.** 2 **17.** −6 **19.** Ident. Prop. of Mult. **21.** Comm. Prop. of Add.

Math Toolbox   **pages 98–99**

3. Use a line graph to show change over time. Use a bar graph to compare quantities.

Lesson 2-8   **pages 100–103**

TRY THIS

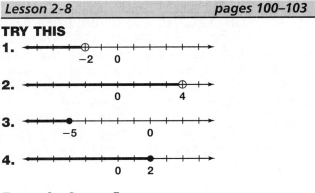

5. $x \geq 3$ **6.** $n < 5$

CHECK UNDERSTANDING **1.** D **2.** A **3.** B **4.** C **5.** $x < 5$ **6.** $y > -3$ **7.** $b \leq 8$

PRACTICE AND PROBLEM SOLVING

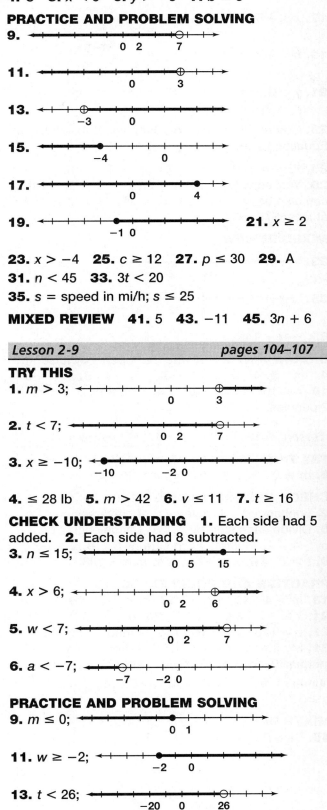

21. $x \geq 2$

23. $x > -4$ **25.** $c \geq 12$ **27.** $p \leq 30$ **29.** A
31. $n < 45$ **33.** $3t < 20$
35. $s = $ speed in mi/h; $s \leq 25$

MIXED REVIEW **41.** 5 **43.** −11 **45.** $3n + 6$

Lesson 2-9   **pages 104–107**

TRY THIS
1. $m > 3$;
2. $t < 7$;
3. $x \geq -10$;

4. ≤ 28 lb **5.** $m > 42$ **6.** $v \leq 11$ **7.** $t \geq 16$

CHECK UNDERSTANDING **1.** Each side had 5 added. **2.** Each side had 8 subtracted.
3. $n \leq 15$;
4. $x > 6$;
5. $w < 7$;
6. $a < -7$;

PRACTICE AND PROBLEM SOLVING
9. $m \leq 0$;
11. $w \geq -2$;
13. $t < 26$;

15. $b > 5.3$;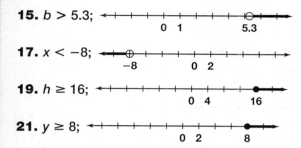

17. $x < -8$;

19. $h \geq 16$;

21. $y \geq 8$;

23. Comm. Prop. of Add.; Simplify.; Subt. Prop. of Equality; Simplify.

25. $13 + n > 15$; $n > 2$ **27.** $b - 11 < -12$; $b < -1$
29. Yes; solving $m + 4 > 2$ gives $m > -2$, which can also be written $-2 < m$.   **31.** $45 + m \geq 120$; at least $75

MIXED REVIEW

33.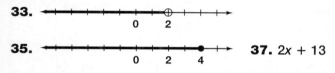

35. **37.** $2x + 13$

39. $-4t - 14$

CHECKPOINT 2   **1.** true   **2.** open   **3.** false
4. -4 **5.** 4   **6.** 6   **7.** -32 **8.** -9 **9.** $m > -9$
10. $r < 19$ **11.** $a \geq 6$ **13.** 1 quarter, 5 dimes, 2 pennies

Lesson 2-10   **pages 108–112**

TRY THIS   **3.** $x > 10$ **4.** $m \leq -7$ **5.** $t \geq -4$
6. $m \geq 8$ **7.** $t > -21$ **8.** $r > 35$

CHECK UNDERSTANDING   **1.** unchanged
2. unchanged   **3.** reverses   **4.** reverses
5. Divide each side by 4.   **6.** Divide each side by -4.   **7.** Multiply each side by 3.   **8.** $x > -7$
9. $t > 7$ **10.** $x < -18$ **11.** $m \leq -108$

PRACTICE AND PROBLEM SOLVING
13. $m > 4$ **15.** $x \leq 3$ **17.** $m < -9$ **19.** $m > 4$
21. $x \geq -6$ **23.** $y > 12$ **25.** $b \geq -93$
27. $v > 120$ **29.** Div. Prop. of Ineq.; Simplify.
31. My friend reversed the direction of the inequality when dividing each side by a positive number.   **33.** $-2a > 10$; $a < -5$ **35.** $\frac{b}{4} \geq 3$; $b \geq 12$

MIXED REVIEW   **41.** $t > 11$ **43.** $r \leq -14$
45. Dist. Prop.   **47.** 41°F

Wrap Up   **pages 114–116**

1. 80   **2.** 700   **3.** 547   **4.** 6,500   **5.** 300   **6.** 105
7. 864   **8.** 496   **9.** 387   **10.** $4w + 36$
11. $24 + 48a$ **12.** $-42 + 14m$ **13.** D   **14.** $7 - 3a$
15. $7w + 9$ **16.** $9 - 3x$ **17.** $15 - 24n$ **18.** k
19. $31 - 17r$ **20.** Check whether the variable parts of the terms are identical.   **21.** $32 + 5 = 6 \cdot 6$; false   **22.** $\frac{t}{17} = -3$; open   **23.** $4 \cdot 20 = 80$; true   **24.** $p + 1.75 = 6.50$ **25.** 11   **26.** 8
27. -5 **28.** 27   **29.** 128   **30.** -8 **31.** $6.50
32.

33.

34.

35.

36. $t < 0$ **37.** $h > 12$ **38.** $n > 14$ **39.** $t \geq -3$
40. $r > -8$ **41.** $k \geq 2$ **42.** $s \leq 3$ **43.** $m < -6$
44. $d < -14$ **45.** $c \leq 36$

Cumulative Review   **page 118**

1. D   **3.** B   **5.** C   **7.** C   **9.** A   **11.** 406
13. 5,010   **15.** $7t + 42$ **17.** $-5s$ **19.** $6b + 2p + 7.59$ **21.** false   **23.** true   **25.** 19   **27.** -12
29. **31.** $x < -5$
33. $s \leq 14$

▶CHAPTER 3

Skills You Need   **page 119**

1. 40   **2.** 10   **3.** 10   **4.** 0   **5.** 50   **6.** 110   **7.** 210
8. 600   **9.** 830   **10.** 6,010   **11.** 0   **12.** 50
13. $>$ **14.** $<$ **15.** $<$ **16.** $<$ **17.** $>$ **18.** $<$
19. $<$ **20.** $>$ **21.** $>$ **22.** $<$ **23.** $<$ **24.** $<$
25. 3.25, 3.8, 4.19, 4.91   **26.** 8.349, 8.35, 8.351, 9.25   **27.** 12.01, 12.09, 12.1, 12.9   **28.** 0.017, 0.02, 0.0201, 0.201   **29.** $-14.1, -1.401, -1.4, -1.04$
30. $-3.2, -3.19, -2.8, -2.3$ **31.** 11.49   **32.** 1.67
33. 14.9   **34.** 3.07   **35.** 2.47   **36.** 0.88
37. 15.217   **38.** 1.206   **39.** 7.14   **40.** 12
41. 6.7067   **42.** 6.5   **43.** 53.07   **44.** 6.9
45. 55.12   **46.** 10.6   **47.** 98.7   **48.** 532   **49.** 300
50. 154,070   **51.** 0.08   **52.** 0.0842   **53.** 0.0161
54. 0.001209   **55.** 0.87   **56.** 15,740   **57.** 143
58. 0.0189

Lesson 3-1   *pages 122–126*

TRY THIS **5.** tenths; 38.4 **6.** ones; 1 **7.** tenths; 7,098.6 **8.** thousandths; 274.943 **9.** tenths; 5.0 **10.** hundredths; 9.85 **11.** about 560 **12.** about 220 **13.** about 18.6 **14.** about $11 **15.** about $15 **16.** about 125

CHECK UNDERSTANDING **1.** 27.39 **2.** 0.912 **3.** 1,046 **4.** 345.7 **5.** about $11 **6.** about 19 **7.** about 45 **8.** about $13.90 **9.** about $10 **10.** about 20.7 **11.** about $129 **12.** about $27 **13.** about 0.60

PRACTICE AND PROBLEM SOLVING **15.** 1.5 **17.** 1 **19.** about $9 **21.** about $28 **23.** about $4 **25.** about 17 **27.** about 93.5 **29.** about 90.4 **31.** about 9.5 **33.** about 10.1 **35.** about $28 **37.** about 3,220 **39.** about $17; rounding **41.** about $40; rounding **43.** about 20; rounding **45.** $37.50; front-end **47.** about 3.4 million **49.** about 44 in.

MIXED REVIEW **53.** $x \le 3$ **55.** $k < 4$ **57.** 4 **59.** −30 **61.** 7 bikes; 3 trucks

Lesson 3-2   *pages 127–130*

TRY THIS **1.** about 10 **2.** about 68 **3.** about 160 **4.** about $40 **5.** about 19 **6.** about 6 **7.** about 20 **8.** yes **9.** no

CHECK UNDERSTANDING **1.** about 35 **2.** about 44 **3.** about 54 **4.** about 100 **5.** about 2 **6.** about 2 **7.** about 20 **8.** about $50

PRACTICE AND PROBLEM SOLVING **11.** about 40 **13.** about 144 **15.** about 400 **17.** about 64 **19.** about $5 **21.** about 4 **23.** about $6 **25.** about 4 **27.** not reasonable; 4.56 **29.** not reasonable; 70.23 **31.** not reasonable; about 0.3168 **33.** about $12 **37.** physical therapist: about $18/h in Dallas; about $16/h in Washington, D.C.; pharmacist: about $20/h in Dallas, about $21/h in Washington, D.C.; nurse: about $15/h in Dallas, about $18/h in Washington, D.C. **39.** about $2 **41.** I rounded to 20 ÷ 4. My friend used compatible numbers, 21 ÷ 3.

MIXED REVIEW **43.** about $39 **45.** about 1,220 **47.** about $2 **49.** Quadrant III **51.** *y*-axis **53.** *x*-axis

Lesson 3-3   *pages 131–135*

TRY THIS **1.** 18.5, 14, 14 **2.** 2.95, 2.8, 2.3 **3.** 3 modes **4.** 1 mode **5.** 31; raises the mean

by 2.6 **6.** 1; lowers the mean by 2.8 **7a.** $25.25, $23.50, $20

CHECK UNDERSTANDING **1.** 11.1, 8, none; outlier: 37 **2.** 122.4, 123, 123; outlier: 115 **3.** 112, 61, none; median; there is no mode, and the outlier (367) affects the mean too much. **4.** 49.1, 50, 50; mean (or mode); there are no outliers.

PRACTICE AND PROBLEM SOLVING **5.** 58.9, 56, 56; outlier: 89 **7.** 2.7, 3, 3; no outliers **9.** Mean; there likely are no outliers. **11.** Mean; there likely are no outliers. **13.** Mean; there likely are no outliers. **15.** 13.5, 14.5, 13.5 and 15; median; the outlier (7) affects the mean too much. **17.** 15, 18, 18; median (or mode); the outlier (1) affects the mean too much. **19.** D

MIXED REVIEW **23.** about 6 **25.** about 6 **27.** $6x + 10$ **29.** $x − 2t + 5$

Math Toolbox   *page 136*

1. 648.5 species; 641.5 species **3.** $5.62; $4.70 **5.** about 159 mi; 127 mi

Lesson 3-4   *pages 137–140*

TRY THIS **1.** $r = 28$ mi/h **2.** $t = 51.5$ yr **3.** 61°F **4.** 59°F **5.** 53.5°F **6.** 88.2 cm **7.** 52 in.

CHECK UNDERSTANDING **1.** 67°F **2.** 57°F **3.** 60°F **4.** 53°F **5.** $d = 481.25$ m **6.** $r = 280$ mi/h **7.** $t = 259.3$ s **8.** $t = 20.4$ h **9.** 5.84 mi

PRACTICE AND PROBLEM SOLVING **11.** 57.2°F **13.** 132.8°F **15.** 21 m **17.** 43.2 yd **19a.** 701.32 ft² **b.** 358.66 ft **21.** 0.425 mi

MIXED REVIEW **23.** 106 min, 123 min, 125 min; median **25.** 33 **27.** 56

CHECKPOINT 1 **1.** 15.66 **2.** 0.891 **3.** 7,023 **4.** 345.7 **5.** about 32 **6.** about 24 **7.** about −1 **8.** about 6 **9.** 56, 57, no mode **10.** 2, 2, 1 **11.** $4.05, $2.25, no mode **12.** B

Math Toolbox   *page 141*

1. 27 in. **3.** 3 in. **5.** 28 h **7.** = 0.5*A2*B2 **9.** = A2*B2+C2

TRY THIS   **1.** 13.9   **2.** 38.96
3. $35.48 + m = 70$; $34.52   **4.** 21.1   **5.** −7.4
6. $x − 14.95 = 12.48$; $27.43

CHECK UNDERSTANDING   **1.** 1.2, 1.2; 13.8
2. 3.33, 3.33; 15.75   **3.** Subtract 8.5 from each
side, or add −8.5 to each side.   **4.** Subtract 54.2
from each side, or add −54.2 to each side.
5. Add 1.9 to each side.   **6.** 3.54   **7.** 0.88
8. 10.73   **9.** 23.7   **10.** 43.2   **11.** −0.8   **12.** No;
the solution of the first equation is −0.9, while the
solution of the second equation is −9.

PRACTICE AND PROBLEM SOLVING   **13.** 1.2
15. 11   **17.** 15.4   **19.** 2.4   **21.** 0   **23.** −23.95
25. 1.1   **27.** 9.502   **29.** 5.3
31. Simplify; Subtraction Property of Equality;
Simplify.   **33.** The student should have *added* 1.6
to each side.   **35.** Add −1.8 to each side.

MIXED REVIEW   **37.** 369.72 in.^{2} **39.** 4   **41.** −9
43. $1.30

TRY THIS   **1.** −2   **2.** 0.5   **3.** 90.9   **4.** $5.5p =$
7.7; $1.40   **5.** −3   **6.** 12.5   **7.** −360   **8.** 12 hits

CHECK UNDERSTANDING   **1.** 0.8, 0.8; 1.875
2. 4.5, 4.5; −13.5   **3.** Divide each side by 0.9.
4. Multiply each side by 0.6.   **5.** Multiply each
side by 15.   **6.** Divide each side by −0.4.   **7.** 1.46
8. 0.56   **9.** −11.04   **10.** −1.94
11a. Harry multiplied the right side by 4 instead of
dividing each side by 4.

PRACTICE AND PROBLEM SOLVING
13. −25.1   **15.** 2.3   **17.** 30   **19.** 1.3   **21.** 0.0804
23. 0.9912   **25.** 3,104.32   **27.** 456   **29.** 13.5
31. 0.048308   **33.** $n \div (−4.5) = 200.6$; −902.7
35a. $f = 3.28\ell$ **b.** 24.6 ft   **c.** about 1.83 m
d. 16.7 m^2 **37a.** 20 hits   **b.** You can have only a
whole number of hits.

MIXED REVIEW   **39.** −5.3   **41.** 26.1   **43.** 7.285
45. yes   **47.** no

TRY THIS   **1.** Centimeter; a meter is too large
unless you use fractional parts of a meter;
millimeters are too small.   **2.** Gram; an energy bar
has a mass of several grams, but it is much less
than 1 kilogram.   **3.** Kilogram; a horse is very
heavy, so grams are too small.   **4.** Liter; a gas tank
holds several liters, so milliliters are too small.
5. 50 km   **6.** 10 mL   **7.** 0.035   **8.** 250,000
9. 6,800   **10.** 3,800 m   **11.** 250 mL

CHECK UNDERSTANDING   **1.** C   **2.** F   **3.** B
4. E   **5.** A   **6.** D   **7.** 5,400   **8.** 0.234   **9.** 0.012
10. 3,010   **11.** 5.18 m

PRACTICE AND PROBLEM SOLVING
13. Meter; the depth is less than a kilometer, so
kilometers are too large.   **15.** Kilogram; a car is
very heavy, so grams are too small.   **17.** Milliliter;
a spoon holds much less than a liter, so a liter is
too large.   **19.** 2,000 mL; 2,000 L is about
2,000 qt and 2,000 mL ≈ 2 qt.   **21.** 150 cm; 150 m
is greater than the length of a football field.
23. 1 g; 1 mg is closer to the mass of a speck of
sawdust.   **25.** m   **27.** 25   **29.** 0.595   **31.** 0.035
33. 9.12   **35.** 0.005   **37.** 5.623   **39.** E   **41.** C
43. A   **45.** 6,008,835 L   **47.** 3.068 kg
49. Camille multiplied by 1,000, so she changed
grams to milligrams.   **51.** A kilometer is 1,000
meters, a kilogram is 1,000 grams, a milliliter is
0.001 liter, and a milligram is 0.001 gram.
53a. 5 to 6 km   **b.** 5,000 to 6,000 m

MIXED REVIEW   **55.** about 80
57. $a \geq 21$ **59.** $r \geq −7$

CHECKPOINT 2   **1.** 0.25   **2.** 130   **3.** 8.55
4. 3.05   **5.** 6.5   **6.** 129.6   **7.** 1.5 m; 1.5 cm is a
little wider than the width of a thumbnail.   **8.** 500
mL; 500 L would have a mass of about 500 kg.
9. 0.095   **10.** 7,650,000   **11.** 0.675   **12.** 7,100
13. 9,100 g

1. 5.2 m   **3.** 8.7 cm   **7.** 14.6 kg   **9.** 7 cm
11. 4 significant digits   **13.** 5 significant digits
15. 15.9 ft^2 **17.** 5,720 cm^2

1. A   **3.** B   **5.** B   **7.** B
9. $d − 40.65 = 182.33$; $222.98

READ   **1.** 1 ft   **2.** 3 ft   **3.** 2 ft

SOLVE   **4.** The number of days it takes to get out
is 1 less than the depth of the well in feet.
5. 9 days

LOOK BACK   6.

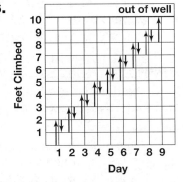

CHECK UNDERSTANDING   1. 107 digits
2. 66 matches   **3.** 13 triangles

PRACTICE AND PROBLEM SOLVING
5. 80 sketches   **7.** 3.25 ft   **9.** 1,320 pieces
11. about 3,095 people/mi²

MIXED REVIEW   13. 0.27   **15.** 2   **17.** 300
19. about $46.50   **21.** 91

Wrap Up   *pages 164–166*

1. about 10; front-end   **2.** about 4; rounding
3. about 24; rounding   **4.** about 10; rounding
5. about 60; clustering   **6.** about 7; rounding
7. about 12; rounding   **8.** about 6; rounding
9. about 18; clustering   **11.** C   **12.** about 48
13. about 4   **14.** about 10   **15.** about 5
16. about 12   **17.** about 6   **18.** about −8
19. about −6   **20.** about 12   **21.** 5.4, 5, 2 and 5;
no outliers   **22.** 16.1, 16.2, 16.3; no outliers
23. 36, 33, none; outlier: 57   **24.** 1.0, 0.2, 0.1;
outlier: 7.9   **28.** 70 mi   **29.** 384 mm²
30. 37.68 in.   **31.** 52 cm   **32.** 7.1   **33.** 9.25
34. −2.01   **35.** −0.8   **36.** −9.1   **37.** 10.6
38. 2.5   **39.** 40.817   **40.** 11.3   **41.** 968.75
42. −19.4   **43.** −185.0125   **44.** C   **45.** Meter; a
kilometer is too large unless you use fractional
parts of a kilometer; centimeters are too small.
46. Kilogram; a bicycle is heavy, so grams are
too small.   **47.** Milliliter; a liter is about the same
as a quart, so liters are too large.   **48.** 85
49. 0.160   **50.** 230   **51.** 1,600   **52.** 620
53. 0.080   **54.** D   **55.** 1, 4, 9, 16, 25, 36, 49, 64,
81, 100

Cumulative Review   *page 168*

1. C   **3.** C   **5.** C   **7.** D   **9.** B   **11.** A
13. B   **15.** C

▶**CHAPTER 4**

Skills You Need   *page 169*

1. 90   **2.** 900   **3.** 22   **4.** 49   **5.** 21   **6.** 45
7. 212   **8.** 27   **9.** 130   **10.** 140   **11.** 91   **12.** 23
13. 1,728   **14.** 512   **15.** 6,561   **16.** 15,625
17. −64   **18.** 64   **34.** $\frac{6}{8}, \frac{3}{4}$ **35.** $\frac{2}{8}, \frac{1}{4}$ **36.** $\frac{3}{9}, \frac{1}{3}$

Lesson 4-1   *pages 172–175*

TRY THIS   1. Yes; 160 ends in 0.   **2.** No; 56 does
not end in 0.   **3.** No; 53 does not end in 0, 2, 4, 6,
or 8.   **4.** Yes; 1,118 ends in 8.   **5.** No; the sum of
the digits, 10, is not divisible by 9.   **6.** No; the sum
of the digits, 13, is not divisible by 3.   **7.** Yes; the
sum of the digits, 12, is divisible by 3.   **8.** Yes; the
sum of the digits, 18, is divisible by 9.   **9.** 1, 2, 5,
10   **10.** 1, 3, 7, 21   **11.** 1, 2, 3, 4, 6, 8, 12, 24
12. 1, 31   **13.** 1 row of 36 students, 2 rows of
18 students, 3 rows of 12 students, 4 rows of
9 students, or 6 rows of 6 students

CHECK UNDERSTANDING   1. 2, 5, 10   **2.** none
3. 3, 5, 9   **4.** 3, 9   **5.** 2, 3, 5, 10   **6.** 3, 9   **7a.** 66
and 4,710   **b.** 66 and 4,710   **c.** An integer is
divisible by 6 if it is divisible by 2 and 3.
8. 1, 2, 4, 8   **9.** 1, 2, 4, 8, 16   **10.** 1, 23
11. 1, 2, 3, 6, 9, 18, 27, 54   **12.** 1, 3, 5, 15, 25, 75
13. 1, 2, 4, 17, 34, 68

PRACTICE AND PROBLEM SOLVING   15. none
17. 2, 3, 5, 9, 10   **19.** none   **21.** 2, 3, 5, 10
23. 3, 9   **25.** 2   **27.** 7   **29.** 2   **31.** 1, 2, 4
33. 1, 2, 3, 6   **35.** 1, 3, 5, 15   **37.** 1, 2, 11, 22
39. 1, 2, 4, 7, 14, 28   **41.** 1, 5, 7, 35   **43.** 1, 2, 5,
10, 25, 50   **45.** 1, 2, 3, 4, 6, 8, 9, 12, 18, 24, 36, 72
47. 1, 2, 3, 4, 6, 8, 9, 12, 16, 18, 24, 36, 48, 72, 144
53a. 2 plates of 21 cookies, 3 plates of 14 cookies,
6 plates of 7 cookies   **b.** 2 plates of 28 cookies,
4 plates of 14 cookies, 7 plates of 8 cookies,
8 plates of 7 cookies   **c.** 2 plates of 30 cookies,
3 plates of 20 cookies, 4 plates of 15 cookies,
5 plates of 12 cookies, 6 plates of 10 cookies

MIXED REVIEW   55. cm   **57.** 27   **59.** 42

Lesson 4-2   *pages 176–179*

TRY THIS   1. 6^3 **2.** $(−3)^4$ **3.** $4xy^2$ **4.** 36
5. −16, 16   **6.** −58   **7.** 81

CHECK UNDERSTANDING   1. 8^3 **2.** r^4s^2
3. $−21a^2b$ **4.** 64   **5.** 0.25   **6.** −9   **7.** 108
8. −15   **9.** 81   **10.** 49   **11.** 22   **12.** No; $−6^2$ is
−36 while $(−6)^2$ is 36.

PRACTICE AND PROBLEM SOLVING **13.** $25a^2$
15. $-15x^2y^2$ **17.** $4b^3c$ **19.** 125 and 243
21. -1 and 1 **23.** 31 **25.** -288 **27.** 35 **29.** 9
31. 0.36 **33.** 1 **35.** -24 **37.** 7.2 **39.** 48
41. 243 **43.** 29 **45.** D **47.** The student didn't
use parentheses around ab. **49.** An even power
of a negative number is positive. An odd power of
a negative number is negative. **51.** 216 in.^{3}
53. 4 in. **55.** No; $5x^2y$ for $x = 1$ and $y = 2$ is 10,
but $5xy^2$ for $x = 1$ and $y = 2$ is 20.

MIXED REVIEW **57.** 3, 5, 9 **59.** 2, 5, 10
61. $4x - 2y$ **63.** $11a - 7$

Lesson 4-3 pages 180–184

TRY THIS **4.** 11, 13, 17, 19; 10, 12, 14, 15,
16, 18, 20 **5.** $2^3 \cdot 3^2$ **6.** $2 \cdot 3 \cdot 5^2$ **7.** $3^2 \cdot 5^2$
8. $2^2 \cdot 59$ **9.** 4 **10.** 3 **11.** $4r$ **12.** $15m$

CHECK UNDERSTANDING **1.** composite; 3^3
2. prime **3.** prime **4.** composite; $2 \cdot 19$
5. composite; $3^2 \cdot 5$ **6.** prime **7.** composite;
$3 \cdot 29$ **8.** composite; $3 \cdot 31$ **9.** composite; 5^3
10. composite; $2^3 \cdot 3^2 \cdot 5$ **11.** 5 **12.** 2 **13.** 1
14. $7c$ **15.** $3y^2$

PRACTICE AND PROBLEM SOLVING
17. composite; 2^3 **19.** prime **21.** neither
23. composite; $5 \cdot 23$ **25.** composite; 7^2
27. composite; $11 \cdot 23$ **29.** 7 **31.** 3 **33.** 4
35. 90 **37.** z **39.** $6c^3$ **41.** $3s$ **43.** x^2y
45. 50, 52 **47.** B **49.** Yes; the GCF is 1.
51. No; the GCF is 13. **53.** No; the GCF is 13.
55. 1, 2, 4, 8, 16; 16 members **57.** 42 chairs

MIXED REVIEW **59.** 50 **61.** 11
63. -8.7 **65.** 9.3

Math Toolbox page 185

1. 17 students **3.** 7 **5.** 36

Lesson 4-4 pages 186–189

TRY THIS **4.** $\frac{3}{4}$ **5.** $\frac{3}{4}$ **6.** $\frac{4}{5}$ **7.** $\frac{1}{ac}$ **8.** $\frac{n}{3}$ **9.** $3x$

CHECK UNDERSTANDING **6.** $\frac{1}{3}$ **7.** $\frac{2}{5}$ **8.** $\frac{1}{4}$
9. $\frac{2}{3}$ **10.** $\frac{m^2}{3}$ **11.** $\frac{2 \cdot 2 \cdot 2 \cdot 3}{2 \cdot 2 \cdot 2 \cdot 2 \cdot 2} = \frac{3}{4}$

PRACTICE AND PROBLEM SOLVING **19.** $\frac{1}{3}$
21. $\frac{3}{5}$ **23.** $\frac{9}{16}$ **25.** $\frac{3}{4}$ **27.** $\frac{3}{5}$ **29.** $\frac{3x}{2}$ **31.** $\frac{7a}{12}$
33. 8 **35.** $\frac{x^2}{3z}$ **37.** 13 **41.** $\frac{1}{3}$ **43.** $\frac{9}{25}$

MIXED REVIEW **45.** 2 **47.** $7a$
49. 2.62 **51.** -6.33

788 Selected Answers

CHECKPOINT 1 **1.** 2, 3, 5, 10 **2.** 2, 3, 9
3. 2, 3 **4.** none **5.** 3, 9 **6.** 64 **7.** 125
8. -18 **9.** $\frac{1}{2}$ **10.** $\frac{2}{3}$ **11.** $\frac{4}{7}$ **12.** $\frac{1}{4}$ **13.** $2y$

Lesson 4-5 pages 190–193

READ **1.** the number of pictures that
must be taken **2.** 7 people **3.** 2 people

SOLVE
4.

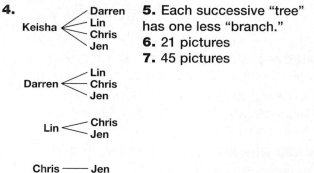

5. Each successive "tree"
has one less "branch."
6. 21 pictures
7. 45 pictures

CHECK UNDERSTANDING **1.** 15 days **2.** 30,
24, 21, 18, 15, 12, 9, 6, 3 **3.** 28 handshakes
4. 15 amounts of money

PRACTICE AND PROBLEM SOLVING
5. 15 pizzas **7.** 12 ways **9.** 6
11a. 60 person-hours **b.** 3 hours

MIXED REVIEW **13.** $\frac{1}{2}$ **15.** $\frac{2a^2}{5}$ **17.** Start with
10; add 10 repeatedly. **19.** Start with 2; multiply
by 3 repeatedly.

Lesson 4-6 pages 194–197

TRY THIS
5–8.

9. $-\frac{1}{3}$ **10.** $\frac{2}{3}$ **11.** -3

CHECK UNDERSTANDING **6.** $\frac{2}{3}$ **7.** $-\frac{5}{6}$
8. $\frac{5}{6}$ **9.** $-\frac{7}{10}$

PRACTICE AND PROBLEM SOLVING **19.** $-\frac{1}{4}$
21. $\frac{5}{7}$ **23.** $-\frac{2}{27}$ **25.** $\frac{4}{-5}, \frac{-12}{15}, -\frac{16}{20}$ **27.** No; if
equivalent, you could multiply the numerator and
denominator of one fraction by the same nonzero
number to get the other, meaning that the
numerator and the denominator of the other
fraction have a common factor. **29.** 64

31. $-\frac{2}{3}, \frac{2}{3}$ **33.** $-\frac{1}{4}, \frac{1}{4}$ **35.** always true

MIXED REVIEW 39. 1 **41.** -2
43. -95 **45.** -34

Lesson 4-7   pages 198–201

TRY THIS 1. 32 **2.** m^{12} **3.** x^5y^5 **4.** $18a^4$
5. $15c^9$ **6.** $12x^6$ **7.** 256 **8.** c^{20} **9.** m^6

CHECK UNDERSTANDING 1. 64 **2.** a^7
3. x^9y^2 **4.** $28b^7$ **5.** $18c^{10}$ **6.** 1,000,000 **7.** x^{12}
8. m^{24} **9.** No; the bases are not the same.

PRACTICE AND PROBLEM SOLVING 11. 128
13. a^{13} **15.** m^{52} **17.** $24y^{11}$ **19.** $144b^4$
21. 64 **23.** c^{16} **25.** m^{25} **27.** 8 **29.** 3 **31.** 4
33. 5 **35.** $<$ **37.** $=$ **39.** $>$ **41.** No; $-(2^3)^2$ is
-64 but $(-2^3)^2$ is 64. **43.** Both $x^8 \cdot x^2$ and
$x^5 \cdot x^5$ are equivalent to x^{10}.
45. $2^{16}; 2^{16} = 2^{1+15} = 2 \cdot 2^{15}$ **47.** $15x^3$

MIXED REVIEW 49. $-\frac{1}{2}$ **51.** -4
53. ![number line] $-2 \quad 0 \quad 2$

55. ![number line] $-2 \quad 0 \quad 2$

Standardized Test Prep   page 202

1. A **3.** B **5.** C **7.** $\frac{7}{12}, \frac{9}{24}$

Lesson 4-8   pages 203–207

TRY THIS 1. 1,000 **2.** x^7 **3.** $4m^4$ **4.** 1 **5.** 5
6. y^3 **7.** 5 **8.** $\frac{1}{16}$ **9.** $\frac{1}{a^2}$ **10.** $\frac{1}{3y^4}$ **11.** b^{-6}
12. $m^{-3}n^{-6}$ **13.** $x^{-4}y^2$

CHECK UNDERSTANDING 1. 8 **2.** h^4 **3.** $\frac{3y^5}{5}$
4. $\frac{n}{m^2}$ **5.** 1 **6.** 5 **7.** $\frac{1}{m^4}$ **8.** $\frac{1}{8}$ **9.** $\frac{1}{5a^3}$ **10.** $\frac{x^3}{y^5}$
11. y^{-3} **12.** $a^{-6}b^2$ **13.** $m^{-2}n^{-2}$ **14.** $x^{-3}y^{-7}$
15. b^6c^{-5}

PRACTICE AND PROBLEM SOLVING 17. 121
19. x^4 **21.** a^8 **23.** $\frac{x^8}{2}$ **25.** $6a^3b^4$ **27.** $\frac{1}{b^3}$
29. $\frac{1}{8}$ **31.** $\frac{1}{a^4}$ **33.** 1 **35.** $\frac{1}{a^5}$ **37.** $\frac{1}{4y^4}$ **39.** $\frac{x^7}{2}$
41. 8 **43.** 2 **45.** -2 **47.** 5 **49.** x^{-2}
51. m^7n^{-7} **53.** b^5c^{-9} **55.** The student thought
that the base was -5. **57.** 900 times as much

MIXED REVIEW 59. x^9 **61.** $16a^{16}$
63. about 20.2 **65.** about 51

CHECKPOINT 2 6. $-\frac{1}{3}$ **7.** $-\frac{1}{2}$ **8.** $\frac{2}{3}$ **9.** $-\frac{5}{8}$
10. $\frac{1}{4}$ **11–15.** ![number line showing points at -0.8, $-\frac{2}{10}$, $\frac{1}{2}$, 0.6, $\frac{9}{10}$ between -1 and 1]
16. 128
17. x^{50}

18. $6a^2$ **19.** $\frac{1}{x^5}$ **20.** $\frac{1}{a^6}$ **21.** C **22.** $\frac{3}{4}$

Lesson 4-9   pages 208–213

TRY THIS 4. 5.45×10^7 **5.** 7.23×10^5
6. 6.02×10^{11} **7.** 2.1×10^{-4} **8.** 5×10^{-8}
9. 8.03×10^{-11} **10.** 32,100,000 **11.** 0.000000059
12. 10,060,000,000 **13.** 1.6×10^6
14. 2.03×10^5 **15.** 7.243×10^{15} **16.** $18.3 \times$
$10^6, 0.098 \times 10^9, 526 \times 10^7$ **17.** 0.22×10^{-10},
$8 \times 10^{-9}, 14.7 \times 10^{-7}$ **18.** 2.4×10^{11}
19. 5.68×10^{-3} **20.** 1.002×10^{-23} kg

CHECK UNDERSTANDING 1. 8.9×10^9
2. 6.31×10^{-4} **3.** 5.559×10^8 **4.** 9×10^{10}
5. 59,400,000 **6.** 0.00000002104 **7.** 120,000
8. 0.00072 **9.** $0.065 \times 10^{11}, 16 \times 10^9, 2.3 \times 10^{12}$
10. $3.7 \times 10^{-8}, 253 \times 10^{-9}, 12.9 \times 10^{-7}$
11. 3×10^9 **12.** 8.6×10^{11} **13.** 6.3×10^{12}

PRACTICE AND PROBLEM SOLVING
15. 6×10^{-6} **17.** 5.28×10^{10} **19.** 1×10^{-9} m
21. 4×10^{-3} in. **23.** 8,430,000 **25.** 0.000000602
27. 0.00714 cm **29.** $10^{-8}, 10^{-6}, 10^0, 10^5, 10^9$
31. $782 \times 10^{-8}, 0.8 \times 10^{-4}, 9.1 \times 10^{-5}$,
$55.8 \times 10^{-5}, 1,009 \times 10^2$ **33.** 6×10^4 **35.** $2 \times$
10^{-4} **37.** 2×10^{10} lb **39.** about 2.18×10^{12}
41a. 3.8×10^8 m **b.** 7.6×10^8 footsteps

MIXED REVIEW 45. x^2 **47.** $\frac{3m^2}{n}$
49. 0.9 ft/h **51.** 78 chimes

Math Toolbox   page 214

1. 1.4976×10^{11} **3.** 2.0196×10^{16}
5. 9.338×10^{23} **7.** 6.19×10^{-5}
9. 1.1907×10^{-12} **11.** 4.2585×10^{-10}

Selected Answers

Wrap Up
pages 216–218

1. 1, 2, 3, 4, 6, 12 **2.** 1, 2, 3, 5, 6, 10, 15, 30 **3.** 1, 2, 3, 6, 7, 14, 21, 42 **4.** 1, 2, 3, 4, 6, 8, 9, 12, 18, 24, 36, 72 **5.** 1, 3, 37, 111 **6.** 1, 2, 3, 4, 6, 7, 9, 12, 14, 18, 21, 28, 36, 42, 63, 84, 126, 252 **7.** 8 **8.** 27 **9.** 172 **10.** −25 **11.** 121 **12.** 58 **13.** 49 **14.** 16 **15.** prime **16.** composite; $2^2 \cdot 5$ **17.** prime **18.** composite; $2 \cdot 5 \cdot 11$ **19.** composite; $3 \cdot 29$ **20.** 4 **21.** 9 **22.** 1 **23.** $3x^2$ **24.** $2ab$ **25.** No factor of a positive integer is greater than the integer. **26.** $\frac{1}{5}$ **27.** $\frac{1}{2}$ **28.** $\frac{4}{13}$ **29.** $\frac{7}{10}$ **30.** $\frac{7}{11}$ **31.** $\frac{1}{6}$ **32.** x **33.** 5 **34.** $\frac{1}{4}$ **35.** $\frac{2}{5}$ **36.** $\frac{x}{3}$ **37.** $4b$ **38.** 24 days

39–42.

43. $\frac{2}{5}$ **44.** $\frac{7}{8}$

45. −1 **46.** $-\frac{4}{5}$ **47.** 128 **48.** $21a^6$ **49.** b^7c^4 **50.** x^{15} **51.** y^{20} **52.** 4,096 **53.** $\frac{1}{b^2}$ **54.** $\frac{7}{8y^5}$ **55.** 2×10^6 **56.** 4.58×10^8 **57.** 7×10^{-7} **58.** 5.9×10^{-9} **59.** 800,000,000,000 **60.** 0.0000032 **61.** 11,190,000 **62.** 0.000000000005 **63.** 4.3×10^{10}, 12×10^{11}, $3,644 \times 10^9$ **64.** 8×10^{-10}, 58×10^{-10}, 716×10^{-10} **65.** 2.4×10^{16} **66.** 1.8×10^{11}

Cumulative Review
page 220

1. B **3.** C **5.** A **7.** D **9.** D **11.** A **13.** B **15.** A **17.** $4a$; 28 **19.** 1, 2, 3, 6, 9, 18, 27, 54

►CHAPTER 5

Skills You Need
page 221

1. $\frac{1}{2}$; $\frac{3}{6}$ **2.** $\frac{8}{12}$; $\frac{2}{3}$ **3.** $\frac{2}{5}$, $\frac{4}{10}$ **4.** $\frac{3}{4}$; $\frac{6}{8}$ **5.** $\frac{5}{6}$ **6.** $\frac{2}{5}$ **7.** −2 **8.** $\frac{1}{8}$ **9.** $-\frac{24}{25}$ **10.** $\frac{1}{3}$ **11.** $\frac{4}{15}$ **12.** $\frac{4}{31}$ **13.** $-\frac{2}{9}$ **14.** $-\frac{2}{13}$ **15.** $\frac{1}{6}$ **16.** $\frac{5}{7}$ **17.** 5.4 **18.** 0.6 **19.** 0.625 **20.** 0.75 **21.** 0.375 **22.** 1.2 **23.** 60 **24.** 23.7 **25.** −45 **26.** −40 **27.** 1.5 **28.** 74 **29.** 8 **30.** −1.78 **31.** 3 **32.** 4 **33.** 12 **34.** 1 **35.** 10 **36.** 5 **37.** 9 **38.** 11 **39.** 10 **40.** 7

Lesson 5-1
pages 224–228

TRY THIS 1. 12 **2.** 20 **3.** 60 **4.** 48 **5.** 45 **6.** 180 **7.** $60xy$ **8.** $56m^4$ **9.** $75xy^2$ **10.** $\frac{2}{9} < \frac{4}{9}$

11. $-\frac{4}{9} < -\frac{2}{9}$ **12.** $-\frac{4}{9} < \frac{2}{9}$ **13.** $\frac{6}{7} > \frac{4}{5}$ **14.** $\frac{2}{3} < \frac{3}{4}$ **15.** $\frac{3}{4} > \frac{7}{10}$ **16.** $\frac{1}{6} < \frac{5}{12} < \frac{8}{12}$ **17.** $\frac{1}{5} < \frac{3}{10} < \frac{1}{2} < \frac{7}{12}$

CHECK UNDERSTANDING 1. 90 **2.** 18 **3.** 60 **4.** 45 **5.** < **6.** < **7.** = **8.** > **9.** $\frac{3}{9} < \frac{5}{9} < \frac{7}{9}$ **10.** $\frac{1}{4} < \frac{1}{3} < \frac{1}{2}$ **11.** $\frac{2}{7} < \frac{2}{5} < \frac{2}{3}$ **12.** $\frac{3}{9}$ or $\frac{1}{3} < \frac{2}{5} < \frac{2}{4}$ **13.** Yes; $\frac{2}{3} > \frac{5}{8}$.

PRACTICE AND PROBLEM SOLVING
15. 180 **17.** 30 **19.** 1,800 **21.** 60 **23.** $200xy$ **25.** $1,008a^2b$ **27.** = **29.** = **31.** > **33.** > **35.** > **37.** > **39.** > **41.** = **43.** < **45.** > **47.** < **49.** = **51.** wood shingle, siding, plywood, asphalt shingle, brick, stucco **53.** you

Mixed Review
page 228

55. 1.394×10^{-3} **57.** 5×10^{-6} **59.** 4 **61.** $45x$

Lesson 5-2
pages 229–233

TRY THIS 1. 0.25 **2.** 1.875 **3.** 3.3 **4.** 0.6 **5.** $0.\overline{7}$; repeating; 7 **6.** $0.9\overline{54}$; repeating; 54 **7.** 1.375; terminating **8.** $0.\overline{72}$; repeating; 72 **9.** 0.2, 0.5, $\frac{7}{10}$, $\frac{4}{5}$ **10.** −0.75, −0.375, $-\frac{1}{4}$, $-\frac{1}{8}$ **11.** $1\frac{3}{4}$ **12.** $3\frac{1}{250}$ **13.** $2\frac{8}{25}$ **14.** $\frac{7}{9}$ **15.** $\frac{6}{11}$ **16.** $\frac{71}{333}$

CHECK UNDERSTANDING 1. 0.28 **2.** 0.6 **3.** −0.625 **4.** $-0.1\overline{6}$ **5.** $0.\overline{2}$ **6.** $0.\overline{6}$ **7.** < **8.** = **9.** > **10.** < **11.** $\frac{1}{10}$ **12.** $5\frac{9}{25}$ **13.** $2\frac{11}{20}$ **14.** $\frac{5}{9}$ **15.** $2\frac{5}{33}$ **16.** $\frac{2}{9}$; $0.\overline{2}$

PRACTICE AND PROBLEM SOLVING 17. 0.45 **19.** 2.3125 **21.** 0.04 **23.** −0.31 **25.** $0.\overline{3}$ **27.** 0.65 **29.** $0.\overline{4}$ **31.** 0.06 **33.** 0.3, $\frac{1}{2}$, $\frac{3}{2}$, $\frac{5}{2}$ **35.** $0.0\overline{6}$, $\frac{2}{5}$, $\frac{2}{3}$, $\frac{5}{6}$ **37.** $\frac{22}{11}$, 2.01, 2.1, $\frac{22}{10}$ **39.** $6\frac{4}{5}$ **41.** $-3\frac{9}{10}$ **43.** $\frac{272,727}{1,000,000}$ **45.** $-\frac{1}{3}$ **47.** 2 **49.** $\frac{91}{495}$ **51.** $\frac{149}{234}$; 0.64

53.

Fraction	$\frac{1}{8}$	$\frac{1}{4}$	$\frac{3}{8}$	$\frac{1}{2}$
Decimal	0.125	0.25	0.375	0.5
Fraction	$\frac{5}{8}$	$\frac{3}{4}$	$\frac{7}{8}$	
Decimal	0.625	0.75	0.875	

Fraction	$\frac{1}{5}$	$\frac{2}{5}$	$\frac{3}{5}$	$\frac{4}{5}$
Decimal	0.2	0.4	0.6	0.8

55. No; there is no block of digits that repeats.

MIXED REVIEW 57. $-\frac{5}{6}, -\frac{1}{3}, \frac{1}{6}, \frac{2}{3}$
59. $-\frac{6}{7}, -\frac{4}{7}, -\frac{3}{14}, -\frac{1}{14}$ **61.** $\frac{11}{6}$ **63.** $\frac{61}{8}$
65. 3.485×10^{10}

1–8. Answers may vary. Sample answers are given. **1.** 2 **3.** 4 **5.** 4 **7.** 2

TRY THIS 4. $\frac{3}{5}$ **5.** $\frac{2}{5}$ **6.** $\frac{6}{y}$ **7.** $\frac{7}{15}$ **8.** $-\frac{1}{8}$
9. $\frac{3m + 14}{7m}$ **10.** $6\frac{5}{8}$ **11.** $29\frac{1}{6}$ **12.** $2\frac{13}{16}$ **13.** $3\frac{1}{2}$ qt
CHECK UNDERSTANDING 1. $\frac{5}{8}$ **2.** $\frac{1}{12}$ **3.** $4m$
4. $\frac{3x}{7}$ **5.** $3\frac{5}{8}$ **6.** $1\frac{5}{8}$ **7.** $13\frac{7}{8}$ **8.** $\frac{5}{6}$ **9.** $1\frac{7}{8}$ in.
PRACTICE AND PROBLEM SOLVING 11. $\frac{1}{3}$
13. $-\frac{2}{5}$ **15.** $\frac{5}{x}$ **17.** $1\frac{3}{10}$ **19.** $\frac{21 + 2d^2}{3d}$ **21.** $\frac{3}{8y}$
23. 6 **25.** $6\frac{5}{24}$ **27.** $-1\frac{1}{8}$ **33.** $1\frac{3}{8}$ **35.** $\frac{x}{2}$ **37.** $\frac{1}{8}$
39. $\frac{9}{98}$ **43.** $1\frac{1}{2}$ lb **45.** $\frac{2}{3}$
MIXED REVIEW 47. $0.6, 0.66, \frac{2}{3}$ **49.** x^3 **51.** x^{12}
CHECKPOINT 1 1. 150 **2.** 100 **3.** 5 **4.** 60
5. 864 **6.** > **7.** < **8.** < **9.** < **10.** =
11. 0.51 **12.** $\frac{3}{250}$ **13.** 1.25 **14.** $\frac{1}{3}$ **15.** $0.8\overline{3}$
16. $\frac{17}{33}$ **17.** B

TRY THIS 6. $\frac{2}{15}$ **7.** $-\frac{5}{9}$ **8.** $\frac{35}{72}$ **9.** $\frac{3}{32}$ **10.** $\frac{4}{7}$
11. $-\frac{3}{10}$ **12.** $\frac{x}{6}$ **13.** $1\frac{1}{2}$ **14.** $\frac{6}{7}$ **15.** $-4\frac{8}{15}$
16. $\frac{15}{16}$ **17.** $-\frac{1}{2}$ **18.** $1\frac{1}{2}$ **19.** $1\frac{3}{5}$ **20.** $-1\frac{1}{3}$
21. $7\frac{1}{2}$
CHECK UNDERSTANDING 1. $\frac{2}{15}$ **2.** $-\frac{3}{16}$
3. $5\frac{1}{28}$ **4.** $3\frac{3}{10}$ **5.** $\frac{7}{10}$ **6.** $5\frac{2}{3}$ **7.** $\frac{2y}{5}$ **8.** $\frac{9x}{2}$
9. $1\frac{1}{2}$ **10.** $\frac{5}{6}$ **11.** $-2\frac{1}{4}$ **12.** $-1\frac{1}{21}$ **13.** $16\frac{8}{9}$
14. $1\frac{7}{9}$ **15.** -2 **16.** $1\frac{1}{2}$ **17.** 9 oz
PRACTICE AND PROBLEM SOLVING 19. $\frac{1}{2}$
21. $\frac{2x}{7}$ **23.** $-8\frac{1}{3}$ **25.** $-\frac{3}{5}$ **27.** $\frac{2a}{15}$ **29.** $\frac{35}{72}$
31. $1\frac{1}{2}$ **33.** $\frac{1}{3}$ **35.** $1\frac{1}{3}$ **37.** $1\frac{7}{8}$ **39.** $-1\frac{1}{5}$
41. $\frac{32}{75}$ **43.** $1\frac{1}{4}$ **45.** 40 **47.** $1\frac{1}{24}$ **49.** $1\frac{1}{6}$
51. 6 days **53.** 5 rest stops **57.** D
MIXED REVIEW 59. $1\frac{23}{35}$ **61.** $\frac{3}{10}$ **63.** $\frac{5}{6}$
65. $4\frac{1}{2}$ **67.** $\frac{2}{3}$ **69.** \$20

TRY THIS 1. Gallons; it is the largest customary unit of capacity smaller than the capacity of a pool. **2.** Pound; it is the largest customary unit of weight smaller than the weight of a baby. **3.** Inch; it is the largest customary unit of length smaller than the length of a pencil. **4.** Fluid ounce; it is the smallest customary unit of capacity. An eyedropper may hold a fraction of a fluid ounce. **5.** $\frac{7}{8}$ **6.** $1\frac{1}{6}$
7. 7 **8.** 56 **9.** $10\frac{1}{2}$ **10.** 7
CHECK UNDERSTANDING 1. C **2.** B **3.** F
4. D **5.** E **6.** A **7.** $\frac{1}{2}$ **8.** $1\frac{1}{2}$ **9.** $\frac{3}{4}$ **10.** 1,000
11. 2,640 **12.** 12 **13.** 56 fl oz, or $3\frac{1}{2}$ pt
PRACTICE AND PROBLEM SOLVING 15. weight
17. weight **19.** volume **21.** Fluid ounce; baby bottles are usually marked in fluid ounces.
23. Yard; it is the largest customary unit of length less than the length of a sports field. **25.** Pound; it is the largest customary unit of weight less than the weight of a medium-sized fish. **27.** no; 10 pt
29. no; 2 in. **31.** A **33.** F **35.** B **37.** 146
39. $2\frac{1}{3}$ **41.** 26,400 **43.** $\frac{1}{2}$ **45.** 168 **47.** 60
49. 25 **51.** 6.5 **53.** 21 **55.** $3\frac{1}{8}$ **57.** 24
59. 48 **61.** ft **63.** t **65.** B **67.** A quarter pound is $\frac{1}{4}$ of 16 oz, or 4 oz, and 4 oz < 6 oz. **69.** $8 \text{ c} \cdot \frac{1 \text{ pt}}{2 \text{ c}} = 4$ pt; the student's answer is not reasonable.

MIXED REVIEW 71. $\frac{9}{29}$ **73.** $1\frac{1}{5}$
75. $x + 3y$ **77.** $-3y$

1. 0.005 mg **3.** 0.05 cm **5.** $\frac{1}{2}$ ft **7.** 0.05 L
9. $\frac{1}{4}$ yd **11.** $\frac{1}{16}$ oz **13.** 0.5 cm, 0.05 cm

READ 1. the time you should leave home
2. 12:30 P.M. **3.** 10 min **4.** $\frac{3}{4}$ h **5.** 10 min
SOLVE 6a. 1:00 P.M. **b.** 12:30 P.M. **c.** 12:20 P.M.
d. 11:35 A.M. **e.** 11:25 A.M.
CHECK UNDERSTANDING 1. 8:30 A.M.
2. 9:00 A.M. **3.** the 12:15 P.M. bus
PRACTICE AND PROBLEM SOLVING
5. 22 stakes **7.** Start with $\frac{2}{3}$ and add $\frac{3}{4}$ repeatedly; $3\frac{2}{3}, 4\frac{5}{12}, 5\frac{1}{6}$.

Selected Answers

MIXED REVIEW   11. $\frac{2}{5}$ **13.** -8 **15.** $\frac{3}{32}$
17. -40 **19.** 1 **21.** -50 **23.** about $48

Lesson 5-7   pages 255–258
TRY THIS   1. $-\frac{1}{3}$ **2.** $\frac{1}{15}$ **3.** $\frac{13}{20}$ **4.** $\frac{4}{5}$ **5.** $1\frac{1}{7}$
6. $7\frac{5}{12}$ **7.** $4\frac{13}{18}$
CHECK UNDERSTANDING   1. $\frac{3}{4}$ **2.** $1\frac{1}{9}$ **3.** $1\frac{7}{30}$
4. $3\frac{1}{2}$ **5.** $2\frac{3}{4}$ **6.** $-2\frac{7}{8}$ **7.** $60\frac{7}{8}$ in.
PRACTICE AND PROBLEM SOLVING   9. 0
11. $5\frac{1}{6}$ **13.** $\frac{1}{5}$ **15.** 5 **17.** $1\frac{5}{24}$ **19.** $5\frac{5}{8}$ **21.** $\frac{1}{8}$
23. $\frac{23}{24}$ **25.** $-3\frac{5}{8}$ **27.** $5\frac{5}{8}$ **35.** A **37.** $4\frac{1}{4}$ lb
39. 10 ft $\frac{1}{4}$ in.
MIXED REVIEW   43. C **45.** pt **47.** yd
49. -152 **51.** 5

Lesson 5-8   pages 259–263
TRY THIS   1. $\frac{5}{56}$ **2.** $\frac{7}{18}$ **3.** $\frac{4}{15}$ **4.** $\frac{15}{4}$, or $3\frac{3}{4}$
5. $\frac{32}{27}$, or $1\frac{5}{27}$ **6.** 1 **7.** $-\frac{7}{8}$ **8.** $\frac{13}{15}$ **9.** $-\frac{1}{14}$ **10.** 8
11. $-\frac{3}{10}$ **12.** $4\frac{6}{11}$
CHECK UNDERSTANDING   1. $\frac{5}{48}$ **2.** $3\frac{1}{3}$ **3.** $1\frac{1}{4}$
4. 4 **5.** $-\frac{4}{27}$ **6.** $\frac{1}{4}$ **7.** $\frac{2}{33}$ **8.** $\frac{7}{15}$ **9.** $\frac{3}{4}s = 9$;
12 sheets
PRACTICE AND PROBLEM SOLVING   11. 6
13. $\frac{7}{3}$ **15.** $-\frac{1}{7}$ **17.** $\frac{4}{25}$ **19.** $\frac{5}{63}$ **21.** 4 **23.** $\frac{2}{3}$
25. $-7\frac{1}{2}$ **27.** $-1\frac{7}{26}$ **29.** $-\frac{2}{9}$ **31.** $3\frac{5}{17}$ **33.** $2\frac{8}{27}$
35. $1\frac{1}{6}$ **37.** $-1\frac{19}{81}$ **39.** Positive; product of
positive and positive is positive. **41.** Positive;
product of negative (-6) and negative $\left(-\frac{4}{3}\right)$ is
positive. **43.** Negative; product of negative $\left(-\frac{3}{5}\right)$
and positive $\left(\frac{-7}{-5}\right)$ is negative. **45.** Zero;
product involving 0 is 0. **47.** 81.75 tons
49. 20 weeks **51.** $1\frac{2}{15}$ mi; 68 mi **53.** 10 min
55. C
MIXED REVIEW   57. $\frac{1}{8}$ **59.** $3\frac{5}{8}$ **61.** $3r^5$
63. $100s^5$ **65.** x^{13}
CHECKPOINT 2   1. 14 **2.** $\frac{1}{2}$ **3.** $-\frac{4}{27}$ **4.** $1\frac{1}{3}$
5. -2 **6.** 34 **7.** $2\frac{1}{4}$ **8.** 90 **9.** $1\frac{1}{2}$ **10.** $\frac{1}{3}$ **11.** $\frac{1}{5}$
12. $1\frac{5}{8}$ **13.** $11\frac{1}{4}$ **14.** $-17\frac{1}{3}$ **15.** $\frac{7}{15}$ **16.** $\frac{6}{35}$
17. $-\frac{27}{40}$ **18.** $3\frac{3}{5}$ **19.** $12

Standardized Test Prep   page 264
1. A **3.** C **5.** B **7.** $9.29

Lesson 5-9   pages 265–268
TRY THIS   1. 216 **2.** $16p^4$ **3.** x^5y^{10} **4.** $25x^6$
5. $16y^4$ **6.** $-16y^4$ **7.** $-125a^6b^3$ **8.** $\frac{1}{8}$ **9.** $\frac{16}{81}$
10. $\frac{8x^6}{27}$
CHECK UNDERSTANDING   1. 225 **2.** $16a^{10}$
3. $8c^6$ **4.** 10,000 x^{12} **5.** $\frac{4}{25}$ **6.** $-\frac{8}{125}$ **7.** $\frac{16}{49y^2}$
8. $\frac{81x^8}{10,000}$ **9.** 2 **10.** 1 **11.** 4 **12.** 3 **13.** 5
14. 3 **15.** $16c^2$ units^2
PRACTICE AND PROBLEM SOLVING   17. 100
19. $8x^6$ **21.** $-9x^2$ **23.** $25c^6$ **25.** $-x^4y^4$
27. m^8n^4 **29.** $\frac{9}{49}$ **31.** $-\frac{32}{x^{15}}$ **33.** $-\frac{27a^3}{b^6}$
35. $\frac{16c^4}{d^8}$ **37.** $-\frac{1}{32y^{15}}$ **39.** $\frac{1}{81x^8}$ **41.** 4 **43.** -8
45. $\frac{1}{64}$ **47.** 216 **49.** 1 **51.** $(3x^2)^2$; $9x^4$
55. $\frac{343}{1,000}$ units^3 **57.** $\frac{343a^3}{8c^3}$ units^3
MIXED REVIEW   59. $\frac{56}{243}$ **61.** $-1\frac{21}{22}$ **63.** E
65. H **67.** B

Wrap Up   pages 270–272
1. 36 **2.** 56 m^2 **3.** 105 **4.** $30xy$ **5.** > **6.** <
7. > **8.** = **9.** 0.6 **10.** $0.1\overline{6}$ **11.** 0.625
12. 0.3 **13.** 0.07 **14.** $\frac{1}{4}$ **15.** $\frac{5}{6}$ **16.** $5\frac{3}{5}$
17. $2\frac{4}{99}$ **18.** $3\frac{1}{12}$ **19.** $7\frac{2}{15}$ **20.** $\frac{30 + 3x}{5x}$ **21.** $\frac{7}{8}$
22. $\frac{7}{12}$ ft, or 7 in. **23.** $\frac{7}{40}$ **24.** $-\frac{4}{5}$ **25.** $1\frac{1}{5}$
26. $2\frac{1}{52}$ **27.** $\frac{1}{2}$ **28.** $2\frac{1}{2}$ **29.** $3\frac{3}{8}$ **30.** 60
31. 24 **32.** 96 **33.** 5,500 **34.** 1:30 P.M.
35. 15 buses **37.** $2\frac{3}{8}$ **38.** $1\frac{2}{15}$ **39.** $1\frac{1}{3}$ **40.** $\frac{1}{54}$
41. $-\frac{8}{21}$ **42.** $\frac{56}{363}$ **43.** $16d^4$ **44.** 36 **45.** $a^{10}b^5$
46. $-\frac{1}{8}$ **47.** $\frac{x^2}{9}$ **48.** $\frac{16a^4}{c^8}$

Cumulative Review   page 274
1. A **3.** A **5.** C **7.** 11 **9.** $\frac{3}{4}$ **11.** $\frac{13}{55}$ **13.** $\frac{13}{36}$
15. $16\frac{1}{2}$ **17.** $\frac{1}{2}$ **19.** 7,920 **21.** $\frac{14}{25}$ **23.** $\frac{9}{50}$
25. 75 **27.** $\frac{4}{7}$ **29.** $-8\frac{5}{8}$ **31.** $9\frac{3}{4}$ **33.** $\frac{16}{25}$
35. $\frac{27x^3}{y^3}$ **37.** $16y^2$

CHAPTER 6

Selected Answers

Skills You Need   **page 275**

1. $\frac{1}{4}$ **2.** $\frac{1}{4}$ **3.** $\frac{4}{5}$ **4.** $\frac{3}{8}$ **5.** $\frac{3}{7}$ **6.** $\frac{1}{8}$ **7.** $\frac{5}{6}$ **8.** $\frac{1}{25}$

9. 16 **10.** 13.5 **11.** $\frac{7}{8}$ **12.** 2.5 **13.** $1\frac{1}{4}$

14. 27.5 **15.** 0.35 **16.** $\frac{3}{50}$ **17.** 3.75 **18.** $\frac{7}{20}$

19. $\frac{7}{8}$ **20.** 3.6 **21.** $1\frac{7}{100}$ **22.** $0.\overline{6}$ **23.** $11.\overline{1}$

24. $\frac{1}{3}$ **25.** 6.25 **26.** $3\frac{49}{50}$ **27.** 5% **28.** 50%

29. 0.5% **30.** 0.17% **31.** 1.7% **32.** 17%

Lesson 6-1   **pages 278–281**

TRY THIS 1. $\frac{2}{5}$ **2.** $\frac{3}{2}$ **3.** \$.9/L **4.** 34 mi/gal
5. 52.5 **6.** 432

CHECK UNDERSTANDING 1. $\frac{1}{3}$ **2.** $\frac{3}{2}$ **3.** $\frac{5}{8}$
4. $\frac{1}{9}$ **5.** $\frac{3}{25}$ **6.** $\frac{1}{10}$ **7.** 8 m/s **8.** 63 words/min
9. $\frac{1}{2}$ **10.** 360 **11.** 15

PRACTICE AND PROBLEM SOLVING 13. $\frac{7}{9}$
15. $\frac{7}{9}$ **17.** $\frac{3}{4}$ **19.** $\frac{4}{3}$ **21.** $\frac{3}{5}$ **23.** $\frac{14}{25}$ **25.** 6 gal/min
27. $4\frac{3}{8}$ mi/h **29.** 5 gal/min **31.** 19.2 **33.** $117.\overline{3}$
35. 81 **37a.** class A, $\frac{6}{30}$ or $\frac{1}{5}$; class B, $\frac{4}{24}$ or $\frac{1}{6}$
b. class A **39.** 19.3 g/cm^3 **41.** 300 : 7, 300 to
7, $\frac{300}{7}$

MIXED REVIEW 43. −1,728 **45.** $-\frac{b^6}{a^3}$ **47.** =
49. 1,239 mi

Math Toolbox   **pages 282–283**

1. 6.3 **3.** 161 **5.** 426 **7.** 30.8 **9.** 2.8 **11.** 1.1
13. 5.3 **15.** 3 packages

Lesson 6-2   **pages 284–288**

TRY THIS 1. 6 **2.** 44 **3.** 77 **4.** yes **5.** no
6. yes **7.** 87 nautical miles

CHECK UNDERSTANDING 1. 16 **2.** 15 **3.** 6
4. no **5.** yes **6.** yes **7.** $\frac{14}{c} = \frac{4}{50}$; 175 calories
8. $\frac{12}{16} = \frac{h}{60}$; 45 heartbeats **9.** Yes; multiply each
side by $\frac{b}{c}$.

PRACTICE AND PROBLEM SOLVING 11. 5
13. 8 **15.** 45 **17.** 5 **19.** 28 **21.** 14 **23.** 6.7
25. 76.5 **27.** 30.3 **29.** 1.5 **31.** 20 **33.** 3
35. 20 **37.** 38 **39.** no **41.** yes **43.** no

45. no **47.** $\frac{20}{27.50} = \frac{12}{x}$; \$16.50 **49.** $\frac{25}{2.5} = \frac{100}{x}$;
10 s **51.** $\frac{4}{1.85} = \frac{16}{t}$; \$7.40 **53.** 12 tea bags
55. \$36.67 **57.** 12.6 cm **59.** 156 francs
63. 15 s **65.** 30 more times

MIXED REVIEW 67. $\frac{1}{100}$ **69.** $\frac{25}{14}$
71. false **73.** \$67.97

Lesson 6-3   **pages 289–293**

TRY THIS 1. 15.75
2.   28 ft **3.** 56 mi

CHECK UNDERSTANDING 1. $2\frac{2}{5}$ **2.** $2\frac{1}{2}$
3. 2 in.; 4.5 in.

PRACTICE AND PROBLEM SOLVING 5. 5 in.
7. 5.7 **9.** 45 km **11.** 7.5 km **13.** 2 in.
15. $1\frac{3}{4}$ in. **17.** 51 cm **21.** 8 in. **23.** N model;
HO model **25.** 4.5 in. **27.** N scale
29. 1 in. : 10 ft **31.** 2.5 ft **33.** Yes; the narrow
section in the drawing is $\frac{3}{4}$ in. by $\frac{3}{4}$ in., representing
a space 7.5 ft by 7.5 ft.

MIXED REVIEW 35. 2 **37.** $2\frac{2}{5}$ **39.** 9, 9.5, 10
41. 0.375 **43.** 0.4375 **45.** 22 mi/gal

Math Toolbox   **page 294**

1b. No; the dilation could lie outside or it could
overlap the original triangle. **c.** △*PQR* lies inside
△*XYZ*. **3.** △*XYZ* lies inside △*PQR*.

Lesson 6-4   **pages 295–299**

TRY THIS 5. $\frac{1}{2}$ **6.** $\frac{1}{6}$ **7.** $\frac{1}{3}$ **8.** $\frac{5}{6}$ **9.** a certain
event **10.** 1 to 4; 4 to 1 **11a.** 2 to 3 **b.** 3 to 2

CHECK UNDERSTANDING 1. $\frac{3}{8}$ **2.** $\frac{5}{8}$ **3.** 0 **4.** $\frac{3}{5}$

PRACTICE AND PROBLEM SOLVING 7. $\frac{1}{3}$
9. 0 **11.** $\frac{2}{3}$ **13.** $\frac{1}{3}$ **15.** $\frac{2}{11}$ **17.** 0 **19.** $\frac{3}{2}$
21. $\frac{3}{2}$ **23.** $\frac{0}{25}$ **25.** 5 to 4 **27.** 5 to 1
29. 25 to 11 **31.** $\frac{3}{14}$ **33a.** 1 to 9 **b.** 9 to 1

MIXED REVIEW 37. $6\frac{2}{3}$ mi **39.** 70 mi
41. $\frac{2}{3}$ **43.** $5\frac{3}{20}$

CHECKPOINT 1 1. 4 mi/h **2.** 6 gal/min
3. 48 ft/s **4.** 4.5 **5.** 42 times **6.** D

Selected Answers

Lesson 6-5 — pages 300–304

TRY THIS **1.** $\frac{29}{50}$ **2.** $\frac{18}{25}$ **3.** $1\frac{11}{25}$ **4.** 0.16
5. 0.625 **6.** 1.2 **7.** 0.45, $\frac{9}{20}$ **8.** 40% **9.** 2.3%
10. 175% **11.** 27%

CHECK UNDERSTANDING **1.** $\frac{2}{5}$, 0.4 **2.** $\frac{7}{25}$,
0.28 **3.** $\frac{39}{100}$, 0.39 **4.** $\frac{11}{20}$, 0.55 **5.** 168%
6. 36% **7.** 70% **8.** 0.2% **9.** 23% **10.** 25%
11. 55% **12.** $16.\overline{6}$%

PRACTICE AND PROBLEM SOLVING **15.** $\frac{3}{50}$
17. $\frac{49}{50}$ **19.** $\frac{9}{25}$ **21.** $\frac{1}{250}$ **23.** 0.1925 **25.** 0.063
27. 0.797 **29.** 0.045 **31.** 85% **33.** 0.75%
35. 259% **37.** 52% **39.** 22.2% **41.** 111%
45. 16.7% **47.** 33.3% **49.** 0.8, 80% **51.** $\frac{1}{2}$,
50% **53.** $\frac{67}{100}$, 0.67 **55.** < **57.** < **59.** <
61. $\frac{1}{10,000}$ **67.** 12.5 **69.** Yes; $\frac{32}{45} \approx 71$%.
71a. $\frac{3}{5}$, 60% **b.** $\frac{7}{40}$, 17.5% **c.** $\frac{9}{40}$, 22.5%

MIXED REVIEW **73.** $\frac{1}{4}$ **75.** $\frac{1}{8}$ **77.** 47
79. 1,320 **81.** 93

Lesson 6-6 — pages 305–309

TRY THIS

1.
2.

$\frac{25}{100} = \frac{n}{124}$; 31 $\frac{43}{100} = \frac{n}{230}$; 98.9

3.

$\frac{12.5}{100} = \frac{n}{80}$; 10
4. 55.2% **5.** 93.3%
6. 25.3 **7.** 313.1
8. about 2,824 screens

CHECK UNDERSTANDING **1.** 16 **2.** 150
3. 75% **4.** 200% **5.** 24 **6.** 37.1 **7.** 32
8. 80 **9.** 20

PRACTICE AND PROBLEM SOLVING **11.** $\frac{n}{100} =$
$\frac{16}{20}$; 80 **13.** $\frac{75}{100} = \frac{420}{n}$; 560 **15.** $\frac{18}{100} = \frac{n}{150}$; 27
17. $\frac{60}{100} = \frac{n}{15}$; 9 **19.** $\frac{92}{100} = \frac{n}{625}$; 575 **21.** $\frac{n}{100} =$
$\frac{17}{92}$; 18.5% **23.** $\frac{98}{100} = \frac{n}{6.1}$; 6.0 **25.** $\frac{35}{100} = \frac{14}{n}$; 40
27. $\frac{35}{100} = \frac{52.5}{n}$; 150 **29.** $\frac{2.5}{100} = \frac{912.5}{n}$; 36,500
31. $\frac{116}{100} = \frac{125}{a}$; 107.8 **33.** 21% **35.** Avocados;
$\frac{1}{3} = 33.\overline{3}$% **37.** A **39.** 50 members

MIXED REVIEW **43.** 52.3% **45.** 456%
47. 2.4×10^3, 2.03×10^4, 2.3×10^4, 2.03×10^5

Lesson 6-7 — pages 310–313

TRY THIS **1.** $n = 0.455 \cdot 20$; 9.1 **2.** $380 =$
$1.25n$; 304 **3.** $.85 **4.** 1,344 people

CHECK UNDERSTANDING **1.** $n = 0.3 \cdot 30$; 9
2. $25 = n \cdot 40$; 62.5% **3.** $120 = 0.15n$; 800
4. $n = 1.5 \cdot 90$; 135 **5.** 4%

PRACTICE AND PROBLEM SOLVING
7. $n \cdot 20 = 11$; 55% **9.** $1.35t = 63$; 46.7
11. $n = 5 \cdot 12$; 60 **13.** $n \cdot 4 = 9$; 225%
15. $n \cdot 150 = 96$; 64% **17.** $n = 0.15 \cdot 150$; 22.5
19. $n = 2.25 \cdot 3.6$; 8.1 **21.** 50% **23.** 100
25. 20% **27.** 1.8 **29.** 300 **31.** about $.50
33. about $3 **35.** 92% **37a.** 76.9 million
households **b.** 66.8 million households
39a. False; 18 is not less than 10% of 63, or 6.3.
b. True; 18 is more than 1,000% of 1, or 10.
41. 0.588x

MIXED REVIEW **43.** $\frac{35}{100} = \frac{n}{60}$; 21
45. 1,000,000 **47.** x^{21}

Lesson 6-8 — pages 314–317

TRY THIS **5.** 14% **6.** 60% **7.** 112.5% **8.** 9%
9. 50% **10.** 5% **11.** 92.9% **12.** 9%

CHECK UNDERSTANDING **1.** 30% increase
2. 220% increase **3.** 25% increase **4.** 20%
decrease **5.** 18.75% decrease **6.** 62.5%
decrease **7.** Eva should compare $8 - 7$ to 7, not 8.

PRACTICE AND PROBLEM SOLVING **9.** 18.8%
increase **11.** 133.3% increase **13.** 166.7%
increase **15.** 62.5% decrease **17.** 55% decrease
19. 70% decrease **21.** 12.5% increase
23. 24.1% increase **25.** 83.1% decrease
27. 44.4% decrease **29.** 64% **31.** 13%
33a. Growtown, 30% increase; Slowtown, 20%
decrease **b.** 3 years

MIXED REVIEW **35.** 75 **37.** 1 **39.** $-1\frac{5}{6}$
41. 94%

Lesson 6-9 **pages 318–321**

TRY THIS **1.** $42 **2.** $8.50

CHECK UNDERSTANDING **1.** $1.05 **2.** $22.04
3. $55.50 **4.** $27 **5.** $4.90 **6.** $210

PRACTICE AND PROBLEM SOLVING **7.** $10.50
9. $299.98 **11.** $12.74 **13.** $8.55 **15a.** $9.80
b. $39.20 **17a.** $y - x$ **b.** $\frac{y - x}{x}(100)$
19. store B; $.11

21. The sweater at the first store; its sale price
($17.50) is less (by $.50).

MIXED REVIEW **23.** 66.7%

CHECKPOINT 2 **1.** = **2.** < **3.** >
4. $0.33 \cdot 120 = n$; 39.6 **5.** $1.25 \cdot 42 = n$; 52.5
6. $n \cdot 5.6 = 1.4$; 25% **7.** $0.15q = 9.75$; 65
8. $n \cdot 500 = 1{,}375$; 275% **9.** $0.8w = 120$; 150
10. $9,600

Standardized Test Prep **page 322**

1. B **3.** D **5.** A **7.** A **9.** Chan's; 70% of 20 =
14, which is greater than 80% of 15 = 12.
11. $21.60 **13.** $815.50 **15.** 19%

Lesson 6-10 **pages 323–326**

READ **1.** the population at the beginning of 2010
2. the population in 2000 and the growth rate

PLAN **5.** No; each year the increase is the same
percent of an increasing amount.

SOLVE
6–7.

	2.5	292.6
292.6	2.5	295.1
295.1	2.5	297.6
297.6		

9. 297.6 million

LOOK BACK **11.** about 299 million

CHECK UNDERSTANDING **1.** 64 microbes
2. 6 orders **3.** 7 ways

PRACTICE AND PROBLEM SOLVING
5. 16 outfits **7.** 1 adult, 5 children; 3 adults,
2 children **9.** 14 cm, 7 cm **11.** 8 qt **13.** 15%

MIXED REVIEW **15.** $3.30 **17.** $127.96
19. $\frac{2}{13}$ **21.** $\frac{1}{2}$

Wrap Up **pages 328–330**

1. $\frac{3}{8}$ **2.** $\frac{4}{7}$ **3.** $\frac{3}{4}$ **4.** $\frac{10}{13}$ **5.** 50 mi/h
6. 90 words/min **7.** $1.89/lb **8.** 35 **9.** 0.7
10. 49 **11.** 126 **12.** 45 **13.** 35 **14.** 0.5 cm
15. $\frac{1}{8}$; 1 to 7 **16.** $\frac{1}{4}$; 1 to 3 **17.** $\frac{3}{8}$; 3 to 5
18. $\frac{6}{25}$; 0.24 **19.** $\frac{18}{25}$; 0.72 **20.** $\frac{2}{25}$; 0.08
21. $\frac{1}{200}$; 0.005 **22.** 30% **23.** 33% **24.** 33.3%
25. 35% **26.** 88.9% **27.** 2.1% **28.** 240%
29. 0.6% **30.** $\frac{15}{100} = \frac{n}{48}$; 7.2 **31.** $\frac{20}{100} = \frac{30}{x}$; 150
32. $\frac{n}{100} = \frac{90}{300}$; 30 **33.** $\frac{125}{100} = \frac{100}{y}$; 80
34. $0.35a = 70$; 200 **35.** $n = 0.68 \cdot 300$; 204
36. $n \cdot 180 = 9$; 5% **37.** $n \cdot 56 = 3.5$; 6.25%
38. 25% decrease **39.** 75% decrease
40. 20% increase **41.** 75% decrease **42.** $8.75
43. $1.70/lb **44.** 30 mi

CUMULATIVE REVIEW **1.** C **3.** B **5.** C **7.** A
9. C **11.** C **13.** $31.90 **15.** 84% **17.** 60%
19. 262% **21.** $\frac{1}{3}$ **23.** 27.5 mi **25.** 48.75 mi
27. 5 **29.** 20 **31.** $\frac{1}{12}$ **33.** $\frac{3}{2}$

▶ CHAPTER 7

Skills You Need **page 333**

1. 11 **2.** −21 **3.** −98 **4.** 5 **5.** 8 **6.** 9.0
7. −32 **8.** −8 **9.** −12 **10.** $4n$ **11.** $-3b + 10$
12. $8x$ **13.** $19c + 13$ **14.** $-7x - 5y$
15. $2a + 6$ **16.** $-36b + 54$ **17.** $9m - 35$
18. $2x - 3y$ **19.** $p + 3$ **20.** $q - 6$ **21.** $12y$
22. $10d$ **23.** $2b$ **24.** $n - 8$

25. $c \geq 1$
26. $y < 2$
27. $a < 10$
28. $b < 4$
29. $x > 0$
30. $x \geq -6$
31. $m < -17$

Selected Answers

32. $x \le 15$

33. $b \le 19$

34. $a > -3$

35. $m \ge 80$

36. $y \ge -1$

Lesson 7-1   pages 336–339

TRY THIS   **1.** 3; subtract 3, divide by 15.   **2.** 16; add 10, multiply by 4.   **3.** −1; subtract 11, divide by 9.   **4.** −2   **5.** 21   **6.** −3   **7.** $16

CHECK UNDERSTANDING   **1.** Subtract 9 from each side.   **2.** Add 4 to each side.   **3.** Subtract −3 from each side.   **4.** 72   **5.** −3   **6.** 15   **7.** $\frac{1}{2}$ **8.** −1   **9.** −3   **10.** 45 muffins

PRACTICE AND PROBLEM SOLVING   **11.** 6 **13.** −9   **15.** −16   **17.** 20   **19.** −6   **21.** −1 **23.** −75   **25.** 98   **27.** −60   **29.** 18   **31.** $20 **33.** $8   **35a.** 34 pickles   **b.** 5 pickles

MIXED REVIEW   **39.** 50%   **41.** 80% **43.** $10a + 3b$ **45.** 3 to 4

Lesson 7-2   pages 340–344

TRY THIS   **3.** 92 points   **4.** 88, 89, 90, 91 **5.** 32, 34   **6.** $\frac{14}{3}$ **7.** −14

CHECK UNDERSTANDING   **1.** $12a$ **2.** $3b + 11$ **3.** $-2x + 14$ **4.** −6   **5.** 6   **6.** −3   **7.** 14   **8.** $-\frac{1}{2}$ **9.** −2   **10.** D

PRACTICE AND PROBLEM SOLVING   **11.** 5 **13.** −5   **15.** −2   **17.** $-\frac{5}{2}$ **19.** 18   **21.** $\frac{17}{8}$ **23.** $\frac{1}{4}$ **25.** 8   **27.** 16, 17   **29.** 22 ft   **31.** 7, 16 **33.** 8, 9, and 10 birdhouses   **35.** 3

MIXED REVIEW   **37.** −5   **39.** $\frac{6}{7}$ **41.** 18.6   **43.** $1\frac{5}{6}$ c

Lesson 7-3   pages 345–349

TRY THIS   **1.** 50   **2.** $\frac{21}{2}$, or $10\frac{1}{2}$ **3.** −38 **4.** $-\frac{5}{2}$, or $-2\frac{1}{2}$ **5.** $\frac{1}{3}$ **6.** $\frac{11}{2}$, or $5\frac{1}{2}$

CHECK UNDERSTANDING   **1.** Subtract 3 from each side.   **2.** Add 1.5 to each side.

---

3. Combine like terms.   **4.** 12   **5.** $14\frac{6}{7}$ **6.** 12 **7.** 9   **8.** 5.5   **9.** 6.5   **10.** 99°F

PRACTICE AND PROBLEM SOLVING   **11.** 8 **13.** 100   **15.** $\frac{5}{2}$ **17.** $\frac{35}{81}$ **19.** $\frac{1}{2}$ **21.** $\frac{2}{5}$ **23.** −7 **25.** 36   **27.** $3.\overline{3}$ or $3\frac{1}{3}$ **29.** 1.2   **31.** $\frac{2}{11}$ **33.** $387.30   **35.** 6 pencils

MIXED REVIEW   **39.** −7   **41.** 0   **43.** $(-7)^2$ **45.** $18a^2$

Lesson 7-4   pages 350–353

READ   **1.** to find how many miles Ms. Smith drove **2.** 2 days   **3.** $29.95 per day   **4.** $.12/mi

LOOK BACK   **5a.** 68.9
71.9, 12, low   **b.** 137 miles

CHECK UNDERSTANDING   **1.** $60 **2.** 16 lessons   **3.** 20 cm, 12 cm

PRACTICE AND PROBLEM SOLVING   **5.** 8 of each coin   **7.** 28 posts   **9a.** 48 person-hours **b.** 4 h   **11.** Jackson, 24 seashells, Petra and Tyrone, 35 seashells apiece

MIXED REVIEW   **13.** 60   **15.** $\frac{13}{25}$, 0.52 **17.** $\frac{1}{200}$, 0.005   **19.** $1.80

CHECKPOINT 1   **1.** 20   **2.** 11   **3.** −18   **4.** 4 **5.** 28   **6.** −42   **7.** 2   **8.** 1.3   **9.** −6   **10.** 0 **11.** 1   **12.** 6   **13.** $84   **14.** 43, 44, 45

Standardized Test Prep   pages 354

1. A   **3.** B   **5.** C   **7.** A   **9.** 35   **11.** 27,300 meals

Lesson 7-5   pages 355–359

TRY THIS   **3.** 16   **4.** 2   **5.** 6 h

CHECK UNDERSTANDING

1. a; $-3a$; $-3a$; $-3a$; $\frac{-3a}{-3}$; 5   **2.** 16; x, x; $3x$; 16, 16; $3x$; $3x$; −7   **3.** −4   **4.** −1   **5.** −8   **6.** $2\frac{1}{4}$ h

PRACTICE AND PROBLEM SOLVING   **7.** 4 **9.** −2   **11.** 6   **13.** 3   **15.** −3   **17.** 3   **19.** −8 **21.** $\frac{1}{3}$ **23.** 4   **27.** 11   **29.** $1\frac{2}{3}$ h   **31.** 84 years **33b.** $\frac{80}{13}$ **35.** The student subtracted $4x$ from the left side of the equation instead of adding $4x$. The correct solution is $-\frac{2}{3}$.

MIXED REVIEW

37. $a \le 27$

39. 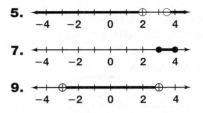 $y \le -6$

41. $28.16   43. $82.50

Lesson 7-6 — pages 360–363

TRY THIS   1. [number line] $a > 4$

2. [number line] $x \le -2$

3. [number line] $c < -6$

4. $m \ge -15$ **5.** $x < 3$ **6.** $b < -22$
7. at least $7,500

CHECK UNDERSTANDING   1. Add 2 to each side, simplify, divide each side by 4, and simplify. **2.** Add 1 to each side, simplify, multiply each side by 2, and simplify.   **3.** Subtract 2 from each side, simplify, divide each side by −3, reverse the inequality sign, and simplify.   **4.** $x > -6$
5. $a < -4$ **6.** $b \ge 7$ **7.** $y \le 2$ **8.** $\frac{x}{-3} - 1 \le 5$; $x \ge -18$

PRACTICE AND PROBLEM SOLVING

9. [number line] $m > -4$

11. [number line] $c \le -2$

13. [number line] $a > 9$

15. [number line] $b < 2$

17. $x \le -2$ **19.** $p > 3$ **21.** $b < 20$ **23.** $m > -7$ **25.** $x > -36$ **27.** $a \ge -2$ **29.** The student simplified $\frac{-36}{-12}$ to −3 instead of 3.   **31.** Letter excerpt: First undo addition and subtraction, and then undo division and multiplication. Remember to reverse the inequality sign when multiplying or dividing by a negative number.   **33.** 5 mi   **35.** at most 9 months

MIXED REVIEW   37. 3
39. 146.25 mi   **41.** 48 cm/h

Math Toolbox — page 364

1. [number line]

3. [number line]

---

5. [number line]

7. [number line]

9. [number line]

Lesson 7-7 — pages 365–368

TRY THIS   1. $s = p + c$ **2.** $k = hj$ **3.** $p = \frac{l}{rt}$
4. $a = \frac{b - 7}{5}$ **5.** $w = \frac{P - 2\ell}{2}$ **6.** $x = 3(y - 8)$
7. $r = \frac{d}{t}$ **8.** $h = an$; 11 hits

CHECK UNDERSTANDING
1. 3; 3; 6, 6; 6, c;   **2.** j; h; g; j   **3.** A   **4.** C   **5.** B
PRACTICE AND PROBLEM SOLVING   7. $s = \frac{P}{4}$
9. $a = 2m - b$ **11.** $b = \frac{2A}{h}$ **13.** $k = \frac{T - 2h}{3}$
15a. $d = \frac{C}{\pi}$ **b.** 5 in.   **17a.** $H = \frac{N}{7L}$ **b.** 9 ft
MIXED REVIEW   19. $x > 2$ **21.** $b > 24$
23. 75%   **25.** 31.3

CHECKPOINT 2   1. −2   **2.** −6   **3.** $\frac{2}{9}$ **4.** 4
5. 3   **6.** 5   **7.** $y > -\frac{9}{10}$ **8.** $x > -56$ **9.** $x > 5$
10. $h = s - g$ **11.** $r = \frac{k - 4}{3}$ **12.** $t = \frac{l}{pr}$
13. $h = 0.375\,M$ **14.** D

Lesson 7-8 — pages 369–373

TRY THIS   1. $30   **2.** $4.38

3.

Bal. at Yr Start	Interest	Bal. at Yr End
$500.00	$15.00	$515.00
$515.00	$15.45	$530.45

4.

Bal. at Yr Start	Interest	Bal. at Yr End
$625.00	$12.50	$637.50
$637.50	$12.75	$650.25
$650.25	$13.01	$663.26
$663.26	$13.27	$676.53

5. $955.09   **6.** $955.37

CHECK UNDERSTANDING   1. $28   **2.** $39.15
3. $577.37   **4.** $1,846.91   **5.** $2,207.63
6. $20,905.49   **7.** $900

PRACTICE AND PROBLEM SOLVING   9. $.88
11.

	Interest	Bal. at Yr End
	$120.00	$3,120.00
$3,120.00	$124.80	$3,244.80
$3,244.80	$129.79	$3,374.59

13. $5,066.88   **15.** $71,250.06   **17a.** $1,181.96
b. $381.96   **21a.** $1,400 and $1,469.33   **b.** 9
c. about 11.1%

MIXED REVIEW   23. $m = \frac{E}{c^2}$ **25.** $k = \frac{8}{5}(d - 1)$

Selected Answers

Math Toolbox
page 374

1a. 13   **b.** $27.41   **c.** $57.42   **3a.** $109.96
b. $88.51   **c.** If you increase the monthly payments, the interest charges will be less.

Wrap Up
pages 376–378

1. -4 **2.** 2   **3.** 48   **4.** 3   **5.** 21   **6.** $\frac{5}{3}$ **7.** $\frac{4}{5}$
8. -2 **9.** $-6\frac{3}{8}$ **10.** 39   **11.** -9 **12.** 8   **13.** -18, $-17, -16, -15$ **14.** $34.99   **15.** 34 tens, 34 twenties   **16.** $1,211.11   **17.** 3   **18.** -4
19. $\frac{6}{5}$ **20.** 4   **21.** -7 **22.** $\frac{2}{3}$ **23.** 2 h

24. $a > 7$

25. $y \le -3$

26. $c \le \frac{2}{3}$

27. $x < -4$

28. $x < -9$

29. $b < 2$

30. $x < 6$

31. $x \ge -\frac{3}{5}$

32. 64 megabytes   **33.** $m = \frac{r}{6k}$ **34.** $y = \frac{4}{3}x$
35. $g = \frac{Q}{p}$ **36.** $b = a + 2c$ **37.** $a = \frac{w - 5n}{3}$
38. $h = 6(e - 11)$ **39.** $27   **40.** $252.50
41. $97.50   **42.** $11,239.42   **43.** $44,890.37
44. $35,303.54   **45.** $80,016.89

Cumulative Review
page 380

1. A   **3.** C   **5.** C   **7.** D   **9.** B   **11.** D   **13.** $320
15. 5   **17.** $-\frac{3}{2}$ **19.** $-\frac{23}{2}$ **21.** -2

▶CHAPTER 8

Skills You Need
page 381

1. $y = -4x + 3$ **2.** $y = -2x + 4$ **3.** $y = 2x - 6$
4. $y = -6x - 8$ **5.** $y = -x + 12$ **6.** $y = -\frac{1}{2}x + \frac{5}{2}$

7. $y = \frac{1}{5}x + 4$ **8.** $y = -\frac{3}{4}x + 3$ **9.** $(5, 2)$
10. $(-3, 4)$ **11.** $(4, 0)$ **12.** $(6, -3)$ **13.** $(-4, -3)$
14. $(0, 3)$
15–20.

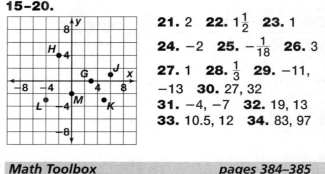

21. 2   **22.** $1\frac{1}{2}$ **23.** 1
24. -2 **25.** $-\frac{1}{18}$ **26.** 3
27. 1   **28.** $\frac{1}{3}$ **29.** -11, -13 **30.** 27, 32
31. $-4, -7$ **32.** 19, 13
33. 10.5, 12   **34.** 83, 97

Math Toolbox
pages 384–385

3a. $2   **b.** $6   **c.** 6h

Lesson 8-1
pages 386–390

TRY THIS   **1.** No; there are two range values for the domain value 2.   **2.** Yes; there is one range value for each domain value.   **3.** No; a specific postage cost (domain value) can mail packages of different weights (range values).   **4.** Yes; for each package weight (domain value) there is one postage cost (range value) to each zip code.

5.   **6.**

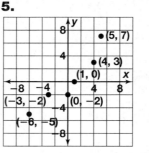 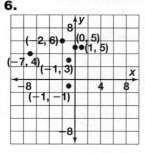

a function   not a function

7.   a function

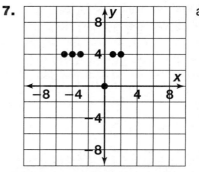

CHECK UNDERSTANDING   **1.** $-\frac{1}{2}, 0, 2, 3; \frac{4}{5}, 1,$ 2, 5   **2.** $-2, -1, 0; 2, 3$ **3.** No; there are three range values for the domain value 3.   **4.** Yes; there is one range value for each domain value.   **5.** Yes; there is one range value for each domain value.

6. No; there are, for example, two range values for the domain value −4.   **7.** Yes; no vertical line passes through two graphed points (vertical-line test).   **8.** Yes; no vertical line passes through two points (vertical-line test).   **9.** no   **10.** yes   **11.** yes

PRACTICE AND PROBLEM SOLVING

13. Yes; there is one range value for each domain value.   **15.** Yes; there is one range value for each domain value.   **17.** Yes; no vertical line passes through two graphed points (vertical-line test).   **19.** Yes; no vertical line passes through two graphed points (vertical line test).

21.
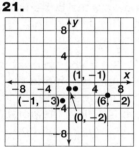

23.
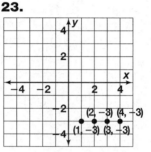

A function; no vertical line passes through two graphed points.

A function; no vertical line passes through two graphed points.

25. Each range value is the absolute value of its domain value.   **27.** Each range value is the square of its domain value.   **29.** Yes; a specific number of students (domain value) requires a particular number of buses (range value).   **31.** For each side length, there is one and only one area of the square.   **33.** A function can have the same y-coordinate with different x-coordinates.

MIXED REVIEW   **35.** 3   **37.** 3

Lesson 8-2   **pages 391–395**

TRY THIS   **1.** (−3, −5)   **2.** (−3, 15)   **3.** (−3, −4)
4. 14°C

5.
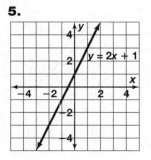

6.
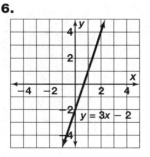

7.
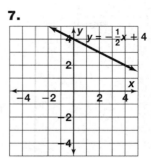

8.
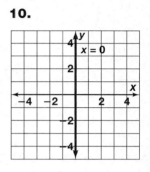
no

9.
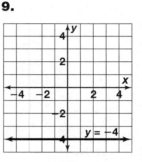

10.
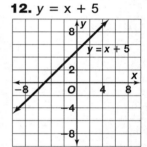

yes   no

11. $y = -2x + 3$
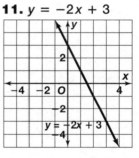

12. $y = x + 5$

13. $y = \frac{3}{2}x + 3$
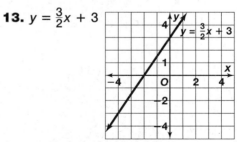

CHECK UNDERSTANDING   **1.** yes   **2.** no
3. no   **4.** no   **5.** yes   **6.** $y = 4x + 16$
7. $y = -x + 3$ **8.** $y = \frac{1}{2}x - 3$

Selected Answers

9.

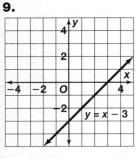

$y = x - 3$

10.

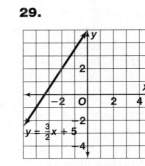

$y = -1$

11.

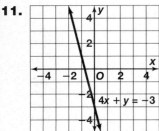

$4x + y = -3$

PRACTICE AND PROBLEM SOLVING

13. $(-2, 4), (1, -2), (4, -8)$ **15.** $(-2, 13), (1, 4),$
$(4, -5)$ **17.** $(-2, 34), (1, 31), (4, 28)$
19. $\left(-2, -7\frac{1}{5}\right), \left(1, -5\frac{2}{5}\right), \left(4, -3\frac{3}{5}\right)$

21.

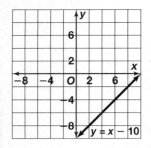

$y = x - 10$

23.

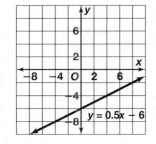

$y = 0.5x - 6$

25.

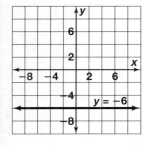

$y = -6$

27.

$-3x = 2y$

29.

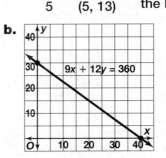

$y = \frac{3}{2}x + 5$

31.

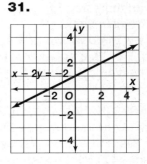

$x - 2y = -2$

33a.

x	(x, y)
1	$(1, 1)$
2	$(2, 4)$
3	$(3, 7)$
4	$(4, 10)$
5	$(5, 13)$

b. Begin with 1 and add 3 repeatedly. **37a.** $(0, 30)$ and $(40, 0)$; You burn 360 cal by swimming only the butterfly stroke for 30 min and only the backstroke for 40 min.

b.

$9x + 12y = 360$

c. $(0, 30)$ is the point at which the graph and the y-axis intercept each other. $(40, 0)$ is the point at which the graph and the x-axis intercept each other.

d. about 27 min

MIXED REVIEW **39.** Yes; there is one range value for each domain value. **41.** 62%
43. 120% **45.** 85% **47.** about 4.86×10^5 mi; about 8.16×10^7 mi

---

Math Toolbox   **page 396**

1. $y = \frac{3}{4}x$ **3.** $y = -\frac{3}{4}x$ **5.** $y = 0.945x$ (y is the number of liters and x is the number of quarts) or $y = 1.058x$ (y is the number of quarts and x is the number of liters); 7.56 L

Lesson 8-3   **pages 397–402**

TRY THIS **2.** $-\frac{5}{4}$ **3.** no slope **4.** 0 **5.** $\frac{3}{4}$ **6.** -1
7.   **8.**

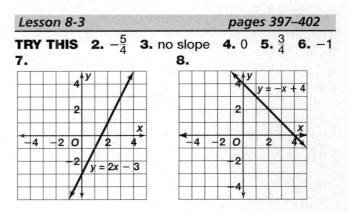

$y = 2x - 3$

$y = -x + 4$

CHECK UNDERSTANDING 1. $\frac{3}{4}$ **2.** -1
3. no slope **4.** $-\frac{5}{6}$ **5.** 0 **6.** $-\frac{2}{3}$ **7.** 7, 3
8. $-1, 4$ **9.** $\frac{1}{2}, -8$

PRACTICE AND PROBLEM SOLVING 11. 0
13. $-\frac{1}{3}$ **15.** $-\frac{3}{5}$ **17.** no slope **19.** -1 **21.** $-\frac{5}{2}$
23. 5, -3 **25.** $-\frac{2}{3}, 1$ **27.** $-\frac{2}{5}, -2$ **29.** 0, -3

31.

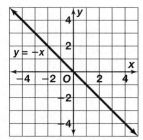

33.

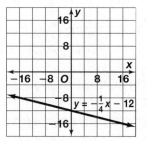

35.

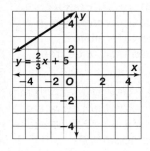

37.

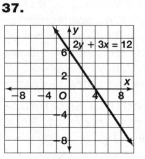

39.

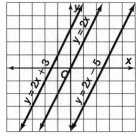

41. The upper roof has the steeper pitch because it has the greater slope.

43a.

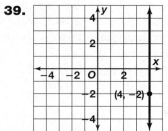

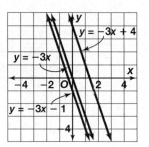

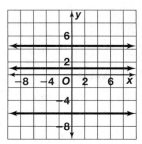

b. The lines are parallel. Explanations may vary. Sample: Their slope ratios are the same, so they never meet. **c.** 0 **45.** B

MIXED REVIEW 49. 10% decrease
51. 25% decrease

Math Toolbox page 403

1.

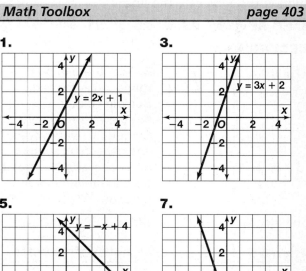

3.

5.

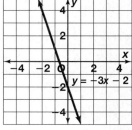

7.

Lesson 8-4 pages 404–408

TRY THIS 1. $c(p) = 3p + 4$; \$19 **2.** $f(x) = 2x$
3. $f(x) = -2x$ **4.** $y = 2x + 1$ **5.** $y = -x + 2$

CHECK UNDERSTANDING 1. $a(c) = 20 - c$
2. $f(x) = x - 9$ **3.** $f(x) = -x$ **4.** $y = -\frac{4}{5}x + 2$

PRACTICE AND PROBLEM SOLVING 5. $k(c) = c - 273.15$ **7a.** $q(p) = \frac{1}{2}p$ **b.** $q(f) = \frac{f}{32}$

Selected Answers

9a. $p(s) = 4s$ **b.** $p(7) = 4(7) = 28$; the perimeter is 28 in.   **11.** $f(x) = -1.2x$ **13.** $f(x) = x - 2$
15. $f(x) = \frac{2}{5}x + 1$ **17.** $f(x) = \frac{1}{4}x + 1$ **19.** $f(x) = x$
23a. $c(k) = 0.04968k + 6.87$ **b.** 315 kWh

25a.

x	$f(x)$
−6	−9
−4	−6
−2	−3
0	0
2	3
4	6

b. increase by 3   **c.** $\dfrac{\text{increase in range values}}{\text{increase in domain values}} = \dfrac{3}{2}$, which is the slope of the line.

MIXED REVIEW **27.** $\frac{2}{3}$ **29.** $\frac{3}{8}$ **31.** $\frac{7}{8}$

CHECKPOINT 1

2.

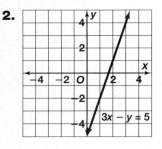

3. Yes; there is one range value for each domain value.
4. Answers may vary. Sample: If every vertical line passes through at most one graphed point, then the relation is a function.   **5.** 5   **6.** −1

7. no slope   **8.** −2, 5   **9.** $p(t) = 2{,}000t$ **10.** C

Lesson 8-5   *pages 409–414*

TRY THIS **4.** has 14 years of education and annual income of $90,000   **5.** 4 people

6.

Climate Data

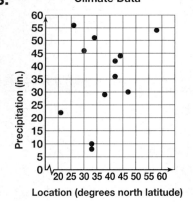

7.

Climate Data

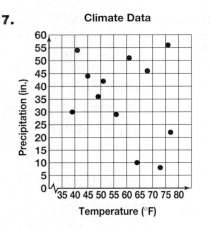

8. Positive correlation; as time goes by, the winning distance has tended to increase.

CHECK UNDERSTANDING **1.** averaged 4 h watching television and 2 h of physical activity daily
2. 8 students   **3.** 6 students   **4.** No correlation; there is no apparent relationship.   **5.** Positive correlation; as one set of values increases, the other set tends to increase.   **6.** Negative correlation; as one set of values increases, the other set tends to decrease.

PRACTICE AND PROBLEM SOLVING **7.** 10 min
9. 3 students   **11.** Positive correlation; as one set of values increases, the other set tends to increase.
13. No correlation; there is no apparent relationship.   **15.** Positive correlation; candles with longer burning times are likely to have greater original heights (assuming equal diameters).
17.

Nutritional Values

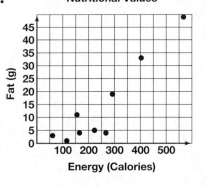

19.

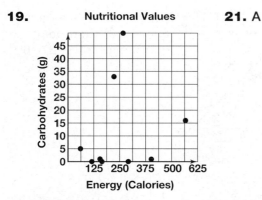

Nutritional Values

21. A

MIXED REVIEW **23.** $y = \frac{5}{2}x$ **25.** $f(x) = -x + 7$
27. $h = \frac{2A}{b + c}$ **29.** $a = S(1 - r)$ **31.** $41.54

Standardized Test Prep page 415

1. A **3.** D **5.** A **7.** B **9.** 3

Lesson 8-6 pages 416–419

READ **1.** the number of wolves and the number of moose **2.** the number of moose when there are 18 wolves

CHECK UNDERSTANDING **1a–b.** Trend lines may vary. Sample is given.

Registered Cars (by State)

c. about 13 million cars **d.** $y = 0.4x + 0.4$; about 3.3 million cars **2.** positive correlation

PRACTICE AND PROBLEM SOLVING **3.** 309 mi
5. 12 ways **7.** 45 ft

MIXED REVIEW **11.** $(-3, 9)$, $(0, 0)$, $(2, -6)$
13. $\left(-3, -3\frac{1}{2}\right)$, $(0, -2)$, $(2, 1)$ **15.** -3
17. about 0.75%

Lesson 8-7 pages 420–425

TRY THIS

1.

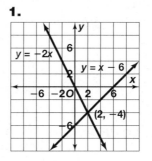

2.

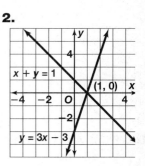

$(2, -4)$

$(1, 0)$

3.

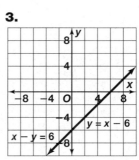

4.

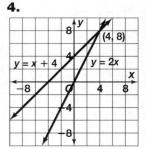

infinitely many solutions $(4, 8)$

5. $-3, -5$

CHECK UNDERSTANDING **1.** $(4, 5)$
2. $(-2, -1)$ **3.** no solution **4.** no **5.** no **6.** yes

7.

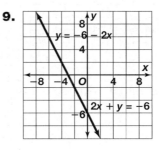

8.

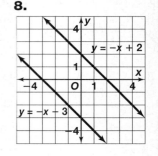

$(-2, -1)$

no solution

9.

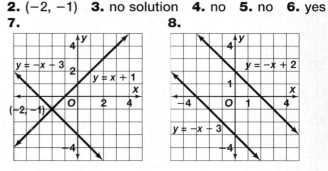

infinitely many solutions

Selected Answers

10a. $x = y + 6$; $x + 2 = 2(y + 2)$

b.

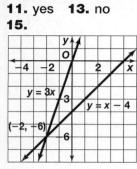

c. Cliff, 10 years; Claire, 4 years

b.

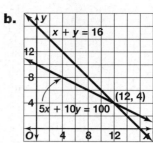

(12, 4)   **c.** 12 five-point questions, 4 ten-point questions   **31.** $-2, -6$
33. 20 ft^2

PRACTICE AND PROBLEM SOLVING

11. yes   **13.** no

15.

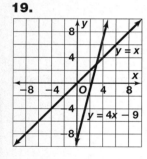

$(-2, -6)$

17.

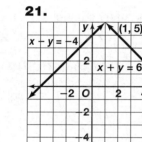

$(2, -1)$

19.

$(3, 3)$

21.

(1, 5)

23.

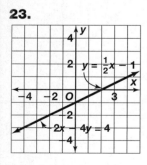

infinitely many solutions

25.

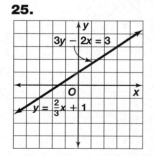

infinitely many solutions

29a. $x + y = 16$
$5x + 10y = 100$

35a.

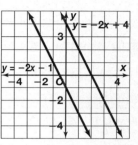

37. $(-3, -1)$

MIXED REVIEW   **41.** $x < -2$ **43.** $t \le 6$

45. $\frac{1}{6}$ **47.** 0

CHECKPOINT 2

1a., 1c.

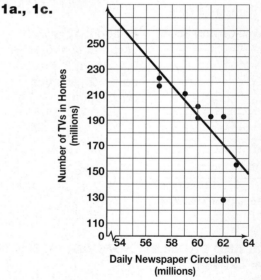

b. Negative correlation; as the number of television sets increases, the newspaper circulation decreases.

2.

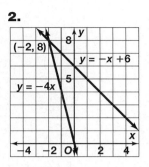

(−2, 8)

3.

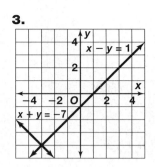

(−3, −4)

5.

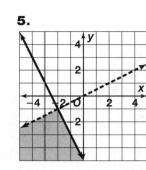

6.

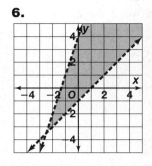

4.

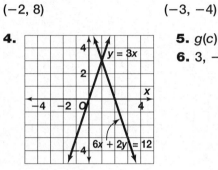

(1, 3)

5. $g(c) = \frac{c}{231}$

6. 3, −7

CHECK UNDERSTANDING   **1.** $y < -4x - 3$

2. $y \geq -2x$ **3.** $y \leq -\frac{2}{3}x + \frac{7}{3}$

4.

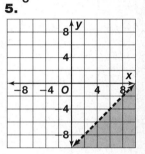

5.

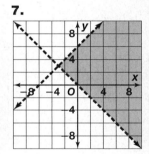

6.

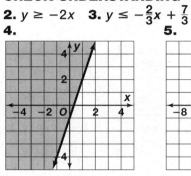

7.

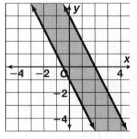

Lesson 8-8   *pages 426–431*

TRY THIS

1.

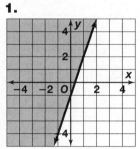

2.

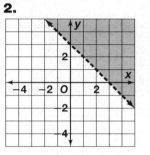

3.

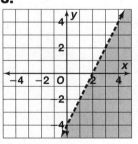

4. Graph $2x + 4y \geq 30$.

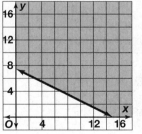

8.

9.

Selected Answers

10a. $6x + 3y \geq 45$

b.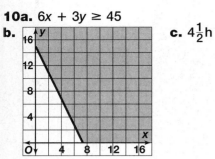

c. $4\frac{1}{2}$ h

PRACTICE AND PROBLEM SOLVING   **11.** C

13. A   **15.** $y = 3x + 2$; dashed   **17.** $y = \frac{1}{2}x$; solid

19. $y = x - 7$; solid   **21.** $y = 2x - 5$; dashed

23. 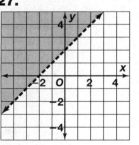   **25.**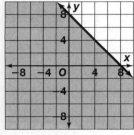

27. 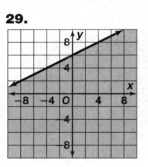   **29.**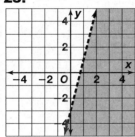

31. 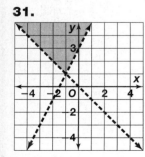   **33.**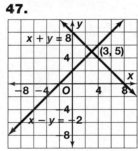

35. 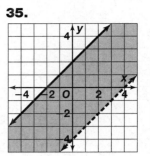   **37.**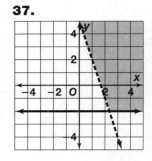

39.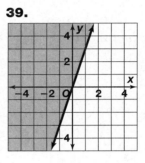

$y \geq 3x$

41.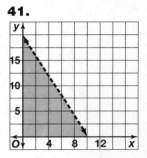

$10x + 5y < 100$

43. B   **45a.** $y > -6$; $x < 2$ **b.** $y \leq x - 1$; $y > -2x - 4$

MIXED REVIEW

47.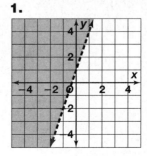

$(3, 5)$

49.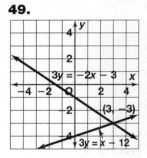

$(3, -3)$

51. $1\frac{1}{5}$ **53.** $\frac{3}{4}$ **55.** $-\frac{7}{2}$ **57.** 6

Math Toolbox   *page 432*

1. 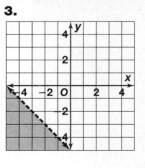   **3.**

5.

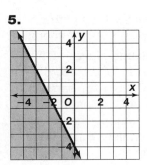

7.

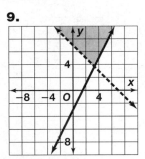

9.

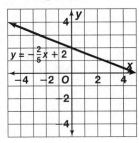

13. -2 **14.** 3   **15.** $-\frac{1}{2}$ **16.** $f(x) = -x$
17. $y = 2x + 1$ **18.** $y = -x + 4$
19. $c(t) = 14t + 2$ **20.** 30 min   **21.** about 620
calories   **22.** Positive correlation; as the time
riding increases, the calories used increases.
23a.

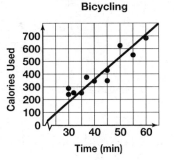

Calories Used While Bicycling

24.

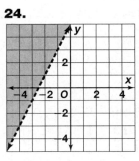

25.

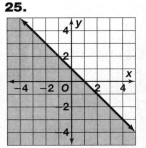

26.

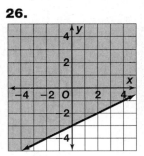

27.

28.

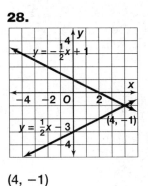

$(4, -1)$

29.

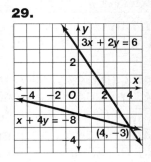

$(4, -2)$

Wrap Up   *pages 434–436*

1. Yes; there is one range value for each domain value.   **2.** Yes; there is one range value for each domain value.   **3.** No; there are domain values for which there are more than one range value.   **4.** No; one length of time (for different distances) could result in different costs.   **5.** $(-3, 2), (0, 5), (2, 7)$
6. $(-3, 12), (0, 0), (2, -8)$ **7.** $\left(-3, 1\frac{1}{2}\right), (0, 3), (2, 4)$
8. $(-3, 12), (0, 6), (2, 2)$
9. $-1, 7$ **10.** 1, 2

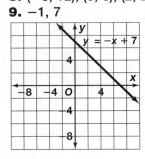

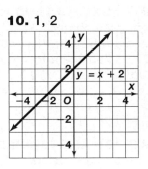

11. $-\frac{2}{5}, 2$ **12.** $\frac{3}{2}, -6$

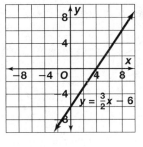

Selected Answers

30.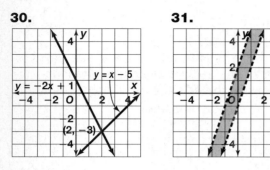

31.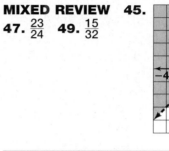

(2, −3)

32. The graphs could be parallel lines, so there is no common solution.

Cumulative Review — page 438

1. C **3.** D **5.** D **7.** D **9.** B **11.** D
13. (−3, −5), (0, −2), (2, 0) **15.** $y = 2x − 2$; 2, −2

▶CHAPTER 9

Skills You Need — page 439

1. D **2.** B **3.** A **4.** C **5.** 6 cm **6.** $\frac{1}{2}$ in.
7. 2.8 cm **8.** 7.5 ft **9.** 6 in. **10.** 2 in. **11.** 7 m
12. $3\frac{1}{2}$ ft

13–22.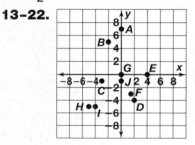

Lesson 9-1 — pages 443–447

TRY THIS 1. C, N, V **2.** $\overline{NC}$, $\overline{NV}$ **3.** $\overrightarrow{NC}$, $\overrightarrow{NV}$
4. $\overline{EH}$, $\overline{FG}$, $\overline{AE}$, $\overline{BF}$ **5.** $\overline{HG}$, $\overline{DC}$, $\overline{AB}$ **6.** $\overline{DH}$, $\overline{CG}$, $\overline{AD}$, $\overline{BC}$

CHECK UNDERSTANDING 2. $\overline{AB}$, $\overline{BC}$, $\overline{AC}$
3. $\overrightarrow{AC}$, $\overrightarrow{BC}$, $\overrightarrow{BA}$, $\overrightarrow{CA}$ **4.** $\overline{KD}$, $\overline{DG}$, $\overline{EH}$, $\overline{EF}$
5. $\overleftrightarrow{GF}$, $\overleftrightarrow{JI}$, $\overleftrightarrow{KH}$ **6.** $\overline{GJ}$, $\overline{FI}$, $\overline{KJ}$, $\overline{HI}$

PRACTICE AND PROBLEM SOLVING 7. Z, R, F; $\overline{ZR}$, $\overline{RF}$, $\overline{ZF}$; $\overrightarrow{ZR}$ (or $\overrightarrow{RF}$ or $\overrightarrow{ZF}$); $\overrightarrow{ZR}$, $\overrightarrow{RF}$, $\overrightarrow{RZ}$, $\overrightarrow{FR}$
9. A, B, C, D; $\overline{AB}$, $\overline{AD}$, $\overline{BD}$, $\overline{BC}$; $\overrightarrow{DA}$; $\overrightarrow{BA}$, $\overrightarrow{BC}$, $\overrightarrow{BD}$, $\overrightarrow{AD}$, $\overrightarrow{DA}$ **11.** R, Q, J, Y, V; $\overline{YQ}$, $\overline{QV}$, $\overline{YV}$, $\overline{RQ}$, $\overline{QJ}$, $\overline{RJ}$; $\overleftrightarrow{QJ}$, $\overrightarrow{QR}$, $\overrightarrow{QJ}$, $\overrightarrow{JR}$, $\overrightarrow{RJ}$
13. N•————•S **15.** •————•→ K E

---

17. •————•———→ O N

23. Parallel; they are in the same plane and do not intersect.
25. Skew; they are not in the same plane. **27.** $\overline{RS}$, $\overline{QP}$, $\overleftrightarrow{LK}$ **29a.** infinitely many **b.** one **33.** 6 + 5x + 4x + 1 = 12x + 1; 6, 10, 9, 25 **35.** sometimes
37. always **39.** sometimes **41.** $\overline{AB}$ is the segment from A to B. AB is a number, the length of $\overline{AB}$. **43a.** intersecting **b.** parallel **c.** parallel
d. intersecting **e.** intersecting

MIXED REVIEW 45.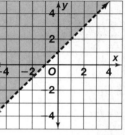
47. $\frac{23}{24}$ **49.** $\frac{15}{32}$

Math Toolbox — page 448

1. **3.** **5.**
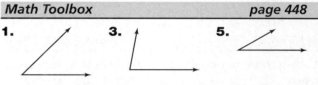

7. 90°, right **9.** 120°, obtuse

Lesson 9-2 — pages 450–453

TRY THIS 1. 160°, 20°, 160° **2.** $\angle 1 \cong \angle 5$, $\angle 4 \cong \angle 8$, $\angle 2 \cong \angle 6$, $\angle 3 \cong \angle 7$; $\angle 4 \cong \angle 6$, $\angle 3 \cong \angle 5$

CHECK UNDERSTANDING 1. 180°
2. complementary **3.** $\angle 3$ is vertical to $\angle 1$. $\angle 2$ is adjacent to $\angle 1$. $m\angle 1 = 40°$ **4.** $\angle 3$ is vertical to $\angle 1$. $\angle 2$ is adjacent to $\angle 1$. $m\angle 1 = 110°$ **5.** $\angle KPL$ is vertical to $\angle 1$. $\angle JPI$ and $\angle HPM$ are adjacent to $\angle 1$. $m\angle 1 = 34°$ **6.** $\angle 1$ and $\angle 5$, $\angle 2$ and $\angle 6$, $\angle 3$ and $\angle 7$, $\angle 4$ and $\angle 8$. **7.** $\angle 2$ and $\angle 8$, $\angle 3$ and $\angle 5$
8. $\angle 6$, $\angle 2$, $\angle 4$

PRACTICE AND PROBLEM SOLVING 9a. $3x = x + 30$, $x = 15$ **b.** 45° **c.** 135° **11.** $m\angle 1 = 80°$, $m\angle 2 = 100°$, $m\angle 3 = 80°$ **13.** $m\angle 1 = 60°$, $m\angle 2 = 60°$ **15.** $m\angle 1 = 55°$, $m\angle 2 = 125°$

MIXED REVIEW 19. •————•→ A B

21. •————•→ D C **23.** 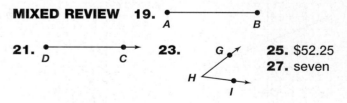 **25.** $52.25
27. seven

Lesson 9-3   pages 454–458

TRY THIS   1. scalene right triangle   **2.** isosceles obtuse triangle   **3.** scalene obtuse triangle
4. rectangles and squares   **5.** $P = 5x$; 80 cm

CHECK UNDERSTANDING   4. 23.1 cm   **5.** 108 yd
6. 20.4 cm   **7.**   **8.**

rhombus

PRACTICE AND PROBLEM SOLVING
9. equilateral acute triangle   **11.** isosceles right triangle   **13.** $P = 4x$; 50 in.   **15.** $P = 5x$; $8\frac{1}{3}$ yd
17. trapezoid, equilateral triangle, rectangle
19.   **21.** trapezoid   **23.** parallelogram, rhombus, square, rectangle

25. parallelogram, rectangle, rhombus, square, trapezoid   **27.** If the congruent sides are 10 cm long, the perimeter is 10 + 10 + 12, or 32 cm. If the congruent sides are 12 cm long, the perimeter is 12 + 12 + 10, or 34 cm.

MIXED REVIEW
29.   **31.** 10   **33.** 8
120°/60°
60°/120°
120°/60°
60°/120°

Math Toolbox   page 459

1. 360°   **3.** 1,080°   **5.** $s = 180(n - 2)$

Lesson 9-4   pages 460–463

READ   1. a polygon with 8 sides
2. a line segment that connects two non-consecutive vertices

PLAN   3. 5   **4.** 4

SOLVE

D	3
E	2
F	1
G	0
H	0
Total	20

CHECK UNDERSTANDING   1. 4 mi   **2.** Jim   **3.** 4

PRACTICE AND PROBLEM SOLVING   5. 8
7. $\frac{1}{4}$ **11.** the dog   **13.** 28, 36, 45; each increase is one greater than the increase before it.   **15.** 5 cm

MIXED REVIEW   17. scalene right triangle
19. scalene obtuse triangle   **21.** $\frac{7}{50}$, 14%
23. $\frac{11}{100}$, 11%   **25.** $\frac{1}{8}$, 12.5%

Lesson 9-5   pages 464–468

TRY THIS   3. $\overline{AB} \cong \overline{DE}$, $\overline{BC} \cong \overline{EC}$, $\overline{AC} \cong \overline{DC}$, $\angle A \cong \angle D$, $\angle B \cong \angle E$, $\angle BCA \cong \angle ECD$, $AC = 50$ m
4. $\overline{FJ} \cong \overline{FG}$, $\overline{FI} \cong \overline{FH}$, $\overline{JI} \cong \overline{GH}$, $\triangle JFI \cong \triangle GFH$ by SSS

CHECK UNDERSTANDING   1. $\overline{AB} \cong \overline{XY}$, $\overline{BC} \cong \overline{YZ}$, $\overline{AC} \cong \overline{XZ}$, $\angle A \cong \angle X$, $\angle B \cong \angle Y$, $\angle C \cong \angle Z$
2. $\overline{AB} \cong \overline{KH}$, $\overline{BC} \cong \overline{HG}$, $\angle B \cong \angle H$, $\triangle ABC \cong \triangle KHG$ by SAS   **3.** $\overline{BC} \cong \overline{EC}$, $\overline{AC} \cong \overline{DC}$, $\angle BCA \cong \angle ECD$, $\triangle ABC \cong \triangle DEC$ by SAS   **4.** $\overline{OM} \cong \overline{RP}$, $\overline{ON} \cong \overline{RQ}$, $\overline{NM} \cong \overline{QP}$, $\triangle ONM \cong \triangle RQP$ by SSS

PRACTICE AND PROBLEM SOLVING   5. $\angle D$
7. $\angle F$ **9.** $m\angle E$ or 90°   **11.** $\overline{DF}$ **13.** $\overline{ED}$ **15.** DF or 5mm   **17.** $\triangle FED$ **19.** $\angle D \cong \angle R$, $\angle DCE \cong \angle RCA$, $\overline{CD} \cong \overline{CR}$, $\triangle ACR \cong \triangle ECD$ by ASA
21. $\overline{RT} \cong \overline{WU}$, $\overline{RS} \cong \overline{WV}$, $\overline{TS} \cong \overline{UV}$, $\triangle RST \cong \triangle WVU$ by SSS   **23.** $\overline{AC} \cong \overline{CA}$, $\overline{AB} \cong \overline{CD}$, $\overline{BC} \cong \overline{DA}$, $\triangle ABC \cong \triangle CDA$ by SSS   **25.** Congruent by SAS. $\angle D \cong \angle K$, so $x = 53°$. Because the sum of the angle measures in a triangle is 180°, $y = 37°$.
27. Incorrect; $\angle R$ does not correspond with $\angle U$.
29. Correct; these are corresponding sides.
31. Correct; these are corresponding angles.
33. 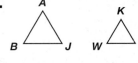 No; $\triangle ABJ$ and $\triangle KWR$ are both equiangular but the sides are not congruent.

35. $\triangle AEB$, $\triangle CDH$, $\triangle MIL$, and $\triangle KJF$ appear to be congruent. $\triangle BDE$, $\triangle HID$, $\triangle LJI$, and $\triangle FEJ$ appear to be congruent. $\triangle CDB$, $\triangle MIH$, $\triangle JKL$, $\triangle AEF$, $\triangle DEG$, $\triangle IDG$, $\triangle IJG$, and $\triangle EJG$ appear to be congruent.

MIXED REVIEW   37. $\frac{3}{8}, \frac{1}{2}, \frac{2}{3}, \frac{5}{6}$ **39.** $\frac{1}{7}, \frac{1}{6}, \frac{1}{5}, \frac{1}{4}$
41. $0.15x = 12$, 80   **43.** 14 students

CHECKPOINT 1   1. ray   **2.** line   **3.** point
4. angle   **5a.** $6x + 16 + 2x + 12 = 180$, $x = 19$
b. 50°   **c.** 130°   **d.** 130°   **6.**   **7.** C

Lesson 9-6   pages 470–473

TRY THIS   **6.** about 628 mi   **7.** about 188.4 mm
8. about $8\frac{4}{5}$ in.

9. Blood Types in The U.S. Population

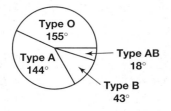

10. Student Jobs at Western High School

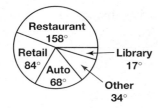

CHECK UNDERSTANDING   **1.** *A, C, D, E, B*
2. about 21.98 cm   **3.** about 314 in.   **4.** about
$29\frac{1}{3}$ m   **5.** about 0.314 m   **6.** about 113.04 in.
7. about 6.28 mi   **8.** 126°   **9.** 180°   **10.** 108°
11. 4°

PRACTICE AND PROBLEM SOLVING
13. 144.44 yd   **15.** 19.782 cm   **17.** $1\frac{4}{7}$ m
19. 3,300   **21.** How Students Travel to School
23. A

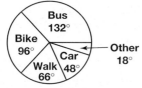

MIXED REVIEW   **25.** $\overline{AD} \cong \overline{CD}$, $\overline{BD} \cong \overline{BD}$,
$\angle ADB \cong \angle CDB$, $\triangle ADB \cong \triangle CDB$ by SAS
27. $\overline{KL} \cong \overline{FE}$, $\overline{KM} \cong \overline{FD}$, $\overline{LM} \cong \overline{ED}$, $\triangle KLM \cong$
$\triangle FED$ by SSS   **29.** No; 1 is paired with more than
one second element.   **31.** 256 times

Lesson 9-7   pages 474–478

TRY THIS

1.

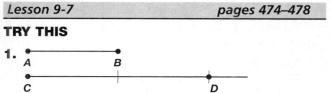

2.

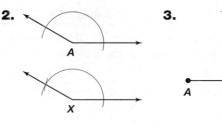

3.

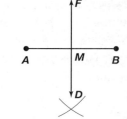

4.

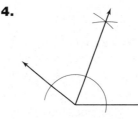

CHECK UNDERSTANDING

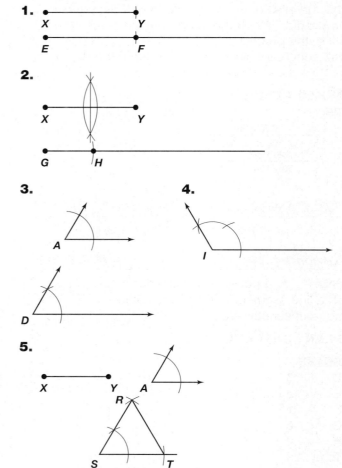

PRACTICE AND PROBLEM SOLVING

7.

9. 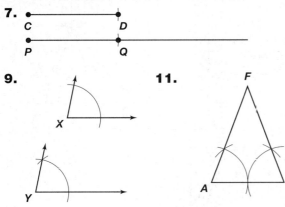 **11.**

13.

15. 110°
17. ∠CDB, ∠BDE

19a.

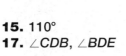

MIXED REVIEW   **21.** 43°   **23.** 18°   **25.** $60
27. 5 and 20

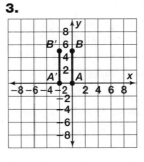
3.

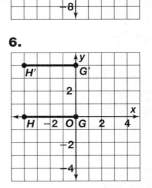
4.

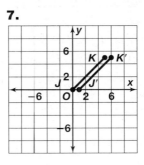
5.

6.

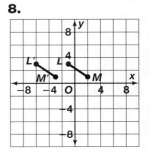
7.

8.

9. $(x, y) \rightarrow (x - 6, y)$ **10.** $(x, y) \rightarrow (x, y + 4)$
11. $(x, y) \rightarrow (x + 4, y - 3)$

PRACTICE AND PROBLEM SOLVING

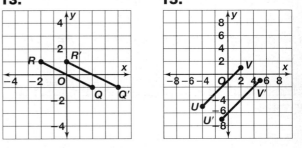
13.   **15.**

17. 5, 7   **19.** $(x, y) \rightarrow (x + 11, y - 2)$ **21.** $(x, y) \rightarrow$
$(x + 3, y + 4)$ **23.** $(x, y) \rightarrow (x + 3, y + 2)$
25. $(x, y) \rightarrow (x + 6, y + 1)$ **27.** $(x, y) \rightarrow (x - 4, y + 1)$
1)   **29.** $(x, y) \rightarrow (x - 6, y - 2)$ **31.** (0, 10)
33. The student subtracted x-coordinates, which
gives the horizontal translation. The student should
have answered *2 units right*.   **35.** D

Lesson 9-8   *pages 479–483*

TRY THIS

1.
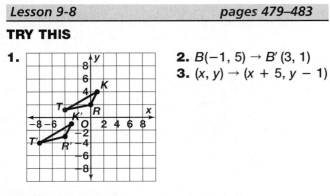

2. $B(-1, 5) \rightarrow B'(3, 1)$
3. $(x, y) \rightarrow (x + 5, y - 1)$

CHECK UNDERSTANDING   **1.** vertical
2. horizontal

Selected Answers

MIXED REVIEW

37.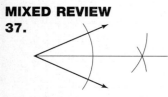

39. $\frac{4}{11}$ **41.** Amanda had salad, Adam had chicken, and Antoine had tofu.

CHECKPOINT 2 1. A is chicken, B is fish, and C is vegetarian. **2.** The central angle for A is 180°, B is 126°, and C is 54°.

3.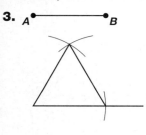

4.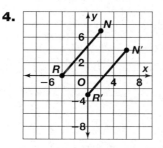

Math Toolbox   page 484

1. $\begin{bmatrix} -5 & -3 & -1 \\ -5 & -1 & -3 \end{bmatrix} + \begin{bmatrix} 6 & 6 & 6 \\ 6 & 6 & 6 \end{bmatrix} = \begin{bmatrix} 1 & 3 & 5 \\ 1 & 5 & 3 \end{bmatrix}$

The vertices of the image are $T'(1, 1)$, $R'(3, 5)$ and $I'(5, 3)$.

3. $\begin{bmatrix} 4 & 7 & 5 \\ 4 & 4 & 0 \end{bmatrix} + \begin{bmatrix} -9 & -9 & -9 \\ -4 & -4 & -4 \end{bmatrix} =$

$\begin{bmatrix} -5 & -2 & -4 \\ 0 & 0 & -4 \end{bmatrix}$ The vertices of the image are

$N'(-5, 0)$, $G'(-2, 0)$ and $L'(-4, -4)$.

5a. $\begin{bmatrix} -1 & -1 & -1 \\ -4 & -4 & -4 \end{bmatrix}$

b. $\begin{bmatrix} 2 & 3 & 3 \\ 2 & 5 & 0 \end{bmatrix} + \begin{bmatrix} -1 & -1 & -1 \\ -4 & -4 & -4 \end{bmatrix} = \begin{bmatrix} 1 & 2 & 2 \\ -2 & 1 & -4 \end{bmatrix}$

The vertices of the image are $A'(1, -2)$, $B'(2, 1)$, and $C'(2, -4)$.

Lesson 9-9   pages 485–488

TRY THIS

1. 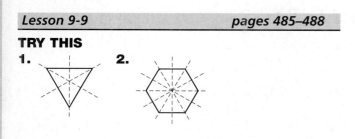   **2.**

3.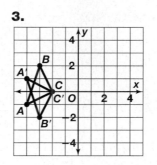

4.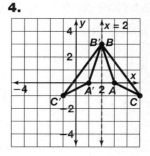

5.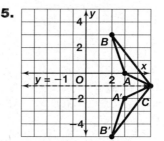

CHECK UNDERSTANDING

1. 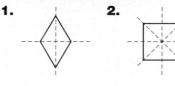   **2.**   **3.**

4. 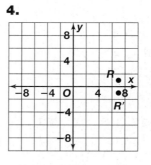   **5.**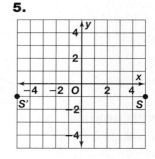

6. 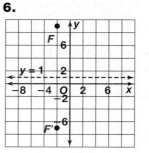   **7.**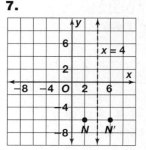

8.

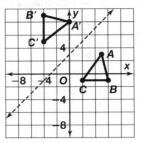

9.

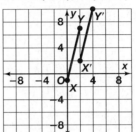

e. $A'(0, 8)$, $B'(-4, 9)$, $C'(-4, 5)$

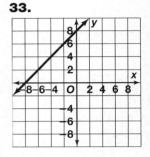

PRACTICE AND PROBLEM SOLVING

11.

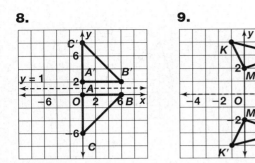

13.

15.

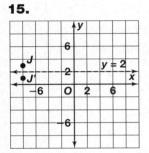

17.

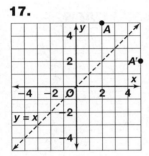

19. $W'(-1, 5)$, $X'(0, 4)$, $Y'(-5, 4)$

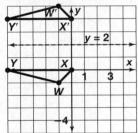

21. No; a figure and its reflection are always congruent. **23.** $(-1, 11)$
25. always **27.** always

29a. and **b.**

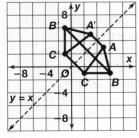

c. They are perpendicular.
d. perpendicular, right

MIXED REVIEW

31. $X'(2, 2)$, $Y'(4, 10)$

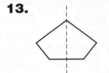

33.

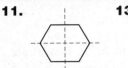

35. 15

Standardized Test Prep   page 489

1. D   **3.** C   **5.** C   **7.** B   **9.** D
11. $X'(3, 1)$, $Y'(2, -2)$, $Z'(4, 2)$

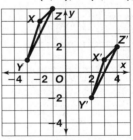

13. If I drive $66.\overline{6}$ miles, $19 + 66.\overline{6}(.15) = 29$, so for driving that distance the two companies charge the same. For a greater distance, Company A charges more.   **14.** 9

Lesson 9-10   pages 491–493

TRY THIS

1.

2. no   **3.** yes, 180°
4. yes, 180°

Selected Answers   **813**

CHECK UNDERSTANDING
1. 90°
2. 270° **3.** 180°
4.

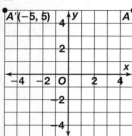

5.

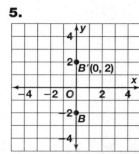

6.

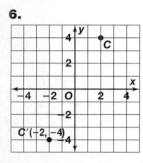

7.

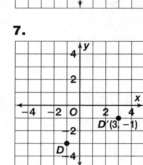

8. yes, 90° **9.** yes, 60° **10.** yes, 60° **11.** no

PRACTICE AND PROBLEM SOLVING
13a.

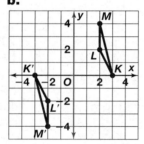

b.

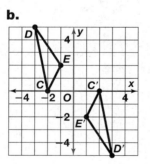

15a.

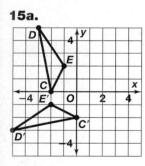

b.

17a.

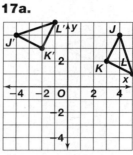

b.

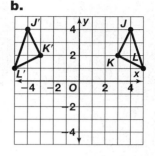

$J'(-4, 4), K'(-2, 3),$
$L'(-1, 5)$
19. yes, 72° **21.** yes, 90° **23.** yes, 120°
25. yes, 72° **27.** yes; yes; yes; yes, if it is
isosceles **29.** No; the reflection of (2, 5) across
the *y*-axis is (−2, 5). A 180° rotation image of (2, 5)
is (−2, −5).

MIXED REVIEW
31.

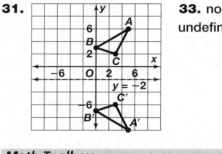

33. no slope or
undefined **35.** $\frac{1}{2}$

Math Toolbox **page 494**

1.

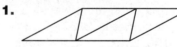

3. Will not
tessellate.

Wrap Up **pages 496–498**

1. $\angle RPD, \angle DPL, \angle RPL$ **2.** $\overrightarrow{PR}, \overrightarrow{PD}, \overrightarrow{PL}$ **3.** $\overline{RP},$
$\overline{PD}, \overline{PL}, \overline{RL}$ **4.** R, P, D, L **5.** $\overleftrightarrow{RL}$ **6.** $\angle 3, \angle 5, \angle 7$
8. $\angle 1$ and $\angle 5$, $\angle 2$ and $\angle 6$, $\angle 3$ and $\angle 7$, $\angle 4$ and $\angle 8$
9. $\angle 4$ and $\angle 6$, $\angle 3$ and $\angle 5$ **10.** $m\angle 1 = 105°$,
$m\angle 3 = 105°, m\angle 4 = 75°, m\angle 5 = 105°, m\angle 6 = 75°,$
$m\angle 7 = 105°, m\angle 8 = 75°$ **11.** equilateral triangle
12. square **13.** isosceles acute triangle
14. trapezoid **15.** $\angle T \cong \angle P$, $\overline{ST} \cong \overline{SP}$,
$\angle RST \cong \angle QSP$, $\triangle RST \cong \triangle QSP$ by ASA
16. $\overline{DE} \cong \overline{FE}$, $\overline{CE} \cong \overline{GE}$, $\angle DEC \cong \angle FEG$,
$\triangle CDE \cong \triangle GFE$ by SAS **17.** 55 ft long, 50 ft wide
18. about 44 cm

19.
Television Programming

20.

21.

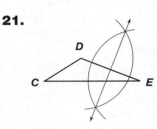

22. $A'(11, 1)$
23. $A'(-7, -2)$
24. $A'(2, 7)$
25. $A'(7, 0)$ **26.** In each case the image is congruent to the original figure. None of these transformations affect size or shape.

Cumulative Review | page 500

1. C **3.** B **5.** C **7.** A **9.** C **11.** B **13.** B
15.

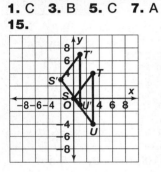

17.

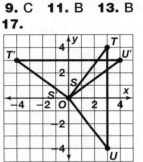

▶CHAPTER 10

Skills You Need | page 501

1. 36 m^2 **2.** 20 in.^{2} **3.** $45y^2$ cm^2 **4.** 6 **5.** $\frac{39}{2}$
6. 9 **7.** $10x$ **8.** $5x^2$ **9.** 55 **10.** 1,364 **11.** 500
12. 8 **13.** 45 **14.** 78.5 **15.** 864 **16.** 48
17. 300 **18.** 452.16 **19.** 157 yd **20.** 628 m
21. 17.27 in.

Lesson 10-1 | pages 504–508

TRY THIS **5.** 1,000 cm^2 **6.** 12 ft^2 **7.** 6 m^2
8. 24 in.^{2}

CHECK UNDERSTANDING **1.** 135 ft^2 or 15 yd^2
2. 1 m^2 or 10,000 cm^2 **3.** 1,000 cm^2 or 0.1 m^2
4. 3 yd^2 or 27 ft^2 **5.** 368 ft^2 **6.** 3 m^2 **7.** 40 ft^2
8. 100 in.^{2} **9.** 15,000 cm^2 or 1.5 m^2

PRACTICE AND PROBLEM SOLVING
11. 14 yd^2 **13.** 10 m^2 or 100,000 cm^2 **15.** 8 in.^{2}

17. 1,400 mm^2 or 14 cm^2
19.

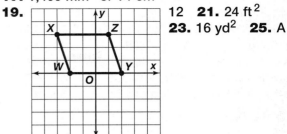

12 **21.** 24 ft^2
23. 16 yd^2 **25.** A

MIXED REVIEW
31.

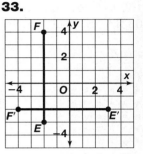

33.

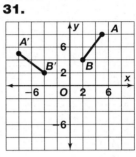

35. $\frac{4}{25}$ **37.** $\frac{44}{9}$

Lesson 10-2 | pages 509–513

TRY THIS **1.** 7.38 ft^2 **2.** 5 m^2 **3.** 24 yd^2
4. 13 ft^2 **5.** 342 mm^2

CHECK UNDERSTANDING **1.** 60 m^2 **2.** 47.6 m^2
3. 36 in.^{2} **4.** 22 cm^2 **5.** 15 in.^{2} **6.** 63 ft^2 **7.** The triangle is two times as high as the parallelogram.

PRACTICE AND PROBLEM SOLVING
9. 37.6 cm^2 **11.** 410 in.^{2} **13.** 1,800 ft^2
15. 412.5 mm^2 **17.** 34 cm^2 **19.** 108 in.^{2}
21. 50 m^2 **25.** A

MIXED REVIEW **27.** 0.5 m^2 or 5,000 cm^2
29. -2 **31.** $1.\overline{54}$ **33.** $10

Lesson 10-3 | pages 514–519

TRY THIS **7.** $2,500\pi$ in.^{2} **8.** 28.26 mi^2
9. 40.2 cm^2

CHECK UNDERSTANDING **1.** 9π ft^2; 28 ft^2
2. 25π m^2; 79 m^2 **3.** 400π cm^2; 1,256 cm^2
4. 144π ft^2; 452 ft^2 **5.** 64π m^2; 201 m^2
6. 900π cm^2; 2,826 cm^2 **7.** 89 in.^{2} **8.** 2,856 yd^2
9. The circle has a greater area. A circle with radius 2 m has an area of 4π m^2, but a square of side length 2 m only has an area of 4 m^2.

PRACTICE AND PROBLEM SOLVING
11. $\frac{1}{4}\pi$ m^2; 0.8 m^2 **13.** 30.25π mi^2; 95 mi^2

Selected Answers

15. 17.64π mm^2; 55.4 mm^2 **17.** 19 cm^2
19. 14 ft^2 **21.** 357 mi^2 **23.** A **25.** C
27a. 392.5 ft^2 **b.** 9 ft^2 **c.** 43.6 yd^2 **29a.** 3 in.
b. 226.08 in.^{2} **c.** 61.92 in.^{2} **31.** The circle with
radius 4 m has greater area because the four circles
will have a total area of 4π m^2, but the circle with
radius 4 m will have an area of 16π m^2. **33.** 4

MIXED REVIEW **35.** 5.25 yd^2 **37.** $10\frac{4}{15}$
39. $1\frac{17}{24}$ **41.** 32

CHECKPOINT 1 **1.** 300 yd^2 **2.** 2,100 cm^2
3. 150 m^2 **4.** 100π yd^2; 314 yd^2 **5.** 625π ft^2;
1,963 ft^2 **6.** $(800 + 50\pi)$ cm^2; 957 cm^2 **7.** D

Math Toolbox	page 520

1. Top   **1.** Front

1. Right Side   **3.** Top

3. Front   **3.** Right Side

Lesson 10-4	pages 521–525

TRY THIS **1.** The figure is a cylinder. **2.** The
figure is a cone. **3.** With a triangular base and
three triangular sides, you can form a triangular
pyramid. **4.** With two square bases and 4 square
lateral sides, you can form a square prism.

CHECK UNDERSTANDING **1.** The base is a
hexagon. The figure is a hexagonal pyramid.
2. The bases are pentagons. The figure is a
pentagonal prism. **3.** The bases are triangles. The
figure is a triangular prism. **4.** square prism

5. triangular pyramid **6.** triangular prism
7.
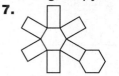

PRACTICE AND PROBLEM SOLVING **9.** The
base is a rectangle. The figure is a rectangular
pyramid. **11.** square pyramid **13.** square prism
15. B **17.** A **19.** The student forgot that there
need to be bases on both sides of the vertical
faces. **21.** triangular prism **23.** The rectangular
pyramid's net will have several triangles attached
to a rectangular base. The rectangular prism's net
will be made entirely of rectangles.
25a. rectangular prism **b.** cone **c.** sphere

MIXED REVIEW **29.** 6.25π m^2; 19.625 m^2
31. 100π m^2; 314 m^2 **33.** $y = x - 5$ **35.** 9

Math Toolbox	page 526

1. square **3.** equilateral triangle
5.   **7.**   **9.** They are
                               all circles.

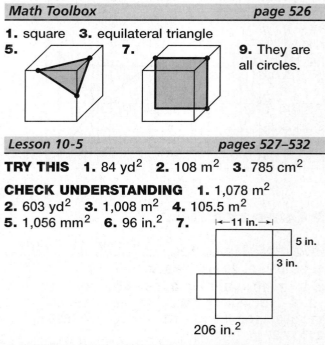

Lesson 10-5	pages 527–532

TRY THIS **1.** 84 yd^2 **2.** 108 m^2 **3.** 785 cm^2

CHECK UNDERSTANDING **1.** 1,078 m^2
2. 603 yd^2 **3.** 1,008 m^2 **4.** 105.5 m^2
5. 1,056 mm^2 **6.** 96 in.^{2} **7.**

206 in.^{2}

PRACTICE AND PROBLEM SOLVING
9. 8,777 cm^2 **11.** 408 cm^2 **13.** 175.8 cm^2
15. 518 m^2 **17.** 10,800 in.^{2} **19a.** 5 **b.** 3,600 ft^2
c. $600 **23.** Doubling the radius has a greater
effect on the surface area because the radius
appears as a higher power than the height in
determining surface area. **25.** The height of the
base is the height of the triangular base, but the
height of the prism is the shortest distance
between the two bases. **27.** 658 ft^2

MIXED REVIEW   29. pentagonal pyramid
31.   **33.**

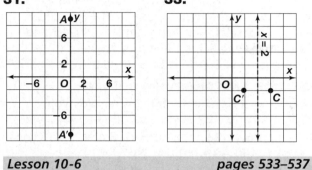

Lesson 10-6   pages 533–537

TRY THIS   1. 720 ft^2 **2.** 1,011.08 ft^2

CHECK UNDERSTANDING   1. 1,256 cm^2
2. 1,017 cm^2 **3.** 60 m^2 **4.** 104 ft^2 **5.** 105 cm^2
6. Both have the same surface area of 16π in.^{2}

PRACTICE AND PROBLEM SOLVING   7. 33 yd^2
9. 540 cm^2 **11.** 49 m^2 **13.** My friend forgot to
add the area of the second base of the prism.
15. 122 m^2 **17a.** 23,766.66 ft^2 **b.** 9.6 ft^2 **19.** B

MIXED REVIEW   21. 52 ft^2 **23.** 848 cm^2
25. 1, 2, 4, 5, 10, 20, 25, 50, 100   **27.** 1, 2, 4, 8,
16, 32   **29.** 5 months

Lesson 10-7   pages 538–541

TRY THIS   1. 216 ft^3 **2.** 1,900 ft^3

CHECK UNDERSTANDING   1. 24 cubic units
2. 54 cm^3 **3.** 480 cm^3 **4.** 628 ft^3 **5.** 603 cm^3
6. 5,341 in.^{3} **7.** 128 ft^3

PRACTICE AND PROBLEM SOLVING
9. 166.4 in.^{3} **11.** 500 m^3 **13.** 6,028.8 m^3
15. 27; $290.37   **17.** The student forgot to
square the radius when making this calculation of
the area of the base.   **19.** 27 in.^{3}

MIXED REVIEW   21. 120 cm^2 **23.** $m\angle$ 4,
$m\angle$ 5, $m\angle$ 8 = $x°$; $m\angle$ 2, $m\angle$ 3, $m\angle$ 6,
$m\angle$ 7 = $(180 - x)°$

Lesson 10-8   pages 542–545

READ   1. The goal is to find the dimensions of
the box that will hold the most popcorn.   **2.** The
size of the piece of cardboard is known as well as
the size of the square corners.

PLAN   3a. $6\frac{1}{2}$ in. by 9 in. by 1 in.   **b.** 58.5 in.^{3}

4. The length and width are decreased by 4 in. and
the height is increased by 2 in.

SOLVE   5. The box with 2-in. by 2-in. corners.
6. No, such a box would require more cardboard
than is actually available in an $8\frac{1}{2}$-in. by 11-in.
piece of cardboard.

LOOK BACK   7. 7, 4.5, 2, 63; 5, 2.5, 3, 37.5; 3,
0.5, 4, 6   **8.** Yes, $5\frac{1}{2}$ in. by 8 in. by $1\frac{1}{2}$ in.

CHECK UNDERSTANDING   1. Use several
different lengths of string and a single weight.
Record the time it takes the weight to swing back
and forth when tied to each of the strings.   **3.** The
shorter side should be the height because it will yield
a volume of 81.8 in.^{3}, and using the longer side as
the height yields a volume of only 63.3 in.^{3}

PRACTICE AND PROBLEM SOLVING
5. C   **7.** 14 cm, 7 cm

MIXED REVIEW   9. 30 cm^3 **11.** 18 ft^3
13. 15, 10, 20   **15.** about 220 cm

CHECKPOINT 2   1. square prism, 56 cm^2
2. cylinder, 207 in.^{2} **3.** square pyramid, 85 cm^2
4. cone, 377 cm^2 **5.** 78.1 cm^3 **6.** 169.6 in.^{3}
7. 0.2 m^3 or 176,625 cm^3

Standardized Test Prep   page 546

1. A   **3.** D   **5.** B   **7.** D   **9.** The area quadruples
and the circumference doubles.

11a.

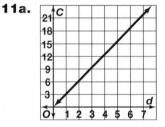

b. π **c.** The slope is
the rate of change of
C per unit d.

Lesson 10-9   pages 547–550

TRY THIS   1. 21 cm^3 **2.** 167 ft^3
3. 14,130 m^3 **4.** 179,503,333,333 mi^3

CHECK UNDERSTANDING   1. 216 in.^{3}
2. 25 yd^3 **3.** 10,467 in.^{3} **4.** 523 in.^{3} **5.** 4 yd^3
6. 87 m^3 **7.** 4

PRACTICE AND PROBLEM SOLVING
9. 819 cm^3 **11.** 65 yd^3 **13.** 7,235 cm^3
15. 447 cm^3 **17a.** 547.8 ft^2 **b.** 1,205.9 ft^3
19. 33.5 cm^3

MIXED REVIEW   21. $27a^3b^6$ **23.** $\frac{9}{64}$
25. 18   **27.** 4

Wrap Up   pages 552–554

1. 189 m² **2.** 14 cm² **3.** 6.25 yd² **4.** 17 in.²
5. 79 m² **6.** 201 mm² **7.** 57 m² **8.** 31 in.²
9. triangular prism **10.** square pyramid
11. cylinder **12.** 164 cm² **13.** 63 in.²
14. 84 cm² **15.** 251,200 m² **16.** 84 cm²
17. 85 cm² **18.** 314 ft² **19.** 27 ft² **20.** 24 in. by
18 in. **21.** Find the area of the walk and garden
and then subtract the area of the garden.
22. 384 cm³ **23.** 18 ft³ **24.** 311 in.³ **25.** 268 m³

Cumulative Review   page 556

1. B **3.** A **5.** B **7.** 28 yd² **9.** 113 in.²
11. 61 in.² **13.** 132 cm² **15.** 1,256 yd²
17. 240 m³ **19.** 117 m³ **21.** 904 yd³

►CHAPTER 11

Skills You Need   page 557

1. 100 **2.** 36 **3.** 4 **4.** 81 **5.** 121 **6.** 0.04
7. 49 **8.** 5.29 **9.** 16 **10.** 25 **11.** G **12.** K
13. H **14.** D **15.** B **16.** F **17.** N **18.** Q
19. (−5, 4) **20.** (−2, −5) **21.** (2, 1) **22.** (7, 0)
23. (−7, 1) **24.** (4, −2) **25.** (8, 6) **26.** (−6, −3)
27. 4 **28.** 4 **29.** 1 **30.** 10 **31.** 2 **32.** 60
33. 77 **34.** 26 **35.** 10 **36.** 32 **37.** 17 **38.** 8
39. 60 **40.** 63 **41.** 3 **42.** 21

Lesson 11-1   pages 560–563

TRY THIS **1.** 10 **2.** −10 **3.** 4 **4.** −4 **5.** 5
6. −8 **7.** 7 **8.** −5 **9.** irrational **10.** rational
11. rational **12.** irrational

CHECK UNDERSTANDING **1.** 2 **2.** −6 **3.** 8
4. 5 **5.** −7 **6.** 3 **7.** −2 **8.** 8 **9.** 4 **10.** −6
11. rational **12.** irrational **13.** irrational
14. rational **15.** x

PRACTICE AND PROBLEM SOLVING **17.** −3
19. 12 **21.** 3 **23.** 6 **25.** 8 **27.** −10 **29.** −7
31. rational **33.** rational **35.** irrational **37a.** In
each repetition of the pattern there is one more
zero than in the previous one. **39.** 3, −3 **41.** 10,
−10 **43.** 9 **45.** 12 **47.** 1 in. **49.** 0.000113 m³
51. 1, 2, 3, 6, 9, 18 **53.** 1, 3, 11, 33 **55.** 1, 2, 5,
10, 25, 50 **57.** yes

Lesson 11-2   pages 564–569

TRY THIS **3.** 5 ft **4.** 9 m **5.** 12.7 m **6.** 8.7 ft
7. No, $7^2 + 8^2 \neq 9^2$. **8.** No, $5^2 + 6^2 \neq 10^2$.

CHECK UNDERSTANDING **1.** 7.9 **2.** 3.5
3. 5.7 **4.** 9.7 **5.** 7.1 **6.** 2.8 **7.** $\overline{XY}$ and $\overline{XZ}$ are
legs, and $\overline{ZY}$ is the hypotenuse. **8.** $\overline{PR}$ and $\overline{QR}$
are legs, and $\overline{PQ}$ is the hypotenuse. **9.** $\overline{AB}$ and
$\overline{BC}$ are legs, and $\overline{AC}$ is the hypotenuse.
10. 15 cm **11.** 9.8 ft **12.** 8 m **13.** yes

PRACTICE AND PROBLEM SOLVING
15. 7.9 in. **17.** 13 cm **19.** 3.5 ft **21.** yes
23. no **25.** no **27.** yes **29.** 4.5 in. **31.** 4 ft
33. $\sqrt{32}$ units **35.** $\sqrt{34}$ units **37.** 6, 8, 10; yes,
36 + 64 = 100 **39.** 10, 24, 26; yes,
100 + 576 = 676

41.

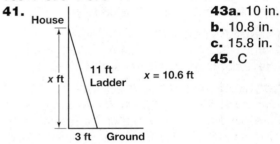

43a. 10 in.
b. 10.8 in.
c. 15.8 in.
45. C

MIXED REVIEW **47.** rational **49.** rational
51. $b^5 c^5$ **53.** $-27b^3$ **55.** $\frac{9m^2}{25}$

Math Toolbox   pages 570–571

1. The perpendicular bisector of a chord of a circle
passes through the center of the circle. **3.** 5.3
5. 11.2 **7.** 8.9 **9.** 5.7 **11.** 25.3

Lesson 11-3   pages 572–576

TRY THIS **1.** 4.1 **2.** 9.5 **3.** 17.5
4. (5, 3) **5.** (−1, 0.5)

CHECK UNDERSTANDING **1.** 5 units
2. 8.9 units **3.** 7.1 units **4.** (7, 1) **5.** (3.5, −5)
6. (−6, 9.5) **7.** No, interchanging x_1 and x_2 will
only affect the sign. Since you will square the
difference, the sign is not important.

PRACTICE AND PROBLEM SOLVING **9.** 13
11. 19.2 **13.** 24.0 **15.** (2.5, −4) **17.** (8.5, −7.5)
19. (0.65, 4.75) **21.** 17 units **23.** (12, 9)
25a. (−0.5, 3)
b. $\sqrt{[-3 - (-0.5)]^2 + (5 - 3)^2} =$
$\sqrt{(-0.5 - 2)^2 + (3 - 1)^2} =$
$\sqrt{(-2.5)^2 + 2^2} = \sqrt{(-2.5)^2 + 2^2}$

MIXED REVIEW **27.** no **29.** 9 **31.** 12.5

33.

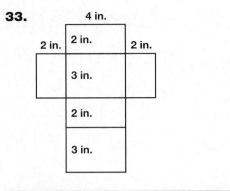

Checkpoint 1   **page 576**
---

1. -2 **3.** 5   **5.** -7 **7.** 10 ft   **9.** 25 yd
11. 9.2; $(-3, -5.5)$ **13.** 21.5; $(-9, 2.5)$

Standardized Test Prep   **page 577**
---

1. B   **3.** A   **5.** B   **7a.** $n(d) = 100d$
b.

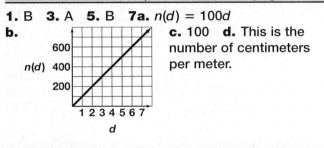

c. 100   **d.** This is the number of centimeters per meter.

Lesson 11-4   **pages 578–581**

READ   **1.** $\overline{RS} \perp \overline{RP}$, $\overline{QT} \perp \overline{RP}$, $\triangle PRS \sim \triangle PQT$, RS, RQ, and QT **2.** QP

LOOK BACK   **3.** $\overline{RQ}$ and $\overline{RP}$, $\overline{ST}$ and $\overline{SP}$
4. It forces you to draw the entire $40 + x$ side to complete the larger triangle.

CHECK UNDERSTANDING   **1.** $\frac{90}{x} = \frac{80}{120}$; 135 m
2. $\frac{x}{10 + x} = \frac{39}{48}$; $43\frac{1}{3}$ ft   **3.** 1.2 mi

PRACTICE AND PROBLEM SOLVING

5. $\frac{x}{60} = \frac{15}{25}$; 36 yd   **7.** 10.5 yd   **9.** 13   **11.** 7:43 A.M.
13. 6.3 ft^2

MIXED REVIEW   **15.** $(3, 5)$ **17.** $(1.5, -6.5)$
19.   **21.** Keith $80, Lucy $40

Lesson 11-5   **pages 582–586**

TRY THIS   **1.** 5.9 cm   **2.** 17 m   **3.** $a \approx 6.9$ cm
$b = 8$ cm   **4.** $e = 6$ in. $f \approx 10.4$ in.

CHECK UNDERSTANDING   **1.** Neither. In a
45°-45°-90° triangle two sides are congruent. In a

30°-60°-90° triangle one leg is twice the other.
2. This is a 45°-45°-90° triangle because two sides are congruent and the hypotenuse is $\sqrt{2}$ times a leg.   **3.** This is a 30°-60°-90° triangle because one side is twice the shortest side and the hypotenuse is $\sqrt{3}$ times the shortest side.   **4.** 4.2 yd
5. $x = 6$ m, $y \approx 5.2$ m   **6.** $x \approx 18.4$ cm, $y = 13$ cm
7. No; the shorter sides are in the ratio $1:\sqrt{3}$.

PRACTICE AND PROBLEM SOLVING   **9.** 9 cm,
12.7 cm   **11.** 3.5 ft, 4 ft   **13.** 12.1 mm, 14 mm
17a. 4 in.   **b.** $2\sqrt{3}$ in.   **c.** $4\sqrt{3}$ in.^{2}
d. $24\sqrt{3}$ in.^{2}

MIXED REVIEW   **19.** Yes, for each domain value there is only one range value.   **21.** 25.1 in.
23. 15.7 ft

Math Toolbox   **page 587**
---

1. $7y$ **3.** $-5x^3$ **5.** a^6 **7.** $9b^4$ **9.** $-x^2y^6$
11. $x^{11}\sqrt{x}$ **13.** $3b^5\sqrt{3b}$

Lesson 11-6   **pages 588–592**

TRY THIS   **4.** $\sin Y = \frac{12}{13}$, $\cos Y = \frac{5}{13}$, $\tan Y = \frac{12}{5}$
5. 0.1736   **6.** 0.2588   **7.** 1.3270   **8.** 0.9272
9. 14.3 ft

CHECK UNDERSTANDING   **1a.** 4   **b.** 3   **c.** 5
2. $\sin A = \frac{4}{5}$, $\cos A = \frac{3}{5}$, $\tan A = \frac{4}{3}$ **3.** 57.2900
4. 0.5   **5.** 0.9703   **6.** 0.9205   **7.** 0.5317   **8.** 1
9. $\frac{1}{2}$ **10.** $\frac{1}{2}$

PRACTICE AND PROBLEM SOLVING   **11.** $\frac{3}{5}$, $\frac{12}{15}$,
$\frac{9}{12}$ **13.** 0.9877   **15.** 0.8290   **17.** 0.3746
19. 0.9925   **21.** 1.7321   **23.** 0.2250
27. The two ratios are equal.   **29.** 4.8 m

MIXED REVIEW   **31.** 14 ft   **33.** $-6, -4, 2$
35. 21, 20, 17   **37.** $\overline{RE} \cong \overline{EA}$

CHECKPOINT 2   **1.** 45°-45°-90°   **2.** 30°-60°-90°
3. 30°-60°-90°   **4.** 0.4848   **5.** 0.5774   **6.** 0.5299
7. 0.9986   **8.** B

Math Toolbox   **page 593**
---

1. $m\angle X \approx 44°$, $m\angle Y \approx 46°$ **3.** $m\angle C \approx 36°$,
$m\angle D \approx 54°$

Selected Answers

Lesson 11-7 — pages 594–598

TRY THIS **1.** 141 m **2.** 16.1 m **3.** 22.7 m

CHECK UNDERSTANDING **1.** angle of elevation = $\angle ADC$, angle of depression = $\angle BAD$ **2.** angle of elevation = $\angle QRS$, angle of depression = $\angle PQR$ **3.** 32.2 m **4.** 95.3 ft **5.** The angle of depression is between the line of sight and the horizontal.

PRACTICE AND PROBLEM SOLVING **7.** 502.4 m **9.** 1,293.8 m **11.** 3.3 km **13.** 17.4 yd

MIXED REVIEW **15.** 0.5543 **17.** 0.8290 **19.** 2.4751 **21.** 3.61π cm^2 $\approx$ 11.3 cm^2 **23.** 20.25π in.^{2} $\approx$ 63.6 in.^{2}

Wrap Up — pages 600–602

1. 1 **2.** −4 **3.** 7 **4.** 8 **5.** −6 **6.** 2 **7.** 3 **8.** 6 **9.** 8 **10.** 10 **11.** rational **12.** rational **13.** rational **14.** irrational **15.** rational **16.** It is irrational because there is not a block of identical repeating digits. **17.** No, $1 + 9 \neq 9$ **18.** Yes, $81 + 144 = 225$ **19.** Yes, $6 + 10 = 16$ **20.** Yes, $900 + 1,600 = 2,500$ **21.** 3.6 **22.** 5 **23.** 12.6 **24.** 2.2 **25.** 9.2 **26.** 13.4 **27.** (2, 4) **28.** (3, 4) **29.** (−2, 2) **30.** (4.5, 10) **31.** (−12, −8) **32.** (2.5, −0.5) **33.** 337.5 ft **34.** $a = 6$ in., $b \approx 10.4$ in **35.** $y \approx 9.9$ m **36.** $f = 4$ ft, $c \approx 3.5$ ft **37.** 0.2756 **38.** 7.1154 **39.** 0.9063 **40.** 0.0524 **41.** 0.9986 **42.** 0.2924 **43.** 0.6947 **44.** 1 **45.** 0.9816 **46.** 0.2309 **47.** 8 ft **48.** about 99 ft

Cumulative Review — page 604

1. C **3.** B **5.** A **7.** D **9.** 0.5592 **11.** 0.1908 **13.** 0.9877 **15.** 2.1 ft

▶CHAPTER 12

Skills You Need — page 605

1. 12 **2.** 52 **3.** 101 **4.** 0.225 **5.** $\frac{1}{6}$ **6.** $\frac{1}{6}$ **7.** $\frac{1}{3}$ **8.** 0 **9.** $\frac{1}{2}$ **10.** $\frac{1}{3}$ **11.** $\frac{5}{6}$ **12.** 0 **13.** $\frac{6}{11}$ **14.** $\frac{5}{11}$ **15.** $\frac{5}{11}$ **16.** $\frac{1}{3}$ **17.** $\frac{3}{4}$ **18.** $\frac{4}{5}$ **19.** $\frac{2}{3}$ **20.** $\frac{1}{2}$ **21.** $\frac{1}{8}$ **22.** $\frac{5}{8}$ **23.** $\frac{1}{10}$ **24.** 0.5 **25.** 0.36 **26.** 0.2 **27.** 0.05 **28.** 20% **29.** 87.5% **30.** 28% **31.** 30%

Lesson 12-1 — pages 608–611

TRY THIS

4.

Number	Frequency
10	5
11	3
12	2
13	2
14	1
15	2

5. Miles to the Mall

; 7 miles

6. $0.19

CHECK UNDERSTANDING

1.

Number	Frequency
0	2
1	2
2	2
3	2
4	2

2.

Number	Frequency
1	1
2	2
3	1
4	3
5	1
6	2
7	1
8	2
9	1

3.

; 4

4.

; 5

PRACTICE AND PROBLEM SOLVING

7.

Number	Frequency
25	2
26	2
27	1
28	3
29	2
30	2

9. Test Scores

Score	Frequency
60	1
65	1
70	4
75	2
80	1
85	2
90	2
95	1
100	2

11. Heights of Plants

Height (in.)	Frequency
16	1
20	2
25	5
26	1
28	1
30	2
31	1

13.

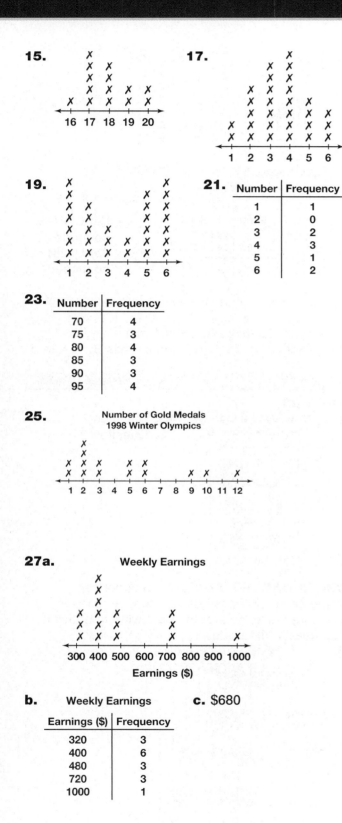

15.

17.

19.

21.

Number	Frequency
1	1
2	0
3	2
4	3
5	1
6	2

23.

Number	Frequency
70	4
75	3
80	4
85	3
90	3
95	4

25.

Number of Gold Medals
1998 Winter Olympics

27a.

Weekly Earnings

b. Weekly Earnings

Earnings ($)	Frequency
320	3
400	6
480	3
720	3
1000	1

c. $680

MIXED REVIEW **29.** 15.5, 16, 16 and 18
31. ∠R **33.** LM

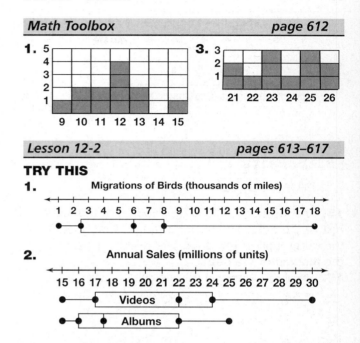

Math Toolbox *page 612*

1.

3.

Lesson 12-2 *pages 613–617*

TRY THIS

1. Migrations of Birds (thousands of miles)

2. Annual Sales (millions of units)

Videos

Albums

3. The values range from 10 to 50. The median is 22.5. At least half of the values are within 2.5 units of the median. **4.** The values range from 15 to 45. The median is 35. At least half of the values are within 10 units of the median. **5.** The women's heights have a median of 71 in. and a range of only 10 in. The men's heights have a median of 79 in. and a range of 12 in. Most of the men are taller than the tallest woman.

CHECK UNDERSTANDING

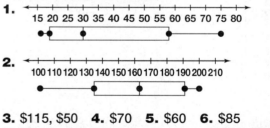

1.

2.

3. $115, $50 **4.** $70 **5.** $60 **6.** $85
7. No; the median is not in the middle of the box.

Selected Answers

PRACTICE AND PROBLEM SOLVING

9.

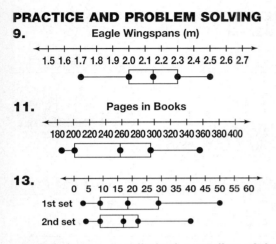

Eagle Wingspans (m)

1.5 1.6 1.7 1.8 1.9 2.0 2.1 2.2 2.3 2.4 2.5 2.6 2.7

11. Pages in Books

180 200 220 240 260 280 300 320 340 360 380 400

13.

0 5 10 15 20 25 30 35 40 45 50 55 60

1st set

2nd set

15. The lower quartile is the median of the lower half of the data; The upper quartile is the median of the upper half of the data. The middle quartile is the median of the data.

17. Maximum Speeds of Animals (mi/h)

0 10 20 30 40 50 60 70 80 90 100

19. The acreages vary considerably, from about 25 acres to about 650 acres. However, most of the parks are between 50 and 250 acres, with a median of 125 acres. **21.** The median can be determined from the line across the box. The mean and mode are not indicated, and the detailed data to calculate them is not shown in the plot.

MIXED REVIEW

23.

Number	Frequency
29	1
30	1
31	3
32	4
33	2
34	0
35	1

25. 11.4 units
27. 20.2 units

Math Toolbox   *pages 618–619*

1a. 0

b. Animal Life Spans

0	1 7
1	0 0 2 2 5 5 5
2	0 5
3	
4	1

1 | 6 means 16

c. 13.5   **d.** 15 years
e. 40 years

3.

4	1 7
5	3 7
6	0
7	5 6 9
8	1 4 5 6

7 | 5 means 75

75.5; no mode; 45

5.

0	2 8 8
1	4
2	6
3	5
4	3 3 5
5	
6	0

4 | 3 means 4.3

3.05; 0.8 and 4.3; 5.8

7.

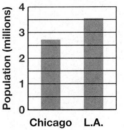

Set D		Set C
	23	6 7
8 3	24	1 2
7 1	25	0
2	26	

means 251 ←—1 | 25 | 0 —→ means 250

Set C: 241, no mode
Set D: 251, no mode

9. Class A: 63 min; Class B: 61 min
11. Class A: 74, 79, and 96 min; Class B: 99 min

Lesson 12-3   *pages 620–625*

TRY THIS

1. Populations of Chicago and Los Angeles

(bar graph: Population (millions) vertical axis 0–4; Chicago and L.A. bars)

4a. Question 3
b. Question 2

CHECK UNDERSTANDING
1. *American Ampersand*   **2.** *Fossil Week*   **3.** One tends to compare the lengths of the bars without noticing the break in the scale.

4. Magazine Circulation

Circuitry Today
American Ampersand
Whiffleball World
Fossil Week

0 2 4 6 8 10 12 14 16
Circulation (millions)

PRACTICE AND PROBLEM SOLVING **7.** nearly 2 to 1; about 1.14 to 1 **9.** It suggests that the percent is rising rapidly, by putting 1989 and 1993 very close together. **11.** That sales more than quadrupled. **13.** No. The break in the vertical axis shows that the presenter is intending to be deceptive.

MIXED REVIEW **19.**

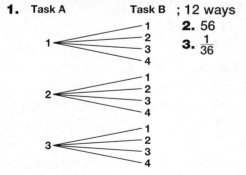

21.

23. $\frac{3}{10}$ **25.** $\frac{1}{5}$

Lesson 12-4   *pages 626–630*

TRY THIS

3.

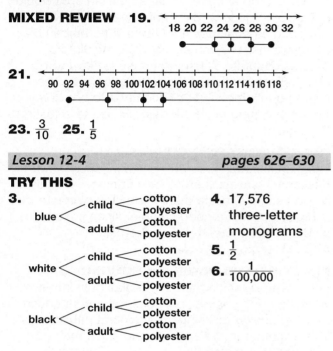

12 choices

4. 17,576 three-letter monograms

5. $\frac{1}{2}$

6. $\frac{1}{100,000}$

CHECK UNDERSTANDING

1. Task A   Task B   ; 12 ways

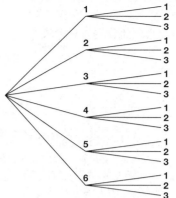

2. 56

3. $\frac{1}{36}$

PRACTICE AND PROBLEM SOLVING

5. Seymour   Clarksville   Belleview   ;18 routes

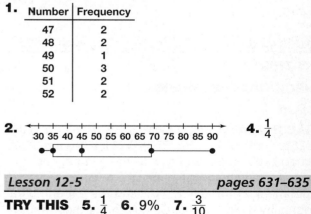

7. 440 cars **9.** HHH, HHT, HTH, THH, HTT, THT, TTH, TTT **11.** Mon. A.M., Mon. P.M., Tue. A.M., Tue. P.M., Wed. A.M., Wed. P.M., Thur. A.M., Thur. P.M., Fri. A.M., Fri. P.M. **13.** $\frac{3}{8}$ **15.** blue cardigan, blue crewneck, blue V-neck, pink cardigan, pink crewneck, pink V-neck, red cardigan, red crewneck, red V-neck, brown cardigan, brown crewneck, brown V-neck, black cardigan, black crewneck, black V-neck; 15 sweaters. **17.** $\frac{1}{3}$

MIXED REVIEW **19.**

X X X   X   range = 4
X X X X X
3 4 5 6 7

21. (0, 2) **23.** While the height of the 1990 bar is $1\frac{2}{3}$ times the height of the 1980 bar, the area is 5 times as great.

CHECKPOINT 1

1.

Number	Frequency
47	2
48	2
49	1
50	3
51	2
52	2

2.
30 35 40 45 50 55 60 65 70 75 80 85 90

4. $\frac{1}{4}$

Lesson 12-5   *pages 631–635*

TRY THIS **5.** $\frac{1}{4}$ **6.** 9% **7.** $\frac{3}{10}$

CHECK UNDERSTANDING **1.** $\frac{2}{25}$ or 8% **2.** $\frac{9}{100}$ or 9% **3.** $\frac{3}{25}$ or 12% **4.** $\frac{3}{50}$ or 6% **5.** $\frac{5}{18}$ **6.** $\frac{5}{18}$ **7.** $\frac{1}{6}$ **8.** $\frac{5}{18}$ **9.** Dependent. The total number of cards has been reduced by 1.

Selected Answers

10. Independent. The total number of cards is unchanged. **11.** Independent. The possibilities on the second roll are the same as on the first.

PRACTICE AND PROBLEM SOLVING 13. $\frac{1}{18}$
15. $\frac{1}{36}$ **17.** $\frac{1}{4}$ **19.** $\frac{2}{45}$ **21.** $\frac{2}{45}$ **23.** $\frac{4}{15}$ **27a.** $\frac{9}{56}$
b. $\frac{3}{28}$ **29.** 83%

MIXED REVIEW 31. $\frac{7}{25}, \frac{24}{25}, \frac{7}{24}$

Lesson 12-6   *pages 636–640*

TRY THIS 1. 120 **2.** 20 **3.** 60 **4.** 120 **5.** 120
6. 20 ways **7.** 28 **8.** 56 **9.** 70 **10.** 56
11. combinations **12.** permutations

CHECK UNDERSTANDING 1. 6 **2.** 120
3. 5,040 **4.** CA, CT, AT; 3 **5.** MA, MT, MH, AT, AH, TH; 6 **6.** VA, VL, VU, VE, AL, AU, AE, LU, LE, UE; 10 **7.** 12 **8.** 360 **9.** 3,024 **10.** 1,814,400
11. 6 **12.** 6 **13.** 15 **14.** 126 **15.** 45 **16.** 3

PRACTICE AND PROBLEM SOLVING 17. 24
19. 336 **21.** SIX; 1 combination **23.** 120
25. 30,240 **27.** 79,833,600 **29.** 2 **31.** 35
33a. 24 **b.** Three: pest, pets, and step **c.** $\frac{1}{8}$
37. permutations **39.** C

MIXED REVIEW 41. $\frac{1}{20}$ **43.** 33.$\overline{3}$%

Standardized Test Prep   *page 641*

1. A **3.** C **5.** D **7.** The height is the length of an altitude. The altitude divides the triangle into two right triangles, both with leg 6 and hypotenuse 12. The altitude is the other leg. $h^2 + 6^2 = 12^2$ and $h = 10.4$

Lesson 12-7   *pages 642–645*

TRY THIS 1. 52%

CHECK UNDERSTANDING 1. $\frac{1}{2}$ **2.** $\frac{1}{8}$
3. $\frac{3}{8}$ **4.** $\frac{7}{8}$

PRACTICE AND PROBLEM SOLVING 7. 16.2%
9. 25% **11.** 0% **13a.** Toss 3 coins repeatedly, perhaps 100 times, and record the results. The percent of the time that you get 3 heads is the experimental probability. **b.** Find the experimental probability as in part (a). Calculate the theoretical probability $\left(\frac{1}{2} \cdot \frac{1}{2} \cdot \frac{1}{2} = \frac{1}{8}\right)$. Compare the probabilities. They will not necessarily be the same. As one performs many experiments, experimental probability will approach theoretical.

MIXED REVIEW 19. 12 **21.** 4
23. $(x, y) \rightarrow (x + 7, y + 4)$ **25.** 0.4 m³

Lesson 12-8   *pages 646–649*

TRY THIS 1. Not a good sample, because these students would be most interested in racing bikes.
2. Not a good sample, because this sample would not include teens who do not rent videos. **3.** This is a good sample, because there is no built-in bias for or against any cereal. **4.** 200 calculators
5. Less accurate. A larger sample is likely to be more representative of the population. **6.** The entire population might be too large to be surveyed. Also, the testing might be destructive, as in testing flash bulbs.

CHECK UNDERSTANDING 1. Not a good sample, since tall students are more likely to be basketball players than other students. **2.** This is a good sample, since there is no bias built into the sample. **3.** Not a good sample, since it excludes students not interested in basketball.
4. 5,760 eggs

PRACTICE AND PROBLEM SOLVING 5. A good sample, since there is no bias built into it.
7. Not a good sample, because restaurant critics may be looking for things the general public pays little attention to. **11.** Write and solve the equation that states that the ratio of defective chips to the 250 chips in the sample is equal to the ratio of defective chips to the 50,000 chips produced.

MIXED REVIEW 13. $\frac{9}{26}$ **15.** $\frac{5}{26}$
17. 576 π cm²; 1,809 cm²
19. 2,500 π mi²; 7,850 mi²

CHECKPOINT 2 1. D **2a.** 380 outcomes
b. 190 committees **3a.** $\frac{2}{15}$ **b.** 3 **c.** No. The player will have off days, and lucky days, and may improve with experience. **4.** 9,444 premium oranges

---

Lesson 12-9   *pages 650–653*

READ 1. $\frac{4}{5}$

PLAN 3. one or two spins **4.** Many—perhaps 100

SOLVE 5a. 69% **b.** 15% **c.** 84%

PRACTICE AND PROBLEM SOLVING 5. $67.50
7. 3 yd × 9 yd **11.** Yes. Since circumference equals πd, $d = \frac{3 \text{ in.}}{\pi} \approx \frac{3 \text{ in.}}{3.14}$, which is less than 1 in.

Math Toolbox page 654

1. 10%; 0 **3.** Let an even digit represent being stopped by a red light. Look for groups with 2 or more even digits.

Wrap Up pages 656–658

1.

Number	Frequency
9	1
10	3
11	3
12	4
13	1

2.

Number	Frequency
45	1
46	3
47	2
48	3
49	2
50	1

3.

; 5

4.

; 5

5.

6.

7. Because the vertical axis is short, the bars appear to be nearly the same height. **9a.** 15 **b.** $\frac{4}{15}$ **10.** $\frac{2}{25}$ **11.** $\frac{1}{20}$ **12.** permutation, since order is important; 120 ways **13.** combination, since order does not matter; 220 groups **14.** $\frac{9}{20}$ **15.** $\frac{1}{2}$ **17.** Not a good sample, because it includes students not in the skating population. **18.** Not a good sample, because it includes students not in the skating population. **19.** A good sample. These people are all in the skating population, and there is not built-in bias.

Cumulative Review page 660

1. B **3.** B **5.** A

7.

9a. $\frac{1}{4}$

11. This is not a good sample, since it excludes men, who are part of the total population.

►CHAPTER 13

Skills You Need page 661

1. −10, −4, 2 **2.** 6, 0, −6 **3.** −10, −2, 6 **4.** −1, 0, 1 **5.** −6$\frac{1}{5}$, −5, −3$\frac{4}{5}$ **6.** 10, 6, 2 **7.** −7$\frac{1}{2}$, −8, −8$\frac{1}{2}$ **8.** 5$\frac{1}{2}$, 6, 6$\frac{1}{2}$ **9.** 5, −1, −7 **10.** 40 **11.** 11 **12.** 208 **13.** 28 **14.** 17 **15.** 25 **16.** 21 **17.** 0.64 **18.** −32 **19.** 2 **20.** 7 **21.** 11a − 4 **22.** 5 **23.** 4 − g **24.** 10t + 5s **25.** 7b + 4d **26.** −45c **27.** 7v + 21 **28.** 3d − 12 **29.** 15x + 5 **30.** 15t − 30 **31.** 3u − 24 **32.** 9p + 72 **33.** 8y + 28 **34.** −12d + 4 **35.** 50 − 30s **36.** −21 + 6w **37.** 6h + 54 **38.** 27 − 6b

Lesson 13-1 pages 664–668

TRY THIS **2.** 5 **3.** −3 **4.** 7, 3, −1; start with 23 and add −4 repeatedly. **5.** −$\frac{2}{3}$, $\frac{2}{3}$, 2; start with −6 and add 1$\frac{1}{3}$ repeatedly. **6.** The common ratio is 3. 162, 486, 1,458; start with 2 and multiply by 3 repeatedly. **7.** The common ratio is $\frac{1}{2}$. 0.25, 0.125, 0.0625; start with 4 and multiply by $\frac{1}{2}$ repeatedly. **8.** geometric; 243, 729, 2,187 **9.** neither; 34, 45, 58 **10.** geometric; −12, 12, −12 **11.** arithmetic; 650, 800, 950

CHECK UNDERSTANDING **1.** −1 **2.** 7 **3.** $\frac{1}{2}$ **4.** −6 **5.** 2 **6.** 2 **7.** $\frac{1}{5}$ **8.** 5 **9.** 256, 1,024, 4,096; start with 1 and multiply by 4 repeatedly. **10.** −9, −6, −3; start with −21 and add 3 repeatedly. **11.** 7.3, 7.5, 7.7; start with 6.5 and add 0.2 repeatedly.

PRACTICE AND PROBLEM SOLVING **13.** 6 **15.** 1.4 **17.** −3 **19.** $\frac{1}{3}$ **21.** 144, 288, 576; start with 9 and multiply by 2 repeatedly. **23.** −3, −9, −15; start with 21 and add −6 repeatedly. **25.** −40, −70, −100; start with 80 and add −30 repeatedly. **27.** 512, 2,048, 8,192; start with 2 and multiply by 4 repeatedly. **29.** arithmetic; −10, −15, −20 **31.** neither; 10, 16, 26 **33.** arithmetic; 1$\frac{5}{6}$, 2$\frac{1}{6}$, 2$\frac{1}{2}$ **35.** neither; 32, 45, 60 **37.** neither; 3, −2, −8 **39.** geometric; −$\frac{1}{80}$, −$\frac{1}{160}$, −$\frac{1}{320}$ **41a.** 12, 11, and 14 million **b.** 1.053, 1.046, 1.056 **c.** geometric **d.** 290 million **43.** 2, 0, 0, 2; neither **45.** −4, −2, 0, 2; arithmetic **47a.** $2,040, $2,080.80, $2,122.42, $2,164.86 **b.** Geometric; each balance is 1.02 times the previous balance. **49.** B

Selected Answers

MIXED REVIEW **51.** 31.4 in. **53.** $\overline{GH} \cong \overline{RP}$, $\overline{IG} \cong \overline{QR}$, $\angle G \cong \angle R$, $\triangle GHI \cong \triangle RPQ$ by SAS

Lesson 13-2 pages 669–672

TRY THIS

3.

x	$\frac{1}{2}x^2 + 3 = y$	(x, y)
−2	$\frac{1}{2}(-2)^2 + 3 = 5$	(−2, 5)
−1	$\frac{1}{2}(-1)^2 + 3 = 3\frac{1}{2}$	$(-1, 3\frac{1}{2})$
0	$\frac{1}{2}(0)^2 + 3 = 3$	(0, 3)
1	$\frac{1}{2}(1)^2 + 3 = 3\frac{1}{2}$	$(1, 3\frac{1}{2})$
2	$\frac{1}{2}(2)^2 + 3 = 5$	(2, 5)

4.

x	$-x^2 + 3 = y$	(x, y)
−2	$-(-2)^2 + 3 = -1$	(−2, −1)
−1	$-(-1)^2 + 3 = 2$	(−1, 2)
0	$-0^2 + 3 = 3$	(0, 3)
1	$-1^2 + 3 = 2$	(1, 2)
2	$-2^2 + 3 = -1$	(2, −1)

5. **6.**

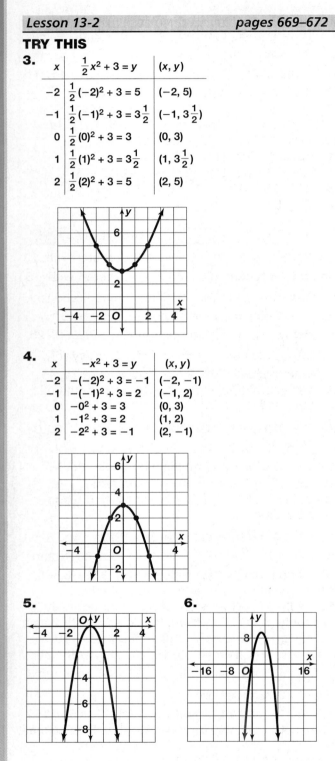

7. **8.**

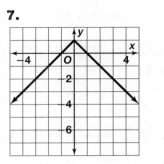
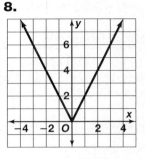

CHECK UNDERSTANDING **1.** V-shape
2. U-shape **3.** U-shape **4.** V-shape

5. **6.**

x	$x^2 + 1$	y	(x, y)
−2	$(-2)^2 + 1$	5	(−2, 5)
−1	$(-1)^2 + 1$	2	(−1, 2)
0	$0^2 + 1$	1	(0, 1)
1	$1^2 + 1$	2	(1, 2)
2	$2^2 + 1$	5	(2, 5)

x	$|x| - 2$	y	(x, y)
−2	$|-2| - 2$	0	(−2, 0)
−1	$|-1| - 2$	−1	(−1, −1)
0	$|0| - 2$	−2	(0, −2)
1	$|1| - 2$	−1	(1, −1)
2	$|2| - 2$	0	(2, 0)

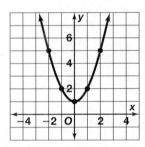
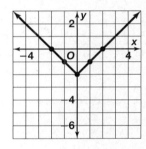

7. **8.**

x	$-x^2 + 2$	y	(x, y)
−2	$-(-2)^2 + 2$	−2	(−2, −2)
−1	$-(-1)^2 + 2$	1	(−1, 1)
0	$-0^2 + 2$	2	(0, 2)
1	$-1^2 + 2$	1	(1, 1)
2	$-2^2 + 2$	−2	(2, −2)

x	$-3|x|$	y	(x, y)
−2	$-3|-2|$	−6	(−2, −6)
−1	$-3|-1|$	−3	(−1, −3)
0	$-3|0|$	0	(0, 0)
1	$-3|1|$	−3	(1, −3)
2	$-3|2|$	−6	(2, −6)

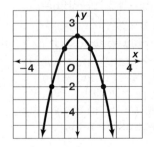
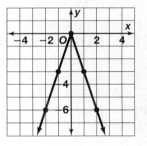

PRACTICE AND PROBLEM SOLVING
9. D **11.** A

13.

x	$x^2 + 4$	y	(x, y)
−2	$(-2)^2 + 4$	8	(−2, 8)
−1	$(-1)^2 + 4$	5	(−1, 5)
0	$0^2 + 4$	4	(0, 4)
1	$1^2 + 4$	5	(1, 5)
2	$2^2 + 4$	8	(2, 8)

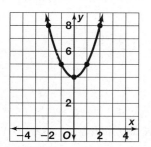

15.

x	$-x^2 + 5$	y	(x, y)
−2	$-(-2)^2 + 5$	1	(−2, 1)
−1	$-(-1)^2 + 5$	4	(−1, 4)
0	$-0^2 + 5$	5	(0, 5)
1	$-1^2 + 5$	4	(1, 4)
2	$-2^2 + 5$	1	(2, 1)

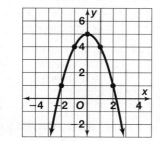

17.

x	$|x| - 4$	y	(x, y)
−2	$|-2| - 4$	−2	(−2, −2)
−1	$|-1| - 4$	−3	(−1, −3)
0	$|0| - 4$	−4	(0, −4)
1	$|1| - 4$	−3	(1, −3)
2	$|2| - 4$	−2	(2, −2)

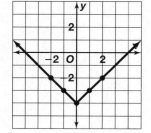

19.

x	$-2|x|$	y	(x, y)
−2	$-2|-2|$	−4	(−2, −4)
−1	$-2|-1|$	−2	(−1, −2)
0	$-2|0|$	0	(0, 0)
1	$-2|1|$	−2	(1, −2)
2	$-2|2|$	−4	(2, −4)

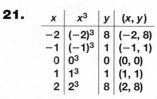

21.

x	x^3	y	(x, y)
−2	$(-2)^3$	8	(−2, 8)
−1	$(-1)^3$	1	(−1, 1)
0	0^3	0	(0, 0)
1	1^3	1	(1, 1)
2	2^3	8	(2, 8)

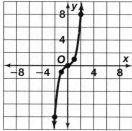

No. In the equation for a quadratic function, the input variable is squared. In this equation it is cubed. Also, the graph of a quadratic function is U-shaped. This one is not.

23a.

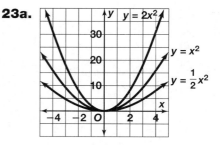

b. The greater the coefficient of x^2, the narrower the graph.

MIXED REVIEW 25. 72, 87, 102; start with 12 and add 15 repeatedly. **27.** A, B, C, $\overline{AB}$, $\overline{BC}$, $\overline{AC}$, $\overleftrightarrow{AC}$ (or $\overleftrightarrow{AB}$), $\overrightarrow{AC}$, $\overrightarrow{BC}$, $\overrightarrow{BA}$, $\overrightarrow{CA}$, $\overrightarrow{CB}$, $\overrightarrow{AB}$

29.

Price	Frequency
$6.00	1
$6.50	2
$7.00	5
$7.50	5
$8.00	3
$8.50	2

Lesson 13-3 *pages 673–676*

TRY THIS

1.

x	3^x	y	(x, y)
1	3^1	3	(1, 3)
2	3^2	9	(2, 9)
3	3^3	27	(3, 27)
4	3^4	81	(4, 81)

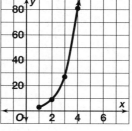

2.

x	$0.5(2)^x$	y	(x, y)
0	$0.5(2)^0$	0.5	(0, 0.5)
1	$0.5(2)^1$	1	(1, 1)
2	$0.5(2)^2$	2	(2, 2)
3	$0.5(2)^3$	4	(3, 4)
4	$0.5(2)^4$	8	(4, 8)
5	$0.5(2)^5$	16	(5, 16)

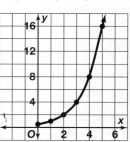

Selected Answers

3.

x	$90(\frac{1}{3})^x$	y	(x, y)
0	$90(\frac{1}{3})^0$	90	(0, 90)
1	$90(\frac{1}{3})^1$	30	(1, 30)
2	$90(\frac{1}{3})^2$	10	(2, 10)
3	$90(\frac{1}{3})^3$	$3\frac{1}{3}$	$(3, 3\frac{1}{3})$
4	$90(\frac{1}{3})^4$	$1\frac{1}{9}$	$(4, 1\frac{1}{9})$
5	$90(\frac{1}{3})^5$	$\frac{10}{27}$	$(5, \frac{10}{27})$

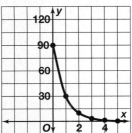

CHECK UNDERSTANDING 1. 1, 2, 8 **2.** 30, $3\frac{1}{3}$, $1\frac{1}{9}$, $\frac{10}{27}$, $\frac{10}{81}$ **3.** 2, $\frac{1}{2}$, $\frac{1}{4}$, $\frac{1}{8}$

4.

x	3^x	y	(x, y)
0	3^0	1	(0, 1)
1	3^1	3	(1, 3)
2	3^2	9	(2, 9)
3	3^3	27	(3, 27)
4	3^4	81	(4, 81)
5	3^5	243	(5, 243)

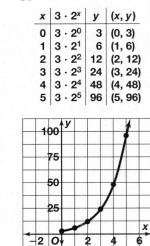

5.

x	$3 \cdot 2^x$	y	(x, y)
0	$3 \cdot 2^0$	3	(0, 3)
1	$3 \cdot 2^1$	6	(1, 6)
2	$3 \cdot 2^2$	12	(2, 12)
3	$3 \cdot 2^3$	24	(3, 24)
4	$3 \cdot 2^4$	48	(4, 48)
5	$3 \cdot 2^5$	96	(5, 96)

6.

x	$100(0.6)^x$	y	(x, y)
0	$100(0.6)^0$	100	(0, 100)
1	$100(0.6)^1$	60	(1, 60)
2	$100(0.6)^2$	36	(2, 36)
3	$100(0.6)^3$	21.6	(3, 21.6)
4	$100(0.6)^4$	13	(4, 13)
5	$100(0.6)^5$	7.8	(5, 7.8)

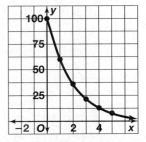

PRACTICE AND PROBLEM SOLVING 7. B
9. A **11.** no **13.** no
15.

x	$\frac{1}{2} \cdot 2^x$	y	(x, y)
0	$\frac{1}{2} \cdot 2^0$	$\frac{1}{2}$	$(0, \frac{1}{2})$
1	$\frac{1}{2} \cdot 2^1$	1	(1, 1)
2	$\frac{1}{2} \cdot 2^2$	2	(2, 2)
3	$\frac{1}{2} \cdot 2^3$	4	(3, 4)
4	$\frac{1}{2} \cdot 2^4$	8	(4, 8)

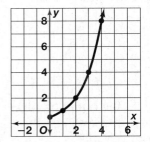

17.

x	$20(\frac{1}{2})^x$	y	(x, y)
0	$20(\frac{1}{2})^0$	20	(0, 20)
1	$20(\frac{1}{2})^1$	10	(1, 10)
2	$20(\frac{1}{2})^2$	5	(2, 5)
3	$20(\frac{1}{2})^3$	2.5	(3, 2.5)
4	$20(\frac{1}{2})^4$	1.25	(4, 1.25)

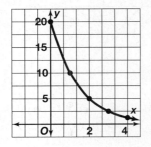

19.

x	$200(0.4)^x$	y	(x, y)
0	$200(0.4)^0$	200	(0, 200)
1	$200(0.4)^1$	80	(1, 80)
2	$200(0.4)^2$	32	(2, 32)
3	$200(0.4)^3$	12.8	(3, 12.8)
4	$200(0.4)^4$	5.12	(4, 5.12)

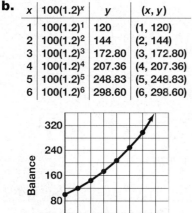

21a. growth, because 5 > 1 **b.** decay, because $\frac{1}{2}$ < 1 **c.** decay, because 0.2 < 1 **d.** growth, because 2 > 1 **23a.** 144; this is the value of the stock after 2 years.

b.

x	$100(1.2)^x$	y	(x, y)
1	$100(1.2)^1$	120	(1, 120)
2	$100(1.2)^2$	144	(2, 144)
3	$100(1.2)^3$	172.80	(3, 172.80)
4	$100(1.2)^4$	207.36	(4, 207.36)
5	$100(1.2)^5$	248.83	(5, 248.83)
6	$100(1.2)^6$	298.60	(6, 298.60)

c. Answers may vary. Sample: 3 years 9 months

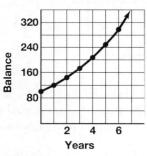

MIXED REVIEW

25.

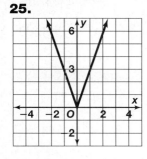

27.

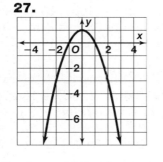

29. (−1, −1) **31.** 12

CHECKPOINT 1 **1.** 40, 25, 10; start with 100 and add −15 repeatedly. **2.** 45, 52, 59; start with 17

and add 7 repeatedly. **3.** 208, 416, 832; start with 13 and multiply by 2 repeatedly.

4.

x	$\frac{1}{4}x^2$	y	(x, y)
0	$\frac{1}{4} \cdot 0^2$	0	(0, 0)
1	$\frac{1}{4} \cdot 1^2$	$\frac{1}{4}$	$(1, \frac{1}{4})$
2	$\frac{1}{4} \cdot 2^2$	1	(2, 1)
3	$\frac{1}{4} \cdot 3^2$	$2\frac{1}{4}$	$(3, 2\frac{1}{4})$
4	$\frac{1}{4} \cdot 4^2$	4	(4, 4)

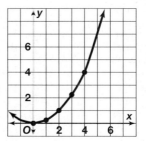

5.

x	$\frac{1}{4}|x|$	y	(x, y)
0	$\frac{1}{4} \cdot |0|$	0	(0, 0)
1	$\frac{1}{4} \cdot |1|$	$\frac{1}{4}$	$(1, \frac{1}{4})$
2	$\frac{1}{4} \cdot |2|$	$\frac{1}{2}$	$(2, \frac{1}{2})$
3	$\frac{1}{4} \cdot |3|$	$\frac{3}{4}$	$(3, \frac{3}{4})$
4	$\frac{1}{4} \cdot |4|$	1	(4, 1)

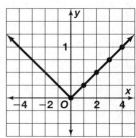

6.

x	$0.25(2)^x$	y	(x, y)
0	$0.25(2)^0$	0.25	(0, 0.25)
1	$0.25(2)^1$	0.5	(1, 0.5)
2	$0.25(2)^2$	1	(2, 1)
3	$0.25(2)^3$	2	(3, 2)
4	$0.25(2)^4$	4	(4, 4)

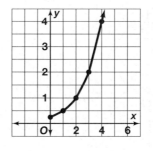

7.

x	$0.5(3)^x$	y	(x, y)
0	$0.5(3)^0$	0.5	(0, 0.5)
1	$0.5(3)^1$	1.5	(1, 1.5)
2	$0.5(3)^2$	4.5	(2, 4.5)
3	$0.5(3)^3$	13.5	(3, 13.5)
4	$0.5(3)^4$	40.5	(4, 40.5)

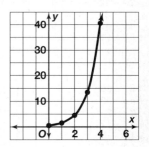

8. C

Math Toolbox   page 677

1.

x	y
−5	10
−4	8
−3	6
−2	4
−1	2
0	0
1	2
2	4
3	6
4	8
5	10

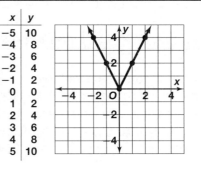

Selected Answers

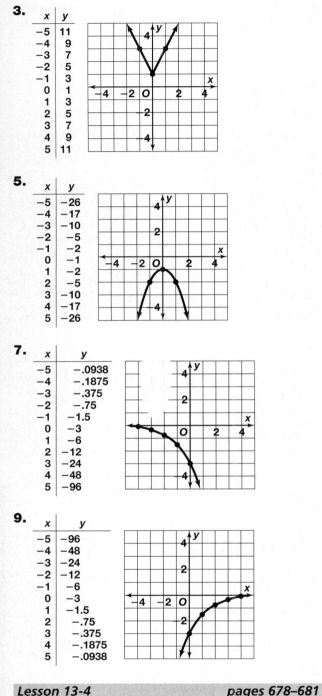

3.

x	y
−5	11
−4	9
−3	7
−2	5
−1	3
0	1
1	3
2	5
3	7
4	9
5	11

5.

x	y
−5	−26
−4	−17
−3	−10
−2	−5
−1	−2
0	−1
1	−2
2	−5
3	−10
4	−17
5	−26

7.

x	y
−5	−.0938
−4	−.1875
−3	−.375
−2	−.75
−1	−1.5
0	−3
1	−6
2	−12
3	−24
4	−48
5	−96

9.

x	y
−5	−96
−4	−48
−3	−24
−2	−12
−1	−6
0	−3
1	−1.5
2	−.75
3	−.375
4	−.1875
5	−.0938

Lesson 13-4 pages 678–681

TRY THIS

1. No; the denominator contains a variable.
2. Yes; it is the product of the variable m and the real number $\frac{1}{6}$. **3.** Yes; it is a real number. **4.** No; it is a sum. **5.** monomial **6.** binomial **7.** binomial **8.** trinomial **9.** −50 **10.** 13 **11.** 13 **12.** 264 ft

---

CHECK UNDERSTANDING 1. No; it is a sum.
2. Yes; it is a product of the real number 18 and the variables a and b. **3.** No; the denominator contains a variable. **4.** Yes; it is a real number.
5. No; a variable has an exponent that is not a whole number. **6.** Yes; it is a product of the real number 0.82 and the variable k. **7.** binomial
8. trinomial **9.** trinomial **10.** monomial **11.** 14
12. −18 **13.** 37 **14.** 16

PRACTICE AND PROBLEM SOLVING 17. Yes; it is a product of the real number −0.3 and the variable y. **19.** Yes; it is a real number. **21.** No; it is a sum. **23.** monomial **25.** binomial
27. binomial **29.** binomial **31.** −4 **33.** 13
35. 4 **37.** 0 **39.** The term $\frac{1}{x}$ contains a variable in the denominator. **41.** The expression is a quotient with a variable in the denominator.
43. binomial **45.** 170

MIXED REVIEW

47.

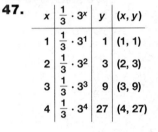 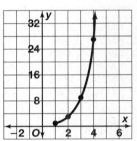

x	$\frac{1}{3} \cdot 3^x$	y	(x, y)
1	$\frac{1}{3} \cdot 3^1$	1	(1, 1)
2	$\frac{1}{3} \cdot 3^2$	3	(2, 3)
3	$\frac{1}{3} \cdot 3^3$	9	(3, 9)
4	$\frac{1}{3} \cdot 3^4$	27	(4, 27)

49. $4m + 5$ **51.** $3a + 10b - 2$

Math Toolbox pages 682–683

1. binomial of degree 1 **3.** trinomial of degree 2
5. binomial of degree 4 **7.** monomial of degree 5
9. $5a + 8$ **11.** $4c^2 + 2c - 7$
13. $b^3 + 2b^2 - b - 2$ **15.** $4x^5 + 4x^4 + 2x^3 + x^2$
17. $6a^3 - 5a^2 + 9a - 5$ **19.** $5a^2 + 5a + 6$
21. $-2p^2 + 10p$ **23.** $x^2 + 2x + 8$
25. $5m^3 + 8m^2 + 11m + 14$ **27.** $-y^2 - 6y - 11$
29. $18x^2 + 26x + 6$

Lesson 13-5 pages 684–688

TRY THIS 1. $9d^2 + 10d$ **2.** $4x^2 + 3x + 17$
3. $7x + 4y$ **4.** $9a^2 - 2a - 4$ **5.** $6g^2 - 2g - 1$
6. $-2t^2 + 3t + 9$ **7.** $2a^2 - 5a$ **8.** $9z^2 + 14z - 2$
9. $-2w^2 + 8v + 11$

CHECK UNDERSTANDING

1. $(2x^2 + x + 2) + (x^2 + 4) = 3x^2 + x + 6$
2. $(x^2 + 2x - 4) + (x^2 + 2x + 2) = 2x^2 + 4x - 2$
3. $2x^2 + 4x + 7$ **4.** $4x^2 + 6x + 3$ **5.** $2a + 9b$
6. $9x^2 + x + 5$ **7.** $3x + 8$ **8.** $-18a^2 - 2a$

PRACTICE AND PROBLEM SOLVING

9. $-x + 5$ **11.** $x^4 + 10x^3 - 4x - 11$
13. $2x^3 + 5x^2 + x + 4$ **15.** $8x + 2y$
17. $-3x^2 + x + 7$ **19.** $15a^2b + 2ab^2$
21. $x^2 + x$ **23.** $10j - 3k + 3m$ **25.** $4y - 15$
27. commutative and associative properties; distributive property; simplify   **29.** $3x + 3x + 3x + 3x = 12x$ **31.** $(m^2 + 1) + (3m - 1) + 2m = m^2 + 5m$
33. $(c + 1) + c + (3c - 1) + c + 4c + 2c = 12c$
37a. $(3x^3 + 9) - (x^3 - 3) = 2x^3 + 12$ **b.** 28 in.^{3}
c. With $x = 2$, the original volume is 33 in.^{3}, so its side is less than 4 in. It will fit into the box.
39. $4x + 1$ **41.** $2m^2 + 2m$ **43.** $2x^2$

MIXED REVIEW   45. -15 **47.** 3
49. 12 in.^{2} **51.** 4.5 cm^2

Lesson 13-6   pages 689–692

TRY THIS   1. $3x^2 + 12x$ **2.** $2x^2 - 3x$
3. $x^3 + 2x^2 + 4x$ **4.** $4a^5 - 6a^4 + 6a^2$
5. $x(2x + 1)$ **6.** $2b(b^2 + 3b - 6)$

CHECK UNDERSTANDING   1. $3x^2 + 3x$
2. $x^2 + 5x$ **3.** $2x^2 + 6x$ **4.** $6x^2 + 2x$
5. $3x^2 + 15x$ **6.** $-8x^2 + 12x$ **7.** $-15x^3 + 10x^2$
8. $5x^3 + x^2 - 4x$ **9.** $3a^3 + 6a^2 + 3a$
10. $6b^3 - 3b^2 + 12b$ **11.** $d^2(3d^2 + 1)$
12. $5x^2(2x^4 - x^2 + 2)$ **13.** $4y(y^2 - 2y - 3)$
14. $3b(-3b - 1)$

PRACTICE AND PROBLEM SOLVING

15. $2x^2 + 12x$ **17.** $6x^2 - 2x$ **19.** $2x^2 + 8x$
21. $3y^2 + 21y$ **23.** $5x^2 + 15x$ **25.** $12y^2 - 3y$
27. $2x^2 - 5x$ **29.** $-16y^2 - 24y$ **31.** $60x^3 + 24x^2$
33. $6y^4 - 12y^3 - 2y^2$ **35.** $4x^5 + 4x^4 - 4x^3$
37. $-14a^3 - 42a^2 + 56a$ **39.** $-6x^3y^2 - 3x^2y^2 - 3xy^3 + 9xy$ **41.** $4a^2 + a$ **43.** $7x(x - 2)$
45. $7(2a^2 + a - 1)$ **47.** $5z(z - 4)$
49. $4x^2(-x^3 - x^2 + 2)$ **51.** $4a(3a^2 - 4a - 1)$
53. $a(2a + b)$ **57.** $w(4w - 5) = 4w^2 - 5w$
59. $\frac{1}{2}b\left(\frac{1}{3}b - 3\right) = \frac{1}{6}b^2 - \frac{3}{2}b$

MIXED REVIEW   61. $-9x^2 - 5x + 13$
63.

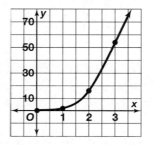

1. C   **3.** D
5b. about 160 ft
  c. 3.5 sec

7.   **9.**

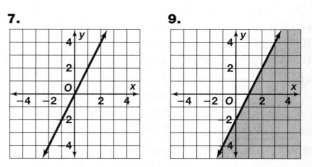

11. It is a positive correlation.
13.

x	$2x^3$	y	(x, y)
0	$2 \cdot 0^3$	0	(0, 0)
1	$2 \cdot 1^3$	2	(1, 2)
2	$2 \cdot 2^3$	16	(2, 16)
3	$2 \cdot 3^3$	54	(3, 54)

Lesson 13-7   pages 694–697

TRY THIS   1. $x^2 + 5x + 6$ **2.** $y^2 + 5y + 4$
3. $x^2 - 3x - 10$ **4.** $2m^2 + 7m + 6$

CHECK UNDERSTANDING   1. $x^2 + 3x + 2$
2. $x^2 + 4x + 4$ **3.** $x^2 + 4x + 3$ **4.** $x^2 + 7x + 12$
5. $x^2 + 9x + 20$ **6.** $x^2 + 12x + 27$ **7.** $x^2 + x - 2$
8. $c^2 + 16c + 63$ **9.** $x^2 - 2x - 15$
10. $a^2 - 6a + 8$ **11.** $x^2 + 10x + 25$
12. $b^2 - 36$ **13.** The student neglected to distribute the 5 to the -3. The third line should read $x^2 - 3x + 5x - 15$.

PRACTICE AND PROBLEM SOLVING

15. $10c^2 + 26c + 12$ **17.** $x^2 + 9x + 18$
19. $m^2 + 7m + 6$ **21.** $x^2 + x - 6$
23. $2x^2 + 9x + 4$ **25.** $x^2 + 10x + 16$
27. $m^2 - 11m + 24$ **29.** $6c^2 - 10c - 4$
31. $2x^2 + 40x + 72$ **33.** $y^2 - 1; y^2 - 4; y^2 - 25$.
The product is a binomial consisting of the square of the first term minus the square of the second term.   **35.** $(w^2 + 8w + 15)$ cm^2

MIXED REVIEW   37. $7a^2 + 35ab + 14ac$
39. $-32m^5 + 8m^3p + 16m^2p^4$
41. Combinations, since the order of the colors is not important. There are 56 possible choices.

CHECKPOINT 2   1. monomial   **2.** binomial
3. monomial   **4.** trinomial   **5.** -8 **6.** 8   **7.** 10
8. 9   **9.** $7a + 4b$ **10.** $2x^2 + 7x + 5$
11. $10p^2q + 16p^2q^2 + 4pq$ **12.** $g^2 + 10g + 24$
13. $-18m^2 - 6m^3p - 30mp$

Math Toolbox	page 698

1. $(x + 1)^2$ **3.** $(x + 2)(x + 5)$ **5.** $(x + 2)^2$
7. $(x + 8)(x + 1)$ **9.** $(2x + 5)(x + 2)$ **11a.** 5 and 6
b. $(x + 5)(x + 6)$

Lesson 13-8	pages 699–702

READ   1. the length of the tail   **2.** The tail is 12 ft plus twice the length of the kite. Together, the two lengths total 21 ft.

LOOK BACK   3a. $18 = 12 + 2 \cdot 3$ **b.** $18 + 3 = 21$

CHECK UNDERSTANDING
1a. 4:30 P.M.   **b.** 180 mi   **2.** 40 rounds   **3.** 30 ft

PRACTICE AND PROBLEM SOLVING   5. 7.5 ft
7. 51 people   **9a.** 31.8 cm^2 **b.** 25 cm^2 **c.** the circle   **11a.** the clerk   **b.** after 5 years   **13.** $24
15. 7

MIXED REVIEW   17. $2d^2 + 9d + 10$ **19.** GO, GA, GT, OA, OT, AT; 6   **21.** HY, HE, HN, HA, YE, YN, YA, EN, EA, NA; 10

Wrap Up	pages 704–706

1. 17, 21, 25; start with 1 and add 4 repeatedly.
2. $-3.75, -1.875, -0.9375$; start with -60 and multiply by $\frac{1}{2}$ repeatedly.   **3.** 128, 135, 142; start with 100 and add 7 repeatedly.   **4.** $-20, -25, -30$; start with 0 and add -5 repeatedly.   **5.** $-18, -29, -40$; start with 26 and add -11 repeatedly.
6. 62.5, 312.5, 1,562.5; start with $\frac{1}{10}$ and multiply by 5 repeatedly.   **7.** arithmetic; 25, 29, 33

---

8. geometric; $-\frac{1}{2}, -\frac{1}{4}, -\frac{1}{8}$ **9.** arithmetic; 7, 8, 9
10. arithmetic; 22, 33, 44   **11.** neither; 30, 3, 40
12. geometric; $\frac{2}{25}, \frac{4}{25}, \frac{8}{25}$

14.

x	$\frac{1}{2}x^2$	y	(x, y)
-2	$\frac{1}{2} \cdot (-2)^2$	2	$(-2, 2)$
-1	$\frac{1}{2} \cdot (-1)^2$	$\frac{1}{2}$	$(-1, \frac{1}{2})$
0	$\frac{1}{2} \cdot (0)^2$	0	$(0, 0)$
1	$\frac{1}{2} \cdot (1)^2$	$\frac{1}{2}$	$(1, \frac{1}{2})$
2	$\frac{1}{2} \cdot (2)^2$	2	$(2, 2)$

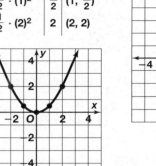

15.

x	$2|x|$	y	(x, y)
-2	$2|-2|$	4	$(-2, 4)$
-1	$2|-1|$	2	$(-1, 2)$
0	$2|0|$	0	$(0, 0)$
1	$2|1|$	2	$(1, 2)$
2	$2|2|$	4	$(2, 4)$

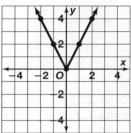

16.

x	$|x| + 1$	y	(x, y)
-2	$|-2| + 1$	3	$(-2, 3)$
-1	$|-1| + 1$	2	$(-1, 2)$
0	$|0| + 1$	1	$(0, 1)$
1	$|1| + 1$	2	$(1, 2)$
2	$|2| + 1$	3	$(2, 3)$

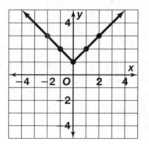

17.

x	$x^2 + 5$	y	(x, y)
-2	$(-2)^2 + 5$	9	$(-2, 9)$
-1	$(-1)^2 + 5$	6	$(-1, 6)$
0	$0^2 + 5$	5	$(0, 5)$
1	$1^2 + 5$	6	$(1, 6)$
2	$2^2 + 5$	9	$(2, 9)$

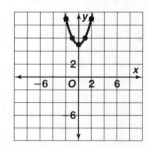

18.

x	$-\lvert x\rvert$	y	(x, y)
-2	$-\lvert -2\rvert$	-2	$(-2, -2)$
-1	$-\lvert -1\rvert$	-1	$(-1, -1)$
0	$-\lvert 0\rvert$	0	$(0, 0)$
1	$-\lvert 1\rvert$	-1	$(1, -1)$
2	$-\lvert 2\rvert$	-2	$(2, -2)$

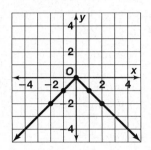

19.

x	$\frac{1}{2}\lvert x\rvert$	y	(x, y)
-2	$\frac{1}{2}\lvert -2\rvert$	1	$(-2, 1)$
-1	$\frac{1}{2}\lvert -1\rvert$	$\frac{1}{2}$	$(-1, \frac{1}{2})$
0	$\frac{1}{2}\lvert 0\rvert$	0	$(0, 0)$
1	$\frac{1}{2}\lvert 1\rvert$	$\frac{1}{2}$	$(1, \frac{1}{2})$
2	$\frac{1}{2}\lvert 2\rvert$	1	$(2, 1)$

22.

x	$\left(\frac{1}{4}\right)^x$	y	(x, y)
0	$\left(\frac{1}{4}\right)^0$	1	$(0, 1)$
1	$\left(\frac{1}{4}\right)^1$	$\frac{1}{4}$	$(1, \frac{1}{4})$
2	$\left(\frac{1}{4}\right)^2$	$\frac{1}{16}$	$(2, \frac{1}{16})$
3	$\left(\frac{1}{4}\right)^3$	$\frac{1}{64}$	$(3, \frac{1}{64})$
4	$\left(\frac{1}{4}\right)^4$	$\frac{1}{256}$	$(4, \frac{1}{256})$

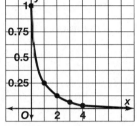

23.

x	$\frac{1}{2}\cdot 2^x$	y	(x, y)
0	$\frac{1}{2}\cdot 2^0$	$\frac{1}{2}$	$(0, \frac{1}{2})$
1	$\frac{1}{2}\cdot 2^1$	1	$(1, 1)$
2	$\frac{1}{2}\cdot 2^2$	2	$(2, 2)$
3	$\frac{1}{2}\cdot 2^3$	4	$(3, 4)$
4	$\frac{1}{2}\cdot 2^4$	8	$(4, 8)$

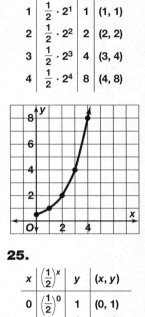

20.

x	$-x^2 - 3$	y	(x, y)
-2	$-(-2)^2 - 3$	-7	$(-2, -7)$
-1	$-(-1)^2 - 3$	-4	$(-1, -4)$
0	$-(0)^2 - 3$	-3	$(0, -3)$
1	$-(1)^2 - 3$	-4	$(1, -4)$
2	$-(2)^2 - 3$	-7	$(2, -7)$

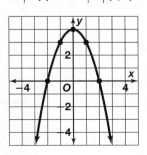

24.

x	3^x	y	(x, y)
0	3^0	1	$(0, 1)$
1	3^1	3	$(1, 3)$
2	3^2	9	$(2, 9)$
3	3^3	27	$(3, 27)$
4	3^4	81	$(4, 81)$

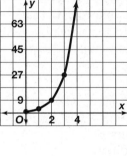

25.

x	$\left(\frac{1}{2}\right)^x$	y	(x, y)
0	$\left(\frac{1}{2}\right)^0$	1	$(0, 1)$
1	$\left(\frac{1}{2}\right)^1$	$\frac{1}{2}$	$(1, \frac{1}{2})$
2	$\left(\frac{1}{2}\right)^2$	$\frac{1}{4}$	$(2, \frac{1}{4})$
3	$\left(\frac{1}{2}\right)^3$	$\frac{1}{8}$	$(3, \frac{1}{8})$
4	$\left(\frac{1}{2}\right)^4$	$\frac{1}{16}$	$(4, \frac{1}{16})$

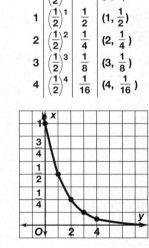

21.

x	$-x^2 + 4$	y	(x, y)
-2	$-(-2)^2 + 4$	0	$(-2, 0)$
-1	$-(-1)^2 + 4$	3	$(-1, 3)$
0	$-(0)^2 + 4$	4	$(0, 4)$
1	$-(1)^2 + 4$	3	$(1, 3)$
2	$-(2)^2 + 4$	0	$(2, 0)$

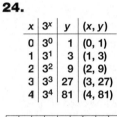

26. monomial **27.** binomial **28.** monomial
29. trinomial **30.** monomial **31.** monomial
32. binomial **33.** binomial **34.** binomial
35. trinomial **36.** 32 **37.** 7 **38.** 6 **39.** -12
40. 9 **41.** $3a^2 + 2a + 8$ **42.** $4m^2 - 2m - 12$
43. $4x^2 - 2x + 2$ **44.** $4p - 7q - 2$
45. $3w^2 + 9w - 5$ **46.** $6x + 6y$ **47.** $2a^2 + 5a$
48. $12c^2 - 28c$ **49.** $-30y^2 - 18y$
50. $3x^3 - 3x^2 - 15x$ **51.** $x^3 + 7x^2$
52. $2x^4 - 6x^3 - 12x^2$ **53.** $x^2 + 7x + 12$
54. $x^2 - 4x - 5$ **55.** $x^2 - 6x + 8$ **56.** $x(x - 1)$
57. $9(p^2 + 3)$ **58.** $3x(x^2 - 3x + 2)$

Selected Answers

59. $5(b^5 + 4b^3 - 6)$ **60.** $2x(4x^2 + x + 2)$
61. $4a(7a - b)$ **62.** $2{,}401 \text{ ft}^2$

Cumulative Review   pages 708–709

1. C **3.** D **5.** C **7.** A **9.** D **11.** D **13.** C
15. A **17.** D **19.** A **21.** A **23.** D
25. $5b + 5b + 5b + 5b = 20b$
27.

x	3^x	y	(x, y)
0	3^0	1	(0, 1)
1	3^1	3	(1, 3)
2	3^2	9	(2, 9)
3	3^3	27	(3, 27)
4	3^4	81	(4, 81)

►Extra Practice

CHAPTER 1 **1.** $x - 6$ **3.** $z + 2$ **5.** $8p$ **7.** 75
9. 9 **11.** 5 **13.** 42 **15.** 11 **17.** 10 **19.** =
21. > **23.** -7 **25.** 24 **27.** -32 **29.** -144
31. Start with -12, and add 9 to the previous term.
33, 42, 51 . . . **33.** Add the two previous terms.
21, 34, 55, . . . **35.** 120 **37.** 24 **39.** -6 **41.** 9

CHAPTER 2
1. $99 + (-99) + (-46) + 45$ Commutative
  Property of Addition
  $0 + (-46) + 45$ Additive Inverse
  -1 Identity Property of Addition
3. $18 + 12 + 13 + (-25)$ Commutative Property
  of Addition
  $18 + -25 + (12 + 13)$ Associative Property of
  Addition
  $18 + -25 + 25$ Commutative Property of
  Addition
  18
5. $2 \cdot 50 \cdot 58$ Commutative Property of
  Multiplication
  $100 \cdot 58$ Multiply from left to right.
  5,800
7. 20 **9.** 96 **11.** $3a - 6c$ **13.** $-17y + 38$
15. $-x + 2$ **17.** $\frac{-3}{-1} = 3$; true **19.** -15
21. -24 **23.** -67 **25.** 24 **27.** -15 **29.** -64

31.

33.

35.

37. $a < -4$ **39.** $x > -13$ **41.** $w \le 47$
43. $c \le -15$ **45.** $0 < r$ **47.** $a > -242$

CHAPTER 3 **7.** about 120 **9.** about 18
11. about 18
13. mean: 12.9   **15.** mean: \$27.30
  median: 12   median: \$29
  modes: 10 and 12   mode: \$30
  outlier: 19   outlier: \$15
17. 130 yd **19.** 175 mi **21.** 12.7 **23.** 93.8
25. 63.6 **27.** 40.95 **29.** 0.1 **31.** 184.3 **33.** 3
35. 32.75 **37.** 0.25 L **39.** 0.060 kg **41.** 562 cm
43. 0.564 m **45.** 0.036g **47.** 0.567 g

CHAPTER 4 **1.** 1, 2, 3, 4, 5, 6, 10, 12, 15, 20, 30,
60 **3.** 1, 2, 4, 8, 16, 32, 64 **5.** 1, 2, 3, 4, 6, 9, 12,
18, 36 **7.** 64 **9.** 76 **11.** 48 **13.** composite; 5^2
15. prime **17.** neither **19.** 10 **21.** $5x$ **23.** $\frac{3}{5}$
25. $\frac{7}{16}$ **27.** $\frac{1}{4}$ **29.** $\frac{8}{25}$ **31.** $\frac{x}{15}$ **33.** $\frac{9x}{4}$
41. $-\frac{2}{5}$ **43.** $\frac{4}{25}$ **45.** $6y^5$ **47.** x^8y **49.** $3t^{15}$
51. 1 **53.** 6.6×10^{16}

CHAPTER 5 **1.** 30 **3.** $24xy$ **5.** > **7.** =
9. 0.875 **11.** $0.\overline{27}$ **13.** -0.7 **15.** $1\frac{3}{10}$ **17.** $\frac{2}{3}$
19. $\frac{7}{20}$ **21.** 1 **23.** $-\frac{3}{8}$ **25.** $-\frac{1}{4}$ **27.** $\frac{20 + 3t}{4t}$
29. $\frac{2}{5}$ **31.** -1 **33.** $\frac{3}{11}$ **35.** $\frac{x}{7}$ **37.** -2 **39.** 5 ft
41. 64 oz **43.** $8\frac{1}{2}$ **45.** $\frac{3}{20}$ **47.** $1\frac{13}{24}$ **49.** x^8y^{12}
51. $a^5b^5c^{15}$ **53.** $8x^3y^3$ **55.** $\frac{4c^2}{d^6}$ **57.** $\frac{1}{64}$

CHAPTER 6 **1.** $\frac{1}{2}$ **3.** $\frac{1}{4}$ **5.** $58.\overline{6}$ ft/s
7. 82.5 gal/h **9.** 84 **11.** 24 **13.** 26.7 **15.** 0.4
17. 34.4 mi **19.** 18.8 mi **21.** 0; 0 to 6 **23.** $\frac{1}{3}$;
1 to 2 **25.** $\frac{2}{1}$; 2 **27.** $\frac{7}{400}$; 0.0175 **29.** 15%
31. 41.7% **33.** 34.5% **35.** 40 **37.** 36.3
39. 150% increase **41.** 12.5% decrease
43. \$45

CHAPTER 7 **1.** -1 **3.** -4 **5.** 15 **7.** -6
9. $-\frac{16}{3}$ **11.** 195 **13.** 1 **15.** 3 **17.** -5 **19.** 28
21. 3
23. $a \ge -3$

25. $x \le 7$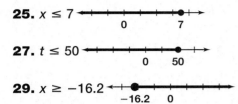

27. $t \le 50$

29. $x \ge -16.2$

31. $p = s - c$ **33.** $a = c + b$ **35.** \$36
37. 4,500   **39.** \$49,744.72   **41.** \$1,480.24
43. \$2,207.63

CHAPTER 8   1. No, 7 and 8 are both mapped
from 4.   **3.** Yes, each y term is mapped from a
different x term.   **5.** $(-3, -11)$, $(0, -2)$, $(2, 4)$
7. $(-3, 6\frac{1}{2})$, $(0, 8)$, $(2, 9)$ **9.** $(-3, -4)$, $(0, -4)$,
$(2, -4)$ **11.** $(-3, -3)$, $(0, -\frac{3}{2})$, $(2, -\frac{1}{2})$ **13.** 5, -4
15. $\frac{3}{2}$, 6   **17.** $\frac{3}{5}$, -1 **19.** 1, $-\frac{1}{2}$

21.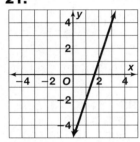

23.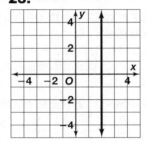

25.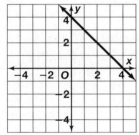

27. $y = 3x - 1$
29. $y = 5x + 4$
31. Positive correlation; as
you move to the right,
most scores increase.

33.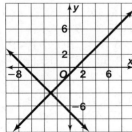

35.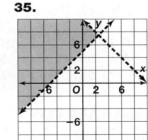

$(-3, -4)$

CHAPTER 9   1. $\overleftrightarrow{AB}$, $\overleftrightarrow{AC}$, $\overleftrightarrow{BC}$ **3.** $\overline{RS}$, $\overline{MQ}$, $\overline{MN}$,
$\overline{UR}$ **5.** $\overline{UT}$, $\overline{NP}$, $\overline{ST}$ **7.** $m\angle 7 = 67°$; $m\angle 4 = 67°$;
$m\angle 1 = 67°$; $m\angle 8 = 113°$; $m\angle 6 = 113°$; $m\angle 2 =$
$113°$; $m\angle 3 = 113°$ **9.** rectangle   **11.** A
13. about 78.5 ft   **15.** about 314 m
17.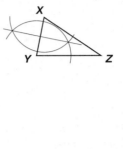

19.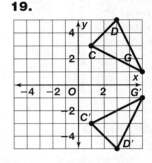

CHAPTER 10   1. 18 ft^2 or 2 yd^2 **3.** 75 m^2
5. 20 ft^2 **7.** 676π m^2, 2,122.6 m^2 **9.** 75π yd^2,
235.5 yd^2 **11.** 45 m^2, 18 m^3 **13.** 803.8 cm^2,
2,143.6 cm^3 **15.** 202 ft^2, 180 ft^3 **17.** 452.12 cm^2,
904.3 cm^3 **19.** 2,940 cm^2, 9,000 cm^3

CHAPTER 11   1. 2   **3.** -6 **5.** 5   **7.** 3   **9.** 10
11. rational   **13.** irrational   **15.** irrational
17. 7.5 yd   **19.** 5.7 units   **21.** 10.4 units
23. $\left(\frac{1}{2}, -\frac{3}{2}\right)$
25. $x = 32\sqrt{2}$ cm, $y = 32$ cm   **27.** $x = 15$ mi,
$y = 15\sqrt{2}$ mi   **29.** 11.4301   **31.** 0.0875
33. 0.4226   **35.** 1.1918

CHAPTER 12
1.

Number	Frequency
20	2
21	5
22	2
23	1

range = 3

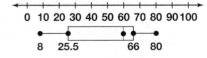

3.

Selected Answers

5.

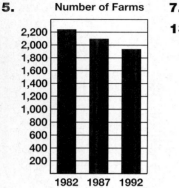
Number of Farms

7. $\frac{4}{121}$ **9.** 3 **11.** 20 **13.** 120 **15.** $\frac{1}{6}$

CHAPTER 13 1. 20, 0, −20, . . . Start with 100 and subtract 20 from the previous term. **3.** 40, 48, 56, . . . Start with 8 and add 8 to the previous term. **5.** −3,125, 15,625, −78,125, . . . Start with −5 and multiply the previous term by −5.

7.
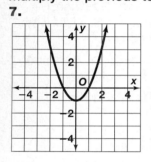

9.
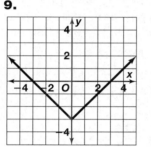

11.
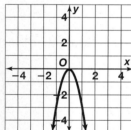

13.
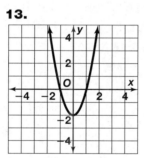

15.
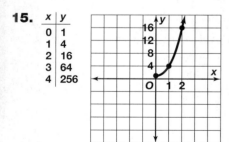

x	y
0	1
1	4
2	16
3	64
4	256

17.

x	y
0	10
1	5
2	2.5
3	1.25
4	0.625

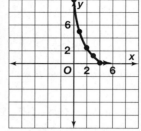

19. trinomial **21.** binomial **23.** monomial
25. trinomial **27.** $7y - 2$ **29.** $-x$
31. $6x^2 + 5x - 12$ **33.** $4b^2 + 8ab$
35. $10x^3 + 12x$ **37.** $12t^4 + 48t^3 - 18t^2$
39. $2y^2 + 16y + 24$ **41.** $4(x^2 - 3)$
43. $2(a^2b - 2a + 3b)$ **45.** $x(6y + 2 + 3xy)$

▶SKILLS HANDBOOK

COMPARING AND ORDERING WHOLE NUMBERS 1. > **3.** > **5.** < **7.** < **9.** >
11. 3,347; 3,474; 3,734; 3,747; 3,774
13. 30,256,403; 30,265,403; 32,056,403; 302,056,403

ROUNDING WHOLE NUMBERS 1. 40 **3.** 670
5. 7,030 **7.** 6,000 **9.** 44,000 **11.** 1,000
13. 6,000 **15.** 82,000 **17.** 35,000 **19.** 68,900
21. 3,407,000 **23.** 71,230,000 **25.** 400,000
27. 3,680 **29.** 69,000 **31.** 566,000
33. 1,400,000

MULTIPLYING WHOLE NUMBERS 1. 444
3. 371 **5.** 392 **7.** 1,536 **9.** 1,350 **11.** 5,712
13. 2,520 **15.** 1,862 **17.** 9,214 **19.** 492
21. 729 **23.** 2,208 **25.** 884 **27.** 4,056
29. 2,478 **31.** 1,440 **33.** 5,467

DIVIDING WHOLE NUMBERS 1. 15 R 1
3. 12 R 6 **5.** 13 R 3 **7.** 217 R 2 **9.** 25 R 6
11. 7 R 41 **13.** 7 R 27 **15.** 3 R 36 **17.** 5 R 21
19. 3 R 7 **21.** 14 R 52 **23.** 37 R 12
25. 21 R 30 **27.** 7 R 3 **29.** 11 R 3 **31.** 64 R 3
33. 50 R 4 **35.** 103 R 1 **37.** 26 R 8 **39.** 7 R 32
41. 5 R 22 **43.** 6 R 21 **45.** 3 R 52 **47.** 15 R 3
49. 22 R 12

DECIMALS AND PLACE VALUE 1. 9 hundred-thousandths **3.** 5 hundredths **5.** 4 hundred millions **7.** 0.0041 **9.** 0.000008 **11.** 0.012
13. six hundredths **15.** eleven hundred-thousandths **17.** twelve thousandths **19.** forty-two ten-thousandths

COMPARING AND ORDERING DECIMALS
1. < **3.** > **5.** < **7.** = **9.** < **11.** >
13. 0.23, 0.231, 2.31, 3.21, 23.1 **15.** 0.002, 0.02,
0.22, 0.222, 2.22 **17.** 0.007, 0.07, 0.7, 0.71, 0.72
19. 7, 7.0324, 7.3, 7.3246, 7.3264

ROUNDING **1.** 105,000 **3.** 79,528,000
5. 4,312,000 **7.** 3 **9.** 101 **11.** 82 **13.** 20.4
15. 130.0 **17.** 96.40 **19.** 4.23 **21.** 7.06
23. 1,520 **25.** 4.2 **27.** 400 **29.** 8.1 **31.** 410
33. 2.58 **35.** 19 **37.** 7,700 **39.** 980,000,000
41. 0.00377 **43.** 12.8 **45.** 21,000

ADDING AND SUBTRACTING DECIMALS
1. 3.67 **3.** 7.312 **5.** 36.127 **7.** 1.6 **9.** 13.95
11. 60.21 **13.** 34.023 **15.** 39.95 **17.** 25.73
19. 31.95 **21.** 7.045 **23.** 6.21 **25.** 7.511
27. 2.825 **29.** 3.55 **31.** 1.434 **33.** 10.37
35. 0.32 **37.** 28.22 **39.** 37.002 **41.** 12.403
43. 747.1109 **45.** 11.36 **47.** 39.101

MULTIPLYING DECIMALS **1.** 5.328 **3.** 2.15
5. 5.168 **7.** 0.38912 **9.** 1.1424 **11.** 2.07828
13. 0.48 **15.** 0.364 **17.** 6.5658 **19.** 41.16
21. 1.26 **23.** 12.15 **25.** 12.05 **27.** 4.8018
29. 18.012

ZEROS IN A PRODUCT **1.** 0.027 **3.** 0.072
5. 0.0025 **7.** 0.00248 **9.** 0.00891 **11.** 0.00165
13. 0.0376 **15.** 0.081 **17.** 0.00072 **19.** 0.0009
21. 0.04 **23.** 0.000376 **25.** 0.012 **27.** 0.092
29. 0.072 **31.** 0.01812 **33.** 0.007

DIVIDING DECIMALS BY WHOLE NUMBERS
1. 2.56 **3.** 0.776 **5.** 8.79 **7.** 0.11 **9.** 0.184
11. 2.07 **13.** 8.76 **15.** 0.0169 **17.** 0.0147
19. 0.561 **21.** 0.868 **23.** 2.551 **25.** 3.9
27. 0.025 **29.** 0.0014

**MULTIPLYING AND DIVIDING BY POWERS OF
TEN** **1.** 560 **3.** 52 **5.** 2,367 **7.** 0.0009 **9.** 8
11. 0.001803 **13.** 13,700 **15.** 0.47 **17.** 0.236
19. 0.00041 **21.** 423 **23.** 502 **25.** 27 **27.** 0.4
29. 0.065 **31.** 26 **33.** 0.0003 **35.** 15.8

DIVIDING DECIMALS BY DECIMALS **1.** 84
3. 452 **5.** 32 **7.** 31.1 **9.** 3.1 **11.** 26 **13.** 31
15. 16 **17.** 44 **19.** 2.8 **21.** 3.6 **23.** 1.24
25. 58.3 **27.** 31.4 **29.** 3.96 **31.** 0.53 **33.** 9.5
35. 1.6 **37.** 3.58 **39.** 0.243 **41.** 3.44 **43.** 1.86
45. 3.77

ZEROS IN DECIMAL DIVISION **1.** 0.046
3. 0.075 **5.** 0.0095 **7.** 0.0025 **9.** 0.085
11. 0.015 **13.** 0.0035 **15.** 0.07 **17.** 0.0021
19. 0.00015 **21.** 0.006 **23.** 0.009 **25.** 0.0035
27. 0.033

WRITING EQUIVALENT FRACTIONS **1.** 2
3. 10 **5.** 12 **7.** 24 **9.** 3 **11.** 16 **13.** 30
15. 21 **17.** $\frac{5}{6}$ **19.** $\frac{3}{4}$ **21.** $\frac{4}{5}$ **23.** $\frac{1}{2}$ **25.** $\frac{3}{7}$
27. $\frac{3}{5}$ **29.** $\frac{11}{12}$ **31.** $\frac{3}{4}$ **33.** $\frac{3}{7}$

**MIXED NUMBERS AND IMPROPER
FRACTIONS** **1.** $1\frac{2}{5}$ **3.** $3\frac{1}{4}$ **5.** $1\frac{3}{10}$ **7.** $2\frac{5}{8}$
9. $3\frac{2}{5}$ **11.** $4\frac{1}{4}$ **13.** $5\frac{2}{5}$ **15.** $3\frac{3}{4}$ **17.** $1\frac{1}{3}$ **19.** $4\frac{1}{2}$
21. $5\frac{1}{2}$ **23.** $4\frac{1}{4}$ **25.** $\frac{3}{2}$ **27.** $\frac{13}{12}$ **29.** $\frac{16}{7}$ **31.** $\frac{23}{8}$
33. $\frac{26}{5}$ **35.** $\frac{37}{4}$ **37.** $\frac{63}{8}$ **39.** $\frac{24}{7}$ **41.** $\frac{31}{10}$

**ADDING AND SUBTRACTING FRACTIONS
WITH LIKE DENOMINATORS** **1.** $1\frac{2}{5}$ **3.** $\frac{4}{7}$
5. $1\frac{1}{5}$ **7.** $\frac{3}{8}$ **9.** $\frac{3}{5}$ **11.** 1 **13.** $4\frac{2}{5}$ **15.** $1\frac{1}{3}$
17. $8\frac{1}{4}$ **19.** $11\frac{1}{2}$ **21.** 11 **23.** $4\frac{3}{5}$ **25.** $\frac{3}{4}$

MULTIPLYING AND DIVIDING FRACTIONS
1. $\frac{9}{20}$ **3.** 4 **5.** $\frac{5}{12}$ **7.** $\frac{1}{25}$ **9.** $\frac{1}{16}$ **11.** $3\frac{5}{9}$ **13.** $7\frac{1}{2}$
15. $43\frac{3}{4}$ **17.** $1\frac{3}{8}$ **19.** $\frac{7}{8}$ **21.** $1\frac{3}{8}$ **23.** $\frac{1}{81}$ **25.** 6
27. $\frac{9}{40}$ **29.** $1\frac{3}{4}$ **31.** $\frac{2}{5}$ **33.** $11\frac{3}{4}$ **35.** $3\frac{4}{7}$

WORKING WITH INTEGERS **1.** 6 **3.** 5 **5.** 3
7. 12 **9.** > **11.** < **13.** < **15.** > **17.** >
19. < **21.** > **23.** > **25.** > **27.** < **29.** >
31. < **33.** >

Index

A

Absolute value, 17–21, 57
  defined, 18, 57
  graphing and, 670–672, 705
  in equations, 91
  in inequalities, 20, 27, 28, 32, 33, 48, 49, 57
  of rational numbers, 197
  of zero, 18, 19

Absolute value function
  graphing, 670–672, 705

***Account for All Possibilities* problem solving strategy,** 190–193, 217

Acute angle, 448

Acute triangle, 454
  isosceles, 458

Addition
  Associative Property of, 64–68, 118, 684
  Commutative Property of, 64–68, 118, 684, 744
  estimating sums in, 122–125
  inverse property of, 23, 744
  of decimals, 122–125
  of fractions, 235–239, 244, 271, 273, 274
  identity property of, 65, 117, 744
  of integers, 23–28, 57
  of matrices, 484
  of mixed numbers, 236–239
  of opposites, 23
  and order of operations, 8–12, 25
  of polynomials, 684–688, 706, 707, 709
  repeated, 44, 47
  solving equations by, 61, 84–88, 103, 107, 117–118, 142–144, 155, 255–258, 272, 273
  solving inequalities by, 104–107, 142–145

Addition Property
  of Equality, 86–88, 143, 145, 744
  of Inequality, 105, 744

Additive identity, 65–68, 744

Additive inverse, 23

Adjacent angles, 449, 497

Algebra and Algebraic expressions. *See* Variable expressions

Algebra tiles, 23, 26, 29–31, 71–72, 75–76, 82–83, 173, 180, 336, 340, 355, 684, 686, 689, 694–695, 698, 706

Alternate exterior angles, 450, 452, 497

Alternate interior angles, 453

Altitude, 505, 509

Angle
  acute, 448

  adjacent, 449, 497
  alternate exterior, 453
  alternate interior, 450–452, 497
  angle-side relationships, 465–468, 497
  bisector of, 476–477, 498
  central, 470–473, 478, 489, 498
  classifying angles, 448
  classifying triangles by, 454, 457–458
  complementary, 449, 452–453
  congruent, 449, 464–465, 475, 497
  corresponding, 289, 450–452, 497
  defined, 448
  of depression, 596–598, 602
  drawing and measuring, 448
  of elevation, 594–598, 602
  naming, 448, 449–453
  obtuse, 448, 475
  of polygon, 459
  right, 448
  in right triangle, 593
  of rotation, 490–493, 498
  straight, 448
  supplementary, 449
  of triangle, 459
  vertex, 448
  vertical, 449, 497

Angle bisector
  constructing, 476–477, 498
  defined, 476

Angle-Side-Angle (ASA), 465

Applications. *See* Connections

Area
  of circle, 514–519, 525, 529, 546, 553, 563, 598, 649
  defined, 504, 552
  of irregular figures, 10, 12, 93, 264, 507, 508, 513, 516–519
  of parallelogram, 504–507, 513, 552, 697
  of rectangle, 10, 12, 69, 96, 139, 149, 167, 168, 193, 201, 241, 344, 349, 354, 365, 425, 501, 504–507, 696
  of square, 179, 266, 267, 354, 390, 501, 563
  of trapezoid, 510–513, 519, 552,
  of triangle, 509–510, 512–513, 519, 552

Arithmetic sequence, 664–668, 704–705

Assessment
  Chapter Assessment, 59, 117, 167, 219, 273, 331, 379, 437, 499, 555, 603, 659, 707
  Chapter Wrap Up, 56–58, 114–116, 164–166, 215–218, 270–272, 328–330, 376–378, 434–436, 496–498, 552–554, 600–602, 656–658, 704–706

Checkpoint, 21, 49, 77, 107, 140, 155, 189, 207, 239, 263, 299, 321, 353, 368, 408, 425, 468, 483, 519, 545, 576, 592, 630, 649, 676, 697
Cumulative Review, 60, 118, 168, 220, 274, 332, 380, 438, 500, 556, 604, 660, 708–709
Journal, 28, 54, 81, 103, 130, 197, 239, 258, 313, 339, 373, 408, 431, 458, 488, 518, 550, 586, 672, 692
Standardized Test Prep, 34, 93, 158, 202, 264, 322, 354, 415, 489, 546, 577, 641, 693
Test Prep Tip, 65, 104, 110, 128, 180, 187, 199, 233, 246, 398, 627
Writing, 7, 12, 16, 21, 27, 31, 33, 39, 48, 54, 57, 59, 73, 77, 81, 88, 92, 99, 103, 107, 112, 115, 117, 118, 126, 129, 135, 145, 149, 154, 161, 164, 167, 168, 175, 178, 183, 188, 196, 200, 206, 213, 217, 219, 233, 244, 249, 250, 258, 262, 268, 272, 273, 283, 287, 292, 299, 304, 309, 313, 321, 330, 331, 339, 344, 349, 359, 363, 364, 367, 373, 378, 379, 390, 394, 397, 401, 407, 408, 424, 430, 434, 436, 437, 446, 453, 459, 462, 463, 467, 472, 477, 482, 487, 493, 498, 499, 507, 513, 518, 524, 532, 537, 540, 554, 555, 562, 585, 591, 598, 601, 603, 616, 623, 624, 630, 634, 639, 645, 648, 652, 654, 657, 659, 667, 672, 675, 680, 697, 706, 707

Assessment exercises, types of
  Free Response, 34, 93, 158, 202, 264, 322, 354, 415, 489, 546, 577, 641, 693
  Multiple Choice, 7, 11, 12, 20, 27, 32, 34, 39, 49, 53, 68, 77, 81, 88, 93, 102, 107, 112, 115, 117, 126, 129, 134, 140, 145, 154, 158, 166, 178, 183, 188, 193, 200, 202, 207, 238, 239, 244, 248, 257, 262, 264, 287, 298, 299, 304, 309, 313, 316, 322, 339, 348, 354, 362, 373, 394, 401, 406, 408, 414, 415, 424, 429, 430, 463, 467, 468, 473, 482, 487, 489, 507, 513, 519, 523, 532, 537, 544, 546, 550, 562, 569, 577, 592, 610, 640, 641, 644, 648, 668, 671, 676, 681, 693, 697
  Open-ended, 12, 19, 20, 27, 32, 33, 34, 48, 49, 54, 73, 77, 87, 92, 93, 103, 107, 112, 125, 129, 135, 141, 145, 158, 175, 184, 188, 196, 197, 200, 202, 206, 213, 244, 249, 263, 264, 268, 292, 299, 303, 309, 321, 339, 354, 358, 373, 390, 395, 402, 412, 423, 425, 430, 437, 457, 458, 468, 477, 483, 489, 494, 499, 508, 513, 518, 524, 531, 540, 545, 555, 562, 576, 616, 625, 629, 630, 634, 640, 645, 648, 671, 677, 680, 692, 697, 705, 707

Index **839**

Index

Index

packaging, 14, 468, 529, 532, 539, 541, 544, 550
parades, 42, 182
pendulum, 544
photography, 127
population, 213, 303, 309, 317, 325, 620
postage, 239
printing, 161
probability, 326, 339, 640
profit, 309, 377
quality control, 287, 647, 648, 653
quilting, 127, 467
real estate, 311
recreation, 16, 349, 358, 531
recycling, 255, 646
sales, 143, 367, 430
sales tax, 309, 363
savings, 668
school, 92, 184, 207, 217, 226, 281, 326, 346, 363, 412, 424, 581, 681
seismology, 207
shopping, 14, 123, 167, 273, 281, 349, 427, 676
space, 317, 352
sports, 24, 27, 48, 64, 97, 117, 128, 161, 192, 224, 233, 251, 254, 304, 309, 341, 356, 366, 397, 408, 411, 462, 549, 580, 583, 591, 596, 611, 615, 617, 665
surveys, 187, 473, 607, 635, 646–649, 653, 655, 668
telephone service, 124, 347
television programming, 498
theater, 94, 402, 428, 436
transportation, 109, 253, 325, 384, 629
travel, 73, 96, 105, 137, 253, 272, 337, 356, 363, 366, 462, 701
urban planning, 10
weather, 30, 32, 43, 97, 112, 126, 239, 262, 348, 366, 391, 410, 597, 635
Consecutive integers, 341, 343, 353, 376, 379
Constant, 74–76
of variation, 396
Constructions, geometric, 474–478, 498
Conversion factors, 245–249, 282–283
Converting
decimals to fractions, 231–233, 271, 299, 463
decimals to percents, 300–304, 329, 463
fractions to decimals, 229–230, 232, 271, 293, 299
units of measure, 151–155, 246–249, 272, 282–283, 396
percents to decimals, 300–304, 329
Cooperative Learning, 8, 44, 69, 108, 122, 180, 208, 235, 240, 295, 314, 340, 355, 397, 409, 464, 469, 504, 514, 564, 588, 626, 631, 664, 669
Coordinate plane
coordinates, 50–54, 58, 381, 492, 557

defined, 50, 58
distances in, 572–576, 601
graphing, 50–54, 58, 268, 321, 373, 381, 388–390, 408, 425, 439, 447, 479, 488, 499
graphing inequalities, 426–431, 447
ordered pairs, 50–54, 58, 439, 506
origin, 50
plotting points, 50–54
polygons in, 506
quadrants on, 50–53, 58, 130
reflections in, 485–488, 499
slope-intercept form, 399–402
transformations, 479–483
translations in, 479–483, 499
x-axis, 50–54, 58
x-coordinate, 50–54, 58, 398, 415, 424, 481, 488
y-axis, 50, 52, 58, 492, 493
y-coordinate, 50, 54, 58, 398, 415, 424, 481, 488
y-intercept, 399–402, 408, 417
See also Graphing
Correlation
negative, 411–414, 425, 437
no trend, 411–414, 425, 437
positive, 411–414, 425, 437
Corresponding angles, 289, 450–452, 497
Corresponding parts, 464–468
Corresponding sides, 289
Cosine, 588–593, 598, 602
Counterexample, 37, 38, 39, 197
Counting
tree diagram for, 626–630
use multiplication, 627–630
Counting Principle, 627, 636, 657
Critical Thinking, 8, 21, 28, 67, 68, 83, 91, 102, 103, 111, 144, 145, 174, 178, 183, 196, 200, 201, 233, 244, 261, 291, 298, 302, 303, 312, 313, 373, 374, 385, 401, 402, 407, 409, 414, 431, 488, 494, 512, 518, 531, 541, 562, 575, 576, 610, 618, 621, 622, 624, 631, 676, 680, 687, 698
See also Error Analysis, Mental Math, *and* Mathematical Reasoning
Cross products
cross products property, 284–288
Cross section
of space figure, 526
trapezoidal, 511
Cube
edges of, 522–525
net of, 522–524
side length of, 179
surface area of, 527–532
volume of, 179, 268
Cubic unit, 538
Cumulative Review, 60, 118, 168, 220, 274, 332, 380, 438, 500, 556, 604, 660, 708–709

Customary system of measurement, 245–249, 272
converting to metric units, 282–283, 396
table of, 742
units in, 246–249
Cylinder
base of, 521–524, 527–532, 539–542
defined, 521, 553
height of, 527–532, 539–541
net of, 522–523
oblique, 527
right, 527
surface area of, 529–532, 553, 555
volume of, 539–541, 554

D

Data
in bar graph, 89, 99, 131, 620–625
in box-and-whisker plot, 613–617, 657
in circle graph, 470–473
choosing appropriate graph for, 98–99, 620–625
collecting, 409, 607, 635, 644, 653
comparing, 620–625
in decision making, 620–625
in double-bar graph, 93, 99
in frequency tables, 608–611
graphing, 98–99, 669
in histogram, 612
in line graph, 98, 620–621, 624–625
in line plot, 609–611
in multiple-line graph, 98
organizing and displaying, 40–41, 98–99, 323–326, 608–625
population, 213, 646
quartile, 613–617
random sample, 646
range of, 609–611
rounding of, 131–135
scale of, 620–625
scatter plot, 409–415
in stem-and-leaf plot, 618–619
in survey, 607, 635, 645, 646–649, 653, 655, 668
trends in, 411–413, 416–419
Data analysis
average. *See* Mean
making estimates, 647–649
misleading information, 620–625
problems involving, 15, 21, 39, 42, 99, 126, 130, 135, 155, 167, 189, 213, 239, 303, 309, 363, 407, 412–414, 418, 425, 431, 436, 438, 623, 624, 625, 644, 672
Data Analysis Connection
average area, 132
biology, 618
currency, 46
drive-in movies, 307
environmental management, 315
jobs, 36, 278

classifying types of, 78–81
combining like terms in, 340–341, 379
cosine ratio, 588–589, 602
defined, 78, 115
distributive property and solving,
  342–344
equivalent, 84
evaluating, 145, 166, 177
graphing, 392–395, 401, 403, 437, 488
graphing in slope-intercept form,
  399–403
graphing systems of equations,
  420–425
linear. See Linear equation
modeling, 340, 355
nonlinear, 669–676, 705
simplifying, 64–68
sine ratio, 588–589, 602
slope-intercept form, 399
solution of, 391–392
solving by adding, 61, 84–88, 103, 107,
  117–118, 143–145, 155, 255–258, 272
solving with decimals, 142–145,
  146–149, 158, 166, 221
solving by dividing, 61, 89–92, 103,
  107, 117–118, 146–149, 155, 275
solving with fractions, 255–263,
  272–273
solving with integers, 221
solving by inverse operations, 84–88,
  89–92, 255–258
solving with mixed numbers, 256–258,
  260, 272
solving with models, 82–83, 336
solving by multiplying, 61, 90–92,
  103, 117–118, 146–149, 155, 259–263,
  272, 273, 275
solving multi-step, 340–349, 353, 376,
  379
  with decimals, 347–349
  with fractions, 345–346, 348–349,
    376
  useful steps for solving, 342
  using the LCM, 346
solving percent problems with,
  310–313
solving by properties of equality,
  84–92, 142–149, 336–339, 346, 355
solving with rational numbers,
  255–263, 272–273
solving by subtracting, 84–88, 103, 107,
  117–118, 140, 142–143, 155, 255–258,
  272
solving systems of linear, 420–425, 436
solving two-step, 336–339, 353, 376, 379
substitution in, 79–81
tangent ratio, 588–589, 602
transforming, 381
with two variables, 391–395, 435, 661
with variables on both sides,
  355–359, 377
Write an Equation problem solving

strategy, 350–353, 377
writing, 80, 81, 87, 92
writing systems of, 421–425
x-intercept, 395
y-intercept, 395, 399
Equilateral triangle, 454–458
Equivalent equations, 84
Equivalent expressions, 187–188, 217
Equivalent fractions, 186–189, 217
Equivalent inequalities, 104
Equivalent ratios, 278–281
Equivalent rational numbers,
  186–189, 217
Error Analysis, 12, 15, 16, 20, 27, 73, 77,
  88, 111, 126, 145, 148, 154, 156, 179,
  188, 200, 206, 238, 248, 258, 262, 268,
  281, 287, 299, 309, 316, 339, 343, 359,
  362, 390, 394, 401, 446, 453, 467, 482,
  524, 531, 536, 541, 550, 576, 585, 597,
  617, 645, 649, 687, 696. See also
  Critical Thinking and Mathematical
  Reasoning
Estimation
  clustering, 124–126, 164
  with compatible numbers, 127–130
  with compensation, 65–68
  with decimals, 122–126, 127–130, 254
  differences, 123, 164
  of distance, 150–155
  exercises that use, 32, 122, 126, 130,
    140, 151, 153, 155, 167, 189, 238, 247,
    254, 286, 302, 312, 561–562, 576, 600,
    603, 647–649, 653
  with fractions, 234
  front-end, 123, 124, 125, 162, 207
  with mixed numbers, 234, 238
  to nearest integer, 561–562, 576, 600,
    603
  with percents, 302, 307, 312
  of products, 127, 129
  of proportions, 286
  of quotients, 128, 129
  by rounding, 32, 122–126. See also
    Rounding
  of sums, 123, 164
  See also Mental Math
Evaluate
  fraction with variable, 195
  variable expression, 13, 57
Even number, 172
Event
  certain event, 296
  complement of, 296
  defined, 295, 329
  dependent, 633–635, 657
  impossible, 296
  independent, 631–635, 657
  odds, 297–299, 329
  probability of, 295–299, 329, 624–652

random, 295
relating graph to, 384–385
simulating, 642–645, 650–652
Exercises. See Assessment
Exchange rate, 121, 135, 149, 155, 163
Experimental probability, 642–645, 649,
  650–653, 654, 658
Exponent
  defined, 176, 216
  dividing expressions containing,
    203–207, 218, 744
  finding power of a power,
    199–201, 218
  multiplying powers with the same
    base, 198–201, 218, 744
  negative exponents, 205–206, 218, 744
  order of operations with, 177, 178, 216
  ordering, 210, 212, 219
  properties of, 218, 744
  scientific notation, 208–213
  simplifying expressions with, 176–179,
    203–207, 218, 501, 557
  using, 176–179, 349
  variable as, 673–677, 705
  variable expressions with, 176–179
  zero as, 204, 206, 744
Exponential decay, 674–676, 705
Exponential growth, 673–676, 705
Expressions
  equivalent, 27, 48, 49, 61, 67, 68, 72
  modeling, 23–26, 29–32, 44
  numerical, 4–7
  ordering, 210, 212, 219
  prime factors in, 238
  simplifying, 8–12, 61, 70, 333
  variable. See Variable expressions
Extra Practice, 710–722

F

Face, of a space figure, 521–525, 527–532,
  533–537, 538–541, 547–551
Factor
  common, 181, 259
  and divisibility, 173–175
  factor tree, 181
  finding, 173, 174, 563
  greatest common, 181–187, 217
  prime factorization, 181–184, 217
Fahrenheit–Celsius formula, 366
Flip, 485–488. See also Reflection
Formulas
  area of circle, 515, 745
  area of parallelogram, 505, 745
  area of rectangle, 365, 504, 670, 745
  area of square, 266, 504, 745
  area of trapezoid, 511, 745
  area of triangle, 509, 745
  batting average, 137–140, 366
  brick laying, 368

Index

evaluating expressions, 15, 67

evaluating products, 47, 69–73, 77, 127–130

evaluating sums and differences, 26, 31, 65–68, 87, 144

fractions and, 227, 234, 238, 248

simple interest, 372

simplifying expressions, 8, 11, 67, 72, 97, 115, 178, 235–238, 243

solving equations, 87, 91, 144, 148, 152–154, 166, 257, 261, 286, 338, 358

with units of measure, 152–154, 247, 248

using properties, 65–68, 69–73, 77

using the Pythagorean theorem, 567

using trigonometric ratios, 591, 747

See also Critical Thinking *and* Mathematical Reasoning

Meter, 150–155, 742

Metric system of measurement

converting to customary units, 282–283

identifying appropriate units, 150–151, 153–154, 167

prefixes in, 151, 154

table of, 742

units in, 150–155, 742

Middle quartile, 613

Midpoint formula, 574, 601

Midpoint, 574–576, 601, 630, 676

Mile, 136, 142, 150, 158, 162, 196, 248–249, 285, 742

Milliliter, 150–155, 373, 742

Milligram, 101, 150–155, 742

Millimeter, 150–155, 742

Mixed numbers

adding, 236–238, 271

dividing, 242–244, 249, 254, 271

estimating with, 234, 238

multiplying, 241, 243, 244, 249, 271

solving equations with, 256–258, 260–262, 263, 268, 272

subtracting, 236–238, 271

writing decimals as, 231

writing in simplest form, 231, 232, 244

writing percents as, 300, 302

Mixed Review *exercises review previous topics and are in every lesson.* 7, 12, 16, 21, 28, 33, 39, 43, 49, 54, 68, 73, 77, 81, 88, 92, 97, 103, 107, 112, 126, 130, 135, 140, 145, 149, 155, 162, 175, 179, 184, 189, 193, 197, 201, 207, 213, 228, 233, 239, 244, 249, 254, 258, 263, 268, 281, 288, 293, 299, 304, 309, 313, 317, 321, 326, 339, 344, 349, 353, 359, 363, 368, 373, 390, 395, 402, 408, 414, 419, 425, 431, 447, 453, 458, 463, 468, 473, 478, 483, 488, 493, 508, 513, 519, 525, 532, 537, 541, 545, 550, 563, 569, 576, 581, 586, 592, 598, 611, 617, 625, 630, 635, 640, 645, 649, 653, 668, 672, 676, 681, 688, 692, 697, 702

Mode, 131–135, 140, 165, 167, 239, 293, 611, 618, 619

Modeling

adding and subtracting integers, 23, 24, 26, 29–31

adding and subtracting polynomials, 684–685

area, 173, 180, 689, 691

equations, 82–83, 340, 355

expressions, 7, 23–26, 29–32, 44, 69, 71

fractions, 169, 221, 235, 240

Make a Model problem solving strategy, 542–544

multiplying binomials, 694–696

multiplying integers, 71, 72

multiplying polynomials, 689, 691

nets, 522–524

number line. *See* Number line

percents, 305–309

scale models, 290–293

simplifying variable expressions, 75–76

solving multi-step equations, 355

solving two-step equations, 336

writing fractions to describe, 169, 186, 221

writing proportions to describe, 305

See also Verbal models, phrases, and descriptions

Money, 7, 19, 27, 42, 43, 46, 73, 96, 143, 268, 279–281

Monomial, 678–681, 705, 707

defined, 678, 705

multiplying polynomials by, 689–692, 706, 707

Multiple

common, 224, 270

least common, 224–228, 239, 270, 273, 346

Multiple Choice, 34, 93, 158, 202, 264, 322, 354, 415, 489, 546, 577, 641, 693

Multiplication

Associative Property of, 64–68, 114, 265, 744

of binomials, 694–697

calculator for, 214

Commutative Property of, 64–68, 114, 176, 265, 744

of decimals, 127–130, 731

estimating products, 127–130

exponents and, 198–201, 218

of fractions, 240–244, 254, 263, 271, 273, 605

Identity Property of, 65–68, 744

of integers, 44–49, 58, 254

by monomial, 689–692

by multiples of ten, 119

and order of operations, 8–12

of mixed numbers, 240–244, 254, 260

of polynomials, 689–697, 706

of powers with same base, 198–201, 218

of rational numbers, 240–241

repeated, 176–177

in scientific notation, 211–213, 218

in solving equations, 90, 91–92, 147, 259–263, 275

in solving inequalities, 109–110

symbols for, 13, 45, 743

of square roots, 582

of three or more factors, 169

Multiplication property

of equality, 90, 284

of inequality, 109

Multiplicative identity, 65–68, 744

Multiplicative inverse, 242

Multi-step equation

solving with decimals, 347–349

solving distributive property in, 342–344

solving with fractions, 345–346, 348–349, 376

N

Negative correlation, 411–414, 425, 437

Negative exponent, 205, 206, 218, 744

Negative number

graphing on number line, 17–21

Net, 522–524, 527, 530, 553

Nonlinear equation, 669–672, 705

Nonlinear function

defined, 669

exponential, 673–677, 705

graphing, 669–676, 677, 705

quadratic, 669–672, 705

Nonzero digit, 156–157

Notation

arrow, 480–482

combination, 637–640

factorial, 743

function, 404–407

permutation, 636–640

scientific, 208–213, 218, 219

See also Table of symbols

Number line

absolute value on, 18

adding integers, 24, 44

comparing fractions, 195–197, 218, 225

inequalities on, 100–102, 107, 116–118, 201, 333, 359, 360–363, 377, 379

graphing integers, 17–21

line plots, 609–611, 656

multiplying integers, 47

opposites on, 18, 197

quartiles on, 613–617

rational numbers on, 195–197, 218, 225

showing repeated addition on, 44, 47

Number patterns, 35–43

describing, 381

See also Patterns

Index

area of, 552
classifying, 454–458, 497
congruent, 497
    corresponding parts of, 464–468
in coordinate plane, 506
defined, 454, 497
diagonal, 460–463
hexagon, 456, 461
measuring angles, 459
naming, 439
octagon, 460
parallelogram. *See* Parallelogram
pentagon, 461
perimeter of, 456
quadrilateral. *See* Quadrilateral
rectangle. *See* Rectangle
regular, 456
rhombus, 455
sides of, 454–458
square. *See* Square
sum of angle measures of, 459
symmetry, 485–488
tessellation and, 494
tiling with, 494
trapezoid. *See* Trapezoid
triangle. *See* Triangle
vertices of, 487

Polygon angle sum, 459

Polynomial
adding, 684–688, 706
area model of, 689
binomial, 678–683, 694–698, 705–706
defined, 678, 705
degree of, 682–683
evaluation of, 679–680, 688
identifying, 678–680
monomial, 678–681, 705
multiplying by a monomial, 689–692
as product, 689–692, 694–697, 706
simplifying, 683
standard form, 683
subtracting, 685–687, 706
trinomial, 678–680, 705
writing, 683

Population, 99, 162, 646, 658

Positive correlation, 411–414, 425, 437

Positive number
graphing, 17, 18
See also Integers

Power
defined, 176
dividing, 203–207, 218
finding a power of a power,
    199–201, 218
multiplying with same base,
    198–201, 218
order of operations, 177
raising product to, 265–266, 272, 273
raising a quotient to, 266, 272, 273
of ten, 208
See also Exponent

Practice and Problem Solving *exercises
give students independent practice and
problem solving in every lesson.*

Precision, 63, 156–157, 158

Predictions, 36–39
based on conjectures, 36–39
scatter plots and, 416–419
trend lines, 416–419

Price, 98, 127, 279–281

Prime factorization, 180–184, 217, 224,
225, 274

Prime factors, 188
using to simplify expressions, 238

Prime notation, 479

Prime number, 180, 217

Principal, 369, 378

Prism
base of, 521–525
cube, 521–525
defined, 521, 553
edges of, 521–525
height of, 527–532
net of, 522–524
pentagonal, 523
oblique, 527
rectangular, 521–525
right, 527
surface area of, 527–528, 553
trapezoidal, 522
volume of, 538–541, 554

Probability, 295–299, 626–635, 642–658
combinations, 636–640
comparing, 643–644
counting outcomes, 295–299, 642–658
defined, 295, 329, 627, 642
dependent events, 632–633
experimental, 642–658
formulas for, 296, 627, 632, 642
independent events, 631–635
permutations, 636–640
odds, 297–299
random numbers, 654
sample space, 627–630
simulating problems, 642–645, 650–653
theoretical, 295–299, 626–635
tree diagrams in, 626–630

Problem Solving *exercises give students
independent practice in every lesson.*
Choose a Method, 10, 110, 124, 182,
    237, 319, 347, 422, 451, 535, 590,
    643, 695
Choose a Strategy, 7, 49, 77, 81, 107,
    126, 130, 135, 162, 184, 193, 197, 207,
    244, 249, 263, 281, 288, 304, 313, 349,
    359, 414, 453, 458, 483, 488, 493, 508,
    513, 525, 541, 692, 702
Different Ways to Solve a Problem,
    10, 110, 124, 182, 237, 319, 347, 422,
    451, 535, 590, 643, 695

Problem Solving Handbook. *See* Tools
for Problem Solving

Problem Solving Strategies
Account for All Possibilities, 190–193,
    217
Choose a Strategy, 7, 49, 77, 81, 107,
    126, 130, 135, 162, 184, 193, 197, 207,
    244, 249, 263, 281, 288, 304, 313, 349,
    359, 414, 453, 458, 483, 488, 493, 508,
    513, 525, 541, 692, 702
Draw a Diagram, 460–463, 498
Look for a Pattern, 40–43, 58
Make a Model, 542–545, 554
Make a Table, 323–326, 330
Simplify a Problem, 159–162, 166
Simulate a Problem, 650–653, 658
Solve by Graphing, 416–419
Try, Test, Revise, 94–97, 116, 351
Use Multiple Strategies, 699–702, 706
Work Backward, 251–254, 272
Write an Equation, 350–353, 377
Write a Proportion, 578–581, 601

Product
cross product, 284–287
estimating, 127, 129
finding, 89–92, 147–149, 169, 243
finding powers of, 265–268, 272, 273
writing polynomials as, 690–692
See also Multiplication

Projects. *See* Chapter Project

Proof
derive a formula,
    30°-60°-90° triangle, 584
    45°-45°-90° triangle, 582
    area of a circle, 515
    area of a parallelogram, 505
    area of a trapezoid, 511
    area of a triangle, 509
    Distance Formula, 572
    Dividing Powers with the Same
        Base, 203
    Finding a Power of a Power, 199
    Midpoint Formula, 574
    Multiplying Powers with the Same
        Base, 198
    Negative exponents, 204–205
    Pythagorean Theorem, 564
    Raising a product to a power, 265
    Raising a quotient to a power, 266
    Surface area of a cone, 534
    Surface area of a cylinder, 529
    Surface area of a prism, 528
    Surface area of a pyramid, 533
    Volume of a cone and pyramid, 547
    Volume of a cylinder, 539
    Volume of a prism, 538
    Zero as an exponent, 204
Justify each step, 68, 75–77, 106, 111,
    144, 196
See also Mathematical Reasoning

Properties
of addition, 64–68, 114, 118, 684, 744
of additive inverse, 23, 744
associative, 64–68, 744
closure, 744
commutative, 64–68, 114, 117, 744
cross product, 744
density, 744
distributive, 69–73
of equality, 86–88, 116, 143, 145, 744
of exponents, 198–207, 218, 744
identity, 65–68, 744
of inequality, 104–105, 116, 744
inverse, 84–88, 744
of multiplication, 64–68, 176, 265, 582, 744
of real numbers, 64–68, 744
of substitution, 13–16
table of, 744
of triangles, 454–458
zero-product, 744
See also Table of properties

Proportion, 284–288
cross products, 284–287
defined, 284
finding measures of central angles, 470–471
indirect measurement and, 290–293, 578–581, 601
percents and, 305–309
as problem solving strategy, 578–581, 601
ratios, 285–287
in scale drawings, 289–294, 329
in similar figures, 289–294, 329, 578–581, 601
solving, 284–288, 305–309, 328, 329–330, 557, 578–580
writing, 285–293, 331, 332, 601

Proportional Reasoning, 278–332, 578–581
See also Mathematical Reasoning

Protractor
drawing and measuring angles, 448
drawing circles, 514

Pyramid
base of, 521–525
defined, 521, 553
edges of, 521–525
face of, 521, 533–537
height of, 547–550
hexagonal, 521–523
net of, 522–523
square, 523
surface area of, 533–536, 554
volume of, 547–550, 554

Pythagorean Theorem
and circles, 570–571
converse of, 566–568
empirical verification, 564
finding distance, 572
in indirect measurement, 564–571, 601

with special right triangles, 582–586
using, 564–571, 601

Pythagorean triple, 568

Q

Quadrants, 50–53, 58, 59, 60, 130, 427
Quadratic function, 669, 705
defined, 669
graphing, 669–672, 705

Quadrilaterals
classifying, 455
defined, 455
diagonals of, 460–461
sides and angles of, 459
sums of angle measures of, 459

Quartile, 613–616

Quick Review, 64, 71, 122, 194, 198, 231, 236, 244, 265, 342, 360, 388, 392, 406, 426, 564, 668, 684, 690

Quotient
estimating, 128, 129
finding, 169, 243
finding powers of, 266–268, 272, 273
simplifying, 46
See also Division

R

Radical sign, 560
Radius
of circle, 439, 563, 571, 577
of cone, 534, 547
of cylinder, 529
of sphere, 548, 534

Random numbers, 654
Random sample, 646–649, 658
Range
of data, 609–611
of function, 386, 434

Rate, 99, 137, 168, 279–281, 299, 328, 363, 366
Ratio
of circumference to diameter, 469, 470
common, 665–668, 704
cosine, 588–592, 602
defined, 278, 328
equivalent, 278–281
of measures of similar space figures, 537
in problem solving, 589–592, 602
in proportions, 284–288
rate. *See* Rate
right triangles, 588–592, 602
scales and scale factors, 290, 294
simplest form of, 278–281, 381
sine, 588–592, 602
tangent, 588–592, 602
trigonometric, 588, 589, 602, 603, 747

writing as fractions, 278–281, 328, 332
writing as unit rates, 279–281, 328

Rational numbers
absolute value of, 197
classifying, 194–197
defined, 194
evaluating fractions with variables, 195–197
graphing, 194–197, 225
identifying, 194, 561–562, 569, 600, 603
simplest form of, 186–189, 217
See also Decimals, Fractions, Integers, Mixed numbers, *and* Whole numbers

Ray, 442, 496, 672
Reading Math
arithmetic sequence, 664
base, 176
bisection, 475
common ratio, 665
discounts, 319
distance formula, 572
distributive property, 71
fraction names, 186
greater than and less than symbols, 100
lateral, 521
lowest common denominator, 226
median, 133
multiplicative inverses, 242
nonlinear functions, 669
number patterns, 35
odds, 297
percent, 300
plural of vertex, 455
powers, 266
power of a power, 199
probabilities, 296
proportions, 284
range, 609
reading equations, 90
reading expressions, 177

Real numbers,
classifying, 561–563
properties of, 744
real world applications. *See* Connections to real world applications

Reasoning. *See* Mathematical Reasoning
Reciprocal, 242, 260, 271
Rectangle
area of, 10, 12, 69, 96, 139, 149, 167, 168, 193, 201, 241, 344, 349, 354, 365, 425, 501, 504–507, 696
classifying, 455
defined, 455
modeling factors, 173, 180, 240
perimeter of, 138, 139, 167, 367, 424, 499

Rectangular prism
net of, 521–525
surface area of, 527–532
volume of, 538–545

Index

as exponent, 673–677, 705
in expressions. *See* Variable
   expressions
inequalities, 104–112, 360–363
powers of, 176–179, 198–201,
   203–207, 218
solving equation with, on both sides,
   355–359, 377
solving formula for a given, 365–368,
   378
substituting values for, 13–16, 79–81,
   137–140

Variable expression, 4–7
binomials, 678, 694–697
coefficient, 74–76
constant, 74–76
defined, 4, 56
Distributive Property, 71–73
dividing, with exponents, 203, 744
evaluating, 13–16, 27, 57, 67,
   177–179, 218
with exponents, 176–179, 198–201,
   203–207, 218
finding greatest common factor of,
   181–184, 217
identifying, 4
identifying parts of, 74, 76
like terms in, 74–77
modeling with algebra tiles, 23, 26,
   29–31, 71–72, 75–76, 82–83, 173, 180,
   336, 340, 355, 686, 691, 695
monomials, 678, 689–692, 705
polynomials, 678–692, 694–698,
   705–706
prime factorization of, 225
simplifying, 8, 12, 16, 19, 21, 28, 47, 49,
   57, 59–60, 74–77, 81, 103, 115, 117,
   118, 177, 198, 200, 203–206, 219, 220,
   239, 243, 263, 267, 273, 274, 313, 333,
   339, 379, 500, 550, 569, 661
unlike terms, 74–77
with square roots, 587
verbal models for. *See* Verbal models,
   phrases, and descriptions
writing, 5, 12, 15, 16, 21, 59, 220, 333

Variation
constant of, 396
direct, 396

Venn diagram, 185

Verbal models, phrases, and descriptions
for addition, 5–7, 12, 14, 16, 21, 27–28,
   33, 56, 59, 77, 85, 87, 255, 333, 341,
   351, 361, 422
for division, 5–7, 12, 16, 21, 27, 56, 87,
   148, 152, 168, 280, 299, 371
for inequality, 101–103, 105–106, 109,
   111, 116–117, 427
for integers, 19–21, 27, 34, 49, 52, 57,
   59, 78, 87, 92, 148

for multiplication, 5–7, 12, 14, 16, 21,
   27, 33, 56, 59, 77–78, 87, 89, 92–93,
   118, 146, 148, 176, 260, 287, 307–308,
   321, 330–331, 351, 356, 361, 368, 378,
   379, 422, 459, 627–628, 636
for subtraction, 5–7, 12, 16, 27–28, 56,
   59–60, 86, 143, 158, 273, 333
for variable expressions, 5–7, 12, 14,
   16, 21, 27, 28, 33, 56, 59, 176, 333
for writing equations, 78–81, 85–89,
   92, 143, 146, 148, 152, 158, 168, 255,
   260, 287, 307–308, 310–312, 321, 330,
   331, 341, 351, 356, 361, 368, 371, 378,
   379, 459, 627–628, 636, 647
for writing linear equations, 404,
   422, 577
for writing rules in function notation,
   404

Vertex
of angle, 448
of parallelogram, 506
of polygon, 455, 487
of space figure, 521
of triangle, 487, 492, 493

Vertical angles, 449, 497

Vertical-line test, 387–388, 392, 408

Vertical translation, 480–481

Views of space figure, 520

Volume
of cone, 547–550, 554
of cube, 179, 268
of cylinder, 539–541, 554
defined, 538, 554
of prism, 538–541, 554
of pyramid, 547–550, 554
of rectangular prism, 538–545
of space figure, 545, 546, 549, 563
of sphere, 548–550, 554
units of, 538

W

Web Extension. *See* Internet

Weight, units of, 245–248

Whole amount
finding, 306–313
finding part of, 305–313

***Work Backward* problem solving
   strategy,** 251–254, 272

***Write an Equation* problem solving
   strategy,** 350–353, 377

***Write a Proportion* problem solving
   strategy,** 578–581, 601

Writing, 7, 12, 16, 21, 27, 31, 33, 39, 48, 54,
   57, 59, 73, 77, 81, 88, 92, 99, 103, 107,
   112, 115, 117, 118, 126, 129, 135, 145,
   149, 154, 161, 164, 167, 168, 175, 178,
   183, 188, 196, 200, 206, 213, 217, 219,
   233, 244, 249, 250, 258, 262, 268, 272,
   273, 283, 287, 292, 299, 304, 309, 313,

321, 330, 331, 339, 344, 349, 359, 363,
364, 367, 373, 378, 379, 390, 394, 397,
401, 407, 408, 424, 430, 434, 436, 437,
446, 453, 459, 462, 463, 467, 472, 477,
482, 487, 493, 498, 499, 507, 513, 518,
524, 532, 537, 540, 554, 555, 562, 585,
591, 598, 601, 603, 616, 623, 624, 630,
634, 639, 645, 648, 652, 654, 657, 659,
667, 672, 675, 680, 697, 706, 707. *See
also* Journal

Writing Math
is equal to, equals, and is, 78
for multiplication, 13, 14, 45
order of, 86
symbols in, 5

X

***x*-axis,** 50–54, 58
***x*-coordinate,** 50, 54, 58, 398, 415,
   424, 481, 488
***x*-intercept,** 395

Y

***y*-axis,** 50, 52, 58, 492, 493
***y*-coordinate,** 50, 54, 58, 398, 415, 424,
   481, 488
***y*-intercept,** 395, 399, 408, 417, 435

Z

Zero
absolute value of, 18, 19
as exponent, 204, 206, 744

Zero pair, 23

Zero-product property, 744

Zero slope, 398

Acknowledgments

STAFF CREDITS

The people who made up the *Pre-Algebra* team—representing editorial, editorial services, design services, market research, marketing, marketing services, project office, on-line services/multimedia development, production services, and publishing processes—are listed below. **Bold type** denotes the core team members.

Barbara A. Bertell, **Judith D. Buice,** Bob Craton, **Kathy Carter,** Sheila DeFazio, **Jo DiGiustini, Frederick Fellows,** Linda Ferreira, Maria Green, Kerri Hoar, Russell Lappa, Catherine Maglio, **Eve Melnechuk,** Paul W. Murphy, Suzanne Schineller, **Dennis Slattery,** Deborah Sommer, **Mark Tricca,** Stuart Wallace, **Diane Walsh,** Joe Will

ADDITIONAL CREDITS

Carolyn Artin, Suzanne Biron, Susan Clare, Jayne Holman, Jerry H. Hooten, Savitri K. Khalsa, Carolyn Langley, Cheryl Mahan, PoYee Oster, Pat Packer-Williams, Sydney Schuster, Angela Sciaraffa

Cover Design: Sweetlight Creative Partners/ David Julian

Cover Image: John de Visser/Masterfile

Technical Illustration: Nesbitt Graphics, Inc.

ILLUSTRATION
Suzanne Biron: 3, 42, 54, 55, 121, 135, 163, 223, 249, 269, 335, 375, 441, 467, 495, 559, 599, 663, 703; photocompositing—7, 32, 51, 120, 123, 156, 250, 252, 444, 448, 451, 454, 464, 465, 468, 480, 485, 491t, 558

John Edwards & Associates: 88

DLF Group: 440, 593

Jared D. Lee: 624br

Ortelius Design, Inc.: 30, 53, 139, 152, 211, 233, 236, 241, 290b, 337, 348, 366, 391, 511, 578t

Pat Packer-Williams: 63, 113, 171, 215, 277, 327, 383, 433, 503, 551, 607, 655; photocompositing—85, 184, 279, 290b, 397, 413, 424, 531, 613, 620, 621

Wendy Simpson: photocompositing—184, 290b, 397, 491b, 531, 611, 613, 617

J/B Woolsey Associates: xxiv, 20, 27, 32, 36, 39, 46, 51, 66, 70, 73, 89, 124, 126, 131, 132, 142, 192, 237, 239, 240, 245, 253, 290t, 302, 307, 311, 315, 322, 343, 363, 407, 447, 453, 456, 471, 480, 494, 507, 514, 516, 518, 549, 563, 566, 568, 578b, 580, 581, 586, 590, 594, 596, 597, 603, 618, 620, 622, 624tl, 625, 644, 689

PHOTOGRAPHY

Picture Research: Toni Michaels

Front Matter

Page v, OAR/National Undersea Research Program (NURP); **vi,** David R. Frazier Photolibrary; **vii,** Russ Lappa; **viii all,** ©Bruce Iverson; **ix,** Alfred Pasieka/Peter Arnold, Inc.; **x,** Cincinnati Zoo; **xi,** James Frank/Stock Connection/PNI; **xii,** Stone/David Young Wolff; **xiii,** Alfred Pasteka/Science Photo Library/Photo Researchers, Inc.; **xiv,** FPG International; **xv,** Stone/Chad Slattery; **xvi,** Lynn Rogers/Peter Arnold, Inc.; **xvii,** Peter Berndt, M.D., P.A.; **xx,** Stone/David Young-Wolff; **xxi t,** Tony Freeman/PhotoEdit; **xxi b,** David Young-Wolff/PhotoEdit; **xxii,** NASA/John F. Kennedy Space Center; **xxv,** Will Hart/PhotoEdit; **xxviii,** Richard Haynes.

Chapter One

Pages 2–3, *Kryptos,* James Sanborn, 1990, 11' x 20', courtesy of the artist; **5,** ©Royal Tyrrell Museum of Palaeontology/Alberta Community Development; **7,** PhotoDisc, Inc.; **10,** Minnesota Dept. of Natural Resources; **14,** Russ Lappa; **16,** Stone/Stuart Westmorland; **25,** Albuquerque Seismological Lab, USGS; **28,** Patrick Somelet/DIAF/The Stock Market; **30,** ©Sowers/Penn State University; **32,** Index Stock Imagery; **40,** Michael Simpson/FPG International; **42,** PhotoDisc, Inc.; **43 all,** Russ Lappa; **44,** OAR/National Undersea Research Program (NURP); **51,** Tom Van Sant/The Stock Market; **54,** Prentice Hall; **55,** *Kryptos,* James Sanborn, 1990, 11' x 20', courtesy of the artist.

Chapter Two

Pages 62–63, Tom Hanson/Liaison Agency; **66,** Russ Lappa; **68,** Mark Kelley/Stock Boston; **70,** Tony Freeman/PhotoEdit; **73,** Russ Lappa; **79,** Stone/Chris Simpson; **81,** Mark Thayer; **82 all,** Ken O'Donoghue; **84 both,** Anthony Neste; **85,** David R. Frazier Photolibrary; **85 inset,** Omni-Photo Communications, Inc.; **94,** Superstock; **97,** Jose L./Palaez; **103 l,** Superstock; **103 m,** Spencer Grant/PhotoEdit; **103 r,** D. & J. Heaton/ Stock Boston; **105,** Russ Lappa; **109,** Andrew Yates/Image Bank; **113,** Tom Hanson/Liaison Agency.

Chapter Three

Pages 120–121, Owen Franken/Stock Boston; **123,** Russ Lappa; **127,** Russ Lappa; **128,** G. Cigolini/Image Bank; **135,** Corel Corp.; **137,** Alvin Staffan/Photo Researchers; **140,** Kevin Schafer/Peter Arnold, Inc.; **142 l,** Lockheed Martin Telecommunications; **142 m, r,** Corel Corp.; **145,** *Dilbert* reprinted by permission of United Features Syndicate, Inc.; **147,** Corbis/Bettmann; **152,** Stone/Ed Simpson; **154,** Stone/Doug Armand; **156 both,** Russ Lappa; **159,** Stone/I. Burgum/P. Boorman; **161,** Russ Lappa; **162,** Bob Daemmrich/Stock Boston; **163,** Owen Franken/ Stock Boston.

Chapter Four

Pages 170–171, Adam Woolfitt/Woodfin Camp & Assoc.; **173,** Russ Lappa; **177 all,** ©Bruce Iverson; **180,** Russ Lappa; **182,** Gary A. Conner/PhotoEdit; **184,** Stone/Michael Rosenfield; **187,** Bob Daemmrich/Stock Boston; **190,** Russ Lappa; **195,** AP/Dusan Vranic/Wide World Photos; **196,** Mehau Kulyk/Science Photo Library/Photo Researchers; **201,** Peggy Yoram Kahana/Peter Arnold, Inc.; **205,** Russell C. Hansen/Peter Arnold, Inc.; **207,** Mark Downey/Liaison Agency; **209,** Tim Barnwell/Stock Boston; **211,** K & G Photo/FPG International; **213,** Stone/Doris De Witt; **215,** Adam Woolfitt/Woodfin Camp & Assoc.

Chapter Five

Pages 222–223, Arthur Tilley/FPG International; **226,** Monkmeyer/Grant Pix; **228,** Alfred Pasieka/Peter Arnold, Inc.; **229 both,** Ken Karp; **236,** Mark Gibson/Corbis; **241,** Alan Schen; **242,** Russ Lappa; **249,** Photri/The Stock Market; **250,** Russ Lappa; **251,** Stone/Jason Hawkes; **252 all,** Russ Lappa; **255,** Dave Davidson/The Stock Market; **258,** Jim Corwim/Photo Researchers; **262,** Daniel Lyons/Bruce Coleman; **266,** Dirk Weisheit/DDB Stock Photo; **269,** Arthur Tilley/FPG International.

Chapter Six

Pages 276–277, David-Young Wolfitt/PhotoEdit; **279,** Russ Lappa; **281,** Stone/Kindra Clineff; **285,** NASA; **287,** REAL LIFE ADVENTURES ©1999 GarLanco. Reprinted with permission of Universal Press Syndicate. All rights reserved.; **288,** Russ Lappa; **292,** Richard Haynes; **294, 295,** Russ Lappa; **297 all,** The United States Mint; **301,** Stone/Renee Lynn; **303,** Jay Syverson/Stock Boston; **304,** Bob Daemmrich/Stock Boston/PNI; **317 t,** Cincinnati Zoo; **317 b,** Spencer Grant/Stock Boston; **320,** Robert Brenner/PhotoEdit; **323,** Joseph Sohm/Stock Boston; **325,** Tek Image/Science Photo Library/Photo Researchers; **326,** Spencer Grant/Stock Boston; **327,** David-Young Wolfitt/PhotoEdit.

Chapter Seven

Pages 334–335, Stone/Hugh Sitton; **337,** Stone/Mark Lewis; **347 t,** Elizabeth Crews/The Image Works; **347 b,** David Young-Wolff/PhotoEdit; **349,** Tim Barnell/ Stock Boston; **350,** The Granger Collection, New York; **356,** James Frank/Stock Connection/PNI; **359,** Michael Heron/The Stock Market; **361,** Jose Carrillo/PhotoEdit; **366,** Stone/David Schultz; **375,** Stone/Hugh Sitton.

Chapter Eight

Pages 382–383, A. Ramey/PhotoEdit; **387,** David Young Wolff; **388,** Corel Corp.; **391,** Lester Lefkowitz/The Stock Market; **397,** Stone/Jess Stock; **401 t,** Bob Daemmrich/The Image Works; **401 b,** Donald Dietz/Stock Boston; **402,** Stone/ Don Smetzer; **413,** Russ Lappa; **416,** Erwin & Peggy Bauer/ Bruce Coleman Inc.; **427,** Joe Sohm/The Image Works; **430,** Ellen Skye/Monkmeyer; **433,** A. Ramey/PhotoEdit.

Chapter Nine

Pages 440–441, Stone/Chad Ehlers; **442,** Photo Researchers; **444,** James Marshall/The Stock Market; **447,** AP/Paul Warner/Wide World Photos; **448,** Jon Chomitz; **451,** Courtesy of J.C. Guillois/Santa Fe Stained Glass; **454,** Gianalberto Cigolini/Image Bank; **456,** Peter Gridley/FPG International; **460,** Alfred Pasteka/Science Photo Library/Photo Researchers; **464,** Georg Gerster/ Photo Researchers; **465,** John Heiney/Sportschrome; **468,** R. Wahhlstrom/Image Bank; **469, 474 t,** Russ Lappa; **474 b,** Jon Chomitz; **480, 485 tl,** Russ Lappa; **485 bl,** Patti Murray/Animals Animals; **485 tr,** Russ Lappa; **485 br,** C. Zeiss/Bruce Coleman; **491 t,** Russ Lappa; **491 b,** Danilo G. Donadoni/Bruce Coleman; **492 l,** Steve Solum/Bruce Coleman; **492 ml,** Adam Peiperl/The Stock Market; **492 mr,** Larry West/Bruce Coleman; **492 r,** John Gerlach/ Tom Stack & Associates; **495,** Stone/Chad Ehlers.

Chapter Ten

Pages 502–503, Ron Stroud/Masterfile; **504,** Leslye Borden/ PhotoEdit; **508,** Ken Chernus/FPG/PNI; **510,** Pascal Quittemelle/Stock Boston; **511,** Corbis-Bettmann; **515,** Alan Carey/Photo Researchers Inc.; **522,** Ellis Herwig/Stock Boston; **524 all, 526, 529,** Russ Lappa; **531,** Keith Gunnar/Bruce Coleman; **533,** FPG International; **535 t,** Russ Lappa; **535 b,** J. Sapinsky/The Stock Market; **537,** Sara Krulwich/NYT Pictures; **539, 541,** Russ Lappa; **542,** Stone/Steven Peters; **548,** Jeff Foott/Bruce Coleman; **550,** Stone/Richard Clintsman; **551,** Ron Stroud/Masterfile.

Chapter Eleven

Pages 558–559, background, Earth Scenes; **558–559 girl,** Richard Haynes; **561,** Alese/Mort PECHTER/The Stock Market; **563,** Telegraph Colour Library/FPG International; **569,** Stone/Chad Slattery; **578,** Stone/Hideo Kurihara; **581,** H.P. Merten/The Stock Market; **583,** Landslides; **592,** Lance Nelson/The Stock Market; **599,** Earth Scenes.

Chapter Twelve

Pages 606–607, Russ Lappa/props, courtesy of Winchester High School, Winchester, MA; **613,** Stone; **614 t,** Marilyn Kazmers/Peter Arnold, Inc.; **614 b,** David Madison/Bruce Coleman; **617,** Gerard Lacz/Peter Arnold, Inc.; **620 l,** Brent Jones/Stock Boston; **620 r,** Nik Wheeler/ Corbis; **621,** Gerard Lacz/Peter Arnold, Inc.; **627,** Russ Lappa; **632,** John Lemker/Earth Scenes; **637,** Corel Corp.; **639,** Russ Lappa; **640,** Lynn Rogers/Peter Arnold, Inc.; **650,** Stone/Greg Pease; **655,** Russ Lappa/props, courtesy of Winchester High School, Winchester, MA.

Chapter Thirteen

Pages 662–663, Stone/Ken Biggs; **665,** Marc Romanelli/ Image Bank; **670,** Sydney Thompson/Animals Animals; **672,** Bob Daemmrich/Stock Boston; **674,** Peter Berndt, M.D., P.A.; **679,** Bob Burch/Bruce Coleman; **699,** John Davenport/Liaison Agency; **703,** Stone/Ken Biggs.